Prentice Hall

LITERATURE
Timeless Voices, Timeless Themes

Copper

Bronze

Silver

Gold

Platinum

The American Experience

The British Tradition

SERIES AUTHORS

The series authors guided the direction and the philosophy of Prentice Hall Literature: Timeless Voices, Timeless Themes. Working closely with the development team, they contributed to the pedagogical integrity of the program and to its relevance for today's teachers and students.

Heidi Hayes Jacobs
Department of Curriculum and Teaching
Teachers College
Columbia University
New York, New York
Heidi Hayes Jacobs has served as an educational consultant to over 1,000 schools nationally and internationally. A frequent contributor to professional journals, she has published two best-selling books through ASCD: Interdisciplinary Curriculum: Design and Implementation and Mapping the Big Picture: Integrating Curriculum and Assessment K–12. She has been on the faculty of Teachers College, Columbia University, since 1981, and her years as a teacher of high-school, middle-school, and elementary-school students in Utah, Massachusetts, and New York provide the fundamental background of her experience.

Richard Lederer
Author, speaker, columnist, and teacher
San Diego, California
Richard Lederer celebrates the English language as the best-selling author of more than ten books, including Anguished English and The Miracle of Language. He writes a syndicated weekly column, "Looking at Language," and he is the Grammar Grappler for Writer's Digest. His work has also appeared in publications such as The New York Times, Sports Illustrated, National Review, and Reader's Digest. Well-known as a speaker and a presenter, Lederer has entertained and informed a wide variety of audiences, including the National Council of Teachers of English. For many years, he taught English at St. Paul's School in Concord, New Hampshire.

Sharon Sorensen
Author, speaker, and consultant
Mt. Vernon, Indiana
An educator with more than thirty years of classroom experience, Sharon Sorensen has taught both secondary language arts and language arts methods at the university level. She has also published over eighty articles and has authored or co-authored more than twenty-five books on writing, writing process, and the teaching of writing, including How to Write Short Stories, How to Write Research Papers, and Webster's New World Student Writing Handbook. She and her husband live in a self-created wildlife sanctuary in rural Indiana, where they are active in the National Audubon Society.

PROGRAM ADVISORS

The program advisors provided ongoing input throughout the development of Prentice Hall Literature: Timeless Voices, Timeless Themes. Their valuable insights ensure that the perspectives of teachers throughout the country are represented within this literature series.

Diane Cappillo
Language Arts Department Chair
Barbara Goleman Senior High School
Miami, Florida
Past President of the Dade County Council of Teachers of English.

Anita Clay
English Instructor
Gateway Institute of Technology
St. Louis, Missouri
Former Middle School Team Leader; Former Chair, High School English Department.

Mary Curfman
Teacher of English
Clark County School District
Las Vegas, Nevada

Ellen Eberly
Teacher of Language Arts
Catholic Memorial
West Roxbury, Massachusetts

Nancy M. Fahner
Language Arts Instructor
Ingham Intermediate School District
Mason, Michigan
Recipient of Charlotte, Michigan, Teacher of the Year Award, 1992. Curriculum Coordinator for School-to-Work Program.

Terri Fields
Language Arts and Communication Arts Teacher, Author
Sunnyslope High School
Phoenix, Arizona
Recipient of Arizona Teacher of the Year and U.S. WEST Outstanding Arizona Teacher awards.

Susan J. Goldberg
Teacher of English
Westlake Middle School
Thornwood, New York
President, Westchester Council of English Educators. President-Elect, New York State English Council.

Argelia Arizpe Guadarrama
Secondary Curriculum Coordinator
Phar–San Juan–Alamo Independent School District
San Juan, Texas
Recognized by Texas Education Agency for work on Texas Assessment of Academic Skills.

V. Pauline Hodges, Ph.D.
Teacher and Educational Consultant
Forgan High School
Forgan, Oklahoma
President, National Rural Education Association. Former Language Arts Coordinator, Jefferson County, Colorado.

Jennifer Huntress
Secondary Language Arts Coordinator
Putnam City Schools
Oklahoma City, Oklahoma
National trainer for writing evaluation, curriculum integration, and alternative assessment strategies.

Angelique McMath Jordan
Teacher of English
Dunwoody High School
Dunwoody, Georgia
Teacher of the Year at Dunwoody High School, 1991.

Thomas S. Lindsay
Assistant Superintendent
Mannheim School District 83
Franklin Park, Illinois

Carol McKee
Middle School Language Arts Research Teacher
Fayette County Public Schools
Lexington, Kentucky
Past President, Kentucky Middle School Association.

Nancy L. Monroe
Teacher of English and ACT Preparation
Bolton High School
Alexandria, Louisiana
Past President of the Rapides Council of Teachers of English and the Louisiana Council of Teachers. National Advanced Placement Consultant.

Rosemary A. Naab
Chair, English Department
Archbishop Ryan High School
Archdiocese of Philadelphia
Philadelphia, Pennsylvania
English Curriculum Committee. Awarded Curriculum Quill Award by the Archdiocese of Philadelphia.

Ann Okamura
Teacher of English
Laguna Creek High School
Elk Grove, California
Participant in the College Board Pacesetters Program. Formerly K–12 District Resource Specialist in Writing, Competency Assessment, Foreign Languages, and the Elk Grove Writing Project. Fellow in the San Joaquin Valley Writing Project and the California Literature Project.

Scott Phillips
Teacher of English
Ford Middle School
Allen, Texas
District Curriculum Committee Member.

Jonathan L. Schatz
Teacher of English/Team Leader
Tappan Zee High School
Orangeburg, New York
Creator of a literacy program to assist students with reading in all content areas.

John Scott
Teacher of English
Hampton High School
Hampton, Virginia
Recipient of the Folger Shakespeare Library Renaissance Forum Award. Participant in four National Endowment for the Humanities teacher programs.

Ken Spurlock
Assistant Principal
Boone County High School
Florence, Kentucky
Former Teacher of English at Holmes High School and District Writing Supervisor. Twice elected President of Kentucky Council of Teachers of English.

Joan West
Teacher of English
Oliver Middle School
Broken Arrow, Oklahoma
Runner-up, Middle Grades Teacher of the Year.

Rick Wormeli
Teacher of English
Rachel Carson Middle School
Herndon, Virginia
Disney's Outstanding English Teacher of the Year, 1996.

Prentice Hall
LITERATURE
Timeless Voices, Timeless Themes

BRONZE

PRENTICE HALL
Upper Saddle River, New Jersey
Needham, Massachusetts

ISBN 0-13-435294-7

6 7 8 9 10   02 01 00

PRENTICE HALL
Upper Saddle River, New Jersey
Needham, Massachusetts

ACKNOWLEDGMENTS

Grateful acknowledgment is made to the following for permission to reprint copyrighted material:

Miriam Altshuler Literary Agency as agent for Walter Dean Myers
"The Treasure of Lemon Brown" by Walter Dean Myers from *Boy's Life Magazine,* March 1983. Copyright © 1983 by Walter Dean Myers. Reprinted by permission of Miriam Altshuler Literary Agency as agent for Walter Dean Myers.

Américas
"Lather and Nothing Else" by Hernando Téllez. Reprinted from *Américas,* a bimonthly magazine published by the General Secretariat of the Organization of American States in English and Spanish. Reprinted by permission of *Américas* magazine.

Arte Publico Press
"Maestro" by Pat Mora is reprinted with permission from the publisher of *Borders* (Houston: Arte Publico Press—University of Houston, 1986).

Susan Bergholz Literary Services, New York
"Four Skinny Trees" from *The House on Mango Street.* Copyright © 1984 by Sandra Cisneros. Published by Vintage Books, a division of Random House Inc., and in hardcover by Alfred A. Knopf, 1994. Reprinted by permission of Susan Bergholz Literary Services, New York. All rights reserved.

Brandt & Brandt Literary Agents, Inc.
"The Third Wish" from *Not What You Expected: A Collection of Short Stories* by Joan Aiken. Copyright © 1974 by Joan Aiken. Reprinted by permission of Brandt & Brandt Literary Agents, Inc.

Broadway Books, a division of Bantam Doubleday Dell Publishing Group
From *Tiger: A Biography of Tiger Woods* by John Strege. Copyright ©1997 by John Strege. Used by permission of Broadway Books, a division of Bantam Doubleday Dell Publishing Group.

Clarion Books/Houghton Mifflin Company
Excerpt from *The Midwife's Apprentice* by Karen Cushman. Copyright © 1995 by Karen Cushman. Reprinted by permission of Clarion Books/Houghton Mifflin Company. All rights reserved.

Don Congdon Associates, Inc.
"The Third Level" by Jack Finney, published in *Collier's,* October 7, 1950. Copyright © 1950 by Crowell Collier, renewed 1977 by Jack Finney. "All Summer In A Day" by Ray Bradbury, published in *The Magazine of Fantasy and Science Fiction,* March 1, 1954. Copyright © 1954, renewed 1982 by Ray Bradbury. Reprinted by permission of Don Congdon Associates, Inc.

Harold Courlander
"All Stories Are Anansi's" from *The Hat-Shaking Dance and Other Ashanti Tales from Ghana* by Harold Courlander with Albert Kofi Prempeh. Copyright © 1957 by Harcourt Brace Jovanovich, Inc.; 1985 by Harold Courlander. Reprinted by permission of the author.

Crown Publishers, Inc.
From *The Iceman* by Don Lessem. Copyright © 1994 by Don Lessem. Reprinted by permission of Crown Publishers, Inc.

Curtis Brown, Ltd.
"Suzy and Leah" by Jane Yolen. Copyright © 1993 by Jane Yolen. First appeared in *American Girl Magazine,* published by The Pleasant Company. Reprinted by permission of Curtis Brown, Ltd.

Delacorte Press, a division of Bantam Doubleday Dell Publishing Group, Inc.
"The Luckiest Time of All" from *The Lucky Stone* by Lucille Clifton. Copyright © 1979 by Lucille Clifton. Used by permission of Delacorte Press, a division of Bantam Doubleday Dell Publishing Group, Inc.

Doubleday, a division of Bantam Doubleday Dell Publishing Group, Inc.
"Two Tankas" from *From the Country of Eight Islands* by Hiroaki Sato and Burton Watson. Copyright © 1981 by Hiroaki Sato and Burton Watson. Used by permission of Doubleday, a division of Bantam Doubleday Dell Publishing Group, Inc. "After Twenty Years" by O. Henry from *The Complete Works of O. Henry.*

Enslow Publishers, Inc.
"Nolan Ryan: Texas Treasure" from *Sports Great Nolan Ryan,* Enslow Publishers, Inc., P.O. Box 699, Springfield, NJ 07081, © 1993 by William W. Lace. Reprinted by permission of the publisher.

(Acknowledgments continue on p. 915.)

Looking at Universal Themes

Unit 1

Finding Yourself

Unit 2

Looking at Universal Themes
Common Threads

Looking at Universal Themes

What Matters

PART 1: RISKING IT ALL

PART 2: MOMENTS OF INSIGHT

Unit

4

Looking at Universal Themes

Resolving Conflicts

Looking at Universal Themes

Just for Fun

Looking at Literary Forms

Short Stories

Unit

8

Poetry

Looking at Literary Forms

Myths, Legends, and Folk Tales

Complete Contents by Genre

SHORT STORY

DRAMA

NONFICTION

Complete Contents by Genre

NONFICTION (CONTINUED)

POETRY

Complete Contents by Genre

POETRY (CONTINUED)

MYTHS, LEGENDS, AND FOLK TALES

Complete Contents by Theme

FINDING YOURSELF

JUST FOR FUN

WHAT MATTERS

Complete Contents by Theme

RESOLVING CONFLICTS

COMMON THREADS

THE WORLD AROUND US

Complete Contents by Theme

Prentice Hall

LITERATURE

Timeless Voices, Timeless Themes

Untitled, Steve Dininno

Finding Yourself

One of the most rewarding searches you'll ever conduct is the discovery of the qualities that make you an individual. The literature in this unit will introduce you to people of all generations who have dedicated themselves to this search. You'll meet a girl who struggles to find who she really is and a boy who imitates his heroes as he creates his own style. You'll encounter a man who travels across the world and another who journeys back in time—each in search of himself. As you read about all of these characters, you may discover something about yourself!

Guide for Reading

Meet the Author:

Isaac Bashevis Singer (1904–1991)

As a boy in Poland, Isaac Bashevis Singer became fascinated with the real-life stories he witnessed in his father's "courtroom." However, his father was neither a lawyer nor a judge. The man was a rabbi, a Jewish religious leader, who settled disputes among the poor Jews of Warsaw, Poland's capital.

The Writer as Judge Later, as a writer, Singer would settle the problems of his own made-up characters. He did this using the language he spoke as a youth and heard in his father's "court": Yiddish. This language, related to German, was spoken by Eastern European Jews and is still used by many Jews.

Far and Not So Far In one way, Singer left his father's world. He came to the United States in 1935 and, over the years, became famous for his novels and stories. Eventually, he won the Nobel Prize for Literature. In another way, though, Singer never really left his father's world. The stories that won him such a wide audience were often based on what he saw and heard as a boy.

THE STORY BEHIND THE STORY

As a religious Jew, Singer's father believed that people should not take pride in their appearance. It is likely that he banned or limited the use of mirrors in his household. You'll see the influence of this attitude in this story.

◆ LITERATURE AND YOUR LIFE

CONNECT YOUR EXPERIENCE

You'd still be yourself in a world without mirrors. However, some part of you would be missing—something that appears often, is as personal as a fingerprint, but weighs nothing: your reflection in the glass! Without that reflection, you couldn't have an accurate mental picture of yourself.

The characters in this story live happily in a mirrorless world and don't know at first that anything is missing.

THEMATIC FOCUS: Finding Yourself

In reading this story, think about whether the image looking out from a mirror is really the same as the self that looks in.

◆ Background for Understanding

SOCIAL STUDIES

The painting on the next page tells you that mirrors have been known for many years. However, the Skibas in this story, peasant farmers from Eastern Europe, regard a mirror as a "luxury."

That's because, as peasants, they have practically no money. They work a small plot of land, producing enough food for their own needs and perhaps a little extra to sell. As a society relies more on technology, peasant farming tends to disappear. However, there are still people in today's world who live much as the Skibas do.

The Cat Who Thought
◆ She Was a Dog and the Dog ◆
Who Thought He Was a Cat

◆ Literary Focus

THE MORAL OF A STORY

A short story is like a magical mirror: It shows you your own life reflected in the lives of others. In other words, a story uses the actions of characters to give you a **moral,** a guide for living, that you can apply to your own life.

Sometimes you have to figure out the moral yourself. However, in Singer's tale and in many others, you can find the moral stated, usually toward the end. It may be spoken by the author or by a character.

Peasant shows his wife up in the mirror, undated painting

◆ Build Vocabulary

PREFIXES: *pro-*

You'll meet a character in this story whose teeth *protruded*. The prefix *pro-* can mean "forward or before in place or time, or in front of," and the word part *-trude* means "to jut out." Teeth that protrude jut out in front of the lip. On your paper, use a graphic organizer like the one at right to help you think of other *pro-* words.

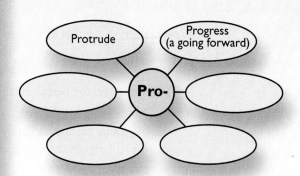

WORD BANK

enthralled
protruded
console
afflicted
vanity
anguish

Look over these words from the story. Which word refers to a quality that causes a person to enjoy looking in a mirror? Check the Build Vocabulary box on page 7 to see if you chose correctly.

Reading for Success

Literal Comprehension Strategies

Reading is not that different from athletics. Just as you need to be light on your feet to play basketball or baseball, you need to be light on your mental feet when you read. The following strategies will get you on your mental toes and moving toward understanding.

Break down long sentences.

▶ Don't read a sentence word by word. Look at groups of meaningful words.
▶ Find the subject, the person, place, or object that the sentence is discussing. Also, find key words that tell you about the subject. The subject and the words that tell you about it don't always appear together:

> subject
>
> The *peddlers* who bought groats, chickens, eggs, honey, calves, and whatever was available from the peasants in the village *never came to Jan Skiba's poor hut.*
>
> tells you about the subject

Apply word identification strategies.

▶ When you come to an unfamiliar word, divide it into syllables and word parts to find familiar elements. When you encounter the word *bedazzled,* break it into its parts:

be + dazzled

You probably know *dazzled,* so you can guess that *bedazzled* means "to be dazzled, or blinded."

Use context to determine meaning.

▶ Use the context, the surroundings, of an unfamiliar word to find clues to its meaning. Nearby words may provide examples of the unfamiliar word:

> From his sack the peddler drew yellow beads, false pearls, tin earrings, rings, brooches, colored kerchiefs, garters, and other such *trinkets.*

If all the items mentioned are examples of *trinkets,* then the word probably means "a small ornament or piece of jewelry."

Reread or read ahead.

▶ If you're confused by passages, reread them to make sense of words or ideas.
▶ Read ahead, keeping in mind any questions. You may find the answers later.

As you read the following story by Isaac Bashevis Singer, look at the notes in the boxes. The notes demonstrate how to apply these strategies to a work of literature.

The Cat Who Thought She Was a Dog and the Dog Who Thought He Was a Cat

Isaac Bashevis Singer

"Then Came a Dog and Bit the Cat" from Had Gadya (Tale of a Goat), 1919, E. Lissitzky, The Jewish Museum, New York, New York

▲ **Critical Viewing** Singer includes humorous touches in his story. What details does this artist use to create humor? Explain. **[Analyze]**

Once there was a poor peasant, Jan Skiba by name. He lived with his wife and three daughters in a one-room hut with a straw roof, far from the village. The house had a bed, a bench bed, and a stove, but no mirror. A mirror was a luxury for a poor peasant. And why would a peasant need a mirror? Peasants aren't curious about their appearance.

But this peasant did have a dog and a cat in his hut. The dog was named Burek and the cat Kot. They had both been born within the same week. As little food as the peasant had for himself and his family, he still wouldn't let his dog and cat go hungry. Since the dog had never seen another dog and the cat had never seen another cat and they saw only each other, the dog thought he was a cat and the cat thought she was a dog. True, they were far from being alike by nature. The dog barked and the cat meowed. The dog chased rabbits and the cat lurked after mice. But must all creatures be exactly like their own kind? The peasant's children weren't exactly alike either. Burek and Kot

> **Break down** this long sentence, and you'll see that its main part is "the dog thought he was a cat and the cat thought she was a dog."

La Cour d'un Ferme (The Farmyard), Marc Chagall

▲ **Critical Viewing** What details in this painting illustrate that Singer's story is set in a rural area far from a village? **[Support]**

lived on good terms, often ate from the same dish, and tried to mimic each other. When Burek barked, Kot tried to bark along, and when Kot meowed, Burek tried to meow too. Kot occasionally chased rabbits and Burek made an effort to catch a mouse.

The peddlers who bought groats,[1] chickens,

eggs, honey, calves, and whatever was available from the peasants in the village never came to Jan Skiba's poor hut. They knew that Jan was so poor he had nothing to sell. But one day a peddler happened to stray there. When he came inside and began to lay out his wares, Jan Skiba's wife and daughters were bedazzled by all the pretty doodads. From his sack the peddler drew yellow beads, false

---

1. groats (grōtz) *n.:* Coarsely cracked grains, especially wheat, buckwheat, oats, or barley.

pearls, tin earrings, rings, brooches, colored kerchiefs, garters, and other such trinkets. But what enthralled the women of the house most was a mirror set in a wooden frame. They asked the peddler its price and he said a half gulden, which was a lot of money for poor peasants. After a while, Jan Skiba's wife, Marianna, made a proposition to the peddler. She would pay him five groshen a month for the mirror. The peddler hesitated a moment. The mirror took up too much space in his sack and there was always the danger it might break. He, therefore, decided to go along, took the first payment of five groshen from Marianna, and left the mirror with the family. He visited the region often and he knew the Skibas to be honest people. He would gradually get his money back and a profit besides.

Use **context clues** to see that *proposition* means "a plan offered for consideration." The next sentence provides the clue; it explains the plan.

Break down *reflections* into its parts: *re + flect- ions.*

The mirror created a commotion in the hut. Until then Marianna and the children had seldom seen themselves. Before they had the mirror, they had only seen their reflections in the barrel of water that stood by the door. Now they could see themselves clearly and they began to find defects in their faces, defects they had never noticed before. Marianna was pretty but she had a tooth missing in front and she felt that this made her ugly. One daughter discovered that her nose was too snub and too broad; a second that her chin was too narrow and too long; a third that her face was sprinkled with freckles. Jan Skiba too caught a glimpse of himself in the mirror and grew displeased by his thick lips and his teeth, which protruded like a buck's. That day, the women of the house became so absorbed in the mirror they didn't cook supper, didn't make up the bed, and neglected all the other household tasks. Marianna had heard of a dentist in the big city who could replace a missing tooth, but such things were expensive. The girls tried to console each

other that they were pretty enough and that they would find suitors, but they no longer felt as jolly as before. They had been afflicted with the vanity of city girls. The one with the broad nose kept trying to pinch it together with her fingers to make it narrower; the one with the too-long chin pushed it up with her fist to make it shorter; the one with the freckles wondered if there was a salve[2] in the city that could remove freckles. But where would the money come from for the fare to the city? And what about the money to buy this salve? For the first time the Skiba family deeply felt its poverty and envied the rich.

Reread this paragraph to understand why the family envied the rich.

But the human members of the household were not the only ones affected. The dog and the cat also grew disturbed by the mirror. The hut was low and the mirror had been hung just above a bench. The first time the cat sprang up on the bench and saw her image in the mirror, she became terribly perplexed. She had never before seen such a creature. Kot's whiskers bristled, she began to meow at her reflection and raised a paw to it, but the other creature meowed back and raised her paw too. Soon the dog jumped up on the bench, and when he saw the other dog he became wild with rage and shock. He barked at the other dog and showed him his teeth, but the other barked back and bared his fangs too. So great was the distress of Burek and Kot that for the first time in their lives they turned on each other. Burek took a bite out of Kot's throat and Kot hissed and spat at him and clawed his muzzle. They both started

---

2. salve (sav) *n.*: Lotion or ointment used to soothe or heal.

◆ Build Vocabulary

enthralled (en thrôld´) *v.*: Fascinated; charmed

protruded (prō trood´ id) *v.*: Stuck out; extended

console (kən sōl´) *v.*: Comfort; make less sad

afflicted (ə flik´ tid) *v.*: Received pain or suffering

vanity (van´ ə tē) *n.*: The quality of being very proud of one's appearance

to bleed and the sight of blood aroused them so that they nearly killed or crippled each other. The members of the household barely managed to separate them. Because a dog is stronger than a cat, Burek had to be tied outside, and he howled all day and all night. In their <u>anguish</u>, both the dog and the cat stopped eating.

When Jan Skiba saw the disruption the mirror had created in his household, he decided a mirror wasn't what his family needed. "Why look at yourself," he said, "when you can see and admire the sky, the sun, the moon, the stars, and the earth, with all its forests, meadows, rivers, and plants?" He took the mirror down from the wall and put it away in the woodshed. When the peddler came for his monthly installment, Jan Skiba gave him back the mirror and in its stead, bought kerchiefs and slippers for the women. After the mirror disappeared, Burek and Kot returned to normal. Again Burek thought he was a cat and Kot was sure she was a dog. Despite all the defects the girls had found in themselves, they made good marriages. The village priest heard what had happened at Jan Skiba's house and he said, "A glass mirror shows only the skin of the body. The real image of a person is in his willingness to help himself and his family and, as far as possible, all those he comes in contact with. This kind of mirror reveals the very soul of the person."

◆ **Build Vocabulary**

anguish (aŋ´ gwish) *n.*: Great suffering; agony

Guide for Responding

◆ LITERATURE AND YOUR LIFE

Reader's Response List some ways in which your life would be different without mirrors.

Thematic Focus What understanding of themselves do the characters lose when they discover their reflections in the mirror?

Skit [Group Activity] Reenact the commotion that occurs in the hut when Marianna and her daughters first see themselves in the mirror.

☑ Check Your Comprehension

1. Briefly describe the Skibas' house and way of life.
2. What is special about their cat and dog?
3. List the events leading up to the purchase of the mirror by the Skibas.
4. What problems does the mirror create for the human and animal characters?
5. How does Jan Skiba solve these problems?

◆ Critical Thinking

INTERPRET

1. What is similar about all the goods that the peddler shows Marianna? **[Connect]**
2. In what way does the mirror, a strange new object, cause the humans and the animals to become strangers to themselves? **[Analyze]**
3. Why are the characters' reactions to the mirror both funny and sad? **[Interpret]**
4. Why does the simple fact that Skiba has removed the mirror have such a dramatic effect on the family? **[Draw Conclusions]**

EVALUATE

5. Could a dog think it's a cat and a cat think it's a dog? Why or why not? **[Criticize]**

APPLY

6. Would it be possible for our society to do without mirrors? Explain. **[Speculate]**

Guide for Responding (continued)

◆ Reading for Success

LITERAL COMPREHENSION STRATEGIES

Review the reading strategies and the notes showing how to understand a writer's words. Then apply them to answer the following.

1. Break down the word *commotion* into its parts and find a familiar word hidden inside it.
2. Break down the sentence on page 7 that begins "So great was the distress . . ." What is the subject? What are the key words that tell you about the subject?
3. Using context clues, find the meaning of *perplexed* on page 7. Explain how you figured out the meaning.

◆ Build Vocabulary

USING THE PREFIX *pro-*

Explain how each italicized *pro-* word includes the meaning "before, ahead, in front of, or forth":

Today, factories *produce* mirrors. Then advertisers *promote* them by showing models *promenading* along a street with mirrors. The ad *promises* people that they will look like models. This system is called *progress*.

SPELLING STRATEGY

The *gw* sound following *n*, as in *anguish,* is spelled *gu.* Write the words containing the *gu* spelling of the *gw* sound that fit the following definitions:

1. Human speech: l _____?_____
2. A black-and-white bird that lives in the Arctic:
   p _____?_____
3. To become weak; to lose energy: l _____?_____

USING THE WORD BANK

On your paper, write the word or phrase whose meaning is closest to that of the first word.

1. enthralled: (a) fascinated, (b) stalled, (c) enjoyed
2. protruded: (a) intruded, (b) stuck out, (c) protected
3. console: (a) help, (b) comfort, (c) go alone
4. afflicted: (a) troubled, (b) calmed, (c) beat
5. vanity: (a) beauty, (b) large mirror, (c) excessive pride
6. anguish: (a) tears, (b) suffering, (c) anger

◆ Literary Focus

THE MORAL OF A STORY

Singer ends his tale with a **moral,** a guide for living, so that the story won't really end with the last printed word. He wants you to keep thinking about this moral and apply it to your own life. In this way, the true ending of the story is you.

To give the full statement of the moral, Singer uses a character who is more educated than the Skibas: the village priest.

1. In your own words, express the moral stated by the priest.
2. Explain how something in your own experience supports or goes against the moral in this story.

◆ Build Grammar Skills

NOUNS

Nouns are words that name a person, animal, place, thing, or idea. Without nouns, we couldn't use language to talk about the world. Singer needs and uses every kind of noun in his story:

Person peasant, daughter	**Thing** mirror, trinket
Animal cat, rabbit	**Idea** soul, rage
	Place village, city

Practice Find the nouns in these sentences and tell what kind of item they name.

1. The peasant had a dog and a cat in his hut.
2. The peddlers never came to the hut.
3. There was a mirror in his sack.
4. All day, the women looked into the mirror.
5. The family felt true distress.

Writing Application Answer the following questions in full sentences. Then, circle the nouns you've used.

1. What kind of home do the Skibas have?
2. Where is their farm located?
3. How does the mirror change life in the house?
4. Which animals use the mirror?
5. What happens to the mirror?

Build Your Portfolio

Idea Bank

Writing

1. **Product Warning** Mirror-makers have taken Singer's story to heart and are attaching a warning to their product. Write a warning they can place in the corner of every mirror.

2. **Advertisements** The Skibas have to sell their quarreling cat and dog. Write two ads for them: one to sell a cat that thinks it's a dog and the other to sell a dog that thinks it's a cat.

3. **Newspaper Article** As a reporter for the local village paper, write an article about the strange events at the Skibas' house. Begin with a lead, a paragraph telling readers *who, what, when, where,* and *how.* **[Career Link]**

Speaking and Listening

4. **Lecture** You're a village teacher who has heard about the Skibas' problems. Using the Skiba household as an example, deliver a lecture to your class on the dangers of vanity. **[Performing Arts Link]**

5. **Humorous Retelling** The peddler in Singer's tale had a funny story to tell his next customers. Retell the story as the peddler might have told it, adding humorous details. **[Performing Arts Link]**

Projects

6. **Report on Eastern Europe** **[Group Activity]** With several classmates, write a report on peasant life in Eastern Europe centuries ago. Divide the work so that one person gathers statistics, another finds out about day-to-day life, and a third weaves the report together. **[Social Studies Link]**

7. **Multimedia Report on Mirrors** Research fantastic facts about the history and uses of mirrors. For example, find out about convex mirrors and funhouse mirrors. Then, including materials like photographs, actual mirrors, diagrams, and video clips, create a presentation for the class. **[Media Link]**

Writing Mini-Lesson

Fable That Teaches a Lesson

Singer's story reads like a fable, a brief tale in which animal characters teach a lesson about life. Write such a fable yourself. Use Singer's cat and dog or other animal characters to teach a lesson, and have a character state the lesson at the end.

**Writing Skills Focus:
Correct Sequence of Events**

Your audience will be confused if they can't follow the **sequence of events.** To hold your audience and teach your lesson, you must tell what happened in the right order. For example, in this passage from his story, Singer uses words that clarify the sequence of events:

Model From the Story
But *one day* a peddler happened to stray there. *When* he came inside . . . *After a while,* Jan Skiba's wife, Marianna, made a proposition to the peddler. . . .

Prewriting Start by choosing the lesson you'll teach at the end of your fable. Then, think of the animal characters you'll use, and jot down the order of events.

Drafting Write the lesson first. Then, tell the events leading up to it, referring to your outline as you draft. Use time words to clarify the sequence of events—words like *after a while, when,* and *then.* Make your fable more than just an outline by having animal characters show silly human weaknesses.

Revising Read your fable to classmates. If they can't follow the events or don't seem amused, add time words to clarify the sequence or exaggerate actions to heighten the humor.

◆ **Grammar Application**
Be sure you've used a variety of kinds of nouns so that readers can picture the world you're describing.

PART 1　*Inventing Yourself*

Untitled, Jean-Francois Podevin

Guide for Reading

Meet the Author:

Amy Tan (1952–)

Amy Tan has struggled to find herself. The author grew up as the second-youngest child in a Chinese American family from California. As a youngster, Tan was pulled between mainstream American culture and the Chinese traditions that her mother kept alive.

Success, Experiments, Success Tan showed early signs of being a writer. At age eight, she published an essay entitled "What the Library Means to Me" in a local paper. However, she went to a number of different colleges and held a variety of jobs—from carhop to educational counselor—before achieving spectacular success with her first novel.

From Book to Movie That first novel, *The Joy Luck Club*, explores life in a Chinese American community. Nominated for a National Book Award, the novel also inspired a movie of the same title.

Finding Herself, Again Tan reports that she struggled with her fear of failure while writing her second novel, *The Kitchen God's Wife*. However, that book and her third, *The Hundred Secret Senses*, have been widely praised.

THE STORY BEHIND THE STORY

Amy Tan used details from her own life to create characters in "Two Kinds." Like the young woman in the story, Tan resisted her Chinese heritage when she was young.

◆ LITERATURE AND YOUR LIFE

CONNECT YOUR EXPERIENCE

You stand at the plate ready to hit a homer or at the microphone ready to dazzle the crowd. Most people love to star in their own daydreams of greatness. However, when you star in a dream that someone else has for you, you may feel divided in half, like the woman on the opposite page. This is the problem that a teenager faces in "Two Kinds."

THEMATIC FOCUS: Inventing Yourself

The mother of the young woman in "Two Kinds" has high hopes for her daughter. Notice what happens when the daughter tries to fulfill her mother's hopes.

◆ Background for Understanding

HISTORY

In 1949, the Communist party seized control of China, following years of civil war. Like the mother in this story, a number of Chinese, who feared the communists, fled to the United States. Many of them had lost everything except their hopes for a better future. They placed these hopes, a heavy but invisible burden, on the shoulders of the children born in the new land.

◆ Build Vocabulary

SUFFIXES: -ness

In "Two Kinds," the narrator describes a girl's "sauciness." *Sauciness* means "the quality of being lively." It combines the adjective *saucy* ("lively") with the suffix *-ness*, meaning "the quality or condition of."

WORD BANK

Which of these words from the story do you think are nouns? Check the Vocabulary Boxes to see if you are right.

prodigy
reproach
mesmerizing
sauciness
conspired
debut
devastated
fiasco

◆ Two Kinds ◆

◆ Literary Focus

CHARACTERS' MOTIVES

It's no accident that **motive** sounds like *motor*. Motives are the engines of personality—the emotions and goals that drive characters this way or that. Some powerful motives are love, anger, hope, and ambition. Acting together, emotional engines like these can sometimes spin characters around or set them on a collision course.

In "Two Kinds," the narrator explains and hints at the different motives that influence her and her mother. On a sheet of paper, keep track of these motives by filling in a chart like the one below.

◆ Reading Strategy

WORD IDENTIFICATION

Sometimes words can look like a secret code. However, by using simple methods of **word identification,** dividing words into syllables and recognizable word parts, you can break the code. The trick is to find something familiar in what at first looks unfamiliar.

In this story, two words that might trip you up are *uneven* and *instructor*. Run your finger over these words, breaking them into syllables and looking for familiar words:

- The first syllable of *uneven* is the prefix *un-*, followed by the word *even*.
- *Instructor* contains the word *instruct*.

Use this strategy to unlock the meaning of other unfamiliar words.

Portrait, Pamela Chin Lee, Courtesy of the artist

	Narrator	**Mother**
Passage from story:	"I was filled with a sense that I would soon become *perfect.* My mother and father would adore me."	"America was where all my mother's hopes lay. She had come here . . . after losing everything in China. . . ."
Motive:	**Need for** *love*	*Hope* **for a better future**
Passage from story: **Motive:**		
Passage from story: **Motive:**		

Two Kinds

from The Joy Luck Club

Amy Tan

My mother believed you could be anything you wanted to be in America. You could open a restaurant. You could work for the government and get good retirement. You could buy a house with almost no money down. You could become rich. You could become instantly famous.

"Of course you can be <u>prodigy</u>, too," my mother told me when I was nine. "You can be best anything. What does Auntie Lindo know? Her daughter, she is only best tricky."

America was where all my mother's hopes lay. She had come here in 1949 after losing everything in China: her mother and father, her family home, her first husband, and two daughters, twin baby girls. But she never looked back with regret. There were so many ways for things to get better.

We didn't immediately pick the right kind of prodigy. At first my mother thought I could be a Chinese Shirley Temple.[1] We'd watch Shirley's old movies on TV as though they were training films. My mother would poke my arm and say, "*Ni kan*"[2]—You watch. And I would see Shirley tapping her feet, or singing a sailor song, or pursing her lips into a very round O while saying, "Oh my goodness."

"*Ni kan*," said my mother as Shirley's eyes flooded with tears. "You already know how. Don't need talent for crying!"

Soon after my mother got this idea about Shirley Temple, she took me to a beauty training school in the Mission district[3] and put me in the hands of a student who could barely hold the scissors without shaking.

◆ Build Vocabulary

prodigy (präd´ ə jē) *n.*: Child of unusually high talent

◀ **Critical Viewing** San Francisco's Chinatown, seen here, uses both the English and Chinese languages. How might such a mix affect the narrator's sense of herself? **[Speculate]**

---

1. **Shirley Temple:** American child star of the 1930's, she starred in her first movie at age three and won an Academy Award at age six.
2. *Ni kan* (nē kän)
3. **Mission district:** Residential district in San Francisco, California.

Instead of getting big fat curls, I emerged with an uneven mass of crinkly black fuzz. My mother dragged me off to the bathroom and tried to wet down my hair.

"You look like Negro Chinese," she lamented, as if I had done this on purpose.

The instructor of the beauty training school had to lop off these soggy clumps to make my hair even again. "Peter Pan is very popular these days," the instructor assured my mother. I now had hair the length of a boy's, with straight-across bangs that hung at a slant two inches above my eyebrows. I liked the haircut and it made me actually look forward to my future fame.

In fact, in the beginning, I was just as excited as my mother, maybe even more so. I pictured this prodigy part of me as many different images, trying each one on for size. I was a dainty ballerina girl standing by the curtains, waiting to hear the right music that would send me floating on my tiptoes. I was like the Christ child lifted out of the straw manger, crying with holy indignity. I was Cinderella stepping from her pumpkin carriage with sparkly cartoon music filling the air.

In all of my imaginings, I was filled with a sense that I would soon become *perfect*. My mother and father would adore me. I would be beyond reproach. I would never feel the need to sulk for anything.

But sometimes the prodigy in me became impatient. "If you don't hurry up and get me out of here, I'm disappearing for good," it warned. "And then you'll always be nothing."

Every night after dinner, my mother and I would sit at the Formica kitchen table. She would present new tests, taking her examples from stories of amazing children she had read in *Ripley's Believe It or Not*, or *Good Housekeeping*, *Reader's Digest*, and a dozen other magazines she kept in a pile in our bathroom. My mother got these magazines from people whose houses she cleaned. And since she cleaned many houses each week, we had a great assortment. She would look through them all, searching for stories about remarkable children.

◆ **Reading Strategy**
What familiar word and common suffix can you find in the word *assortment*?

The first night she brought out a story about a three-year-old boy who knew the capitals of all the states and even most of the European countries. A teacher was quoted as saying the little boy could also pronounce the names of the foreign cities correctly.

"What's the capital of Finland?" my mother asked me, looking at the magazine story.

All I knew was the capital of California, because Sacramento was the name of the street we lived on in Chinatown. "Nairobi!"[4] I guessed, saying the most foreign word I could think of. She checked to see if that was possibly one way to pronounce "Helsinki"[5] before showing me the answer.

The tests got harder—multiplying numbers in my head, finding the queen of hearts in a deck of cards, trying to stand on my head without using my hands, predicting the daily temperatures in Los Angeles, New York, and London.

One night I had to look at a page from the Bible for three minutes and then report everything I could remember. "Now Jehoshaphat had riches and honor in abundance and . . . that's all I remember, Ma," I said.

And after seeing my mother's disappointed face once again, something inside of me began to die. I hated the tests, the raised hopes and failed expectations. Before going to bed that night, I looked in the mirror above the bathroom sink and when I saw only my face staring back—and that it would always be

---

◆ **Build Vocabulary**

reproach (ri prōch´) *n.*: Disgrace; blame

mesmerizing (mez´ mər īz´ iŋ) *adj.*: Hypnotizing

sauciness (sô´ sē nes) *n.*: Liveliness; boldness; spirit

---

4. **Nairobi** (nī rō´ bē): Capital of Kenya, a country in east central Africa.
5. **Helsinki** (hel siŋ´ kē)

this ordinary face—I began to cry. Such a sad, ugly girl! I made high-pitched noises like a crazed animal, trying to scratch out the face in the mirror.

And then I saw what seemed to be the prodigy side of me—because I had never seen that face before. I looked at my reflection, blinking so I could see more clearly. The girl staring back at me was angry, powerful. This girl and I were the same. I had new thoughts, willful thoughts, or rather thoughts filled with lots of won'ts. I won't let her change me, I promised myself. I won't be what I'm not.

So now on nights when my mother presented her tests, I performed listlessly, my head propped on one arm. I pretended to be bored. And I was. I got so bored I started counting the bellows of the foghorns out on the bay while my mother drilled me in other areas. The sound was comforting and reminded me of the cow jumping over the moon. And the next day, I played a game with myself, seeing if my mother would give up on me before eight bellows. After a while I usually counted only one, maybe two bellows at most. At last she was beginning to give up hope.

Two or three months had gone by without any mention of my being a prodigy again. And then one day my mother was watching *The Ed Sullivan Show* [6] on TV. The TV was old and the sound kept shorting out. Every time my mother got halfway up from the sofa to adjust the set, the sound would go back on and Ed would be talking. As soon as she sat down, Ed would go silent again. She got up, the TV broke into loud piano music. She sat down. Silence. Up and down, back and forth, quiet

Mandarin Square: Badge with peacock-insignia-3rd civil rank. China, 17th–20th century, Unknown artist, Yale University Art Gallery

▲ **Critical Viewing** Which characters in the story are best suggested by this peacock, a symbol of arrogance and pride? **[Connect]**

and loud. It was like a stiff embraceless dance between her and the TV set. Finally she stood by the set with her hand on the sound dial.

She seemed entranced by the music, a little frenzied piano piece with this <u>mesmerizing</u> quality, sort of quick passages and then teasing lilting ones before it returned to the quick playful parts.

"*Ni kan,*" my mother said, calling me over with hurried hand gestures. "Look here."

I could see why my mother was fascinated by the music. It was being pounded out by a little

◆ **Literature and Your Life**
Have you ever dreamed of being a television star? Explain.

Chinese girl, about nine years old, with a Peter Pan haircut. The girl had the <u>sauciness</u> of a Shirley Temple. She was proudly modest like a proper Chinese child. And she also did this fancy sweep of a curtsy, so that the fluffy

---

6. *The Ed Sullivan Show:* Popular variety show, hosted by Ed Sullivan, that ran from 1955 to 1971.

skirt of her white dress cascaded slowly to the floor like the petals of a large carnation.

In spite of these warning signs, I wasn't worried. Our family had no piano and we couldn't afford to buy one, let alone reams of sheet music and piano lessons. So I could be generous in my comments when my mother bad-mouthed the little girl on TV.

"Play note right, but doesn't sound good! No singing sound," complained my mother.

"What are you picking on her for?" I said carelessly. "She's pretty good. Maybe she's not the best, but she's trying hard." I knew almost immediately I would be sorry I said that.

"Just like you," she said. "Not the best. Because you not trying." She gave a little huff as she let go of the sound dial and sat down on the sofa.

The little Chinese girl sat down also to play an encore of "Anitra's Dance" by Grieg.[7] I remember the song, because later on I had to learn how to play it.

Three days after watching *The Ed Sullivan Show*, my mother told me what my schedule would be for piano lessons and piano practice. She had talked to Mr. Chong, who lived on the first floor of our apartment building. Mr. Chong was a retired piano teacher and my mother had traded housecleaning services for weekly lessons and a piano for me to practice on every day, two hours a day, from four until six.

When my mother told me this, I felt as though I had been sent to hell. I whined and then kicked my foot a little when I couldn't stand it anymore.

"Why don't you like me the way I am? I'm *not* a genius! I can't play the piano. And even if I could, I wouldn't go on TV if you paid me a million dollars!" I cried.

---

7. **Grieg** (grēg): Edvard Grieg (1843–1907), Norwegian composer.

▶ **Critical Viewing** What details in the photograph and the story tell you that the action takes place in an earlier time? [Infer]

My mother slapped me. "Who ask you be genius?" she shouted. "Only ask you be your best. For you sake. You think I want you be genius? Hnnh! What for! Who ask you!"

"So ungrateful," I heard her mutter in Chinese. "If she had as much talent as she has temper, she would be famous now."

Mr. Chong, whom I secretly nicknamed Old Chong, was very strange, always tapping his fingers to the silent music of an invisible orchestra. He looked ancient in my eyes. He had lost most of the hair on top of his head and he wore thick glasses and had eyes that always looked tired and sleepy. But he must have been younger than I thought, since he lived with his mother and was not yet married.

I met Old Lady Chong once and that was enough. She had this peculiar smell like a baby that had done something in its pants. And her fingers felt like a dead person's, like an old peach I once found in the back of the refrigerator; the skin just slid off the meat when I picked it up.

I soon found out why Old Chong had retired from teaching piano. He was deaf. "Like Beethoven!"[8] he shouted to me. "We're both listening only in our head!" And he would start to conduct his frantic silent sonatas.

Our lessons went like this. He would open the book and point to different things, explaining their purpose: "Key! Treble! Bass! No sharps or flats! So this is C major! Listen now and play after me!"

And then he would play the C scale a few times, a simple chord, and then, as if inspired by an old, unreachable itch, he gradually added more notes and running trills and a pounding bass until the music was really something quite grand.

I would play after him, the simple scale, the simple chord, and then I just played some nonsense that sounded like a cat running up and down on top of garbage cans.

---

8. **Beethoven** (bā′ tō′ vən): Ludwig van Beethoven (1770–1827), German composer who began to lose his hearing in 1801. By 1817 he was completely deaf. Some of his greatest pieces were written when he was deaf.

Chinese Girl Under Lanterns, Winson Trang

▲ **Critical Viewing** How does the contrast between the modern and the traditional in this painting reflect the title of Tan's story? [**Connect**]

Old Chong smiled and applauded and then said, "Very good! But now you must learn to keep time!"

So that's how I discovered that Old Chong's eyes were too slow to keep up with the wrong notes I was playing. He went through the motions in half-time. To help me keep rhythm, he stood behind me, pushing down on my right shoulder for every beat. He balanced pennies on top of my wrists so I would keep them still as I slowly played scales and arpeggios.[9] He had me curve my hand around an apple and keep that shape when playing chords. He marched stiffly to show me how

to make each finger dance up and down, staccato[10] like an obedient little soldier.

He taught me all these things, and that was how I also learned I could be lazy and get away with mistakes, lots of mistakes. If I hit the wrong notes because I hadn't practiced enough, I never corrected myself. I just kept playing in rhythm. And Old Chong kept conducting his own private reverie.

So maybe I never really gave myself a fair chance. I did pick up the basics pretty quickly, and I might have become a good pianist at that young age. But I was so determined not to try, not to be anybody different that I

---

9. arpeggios (är pej´ ē ōz) *n.*: Notes in a chord played in quick succession instead of at the same time.

10. staccato (stə kät´ ō) *adv.*: Played crisply, with distinct breaks between notes.

learned to play only the most ear-splitting preludes, the most discordant hymns.

Over the next year, I practiced like this, dutifully in my own way. And then one day I heard my mother and her friend Lindo Jong both talking in a loud bragging tone of voice so others could hear. It was after church, and I was leaning against the brick wall wearing a dress with stiff white petticoats. Auntie Lindo's daughter, Waverly, who was about my age, was standing farther down the wall about five feet away. We had grown up together and shared all the closeness of two sisters squabbling over crayons and dolls. In other words, for the most part, we hated each other. I thought she was snotty. Waverly Jong had gained a certain amount of fame as "Chinatown's Littlest Chinese Chess Champion."

"She bring home too many trophy," lamented Auntie Lindo that Sunday. "All day she play chess. All day I have no time do nothing but dust off her winnings." She threw a scolding look at Waverly, who pretended not to see her.

> ◆ Literary Focus
> What motivates the mother to brag about her daughter?

"You lucky you don't have this problem," said Auntie Lindo with a sigh to my mother.

And my mother squared her shoulders and bragged: "Our problem worser than yours. If we ask Jing-mei wash dish, she hear nothing but music. It's like you can't stop this natural talent."

And right then, I was determined to put a stop to her foolish pride.

A few weeks later, Old Chong and my mother conspired to have me play in a talent show which would be held in the church hall. By then, my parents had saved up enough to buy me a secondhand piano, a black Wurlitzer spinet[11] with a scarred bench. It was the showpiece of our living room.

For the talent show, I was to play a piece

---

11. **spinet** (spin´ it) *n.*: Small, upright piano.

---

called "Pleading Child" from Schumann's[12] *Scenes from Childhood*. It was a simple, moody piece that sounded more difficult than it was. I was supposed to memorize the whole thing, playing the repeat parts twice to make the piece sound longer. But I dawdled over it, playing a few bars and then cheating, looking up to see what notes followed. I never really listened to what I was playing. I daydreamed about being somewhere else, about being someone else.

The part I liked to practice best was the fancy curtsy: right foot out, touch the rose on the carpet with a pointed foot, sweep to the side, left leg bends, look up and smile.

My parents invited all the couples from the Joy Luck Club[13] to witness my debut. Auntie Lindo and Uncle Tin were there. Waverly and her two older brothers had also come. The first two rows were filled with children both younger and older than I was. The littlest ones got to go first. They recited simple nursery rhymes, squawked out tunes on miniature violins, twirled Hula Hoops, pranced in pink ballet tutus, and when they bowed or curtsied, the audience would sigh in unison, "Awww," and then clap enthusiastically.

When my turn came, I was very confident. I remember my childish excitement. It was as if I knew, without a doubt, that the prodigy side of me really did exist. I had no fear whatsoever, no nervousness. I remember thinking to myself, This is it! This is it! I looked out over the audience, at my mother's blank face, my father's yawn, Auntie Lindo's stiff-lipped smile, Waverly's sulky expression. I had on a white dress layered with sheets of lace, and a pink bow in my Peter Pan haircut. As I sat down I

---

12. **Schumann** (shoo´ män): Robert Alexander Schumann (1810–1856), German composer.
13. **Joy Luck Club:** Four Chinese women who have been meeting for years to socialize, play games, and tell stories from the past.

◆ Build Vocabulary

conspired (kən spīrd´) *v.*: Planned together secretly

debut (dā byoo´) *n.*: First performance in public

◆ **Reading Strategy**

Break the word *envisioned* into syllables. What familiar word is hidden inside?

envisioned people jumping to their feet and Ed Sullivan rushing up to introduce me to everyone on TV.

And I started to play. It was so beautiful. I was so caught up in how lovely I looked that at first I didn't worry how I would sound. So it was a surprise to me when I hit the first wrong note and I realized something didn't sound quite right. And then I hit another and another followed that. A chill started at the top of my head and began to trickle down. Yet I couldn't stop playing, as though my hands were bewitched. I kept thinking my fingers would adjust themselves back, like a train switching to the right track. I played this strange jumble through two repeats, the sour notes staying with me all the way to the end.

When I stood up, I discovered my legs were shaking. Maybe I had just been nervous and the audience, like Old Chong, had seen me go through the right motions and had not heard anything wrong at all. I swept my right foot out, went down on my knee, looked up and smiled. The room was quiet, except for Old Chong, who was beaming and shouting, "Bravo! Bravo! Well done!" But then I saw my mother's face, her stricken face. The audience clapped weakly, and as I walked back to my chair, with my whole face quivering as I tried not to cry, I heard a little boy whisper loudly to his mother, "That was awful," and the mother whispered back, "Well, she certainly tried."

And now I realized how many people were in the audience, the whole world it seemed. I was aware of eyes burning into my back. I felt the shame of my mother and father as they sat stiffly throughout the rest of the show.

We could have escaped during intermission. Pride and some strange sense of honor must have anchored my parents to their chairs. And so we watched it all: the eighteen-year-old boy with a fake mustache who did a magic show and juggled flaming hoops while riding a unicycle. The breasted girl with white makeup who sang from *Madama Butterfly* and got honorable mention. And the eleven-year-old boy who won first prize playing a tricky violin song that sounded like a busy bee.

After the show, the Hsus, the Jongs, and the St. Clairs from the Joy Luck Club came up to my mother and father.

"Lots of talented kids," Auntie Lindo said vaguely, smiling broadly.

"That was somethin' else," said my father, and I wondered if he was referring to me in a humorous way, or whether he even remembered what I had done.

Waverly looked at me and shrugged her shoulders. "You aren't a genius like me," she said matter-of-factly. And if I hadn't felt so bad, I would have pulled her braids and punched her stomach.

But my mother's expression was what devastated me: a quiet, blank look that said she had lost everything. I felt the same way, and it seemed as if everybody were now coming up, like gawkers at the scene of an accident, to see what parts were actually missing. When we got on the bus to go home, my father was humming the busy-bee tune and my mother was silent. I kept thinking she wanted to wait until we got home before shouting at me. But when my father unlocked the door to our apartment, my mother walked in and then went to the back, into the bedroom. No accusations. No blame. And in a way, I felt disappointed. I had been waiting for her to start shouting, so I could shout back and cry and blame her for all my misery.

I assumed my talent-show fiasco meant I never had to play the piano again. But two days later, after school, my mother came out of the kitchen and saw me watching TV.

"Four clock," she reminded me as if it were any other day. I was stunned, as though she were asking me to go through the talent-show torture again. I wedged myself more tightly in front of the TV.

"Turn off TV," she called from the kitchen five minutes later.

I didn't budge. And then I decided. I didn't have to do what my mother said anymore. I wasn't her slave. This wasn't China. I had listened to her before and look what happened. She was the stupid one.

She came out from the kitchen and stood in the arched entryway of the living room. "Four clock," she said once again, louder.

"I'm not going to play anymore," I said nonchalantly. "Why should I? I'm not a genius."

She walked over and stood in front of the TV. I saw her chest was heaving up and down in an angry way.

◆ **Literary Focus**
What word in this paragraph gives you a clue to the mother's motive?

"No!" I said, and I now felt stronger, as if my true self had finally emerged. So this was what had been inside me all along.

"No! I won't!" I screamed.

She yanked me by the arm, pulled me off the floor, snapped off the TV. She was frighteningly strong, half pulling, half carrying me toward the piano as I kicked the throw rugs under my feet. She lifted me up and onto the hard bench. I was sobbing by now, looking at her bitterly. Her chest was heaving even more and her mouth was open, smiling crazily as if she were pleased I was crying.

"You want me to be someone that I'm not!" I sobbed. "I'll never be the kind of daughter you want me to be!"

"Only two kinds of daughters," she shouted in Chinese. "Those who are obedient and those who follow their own mind! Only one kind of daughter can live in this house. Obedient daughter!"

"Then I wish I wasn't your daughter. I wish you weren't my mother," I shouted. As I said these things I got scared. It felt like worms and toads and slimy things crawling out of my chest, but it also felt good, as if this awful

Portrait, Pamela Chin Lee, Courtesy of the artist

▲ **Critical Viewing** Do you think this image accurately portrays the "two kinds" of daughters the mother describes? [Evaluate]

side of me had surfaced, at last.

"Too late change this," said my mother shrilly.

And I could sense her anger rising to its breaking point. I wanted to see it spill over. And that's when I remembered the babies she

◆ **Build Vocabulary**

devastated (dev´ ə stā tid) *v.:* Destroyed; completely upset

fiasco (fē as´ cō) *n.:* Complete failure

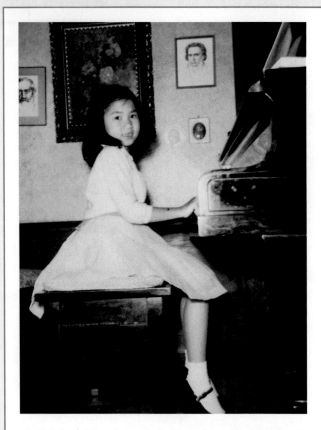

▲ Critical Viewing How does this photograph of the author compare with the story's narrator? [Compare and Contrast]

had lost in China, the ones we never talked about. "Then I wish I'd never been born!" I shouted. "I wish I were dead! Like them."

It was as if I had said the magic words. Alakazam!—and her face went blank, her mouth closed, her arms went slack, and she backed out of the room, stunned, as if she were blowing away like a small brown leaf, thin, brittle, lifeless.

It was not the only disappointment my mother felt in me. In the years that followed, I failed her so many times, each time asserting my own will, my right to fall short of expectations. I didn't get straight A's. I didn't become class president. I didn't get into Stanford. I dropped out of college.

For unlike my mother, I did not believe I could be anything I wanted to be. I could only be me.

And for all those years, we never talked

about the disaster at the recital or my terrible accusations afterward at the piano bench. All that remained unchecked, like a betrayal that was now unspeakable. So I never found a way to ask her why she had hoped for something so large that failure was inevitable.

And even worse, I never asked her what frightened me the most: Why had she given up hope?

For after our struggle at the piano, she never mentioned my playing again. The lessons stopped. The lid to the piano was closed, shutting out the dust, my misery, and her dreams.

So she surprised me. A few years ago, she offered to give me the piano, for my thirtieth birthday. I had not played in all those years. I saw the offer as a sign of forgiveness, a tremendous burden removed.

◆ Literary Focus
What is the mother's motive in offering the piano?

"Are you sure?" I asked shyly. "I mean, won't you and Dad miss it?"

"No, this your piano," she said firmly. "Always your piano. You only one can play."

"Well, I probably can't play anymore," I said. "It's been years."

"You pick up fast," said my mother, as if she knew this was certain. "You have natural talent. You could been genius if you want to."

"No I couldn't."

"You just not trying," said my mother. And she was neither angry nor sad. She said it as if to announce a fact that could never be disproved. "Take it," she said.

But I didn't at first. It was enough that she had offered it to me. And after that, every time I saw it in my parents' living room, standing in front of the bay windows, it made me feel proud, as if it were a shiny trophy I had won back.

Last week I sent a tuner over to my parents' apartment and had the piano reconditioned, for purely sentimental reasons. My mother had died a few months before and I had been getting things in order for my father, a little bit at a time. I put the jewelry in special silk pouches. The sweaters she had knitted in yellow, pink, bright orange—all the colors I hated—I put those in moth-proof boxes. I found some old Chinese silk dresses, the kind with little slits up the sides. I rubbed the old silk against my skin, then wrapped them in tissue and decided to take them home with me.

After I had the piano tuned, I opened the lid and touched the keys. It sounded even richer than I remembered. Really, it was a very good piano. Inside the bench were the same exercise notes with handwritten scales, the same secondhand music books with their covers held together with yellow tape.

I opened up the Schumann book to the dark little piece I had played at the recital. It was on the left-hand side of the page, "Pleading Child." It looked more difficult than I remembered. I played a few bars, surprised at how easily the notes came back to me.

And for the first time, or so it seemed, I noticed the piece on the right-hand side. It was called "Perfectly Contented." I tried to play this one as well. It had a lighter melody but the same flowing rhythm and turned out to be quite easy. "Pleading Child" was shorter but slower; "Perfectly Contented" was longer, but faster. And after I played them both a few times, I realized they were two halves of the same song.

Guide for Responding

◆ LITERATURE AND YOUR LIFE

Reader's Response What advice would you have given the mother and daughter?

Thematic Focus In what ways can parents' hopes and expectations *help* children to create their own identities?

Gift Exchange With several classmates, choose presents for the mother and grown-up daughter to exchange in order to restore harmony.

☑ Check Your Comprehension

1. List the ways in which the mother tries to make her daughter into a prodigy.
2. Describe what happens at the talent show.
3. After the show, what occurs when the mother forces the daughter to practice?
4. How does the mother surprise the daughter years later?
5. What does the daughter finally discover about the piano piece she had played at the recital?

◆ Critical Thinking

INTERPRET

1. What do the daughter's failures on the nightly tests reveal about her abilities? **[Infer]**
2. Compare and contrast the daughter's use of the word *prodigy* with her mother's. **[Compare and Contrast]**
3. In the argument after the recital, why do the daughter's final words have such a powerful effect on her mother? **[Analyze]**
4. What have the mother and daughter learned from their conflict? **[Draw Conclusions]**

EVALUATE

5. Do you agree with the daughter's statement that people can't be anything they want to be? Why or why not? **[Criticize]**

EXTEND

6. What does this story suggest about differences between some immigrant parents and their American-born children? **[Social Studies Link]**

◆ Reading Strategy

APPLY WORD IDENTIFICATION STRATEGIES

Some words in this story may seem odd until you use **word identification** to break them into syllables and familiar word parts. The word *expectation,* for example, might look too big for anyone's good. Inside it, however, you'll find the two-syllable word *expect* combined with the word ending *-ation.* You can guess that *expectation* means "the action of expecting or waiting for something."

Explain how word identification can help you make sense of these words from the story:

1. assortment   3. applauded
2. crazed   4. embraceless

◆ Build Vocabulary

USING THE SUFFIX *-ness*

Use the suffix *-ness* to change the adjectives describing each character into the qualities that each character possesses:

1. Mother: stubborn; hopeful
2. Daughter: rebellious; saucy; sad

SPELLING STRATEGY

If the final *y* in a word is preceded by a consonant, change the *y* to *i* when adding a suffix like *-ness:* saucy + -ness = sauciness. Write the following words correctly.

1. happy + -ness   3. filthy + -ness
2. messy + -ness   4. silly + -ness

USING THE WORD BANK

Replace each italicized word or phrase with the word from the Word Bank that has the same meaning.

The *child genius* sat down at the piano for her *first appearance* on stage. Her *hypnotic* performance was beyond *blame,* and her *boldness* won her admirers. The clarinetist sensed that his own efforts were a *failure.* Everything and everyone had *plotted* against him, and he felt *destroyed.*

◆ Literary Focus

CHARACTERS' MOTIVES

In this story, the **characters' motives**—the reasons for their actions—power them into a head-on collision. The daughter reveals some of her motives directly. Looking in the mirror, she sees the anger she feels toward her mother. She also reveals her mother's motives, especially when describing what her mother lost in China and hopes for in America.

1. How do Chinese losses and American hopes explain why the mother pressures her daughter?
2. Why is the daughter careless when she practices at the piano?
3. Why does the daughter no longer wish to please her mother after the recital?

◆ Build Grammar Skills

COMMON AND PROPER NOUNS

This story contains **common nouns,** which name people, places, things, and ideas in general, and **proper nouns,** which refer to specific people, places, things, and ideas. As this sentence indicates, common nouns are not capitalized, but proper nouns are:

      proper   common
   Sacramento was the *name* of
   common   proper
the *street* we lived on in *Chinatown.*

Practice On your paper, identify common and proper nouns in these sentences.

1. She said that she couldn't play the piano.
2. The name of her teacher was Mr. Chong.
3. At the recital, she played a piece by Schumann.
4. Her mother competed with Auntie Lindo, whose daughter played chess.
5. Because they weren't living in China, she felt that she didn't have to do what her mother said.

Writing Application Rewrite these sentences, replacing the proper nouns with common nouns.

1. I met Old Lady Chong once in the Mission district and that was enough.
2. Auntie Lindo and Uncle Tin were there.

Build Your Portfolio

 Idea Bank

Writing

1. **Job Description** Briefly describe what the mother believes a prodigy should be able to do. Write your descriptions under these words: *Wanted! A Prodigy Who Can . . .*

2. **Music Review** Using details provided in the story, write a review of the daughter's performance at the recital. Imagine you are writing the review for a local newspaper. **[Career Link]**

3. **Prequel** Write an episode that comes before the events of this story. Briefly describe the mother's experiences in fleeing China. Base your account on details from the story's third paragraph and on your own imagination.

Speaking and Listening

4. **Counseling Conference [Group Activity]** Role-play a meeting of the daughter, the mother, and a guidance counselor. Have the mother and daughter express their disagreements, and have the counselor try to resolve them. **[Health Link]**

5. **Monologue** The daughter in the story has a moment alone in the bathroom after failing her mother's tests. Perform the speech that she might give as she looks at her face in the mirror. **[Performing Arts Link]**

Projects

6. **Television Soundtrack** You're producing a teleplay based on "Two Kinds." Choose two musical themes for the soundtrack—one for the daughter and one for the mother. Record your choices, and play them for the class. **[Music Link; Media Link]**

7. **Report on Chinese Customs** Use encyclopedias and books on China to learn what the Chinese believe about raising children. Write a report that will help students understand why the mother in the story insists on obedience. **[Social Studies Link]**

 Writing Mini-Lesson

Mother's Diary Entry

You may feel closer to the daughter in this story than to the mother. However, stretch your imagination by looking at events through the mother's eyes. Choose an episode and write a diary entry about it as if you were the mother. Assume that the mother writes English well.

Writing Skills Focus: Elaborate to Add Emotional Depth

In writing diary entries and remembrances, it's important to reveal emotions. **Elaborate** to add emotional depth by stating how you feel about people and events. Also, use words that convey strong feelings, like *frenzied* rather than *hurried*. Notice how Amy Tan uses statements of emotion and emotional words in this passage:

Model From the Story

I began to cry. Such a sad, ugly girl! I made high-pitched noises like a crazed animal, trying to scratch out the face in the mirror.

Prewriting Choose an event that prompted strong feelings in the mother. Then, recall her experiences in China and her goals for her daughter. Keeping these in mind, jot down words that reflect the mother's feelings about the event.

Drafting As the mother, describe what happened. Elaborate on your factual account by stating how you feel about your daughter's behavior and including emotional words from your Prewriting list.

◆ **Grammar Application**
Use proper nouns that give a Chinese flavor to the diary entry.

Revising Have a classmate read the entry to see whether it is true to the mother's character and expresses strong feelings. If your entry is emotionally boring, replace flat words like *unpleasant* with crackling words like *hateful*.

Guide for Reading

Meet the Authors:

Walt Whitman (1819–1892)

There are two Walt Whitmans, related but different. One is a real person, and the other is the self he invented. The real Whitman grew up in Brooklyn, New York, and tried many jobs—from teaching to news reporting. During the Civil War, he traveled to Washington, D.C., to nurse his wounded brother and stayed to help other wounded soldiers.

All this time, the real Whitman was inventing a character based on himself. This character first appears in "Song of Myself." Striding out from the poem's free-flowing lines, the invented Whitman is confident and larger than life. [For more information on Whitman, see page 258.]

Emily Dickinson (1830–1886)

Walt Whitman traveled around, but Emily Dickinson hardly ever ventured outside Amherst, Massachusetts, where she was born. Quietly, however, she was writing the 1,775 poems that would make her famous after her death. In these brief lyrics, she created a poetic self that flashes with humor and intelligence.

Walter de la Mare (1873–1956)

While still a teenager, Walter de la Mare began working on statistics in a London office. Numbers were part of his daily life. By night, however, he escaped into the world of his imagination, writing poems for adults and children. In the poem "Me," De la Mare writes about the mystery of being one of a kind, not a statistic.

◆ Literature and Your Life

Connect Your Experience

Standing alone, like the man in the photograph on the opposite page, you may feel like a small part of a large world. With friends, you may feel just the right size, an important member of the group. When you look at objects under a microscope, you may suddenly feel like a giant. These poets explore what it means to be unique—whether you're feeling large or small.

Thematic Focus: Inventing Yourself

As you read these poems, think about the self that is you. How much of it did you create?

◆ Background for Understanding

Literature

Just as each individual creates a special self, every country creates a unique set of literary works. Walt Whitman and Emily Dickinson both contributed to the special character of American literature. Whitman used free verse, poems without regular rhythms to capture the American spirit. Dickinson gave American poetry the gift of looking inward.

◆ Build Vocabulary

Related Words: Forms of equal

In math, equal quantities are "the same as each other." Whitman also uses the word equal to mean "the same" when he says "with equal cheerfulness I can wait." A related form of this word is unequal, meaning "not the same."

Word Bank

Look over these words from the poems. Describe a place where you might loaf. Check the Build Vocabulary box on page 30 to see if loafing is something you really can do in the place you described.

assume
loaf
content
equal
banish
bog
forlorn

◆ Song of Myself ◆ I'm Nobody ◆ Me ◆

◆ Literary Focus

THE SPEAKER IN POETRY

Starting to read a poem is like answering a telephone call. Suddenly you "hear" a voice saying the words of the poem—the voice of the **speaker.** This speaker might be the poet or a character that the poet has created.

In these poems, the poets seem to be speaking as themselves. Listen to the words they stress and the rhythms of their speech, just as you would listen to an unknown voice on the telephone. These clues will help you understand who the speakers are and what they are telling you.

◆ Reading Strategy

READ POETRY ACCORDING TO PUNCTUATION

By **reading according to punctuation,** pausing with commas and stopping with end marks, you'll hear a human voice in a poem. Otherwise, the speaker will sound like a weird computer voice, halting along.

In reading each poem, pause at commas, ellipsis marks (three dots), and dashes. Stop longer at end marks, making questions sound like questions and stressing statements that end with exclamation points. Don't stop at the ends of lines if there is no punctuation. Create a reading copy of each poem with notes like these:

Stress first statement.   Read as question.
Full pause. ⟍   Full pause. ⟋

I'm nobody! Who are you?

from Song of Myself
Walt Whitman

I celebrate myself,
And what I <u>assume</u> you shall assume,
For every atom belonging to me as good belongs to you.

I <u>loaf</u> and invite my soul,
5   I lean and loaf at my ease . . . . observing a spear of summer grass.

                    *   *   *

I exist as I am, that is enough,
If no other in the world be aware I sit <u>content</u>,
And if each and all be aware I sit content.

One world is aware, and by far the largest to me, and that is myself,
10   And whether I come to my own today or in ten thousand or ten million years,
I can cheerfully take it now, or with <u>equal</u> cheerfulness I can wait.

◆ Build Vocabulary

assume (ə sōōm´) *v.*: Believe to be a fact

loaf (lōf) *v.*: Spend time idly

content (kən tent´) *adj.*: Happy enough

equal (ē´ kwəl) *adj.*: Of the same amount

banish (ban´ ish) *v.*: Send away; exile

bog (bäg) *n.*: Small marsh or swamp

I'm Nobody

Emily Dickinson

I'm Nobody! Who are you?
Are you—Nobody—too?
Then there's a pair of us!
Don't tell! they'd <u>banish</u> us—you know!

5   How dreary—to be—Somebody!
How public—like a Frog—
To tell your name—the livelong June—
To an admiring <u>Bog</u>!

Guide for Responding

◆ LITERATURE AND YOUR LIFE

Reader's Response Which of these poets would make a better companion on a hike? At a school basketball game? Explain.

Thematic Focus What is unusual or surprising about the selves that these poets present?

Sketch Make a quick line drawing of Whitman loafing or of a secret meeting between two Nobodies.

☑ Check Your Comprehension

1. Describe three things Whitman does in the first five lines of "Song of Myself."
2. What fact is "enough" for Whitman?
3. What does Dickinson ask and tell the reader in the first stanza of "I'm Nobody"?
4. In "I'm Nobody," how do Somebodies behave like frogs?

◆ Critical Thinking

INTERPRET

1. How can Whitman's loafing be a celebration of himself? **[Infer]**
2. What advice about living is Whitman passing on to readers? **[Draw Conclusions]**
3. Name three traits that Dickinson's Somebodies share, and explain your choices. **[Deduce]**
4. For Dickinson, what two key differences make Nobodies better than Somebodies? Explain. **[Draw Conclusions]**

EVALUATE

5. Do you agree with Dickinson that it's better to be Nobody than Somebody? Explain. **[Criticize]**

COMPARE LITERARY WORKS

6. In what ways do both of these poets create a special bond with the reader? **[Connect]**

Me

Walter de la Mare

As long as I live
I shall always be
My Self—and no other,
Just me.

5   Like a tree.

Like a willow or elder,
An aspen, a thorn,
Or a cypress[1] forlorn.

Like a flower,
10   For its hour
A primrose, a pink,
Or a violet—
Sunned by the sun,
And with dewdrops wet.

15   Always just me.

---

1. **cypress** (sī′ prəs) *n.*: Evergreen, cone-bearing tree whose branches or sprigs are used as a symbol of grief or mourning.

◆ **Build Vocabulary**

forlorn (fôr lôrn′) *adj.*: Alone and miserable

Beyond Literature

Science Connection

Nature's One-of-a-Kind Creations

In "Me," De la Mare compares his own uniqueness to that of various trees and flowers. Did you know that for every kind of tree and flower, there may be dozens—or even hundreds—of unique variations? Botanists are scientists who study and classify plants according to their characteristics. For most of us, a rose is a rose, but for botanists, there are actually hundreds of different types of roses—each one unlike every other one.

Cross-Curricular Activity

Classifying Plants Choose a plant, and do research to find out how many variations of it exist. Visit a local nursery or consult Internet and library resources. Then, use your findings to create an illustrated chart that shows your plant and the characteristics botanists use to classify it. Post your chart in the classroom or the school library.

Guide for Responding

◆ LITERATURE AND YOUR LIFE

Reader's Response Would you like to meet the speaker of this poem? What do you think he or she would be like?

Thematic Focus Does De la Mare give you the feeling that people are able to create their own identities? Why or why not?

Comparison Game With a group of classmates, take turns writing sentences that compare people to trees, flowers, or animals. Each person should complete the statement "I am most like a ..." and then explain the comparison. Be original in your responses.

☑ Check Your Comprehension

1. What will the poet be as long as he lives?
2. To what trees and flowers does he compare himself?

◆ Critical Thinking

INTERPRET
1. What is similar about the things to which De la Mare compares himself? **[Connect]**
2. How is the message of "Me" both comforting and limiting? **[Draw Conclusions]**

EVALUATE
3. Is "Me" successful in suggesting the mystery of being a "Self"? Explain. **[Criticize]**

EXTEND
4. In what way is a person in society "Just me" and more than "Just me"? **[Social Studies Link]**

Guide for Responding (continued)

◆ Reading Strategy

READ POETRY ACCORDING TO PUNCTUATION

You heard the human voices in these poems by **reading poetry according to punctuation,** pausing briefly at commas and longer at end marks. You didn't make the voices sound stiff by pausing at the ends of lines where there was no punctuation.

1. In the last three lines of "Song of Myself," find six places where you should pause.
2. Which place requires the longest pause? Why?
3. How many brief pauses are there in lines 5–8 of "I'm Nobody"? How many longer pauses?
4. Where is the first brief pause in "Me"?

◆ Build Vocabulary

USING FORMS OF *equal*

Equal means "the same as," but related forms of the word express this sameness in different ways. Using each word only once, choose the form of *equal* that fits best in each blank.

    unequal   equals   equality

Because poetry is so personal, one poet never exactly ___?___ another. Also, poets are ___?___ in their achievements. However, these three poets, like all fine writers, display an ___?___ of spirit.

SPELLING STRATEGY

The *kw* sound following the *e* in *equal* is spelled *qu.* Fill in the blanks with a suitable word containing the *qu* spelling of the *kw* sound:

1. Often Dickinson's poems ask ___?___ that are hard to answer.
2. Living many years ago, Whitman and Dickinson probably wrote with a ___?___ and ink.

USING THE WORD BANK

On your paper, match each word in the first column with the word that is closest in meaning to it in the second column.

1.	assume	a.	identical
2.	loaf	b.	sad
3.	equal	c.	suppose
4.	bog	d.	swamp
5.	forlorn	e.	relax
6.	banish	f.	remove

◆ Literary Focus

THE SPEAKER IN POETRY

The **speaker** is the voice or character who narrates a poem. The speakers of these poems reveal themselves in the words and rhythms they use. De la Mare, for example, repeats the phrase "just me" and uses lines that are very brief. These clues suggest that the speaker feels both special and small.

1. In "Song of Myself," what do the long lines and long sentences indicate about the speaker?
2. In "I'm Nobody," how does the speaker stress words in a humorous way to show that Nobodies are special but Somebodies are not?

◆ Build Grammar Skills

GENERAL AND SPECIFIC NOUNS

In using nouns to refer to people, places, or things, imagine that you're operating a movie camera. A **general noun,** like *tree,* is a wide-angle shot that takes in a group of related items. There are many kinds of trees in the group. A **specific noun,** like *oak,* is a close-up shot of a single item. An oak is one type of tree.

Notice how De la Mare follows a wide-angle shot (general noun) with a series of quick close-ups (specific nouns):

Like a tree.

Like a willow or elder,
An aspen, a thorn,
Or a cypress forlorn.

Practice On your paper, indicate whether each italicized noun is general or specific.

1. De la Mare compares human life to that of a *flower.*
2. The poet doesn't mention a *daisy.*
3. For Dickinson, a Somebody is like a *frog.*
4. Whitman writes about many types of *vehicles.*
5. For Whitman, each *person* was special.

Writing Application On your paper, fill in a plural general noun in the first blank and three specific nouns in the following blanks: Three examples of ___?___ are a ___?___, a ___?___, and a ___?___ .

Build Your Portfolio

 Idea Bank

Writing

1. **Rules for a Club** Dickinson's poem "I'm Nobody" reads like an invitation to a club. Write the rules for a Happy-to-Be-Nobody Club. Include entrance requirements and procedures for meetings.

2. **Plan for a Celebration** Your school is honoring Whitman with a Self-Celebration Day. Write the plan for a day on which all students can express and celebrate what makes them special.

3. **Comparison and Contrast** In an essay, compare two of these poems, focusing on their ideas about a person's self. For example, what elements are similar and different about Dickinson's "Nobody" and De la Mare's "just me"?

Speaking and Listening

4. **Telephone Conversation** With a partner, improvise a phone conversation between any two of these poets. Make the poets sound as they do in their poems. **[Performing Arts Link]**

5. **Three-Way Poetry Contest** Stage a competition among these poets as they read from their work. A panel can rate the performances based on the quality of the poems and the drama of the presentation. **[Performing Arts Link]**

Projects

6. **Multimedia Presentation** Dramatize the life of Whitman or Dickinson in a multimedia presentation. Research the poet's life, gathering film clips, slides, photographs, and books. Then, weave these materials into a script and present it to the class. **[Media Link]**

7. **Science Fair [Group Activity]** What do scientists think is special about each person? Stage a fair to answer this question. One student can demonstrate fingerprinting, and others can present information on genes and DNA. **[Science Link]**

 Writing Mini-Lesson

Personal Creed

Each of these poems is a kind of personal creed, a statement of the poet's deepest beliefs. In prose, write your own personal creed. Think of it as a statement of your beliefs that could appear under your photograph in a school yearbook. It will tell your classmates and teachers about the ideas and loyalties that guide your life.

Writing Skills Focus: Using Connotations

Because your creed will express deep feelings, you must focus on the **connotations** of words—the emotions and ideas they stir up. Even when two words have the same dictionary meaning, they often have different connotations. For example, *to celebrate* sounds grander and more festive than *to honor* in the following:

Model From the Poem
I celebrate myself,
And what I assume you shall assume . . .

Prewriting Write "I believe _____" several times on a sheet of paper and fill in the blanks with words and phrases. Then, substitute words with similar dictionary meanings and different connotations to see which ones you prefer.

Drafting Imagine that you're answering a close friend who has just asked, "What do you believe in?" Refer to your prewriting notes for key words and phrases.

> ◆ **Grammar Application**
> Where possible, replace general nouns like *relative* with specific nouns that have more feeling, like *father* or *mother*.

Revising Have classmates look over your creed and describe the feelings that key words stir up in them. If a word's connotations aren't right for your purpose, replace the word with a synonym.

Guide for Reading

Meet the Author:

Alex Haley (1921–1992)

Alex Haley grew up in Tennessee and Alabama. As a teenager, he wanted to see more of the world, so he joined the Coast Guard. It was while aboard ships, lying in his bunk at night, that he started to imagine and write sea adventure stories.

A Writer on His Own After twenty years with the Coast Guard, Haley retired to begin a full-time career as a writer. He wrote several books, but his best-known work is *Roots: The Saga of an American Family.* "My Furthest-Back Person" explains how he began this book.

A Television Mini-Series Haley's *Roots* tells about the history of his family in Africa and the United States. An immediate bestseller, it led to a television mini-series that was viewed by 130 million people. The book and the mini-series inspired many people to research their own family histories.

THE STORY BEHIND THE ESSAY

As a boy in Tennessee, Haley would sit on the porch, listening to his grandmother and great aunts tell stories about the family's "furthest-back person." These stories prompted him to find out more about the mysterious African named "Kin-tay."

◆ LITERATURE AND YOUR LIFE

CONNECT YOUR EXPERIENCE

Photographs, family stories, and heirlooms such as the quilt on the facing page can help people re-create their family's history. However, most of us can't trace our family's roots for more than a few generations. This was true of Alex Haley, whose distant relatives were brought to the United States as slaves. In this essay, he describes how he struggled to find his missing roots.

THEMATIC FOCUS: Inventing Yourself

Sometimes you learn who you are by discovering who your ancestors were. Notice how Haley's research gives him a new sense of himself.

◆ Background for Understanding

SOCIAL STUDIES

Alex Haley began his research at the National Archives in Washington, D.C. This agency was established in 1934 to store government records. There, Haley found population lists with the names of his great-grandparents. In Africa, he found another way to keep records: in the memory of a tribal "historian" who could recite centuries of history!

◆ Build Vocabulary

PREFIXES: *un-*

Haley uses the word "*uncanny*." The prefix *un-* means "not or the opposite of." Combined with *canny,* which can mean "comfortable," it creates a word meaning "strange, in a way that is not comfortable."

WORD BANK

Which of these words from the essay might be related to the word *question?*

intrigue
uncanny
cherished
queried
eminent
destination

My Furthest-Back Person
(*The Inspiration for* Roots)

The Purple Quilt (detail), 1986: acrylic on canvas, tie-dyed and printed fabric, 91 x 72, Faith Ringgold, Courtesy of Bernice Steinbaum

◆ Literary Focus

PERSONAL ESSAY

The word *essay*, which means "a brief, non-fiction discussion of a topic," sounds cold and distant. However, imagine sitting on a porch with a writer who talks to you like a friend. That's just what **personal essays** do—they place you close to authors who tell you about their lives.

From the first sentence, Haley's writing reveals the elements of a personal essay. With its conversational style, its use of the pronoun "I," and its focus on Haley's own life, it speaks to you like a porch companion: "One Saturday in 1965 I happened to be walking...."

◆ Reading Strategy

BREAK DOWN LONG SENTENCES

When you read, you create meaning from words. To build up meaning, you must sometimes **break down long sentences**—find the subject of the sentence (what it is about) and what the sentence is saying about the subject.

You can break down this sentence by Haley by placing the subject at the beginning:

Haley's Sentence: One Saturday in 1965 I happened to be walking past the National Archives....

Rearranged Sentence: I happened to be walking past the National Archives one Saturday in 1965.

My Furthest-Back Person

(The Inspiration for Roots) Alex Haley

As a boy, Alex Haley spent his summers on his grandmother's front porch in Henning, Tennessee, listening to her and her sisters tell stories of the family's history back through the days of slavery. The "furthest-back person" they spoke of was an ancestor they called "The African," who was kidnapped in his native country, shipped to Annapolis, Maryland, and sold into slavery. These stories stayed with young Alex throughout his life.

One Saturday in 1965 I happened to be walking past the National Archives building in Washington. Across the interim years I had thought of Grandma's old stories—otherwise I can't think what diverted me up the Archives' steps. And when a main reading room desk attendant asked if he could help me, I wouldn't have dreamed of admitting to him some curiosity hanging on from boyhood about my slave forebears. I kind of bumbled that I was interested in census records of Alamance County, North Carolina, just after the Civil War.

The microfilm rolls were delivered, and I turned them through the machine with a building sense of intrigue, viewing in different census takers' penmanship an endless parade of names. After about a dozen microfilmed rolls, I was beginning to tire, when in utter astonishment I looked upon the names of Grandma's parents: Tom Murray, Irene Murray . . . older sisters of Grandma's as well—every one of them a name that I'd heard countless times on her front porch.

It wasn't that I hadn't believed Grandma. You just *didn't* not believe my Grandma. It was simply so uncanny actually seeing those names in print and in official U.S. Government records.

◆ **Build Vocabulary**
intrigue (in´ trēg) *n.*: Curiosity and interest
uncanny (un kan´ ē) *adj.*: Strange; eerie

During the next several months I was back in Washington whenever possible, in the Archives, the Library of Congress, the Daughters of the American Revolution Library. (Whenever black attendants understood the idea of my search, documents I requested reached me with miraculous speed.) In one source or another during 1966 I was able to document at least the highlights of the <u>cherished</u> family story. I would have given anything to have told Grandma, but, sadly, in 1949 she had gone. So I went and told the only survivor of those Henning front-porch storytellers: Cousin Georgia Anderson, now in her 80's in Kansas City, Kan. Wrinkled, bent, not well herself, she was so overjoyed, repeating to me the old stories and sounds; they were like Henning echoes: "Yeah, boy, that African say his name was 'Kin-tay'; he say the banjo was 'ko,' an' the river 'Kamby Bolong,' an' he was off choppin' some wood to make his drum when they grabbed 'im!" Cousin Georgia grew so excited we had to stop her, calm her down, "You go 'head, boy! Your grandma an' all of 'em—they up there watching what you do!"

That week I flew to London on a magazine assignment. Since by now I was steeped in the old, in the past, scarcely a tour guide missed me—I was awed at so many historical places and treasures I'd heard of and read of. I came upon the Rosetta stone in the British Museum, marveling anew at how Jean Champollion, the French archaeologist, had miraculously deciphered its ancient demotic and hieroglyphic texts[1] . . .

The thrill of that just kept hanging around in my head. I was on a jet returning to New York when a thought hit me. Those strange, unknown-tongue sounds, always part of our family's old story . . . they were obviously bits of our original African *"Kin-tay's"* native tongue. What specific tongue? Could I somehow find out?

Back in New York, I began making visits to the United Nations Headquarters lobby; it wasn't hard to spot Africans. I'd stop any I could, asking if my bits of phonetic sounds held any meaning for them. A couple of dozen Africans quickly looked at me, listened, and took off—understandably dubious about some Tennesseean's accent alleging "African" sounds.

My research assistant, George Sims (we grew up together in Henning), brought me some names of ranking scholars of African linguistics. One was particularly intriguing: a Belgian- and English-educated Dr. Jan Vansina; he had spent his early career living in West African villages, studying and tape-recording countless oral histories that were narrated by certain very old African men; he had written a standard textbook, "The Oral Tradition."

So I flew to the University of Wisconsin to see Dr. Vansina. In his living room I told him every bit of the family story in the fullest detail that I could remember it. Then, intensely, he <u>queried</u> me about the story's relay across the generations, about the gibberish of "*k*" sounds Grandma had fiercely muttered to herself while doing her housework, with my brothers and me giggling beyond her hearing at what we had dubbed "Grandma's noises."

Dr. Vansina, his manner very serious, finally said, "These sounds your family has kept sound very probably of the tongue called 'Mandinka.'"

I'd never heard of any "Mandinka." Grandma just told of the African saying "*ko*" for banjo, or "*Kamby Bolong*" for a Virginia river.

---

1. **demotic and hieroglyphic texts** (dē mät´ ik and hī´ ər ō´ glif ik) *adj.*: Ancient Egyptian writing, using symbols and pictures to represent words.

◆ **Build Vocabulary**

cherished (cher´ ishd) *adj.*: Beloved; valued

queried (kwir´ ēd) *v.*: Asked

eminent (em´ ə nənt) *adj.*: Distinguished or outstanding

Among Mandinka stringed instruments, Dr. Vansina said, one of the oldest was the "*kora.*"

"*Bolong,*" he said, was clearly Mandinka for "river." Preceded by "*Kamby,*" it very likely meant "Gambia River."

Dr. Vansina telephoned an eminent Africanist colleague, Dr. Philip Curtin. He said that the phonetic "*Kin-tay*" was correctly spelled "*Kinte,*" a very old clan that had originated in Old Mali. The Kinte men traditionally were blacksmiths, and the women were potters and weavers.

I knew I must get to the Gambia River.

The first native Gambian I could locate in the U.S. was named Ebou Manga, then a junior attending Hamilton College in upstate Clinton, N.Y. He and I flew to Dakar, Senegal, then took a smaller plane to Yundum Airport, and rode in a van to Gambia's capital, Bathurst. Ebou and his father assembled eight Gambia government officials. I told them Grandma's stories, every detail I could remember, as they listened intently, then reacted. "'*Kamby Bolong*' of course is Gambia River!" I heard. "But more clue is your forefather's saying his name was '*Kinte.*'" Then they told me something I would never ever have fantasized—that in places in the back country lived very old men, commonly called *griots*, who could tell centuries of the histories of certain very old family clans. As for *Kintes*, they pointed out to me on a map some family villages, Kinte-Kundah, and Kinte-Kundah Janneh-Ya, for instance.

The Gambian officials said they would try to help me. I returned to New York dazed. It is embarrassing to me now, but despite Grandma's stories, I'd never been concerned much with Africa, and I had the routine images of African people living mostly in exotic jungles. But a compulsion now laid hold of me to learn all I could, and I began devouring books about Africa, especially about the slave trade. Then one Thursday's mail contained a letter from one of the Gambian officials, inviting me to return there.

Monday I was back in Bathurst. It galvanized me when the officials said that a *griot* had been located who told the *Kinte* clan history—his name was Kebba Kanga Fofana. To reach him, I discovered, required a modified safari: renting a launch to get upriver, two land vehicles to carry supplies by a round-about land route, and employing finally 14 people, including three interpreters and four musicians, since a *griot* would not speak the revered clan histories without background music.

◆ **Reading Strategy**
Break down this sentence to explain what "galvanized" Haley, making him pay attention.

▶ **Critical Viewing** This photograph and the one on page 43 are stills from the television mini-series about Haley's experience. What does the posture of the actors reveal about the relationship between their characters? **[Analyze]**

The boat Baddibu vibrated upriver, with me acutely tense: Were these Africans maybe viewing me as but another of the pith-helmets?[2] After about two hours, we put in at James Island, for me to see the ruins of the once British-operated James Fort. Here two centuries of slave ships had loaded thousands of cargoes of Gambian tribes-people. The crumbling stones, the deeply oxidized swivel cannon, even some remnant links of chain seemed all but impossible to believe. Then we continued upriver to the left-bank village of Albreda, and there put ashore to continue on foot to Juffure,[3] village of the *griot*. Once more we stopped, for me to see *toubob kolong*, the "white man's well," now almost filled in, in a swampy area with abundant, tall, saw-toothed grass. It was dug two centuries ago to "17 men's height deep" to insure survival drinking water for long-driven, famishing coffles[4] of slaves.

Walking on, I kept wishing that Grandma could hear how her stories had led me to the "*Kamby Bolong*." (Our surviving storyteller Cousin Georgia died in a Kansas City hospital during this same morning, I would learn later.) Finally, Juffure village's playing children, sighting us, flashed an alert. The 70-odd people came rushing from their circular, thatch-roofed, mud-walled huts, with goats bounding up and about, and parrots squawking from up in the palms. I sensed him in advance somehow, the small man amid them, wearing a pillbox cap and an off-white robe—the *griot*. Then the interpreters went to him, as the villagers thronged around me.

And it hit me like a gale wind: every one of them, the whole crowd, was *jet black*. An enormous sense of guilt swept me—a sense of being some kind of hybrid . . . a sense of being impure among the pure. It was an awful sensation.

The old *griot* stepped away from my interpreters and the crowd quickly swarmed around him—all of them buzzing. An interpreter named A.B.C. Salla came to me; he whispered: "Why they stare at you so, they have never seen here a black American." And that hit me: I was symbolizing for them twenty-five millions of us they had never seen. What did they think of me—of us?

Then abruptly the old *griot* was briskly walking toward me. His eyes boring into mine, he spoke in Mandinka, as if instinctively I should understand—and A.B.C. Salla translated:

"Yes . . . we have been told by the forefathers . . . that many of us from this place are in exile . . . in that place called America . . . and in other places."

I suppose I physically wavered, and they thought it was the heat; rustling whispers went through the crowd, and a man brought me a low stool. Now the whispering hushed—the musicians had softly begun playing *kora* and *balafon*, and a canvas sling lawn seat was taken by the *griot*, Kebba Kanga Fofana, aged 73 "rains" (one rainy season each year). He seemed to gather himself into a physical rigidity, and he began speaking the *Kinte* clan's ancestral oral history; it came rolling from his mouth across the next hours . . . 17th- and 18th-century *Kinte* lineage details, predominantly what men took wives; the children they "begot," in the order of their births; those children's mates and children.

Events frequently were dated by some proximate[5] singular physical occurrence. It was as if some ancient scroll were printed indelibly within the *griot's* brain. Each few sentences or so, he would pause for an interpreter's translation to me. I distill here the essence:

The *Kinte* clan began in Old Mali, the men generally blacksmiths ". . . who conquered fire," and the women potters and weavers.

---

2. **pith-helmets** *jargon:* Tourists or hunters on safari, who traditionally wore this type of fabric-covered hard hat.

3. **Juffure** (jo͞o′ fo͞o rā)

4. **coffles** (kôf′ əlz) *n.:* Groups of animals or slaves chained or tied together in a line.

---

5. **proximate** (präks′ ə mət) *adj.:* Near in time.

► **Critical Viewing**
Which paragraph of the essay does this photograph bring to life? [Identify]

One large branch of the clan moved to Mauretania from where one son of the clan, Kairaba Kunta Kinte, a Moslem Marabout holy man, entered Gambia. He lived first in the village of Pakali N'Ding; he moved next to Jif-farong village; ". . . and then he came here, into our own village of Juffure."

In Juffure, Kairaba Kunta Kinte took his first wife, ". . . a Mandinka maiden, whose name was Sireng. By her, he begot two sons, whose names were Janneh and Saloum. Then he got a second wife, Yaisa. By her, he begot a son, Omoro."

The three sons became men in Juffure. Janneh and Saloum went off and found a new village, Kinte-Kundah Janneh-Ya. "And then Omoro, the youngest son, when he had 30 rains, took as a wife a maiden, Binta Kebba.

"And by her, he begot four sons—Kunta, Lamin, Suwadu, and Madi . . ."

Sometimes, a "begotten," after his naming, would be accompanied by some later-occurring detail, perhaps as ". . . in time of big water (flood), he slew a water buffalo." Having named those four sons, now the *griot* stated such a detail.

"About the time the king's soldiers came, the eldest of these four sons, Kunta, when he had about 16 rains, went away from his village, to chop wood to make a drum . . . and he was never seen again . . ."

◆ **Reading Strategy**
Who is the subject of the sentence, and what did he do?

Goose-pimples the size of lemons seemed to pop all over me. In my knapsack were my cumulative notebooks, the first of them including how in my boyhood, my Grandma, Cousin Georgia and the others told of the African "*Kin-tay*" who always said he was kidnapped near his village—while chopping wood to make a drum . . .

I showed the interpreter, he showed and told the *griot*, who excitedly told the people; they grew very agitated. Abruptly then they formed a human ring, encircling me, dancing and chanting. Perhaps a dozen of the women carrying their infant babies rushed in toward me, thrusting the infants into my arms conveying, I would later learn, "the laying on of hands . . . through this flesh which is us, we are you, and you are us." The men hurried me into their mosque, their Arabic praying later being translated outside: "Thanks be to Allah for returning the long lost from among us." Direct descendants of Kunta Kinte's blood brothers were hastened, some of them from nearby villages, for a family portrait to be taken with me, surrounded by actual ancestral sixth cousins. More symbolic acts filled the remaining day.

When they would let me leave, for some reason I wanted to go away over the African land. Dazed, silent in the bumping Land Rover, I heard the cutting staccato of talking drums. Then when we sighted the next village, its people came thronging to meet us. They were all—little naked ones to wizened elders—waving, beaming; amid a cacophony of crying out; and then my ears identified their words: "*Meester Kinte! Meester Kinte!*"

Let me tell you something: I am a man. But I remember the sob surging up from my feet, flinging up my hands before my face and bawling as I had not done since I was a baby . . . the jet-black Africans were jostling,[6] staring . . . I didn't care, with the feelings surging. If you really knew the odyssey of us millions of black Americans, if you really knew how we came in the seeds of our forefathers, captured, driven, beaten, inspected, bought, branded, chained in foul ships, if you really knew, you needed weeping . . .

◆ **Literary Focus**
How do these details of his reaction create a close bond between you and Haley?

Back home, I knew that what I must write, really, was our black saga, where any individual's past is the essence of the millions'. Now flat broke, I went to some editors I knew, describing the Gambian miracle, and my desire to pursue the research; Doubleday contracted to publish, and Reader's Digest to condense the projected book; then I had advances to travel further.

What ship brought Kinte to Grandma's "'Naplis" (Annapolis, Md., obviously)? The old *griot's* time reference to "king's soldiers" sent me flying to London. Feverish searching at last identified, in British Parliament records, "Colonel O'Hare's Forces," dispatched in mid-1767 to protect the then British-held James Fort whose ruins I'd visited. So Kunta Kinte was down in some ship probably sailing later that summer from the Gambia River to Annapolis.

Now I feel it was fated that I had taught myself to write in the U.S. Coast Guard. For the sea dramas I had concentrated on had given me years of experience searching among yellowing old U.S. maritime records. So now in English 18th Century marine records I finally tracked ships reporting themselves in and out to the Commandant of the Gambia River's James Fort. And then early one afternoon I found that a Lord Ligonier under a Captain Thomas Davies had sailed on the Sabbath of July 5, 1767. Her cargo: 3,265 elephants' teeth, 3,700 pounds of beeswax, 800 pounds of cotton, 32 ounces of Gambian gold and 140 slaves; her <u>destination</u>: "Annapolis."

That night I recrossed the Atlantic. In the Library of Congress the Lord Ligonier's arrival was one brief line in "Shipping In The Port Of Annapolis—1748–1775." I located the author, Vaughan W. Brown, in his Baltimore brokerage office. He drove to Historic

Beyond Literature

Technology Connection

Genealogy on the Internet If you wanted to find your "furthest-back person," how would you do it? The Internet is a great place to start. A net search of the key word *genealogy* will give you links to organizations and journals that specialize in genealogy, like the National Genealogical Society. Their home pages have lists of resources and tips for how to use them. Or you can do a more specific search based on where your family came from or your family's ethnic group.

Cross-Curricular Activity
Digging Up Your Roots Use the Internet to learn about your family history. Then, create a family tree based on what you discover. Share your results with classmates, describing the steps you took to get the information.

---

6. **jostling** (jäs´ ling) *v.*: Bumping and pushing, as in a crowd.

Annapolis, the city's historical society, and found me further documentation of her arrival on Sept. 29, 1767. (Exactly two centuries later, Sept. 29, 1967, standing, staring seaward from an Annapolis pier, again I knew tears.) More help came in the Maryland Hall of Records. Archivist Phebe Jacobsen found the Lord Ligonier's arriving customs declaration listing, "98 Negroes"—so in her

86-day crossing, 42 Gambians had died, one among the survivors being 16-year-old Kunta Kinte. Then the microfilmed Oct. 1, 1767, Maryland Gazette contained, on page two, an announcement to prospective buyers from the ship's agents, Daniel of St. Thos. Jenifer and John Ridout (the Governor's secretary): "from the River GAMBIA, in AFRICA . . . a cargo of choice, healthy SLAVES . . ."

◆ **Literature and Your Life**
What feelings do you think people have as they research family records in this way? Explain.

◆ **Build Vocabulary**
destination (des´ tə nā´ shən) *n.:* The place to which something is being sent

Guide for Responding

◆ LITERATURE AND YOUR LIFE

Reader's Response What questions would you like to ask Haley about his experience?

Thematic Focus Some people say that our identity is the story we tell about ourselves. How did Haley's research help him tell a better story about himself?

Journal Writing Jot down what you know about your own family's ancestry and what you'd like to learn. List possible sources of information, like family photographs, letters and diaries, and government records.

☑ Check Your Comprehension

1. What does Haley discover "One Saturday in 1965"?
2. Tell how clues from the "family's old story" lead Haley to Gambia as the family's original home.
3. Summarize what Haley learns on his second trip to Gambia.
4. Describe Haley's reaction to villagers calling him *"Meester Kinte!"*
5. What does Haley decide to write?

◆ Critical Thinking

INTERPRET

1. How is Haley's quest, from the very beginning, both a mental puzzle and an emotional thrill? **[Interpret]**
2. What is similar and different about the African sounds in Haley's family stories and the writing on the Rosetta stone? **[Compare and Contrast]**
3. In what way are the tales of the *griot* and the tales of Haley's family like two parts of the same puzzle? **[Connect]**
4. When villagers greeted Haley as *"Meester Kinte,"* what did he find that had been lost for 200 years? **[Draw Conclusions]**

EVALUATE

5. Was it "fated" that Haley would solve the mystery of "the African," or was it just chance? Explain. **[Make a Judgment]**

EXTEND

6. This essay suggests that, in addition to being special, a person needs to feel part of a larger group. Explain why you agree or disagree. **[Social Studies Link]**

*G*uide for Responding (continued)

◆ Reading Strategy

BREAK DOWN LONG SENTENCES

When you **break down long sentences,** you find the subject and what the sentence tells about it. Now test your skills again. On your paper, underline the subject of each sentence, and circle the words that tell you about the subject.

1. Back in New York, I began making visits to the United Nations Headquarters lobby....
2. When they would let me leave, for some reason I wanted to go away over the African land.

◆ Build Vocabulary

USING THE PREFIX *un-*

Use your knowledge of the prefix un- ("not" or "the opposite of") to answer these questions.

1. Why was Africa *unmapped* territory for Haley before he began his research?
2. What incident in Gambia proves that Haley was *unafraid* of showing his emotions?

SPELLING STRATEGY

When you add a prefix to a word, you don't change the spelling of the original word:

    un- + canny = uncanny

Write the following words correctly.

1. un- + even   3. un- + necessary
2. re- + place   4. re- + elect

USING THE WORD BANK

Answer each question yes or no. Then explain your responses.

1. If a project is *cherished*, is it valued?
2. Was Alex Haley an *eminent* writer?
3. Was Ghana Haley's *destination* in Africa?
4. Did the *intrigue* of the quest decrease for Haley?
5. Did seeing his great-grandparents' names in census records give Haley an *uncanny* feeling?
6. Is it likely that people *queried* Haley about how to find their own roots?

◆ Literary Focus

PERSONAL ESSAY

A **personal essay** is a brief nonfiction account about a memorable event from the writer's life. Haley's essay gives you the feeling of sitting comfortably with him as he tells you about his life. To create that special bond with you, he uses phrases from casual conversation, such as "I wouldn't have dreamed of ..." and "I kind of bumbled that I was interested. ..." He also includes precise details, like his cousin's words, that help you experience what he did. Finally, he expresses emotions that you can share with him.

Reread the last six paragraphs of the essay. Find these elements in the passage you've read, and explain how each makes the essay more personal.

1. conversational phrases
2. people's exact words
3. expressions of emotion

◆ Build Grammar Skills

COLLECTIVE NOUNS

Haley's essay is about individuals and the groups from which they come. Therefore, it isn't surprising that he uses **collective nouns,** words whose singular form names a group of persons, animals, or objects. *Crowd,* for example, is a collective noun:

    The *crowd* surrounded him.

Other examples are *team, jury, herd,* and *audience.*

Practice On your paper, write these sentences. Then underline the collective noun in each.

1. Haley was interested in the history of his family.
2. In Africa, the crew of the boat took him upriver.
3. He saw the flock circling over the boat.
4. He met many people, and the majority were nice.
5. A dozen of the African musical instruments were unknown to him.

Writing Application Write sentences with each of the following collective nouns: *orchestra, team, army.*

Build Your Portfolio

 ## Idea Bank

Writing

1. **Captions** Write brief but informative captions for three or four photographs in your family's album. Identify the people in each picture, the occasion on which it was taken, and the date.

2. **Book Jacket** A jacket, the paper cover of a book, contains interesting information about the book and the author. Write jacket copy for *Roots*, the book that came out of Haley's experiences in "My Furthest-Back Person."

3. **Proposal** As Haley, write a proposal that will interest a publisher to want to publish your book. Explain what you'll include and what you've done so far. Also, explain why your book will appeal to a wide audience.

Speaking and Listening

4. **Speaker's Introduction** Suppose that Alex Haley could speak to your class. Briefly introduce him to your classmates, telling them who he is and what he'll discuss. **[Performing Arts Link]**

5. **Storytellers' Circle** Get together with two or three classmates and tell one another stories about your families. Record your performance, and play the recording for the class. **[Performing Arts Link; Social Studies Link]**

Projects

6. **Family Chart** Ask your teacher how to chart family births, marriages, and deaths. Then, create a chart for your own family or for one that is famous in history. Interview people, research family records, or study history books to gather facts. **[Social Studies Link; Art Link]**

7. **Film Review [Group Activity]** Rent one or more of the episodes in the television mini-series *Roots*. Then, with a group, review the film for classmates. Each group member can discuss a different element of the film, including the acting, directing, setting, camera work, soundtrack, and story. **[Social Studies Link; Media Link]**

 ## Writing Mini-Lesson

I-Search Paper

Haley's personal essay is in some ways very much like an I-Search paper. This type of paper not only reports on a topic but also describes the adventure involved in the research itself. Write an I-Search paper about a topic that interests you. As Haley does in his essay, include the story of *how* you learned as you report on *what* you learned.

Writing Skills Focus: Elaborate With Precise Details

You can bring writing to life by giving readers **precise details** rather than general statements. Haley uses such details to make you a partner in his discoveries. For example, his remark about the varying penmanship of census takers is a detail that helps you *see* the microfilmed rolls:

Model From the Essay

. . . I turned them through the machine with a building sense of intrigue, viewing in different census takers' penmanship an endless parade of names.

Prewriting Research a topic that interests you by reading books and encyclopedia articles. Also, interview people who know about the subject. Besides taking notes on the facts you learn, record details of your research adventure: people you meet and places to which you travel.

Drafting Using precise details, weave your research adventure into your report on the facts.

Revising Scan your paper for dull, general statements, like "I read the rolls of microfilm and found the names." Spice them up with precise details: "There, *hovering in and out of focus,* were the names for which I was looking."

◆ **Grammar Application**
With a highlighter pen, identify any collective nouns you've used.

Guide for Reading

Meet the Author:

Jack Finney (1911–1995)

When you read the writings of Jack Finney, you have to wonder whether he really did learn the secret of time travel. This fantastic idea is at the heart of many of his works, including "The Third Level" and the novel *Time and Again*. When Finney explores the idea of moving through time, he maps out an escape route for travel from a harsh present to an appealing past.

Finney was born in Milwaukee, Wisconsin. After graduating from college, he went to New York City to seek his fortune. While working in advertising, Finney began a second career writing short stories and novels. His science-fiction novel *The Body Snatchers* brought him wider recognition and eventually inspired two film versions.

THE STORY BEHIND THE STORY

Even though "The Third Level" deals with time travel—a fictional and to-date impossible occurrence—the story's characters and setting are drawn from Finney's own experience. Like the writer, the main character has come from the Midwest to New York City. In the story, he makes a reverse trip.

◆ LITERATURE AND YOUR LIFE

CONNECT YOUR EXPERIENCE

You've probably gotten a glimpse of life in the late 1800's from movies and television. Based on what you know or what you can assume from the photograph on the facing page, what might you like about life in that time? Compare your thoughts to the reactions of this story's narrator, as he travels back to 1894 and finds that time period strangely appealing.

THEMATIC FOCUS: Inventing Yourself

How do the time and place in which you live help to shape you? What might happen if your likes and dislikes didn't fit well with your surroundings?

◆ Background for Understanding

HISTORY

"The Third Level" is set in New York City's Grand Central Station. Completed in 1913, Grand Central is one of the world's most famous train stations. The huge main room of the station is connected to railroad platforms, subways, and streets by a series of tunnels. In "The Third Level," a tunnel takes an unexpected turn.

◆ Build Vocabulary

SUFFIXES: -ist

The character in "The Third Level" frequently mentions his *psychiatrist*. The word *psychiatrist* ends with the suffix *-ist*, meaning "someone who is skilled in." *Psychiatry* deals with illnesses of the mind, so a *psychiatrist* is skilled in curing these illnesses.

WORD BANK

Which of these words might describe the shape of a doorway? Check the Build Vocabulary boxes to see if you chose correctly.

psychiatrist
arched
currency
premium

◆ The Third Level ◆

◆ Literary Focus

TIME IN A SETTING

Setting is the time and place in which a story's events occur. In Finney's story, time plays an especially important role, as the main character walks down a corridor in Grand Central Station and discovers that he has been transported back to 1894. As you read, record the details of 1894 that contrast with the details of the contemporary setting on a chart like the following:

Clues That Show Charley Is in Present	Clues That Show Charley Is in 1894

◆ Reading Strategy

USE CONTEXT TO UNLOCK MEANING

In a story like "The Third Level" with an unusual or unfamiliar setting, you'll come across place names, slang, or other words that you don't recognize. When you encounter a name or a word you don't know, use its **context**—the words, phrases, and sentences around it—to figure out its meaning. Look at this example:

> I . . . glanced at the stack of papers at his feet. It was the *World*; and the *World* hasn't been published for years.

At first glance, you might wonder why a stack of papers would be called the *World*. The capitalization and italics indicate the title of a published work. Context clues such as "papers" and "published" provide further information to help you conclude that the *World* was a newspaper.

The Third Level

Jack Finney

he presidents of the New York Central and the New York, New Haven and Hartford railroads will swear on a stack of time-tables that there are only two. But I say there are three, because I've *been* on the third level at Grand Central Station.[1] Yes, I've taken the obvious step: I talked to a psychiatrist friend of mine, among others. I told him about the third level at Grand Central Station, and he said it was a waking-dream wish fulfillment. He said I was unhappy. That made my wife kind of mad, but he explained that he meant the modern world is full of insecurity, fear, war, worry and all the rest of it, and that I just want to escape. Well, who doesn't? Everybody I know wants to escape, but they don't wander down into any third level at Grand Central Station.

But that's the reason, he said, and my friends all agreed. Everything points to it, they claimed. My stamp collecting, for example; that's a "temporary refuge from reality." Well, maybe, but my grandfather didn't need any refuge from reality; things were pretty nice and peaceful in his day, from all I hear, and he started my collection. It's a nice collection, too, blocks of four of practically every U.S. issue, first-day covers, and so on. President Roosevelt collected stamps, too, you know.

Anyway, here's what happened at Grand Central. One night last summer I worked late at the office. I was in a hurry to get uptown to my apartment so I decided to take the subway from Grand Central because it's faster than the bus.

Now, I don't know why this should have happened to me. I'm just an ordinary guy named Charley, thirty-one years old, and I was wearing a tan gabardine[2] suit and a straw hat with a fancy band; I passed a dozen men who looked just like me. And I wasn't trying to escape from anything; I just wanted to get home to Louisa, my wife.

I turned into Grand Central from Vanderbilt Avenue, and went down the steps to the first level, where you take trains like the Twentieth Century. Then I walked down another flight to the second level, where the suburban trains leave from, ducked into an arched doorway heading for the subway—and got lost. That's easy to do. I've been in and out of Grand Central hundreds of times, but I'm always bumping into new doorways and stairs and corridors. Once I got into a tunnel about a mile long and came out in the lobby of the Roosevelt Hotel. Another time I came up in an office building on Forty-sixth Street, three blocks away.

Sometimes I think Grand Central is growing like a tree, pushing out new corridors and staircases like roots. There's probably a long tunnel that nobody knows about feeling its way under the city right now, on its way to Times Square, and maybe another to Central Park. And maybe—because for so many people through the years Grand Central *has* been an exit, a way of escape—maybe that's how the tunnel I got into . . . But I never told my psychiatrist friend about that idea.

The corridor I was in began angling left and slanting downward and I thought that was wrong, but I kept on walking. All I could hear was the empty sound of my own footsteps and I didn't pass a soul. Then I heard that sort of

◆ Literary Focus
What details of setting does this paragraph provide?

---

1. **Grand Central Station:** Large train station in New York City.

2. **gabardine** (gab´ ər dēn´): Cloth of wool, cotton, rayon, or other material used for suits and dresses.

◆ Build Vocabulary

psychiatrist (sī kī´ ə trist) *noun used as adj.*: Medical doctor specializing in illnesses of the mind

arched (ärcht) *adj.*: Curved

hollow roar ahead that means open space and people talking. The tunnel turned sharp left; I went down a short flight of stairs and came out on the third level at Grand Central Station. For just a moment I thought I was back on the second level, but I saw the room was smaller, there were fewer ticket windows and train gates, and the information booth in the center was wood and old-looking. And the man in the booth wore a green eyeshade and long black sleeve protectors. The lights were dim and sort of flickering. Then I saw why; they were open-flame gaslights.

There were brass spittoons[3] on the floor, and across the station a glint of light caught my eye; a man was pulling a gold watch from his vest pocket. He snapped open the cover, glanced at his watch, and frowned. He wore a derby hat,[4] a black four-button suit with tiny lapels, and he had a big, black, handle-bar mustache. Then I looked around and saw that everyone in the station was dressed like eighteen-ninety-some-thing; I never saw so many beards, sideburns and fancy mustaches in my life. A woman walked in through the train gate; she wore a dress with leg-of-mutton sleeves[5] and skirts to the top of her high-buttoned shoes. Back of her, out on the tracks, I caught a glimpse of a locomotive, a very small Currier & Ives[6]

◆ Reading Strategy
Using the beards and mustaches as a clue, what do you think *sideburns* are?

---

3. **spittoons** (spi tōōnz′): Jarlike containers into which people spit. Spitting in public was a more accepted habit in the past.

▼ Critical Viewing List three specific details to prove this photograph was taken in modern New York City. [Support]

---

4. **derby hat:** Stiff felt hat with a round crown and curved brim.
5. **leg-of-mutton sleeves:** Sleeves that puff out toward the shoulder and resemble a leg of mutton (lamb or sheep).
6. **Currier & Ives:** These nineteenth-century American printmakers became famous for their pictures of trains, yachts, horses, and scenes of nature.

locomotive with a funnel-shaped stack. And then I knew.

To make sure, I walked over to a newsboy and glanced at the stack of papers at his feet. It was the *World;* and the *World* hasn't been published for years. The lead story said something about President Cleveland. I've found that front page since, in the Public Library files, and it was printed June 11, 1894.

I turned toward the ticket windows knowing that here—on the third level at Grand Central—I could buy tickets that would take Louisa and me anywhere in the United States we wanted to go. In the year 1894. And I wanted two tickets to Galesburg, Illinois.

Have you ever been there? It's a wonderful town still, with big old frame houses, huge lawns and tremendous trees whose branches meet overhead and roof the streets. And in

1894, summer evenings were twice as long, and people sat out on their lawns, the men smoking cigars and talking quietly, the women waving palm-leaf fans, with the fireflies all around, in a peaceful world. To be back there with the First World War still twenty years off, and World War II over forty years in the future . . . I wanted two tickets for that.

The clerk figured the fare—he glanced at my fancy hatband, but he figured the fare—and I had enough for two coach tickets, one way. But when I counted out the money and looked up, the clerk was staring at me. He nodded at the bills. "That ain't money, mister," he said, "and if you're trying to skin me you won't get very far," and he glanced at the cash drawer beside him. Of course the money in his drawer was old-style bills, half again as big as the money we use nowadays, and different-looking. I turned away and got out fast. There's nothing nice about jail, even in 1894.

And that was that. I left the same way I came, I suppose. Next day, during lunch hour, I drew three hundred dollars out of the bank, nearly all we had, and bought old-style <u>currency</u> (that *really* worried my psychiatrist friend). You can buy old money at almost any coin dealer's, but you have to pay a <u>premium</u>. My three hundred dollars bought less than two hundred in old-style bills, but I didn't care; eggs were thirteen cents a dozen in 1894.

But I've never again found the corridor that leads to the third level at Grand Central Station, although I've tried often enough.

Louisa was pretty worried when I told her all this, and didn't want me to look for the third level any more, and after a while I stopped; I went back to my stamps. But now we're *both* looking, every weekend, because now we have proof that the third level is still there. My friend

▼ **Critical Viewing** List three specific details to prove this photograph was taken in New York City at an earlier time. **[Support]**

◆ **Build Vocabulary**

currency (kʉr´ ən sē) *n.:* Money

premium (prē´ mē əm) *n.:* Additional charge

Sam Weiner disappeared! Nobody knew where, but I sort of suspected because Sam's a city boy, and I used to tell him about Galesburg—I went to school there—and he always said he liked the sound of the place. And that's where he is all right. In 1894.

Because one night, fussing with my stamp collection, I found—well, do you know what a first-day cover is? When a new stamp is issued, stamp collectors buy some and use them to mail envelopes to themselves on the very first day of sale; and the postmark proves the date. The envelope is called a first-day cover. They're never opened; you just put blank paper in the envelope.

That night, among my oldest first-day covers, I found one that shouldn't have been there. But there it was. It was there because someone had mailed it to my grandfather at his home in Galesburg; that's what the address on the envelope said. And it had been there since July 18, 1894—the postmark showed that—yet I didn't remember it at all. The stamp was a six-cent, dull brown, with a picture of President Garfield. Naturally, when the envelope came to Granddad in the mail, it went right into his collection and

stayed there—till I took it out and opened it.

The paper inside wasn't blank. It read:

> 941 Willard Street
> Galesburg, Illinois
> July 18, 1894

Charley:

I got to wishing that you were right. Then I got to believing you were right. And, Charley, it's true; I found the third level! I've been here two weeks, and right now, down the street at the Daly's, someone is playing a piano, and they're all out on the front porch singing, "Seeing Nellie home." And I'm invited over for lemonade. Come on back, Charley and Louisa. Keep looking till you find the third level! It's worth it, believe me!

The note was signed *Sam*.

At the stamp and coin store I go to, I found out that Sam bought eight hundred dollars' worth of old-style currency. That ought to set him up in a nice little hay, feed and grain business; he always said that's what he really wished he could do, and he certainly can't go back to his old business. Not in Galesburg, Illinois, in 1894. His old business? Why, Sam was my psychiatrist.

Guide for Responding

◆ LITERATURE AND YOUR LIFE

Reader's Response As it is described, is Galesburg in 1894 a place to which you would like to go? Why or why not?

Thematic Focus What advice would you give Charley and Louisa about reinventing themselves to fit into an 1894 world?

☑ Check Your Comprehension

1. According to Charley's psychiatrist, how can Charley's visit to the third level be explained?
2. What makes Charley think he has traveled to another time?
3. What proof does Charley get that the third level exists?

◆ Critical Thinking

INTERPRET

1. Contrast life in the modern world and life in Galesburg in 1894. **[Compare and Contrast]**
2. What evidence suggests that Charley feels out of place in modern times? **[Support]**
3. In what two ways does the stamp collection provide a link to life in Galesburg? **[Connect]**
4. How does Sam's attitude toward the third level change during the story? **[Analyze]**

APPLY

5. What leads some people to believe that life in previous times was simpler or better than life in the present? Do you agree or disagree with this view? **[Explain]**

Guide for Responding (continued)

◆ Reading Strategy

USE CONTEXT TO UNLOCK MEANING

Using **context**—the surrounding words, phrases, and sentences—can help you determine the meaning of unfamiliar words, objects, or slang from another time period. There are many types of context clues, including description, example, restatement, and comparison or contrast.

Use context to define the italicized words. Identify the clues you used and explain your answer.

1. "... where you take trains like the *Twentieth Century.*"
2. "That ain't money, mister, " he said, "and if you're trying to *skin* me you won't get very far."

◆ Build Vocabulary

USING THE SUFFIX *-ist*

The suffix *-ist* means "someone who is skilled in or practices." Write a definition explaining what each of the following people practices.

1. artist   3. novelist   5. dentist
2. chemist   4. scientist

SPELLING STRATEGY

Follow these rules when adding *-ist* to words:

If the word ends in a silent *e* preceded by a consonant, drop the *e:*

manicure + -ist = manicurist

If the word ends in *y,* drop the *y* when the *y* sounds like a long *e:*

psychiatry + -ist = psychiatrist

On your paper, add *-ist* to the following words.

1. botany   2. hairstyle   3. zoology   4. type

USING THE WORD BANK

On your paper, complete each sentence with a word from the Word Bank.

1. An _____?_____ window offers a better view of the cityscape than a narrow, square one.
2. When you visit another country, you have to exchange American dollars for foreign _____?_____.
3. A _____?_____ may help those experiencing extreme sadness or anger.
4. Tickets for the hottest concert of the year were available only at a _____?_____.

◆ Literary Focus

TIME IN A SETTING

Setting is the time and place of a story's action. When a story shifts from the present to the past, as "The Third Level" does, you have to determine when the action is taking place. You also have to consider how that changing time affects the characters. Answer the following questions. You may refer to your chart to help you.

1. What detail first hints that Charley has entered the Grand Central Station of 1894?
2. Identify at least three other details that show that the third level is in the past.
3. How does travel to 1894 change Sam?
4. What does Sam's letter say that suggests life in Galesburg in 1894 is better than life in modern-day New York City?

◆ Build Grammar Skills

CONCRETE AND ABSTRACT NOUNS

Concrete nouns refer to physical things that can be seen, heard, tasted, smelled, or touched. **Abstract nouns** refer to ideas, qualities, or feelings that can't be experienced through the five senses. Look at these nouns from the story:

Concrete: apartment, president, ticket
Abstract: insecurity, war, worry

An *apartment* can be touched or seen. *Insecurity* can only be described or experienced.

Practice Identify each of the following as either a concrete or an abstract noun.

1. wish   3. mustache   5. fear
2. corridor   4. envelope   6. reality

Writing Application Copy and complete the following sentences on your paper. Use either a concrete or an abstract noun as indicated.

1. Louisa explained her _____?_____ about how to reach the third level. (abstract)
2. They dressed in _____?_____ from 1894. (concrete)
3. The clerk gave Charley two _____?_____ to Galesburg. (concrete)
4. Sam and Charley were filled with _____?_____ when they saw each other again. (abstract)

Build Your Portfolio

 ## Idea Bank

Writing

1. Letters Write a letter from Charley asking Sam about Galesburg and the third level. Then, write Sam's response, with details about the 1890's.

2. Time-Travel Story Like Charley, you make a turn down an unfamiliar corridor and step into the past. Write a story to describe your experience.

3. Psychiatrist's Report Imagine you are a psychiatrist who believes the third level is a product of Charley's imagination. Using examples from the story, write a report explaining your opinion.

Speaking and Listening

4. Oral History Interview an older relative or friend about the time period of his or her childhood. Find out about fashion, fun, and issues of concern. Record the oral history, and present it with visuals from the period. **[Social Studies Link]**

5. Leisure Time Presentation **[Group Activity]** In a group, learn more about leisure activities in the late nineteenth century. Each group member should research a different topic, such as sports, games, and music. Then, describe to the class the activities the people of Galesburg might have enjoyed. **[Performing Arts Link; Social Studies Link]**

Projects

6. Poster Series on Train Travel In 1894, passenger train travel was far more important than it is today. Using the Internet or reference books, research train travel in the late 1800's. Present your findings in several colorful posters. **[Art Link; Social Studies Link]**

7. Survey Write a survey about time travel, providing three or four answer choices for each question. For example, you might ask people whether they believe in the possibility of time travel or what time period they might choose to visit if it were possible. Conduct the survey, and plot the results on a bar graph. **[Math Link]**

 ## Writing Mini-Lesson

Description of a Place

Jack Finney uses vivid description to re-create the atmosphere, or mood, of a time long gone. Like Finney's 1894 Grand Central Station, the locations you visit today will become a later generation's "ancient history." Write a description to help readers of the distant future see the physical details and experience the mood of a place in today's world.

Writing Skills Focus: Spatial Details

Help readers picture the place you are describing by using **spatial details**. Use such words and phrases as *above, behind,* and *in front of* that tell where things are located in space. Notice how Finney organizes his spaces to lead readers through Grand Central Station.

Model From the Story

Then I heard that sort of hollow roar *ahead* that means open space and people talking. The tunnel turned sharp *left*; I went *down* a short flight of stairs and came *out* on the *third level*. . . .

Prewriting If possible, visit the place you've chosen, and take notes on its physical details. Jot down words such as *bustling, tense,* or *dim* to describe the atmosphere.

Drafting Begin with a vivid detail of atmosphere, such as the sounds or movement in the place. Then, use your notes to build a complete picture of the scene.

> ◆ **Grammar Application**
> Use concrete nouns, such as *scoreboard,* to show a space's physical elements. Use abstract nouns, such as *excitement,* to convey emotions.

Revising Review your description, noting places where additional vivid details could make the atmosphere more realistic.

CONNECTING LITERATURE TO SOCIAL STUDIES
MEDIEVAL TIMES

King Arthur: The Marvel of the Sword by Mary MacLeod

TEENAGER ELECTED PRESIDENT. You may have wondered if a headline like this could ever appear in a newspaper. Actually, an event like this did happen—in another country and another time. The story is part of English legend.

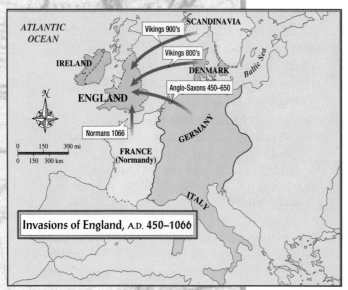

Invasions of England, A.D. 450–1066

The Making of a Legend Legends are tales that are loosely based on historical facts. These stories may not be entirely true, but they do reflect a group's identity: what it wishes for and values.

Campfires and Castles The legend of King Arthur began to be told more than a thousand years ago. Whispered over open campfires and recited in drafty castles, it reflected the yearning of the English people to be united under a wise and brave ruler. The details changed with every telling, but the legend always expressed this same yearning.

Wars and Invasions This story gathered power during a perilous time in English history. In the middle of the fifth century A.D., tribes of sea-rovers began invading England from Northern Europe. These invaders gradually settled in England, but fresh dangers threatened the English people. The land was divided by warring kingdoms as noblemen struggled for power. Also, new invaders kept coming from across the water: Vikings from Scandinavia and Denmark in the ninth century, and Normans from France in 1066.

A King Who Never Was? Maybe King Arthur really lived during the time of the first invaders. Maybe he won victories against these sea-rovers. These maybes don't add up to historical fact, but people needed to hear about a great king like Arthur as long as times remained perilous. In "The Marvel of the Sword," you'll meet this legendary king when he is a teenager.

King Arthur:
The Marvel of the Sword

Mary MacLeod

When Uther[1] Pendragon, King of England, died, the country for a long while stood in great danger, for every lord that was mighty gathered his forces, and many wished to be king. For King Uther's own son, Prince Arthur, who should have succeeded him, was but a child, and Merlin, the mighty magician, had hidden him away.

Now a strange thing had happened at Arthur's birth.

Some time before, Merlin had done Uther a great service, on condition that the King should grant him whatever he wished for. This the King swore a solemn oath to do. Then Merlin made him promise that when his child was born it should be delivered to Merlin to bring up as he chose, for this would be to the child's own great advantage. The King had given his promise so he was obliged to agree. Then Merlin said he knew a very true and faithful man, one of King Uther's lords, by name Sir Ector,[2] who had large posses-sions in many parts of England and Wales, and that the child should be given to him to bring up.

On the night the baby was born, while it was still unchristened, King Uther commanded two knights and two ladies to take it, wrapped in a cloth of gold, and deliver it to a poor man whom they would find waiting at the postern gate of the Castle. This poor man was Merlin in disguise, although they did not know it. So the child was delivered unto Merlin and he carried him to Sir Ector, and made a holy man christen him, and named him Arthur; and Sir Ector's wife cherished him as her own child.

Within two years King Uther fell sick of a great malady, and for three days and three nights he was speechless. All the Barons[3]

---

3. **Barons** (bar´ ənz) n.: Members of the lowest rank of British nobility.

◆ **Build Vocabulary**
malady (mal´ ə dē) n.: Illness; disease

---

1. **Uther** (yōō thər)
2. **Ector** (ek´ tôr)

MERLIN TAKETH THE CHILD ARTHVR INTO HIS KEEPING

Drawing from an 1894 edition of Sir Thomas Malory's Le Morte d'Arthur, Aubrey Beardsley

▲ **Critical Viewing** Identify in the picture these details from the story: "two knights and two ladies," the baby "wrapped in a cloth of gold," and Merlin disguised as a "poor man." [**Connect**]

were in sorrow, and asked Merlin what was best to be done.

"There is no remedy," said Merlin. "God will have His Will. But look ye all, Barons, come before King Uther tomorrow, and God will make him speak."

So the next day Merlin and all the Barons came before the King, and Merlin said aloud to King Uther:

"Sir, after your days shall your son Arthur be King of this realm and all that belongs to it?"

Then Uther Pendragon turned and said in hearing of them all: "I give my son Arthur God's blessing and mine, and bid him pray for my soul, and righteously and honorably claim the crown, on forfeiture of my blessing."

And with that, King Uther died.

But Arthur was still only a baby, not two years old, and Merlin knew it would be no use yet to proclaim him King. For there were many powerful nobles in England in those days, who were all trying to get the kingdom for themselves, and perhaps they would kill the little Prince. So there was much strife and debate in the land for a long time.

When several years had passed, Merlin went to the Archbishop of Canterbury[4] and counseled him to send for all the lords of the realm,[5] and all the gentlemen of arms, that they should come to London at Christmas, and for this cause—that a miracle would

show who should be rightly King of the realm. So all the lords and gentlemen made themselves ready, and came to London, and long before dawn on Christmas Day they were all gathered in the great church of St. Paul's to pray.

When the first service was over, there was seen in the churchyard a large stone, four-square, like marble, and in the midst of it was like an anvil of steel, a foot high. In this was stuck by the point a beautiful sword, with naked blade, and there were letters written in gold about the sword, which said thus:

Whoso pulleth this sword out of this stone and anvil is rightly King of all England.

Then the people marveled, and told it to the Archbishop.

"I command," said the Archbishop, "that you keep within the church, and pray unto God still; and that no man touch the sword till the service is over."

So when the prayers in church were over, all the lords went to behold the stone and the sword; and when they read the writing some of them—such as wished to be king—tried to pull the sword out of the anvil. But not one could make it stir.

"The man is not here, that shall achieve the sword," said the Archbishop, "but doubt not God will make him known. But let us provide ten knights, men of good fame, to keep guard over the sword."

So it was ordained, and proclamation was made that everyone who wished might try to win the sword. And upon New Year's Day the Barons arranged to have a great tournament, in which all knights who would joust[6] or tourney[7] might take a part. This was ordained to keep together the Lords and Commons, for

---

4. **Canterbury** (kan´ tər ber´ ē) n.: Cathedral and sacred shrine in Canterbury, a town southeast of London. In medieval times, many English people made pilgrimages or journeys to Canterbury.
5. **realm** (relm) n.: Kingdom.

◆ Build Vocabulary

remedy (rem´ ə dē) n.: Medicine or treatment that cures illness

strife (strīf) n.: Trouble; conflict; struggle

ordained (ôr dān´ əd) v.: Ordered; decreed

---

6. **joust** (jowst) v.: To take part in a combat between two knights on horseback with lances.
7. **tourney** (toor´ nē) v.: To compete; to take part in a tournament.

the Archbishop trusted that it would be made known who should win the sword.

On New Year's Day, after church, the Barons rode to the field, some to joust, and some to tourney, and so it happened that Sir Ector, who had large estates near London, came also to the tournament; and with him rode Sir Kay, his son, with young Arthur, his foster brother.

As they rode, Sir Kay found he had lost his sword, for he had left it at his father's lodging, so he begged young Arthur to go and fetch it for him.

"That will I, gladly," said Arthur, and he rode fast away.

But when he came to the house, he found no one at home to give him the sword, for everyone had gone to see the jousting. Then Arthur was angry and said to himself:

> **Connecting Literature to Social Studies**
> What qualities does Arthur display that suggest he will be a good ruler?

"I will ride to the churchyard, and take the sword with me that sticketh in the stone, for my brother, Sir Kay, shall not be without a sword this day."

When he came to the churchyard he alighted,[8] and tied his horse to the stile, and went to the tent. But he found there no knights, who should have been guarding the sword, for they were all away at the joust. Seizing the sword by the handle he lightly and fiercely pulled it out of the stone, then took his horse and rode his way, till he came to Sir Kay his brother, to whom he delivered the sword.

As soon as Sir Kay saw it, he knew well it was the sword of the Stone, so he rode to his father Sir Ector, and said:

"Sir, lo, here is the Sword of the Stone,

wherefore[9] I must be King of this land."

When Sir Ector saw the sword he turned back, and came to the church, and there they all three alighted and went into the church, and he made his son swear truly how he got the sword.

"By my brother Arthur," said Sir Kay, "for he brought it to me."

"How did you get this sword?" said Sir Ector to Arthur.

And the boy told him.

"Now," said Sir Ector, "I understand you must be King of this land."

"Wherefore I?" said Arthur. "And for what cause?"

"Sir," said Ector, "because God will have it so; for never man could draw out this sword but he that shall rightly be King. Now let me see whether you can put the sword there as it was, and pull it out again."

"There is no difficulty," said Arthur, and he put it back into the stone.

Then Sir Ector tried to pull out the sword, and failed; and Sir Kay also pulled with all his might, but it would not move.

"Now you shall try," said Sir Ector to Arthur.

"I will, well," said Arthur, and pulled the sword out easily.

At this Sir Ector and Sir Kay knelt down on the ground.

"Alas," said Arthur, "mine own dear father and brother, why do you kneel to me?"

"Nay, nay, my lord Arthur, it is not so; I was never your father, nor of your blood; but I know well you are of higher blood than I thought you were."

> **Connecting Literature to Social Studies**
> Why was it important to keep Arthur's true identity a secret even from him?

Then Sir Ector told him all, how he had taken him to bring up, and by whose

---

8. **alighted** (ə lit′ əd) v.: Dismounted; got down off a horse.

9. **wherefore:** Why.

CONNECTING LITERATURE TO SOCIAL STUDIES

◀ **Critical Viewing** In what ways does this picture explain the respect that Merlin seems to command throughout the story? [Interpret]

MERLIN

Free Public Library of Philadelphia

command; and how he had received him from Merlin. And when he understood that Ector was not his father, Arthur was deeply grieved.

"Will you be my good, gracious lord, when you are King?" asked the knight.

"If not, I should be to blame," said Arthur, "for you are the man in the world to whom I am the most beholden, and my good lady and mother your wife, who has fostered and kept me as well as her own children. And if ever it be God's will that I be King, as you say, you shall desire of me what I shall do, and I shall not fail you: God forbid I should fail you."

"Sir," said Sir Ector, "I will ask no more of you but that you will make my son, your foster brother Sir Kay, seneschal[10] of all your lands."

"That shall be done," said Arthur, "and by my faith, never man but he shall have that office while he and I live."

Then they went to the Archbishop and told him how the sword was achieved, and by whom.

On Twelfth Day all the Barons came to the stone in the churchyard, so that anyone who wished might try to win the sword. But not one of them all could take it out, except Arthur. Many of them therefore were very angry, and said it was a great shame to them and to the country to be governed by a boy not of high blood, for as yet none of them knew that he was the son of King Uther Pendragon. So they agreed to delay the decision till Candlemas, which is the second day of February.

But when Candlemas came, and Arthur once more was the only one who could pull

---

10. seneschal (sen´ ə shəl) *n.*: Person in charge of household arrangements.

◆ **Build Vocabulary**

grieved (grēvd) *adj.*: Saddened; overcome by grief

out the sword, they put it off till Easter; and when Easter came, and Arthur again prevailed in the presence of them all, they put it off till the Feast of Pentecost.

Then by Merlin's advice the Archbishop summoned some of the best knights that were to be—such knights as in his own day King Uther Pendragon had best loved, and trusted most—and these were appointed to attend young Arthur, and never to leave him night or day till the Feast of Pentecost.

When the great day came, all manner of men once more made the attempt, and once more not one of them all could prevail but Arthur. Before all the Lords and Commons there assembled he pulled out the sword, whereupon all the Commons cried out:

> **Connecting Literature to Social Studies**
> What conclusion can you draw from the fact that the common people, rather than the nobles, demand that Arthur be crowned?

"We will have Arthur for our King! We will put him no more in delay, for we all see that it is God's will that he shall be our King, and he who holdeth against it, we will slay him."

And therewith they knelt down all at once, both rich and poor, and besought pardon of Arthur, because they had delayed him so long.

And Arthur forgave them, and took the sword in both his hands, and offered it on the altar where the Archbishop was and so he was made knight by the best man there.

After that, he was crowned at once, and there he swore to his Lords and Commons to be a true King, and to govern with true justice from thenceforth all the days of his life.

◆ LITERATURE AND YOUR LIFE

Reader's Response If you were Arthur, how would you feel about suddenly discovering you were king? Why?

Thematic Focus Why does the deed by which Arthur discovers his identity have to be witnessed by others?

☑ Check Your Comprehension

1. How does Arthur become part of Sir Ector's family?
2. What surprising event occurs on New Year's Day?
3. Describe the reaction of the Barons to this event.
4. In what way does Arthur finally become king?

◆ Critical Thinking

INTERPRET

1. Why do Sir Ector and then the Barons ask Arthur to pull the sword out again and again? **[Infer]**
2. What message does this tale convey about division and unity in a kingdom? **[Draw Conclusions]**
3. Does Arthur seem like a hero to you? Why or why not? **[Make a Judgment]**
4. Arthur is recognized as king after pulling a magic sword from a stone. In what ways do we choose and test our leaders today? **[Social Studies Link]**

Meet the Author

Mary MacLeod (? –1914) made legendary heroes come alive for children by rewriting Shakespeare's plays and the classic tales of Robin Hood and King Arthur. Like many people who have retold the tales of King Arthur, MacLeod based her stories on those of Sir Thomas Malory, who wrote *Le Morte d'Arthur* (French for "The Death of Arthur"), which was published in 1485. It was Malory who first compiled the tales of King Arthur and his Knights of the Round Table.

CONNECTING LITERATURE TO SOCIAL STUDIES

The King Arthur of legend is a national hero of the English people. He may have been loosely modeled on a real leader, but many details of his story were made up and revised in constant retellings.

Although these retellings varied, certain details stayed the same: The teenage Arthur goes on to establish his court at Camelot. There he assembles the greatest knights of the day, who sit as equals at the famous Round Table. Often, these knights go out on adventures, rescuing ladies in distress and righting wrongs.

To people living during the Middle Ages (1066–1485) and after, Arthur and his knights came to represent the gentlemanly traits that nobles were supposed to have: loyalty, bravery, courtesy, and honor. Even in this story about the young Arthur, you can see evidence of these traits.

1. What is the chief detail that makes this story a legend rather than a historical account? Explain.
2. Identify two gentlemanly traits displayed by young Arthur, and support your choices.
3. Why might this account of young Arthur have comforted people during times of danger?

 Idea Bank

Writing

1. **Job Description** As a nobleman of England, write a job description for a king. First, briefly describe the job and its duties. Then, list the physical and mental traits that an applicant for the throne should demonstrate.

2. **Speech** Arthur will have to give a speech to present himself and his policies to his people. Write such a speech for him. Include one or two things he plans to do in order to protect the country.

3. **Legend** Extend the legend of King Arthur by creating another adventure for him. For example, you may want to describe how he passes a different kind of test. Among the characters you can include are the magician Merlin.

Speaking and Listening

4. **Debate** Role-play the debate that the Barons might have had while deciding whether Arthur should be king. Have one side support him and the other argue against him. Present your debate to a small group of classmates.

Projects

5. **Timeline** Create a timeline showing the wars and invasions that troubled English history, which may have helped to foster the legend of King Arthur. Cover the years A.D. 500–1500.

6. **Coat of Arms** Create a coat of arms for Arthur, a special decoration that he can display on his shield. To find out more about coats of arms, research the topic heraldry in an encyclopedia. Then use what you learn—and what you already know about Arthur—to design his coat of arms.

Further Reading, Listening, and Viewing

- Graeme Fife's *Arthur the King* (1991) explains the mysteries of the Arthurian legend.
- T. H. White's *The Once and Future King* (1958) is a humorous retelling of the legend.
- Persia Woolley's *Queen of the Summer Stars* (1990) is about Guinevere, Arthur's queen.
- Alan Jay Lerner and Frederick Loewe's *Camelot* (1960) is a musical based on the legend.

Personal Narrative

Writing Process Workshop

Life is full of memorable events—joyous or miserable, terrifying or enlightening, humorous, wonderful, or just plain exciting. A **personal narrative** is a written account of a memorable event from your own life. Re-create an event that shaped your image of yourself by writing a personal narrative about it. The following skills, introduced in this part's Writing Mini-Lessons, will help you write your personal narrative.

Writing Skills Focus

▶ **Show a clear sequence of events** to help your readers see what happened first, next, and last. (See p. 10.)

▶ **Add emotional depth** by providing details that show what you thought during the event. (See p. 27.)

▶ **Use the power of connotations** by considering the ideas associated with the words you choose. (See p. 35.)

▶ **Supply precise details** that describe your experience accurately and completely. (See p. 47.)

▶ **Let spatial details create the setting.** To help readers picture the event, provide information about where objects and people are located. (See p. 55.)

Alex Haley uses these skills to describe how he discovered a key to his identity. In this passage, Haley shares his notebook with an African, and both realize they are distantly related.

MODEL FROM LITERATURE

from "My Furthest-Back Person" by Alex Haley

I showed the interpreter, he showed and told the *griot,* who excitedly told the people; they grew very agitated. ①
Abruptly then they formed a human ring, encircling me, dancing and chanting. ②
Perhaps a dozen of the women carrying their infant babies rushed in toward me, thrusting the infants into my arms conveying, I would later learn, "the laying on of hands . . . through this flesh which is us, we are you, and you are us." ③

① The author makes the sequence of events clear by listing them in the order in which they occurred.

② By describing the circle of dancers, Haley offers spatial information to help readers see the action.

③ Haley's precise details help bring the events to life.

Prewriting

Interview a Partner Generate a list of questions that will spark ideas for personal narratives. With a partner, take turns asking and answering the questions on the list. Use your answers or the ideas below to help you choose your topic.

Topic Ideas

- Taking a family vacation
- Enduring a storm
- Planning a surprise party
- Winning—or losing—an important game

Play a Mental Video Prepare for writing your personal narrative by replaying the event in your mind. Write down key words and phrases to help you remember the order in which events occurred. Jot down ideas about your emotions at each stage of the event, too.

Draw a Map To help you remember details about where people, objects, and occurrences were located, draw maps or pictures. On your maps, show key moments in your memorable event. You can use your maps to help you provide spatial details as you draft your personal narrative.

Drafting

Use Dialogue Showing, rather than telling, your readers what people say will bring your narrative to life. Through dialogue, you can reveal people's personalities and create a moving picture in your readers' minds. Look at these examples.

Telling	Showing (Dialogue)
My sister and I argued until Dad, thoroughly fed up, yelled at us.	"Did not." "Did so." "Did not!" "Kids!" Dad yelled, thoroughly fed up with us. "Knock it off!"
The phone woke him at three in the morning.	"Uh . . . hello?" he said, rubbing his eyes and squinting at the alarm. "Who?—what *time* is it? Do you know what time it is?!"

DRAFTING/REVISING

APPLYING LANGUAGE SKILLS: Direct and Indirect Quotations

A direct quotation is the exact statement of a speaker. Quotation marks show where a speaker's words begin and end. An indirect quotation is a restatement or paraphrase of what somebody said.

Direct: He said, "I discovered a lot about myself that day."

Indirect: He said he discovered a lot about himself that day.

Practice Rewrite these sentences to change direct quotations into indirect quotations and vice versa.

1. "What is your most memorable birthday?" I asked.
2. She said it was her tenth and that she would always remember it.
3. "On that day, I got Sherman, the puppy who changed my life," she said.

Writing Application As you draft your personal narrative, use both indirect and direct quotations.

Writer's Solution Connection
Writing Lab

For help choosing a topic, use the Inspirations in the Narration Tutorial.

APPLYING LANGUAGE SKILLS: Punctuating Dialogue

Dialogue is conversation between speakers. It needs special punctuation.

• Place quotation marks around a speaker's exact words.

• Begin the first word of a quotation with a capital letter.

• Use a comma to separate the quotation from the rest of the sentence.

• Place a closing period, question mark, or exclamation point inside the quotation marks.

Example: "I feel strange when people call me a hero," she admitted.

Practice On your paper, punctuate these sentences.

1. I'm not brave she said.
2. She explained I just reacted to the danger.
3. It wasn't courage she said. It was adrenaline.
4. I only hope someone will do the same for you! he said.

Writing Application Review your narrative, and correct punctuation in dialogue.

Writer's Solution Connection Language Lab

For more practice with quotations, complete the Language Lab lesson on Quotation Marks, Colons, and Semicolons.

Elaborate About Thoughts and Feelings Provide information about how each stage of the events affected you at the time and how the whole experience has affected you since. Provide enough details so that readers can understand and share your emotions.

Revising

Fill in the Gaps As you revise, look for places in your personal narrative where you need to add details. Review the notes you made when you replayed the event in your mind, and use the items as a checklist. Insert any information you may have missed.

Replace Weak Words With Strong Words Take another look at the words you've used. Replace vague words like *player* with precise words like *goalie*. Consider the connotation of words, and replace those that may provoke the wrong response.

REVISION MODEL

After the two-hour hike, I stood in the clearing marveling at the exhilarating view. The ① creatures sparkled [*hummingbirds*] in the sunlight like tiny jewels. They stood for a moment [*hovered*] in midair, and then moved off in a flash of ② blue, green, and purple. [*sapphire, emerald, and amethyst.*]

① The writer replaces a vague word with a precise word.
② Carefully chosen words help suggest preciousness as well as color.

Publishing and Presenting

▶ **Class Book** With your classmates, create a class book of personal narratives. Each writer may wish to illustrate his or her personal narrative. Display your book in the school library so that others can enjoy your writing.

▶ **Dramatization** Adapt your personal narrative or a section of it as a dramatic performance. Working solo or in a group, act out the event you have adapted from your personal narrative.

Real-World Reading Skills Workshop

Understanding an Author's Purpose

Strategies for Success

You probably read the cartoon pages of the newspaper differently from the way you read the guidelines for behavior at the local pool. While a cartoonist usually works to amuse, the director of a community pool creates a list of rules to establish and maintain order and safety—a completely different purpose. As these examples illustrate, each piece of writing you encounter has a unique purpose. Some common purposes are to entertain, to inform, and to persuade. As a reader, if you can identify a writer's purpose, you can get more out of what you read.

Scan Writing for Clues to Purpose Before you read an essay or article thoroughly, quickly scan the pages for clues to help you identify the author's purpose. The title, language, style, and form the author chooses are important clues to his or her purpose. For example, descriptive essays use more poetic language than police reports do. Make a guess about the author's intention, and adjust your reading to suit that purpose.

Adjust Your Expectations Once you have identified the author's probable purpose, you can prepare yourself mentally. If the author's purpose is to describe or to tell a story, get ready to enjoy the images and events the author creates. If the author's purpose is to inform or explain, prepare yourself to gather useful information from your reading.

✔ Here are other situations in which it's important to recognize the author's purpose:
  ▶ Newspaper articles
  ▶ Political campaigns
  ▶ Advertisements

Apply the Strategies

An inventory is usually a detailed list of items that catalogs the stock of a business. However, in "Thanksgiving Inventory," the writer takes stock of a different kind. Read this section to determine the writer's purpose.

from Thanksgiving Inventory
by Roger Rosenblatt, *Time* Magazine

Then I drive home, where I make more entries still. In the mail are new pictures of the children; I share a cup of hot chocolate with the dog; the wind kicks up; the fat pine on the front lawn trembles its skirts in the late afternoon; shadows smudge the hedges; day hookslides into night. I think of high school baseball, then basketball. The orange moon hangs so low it looks as if it is about to fall to earth and bounce.

This inventory is getting out of hand. Last week alone I made more than a thousand new entries, and I never erase the old ones. If this keeps up, I will require a dozen ledgers, and even then my accounts will be woefully incomplete. Every year is the same. I prepare my inventory for Thanksgiving, to say grace, and always come up short.

1. What is unusual about the items in the writer's inventory?
2. What is the writer's attitude toward his inventory?
3. What is the writer's purpose? How do you know?
4. (a) How would the details be different if the writer were trying to persuade you that you have much to be thankful for? (b) Rewrite the article to reflect this purpose.

Grammar Review

Nouns are the words that name. They name persons, places, things, and ideas or qualities.

Person	peddler, author, Walt Whitman
Thing	city, mirror, money, Grand Central Station
Idea or quality	loveliness, knowledge, luck, freedom

Nouns fall into these categories:

Common (See p. 26.)	writer, town, river
Proper (See p. 26.)	Jack Finney, Galesburg, Columbia River
Concrete (See p. 54.)	piano, library, finger, San Francisco
Abstract (See p. 54.)	humor, jealousy, anger
Collective (See p. 46.)	family, crowd, herd, team, jury

Practice 1 List the nouns in the sentences that follow. Next to each, identify the noun as common or proper; then label any nouns that are collective or abstract.

1. Amy Tan loses her confidence during a disaster at a recital.

2. The audience claps, but the people see her embarrassment as she walks to her chair.

3. While touring Africa, Alex Haley discovers a connection to his family.

4. The writer realizes the truth behind the stories he loved as a child.

5. Charley's visit to Grand Central Station leads him on a fantastic journey.

Practice 2
Rewrite the following paragraph, filling in each blank with a noun.

We share many _____ in common, but we all have our own special qualities that set us apart. Your unique _____ is affected by many factors. Your _____, your _____, and your _____ all shape the things you think, the _____ you like, even the _____ you wear. While some parts of your "self" stay constant over time, other _____ are always changing. Every new _____ you have adds to your own particular values and beliefs.

Grammar in Writing

✔ *When you write, let nouns work for you. Use specific nouns to help your reader see precisely what you are describing.*

General noun: The peddler in Jan Skiba's village sold many *items*.

Specific nouns: The peddler in Jan Skiba's village sold *beads, false pearls, rings,* and *kerchiefs*.

Use a thesaurus—a reference book containing synonyms—to help you select specific nouns.

PART 2 *Testing Yourself*

Racer, Diana Ong

Guide for Reading

Meet the Author:

Ernest Hemingway (1899–1961)

Ernest Hemingway earned international fame for his gripping tales of war and adventure. Amazingly, most of his writing was based on his own true-life experiences.

Restless for excitement, Hemingway left home as soon as he graduated from high school. Just before his nineteenth birthday, he was wounded in World War I. While hospitalized in Italy, he received a medal for heroism. These experiences became the basis for a number of short stories and the novel *A Farewell to Arms*.

A Life of Adventure Hemingway went on to travel the world, using his experiences as material for his writing. African safaris inspired stories like "The Snows of Kilimanjaro." Involvement with the Spanish Civil War sparked the novel *For Whom the Bell Tolls*. His observations of bullfighting in Spain provided material for *The Sun Also Rises*.

THE STORY BEHIND THE STORY

Hemingway's writing celebrates heroes and explores the nature of courage. In much of his writing, he dramatizes the importance of bravery in the face of death and of life's everyday problems. "A Day's Wait" is not about war or outdoor adventures, but it still deals with the quiet courage needed to face fear.

◆ LITERATURE AND YOUR LIFE

CONNECT YOUR EXPERIENCE

When you're waiting for a party, time seems to drag. When you're waiting to have a tooth drilled, time races by. As the photograph on the next page suggests, lying in bed when you're sick can be the worst kind of waiting. In addition to the fact that you feel bad and you're bored, you have plenty of time to worry. In "A Day's Wait," a young boy experiences this worst kind of waiting.

THEMATIC FOCUS: Testing Yourself

Major problems in our lives force us to examine who we are. In "A Day's Wait," an illness causes a boy to discover his inner reserve of courage.

◆ Background for Understanding

SCIENCE

In this story, a doctor measures a boy's temperature in degrees Fahrenheit (°F). On this scale, water freezes at 32°F and boils at 212°F. Although Fahrenheit is used in the United States, most of the world measures temperature in degrees Celsius (°C). In that system, water freezes at 0°C and boils at 100°C. A confusion about these scales sets off part of the trouble in "A Day's Wait."

◆ Build Vocabulary

WORD ROOTS: -vid-

In this story, you'll encounter the word *evidently*, which contains the root *-vid-*, meaning "to see." *Evidently* means "obviously" or "easily able to be seen."

WORD BANK

Which of these words from the story do you think tells how something is done? Check the Build Vocabulary boxes on pages 73 and 74 to see whether you chose the correct word.

| epidemic |
| evidently |

A Day's Wait

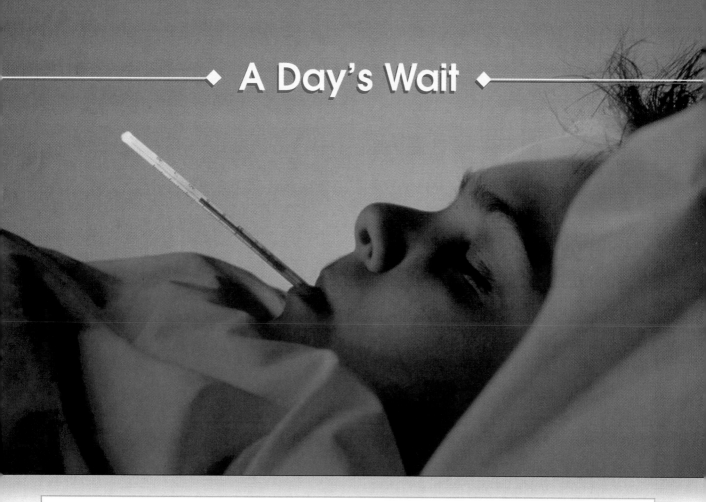

◆ Literary Focus

INTERNAL CONFLICT

Most fiction centers around a **conflict,** which is a struggle between opposing forces. An **internal conflict** is one that takes place inside a character's mind. The struggle may be to overcome a fear, learn how to manage anger, or decide between two options of equal value. "A Day's Wait" is a story of a boy's internal conflict. Because you do not know the boy's thoughts, you discover his conflict through his actions and words.

◆ Reading Strategy

REREAD

Reading can be a many-step process. When you **reread,** you read again for a particular purpose. You might pause to reread a passage that's unclear, or reread an entire story to find answers to unresolved questions. Through this process, you can gain new understanding. For example, you might find clues that explain why the boy in this story is so worried. Use a chart like the one below to record questions that come to mind or details that seem unclear as you read for the first time. Then, reread all or part of the story, focusing on finding answers to your questions.

Reading Questions	Rereading Answers
Why won't the boy stay in bed if he is sick?	

A Day's Wait

ERNEST HEMINGWAY

He came into the room to shut the windows while we were still in bed and I saw he looked ill. He was shivering, his face was white, and he walked slowly as though it ached to move.

"What's the matter, Schatz?"[1]

"I've got a headache."

"You better go back to bed."

"No. I'm all right."

"You go to bed. I'll see you when I'm dressed."

But when I came downstairs he was dressed, sitting by the fire, looking a very sick and miserable boy of nine years. When I put my hand on his forehead I knew he had a fever.

"You go up to bed," I said, "you're sick."

"I'm all right," he said.

When the doctor came he took the boy's temperature.

"What is it?" I asked him.

"One hundred and two."

Downstairs, the doctor left three different medicines in different colored capsules with instructions for giving them. One was to bring down the fever, another a purgative, the third to overcome an acid condition. The germs of influenza can only exist in an acid condition, he explained. He seemed to know all about influenza and said there was nothing to worry about if the fever did not go above one hundred and four degrees. This was a light epidemic of flu and there was no danger if you avoided pneumonia.

Back in the room I wrote the boy's temperature down and made a note of the time to give the various capsules.

---

1. **Schatz** (shäts): German term of affection, used here as a loving nickname.

▲ **Critical Viewing** In this story, a father and son spend time apart. How might time in a natural setting like this one help the father to stay calm? **[Speculate]**

"Do you want me to read to you?"

"All right. If you want to," said the boy. His face was very white and there were dark areas under his eyes. He lay still in the bed and seemed very detached from what was going on.

I read aloud from Howard Pyle's *Book of Pirates;* but I could see he was not following what I was reading.

"How do you feel, Schatz?" I asked him.

"Just the same, so far," he said.

I sat at the foot of the bed and read to

◆ **Build Vocabulary**

epidemic (ep′ ə dem′ ik) *n.:* Outbreak of a contagious disease

myself while I waited for it to be time to give another capsule. It would have been natural for him to go to sleep, but when I looked up he was looking at the foot of the bed, looking very strangely.

"Why don't you try to go to sleep? I'll wake you up for the medicine."

"I'd rather stay awake."

After a while he said to me, "You don't have to stay in here with me, Papa, if it bothers you."

"It doesn't bother me."

"No. I mean you don't have to stay if it's going to bother you."

I thought perhaps he was a little lightheaded

and after giving him the prescribed capsules at eleven o'clock I went out for a while. It was a bright, cold day, the ground covered with a sleet that had frozen so that it seemed as if all the bare trees, the bushes, the cut brush and all the grass and the bare ground had been varnished with ice. I took the young Irish setter for a little walk up the road and along a frozen creek, but it was difficult to stand or walk on the glassy surface and the red dog slipped and slithered and I fell twice, hard, once dropping my gun and having it slide away over the ice.

We flushed[2] a covey[3] of quail under a high clay bank with overhanging brush and I killed two as they went out of sight over the top of the bank. Some of the covey lit in trees but most of them scattered into brush piles and it was necessary to jump on the ice-coated mounds of brush several times before they would flush. Coming out while you were poised unsteadily on the icy, springy brush they made difficult shooting, and I killed two, missed five, and started back pleased to have found a covey close to the house and happy there were so many left to find on another day.

At the house they said the boy had refused to let anyone come into the room.

"You can't come in," he said. "You mustn't get what I have."

I went up to him and found him in exactly the position I had left him, white-faced, but with the tops of his cheeks flushed by the fever, staring still, as he had stared at the foot of the bed.

I took his temperature.

"What is it?"

"Something like a hundred," I said. It was one hundred and two and four tenths.

"It was a hundred and two," he said.

"Who said so?"

"The doctor."

"Your temperature is all right," I said. "It's nothing to worry about."

"I don't worry," he said, "but I can't keep from thinking."

"Don't think," I said. "Just take it easy."

"I'm taking it easy," he said and looked straight ahead. He was <u>evidently</u> holding tight on to himself about something.

"Take this with water."

"Do you think it will do any good?"

"Of course it will."

I sat down and opened the *Pirate* book and commenced to read, but I could see he was not following, so I stopped.

"About what time do you think I'm going to die?" he asked.

"What?"

"About how long will it be before I die?"

"You aren't going to die. What's the matter with you?"

"Oh, yes, I am. I heard him say a hundred and two."

"People don't die with a fever of one hundred

◆ **Literary Focus**
How does Schatz's response hint at an inner conflict?

---

2. **flushed** (flusht) *v.*: Drove from hiding.
3. **covey** (kuv′ ē) *n.*: Small flock of birds.

◆ **Build Vocabulary**

evidently (ev′ ə dent′ lē) *adv.*: Clearly; obviously

and two. That's a silly way to talk."

"I know they do. At school in France the boys told me you can't live with forty-four degrees. I've got a hundred and two."

◆ **Reading Strategy**
Reread the first two pages of the story to see why Schatz thought he was going to die.

He had been waiting to die all day, ever since nine o'clock in the morning.

"You poor Schatz," I said. "Poor old Schatz. It's like miles and kilometers.[4] You aren't going to die. That's a

different thermometer. On that thermometer thirty-seven is normal. On this kind it's ninety-eight."

"Are you sure?"

"Absolutely," I said. "It's like miles and kilometers. You know, like how many kilometers we make when we do seventy miles in the car?"

"Oh," he said.

But his gaze at the foot of the bed relaxed slowly. The hold over himself relaxed too, finally, and the next day it was very slack and he cried very easily at little things that were of no importance.

---

4. **kilometers** (ki läm′ ə tərz) *n.*: A kilometer is 1,000 meters or about 5/8 of a mile.

Guide for Responding

◆ LITERATURE AND YOUR LIFE

Reader's Response Do you find the boy's actions courageous, touching, or silly? Explain.

Thematic Focus How does the boy's illness cause him to test his image of himself? What does he discover?

Journal Entry What do people learn from their experiences with anxiety? Write about a time when you worried about something that turned out to be less of a problem than you originally imagined. What lesson did you take away from the experience?

☑ Check Your Comprehension

1. What starts the boy's concern over dying?
2. How does the boy spend his day of illness?
3. What does the boy's father do while the boy is ill?
4. Why does the boy think he will die?
5. How does the father explain the mistake to his son?

◆ Critical Thinking

INTERPRET

1. What is the meaning of the story's title? **[Interpret]**
2. Describe two ways in which the boy shows courage or concern for others. **[Connect]**
3. Why does the boy cry easily the next day? **[Analyze Cause and Effect]**
4. How do you think the confusion over the boy's illness will change the relationship between the boy and his father? **[Speculate]**
5. What long-term effect might this "day's wait" have on the boy? **[Analyze Cause and Effect; Speculate]**

APPLY

6. In his novels, Hemingway often celebrated bravery. How does the boy's behavior in "A Day's Wait" illustrate Hemingway's ideal of courage? **[Draw Conclusions]**

EXTEND

7. Name two jobs in which the boy's quiet bravery would be valuable. Explain how this quality would be useful in each job. **[Career Link]**

Guide for Responding (continued)

◆ Reading Strategy

REREAD

Rereading passages of text will help you answer questions and clear up areas of confusion. You can truly appreciate the behavior of the boy in "A Day's Wait," for example, once you understand what triggers his fear. Rereading may also reveal that an author has omitted certain information for a reason. Reread "A Day's Wait" to answer each of the following questions.

1. Why doesn't the boy's father notice his son's fear?
2. How did the boy become confused about his condition?
3. What information has the author not included that would have improved your understanding of the story?

◆ Build Vocabulary

USING THE WORD ROOT -vid-

The following words contain the root -vid-, meaning "to see." Complete the sentences with one of these words:

    video   evidence

1. Sports analysts review the ____?____ to get a better look at close plays.
2. His white face and tense expression were ____?____ of the boy's fear.

SPELLING STRATEGY

The -ent in evident makes the word an adjective, a word that describes a noun. Many words that end in -ent have a related noun form that ends in -ence, like evidence. Write the related noun form of these words:

1. resident   3. insistent
2. patient   4. different

USING THE WORD BANK

On your paper, complete the paragraph with words from the Word Bank.

    People in the tiny Italian village were terrified. A terrible ____?____ had caused dozens of people to fall ill. ____?____, a germ had made its way into the water supply.

◆ Literary Focus

INTERNAL CONFLICT

An **internal conflict** is a struggle within a character's mind. In "A Day's Wait," the boy's statements and actions suggest that he is responding to an inner conflict rather than to the actual situation.

1. What conflicting feelings does the boy have?
2. List two examples of unusual statements or actions that point to the boy's internal conflict.

◆ Build Grammar Skills

PRONOUNS

A **pronoun** is a word that takes the place of a noun or a group of words acting as a noun. Pronouns offer writers another way to identify people, places, and things. For instance, Hemingway uses the nouns "boy" and "Schatz" to refer to his main character, and he uses the pronouns "he" and "him" in place of these nouns. Here are the most common pronouns:

I	me	my	hers	herself
she	us	mine	its	themselves
he	you	our	their	who
it	them	ours	myself	whose
we	him	your	ourselves	which
they	her	his	himself	

Practice Write the following sentences. Circle the pronouns.

1. As readers, we understand the father's actions.
2. How would you explain it to the boy?
3. The boy finally tells himself he will survive.
4. It makes him feel much better.
5. Who will research Hemingway's life?

Writing Application Copy the following sentences, replacing the italicized words with pronouns.

1. The boy believes *the boy* is going to die.
2. The boy wonders how *the boy's* father could hunt now.
3. His temperature is high; *the temperature* is 102°F.
4. When readers understand his fears, *readers* can appreciate his behavior.

Build Your Portfolio

 ## Idea Bank

Writing

1. **Internal Monologue** Describe the thoughts running through the boy's mind as he waits to die. Write a monologue—the speech or thoughts of a single character—that captures his feelings.

2. **Film Director's Memo** Imagine that you are directing a movie based on this story. Choose a scene, and describe camera shots that will capture the boy's internal conflict. Explain why each shot would be effective. **[Career Link]**

3. **Definition** "A Day's Wait" shows that courage is sometimes tested in the most unexpected ways. Write a definition of courage. Use your own experiences or those of people you know to illustrate your definition.

Speaking and Listening

4. **Medal Presentation Speech** Deliver a speech in which you award the boy a medal for courage. Explain how his behavior in the face of fear has earned him this medal.

5. **Panel Discussion** Organize an information session about children's health. Invite outside speakers or the school nurse to speak about common childhood illnesses. Prepare a list of specific questions. Then, host the visit, welcoming your guests and directing the conversation. **[Health Link]**

Projects

6. **Comparison Chart** Many Americans know that cakes bake at 350°F and that kids wear shorts if the weather hits 70°F. List significant temperatures like these, and calculate their Celsius equivalents. Use the formula °C= ⅝ × (°F −32). Show results in an illustrated chart. **[Math Link]**

7. **Advice Pamphlet** **[Group Activity]** With classmates, develop a pamphlet to help parents deal with common childhood ailments. One person can research the symptoms children may experience, while others can list tips for keeping children comfortable. **[Health Link]**

 ## Writing Mini-Lesson

A Day of Anticipation

In "A Day's Wait," a boy fearfully anticipates his own death. Imagine how different the story would have been if the boy had been looking forward to a happy occasion. The boy probably would have been anxious for time to pass as quickly as possible, and he might have struggled to contain his excitement. Recall a day you spent anticipating an event or decision. Write a narrative telling the story of that day.

Writing Skills Focus: Elaborate to Make Writing Personal

Draw readers into your personal experience. Provide details to show how the events of that anxious day made you feel. Tell readers, for example, that your heart jumped every time the phone rang, that time seemed to stand still, or that you were surprised at how calm you became as the event drew near.

Prewriting Choose the day about which you will write. Then write an hour-by-hour list of events that occurred during the day. Next to each event, list the emotion it triggered.

Drafting Begin by identifying the anticipated event or by providing a vivid example of your emotions. Then, unfold the day's story, showing the events and your reactions. Conclude your essay by describing what finally happened and the impact the event had on your feelings.

Revising Review your story to identify places where you simply recount events. In these spots, elaborate by adding details that explain how the events made you feel.

◆ Grammar Application

Find the places where your use of nouns is repetitive. Replace some nouns, especially names, with pronouns. Pronouns will make your story flow more smoothly.

Guide for Reading

Meet the Authors:

Richard Wilbur (1921–)

Although Richard Wilbur is known for his writing, he originally planned to be a cartoonist. He created cartoons for his college magazine and later secretly thought that if he failed at other things, he could always be a comic-strip artist. Instead, he has become an award-winning poet.

By the time he reached 30, Wilbur had published two collections of poetry and established himself as an important young writer. In 1987, Wilbur was appointed poet laureate of the United States.

Christina Rossetti (1830–1894)

Poor health forced Christina Rossetti to live a quiet life, but it did not keep her from writing. When she was twenty, Rossetti published her first poems in a magazine produced by her brother. She went on to write many volumes of prose and poetry, including verses for young people, of which "Flint" is an example.

Gary Soto (1952–)

Gary Soto grew up in an industrial neighborhood in Fresno, California. Although the neighborhood was poor, Soto loved it and was deeply saddened when the old buildings were torn down in the 1960's. He says that much of his writing is a reaction to the loss of this happy childhood place.

In fact, Soto's short-story collection *Baseball in April* and his poetry collection *Living Up the Street* reflect his fondness for youth. [For more information about Soto, see page 120.]

◆ LITERATURE AND YOUR LIFE

CONNECT YOUR EXPERIENCE

Like the geode pictured on the opposite page, everyone has an outer appearance that often conceals an inner drama. Think how exciting it is when you see the inner core of someone else or when someone sees what matters to you. In these poems, look for strength waiting just below the surface.

THEMATIC FOCUS: TESTING YOURSELF

When situations test you, you may find your strength somewhere beyond the public part of your personality. These poems remind you that the same applies to others—sometimes you need to look past appearances to find their true identity, too.

◆ Background for Understanding

SCIENCE

Christina Rossetti's poem is about flint—a hard, gray rock. If you strike a piece of flint sharply against steel, sparks will fly, and you can start a fire. Centuries before the invention of matches, flint was an everyday necessity. To start a fire, a person would put a small pile of twigs on pieces of wood. Sparks from the flint and steel would then ignite a fire.

◆ Build Vocabulary

WORDS FROM FRENCH

English has borrowed many words from French. In "Oranges," Gary Soto refers to *rouge*, a French word meaning "red." In English, *rouge* describes a cosmetic, now known as *blusher*, used to color the cheeks.

WORD BANK

Which of these words from the poems sounds like the noise it might describe?

commotion
clamor
iridescent
rouge
tiered
hissing

◆ Literary Focus

SENSORY LANGUAGE

Sensory language appeals to your sense of sight, hearing, taste, smell, or touch. Poets use sensory language to make the world of a poem come alive. To appreciate a poem fully, read with your senses as well as your mind. For example, when you read Soto's description of cars "hissing by," call up your memories of this noise. When Soto and Rossetti describe fire, remember how a fire sounds and smells. Use a chart like the one below to record words and phrases appealing to each sense.

◆ Reading Strategy

RECOGNIZE SIGNAL WORDS

Poets use language in creative ways. They may include different ideas, jumping from one thought or image to another. One way to follow the flow of ideas is to pay attention to words such as *first*, *but*, and *then* that **signal** relationships between the elements in a poem. As you read the poetry of Wilbur, Rossetti, and Soto, find signal words to help you make connections among the words and ideas.

	Sight	Sound	Smell	Taste	Touch
"Flint"	Emerald green grass		grass		

The Writer

Richard Wilbur

In her room at the prow[1] of the house
Where light breaks, and the windows are tossed with linden,[2]
My daughter is writing a story.

I pause in the stairwell, hearing
5   From her shut door a <u>commotion</u> of typewriter-keys
Like a chain hauled over a gunwale.[3]

Young as she is, the stuff
Of her life is a great cargo, and some of it heavy:
I wish her a lucky passage.

10   But now it is she who pauses,
As if to reject my thought and its easy figure.
A stillness greatens, in which

The whole house seems to be thinking,
And then she is at it again with a bunched <u>clamor</u>
15   Of strokes, and again is silent.

I remember the dazed starling[4]
Which was trapped in that very room, two years ago;
How we stole in, lifted a sash

And retreated, not to affright it;
20   And how for a helpless hour, through the crack of the door,
We watched the sleek, wild, dark

And <u>iridescent</u> creature
Batter against the brilliance, drop like a glove
To the hard floor, or the desk-top,

25   And wait then, humped and bloody,
For the wits to try it again; and how our spirits
Rose when, suddenly sure,

It lifted off from a chair-back,
Beating a smooth course for the right window
30   And clearing the sill of the world.

It is always a matter, my darling,
Of life or death, as I had forgotten. I wish
What I wished you before, but harder.

▶ **Critical Viewing** Which lines from "The Writer" might this image illustrate? Explain. **[Interpret]**

◆ **Build Vocabulary**

commotion (kə mō´ shən) *n.*: Noisy rushing about

clamor (klam´ ər) *n.*: Loud, sustained noise

iridescent (ir´ i des´ ənt) *adj.*: Shimmering with colors; having shifting rainbow colors, like a soap bubble

---

1. **prow** (prou) *n.*: Front part of a ship or boat.
2. **linden** (lin´ dən) *n.*: Type of tree.
3. **gunwale** (gun´ əl) *n.*: Upper edge of the sides of a ship or boat.
4. **starling** (stär´ liŋ) *n.*: Bird with black feathers that shine in a greenish or purplish way.

nde Famille *(The Great Family),* Rene Magritte, Private Collection/Lauros-Giraudon, Paris

FLINT

Christina Rossetti

An emerald is as green as grass;
    A ruby red as blood;
A sapphire shines as blue as heaven;
    A flint lies in the mud.

5   A diamond is a brilliant stone,
        To catch the world's desire;
An opal holds a fiery spark;
    But a flint holds fire.

Beyond Literature

Workplace Connection

Opportunities for Young Writers Like many young people, the girl in "The Writer" takes her creativity seriously. Most writers, young or old, dream of publishing their work. But where do you publish when you're twelve or thirteen years old? There are a number of publications and contests for student writers. "Creative Kids," "READ," "Skipping Stones," and *Merlyn's Pen* are among the most well known, but there are many others.

Activity
Go for It! Use the library or the Internet to compile a list of names and addresses of publications and contests that specialize in student writing. Then, choose one and submit your best work. Most publications list submission guidelines in each issue. For contests, contact sponsoring organizations for submission rules.

Oranges

GARY SOTO

Three Fruit, Ashton Hinrichs

▲ **Critical Viewing** This painting of oranges seems to suit Gary Soto's poem. What other image might you suggest? Defend your choice. **[Extend]**

The first time I walked
With a girl, I was twelve,
Cold, and weighted down
With two oranges in my jacket.
5   December. Frost cracking
Beneath my steps, my breath
Before me, then gone,
As I walked toward
Her house, the one whose
10   Porchlight burned yellow
Night and day, in any weather.
A dog barked at me, until
She came out pulling
At her gloves, face bright
15   With rouge. I smiled,
Touched her shoulder, and led
Her down the street, across
A used car lot and a line
Of newly planted trees,
20   Until we were breathing
Before a drug store. We
Entered, the tiny bell
Bringing a saleslady
Down a narrow aisle of goods.
25   I turned to the candies
Tiered like bleachers,
And asked what she wanted—
Light in her eyes, a smile
Starting at the corners
30   Of her mouth. I fingered
A nickel in my pocket,
And when she lifted a chocolate
That cost a dime,
I didn't say anything.
35   I took the nickel from
My pocket, then an orange,
And set them quietly on
The counter. When I looked up,
The lady's eyes met mine,
40   And held them, knowing
Very well what it was all
About.

Outside,
A few cars hissing past,
45 Fog hanging like old
Coats between the trees.
I took my girl's hand
In mine for two blocks,
Then released it to let
50 Her unwrap the chocolate.
I peeled my orange
That was so bright against
The gray of December
That, from some distance,
55 Someone might have thought
I was making a fire in my hands.

◆ **Build Vocabulary**

rouge (roozh) *n.*: Reddish cosmetic used to color cheeks

tiered (tird) *adj.*: Stacked in rows

hissing (his´ in) *adj.*: Making a sound like a prolonged *s*

Guide for Responding

◆ LITERATURE AND YOUR LIFE

Reader's Response Do you think that you are most like the speaker in "The Writer," "Flint," or "Oranges"? Explain.

Thematic Focus Explain how these poems celebrate qualities that are revealed only through careful examination.

☑ Check Your Comprehension

1. Describe the daughter's actions in "The Writer."
2. In "The Writer," how do the speaker and his daughter respond to the starling's situation?
3. What objects are the subject of "Flint"?
4. Where does Rossetti say that flint can be found?
5. Describe the girl in "Oranges" when she first comes out of her house.
6. Why does the speaker in "Oranges" pay for the candy with a nickel and an orange?

◆ Critical Thinking

INTERPRET

1. According to the speaker of "The Writer," how are his daughter and the starling similar? **[Compare and Contrast]**
2. What does the speaker of "The Writer" conclude about the ways he can affect his daughter's life? **[Synthesize]**
3. What comparision does the speaker of "Flint" see between flint and precious gems? **[Infer]**
4. Explain the saleslady's reaction in "Oranges" when the speaker offers an orange. **[Analyze]**
5. What does the remaining orange come to represent to the speaker in "Oranges"? **[Infer]**

APPLY

6. How might "Flint" help people better understand one another? **[Relate]**

COMPARE LITERARY WORKS

7. Which poem do you think is most successful in describing the need to see beyond initial expectations? Explain. **[Evaluate]**

Guide for Responding (continued)

◆ Reading Strategy

RECOGNIZE SIGNAL WORDS

By acting as road signs that direct the flow of ideas, **signal words**—like *then, now, next, after,* and *but*—help you follow a poet's ideas. In "Oranges," for example, the word *as* links two actions happening at the same time: *As* he walked, he heard a dog bark. He hears this sound *until* he sees his date. In "The Writer," the words "I remember" tell you that the speaker is about to describe a memory of a past event.

1. Identify a key signal word in "Flint," and explain the relationship to the ideas it suggests.
2. List two signal words each from "The Writer" and "Oranges." Explain how each word links the ideas around it.

◆ Build Vocabulary

USING WORDS FROM FRENCH

The word *rouge,* which appears in "Oranges," comes from French. Other French words, now common in English, are listed below. With a partner, discuss each one. Jot down a definition for each word you recognize. Check your definition in an English dictionary.

1. bureau
2. physique
3. chic
4. boutique
5. rendezvous
6. cliché

SPELLING STRATEGY

The rule "Use *i* before *e* except after *c*" also holds true when *i* and *e* appear before *r*. For example, *i* comes before *e* in *tier.* On your paper, complete the following words by filling in the blanks with *i* and *e*.

1. p_ _ r
2. f _ _ rce
3. cash _ _ r
4. p _ _ rce

USING THE WORD BANK

Write sentences according to the directions below. Provide enough context to demonstrate the meaning of the italicized words.

1. Use the words *hissing, clamor,* and *commotion* to describe a scary scene.
2. Use the word *tiered* to describe a wedding cake.
3. Use the word *iridescent* to describe a lake.
4. Use the word *rouge* to describe a model's face.

◆ Literary Focus

SENSORY LANGUAGE

Sensory language refers to words and phrases that appeal to the senses. The sensory language in these poems helps you experience the ideas and images in them. For example, "Flint" includes sensory language that displays the jewels in vivid color. "Oranges" lets you experience the street sounds and the feel of a nickel. The vivid description of the starling in "The Writer" enables you to picture the trapped bird.

1. List three sensory details that help you see specific images in these poems.
2. List three sensory details that help you hear the images in these poems.
3. To which of your senses do the following words appeal? (a) salty, (b) purple, (c) fragrant, (d) silky, (e) squeak

◆ Build Grammar Skills

PRONOUNS AND ANTECEDENTS

A **pronoun** takes the place of a noun. The noun that a pronoun replaces is called its **antecedent**. Most antecedents come before the pronouns that take their place. Look at this example:

antecedent   pronoun

The first time I walked with a *girl* . . . *She* came out pulling at her gloves.

Practice In the following sentences, pronouns are italicized. Identify the antecedent for each one.

1. My daughter is writing in *her* room.
2. Trapped inside, the bird hit the window again. *It* finally escaped after many tries.
3. Rubies, emeralds, and sapphires are jewels. *They* are brightly colored.
4. The saleslady accepted the offer. *She* traded the candy bar for the orange.
5. As my girl and I left the store, *we* smiled.

Writing Application Using "Oranges" as an inspiration, describe the first time you met someone. In a paragraph, use at least three pronouns and identify the antecedent for each one.

Build Your Portfolio

 ## Idea Bank

Writing

1. **Jewelry Description** Write descriptions of jewelry for a humorous catalogue. Besides items containing traditional diamonds and rubies, include some pieces of flint jewelry. The more outrageous your descriptions, the better.

2. **He Said, She Said** Rewrite "Oranges" from the girl's point of view. Describe her feelings as she waits for the boy, walks with him, picks out the candy, and watches him pay for it.

3. **Poetry Critique** In a review for a poetry magazine, write a critique of "The Writer." Tell readers what message you think the poet conveys and whether you think he conveys it effectively.

Speaking and Listening

4. **Dialogue** In "Oranges," the speaker and the saleswoman communicate silently when he hands her the nickel and the orange. With a partner, create a dialogue that expresses their thoughts.

5. **Song Lyrics [Group Activity]** With a group, work to make "Flint" into a song. One person can choose or create music for the poem, while another can write additional verses with the same length and rhythm. A third person can direct a rehearsal or recording. **[Music Link]**

Projects

6. **Informative Brochure** By letter or telephone, contact experts such as veterinarians and wildlife rehabilitators to find out how to care for injured wild birds and animals. Ask for tips on avoiding potentially dangerous animals. Turn your findings into a brochure. **[Science Link; Health Link]**

7. **Illustrated Chart** Research the list of precious and semiprecious stones in "Flint." In addition to the scientific characteristics of each one, find out the cultural meaning of each one. For example, emerald is the May birthstone, and diamonds are often set in engagement rings. Present your findings in a colorful chart. **[Science Link]**

 ## Writing Mini-Lesson

Description of a Fire

Two of these poets use the power of fire in their writing. A fire is one of the most captivating things in the world. It can be comforting or terrifying, but it is always powerful. Write a description that captures the energy of a fire.

> **Writing Skills Focus: Sensory Language**
>
> A fire appeals to many senses. Therefore, to make your description complete, include vivid details about how it looks, sounds, feels, and smells. Describe its color, size, and shape. Imagine how it sounds, how it smells, how hot it is, and how the smoke makes you feel.

Prewriting Decide what kind of fire you want to describe. For example, you might choose a bonfire, forest fire, fire in a fireplace, or fire in an outdoor grill. Imagine how that fire would look, smell, feel, and sound. Jot down words to help describe the fire.

Drafting Write your first draft. Organize your details according to the senses to which they appeal. For example, you might begin with how the fire smells and move on to how it looks.

Revising Review your sensory details. Are they varied and precise? Can you replace any of your descriptive words and phrases with more vivid and original alternatives?

> ◆ **Grammar Application**
>
> Look at all the pronouns in your description. For each one, be sure the antecedent is obvious. If necessary, replace a pronoun with a noun or clarify the context so that the antecedent is clear.

Guide for Responding (continued)

◆ Reading Strategy

CONTEXT CLUES

When you study the **context** of a word—the words and ideas surrounding it—you can uncover clues to its meaning. Use the context to determine the meaning of each italicized word in the following passages. Then, explain what clue the context provided.

1. "our real heroes were the famous prize fighters, and the way to *emulate* a fighter was to walk around with a Band-Aid over one eye."
2. "the toughest guys of all wore tourniquets around their necks. We were capable of such *attire*. . . ."

◆ Build Vocabulary

USING THE SUFFIX -ly

The suffix -ly, meaning "in this way," usually indicates that the word is an adverb. Add -ly to each word listed here to create an adverb. Then write a sentence using the new word.

1. ridiculous
2. stupid
3. painful

SPELLING STRATEGY

In certain words that come from French, the k sound is spelled qu, as in tourniquet. On your paper, use the definitions provided to fill in the missing letters of the words containing the qu spelling of the k sound.

1. Bunch of flowers held together: b _ _ _ _ _ t
2. Sports equipment used to hit a tennis ball: r _ c _ _ _ t
3. A very old and valuable piece of furniture: a _ _ _ _ _ e

USING THE WORD BANK

On your paper, answer these questions. Explain each answer.

1. Which would be a more effective *tourniquet* for a deep cut on the leg—a chair or a belt?
2. Would you describe someone at a funeral as "walking *dejectedly* to the car"?
3. If you wanted to expand your car-washing business, might you *incorporate* it?

◆ Literary Focus

HUMOROUS ANECDOTE

A **humorous anecdote,** such as Bill Cosby's story, relates a brief, funny, and often true experience to make a point. Techniques of comedy, including exaggeration and contrast, can help writers bring out the humor in otherwise ordinary stories.

1. Identify a scene in which Cosby uses exaggeration.
2. Identify a scene in which Cosby uses contrast.
3. (a) What message do you think Cosby conveys? (b) How does humor add to his message?

◆ Build Grammar Skills

PERSONAL PRONOUNS

Writers use **personal pronouns** to identify the person speaking (first person), the person spoken to (second person), or the person, place, or thing spoken about (third person). This chart shows the most common personal pronouns:

	SINGULAR	PLURAL
First person	I, me, mine	we, us, our, ours
Second person	you, your, yours	you, your, yours
Third person	he, she, him, her, his, it, its	they, them, their, theirs

Notice that Cosby uses the first-person pronouns *us* and *our* to identify himself and his friends:

Although . . . football stars inspired *us, our* real heroes were . . . prize fighters.

Practice Write the personal pronouns in each sentence on your paper. Then, identify each as first, second, or third person.

1. Cosby and his friends try to act like their heroes.
2. A boxer is popular with them for a while.
3. They switch favorites every week.
4. We also admire actors and celebrities.
5. Who is inspiring to you?

Writing Application Answer the following questions using personal pronouns. For each, identify the type of personal pronoun you used.

1. What does Junior wear every day?
2. How did Bill like to walk?
3. Whom did Bill and his friends idolize?

Build Your Portfolio

 ## Idea Bank

Writing

1. **Letter of Recommendation** Write a letter recommending one of your heroes for a teen role model award. Explain why your hero deserves this award.

2. **Definition of a Hero** Describe the qualities or behaviors you admire most in others. Write a few paragraphs giving your personal definition of a hero.

3. **Humorous Story** Write a funny story about a teenager who trades places for a day with a personal hero. Use exaggeration and contrast to increase the humor of your story.

Speaking and Listening

4. **Stand-up Routine** Jot down a few of the techniques used by your favorite comedians. Then, use your notes to help you develop, rehearse, and stage an original comedy routine or perform an already published one. **[Performing Arts Link]**

5. **Role Play** With a partner, discuss what makes the scenes between Bill and his mother authentic. Then, role-play the scenes for classmates using gestures and body language. **[Performing Arts Link]**

Projects

6. **Comic Strip** Choose an incident from your own life and present it humorously in comic-strip form. Create at least three panels, and include captions or speech balloons to help communicate the action. **[Art Link]**

7. **Scrapbook of Heroes** **[Group Activity]** Working with a group, identify public figures you think might make good role models. Each group member should research at least one person's accomplishments and personal life. Then, organize the group's findings in a scrapbook, with group members contributing photographs and informative captions for their chosen role models. Share your scrapbook with the class.

 ## Writing Mini-Lesson

Essay of Opinion

In his writing, Bill Cosby pokes fun at his boyhood practice of idolizing his sports heroes. He also raises an important question: Are stars worthy of young people's admiration and respect? Write an opinion essay in which you explain whether you think athletes make good role models.

Writing Skills Focus: Provide Reasons

Make your essay effective by **providing concrete and convincing reasons** to support your opinion. Don't simply write: "I think sports figures are good role models." Add impact with a clearly stated reason. For example, when asked why he is imitating Jackie Robinson's walk, Bill Cosby replies: "He's the fastest man in baseball." The reason—Robinson's speed—helps readers understand *why* Cosby wants to imitate Robinson.

Prewriting Make a chart of the pros and cons of holding athletes up as role models. Jot down the names of athletes whose behavior supports each side. Then study your list to decide where you stand.

Drafting Begin your essay by stating your opinion. Follow with two or three supporting reasons. If you can, give a real-life example for each reason. You might put each reason and its example in a separate paragraph. End by forcefully restating your opinion.

> ◆ **Grammar Application**
>
> Avoid repeating names of people too often. Create connections by using personal pronouns—such as *he, she, I,* or *they*—after you have named people or groups.

Revising Review your essay to be sure that your argument makes sense. Strengthen weak reasons and replace boring examples with more vivid or convincing situations.

CONNECTIONS TO TODAY'S WORLD

Tiger: A Biography of Tiger Woods
John Strege

Thematic Connection

TESTING YOURSELF

Have you ever wondered what it would be like to be a world-famous athlete? Competitors like golf professional Tiger Woods must perform at their best over and over—even when they don't feel their best. Each time Tiger plays, he puts himself to the test. He has been doing this regularly since he was thirteen years old.

Woods is just one of many athletes who have dedicated themselves to their sport at a young age. Some, like Woods, have achieved national and even world recognition. In 1998, Tara Lipinski became the youngest figure skater to win an Olympic gold medal. She was fifteen years old at the time.

BEING THE BEST IN YOUR FIELD

Most young athletes never become as well known as Woods and Lipinski, but many do get noticed within their sport. The three Sanderson brothers of Heber City, Utah, all won awards at wrestling's important regional Junior Olympics. At age thirteen, Angela Moscarelli held fifteen national archery records. At age twelve, Kelly Quinn broke new ground as the only female ice hockey player in her league and hoped to be ready for the 2002 women's Olympic ice hockey team. Ten-year-old fly fisherman Jake Howard even received a $5,000 scholarship for winning the Casting Kids national championship.

THE COST OF SUCCESS

These young athletes take competition very seriously. Most train very hard, sometimes for several hours each day. They all learn, as Tiger Woods does, the importance of commitment—of never quitting.

This section from Tiger Woods's biography focuses on a personal test. As you read, think about the tests you face in your life—preparing for a music performance, winning a key basketball game, earning money for a group or school trip, showing your readiness for a new responsibility at home. Consider how these tests ask of you the same blend of dedication and perspective successful young athletes must develop.

JOHN STREGE
(1939–   )

As a reporter, John Strege met Tiger Woods when the golfer was making news at the age of fourteen. Through attendance at many golf tournaments, Strege came to know Woods and his family, and the writer and the golfer became friends. This familiarity paid off. Strege's biography of Tiger Woods, released in 1997, was noted for its author's knowledge of the family.

from

Tiger: A Biography of Tiger Woods

John Strege

He was as thin as a steel shaft and lighter than graphite.[1] He stood five-feet-five and weighed one hundred seven pounds, which, if a fair fight was the objective, would have required he be matched against a 4-iron. In this instance, his opponent was a heavyweight, John Daly, the Arkansas Player of the Year in 1986 and 1987, and already a legend, on a local scale, for his prodigious length.

The site was Texarkana Country Club in Texarkana, Arkansas, on a golf course that, according to a local newspaper, had never before been played by a black. Until then Woods had considered himself only a golfer. Suddenly, he had become a black golfer,

which puzzled him. He was thirteen and only vaguely aware of the social impact a talented black player might have on the game.

Tiger was there to play in the Big I, short for the Insurance Youth Golf Classic, a prestigious event on the American Junior Golf Association tour. The Big I created excitement among the juniors: in the final round they were paired with professional golfers. Daly was among the twenty pros recruited to participate with the sixty juniors,

◆ **Build Vocabulary**

objective (əb jek´ tiv) *n.*: Goal

prodigious (prō dij´ əs) *adj.*: Amazing

prestigious (pres tij´ əs) *adj.*: Having an impressive reputation

---

1. **graphite** (graf´ ĭt) *n.*: Lightweight material used to make golf clubs.

and he was paired with Woods. Through four holes, Woods was ahead of Daly, who turned to a friend and said loud enough to be heard by those in the gallery, "I can't let this thirteen-year-old beat me."

Tiger remained ahead at the turn, three-under par to Daly's one-under par. But Daly's four birdies on the back nine and three on the last four holes enabled him to defeat Woods. Still, Tiger's score was better than those posted by eight of the twenty professionals, and he finished second in the tournament.

Three years later, Tiger was asked what he recalled about playing with Daly that day. "I don't remember too much, except he wasn't a smart player," he said. "He'd take his driver and go over trees. He's got to throttle back."[2]

Daly, conversely, had been indelibly[3] impressed. "That kid is great," he said. "Everybody was applauding him and nobody applauded me. He's better than I'd heard."

Few people knew of Daly then, but Tiger's

legend had already begun to blossom and was steadily expanding. He was still only thirteen when his first college recruiting letter arrived in the mail. Dated March 28, 1989, it read in part:

> Dear Tiger,
> Here at Stanford I'm finding that it is never too early to get word out to you exceptional young men.

It had been sent by Wally Goodwin, the golf coach at Stanford, who a few years before had been tipped off about Woods by Tom Sargent, the professional at Yorba Linda Country Club. Goodwin was reintroduced to the name when he had seen Woods featured in *Sports Illustrated*'s "Faces in the Crowd." He sent off the first of several letters he would mail to Woods in the next five years. Tiger wrote back to him in April:

> Dear Coach Goodwin,
> Thank you for your recent letter expressing Stanford's interest in me as a

---

2. **throttle back:** Ease up.
3. **indelibly** (in del´ ə blē) *adv.*: Lastingly; permanently.

GOLF GLOSSARY

THE COURSE:

tee: Flat area from which the golfer takes the first stroke, or shot, for a given hole

fairway: Path between the tee and the green

green: Area of closely mown grass around the hole

THE CLUBS:

Clubs are numbered from 1 to 9 to indicate the angle of a club. Clubs with a greater number will produce higher and shorter shots.

irons: Clubs with thin, bladelike heads; used for accuracy

woods: Clubs with large, thick heads; used for long shots

driver: Number 1 wood; used off the tee

THE SCORING:

par: Number of strokes assigned to a specific hole or course for comparative purposes

three-under par: Score of three strokes less than par

bogey (bō´ gē): Score of one-over par on a hole

birdie: Score of one-under par on a hole

eagle: Score of two-under par on a hole

ace: Hole in one; when the tee shot goes into the hole

future student and golfer. At first it was hard for me to understand why a university like Stanford was interested in a thirteen-year-old seventh grader. But after talking with my father I have come to better understand and appreciate the honor you have given me. I further appreciate Mr. Sargent's interest in my future development by recommending me to you.

I became interested in Stanford's academics while watching the Olympics and Debi Thomas. My goal is to obtain a quality business education. Your guidelines will be most helpful in preparing me for college life. My GPA this year is 3.86 and I plan to keep it there or higher when I enter high school.

I am working on an exercise program to increase my strength. My April USGA handicap is 1 and I plan to play in SCPGA and maybe some AJGA tournaments this summer. My goal is to win the Junior World in July for the fourth time and to become the first player to win each age bracket. Ultimately I would like to be a PGA professional. Next February I plan to go to Thailand and play in the Thai Open as an amateur.

I've heard a lot about your golf course and I would like to play it with my dad some time in the future.

Hope to hear from you soon.

Sincerely,
Tiger Woods 5-5/100
(*his weight and height*)

"There's no way this youngster wrote the letter," a disbelieving Goodwin said. "It was absolutely a perfect letter. I called Tida[4] after that. I said, 'It's hard for me to believe that Tiger wrote that letter himself.' She said, 'Coach, he wrote every word himself.'

"I was having a team meeting in my office. There were three academic All-Americans.

One guy was being a smart aleck. I said, 'Listen, buster, I got a letter from a little black kid in Los Angeles that writes a letter better than any of you guys in this room can write. It's got capital letters, punctuation, every sentence has a verb in it. It's perfect.' They said, 'Come on, coach.' So I got the letter, made copies and gave one to each guy. Dead silence."

Later that year, Tiger admitted that he was 90 percent certain that he would attend Stanford, although he had not yet even started the eighth grade. He intended to earn a college degree, as a safeguard against failing to earn a living from golf. It was only a contingency plan[5] as he fully expected to excel at the game and to some day win the Masters and the U.S. Open. He already rated his game an A, primarily because he seldom

made mental mistakes. On the golf course, he likened himself to a thirty-year-old in a thirteen-year-old body.

His maturity at such a young age led to countless charges that Earl was a stage father living vicariously[6] through his son's success and applying undue pressure on Tiger to measure up to unrealistic standards. But the Woodses simply presented professional golf as an option to Tiger, never a requirement.

---

4. Tida: Tiger's mother.

5. contingency (kən tin´ jən sē) **plan:** Plan to cover the possibility of an unexpected event.
6. vicariously (vī ker´ ē əs lē) *adv.*: Imagined participation in another's experience.

"He isn't living anyone else's expectations," said Jay Brunza, a long-time family friend and Woods's sports psychologist. "He plays the game for the joy and passion within himself. If he said, 'I'm tired of golf. I want to collect stamps,' his parents would say, 'Fine, son,' and walk him down to the post office."

Overbearing stage parents were not in short supply on the American Junior Golf Association tour.

The AJGA is comprised of the best junior golfers in the country, male and female, and conducts tournaments throughout the year. At one such event, Earl witnessed a father berating his son for playing poorly, leaving Earl shaking his head in disgust. Similar scenes played out at other tournaments, with children frequently walking away from parents in mid-scolding.

"It's not necessary for Tiger to play professionally," Earl said. "If he wants to be a fireman in Umpity-Ump, Tennessee, that's fine as long as he's an upright citizen. There's no pressure. He doesn't have to provide for Dad's welfare. He doesn't have to buy me a home. I already have a home. He doesn't have to buy me a car. I have four cars. I'm set for life. My goal for Tiger is for him to be an upright, contributing citizen."

When Tiger lost to Dennis Hillman in the semifinal of the U.S. Junior Amateur in 1990, his disappointment was apparent. He stared impassively ahead as he and Earl began driving away from the club. Moments later, Tiger reached over and hugged his father and said, "Pop, I love you."

"That made the whole thing worthwhile for me," Earl said. "I'm very proud that Tiger is a better person than he is a golfer."

His mother and father were atypical of the parents of athletic prodigies in that, though Tiger rarely lost a junior tournament, he received the same postround reception from his parents as he did when he won. So Tiger, unafraid of failing and disappointing his parents, had a psychological advantage over those who shied away from pressure and tended to play not to lose.

After a tournament, he and his dad would discuss the round and identify the problem areas that needed work, but his mother stressed that, "he doesn't have to be Jack Nicklaus."

Once when Tiger was ten, he was on the course and was faced with several options on a particular shot. He chose a peculiar one from Earl's perspective. After the round, Earl asked him why he had hit that shot.

"Because that's what I thought you wanted me to do," Tiger said.

"Tiger," Earl said, "you're not out there playing for me. You're out there playing for yourself. On the golf course you're the boss. You do what you want to do."

From then on he understood that he had to perform only to the standards he had established for himself. There was never parental pressure on Tiger to win; anything was an acceptable outcome as long as an appropriate effort was made to avoid losing. Once, his effort failed to measure up, a mistake compounded by the fact that his father was a witness: At the Orange Bowl Junior Classic in Miami, Tiger was leading when he missed a short putt, which ignited a short fuse. He sulked the rest of the round, losing his lead and eventually the tournament. It was apparent that he had quit on himself, the one mistake Earl would not tolerate, and it exposed Earl's military expertise at upbraiding a subordinate.

Earl's lecture, delivered at decibels with which Tiger was unfamiliar, centered on the theme that golf owes no one anything, least of all success, and that quitting is a flagrant foul, intolerable. Even golf's most prolific winner, Jack Nicklaus, was renowned in part for the manner in which he accepted defeat. Even when he was losing, when he was far removed from contention, he continued to grind, as if a U.S. Open victory hung in the balance with each shot. From Earl's lesson, Tiger learned the importance of behaving similarly if he wanted to achieve the same level of greatness.

Thematic Connection

TESTING YOURSELF

Like the other selections in this unit, this section from Tiger Woods's biography highlights the importance of testing your own ideas and pushing yourself to the limits of your abilities.

1. Jot down a few words that describe each of the following characters in the face of a challenge: (a) the daughter in "Two Kinds," (b) Alex Haley in "My Furthest-Back Person," (c) the boy in "A Day's Wait," (d) young Bill Cosby in "Was Tarzan a Three-Bandage Man?"
2. (a) What qualities do the people named in question 1 share? (b) How does Tiger Woods demonstrate these qualities?
3. For centuries, human beings have been challenging themselves—to climb mountains, win races, walk on the moon. Why do you think people are so drawn to tests or challenges? Explain.

◆ Critical Thinking

INTERPRET

1. What does Tiger's letter to Coach Goodwin show about his character? **[Analyze]**
2. How do Earl Woods's responses affect his son? **[Analyze Causes and Effects]**
3. How does Tiger's personal development affect his golf game? Be specific. **[Connect]**
4. What can you conclude from this article about the qualities necessary to become a successful competitive athlete? **[Draw Conclusions]**

APPLY

5. How can you apply the lessons Tiger Woods learned to the tests in your life? **[Relate]**

EXTEND

6. In sports, accomplishments may be easy to see. How is accomplishment measured in fields such as the performing or fine arts? **[Art Link]**

Firsthand Biography

Writing Process Workshop

How do people become who they are? One way of exploring this question is to examine the life of someone you know. You can do this by writing a firsthand biography. This is a life story written by someone who has a close relationship with the subject of the biography. Because you are writing about someone you know personally, you can provide insights not found in biographies based on research. Use the following skills, introduced in this section's Writing Mini-Lessons, as you write your firsthand biography.

Writing Skills Focus

▶ **Elaborate** to make your writing personal by providing details about how you feel about the subject. (See p. 77.)

▶ **Use sensory language**—details that appeal to the senses—to create vivid images. (See p. 85.)

▶ **Supply reasons or examples** to support the statements you make about the subject. (See p. 91.)

▶ **Make sure that your facts are accurate.**

▶ **Provide necessary context** so readers have enough background to understand your subject.

The writer uses these skills in the following firsthand biography of her grandfather.

WRITING MODEL

I yelp as a spray of icy lake water splashes me and the rough, warm boards of the swimming dock. Above the roar of the motorboat, I hear a triumphant whoop. ① Grandpa has just learned to water-ski.

Grandpa is the most amazing person I know. He can repair a car, play the banjo, and bake the world's best chocolate-chip cookies. ② Curious and full of energy, he is always eager to learn new things. Grandma teases him about either behaving himself or getting more insurance, but she loves him just the way he is. ③ Grandpa is my oldest friend—and maybe my best friend.

① Sensory details in these sentences appeal to the senses of touch and hearing.

② Here, the writer provides reasons why the subject is "amazing."

③ Elaboration helps reveal the writer's affection for the subject.

Prewriting

Take Stock of Your Choices To help you think of potential subjects for your firsthand biography, create a list of people whom you know personally whose achievements or experiences make them interesting. Use your list or the topic ideas below to help you choose your subject.

Topic Ideas
- My most unusual relative
- An everyday hero
- An outstanding achiever

Conduct Interviews Gather details for your firsthand biography by interviewing your subject and the people who know him or her well. Before each interview, make a list of questions that will help you get a good picture of the subject's childhood, achievements, or goals and dreams.

Develop a Timeline Use a timeline similar to this one to organize the information you have gathered about your subject. This will give you a clear idea of when important events took place in your subject's life.

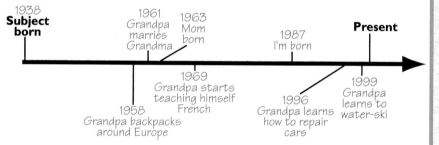

Drafting

Use Your Notes Refer to your interview notes as you draft your firsthand biography. The information in your notes will help you provide necessary background and ensure accuracy when you report facts or quote words from your interviews.

Share Your Feelings Instead of just recounting important dates and events, supply the details and feelings that will add a personal touch to your biography.

Finish With a Flourish Wrap up your firsthand biography by summarizing the most important ideas about your subject. Briefly touch upon the reasons for your opinions about your subject. Finally, explain what conclusions you think people can draw from the subject's life and achievements.

APPLYING LANGUAGE SKILLS: Varying Sentence Beginnings

You can make your writing more lively and interesting by varying your sentence structure. Start some sentences with a subject. Start other sentences with phrases.

Start with a subject:

The man is an inspiration.

He always tries new ideas and activities.

Start with a phrase:

Skilled and patient, the man is an inspiration.

Even at sixty, he always tries new activities.

Practice Rewrite the following sentences so that they start with a phrase.

1. Grandpa patiently explained what he was doing as he fussed with poles, pegs, and ropes.
2. The process suddenly began to make sense.

Writing Application As you draft your firsthand biography, make sure you vary your sentences.

Writer's Solution Connection
Language Lab

For instruction in sentence beginnings and types of sentences, see the lesson on Varying Sentence Structure.

APPLYING LANGUAGE SKILLS: AVOID RUN-ON SENTENCES

A **run-on sentence** is two or more complete sentences written as if they were a single sentence. There are two kinds of run-on sentences:

No punctuation: It was 1965 he was on his own in Europe.

Separation by comma: It was 1965, he was on his own in Europe.

To correct a run-on sentence:

• Use a comma and a coordinating conjunction: It was 1965, and he was on his own in Europe.

• Use a semicolon: It was 1965; he was on his own in Europe.

• Use a period and begin a new sentence: It was 1965. He was on his own in Europe.

Practice Correct these run-on sentences.

1. Grandpa loved dinosaurs he went to the museum.

2. He knows a lot he still studies.

Writing Application Correct run-on sentences you see in your firsthand biography.

Writer's Solution Connection Language Lab

For more help punctuating run-on sentences, see the lessons on Sentence Errors.

Revising

Use a Checklist The following checklist will help you revise your firsthand biography.

▶ Is my writing interesting and vivid?
  As you revise, look for places where you can add sensory details or elaborate to make the biography more personal.

▶ Are events listed in the proper sequence?
  Consult the timeline you prepared earlier.

▶ Is my biography accurate?
  Check your notes to make sure that you haven't made any mistakes.

REVISION MODEL

Grandpa's oldest brother recalls, "He was into everything, even as a baby. He never walked when he could run. Some things never change." Grandpa was born in ② 1937, ① the youngest of three boys. His family lived in a ③ house at what was then the edge of town.

1938
cozy red brick

① Changing the order of the sentences puts events in the proper sequence.
② The writer revised this date to ensure accuracy.
③ More sensory details make objects and events easier to picture.

Publishing and Presenting

▶ **Hall of Fame** With classmates, prepare a bulletin board display that shows photographs or portraits of the subjects of your firsthand biographies. Write captions that let viewers identify each person and preview the essays. Then, arrange your biographies on a shelf beneath the bulletin board so that visitors to your "hall of fame" can learn more about the people featured there.

▶ **Oral Tribute** Using the information in your firsthand biography, prepare a short speech that explains why you selected the subject and what that person means to you.

Real-World Reading Skills Workshop

Strategies for Success

If a writer tried to spell out every single bit of background information about a topic, the resulting writing wouldn't be very interesting and would take too much time and concentration to dig through it! Instead, authors expect you to **make inferences**—to use your own knowledge and imagination to supply information that they don't state directly. When you make inferences in your reading, you're using a skill that you use just about every day in real life, without even realizing it. For example, if you see puddles outside, you infer that it has rained. Or, if you see your friend slam her books down, you can infer she's angry about something.

Look for Clues Read the text carefully. Take note of the information that the author provides, such as time and place and the people's actions, opinions, and reactions. Consider this example: *Spike Johnson walked to the plate slowly, as a hush fell over the crowd.* The detail that he's walking to the plate helps you infer that the author is writing about a baseball game. The facts that Spike is walking slowly and that the crowd is hushed are good clues that it's a crucial moment in the game.

Use Your Experience To make inferences, readers must combine their own knowledge with the information given by the author. In some cases, it may be helpful to think about a similar situation that you have experienced. Consider another example: *Alex wrung his hands and his voice was shaky as he talked to the coach.* Using the details provided (Alex's hand-wringing and his shaky voice) along with your knowledge of what this behavior means, you can infer that Alex is nervous.

Apply the Strategies

Read the article at the bottom of the first column, and make inferences to answer the questions that follow. List the clues in the article that helped you make each inference.

1. What sport is the article about?
2. What part of the game does the writer describe?
3. What is the player about to do?
4. What has the player done to prepare for the game?
5. What does the player always do before his shot?

The Moment of Truth
by Don Pollero

Many lonely practice hours in the gym lead up to the moment when the game clock is down to the last few seconds. A player stands alone on the line, pounding the ball a routine three bounces. Was all that practice enough to make the shot with the game on the line? The crowd holds its breath, waiting for his shot.

> ✔ Here are other situations in which you can use the strategies for making inferences:
> ▶ Watching television
> ▶ Looking at a painting
> ▶ Listening to music

Grammar Review

A **pronoun** is a word that takes the place of a noun or a group of words acting as a noun (see page 76). Pronouns provide another way to identify the people, places, and things in writing.

The pronoun's **antecedent** is the noun (or group of words acting as a noun) to which the pronoun refers (see page 84).

antecedent   pronoun

Even though *flint* is a dull, gray rock, *it* contains fire.

Personal pronouns (see page 90) refer to the person speaking (first person), the person spoken to (second person), or the person or thing spoken about (third person).

	Singular	Plural
First Person	I, me, my, mine	we, us, our, ours
Second Person	you, your, yours	you, your, yours
Third Person	he, him, his, she, her, hers, it, its	they, them, their, theirs

Practice 1 Write the personal pronouns in these sentences. Identify each pronoun as being in the first, second, or third person.

1. Ernest Hemingway's writing shows his belief in courage.

2. When people first read Hemingway, they immediately notice his short sentences.

3. If you could ask him, he might explain it.

4. Which style do you prefer?

5. I guess we all have our own preferences.

Practice 2 Rewrite the paragraph below, replacing repeated nouns with pronouns.

The writing in this section deals with testing yourself—an important part of life. As young people try to figure out what is important, *young people* try many things. Bill Cosby had several sports heroes, yet *Cosby* has become not an athlete but a comedian. Tiger Woods, however, has shown that his own athletic work pays off. Tiger Woods's determination helped *Tiger Woods* compete in golf on a professional level. Woods and Cosby can teach all of us about personal tests. *Woods* and *Cosby* may be heroes to the next generation.

Grammar in Writing

✔ *Pronouns make your writing flow smoothly. However, look out for pronouns that could refer to more than one antecedent.*

Vague: When the boy explained his confusion to his father, he laughed.

(He could refer to the boy or his father.)

Clear: When the boy explained his confusion to his father, his father laughed.

Be sure that the pronouns you use have a definite and clear antecedent.

Speaking, Listening, and Viewing Workshop

According to an old expression, "many hands make light work." This means that a job is easier when you have lots of people to help. The idea holds true whether you are moving a sofa or developing a project for class. When you follow a few simple rules, you can allow the group to benefit from everyone's ideas and talents. In addition, the basic rules of group participation can help build respect, prevent arguments, and protect people's feelings.

Tips for Participating in a Group

✔ *Use these strategies to get more out of participating in a group:*

▶ Take turns speaking during a group discussion. Listen attentively when it is not your turn to speak.

▶ Speak clearly and get to the point. If others want to speak, wrap up quickly, and give the next person a turn.

▶ Listen courteously. Acknowledge other people's contributions and their right to participate.

▶ If you have a problem with someone's ideas, provide constructive criticism and be sensitive to the other person's feelings. Explain why you disagree, and suggest what could be done to address your concerns. Criticize the idea, action, or product—never the person.

▶ As a group, decide first on the tasks that need to be done and how to divide them up fairly. Then, come to an agreement on who will be responsible for each task.

▶ At the end of a meeting, make sure everyone agrees on what was decided and what actions need to be taken.

▶ For complicated projects, make a schedule so everyone knows what needs to be done and when.

Apply the Strategies

With a group of four to six classmates, work through these stages of a project:

1. Brainstorm for ways to raise money for your school or for a charity.

2. Review your list, and decide on one fund-raising idea that you can all support.

3. List the tasks that need to be done, and divide them fairly.

4. Develop a schedule for doing the tasks and assign them.

5. If possible, obtain permission to do your project and carry out your plan.

What's Behind the

Words

Vocabulary Adventures with Richard Lederer

Words From Names

The Greeks had a word for a person who lives on in our everyday conversations—*eponym*, meaning "after or upon a name." Stories of the origins of words made from people or places, real or imaginary, are among the most entertaining about the English language. Such words gradually lose their reference to specific persons and usually shed their capital letters. These additions to our vocabulary help our language to remain alive and energetic. Here are some colorful examples of common words in our language that were born from proper names.

Maverick

Samuel Augustus Maverick, a San Antonio rancher, acquired vast tracts of land and dabbled in cattle raising. When he neglected to brand the calves born into his herd, his neighbors began calling the unmarked offspring by his name. Over time, Maverick's surname lost its capitalization and came to designate any nonconformist—one who is not part of the herd.

Boycott

Charles Cunningham Boycott, an Irish land agent, so enraged his tenants with his rent collection practices that they threatened his life and property and burned his figure in effigy. Thus, from Ireland comes the verb *boycott,* which means "to refuse as a group to deal with someone."

Mesmerize

Franz Anton Mesmer, a Viennese physician, attempted to treat his patients by fixing them with a piercing gaze, questioning them about their ailments, and waving a wand over them. Today, a verb form of his name—*mesmerize*—means "to hypnotize" or "to fascinate."

ACTIVITY 1 Here is a list of ten words that have descended from people's names. Define each word, and find out about the person whose name inspired it.

1. silhouette
2. chauvinist
3. galvanize
4. graham cracker
5. leotards
6. pasteurize
7. poinsettia
8. pompadour
9. sideburns
10. bloomers

ACTIVITY 2 Using their names as clues, identify the inventions of each of these people. Then with a partner, research the story behind the word. Share your findings with the class.

1. George Ferris
2. Robert Bunsen
3. Rudolph Diesel
4. George Pullman
5. Joseph Guillotin
6. Ferdinand Count von Zeppelin

ACTIVITY 3 Make up and clearly define a new word from a person's name. It can be a famous person or a person you know.

Extended Reading Opportunities

Because finding yourself is a lifelong process, the search is a popular topic for writers and readers alike. Here are suggestions for your further exploration of the subject.

Suggested Titles

Bearstone
Will Hobbs

Will Hobbs tells the tale of Cloyd, a Native American boy who struggles to build a future for himself. His people, the Utes, once lived among the stark peaks and lush valleys of southwestern Colorado, the region where this modern-day story takes place.

Cloyd's knowledge of his ancestors helps him deal with his problems in the present. His broken family and his bitterness make it hard for him to accept help until he meets an older white man named Walter Landis.

Where the Red Fern Grows
Wilson Rawls

Although still a ten-year-old, Billy is desperate for a hunting dog, and he sets his mind on getting one. From the day he raises enough money and hikes twenty miles to town, he begins his own journey to adulthood. Billy's experiences with his dogs, Old Dan and Little Ann, teach him about fear, responsibility, ingenuity, friendship, strength, and death.

Child of the Owl
Laurence Yep

After her father is hospitalized, twelve-year-old Casey is sent to live with her grandmother in San Francisco's bustling Chinatown. While adjusting to her colorful new home, she begins to discover aspects of her family history and Chinese heritage she never knew before. In this novel, a grandmother's wisdom helps change a tough, independent girl with no real sense of home to a young woman with a new sense of who she is and where she belongs.

Other Possibilities

Missing Pieces	Norma Fox Mazer
Maniac McGee	Jerry Spinelli
My Brother, My Sister, and I	Yoko Kawashima Watkins
Hold Fast to Dreams	Andrea Davis Pinkney

Guide for Reading

Meet the Author:

Alice Walker (1944–   )

Since her childhood in rural Georgia, Alice Walker's life has been shaped by the love and power of women. First, there was Walker's mother, who stood at the center of her large family. An African American woman with limited education and income, she shared her artistic spirit and creations with her family and community. Later, there were the many African and African American ancestors Walker discovered. Characters based on these women appear in many of Walker's works.

Becoming a Writer Despite her family's size and limited financial resources, Walker went to college. There, she wrote her first book of poems— about a summer trip to Africa and her work in the civil rights movement. Walker's work blossomed from there, and she became very popular. *The Color Purple,* for example, won the Pulitzer Prize and became a successful movie.

THE STORY BEHIND THE ESSAY

This essay is a tribute to Alice Walker's mother, who, in Walker's words, "made a way out of no way." Walker wrote the essay in 1983 as a way to honor the creative influence that helped her achieve great success with *The Color Purple* and other works. This essay has turned out to be a creative influence, too, inspiring Walker's fictional story *Everyday Use.*

[For more on Alice Walker, see page 228.]

◆ LITERATURE AND YOUR LIFE

CONNECT YOUR EXPERIENCE

Think about a special someone—your older brother, a grandparent, or maybe your fourth grade teacher. Somehow this special person may have changed your life or shaped who you are today. In this essay, Alice Walker shares her memories of the person who had the strongest impact on her life, her mother.

THEMATIC FOCUS: Common Threads

As you read, think about how the talents of one generation reappear in the next generation.

◆ Background for Understanding

HISTORY

Like many African American families in the South just after the Civil War, Alice Walker's ancestors lived the difficult life of sharecroppers—working on plantations for landowners who no longer had slaves to work the fields. In return for land, seed, and tools, these former slaves and poor whites gave the landowners a percentage of their crops at harvest time. Sharecroppers worked long hours and dreamed of buying land of their own eventually. However, many fell into debt and were fortunate if they had enough food for their families.

from In Search of Our Mothers' Gardens

◆ Literary Focus

TRIBUTE

The piece you're about to read is a **tribute,** a literary expression of gratitude or admiration, to honor a special person. A tribute often contains anecdotes, or brief stories, that show the qualities of the honored person and includes an explanation of the subject's importance to the writer. As you read, you get to know both the subject and the writer. Use a graphic organizer like the one below to note what you learn about Walker and her mother.

◆ Build Vocabulary

WORD ROOTS: *-nym-*

Alice Walker describes an extraordinary quilt created by an "anonymous Black woman in Alabama." The word *anonymous* contains the root *-nym-*, meaning "name." *Anonymous* means "without name." No one knows who made the quilt.

WORD BANK

Look over these words from the essay. Can you identify which two words have to do with light?

mutilated
vibrant
anonymous
profusely
radiant
illuminates
hindered

Reading for Success

Interactive Reading Strategies

Whether you're watching a horror movie, singing in a chorus, or learning about ancient cultures, you have to be involved to get the most from your experience. Reading is no different—you must actively participate to get the most from your reading. By interacting with literature, you'll better understand what you read. These strategies will help you read interactively.

Set a purpose for reading.
▶ For every piece of writing you encounter, determine your purpose for reading. For example, you may read:
  • To learn about history
  • To study a writer's work
  • To find out more about someone you respect
You might read Alice Walker's essay to see why she honors a special person.
▶ Look for details in your reading that help you meet your purpose. For example, look for Walker's ideas about her mother. Find examples of experiences the two women share.

Relate to your own experience.
▶ People, even in very different settings, often share emotions and ideas. Find ways that your experiences relate to those of the writer or the character.

Ask questions.
▶ Make the reading an active experience by asking questions like these:
  • Why do the characters behave as they do?
  • What causes events to happen?
  • Why does the writer include certain information?
Look for answers to your questions as you read.

Paraphrase.
▶ Paraphrasing is simply restating in your own words. When you paraphrase sentences or paragraphs, you make their meaning clear to yourself.
  Walker's Words: For stories, too, were subject to being distracted, to dying without conclusion.
  Paraphrase: Stories could be interrupted or not even finished.

As you read the following essay by Alice Walker, look at the notes in the boxes. The notes show you how to apply these strategies to your reading.

In Search of Our Mothers' Gardens

Alice Walker

My mother made all the clothes we wore, even my brothers' overalls. She made all the towels and sheets we used. She spent the summers canning vegetables and fruits. She spent the winter evenings making quilts enough to cover all our beds.

During the "working" day, she labored beside—not behind—my father in the fields. Her day began before sunup, and did not end until late at night. There was never a moment for her to sit down, undisturbed, to unravel her own private thoughts; never a time free from interruption—by work or the noisy inquiries of her many children. And yet, it is to my mother—and all our mothers who were not famous—that I went in search of the secret of what has fed that muzzled[1] and often mutilated, but vibrant, creative spirit that the black woman has inherited, and that pops out in wild and unlikely places to this day.

But when, you will ask, did my overworked mother have time to know or care about feeding the creative spirit?

The answer is so simple that many of us have spent years discovering it. We have constantly looked high, when we should have looked high—and low.

For example: in the Smithsonian Institution[2] in Washington, D.C., there hangs a quilt unlike any other in the world. In fanciful,[3] inspired, and yet simple and identifiable figures, it portrays the story of the Crucifixion.[4] It is considered rare, beyond price. Though it follows no known pattern of quilt-making, and though it is made of bits and pieces of worthless rags, it is obviously the work of a person of powerful imagination and deep spiritual feeling. Below this quilt I saw a note that says it was made by "an anonymous Black woman in Alabama, a hundred years ago."

If we could locate this "anonymous" black woman from Alabama, she would turn out to be one of our grandmothers—an artist who left her mark in the only materials she could afford, and in the only medium her position in society allowed her to use.

> The statement beginning with "And yet" identifies Alice Walker's main idea. You can now **set a purpose** to find supporting ideas throughout the essay.

2. **Smithsonian Institution:** Group of museums with exhibits in the fields of science, art, and history.
3. **fanciful** (fan´ si fəl) *adj.:* Playfully imaginative.
4. **the Crucifixion** (kro͞o´ sə fik´ shən): Jesus Christ's suffering and death on the cross.

◆ Build Vocabulary

mutilated (myo͞ot´ əl āt´ id) *adj.:* Damaged or injured

vibrant (vī´ brənt) *adj.:* Lively and energetic

anonymous (ə nän´ ə məs) *adj.:* With no name known

1. **muzzled** (muz´ əld) *adj.:* Prevented from expressing itself.

And so our mothers
and grandmothers have,
more often than not
anonymously, handed
on the creative spark,
the seed of the flower
they themselves never
hoped to see: or like a sealed letter they could
not plainly read.

And so it is, certainly, with my own mother.
Unlike "Ma" Rainey's songs,[5] which retained
their creator's name even while blasting forth
from Bessie Smith's mouth,[6] no song or poem
will bear my mother's name. Yet so many of
the stories that I write, that we all write, are
my mother's stories. Only recently did I fully
realize this: that through years of listening to
my mother's stories of her life, I have absorbed
not only the stories themselves, but something
of the manner in which she spoke, something
of the urgency that involves the knowledge
that her stories—like her life— must be
recorded. It is probably for this reason that so
much of what I have written is about characters whose counterparts in real life are so
much older than I am.

But the telling of these stories, which came
from my mother's lips as naturally as breathing, was not the only way my mother showed
herself as an artist. For stories, too, were subject to being distracted, to dying without conclusion. Dinners must be started, and cotton
must be gathered before the big rains. The
artist that was and is my mother showed itself
to me only after many years. This is what I
finally noticed:

Like Mem, a character in *The Third Life of
Grange Copeland*,[7] my mother adorned with

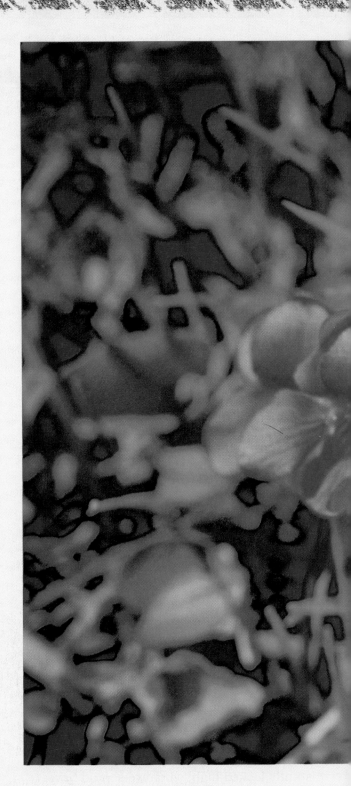

---

5. "Ma" Rainey's songs: Gertrude ("Ma") Rainey, one of
America's first blues singers, lived during the early years
of this century.
6. Bessie Smith's mouth: Bessie Smith was a well-
known blues singer (1898?–1937), who knew and learned
from "Ma" Rainey.
7. *The Third Life of Grange Copeland:* The title of a
novel by Alice Walker.

▲ **Critical Viewing** This essay describes a woman's love of gardening. How can planting and caring for a garden be a creative process? **[Support]**

▲ **Critical Viewing** Gardens like this one and the one Walker's mother kept include many varieties of plants. How might such a blend make a garden more difficult to maintain? **[Analyze]**

flowers whatever shabby house we were forced to live in. And not just your typical straggly[8] country stand of zinnias, either. She planted ambitious gardens—and still does—with over fifty different varieties of plants that bloom <u>profusely</u> from early March until late November. Before she left home for the fields, she watered her flowers, chopped up the grass, and laid out new beds. When she returned from the fields she might divide clumps of bulbs, dig a cold pit,[9] uproot and replant roses, or prune branches from her taller bushes or trees—until night came and it was too dark to see.

---

8. straggly (strag´ lē) *adj.*: Spread out in an irregular way.
9. cold pit: Hole in which seedlings are planted at the beginning of the spring.

Whatever she planted grew as if by magic, and her fame as a grower of flowers spread over three counties. Because of her creativity with her flowers, even my memories of poverty are seen through a screen of blooms—sunflowers, petunias, roses, dahlias, forsythia, spirea, delphiniums, verbena . . . and on and on.

And I remember people coming to my mother's yard to be given cuttings from her flowers; I hear again the praise showered on her because whatever rocky soil she landed on, she turned into a garden. A garden so

> **Paraphrase** this paragraph in this way: "She was a talented gardener whose ability to create beauty softened my experience of our poverty."

brilliant with colors, so original in its design, so magnificent with life and creativity, that to this day people drive by our house in Georgia—perfect strangers and imperfect strangers—and ask to stand or walk among my mother's art.

Relate this passage to your own experience by recalling your own excitement over a colorful sunset or a sleek new skateboard.

I notice that it is only when my mother is working in her flowers that she is radiant, almost to the point of being invisible—except as Creator: hand and eye. She is involved in work her soul must have. Ordering the universe in the image of her personal conception of Beauty.

When you ask why Walker includes this information, you may see her love and appreciation for her mother.

Her face, as she prepares the Art that is her gift, is a legacy[10] of respect she leaves to me, for all that illuminates and cherishes life. She has handed down respect for the possibilities—and the will to grasp them.

For her, so hindered and intruded upon in so many ways, being an artist has still been a daily part of her life. This ability to hold on, even in very simple ways, is work black women have done for a very long time.

This poem is not enough, but it is something, for the woman who literally covered the holes in our walls with sunflowers:

Ask what qualities Walker emphasizes in the poem.

They were women then
My mama's generation
Husky of voice—Stout of
Step
With fists as well as
Hands

How they battered down
Doors
And ironed
Starched white
Shirts
How they led
Armies
Headragged[11] Generals
Across mined[12]
Fields
Booby-trapped[13]
Kitchens
To discover books
Desks
A place for us
How they knew what we
Must know
Without knowing a page
Of it
Themselves.

Guided by my heritage of a love of beauty and a respect for strength—in search of my mother's garden, I found my own.

And perhaps in Africa over two hundred years ago, there was just such a mother; perhaps she painted vivid and daring decorations in oranges and yellows and greens on the walls of her hut; perhaps she sang—in a voice

---

11. headragged (hed´ ragd) *adj.*: With head wrapped around by a rag or kerchief.
12. mined (mīnd) *adj.*: Filled with buried explosives that are set to go off when stepped on.
13. booby-trapped (boo´ bē trapt) *adj.*: With bombs or mines hidden and set to go off when someone touches or lifts an object.

◆ **Build Vocabulary**

profusely (prō fyoos´ lē) *adv.*: Freely or plentifully

radiant (rā´ dē ənt) *adj.*: Filled with light; shining brightly

illuminates (i loo´ mə nāts´) *v.*: Brightens; sheds light on

hindered (hin´ dərd) *adj.*: Held back

---

10. legacy (leg´ ə sē) *n.*: Something handed down by a parent or an ancestor.

from *In Search of Our Mothers' Gardens* ◆ 115

like Roberta Flack's[14]—*sweetly* over the compounds of her village; perhaps she wove the most stunning mats or told the most ingenious[15] stories of all the village storytellers. Perhaps she was herself a poet—though only her daughter's name is signed to the poems that we know.

Perhaps Phillis Wheatley's[16] mother was also an artist.

Perhaps in more than Phillis Wheatley's biological life is her mother's signature made clear.

---

14. Roberta Flack's: Roberta Flack is a contemporary African American singer.
15. ingenious (in jēn′ yəs) *adj.*: Clever and inventive.

16. Phillis Wheatley's: Phillis Wheatley (1753?–1784) was a poet, considered the first important black writer in America.

◇ Guide for Responding

◆ LITERATURE AND YOUR LIFE

Reader's Response Which of Walker's mother's personal qualities do you most admire? Why?

Thematic Focus Walker says that our skills and creativity are passed on to us from our parents. Do you agree with her? Why or why not?

Journal Writing Each person finds his or her own ways to express creativity—from experimenting with clothing styles to writing original music. List some ways in which you are creative. What do these creative expressions mean to you?

☑ Check Your Comprehension

1. Briefly describe the home and setting of Alice Walker's childhood.
2. What role does Walker's mother play in the household?
3. In what two ways did Walker's mother reveal herself as an artist?
4. Why do people visit the garden Walker's mother created?
5. What legacies, or gifts, has Walker's mother given her daughter?

◆ Critical Thinking

INTERPRET

1. What does Walker mean when she writes, "We have constantly looked high, when we should have looked high—and low"? **[Interpret]**
2. How does the anecdote of the quilt hanging in the Smithsonian Institution clarify Walker's point? **[Support]**
3. For Walker, how does the setting emphasize the power of her mother's creative spirit? **[Connect]**
4. If Walker were to summarize what makes her mother an artist, what would she say? **[Synthesize]**
5. Why does Walker call this essay "In Search of *Our* Mothers' Gardens" instead of "In Search of *My* Mother's Garden"? **[Analyze]**

EVALUATE

6. Do you think Walker's poem is a fitting tribute to her mother? Explain. **[Criticize]**

EXTEND

7. (a) What does this story suggest about the importance of practical arts like gardening and quilting compared with fine arts like painting and sculpting? (b) Explain whether you agree with that suggestion. **[Art Link]**

Guide for Responding (continued)

◆ Reading Strategy

INTERACTIVE READING STRATEGIES

When you **read interactively,** you increase your participation in the experience of reading. Review the strategies and the notes showing how to interact with the text. Then, apply them to answer the following.

1. List some questions that came to you while reading. Tell whether you found answers as you read.
2. Find and paraphrase the sentence near the end of the essay, beginning "Guided by my heritage ..."
3. How did your own knowledge or experience help you appreciate Walker's tribute to her mother?

◆ Build Vocabulary

USING THE WORD ROOT -nym-

The word *anonymous* is built around the word root -nym-, meaning "name." On your paper, complete these word equations containing the root -nym-. Then, use the examples to help you define each word.

1. homo (the same) + -nym- = _____?_____
   Example: there/they're/their
2. anto (the opposite) + -nym- = _____?_____
   Example: here/there
3. pseudo (fake) + -nym- = _____?_____
   Example: William Sydney Porter/O. Henry

SPELLING STRATEGY

In the -nym- root, always spell the short *i* sound with *y*. Add -nym to the end of each word part. Write the complete word correctly on your paper.

1. acro +   2. hetero +   3. syno +

USING THE WORD BANK

Identify the word that means the opposite of the first word.

1. radiant: (a) dull, (b) joyful, (c) shining
2. vibrant: (a) alive, (b) weak, (c) eager
3. illuminates: (a) lights, (b) darkens, (c) explains
4. anonymous: (a) unknown, (b) evil, (c) credited
5. profusely: (a) scarcely, (b) frequently, (c) loudly
6. mutilated: (a) damaged, (b) whole, (c) silly
7. hindered: (a) aided, (b) delayed, (c) frustrated

◆ Literary Focus

TRIBUTE

A **tribute** is a literary expression of admiration. In her essay, Alice Walker shows appreciation for her mother's strength and creativity through a vivid and admiring portrait of the woman. Using anecdotes (brief stories) and description, she says "thank you" and "you're wonderful." Through the process of sharing her memories of her mother, Walker also provides readers a glimpse of her own personality.

1. What qualities does Walker admire about her mother?
2. Identify one anecdote Walker uses to describe her mother. How does this story support Walker's tribute?
3. How would you describe Walker's attitude toward her mother?

◆ Build Grammar Skills

VERBS

Verbs are words that express action or state of being. Some verbs show physical action, like *throwing*. Others show mental action, like *thinking*. Verbs like *am*, *is*, *are*, *was*, or *were* show a state of being.

My mother *made* all the clothes we *wore*. . . .
The artist that *was* and *is* my mother . . .

Practice Identify the verbs in these sentences. Then, explain whether each verb expresses a physical action, mental action, or state of being.

1. People drive by our house in Georgia.
2. All my mother's plants grew as if by magic.
3. I admire my mother's courage and strength.
4. Today, my mother might be a professional artist.
5. They handed on the creative spark.

Writing Application Use the following verbs in sentences.

1. create
2. believe
3. express
4. honor
5. remember

Build Your Portfolio

 Idea Bank

Writing

1. **Slogans** Use Walker's essay to create five to ten slogans about mothers. You might begin each with the words *A good mother . . .*

2. **Walker Family Story** Write one of the stories Alice Walker's mother might have told. Use details from the essay and aspects of her personality to choose a plot and theme.

3. **Literary Analysis** For Alice Walker and her mother, a garden is more than just a collection of plants. In an essay, use the details in Walker's writing to discuss the symbolic meaning that gardens hold for the Walkers.

Speaking and Listening

4. **Television Commercial** Write and present the introduction you would give if Alice Walker were speaking to students at your school. Use the information in the material on page 108 as well as what you've learned about Walker from her essay. **[Media Link]**

5. **How-to Speech** Like gardening and quilting, many daily chores can bring out a person's creative talents. Choose a skill that requires an artistic flair—such as gift wrapping or food preparation. In a brief how-to speech, explain the activity and show how creativity can improve the products.

Projects

6. **Sharecropping Report** Walker's parents, grandparents, and great-grandparents lived the life of sharecroppers. Find out more about the living and working conditions sharecropping produced. Share your findings in a written report. **[Social Studies Link]**

7. **Garden Plan [Group Activity]** Plan a garden using the plants named in Walker's essay or others of your choosing. Use graph paper to sketch your plan. If possible, create the garden at home or in the classroom. **[Science Link]**

 Writing Mini-Lesson

Tribute

By the time you've finished reading Alice Walker's tribute, her mother seems like an old friend. You learn about the strong connection between mother and daughter and between artist and teacher. Choose an important person in your life, and write a tribute to that person. Think of it as a way to thank someone for help, guidance, or concern.

Writing Skills Focus: Vivid Words

For a tribute to be effective, your readers must feel as if they know the subject personally. Describe the person with words that add precise detail and help readers "see" the action. Notice how Walker creates an image of the garden.

Model From the Selection

A garden so brilliant with colors, so original in its design, so magnificent with life and creativity, that to this day . . . perfect strangers and imperfect strangers . . . ask to stand or walk among my mother's art.

Prewriting List people who have been important in your life. Choose the person you think you can describe most fully. Jot down vivid details about this person's appearance, traits, special quirks, and—most important—what this person means to you.

Drafting Develop your tribute with anecdotes that capture your subject's qualities and interactions with you. Make the stories believable with vivid descriptions of your subject's behavior.

Revising Review your essay. If your tribute doesn't read as if it honors a real person, replace ordinary verbs, nouns, and adjectives with vivid words that bring the portrait to life.

◆ **Grammar Application**

Use specific verbs in your tribute. When possible, replace forms of *be* with action verbs.

PART 1 *Fitting In*

Friends, Diana Ong

$\mathcal{G}$uide for Reading

Meet the Authors:

Gary Soto (1952–   )

Gary Soto has a lot in common with Victor, a character in "Seventh Grade." Soto grew up in Fresno and once harvested crops in the fields of California.

Finding His Place
Soto began writing while in college. In the fiction and poetry he's written since, he reaches back to the sense of belonging he felt in Fresno. He often writes for young adults—who he knows are also searching for their community, their place. [For more on Soto, see page 78.]

Anna Quindlen (1953–   )

Anna Quindlen spent five years reporting for *The New York Times*, covering issues relating to her family and her neighborhood.

As a reporter, Quindlen wrote regular columns and earned a Pulitzer Prize. She left the newspaper to write novels and has published two bestsellers, *One True Thing* and *Black and Blue*.

THE STORY BEHIND THE ESSAY

"Melting Pot" originally appeared in "Life in the 30's," a popular column that Quindlen wrote for five years. In the column, she spoke from her perspective as a working mother. She addressed issues of concern to other people in her age group.

◆ LITERATURE AND YOUR LIFE

CONNECT YOUR EXPERIENCE

You're wearing the perfect outfit, you've found the coolest way to walk, and you're ready to amaze your friends. Then, you freeze in horror when a classmate gives your shoes an odd look. Now you feel like two people— the one you think you present and the one others are seeing. When the main character in "Seventh Grade" feels these pangs, he wonders what he needs to do to belong.

THEMATIC FOCUS: Fitting In

What do these selections reveal about the ways people try to fit in to their schools and communities?

◆ Background for Understanding

SOCIAL STUDIES

Since the 1970's, immigrants have been coming to the United States at a faster rate than at any time since the start of the twentieth century. Many of the new arrivals come from Asia, the Pacific Islands, and Latin America. As Quindlen's essay describes, neighborhoods in and around large cities are often most strongly affected by the constant arrival of new citizens.

◆ Build Vocabulary

PREFIXES: *inter-*

Anna Quindlen says she fears some people see her as an *interloper*. Understanding that the prefix *inter-* means "among or between" can help you see that *interloper* means "someone who pushes in between others."

WORD BANK

Which of these words from the selections do you think might describe an angry expression? Check the Build Vocabulary boxes to see if you were right.

elective
scowl
ferocity
conviction
sheepishly
fluent
bigots
interloper

◆ Literary Focus

TONE

The **tone** of a literary work is the writer's attitude toward the subject and characters. The tone can often be described in one word, such as *formal, playful,* or *serious.* Tone is revealed in a writer's choice of words and details and even in the sentence structure. For example, Anna Quindlen says that her children are having dinner with her Ecuadorian neighbors and that her neighbors' choice to teach their son only English seems natural to her. These details show Quindlen's affection toward her neighbors.

◆ Reading Strategy

RELATE TO YOUR EXPERIENCES

Once you grasp the tone of a literary work, you'll probably find yourself comparing your own attitude toward the subject and characters with the writer's attitudes. Doing so will help draw you into the literature. To become even more involved with your reading, try to **relate** the literature **to your own experiences**— look for common ground between the characters' lives and your own. For example, you may have had an experience similar to a character's or met someone who reminded you of a character. Use a chart like the one below to note such connections.

Experiences in Story	→	My Experiences
Victor is in the seventh grade.	→ → → →	I am in the seventh grade.

Seventh Grade

Gary Soto

On the first day of school, Victor stood in line half an hour before he came to a wobbly card table. He was handed a packet of papers and a computer card on which he listed his one <u>elective</u>, French. He already spoke Spanish and English, but he thought some day he might travel to France, where it was cool; not like Fresno, where summer days reached 110 degrees in the shade. There were rivers in France and huge churches, and fair-skinned people everywhere, the way there were brown people all around Victor.

Besides, Teresa, a girl he had liked since they were in catechism classes at Saint Theresa's, was taking French, too. With any luck they would be in the same class. Teresa is going to be my girl this year, he promised himself as he left the gym full of students in their new fall clothes. She was cute. And good in math, too, Victor thought as he walked down the hall to his homeroom. He ran into his friend, Michael Torres, by the water fountain that never turned off.

They shook hands, *raza*-style, and jerked their heads at one another in a *saludo de vato*.[1] "How come you're making a face?"

---

1. ***raza*-style . . . *saludo de vato*** (säl o͞o′ dō dä bä′ tō): Spanish gestures of greeting between friends.

◆ **Literary Focus**
What is Soto's attitude toward Victor? Explain.

asked Victor.

"I ain't making a face, *ese*.[2] This *is* my face." Michael said his face had changed during the summer. He had read a *GQ* magazine that his older brother had borrowed from the Book Mobile and noticed that the male models all had the same look on their faces. They would stand, one arm around a beautiful woman, and *scowl*. They would sit at a pool, their rippled stomachs dark with shadow, and *scowl*. They would sit at dinner tables, cool

---

2. *ese* (es´ ā): Spanish word for "man."

drinks in their hands, and *scowl*.

"I think it works," Michael said. He scowled and let his upper lip quiver. His teeth showed along with the ferocity of his soul. "Belinda Reyes walked by a while ago and looked at me," he said.

Victor didn't say anything, though he

◆ **Build Vocabulary**

elective (ē lek´ tiv) *n.:* Optional course or subject in a school or college curriculum

scowl (skoul) *v.:* Lower eyebrows and corners of the mouth; look angry or irritated

ferocity (fə räs´ ə tē) *n.:* Fierceness; wild force

thought his friend looked pretty strange. They talked about recent movies, baseball, their parents, and the horrors of picking grapes in order to buy their fall clothes. Picking grapes was like living in Siberia,[3] except hot and more boring.

"What classes are you taking?" Michael said, scowling.

"French. How 'bout you?"

"Spanish. I ain't so good at it, even if I'm Mexican."

"I'm not either, but I'm better at it than math, that's for sure."

A tinny, three-beat bell propelled students to their homerooms. The two friends socked each other in the arm and went their ways, Victor thinking, man, that's weird. Michael thinks making a face makes him handsome.

On the way to his homeroom, Victor tried a scowl. He felt foolish, until out of the corner of his eye he saw a girl looking at him. Umm, he thought, maybe it does work. He scowled with greater <u>conviction</u>.

In homeroom, roll was taken, emergency cards were passed out, and they were given a bulletin to take home to their parents. The principal, Mr. Belton, spoke over the crackling loudspeaker, welcoming the students to a new year, new experiences, and new friendships. The students squirmed in their chairs and ignored him. They were anxious to go to first period. Victor sat calmly, thinking of Teresa, who sat two rows away, reading a paperback novel. This would be his lucky year. She was in his homeroom, and would probably be in his English and math classes. And, of course, French.

The bell rang for first period, and the students herded noisily through the door. Only Teresa lingered, talking with the homeroom teacher.

"So you think I should talk to Mrs.

---

3. **Siberia** (sī bir′ ē ə): Region in northern Asia known for its harsh winters.

▼ **Critical Viewing** Soto describes the students' mood as "sunny" on the first day of school. How does this photograph convey that feeling? **[Connect]**

Gaines?" she asked the teacher. "She would know about ballet?"

"She would be a good bet," the teacher said. Then added, "Or the gym teacher, Mrs. Garza."

Victor lingered, keeping his head down and staring at his desk. He wanted to leave when she did so he could bump into her and say something clever.

He watched her on the sly. As she turned to leave, he stood up and hurried to the door, where he managed to catch her eye. She smiled and said, "Hi, Victor."

He smiled back and said, "Yeah, that's me." His brown face blushed. Why hadn't he said, "Hi, Teresa," or "How was your summer?" or something nice?

As Teresa walked down the hall, Victor walked the other way, looking back, admiring how gracefully she walked, one foot in front of the other. So much for being in the same class, he thought. As he trudged to English, he practiced scowling.

In English they reviewed the parts of speech. Mr. Lucas, a portly man, waddled down the aisle, asking, "What is a noun?"

"A person, place, or thing," said the class in unison.

"Yes, now somebody give me an example of a person—you, Victor Rodriguez."

"Teresa," Victor said automatically. Some of the girls giggled. They knew he had a crush on Teresa. He felt himself blushing again.

"Correct," Mr. Lucas said. "Now provide me with a place."

Mr. Lucas called on a freckled kid who answered, "Teresa's house with a kitchen full of big brothers."

After English, Victor had math, his weakest subject. He sat in the back by the window, hoping that he would not be called on. Victor understood most of the problems, but some of the stuff looked

like the teacher made it up as she went along. It was confusing, like the inside of a watch.

After math he had a fifteen-minute break, then social studies, and, finally, lunch. He bought a tuna casserole with buttered rolls, some fruit cocktail, and milk. He sat with Michael, who practiced scowling between bites.

Girls walked by and looked at him.

"See what I mean, Vic?" Michael scowled. "They love it."

"Yeah, I guess so."

They ate slowly, Victor scanning the horizon for a glimpse of Teresa. He didn't see her. She must have brought lunch, he thought, and is eating outside. Victor scraped his plate and left Michael, who was busy scowling at a girl two tables away.

The small, triangle-shaped campus bustled with students talking about their new classes. Everyone was in a sunny mood. Victor hurried to the bag lunch area, where he sat down and opened his math book. He moved his lips as if he were reading, but his mind was somewhere else. He raised his eyes slowly and looked around. No Teresa.

He lowered his eyes, pretending to study, then looked slowly to the left. No Teresa. He turned a page in the book and stared at some math problems that scared him because he knew he would have to do them eventually. He looked to the right. Still no sign of her. He stretched out lazily in an attempt to disguise his snooping.

Then he saw her. She was sitting with a girlfriend under a plum tree. Victor moved to a table near her and daydreamed about taking her to a movie. When the bell sounded, Teresa looked up, and their eyes met. She smiled sweetly and gathered her books. Her next class was French, same as Victor's.

They were among the last students to arrive in class, so all the good desks in the back had already been taken. Victor

◆ **Build Vocabulary**

conviction (kən vik´ shən) *n*.: Belief

was forced to sit near the front, a few desks away from Teresa, while Mr. Bueller wrote French words on the chalkboard. The bell rang, and Mr. Bueller wiped his hands, turned to the class, and said, "*Bonjour.*"[4]

"*Bonjour*," braved a few students.

"*Bonjour*," Victor whispered. He wondered if Teresa heard him. Mr. Bueller said that if the students studied hard, at the end of the year they could go to France and be understood by the populace.

One kid raised his hand and asked, "What's 'populace'?"

"The people, the people of France."

Mr. Bueller asked if anyone knew French. Victor raised his hand, wanting to impress Teresa. The teacher beamed and said, "*Trés bien. Parlez-vous français?*"[5]

Victor didn't know what to say. The teacher wet his lips and asked something else in French. The room grew silent. Victor felt all eyes staring at him. He tried to bluff his way out by making noises that sounded French.

"La me vave me con le grandma," he said uncertainly.

Mr. Bueller, wrinkling his face in curiosity, asked him to speak up.

Great rosebushes of red bloomed on Victor's cheeks. A river of nervous sweat ran down his palms. He felt awful. Teresa sat a few desks away, no doubt thinking he was a fool. Without looking at Mr. Bueller, Victor mumbled, "Frenchie oh wewe gee in September."

Mr. Bueller asked Victor to repeat what he had said.

"Frenchie oh wewe gee in September," Victor repeated.

Mr. Bueller understood that the boy didn't know French and turned away. He walked to the blackboard and pointed to the words on the board with his steel-edged ruler.

"*Le bateau*," he sang.

"*Le bateau*," the students repeated.

"*Le bateau est sur l'eau*,"[6] he sang.

"*Le bateau est sur l'eau*."

Victor was too weak from failure to join the class. He stared at the board and wished he had taken Spanish, not French. Better yet, he wished he could start his life over. He had never been so embarrassed. He bit his thumb until he tore off a sliver of skin.

The bell sounded for fifth period, and Victor shot out of the room, avoiding the stares of the other kids, but had to return for his math book. He looked sheepishly at the teacher, who was erasing the board, then widened his eyes in terror at Teresa who stood in front of him. "I didn't know you knew French," she said. "That was good."

Mr. Bueller looked at Victor, and Victor looked back. Oh please, don't say anything, Victor pleaded with his eyes. I'll wash your car, mow your lawn, walk your dog—anything! I'll be your best student and I'll clean your erasers after school.

Mr. Bueller shuffled through the papers on his desk. He smiled and hummed as he sat down to work. He remembered his college years when he dated a girlfriend in borrowed cars. She thought he was rich because each time he picked her up he had a different car. It was fun until he had spent all his money on her and had to write home to his parents because he was broke.

Victor couldn't stand to look at Teresa. He was sweaty with shame. "Yeah, well, I

◆ Literary Focus

How do Mr. Bueller's thoughts and actions create a sympathetic tone?

---

4. *Bonjour* (bōn zhōor´): French for "Hello"; "Good day."

5. *Trés bien. Parlez-vous français?* (trā byan pär lā´ vōō frän sā´): French for "Very well. Do you speak French?"

6. *Le bateau est sur l'eau.* (lə bä tō´ ā sŏor lō): French for "The boat is on the water."

picked up a few things from movies and books and stuff like that." They left the class together. Teresa asked him if he would help her with her French.

"Sure, anytime," Victor said.

"I won't be bothering you, will I?"

"Oh no, I like being bothered."

"*Bonjour*," Teresa said, leaving him outside her next class. She smiled and pushed wisps of hair from her face.

"Yeah, right, *bonjour*," Victor said. He turned and headed to his class. The rosebushes of shame on his face became bouquets of love. Teresa is a great girl, he thought. And Mr. Bueller is a good guy.

He raced to metal shop. After metal shop there was biology, and after biology a long sprint to the public library, where he checked out three French textbooks.

He was going to like seventh grade.

◆ **Reading Strategy**
Recall a time when you pretended to know something you did not in order to impress someone. How did you feel?

◆ **Build Vocabulary**

sheepishly (shēp´ ish lē) *adv.*: In a shy or embarrassed way

Guide for Responding

◆ LITERATURE AND YOUR LIFE

Reader's Response What would you say to Victor about the way he tries to impress Teresa? What advice would you give him?

Thematic Focus Deciding how to "fit in" may be one of the biggest choices the characters in "Seventh Grade" make. How do Victor and Michael change themselves in an effort to belong?

Journal Writing Although he may be your age, Victor might handle his life very differently from the way you approach yours. In your journal, identify the ways in which you and Victor are alike and different. What would you have done in his place?

☑ Check Your Comprehension

1. At what time of year does the story take place?
2. What are Victor's goals for seventh grade?
3. Why does Michael scowl?
4. What does Victor do to try to impress Teresa?
5. What does Mr. Bueller do to help Victor?

◆ Critical Thinking

INTERPRET

1. Why does Victor pretend to know French? **[Analyze]**
2. How do Michael's scowls really affect the girls? **[Analyze Cause and Effect]**
3. How do the impressions Victor, Michael, and Mr. Bueller create prevent people from seeing their real selves? **[Draw Conclusions]**
4. Using examples from the story to support your answer, describe Teresa. **[Support]**
5. What do you predict will happen when Victor tries to tutor Teresa? **[Speculate]**
6. What lesson can you learn from Victor's experiences? **[Draw Conclusions]**

APPLY

7. Why do you think people try so hard to create a good impression? **[Synthesize]**

EXTEND

8. Though his reason is purely social, Victor does choose to study a third language. Do you think young Americans should speak more than one language? Why or why not? **[Social Studies Link]**

Melting Pot

Anna Quindlen

My children are upstairs in the house next door, having dinner with the Ecuadorian family that lives on the top floor. The father speaks some English, the mother less than that. The two daughters are <u>fluent</u> in both their native and their adopted languages, but the youngest child, a son, a close friend of my two boys, speaks almost no Spanish. His parents thought it would be better that way. This doesn't surprise me; it was the way my mother was raised, American among Italians. I always suspected, hearing my grandfather talk about the "No Irish Need Apply" signs outside factories, hearing my mother talk about the neighborhood kids, who called her greaseball, that the American fable of the melting pot was a myth. Here in our neighborhood it exists, but like so many other things, it exists only person-to-person.

The letters in the local weekly tabloid[1] suggest that everybody hates everybody else here, and on a macro level they do. The old-timers are

---

1. **tabloid** (tab´ loid´) *n.*: Small newspaper.

angry because they think the new moneyed professionals are taking over their town. The professionals are tired of being blamed for the neighborhood's rising rents, particularly since they are the ones paying them. The old immigrants are suspicious of the new ones. The new ones think the old ones are <u>bigots</u>. Nevertheless, on a micro level most of us get along. We are friendly with the Ecuadorian family, with the Yugoslavs across the street, and with the Italians next door, mainly by virtue of our children's sidewalk friendships. It took awhile. Eight years ago we were the new people on the block, filling dumpsters with old plaster and lath, . . . (sitting) on the stoop with our demolition masks hanging around our necks like goiters.[2] We thought we could feel people staring at us from behind the sheer curtains on their windows. We were right.

My first apartment in New York was in a gritty warehouse district, the kind of place that makes your parents wince. A lot of old Italians lived around me, which suited me just fine because I was the granddaughter of old Italians. Their own children and grandchildren had moved to Long Island and New Jersey. All they had was me. All I had was them.

I remember sitting on a corner with a group of half a dozen elderly men, men who had known one another since they were boys sitting together on this same corner, watching a glazier install a great spread of tiny glass panes to make one wall of a restaurant in the ground floor of an old building across the street. The men laid bets on how long the panes, and the restaurant, would last. Two years later two of the men were dead, one had moved in with his married daughter in the suburbs, and the three remaining sat and watched dolefully as people waited each night for a table in the restaurant. "Twenty-two dollars for a piece of veal!" one of

---

2. **goiters** (goit´ ərz) *n.*: Swellings in the lower front of the neck caused by an enlarged thyroid gland.

◆ Build Vocabulary

fluent (floo´ ənt) *adj.*: Able to write or speak easily and smoothly

bigots (big´ əts) *n.*: Narrow-minded, prejudiced people

them would say, apropos of nothing.[3] But when I ate in the restaurant they never blamed me. "You're not one of them," one of the men explained. "You're one of me." It's an argument familiar to members of almost any embattled race or class: I like you, therefore you aren't like the rest of your kind, whom I hate.

Change comes hard in America, but it comes constantly. The butcher whose old shop is now an antiques store sits day after day outside the pizzeria here like a lost child. The old people across the street cluster together and discuss what kind of money they might be offered if the person who bought their building wants to turn it into condominiums. The greengrocer stocks yellow peppers and fresh rosemary for the gourmands, plum tomatoes and broadleaf parsley for the older Italians, mangoes for the Indians. He doesn't carry plantains, he says, because you can buy them in the bodega.[4]

Sometimes the baby slips out with the bath water. I wanted to throw confetti the day that a family of rough types who propped their speakers on their station wagon and played heavy metal music at 3:00 A.M. moved out. I stood and smiled as the seedy bar at the corner was transformed into a slick Mexican restaurant. But I liked some of the people who moved out at the same time the rough types did. And I'm not sure I have that much in common with the

▲ **Critical Viewing** In what ways do the doors accompanying this essay illustrate its title? **[Connect]**

singles who have made the restaurant their second home.

Yet somehow now we seem to have reached a nice mix. About a third of the people in the neighborhood think of squid as calamari, about a third think of it as sushi, and about a third think of it as bait. Lots of the single people who have moved in during the last year or two are easygoing and good-tempered about all the kids. The old Italians have become philosophical about the new Hispanics, although they still think more of them should know English. The firebrand community organizer with the storefront on the block, the one who is always talking about people like us as though we stole our houses out of the open purse of a ninety-year-old blind widow, is pleasant to my boys.

Drawn in broad strokes, we live in a pressure cooker: oil and water, us and them. But if you come around at exactly the right time, you'll find members of all these groups gathered around complaining about the condition of the streets, on which everyone can agree. We melt together, then draw apart. I am the granddaughter of immigrants, a young professional—either an interloper or a longtime resident, depending on your concept of time. I am one of them, and one of us.

◆ **Build Vocabulary**

interloper (in´ tər lō´ pər) n.: Person who intrudes on another's rights or territory

---

3. **apropos** (ap´ rə pō´) **of nothing:** Without connection.
4. **bodega** (bō dā´ gə) n.: Small Hispanic grocery store.

Beyond Literature

Social Studies Connection

The Immigrant Experience Like Anna Quindlen's Ecuadorian neighbors, the hundreds of thousands of people who emigrate to the United States each year face tough choices. Should they learn English and teach their children American ways, or should they keep to the old traditions? How can they create a home in their adopted country without missing the community they left behind? Pulled in opposite directions, immigrants may feel unsure of who they are or where they belong.

Cross-Curricular Activity

Get to Know an Immigrant In your family or community, locate someone who emigrated to the United States. With an adult's help, ask at neighborhood churches or temples, local senior citizen centers, or even ethnic restaurants. Interview an immigrant about his or her experiences. Find out the easiest and most difficult things about settling in a new country. Share your findings with the class.

Guide for Responding

◆ LITERATURE AND YOUR LIFE

Reader's Response Would you like to live in Anna Quindlen's neighborhood? Why or why not?

Thematic Focus Why do you think Anna Quindlen is accepted by the long-time residents of her neighborhood?

Cultural Catalog With a partner, list the cultures represented in the "Melting Pot" neighborhood. Compare these with the cultures represented in your classroom, school, or neighborhood.

☑ Check Your Comprehension

1. What countries and ethnic groups do the people in Anna Quindlen's neighborhood represent?
2. What role did Quindlen's children play in helping the family fit into the neighborhood?
3. How does Quindlen get along with her neighbors?
4. How do the people in the neighborhood get along "on a micro level"?

◆ Critical Thinking

INTERPRET

1. What beliefs do most of the neighborhood residents share? **[Connect]**
2. How do these shared beliefs both unite and divide the residents? **[Interpret]**
3. What does Quindlen's choice of neighborhood reveal about what she finds important? **[Analyze]**
4. What advice would Quindlen give on how people of different cultures can get along with one another? **[Draw Conclusions]**

EVALUATE

5. Do you think it's possible to be "one of them" and "one of us"? Explain. **[Make a Judgment]**
6. What does this story suggest about the way people live in American city neighborhoods? **[Social Studies Link]**

COMPARE LITERARY WORKS

7. In what ways do "Seventh Grade" and "Melting Pot" remind us to look beyond people's appearances before making any judgments? **[Connect]**

Guide for Reading

Meet the Authors:

Ralph Waldo Emerson (1803–1882)

Ralph Waldo Emerson had a lifelong motto. This phrase, "*Trust yourself*," helped direct many of his decisions and actions. Emerson believed in people's inborn judgment—their ability to evaluate the world and make the right choices. From his Boston boyhood to his years as a minister, Emerson worked hard at understanding his world. In writing about his ideas, he changed the way many people viewed their place in the world.

Eve Merriam (1916–1992)

"Words are fun!" might have been Eve Merriam's motto. Merriam found the world an entertaining place. She especially enjoyed words—for what they mean, how they look on a page, how they sound. Even as a child in Philadelphia, Merriam loved to make up rhymes. [For more on Eve Merriam, see page 780.]

Rudyard Kipling (1865–1936)

"Be brave, and do what needs to be done" would be a suitable motto for Rudyard Kipling. His approach to life may have dated back to growing up in India at a time when it was ruled by the British. In that time and place, a British boy was expected to be brave and to know where he was going. The poem "If—" outlines some of these expectations. "If—" is a tiny part of Kipling's work. His novels, plays, and other writings won him a Nobel Prize for Literature in 1907. [For more on Kipling, see page 462.]

◆ LITERATURE AND YOUR LIFE

CONNECT YOUR EXPERIENCE

There are moments in our lives when we feel a great sense of accomplishment—imagine passing a tough exam, mastering a rollerblading trick, or getting the lead role in a play. At these times, we celebrate our achievements, our determination, and our own special abilities. The memory of these successes may even help us through difficult times later in life.

THEMATIC CONNECTION: Fitting In

These poems show how even the successful feeling of being an individual gives people shared experiences and helps them to fit in.

◆ Background for Understanding

SCIENCE

Eve Merriam's poem takes a scientific approach to the concept of individuality. Every person—even an identical twin—is different from everyone else. This difference is evident not just in personality or appearance, but in actual scientific ways. For example, no two human beings have the same fingerprint. The pattern of ridges in the skin is different on each person's fingertips. That is why fingerprints can be used to identify people, even when their appearance has changed.

◆ Build Vocabulary

PREFIXES: *uni-*

These poets explore individuality. Once you know that the prefix *uni-* means "one," you can see why Eve Merriam uses the word *unique*, meaning "like no other," in her exploration.

WORD BANK

Which word from the poems might describe people who aren't who they appear to be?

spry
unique
base
impostors
virtue

◆ Literary Focus

RHYME

Rhyme is the repetition of sounds at the ends of words. Rhyme that occurs at the end of lines is called **end rhyme. Exact rhyme** refers to words that sound exactly alike except for the beginning consonant, like *disgrace* and *place*. **Half rhymes** are words whose sounds are similar but not identical, like *squirrel* and *quarrel*.

Rhyme is important for several reasons. You begin to listen for it, and the expectation of sounds repeated keeps you interested. A poet may also vary the **rhyme scheme,** or pattern of rhymes, to call your attention to a passage.

◆ Reading Strategy

PARAPHRASE

Poets may use words in unusual ways, or they may play with sentence order. One way to help you get to the meaning of a poem is to **paraphrase** it. When you paraphrase, you restate lines in your own words. Look at this example:

Kipling's Version: If you can trust yourself when all men doubt you, / But make allowance for their doubting too . . .

Paraphrased: If you can be confident when others question you, / while understanding why they doubt you . . .

Use a chart like the one below to paraphrase passages from these poems.

Poet's Words	Paraphrase

Fable

Ralph Waldo Emerson

The mountain and the squirrel
Had a quarrel;
And the former called the latter 'Little Prig.'
Bun replied,
5 'You are doubtless very big;
But all sorts of things and weather
Must be taken in together,
To make up a year
And a sphere.
10 And I think it no disgrace
To occupy my place.
If I'm not so large as you,
You are not so small as I,
And not half so spry.
15 I'll not deny you make
A very pretty squirrel track;
Talents differ; all is well and wisely put;
If I cannot carry forests on my back,
Neither can you crack a nut.'

◆ **Build Vocabulary**

spry (sprī) *adj.*: Full of life; active; nimble

Thumbprint
Eve Merriam

On the pad of my thumb
are whorls, whirls, wheels
in a <u>unique</u> design:
mine alone.
5 What a treasure to own!
My own flesh, my own feelings.
No other, however grand or <u>base</u>,
can ever contain the same.
My signature,
10 thumbing the pages of my time.
My universe key,
my singularity.

Impress, implant,
I am myself,
15 of all my atom parts I am the sum.
And out of my blood and my brain
I make my own interior weather,
my own sun and rain.
Imprint my mark upon the world,
20 whatever I shall become.

◆ Build Vocabulary

unique (yoo nēk´) *adj.*: Unlike any
other; singular

base (bās) *adj.*: Lowly; inferior

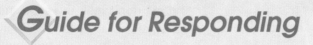

Guide for Responding

◆ LITERATURE AND YOUR LIFE

Reader's Response Which of these poems
comes closest to stating your life motto? Explain.

Thematic Focus Based on the ideas in their
poems, which of these poets might be a better
team member? Which might be more successful
in an individual effort? Explain.

Read Aloud Read these poems aloud. For
"Fable," use voice and gesture to capture the
personalities of the mountain and the squirrel.

✓ Check Your Comprehension

1. Summarize the conversation in "Fable."
2. What does Eve Merriam describe in
   "Thumbprint"?
3. What are the "whorls, whirls, wheels"
   Merriam describes?

◆ Critical Thinking

INTERPRET
1. Why does the squirrel compare its place in
   the world to the parts of a year? **[Interpret]**
2. What does Emerson suggest about the value
   of the individual? **[Draw Conclusions]**
3. Why is the speaker's thumbprint so precious
   to her? **[Analyze]**
4. How does a thumbprint help Merriam make a
   point about individuality ? **[Infer]**

EXTEND
5. How might these poems help family members,
   classmates, or co-workers understand one another better? **[Social Studies Link]**

COMPARE LITERARY WORKS
6. What message do these poems share?
   [Compare and Contrast]

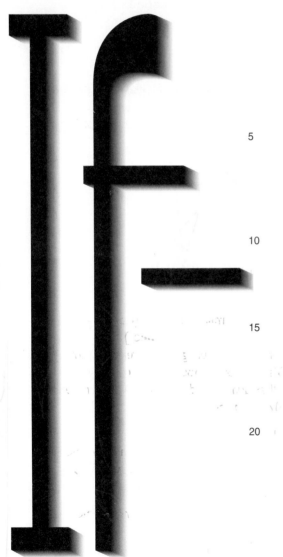

Rudyard Kipling

If you can keep your head when all about you
　Are losing theirs and blaming it on you,
If you can trust yourself when all men doubt you,
　But make allowance for their doubting too;
5　If you can wait and not be tired by waiting,
　Or being lied about, don't deal in lies,
Or being hated, don't give way to hating,
　And yet don't look too good, nor talk too wise:

If you can dream—and not make dreams your master;
10　If you can think—and not make thoughts your aim;
If you can meet with Triumph and Disaster
　And treat those two impostors just the same;
If you can bear to hear the truth you've spoken
　Twisted by knaves to make a trap for fools,
15　Or watch the things you gave your life to, broken,
　And stoop and build 'em up with worn-out tools:

If you can make one heap of all your winnings
　And risk it on one turn of pitch-and-toss,
And lose, and start again at your beginnings
20　And never breathe a word about your loss;
If you can force your heart and nerve and sinew
　To serve your turn long after they are gone,
And so hold on when there is nothing in you
　Except the Will which says to them: "Hold on!"

<blockquote>
25   If you can talk with crowds and keep your <u>virtue</u>,
        Or walk with Kings—nor lose the common touch,
      If neither foes nor loving friends can hurt you,
        If all men count with you, but none too much;
      If you can fill the unforgiving minute
30   With sixty seconds' worth of distance run,
      Yours is the Earth and everything that's in it,
        And—which is more—you'll be a Man, my son!
</blockquote>

◆ Build Vocabulary

impostors (im päs′ tərz) *n.*: People who trick or deceive others by pretending to be what they are not

virtue (vʉr′ chōō) *n.*: Moral goodness

Guide for Responding

◆ LITERATURE AND YOUR LIFE

Reader's Response Which of the conditions described in this poem would you find hardest to fulfill? Which might be easiest to fulfill? Explain.

Thematic Focus According to "If—," what does an individual need to do to fit in with the group?

Journal Writing Choose a line or two from Kipling's poem that reminds you of an experience you've had. In a brief journal entry, explain what happened and what you learned from the experience.

☑ Check Your Comprehension

1. List three situations and behaviors the speaker includes in "If—."
2. What happens if all the conditions are met?

◆ Critical Thinking

INTERPRET

1. What is similar about many of the conditions Kipling describes? **[Connect]**
2. Why does Kipling advise treating Triumph and Disaster as impostors? **[Interpret]**
3. What qualities does Kipling value in people? **[Draw Conclusions]**

APPLY

4. How does the poem celebrate the individual while acknowledging the group? **[Support]**

EXTEND

5. Which jobs might suit a person who meets the conditions of the poem? **[Career Link]**

beard, broad face, and small piggish eyes; the face of another seemed to consist entirely of nose, and was surmounted by a white sugar-loaf hat,[24] set off with a little red cock's tail. They all had beards, of various shapes and colors. There was one who seemed to be the commander. He was a stout old gentleman, with a weather-beaten countenance,[25] he wore a laced doublet, broad belt and hanger,[26] high-crowned hat and feather, red stockings, and high-heeled shoes, with roses in them. The whole group reminded Rip of the figures in an old Flemish[27] painting, in the parlor of Dominie Van Shaick, the village parson, and which had been brought over from Holland at the time of the settlement.

What seemed particularly odd to Rip was, that though these folks were evidently amusing themselves, yet they maintained the gravest face, the most mysterious silence, and were, withal, the most melancholy party of pleasure he had ever witnessed. Nothing interrupted the stillness of the scene but the noise of the balls, which, whenever they were rolled, echoed along the mountains like rumbling peals of thunder.

As Rip and his companion approached them, they suddenly desisted from their play, and stared at him with such fixed, statuelike gaze, and such strange, lackluster[28] countenances, that his heart turned within him, and his knees smote together. His companion, now emptied the contents of the keg into large flagons,[29] and made signs to him to wait upon the company. He obeyed with fear and trembling; they quaffed[30] the liquor in profound silence, and then returned to their game.

By degrees Rip's awe and apprehension subsided. He even ventured, when no eye was fixed upon him, to taste the beverage, which he found had much of the flavor of excellent Hollands.[31] He was naturally a thirsty soul, and was soon tempted to repeat the draft. One taste provoked another; and he reiterated his visits to the flagon so often that at length his senses were overpowered, his eyes swam in his head, his head gradually declined, and he fell into a deep sleep.

On waking, he found himself on the green knoll whence he had first seen the old man of the glen. He rubbed his eyes—it was a bright sunny morning. The birds were hopping and twittering among the bushes, and the eagle was wheeling aloft, and breasting the pure mountain breeze. "Surely," thought Rip, "I have not slept here all night." He recalled the occurrences before he fell asleep. The strange man with a keg of liquor—the mountain ravine—the wild retreat among the rocks—the woebegone party at ninepins—the flagon— "Oh! that flagon! that wicked flagon!" thought Rip— "what excuse shall I make to Dame Van Winkle?"

He looked round for his gun, but in place of the clean, well-oiled fowling piece, he found an old firelock lying by him, the barrel incrusted with rust, the lock falling off, and the stock worm-eaten. He now suspected that the grave roysters[32] of the mountain had put a trick upon him, and having dosed him with liquor, had robbed him of his gun. Wolf, too, had disappeared, but he might have strayed away after a squirrel or partridge. He whistled after him and shouted his name, but all in vain; the echoes repeated his whistle and shout, but no dog was to be seen.

He determined to revisit the scene of the last evening's gambol,[33] and if he met with any of

---

24. **sugar-loaf hat:** Hat shaped like a cone.
25. **countenance** (koun´ tə nəns) *n.*: Face.
26. **hanger** (haŋ´ ər) *n.*: Short sword that hangs from the belt.
27. **Flemish** (flem´ ish) *adj.*: Referring to the former country of Flanders in northwest Europe.
28. **lackluster** (lak´ lus´ tər) *adj.*: Lacking brightness; dull.
29. **flagons** (flag´ ənz) *n.*: Containers for liquids with a handle, narrow neck, spout, and sometimes a lid.
30. **quaffed** (kwäft) *v.*: Drank in a thirsty way.

31. **Hollands** *n.*: Drink made in the Netherlands.
32. **roysters** (rois´ tərs) *n.*: People who are having a good time at a party.
33. **gambol** (gam´ bəl) *n.*: Play; frolic.

the party, to demand his dog and gun. As he rose to walk, he found himself stiff in the joints, and wanting in his usual activity. "These mountain beds do not agree with me," thought Rip, "and if this frolic should lay me up with a fit of the rheumatism, I shall have a blessed time with Dame Van Winkle." With some difficulty he got down into the glen: he found the gully up which he and his companion had ascended the preceding evening; but to his astonishment a mountain stream was now foaming down it, leaping from rock to rock, and filling the glen with babbling murmurs. He, however, made shift to scramble up its sides, working his toilsome way through thickets of birch, sassafras, and witch hazel, and sometimes tripped up or entangled by the wild grapevines that twisted their coils or tendrils from tree to tree, and spread a kind of network in his path.

At length he reached to where the ravine had opened through the cliffs to the amphitheater; but no traces of such opening remained. The

▼ **Critical Viewing** What has changed about Rip's appearance in this painting? **[Analyze]**

◆ **Build Vocabulary**

melancholy (mel′ ən käl′ ē) *adj.*: Sad; gloomy
declined (dē klīnd′) *v.*: Bent or sank downward

rocks presented a high impenetrable wall, over which the torrent came tumbling in a sheet of feathery foam, and fell into a broad deep basin, black from the shadows of the surrounding forest. Here, then, poor Rip was brought to a stand. He again called and whistled after his dog; he was only answered by the cawing of a flock of idle crows, sporting high in air about a dry tree that overhung a sunny precipice; and who, secure in their elevation, seemed to look down and scoff at the poor man's perplexities. What was to be done? The morning was passing away, and Rip felt famished for want of his breakfast. He grieved to give up his dog and gun; he dreaded to meet his wife; but it would not do to starve among the mountains. He shook his head, shouldered the rusty firelock, and with a heart full of trouble and anxiety, turned his steps homeward.

As he approached the village he met a number of people, but none whom he knew, which somewhat surprised him, for he had thought himself acquainted with everyone in the country round. Their dress, too, was of a different fashion from that to which he was accustomed. They all stared at him with equal marks of surprise,

▼ **Critical Viewing** Which details in this painting relate to details in the story? [**Connect**]

Return of Rip Van Winkle, 1849, John Quidor, National Gallery of Art, Washington, DC

and whenever they cast their eyes upon him, invariably stroked their chins. The constant recurrence of this gesture induced Rip, involuntarily, to do the same, when, to his astonishment, he found his beard had grown a foot long!

He had now entered the outskirts of the village. A troop of strange children ran at his heels, hooting after him, and pointing at his gray beard. The dogs, too, not one of which he recognized for an old acquaintance, barked at him as he passed. The very village was altered; it was larger and more populous. There were rows of houses which he had never seen before, and those which had been his familiar haunts had disappeared. Strange names were over the doors—strange faces at the windows—every thing was strange. His mind now misgave him; he began to doubt whether both he and the world around him were not bewitched. Surely this was his native village, which he had left but the day before. There stood the Catskill mountains—there ran the silver Hudson at a distance—there was every hill and dale precisely as it had always been—Rip was sorely perplexed—"That flagon last night," thought he; "has addled[34] my poor head sadly!"

It was with some difficulty that he found the way to his own house, which he approached with silent awe, expecting every moment to hear the shrill voice of Dame Van Winkle. He found the house gone to decay—the roof fallen in, the windows shattered, and the doors off the hinges. A half-starved dog that looked like Wolf was skulking about it. Rip called him by name, but the cur snarled, showed his teeth, and passed on. This was an unkind cut indeed—"My very dog," sighed poor Rip, "has forgotten me!"

He entered the house, which, to tell the truth, Dame Van Winkle had always kept in neat order. It was empty, forlorn, and apparently abandoned. This desolateness overcame all his fears—he called loudly for his wife and children —the lonely chambers rang for a moment with his voice, and then all again was silence.

He now hurried forth, and hastened to his old resort, the village inn—but it too was gone. A large rickety wooden building stood in its place, with great gaping windows, some of them broken and mended with old hats and petticoats, and over the door was painted, "The Union Hotel, by Jonathan Doolittle." Instead of the great tree that used to shelter the quiet little Dutch inn of yore, there now was reared a tall, naked pole, with something on the top that looked like a red nightcap,[35] and from it was fluttering a flag, on which was a singular assemblage of stars and stripes—all this was strange and incomprehensible. He recognized on the sign, however, the ruby face of King George, under which he had smoked so many a peaceful pipe; but even this was singularly metamorphosed.[36] The red coat was changed for one of blue and buff, a sword was held in the hand instead of a scepter, the head was decorated with a cocked hat, and underneath was painted in large characters, GENERAL WASHINGTON.

> ◆ **Literary Focus**
> What historical changes seem to have taken place since Rip was here last? How do you know?

There was, as usual, a crowd of folk about the door, but none that Rip recollected. The very character of the people seemed changed. There was a busy, bustling, disputatious tone about it, instead of the accustomed drowsy tranquillity. He looked in vain for the sage Nicholas Vedder, with his broad face, double chin, and fair long pipe, uttering clouds of tobacco smoke instead of idle speeches; or Van Bummel, the schoolmaster, doling forth the contents of an ancient newspaper. In places of these, a lean, bilious-looking[37] fellow, with his pockets full

---

34. addled (ad´ əld) *v.*: Muddled and confused.

35. red nightcap: Liberty cap, used by colonists to symbolize their freedom from Great Britain.
36. metamorphosed (met´ ə môr´ fōzd) *v.*: Changed.
37. bilious (bil´ yəs) **-looking** *adj.*: Looking cross or bad-tempered.

of handbills, was speaking vehemently about rights of citizens—elections—members of Congress—liberty—Bunker's Hill—heroes of seventy-six—and other words, which were a perfect Babylonish jargon[38] to the bewildered Van Winkle.

The appearance of Rip, with his long grizzled beard, his rusty fowling piece, his uncouth dress, and an army of women and children at his heels, soon attracted the attention of the tavern politicians. They crowded round him, eyeing him from head to foot with great curiosity. The orator bustled up to him, and, drawing him partly aside, inquired "on which side he voted?" Rip stared in vacant stupidity. Another short but busy little fellow pulled him by the arm, and, rising on tiptoe, inquired in his ear, "whether he was Federal or Democrat?"[39] Rip was equally at a loss to comprehend the question; when a knowing, self-important old gentleman in a sharp cocked hat made his way through the crowd, putting them to the right and left with his elbows as he passed, and planting himself before Van Winkle, with one arm akimbo,[40] the other resting on his cane, his keen eyes and sharp hat penetrating, as it were, into his very soul, demanded, in an austere tone, "what brought him to the election with a gun on his shoulder, and a mob at his heels, and whether he meant to breed a riot in the village?" "Alas! gentlemen," cried Rip, somewhat

> "Rip's heart died away at hearing of these sad changes in his home and friends, and finding himself thus alone in the world."

dismayed, "I am a poor, quiet man, a native of the place, and a loyal subject of the king, God bless him!"

Here a general shout burst from the bystanders— "A tory![41] a tory! a spy! a refugee! hustle him! away with him!" It was with great difficulty that the self-important man in the cocked hat restored order; and, having assumed a tenfold austerity of brow, demanded again of the unknown culprit, what he came there for, and whom he was seeking. The poor man humbly assured him that he meant no harm, but merely came there in search of some of his neighbors, who used to keep about the tavern.

"Well, who are they? Name them."

Rip bethought himself a moment, and inquired, "Where's Nicholas Vedder?"

There was a silence for a little while, when an old man replied, in a thin, piping voice, "Nicholas Vedder! why, he is dead and gone these eighteen years! There was a wooden tombstone in the churchyard that used to tell all about him, but that's rotten and gone too."

"Where's Brom Dutcher?"

"Oh, he went off to the army in the beginning of the war; some say he was killed at the storming of Stony Point[42]—others say he was drowned in a squall at the foot of Antony's Nose.[43] I don't know—he never came back again."

"Where's Van Bummel, the schoolmaster?"

---

38. Babylonish (bab´ ə lō´ nish) **jargon:** Language he could not understand.

39. Federal or Democrat: Two political parties.

40. akimbo (ə kim´ bō) *adj.*: Hand on hip, with elbow pointing outward.

41. tory (tôr´ ē): Person who supported the British during the American Revolution.

42. Stony Point: Town on the Hudson River where a Revolutionary War battle was fought in 1779.

43. Antony's Nose: Mountain on the Hudson River.

"He went off to the wars, too, was a great militia general, and is now in Congress."

Rip's heart died away at hearing of these sad changes in his home and friends, and finding himself thus alone in the world. Every answer puzzled him too, by treating of such enormous lapses of time, and of matters which he could not understand; war—Congress—Stony Point—he had no courage to ask after any more friends, but cried out in despair, "Does nobody here know Rip Van Winkle?"

"Oh, Rip Van Winkle!" exclaimed two or three, "Oh, to be sure! that's Rip Van Winkle yonder, leaning against the tree."

Rip looked, and beheld a precise counterpart of himself, as he went up the mountain: apparently as lazy, and certainly as ragged. The poor fellow was now completely confounded. He doubted his own identity, and whether he was himself or another man. In the midst of his bewilderment, the man in the cocked hat demanded who he was, and what was his name.

"Goodness knows," exclaimed he, at his wit's end; "I'm not myself—I'm somebody else—that's me yonder—no—that's somebody else got into my shoes—I was myself last night, but I fell asleep on the mountain, and they've changed my gun, and everything's changed, and I'm changed, and I can't tell what's my name, or who I am!"

The bystanders began now to look at each other, nod, wink significantly, and tap their fingers against their foreheads. There was a whisper, also, about securing the gun, and keeping the old fellow from doing mischief, at the very suggestion of which the self-important man in the cocked hat retired with some precipitation. At this critical moment a fresh, comely[44] woman pressed through the throng to get a peep at the gray-bearded man. She had a chubby child in her arms, which, frightened at his looks, began to cry, "Hush, Rip," cried she, "hush, you little

fool; the old man won't hurt you." The name of the child, the air of the mother, the tone of her voice, all awakened a train of recollections in his mind. "What is your name, my good woman?" asked he.

"Judith Gardenier."

"And your father's name?"

"Ah! poor man, Rip Van Winkle was his name, but it's twenty years since he went away from home with his gun and never has been heard of since—his dog came home without him; but whether he shot himself, or was carried away by the Indians, nobody can tell. I was then but a little girl."

Rip had but one question more to ask; but he put it with a faltering voice:

"Where's your mother?"

"Oh, she too had died but a short time since; she broke a blood vessel in a fit of passion at a New England peddler."

> ◆ **Literature and Your Life**
> Why do you think Rip asks about his wife in a "faltering" voice?

There was a drop of comfort, at least, in this intelligence.[45] The honest man could contain himself no longer. He caught his daughter and her child in his arms. "I am your father!" cried he— "Young Rip Van Winkle once—old Rip Van Winkle now! Does nobody know poor Rip Van Winkle?"

All stood amazed, until an old woman, tottering out from among the crowd, put her hand to her brow, and peering under it in his face for a moment, exclaimed, "Sure enough! it is Rip Van Winkle—it is himself! Welcome home again, old neighbor. Why where have you been these twenty long years?"

Rip's story was soon told, for the whole twenty long years had been to him but as one night. The neighbors stared when they heard it; some were seen to wink at each other, and put their tongues in their cheeks: and the self-important man in the cocked hat, who, when

---

44. **comely** (kum´ lē) *adj.*: Attractive; pretty.

45. **intelligence** (in tel´ ə jəns) *n.*: News.

the alarm was over, had returned to the field, screwed down the corners of his mouth, and shook his head—upon which there was a general shaking of the head throughout the assemblage.

It was determined, however, to take the opinion of old Peter Vanderdonk, who was seen slowly advancing up the road. He was a descendant of the historian of that name, who wrote one of the earliest accounts of the province. Peter was the most ancient inhabitant of the village, and well versed in all the wonderful events and traditions of the neighborhood. He recollected Rip at once, and corroborated his story in the most satisfactory manner. He assured the company that it was a fact, handed down from his ancestor the historian, that the Catskill mountains had always been haunted by strange beings. That it was affirmed that the great Henry Hudson, the first discoverer of the river and country,[46] kept a kind of vigil there every twenty years, with his crew of the *Half-Moon;* being permitted in this way to revisit the scenes of his enterprise, and keep a guardian eye upon the river, and the great city called by his name. That his father had once seen them in their old Dutch dresses playing at ninepins in a hollow of the mountain; and that he himself had heard, one summer afternoon, the sound of their balls, like distant peals of thunder.

To make a long story short, the company broke up, and returned to the more important concerns of the election. Rip's daughter took him home to live with her; she had a snug, well-furnished house, and a stout, cheery farmer for a husband, whom Rip recollected for one of the urchins that used to climb upon his back. As to Rip's son and heir, who was the ditto of himself, seen leaning against the tree, he was employed to work on the farm; but evinced an hereditary disposition to attend to anything else but his business.

---

46. **country:** Area around the Catskills.

Rip now resumed his old walks and habits; he soon found many of his former cronies, though all rather the worse for the wear and tear of time; and preferred making friends among the rising generation, with whom he soon grew into great favor.

Having nothing to do at home, and being arrived at that happy age when a man can be idle with impunity, he took his place once more on the bench at the inn door, and was reverenced as one of the patriarchs of the village, and a chronicle of the old times "before the war." It was some time before he could get into the regular track of gossip, or could be made to comprehend the strange events that had taken place during his torpor. How that there had been a revolutionary war—that the country had thrown off the yoke of old England—and that, instead of being a subject of his Majesty George the Third, he was now a free citizen of the United States. Rip, in fact, was no politician; the changes of states and empires made but little impression on him; but there was one species of despotism under which he had long groaned, and that was—petticoat government. Happily that was at an end; he had got his neck out of the yoke of matrimony, and could go in and out whenever he pleased, without dreading the tyranny of Dame Van Winkle. Whenever her name was mentioned, however, he shook his head, shrugged his shoulders, and cast up his eyes; which might pass either for an expression of resignation to his fate, or joy at his deliverance.

He used to tell his story to every stranger that arrived at Mr. Doolittle's hotel. He was observed, at first, to vary on some points every time he told it, which was, doubtless, owing to his having so recently awaked. It at last settled down precisely to the tale I have related, and not a man, woman, or child in the neighborhood, but

> ◆ **Literary Focus**
> What clues in this passage show the story's historical setting?

knew it by heart. Some always pretended to doubt the reality of it, and insisted that Rip had been out of his head, and that this was one point on which he always remained flighty. The old Dutch inhabitants, however, almost universally gave it full credit. Even to this day they never hear a thunderstorm of a summer afternoon about the Catskills, but they say Henry Hudson and his crew are at their game of ninepins; and it is a common wish of all henpecked husbands in the neighborhood, when life hangs heavy on their hands, that they might have a quieting draft out of Rip Van Winkle's flagon.

Guide for Responding

◆ LITERATURE AND YOUR LIFE

Reader's Response Which part of the story did you find the most entertaining? Explain.

Thematic Focus Rip was well liked before he disappeared for twenty years. How did his absence affect his relationships with other people?

Journal Writing At the end of the story, Rip fits in better with young people than he does with his old friends. Write a journal entry to explore why this may have been so.

☑ Check Your Comprehension

1. Describe the "great error" in Rip's character.
2. Why does Rip go for a walk in the mountains?
3. Summarize what happens between the time Rip sets out and the time he returns to the village.
4. (a) What is Rip's reaction when he reenters the village? (b) How do the villagers react to Rip?
5. According to the story, what really happened to Rip in the mountains?

◆ Critical Thinking

INTERPRET

1. Why do Rip and his wife have such a stormy marriage? **[Analyze]**
2. A sentence in the story says that a quarrelsome wife may be considered a blessing. What does this mean? **[Interpret]**
3. How do Dame Van Winkle's personality and Rip's personality differ? **[Contrast]**
4. Compare and contrast Rip's life after his long sleep with his earlier life. **[Compare and Contrast]**
5. Reread the last sentence of the story. What might be Irving's purpose in ending the story with this statement? **[Analyze]**

EVALUATE

6. How might Rip's life have been different if his wife and he had been more suited to each other? **[Hypothesize]**

APPLY

7. Major historic changes take place while Rip is asleep. Imagine that you were to fall into a similar sleep. What changes in the country and in the world do you think you would discover when you awoke? **[Social Studies Link]**

Guide for Responding (continued)

◆ Reading Strategy

BREAK DOWN LONG SENTENCES

In reading "Rip Van Winkle," you may have had to go back and reread some of the long sentences, **breaking them down** into shorter parts in order to understand them better.

1. Choose two long sentences from the story, and write them out. Use brackets and slashes to show how you broke each one down.
2. Write the meaning of each sentence as you understand it.

◆ Build Vocabulary

USING THE WORD ROOT -cline-

The word root -cline- means "lean, bend, or turn." Knowing this can help you figure out the meaning of words that contain -cline-. On a piece of paper, write a definition for each italicized word.

1. Watching television, he dozed off in his *recliner.*
2. She was forced to push her bike up the *incline.*
3. He *declined* her invitation to the party.

SPELLING STRATEGY

When you add the suffix -able to most words, do not change the spelling of the original word:

wash + -able = washable

If the word ends in silent e, drop the e:

like + -able = likable

If the word ends in a consonant preceded by a single vowel, you usually double the final consonant:

swim + -able = swimmable

On your paper, write the word that results when -able is added to each of the following words.

1. comfort	3. use	5. do
2. value	4. win	6. laugh

USING THE WORD BANK

Decide whether the following word pairs are synonyms, which mean the same thing, or antonyms, which mean opposite things. On your paper, write *S* for synonym and *A* for antonym.

1. martial, warlike
2. wistfully, longingly
3. melancholy, cheerful
4. incomprehensible, understandable
5. domestic, foreign
6. majestic, regal
7. declined, wilted

◆ Literary Focus

HISTORICAL SETTING

Every story has a **setting,** a time and place in which the action occurs. Some stories have a **historical setting** that places them in a specific period from the past. "Rip Van Winkle," for example, is set in New York's Hudson River valley both before and after the American Revolution.

1. When the story opens, what details of the village reflect the story's historical setting?
2. What details indicate that the American Revolution has been fought and won while Rip has slept?

◆ Build Grammar Skills

VERB TENSES

In addition to the simple present, past, and future tenses, verbs have **perfect tenses.** Perfect verb tenses use *have, has,* or *had* added to the past form of the verb, which is usually made by adding -d or -ed to the main part of the verb.

The **present perfect tense** shows an action that began in the past and continues into the present:

Whoever *has voyaged* up the Hudson must remember the Catskill Mountains.

The **past perfect tense** shows a past action that ended before another began:

Rip *had* unconsciously *scrambled* to one of the highest parts of the Catskill Mountains.

The **future perfect tense** shows a future action that will have ended before another begins. This tense also uses the helping verb *will:*

By the time Rip awakens, his wife *will have died.*

Practice Indicate whether the verb tenses below are present perfect, past perfect, or future perfect.

1. Rip had argued with his wife.
2. She has scolded him all day.
3. The villagers will have forgotten Rip.
4. He had slept for a long time.
5. Have you climbed the Catskills?

Writing Application Write a paragraph in which you use all three perfect verb tenses.

Build Your Portfolio

 ## Idea Bank

Writing

1. **Memoir** Write a passage that Rip might have composed for his memoirs. In it, describe Rip's encounter with the ghosts of Hudson's crew.

2. **Newspaper Article** Imagine that you are a reporter in the square when Rip returns. Write an article about him for the village newspaper.

3. **Comparison-and-Contrast Essay** The action of "Rip Van Winkle" takes place within a few miles, but the story spans twenty years. In an essay, compare and contrast Rip's surroundings before and after his twenty-year sleep.

Speaking and Listening

4. **Talk Show Appearance** [Group Activity] Imagine that Rip or his wife were invited to appear on a talk show. With a group, write and perform the show. Divide these roles in your group: host, audience members, and Dame or Rip Van Winkle. Use details from the story to help you create believable characters.

5. **Dramatization** With a group, choose a scene from the story and act it out. Feel free to add dialogue not included in Irving's story to bring the scene to life. **[Performing Arts Link]**

Projects

6. **Oral Presentation** Settings that inspired Washington Irving also captured the imaginations of many painters, most notably, Thomas Cole and Frederick Church, whose work came to be known as the Hudson River School. Find out more about these artists, and prepare a brief presentation about their work. **[Art Link]**

7. **Geography Update** Conduct research to find out how the Catskills have changed since the early 1700's to the present. Investigate changes caused by exploration, settlement, and land use. Create a report using the maps and photographs you have found. **[Social Studies Link]**

 ## Writing Mini-Lesson

Description of a Trip Through Time

Much can happen in twenty years. When Rip wakes up after his long, long nap, he barely recognizes his own village. Not a face looks familiar. People are strangely dressed. Only the mountains are unchanged. Imagine that you wake up tomorrow morning to find that twenty years have passed. What would it be like? Write a short description of your experience.

Writing Skills Focus: Engage the Senses

Description can be most effective when it **engages the senses.** A vague statement like "Everything was different" doesn't let a reader see what you're describing. "The saplings we had planted were now leafy maples" provides a better image. Notice how Irving engages the sense of hearing as he describes an empty house:

Model From the Story
. . . the lonely chambers *rang* for a moment with his voice, and then all again was *silence.*

Prewriting Spend some time jotting down ideas about what the world might look like in twenty years. In a five-column chart, list words that appeal to each sense: sight, hearing, taste, smell, and touch.

Drafting As you write, form a mental picture of what you are describing. Use your chart to choose words that convey images of your future world.

> ◆ **Grammar Application**
> Since your description is set in the future, there may be many actions that begin in the past, present, or future and continue. Be sure that you have used perfect tenses correctly.

Revising Check to make sure your description tells a clear story. Then, improve your writing by replacing vague words with more vivid ones.

Descriptive Essay

Writing Process Workshop

Have words ever caused you to think, "Wow, I feel like I'm there!" Good description can transport readers to another place. When you write a long description in which several paragraphs contribute to one mood, you're writing a **descriptive essay.** For this assignment, choose a real place that inspires a definite mood. The following skills, introduced in this section's Writing Mini-Lessons, will help you write your descriptive essay.

Writing Skills Focus

▶ **Use vivid words.** Paint a word picture that's sharp, precise, and in focus. (See page 118.)

▶ **Develop each point** by moving slowly through the topic of your description. (See page 133.)

▶ **Grab your readers' interest.** Make your first detail a strong one. (See page 141.)

▶ **Engage many senses.** Think about all five senses—and don't forget to use your imagination. (See page 159.)

Washington Irving uses these writing skills to make you feel as if you're hiking into Sleepy Hollow.

MODEL FROM LITERATURE

from *The Legend of Sleepy Hollow* by Washington Irving

. . . the voyager may have seen the light smoke curling up from a village, ① whose shingle roofs gleam among the trees, just where the blue tints of the upland melt away into the fresh green of the nearer landscape. It is a little village, of great antiquity, having been founded by some of the Dutch colonists, in the early times of the province, just about the beginning of the government of the good Peter Stuyvesant, . . . and there were some of the houses of the original settlers ② standing within a few years, built of small yellow bricks brought from Holland, ③ having latticed windows and gable fronts, surmounted with weathercocks.

① The smoke appeals to two senses: sight and smell.

② The writer zooms in— bringing a wide description of the landscape into a closer focus on the houses.

③ Instead of using a vague word like *stones*, the writer calls them *small yellow bricks from Holland.* Now that's precise!

Prewriting

Use Photographs and Memories To help you choose a topic, remember recent vacations or special days that were filled with excitement. If you have photographs, dig them out. Look through yearbooks or flip through a calendar to jump start your memory. If you still can't find a place or event you'd like to describe, consider these topic ideas:

> ### Topic Ideas
> - A corner of your room
> - Your favorite camping site
> - A movie theater just before the lights go down

Make a Sensory Chart One of the easiest ways to explore all five senses is to make a sensory chart. Can you guess what kind of place this chart describes?

SIGHT	SMELL	SOUND	TASTE	TOUCH
Roller coaster	Sausage frying	Screams	Fried dough	Soft tickets
Babies in strollers	Horse stalls	Rock music	Candy apples	Cold metal railings
Games of chance	Cotton candy	"Tickets, please!"	Lemonade	Drizzle in air

Convey a Mood What feeling do you want to convey about this place? Once you've named it, make a list of details that work together to support that feeling.

Choose Your Order Should you begin at the bottom and move to the top? How about top to bottom—or left to right? Choose a spatial order that makes sense. Don't confuse your audience by wandering around aimlessly or jumping from point to point.

Drafting

Hook Your Readers Make your first detail strong and impressive. Hook your readers' interest from the very first sentence.

Vary Your Sentences Descriptions can get boring if sentences all sound the same. Try using questions, exclamations, and quotations. Mix short sentences with long ones. Don't be afraid to experiment.

DRAFTING/REVISING

APPLYING LANGUAGE SKILLS: Using Precise Nouns

A **general noun,** which names a broad class of people, places, or things, is vague. A **precise noun** is the opposite; it is specific, concrete, and clear. Make your nouns as precise as possible.

General:
The *animal* ran up the *tree* with *something* in his mouth.

Precise:
The *raccoon* ran up the *sycamore* tree with a *trout* in his teeth.

Practice On your paper, rewrite these sentences to make the nouns more precise.

1. The place was full of plants.
2. Put your clothes in the room.
3. Let's build something with this stuff.
4. The man held a toy.

Writing Application As you write your descriptive essay, make your nouns precise.

Writer's Solution Connection Language Lab

For more practice with precise nouns, complete the Language Lab lesson on Exact Nouns.

EDITING/PROOFREADING

APPLYING LANGUAGE SKILLS: Spelling Noun Plurals

Singular nouns name one person, place, or thing. **Plural** nouns name more than one person, place, or thing. Usually, to make a singular noun plural, you add -s or -es. Add -es to words that end in s (glasses), ch (churches), and x (mixes). If a noun ends in y, change the y to an i and add -es (candies).

A few nouns stay the same whether they are singular or plural: deer, deer. Other plurals don't seem to follow any rules: children; mice; teeth.

Practice Make these singular noun phrases plural. If necessary, use a dictionary for reference.

1. sharp wit
2. pretty lady
3. blueberry patch
4. fancy store

Writing Application As you edit your descriptive essay, check that you have spelled all plural nouns correctly.

Writer's Solution Connection Writing Lab

For help revising vague adjectives in your description, use the Word Bins in the tutorial for Description in the Writing Lab CD-ROM.

Mark Places to Use Precise Details Avoid pausing in your first draft to fill in the precise details you don't have. Just mark the place where you can go back and insert details, like a player's name or uniform number.

Revising

Whittle Wordiness Good descriptions don't use unnecessary words. They don't repeat. For example, you could whittle "a mouth that looked really dangerous, like it could really hurt you" to "sharp teeth." The more you say with fewer words, the stronger your writing will be.

Use Action Verbs It might be a temptation to write sentences that use the verb to be. (Her hat *was* red. His face *is* leathery.) As you revise, circle forms of to be and replace them with action verbs.

REVISION MODEL

① ② crashed
~~The beach was nice.~~ As the waves ̷moved onto the beach,
③ that tasted salty and smelled vaguely of seaweed
they sent up a fine cool spray. The sand, soft and warm

under our feet, was sprinkled with shells and smooth

pebbles.

① Deleting a weak first sentence allows the writer to begin with a strong detail.
② The writer uses a more vivid word.
③ These details appeal to the senses of taste and smell.

Publishing and Presenting

Musical Descriptions Make a tape recording of your descriptive essay accompanied by music that reflects the mood of your writing. Play your recording for a friend who has never been to the place you describe.

Book of Places With a group of classmates, create a collection of descriptive essays that are illustrated by photographs or drawings. Display the finished collection in your school library.

Real-World Reading Skills Workshop

Reading a Map

Strategies for Success

Being able to read a map can be extremely useful when you're visiting a new city. To get to the places you want to visit, you may need to use special maps that show the city's public transportation system.

Locate Your Stops The first step in using a bus or subway map is to determine the stop that's nearest your starting location. The next step is to figure out which stop is closest to where you want to go. These steps may involve looking at a street map on which the stops are marked. Keep in mind that maps of bus routes and subways are simplified. They do not show the geographic layout of the stops.

Look at the Lines Different routes have different colors. If your starting location and your destination are lines of different colors, then you will have to switch to a different bus or train—perhaps more than once.

Trace Possible Paths Follow the lines that connect your location to your destination. Find the paths that minimize the number of times you have to switch buses or trains. Then, determine which path has the fewest number of stops. This will be your best route.

Note the Direction Look at the ends of the routes to make sure you catch the bus or train that is headed in the correct direction. For example, if you were going from Central to Park Street on Boston's subway, you'd take the train that is traveling toward Braintree, not the one that's heading to Alewife.

Apply the Strategies

Imagine that you're visiting Boston for the first time, and you want to use the subway system to get from place to place. Use the map below to answer these questions.

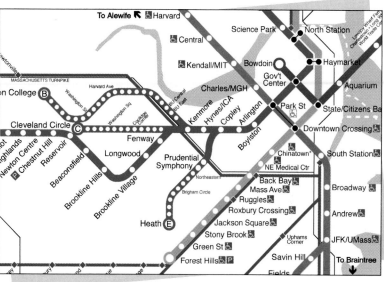

1. On what line is Fenway?

2. How would you get from South Station to Cleveland Circle?

3. How many times do you have to change trains to get from Park Street to the Aquarium?

✔ Here are some other situations in which reading a map can be helpful:
▶ Helping a driver find the way to a new place
▶ Providing directions to your home
▶ Planning a walking tour
▶ Reading news magazines

Grammar Review

A **verb** tells what the subject of a sentence does or is. Verbs that tell what the subject *does* are **action verbs**. Verbs that tell what the subject *is* are **linking verbs.** (See page 132.)

Verbs change form to show time. The six tenses of verbs are given in the following chart. Note that some tenses add helping verbs—such as *have, has, had,* and *will*—to the main verb.

verb (vurb) *n.* a word that shows action or a condition of being: some verbs are used to link a subject with words that tell about the subject, or to help other verbs show special features. In "The children ate early" and "Cactuses grow slowly," the words "ate" and "grow" are *verbs.* In "He is asleep," the word "is" is a linking *verb.* In "Where have you gone?", the word "hav..."

Verb Tense	Helping Verb	Verb Ending	Examples
Simple Tenses (See page 140.)			
Present	none	none or -s, -es	I look; he looks
Past	none	-ed (for regular verbs)	You looked
Future	will or shall	none	We will look
Perfect Tenses (See page 158.)			
Present Perfect	have or has	-ed (for regular verbs)	They have looked; she has looked
Past Perfect	had	-ed (for regular verbs)	I had looked
Future Perfect	will have or shall have	-ed (for regular verbs)	It will have looked

Practice 1 Copy the numbered sentences on a piece of paper. Underline main verbs twice. Underline helping verbs once. Then, identify the verb tense, and indicate whether the main verb is a linking verb or an action verb.

   1. Alice Walker remembers her mother's garden.
   2. Victor will be more careful and will not boast anymore.
   3. The people in Quindlen's neighborhood have changed.

   4. The squirrel collected and ate nuts.
   5. Rip Van Winkle had gone hunting in the mountains.

Practice 2 Rewrite the following paragraph, putting the given verb into the tense indicated in parentheses.

When I first (meet, *past*) Caroline, I (think, *past*) we (have, *past*) nothing at all in common. Until that year, she (spend, *past perfect*) all her life in London. In contrast, I (grow, *past*) up on a ranch that (is, *present*) far away from any city. After I (learn, *past perfect*) more about Caroline, however, I (find, *past*) that we (share, *past*) many interests. For example, we (is, *present*) both crazy about horses. After we (finish, *present perfect*) high school, we (hope, *present*) to start a riding school. By that time, we (gain, *future perfect*) a lot of experience from working at my aunt's stable during school vacations.

Grammar in Writing

✔ *When you write, be careful to use verb tenses correctly. Avoid changing tenses when events occur at the same time, but do change tenses when you want to show that events did not occur at the same time.*

PART 2 *Shared Dreams*

Untitled (Two Girls Talking), Pierre-Auguste Renoir

Guide for Reading

Meet the Authors:

Langston Hughes (1902–1967)

Langston Hughes was one of the main figures in the Harlem Renaissance, a creative movement that took place in the 1920's in the New York City community of Harlem. Hughes and other artists and writers used their talents to celebrate their African American heritage.

Edna St. Vincent Millay (1892–1950)

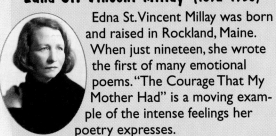

Edna St. Vincent Millay was born and raised in Rockland, Maine. When just nineteen, she wrote the first of many emotional poems. "The Courage That My Mother Had" is a moving example of the intense feelings her poetry expresses.

Henry Wadsworth Longfellow (1807–1882)

Henry Wadsworth Longfellow's poetry was just as popular in his time as the best-loved television programs are today. Longfellow was part of a group that was called the Fireside Poets because their family audiences would read poems, including "The Village Blacksmith," aloud while sitting around their fireplaces.

William Saroyan (1908–1981)

William Saroyan's childhood was a difficult time. He spent part of it in an orphanage and left school at twelve. Saroyan writes often about the Armenian immigrants he knew as a boy.

◆ LITERATURE AND YOUR LIFE

CONNECT YOUR EXPERIENCE

You look to adults to provide guidance and to set an example. As you grow into adulthood, you'll probably continue to draw upon the wisdom of those who are older or more experienced. In these selections, writers celebrate the inspiring strength and wisdom of mothers, fathers, and neighbors.

THEMATIC FOCUS: Shared Dreams

As you read about the values these writers find important, consider whether you share their hopes and goals for life.

◆ Background for Understanding

HISTORY

In his poem, Longfellow describes in vivid detail the work of a blacksmith in a small New England village in the 1800's. At the time, blacksmiths played a key role in village life, making and repairing horseshoes and iron tools used in the fireplace. The blacksmith would heat the iron until it was red-hot and then shape it with a heavy hammer. Because horses were the main means of transportation and because people used a fireplace to cook their meals, blacksmiths were in high demand at the time.

◆ Build Vocabulary

PREFIXES: *trans-*

The hummingbird in Saroyan's story completes a *transformation*. The prefix *trans-* means "across, over, or beyond." A *transformation* is a change from one form to another.

WORD BANK

Which of these words from the selections might describe a strong and muscular person?

quarried
brooch
brawny
pathetic
transformation

Mother to Son ◆ The Courage That My Mother Had
◆ The Village Blacksmith ◆
The Hummingbird That Lived Through Winter

◆ Literary Focus

SYMBOL

A **symbol** is an object that conveys an idea beyond itself. For example, a dove with an olive branch is a symbol of peace. A crown is a symbol of a king's authority. Symbols are frequently used to express an idea in a concrete and memorable way. To identify symbols, look for objects that call to mind specific associations or seem to take on extra importance in a literary work. For each selection, record details relating to such objects. Use the organizer below as you read "Mother to Son." On each step, note a detail about the staircase. Create similar organizers for the other selections.

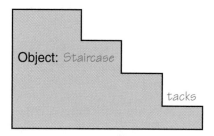

Object: Staircase

tacks

◆ Reading Strategy

QUESTION

One way to get a better understanding of what you read is to create questions based on the text and then see if you can answer them. Begin with the common question words *who, what, where, when, why,* and *how.* For example, when Edna St. Vincent Millay uses the image of New England rock, you might ask what the rock represents to the poet. Search for the answers to your questions as you read, and you'll find an understanding of the selection easy to reach.

Mother to Son

Langston Hughes

Well, son, I'll tell you:
Life for me ain't been no crystal stair.
It's had tacks in it,
And splinters,
5 And boards torn up,
And places with no carpet on the floor—
Bare.
But all the time
I'se been a-climbin' on,
10 And reachin' landin's,
And turnin' corners,
And sometimes goin' in the dark
Where there ain't been no light.
So boy, don't you turn back.
15 Don't you set down on the steps
'Cause you finds it's kinder hard.
Don't you fall now—
For I'se still goin', honey,
I'se still climbin',
20 And life for me ain't been no crystal stair.

Organdy Collar, 1936, Edmund Archer, Whitney Museum of American Art

▲ **Critical Viewing** What details of
the painting on this page convey the
emotion of the poem? **[Connect]**

The Courage That My Mother Had

Edna St. Vincent Millay

The courage that my mother had
Went with her, and is with her still:
Rock from New England quarried;
Now granite in a granite hill.

5   The golden brooch my mother wore
She left behind for me to wear;
I have no thing I treasure more:
Yet, it is something I could spare.

Oh, if instead she'd left to me
10 The thing she took into the grave!—
That courage like a rock, which she
Has no more need of, and I have.

◆ Build Vocabulary

quarried (kwôr´ ēd) *adj.*: Carved out of the ground

brooch (brōch) *n.*: Large ornamental pin worn on a blouse or dress

Guide for Responding

◆ LITERATURE AND YOUR LIFE

Reader's Response Would you like to know the mothers described in these poems? Why or why not?

Thematic Focus How can a parent's courage or endurance help children achieve their dreams?

☑ Check Your Comprehension

1. In "Mother to Son," what advice does the mother give to her son?
2. Where is the speaker's mother in "The Courage That My Mother Had"?
3. For what quality does the speaker of "The Courage That My Mother Had" wish?

◆ Critical Thinking

INTERPRET

1. (a) In "Mother to Son," what does the mother say about her life? (b) What comparison does she make to develop this point? **[Analyze]**
2. In lines 14–17 of "Mother to Son," what does the mother say about how to live? **[Synthesize]**
3. Explain lines 3–4 in "The Courage That My Mother Had." **[Analyze]**
4. Why does Millay compare her mother to New England granite? **[Interpret]**
5. Why would Millay rather have her mother's character than a brooch made of gold? **[Infer]**
6. Describe the feeling that the speaker expresses in "The Courage That My Mother Had." **[Interpret]**

EVALUATE

7. The speaker in Millay's poem implies that courage is a quality you either have or don't have. Can we learn qualities such as courage or perseverance? Explain. **[Criticize]**

COMPARE LITERARY WORKS

8. What qualities do you think the women in "Mother to Son" and "The Courage That My Mother Had" share? **[Connect]**

The Village Blacksmith

Henry Wadsworth Longfellow

Under a spreading chestnut tree
    The village smithy[1] stands;
The smith, a mighty man is he,
    With large and sinewy[2] hands;
5 And the muscles of his brawny arms
    Are strong as iron bands.

His hair is crisp,[3] and black, and long,
    His face is like the tan;
His brow is wet with honest sweat,
10   He earns whate'er he can,
And looks the whole world in the face,
    For he owes not any man.

Week in, week out, from morn till night,
    You can hear his bellows[4] blow;
15 You can hear him swing his heavy sledge,[5]
    With measured beat and slow,
Like a sexton[6] ringing the village bell,
    When the evening sun is low.

And children coming home from school
20   Look in at the open door;
They love to see the flaming forge,
    And hear the bellows roar,
And catch the burning sparks that fly
    Like chaff from a threshing floor.

25 He goes on Sunday to the church,
    And sits among his boys;
He hears the parson pray and preach,
    He hears his daughter's voice,

1. **smithy** (smith´ ē) *n.*: Workshop of a blacksmith.
2. **sinewy** (sin´ yo͞o wē) *adj.*: Tough and strong.
3. **crisp** (krisp) *adj.*: Closely curled and wiry.
4. **bellows** (bel´ ōz) *n.*: Device for quickening the fire by blowing air on it.
5. **sledge** (slej) *n.*: Sledgehammer; a long, heavy hammer, usually held with both hands.
6. **sexton** (seks´ tən) *n.*: Church official in charge of ringing the bells.

Singing in the village choir,
30 And it makes his heart rejoice.

It sounds to him like her mother's voice,
    Singing in Paradise!
He needs must think of her once more,
    How in the grave she lies;
35 And with his hard, rough hand he wipes
    A tear out of his eyes.

Toiling—rejoicing—sorrowing,
    Onward through life he goes;
Each morning sees some task begin,

40   Each evening sees it close;
    Something attempted, something done,
    Has earned a night's repose.

Thanks, thanks to thee, my worthy friend,
    For the lesson thou hast taught!
45 Thus at the flaming forge of life
    Our fortunes must be wrought;
Thus on its sounding anvil shaped
    Each burning deed and thought.

◆ **Build Vocabulary**

brawny (brôn′ ē) *adj.*: Strong and muscular

Guide for Responding

Beyond Literature

Career Connection

Modern Metalwork The intense manual effort that Longfellow describes has been eased by new technology. Now, machines do most of the work. Instead of a hammer and an anvil, forging presses force red-hot metal into shape by squeezing it into molds called dies. This process creates such common products as tools and engine parts.

Cross-Curricular Activity
Career Profile Today, there are plenty of jobs involving metalwork. Discover what you can about these careers. Research the metalwork at nearby factories, repair shops, or industrial centers. Interview someone who works with metal to find out about educational requirements and job responsibilities. Then, share your findings with the class.

◆ LITERATURE AND YOUR LIFE

Reader's Response Do you admire the blacksmith? Explain.

Thematic Focus How do the blacksmith's actions reflect the values and beliefs he shares with his community?

☑ Check Your Comprehension

1. Describe the blacksmith's appearance.
2. Why is the blacksmith able to look the whole world in the face?

◆ Critical Thinking

INTERPRET
1. Which details tell you that the blacksmith is an honest, hard-working man? **[Connect]**
2. What does the tear in his eye reveal about him? **[Infer]**
3. Based on this poem, what is Longfellow's philosophy of life? **[Draw Conclusions]**

EXTEND
4. The village blacksmith symbolized the hard work that Americans prized in Longfellow's time. What occupations do you think symbolize the values of the United States today? **[Career Link]**

The Hummingbird That Lived Through Winter

William Saroyan

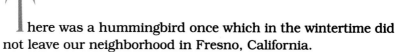

There was a hummingbird once which in the wintertime did not leave our neighborhood in Fresno, California.

I'll tell you about it.

Across the street lived old Dikran,[1] who was almost blind. He was past eighty and his wife was only a few years younger. They had a little house that was as neat inside as it was ordinary outside—except for old Dikran's garden, which was the best thing of its kind in the world. Plants, bushes, trees—all strong, in sweet black moist earth whose guardian was old Dikran. All things from the sky loved this spot in our poor neighborhood, and old Dikran loved *them.*

One freezing Sunday, in the dead of winter, as I came home from Sunday School I saw old Dikran standing in the middle of the street trying to distinguish what was in his hand. Instead of going into our house to the fire, as I had wanted to do, I stood on the steps of the front porch and watched the old man. He would turn around and look upward at his trees and then back to the palm of his hand. He stood in the street at least two minutes and then at last he came to me. He held his hand out, and in Armenian[2] he said, "What is this in my hand?"

I looked.

"It is a hummingbird," I said half in English and half in Armenian. Hummingbird I said in English because I didn't know its name in Armenian.

"What is that?" old Dikran asked.

"The little bird," I said. "You know. The one that comes in the summer and stands in the air and then shoots away. The one with the wings that beat so fast you can't see them. It's in your hand. It's dying."

"Come with me," the old man said. "I can't see, and the old lady's at church. I can feel its heart beating. Is it in a bad way? Look again, once."

I looked again. It was a sad thing to behold. This wonderful little creature of summertime in the big rough hand of the old peasant. Here it was in the cold of winter, absolutely helpless and pathetic, not suspended in a shaft of summer light, not the most

---

1. **Dikran** (dēk´ rän)
2. **Armenian** (är mē´ nē ən): Language spoken in Armenia, a country in southwestern Asia, bordering Georgia, Turkey, Iran, and Azerbaijan.

◆ Build Vocabulary

pathetic (pə thet´ ik) *adj.*: Arousing pity, sorrow, and sympathy

---

◀ **Critical Viewing** What information in the Beyond Literature Connection on page 175 helps you understand this photograph of a hummingbird? Explain. **[Connect]**

alive thing in the world, but the most helpless and heartbreaking.

"It's dying," I said.

The old man lifted his hand to his mouth and blew warm breath on the little thing in his hand which he could not even see. "Stay now," he said in Armenian. "It is not long till summer. Stay, swift and lovely."

We went into the kitchen of his little house, and while he blew warm breath on the bird he told me what to do.

"Put a tablespoonful of honey over the gas fire and pour it into my hand, but be sure it is not too hot."

This was done.

After a moment the hummingbird began to show signs of fresh life. The warmth of the room, the vapor of the warm honey—and, well, the will and love of the old man. Soon the old man could feel the change in his hand, and after a moment or two the hummingbird began to take little dabs of the honey.

"It will live," the old man announced. "Stay and watch."

The <u>transformation</u> was incredible. The old man kept his hand generously open, and I expected the helpless bird to shoot upward out of his hand, suspend itself in space, and scare the life out of me—which is exactly what happened. The new life of the little bird was magnificent. It spun about in the little kitchen, going to the window, coming back to the heat, suspending, circling as if it were summertime and it had never felt better in its whole life.

The old man sat on the plain chair, blind but attentive. He listened carefully and tried to see, but of course he couldn't. He kept asking about the bird, how it seemed to be, whether it showed signs of weakening again, what its spirit was, and whether or not it appeared to be restless; and I kept describing the bird to him.

When the bird was restless and wanted to go, the old man said, "Open the window and let it go."

"Will it live?" I asked.

"It is alive now and wants to go," he said. "Open the window."

I opened the window, the hummingbird stirred about here and there, feeling the cold from the outside, suspended itself in the area of the open window, stirring this way and that, and then it was gone.

"Close the window," the old man said.

We talked a minute or two and then I went home.

The old man claimed the hummingbird lived through that winter, but I never knew for sure. I saw hummingbirds again when

◆ **Build Vocabulary**

transformation (trans´ fər māˊ shən) *n*.: Change in condition or outward appearance

summer came, but I couldn't tell one from the other.

One day in the summer I asked the old man.

"Did it live?"

"The little bird?" he said.

"Yes," I said. "That we gave the honey to. You remember. The little bird that was dying in the winter. Did it live?"

"Look about you," the old man said. "Do you see the bird?"

"I see humming*birds*," I said.

"Each of them is our bird," the old man said. "Each of them, each of them," he said swiftly and gently.

Beyond Literature

Science Connection

Hummingbirds—Nature's Wonder

Saroyan's narrator is fascinated by the hummingbird, a tiny bird that can suspend itself in midair by beating its wings 50 times each second! Hummingbirds hover over flowers long enough to feed on their nectar before darting away—at speeds of up to 60 miles per hour. Since this motion expends energy, the birds spend nights in deep sleep.

Cross-Curricular Activity

Multimedia Report With classmates, learn more about hummingbirds. Check the Internet, read books, or speak with bird specialists at a local college or zoo. Then, create a multimedia presentation using artwork, models, or videos to accompany an oral report that captures this amazing bird's spirit.

Guide for Responding

◆ LITERATURE AND YOUR LIFE

Reader's Response Would you have let the hummingbird go again, or would you have tried to keep it inside until spring? Explain.

Thematic Focus How does working together to save the hummingbird change the relationship between the boy and the old man?

☑ Check Your Comprehension

1. Describe "old Dikran's" personality and appearance.
2. What do the narrator and Dikran do to help the hummingbird?
3. What happens to the hummingbird while it is in Dikran's house?
4. How does Dikran respond to the narrator's question about whether the bird lived?

◆ Critical Thinking

INTERPRET

1. How does Dikran feel about nature and living creatures? **[Infer]**
2. What does the narrator think about the old man's efforts to save the bird? **[Interpret]**
3. Why does Dikran let the bird go? **[Analyze]**
4. Compare and contrast the two characters' ways of looking at the world. **[Compare and Contrast]**

APPLY

5. The narrator says the bird "began to show signs of life." What does he mean by this expression? Whom do you know who fits this description? **[Relate]**

EXTEND

6. From a scientist's view, is it likely that the hummingbird survived the winter? Why or why not? **[Science Link]**

Guide for Responding (continued)

◆ Reading Strategy

QUESTION

When you **question** as you read, you can often unlock the meaning of a work of literature. You can ask why a character says or does something or wonder about a writer's choices of details or plot. For example, if you asked why Millay used the image of a rock, you might have concluded that rocks are strong and enduring. These, in turn, are qualities that Millay links to her mother's courage. Consider these questions, and then explain how answering them adds to your reading.

1. In "The Village Blacksmith," how and when do you think the blacksmith's wife died?
2. In "Mother to Son," why might the speaker want to give this advice to her son?
3. Why does Dikran feel so strongly about nature?

◆ Build Vocabulary

USING THE PREFIX *trans-*

Words that include the prefix *trans-* involve change or movement. They tell about moving people, ideas, or objects "across, over, through, and beyond." Add *trans-* to these words or word parts to create a word fitting the definition supplied. Then, use each word in a sentence.

1. *-late*: Change from one language into another
2. *-continental*: Extending across a continent
3. *-lucent*: Something that light can shine through

SPELLING STRATEGY

To make the plural of words ending in *ch*, always add *-es*, as in brooches. On your paper, make these words plural.

1. watch   2. church   3. ditch   4. sketch

USING THE WORD BANK

On your paper, complete each sentence with the correct word from the Word Bank.

1. She was ____?____ in her grief over the old man's death.
2. After weight-training, his body became ____?____ .
3. The gravestones are ____?____ nearby.
4. Millay remembers her mother's gold ____?____ .
5. The man's efforts caused a ____?____ in the bird.

◆ Literary Focus

SYMBOL

A **symbol** is an object that conveys an idea or message beyond itself. The writers in this grouping use symbols to suggest important ideas. For example, in "Mother to Son," the "dark" symbolizes confusion and "light" stands for knowledge. Because they give you simple and concrete pictures, these symbols let you get closer to Hughes's ideas about life's struggles.

1. (a) What does the brooch in "The Courage That My Mother Had" represent? (b) How do you know?
2. (a) What does the hummingbird symbolize for Dikran? (b) What details help you decide?
3. In "The Village Blacksmith," why is a blacksmith an effective symbol for the strength to keep going and the value of hard work?

◆ Build Grammar Skills

PRINCIPAL PARTS OF VERBS

Every verb (word expressing an action or state of being) has four main forms, called its **principal parts.** These parts are used to form verb tenses, the forms that show time. Regular verbs, such as *climb*, form their past tense and past participles by adding *-ed* or *-d.* Irregular verbs, such as *be*, form their past tense and/or past participles in different ways.

Base (present)	Present Participle	Past	Past Participle
reach	reaching	reached	(have, has, had) reached
earn	earning	earned	(have, has, had) earned
am, be	being	was, were	(have, has, had) been
go	going	went	(have, has, had) gone

Practice On your paper, complete the following chart.

Base (present)	Present Participle	Past	Past Participle
	talking	talked	
	choosing		(have, has, had) chosen
find			(have, has, had) found

Writing Application Write four sentences about one of the selections in this grouping. In each sentence, use a different principal part of the verb *try*.

Build Your Portfolio

 Idea Bank

Writing

1. **Response Poem** Write a poem that could be called "Son to Mother." Answer the mother's advice, using speech patterns that a real boy would use. Follow Hughes's example by using a comparison to describe the son's life.

2. **Public-Service Announcement** A public-service announcement, or PSA, is a message that attempts to educate, advise, or persuade the public to respond to an issue of public concern. Write the text of a PSA intended to encourage respect for adults and the older generation.

3. **Analysis of a Symbol** Choose a symbol in one of the works you just read. In an essay, explain what the symbol represents. Use evidence from the text to support your interpretation.

Speaking and Listening

4. **Song** Using "The Courage That My Mother Had" as an inspiration, write a song in which you explain the importance of courage. Add music to your lyrics. **[Music Link]**

5. **An Unexpected Meeting** Role-play a meeting among the writers whose work is presented here. Have each writer give the others advice about life. Use the poems and story plus what you know about the writers' lives to make them sound realistic. **[Performing Arts Link]**

Projects

6. **Survey [Group Activity]** Ask adults in your community to identify the one quality in people that they most value. Divide these tasks among a group: collect the data, tabulate results on a chart or graph, and write a brief summary of the conclusions you draw from the information. **[Math Link]**

7. **Internet Research** Go on-line to learn about one of the authors presented here. Collect facts about the writer's life and work. If possible, share examples of his or her writing with the class.

 Writing Mini-Lesson

Pep Talk

Like a coach giving a pep talk before the big game, each of these writers—Longfellow, Hughes, Millay, and Saroyan—offers encouragement about facing life's challenges. Imagine that you have to give a similar pep talk—to a friend with a problem, to your teammates before the debate finals, to a younger brother or sister entering a new school. Choose a situation, and write the pep talk that you might give to encourage extra effort or to inspire bravery.

Writing Skills Focus: Stress Main Idea

Because you give a pep talk when there's a problem to be solved, you want listeners to remember your advice. If you **stress the main idea**—by repeating it, restating it several ways, or putting it in your opening and concluding paragraphs—your message is sure to be received. Notice how Langston Hughes restates the main idea that life isn't easy.

> ***Model From the Poem***
> Life for me ain't been no crystal stair.
> It's had tacks in it,
> And splinters,
> And boards torn up,

Prewriting Once you've chosen a situation, list the problems your audience might face. For each, explain why your audience is up for the challenge.

Drafting Address each problem individually, but always return to your main point—that no problem is impossible to conquer.

Revising Read your draft to classmates, and ask whether they feel encouraged or inspired by it. If the talk is not working, go back to your draft, and find places to stress your main idea more strongly.

◆ **Grammar Application**
Make sure you have correctly formed the past and past participle forms of irregular verbs.

In the following article, sportswriter Johnette Howard tells the story of the dream shared by teammates. Showing the courage and determination that Hughes and Longfellow celebrate, the members of the U.S. Women's Hockey Team worked together to achieve their dream—winning a gold medal at the 1998 Winter Olympics.

From golden girls:
The 1998 U.S. Women's Hockey Team

Johnette Howard

By the time the clock struck midnight and the pop of champagne corks was heard at the victory party, the game's particulars had begun to fade from conversation. The feelings were what the U.S. women ice hockey players wanted to review: the lumps in their throats, the chills that ran down their spines, the eye-dampening sight of goalie Sarah Tueting high-stepping around the ice like a crazed drum major after the U.S. won the gold medal game 3–1 against archnemesis Canada. Sandra Whyte, Tueting's onetime housemate in Boston, had sealed the victory, nudging in a 40-foot empty-net goal that the sellout crowd in Nagano's Big Hat stadium traced on its excruciatingly slow path to the net with a steadily building roar of *oh-oh-ooOOHH!* "I'm sure all of us will see ourselves celebrating on tape tomorrow and say, 'I did *what?*' said U.S. forward A.J. Mleczko.

"All I could think was, We just won a gold medal—did we not just win a gold medal?" said Tueting, an apple-cheeked Dartmouth junior-to-be who made 21 saves, many of them spectacular, in the final, and then floated into both the postgame press conference and the victory party wearing a two-foot-tall foam-rubber Uncle Sam hat that her brother, Jonathon, had tossed onto the ice. Suddenly those despair-filled months in 1996, when Tueting was ready to quit hockey at age 19 because she'd never been invited to a U.S. national team tryout, seemed long, long ago. "I had gone home that summer, taken the Olympic posters off my bedroom wall and told everyone I was through," Tueting said. "Then August came, and I got a letter inviting me to camp. I made the national team. In the space of two weeks I went from quitting hockey to putting my life on hold to chase this dream. And now look."

In winning the six-team inaugural women's Olympic tournament with a 6–0 record, the U.S. team eclipsed Picabo Street[1] as America's feel-good story of the Winter Games. On Sunday, General Mills announced that it had chosen Tueting and her teammates to adorn its post-Olympics

---

1. **Picabo** (pēk´ ə bōō) **Street:** Member of the U.S. Women's Ski Team who came back from a serious injury to win two gold medals at the 1998 Olympic Winter Games.

▲ Critical Viewing This photograph was taken moments after the medal ceremony at the 1998 Olympic Winter Games. What details show the women saw their victory as a team effort? [Analyze]

Wheaties box. Just hours after the gold medal game on Feb. 17, the *Late Show with David Letterman* rushed 10 of the U.S. players to a Nagano TV studio to read a Top Ten List titled "Cool Things About Winning an Olympic Gold Medal."

Sportswriters walked into the final grousing about having to cover it and walked out gushing that it was the best thing they'd ever seen. A felicitous[2] line by *Washington Post* columnist Michael Wilbon, who called Mleczko "the first leftwinger I've ever had a crush on," was typical.

That stretching sound you hear is attitudes about women athletes continuing to expand. After the 1996 Atlanta Summer Olympics and now the Nagano Games, it's clear that the U.S.'s female athletic heroes don't have to play what Billie Jean King has

jokingly called the "good clothes sports"—figure skating, tennis and golf. Women never lacked the strength or will to compete in the grittier sports, just the opportunity. When they get the chance, they can produce stirring results. As the U.S. men's Olympic goalie, Mike Richter of the New York Rangers, said admiringly after watching the U.S. women play Canada, "You felt so good for them, the way they were just bleeding for each other to win every game."

2. **felicitous** (fə lis′ i təs) *adj.*: Appropriate or well-chosen.

1. (a) What was Sarah Tueting's dream in college? (b) Why did she nearly give up on this dream?
2. (a) Why did sportswriters complain about covering the finals? (b) Why did they "walk out gushing"?
3. Drawing on your reading of this article and the other selections in this part, describe what it takes to make shared dreams come true.

CONNECTING LITERATURE TO SOCIAL STUDIES

MEDIEVAL TIMES

The Midwife's Apprentice *by Karen Cushman*

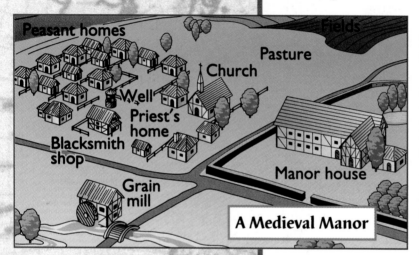

Peasant homes **Fields** **Pasture** **Church** **Well** **Priest's home** **Blacksmith shop** **Grain mill** **Manor house**

A Medieval Manor

FIRST BATH IN MONTHS! Believe it or not, such an occurrence wouldn't be unusual in the England of six hundred years ago. People bathed very rarely—some doctors even believed dangerous diseases could get through uncovered skin.

Peasants and Lords In England in the fourteenth century, people spent their days just trying to survive. If they lived in the country, their lives centered around a manor house, like the one pictured here—usually the home of a lord, a member of a class just below the king in importance. The manor functioned as a complete community, inhabited not only by the lord and his family, but also by peasants who worked for the lord in return for protection from roving gangs.

Village Life The peasants led simple lives. The men plowed fields and grew crops. Many raised sheep for wool and milk. Women walked to the village well to get fresh water. They spun yarn and wove cloth from sheep's wool to make clothing. Food was simple—bread made from local grains and vegetables from the garden.

At the Manor Children helped in the fields or at home. Like the boy in this story, some worked in the manor at such chores as roasting meat over a fire with a hand crank. When the lord was home—for he might be away in the king's service—the manor would fill with parties. Though a boy would then work harder, he might enjoy the excitement in the manor's hall.

Shared Dreams Life was hard, and young people grew up very fast. Still, just like you, children of the time yearned for friendship and wondered if others found them attractive. In *The Midwife's Apprentice*, you'll meet two fictional young people whose lives are set during this distant age.

from *The Midwife's Apprentice*

Karen Cushman

Alyce, a homeless child, is taken in by a sharp-tongued midwife (a woman who helps others with childbirth). She makes the girl her apprentice. One day, Alyce finds Edward, another homeless child. Although she is not able to care for him herself, Alyce persuades the cook at the local baron's manor to give the boy a job and a place to stay. Alyce promises Edward that she will return for him when she can. Months pass. Alyce has an argument with the midwife and takes a job working at an inn. Now that she has an income of her own and a place to live, Alyce returns to the manor to reclaim Edward.

While they ate their bread-and-bacon supper, while Alyce helped Edward mound up straw in a corner of the kitchen, while she sat by watching for him to go to sleep, all the while Edward talked of life on the manor. He told her of the silken-robed lords and ladies who came for feasts and rode out to hunt and danced like autumn leaves in the candlelit great hall, of the visiting knights who clanked their swords against each other as they practiced in the school yard, of the masons who slapped mortar and bricks together to build a great new tower at the corner of the hall that looked to stretch near all the way to heaven. He described the excitement of buying and selling at the great autumn horse fair, the nervous preparations accompanying the arrival of some velvet-shod bishop or priest, and the thrill of watching the baron's

men ride out to confront a huge maddened boar who had <u>roamed</u> too close to the village. And he complained at his lot, doing all the smallest tasks, not being allowed to help with the threshing and ploughing, being teased for being so little and <u>frail</u> and tied to Cook's skirts and fit for nothing but gathering eggs. Finally as his eyes looked near to closing, he said, "Tell me a story, Alyce."

"I don't know any stories."

"For sure you do. Everyone does."

"Well, Jennet told me that one night a visiting mayor fell out of bed, hit his head, and thought he was a cat, so he slept all night on the floor watching the mouseholes."

"That is no story, Alyce. Cook tells me stories. A story should have a hero and brave deeds."

"Well then, once there was a boy who for all he was so small and puny was brave enough to do what he must although he didn't like it and was sometimes teased. Is that a story?"

"Close enough, Alyce." And he closed his eyes.

When the moon shone through the misty clouds and two owls hooted in the manor yard, Edward and Alyce slept, each comforted

> **Connecting Literature to Social Studies**
> How is Edward's life at the manor different from that of a peasant boy living in the village?

◆ **Build Vocabulary**

roamed (rōmd) *v.*: Wandered

frail (frāl) *adj.*: Delicate or weak

Farmyard with woman milking cow, from the Da Costa Book of Hours, Bruges, c. 1515

▲ **Critical Viewing** What can you infer about medieval life from this painting? **[Infer]**

by knowing the other was safe and warm and sheltered and not too very far away.

The next day being the day the woolly black-faced sheep were washed before shearing, Alyce and Edward ate their breakfast down by the river to watch the great event.

Edward finished his breakfast first. "I'm still hungry, Alyce, and there is nothing about here to eat but grass. Do you know if grass is good for people to eat?"

"Try it."

He did. "It be good for exercising my teeth and making my mouth taste better, but it tastes like . . . grass, I would say."

"Then do not eat it."

"What is the best thing you ever ate, Alyce?"

"Hot soup on a cold day, I think."

"Once long ago a monk gave me a fig. It was a wonderful thing, Alyce, soft and sweet. After that I had nothing to eat for three days but the

smell of the fig on my fingers. Are you ever going to finish that bread, Alyce?"

And Alyce gave him her bread, which is what Edward wanted and Alyce intended all along.

Connecting Literature to Social Studies
What conclusion about his life experience can you draw from Edward's reaction to eating a fig?

Part of the river had been dammed to form a washing pool. Men stood in the waist-deep water while the hairy shepherds, looking much like sheep themselves, drove the woolly beasts into the water to have their loose fleeces pulled off and then be scrubbed with the strong yellow soap. The river was noisy with the barking of dogs, the bleating of sheep, the calling and cursing of men, and the furious bawling[1] of those lambs separated from their mothers. Edward soon took on the job of matching mothers and babies. He snatched up the bawling lambs and ran from mother to mother until he made up the right pair, whereupon they would knock him out of the way in their hurry to nuzzle each other.

As the day grew hotter the river looked cooler, and finally Alyce tucked her skirt up into her belt and waded in. The weary men were glad of another pair of hands and soon had Alyce helping. First she held the woolly black faces while they were scrubbed, but one old ewe took offense at Alyce's handling and, standing up with her front feet on Alyce's chest, pushed the girl into the water. Alyce, coughing and sputtering, traded jobs with the man who was lathering their backs. Fleeces clean, the sheep swam to the bank and scrambled out of the water, <u>nimble</u> as goats and hungry as pigs.

By midafternoon they were finished. While Edward and the shepherds drove the sheep to their pens across the field, Alyce stretched and wiped her wet hands on her wet skirt. What a

---

1. **bawling** (bôl´ iŋ) *n.:* Loud or angry cries.

◆ **Build Vocabulary**

nimble (nim´ bəl) *adj.:* Moving quickly and lightly

wonder, she thought, looking at her hands. How white they were and how soft. The hours of strong soap and sudsy fleece had accomplished what years of cold water never had—her hands were really clean. There was no dirt between her fingers, around her nails, or ground into the lines on her palms. She sat back against a tree, held her hands up before her, and admired them. How clean they were. How white.

Suddenly she sat forward. Was the rest of her then that white and clean under all the dirt? Was her face white and clean? Was Will Russet right—was she even *pretty* under the dirt? There never had been one pretty thing about her, just skinny arms and big feet and dirt, but lately she had been told her hair was black and curly and her eyes big and sad and she was mayhap even pretty.

Alyce looked about. The washing was done and the sheep driven to the barn to dry off for tomorrow's shearing. The

Connecting Literature to Social Studies
Why does Alyce look around before she begins to bathe?

river was empty but for great chunks of the greasy yellow soap floating here and there. Alyce found a spot a bit upriver from the befouled[2] washing pool, pulled off her clothes, and waded in. She rubbed her body with the yellow soap and a handful of sandy gravel until she tingled. Squatting down until the

water reached her chin, she washed her hair and watched it float about her until she grew chilled.

Alyce stood up in the shallow water and looked at herself. Much cleaner, although a

---

▼ **Critical Viewing** Judging from their clothing, which of the women in this painting do you think is of higher social rank? Explain. **[Compare and Contrast; Support]**

Garden in the interior of a palace: a young lady and her servant, from Recueil de miniatures

---

2. **befouled** (bē fould´) *adj.*: Dirty.

Guide for Reading

Meet the Author:

Joan Aiken (1924–)

As a child, Joan Aiken loved to take walks in the fields by her house, creating stories to amuse herself. Aiken was strongly influenced by her father, the American poet Conrad Aiken. Her mother contributed to her imagination by reading aloud from the works of Charles Dickens, Jane Austen, and countless other classic English writers.

English Roots

Born and schooled in England, Aiken continues to live both there and in the United States. She has received awards for her writing from both countries, including the Lewis Carroll Shelf Award and the Edgar Allan Poe Award from the Mystery Writers of America.

The Story Behind the Story

Joan Aiken has the special ability to bring new life to traditional literary forms. Her imaginative stories combine pieces of historical fiction, fairy tales, and horror stories and usually deal with fantastic or mysterious events. As you'll see, "The Third Wish" gives a twist to the predictable fairy-tale form. In fact, the story comes from a collection whose title sums up the appeal of Aiken's work—*Not What You Expected.*

◆ LITERATURE AND YOUR LIFE

CONNECT YOUR EXPERIENCE

Imagine that you could have three wishes granted to you. Do you know what your wishes would be? This is the situation of Mr. Peters in "The Third Wish," a person whose life has always been routine, even humdrum. As you read, think about how Mr. Peters's wishes compare with wishes you might make in a similar situation.

THEMATIC FOCUS: What Matters

When Mr. Peters has to decide whose happiness is most important, he must weigh everything that matters to him. You may be surprised at the values he reveals.

◆ Background for Understanding

LITERATURE

"The Third Wish" features the swan, a long-necked water bird known for its grace. Joan Aiken enhances the physical characteristics of swans by adding magical qualities. She is not the first writer to transform a swan into a mystical creature. Throughout time, swans have appeared in myths and legends. In some legends, swans represent feminine qualities. In others, they lead a wanderer on a mysterious journey. Aiken picks up this mythical pattern as she describes the mysterious journey of her main character in "The Third Wish."

◆ The Third Wish ◆

◆ Literary Focus

MODERN FAIRY TALE

The elements of a **modern fairy tale** are the same as those in traditional fairy tales: mysterious and fantastic events, magic and wishes, and animals with unusual abilities. Modern fairy tales also include details and concerns related to contemporary life.

In "The Third Wish," a lonely Englishman stumbles into the realm of fantasy one evening while driving home in his car. As you read the story, record the elements of a modern fairy tale in a chart like the one below.

◆ Build Vocabulary

SUFFIXES: *-ous*

A character in "The Third Wish" describes Mr. Peters as being "presumptuous." This word is derived from the word *presume*. The suffix *-ous* means "full of" or "characterized by." *Presumptuous* means "characterized by presuming or taking too much for granted"—in other words, being too bold or daring for your own good.

WORD BANK

Which of these words from the selection describes a person who is full of bad intent, or malice? Check the Build Vocabulary boxes to see if you are correct.

extricate
presumptuous
composure
rash
remote
malicious

Mysterious and Fantastic Events	Magic and Wishes	Unusual Animals	Details About Contemporary Life
		Talking swan	

Reading for Success

Interactive Reading Strategies

Reading is like many activities in our lives—the more actively we participate, the more we get out of it. When you get truly involved in your reading, or read interactively, you'll better remember what you read. These strategies will help you become an interactive reader:

Predict what will happen.

When you read a story, your mind may race ahead, predicting what a character might do or how a conflict might be resolved. Look for clues or hints in the story to help you predict what is likely to occur. Look at this example:

Title: "The Third Wish"
Predictions: This story will be about a person granted three wishes. The last wish will be most important.

As you read, revise your predictions according to events in the story.

Clarify.

Only you know what you don't understand. When you read a passage you find difficult or confusing, take the time to pause to clarify the meaning. Try these strategies:

▶ Reread a section slowly to find out what the author is really saying.
▶ Ask questions to resolve the confusion.
▶ Look up a word in the dictionary, or get information from another source.

Summarize what you have read.

As you read a selection, pause occasionally to review and restate what has happened so far. This will help you to identify the most important ideas.

Respond.

You may understand a work of literature best when it evokes strong feelings. Get to know your own reactions by asking yourself what the selection meant to you. Use these questions to get you started:

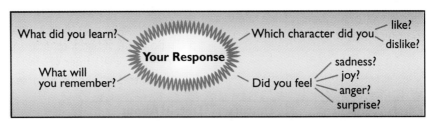

As you read "The Third Wish," look at the notes in the boxes. The notes demonstrate how to apply these strategies to a work of literature.

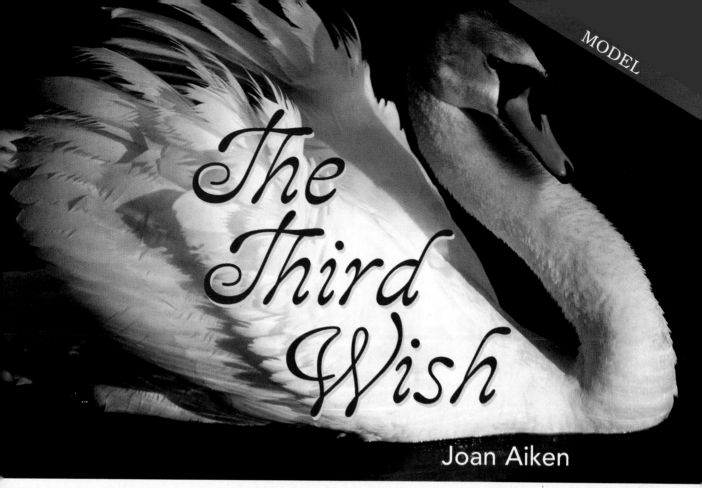

The Third Wish

Joan Aiken

▲ **Critical Viewing** In this story, a swan has magical powers. What details of the photograph make this swan look powerful? **[Relate]**

Once there was a man who was driving in his car at dusk on a spring evening through part of the forest of Savernake. His name was Mr. Peters. The primroses were just beginning but the trees were still bare, and it was cold; the birds had stopped singing an hour ago.

As Mr. Peters entered a straight, empty stretch of road he seemed to hear a faint crying, and a struggling and thrashing, as if somebody was in trouble far away in the trees. He left his car and climbed the mossy bank beside the road. Beyond the bank was an open slope of beech trees leading down to thorn bushes through which he saw the gleam of water. He stood a moment waiting to try and discover where the noise was coming from, and presently heard a rustling and some strange cries in a voice which was almost human—and yet there was something too hoarse about it at one time and too clear and sweet at another. Mr. Peters ran down the hill and as he neared the bushes he saw something white among them which was trying to <u>extricate</u> itself; coming closer he found that it was a swan that had become

> From these details, you can **predict** that this swan will become important in the story.

◆ **Build Vocabulary**

extricate (eks´ tri kāt´) v.: To set free

entangled in the thorns growing on the bank of the canal.

The bird struggled all the more frantically as he approached, looking at him with hate in its yellow eyes, and when he took hold of it to free it, it hissed at him, pecked him, and thrashed dangerously with its wings which were powerful enough to break his arm. Nevertheless he managed to release it from the thorns, and carrying it tightly with one arm, holding the snaky head well away with the other hand (for he did not wish his eyes pecked out), he took it to the verge of the canal and dropped it in.

The swan instantly assumed great dignity and sailed out to the middle of the water, where it put itself to rights with much dabbling and preening, smoothing its feathers with little showers of drops. Mr. Peters waited, to make sure that it was all right and had suffered no damage in its struggles. Presently the swan, when it was satisfied with its appearance, floated in to the bank once more, and in a moment, instead of the great white bird, there was a little man all in green with a golden crown and long beard, standing by the water. He had fierce glitter-ing eyes and looked by no means friendly.

"Well, Sir," he said threateningly, "I see you are presumptuous enough to know some of the laws of magic. You think that because you have rescued—by pure good fortune—the King of the Forest from a difficulty, you should have some fabulous reward."

"I expect three wishes, no more and no less," answered Mr. Peters, looking at him steadily and with composure.

"Three wishes, he wants, the clever man! Well, I have yet to hear of the human being who made any good use of his three wishes—they mostly end up worse off than they started. Take your three wishes then"— he flung three dead leaves in the air—"don't blame me if you spend the last wish in un-doing the work of the other two."

◆ **Build Vocabulary**

presumptuous (prē zump´ chŏō əs) *adj.*: Overconfident; arrogant

composure (kəm pō´ zhər) *n.*: Calmness of mind

rash (rash) *adj.*: Thoughtless

remote (ri mōt´) *adj.*: Far away from everything else

Mr. Peters caught the leaves and put two of them carefully in his briefcase. When he looked up, the swan was sailing about in the middle of the water again, flicking the drops angrily down its long neck.

Mr. Peters stood for some minutes reflecting on how he should use his reward. He knew very well that the gift of three magic wishes was one which brought trouble more often than not, and he had no intention of being like the forester who first wished by mistake for a sausage, and then in a rage wished it on the end of his wife's nose, and then had to use his last wish in getting it off again. Mr. Peters had most of the things which he wanted and was very content with his life. The only thing that troubled him was that he was a little lonely, and had no companion for his old age. He decided to use his first wish and to keep the other two in case of an emergency. Taking a thorn he pricked his tongue with it, to remind himself not to utter <u>rash</u> wishes aloud. Then holding the third leaf and gazing round him at the

> You might **respond** with amusement to the story of the forester.

dusky undergrowth, the primroses, great beeches and the blue-green water of the canal, he said:

"I wish I had a wife as beautiful as the forest."

A tremendous quacking and splashing broke out on the surface of the water. He thought that it was the swan laughing at him. Taking no notice he made his way through the darkening woods to his car, wrapped himself up in the rug and went to sleep.

When he awoke it was morning and the birds were beginning to call. Coming along the track towards him was the most beautiful creature he had ever seen, with eyes as blue-green as the canal, hair as dusky as the bushes, and skin as white as the feathers of swans.

"Are you the wife that I wished for?" asked Mr. Peters.

"Yes, I am," she replied. "My name is Leita."

She stepped into the car beside him and they drove off to the church on the outskirts of the forest, where they were married. Then he took her to his house in a <u>remote</u> and lovely valley and showed her all his treasures —the bees in their white hives, the Jersey

Summarize the events of the story this way: When Mr. Peters rescued a swan who turned out to be the King of the Forest, he was granted three wishes. Mr. Peters used one wish to ask for a wife, and Leita appeared.

cows, the hyacinths, the silver candlesticks, the blue cups and the luster bowl for putting primroses in. She admired everything, but what pleased her most was the river which ran by the foot of his garden.

"Do swans come up there?" she asked.

"Yes, I have often seen swans there on the river," he told her, and she smiled.

Leita made him a good wife. But as time went by Mr. Peters began to feel that she was not happy. She seemed restless, wandered much in the garden, and sometimes when he came back from the fields he would find the house empty and she would return after half an hour or so with no explanation of where she had been. On these occasions she was always especially tender and would put out his slippers to warm and cook his favorite dish—Welsh rarebit[1] with wild strawberries—for supper.

One evening he was returning home along the river path when he saw Leita in front of him, down by the water. A swan had sailed up to the verge and she had her arms round its

You might respond to Leita's crying by remembering a time when you felt very sad.

neck and the swan's head rested against her cheek. She was weeping, and as he came nearer he saw that tears were rolling, too, from the swan's eyes.

"Leita, what is it?" he asked, very troubled.

"This is my sister," she answered. "I can't bear being separated from her."

Now he understood that Leita was really a swan from the forest, and this made him very

---

1. **Welsh rarebit:** A dish of melted cheese served on crackers or toast.

◆ **Build Vocabulary**

malicious (mə lish′ əs) *adj.*: Spiteful; hateful

sad because when a human being marries a bird it always leads to sorrow.

"I could use my second wish to give your sister human shape, so that she could be a companion to you," he suggested.

"No, no," she cried, "I couldn't ask that of her."

"Is it so very hard to be a human being?" asked Mr. Peters sadly.

"Very, very hard," she answered.

"Don't you love me at all, Leita?"

"Yes, I do, I do love you," she said, and there were tears in her eyes again. "But I missed the old life in the forest, the cool grass and the mist rising off the river at sunrise and the feel of the water sliding over my feathers as my sister and I drifted along the stream."

"Then shall I use my second wish to turn you back into a swan again?" he asked, and his tongue pricked to remind him of the old King's words,

Clarify that Mr. Peters pricked his tongue when he made his first wish, to remind himself not to make rash wishes.

and his heart swelled with grief inside him.

"Who will take care of you?"

"I'd do it myself as I did before I married you," he said, trying to sound cheerful.

She shook her head. "No, I could not be as unkind to you as that. I am partly a swan, but I am also partly a human being now. I will stay with you."

Poor Mr. Peters was very distressed on his wife's account and did his best to make her life happier, taking her for drives in the car, finding beautiful music for her to listen to on the radio, buying clothes for her and even suggesting a trip round the world. But she said no to that; she would prefer to stay in their own house near the river.

He noticed that she spent more and more time baking wonderful cakes—jam puffs, petits fours, eclairs and meringues. One day he saw her take a basketful down to the river and he guessed that she was giving them to her sister.

He built a seat for her by the river, and the two sisters spent hours together there, communicating in some wordless manner. For a time he thought that all would be well, but then he saw how thin and pale she was growing.

One night when he had been late doing the account he came up to bed and found her weeping in her sleep and calling:

"Rhea! Rhea! I can't understand what you say! Oh, wait for me, take me with you!"

Then he knew that it was hopeless and she would never be happy as a human. He stooped down and kissed her goodbye, then took another leaf from his notecase, blew it out of the window, and used up his second wish.

Next moment instead of Leita there was a sleeping swan lying across the bed with its head under its wing. He carried it out of the house and down to the brink of the river, and then he said, "Leita! Leita!" to waken her, and gently put her into the water. She gazed round her in astonishment for a moment, and then came up to him and rested her head lightly against his hand; next instant she was flying away over the trees towards the heart of the forest.

He heard a harsh laugh behind him, and turning round saw the old King looking at him with a <u>malicious</u> expression.

"Well, my friend! You don't seem to have managed so wonderfully with your first two wishes, do you? What will you do with the last? Turn yourself into a swan? Or turn Leita back into a girl?"

"I shall do neither," said Mr. Peters calmly. "Human beings and swans are better in their own shapes."

But for all that he looked sadly over towards the forest where Leita had flown, and walked slowly back to his house.

Next day he saw two swans swimming at the bottom of the garden, and one of them wore the gold chain he had given Leita after their marriage; she came up and rubbed her

> The story events lead you to **predict** what must happen to Leita.

◀ **Critical Viewing** What experiences pictured here might Leita miss as a human? [**Analyze**]

head against his hand.

Mr. Peters and his two swans came to be well known in that part of the country; people used to say that he talked to swans and they understood him as well as his neighbors.

Many people were a little frightened of him. There was a story that once when thieves tried to break into his house they were set upon by two huge white birds which carried them off bodily and dropped them into the river.

Compare the story's ending with your **prediction** to see if you were right.

As Mr. Peters grew old everyone wondered at his contentment. Even when he was bent with rheumatism[2] he would not think of

---

2. **rheumatism** (roo´ me tiz əm) *n.*: Pain and stiffness of the joints and muscles.

moving to a drier spot, but went slowly about his work, with the two swans always somewhere close at hand.

Sometimes people who knew his story would say to him:

"Mr. Peters, why don't you wish for another wife?"

"Not likely," he would answer serenely. "Two wishes were enough for me, I reckon. I've learned that even if your wishes are granted they don't always better you. I'll stay faithful to Leita."

One autumn night, passers-by along the road heard the mournful sound of two swans singing. All night the song went on, sweet and harsh, sharp and clear. In the morning Mr. Peters was found peacefully dead in his bed with a smile of great happiness on his face. In his hands, which lay clasped on his breast, were a withered leaf and a white feather.

Guide for Responding

◆ LITERATURE AND YOUR LIFE

Reader's Response If you could give advice to Mr. Peters about how to use his third wish, what would you tell him?

Thematic Focus As the story unfolds, what does Mr. Peters learn about the things that matter to him?

☑ Check Your Comprehension

1. How does Mr. Peters get an opportunity to ask for three wishes?
2. How is his first wish granted?
3. What is Mr. Peters's second wish?
4. Describe Mr. Peters's life after his second wish is granted.
5. What is his third wish?

◆ Critical Thinking

INTERPRET

1. Mr. Peters turns his wife back into a swan. What does this show about him? **[Infer]**
2. Why does Mr. Peters die with a look of happiness on his face? **[Analyze]**
3. Explain the story's ending. **[Draw Conclusions]**

EVALUATE

4. Do you think Mr. Peters wisely used the three wishes granted to him? **[Evaluate]**

APPLY

5. If Mr. Peters were alive today, do you think he would have used his third wish? Why or why not? **[Speculate]**

Guide for Responding (continued)

◆ Reading for Success

INTERACTIVE READING STRATEGIES

Review the reading strategies and the notes showing how to interact with the story. Then apply them to answer the following questions.

1. Summarize the events that lead up to Mr. Peters's three wishes.
2. At what point in this story would you predict what each of the three wishes might be? Why?
3. Do you think Mr. Peters used his second wish wisely? Explain.

◆ Build Vocabulary

USING THE SUFFIX -OUS

The suffix -ous, meaning "full of" or "characterized by," makes a noun an adjective. On a sheet of paper, add -ous to the word in parentheses to complete each sentence.

1. She looked ____?____ in that silly outfit. (ridicule)
2. The ____?____ firefighter rescued the child. (courage)
3. With her diamond barrettes and her dark glasses, the actress looked very ____?____. (glamour)

SPELLING STRATEGY

When you add -ous to words that end with ce pronounced like s, change the final e to i before adding the suffix: malice + -ous = malicious.

Add -ous to these nouns to create adjectives. Then, write sentences using each new word.

   1. space
   2. grace
   3. vice

USING THE WORD BANK

On your paper, match each word in the first column with a word that means the same in the second column.

1. extricate   a. far
2. composure   b. thoughtless
3. presumptuous c. free
4. rash   d. calmness
5. remote   e. spiteful
6. malicious   f. arrogant

◆ Literary Focus

MODERN FAIRY TALE

Because it contains both old-fashioned and contemporary elements, "The Third Wish" is a **modern fairy tale.** Aiken uses such classic fairy-tale elements as magic, wishes, and the unexpected behavior of animals. She also incorporates contemporary twists and issues in the setting, characters, and plot of the story.

1. What details of the setting in "The Third Wish" make it a modern fairy tale?
2. (a) In what ways is Mr. Peters like the main character in a traditional fairy tale? (b) How is he different and more contemporary?
3. How does Leita represent a character specific to a modern fairy tale?

◆ Build Grammar Skills

ADJECTIVES

Adjectives are words that modify or describe nouns or pronouns. They tell more about the nouns or pronouns they modify by answering the questions *what kind*, *which one*, *how many*, and *how much*. In the following sentence, Aiken uses adjectives to inform the reader about "how many" wishes Mr. Peters expects. She also tells "what kind" of man Mr. Peters is.

"*Three* wishes, he wants, the *clever* man!"

Practice Copy these sentences. Underline each adjective, and draw an arrow to the word it modifies. Then, tell what question it answers.

1. He climbed the mossy bank beside the road.
2. He had fierce glittering eyes and powerful white wings.
3. Leita made him a good wife.
4. He heard a harsh laugh behind him.
5. Next day he saw two swans.

Writing Application On your paper, write a paragraph using the following adjectives.

1. careful   3. happy
2. vivid   4. astonished

Build Your Portfolio

 ## Idea Bank

Writing

1. **Journal Entry** As the King of the Forest, write a journal entry describing how you were rescued by Mr. Peters.

2. **Obituary** An obituary is a notice of someone's death. Write an obituary for Mr. Peters, including facts about his death. Add colorful details of Mr. Peters's life to make the obituary interesting.

3. **Analysis** "The Third Wish" has a message for readers. In an essay, identify the message and cite story details to support your interpretation. Include your reaction to the idea the story stresses.

Speaking and Listening

4. **Song Lyrics [Group Activity]** If Leita were to sing a song about her experiences as a swan, what would the lyrics of her song say? With one or two classmates, write the music and lyrics of Leita's song and perform it for your class. **[Music Link]**

5. **Radio Drama** Mr. Peters had an extraordinary experience when he saved the King of the Forest. Create a radio script that portrays the rescue, and act it out for your class. Add sound effects to bring the action to life. **[Performing Arts Link]**

Projects

6. **Poster on the Number Three** Like Aiken's story, many fairy tales include three wishes. Common wisdom says that good things happen in threes. The ancient Greeks had three major gods. The Greek philosopher Pythagoras considered three perfect because it represents a beginning, middle, and an end. Compile a poster of mathematical data about the number three: its square root, its factors, and its relationship to geometric shapes. **[Math Link]**

7. **Multimedia Report** Research fairy tales from different cultures. Note their countries of origin, characters, magic elements, and messages. Gather maps, book jackets, illustrations, and videos to create a multimedia report. **[Media Link]**

 ## Writing Mini-Lesson

Modern Fairy Tale

"The Third Wish" takes place in the modern world, but it contains fantasy and magic—elements of traditional fairy tales. Choose a traditional fairy tale with which you're familiar, and write a retelling of it in a modern setting.

> **Writing Skills Focus: Elaborate on Key Ideas**
>
> Let your readers know you've updated your story by **elaborating on key ideas.** For example, if you decide to include an electronic fairy godmother who appears via e-mail, you might provide supporting details such as these:
> - The hero spends a lot of time at the computer.
> - A computer crash and restart signals the appearance and disappearance of the fairy godmother.
> - At the end of the story, the computer seems strangely normal again.

Prewriting List the events in your story. Brainstorm for ways to update the setting, and jot down your best ideas.

Drafting Begin with the traditional opening sentence of a fairy tale: "Once upon a time . . ." As you draft your story, refer to your list of events, and include the details of the setting you've planned.

> ◆ **Grammar Application**
> Look for places in your story where adjectives can provide more information.

Revising Check that the events of your story lead smoothly from one point to the next. If necessary, add more information to make the characters, plot, and setting easier for your readers to understand.

Part 1 *Risking It All*

Guide for Reading

Meet the Authors:

James Ramsey Ullman (1907–1971)

Born in the shadow of the mountain-like skyscrapers of New York City, James Ramsey Ullman developed a love for climbing that made him feel more at home in Tibet than on New York's crowded streets. Although he personally did not climb Mt. Everest, he was a member of the first American expedition to the mountain.

Climbing and Writing Ullman was also a talented writer who worked as a reporter and wrote fiction and plays. He combined his love of climbing and his writing skill in *Banner in the Sky*, which won a Newbery Honor award. Five of Ullman's books became films, including *The White Tower, River of the Sun,* and *Banner in the Sky.*

Jon Krakauer (1954–   )

Family outings in Oregon set the stage for Jon Krakauer's interest in mountaineering. By his early twenties, he had attempted several difficult mountain ascents. His first book-length publication, *Eiger Dreams: Ventures Among Men and Mountains,* was a collection of essays about climbing the Eiger, one of the toughest peaks of the Alps. He was well prepared for the challenge of climbing Mt. Everest and writing about it in his best-selling book *Into Thin Air.*

◆ LITERATURE AND YOUR LIFE

CONNECT YOUR EXPERIENCE

You may have felt your heart race as you experienced the risks and rewards of downhill skiing, extreme skateboarding, or white-water rafting. These selections describe the heart-pounding danger and excitement of mountaineering—a challenge most of us may never have the courage or opportunity to experience firsthand.

THEMATIC FOCUS: Risking It All

Characters in these narratives risk it all to reach a goal, help someone in trouble, and overcome their fear.

◆ Background for Understanding

GEOGRAPHY

In "Into Thin Air," Jon Krakauer describes a dangerous hike across a glacier. Glaciers are huge ice chunks that develop where more snow falls than melts. Snow builds in layers until the glacier's crushing weight pushes it across the land. Since the surface of a glacier is rigid and it cannot flow like the compacted layers below, the layers do not move at the same speed. Stress builds until the surface cracks and deep crevasses appear. In addition to these dangerous cracks, those hiking across glaciers face deadly icefalls—avalanches of glacial ice.

◆ Build Vocabulary

PREFIXES: *mal-*

The word *malevolent* combines the prefix *mal-,* meaning "bad or evil" and *-volence,* meaning "to wish." *Malevolent* means "wishing harm to others." You can see how these writers might call the mountains *malevolent,* since each could harm the climbers.

WORD BANK

Which of these words from the selections do you think are verbs? Why?

prone
taut
pummeled
reconnoiter
malevolent
denigrate

◆ A Boy and a Man ◆ *from* Into Thin Air ◆

◆ Literary Focus

CONFLICT WITH NATURE

Conflict is a struggle between opposing sides or forces. Most stories are built around a conflict. Conflicts may occur between characters, with nature, with society, or within an individual. Both these stories feature a conflict with nature in which people are pitted against the elements. In each case, the conflict focuses specifically on a struggle against an icy glacier, resulting in a chilling, life-or-death adventure.

◆ Reading Strategy

PREDICT

Gripping stories such as these keep you wondering what's going to happen next. Based on information the author provides, you can **predict,** or make an informed guess about, the events to follow. When you come to a place where the action could go in several directions, ask yourself: What details does the author provide about the conflict that suggest what will happen? Then, read to find out whether your prediction is correct. Keep track of your predictions by filling in a chart like the one below.

Detail or Hint	My Prediction	Actual Outcome
Rudi hears the voice in the crevasse.	He will try to rescue the man.	

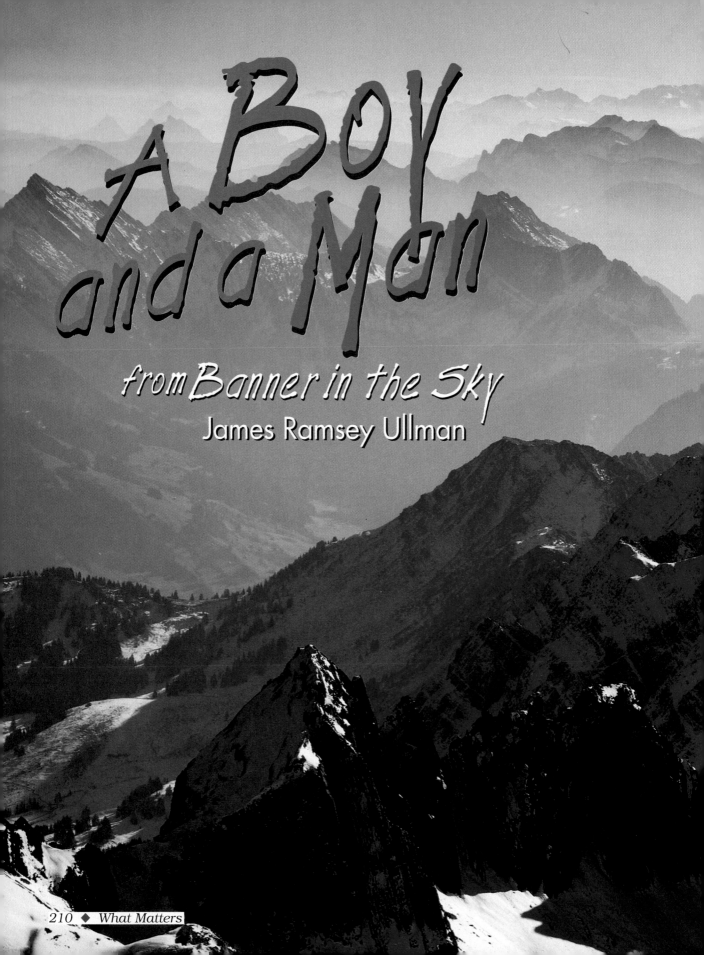

A Boy and a Man

from Banner in the Sky

James Ramsey Ullman

The crevasse[1] was about six feet wide at the top and narrowed gradually as it went down. But how deep it was Rudi could not tell. After a few feet the blue walls of ice curved away at a sharp slant, and what was below the curve was hidden from sight.

"Hello!" Rudi called.

"Hello—" A voice answered from the depths.

"How far down are you?"

"I'm not sure. About twenty feet, I'd guess."

"On the bottom?"

"No. I can't even see the bottom. I was lucky and hit a ledge."

The voice spoke in German, but with a strange accent. Whoever was down there, Rudi knew, it was not one of the men of the valley.

"Are you hurt?" he called.

"Nothing broken—no," said the voice. "Just shaken up some. And cold."

"How long have you been there?"

"About three hours."

Rudi looked up and down the crevasse. He was thinking desperately of what he could do.

"Do you have a rope?" asked the voice.

"No."

"How many of you are there?"

"Only me."

There was a silence. When the voice spoke again, it was still quiet and under strict control. "Then you'll have to get help," it said.

Rudi didn't answer. To get down to Kurtal

would take at least two hours, and for a party to climb back up would take three. By that time it would be night, and the man would have been in the crevasse for eight hours. He would be frozen to death.

"No," said Rudi, "it would take too long."

"What else is there to do?"

Rudi's eyes moved over the ice-walls: almost vertical, smooth as glass. "Have you an ax?" he asked.

"No. I lost it when I fell. It dropped to the bottom."

"Have you tried to climb?"

"Yes. But I can't get a hold."

There was another silence. Rudi's lips tightened, and when he spoke again his voice was strained. "I'll think of something." he cried. "I'll think of *something*!"

"Don't lose your head." the voice said. "The only way is to go down for help."

"But you'll—"

"Maybe. And maybe not. That's a chance we'll have to take."

The voice was as quiet as ever. And, hearing it, Rudi was suddenly ashamed. Here was he, safe on the glacier's surface, showing fear and despair, while the one below, facing almost certain death, remained calm and controlled. Whoever it was down there it was a real man. A brave man.

Rudi drew in a long, slow breath. With his climbing-staff he felt down along the smooth surface of the ice walls.

"Are you still there?" said the voice.

"Yes," he said.

"You had better go."

---

1) **crevasse** (krə vas′) *n.*: Deep crack, especially in a glacier.

mountaineer of his day, and during the past ten years had made more first ascents of great peaks than any other man alive. Rudi had heard that he had come to Kurtal a few days before. He had hoped that at least he would see him in the hotel or walking by in the street. But actually to meet him—and in this way! To pull him from a crevasse—save him . . . . It was incredible!

Captain Winter was watching him. "And you, son." he asked. "What is your name?"

Somehow the boy got his voice back. "Rudi," he said. "Rudi Matt."

"Matt?" Now it was the man's turn to be impressed. "Not of the family of the great Josef Matt?"

"He was my father," Rudi said.

Captain Winter studied him with his gray eyes. Then he smiled again. "I should have known," he said. "A boy who could do what you've done—"

"Did you know my father, sir?"

"No, unfortunately I didn't. He was before my day. But ever since I was a boy I have heard of him. In twenty years no one has come to the Alps and not heard of the great guide, Josef Matt."

Rudi's heart swelled. He looked away. His eyes fixed on the vast mountain that rose before them, and then he saw that Captain Winter was watching it too.

Unconsciously the Englishman spoke his thoughts. "Your father was—" He caught himself and stopped.

"Yes," said Rudi softly. "he was killed on the Citadel."

There was a silence. Captain Winter reached into a pocket and brought out an unbroken bar of chocolate. "Lucky I fell on the other side," he grinned.

He broke the bar in two and handed half to Rudi.

"Oh, no, sir, thank you. I couldn't."

"When I meet a boy your age who can't eat chocolate," said Winter. "I'll be glad to stay in a crevasse for good."

Rudi took it, and they sat munching. The sun was warm on their thawing bodies. Far above, it struck the cliffs and snowfields of the Citadel, so brightly that they had to squint against the glare.

Then there was Winter's quiet voice again. "What do you think, Rudi?"

"Think. sir?"

"Can it be climbed?"

"Climbed? The Citadel?"

"Your father thought so. Alone among all the guides of Switzerland, he thought so." There was another pause. "And I think so too." said Captain Winter.

The boy was peering again at the shining heights. And suddenly his heart was pounding so hard that he was sure the Englishman must be able to hear it. "Is—is that why you have come here, sir?" he asked. "To try to climb the Citadel?"

"Well, now—" Winter smiled. "It's not so simple, you know. For one thing, there's not a guide in the valley who would go with me."

"I have an uncle, sir. He is—"

"Yes, I know your uncle. Franz Lerner. He is the best in Kurtal, and I've spoken to him. But he would not go. Anything but that, he said. Any other peak, any route, any venture. But not *that*, he said. Not the Citadel."

"He remembers my father—"

"Yes, he remembers your father. They all remember him. And while they love and respect his memory, they all think he was crazy." Winter chuckled softly. "Now they think *I'm* crazy," he added. "And maybe they're right too," he said.

◆ **Literature and Your Life**

Have you ever had a goal others called "crazy"? Did this make you think twice?

"What will you do. sir?" asked Rudi. "Not try it alone?"

"No, that crazy I'm not." Winter slowly stroked his long jaw. "I'm not certain what I'll do." he went on. "Perhaps I'll go over to the next valley. To Broli. I've been told there is a guide there—a man called Saxo. Do you know him?"

"Yes—Emil Saxo. I have never met him. but I have heard of him. They say he is a very

▲ **Critical Viewing** What details of this photograph might inspire Rudi? Explain. **[Speculate]**

great guide."

"Well, I thought perhaps I'd go and talk with him. After a while. But first I must <u>reconnoiter</u> some more. Make my plans. Pick the route. If there *is* a route."

"Yes, there is! Of course there is!"

Rudi had not thought the words. They simply burst out from him. And now again he was embarrassed as the man looked at him curiously.

"So?" said Captain Winter. "That is interesting, Rudi. Tell me why you think so."

"I have studied the Citadel many times, sir."

"Why?"

◆ **Build Vocabulary**

reconnoiter (rē kə nɔɪt´ ər) *v.*: Look around

"Because—because—" He stopped. He couldn't say it.

"Because you want to climb it yourself?"

"I am not yet a grown man. sir. I know I cannot expect—"

"I wasn't a grown man either," said the Captain, "when I first saw the Citadel. I was younger than you—only twelve—and my parents had brought me here for a summer holiday. But I can still remember how I felt when I looked up at it, and the promise I made myself that some day I was going to climb it." He paused. His eyes moved slowly upward. "Youth is the time for dreams, boy," he murmured. "The trick is, when you get older, not to forget them."

Rudi listened, spellbound. He had never heard anyone speak like that. He had not known a grown man could think and feel like that.

Then Winter asked:

from
Into Thin Air

Jon Krakauer

In April 1996, writer John Krakauer joined an expedition to the top of Mount Everest. Krakauer survived to write a book about his experience, but before the trip was over, eight climbers had lost their lives. Here, Krakauer describes one of the terrifying ordeals of his climb.

If the Icefall required few orthodox climbing techniques, it demanded a whole new repertoire of skills in their stead—for instance, the ability to tiptoe in mountaineering boots and crampons[1] across three wobbly ladders lashed end to end, bridging a heart-stopping chasm. There were many such crossings, and I never got used to them.

At one point I was balanced on an unsteady ladder in the predawn gloaming, stepping tenuously from one bent rung to the next, when the ice supporting the ladder on either end began to quiver as if an earthquake had struck. A moment later came an explosive roar as a large serac[2] somewhere close above came crashing down. I froze, my heart in my throat, but the avalanching ice passed fifty yards to the left, out of sight, without doing any damage. After waiting a few minutes to regain my composure I resumed my herky-jerky passage to the far side of the ladder.

The glacier's continual and often violent state of flux added an element of uncertainty to every ladder crossing. As the glacier moved, crevasses would sometimes compress, buckling ladders like toothpicks; other times a crevasse might expand, leaving a ladder dangling in the air, only tenuously supported, with neither end mounted on solid ice. Anchors securing the ladders and lines routinely melted out when the afternoon sun warmed the surrounding ice and snow. Despite daily maintenance, there was a very real danger that any given rope might pull loose under body weight.

But if the Icefall was strenuous and terrifying, it had a surprising allure as well. As dawn washed the darkness from the sky, the shattered glacier was revealed to be a three-dimensional landscape of phantasmal beauty. The temperature was six degrees

---

1. **crampons** (kram´ pənz) *n.*: Iron spikes on shoes to prevent slipping.
2. **serac** (sə rak´) *n.*: High, pointed mass of ice.

◀ **Critical Viewing** What impression of the climb does this photograph give you? [Respond]

Fahrenheit. My crampons crunched reassuringly into the glacier's rind. Following the fixed line, I meandered through a vertical maze of crystalline blue stalagmites.[3] Sheer rock buttresses seamed with ice pressed in from both edges of the glacier, rising like the shoulders of a malevolent god. Absorbed by my surroundings and the gravity of the labor, I lost myself in the unfettered pleasures of ascent, and for an hour or two actually forgot to be afraid.

Three-quarters of the way to Camp One, Hall remarked at a rest stop that the icefall was in better shape than he'd ever seen it: "The route's a bloody freeway this season." But only slightly higher, at 19,000 feet, the ropes brought us to the base of a gargantuan, perilously balanced serac. As massive as a twelve-story building, it loomed over our

---

3. **stalagmites** (stə lag´ mīts´) *n.*: Cone-shaped mineral deposits.

◆ Build Vocabulary

malevolent (mə lev´ ə lənt) *adj.*: Wishing evil or harm to others

denigrate (den´ ə grāt´) *n.*: Discredit; put down; belittle

heads, leaning 30 degrees past vertical. The route followed a natural catwalk that angled sharply up the overhanging face: we would have to climb up and over the entire off-kilter tower to escape its threatening tonnage.

Safety, I understood, hinged on speed. I huffed toward the relative security of the serac's crest with all the haste I could muster, but since I wasn't acclimatized my fastest pace was no better than a crawl. Every four or five steps I'd have to stop, lean against the rope, and suck desperately at the thin, bitter air, searing my lungs in the process.

I reached the top of the serac without it collapsing and flopped breathless onto its flat summit, my heart pounding like a jackhammer. A little later, around 8:30 A.M., I arrived at the top of the Icefall itself, just beyond the last of the seracs. The safety of Camp One didn't supply much peace of mind, however: I couldn't stop thinking about the ominously tilted slab a short distance below, and the fact that I would have to pass beneath its faltering bulk at least seven more times if I was going to make it to the summit of Everest. Climbers who snidely denigrate this as the Yak Route, I decided, had obviously never been through the Khumbu Icefall.

Guide for Responding

◆ LITERATURE AND YOUR LIFE

Reader's Response What thoughts might you have had if you were crossing the Icefall?

Thematic Focus Jon Krakauer and his fellow climbers risked their lives to climb Mount Everest. Why do you think Krakauer was willing to risk everything to make it to the top?

☑ Check Your Comprehension

1. Give two reasons why the ladder crossings on the Icefall were dangerous.
2. Why did the Icefall attract Krakauer in spite of its dangers?
3. Why did Krakauer have difficulty climbing the twelve-story serac?

◆ Critical Thinking

INTERPRET

1. Why do you think Krakauer never got used to crossing the chasms? **[Analyze]**
2. From what you have read, how would you rate Krakauer's skills as a mountaineer? **[Infer]**
3. Despite fear, Krakauer continued across the Icefall. What does this tell you about his character? **[Draw Conclusions]**

COMPARE LITERARY WORKS

4. Compare the environment of "A Boy and a Man" and the environment of the excerpt from *Into Thin Air*. **[Compare and Contrast]**

Guide for Responding (continued)

◆ Reading Strategy

PREDICT

When you **predict,** you make a guess about the outcome of a story using details the author provides. Making and revising your predictions based on the information in each paragraph keeps you an active participant in the reading process.

1. (a) Did you predict that Rudi in "A Boy and a Man" would successfully rescue Captain Winter? (b) On what facts or beliefs did you base this prediction?
2. (a) Do you predict that Rudi will climb the Citadel? (b) What details in "A Boy and a Man" support your prediction?
3. Krakauer reaches the summit of Mount Everest and safely returns. What details in this passage from *Into Thin Air* help you predict his success?

◆ Build Vocabulary

USING THE PREFIX *mal-*

The prefix *mal-* means "bad" or "badly." On a sheet of paper, write the words formed by adding *mal- to* these words. Then, write a definition for the new word.

1. functioned   2. nourished   3. formed

SPELLING STRATEGY

When you break a word with double consonants at the end of a line, divide it between the two consonants: *pum-meled.*

Copy the following words on your paper, dividing them as if you reached the end of a line.

1. reconnoiter   3. allure
2. beginning   4. innocent

USING THE WORD BANK

Replace each italicized word or phrase with the word from the Word Bank that means the same.

The lieutenant was in the field to **(1)** *investigate* the area which was to be attacked. His body was **(2)** *tense.* He thought that the situation was potentially dangerous, even though he had heard others **(3)** *belittle* the threat. As he lay in a **(4)** *flat* position on the ground, he saw where the **(5)** *evil* enemy had been **(6)** *beaten up* by cannon fire. Knowing the enemy was retreating, the lieutenant felt reassured.

◆ Literary Focus

CONFLICT WITH NATURE

Conflict is a struggle between two opposing forces. In both fiction and nonfiction, conflict provides interest, suspense, and tension. Both of these narratives feature a **conflict with nature** in which characters face the elements in a fierce struggle for survival. The main characters struggle against high, forbidding mountain environments.

1. Identify three details in "A Boy and a Man" that show that a conflict with nature can be brutal.
2. Describe the most terrifying environmental threat in *Into Thin Air.*
3. What protection do characters in both narratives use against the elements?

◆ Build Grammar Skills

PLACEMENT OF ADJECTIVES

Both Ullman and Krakauer make their writing more descriptive by using **adjectives,** words that modify nouns or pronouns. Adjectives can be placed in several different parts of a sentence. Sometimes, they come directly before the noun they modify. Sometimes, they follow linking verbs such as *am, is, are, was,* and *were* to modify the subject of the sentence.

Before a Noun: Captain Winter brought out an *unbroken* bar of chocolate.

After a Linking Verb: The Icefall was *strenuous.*

Practice Copy these sentences on your paper. Underline each adjective, and draw an arrow to the word it modifies.

1. Again he could hear a scraping sound below.
2. I was lucky and hit a ledge.
3. You can see that she is afraid.
4. The climb was terrifying.
5. I meandered through a vertical maze of crystalline stalagmites.

Writing Application Write a paragraph describing a time when you faced extreme cold, extreme heat, or another serious weather condition. In your paragraph, use three adjectives before nouns and three adjectives following linking verbs.

Build Your Portfolio

 ## Idea Bank

Writing

1. **Advertisement** Imagine Jon Krakauer has started a travel agency for mountaineers. Write an advertisement for his new business.

2. **Movie Proposal** A mountaineering movie based on either of these narratives could be very successful. Choose one of the pieces and write a proposal to a film studio to convince them that the story would make a successful film.

3. **Autobiographical Incident** Even though you may not have climbed Mount Everest yet, you've probably pushed yourself to reach a difficult goal. In an essay, describe the challenge you faced and the steps you took to succeed.

Speaking and Listening

4. **Dialogue [Group Activity]** Pretend that Rudi, Captain Winter, and Jon Krakauer have met at a mountaineering convention. With two classmates, prepare and present the conversation that takes place among the three climbers.

5. **Rescue Interview** "A Boy and a Man" describes a dramatic rescue. Interview your local fire chief to find out how professional rescue teams work where you live. Prepare your questions in advance and share the information you discover with the class. **[Community Link]**

Projects

6. **Glacier Research** "A Boy and a Man" takes place on a glacier, a huge mass of ice. Use library resources to learn more about glaciers. For example, prepare a report explaining how glaciers are formed, how far they travel in a year, or how they affect the Earth's surface. **[Science Link]**

7. **How-to Guide** The characters in these narratives put themselves in danger's path. However, most people are unprepared when nature's fury strikes home. In a brochure, outline the ways people can prepare for such unexpected natural events as hurricanes, floods, or blizzards.

 ## Writing Mini-Lesson

Persuasive Letter

You want Rudi to be part of the group you are organizing to climb the Citadel. However, his family wants him to choose a safer life. Write a letter to Rudi's mother persuading her to let her son join you.

> ### Writing Skills Focus: Order of Importance
>
> When you write to persuade, you want to convince your reader that your position is right. To make your argument most effective, arrange your ideas in **order of importance.** Build from your least important to your most important reason or piece of evidence. This strategy will leave your reader thinking about your strongest point.

Prewriting Review "A Boy and a Man" to gather details that support your opinion. Jot down a list of reasons that prove that Rudi should become part of the team. Next, rank the items on your list from the least important to the most important.

Drafting Your persuasive letter should begin with your opinion—Rudi should be part of your team. Then, write your reasons beginning with the least important and ending with the most important. For each reason you cite, give examples or details to support your idea. Remember you are writing to Rudi's mother, so use reasonable and polite language. Let your argument speak for itself.

Revising Check your letter to be sure that you have used the proper form, heading, and salutation. If you have not concluded with your strongest point, adjust your ending. Don't forget to sign your letter.

◆ **Grammar Application**

Add specific adjectives to make your arguments more powerful.

CONNECTING LITERATURE TO SOCIAL STUDIES
PREHISTORIC TIMES

from **The Iceman** *by Don Lessem*

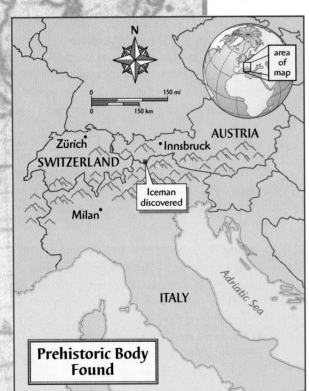

N

area of map

0   150 mi
0   150 km

Zürich
SWITZERLAND
AUSTRIA
•Innsbruck

Iceman discovered

Milan•

ITALY

Adriatic Sea

Prehistoric Body Found

SCIENCE FICTION In the movie *Jurassic Park,* scientists discover a tiny piece of a dinosaur's body. It had been preserved in amber for millions of years. These Hollywood scientists use it to clone several living dinosaurs. The movie was science fiction—a made-up story based on scientific knowledge of things that could happen.

Scientific Fact In the real world, scientists actually do discover remains of the world as it existed long before history was recorded and passed down from one generation to another. This period is known as the *prehistoric* era.

Tools, Artifacts, and Art If a period precedes written history, how do we know anything about it? We know from the many discoveries scientists have made in various parts of the world. Some scientists dig in places where they believe people once lived. They uncover tools and other artifacts that prehistoric people used in their daily lives. They discover drawings on the walls of caves. Once in a great while, the search uncovers the remains of a human being.

Preserved in Ice When a creature dies, its body slowly changes into the elements that make up the Earth. This process is called *decomposition.* One way to stop decomposition is to freeze the dead body. Sometimes this freezing happens naturally. If an animal or a person dies in a very cold climate, the dry, icy air will keep the body from decomposing. Suppose this happens in a place where the climate is always very cold. How long do you think the body of a dead person could be preserved? You'll find an answer in "The Iceman."

from THE
ICEMAN

by Don Lessem

In 1991, hikers in the mountains of northern Europe found the body of a 5,300-year-old man. It was perfectly preserved by the snow that had covered it for so long. Scientists of many kinds used information gathered from the man, whom they named Ötzi, to create a picture of European life in the Copper Age.

Ötzi and the everyday objects that were found beside him are unique and wonderfully preserved clues to daily life in a time that has long been mysterious. With their help, we can imagine what life might have been like in the Copper Age[1] and how Ötzi lived and died. We can never be certain, but it may have been something like this:

Ötzi may have been a shepherd herding sheep, a trader trading stone and metal for tools, or even a medicine man in search of messages from gods. Whatever the reason, Ötzi had hiked high into the mountains. He was strong and well equipped, perhaps a leader among his people.

---

1. Copper Age (käp´ ər) *n.*: Period lasting from 5,000 B.C. to 3,500 B.C., when copper was the most advanced metal in use.

The tattoo lines on his knee, foot, and back may have been religious emblems or a sign of his bravery or status.

Ötzi was a welcome visitor to the villages along his route. If he was a shepherd, he would have brought the villagers meat (since wool was not yet used for clothing). If he was a trader, he would have brought them flint for tools or copper for weapons.

Ötzi may have admired the villagers' talents. They used wheeled wagons and plows to farm. They sewed linen clothes and shoes expertly. They fed him butter and other delicacies.

The villagers may have been impressed with the hard flints Ötzi had brought—wonderful stones for making daggers and knives—and with his fine ax. But Ötzi would not part with the ax. He had traveled far to the south and traded away many of his belongings to the copper workers for his ax.

> **Connecting Literature to Social Studies**
> What objects did Ötzi have with him on his trip into the mountains?

Ötzi was handy and so found many uses for his ax. He had been wielding it lately to make a new bow to replace the one he'd traded away or broken. It was a huge bow, taller than he was. It took all his strength to pull the bowstring.

Ötzi had been hunting since he was a child. He had learned to feather his arrows at an angle to make them spin in flight and hold their course. After crossing the mountains, Ötzi planned to finish his new bow and arrows. Then he could hunt in the woods for ibex,[2] deer, and boar, and kill threatening bears and wolves. But for now, his mind was on traveling across the treeless high mountains in the thin, cold air.

> **Connecting Literature to Social Studies**
> What clues did scientists use to support their conclusion about the cold temperature Ötzi faced?

In the soft deerskin suit and grass cape made for him by the village tailors, Ötzi was dressed for chill mountain weather. He had stuffed his shoes with mountain grass to protect his feet from the cold. He wore a fur cap on his head.

But the autumn air turned even colder than Ötzi had expected. He huddled in the shelter of a rock hollow. He was too cold and tired to eat the last of the antelope meat and berries he had brought with him.

Ötzi tried to start a fire. He had flint to strike a spark and strips of felt to help the fire along. But far above the tree line,[3] Ötzi could

---

2. **ibex** (ī′ beks′) *n.*: European wild goats.
3. **tree line** *n.*: Line above which trees will not grow.

◆ **Build Vocabulary**

emblems (em′ bləmz) *n.*: Symbols, signs, or badges

delicacies (del′ i ke sēz) *n.*: Foods that are rare and tasty

wielding (wēld′ in) *v.*: Using with skill

▶ **Critical Viewing** John Gurche (left) of the Denver Museum used a copy of the Iceman's skull (right) to reconstruct a head (center). Why do you think he gave his model a ruddy complexion and a beard? **[Infer]**

find no branches to keep a fire going. Perhaps falling snow snuffed out the few sparks he had created.

Ötzi's only hope for survival was to move on through the mountain pass and down into the valley. But he was too weak to move. Maybe he was sick or injured.

Ötzi carefully laid his belongings, including his beautiful ax, against the rocks around him. He lay down to sleep on his left side atop a large stone as the snow fell through the frigid air.

> **Connecting Literature to Social Studies**
> How do scientists know Ötzi rested on his left side?

Days later, when Ötzi did not appear, other shepherds, or friends from the village, may have come looking for him. If they came upon the spot where he lay down, they would have found only a blanket of snow.

In cold isolation, Ötzi had quietly died. Five thousand years later, his snow blanket was finally removed. At last Ötzi was found, along with his treasures. Their value is beyond measure, for they give us our best view yet of the lost world of our Copper Age ancestors.

Guide for Responding

◆ LITERATURE AND YOUR LIFE

Reader's Response Suppose that you lived in one of the villages that Ötzi visited. Would you have joined the search party that went out to look for him? Why or why not?

Thematic Focus What risks did Ötzi face during his travels?

Journal Writing How would you feel if you were one of the archaeologists or scientists who initially studied Ötzi? Write a journal entry to describe your first day's findings.

☑ Check Your Comprehension

1. What are some possible explanations for Ötzi's traveling so far from home?
2. What evidence is there that Ötzi was probably very strong?
3. Why was Ötzi unable to build a fire to protect himself from the cold?
4. Why did the villagers have trouble finding Ötzi when they went looking for him?

◆ Critical Thinking

INTERPRET

1. Do you think Ötzi would have felt free to enter a village where he was a stranger? Why or why not? **[Infer]**
2. What could Ötzi have done to avoid dying in the snowstorm? **[Speculate]**

APPLY

3. Why do scientists find the details of Ötzi's life useful? **[Assess]**
4. Why was Ötzi more at risk than a traveler along the same route would be today? **[Apply]**

Meet the Author

Don Lessem (1952–   ) has explained prehistoric times in more than a dozen books. He is best known as a dinosaur expert who edits a newspaper called *Dino Times*. It includes a column he writes using the name of Dino Don.

Lessem was a consultant on the movie *Jurassic Park,* and he is the host of a Microsoft CD-ROM about dinosaurs. *The Iceman* is Lessem's book about the discovery and study of the man who came to be called Ötzi.

Connecting Literature to Social Studies

The Iceman's remains were not discovered by scientists. They were found by two people who were hiking in the mountains on the border between Italy and Austria. The local police used a jackhammer to break up the ice surrounding the body. Other people tried digging it out with axes. All this digging ruined some of the artifacts lying near the body. It took several days before a scientist examined the body and realized it was old, deciding that it was probably more than 1,000 years old. The body was then flown by helicopter to a place where it could be studied. Only after more study did scientists learn that the body was actually 5,000 years old. The local people began calling it Ötzi because it was found near a valley named Ötzal.

1. Why was Ötzi's ax so important to him?
2. Identify three details from the selection that reveal how people probably lived during Ötzi's time.
3. Why are scientists interested in the remains of someone who lived thousands of years ago?

 Idea Bank

Writing

1. **Journal Entry** If Ötzi could read and write, he might have kept a journal of his travels. Write the entry he might have made just before going to sleep the night he could not build a fire.
2. **TV News Story** Imagine that a TV camera crew has taped the police and the scientists digging up Ötzi's remains. Write a script to be read by the anchorperson of a news program that will show the tape.
3. **Letter** Write a letter to the editor of a newspaper. Tell why you think the discovery and study of Ötzi's remains are important to the world.

Speaking and Listening

4. **Telephone Interview** Learn more about the fields of science that study prehistory. Find an expert at a local museum or university, and arrange a telephone interview. Prepare questions in advance. Then, share what you learn with classmates. **[Career Link]**

Projects

5. **Research** Use an encyclopedia and other library resources to research the Copper Age and the Bronze Age. Report to the class on how metals were made and used during those two periods.
6. **Model Tools** Find out more about the technology of the Copper and Bronze ages. Use what you discover to make models of several tools used during the Copper and Bronze ages.

Further Reading

- John Napier's *The Origins of Man* (1968) gives information about the earliest humans.
- William Jaspersohn's *How People First Lived* (1985) is about prehistoric communities.
- Isaac Asimov's *How Did We Find Out About Our Human Roots?* (1979) explains some of the methods scientists use to study prehistory.

Guide for Reading

Meet the Authors:

Alfred, Lord Tennyson (1809–1892)

Alfred, Lord Tennyson was the most popular British poet of his day. Many of his poems focused on nature. Others dealt with significant historical events. In "The Charge of the Light Brigade," a poem based on a newspaper account of a battle between English and Russian troops, he honored the courage of the English cavalry who fought against overwhelming odds.

William Shakespeare (1564–1616)

We are sure that William Shakespeare was born in Stratford-on-Avon, England, but no one knows much about his early life. He became England's greatest poet and foremost playwright. Shakespeare wrote thirty-seven plays. His historical dramas, such as *Henry V,* instilled the English people with pride in their heritage and provided them with a model of patriotism. [For more information on Shakespeare, see page 780.]

Alice Walker (1944–   )

Alice Walker was born the eighth and last child in a poor family in Eatonton, Georgia. She developed a love of reading and writing at an early age, and she has gone on to establish herself as one of today's best-known and most-loved writers. In many of her works, she expresses her concerns about social injustice. [For more information on Walker, see page 108.]

◆ LITERATURE AND YOUR LIFE

CONNECT YOUR EXPERIENCE

You may have heard the battle stories of people who have fought for our country in a war. Yet you probably have a hard time imagining what it is like to be in battle. The pieces you're about to read will bring the experiences of battle to life and give you an appreciation of the sacrifices that soldiers make.

THEMATIC FOCUS: Risking It All

As you read, think about the courage it takes for soldiers to risk their lives in battle.

◆ Background for Understanding

HISTORY

Fought between 1853 and 1856, the Crimean War pitted Russia against the combined armies of Great Britain, France, and what is now Turkey. It was the first war to be covered by journalists at the front line, and citizens at home learned about it in a graphic way. "The Charge of the Light Brigade" commemorates the Battle of Balaklava, in which a confusion in orders led 600 lightly armed British troops to charge a heavily armed Russian fortification. Three fourths of the British were killed.

◆ Build Vocabulary

HOMOPHONES

Homophones, words that sound the same but have different meanings, can cause confusion. For example, *real* means "genuine" or "true," but *reel* can mean to "stagger" or "sway."

WORD BANK

Which of these words from the poems might mean "made a foolish mistake"?

dismayed
blundered
volleyed
reeled
sundered

The Charge of the Light Brigade
from Henry V ◆ Lonely Particular ◆ The Enemy

◆ Literary Focus

REPETITION

Repetition is the repeated use of words, phrases, or rhythms. Poets use repetition to add to the music of poetry, to emphasize ideas, and to help establish mood or atmosphere. Look at these famous lines from Tennyson's poem:

> *Theirs not to* make reply,
> *Theirs not to* reason why,
> *Theirs* but to do and die.

Notice how the use of repetition in this example creates rhythm and adds emphasis to the ideas Tennyson is expressing.

◆ Reading Strategy

READING POETIC CONTRACTIONS

To achieve a specific rhythm, or pattern of sound, poets often use **poetic contractions.** These words, which appear mostly in poetry, are abbreviated versions of common words. Remember that in a contraction, an apostrophe replaces missing letters. For example, you may see the contraction *ne'er* for "never" or *o'er* for "over." To understand these words, supply the missing letters. Use a chart like the following to clarify the contractions in these poems.

Contraction	Meaning
Sab'ring	sabering
call'd	
rememb'red	
ne'er	
accurs'd	

The Charge of the Light Brigade

Alfred, Lord Tennyson

Charge of the Light Brigade at the Battle of Balaklava, 1854, Artist Unknown

▲ **Critical Viewing** The Charge of the Light Brigade led to
tremendous losses for the British. What in this painting
confirms that the battle was unbalanced? **[Analyze]**

1

Half a league,[1] half a league,
Half a league onward,
All in the valley of Death
    Rode the six hundred.
5 "Forward, the Light Brigade!
Charge for the guns!" he said:
Into the valley of Death
    Rode the six hundred.

2

  "Forward, the Light Brigade!"
10 Was there a man dismayed?
Not though the soldier knew
    Someone had blundered:
Theirs not to make reply,
Theirs not to reason why,
15 Theirs but to do and die,
Into the valley of Death
    Rode the six hundred.

3

Cannon to right of them,
Cannon to left of them,
20 Cannon in front of them
    Volleyed and thundered;
Stormed at with shot and shell,
Boldly they rode and well,
Into the jaws of Death,
25 Into the mouth of Hell
    Rode the six hundred.

4

Flashed all their sabers bare,
Flashed as they turned in air,
Sab'ring the gunners there,
30 Charging an army, while
    All the world wondered:
Plunged in the battery[2] smoke
Right through the line they broke:
Cossack[3] and Russian
35 Reeled from the saber stroke
    Shattered and sundered.
Then they rode back, but not,
    Not the six hundred.

5

Cannon to right of them,
40 Cannon to left of them,
Cannon behind them
    Volleyed and thundered;
Stormed at with shot and shell,
While horse and hero fell,
45 They that had fought so well
Came through the jaws of Death,
Back from the mouth of Hell,
All that was left of them,
    Left of six hundred.

6

50 When can their glory fade?
O the wild charge they made!
    All the world wondered.
Honor the charge they made!
Honor the Light Brigade,
55   Noble six hundred!

---

1. **league** (lēg) *n.*: Three miles.

2. **battery:** Fortification equipped with heavy guns.
3. **Cossack** (käs´ ak´): People of southern Russia famous as horsemen and cavalrymen.

◆ Build Vocabulary

dismayed (dis mād´) *adj.*: Afraid; without confidence
blundered (blun´ dərd) *v.*: Made a foolish mistake
volleyed (väl´ ēd) *v.*: Fired together
reeled (rēld) *v.*: Fell back from a blow
sundered (sun´ dərd) *v.*: Broken apart

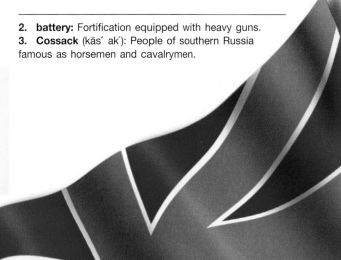

from Henry V, St. Crispian's Day Speech

❧ William Shakespeare ❧

This day is call'd the feast of Crispian:[1]
He that outlives this day, and comes safe home,
Will stand a' tiptoe when this day is named,
And rouse him at the name of Crispian.
5   He that shall live this day, and see old age,
Will yearly on the vigil feast his neighbors,
And say, "To-morrow is Saint Crispian."
Then will he strip his sleeve and show his scars,
[And say, "These wounds I had on Crispin's day."]
10   Old men forget; yet all shall be forgot,
But he'll remember with advantages
What feats he did that day. Then shall our names,
Familiar his mouth as household words,
Harry the King,[2] Bedford and Exeter,
15   Warwick and Talbot, Salisbury and Gloucester,[3]
Be in their flowing cups freshly rememb'red.
This story shall the good man teach his son;
And Crispin Crispian shall ne'er go by,
From this day to the ending of the world,
20   But we in it shall be remembered—
We few, we happy few, we band of brothers;
For he to-day that sheds his blood with me
Shall be my brother; be he ne'er so vile,
This day shall gentle his condition;
25   And gentlemen in England, now a-bed,
Shall think themselves accurs'd they were not here;
And hold their manhoods cheap whiles any speaks
That fought with us upon Saint Crispin's day.

---

1. **feast of Crispian:** St. Crispin's (kris′ pinz) Day, October 25, a religious holiday celebrating two early Christian martyrs.
2. **Harry the King:** King Henry V, ruler of England, 1413–1422.
3. **Bedford and Exeter** (eks′ ə tər), **Warwick** (wôr′ ik) **and Talbot** (tôl′ bət), **Salisbury** (sôlz′ ber′ e) **and Gloucester** (gläs′ tər): Lords in King Henry V's army.

◀ **Critical Viewing** Laurence Olivier, pictured in armor here, had the title role in the 1944 film version of *Henry V*. What elements of his body language suggest the royalty and leadership the speech conveys? **[Connect]**

Guide for Responding

◆ LITERATURE AND YOUR LIFE

Reader's Response Would Alfred, Lord Tennyson or William Shakespeare make a better war correspondent for television news? Explain.

Thematic Focus In what ways are the soldiers asked to risk it all in "The Charge of the Light Brigade" and in the St. Crispian's Day speech?

Journal Writing What advice might a member of the Light Brigade give to a soldier who had just heard Henry's St. Crispian's Day speech? In a journal entry, explore this question.

✓ Check Your Comprehension

1. The soldiers in "The Charge of the Light Brigade" realize someone had blundered. Why do they still go into battle?
2. What was the outcome of the battle?
3. Why does Henry V say that the world will always remember St. Crispian's Day?

◆ Critical Thinking

INTERPRET

1. What is the spirit of the Light Brigade's cavalrymen as they make their charge? **[Infer]**
2. Describe the speaker's feelings about the cavalrymen. **[Speculate]**
3. What reasons might Henry V have had for calling all the soldiers, both noble and common, his brothers? **[Analyze]**
4. What does the St. Crispian's Day speech tell you about the character of Henry V? **[Infer]**

EVALUATE

5. Henry V's St. Crispian's Day speech is considered by many to be one of the greatest speeches an actor can perform. Based on your reading, why do you think this is so? **[Assess]**
6. Could a poem like "The Charge of the Light Brigade" be written today about a modern battle? **[Make a Judgment]**

COMPARE LITERARY WORKS

7. How does the representation of courage presented in these two selections differ? **[Contrast]**

Beyond Literature

History Connection

Who Was Henry V? Henry V was one of England's greatest leaders, a soldier-king who conquered a large part of France. His first military campaign in 1415 led England against France and ended in the crushing defeat of the French at the Battle of Agincourt, where a starving English army defeated a well-rested French one several times its size. Shakespeare dramatized this battle in his play *Henry V*. Long marches and several battles finally took their toll on King Henry. He died in 1422 at the height of his power. His nine-month-old son, Henry VI, succeeded him to the throne. Not long after, the English lost all the land they had taken from the French.

Cross-Curricular Activity
History at the Movies William Shakespeare's depiction of Henry V did more to immortalize this ambitious king than any history book ever could. Hollywood has taken the playwright's work to the silver screen, producing several versions of Shakespeare's play. Read at least two reviews of a recent making of *Henry V*. What did the reviewers think of it? Share your findings with the class.

LONELY PARTICULAR
Alice Walker

When the people knew you
That other time
You were not as now
A crowding General.
5   Firing into your own
Ranks;
Forcing the tender skin
Of men
Against the guns
10 The very sun
To mangled perfection
For your cause.

Not General then
But frightened boy.
15 The cheering fell
Within the quiet
That fed your
Walks
Across the mines.
20 A mere foot soldier,
Marching the other way:
A lonely Particular.

THE ENEMY

Alice Walker

in gray, battle-scarred Leningrad[1]
a tiny fist unsnapped to show
crumpled heads
of pink and yellow flowers
5 snatched hurriedly on the go
in the cold spring shower—

consent or not
countries choose
cold or hot
10 win or lose
to speak of wars
yellow and red
but there is much
let it be said
15 for children.

_____
1. Leningrad (len´ in grad´) *n.*: Important city in the former Soviet Union, renamed St. Petersburg, in 1991.

Guide for Responding

◆ LITERATURE AND YOUR LIFE

Reader's Response What would you like to say to the General in "Lonely Particular"? What questions would you ask "The Enemy"?

Thematic Focus A loyal and courageous soldier risks everything fighting the enemy. Do you think Alice Walker believes soldiers should be asked to risk their lives for their country?

☑ Check Your Comprehension

1. Why is the General in "Lonely Particular" firing?
2. How has the General changed since his youth?
3. What is the setting of "The Enemy"?
4. In "The Enemy," who is holding the pink and yellow flowers?

◆ Critical Thinking

INTERPRET

1. How does the relationship between the words "general" and "particular" help you interpret the meaning of "Lonely Particular"? **[Connect]**
2. What might have caused the General to fire into his own ranks? **[Analyze Cause and Effect]**
3. What do you think Walker thinks about war? Explain. **[Draw Conclusions]**

EVALUATE

4. Explain whether the General in "Lonely Particular" is fit to lead soldiers. **[Assess]**

COMPARE LITERARY WORKS

5. Which poem presents a stronger case for Walker's position on war? Explain. **[Distinguish]**

Guide for Responding (continued)

◆ Reading Strategy

READING POETIC CONTRACTIONS

Henry V's St. Crispian's Day speech includes **poetic contractions** that help maintain the poetic rhythm. Practice reading the speech aloud. Read *accurs'd (accursed)* as two syllables, *rememb'red* as three syllables, *remembered* as four, and *ne'er (never)* as one syllable. When you are ready, read the speech aloud for your class.

◆ Build Vocabulary

USING HOMOPHONES

Homophones are words that sound alike but have different spellings and meanings. On a sheet of paper, write the proper word in the following sentences. Use a dictionary to help you.

1. His ring was made of _____?_____ gold. (real, reel)
2. The cowboy and his horse began to _____?_____ as they chased the calf. (real, reel)
3. The doctor gave the _____?_____ of medicine to his patient. (vile, vial)
4. Rotting meat gives off a _____?_____ smell. (vile, vial)

SPELLING STRATEGY

When you add -*ed* to a verb whose last syllable is stressed, double the final consonant if it is preceded by a vowel:

    commit + -ed = committed

Exceptions include words ending in *r, w, x,* and *y.* In those cases, do not double the final letter:

    follow + -ed = followed   dismay + -ed = dismayed

Write the following words correctly on a sheet of paper:

1. volley + -ed =   3. wonder + -ed =
2. blunder + -ed =   4. regret + -ed =

USING THE WORD BANK

On your paper, match each word in the first column with the word or words closest in meaning in the second column.

1. dismayed   **a.** bungled
2. blundered   **b.** barraged; attacked
3. volleyed   **c.** separated
4. reeled   **d.** wavered
5. sundered   **e.** frightened

◆ Literary Focus

REPETITION

Repetition in poetry is the repeated use of words, phrases, or rhythmic patterns. Poets use repetition to emphasize key ideas. For example, in his poem, Tennyson uses repetition to leave readers with an unforgettable impression of the sights and sounds of actual battle.

1. What is the effect of the repetition in these lines: "Cannon to right of them,/Cannon to left of them,/Cannon in front of them"?
2. In the first stanza, Tennyson repeats the line "Rode the six hundred." (a) Scan the rest of the poem to identify the lines that repeat the words "six hundred." (b) What is the effect of the repetition of these words? (c) What is the effect of the changing of the line as the battle progresses?

◆ Build Grammar Skills

POSSESSIVE ADJECTIVES

While all **adjectives** modify nouns or pronouns, some adjectives show ownership by answering the question *whose.* The personal pronouns *my, your, his, her, our, their,* and *its* modify nouns and tell *whose.* These pronouns are therefore sometimes called **possessive adjectives.** Notice that the pronoun *his* functions as an adjective in this line spoken by Henry V:

    "Then will he strip *his* sleeve and show *his* scars."

Practice On your paper, identify the possessive adjectives in the following lines from the poems. Then, indicate which noun each modifies.

1. Flashed all their sabers bare, . . .
2. When can their glory fade?
3. Then shall our names,/Familiar his mouth as household words, . . .
4. For he to-day that sheds his blood with me/Shall be my brother; . . .
5. Within the quiet/That fed your/Walks . . .

Writing Application On your paper, write three sentences or a short poem using the following possessive adjectives.

1. my   **2.** our   **3.** his   **4.** their

Build Your Portfolio

 ## Idea Bank

Writing

1. **Letter for Future Generations** As one of King Henry's soldiers, you are moved by his St. Crispian's Day speech. In a letter for future generations of your family, describe how Henry V's words made you feel that fateful day.

2. **Eyewitness Report** As one of the British reporters on the front lines of the battle described in "The Charge of the Light Brigade," provide a description for readers back home. Use vivid language that will help readers "see" the event.

3. **Evaluation of a Poet's Message** These poems present different views of the responsibilities of soldiers and leaders. Choose one of the poems. Analyze the message it conveys about war. Then, in an essay identify the message of the poem, and tell whether you agree or disagree with it.

Speaking and Listening

4. **Poetry Reading** With a group, present a dramatic reading of each of the poems in this section. Add appropriate music or visuals to enhance your presentation. **[Performing Arts Link]**

5. **Debate [Group Activity]** With a small group, conduct a debate among the three writers that explores their positions on courage, loyalty, honor, or war. Each group member can take the part of a writer. Present the debate to your class.

Projects

6. **Museum Exhibit [Group Activity]** Create an exhibit about an important war in history. Decide which conflict your group will study. Use the library and the Internet for research. Create dioramas, three-dimensional maps, and posters to present your information. **[Media Link]**

7. **Oral History** Conduct an interview with someone who has served in the armed forces. Prepare questions in advance, and take notes or tape record the interview. Present your findings to your class. **[History Link]**

 ## Writing Mini-Lesson

Report

Tennyson uses poetry to describe a battle that occurred during his lifetime. However, you can find more factual information about the Crimean War in encyclopedias and history books. Choose an important historical battle, and write a factual report about the causes of the battle and its outcome.

Writing Skills Focus: Accuracy

While Tennyson's language tugs at reader's emotions, you should strive to inform your audience. To achieve this purpose, concentrate on **accuracy**—provide a true, fair report of the events. Use these tips to guide you:

- Use as many sources as possible. If a detail appears in two sources, you can generally be assured of its accuracy.
- Be careful as you take notes. Copy statistics exactly. Avoid changing the meaning when you put information into your own words.

Prewriting Begin with a source such as an encyclopedia, which will give an overview of the battle. Find two other books to give you further information. As you read, note the countries involved, the dates of the battle, the numbers of soldiers killed, and the reason for the fight.

Drafting Devote each paragraph in your essay to a specific topic. For example, in one paragraph, address the causes of the battle; in another, describe the location and duration of the fighting; and in another, describe the weapons and technology used.

Revising When you revise, check your draft against your notes to be sure you have accurately reported the facts.

> ◆ **Grammar Application**
> Check your use of possessive adjectives. Do they show ownership or a clear relationship?

Persuasive Letter

Writing Process Workshop

If you've ever tried to convince your parents to let you get a pet or argued with a friend that one musical group is better than another, you've used persuasion. Persuasion is writing or speaking that tries to convince people to agree with a writer's perspective. Write a **persuasive letter** about something that really matters to you. Your letter should try to get someone to see things your way or to take a certain action. The following skills, introduced in this section's Writing Mini-Lessons, will help you write your persuasive letter.

Writing Skills Focus

▶ **Elaborate on key ideas.** To really convince your reader, include facts and details that prove your arguments are sound. (See p. 206.)

▶ **Organize your main points by order of importance.** Begin with your least important point and work up to the most important one, or do just the opposite. (See p. 221.)

▶ **Be accurate.** Double-check the facts you use, and document your sources. (See p. 237.)

In this model, a girl who wants to convince her parents to let her learn a potentially dangerous activity uses these skills in her request.

MODEL

Dear Mom and Dad,
    The YMCA is offering a rock-climbing course, and I really want to sign up. You'll be happy to know that the motto of the program is "Safety First." In fact, there are only three students to every instructor. ① The course brochure says the class is designed for beginners with a "taste for adventure." That sounds just like me!
    Classes meet from 10:00 to 12:30 on Saturday mornings beginning the first of next month. . . . ②

① The writer begins with her most important point: the course is safe. Then, she supports this point with details.

② The writer should double-check these facts for accuracy.

Prewriting

Choose Your Topic The topic of your letter should be something that really matters to you. Get your ideas into focus by completing this sentence: "I want to persuade _____ to _____." For example, you might want to persuade a friend to support a worthy cause, or convince an employer to offer you a job. If you'd like, consider these ideas:

Topic Ideas

Young people should/should not
- Get a driver's license at 15
- Wear a uniform to school
- Eat a vegetarian diet

Conduct Research Look for support beyond your own ideas. At the library, check nonfiction books, encyclopedias, magazine articles, CD-ROM references, and the Internet. Double-check your facts by consulting at least two sources.

Prepare Counterarguments To strengthen your letter, be aware of arguments against your position, and decide how to address them. Use a chart like the one below to jot down arguments for both sides.

Rock Climbing	
Pros	**Cons**
Rock climbing builds strength and stamina.	It can be dangerous.
Learning rock climbing will build confidence.	A class might be expensive.

Drafting

Write a Strong Beginning Even if you save your most powerful argument for the end of your letter, begin in a way that will really grab your readers' attention. Consider using a snappy statistic, an emotional appeal, a question, or a strong statement.

Keep to a Planned Organization Whether you decide to begin with your strongest argument or build up to a grand finale, be sure your arguments follow the pattern you decide.

DRAFTING/REVISING

APPLYING LANGUAGE SKILLS: Friendly Letter Format

Follow these pointers when you write a friendly letter.

- Use correct state abbreviations.
- Use a comma after the greeting.
- Begin the closing with a capital letter and follow it with a comma.

A friendly letter includes these five parts:

Heading	48 Plains Road Harrison, TX 74040
Greeting	Dear Mr. Backman,
Body	I would like to go to the Art Museum on our field trip.
Closing	Your student,
Signature	Sam Scribner

Practice Write these parts of a friendly letter correctly.

1. dover Ohio 44622
2. sincerely yours
3. dear michelle

Writing Application In your friendly letter, follow the proper format.

Writer's Solution Connection Writing Lab

To help you follow the proper format, draft your letter in the Letter Shell in the tutorial on Expression.

APPLYING LANGUAGE SKILLS:
Formal and Informal Language

The language in your writing should depend on your audience and purpose. When you use **formal language,** you write in full sentences, follow all rules of grammar, and avoid slang. Use formal language for serious letters to people you do not know. **Informal language** sounds like speech—relaxed and casual. Use it with friends and family.

Formal:

Please consider me for the position of lifeguard. I am well qualified and dependable.

Informal:

I'd love to land the lifeguard job.

Practice On your paper, make the formal sentences informal—and vice versa.

1. Check out the show at 7.
2. This rule is such a drag.
3. I hereby protest that you did not return my note.

Writing Application In your persuasive letter, use the language that best suits your audience and purpose.

Writer's Solution Connection
Language Lab

For additional instruction and practice, see the unit on Composing.

Revising

Listen to Your Letter Ask a classmate to read your letter aloud to you. You may hear something that you missed with your eyes. When your classmate has finished reading, ask questions such as these:

▶ Which of my reasons was strongest? Weakest?
▶ Did I offer enough evidence to convince you of my argument?
▶ Can you think of any way a reader could disagree?

Revise according to the feedback you receive.

Check Your Facts Check all the facts, quotations, and statistics you used in your letter. Make sure they are accurate and that they support your position directly and clearly.

REVISION MODEL

Since I know I'll want to pursue rock climbing when I get older, I think taking this class now ⓵, in the safety of a gymnasium, will help give me the knowledge I'll need. The instructor has ⓶ five/two years of climbing experience, including climbs at Glacier National Park and Yosemite.

⓵ The writer adds more details to convince an anxious reader.
⓶ To be completely accurate, the writer corrects a fact.

Publishing and Presenting

Make It a Speech Deliver your letter as a speech to the class. Use the tone of your voice, gestures, and even visual aids or props as added persuasive details.

Mail It Hand deliver, mail, or send your letter via computer e-mail. Ask for a reply, to see if your persuasion worked.

Real-World Reading Skills Workshop

Strategies for Success

When a writer's personal opinions come through in a story or news report, he or she is revealing a *bias*. Certain types of writers—reporters, for instance—are supposed to be objective. They are expected to stick to the facts and keep their personal opinions out of their writing. Recognizing bias while you read will help you sort out fact from opinion.

Watch for Loaded Words Loaded words do more than just state the facts. They reveal the writer's personal opinion. For instance, one sports reporter may write about a "losing pitcher," while another describes the same athlete as a "sloppy losing pitcher." The word *sloppy* is a loaded word that shows the writer's bias.

Look Out for Stereotypes Stereotypes label an entire group as being a certain way without looking at the different members of that group. For instance, a writer who reports that "men are reckless drivers" creates a stereotype about male drivers. If the writer had done more research, he or she might have learned that some men—and some women—drive recklessly, but not all. Stereotypes like this one reveal bias.

Be Aware of One-Sided Arguments Bias is also revealed when a writer presents only one side of an argument. For instance, a reporter who reports only the views of one political candidate presents a one-sided argument. The reader does not get the whole story.

Apply the Strategies

Read the newspaper article on this page. Then, answer the questions that follow.

1. Do you see any loaded words in the article? List them.

2. Has the writer created a stereotype? Explain.

3. Did the writer present any one-sided arguments? If so, what might be the other side of that argument?

Skateboard Madness

On Saturday, the warm spring weather brought out crowds of inconsiderate kids with skateboards. Wild skateboarders clogged sidewalks and made walking difficult. The town should allow skateboarding only in parks and playgrounds.

✔ *Here are other places to be on the lookout for bias:*
- ▶ *A letter written to a newspaper's editorial page*
- ▶ *A candidate's speech about an opponent*
- ▶ *A hometown sports report about a rival team*
- ▶ *An eyewitness account of an automobile accident*

Grammar Review

An **adjective** is a word that modifies or describes a noun or a pronoun. (See page 205.) By answering the questions *what kind, which one, how many, how much,* and *whose,* adjectives make the words they modify more vivid and precise.

Placement of Adjectives An adjective may come before the word it modifies or after a linking verb, modifying the subject. (See page 220.)

Position	Example
Before the Word It Modifies	The *graceful* swan glided by.
After a Linking Verb	The swan was *graceful.*

Possessive Adjectives The personal pronouns *my, your, his, her, its, our,* and *their* modify nouns and tell *whose.* These pronouns are sometimes called **possessive adjectives.** (See page 236.)

His speech was inspiring.

Practice 1 Copy these sentences. Underline each adjective, and draw an arrow to the word it modifies.

1. His wish was for a beautiful and gentle wife.

2. The snow-capped mountains are beautiful but dangerous.

3. Many climbers have lost their lives while attempting to scale the rugged peaks.

4. The brigade was brave but outnumbered.

5. Some of the courageous men who fought with Henry V lived to tell their grandchildren about the fierce battle.

Practice 2 Rewrite the following paragraph, putting adjectives into the blanks.

_____?_____ people think that the _____?_____ way to discover what really matters is to engage in activities that push your _____?_____ and _____?_____ abilities to the limit. Such activities can be risky, even _____?_____. However, by paying attention to safety and taking _____?_____ precautions, you can avoid taking _____?_____ risks.

Grammar in Writing

✔ *Some adjectives have been overused to the point where they are empty, or meaningless. Empty adjectives— nice, cute, special, awful, and interesting, to name a few—do little to make meanings stronger or clearer. When revising, replace empty adjectives with precise adjectives.*

PART 2 *Moments of Insight*

The Voice, 1930, Agnes Pelton, Collection of the Jonson Gallery of the University of New Mexico Art Museum, Albuquerque

Guide for Reading

Mark Twain (1835–1910)

In his youth, Mark Twain worked as a Mississippi riverboat pilot before heading west to prospect for gold. He never struck it rich through gold, but Twain's experiences in the camps gave him the raw material for success in writing. Soon, he was penning humorous reports for a local newspaper. He was on his way to becoming one of America's most popular storytellers.

THE STORY BEHIND THE STORY

Because Twain loved meeting colorful characters and studying the way that people fool even themselves, life in the prospectors' camps provided him with the material to make great stories. You'll see both these elements at work in "The Californian's Tale."

Seamus Heaney (1939–   )

Seamus Heaney is one of Ireland's most beloved contemporary poets. Much of his early work focuses on everyday life in the Irish countryside where he was born. His most recent poetry deals with Irish history, culture, and politics.

Nobel Prize Winner

Heaney has won numerous awards and honors, including the 1995 Nobel Prize for Literature.

◆ LITERATURE AND YOUR LIFE

CONNECT YOUR EXPERIENCE

Open a school yearbook, and you'll see rows of smiling young faces. In truth, you know little of the lives that go with the faces. As you read Twain's tale and Heaney's poem, remember that behind every picture lies a story—but it's not necessarily the story you imagine.

THEMATIC FOCUS: Moments of Insight

In "The Californian's Tale," the narrator tries to piece together a strange situation. As you read, you may reach a moment of insight before he does.

◆ Background for Understanding

HISTORY

The California Gold Rush of 1849 brought thousands to California, eager to strike it rich. Often, men left wives and family behind to make their fortunes. They lived in terrible conditions. In the first year of the Gold Rush, nearly 10,000 died. There were few women present to nurse the sick, prepare healthy food, and keep a home. No wonder the prospector in this story saw a woman's presence as a treasure worth more than gold!

◆ Build Vocabulary

SUFFIXES: -ify

The narrator of "The Californian's Tale" seeks to *gratify* his host by admiring various objects in his house. *Gratify* means "to please." The suffix *-ify* indicates that *gratify* is a verb.

WORD BANK

Which of these words from the selections do you think might mean "those who came before"? What in the word suggests "before"? Check the Build Vocabulary boxes to see if you are correct.

balmy
predecessors
humiliation
abundant
desolation
furtive
gratify
apprehensions

The Californian's Tale ◆ Valediction

◆ Literary Focus

LOCAL COLOR

Local color, the use of detail specific to a region, adds authenticity to a story. To help readers see the mining camp of his story, Twain includes descriptions of the people, places, and customs of these makeshift towns. For example, Twain provides these details of the cabins: "dirt floor, never-made beds, tin plates and cups, bacon and beans and black coffee, and nothing of ornament but war pictures . . . tacked to the log walls."

As you read, keep a chart like the one below to note details of local color that bring "The Californian's Tale" to life.

◆ Reading Strategy

SUMMARIZE

If you want to describe a story to someone who hasn't read it or a movie to someone who hasn't seen it, you'd probably do so by summarizing. When you **summarize,** you state briefly in your own words the main points and key details of the action. If you summarize as you read by stopping after each paragraph, page, or episode to note key events, you will improve your understanding of the story.

California Mining Camp

dirt floors, tin plates, bacon & beans

The Californian's Tale

Mark Twain

Thirty-five years ago I was out prospecting on the Stanislaus,[1] tramping all day long with pick and pan and horn, and washing a hatful of dirt here and there, always expecting to make a rich strike, and never doing it. It was a lovely region, woodsy, balmy, delicious, and had once been populous, long years before, but now the people had vanished and the charming paradise was a solitude. They went away when the surface diggings gave out. In one place, where a busy little city with banks and newspapers and fire companies and a mayor and aldermen had been, was nothing but a wide expanse of emerald turf, with not even the faintest sign that human life had ever been present there. This was down toward Tuttletown. In the country neighborhood thereabouts, along the dusty roads, one found at intervals the prettiest little cottage homes, snug

---

1. **Stanislaus** (stå´ ni slôws) *n.*: County, river, and mountain, all located in California.

▲ **Critical Viewing** Based on the clothing in this illustration, what conclusions can you draw about life in the mining camp? **[Draw Conclusions]**

and cozy, and so cobwebbed with vines snowed thick with roses that the doors and windows were wholly hidden from sight—sign that these were deserted homes, forsaken years ago by defeated and disappointed families who could neither sell them nor give them away. Now and then, half an hour apart, one came across solitary log cabins of the earliest mining days, built by the first gold-miners, the <u>predecessors</u> of the cottage-builders. In some few cases these cabins were still occupied; and when this was so, you could depend upon it that the occupant was the very pioneer who had built the cabin; and you could depend on another thing, too—that he was there because he had once had his opportunity to go home to the States rich, and had not done it; had rather lost his wealth, and had then in his <u>humiliation</u> resolved to sever all communication with his home relatives and friends, and be to them thenceforth as one dead. Round about California in that day were scattered a host of these living dead men—pride-smitten poor fellows, grizzled and old at forty, whose secret thoughts were made all of regrets and longings—regrets for their wasted lives, and longings to be out of the struggle and done with it all.

It was a lonesome land! Not a sound in all those peaceful expanses of grass and woods but the drowsy hum of insects; no glimpse of man or beast; nothing to keep up your spirits and make you glad to be alive. And so, at last, in the early part of the afternoon, when I caught sight of a human creature, I felt a most grateful uplift. This person was a man about forty-five years old, and he was standing at the gate of one of those cozy little rose-clad cottages of the sort already referred to. However, this one hadn't a deserted look; it had the look of being lived in and petted and cared for and looked after; and so had its front yard, which was a garden of flowers, <u>abundant</u>, gay, and flourishing. I was invited in, of course, and required to make myself at home—it was the custom of the country.

It was delightful to be in such a place, after

◆ **Reading Strategy**
Summarize the narrator's main reasons for liking the cottage so much.

long weeks of daily and nightly familiarity with miners' cabins—with all which this implies of dirt floor, never-made beds, tin plates and cups, bacon and beans and black coffee, and nothing of ornament but war pictures from the Eastern illustrated papers tacked to the log walls. That was all hard, cheerless, materialistic <u>desolation</u>, but here was a nest which had aspects to rest the tired eye and refresh that something in one's nature which, after long fasting, recognizes, when confronted by the belongings of art, howsoever cheap and modest they may be, that it has unconsciously been famishing and now has found nourishment. I could not have believed that a rag carpet could feast me so, and so content me; or that there could be such solace to the soul in wall-paper and framed lithographs,[2] and bright-colored tidies[3] and lamp-mats, and Windsor chairs,[4] and varnished what-nots, with sea-shells and books and china vases on them, and the score of little unclassifiable tricks and touches that a woman's hand distributes about a home, which one sees without knowing he sees them, yet would miss in a moment if they were taken away. The delight that was in my heart showed in my face, and the man saw it and was pleased; saw it so plainly that he answered it as if it had been spoken.

"All her work," he said, caressingly; "she did it all herself—every bit," and he took the room in with a glance which was full of affectionate

---

2. **lithographs** (li*th*′ ə grafs′) *n.*: Type of print.
3. **tidies** (tīd′ ēz) *n.*: Ornamental chair coverings that protect the back, armrests, and headrest.
4. **Windsor chairs** (win′ zər) *n.*: Wooden chairs popular in the 18th century. They had spreading legs, a back of spindles, and usually a saddle seat.

◆ Build Vocabulary

balmy (bäm′ ē) *adj.*: Soothing; mild; pleasant

predecessors (pred′ ə ses′ ərz) *n.*: Those who came before

humiliation (hyo͞o mil′ ē ā′ shən) *n.*: Embarrassment; feeling of hurt pride

abundant (ə bun′ dənt) *adj.*: Plentiful

desolation (des′ ə lā′ shən) *n.*: Loneliness; emptiness; misery

worship. One of those soft Japanese fabrics with which woman drape with careful negligence the upper part of a picture-frame was out of adjustment. He noticed it, and rearranged it with cautious pains, stepping back several times to gauge the effect before he got it to suit him. Then he gave it a light finishing pat or two with his hand, and said: "She always does that. You can't tell just what it lacks, but it does lack something until you've done that—you can see it yourself after it's done, but that is all you know; you can't find out the law of it. It's like the finishing pats a mother gives the child's hair after she's got it combed and brushed, I reckon. I've seen her fix all these things so much that I can do them all just her way, though I don't know the law of any of them. But she knows the law. She knows the why and the how both; but I don't know the why; I only know the how."

He took me into a bedroom so that I might wash my hands; such a bedroom as I had not seen for years: white counterpane, white pillows, carpeted floor, papered walls, pictures, dressing-table, with mirror and pin-cushion and dainty toilet things; and in the corner a wash-stand, with real china-ware bowl and pitcher,[5] and with soap in a china dish, and on a rack more than a dozen towels—towels too clean and white for one out of practice to use without some vague sense of profanation. So my face spoke again, and he answered with gratified words:

◆ Literary Focus
What details in this passage develop the local color?

"All her work; she did it all herself—every bit. Nothing here that hasn't felt the touch of her hand. Now you would think—But I mustn't talk so much."

By this time I was wiping my hands and glancing from detail to detail of the room's belongings, as one is apt to do when he is in a new place, where everything he sees is a comfort to his eye and his spirit; and I became conscious, in one of those unaccountable ways,

you know, that there was something there somewhere that the man wanted me to discover for myself. I knew it perfectly, and I knew he was trying to help me by furtive indications with his eye, so I tried hard to get on the right track, being eager to gratify him. I failed several times, as I could see out of the corner of my eye without being told; but at last I know I must be looking straight at the thing—knew it from the pleasure issuing in invisible waves from him. He broke into a happy laugh, and rubbed his hands together, and cried out:

"That's it! You've found it. I knew you would. It's her picture."

I went to the little black-walnut bracket on the farther wall, and did find there what I had not yet noticed—a daguerreotype-case. It contained the sweetest girlish face, and the most beautiful, as it seemed to me, that I had ever seen. The man drank the admiration from my face, and was fully satisfied.

"Nineteen her last birthday," he said, as he put the picture back; "and that was the day we were married. When you see her—ah, just wait till you see her!"

"Where is she? When will she be in?"

"Oh, she's away now. She's gone to see her people. They live forty or fifty miles from here. She's been gone two weeks to-day."

"When do you expect her back?"

"This is Wednesday. She'll be back Saturday, in the evening—about nine o'clock, likely."

I felt a sharp sense of disappointment.

"I'm sorry, because I'll be gone by then," I said, regretfully.

"Gone? No—why should you go? Don't go. She'll be so disappointed."

She would be disappointed—that beautiful creature! If she had said the words herself they could hardly have blessed me more. I was feeling a deep, strong longing to see her—a longing so supplicating, so insistent, that it made me afraid. I said to myself: "I will go straight away from this place, for my peace of mind's sake."

"You see, she likes to have people come and

---

5. **wash-stand, with real china-ware bowl and pitcher:** Items used for washing before sinks and indoor plumbing were available.

◆ **Build Vocabulary**

furtive (fur´ tiv) *adj.*: Sneaky

gratify (grat´ i fī´) v.: To please

stop with us—people who know things, and can talk—people like you. She delights in it; for she knows—oh, she knows nearly everything herself, and can talk, oh, like a bird—and the books she reads, why, you would be astonished. Don't go; it's only a little while, you know, and she'll be so disappointed."

I heard the words, but hardly noticed them, I was so deep in my thinkings and strugglings. He left me, but I didn't know. Presently he was back, with the picture-case in his hand, and he held it open before me and said:

"There, now, tell her to her face you could have stayed to see her, and you wouldn't."

That second glimpse broke down my good resolution. I would stay and take the risk. That night we smoked the tranquil pipe, and talked till late about various things, but mainly about her; and certainly I had had no such pleasant and restful time for many a day. The Thursday followed and slipped comfortably away. Toward

twilight a big miner from three miles away came—one of the grizzled, stranded pioneers—and gave us warm salutation, clothed in grave and sober speech. The he said:

"I only just dropped over to ask about the little madam, and when is she coming home. Any news from her?"

"Oh yes, a letter. Would you like to hear it, Tom?"

"Well, I should think I would, if you don't mind, Henry!"

Henry got the letter out of his wallet, and said he would skip some of the private phases, if we were willing; then he went on and read the bulk of it—a loving, sedate, and altogether charming and gracious piece of handiwork, with a postscript full of affectionate regards and messages to Tom, and Joe, and Charley, and other close friends and neighbors.

As the reader finished, he glanced at Tom, and cried out:

"Oho, you're at it again! Take your hands away, and let me see your eyes. You always do that when I read a letter from her. I will write and tell her."

▼ Critical Viewing Why would a cabin such as the one pictured here be unusual in the mining camps? [Connect]

"Oh no, you mustn't, Henry. I am getting old, you know, and any little disappointment makes me want to cry. I thought she'd be here herself, and now you've got only a letter."

"Well, now, what put that in your head? I thought everybody knew she wasn't coming till Saturday."

"Saturday! Why, come to think, I did know it. I wonder what's the matter with me lately? Certainly I knew it. Ain't we all getting ready for her? Well, I must be going now. But I'll be on hand when she comes, old man!"

Late Friday afternoon another gray veteran tramped over from his cabin a mile or so away, and said the boys wanted to have a little gaiety and a good time Saturday night, if Henry thought she wouldn't be too tired after her long journey to be kept up.

"Tired? She tired! Oh, hear the man! Joe, *you* know she'd sit up six weeks to please any one of you!"

When Joe heard that there was a letter, he asked to have it read, and the loving messages in it for him broke the old fellow all up; but he said he was such an old wreck that *that* would happen to him if she only just mentioned his name. "Lord, we miss her so!" he said.

Saturday afternoon I found I was taking out my watch pretty often. Henry noticed it, and said, with a startled look:

"You don't think she ought to be here so soon, do you?"

I felt caught, and a little embarrassed; but I laughed, and said it was a habit of mine when I was in a state of expectancy. But he didn't seem quite satisfied; and from that time on he began to show uneasiness. Four times he walked me up the road to a point whence we could see a long distance; and there he would stand, shading his eyes with his hand, and looking. Several times he said:

"I'm getting worried, I'm getting right down worried. I know she's not due till about nine o'clock, and yet something seems to be trying to warn me that something's happened. You don't think anything has happened, do you?"

I began to get pretty thoroughly ashamed of him for his childishness; and at last, when he repeated that imploring question still another time, I lost my patience for the moment, and spoke pretty brutally to him. It seemed to shrivel him up and cow him; and he looked so wounded and so humble after that, that I detested myself for having done the cruel and unnecessary thing. And so I was glad when Charley, another veteran, arrived toward the edge of the evening, and nestled up to Henry to hear the letter read, and talked over the preparations for the welcome. Charley fetched out one hearty speech after another, and did his best to drive away his friend's bodings and apprehensions.

"Anything *happened* to her? Henry, that's pure nonsense. There isn't anything going to happen to her; just make your mind easy as to that. What did the letter say? Said she was well, didn't it? And said she'd be here by nine o'clock, didn't it? Did you ever know her to fail of her word? Why, you know you never did. Well, then, don't you fret; she'll *be* here, and that's absolutely certain, and as sure as you are born. Come, now, let's get to decorating—not much time left."

◆ Literary Focus
Which words in the dialogue here help to show local color?

Pretty soon Tom and Joe arrived, and then all hands set about adorning the house with flowers. Toward nine the three miners said that as they had brought their instruments they might as well tune up, for the boys and girls would soon be arriving now, and hungry for a good, old-fashioned break-down. A fiddle, a banjo, and a clarinet—these were the instruments. The trio took their places side by side, and began to play some rattling dance-music, and beat time with their big boots.

It was getting very close to nine. Henry was standing in the door with his eyes directed up the road, his body swaying to the torture of his mental distress. He had been made to drink his wife's health and safety several times, and now Tom shouted:

◆ Build Vocabulary

apprehensions (ap´ rē hen´ shənz) *n*.: Fears; anxious feelings

"All hands stand by! One more drink, and she's here!"

Joe brought the glasses on a waiter, and served the party. I reached for one of the two remaining glasses, but Joe growled, under his breath:

"Drop that! Take the other."

Which I did. Henry was served last. He had hardly swallowed his drink when the clock began to strike. He listened till it finished, his face growing pale and paler; then he said:

"Boys, I am sick with fear. Help me—I want to lie down!"

They helped him to the sofa. He began to nestle and drowse, but presently spoke like one talking in his sleep, and said: "Did I hear horses' feet? Have they come?"

One of the veterans answered, close to his ear: "It was Jimmy Parrish come to say the party got delayed, but they're right up the road a piece, and coming along. Her horse is lame, but she'll be here in half an hour."

"Oh, I'm *so* thankful nothing has happened!"

He was asleep almost before the words were out of his mouth. In a moment those handy men had his clothes off, and had tucked him into his bed in the chamber where I had washed my hands. They closed the door and came back. Then they seemed preparing to leave; but I said: "Please don't go, gentlemen. She won't know me; I am a stranger."

They glanced at each other. Then Joe said:

"She? Poor thing, she's been dead nineteen years!"

"Dead?"

"That or worse. She went to see her folks half a year after she was married, and on her way back, on a Saturday evening, the Indians captured her within five miles of this place, and she's never been heard of since."

"And he lost his mind in consequence?"

"Never has been sane an hour since. But he only gets bad when that time of the year comes round. Then we begin to drop in here, three days before she's due, to encourage him up, and ask if he's heard from her, and Saturday we all come and fix up the house with flowers, and get everything ready for a dance. We've done it every year for nineteen years. The first Saturday there was twenty-seven of us, without counting the girls; there's only three of us now, and the girls are all gone. We drug him to sleep, or he would go wild; then he's all right for another year—thinks she's with him till the last three or four days come round; then he begins to look for her, and gets out his poor old letter, and we come and ask him to read it to us. Lord, she was a darling!"

Beyond Literature

Geography Connection

The Rise of the Gold Rush Towns
"Gold!" The cry rang out across the country. Discovered in 1848 at Sutter's Mill, California, gold—and the chance at immediate wealth— was the reason more than 80,000 people rushed west. Boom towns sprang up overnight, as settlements were founded to support prospecting activities. Dirty and often overcrowded, these towns were composed mostly of men. They were dangerous, lawless places. To create a sense of order, the residents in the towns established small, grassroots democracies. Eventually, the gold would be depleted at each of the sites. With the gold gone, most of the people left, the streets grew bare, and the buildings empty. How do you think it would feel to be the last person living in such a ghost town?

Cross-Curricular Activity
Gold Rush Towns Map Conduct research on the locations of several gold rush towns in the West during the middle of the nineteenth century. Draw a map that shows the locations of these towns. Share your map with the class, and discuss what happened to these towns.

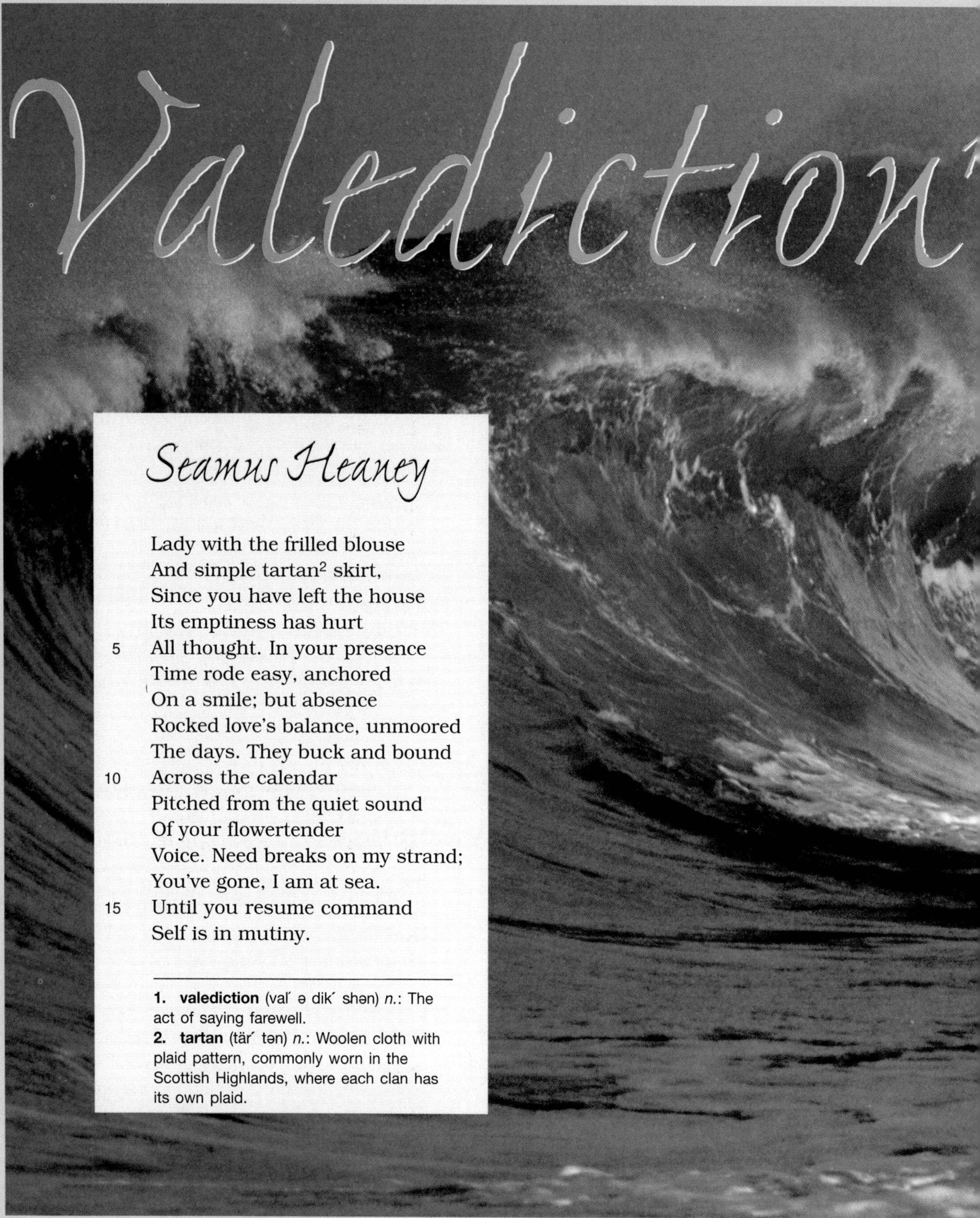

Valediction[1]

Seamus Heaney

Lady with the frilled blouse
And simple tartan[2] skirt,
Since you have left the house
Its emptiness has hurt

5   All thought. In your presence
Time rode easy, anchored
On a smile; but absence
Rocked love's balance, unmoored
The days. They buck and bound

10   Across the calendar
Pitched from the quiet sound
Of your flowertender
Voice. Need breaks on my strand;
You've gone, I am at sea.

15   Until you resume command
Self is in mutiny.

---

1. valediction (val´ ə dik´ shən) *n.*: The act of saying farewell.

2. tartan (tär´ tən) *n.*: Woolen cloth with plaid pattern, commonly worn in the Scottish Highlands, where each clan has its own plaid.

Guide for Responding

◆ LITERATURE AND YOUR LIFE

Reader's Response Were you surprised by the ending of "The Californian's Tale," or did you guess what was coming? Explain your response.

Thematic Focus At the end of "The Californian's Tale," the narrator understands the true nature of Henry's situation. How do you think he felt about Henry and the other men once he understood? Explain.

☑ Check Your Comprehension

1. In "The Californian's Tale," what is special about Henry's house?
2. Where does Henry say his wife is?
3. Why do Tom, Joe, and Charley come to Henry's house?
4. What has happened to Henry's wife?
5. Explain the speaker's situation in "Valediction."

◆ Critical Thinking

INTERPRET

1. Why is Henry's cottage so appealing to the narrator in "The Californian's Tale"? **[Analyze]**
2. Henry's wife was just nineteen when she disappeared. What do you think she was like? **[Speculate]**
3. (a) Why do the miners go to such lengths to help Henry? (b) What does their behavior say about their own lives? **[Infer]**
4. What can you infer about the relationship between the speaker and the "Lady with the frilled blouse" in "Valediction"? **[Infer]**

APPLY

5. (a) What does "The Californian's Tale" say about the value of a woman in the home? (b) Explain whether this idea has changed since the time when the story takes place. **[Synthesize]**

COMPARE LITERARY WORKS

6. "The Californian's Tale" and "Valediction" are about men who are at a loss when the women in their lives leave. Compare and contrast the ways in which each man deals with his loss. **[Compare and Contrast]**

Guide for Responding (continued)

◆ Reading Strategy

SUMMARIZE

When you **summarize** as you read, you stop to restate the main events of the action so far. As you do so, it is important to note the key points and important details, but keep your summary short by leaving out any descriptive information.

1. Summarize the events that lead Henry to beg the narrator to stay to meet his wife.
2. Summarize the events that take place between Wednesday and Saturday.
3. Summarize the events of Saturday night.

◆ Build Vocabulary

USING THE SUFFIX -ify

The suffix -ify indicates that a word is a verb showing action. Use -ify to create a verb from the word in italics in each sentence below. Write your answers on a sheet of paper.

1. As a witness, you may be asked to give testimony in a trial. Be prepared to ____?____.
2. Ice is water in a solid state. If you cool water to the freezing point, it will ____?____.

SPELLING STRATEGY

In the word balmy, the l is silent. Fill in the blanks with other common words that include this silent letter.

Though he tried to remain c____?____, Henry was anxious and upset. The p____?____ of his hands were sweaty. He w____?____ to the end of the road and back, t____?____ to himself about his absent wife.

USING THE WORD BANK

Answer these questions. Explain each response.

1. How long might a furtive glance take?
2. Would a farmer be happy with an abundant crop?
3. How could you calm your friend's apprehensions?
4. What was the predecessor to digital watches?
5. Would you need mittens on a balmy night?
6. What could you do to gratify your sister?
7. What is a good way to overcome humiliation?
8. Where would you expect to find desolation?

◆ Literary Focus

LOCAL COLOR

Mark Twain creates **local color** by providing details specific to the California mining region where his story is set. These details include the look of the landscape, the colorful language of the people who live there, and the style of clothing and furniture.

1. Review the second and third paragraphs of the story to identify three details of local color.
2. Find two examples of unusual language that add to the local color.
3. Name five details of local color you would expect to find if this story were set in a busy city.

◆ Build Grammar Skills

ADVERBS

An **adverb** is a word that modifies or describes a verb, an adjective, or another adverb. Adverbs provide information by answering the questions how, when, where, how often, or to what extent. Many adverbs end in the suffix -ly. Here are examples from "The Californian's Tale":

They went away. (Where did they go?)
"All her work," he said caressingly. (How did he say it?)
"She always does that." (When does she do that?)
Certainly I had had no such pleasant time. (To what extent had he not had a pleasant time?)

Practice On your paper, identify each adverb and the word it modifies. Tell what question it answers.

1. Doors were wholly hidden from sight.
2. Thursday followed and slipped comfortably away.
3. "Well, I must be going now."
4. He rose hourly to pace the floor.
5. I began to get pretty thoroughly ashamed of him.

Writing Application Write sentences using each of the following adverbs. For each sentence, identify the verb modified.

1. completely
2. unfortunately
3. sadly
4. nearly
5. wisely

Build Your Portfolio

 ## Idea Bank

Writing

1. **Journal Entry** Write a journal entry telling about a day in the life of one of Henry's friends, a miner.

2. **Letter Home** Imagine that Henry's wife has spent the last nineteen years living with the Indian tribe that captured her. Write a letter that she might have written to Henry, telling about her life and explaining why she could not return to the mining camp.

3. **Behavior Analysis** The miners in "The Californian's Tale" believe their deception protects Henry. In an essay, defend or criticize their behavior. Refer to "Valediction" if it helps your argument.

Speaking and Listening

4. **Public Reading** Mark Twain was a performer as well as a writer. He toured the country giving public readings from his work. Appearing as Twain, read an excerpt to your class from "The Californian's Tale." **[Performing Arts Link]**

5. **Dramatization [Group Activity]** With a group, dramatize the ending of "The Californian's Tale," beginning with the miners' arrival for the party. Add dialogue to make your scene sound as much like Twain's writing as possible. **[Performing Arts Link]**

Projects

6. **Portrait of a Lady** Draw, paint, or make a collage to convey a portrait of the lady in "Valediction." Place her in a setting suggested by the poet's language. **[Art Link]**

7. **Multimedia Presentation** With a group, create a multimedia presentation about the California Gold Rush. In addition to explaining what you learn from research, use maps, photographs, newspaper reports, music, and diary entries to bring the subject to life. Present your report to the class. **[Social Studies Link; Technology Link]**

 ## Writing Mini-Lesson

Character Sketch

Mark Twain uses actions, dialogue, and descriptive details to paint a word picture of the characters in his story. However, he leaves readers to piece together these elements of his narrator. Write a character sketch of the narrator of "The Californian's Tale," based on details in the text that show what kind of person he is.

Writing Skills Focus: Specific Examples

Bring the character to life by showing **specific examples** of his actions, gestures, and attitudes. Instead of telling that he is a tall man, for example, show him stooping to pass through a doorway. Notice how much Twain conveys about Henry in this description.

Model From the Story

"All her work," he said, caressingly; "she did it all herself—every bit," and he took the room in with a glance which was full of affectionate worship.

Prewriting Review the story, jotting down what you know about the narrator. Where did he come from? Why is he prospecting? How does he walk and talk?

Drafting Show the character in action. Describe how he looked, acted, and talked. End with a statement revealing your impression of him, such as, "He was one of the ____?____est men I'd ever met."

> ◆ **Grammar Application**
>
> Look for places where you might add an adverb to explain *where, when,* or *how* action takes place.

Revising Check to see that you include specific examples to show what the character is like. Add more action and dialogue, if necessary, to bring him to life.

CONNECTIONS TO TODAY'S WORLD

Mark Twain's "The Californian's Tale" and Seamus Heaney's "Valediction" show us that loss and the loneliness it creates can be paralyzing. In fact, such topics have provided rich sources of inspiration through the ages. In 1862, the French writer Victor Hugo wrote *Les Misérables* ("The Miserable Ones"), a gripping novel based on the French riots of 1832. During the 1980's, the book was transformed into a musical play so appealing that it has been translated into at least seven languages. In this song from the musical, the character Eponine sings of her love for the rebel Marius.

from
Les Misérables

On My Own

Alain Bloubil

Herbert Kretzmer

John Caird

Trevor Nunn

Jean-Marc Natel

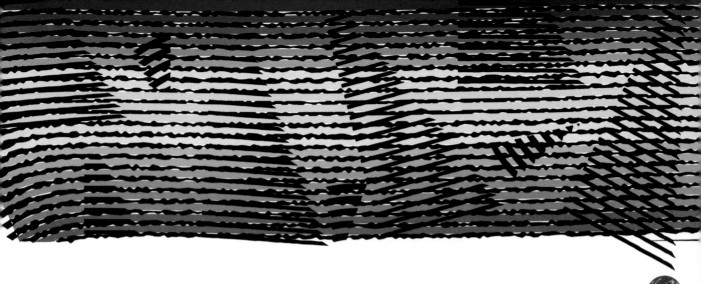

And now I'm all alone again
Nowhere to turn, no one to go to
Without a home, without a friend,
Without a face to say hello to.
5   And now the night is near
Now I can make believe he's here.

Sometimes I walk alone at night
When everybody else is sleeping
I think of him and then I'm happy
10 With the company I'm keeping
The city goes to bed
And I can live inside my head.

On my own
Pretending he's beside me
15 All alone, I walk with him till morning
Without him
I feel his arms around me
And when I lose my way I close my eyes
And he has found me

20 In the rain the pavement shines like silver
All the lights are misty in the river
In the darkness, the trees are full of starlight
And all I see is him and me for ever and
     forever

And I know it's only in my mind
25 That I'm talking to myself and not to him
And although I know that he is blind
Still I say, there's a way for us

I love him
But when the night is over
30 He is gone, the river's just a river
Without him the world around me changes
The trees are bare and everywhere
The streets are full of strangers

I love him
35 But every day I'm learning
All my life I've only been pretending
Without me his world will go on turning
A world that's full of happiness
That I have never known!

40 I love him
I love him
I love him
But only on my own.

---

1. What does Eponine do to relieve her loneliness?
2. What lines of the song convey Eponine's "moment of insight"? Explain.
3. Compare and contrast what you know of Eponine in *Les Misérables* and Henry in "The Californian's Tale." In what ways are they similar? In what ways are they different?

Guide for Reading

Meet the Authors:

Robert Frost (1875–1963)

Robert Frost was born in San Francisco but moved to New England when he was only ten. This region would prove to be most inspirational to him. Frost's most popular poetry describes New England country life and landscapes. Of these, "Stopping by Woods on a Snowy Evening" is considered one of his best. Frost won the Pulitzer Prize four times—more than any other poet. [For more information on Frost, see page 752.]

Sandra Cisneros (1954–   )

Sandra Cisneros was born and raised in Chicago. Because her parents were born in Mexico, she grew up speaking English and Spanish. She writes both poetry and fiction about subjects she knows best— memories of her childhood and her Mexican heritage. Her feelings about growing up in the city are reflected in "Four Skinny Trees."

Walt Whitman (1819–1892)

Walt Whitman worked at many occupations during his life. He was a printer, carpenter, teacher, and newspaper reporter. Known by many as the father of modern American poetry, Whitman abandoned regular rhythm and rhyme in favor of free verse that followed no set pattern. Because of his unusual style, publishers refused to publish *Leaves of Grass*, his long poem about America. Undiscouraged, Whitman published the first edition himself. [For more information on Whitman, see page 28.]

◆ LITERATURE AND YOUR LIFE

CONNECT YOUR EXPERIENCE

Whether you live on a farm, in a tree-lined neighborhood, or in a crowded city, where you live probably has a big influence on the way you see the world. In the pieces that follow, Frost, Cisneros, and Whitman describe the settings that surround them and express how these places shape their thoughts and feelings.

THEMATIC FOCUS: Moments of Insight

As you read, consider how each unique setting leads a narrator to a moment of insight.

◆ Background for Understanding

LITERATURE

Robert Frost is one of America's best loved poets. Most frequently, Frost sets his work in the stark natural landscape of rural northern New England. This region is known for its natural beauty, harsh winters, and picture-postcard villages. There, isolated from America's bustling cities, Frost's speakers confront difficult and life-changing choices—which road to take, what commitments to honor, how connected each person should be to others.

◆ Build Vocabulary

RELATED WORDS: FORMS OF *ferocious*

Cisneros uses the word *ferocious* to describe trees: "They send ferocious roots beneath the ground." *Ferocious* is an adjective meaning "fierce" or "savage." The noun form *ferocity* refers to the state of being ferocious.

WORD BANK

Which of these words from the selections do you think means "as light and fluffy as goose feathers"?

downy
ferocious
exquisite
distinct

Stopping by Woods on a Snowy Evening
Four Skinny Trees ◆ Miracles

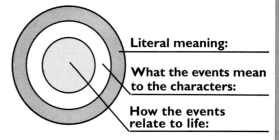

White Veil, 1909, William L. Metcalf, Museum of Art, Rhode Island School of Design

◆ Literary Focus
LEVELS OF MEANING

Many works of literature contain different **levels of meaning.** Beyond the literal meaning —what the words actually say—the work may contain deeper meanings that relate more broadly to life. "Four Skinny Trees," for example, is literally about four trees that grow outside a young woman's home. On a deeper level, it is about how she identifies with these trees. On the deepest level, it is about all young people and their struggle to make a place for themselves. Use a chart like the one below to identify the levels of meaning in these selections.

Literal meaning:

What the events mean to the characters:

How the events relate to life:

◆ Reading Strategy
RESPOND TO LEVELS OF MEANING

Whenever you read a work of literature, you **respond to each level of meaning** in a personal way. Something the author says—at a literal level or at a deeper level—triggers an emotional response in you. You may relate what the writer says to your own experience. Or you may simply agree or disagree with the message.

As you read these selections, ask yourself how they relate to you personally. What does each writer say that connects to you?

Stopping by Woods on a Snowy Evening

Robert Frost

Whose woods these are I think I know.
His house is in the village, though;
He will not see me stopping here
To watch his woods fill up with snow.

5 My little horse must think it queer
To stop without a farmhouse near
Between the woods and frozen lake
The darkest evening of the year.

He gives his harness bells a shake
10 To ask if there is some mistake.
The only other sound's the sweep
Of easy wind and downy flake.

The woods are lovely, dark, and deep,
But I have promises to keep,
15 And miles to go before I sleep,
And miles to go before I sleep.

Four Skinny Trees

Sandra Cisneros

They are the only ones who understand me. I am the only one who understands them. Four skinny trees with skinny necks and pointy elbows like mine. Four who do not belong here but are here. Four raggedy excuses planted by the city. From our room we can hear them, but Nenny just sleeps and doesn't appreciate these things.

Their strength is secret. They send <u>ferocious</u> roots beneath the ground. They grow up and they grow down and grab the earth between their hairy toes and bite the sky with violent teeth and never quit their anger. This is how they keep.

Let one forget his reason for being, they'd all droop like tulips in a glass, each with their arms around the other. Keep, keep, keep, trees say when I sleep. They teach.

When I am too sad and too skinny to keep keeping, when I am a tiny thing against so many bricks, then it is I look at trees. When there is nothing left to look at on this street. Four who grew despite concrete. Four who reach and do not forget to reach. Four whose only reason is to be and be.

◆ Build Vocabulary

downy (dȯun´ ē) *adj.*: Soft and fluffy

ferocious (fə rō´ shəs) *adj.*: Fierce; savage

◀ Critical Viewing What emotions does a wintry scene like the one pictured here bring out in the speaker of "Stopping by Woods . . ."? [Infer]

◆ LITERATURE AND YOUR LIFE

Reader's Response Which selection more closely reflects the setting where you live? Explain.

Thematic Focus How do the physical settings of the selections contribute to each narrator's insights into life?

☑ Check Your Comprehension

1. Describe the setting—both the time and the place—of "Stopping by Woods . . . ."
2. Why has the speaker in "Stopping by Woods . . ." stopped here?
3. Where are the "Four Skinny Trees" described in this selection?
4. What physical characteristics do the trees and the speaker share?

◆ Critical Thinking

INTERPRET

1. "Stopping by Woods on a Snowy Evening" takes place on "The darkest evening of the year." How does this description affect the meaning of the poem? **[Connect]**
2. What comment about life is Frost making when he writes, "But I have promises to keep, /And miles to go before I sleep"? **[Draw Conclusions]**
3. In "Four Skinny Trees," the speaker says that she can "hear" the trees from her room. What does this reveal about her relationship with the trees? **[Infer]**
4. (a) According to "Four Skinny Trees," what lessons can the trees teach? (b) Who can learn these lessons? **[Generalize]**

EVALUATE

5. Do you think the speaker in "Stopping by Woods . . ." honors his promises? Explain. **[Deduce]**

COMPARE LITERARY WORKS

6. Compare and contrast the role of nature in these two selections. **[Compare and Contrast]**

Miracles

Walt Whitman

Why, who makes much of a miracle?
As to me I know of nothing else but miracles,
Whether I walk the streets of Manhattan,
Or dart my sight over the roofs of houses toward the sky,
5   Or wade with naked feet along the beach just in the edge of the water,
Or stand under trees in the woods,
Or talk by day with any one I love . . .
Or sit at table at dinner with the rest.
Or look at strangers opposite me riding in the car,
10   Or watch honeybees busy around the hive of a summer forenoon[1]
Or animals feeding in the fields,
Or birds, or the wonderfulness of insects in the air,
Or the wonderfulness of the sundown, or of stars shining so quiet and bright,
Or the exquisite delicate thin curve of the new moon in spring;
15   These with the rest, one and all, are to me miracles,
The whole referring, yet each distinct and in its place.

To me every hour of the light and dark is a miracle,
Every cubic inch of space is a miracle,
Every square yard of the surface of the earth is spread with the same,
20   Every foot of the interior swarms[2] with the same.

To me the sea is a continual miracle,
The fishes that swim—the rocks—the motion of the waves—
    the ships with men in them,
What stranger miracles are there?

---

1. **forenoon** (fôr′ nōōn′) *n.*: Morning.
2. **swarms** (swôrmz) *v.*: Is filled or crowded.

La Bonne Aventure (Good Fortune), 1939, Rene Magritte, Museum Boymans-van Beuningen, Rotterdam

▶ Critical Viewing
Identify a line in the poem that relates to this painting. Explain your choice. [Connect]

Guide for Responding

◆ LITERATURE AND YOUR LIFE

Reader's Response Name something in your environment that is a miracle to you.

Thematic Focus How does the speaker's attitude reflect a moment of insight?

Journal Writing The speaker says that every experience is a miracle. In your journal, discuss the way this attitude could change the way you live.

☑ Check Your Comprehension

1. Which people does the speaker consider to be miracles?
2. List five of the physical settings, or places, mentioned in the poem.
3. Name four events that Whitman calls miracles.

◆ Critical Thinking

INTERPRET
1. "Miracles" begins and ends with a question. What impact does this have on you? [Connect]
2. In what way is the sea a "continual miracle"? [Infer]
3. How does your definition of "miracle" contrast with the speaker's definition? [Compare and Contrast]

EVALUATE
4. From what you know about the speaker in "Miracles," do you think he is a contented person? Explain. [Evaluate]

APPLY
5. Do you think that people today see the world around them as full of miracles? Explain. [Relate]

Guide for Responding (continued)

◆ Literary Focus

LEVELS OF MEANING

Each of these selections has several **levels of meaning.** The literal meaning consists simply of the details and events in each work. Another level of meaning can be found in the insights that the characters have as a result of the events in each work. On the deepest level, the events lead readers to a general understanding of all people or of life.

1. (a) What is the literal meaning of "Stopping By Woods on a Snowy Evening"? (b) Of what do the events of the poem remind the speaker? (c) How can his experience apply to the experiences of people everywhere?
2. (a) What is the literal meaning of "Miracles"? (b) What does the poem's list remind the speaker? (c) How can his feelings and ideas apply to people everywhere?

◆ Build Vocabulary

USING FORMS OF *ferocious*

Ferocious is an adjective meaning "fierce" or "savage." Related forms of the word express the same meaning as different parts of speech. Use these forms of *ferocious* to complete each sentence.

ferocious   ferociously   ferocity

1. The roots grew ____?____.
2. The ____?____ roots grew under the concrete.
3. Their ____?____ caused the concrete to crack.

SPELLING STRATEGY

The z sound you hear in *exquisite* is spelled with an s. For each clue below, write a word that uses an s spelling for a z sound.

1. A dry, sandy region: d____?____
2. A loud, disturbing sound: n____?____
3. To create a piece of writing or music: c____?____

USING THE WORD BANK

On your paper, write the word that best defines the first word.

1. downy: (a) below, (b) crusty, (c) fluffy
2. ferocious: (a) fat, (b) fierce, (c) famous
3. exquisite: (a) small, (b) beautiful, (c) extra
4. distinct: (a) separate, (b) loud, (c) similar

◆ Reading Strategy

RESPOND TO LEVELS OF MEANING

Once you've identified all the **levels of meaning** in a work of literature, decide whether you agree with the message the work sends. Your response may be different from that of your classmates because your experiences, memories, and attitudes are different from one another.

1. For one of these selections, write down two or three lines or passages that moved you or meant something to you. Explain your response.
2. You probably found that the more you read a selection and thought about it, the more it meant to you. What might be some reasons for this?

◆ Build Grammar Skills

ADVERBS MODIFYING ADJECTIVES AND ADVERBS

Often, **adverbs** modify or describe a verb. They can also modify an adjective or another adverb. The following adverbs are commonly used to modify adjectives and other adverbs: *too, so, very, quite, much, more, rather, usually, almost.* Look at these examples:

Modifiying Adjectives: When I am *too* sad and *too* skinny to keep keeping . . . (How sad and how skinny?)

Modifiying Adverbs: The snow falls *more* silently in the forest. (How silently?)

Practice Copy the sentences below. Underline each adverb. Then, identify whether the adverb modifies an adjective, another adverb, or a verb.

1. Frost's poems are extremely popular.
2. Cisneros's piece makes one feel quite lonely.
3. I read Whitman's poem very carefully.
4. Miracles almost never happen to me!
5. The three poets write rather eloquently.

Writing Application Copy the sentences below, adding an adverb to each one.

1. The tree grows slowly. (How slowly?)
2. Cisneros lived happily in Chicago. (How happily?)
3. That night, he was tired. (How tired?)
4. He greets strangers warmly. (How warmly?)
5. We walked quickly through the snow. (How quickly?)

Build Your Portfolio

Idea Bank

Writing

1. **Reminiscence** Sandra Cisneros describes an important element of the setting in which she grew up. In a description, explain how a place or a scene holds special meaning for you.

2. **Travel Brochure** Imagine that you have chosen "Stopping by Woods on a Snowy Evening" and the photograph on page 260 to appear in a travel brochure. Write the text you would include to encourage visitors to travel to New England.

3. **Letter to the Author** In a letter to the writer, respond to one of the works in this grouping. For example, tell Whitman whether you agree with his philosophy, or explain to Frost whether you might have made the same decision he did. Support your ideas with lines from the work.

Speaking and Listening

4. **Weather Commentary** Many of nature's "miracles" are observable each day. Others, like rainbows and lunar eclipses, are not quite as common. Give a brief presentation to explain one of nature's usual or unusual miracles. **[Science Link]**

5. **"Sounds of Home" Tape [Group Activity]** The street scene that Cisneros describes would sound much different from Frost's wintry forest. With a group, collect audio material to convey the environment in which you live. Use an audiotape to record the sounds that are "home" to you and your neighbors. **[Social Studies Link]**

Projects

6. **A Picture of Miracles** Create a collage of images that reflect what you consider to be miracles. Consider the wonders of nature and those of human creation. **[Art Link]**

7. **Survey and Chart** Ask friends and neighbors to identify the everyday events that they consider miracles. Chart their responses to create a mathematical response to Whitman's poem. **[Mathematics Link]**

Writing Mini-Lesson

Poem About Your Environment

Imagine that, like Frost, you are stopping to watch something on your way home from school or that, like Cisneros, you are looking out of a window from your room at home. Write a poem about where you are and what you see. As part of your description, tell something about yourself.

Writing Skills Focus: Precise Words

Choose **precise words** to convey exactly what you mean. A well-chosen word can clinch a description or bring a feeling into clear focus. Notice, for example, how Frost chooses a single word to describe the lake and a single word to describe the evening. What do these words tell you about winter at the time the poem is set?

Model From the Poem
My little horse must think it queer
To stop without a farmhouse near
Between the woods and *frozen* lake
The *darkest* evening of the year.

Prewriting Decide where you are. Jot down some descriptive words about the setting and what you see. Then, jot down some words that describe how you feel at this time.

Drafting Write a few lines or verses, sketching out your poem with words or phrases from your list. As you draft, be open to a variety of structures your poem might take. Reread what you have written to develop patterns you want to use.

◆ Grammar Application
Look for places where you can use an adverb to clarify an adjective or another adverb to make a description precise.

Revising Change individual words to describe the environment more accurately. Also, change words, phrases, or lines to suit the patterns of rhyme or rhythm you've chosen.

The Fight Interrupted, William Mulready, Victoria & Albert Museum

Resolving Conflicts

Conflicts are a fact of life. The trick to living graciously is to find a way to solve these problems without compromising your beliefs or hurting someone else. The selections in this unit show you a range of problem-solving behaviors. As you read about two boys who must face each other in the boxing ring, a detective who cleverly solves a crime, and a bicycle rider who speeds away from loneliness, decide what techniques you might use to resolve the same problems.

Reading for Success

Strategies for Constructing Meaning

To understand a work of literature fully, you must go beyond a simple scan of the page to put the writer's ideas together in your own mind. What idea does he or she want to communicate? What does the work mean to you? In looking for answers to these questions, you construct the meaning of the work for you. Use these strategies to help you construct meaning:

Envision.

▶ Use details that the author provides to help you picture in your mind the places, people, and events in a piece of writing. Don't limit yourself to just your sense of sight, however. Use your imagination to experience sounds, tastes, smells, and physical sensations as well. For example, use your sense of hearing to experience this detail from Thurber's essay:

> We later heard *ominous creakings* as he crawled into bed.

Make inferences.

▶ It's a reader's job to fill in details the author doesn't provide. You can do so by making inferences based on the details that *are* provided, combined with your own knowledge and experience. For example, from the descriptions in the essay, you can infer that Thurber's house and family are large.

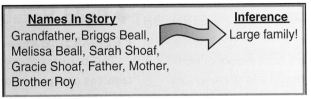

Names In Story	Inference
Grandfather, Briggs Beall, Melissa Beall, Sarah Shoaf, Gracie Shoaf, Father, Mother, Brother Roy	Large family!

Draw conclusions.

▶ A conclusion is a general statement that you can support with details from the text. A series of inferences can lead you to a conclusion. For example, if a character behaves badly and suffers as a result of his actions, you can conclude that the writer is making a point about how this type of behavior should be avoided.

Identify causes and effects.

▶ Look carefully at the relationship of events. Identify causes and effects. Notice how the cause—an action, feeling, or situation—brings about a result—the effect. Look at this example:

> *Cause:* The speaker's cousin believes he will stop breathing in his sleep.
>
> *Effect:* He gets up every hour during the night to check his breathing.

As you read the following essay by James Thurber, look at the notes in the boxes. These notes model how to use the strategies.

The Night the Bed Fell

James Thurber

I suppose that the high-water mark of my youth in Columbus, Ohio, was the night the bed fell on my father. It makes a better recitation (unless, as some friends of mine have said, one has heard it five or six times) than it does a piece of writing, for it is almost necessary to throw furniture around, shake doors, and bark like a dog, to lend the proper atmosphere and verisimilitude[1] to what is admittedly a somewhat incredible tale. Still, it did take place.

It happened, then, that my father had decided to sleep in the attic one night, to be away where he could think. My mother opposed the notion strongly because, she said, the old wooden bed up there was unsafe: it was wobbly and the heavy headboard would crash down on father's head in case the bed fell, and kill him. There was no dissuading him, however, and at a quarter past ten he closed the attic door behind him and went up the narrow twisting stairs. We later heard ominous creakings as he crawled into bed. Grandfather, who usually slept in the attic bed when he was with us, had disappeared some days before. On these occasions he was usually gone six or eight days and returned growling and out of temper, with the news that the Federal Union[2] was run by a passel of blockheads and that the Army of the Potomac[3] didn't have a chance.

We had visiting us at this time a nervous first cousin of mine named Briggs Beall, who believed that he was likely to cease breathing when he was asleep. It was his feeling that if he were not awakened every hour during the night, he might die of suffocation. He had been accustomed to setting an alarm clock to ring at intervals until morning, but I persuaded him to abandon this. He slept in my room and I told him that I was such a light sleeper that if anybody quit breathing in the same room with me, I would wake instantly. He tested me the first night—which I had suspected he would—by holding his breath after my regular breathing had convinced him I was asleep. I was not asleep, however, and called to him. This seemed to allay his fears a little, but he took the precaution of putting a glass of spirits of camphor[4] on a little table at the head of his bed. In case I didn't arouse him until he was almost gone, he said, he would sniff the camphor, a powerful reviver. Briggs was not the only member of his family who had his crotchets.[5] Old Aunt Melissa Beall (who could whistle like a man, with two fingers in her mouth) suffered under the premonition that she was destined to die on South High Street, because she had been born on South High Street and married on South

> Read this paragraph to **draw a conclusion** about the subject and tone of the essay. It will be about an incredible night in his family's history. The story contains funny, hard-to-believe but true events.

---

1. **verisimilitude** (ver´ ə si mil´ ə t$\overline{oo}$d´) *n.*: Appearance of being true or real.

◆ **Build Vocabulary**

ominous (äm´ ə nəs) *adj.*: Threatening

allay (a lā´) *v.*: Put to rest; calm

---

2. **Federal Union:** Northern side during the Civil War. He is under the illusion that the Civil War has not yet ended.
3. **Army of the Potomac:** One of the northern armies during the Civil War.
4. **spirits of camphor:** Liquid with a powerful odor.
5. **crotchets** (kräch´ əts) *n.*: Peculiar or stubborn ideas.

High Street. Then there was Aunt Sarah Shoaf, who never went to bed at night without the fear that a burglar was going to get in and blow chloroform[6] under her door through a tube. To avert this calamity—for she was in greater dread of anesthetics than of losing her household goods—she always piled her money, silverware, and other valuables in a neat stack just outside her bedroom, with a note reading: "This is all I have. Please take it and do not use your chloroform, as this is all I have." Aunt Gracie Shoaf also had a burglar phobia, but she met it with more <u>fortitude</u>. She was confident that burglars had been getting into her house every night for forty years. The fact that she never missed any thing was to her no proof to the contrary. She always claimed that she scared them off before they could take anything, by throwing shoes down the hallway. When she went to bed she piled, where she could get at them handily, all the shoes there were about her house. Five minutes after she had turned off the light, she would sit up in bed and say "Hark!" Her husband, who had learned to ignore the whole situation as long ago as 1903, would either be sound asleep or pretend to be sound asleep. In either case he would not respond to her tugging and pulling, so that presently she would arise, tiptoe to the door, open it slightly and heave a shoe down the hall in one direction, and its mate down the hall in the other direction. Some nights she threw them all, some nights only a couple of pair.

> Use details about Aunt Sarah to **picture** her daily before-bed antics.

But I am straying from the remarkable incidents that took place during the night that the bed fell on father. By midnight we were all in bed. The layout of the rooms and the disposition[7] of their occupants is important to an understanding of what later occurred. In the front room upstairs (just under father's attic bedroom) were my mother and my brother Herman, who sometimes sang in his sleep,

"Aunt Gracie Shoaf Throwing Shoes" by James Thurber

▲ **Critical Viewing** How would Gracie Shoaf defend the actions shown in this drawing? **[Analyze]**

usually "Marching Through Georgia" or "Onward, Christian Soldiers." Briggs Beall and myself were in a room adjoining this one. My brother Roy was in a room across the hall from ours. Our bull terrier, Rex, slept in the hall.

My bed was an army cot, one of those affairs which are made wide enough to sleep on comfortably only by putting up, flat with the middle section, the two sides which ordinarily hang down like the sideboards of a drop-leaf table. When these sides are up, it is <u>perilous</u> to roll too far toward the edge, for then the cot is likely to tip completely over, bringing the whole bed down on top of one, with a tremendous banging crash. This, in fact, is precisely what happened about two o'clock in the morning. (It was my mother who, in recalling the scene later, first referred to it as "the night the bed fell on your father.")

Always a deep sleeper, slow to arouse (I had lied to Briggs), I was at first unconscious of what

---

6. **chloroform** (klôr´ ə fôrm´) *n.*: Substance used at one time as an anesthetic, or pain-killer, during operations because it can cause a person to pass out.

7. **disposition** (dis´ pə zish´ ən) *n.*: Arrangement.

had happened when the iron cot rolled me onto the floor and toppled over on me. It left me still warmly bundled up and unhurt, for the bed rested above me like a canopy. Hence I did not wake up, only reached the edge of consciousness and went back. The racket, however, instantly awakened my mother, in the next room, who came to the immediate conclusion that her worst dread was realized: the big wooden bed upstairs had fallen on father. She therefore screamed, "Let's go to your poor father!" It was this shout, rather than the noise of my cot falling, that awakened Herman, in the same room with her. He thought that mother had become, for no apparent reason, hysterical. "You're all right, Mamma!" he shouted, trying to calm her. They exchanged shout for shout for perhaps ten seconds: "Let's go to your poor father!" and "You're all right!" That woke up Briggs. By this time I was conscious of what was going on, in a vague way, but did not yet realize that I was under my bed instead of on it. Briggs, awakening in the midst of loud shouts of fear and apprehension, came to the quick conclusion that he was suffocating and that we were all trying to "bring him out." With a low moan, he grasped the glass of

> **Identify cause and effect**—the noise made by young Thurber falling out of and under his bed awakens his mother. This causes her to think that her husband has fallen out of his bed.

> **Use Briggs's assumption that everyone is worried about him, along with the earlier details about his anxiety about going to sleep, to make the inference that he thinks mostly about his own situation.**

camphor at the head of his bed and instead of sniffing it poured it over himself. The room reeked of camphor. "Ugf, ahfg," choked Briggs, like a drowning man, for he had almost succeeded in stopping his breath under the <u>deluge</u> of <u>pungent</u> spirits. He leaped out of bed and groped toward the open window, but he came up against one that was closed. With his hand, he beat out the glass, and I could hear it crash and tinkle on the alleyway below. It was at this juncture that I, in trying to get up, had the uncanny sensation of feeling my bed above me! Foggy with sleep, I now suspected, in my turn, that the whole uproar was being made in a frantic endeavor to <u>extricate</u> me from what must be an unheard-of and perilous situation. "Get me out of this!" I bawled. "Get me out!" I think I had the nightmarish belief that I was entombed in a mine. "Gugh," gasped Briggs, floundering in his camphor.

By this time my mother, still shouting, pursued by Herman, still shouting, was trying to open the door to the attic, in order to go up and get my father's body out of the wreckage. The door was stuck, however, and wouldn't yield. Her frantic pulls on it only added to the general banging and confusion. Roy and the

▶ **Critical Viewing**
Everyone, including the dog, jumped into action the night the bed fell. How does this make the events even funnier? [**Assess**]

dog were now up, the one shouting questions, the other barking.

Father, farthest away and soundest sleeper of all, had by this time been awakened by the battering on the attic door. He decided that the house was on fire. "I'm coming, I'm coming!" he wailed in a slow, sleepy voice—it took him many minutes to regain full consciousness. My mother, still believing he was caught under the bed, detected in his "I'm coming!" the mournful, resigned note of one who is preparing to meet his Maker. "He's dying!" she shouted.

"I'm all right!" Briggs yelled to reassure her. "I'm all right!" He still believed that it was his own closeness to death that was worrying mother. I found at last the light switch in my room, unlocked the door, and Briggs and I joined the others at the attic door. The dog, who never did like Briggs, jumped for him—assuming that he was the <u>culprit</u> in whatever was going on—and Roy had to throw Rex and hold him. We could hear father crawling out of bed upstairs. Roy pulled the attic door open, with a mighty jerk, and father came down the stairs, sleepy and irritable but safe and sound. My mother began to weep when she saw him. Rex began to howl. "What in the name of heaven is going on here?" asked father.

The situation was finally put together like a gigantic jigsaw puzzle. Father caught a cold from prowling around in his bare feet but there were no other bad results. "I'm glad," said mother, who always looked on the bright side of things, "that your grandfather wasn't here."

◆ **Build Vocabulary**

culprit (kul´ prit) *n.*: Guilty person

Guide for Responding

◆ LITERATURE AND YOUR LIFE

Reader's Response Do you think you would enjoy living with, or even visiting, a family like James Thurber's? Explain.

Thematic Focus Several characters in the story worry about the night. How do these fears contribute to the problems that develop?

Journal Writing In a journal entry, describe a time when confusion led to comedy in your home or school.

☑ Check Your Comprehension

1. Who is in the house on the night described?
2. Describe the layout of the rooms. Why is their placement important to the plot of the story?
3. What is Briggs's crotchet, or peculiar idea?
4. In chronological, or time, order, list the actions that occur after Thurber's bed collapses.

◆ Critical Thinking

INTERPRET

1. Why does Thurber begin the essay with a description of his relatives? **[Interpret]**
2. In what ways are Thurber's relatives similar? **[Compare and Contrast]**
3. How does the fact that all the characters were asleep when Thurber's bed fell cause them to act especially strangely? **[Analyze]**
4. Why does the collapse of Thurber's bed lead to such confusion and odd behavior among his family? **[Draw Conclusions]**
5. What evidence is there that Thurber felt affection for his family? **[Support]**

APPLY

6. What changes can you suggest to avoid future confusion in the Thurber household? **[Resolve]**

EXTEND

7. What does this story suggest about the importance of being fully awake before joining in the events around you? **[Health Link]**

Guide for Responding (continued)

◆ Reading for Success

STRATEGIES FOR CONSTRUCTING MEANING

Review the reading strategies and the notes showing how to construct meaning. Then, apply them to answer the questions.

1. List three sensory details that show the night's confusion.
2. What event causes Briggs Beall to awaken?
3. (a) What experiences from your own life might relate to this story? (b) How does such a connection help you understand the essay?

◆ Build Vocabulary

USING THE PREFIX ex-

The common prefix ex- means "out." For example, *exclude* means "to leave out," and *expand* means "to spread out." Match each word to its definition.

1. exalt
2. exceed
3. exhale

a. to go beyond the limit
b. to breathe out
c. to raise high

SPELLING STRATEGY

You often spell the *j* sound with a *g*, as in *pungent*. When this sound appears at the end of a word, as in *deluge*, always use *ge*. Use the definitions below to write words containing *j* spelled with *g*.

1. the trick of pulling a rabbit out of a hat: ma____?____
2. a larger-than-life figure: le____?____
3. photograph, painting, or moving picture: im____?____
4. a number indicating the amount of years you've lived: ag____?____

USING THE WORD BANK

On your paper, write the letter of the word that is most opposite in meaning to the first word.

1. fortitude: (a) strength, (b) weakness, (c) courage
2. ominous: (a) favorable, (b) dull, (c) scary
3. deluge: (a) flood, (b) drought, (c) shower
4. extricate: (a) rescue, (b) revolve, (c) capture
5. culprit: (a) lawyer, (b) offender, (c) victim
6. perilous: (a) risky, (b) exciting, (c) secure
7. allay: (a) partner, (b) irritate, (c) calm
8. pungent: (a) moldy, (b) tangy, (c) bland

◆ Literary Focus

HUMOROUS ESSAY

A **humorous essay** is a brief work of non-fiction meant to amuse. In "The Night the Bed Fell," Thurber creates the fun by showing both what is really happening and what each character thinks is happening. For example, Thurber's mother believes that her husband lies crushed in the wreckage of his bed, but he is really safely asleep.

1. Contrast what actually happens when the bed falls with what each character thinks happens.
2. Would the essay be as funny if you were as confused about what happened as the characters were? Why or why not?
3. At the beginning of the essay, Thurber writes that he prefers to tell the story orally because he can add physical effects. Do you think such antics would make this funny tale even funnier? Explain.

◆ Build Grammar Skills

PREPOSITIONS

A **preposition** is a word that relates a noun or pronoun that follows it to another word in the sentence. Here are some common prepositions: *above, behind, below, near, into, through, outside, inside, beyond, off, on, over, to, up,* and *with.* Some prepositions—such as *ahead of, because of,* and *in addition to*—consist of more than one word. Look at these examples:

> *On* these occasions he returned *out of* temper.
> Father had been awakened *by* the noise.
> I didn't realize I was *under* my bed not *on* it.

Practice On your paper, write the prepositions in each sentence.

1. The room was underneath the attic bedroom.
2. Mrs. Thurber slept in that room, too.
3. Two were in the room next to Herman's.
4. Roy slept in a room across the hall from them.
5. The dog, Rex, slept in front of Roy's door.

Writing Application Rewrite each practice sentence using a different preposition. Explain how the meaning of the sentence changes.

Build Your Portfolio

 Idea Bank

Writing

1. **Invitation** The Thurbers are planning a party. Write an invitation describing the amusements in store for guests. If you like, decorate your invitation with Thurberlike cartoons. **[Art Link]**

2. **Home Name Proposal** In some communities, homes are named to reflect the personality or interest of the occupants. Given the goings-on that Thurber reports, suggest a name for his home. Present your idea in a written proposal.

3. **News Report** As a local journalist, write a news report of the events at Thurber's house. Include important facts about who was involved, what happened, when the events occurred, and where the action took place. **[Media Link]**

Speaking and Listening

4. **Skit [Group Activity]** With a few classmates, dramatize the confusion at the Thurber home. In preparation for a performance, one student can write the final script, another can select or create music to fit the mood, and another can direct a rehearsal. **[Performing Arts Link]**

5. **Guided Tour** Draw a plan of the Thurber house as it is described in the essay. Then, present a tour of the evening's events, using a pointer to explain each character's movements. **[Art Link]**

Projects

6. **Sleep Research** Some of the confusion in the essay grows out of the fact that the characters are half asleep. Research the effect of sleep on the senses. Find out how sensory information can be distorted by the sleeping state. Share your findings with the class. **[Science Link]**

7. **Game Collection** Learn about games such as Telephone, in which the fun and humor come from misunderstandings. Consult game books and exchange ideas with classmates. Then, play several games in class, analyzing how the confusion leads to humor.

 Writing Mini-Lesson

Humorous Essay

You may think that your life experiences could never be as funny as Thurber's. However, though you may not have an aunt as unusual as Melissa Beall, you've surely had an especially funny experience. Write an essay telling the story of your experience. Use some of Thurber's techniques to get the most humor out of the events.

Writing Skills Focus: Punchy Conclusion

There's nothing worse than knowing your audience "doesn't get the joke." To avoid this fate, end your story with a **punchy conclusion.** This might be a joke or a summarizing comment that ties all the pieces together. Notice how Thurber ends his essay with a clinching reminder of his family's unusual outlook on life.

Model From the Story

"I'm glad," said mother, who always looked on the bright side of things, "that your grandfather wasn't here."

Prewriting Brainstorm with family or friends to recall favorite amusing stories. Once you've chosen your story, list the main events in sequence. Find the funniest sequence, experimenting with the most effective concluding element.

Drafting Write the conclusion first. Get the punch line—the clincher—down, and then go back to the beginning to narrate the events. Add exaggeration and contrast where it will create humor.

> ◆ **Grammar Application**
> Make sure your prepositions describe the relationships between words accurately.

Revising Read your essay aloud. Do listeners laugh in the places you expected? If the concluding punch line doesn't tie it all together for them, reorganize events or add more exaggeration and contrast.

PART 1 *Trouble Brewing*

View of Toledo, Domenikos Theotokopoulos, The Metropolitan Museum of Art

Trouble Brewing ◆ 285

Guide for Reading

Meet the Author:

Ray Bradbury (1920–)

As a boy, Ray Bradbury loved magicians, circuses, and the stories of science-fiction novelist Edgar Rice Burroughs.

Bradbury began his own writing almost by accident. He couldn't afford to buy the sequel to a Burroughs novel, so he invented a sequel. Writing his own story ending proved to be the beginning of an award-winning career as a science-fiction writer.

THE STORY BEHIND THE STORY

In 1950, Bradbury published a story about a group of Earthmen struggling through the rainy world of Venus. This story made him wonder how a child would react to the sun's brief appearances on Venus. To answer this question, he wrote "All Summer in a Day."

Carl Sandburg (1878–1967)

Carl Sandburg is one of America's most beloved poets. When his poetry first appeared, however, it created a stir because it lacked set rhyme and rhythm. In addition, because Sandburg used the language of the common people, some critics thought his poetry was rough and crude. [For more information on Sandburg, see page 788.]

◆ LITERATURE AND YOUR LIFE

CONNECT YOUR EXPERIENCE

Watching the sun break through the clouds after a storm, you may feel as if you're welcoming back a good friend. Imagine how you'd feel to see the sun if it had been raining for seven years! This is the situation for schoolchildren in Ray Bradbury's story. How do you think they'll act as the rain ends and the sun finally appears?

THEMATIC FOCUS: Trouble Brewing

One child in "All Summer in a Day" remembers seeing the sun before. Why might its appearance be different for her? Why is it important for others to respect her feelings?

◆ Background for Understanding

SCIENCE

"All Summer in a Day" is set on Venus, the second planet from the sun. Today, we know that Venus has a surface temperature of almost 900°F, more than twice the oven temperature for roasting chicken. In 1950, when Bradbury wrote his story, Venus was a mystery planet. Some scientists believed that its clouds concealed a watery world. That's probably why Bradbury describes Venus as a place of soggy jungles and almost continuous rain.

◆ Build Vocabulary

WORD ROOTS: -vita-

A girl in this story is not doing well on Venus, where she lives. Her parents feel that it is *vital* that they take her back to Earth. The word *vital*, which means "necessary for life," contains the root -vita-, meaning "life."

WORD BANK

Look over these words from the story. Which two words are past tense verbs?

concussion
slackening
vital
surged
tumultuously
resilient
savored

All Summer in a Day
◆ Primer Lesson ◆

◆ Literary Focus

SETTING

A story's **setting,** its place and time, is the world in which its characters live. That world can be anywhere and any time—a sunny street in a modern city or another planet whose sky is always torn by lightning. In some stories, the setting is just a background for the events. In others, like this story, the setting drives the characters' actions. The children on Bradbury's rainy Venus, for instance, would give almost anything for a glimpse of the sun.

◆ Reading Strategy

ENVISION SETTING AND ACTIONS

You can live in a story's setting just as the characters do. All you need are your senses. Practice using them by imagining that the picture above is a window. As you look through it, watch the dark clouds fly by and listen for the wind that carries them. Apply this same technique to the story. **Envision** the setting and the actions by finding details that help you sense the world that Bradbury creates. Then, as you read, fill out a chart like the one below to capture sensory details.

Situation	Sights, Sounds, Smells, Physical Sensations
At the classroom window	
In the tunnels	
In the sun-filled jungle	
In the closet	

All Summer in a Day

RAY BRADBURY

R eady?"

"Ready."

"Now?"

"Soon."

"Do the scientists really know? Will it happen today, will it?"

"Look, look; see for yourself!"

The children pressed to each other like so many roses, so many weeds, intermixed, peering out for a look at the hidden sun.

It rained.

It had been raining for seven years; thousands upon thousands of days compounded and filled from one end to the other with rain, with the drum and gush of water, with the sweet crystal fall of showers and the <u>concussion</u> of storms so heavy they were tidal waves come over the islands. A thousand forests had been crushed under the rain and grown up a thousand times to be crushed again. And this was the way life was forever on the planet Venus and this was the schoolroom of the children of the rocket men and women who had come to a raining world to set up civilization and live out their lives.

"It's stopping, it's stopping!"

"Yes, yes!"

Margot stood apart from them, from these children who could never remember a time when there wasn't rain and rain and rain. They were all nine years old, and if there had been a day, seven years ago, when the sun came out for an hour and showed its face to the stunned world, they could not recall. Sometimes, at night, she heard them stir, in remembrance, and she knew they were dreaming and remembering gold or a yellow crayon or a coin large enough to buy the world with. She knew they thought they remembered a warmness, like a blushing in the face, in the

> ◆ Literary Focus
> How might the setting described in these opening paragraphs affect the characters?

◆ **Build Vocabulary**

concussion (kən kush′ ən) *n.:* Violent shaking

▲ **Critical Viewing** What aspects of the story's setting do you see in this picture? **[Distinguish]**

body, in the arms and legs and trembling hands. But then they always awoke to the tatting drum, the endless shaking down of clear bead necklaces upon the roof, the walk, the gardens, the forests, and their dreams were gone.

All day yesterday they had read in class about the sun. About how like a lemon it was, and how hot. And they had written small stories or essays or poems about it:

> *I think the sun is a flower,*
> *That blooms for just one hour.*

That was Margot's poem, read in a quiet voice in the still classroom while the rain was falling outside.

"Aw, you didn't write that!" protested one of the boys.

"I did," said Margot. "I *did.*"

"William!" said the teacher.

But that was yesterday. Now the rain was <u>slackening</u>, and the children were crushed in the great thick windows.

"Where's teacher?"

"She'll be back."

"She'd better hurry, we'll miss it!"

They turned on themselves, like a feverish wheel, all fumbling spokes.

Margot stood alone. She was a very frail girl who looked as if she had been lost in the rain for years and the rain had washed out the blue from her eyes and the red from her mouth and the yellow from her hair. She was an old photograph dusted from an album, whitened away, and if she spoke at all her voice would be a ghost. Now she stood, separate, staring at the rain and the loud wet world beyond the huge glass.

"What're *you* looking at?" said William.

Margot said nothing.

"Speak when you're spoken to." He gave her a shove. But she did not move; rather she let herself be moved only by him and nothing else.

They edged away from her, they would not look at her. She felt them go away. And this was because she would play no games with them in the echoing tunnels of the underground city. If they tagged her and ran, she stood blinking after them and did not follow. When the class sang songs about happiness and life and games her lips barely moved. Only when they sang about the sun and the summer did her lips move as she watched the drenched windows.

And then, of course, the biggest crime of all was that she had come here only five years ago from Earth, and she remembered the sun and the way the sun was and the sky was when she was four in Ohio. And they, they had been on Venus all their lives, and they had been only two years old when last the sun came out and had long since forgotten the color and heat of it and the way it really was. But Margot remembered.

"It's like a penny," she said once, eyes closed.

"No, it's not!" the children cried.

"It's like a fire," she said, "in the stove."

"You're lying, you don't remember!" cried the children.

But she remembered and stood quietly apart from all of them and watched the patterning windows. And once, a month ago, she had refused to shower in the school shower rooms, had clutched her hands to her ears and over her head, screaming the water mustn't touch her head. So after that, dimly, dimly, she sensed it, she was different and they knew her difference and kept away.

There was talk that her father and mother were taking her back to Earth next year; it seemed vital to her that they do so, though it would mean the loss of thousands of dollars to her family. And so, the children hated her for all these reasons of big and little consequence. They hated her pale snow face, her waiting silence, her thinness, and her possible future.

"Get away!" The boy gave her another push. "What're you waiting for?"

Then, for the first time, she turned and looked at him. And what she was waiting for was in her eyes.

"Well, don't wait around here!" cried the boy savagely. "You won't see nothing!"

Her lips moved.

"Nothing!" he cried. "It was all a joke, wasn't it?" He turned to the other children. "Nothing's happening today. *Is* it?"

They all blinked at him and then, understanding, laughed and shook their heads. "Nothing, nothing!"

"Oh, but," Margot whispered, her eyes helpless. "But this is the day, the scientists predict, they say, they *know*, the sun . . ."

"All a joke!" said the boy, and seized her roughly. "Hey, everyone, let's put her in a closet before teacher comes!"

"No," said Margot, falling back.

They surged about her, caught her up and bore her, protesting, and then pleading, and then crying, back into a tunnel, a room, a closet, where they slammed and locked the door. They stood looking at the door and saw it tremble from her beating and throwing herself against it. They heard her muffled cries. Then, smiling, they turned and went out and back down the tunnel, just as the teacher arrived.

"Ready, children?" She glanced at her watch.

◆ **Build Vocabulary**

slackening (slak´ ən iŋ) v.: Easing; becoming less active

vital (vīt´ əl) adj.: Necessary to life; critically important

surged (surjd) v.: Moved in a violent swelling motion

A New Planet, K.F. Yuon, Tretiakov Gallery, Moscow, Russia

▲ **Critical Viewing** How do the emotions of the people in this painting compare with those of the characters in the story? **[Connect]**

"Yes!" said everyone.
"Are we all here?"
"Yes!"
The rain slackened still more.
They crowded to the huge door.
The rain stopped.

It was as if, in the midst of a film concerning an avalanche, a tornado, a hurricane, a volcanic eruption, something had, first, gone wrong with the sound apparatus, thus muffling and finally cutting off all noise, all of the blasts and repercussions and thunders, and then, second, ripped the film from the projector and inserted in its place a peaceful tropical slide which did not move or tremor. The world ground to a standstill. The silence was so immense and unbelievable that you felt your ears had been stuffed or you had lost your hearing altogether. The children put their hands to their ears. They stood apart. The door slid back and the smell of the silent, waiting world came in to them.

The sun came out.

It was the color of flaming bronze and it was very large. And the sky around it was a blazing blue tile color. And the jungle burned with sunlight as the children, released from their spell, rushed out, yelling, into the springtime.

◆ **Reading Strategy**
How do you picture the sun based on this description?

"Now, don't go too far," called the teacher after them. "You've only two hours, you know. You wouldn't want to get caught out!"

But they were running and turning their faces up to the sky and feeling the sun on their cheeks like a warm iron; they were taking off their jackets and letting the sun burn their arms.

"Oh, it's better than the sun lamps, isn't it?"

"Much, much better!"

They stopped running and stood in the great jungle that covered Venus, that grew and never stopped growing, <u>tumultuously</u>, even as you watched it. It was a nest of octopi, clustering up great arms of flesh-like weed, wavering, flowering in this brief spring. It was the color of rubber and ash, this jungle, from the many years without sun. It was the color of stones and white cheeses and ink, and it was the color of the moon.

The children lay out, laughing, on the jungle mattress, and heard it sigh and squeak under them, <u>resilient</u> and alive.

◆ **Literature and Your Life**

Describe a time when your experience of something was much better than what you'd expected.

They ran among the trees, they slipped and fell, they pushed each other, they played hide-and-seek and tag, but most of all they squinted at the sun until tears ran down their faces, they put their hands up to that yellowness and that amazing blueness and they breathed of the fresh, fresh air and listened and listened to the silence which suspended them in a blessed sea of no sound and no motion. They looked at everything and <u>savored</u> everything. Then, wildly, like animals escaped from their caves, they ran and ran in shouting circles. They ran for an hour and did not stop running.

And then—

In the midst of their running one of the girls wailed.

Everyone stopped.

The girl, standing in the open, held out her hand.

"Oh, look, look," she said, trembling.

They came slowly to look at her opened palm.

In the center of it, cupped and huge, was a single raindrop.

She began to cry, looking at it.

They glanced quietly at the sky.

"Oh, Oh."

A few cold drops fell on their noses and their cheeks and their mouths. The sun faded behind a stir of mist. A wind blew cool around them. They turned and started to walk back toward the underground house, their hands at their sides, their smiles vanishing away.

A boom of thunder startled them and like leaves before a new hurricane, they tumbled upon each other and ran. Lightning struck ten miles away, five miles away, a mile, a half mile. The sky darkened into midnight in a flash.

They stood in the doorway of the underground for a moment until it was raining hard. Then they closed the door and heard the gigantic sound of the rain falling in tons and avalanches, everywhere and forever.

"Will it be seven more years?"

"Yes. Seven."

Then one of them gave a little cry.

"Margot!"

"What?"

"She's still in the closet where we locked her."

"Margot."

They stood as if someone had driven them, like so many stakes, into the floor. They looked at each other and then looked away. They glanced out at the world that was raining now and raining and raining

◆ **Build Vocabulary**

tumultuously (too mul′ choo əs lē) *adv.*: Noisily and violently

resilient (ri zil′ yənt) *adj.*: Springing back into shape

savored (sā′ vərd) *v.*: Enjoyed

Sunrise IV, Arthur Dove, Hirshhorn Museum and Sculpture Garden, Smithsonian Institution

▲ **Critical Viewing** How well does the painting fit the story? **[Evaluate]**

steadily. They could not meet each other's glances. Their faces were solemn and pale. They looked at their hands and feet, their faces down.

"Margot."

One of the girls said, "Well . . .?"

No one moved.

"Go on," whispered the girl.

They walked slowly down the hall in the sound of cold rain. They turned through the doorway to the room in the sound of the storm and thunder, lightning on their faces, blue and terrible. They walked over to the closet door slowly and stood by it.

Behind the closet door was only silence.

They unlocked the door, even more slowly, and let Margot out.

Primer¹ Lesson

Carl Sandburg

Look out how you use proud words.
When you let proud words go, it is
    not easy to call them back.
They wear long boots, hard boots; they
5   walk off proud; they can't hear you
        calling—
Look out how you use proud words.

---

1. primer (prim´ ər) *adj.*: From a simple text-book for teaching basic reading and morals.

Science Connection

Exploring Venus Venus is the closest planet to Earth and is a near twin in size. However, that's where the similarity ends. The average surface temperature on Venus is 887 degrees Fahrenheit, eight times hotter than any region on Earth. In addition, its atmosphere is dramatically different from that of Earth, consisting mostly of sulfuric acid and sulfur dioxide. Finally, Venus rotates only once every 243 days, in contrast to Earth, which rotates once every 24 hours.

Cross-Curricular Activity
Museum Exhibit With a group of classmates, search the Internet or use library resources to learn more about Venus. Gather maps, charts, photographs, and other materials. Label each of the visuals you gather. Then, assemble the materials you gather into a museum exhibit that you can display in the classroom.

Guide for Responding

◆ LITERATURE AND YOUR LIFE

Reader's Response What is your reaction to how Margot is treated by the other students? Why?

Thematic Focus The other children's impulsive actions kept Margot from seeing the sun, which mattered very much to her. What would you like to say to the other children?

Journal Writing This story takes place in a world that is almost completely sunless. In a journal entry, jot down some ways in which you would adjust to life on Venus.

☑ Check Your Comprehension

1. Why are all the students excited at the start of the story?
2. Why does Margot know more about the sun than her classmates do?
3. What do the children do to Margot just before the rain stops?
4. What do the children do during the two hours that they are outdoors?
5. What happens to Margot at the very end?
6. In "Primer Lesson," what makes "proud words" dangerous?

◆ Critical Thinking

INTERPRET

1. Why are the children unkind to Margot? **[Infer]**
2. Why do the children reject Margot's descriptions of what the sun is like? **[Infer]**
3. Why do you think that all of the children go along with the prank that is played against Margot? **[Draw Conclusions]**
4. How do you think the children intend for their prank to end? **[Speculate]**
5. How do they feel when they remember what they have done to Margot? **[Analyze]**
6. What lessons does this story teach that can be applied to life in our world? **[Generalize]**
7. What quality of "proud words" does Sandburg stress in saying they wear "hard boots"? **[Interpret]**
8. Read the footnoted definition of *primer*. Why do you think Sandburg called his poem "Primer Lesson"? **[Generalize]**

EXTEND

9. How do you think the other children will treat Margot in the future? **[Predict]**

COMPARE LITERARY WORKS

10. How can you apply the message of "Primer Lesson" to "All Summer in a Day"? **[Connect]**

Guide for Responding (continued)

◆ Reading Strategy

ENVISION SETTING AND ACTIONS

Envisioning details that appeal to your senses in various scenes will help you to participate in the story. You can better understand the struggle between Margot and her classmates by contrasting the rainy period and the few hours of sunlight.

1. List three sensory details that show why living on Venus is difficult.
2. List three sensory details that show how the students enjoy the rare appearance of the sun.
3. What details in "Primer Lesson" help you envision "proud words"?

◆ Build Vocabulary

USING THE WORD ROOT -vita-

You will recognize the word root -vita-, meaning "life," in these words and expressions:

vitamins   vitality   vital signs

On your paper, match the words with their meanings.

1. A feeling of being alive: _____?_____
2. Elements in food that are essential for life: _____?_____
3. The body's indicators of life: _____?_____

SPELLING STRATEGY

In some words, like *tumultuously*, the *choo* sound is spelled *tu*. Write the following sentences, completing the spelling of the *choo* sound.

1. Constant rains sa__rated Bradbury's Venus.
2. In ac__ality, there is no rain on Venus.
3. The fictional si__ation makes a good story.

USING THE WORD BANK

Answer the following questions. Explain each answer.

1. Is water *vital* to life?
2. Is a meal that you *savored* one that you liked?
3. Is *slackening* rain increasing or decreasing?
4. When a feather lands on the floor, does it produce a *concussion?*
5. Would you describe a baseball as *resilient?*
6. If electricity *surged* through your computer, what effect would it have?
7. If children play *tumultuously*, are they quiet?

◆ Literary Focus

SETTING

The **setting** of "All Summer in a Day"—the time and place in which events occur—plays a key role in the characters' actions and the events in the plot.

1. What details of the setting are most essential?
2. How is Margot affected by the story's setting?
3. How are the other children affected by it?
4. Could events similar to those in this story occur in a different setting? Explain.

◆ Build Grammar Skills

PREPOSITIONAL PHRASES

A **preposition** relates a noun or pronoun that appears with it to another word in the sentence. A **prepositional phrase** is a group of words that begins with a preposition and ends with a noun or pronoun. The noun or pronoun following a preposition is called the **object of the preposition.**

Common Prepositions				
about	behind	during	off	to
above	below	except	on	toward
across	beneath	for	onto	under
after	beside	from	outside	until

In this example, the prepositional phrases are in italics. The prepositions are printed in boldface, and the objects of the prepositions are underlined:

> The children pressed **to** *each other,* **like** *so many roses* . . . peering out **for** *a look* **at** *the hidden sun.*

Practice Copy the following sentences, and underline the prepositional phrases. Identify the preposition and the object of each preposition.

1. It had been raining for seven years.
2. Margot stood apart from these children.
3. They had read in class about the sun.
4. She would play no games with them in the echoing tunnels of the underground city.
5. The sky darkened into midnight in a flash.

Writing Application Add at least two prepositional phrases to each of the following sentences.

1. It rains heavily.
2. One boy spoke.

Build Your Portfolio

 ## Idea Bank

Writing

1. **Diary Entry** Write a diary entry that Margot might have composed on the night following the events in the story.

2. **Travel Brochure** Write a pamphlet for tourists who want to visit Venus. Advertise interesting sights, fun activities, and cultural institutions. Also, say something favorable about the weather.

3. **Teacher's Report** As Margot's teacher, write a report on the incident described in the story. Keep your report as objective as possible. Include statements from the children involved and suggest appropriate discipline.

Speaking and Listening

4. **Lecture** If you were the teacher, what would you say to your class after discovering what they had done to Margot? Reread "Primer Lesson," and then deliver a lecture to the class in response to their treatment of Margot.

5. **Dramatization [Group Activity]** With a group, act out the scene in which Margot is locked in the closet. Feel free to add dialogue not included in Bradbury's story. **[Performing Arts Link]**

Projects

6. **Internet Research** Use the Internet to find out about weather conditions on different planets. Investigate temperature, atmosphere, and the length of a year. Share your findings, and identify the Web sites you used. **[Science Link]**

7. **Multimedia Report** Create a multimedia report on life in a place with a large average rainfall. Gather maps, charts, photographs, and, if possible, video. Put these materials together, along with written text, in a report that you can present to the class. **[Media Link]**

 ## Writing Mini-Lesson

Remembrance

As time passes, our feelings about key events often change. Imagine how the children in Bradbury's story might have felt years later when they looked back on how they had treated Margot. Put yourself in the place of one of the characters, and write a **remembrance**—a piece of writing that describes people, places, and events from the past.

Writing Skills Focus: Show, Don't Tell

As you develop your remembrance, **show** the events instead of **telling** readers about them. Dramatize the situation through dialogue and detailed description. Instead of simply writing, "The other students picked on Margot," Bradbury dramatizes how the students picked on her. Look at the following example:

Model From the Story

"What're *you* looking at?" said William. Margot said nothing.

"Speak when you're spoken to." He gave her a shove. But she did not move. . . .

Prewriting Choose the character from whose point of view you will write. Then, jot down how that character might feel years after the incident.

Drafting Begin your remembrance by revealing how you feel now about the event. Then, follow with a detailed description of what happened. In your description, focus on dramatizing the events, rather than simply telling what happened. End by revealing what you learned from the experience.

Revising Revise your remembrance by looking for places where you can improve your descriptions. Replace vague words with more vivid ones, or add dialogue or other details.

◆ Grammar Application

Use prepositional phrases to add descriptive or informative details to your remembrance.

Guide for Reading

Meet the Authors:

Alfred Noyes (1880–1958)

Alfred Noyes, born in Staffordshire, England, was both a poet and a critic. He wrote frequently about the English countryside and legends. Despite his great love for England's history, Noyes moved to New Jersey to teach at Princeton University. This new location did not stop him from writing poems about English history, especially of legendary figures like Robin Hood.

Geoffrey C. Ward (1940–   )

From *The Civil War* to *The West* and *Baseball,* historian Geoffrey C. Ward balances legend against fact to bring the American past to life in successful television documentaries. Ward has combined his own writing talent and knowledge of history with Ken Burns's distinctive film-making style to co-create these award-winning PBS series.

Folk Ballads

Before printed books were easily available, stories were passed along orally. Told around an evening fire, some stories became songs, called ballads. Today, these ballads carry on the legends of the American West. Many focus on larger-than-life heroes. Some, like "The Dying Cowboy," tell a tragic tale with a twist of humor.

◆ LITERATURE AND YOUR LIFE

CONNECT TO YOUR EXPERIENCE

Who's your favorite athlete, film character, or figure from history? These people—who can perform amazing physical tasks or think fast to get out of a tight spot—seem bigger than the rest of us. They mix independence, strength, and determination. As you read these selections, think about how personalities from history and legend compare with today's giants.

THEMATIC FOCUS: Trouble Brewing

As you encounter the larger-than-life personalities in these selections, ask yourself whether they attract difficulty or are just better able to cope with it.

◆ Background for Understanding

HISTORY

Like Bess, a main character in "The Highwayman," Englishman Alfred Noyes saw British outlaws as dashing, romantic figures. So when Noyes visited Bagshot, Heath, England—a lonely region once terrorized by these highway thieves—perhaps a local legend caught his imagination and inspired him to write his famous poem.

◆ Build Vocabulary

COMPOUND NOUNS

The word *landlord,* which appears in "The Highwayman," is a compound noun combining two words, *land* and *lord.* A landlord is the owner of a business or property.

WORD BANK

Which two of these words from the selections might describe a waterfall?

torrent
landlord
cascade
tawny
bound
strive
brandished

The Highwayman
◆ The Dying Cowboy ◆
The Real Story of a Cowboy's Life

◆ Literary Focus

SUSPENSE

When you find yourself inching toward the edge of your seat in a movie theater, **suspense** is at work. This sense of uncertainty about how events will unfold also plays an important role in works of literature. Suspense makes you want to keep reading. Writers create suspense by presenting life-or-death danger or by building tension before a problem is resolved. In "The Highwayman," a stormy setting and the character's fear help build the poem's suspense.

◆ Reading Strategy

IDENTIFY CAUSE AND EFFECT

Trouble usually has a **cause,** a reason that explains why it occurs. In "The Highwayman," an outlaw goes "after a prize," knowing the dangers he's up against. What he may not anticipate, how-ever, is the **effect,** or result of his decision. Each event becomes a cause for the next event, linking causes and effects and propelling the action forward. Use a chart like the one below to record causes and effects as you read these selections.

| Highwayman tells Bess of his plan. | → | ☐ | → | ☐ | → | ☐ | → | ☐ |

The Highwayman

Alfred Noyes

▲ Critical Viewing What elements of the poem's setting does this illustration capture? [Connect]

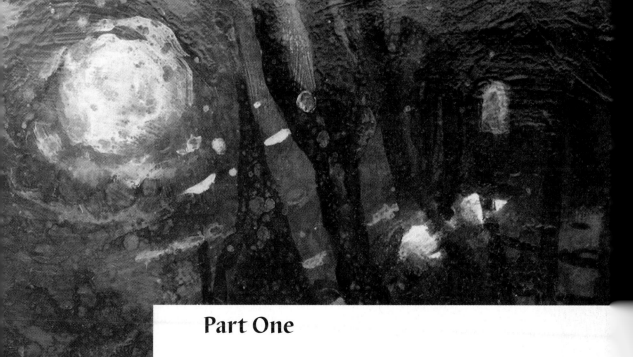

Part One

The wind was a <u>torrent</u> of darkness among the gusty trees.
The moon was a ghostly galleon[1] tossed upon cloudy seas.
The road was a ribbon of moonlight over the purple moor,[2]
And the highwayman came riding—
5   Riding—riding—
The highwayman came riding, up to the old inn door.

He'd a French cocked-hat on his forehead, a bunch of lace at
     his chin,
A coat of the claret velvet, and breeches[3] of brown doeskin.
They fitted with never a wrinkle. His boots were up to the
     thigh.
10   And he rode with a jeweled twinkle,
          His pistol butts a-twinkle,
His rapier hilt[4] a-twinkle, under the jeweled sky.

Over the cobbles he clattered and clashed in the dark innyard.
He tapped with his whip on the shutters, but all was locked
     and barred.
15   He whistled a tune to the window, and who should be waiting
     there

---

1. **galleon** (gal´ ē ən) *n.*: Large Spanish sailing ship.
2. **moor** (moor) *n.*: Open, rolling land with swamps.
3. **breeches** (brich´ iz) *n.*: Trousers that reach to or just below the knee.
4. **rapier** (rā´ pē ər) **hilt**: Large cup-shaped handle of a rapier, which is a type of sword.

◆ **Build Vocabulary**
torrent (tôr´ ənt) *n.*: Flood

But the <u>landlord's</u> black-eyed daughter,
    Bess, the landlord's daughter,
Plaiting[5] a dark red love knot into her long black hair.

And dark in the dark old innyard a stable wicket[6] creaked
20 Where Tim the ostler[7] listened. His face was white and peaked.
His eyes were hollows of madness, his hair like moldy hay,
But he loved the landlord's daughter,
    The landlord's red-lipped daughter.
Dumb as a dog he listened, and he heard the robber say—
25 "One kiss, my bonny[8] sweetheart, I'm after a prize to-night,
But I shall be back with the yellow gold before the morning
    light;
Yet, if they press me sharply, and harry[9] me through the day.
Then look for me by moonlight,
    Watch for me by moonlight,
30 I'll come to thee by moonlight, though hell should bar the
    way."

He rose upright in the stirrups. He scarce could reach her
    hand,
But she loosened her hair in the casement.[10] His face burnt
    like a brand[11]
As the black <u>cascade</u> of perfume came tumbling over his
    breast;
And he kissed its waves in the moonlight,
35   (O, sweet black waves in the moonlight!)
Then he tugged at his rein in the moonlight, and galloped
    away to the west.

Part Two

He did not come in the dawning. He did not come at noon;
And out of the <u>tawny</u> sunset, before the rise of the moon,
When the road was a gypsy's ribbon, looping the purple moor,
40 A redcoat troop came marching—
    Marching—marching—
King George's men[12] came marching, up to the old inn door.

---

5. **plaiting** (plāt´ iŋ) *adj.*: Braiding.
6. **stable wicket** (stā´ bəl wik´ ət): Small door or gate to a stable.
7. **ostler** (äs´ lər) *n.*: Person who takes care of horses at an inn or a stable.
8. **bonny** (bän´ ē) *adj.*: Scottish for "pretty."
9. **harry** (har´ ē) *v.*: To disturb by constant attacks.
10. **casement** (kās´ mənt) *n.*: Window frame that opens on hinges.
11. **brand** (brand) *n.*: Piece of burning wood.
12. **King George's men:** Soldiers serving King George of England.

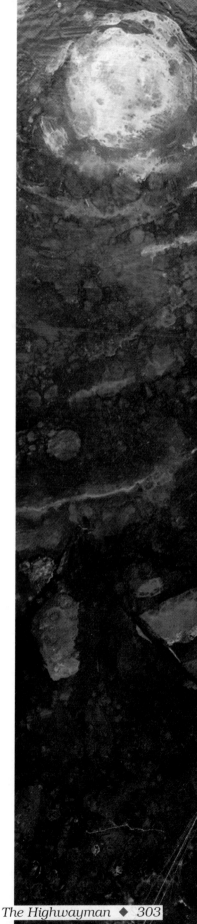

They said no word to the landlord. They drank his ale instead
But they gagged his daughter, and <u>bound</u> her, to the foot of
her narrow bed.
45 Two of them knelt at her casement, with muskets at their
side!
There was death at every window;
And hell at one dark window;
For Bess could see, through her casement, the road that *he*
would ride.

They had tied her up to attention, with many a sniggering
jest.[13]
50 They had bound a musket beside her, with the muzzle
beneath her breast!
"Now, keep good watch!" and they kissed her. She heard the
doomed man say—
Look for me by moonlight;
Watch for me by moonlight;
I'll come to thee by moonlight, though hell should bar the
way!

55 She twisted her hands behind her; but all the knots held
good!
She writhed her hands till her fingers were wet with sweat or
blood!
They stretched and strained in the darkness, and the hours
crawled by like years,
Till, now, on the stroke of midnight,
Cold, on the stroke of midnight,
60 The tip of one finger touched it! The trigger at least was hers!

The tip of one finger touched it. She strove no more for the
rest.
Up, she stood up to attention, with the muzzle beneath her
breast.
She would not risk their hearing; she would not <u>strive</u> again;
For the road lay bare in the moonlight;
65 Blank and bare in the moonlight;

---

13. sniggering (snig´ ər iŋ) **jest:** Sly joke.

◆ Build Vocabulary

landlord (land´ lôrd) *n.*: Person who keeps a rooming house, inn, etc.
cascade (kas kād´) *n.*: Waterfall or anything tumbling like water
tawny (tô´ nē) *adj.*: Tan; yellowish brown
bound (bound) *v.*: Tied
strive (strīv) *v.*: Struggle

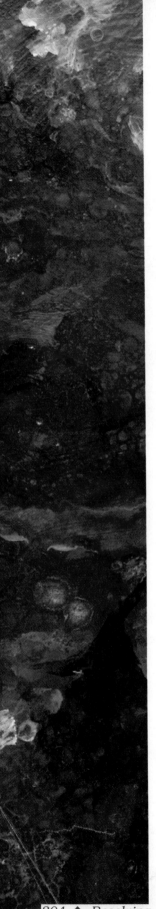

And the blood of her veins, in the moonlight, throbbed to
    her love's refrain.

Tlot-tlot; tlot-tlot! Had they heard it? The horsehoofs ringing
    clear;
Tlot-tlot, tlot-tlot, in the distance? Were they deaf that they
    did not hear?
Down the ribbon of moonlight, over the brow of the hill,
70   The highwayman came riding—
        Riding—riding—
The redcoats looked to their priming![14] She stood up, straight
    and still.

Tlot-tlot, in the frosty silence! *Tlot-tlot,* in the echoing night!
Nearer he came and nearer. Her face was like a light.
75   Her eyes grew wide for a moment; she drew one last deep
    breath,
Then her finger moved in the moonlight,
        Her musket shattered the moonlight,
Shattered her breast in the moonlight and warned him—
    with her death.

He turned. He spurred to the west; he did not know who stood
80   Bowed, with her head o'er the musket, drenched with her own
    blood!
Not till the dawn he heard it, and his face grew gray to hear
How Bess, the landlord's daughter,
        The landlord's black-eyed daughter,
Had watched for her love in the moonlight, and died in the
    darkness there.

85   Back, he spurred like a madman, shouting a curse to the sky,
With the white road smoking behind him and his rapier
      brandished high.
Blood-red were his spurs in the golden noon; wine-red was his
    velvet coat;
When they shot him down on the highway,
        Down like a dog on the highway,
90   And he lay in his blood on the highway, with a bunch of lace
    at his throat.

. . . .

---

14. **priming** (prī′ miŋ) *n.*: Explosive used to set off the charge in a gun.

◆ **Build Vocabulary**

brandished (bran′ dishd) *adj.*: Waved in a threatening way

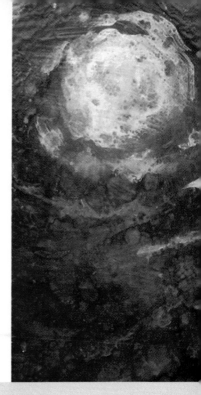

And still of a winter's night, they say, when the wind is in
     the trees,
When the moon is a ghostly galleon tossed upon cloudy
     seas,
When the road is a ribbon of moonlight over the purple moor,
A highwayman comes riding—
95   Riding—riding—
A highwayman comes riding, up to the old inn door.

Over the cobbles he clatters and clangs in the dark innyard.
He taps with his whip on the shutters, but all is locked and
     barred.
He whistles a tune to the window, and who should be
     waiting there
100 But the landlord's black-eyed daughter,
        Bess, the landlord's daughter,
Plaiting a dark red love knot into her long black hair.

Guide for Responding

◆ LITERATURE AND YOUR LIFE

Reader's Response Who do you think was more brave—Bess or the highwayman? Why?

Thematic Focus What choices do Bess and the highwayman make that lead to trouble?

Poll Ask several classmates to supply three adjectives to describe the highwayman. Identify the adjectives most frequently used. What conclusion can you draw about this larger-than-life figure based on the results?

☑ Check Your Comprehension

1. Describe the two main characters of the poem.
2. Where and when does most of the action take place?
3. Use lines 25–30 to explain the highwayman's plans.
4. Why does Bess think she needs to warn the highwayman?
5. Use lines 75–80 to summarize how she communicates her warning.

◆ Critical Thinking

INTERPRET

1. What evidence is there to suggest that Bess and the highwayman have met on many moon-lit nights? **[Infer]**
2. Find three details that make the highwayman appear a romantic, or dashing, figure. **[Connect]**
3. How does the repetition of the color red add to the poem's romantic quality? **[Support]**
4. What elements of the setting add to the poem's romantic quality? **[Support]**
5. What do the last two stanzas suggest about the love between Bess and her highwayman? **[Draw Conclusions]**

EVALUATE

6. Would the poem have been as effective if it had ended at line 90? Explain. **[Evaluate]**

EXTEND

7. What can you learn from this poem about life in eighteenth-century England? **[Social Studies Link]**

The Dying Cowboy

Traditional

"Oh, bury me not on the lone prairie."
These words came low and mournfully
From the pallid[1] lips of a youth who lay
On his dying bed at the close of day.

5   He had wailed in pain till o'er his brow
Death's shadows fast were gathering now;
He thought of his home and his loved ones nigh
As the cowboys gathered to see him die.

    "Oh, bury me not on the lone prairie
10   Where the wild coyotes will howl o'er me,
    In a narrow grave just six by three.
    Oh, bury me not on the lone prairie.

"In fancy I listen to the well known words
Of the free, wild winds and the song of the birds;
15   I think of home and the cottage in the bower[2]
And the scenes I loved in my childhood's hour.

"It matters not, I've oft been told,
Where the body lies when the heart grows cold;
Yet grant, oh, grant this wish to me:
20   Oh, bury me not on the lone prairie.

---

1. **pallid** (pal′ id) *adj.*: Faint in color; pale.
2. **bower** (bou′ ər) *n.*: Place enclosed by tree limbs.

"Oh, then bury me not on the lone prairie,
In a narrow grave six foot by three,
Where the buffalo paws o'er a prairie sea.
Oh, bury me not on the lone prairie.

25 "I've always wished to be laid when I died
In the little churchyard on the green hillside;
By my father's grave there let mine be,
And bury me not on the lone prairie.

"Let my death slumber be where my mother's prayer
30 And a sister's tear will mingle there,
Where my friends can come and weep o'er me;
Oh, bury me not on the lone prairie.

"Oh, bury me not on the lone prairie
In a narrow grave just six by three,
35 Where the buzzard waits and the wind blows free;
Then bury me not on the lone prairie.

"There is another whose tears may be shed
For one who lies on a prairie bed;
It pained me then and it pains me now—
40 She has curled these locks, she has kissed this brow.

"These locks she has curled, shall the rattlesnake kiss?
This brow she has kissed, shall the cold grave press?
For the sake of the loved ones that will weep for me,
Oh, bury me not on the lone prairie.

45 "Oh, bury me not on the lone prairie
Where the wild coyotes will howl o'er me,
Where the buzzards sail and wind goes free.
Oh, bury me not on the lone prairie.

"Oh, bury me not—" And his voice failed there.
50 But we took no heed of his dying prayer;
In a narrow grave just six by three
We buried him there on the lone prairie.

Where the dewdrops glow and the butterflies rest,
And the flowers bloom o'er the prairie's crest;
55 Where the wild coyote and winds sport free
On a wet saddle blanket lay a cowboy-ee.

◄ **Critical Viewing** What aspects of a cowboy's
life do the photograph and "The Dying Cowboy"
suggest? [Connect]

"Oh, bury me not on the lone prairie
    Where the wild coyotes will howl o'er me,
    Where the rattlesnakes hiss and the crow flies free.
60   Oh, bury me not on the lone prairie."

    Oh, we buried him there on the lone prairie
    Where the wild rose blooms and the wind blows free;
    Oh, his pale young face nevermore to see—
    For we buried him there on the lone prairie.

65 Yes, we buried him there on the lone prairie.
    Where the owl all night hoots mournfully,
    And the blizzard beats and the winds blow free
    O'er his lowly grave on the lone prairie.

    And the cowboys now as they roam the plain—
70 For they marked the spot where his bones were lain—
    Fling a handful of roses o'er his grave,
    With a prayer to Him who his soul will save.

    "Oh, bury me not on the lone prairie
    Where the wolves can howl and growl o'er me;
75 Fling a handful of roses o'er my grave
    With a prayer to Him who my soul will save."

Guide for Responding

◆ LITERATURE AND YOUR LIFE

Reader's Response Were you surprised by this song's ending? Explain.

Thematic Focus The main speaker in "The Dying Cowboy" regrets some of his life choices. How can people identify decisions that may lead to trouble—before it's too late?

Journal Writing In a journal entry, explain the images that the word *cowboy* sparks in your mind.

☑ Check Your Comprehension

1. Summarize the wishes expressed by "The Dying Cowboy."
2. What three reasons does he provide to support his wishes?

◆ Critical Thinking

INTERPRET

1. How does the cowboy's view of the prairie differ from his companions' view of it? **[Compare and Contrast]**
2. How does the cowboy feel about his family and friends back home? **[Infer]**
3. What messages about life can you find in this song? **[Draw Conclusions]**

EVALUATE

4. (a) What impression of a cowboy's life does the song convey? (b) What details contribute to this impression? **[Assess]**

The Real Story of a Cowboy's Life

Geoffrey C. Ward

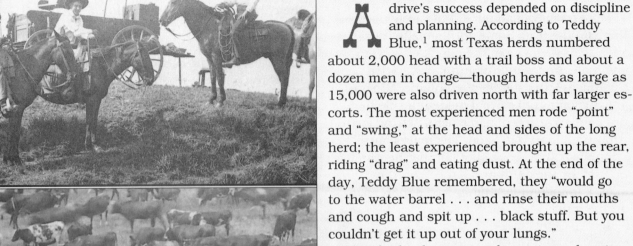

A drive's success depended on discipline and planning. According to Teddy Blue,[1] most Texas herds numbered about 2,000 head with a trail boss and about a dozen men in charge—though herds as large as 15,000 were also driven north with far larger escorts. The most experienced men rode "point" and "swing," at the head and sides of the long herd; the least experienced brought up the rear, riding "drag" and eating dust. At the end of the day, Teddy Blue remembered, they "would go to the water barrel . . . and rinse their mouths and cough and spit up . . . black stuff. But you couldn't get it up out of your lungs."

They had to learn to work as a team, keeping the herd moving during the day, resting peacefully at night. Twelve to fifteen miles a day was a good pace. But such steady progress could be interrupted at any time. A cowboy had to know how to gauge the temperament of his cattle, how to chase down a stray without alarming the rest of the herd, how to lasso[2] a steer using the horn of his saddle as a tying post. His saddle was his most prized possession; it served as his chair, his workbench, his pillow at night. Being dragged to death was the most common death for a cowboy, and so the most feared occurrence on the trail was the nighttime stampede.[3] As Teddy Blue recalled, a sound, a smell, or simply the sudden movement of a jittery cow could set off a whole herd.

> If . . . the cattle started running—you'd hear that low rumbling noise along the ground and the men on herd wouldn't need to come in and tell you, you'd know—then you'd jump for your horse and get out there in the lead,

---

1. **Teddy Blue:** Edward C. Abbot; a cowboy who rode in a successful trail drive in the 1880's.
2. **lasso** (las´ ō´) v.: To throw a long rope with a sliding noose at one end over something, then pulling the noose tight and catching it.
3. **stampede** (stam pēd´) n.: Sudden rush of panicked animals.

trying to head them and get them into a mill before they scattered. It was riding at a dead run in the dark, with cut banks and prairie dog holes all around you, not knowing if the next jump would land you in a shallow grave.

Most cowboys had guns, but rarely used them on the trail. Some outfits made them keep their weapons in the chuck wagon[4] to eliminate any chance of gunplay. Charles Goodnight[5] was still more emphatic: "Before starting on a trail drive, I made it a rule to draw up an article of agreement, setting forth what each man was to do. The main clause stipulated[6] that if one shot another he was to be tried by the outfit and hanged on the spot, if found guilty. I never had a man shot on the trail."

Regardless of its ultimate destination, every herd had to ford[7] a series of rivers—the Nueces, the Guadalupe, the Brazos, the Wichita, the Red. A big herd of longhorns swimming across a river, Goodnight remembered, "looked like a million floating rocking chairs," and crossing those rivers one after another, a cowboy recalled, was like climbing the rungs of a long ladder reaching north.

"After you crossed the Red River and got out on the open plains," Teddy Blue remembered, "it was sure a pretty sight to see them strung out for almost a mile, the sun shining on their horns." Initially, the land immediately north of the Red River was Indian territory, and some tribes charged tolls for herds crossing their land—payable in money or beef. But Teddy Blue remembered that the homesteaders,[8] now pouring onto the Plains by railroad, were far more nettlesome:

There was no love lost between settlers

---

4. **chuck wagon** *n.*: Wagon equipped like a kitchen to feed cowboys or other outdoor workers.
5. **Charles Goodnight:** Cowboy who rode successful trail drives in the 1880's.
6. **stipulated** (stip′ yoō lāt′ id) *v.*: Stated as a rule.
7. **ford** (fôrd) *v.*: To cross a river at its low point.
8. **homesteaders** *n.*: Settlers who obtained land from the government in exchange for a commitment to farm it for at least five years.

and cowboys on the trail. Those jay-hawkers would take up a claim right where the herds watered and charge us for water. They would plant a crop alongside the trail and plow a furrow around it for a fence, and then when the cattle got into their wheat or their garden patch, they would come cussing and waving a shotgun and yelling for damages. And the cattle had been coming through there when they were still raising punkins in Illinois.

The settlers' hostility was entirely understandable. The big herds ruined their crops, and they carried with them a disease, spread by ticks and called "Texas fever," that devastated domestic livestock. Kansas and other territories along the route soon established quarantine[9] lines, called "deadlines," at the western fringe of settlement, and insisted that trail drives not cross them. Each year, as settlers continued to move in, those deadlines moved farther west.

<table>
<tr><td>◆ **Reading Strategy**
Identify two effects the cattle drives had on settlers.</td></tr>
</table>

Sometimes, farmers tried to enforce their own, as John Rumans, one of Charles Goodnight's hands, recalled:

Some men met us at the trail near Canyon City, and said we couldn't come in. There were fifteen or twenty of them, and they were not going to let us cross the Arkansas River. We didn't even stop. . . . Old man [Goodnight] had a shotgun loaded with buckshot and led the way, saying: "John, get over on that point with your Winchester and point these cattle in behind me." He slid his shotgun across the saddle in front of him and we did the same with our Winchesters. He rode right across, and as he rode up to them, he said: "I've monkeyed as long as I want to with you," and they fell back to the sides, and went home after we had passed.

---

9. **quarantine** (kwôr′ ən tēn) **lines** *n.*: Boundaries created to prevent the spread of disease.

There were few diversions on the trail. Most trail bosses banned liquor. Goodnight prohibited gambling, too. Even the songs for which cowboys became famous grew directly out of doing a job, remembered Teddy Blue:

The singing was supposed to soothe [the cattle] and it did; I don't know why, unless it was that a sound they was used to would keep them from spooking at other noises. I know that if you wasn't singing, any little sound in the night—it might be just a horse shaking himself—could make them leave the country; but if you were singing, they wouldn't notice it.

The two men on guard would circle around with their horses on a walk, if it was a clear night and the cattle was bedded down and quiet, and one man would sing a verse of song, and his partner on the other side of the herd would sing another verse; and you'd go through a whole song that way. . . . "Bury Me Not on the Lone Prairie" was a great song for awhile, but . . . they sung it to death. It was a saying on the range that even the horses nickered it and the coyotes howled it; it got so they'd throw you in the creek if you sang it.

The number of cattle on the move was sometimes staggering: once, Teddy Blue rode to the top of a rise from which he could see seven herds strung out behind him; eight more up ahead; and the dust from an additional thirteen moving parallel to his. "All the cattle in the world," he remembered, "seemed to be coming up from Texas."

At last, the herds neared their destinations. After months in the saddle—often wearing the same clothes every day, eating nothing but biscuits and beef stew at the chuck wagon, drinking only water and coffee, his sole companions his fellow cowboys, his herd, and his horse—the cowboy was about to be paid for his work, and turned loose in town.

Guide for Responding

◆ LITERATURE AND YOUR LIFE

Reader's Response Which detail in "The Real Story of a Cowboy's Life" surprised you the most? Why?

Thematic Focus What facts in this essay show that a cowboy's life was dangerous?

✓ Check Your Comprehension

1. Use the information in "The Real Story of a Cowboy's Life" to identify four uses of a cowboy's saddle.
2. What was the most common cause of death on the trail?
3. Identify two details that explain how violence was kept to a minimum on the trail.
4. According to "The Real Story of a Cowboy's Life," why were songs like "The Dying Cowboy" sung?

◆ Critical Thinking

INTERPRET

1. (a) What challenges did the landscape present to cowboys on a drive? (b) What challenges did people present? **[Analyze]**
2. What qualifies Teddy Blue as a reliable source of information about cattle drives? **[Infer]**
3. What evidence suggests Teddy Blue liked cattle driving? **[Support]**

APPLY

4. Based on "The Real Story of a Cowboy's Life," what kind of person do you think would succeed as a cowboy? **[Apply]**

COMPARE LITERARY WORKS

5. "The Dying Cowboy" and "The Real Story of a Cowboy's Life" present very different versions of life on the prairie. What is the value of each one? **[Evaluate]**

Guide for Responding (continued)

◆ Reading Strategy

IDENTIFY CAUSE AND EFFECT

A **cause** makes something happen. An **effect** is what happens. Noting cause-and-effect relationships will help you get at the meaning of a selection. For example, Tim's betrayal of the outlaw's plans in "The Highwayman" gains importance when you realize that it eventually causes Bess's death.

1. Identify two other causes and their effects in "The Highwayman."
2. (a) What causes can you find for the wishes of the "Dying Cowboy"? (b) What effect do his wishes have on the other cowboys' actions?

◆ Build Vocabulary

COMPOUND NOUNS

The word *moonlight* is a compound noun—one made by combining two smaller words. With a partner, piece together the words below into as many compound nouns as you can.

lord	way	lamp	land	high
light	ache	heart	quarters	head

SPELLING STRATEGY

When you make compound adjectives, use a hyphen to separate an adjective and the *-ed* form of a noun: *black* + *eye* become the adjective *black-eyed*. Use the details below to create compound adjectives that describe Bess or the highwayman.

1. red lips   3. velvet coat
2. black hair   4. sharp eye

USING THE WORD BANK

In your notebook, label each word pair with *A* for *antonyms* (words with opposite meanings) and *S* for *synonyms* (words with similar meanings).

1. torrent, flood
2. cascade, trickle
3. brandished, hid
4. bound, unlocked
5. tawny, tan
6. landlord, tenant
7. strive, try

◆ Literary Focus

SUSPENSE

By creating **suspense,** or story tension, writers draw readers into a literary work and lead them to anxiously anticipate the outcome. Suspense often surrounds dangerous or uncertain situations. For example, the secrecy of the meeting between Bess and the highwayman increases the suspense.

1. Identify three details Noyes uses to increase the suspense in "The Highwayman."
2. How does "The Dying Cowboy" build suspense?
3. How do the repeated lines in both poems increase the suspense?
4. What details in "The Real Story of a Cowboy's Life" might be used to create suspenseful writing?

◆ Build Grammar Skills

ADJECTIVE AND ADVERB PHRASES

A **preposition** relates the noun or pronoun following it to another word in the sentence. A **prepositional phrase** includes a preposition and its object. Prepositional phrases can act as **adjectives** modifying nouns or as **adverbs** modifying verbs.

noun   prep. phrase

Adjective: The wind was a *torrent* of darkness.

verb   prep. phrase

Adverb: They *fitted* with never a wrinkle.

Practice Copy the following sentences. Bracket each prepositional phrase, and identify the word it modifies. Then, tell whether it functions as an adjective or an adverb.

1. The moors shone in the blinding moonlight.
2. He kissed the tumbling waves of Bess's hair.
3. The dying cowboy died on the lonely prairie.
4. All of the buzzards landed on the cowboy's grave.
5. Experienced men rode at the head of the herd.

Writing Application Write sentences that include these prepositional phrases, used as shown.

1. of his home far away (as an adverb)
2. on the prairie (as an adverb)
3. from the window (as an adjective)

Build Your Portfolio

 ## Idea Bank

Writing

1. **Wanted Poster** Write a wanted poster offering a reward for the highwayman's capture. Include a vivid description of him, and mention his known associates and hangouts.

2. **Letter of Appeal** As a loved one of "The Dying Cowboy," write a letter to his companions asking them to send the cowboy home for his burial. Use reasons and details from the song to make your letter effective.

3. **Narrative Poem** Use the events in "The Dying Cowboy" or "The Real Story of a Cowboy's Life" to write a narrative poem—a poem that tells a story. Study "The Highwayman" for tips on structure and technique.

Speaking and Listening

4. **Poetry Reading** Read "The Highwayman" to classmates. To bring out the meaning of the poem, change the speed and volume of your voice, and let punctuation determine your pauses.

5. **Ballad Collection** In recordings or books of musical history, find examples of western and English ballads to share with the class. Then, discuss the stories told by the songs, and identify any elements of suspense. **[Music Link]**

Projects

6. **Oral Report on Legendary Figures [Group Activity]** In a group, research such legendary western figures as Davy Crockett, Kit Carson, or Jesse James. Watch episodes of Geoffrey C. Ward and Ken Burns's series *The West* or consult the companion book. Identify the information each group member will seek. Then, include all the findings in an oral report. **[Social Studies Link]**

7. **Geography Comparison** Using the settings of "The Highwayman" and "The Real Story of a Cowboy's Life," make a chart comparing and contrasting the natural features described. **[Social Studies Link]**

 ## Writing Mini-Lesson

Police Report

"The Highwayman" and "The Dying Cowboy" describe events from a particular point of view—almost as an eyewitness would. However, what would the same events look like through the eyes of an observer who was not involved? Choose a selection, and write a police report recounting its events. To make your report realistic, use a detective's technique: include information from interviews with participants or eyewitnesses.

Writing Skills Focus:
Facts and Examples

To explain the events reported, use **facts and examples** to provide the details. Answer the question "*Who* was *where when?*" by saying, for example, "The landlord's daughter met the suspect early on the night of the robbery." Also, use examples to describe the participants' behavior—"The highwayman avoided arrest by shooting at officers, hiding in a wooded area, and adopting a disguise."

Prewriting After choosing your selection, list its events in chronological order. Highlight the places in the sequence where an eyewitness interview or a specific fact would be useful.

Drafting Build on your timeline, adding details about *who*, *what*, *when*, *where*, and *how* to show the key facts of each event. Use eyewitness reports to show different interpretations of the events.

◆ **Grammar Application**
Make your report more specific by providing details in adjective and adverb phrases.

Revising Make sure your report objectively details what happened. If necessary, add information to help readers understand the *who*, *what*, *when*, *where*, and *how* of the events.

Guide for Reading

Meet the Authors:

Sir Arthur Conan Doyle (1859–1930)

Almost like a combination of his two most famous characters—Sherlock Holmes and Dr. Watson—Sir Arthur Conan Doyle was both a mystery solver *and* a trained medical doctor.

Success as a Writer Doyle was born in Edinburgh, Scotland. When his medical practice struggled, he turned to mystery writing as a way to earn money, achieving immediate success with his Sherlock Holmes stories. In addition to detective stories, Doyle wrote historical and fantasy novels.

Although Holmes was a great success, Doyle often considered killing off the famous detective. Readers protested so wildly to one attempt that Doyle brought Holmes back to life.

Michael Hardwick (1924–1991)
Mollie Hardwick

Fortunately for Michael Hardwick, Doyle wrote many Sherlock Holmes stories. Studying Doyle and writing materials to go with his stories kept Michael Hardwick busy writing for years. Together with his wife, Mollie, he wrote this dramatic version of "The Dying Detective." Michael once said their styles were so similar that even they couldn't tell later who wrote specific passages.

◆ Literature and Your Life

Connect Your Experience

Somewhere in your life there's probably a person whom you know really well. You can finish each other's sentences and predict each other's emotions. What would you do if this person started acting strangely? What if he or she suddenly seemed to dislike you and, although unhappy, insisted on suffering alone? This is the problem Dr. Watson faces in "The Dying Detective."

Thematic Focus: Finding Solutions

In "The Dying Detective," the characters each try to solve different problems. Think about how each man's actions can help the other solve his problem.

◆ Background for Understanding

Mathematics

Detectives solve mysteries with logical deductions—conclusions reached by reasoning from a general statement to a specific one. Look at these two sentences:

Holmes usually speaks clearly and logically.
Today, Holmes is not making sense.

From these statements, you can draw this conclusion:

Something is wrong with Holmes.

As you read, think about how Dr. Watson might use logic to solve the problem of Holmes's strange behavior.

◆ Build Vocabulary

Suffixes: *-ology*

Sherlock Holmes describes a disease as *pathological.* The related word *pathology* is formed from the root *path,* meaning "feeling or suffering," and the suffix *-ology,* meaning "the science or study of disease."

Word Bank

Which of these words do you think might describe a careful and very organized person?

agitated
pathological
implore
methodical
irksome

◆ The Dying Detective ◆

Sherlock Holmes, Frederic Dorr Steele

◆ Reading Strategy

DRAW CONCLUSIONS

A mystery like "The Dying Detective" is built around the facts the author includes and the information that is held back. When you **draw conclusions,** you use details in the text to make general statements. By identifying the clues Doyle presents, you might unravel the mystery. As you read, be aware of the characters' actions and any unusual remarks. Note the topics that the main characters think are important. With these clues, you may solve a crime before the characters do.

◆ Literary Focus

STAGING

The techniques that bring a drama to life—movements, costumes, scenery, lighting, and sound—are called **staging.** Playwrights provide staging directions in brackets that appear in the script. Directors use this information as they plan productions. Readers use the information to visualize the action. The staging directions at the beginning of "The Dying Detective" describe the appearance of Holmes's room. As you read, create a staging chart like the one below for each scene.

	Actors' Movements	Scenery	Lighting and Sound Effects	Costumes
Scene 1:				
Scene 2:				
Scene 3:				

The Dying Detective

FROM A STORY BY SIR ARTHUR CONAN DOYLE

Michael and Mollie Hardwick

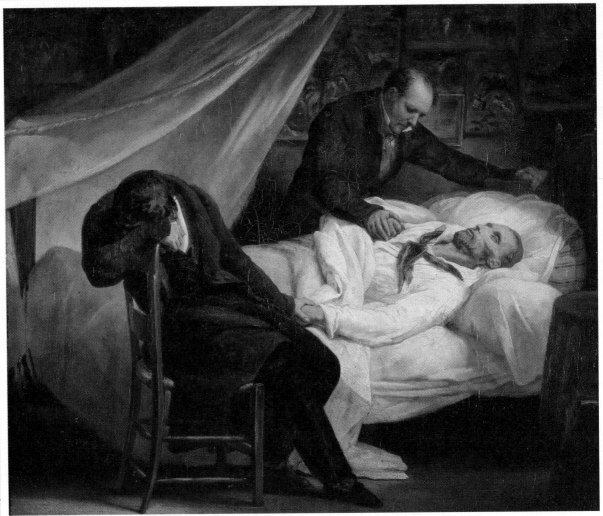

The Death of Theodore Gericault (1791–1824) with his friends Colonel Bro de Comeres and the painter Pierre-Joseph Dedreux-Dorcy (1789–1874), 1824, Ary Scheffer, Louvre, Paris, France

▲ **Critical Viewing** If you went to see a production of "The Dying Detective," the curtain might rise on a scene like the one in this painting. How would you expect the audience to respond? **[Hypothesize]**

Scene 1: Sherlock Holmes's bedroom, *afternoon*

Scene 2: The same, *dusk*

Scene 3: The same, *evening*

Scene 1

[SHERLOCK HOLMES's *bedroom at 221B Baker Street. The essential features are: a bed with a large wooden head, placed crosswise on the stage, the head a foot or two from one side wall; a small table near the bed-head, on the audience's side, on which stand a carafe of water and a glass, and a tiny metal or ivory box; a window in the back wall, the curtains parted; and, under the window, a table or chest of drawers, on which stand a green wine bottle, some wine-glasses, a biscuit-barrel,[1] and a lamp. Of course, there may be further lamps and any amount of furnishing and clutter: Holmes's bedroom was adorned with pictures of celebrated criminals and littered with everything from tobacco pipes to revolver cartridges.*]

[*There is daylight outside the window.* SHERLOCK HOLMES *lies in the bed on his back, tucked up to the chin and evidently asleep. He is very pale.* MRS. HUDSON *enters followed by* DR. WATSON, *who is wearing his coat and hat and carrying his small medical bag.* MRS. HUDSON *pauses for a moment.*]

----

1. **biscuit-barrel** (bis´ kit bar´ əl) *n.:* British term for a container holding cookies or crackers.

MRS. HUDSON. He's asleep, sir.

[*They approach the bed.* WATSON *comes round to the audience's side and looks down at* HOLMES *for a moment. He shakes his head gravely, then he and* MRS. HUDSON *move away beyond the foot of the bed.* WATSON *takes off his hat and coat as they talk and she takes them from him.*]

> ◆ **Literary Focus**
> What information about the actors and their appearance do these staging directions provide?

WATSON. This is dreadful, Mrs. Hudson. He was perfectly hale and hearty when I went away only three days ago.

MRS. HUDSON. I know, sir. Oh, Dr. Watson, sir, I'm glad that you've come back. If anyone can save Mr. Holmes, I'm sure you can.

WATSON. I shall have to know what is the matter with him first. Mrs. Hudson, please tell me, as quickly as you can, how it all came about.

MRS. HUDSON. Yes, sir. Mr. Holmes has been working lately on some case down near the river—Rotherhithe, I think.

WATSON. Yes, yes. I know.

MRS. HUDSON. Well, you know what he is for coming in at all hours. I was just taking my lamp to go to my bed on Wednesday night when I heard a faint knocking at the street door. I . . . I found Mr. Holmes there. He could hardly stand. Just muttered to me to help him up to his bed here, and he's barely spoken since.

WATSON. Dear me!

MRS. HUDSON. Won't take food or drink. Just lies there, sleeping or staring in a wild sort of way.

WATSON. But, goodness gracious, Mrs. Hudson, why did you not send for another doctor in my absence?

MRS. HUDSON. Oh, I told him straightaway I was going to do that, sir. But he got so agitated—almost shouted that he wouldn't allow any

◆ **Build Vocabulary**
agitated (aj´ i tāt´ id) *adj.:* Shaken or upset

doctor on the premises. You know how masterful he is, Dr. Watson.

WATSON. Indeed. But you could have telegraphed[2] for me.

[MRS. HUDSON *appears embarrassed*.]

MRS. HUDSON. Well, sir . . .

WATSON. But you didn't. Why, Mrs. Hudson?

MRS. HUDSON. Sir, I don't like to tell you, but . . . well, Mr. Holmes said he wouldn't even have you to see him.

WATSON. What? This is monstrous! I, his oldest friend, and . . .
[HOLMES *groans and stirs slightly*.]

Ssh! He's waking. You go along, Mrs. Hudson, and leave this to me. Whether he likes it or not, I shall ensure that everything possible is done.

MRS. HUDSON. Thank you, sir. You'll ring if I can be of help.
[*She exits with* WATSON'S *things.* HOLMES *groans again and flings out an arm restlessly.* WATSON *comes to the audience's side of the bed and sits on it.*]

WATSON. Holmes? It's I—Watson.

HOLMES. [*Sighs*] Ahh! Well, Watson? We . . . we seem to have fallen on evil days.

WATSON. My dear fellow!
[*He moves to reach for* HOLMES'S *pulse.*]

HOLMES. [*Urgently*] No, no! Keep back!

WATSON. Eh?

HOLMES. Mustn't come near.

WATSON. Now, look here, Holmes . . . !

HOLMES. If you come near . . . order you out of the house.

WATSON. [*Defiantly*] Hah!

HOLMES. For your own sake, Watson. Contracted . . . a disease—from Sumatra.[3] Very

little known, except that most deadly. Contagious by touch. So . . . must keep away.

WATSON. Utter rubbish. Holmes! Mrs. Hudson tells me she helped you to your bed. There's nothing the matter with her.

HOLMES. Period of . . . incubation.[4] Only dangerous after two or three days. Deadly by now.

WATSON. Good heavens, do you suppose such a consideration weighs with me? Even if I weren't a doctor, d'you think it would stop me doing my duty to an old friend? Now, let's have a good look at you. [*He moves forward again.*]

HOLMES. [*Harshly*] I tell you to keep back!

WATSON. See here, Holmes . . .

HOLMES. If you will stay where you are, I will talk to you. If you will not, you can get out.

WATSON. Holmes! [*Recovering*] Holmes, you aren't yourself. You're sick and as helpless as a child.
Whether you like it or not, I'm going to examine you and treat you.

◆ Reading Strategy
What conclusions can you draw based on Holmes's unusual behavior?

HOLMES. [*Sneering*] If I'm to be forced to have a doctor, let him at least be someone I've some confidence in.

WATSON. Oh! You . . . After all these years, Holmes, you haven't . . . confidence in me?

HOLMES. In your friendship, Watson—yes. But facts are facts. As a medical man you're a mere general practitioner, of limited experience and mediocre[5] qualifications.

WATSON. Well . . . ! Well, really!

HOLMES. It is painful to say such things, but you leave me no choice.

WATSON. [*Coldly*] Thank you. I'll tell you this, Holmes. Such a remark, coming from you, merely serves to tell me what state your nerves are in. Still, if you insist that you have no

---

2. **telegraphed** (tel′ ə grafd′) *v.*: Sent a message by telegraph, a system that changes codes into electrical impulses and sends them into a distant receiver.
3. **Sumatra** (soo mä′ trə): Large island of Indonesia.

4. **incubation** (in′ kyoo bā′ shən) *n.*: The phase of a disease between infection and the first appearance of symptoms.
5. **mediocre** (mē′ dē ō′ kər) *adj.*: Neither very good nor very bad.

confidence in me, I will not intrude my services. But what I shall do is to summon Sir Jasper Meek or Penrose Fisher, or any of the other best men in London.

HOLMES. [*Groans*] My . . . dear Watson. You mean well. But do you suppose they—any of them—know of the Tapanuli Fever?

WATSON. The Tap . . . ?

HOLMES. What do you yourself know of the Black Formosa Corruption?

WATSON. Tapanuli Fever? Black Formosa Corruption? I've never heard of either of 'em.

HOLMES. Nor have your colleagues.[6] There are many problems of disease, many pathological possibilities, peculiar to the East. So I've learned during some of my recent researches. It was in the course of one of them that I contracted this complaint. I assure you, Watson, you can do nothing.

WATSON. Can't I? I happen to know, Holmes, that the greatest living authority on tropical disease, Dr. Ainstree, is in London just now.

HOLMES. [*Beseeching*] Watson!

WATSON. All remonstrance[7] is useless. I am going this instant to fetch him. [*He gets up*]

HOLMES. [*A great cry*] No!

WATSON. Eh? Holmes . . . my dear fellow . . .

HOLMES. Watson, in the name of our old friendship, do as I ask.

WATSON. But . . .

---

6. **colleagues** (käl´ ēgz) *n.:* Fellow workers.
7. **remonstrance** (ri män´ strəns) *n.:* Act of protesting or complaining.

◆ **Build Vocabulary**

pathological (path´ ə läj´ i kəl) *adj.:* Due to or related to disease

HOLMES. You have only my own good at heart. Of course, I know that. You . . . you shall have your way. Only . . . give me time to . . . to collect my strength. What is the time now? [WATSON *sits again and consults his watch.*]

WATSON. Four o'clock.

HOLMES. Then at six you can go.

WATSON. This is insanity!

HOLMES. Only two hours, Watson. I promise you may go then.

WATSON. Hang it, this is urgent, man!

HOLMES. I will see no one before six. I will not be examined. I shall resist!

WATSON. [*Sighing*] Oh, have it your own way, then. But I insist on staying with you in the meantime. You need an eye keeping on you, Holmes.

HOLMES. Very well, Watson. And now I must sleep. I feel exhausted. [*Drowsily*] I wonder how a battery feels when it pours electricity into a non-conductor?

WATSON. Eh?

HOLMES. [*Yawning*] At six, Watson, we resume our conversation. [*He lies back and closes his eyes.* WATSON *makes as though to move, but thinks better of it. He sits still, watching* HOLMES. *A slow black-out*]

Scene 2

[*The stage lights up again, though more dimly than before, to disclose the same scene. Twilight is apparent through the window.* HOLMES *lies motionless.* WATSON *sits as before, though with his head sagging, half asleep. His chin drops suddenly and he wakes with a jerk. He glances*

◀ **Critical Viewing** Why is a magnifying glass like the one pictured here an important tool for Sherlock Holmes? [**Assess**]

around, sees the twilight outside, and consults his watch. He yawns, flexes his arms, then proceeds to glance idly about him. His attention is caught by the little box on the bedside table. Stealthily, he reaches over and picks it up.]

HOLMES. [*Very loudly and urgently*] No! No, Watson, no!

WATSON. [*Startled*] Eh? What?
[HOLMES *starts up onto his elbow.*]

HOLMES. Put it down! Down this instant! Do as I say, Watson!

WATSON. Oh! All right, then. [*Putting the box down.*] Look here, Holmes, I really think . . .

HOLMES. I hate to have my things touched. You know perfectly well I do.

WATSON. Holmes . . . !

HOLMES. You fidget[8] me beyond endurance. You, a doctor—you're enough to drive a patient into an asylum!

WATSON. Really!

HOLMES. Now, for heaven's sake, sit still, and let me have my rest.

WATSON. Holmes, it is almost six o'clock, and I refuse to delay another instant. [*He gets up determinedly.*]

HOLMES. Really? Watson, have you any change in your pocket?

WATSON. Yes.

HOLMES. Any silver?

WATSON. [*Fishing out his change*] A good deal.

HOLMES. How many half-crowns?

WATSON. Er, five.

HOLMES. [*Sighing*] Ah, too few, too few. However, such as they are, you can put them in your watch-pocket—and all the rest of your money in your left trouser-pocket. It will balance you so much better like that.

WATSON. Balance . . . ? Holmes, you're raving! This has gone too far . . . !

---

8. **fidget** (fij´ it) *v.*: Used here to mean the same as "to irritate."

HOLMES. You will now light that lamp by the window, Watson, but you will be very careful that not for one instant shall it be more than at half flame.

WATSON. Oh, very well. [WATSON *goes to the lamp and strikes a match.*]

HOLMES. I implore you to be careful.

◆ **Literary Focus**
How does the stage lighting change during this passage?

WATSON. [*As though humoring him*] Yes, Holmes.
[*He lights the lamp, carefully keeping the flame low. He moves to draw the curtains.*]

HOLMES. No, you need not draw the curtains. [WATSON *leaves them and comes back round the bed.*]

So! Good. You may now go and fetch a specialist.

WATSON. Well, thank heaven for that.

HOLMES. His name is Mr. Culverton Smith, of 13 Lower Burke Street.

WATSON. [*Staring*] Eh?

HOLMES. Well, go on, man. You could hardly wait to fetch someone before.

WATSON. Yes, but . . . Culverton Smith? I've never heard the name!

HOLMES. Possibly not. It may surprise you to know that the one man who knows everything about this disease is not a medical man. He's a planter.

WATSON. A planter!

HOLMES. His plantation is far from medical aid. An outbreak of this disease there caused him to study it intensely. He's a very methodical man, and I asked you not to go before six because I knew you wouldn't find him in his study till then.

WATSON. Holmes, I . . . I never heard such a . . . !

◆ **Build Vocabulary**
implore (im plôr´) *v.*: Ask or beg earnestly
methodical (mə thäd´ i kəl) *adj.*: Orderly; organized

HOLMES. You will tell him exactly how you have left me. A dying man.

WATSON. No, Holmes!

HOLMES. At any rate, delirious. Yes, not dying, delirious. [*Chuckles*] No, I really can't think why the whole ocean bed isn't one solid mass of oysters.

WATSON. Oysters?

HOLMES. They're so prolific,[9] you know.

WATSON. Great Heavens! Now, Holmes, you just lie quiet, and . . .

HOLMES. Strange how the mind controls the brain. Er, what was I saying, Watson?

WATSON. You were . . .

HOLMES. Ah, I remember. Culverton Smith. My life depends on him, Watson. But you will have to plead with him to come. There is no good feeling between us. He has . . . a grudge. I rely on you to soften him. Beg, Watson. Pray. But get him here by any means.

◆ **Reading Strategy**
What conclusions can you draw based on the change in Holmes's manner?

WATSON. Very well. I'll bring him in a cab, if I have to carry him down to it.

HOLMES. You will do nothing of the sort. You will persuade him to come—and then return before him. [*Deliberately*] Make any excuse so as not to come with him. Don't forget that, Watson. You won't fail me. You never did fail me.

WATSON. That's all very well, Holmes, but . . .

HOLMES. [*Interrupting*] Then, shall the world be overrun by oysters? No doubt there are natural enemies which limit their increase. And yet . . . No, horrible, horrible!

WATSON. [*Grimly*] I'm going, Holmes. Say no more, I'm going!
[*He hurries out.* HOLMES *remains propped up for a moment, staring after* WATSON, *then sinks back into a sleeping posture as the stage blacks out.*]

---

9. **prolific** (prō lif′ ik) *adj.:* Producing many young.

Scene 3

[*The stage lights up on the same scene.* HOLMES *lies still. It is now quite dark outside. After a moment* WATSON *bustles in, pulling off his coat. He pauses to hand it to* MRS. HUDSON, *who is behind him.*]

WATSON. Thank you, Mrs. Hudson. A gentleman will be calling very shortly. Kindly show him up here immediately.

MRS. HUDSON. Yes, sir.
[*She exits.* WATSON *approaches the bed.*]

HOLMES. [*Drowsily*] Watson?

WATSON. Yes, Holmes. How are you feeling?

HOLMES. Much the same, I fear. Is Culverton Smith coming?

WATSON. Should be here any minute. It took me some minutes to find a cab, and I almost expected him to have got here first.

HOLMES. Well done, my dear Watson.

WATSON. I must say, Holmes, I'm only doing this to humor you. Frankly, I didn't take to your planter friend at all.

HOLMES. Oh? How so?

WATSON. Rudeness itself. He almost showed me the door before I could give him your message. It wasn't until I mentioned the name, Sherlock Holmes . . .

HOLMES. Ah!

WATSON. Quite changed him—but I wouldn't say it was for the better.

HOLMES. Tell me what he said.

WATSON. Said you'd had some business dealings together, and that he respected your character and talents. Described you as an amateur of crime, in the way that he regards himself as an amateur of disease.

HOLMES. Quite typical—and surely, quite fair?

WATSON. Quite fair—if he hadn't put such sarcasm into saying it. No, Holmes, you said he bears you some grudge. Mark my words, as soon as he has left this house I insist upon calling a recognized specialist.

HOLMES. My dear Watson, you are the best of messengers. Thank you again.

WATSON. Not at all. Holmes, Holmes—let me help you without any of this nonsense. The whole of Great Britain will condemn me otherwise. Why, my cabmen both inquired anxiously after you; and so did Inspector Morton . . .

HOLMES. Morton?

WATSON. Of the Yard. He was passing our door just now as I came in. Seemed extremely concerned.

HOLMES. Scotland Yard[10] concerned for me? How very touching! And now, Watson, you may disappear from the scene.

WATSON. Disappear! I shall do no such thing. I wish to be present when this Culverton Smith

---

10. **Scotland Yard:** The London police, especially the detective bureau.

---

arrives. I wish to hear every word of this so-called medical expert's opinion.

HOLMES. [*Turning his head*] Yes, of course. Then I think you will just find room behind the head of the bed.

WATSON. What? Hide?

HOLMES. I have reason to suppose that his opinion will be much more frank and valuable if he imagines he is alone with me. [*We hear the murmur of* MRS. HUDSON'S *and* CULVERTON SMITH'S *voices off-stage.*]

Listen! I hear him coming. Get behind the bed, Watson, and do not budge, whatever happens. *Whatever* happens, you understand?

WATSON. Oh, all right, Holmes. Anything to please you. But I don't like this. Not at all. [*He goes behind the bedhead and conceals himself.* MRS. HUDSON *enters, looks round the room and then at* HOLMES. SMITH *enters behind her.*]

◆ Literary Focus
What is the result of this staging direction?

MRS. HUDSON. [*To* SMITH] Oh, Dr. Watson must have let himself out. No doubt he'll be back directly, sir.

SMITH. No matter, my good woman. [MRS. HUDSON *bristles at this form of address.*]

You may leave me alone with your master.

MRS. HUDSON. As you wish—*sir.* [*She sweeps out.* SMITH *advances slowly to the bed and stands at the foot, staring at the recumbent* HOLMES.]

SMITH. [*Almost to himself*] So, Holmes. It has come to this, then. [HOLMES *stirs.* SMITH *chuckles and leans his arms on the bed-foot and his chin on them, continuing to watch* HOLMES.]

▲ **Critical Viewing** How does the formal clothing of the men compare with the costumes you would expect to see in a production of "The Dying Detective"? [Compare and Contrast]

HOLMES. [*Weakly*] Watson? Who . . . ? Smith? Smith, is that you?

SMITH. [*Chuckles*]

HOLMES. I . . . I hardly dared hope you would come.

SMITH. I should imagine not. And yet, you see, I'm here. Coals of fire,[11] Holmes—coals of fire!

HOLMES. Noble of you . . .

SMITH. Yes, isn't it?

HOLMES. I appreciate your special knowledge.

SMITH. Then you're the only man in London who does. Do you know what is the matter with you?

HOLMES. The same as young Victor—your cousin.

SMITH. Ah, then you recognize the symptoms. Well, then, it's a bad look-out for you. Victor was a strong, hearty young fellow—but a dead man on the fourth day. As you said at the time, it *was* rather surprising that he should contract an out-of-the-way Asiatic[12] disease in the heart of London—a disease of which I have made such a very special study. [*Chuckles*] And now, you, Holmes. Singular coincidence, eh? Or are you going to start making accusations once again—about cause and effect and so on?

HOLMES. I . . . I knew you caused Victor Savage's death.
[SMITH *comes round the bed.*]

SMITH. [*Snarling*] Did you? Well, proving it is a different matter, Holmes. But what sort of a game is this, then—spreading lying reports about me one moment, then crawling to me for help the next?

HOLMES. [*Gasping*] Give . . . give me water. For . . . pity's sake, Smith. Water!
[SMITH *hesitates momentarily, then goes to the table and pours a glass from the carafe.*]

---

11. **Coals of fire:** Reference to a biblical passage, Proverbs 25:21–22, about revenging oneself on an enemy.
12. **Asiatic** (ā zhē at´ ik): Related to Asia, largest continent in the Eastern Hemisphere.

SMITH. You're precious near your end, my friend, but I don't want you to go till I've had a word with you.
[*He holds out the glass to* HOLMES, *who struggles up feebly to take it and drinks.*]

HOLMES. [*Gulping water*] Ah! Thank . . . thank you. Please . . . do what you can for me. Only cure me, and I promise to forget.

SMITH. Forget what?

HOLMES. About Victor Savage's death. You as good as admitted just now that you had done it. I swear I will forget it.

SMITH. [*Laughs*] Forget it, remember it—do as you like. I don't see you in any witness-box, Holmes. Quite another shape of box, I assure you. But you must hear first how it came about.

HOLMES. Working amongst Chinese sailors. Down at the docks.

SMITH. Proud of your brains, aren't you? Think yourself smart? Well, you've met a smarter one this time.
[HOLMES *falls back, groaning loudly.*]

Getting painful, is it?
[HOLMES *cries out, writhing in agony.*]

SMITH. That's the way. Takes you as cramp, I fancy?

HOLMES. Cramp! Cramp!

SMITH. Well, you can still hear me. Now, can't you just remember any unusual incident—just about the time your symptoms began?

HOLMES. I . . . can't think. My mind is gone! Help me, Smith!

SMITH. Did nothing come to you through the post, for instance?

HOLMES. Post? Post?

SMITH. Yes. A little box, perhaps?

HOLMES. [*A shuddering groan*]

SMITH. [*Closer; deadly*] Listen! You *shall* hear me! Don't you remember a box—a little ivory box? [*He sees it on the table and holds it up.*] Yes, here it is on your bedside table. It came on

Wednesday. You opened it—do you remember?

HOLMES. Box? Opened? Yes, yes! There was . . . sharp spring inside. Pricked my finger. Some sort of joke . . .

SMITH. It was no joke, Holmes. You fool! Who asked you to cross my path? If you'd only left me alone I would never have hurt you.

HOLMES. Box! Yes! Pricked finger. Poison!

SMITH. [*Triumphantly*] So you do remember. Good, good! I'm glad indeed. Well, the box leaves this room in my pocket, and there's your last shred of evidence gone. [*He pockets it.*] But you have the truth now, Holmes. You can die knowing that I killed you. You knew too much

▼ **Critical Viewing** What does this photograph suggest about the importance of close examination? What role might such an examination play in this drama? [**Connect**]

about what happened to Victor Savage, so you must share his fate. Yes, Holmes, you are very near your end now. I think I shall sit here and watch you die. [*He sits on the bed.*]

HOLMES. [*Almost a whisper*] The . . . shadows . . . falling. Getting . . . so dark. I can't see. Smith! Smith, are you there? The light . . . for charity's sake, turn up the light!
[SMITH *laughs, gets up and goes to the light.*]

SMITH. Entering the valley of the shadow, eh, Holmes? Yes, I'll turn up the light for you. I can watch your face more plainly, then. [*He turns the flame up full.*] There! Now, is there any *further* service I can render you?

HOLMES. [*In a clear, strong voice*] A match and my pipe, if you please.
[*He sits bolt upright.* SMITH

◆ **Reading Strategy**
Notice how eager Holmes is to see Culverton Smith. Draw a conclusion based on this detail.

spins round to see him.]

SMITH. Eh? What the devil's the meaning of this?

HOLMES. [*Cheerfully*] The best way of successfully acting a part is to *be* it. I give you my word that for three days I have neither tasted food nor drink until you were good enough to pour me out that glass of water. But it's the tobacco I find most <u>irksome</u>.
[*We hear the thud of footsteps running upstairs off-stage.*]

Hello, hello! Do I hear the step of a friend?
[INSPECTOR MORTON *hurries in.*]

MORTON. Mr. Holmes?

HOLMES. Inspector Morton, this is your man.

SMITH. What is the meaning of . . . ?

MORTON. Culverton Smith, I arrest you on the charge of the murder of one Victor Savage, and I must warn you that anything you say . . .

SMITH. You've got nothing on me! It's all a trick! A pack of lies!
[*He makes to escape.* MORTON *restrains him.*]

MORTON. Keep still, or you'll get yourself hurt!

SMITH. Get off me!

MORTON. Hold your hands out!
[*They struggle.* MORTON *gets out handcuffs and claps them on* SMITH'S *wrists.*]

That'll do.

HOLMES. By the way, Inspector, you might add the attempted murder of one Sherlock Holmes to that charge. Oh, and you'll find a small box in the pocket of your prisoner's coat. Pray, leave it on the table, here. Handle it gingerly, though. It may play its part at his trial.
[MORTON *retrieves the box and places it on the table.*]

SMITH. Trial! You'll be the one in the dock,[13] Holmes. Inspector, he asked me to come here. He was ill, and I was sorry for him, so I came. Now he'll pretend I've said anything he cares to invent that will corroborate[14] his insane

suspicions. Well, you can lie as you like, Holmes. My word's as good as yours.

HOLMES. Good heavens! I'd completely forgotten him!

MORTON. Forgotten who, sir?

HOLMES. Watson, my dear fellow! Do come out!
[WATSON *emerges with cramped groans.*]

I owe you a thousand apologies. To think that I should have overlooked you!

WATSON. It's all right, Holmes. Would have come out before, only you said, whatever happened, I wasn't to budge.

SMITH. What's all this about?

HOLMES. I needn't introduce you to my witness, my friend Dr. Watson. I understand you met somewhat earlier in the evening.

SMITH. You . . . you mean you had all this planned?

HOLMES. Of course. To the last detail. I think I may say it worked very well—with your assistance, of course.

SMITH. Mine?

HOLMES. You saved an invalid trouble by giving my signal to Inspector Morton, waiting outside. You turned up the lamp.
[SMITH *and* WATSON *are equally flabbergasted.*]

MORTON. I'd better take him along now, sir. [*To* SMITH] Come on.
[*He bundles* SMITH *roughly toward the door.*]

We'll see you down at the Yard tomorrow, perhaps, Mr. Holmes?

HOLMES. Very well, Inspector. And many thanks.

WATSON. Goodbye, Inspector.
[MORTON *exits with* SMITH.]

[*Chuckles*]

Well, Holmes?

---

13. **dock** (däk) *n.:* Place where the accused sits or stands in court.
14. **corroborate** (kə räb′ ə rāt′) *v.:* Support; strengthen.

◆ **Build Vocabulary**

irksome (ʉrk′ səm) *adj.:* Tiresome or annoying

HOLMES. Well, Watson, there's a bottle of claret over there—it is uncorked—and some biscuits in the barrel. If you'll be so kind, I'm badly in need of both.
[WATSON *goes to fetch them.*]

WATSON. Certainly. You know, Holmes, all this seems a pretty, well, elaborate way to go about catching that fellow. I mean, taking in Mrs. Hudson—*and me*—like that. Scared us half to death.

HOLMES. It was very essential that I should make Mrs. Hudson believe in my condition. She was to convey it to you, and you to him.

WATSON. Well . . .

HOLMES. Pray do not be offended, my good Watson. You must admit that among your many talents, dissimulation scarcely finds a place. If you'd shared my secret, you would never have been able to impress Smith with the urgent necessity of coming to me. It was the vital point of the whole scheme. I knew his vindictive nature, and I was certain he would come to gloat over his handiwork.
[WATSON *returns with the bottle, glasses and barrel.*]

WATSON. But . . . but your appearance, Holmes. Your face! You really do look ghastly.

HOLMES. Three days of absolute fast does not improve one's beauty, Watson. However, as you know, my habits are irregular, and such a feat means less to me than to most men. For the rest, there is nothing that a sponge won't cure. Vaseline to produce the glistening forehead; belladonna[15] for the watering of the eyes; rouge over the cheekbones and crust of beeswax round one's lips. . . .

WATSON. [*Chuckling*] And that babbling about oysters! [*He begins pouring the wine.*]

◆ **Literature and Your Life**
Holmes explains his scheme here. How would you feel to have tricked Smith this way?

15. **belladonna** (bel ə dän´ ə) *n.:* Poisonous European plant.

HOLMES. Yes. I've sometimes thought of writing a monograph on the subject of malingering.[16]

WATSON. But why wouldn't you let me near you? There was no risk of infection.

HOLMES. Whatever I may have said to the contrary in the grip of delirium, do you imagine that I have no respect for your medical talents? Could I imagine that you would be deceived by a dying man with no rise of pulse or temperature? At four yards' distance I *could* deceive you.
[WATSON *reaches for the box.*]

WATSON. This box, then . . .

HOLMES. No, Watson. I wouldn't touch it. You can just see, if you look at it sideways, where the sharp spring emerges as you open it. I dare say it was by some such device that poor young Savage was done to death. He stood between that monster and an inheritance, you know.

WATSON. Then it's true, Holmes! You . . . you might have been killed, too!

HOLMES. As you know, my correspondence is a varied one. I am somewhat on my guard against any packages which reach me. But I saw that by pretending he had succeeded in his design I might be enabled to surprise a confession from him. That pretense I think I may claim to have carried out with the thoroughness of a true artist.

WATSON. [*Warmly*] You certainly did, Holmes. Er, a biscuit? [*He holds out the barrel.*]

HOLMES. On second thought, Watson, no thank you. Let us preserve our appetite. By the time I have shaved and dressed, I fancy it will just be a nice time for something nutritious at our little place in the Strand.[17]
[*They raise their glasses to one another and drink. The curtain falls.*]

16. **monograph on . . . malingering:** Study on the subject of pretending to be ill in order to avoid work.
17. **the Strand:** London's main shopping and entertainment district; also, the name of a specific street within this district.

Beyond Literature

Science Connection

Catching Criminals With Science

Unlike Sherlock Holmes, who catches Culverton Smith with a clever trick, today's detectives often use scientific evidence. They analyze this evidence with the help of forensic experts, who study the chemical makeup of tiny pieces of material—hair, fabric, or soil, for example—from a crime scene to link it with an accused criminal. They may also evaluate fingerprints, blood, and teeth to help identify crime victims and criminals or to study a victim's body for clues that reveal how a crime was committed.

Cross-Curricular Activity

Can You Make a Match? Two ways in which forensic experts can trace who has been at a crime scene is by matching hair samples and shoe impressions. With a group of classmates, conduct the following experiment. At home or in another classroom, have each group member make an ink print of his or her shoe. Then, work together to match the prints to the shoes that each of you is wearing. Finally, discuss the experience.

Guide for Responding

◆ LITERATURE AND YOUR LIFE

Reader's Response If you were Watson, how would you feel about Holmes at the end of this play? Why?

Thematic Focus Holmes traps a murderer through deception. Why do you think Holmes chose this method for catching Culverton Smith?

List If Culverton Smith didn't visit, the outcome of the story would have changed drastically. With a partner, make a list of the possible outcomes of Holmes's risky trap.

☑ Check Your Comprehension

1. What kind of disease does Holmes claim to have?
2. What reasons does Sherlock Holmes give for not letting Dr. Watson treat him?
3. How does this deception suit Holmes's plan to bring Culverton Smith to justice?
4. What criminal doings does Holmes trick Smith into revealing?
5. What is the real reason that Holmes asks Culverton Smith to turn up the light?

◆ Critical Thinking

INTERPRET

1. Why does Sherlock Holmes make wild statements to Watson about batteries, coins, and oysters? **[Infer]**
2. Why doesn't Holmes tell Watson of his plan for proving Smith a murderer? **[Analyze Cause and Effect]**
3. Explain the importance of Watson's hiding place in Holmes's plot against Smith. **[Interpret]**
4. How do Watson's feelings about Holmes change during the play? **[Connect]**
5. What qualities does Holmes value in his friends? Support your answer. **[Draw Conclusions]**

EVALUATE

6. (a) In what ways is Watson suited to deceiving Smith? (b) In what ways is Watson suited to being deceived by Holmes? **[Assess]**

EXTEND

7. Compare and contrast Holmes's methods to those of modern crime fighters, real or fictional. **[Literature Link; Career Link]**

Guide for Responding (continued)

◆ Reading Strategy

DRAW CONCLUSIONS

As in any other mystery, certain key pieces of information aren't revealed until the end of this play. If you **drew conclusions** by making general statements that the facts of the play could support, you may have solved the mystery before the final scene. For example, Holmes recovers strength every time Watson's actions lead away from the plan. You could use this fact to conclude that the detective is not really dying.

1. (a) List three facts about Holmes's condition that might fool the audience into believing he's ill.
   (b) List one detail that hints he is not truly dying.
2. At what exact moment would an audience understand the true situation?
3. (a) What can you conclude about the relationship between Holmes and Watson? (b) What details support this conclusion?

◆ Build Vocabulary

USING THE SUFFIX -ology

Knowing that -ology means "the study or science of" can help you solve the mystery behind some unfamiliar words. Use the clues provided to define these words. Check a dictionary to adjust your definition.

1. biology (*bio-* means "life")
2. theology (*theo-* means "God")
3. anthropology (*anthropo-* means "human")

SPELLING STRATEGY

When you add the suffix -ing to verbs ending in silent e, drop the e: *implore* + -ing = *imploring*. On your paper, add -ing to each of these verbs:

1. agitate   2. examine   3. disclose   4. balance

USING THE WORD BANK

Identify the word from the Word Bank that has the same meaning as each word or phrase following.

1. beg strongly: _____?_____
2. organized: _____?_____
3. upset: _____?_____
4. annoying: _____?_____
5. concerning disease: _____?_____

◆ Literary Focus

STAGING

In this play, **staging**—the scenery, lighting, sound, special effects, costumes, props, and stage directions—plays a key role in getting you to the edge of your seat. For example, all the action of the play takes place in one room. This increases the suspense because the audience does not know what the characters who leave the room may be saying to each other.

1. Describe the set of "The Dying Detective."
2. How are the bed, window, and box important to the plot?
3. Picture Watson in his hiding place behind the bed. How does this use of staging create suspense?

◆ Build Grammar Skills

INTERJECTIONS

Because they use dialogue, plays often contain **interjections**—words that express feeling and emotion. Interjections function independently of a sentence. Exclamation points often follow interjections, which are also capitalized if they appear at the beginning of a sentence. Interjections can express a variety of emotions—from surprise to pain to disapproval.

Concern: *Dear me!*
Urgency: *No, no!* Keep back!
Hurt: *Oh!* Don't you have any confidence in me?
Surprise: *Good heavens!* I completely forgot him!

Practice Rewrite these sentences. Underline the interjections, and correct punctuation when necessary.

1. Ouch. That box has a sharp spring in it.
2. Oh no. The spring seems to contain poison.
3. Ah, uh, what do we do now?
4. Look. It never actually pricked your skin.
5. Phew. What a close call.

Writing Application Complete each sentence with an interjection that fits the emotion indicated.

1. (joy) You are lucky Smith agreed to come.
2. (surprise) Did you think I'd leave it to chance?
3. (impatience) I knew I could count on you.

Build Your Portfolio

 ## Idea Bank

Writing

1. **Monologue** Without giving away too much of the action, write a speech that Holmes can deliver to the audience at the beginning of the play. Have him give readers or viewers a few clues about the outcome. **[Performing Arts Link]**

2. **Scene** Write a scene that takes place outside Holmes's bedroom, to give viewers at least a few clues to what is really going on. If necessary, invent new characters. **[Performing Arts Link]**

3. **Memo to a Drama Coach** Recall a short story you have recently enjoyed. Write a memo to the drama club coach describing in detail how you would stage the story. Specify sets and props you'd use. **[Art Link]**

Speaking and Listening

4. **Dramatic Scene [Group Activity]** With a few classmates, perform a scene from the play. In rehearsal, discuss how each role should be played, and practice the lines. Design costumes and scenery. **[Performing Arts Link]**

5. **Lawyer's Argument** Present an opening argument at Culverton Smith's trial. Use facts from the play and your own knowledge from movies or television of suspected criminals' rights. Then, outline the strategy you would use to defend—or prosecute—Smith. **[Career Link]**

Projects

6. **Multimedia Biography** Research Sherlock Holmes to learn more about this popular literary character. Tell his life story to the class, using maps, music, or video clips to enhance your presentation. **[Media Link]**

7. **Crime-Solvers' Club [Group Activity]** With a group, gather facts about popular crime solvers from television, books, and movies. Discuss how they solve crimes—with special gadgets or talents, with strength or mental quickness. Share your observations with the class.

 ## Writing Mini-Lesson

Critical Review

Would you recommend "The Dying Detective" to a friend? That is the question a drama critic answers when reviewing a play. Imagine that you have just seen the play performed. Write a critical review in which you identify what worked about the performance and what didn't. Focus on the plot, dialogue, and staging as they appear in the script.

Writing Skills Focus: Language to Evaluate

In a critical review, you express an opinion. **Language to evaluate**—words that praise or criticize—conveys that opinion. Make these words as specific as possible. For example, *splendid* reflects stronger praise than *good*. Use words that show precisely how you feel.

   Mild Dislike: It was *disappointing*.
   Strong Dislike: It was *horrible*.
   Mild Praise: It was *well written*.
   High Praise: It was *brilliant*.

Prewriting Start by making a two-column chart of elements you liked and those you disliked in the written script. Highlight those elements about which you feel most strongly.

Drafting Picture yourself in the emptying theater, just after the show has ended. Describe your reactions to the plot, staging, and acting. You could begin with a feature you loved—or hated. Use evaluating words to make your feelings clear.

> ◆ **Grammar Application**
> Where possible, use interjections like *Wow!* or *No!* to express your reactions to the play. However, avoid using too many of these words.

Revising Reread your review, and identify opinions that are not well supported or don't clearly communicate your feelings. If necessary, add details from the play. Replace general words, like *interesting*, with more precise words, like *suspenseful*.

Guide for Reading

Meet the Authors:

Phillip Hoose

Phillip Hoose was inspired to write about people making a difference in their communities. The energy and compassion he saw led him to write *It's Our World, Too,* a collection of essays about young people working to help others. "Justin Lebo" comes from that book.

Naomi Shihab Nye (1952–   )

As a teenager, Naomi Shihab Nye probably felt the loneliness she discusses in her poem. Her family moved from its home in St. Louis, Missouri, to Jerusalem, Israel, when she was fourteen. While Nye now values the chance to learn about her Arab heritage, the move wasn't easy. Nye's poems often focus on such real-life experiences—what she calls "true things."

Piri Thomas (1928–   )

Reading Piri Thomas's autobiography, *Down These Mean Streets,* you know that growing up in New York City's Spanish Harlem was a challenge. Like the boys he creates in "Amigo Brothers," Thomas had to overcome the problems of his surroundings. The road was bumpy before Thomas "dreamt positive."

Thomas Hardy (1840–1928)

Thomas Hardy lived during the Victorian Era, a time when writers spun stories of morals, manners, and money. Hardy, considered to be the greatest novelist of his time, was buried in London's Westminster Abbey when he died.

◆ LITERATURE AND YOUR LIFE

CONNECT YOUR EXPERIENCE

Sometimes your energy overflows. You think of exciting projects and feel sure you can conquer any challenge. What happens, though, when solving one problem creates another? That is what the characters in "Amigo Brothers" and "Justin Lebo" face.

THEMATIC FOCUS: Finding Solutions

The characters in these selections confront loneliness, isolation, and boredom—problems that face many of us at one time or another. As you read, notice how they solve the problems that might limit freedom.

◆ Background for Understanding

SPORTS

"Amigo Brothers" is the story of two teenage boxers with championship dreams. Competing against each other, they both want to represent their club in the annual Golden Gloves tournament. In this tournament—probably the most famous amateur boxing event in the United States—local and regional elimination bouts lead to the final championship matches.

◆ Build Vocabulary

PREFIXES: *re-*

Justin Lebo *realigns* the wheels of his bikes. If you know that *aligns* means "puts in line" and that the prefix *re-* means "again," you can easily determine the meaning of this word.

WORD BANK

Which of these words from the selections might refer to a group working toward a common goal? What word clue helps you decide?

realign
yield
coalition
devastating
superimposed
perpetual
dispelled
evading

Justin Lebo ◆ The Rider
Amigo Brothers ◆ The Walk

◆ Literary Focus

THIRD-PERSON POINT OF VIEW

Point of view refers to the angle or position from which a writer tells a story. When using a **third-person point of view,** a writer or narrator stands outside the action to describe it. From this position, the narrator gives you information about characters that even they don't know. Narrators in "Amigo Brothers" and "Justin Lebo" tell you about the thoughts, feelings, and actions of many people. As you read, look for details that only the third-person point of view could provide.

◆ Reading Strategy

MAKE INFERENCES

When you **make inferences**—guesses based on evidence—you supply information an author omits. Making inferences allows you to get a fuller understanding of the people and situations writers present. For example, since Justin Lebo loves to fix bikes, you can infer that he has mechanical ability. As you read, use an organizer like this one to record key details and to make inferences based on each detail.

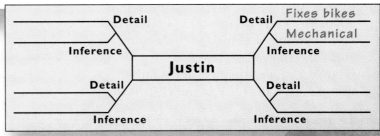

JUSTIN LEBO

Phillip Hoose

Something about the battered old bicycle at the garage sale caught ten-year-old Justin Lebo's eye. What a wreck! It was like looking at a few big bones in the dust and trying to figure out what kind of dinosaur they had once belonged to.

It was a BMX bike with a twenty-inch frame. Its original color was buried beneath five or six coats of gunky paint. Now it showed up as sort of a rusted red. Everything—the grips, the pedals, the brakes, the seat, the spokes—was bent or broken, twisted and rusted. Justin stood back as if he were inspecting a painting for sale at an auction. Then he made his final judgment: perfect.

Justin talked the owner down to $6.50 and asked his mother, Diane, to help him load the bike into the back of their car.

When he got it home, he wheeled the junker into the garage and showed it proudly to his father. "Will you help me fix it up?" he asked. Justin's hobby was bike racing, a passion the two of them shared. Their garage barely had room for the car anymore. It was more like a bike shop. Tires and frames hung from hooks on the ceiling, and bike wrenches dangled from the walls.

At every race, Justin and his father would adjust the brakes and realign the wheels of his two racing bikes. This was a lot of work, since Justin raced flat out, challenging every gear and part to perform to its fullest. He had learned to handle almost every repair his father could and maybe even a few things he couldn't. When Justin got really stuck, he went to see Mel, the owner of the best bike shop in town. Mel let him hang out and watch, and he even grunted a few syllables of advice from between the spokes of a wheel now and then.

Now Justin and his father cleared out a work space in the garage and put the old junker up on a rack. They poured alcohol on the frame and rubbed until the old paint began to yield, layer by layer. They replaced the broken pedal, tightened down a new seat, and restored the grips. In about a week, it looked brand new.

◆ Build Vocabulary

realign (rē´ ə līn´) v.: Readjust into a straight line or into proper coordination

yield (yēld) v.: Give way to pressure or force

▲ **Critical Viewing** Like the father and son in this photograph, Justin and his father fix bicycles together. How might such a hobby bring two people together? [**Connect**]

Justin wheeled it out of the garage, leapt aboard, and started off around the block. He stood up and mashed down on the pedals, straining for speed. It was a good, steady ride, but not much of a thrill compared to his racers.

Soon he forgot about the bike. But the very next week, he bought another junker at a yard sale and fixed it up, too. After a while it bothered him that he wasn't really using either bike. Then he realized that what he loved about the old bikes wasn't riding them: it was the challenge of making something new and useful out of something old and broken.

Justin wondered what he should do with them. They were just taking up space in the garage. He remembered that when he was younger, he used to live near a large brick building called the Kilbarchan Home for Boys. It was a place

for boys whose parents couldn't care for them for one reason or another.

He found "Kilbarchan" in the phone book and called the director, who said the boys would be thrilled to get two bicycles. The next day when Justin and his mother unloaded the bikes at the home, two boys raced out to greet them. They leapt aboard the bikes and started tooling around the semicircular driveway, doing wheelies and pirouettes, laughing and shouting.

The Lebos watched them for a while, then started to climb into their car to go home. The boys cried after them, "Wait a minute! You forgot your bikes!" Justin explained that the bikes were for them to keep. "They were so happy," Justin remembers. "It was like they couldn't believe it. It made me feel good to see them happy."

On the way home, Justin was silent. His mother assumed he was lost in a feeling of satisfaction. But he was thinking about what would happen once those bikes got wheeled inside and everyone saw them.

How would all those kids decide who got the bikes? Two bikes could cause more trouble than they would solve. Actually, they hadn't been that hard to build. It was fun. Maybe he could do more. . . .

"Mom," Justin said as they turned onto their street, "I've got an idea. I'm going to make a bike for every boy at Kilbarchan for Christmas." Diane Lebo looked at Justin out of the corner of her eye. She had rarely seen him so determined.

When they got home, Justin called Kilbarchan to find out how many boys lived there. There were twenty-one. It was already June. He had six months to make nineteen bikes. That was almost a bike a week. Justin called the home back to tell them of his plan. "I could tell they didn't think I could do it," Justin remembers. "I knew I could."

Justin knew his best chance was to build bikes almost the way GM or Ford builds cars: in an assembly line. He would start with frames from three-speed, twenty-four-inch BMX bicycles. They were common bikes, and all the parts were interchangeable. If he could find enough decent frames, he could take parts off broken bikes and fasten them onto the good frames. He figured it would take three or four junkers to produce enough parts to make one good bike. That meant sixty to eighty bikes. Where would he get them?

Garage sales seemed to be the only hope. It was June, and there would be garage sales all summer long. But even if he could find that many bikes, how could he ever pay for them? That was hundreds of dollars.

He went to his parents with a proposal. "When Justin was younger, say five or six," says his mother, "he used to give some of his allowance away to help others in need. His father and I would donate a dollar for every dollar Justin donated. So he asked us if it could be like the old days, if we'd match every dollar he put into buying old bikes. We said yes."

Justin and his mother spent most of June and July hunting for cheap bikes at garage sales and thrift shops. They would haul the bikes home, and Justin would start stripping them down in the yard.

But by the beginning of August, he had managed to make only ten bikes. Summer vacation was almost over, and school and homework would soon cut into his time. Garage sales would dry up when it got colder, and Justin was out of money. Still, he was determined to find a way.

At the end of August, Justin got a break. A neighbor wrote a letter to the local newspaper describing Justin's project, and an editor thought it would make a good story. One day a reporter entered the Lebo garage. Stepping gingerly through the tires and frames that covered the floor, she found a boy with cut fingers and dirty nails, banging a seat onto a frame. His clothes were covered with grease. In her admiring article about a boy who was devoting his summer to help kids he didn't even know, she said Justin needed bikes and money, and she printed his home phone number.

Overnight, everything changed. "There must have been a hundred calls," Justin says. "People would call me up and ask me to come over and pick up their old bike. Or I'd be working in the garage, and a station wagon would pull up. The driver

Bicycles, Robert Vickrey, 32 1/2" x 46" © Robert Vickrey/Licensed by VAGA, New York, NY

▲ **Critical Viewing** How does the mood of this photograph compare with the mood at the Kilbarchan Home when Justin brings his bicycles? [**Compare and Contrast**]

would leave a couple of bikes by the curb. It just snowballed."

By the start of school, the garage was overflowing with BMX frames. Pyramids of pedals and seats rose in the corners. Soon bike parts filled a toolshed in the backyard and then spilled out into the small yard itself, wearing away the lawn.

More and more writers and television and radio reporters called for interviews. Each time he told his story, Justin asked for bikes and money. "The first few interviews were fun," Justin says, "but it reached a point where I really didn't like

doing them. The publicity was necessary, though. I had to keep doing interviews to get the donations I needed."

By the time school opened, he was working on ten bikes at a time. There were so many calls now that he was beginning to refuse offers that weren't the exact bikes he needed.

As checks came pouring in, Justin's money problems disappeared. He set up a bank account and began to make bulk orders of common parts from Mel's bike shop. Mel seemed delighted to see him. Sometimes, if Justin brought a bike by the shop, Mel would help him fix it. When Justin tried to talk him into a lower price for big orders, Mel smiled and gave in. He respected another good businessman. They became friends.

The week before Christmas Justin delivered the last of the twenty-one bikes to Kilbarchan. Once again, the boys poured out of the home and leapt aboard the bikes, tearing around the snow.

And once again, their joy inspired Justin. They reminded him how important bikes were to him. Wheels meant freedom. He thought how much more the freedom to ride must mean to boys like these who had so little freedom in their lives. He decided to keep on building.

"First I made eleven bikes for the children in a foster home my mother told me about. Then I made bikes for all the women in a battered women's shelter. Then I made ten little bikes and tricycles for the kids in a home for children with AIDS. Then I made twenty-three bikes for the Paterson Housing Coalition."

In the four years since he started, Justin Lebo has made between 150 and 200 bikes and given them all away. He has been careful to leave time for his homework, his friends, his coin collection, his new interest in marine biology, and of course his own bikes.

Reporters and interviewers have asked Justin Lebo the same question over and over: "Why do you do it?" The question seems to make him uncomfortable. It's as if they want him to say what a great person he is. Their stories always make him seem like a saint, which he knows he isn't. "Sure it's nice of me to make the bikes," he says, "because I don't have to. But I want to. In part, I do it for myself. I don't think you can ever really do anything to help anybody else if it doesn't make you happy.

"Once I overheard a kid who got one of my bikes say, 'A bike is like a book; it opens up a whole new world.' That's how I feel, too. It made me happy to know that kid felt that way. That's why I do it."

◆ **Build Vocabulary**

coalition (kō′ ə lish′ ən) *n.*: Association or organization formed for a specific purpose

Beyond Literature

Community Connection

Making a Difference Justin Lebo isn't the only young person to help others, finding personal satisfaction through the process. In communities across the nation, people volunteer and improve the lives of others. Some volunteering opportunities can be found through organizations—serving food in a soup kitchen, working with a group to teach adults to read, or joining others to build houses for those who might not otherwise be able to afford them. In contrast, some volunteering opportunities are not organized: People may bring home groceries for their elderly neighbors, or a few adults might get together to help a mother of triplets manage her newborns.

Cross-Curricular Activity
Community Project In discussion with a group, identify some problems in your community. Consider the environment, housing, or the condition of public spaces, for example. Talk with parents and teachers to find out what problems residents may have already identified. After choosing an issue, look for ways that your group can get involved. Make your plans as specific as possible. With your teacher's help, offer your help to an appropriate organization.

The Rider
Naomi Shihab Nye

◆ LITERATURE AND YOUR LIFE

Reader's Response What does riding a bicycle mean to you? Explain.

Thematic Focus How do bicycles help Justin Lebo and the speaker of "The Rider" to solve problems?

Journal Writing What skills could you share, as Justin Lebo shares his mechanical abilities? In a journal entry, describe the talents you have that could help others.

☑ **Check Your Comprehension**

1. What special talent does Justin Lebo have?
2. How does he use his talent to help the boys at Kilbarchan?
3. What obstacles must Justin overcome to accomplish his plan?
4. In the first stanza of "The Rider," against whom or what is the boy racing?
5. What is the speaker of the poem doing?

A boy told me
if he rollerskated fast enough
his loneliness couldn't catch up to him,

the best reason I ever heard
5   for trying to be a champion.

What I wonder tonight
pedaling hard down King William Street
is if it translates to bicycles.

A victory! To leave your loneliness
10   panting behind you on some
        street corner
while you float free into a cloud
        of sudden azaleas,
luminous pink petals that have
        never felt loneliness,
no matter how slowly they fell.

▲ **Critical Viewing** What details of this photograph convey the feelings the poem describes? **[Analyze]**

◆ **Critical Thinking**

INTERPRET

1. Find two examples that show Justin Lebo likes a challenge. **[Connect]**
2. In accomplishing his goal, how does Justin give inspiration to others and receive it from them? **[Analyze Cause and Effect]**
3. What does Justin learn from his project? **[Draw Conclusions]**
4. What words in "The Rider" help communicate the idea of freedom? **[Support]**
5. What do the two activities described in "The Rider" have in common? **[Compare]**

APPLY

6. What are some ways in which the speaker of "The Rider" could help others? **[Apply]**

COMPARE LITERARY WORKS

7. Do you think Justin Lebo would agree with the ideas presented in "The Rider"? Why or why not? **[Connect]**

Amigo Brothers

Piri Thomas

Antonio Cruz and Felix Vargas were both seventeen years old. They were so together in friendship that they felt themselves to be brothers. They had known each other since childhood, growing up on the lower east side of Manhattan in the same tenement building on Fifth Street between Avenue A and Avenue B.

Antonio was fair, lean, and lanky, while Felix was dark, short, and husky. Antonio's hair was always falling over his eyes, while Felix wore his black hair in a natural Afro style.

Each youngster had a dream of someday becoming lightweight champion of the world. Every chance they had the boys worked out, sometimes at the Boys Club on 10th Street and Avenue A and sometimes at the pro's gym on 14th Street. Early morning sunrises would find them running along the East River Drive, wrapped in sweat shirts, short towels around their necks, and handkerchiefs Apache style around their foreheads.

While some youngsters were into street negatives, Antonio and Felix slept, ate, rapped, and dreamt positive. Between them, they had a collection of *Fight* magazines second to none, plus a scrapbook filled with torn tickets to every boxing match they had ever attended, and some clippings of their own. If asked a question about any given fighter, they would immediately zip out from their memory banks divisions, weights, records of fights, knock-outs,

◆ **Literary Focus**
Who is telling this story? How can you tell?

technical knock-outs,[1] and draws or losses.

Each had fought many bouts representing their community and had won two gold-plated medals plus a silver and bronze medallion. The difference was in their style. Antonio's lean form and long reach made him the better boxer, while Felix's short and muscular frame made him the better slugger. Whenever they had met in the ring for sparring sessions, it had always been hot and heavy.

Now, after a series of elimination bouts,[2] they had been informed that they were to meet each other in the division finals that were scheduled

---

1. **technical knock-outs:** Occasions when a fight is stopped because one of the fighters is too hurt to continue, even though he is on his feet.
2. **elimination bouts:** Matches in which only the winners go on to fight in other matches.

for the seventh of August, two weeks away—the winner to represent the Boys Club in the Golden Gloves Championship Tournament.

The two boys continued to run together along the East River Drive. But even when joking with each other, they both sensed a wall rising between them.

One morning less than a week before their bout, they met as usual for their daily workout. They fooled around with a few jabs at the air, slapped skin, and then took off, running lightly along the dirty East River's edge.

Antonio glanced at Felix who kept his eyes purposely straight ahead, pausing from time to time to do some fancy leg work while throwing one-twos followed by upper cuts to an imaginary jaw. Antonio then beat the air with a barrage of body blows and short <u>devastating</u> lefts with an overhand jaw-breaking right. After a mile or so, Felix puffed and said, "Let's stop a while, bro. I think

we both got something to say to each other." Antonio nodded. It was not natural to be acting as though nothing unusual was happening when two ace-boon buddies were going to be blasting each other within a few short days.

They rested their elbows on the railing separating them from the river. Antonio wiped his face with his short towel. The sunrise was now creating day.

Felix leaned heavily on the river's railing and stared across to the shores of Brooklyn. Finally, he broke the silence.

"Man, I don't know how to come out with it."

Antonio helped. "It's about our fight, right?"

"Yeah, right." Felix's eyes squinted at the rising orange sun.

"I've been thinking about it too, *panín*. In fact, since we found out it was going to be me and you, I've been awake at night, pulling punches on you, trying not to hurt you."

"Same here. It ain't natural not to think about the fight. I mean, we both are *cheverote* fighters and we both want to win. But only one of us can win. There ain't no draws in the eliminations."

Felix tapped Antonio gently on the shoulder. "I don't mean to sound like I'm bragging, bro. But I wanna win, fair and square."

◆ **Reading Strategy**
What can you infer about Felix and Antonio's relationship from this conversation?

Antonio nodded quietly. "Yeah. We both know that in the ring the better man wins. Friend or no friend, brother or no . . ."

Felix finished it for him. "Brother. Tony, let's promise something right here. Okay?"

"If it's fair, *hermano*, I'm for it." Antonio admired the courage of a tugboat pulling a barge five times its welterweight size.

◆ **Build Vocabulary**
devastating (dev´ əs tāt´ iŋ) *adj.*: Destructive; overwhelming

◀ **Critical Viewing** Felix and Antonio box against each other in "Amigo Brothers." What does the protective gear in this photograph suggest about boxing? [Analyze Cause and Effect]

The loudspeakers blared into the open windows of the school. There were speeches by dignitaries, community leaders, and great boxers of yesteryear. Some were well prepared, some improvised on the spot. They all carried the same message of great pleasure and honor at being part of such a historic event. This great day was in the tradition of champions emerging from the streets of the lower east side.

Interwoven with the speeches were the sounds of the other boxing events. After the sixth bout, Felix was much relieved when his trainer Charlie said, "Time change. Quick knock-out. This is it. We're on."

Waiting time was over. Felix was escorted from the classroom by a dozen fans in white T-shirts with the word FELIX across their fronts.

Antonio was escorted down a different stairwell and guided through a roped-off path.

As the two climbed into the ring, the crowd exploded with a roar. Antonio and Felix both bowed gracefully and then raised their arms in acknowledgment.

Antonio tried to be cool, but even as the roar was in its first birth, he turned slowly to meet Felix's eyes looking directly into his. Felix nodded his head and Antonio responded. And both as one, just as quickly, turned away to face his own corner.

Bong—bong—bong. The roar turned to stillness.

"Ladies and Gentlemen. *Señores y Señoras.*"

The announcer spoke slowly, pleased at his bilingual efforts.

"Now the moment we have all been waiting for—the main event between two fine young Puerto Rican fighters, products of our lower east side. In this corner, weighing 134 pounds, Felix Vargas. And in this corner, weighing 133 pounds, Antonio Cruz. The winner will represent the Boys Club in the tournament of champions, the Golden Gloves. There will be no draw. May the best man win."

The cheering of the crowd shook the window panes of the old buildings surrounding Tompkins Square Park. At the center of the ring, the referee was giving instructions to the youngsters. "Keep your punches up. No low blows. No punching on the back of the head. Keep your heads up. Understand. Let's have a clean fight. Now shake hands and come out fighting."

Both youngsters touched gloves and nodded. They turned and danced quickly to their corners. Their head towels and dressing gowns were lifted neatly from their shoulders by their trainers' nimble fingers. Antonio crossed himself. Felix did the same.

BONG! BONG! ROUND ONE. Felix and Antonio turned and faced each other squarely in a fighting pose. Felix wasted no time. He came in fast, head low, half hunched toward his right shoulder, and lashed out with a straight left. He missed a right cross as Antonio slipped the punch and countered with one-two-three lefts that snapped Felix's head back, sending a mild shock coursing through him. If Felix had any small doubt about their friendship affecting their fight, it was being neatly dispelled.

◆ Literary Focus
How does the narrator help you learn about the announcer?

▲ Critical Viewing In boxing matches, as in many other sporting events, competitors wear contrasting colors. Why do you think this is true? [Hypothesize]

Antonio danced, a joy to behold. His left hand was like a piston pumping jabs one right after another with seeming ease. Felix bobbed and weaved and never stopped boring in. He knew that at long range he was at a disadvantage. Antonio had too much reach on him. Only by coming in close could Felix hope to achieve the dreamed-of knockout.

Antonio knew the dynamite that was stored in his *amigo* brother's fist. He ducked a short right and missed a left hook. Felix trapped him against the ropes just long enough to pour some punishing rights and lefts to Antonio's hard midsection. Antonio slipped away from Felix, crashing two lefts to his head, which set Felix's right ear to ringing.

Bong! Both *amigos* froze a punch well on its way, sending up a roar of approval for good sportsmanship.

Felix walked briskly back to his corner. His right ear had not stopped ringing. Antonio gracefully danced his way toward his stool none the worse, except for glowing glove burns, showing angry red against the whiteness of his midribs.

"Watch that right, Tony." His trainer talked into his ear. "Remember Felix always goes to the body. He'll want you to drop your hands for his overhand left or right. Got it?"

♦ **Build Vocabulary**

dispelled (dis peld´) *v.*: Driven away; made to disappear

Antonio nodded, spraying water out between his teeth. He felt better as his sore midsection was being firmly rubbed.

Felix's corner was also busy.

"You gotta get in there, fella." Felix's trainer poured water over his curly Afro locks. "Get in there or he's gonna chop you up from way back."

Bong! Bong! Round two. Felix was off his stool and rushed Antonio like a bull, sending a hard right to his head. Beads of water exploded from Antonio's long hair.

Antonio, hurt, sent back a blurring barrage of lefts and rights that only meant pain to Felix, who returned with a short left to the head followed by a looping right to the body. Antonio countered with his own flurry, forcing Felix to give ground. But not for long.

Felix bobbed and weaved, bobbed and weaved, occasionally punching his two gloves together.

Antonio waited for the rush that was sure to come. Felix closed in and feinted[4] with his left shoulder and threw his right instead. Lights suddenly exploded inside Felix's head as Antonio slipped the blow and hit him with a piston-like left catching him flush on the point of his chin. Bedlam[5] broke loose as Felix's legs momentarily buckled. He fought off a series of rights and lefts and came back with a strong right that taught Antonio respect.

Antonio danced in carefully. He knew Felix had the habit of playing possum when hurt, to

4. **feinted** (fānt´ əd) *v.*: Pretended to make a blow.
5. **Bedlam** (bed´ ləm) *n.*: Condition of noise and confusion.

sucker an opponent within reach of the powerful bombs he carried in each fist.

A right to the head slowed Antonio's pretty dancing. He answered with his own left at Felix's right eye that began puffing up within three seconds.

Antonio, a bit too eager, moved in too close and Felix had him entangled into a rip-roaring, punching toe-to-toe slugfest that brought the whole Tompkins Square Park screaming to its feet.

Rights to the body. Lefts to the head. Neither fighter was giving an inch. Suddenly a short right caught Antonio squarely on the chin. His long legs turned to jelly and his arms flailed out desperately. Felix, grunting like a bull, threw wild punches from every direction. Antonio, groggy, bobbed and weaved, evading most of the blows. Suddenly his head cleared. His left flashed out hard and straight catching Felix on the bridge of his nose.

◆ **Reading Strategy**
What do the fierce fighting efforts of Antonio and Felix tell you about their feelings?

Felix lashed back with a haymaker,[6] right off the ghetto streets. At the same instant, his eye caught another left hook from Antonio. Felix swung out trying to clear the pain. Only the frenzied screaming of those along ringside let him know that he had dropped Antonio. Fighting off the growing haze, Antonio struggled to his feet, got up, ducked, and threw a smashing right that dropped Felix flat on his back.

Felix got up as fast as he could in his own corner, groggy but still game. He didn't even hear the count. In a fog, he heard the roaring of the crowd, who seemed to have gone insane. His head cleared to hear the bell sound at the end of the round. He was very glad. His trainer sat him down on the stool.

In his corner, Antonio was doing what all fighters do when they are hurt. They sit and smile at everyone.

The referee signaled the ring doctor to check the fighters out. He did so and then gave his okay. The cold water sponges brought clarity to both *amigo* brothers. They were rubbed until their circulation ran free.

Bong! Round three—the final round. Up to now it had been tic-tac-toe, pretty much even. But everyone knew there could be no draw and this round would decide the winner.

This time, to Felix's surprise, it was Antonio who came out fast, charging across the ring. Felix braced himself but couldn't ward off the barrage of punches. Antonio drove Felix hard against the ropes.

The crowd ate it up. Thus far the two had fought with *mucho corazón.* Felix tapped his gloves and commenced his attack anew. Antonio, throwing boxer's caution to the winds, jumped in to meet him.

Both pounded away. Neither gave an inch and neither fell to the canvas. Felix's left eye was tightly closed. Claret red blood poured from Antonio's nose. They fought toe-to-toe.

The sounds of their blows were loud in contrast to the silence of a crowd gone completely mute. The referee was stunned by their savagery.

Bong! Bong! Bong! The bell sounded over and over again. Felix and Antonio were past hearing. Their blows continued to pound on each other like hailstones.

Finally the referee and the two trainers pried Felix and Antonio apart. Cold water was poured over them to bring them back to their senses.

They looked around and then rushed toward each other. A cry of alarm surged through Tompkins Square Park. Was this a fight to the death instead of a boxing match?

The fear soon gave way to wave upon wave of cheering as the two *amigos* embraced.

No matter what the decision, they knew they would always be champions to each other.

BONG! BONG! BONG! "Ladies and Gentlemen. *Señores* and *Señoras.* The winner and representative to the Golden Gloves Tournament of Champions is . . ."

The announcer turned to point to the winner and found himself alone. Arm in arm the champions had already left the ring.

◆ **Build Vocabulary**

evading (ē vād′ iŋ) *adj.*: Keeping away from or avoiding

---

6. **haymaker:** Punch thrown with full force.

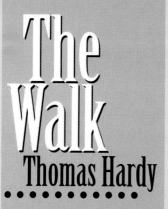

The Walk
Thomas Hardy

You did not walk with me
Of late to the hilltop tree
    By the gated ways,
    As in earlier days;
5   You were weak and lame,
So you never came,
And I went alone, and I did not mind,
Not thinking of you as left behind.

    I walked up there today
10   Just in the former way;
    Surveyed[1] around
    The familiar ground
    By myself again:
    What difference, then?
15 Only that underlying sense
Of the look of a room on returning thence.

---

1. **surveyed** (sər vād′) *v*.: Looked at in a careful and thorough way.

*G*uide for Responding

◆ LITERATURE AND YOUR LIFE

Reader's Response How do you feel when you have to be separated from a friend for a time? Explain.

Thematic Focus Antonio thinks that at the fight, he and Felix should imagine they're strangers. In what other ways might he solve this problem?

Discussion What might have happened had the fight ended differently? With a small group, discuss the connection between "The Walk" and such an ending.

☑ Check Your Comprehension

1. What dream do the boys share?
2. What event creates a wall between them?
3. What agreement do they make while jogging?
4. Describe the way the boys leave the ring at the end of the fight.
5. Why is the speaker of "The Walk" alone?

◆ Critical Thinking

INTERPRET

1. Why is boxing so important to Antonio and Felix? **[Infer]**
2. Why do the boys decide not to see each other until the fight? **[Interpret]**
3. How does their relationship both help and hurt the boys during the fight? **[Analyze]**
4. What do the boys discover they value as much as or more than winning? **[Draw Conclusions]**
5. Why is the event described in "The Walk" different from the way it used to be? **[Interpret]**
6. How does the speaker of "The Walk" feel about this change? **[Infer]**

APPLY

7. What lesson from "Amigo Brothers" could you apply to your own life? Explain. **[Apply]**

COMPARE LITERARY WORKS

8. What advice would the speaker of "The Walk" give to the boys of "Amigo Brothers"? Explain. **[Speculate; Connect]**

Guide for Responding (continued)

◆ Reading Strategy

MAKE INFERENCES

When you **make inferences,** you use the information the writers tell you to draw conclusions about details that are left out. This strategy helps you more fully understand the characters in the literature you read.

1. (a) Describe Justin Lebo's relationship with Mel.
   (b) What inferences about Justin can you make based on this relationship?
2. What can you infer about the speaker of "The Rider"?
3. (a) How do the boys in "Amigo Brothers" feel about their neighborhood? (b) What details help you answer?
4. What do you learn about the relationship between the speaker and the person being addressed in "The Walk"?

◆ Build Vocabulary

USING THE PREFIX *re-*

The prefix *re-* means "again." Use these words in sentences to demonstrate each word's meaning.

1. review   3. renew   5. reappear
2. recall   4. recycle   6. reheat

SPELLING STRATEGY

In most cases, you do not use a hyphen when adding the prefix *re-* to a word: *realign* not *re-align.* On your paper, add *re-* to the following words:

1. paint 2. live 3. build 4. new 5. act 6. enter

USING THE WORD BANK

On your paper, match the word on the left with its definition on the right.

1. realign   a. put on top of something
2. yield   b. made to disappear
3. coalition   c. adjust so the parts work together
4. devastating   d. avoiding
5. superimposed   e. give way to pressure
6. perpetual   f. group formed for a common goal
7. dispelled   g. overwhelming; damaging
8. evading   h. never stopping

◆ Literary Focus

THIRD-PERSON POINT OF VIEW

When a writer uses the **third-person point of view,** the narrator speaks from outside the events to communicate the thoughts, feelings, and actions of many different characters. Characters are referred to by name or as "he" or "she." This point of view lets writers provide details you'd miss if one of the characters narrated the story. For example, you couldn't know how both boys in "Amigo Brothers" feel if either one of them were telling the story.

1. Justin Lebo is silent as he and his mom drive away from Kilbarchan for the first time. (a) What does his mother think about this silence? (b) What is Justin thinking?
2. In what ways would "Amigo Brothers" be different if Felix or Anthony told the story?

◆ Build Grammar Skills

COORDINATING CONJUNCTIONS

Coordinating conjunctions —including *and, but, for, nor, or, so,* and *yet*—connect words of a similar kind. They can also connect larger groups of words, such as phrases or even entire sentences. In these examples, the coordinating conjunctions are circled. The words they connect are italicized.

Nouns: Everyone could view the fight, whether from *ringside* or *fire escapes* or *rooftops.*

Verbs: Mel let him *hang out* and *watch.*

Prepositional Phrases: He stored bicycles *in the garage* and *on the driveway.*

Practice On your paper, circle the coordinating conjunction in each sentence. Then, underline the words or phrases connected by the conjunction.

1. Which do you prefer, bicycling or roller skating?
2. Odds were against him, but Justin wouldn't quit.
3. The two friends had to fight each other, so they decided to stay apart until the big day.
4. Before and after the fight, they were friends.
5. Justin used old or new parts.

Writing Application Write a paragraph summarizing one of the selections. In it, use and identify three different coordinating conjunctions.

Build Your Portfolio

 ## Idea Bank

Writing

1. **Journal Entry** Imagine that you're one of the "Amigo Brothers." In a journal entry, describe your thoughts and feelings when you discover that you will fight your best friend.

2. **Citizenship Award** Using Justin Lebo's actions as a model, create the criteria for a student citizenship award. Consider the achievements or personal characteristics a person would need in order to win. **[Social Studies Link]**

3. **Comparison-and-Contrast Essay** Compare and contrast two characters from the selections presented here. For example, you might consider comparing Felix to Justin Lebo. In an essay, identify the character's similarities and differences.

Speaking and Listening

4. **School Interviews** Interview classmates who do something to make a difference or who have displayed a special skill. Learn about their accomplishments, and gather advice for other students. Share your findings with the class.

5. **How-to Fair [Group Activity]** Justin Lebo uses his talents to help his community. The people in "The Rider" help themselves through physical activity. Organize a fair in which students demonstrate their skills. Each presenter should explain how his or her talent could help other members of the community. **[Social Studies Link]**

Projects

6. **Community Participation** The "Amigo Brothers" made use of a Boys Club program. Find out about organizations that offer activities for young people in your area. Describe the programs in a list for the class.

7. **Flowchart** Justin Lebo modeled his small business on the big-business ideas of a very successful man. Research the ideas of Henry Ford, and create a flowchart that outlines his assembly-line process.

 ## Writing Mini-Lesson

Volunteering Handbook

Justin Lebo worked by himself, but your classmates might prefer to join an organization that helps others. To help others choose the group that works best for them, research and write a handbook of volunteer opportunities. Include basic information about each organization.

Writing Skills Focus: Address Your Audience

You are writing for classmates, not Wall Street investors. It is important to **keep your audience in mind** and to choose information that readers can use. Consider these tips:
- Include material to help readers make a wise decision. A group's policies about teen volunteers is more useful than its policies on charitable contributions.
- Use language your audience will understand.
- Avoid overly technical information.

Prewriting Gather organizations from library or other sources and through your guidance counselor. For each organization you find interesting, record the name, address, phone number, volunteer requirements, goals, and projects in process.

Drafting Arrange the entries alphabetically or by topic. List the same information about every entry, in the same order. For each entry, briefly explain the appeal to your audience.

◆ **Grammar Application**
Combine short, choppy sentences gracefully using coordinating conjunctions.

Revising Read your handbook to make sure that entries contain the necessary facts. Double-check that entries are chosen and written for an audience of young volunteers. If necessary, replace "grown-up" entries like a driving service for older residents with "kid friendly" entries like a park cleanup group.

Persuasive Essay

Writing Process Workshop

Persuasion is everywhere. Commercials persuade us to buy new products. Billboards persuade us to see new films. Politicians give speeches to persuade voters to elect them to office. In a **persuasive essay,** a writer attempts to persuade an audience to take action or to think a certain way. The following skills, introduced in the Writing Mini-Lessons, will help you write an effective persuasive essay.

Writing Skills Focus

▶ **Use language to evaluate**—words that praise or criticize—to convey your opinions precisely. (See p. 341.)

▶ **Address your audience.** Make sure your word choices, tone, and style are suitable for the person or people for whom you are writing. (See p. 361.)

▶ **Provide facts and examples to support your opinions.**

After reading the essay "Justin Lebo," one writer decided to persuade other young people to do something to make others happy.

MODEL

Sure, the residents of Montello Manor were born many years before we were, but most of them are lively, funny, and interested in the same things we are. ① They just need someone to be with. ② They love to tell stories, but they need someone who will listen. Many of them have trouble seeing well enough to read, but they love to be read to. They also enjoy walking in the gardens outside and playing cards and board games. You could help them write a letter or tape-record a memory for their family. ③

① Evaluative words like *lively* and *funny* show the writer's positive evaluation of the residents.

② This sentence is an opinion, which the writer supports with examples.

③ The essay's informal tone is appropriate for an audience of teenagers.

Prewriting

Choose a Cause With a partner, discuss actions that you might want to persuade others to take. Consider national and local issues, and choose a topic that's important to you. Then, identify your position. Here are some suggestions to get you started:

Topic Ideas
- Volunteerism
- Endangered species
- Required military service

Make a Plan Organize your ideas by creating an outline, a web, or other type of plan for your essay. Here's an example:

```
I. Introduction
        A. Montello Manor
        B. Mrs. Campbell
O  II. The Residents
        A. Need social interaction
        B. Examples of activities
                1. reading
                2. playing games
                3. going for walks
   III. The Rewards
        A. Personal satisfaction
        B. Lasting friendships
        C. Experience for future jobs
   IV. Conclusion
        A. Statistics about Montello Manor
O       B. Quotation by Mrs. Campbell
```

Drafting

Use Emotion, Reason, or Both As you write your essay, keep in mind the "angle" that will best suit your audience. Here are some different types of appeals you might use:

TYPE OF APPEAL	EXAMPLE
Feelings and Emotions	Imagine being old, lonely, and confined to one place.
Sense of Right and Wrong	Helping others is the right thing to do.
Self-Interest	You can learn a lot from an older person.

APPLYING LANGUAGE SKILLS: Connotations

If you look up a word in a dictionary, you find its denotation. **Denotation** is the exact meaning (or meanings) of a word. However, words also create feelings and associations, called **connotations.** Although some pairs of words mean basically the same thing, some words have positive connotations and others have negative connotations.

Positive	Negative
mellow	lazy
joking	mocking
assertive	bossy

Practice From each pair in parentheses, choose the word with the positive connotation.

1. These hats are (cheap, inexpensive).
2. My uncle is (clever, conniving).
3. The music was (calming, boring).
4. My little sister is (active, wild).

Writing Application Pay close attention to the connotations of the words you choose for your persuasive essay.

Writer's Solution Connection Writing Lab

To learn more about distinguishing fact from opinion, see the Prewriting section in the tutorial on Persuasion.

APPLYING LANGUAGE SKILLS: Frequently Confused Words

Some words are frequently confused with other words that sound similar or are related in meaning. Here are some examples:

Accept is a verb that means *to receive* or *to agree to.*

Except is a preposition that means *other than* or *leaving out.*

Among is used with three or more items.

Between is used with only two items.

Can refers to the ability to do something.

May refers to having permission to do something.

Practice Correct the commonly confused words in these sentences.

1. Can I bring flowers when I visit?

2. Bill excepted my birthday card.

3. Let's keep this secret between the three of us.

Writing Application As you write your persuasive essay, be careful to use the correct word.

Writer's Solution Connection Language Lab

For more help with revision, use the Revision Checkers in the tutorial on Persuasion.

Appeal to Your Audience Use words that your audience will know. If you're writing for teenagers, your language should be informal and fun. If you're writing to a government official, your language should be formal and serious.

Present One Opinion; Many Facts The point you are trying to make is your opinion. It's the only opinion that should appear in your essay. The rest of your essay should contain facts: details, statistics, evidence, or descriptions. Facts will make your case strong and persuade your audience.

Revising

Use a Checklist Use a checklist to help you determine places that need revision. Your checklist might include these questions:
- ▶ Are the words I use appropriate for my audience?
- ▶ Would I be convinced by this essay?
- ▶ Are my opinions supported by facts, statistics, and examples?

REVISION MODEL

① *protect the places where these nearly extinct birds live*

It is important that we take measures to ~~conserve the~~

~~remaining habitats of these endangered species.~~ This

② *fascinating*

can help preserve these ~~interesting~~ and unusual birds

for future generations.

① The writer simplified this phrase so it was better suited for the intended audience.
② Stronger language of evaluation reveals how the writer feels.

Publishing and Presenting

▶ **Give a Speech** Like written essays, persuasive speeches are delivered to motivate the audience to take up an action or change their opinions. Deliver your essay as a speech. Use gestures, tone, and volume to make your point dramatic and clear.

▶ **Spread the Word** Most newspapers will publish well-written persuasive essays if they appeal to the newspaper's audience. Submit your essay to a school, local, or big-city newspaper, and see what happens.

Strategies for Success

Language can be very powerful. Some words are meant to strike the reader or listener as funny, inspirational, or hurtful. Certain words, chosen for their power, can cause strong reactions. Recognizing when such *charged words* are being used helps you better understand why they are being used.

Be on the Lookout Charged words are often used as attention-getters. This is especially true in advertising. Words or phrases like *big savings, going fast,* and *act now* are used to grab your attention. It's important to be able to tell the difference between words that are just trying to hook your interest and those that give important information.

Distinguish Between Fact and Opinion A fact is a statement that can be proved: *The mayor raised taxes.* However, when a charged word is added, a basic fact becomes an opinion—something that reveals beliefs or attitudes and that cannot be proved. *The mayor sneakily raised taxes.* In this revised sentence, the word *sneakily* shows that the writer has an opinion about the mayor's action.

Don't Be Tricked by Stereotypes Charged words are often used to label an entire group of individuals. In these cases, the charged words create stereotypes and prevent the reader or listener from getting a true picture. Charged words can be hurtful when they are used unfairly to label people.

Apply the Strategies

Read the poster below. Then, answer the questions that follow.

Stop Night Swimming!

The public pool should be closed at night. Rowdy teenagers cannot be trusted to swim safely. They make too much noise and never follow rules. Join smart people who want to stop nighttime swimming.

1. Identify the charged words used on the poster.
2. Why do you think these charged words are being used?
3. How much of what is on the poster do you think is fact? How much is opinion?
4. Rewrite the poster without using charged words.

✔ Here are some other places where charged words may show up:
 ▶ Newspaper editorials
 ▶ Political advertisements
 ▶ Letters to the editor of a newspaper or magazine

An **interjection** is a word or phrase that expresses emotion and has no grammatical relation to the rest of the words in a sentence. (See page 340.) Use an exclamation point after an interjection that expresses strong feeling; use a comma after one that expresses mild emotion.

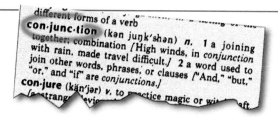

different forms of a verb
con·junc·tion (kən juŋk′shən) *n.* 1 a joining together; combination /High winds, in conjunction with rain, made travel difficult./ 2 a word used to join other words, phrases, or clauses /"And," "but," "or," and "if" are conjunctions./
con·jure (kän′jər) *v.* to ~~practice~~ magic or wi~~tchcraft~~

Emotion	Strength of Emotion	Example
Agreement	Mild	*Yes,* I would like to go with you.
Excitement	Strong	*Wow!* Look at all this stuff.
Alarm	Mild	*Uh, oh,* I think those boxes are falling.
Urgency	Strong	*Hey!* Watch out!
Concern	Strong	*Goodness!* Are you okay?
Relief	Strong	*Whew!* I'm glad we didn't break anything.

A **conjunction** is a word that links two or more words or groups of words. **Coordinating conjunctions**—including *and, but, for, nor, or, so,* and *yet*—connect words of a similar kind. They can also connect phrases, clauses, or entire sentences. (See page 360.)

Practice 1 Copy these sentences. Circle each interjection. Underline each conjunction, and identify the words, phrases, or clauses each connects.

1. Holmes is both clever and a good actor.

2. He pretended to be dying so the murderer would confess.

3. Well, I was amazed and inspired by Justin, but I had to wonder what his friends thought about his bike project.

4. After fighting their boxing match, Felix and Anthony remained good friends.

5. No, I don't think the speaker in "The Walk" will change his habits or visit his friend.

Practice 2 Rewrite each of the following pairs of sentences as a single sentence, following the directions given in parentheses.

1. Ellen loves mysteries. She reads them often. (*Add a coordinating conjunction.*)

2. Holmes wanted to trap a killer. Holmes wanted to avoid hurting Watson. (*Add a coordinating conjunction.*)

3. Are you listening to me? Are you ignoring me? (*Add an interjection and a coordinating conjunction.*)

Grammar in Writing

✔ *Even when writing dialogue, avoid overusing interjections. Using them too often lessens their dramatic impact and can be annoying.*

Disagreement can be healthy. If everyone always agreed, we'd never have new ideas. When a disagreement turns to confrontation, however, it's time to think carefully about how you listen and speak. Try to take the anger out of the situation.

Listen Actively Sometimes we think we know what someone is going to say. We hear a few words, stop listening, and begin planning what we're going to say next. Break this dangerous habit. Instead, make sure you understand what someone really means before you respond. Ask questions to get him or her to explain. Ask for examples, if that will help.

This is the first step in handling a potential confrontation—trying to avoid it in the first place. People like to be heard. Even when you disagree, if you give the speaker respect in listening, you can have a healthy disagreement, not a confrontation.

Use "I" When you speak or respond, say things you can be certain of: what *you* think and feel. In other words, don't say, "You're wrong!" but say, "I still don't understand why that's important to you," or even, "I can't agree." Name-calling and blaming just make people emotional. The real point gets lost.

Seek Common Ground Find ways to be on the same side. If a conflict arises out of an athletic competition, for example, remember that both sides love the game. Make sure to tell the other person whenever you agree with something he or she is saying.

Apply the Strategies

As a group, share stories of confrontations you have witnessed—in real life, in books, or in movies. Choose three of those confrontations to evaluate. Discuss the following:

1. What was the disagreement?
2. Why did the disagreement escalate into a confrontation?
3. How was the confrontation resolved?
4. What should or could have been done differently?

Tips for Handling a Confrontational Situation

✔ *If you want to keep your cool during a tense situation, use these strategies:*

▶ The best response to an insult can be a shrug. It helps defuse the situation and shows your strength or confidence.
▶ If you feel yourself getting angry, take a deep breath and be still for a few seconds.
▶ If all else fails, walk away. You can return to express your feelings when you are calmer.

What's Behind the Words

Vocabulary Adventures With Richard Lederer

The Sports Origins of Common Phrases

A teacher once asked a student, "What's a metaphor?" The student answered, "For cows to eat grass in." Well . . . actually, a metaphor (met-uh-for) is a figure of speech that compares one thing to another, blending ideas in creative ways. Did you know that you speak in metaphors every day?

The metaphors that are common in a culture tell us a lot. With many of the expressions we use every day, we honor the prominent place of sports in our society.

Take Me Out to the Ballgame

In the early days of the twentieth century, a college professor explained, "To understand America, you must first understand baseball." Baseball is not only America's pastime but the most popular athletic metaphor in the American language. Right off the bat, we bat around a few ideas and then go to bat for someone. If we don't touch base with others, we may find ourselves way off base or not able to get to first base.

Please don't think me a screwball who's out in left field with two strikes against me. I'm playing vocabulary hardball here, and I call 'em as I see 'em. And what I see are ballpark figures (of speech) like *in there pitching, bush league operation, major league performance, play the field, a smash hit, safe by a mile, take a rain check, hit and run,* and *pinch-hit for somebody.*

Sportspeak

Here are the origins of some sporty words and expressions that have moved into our general vocabulary:

To hold the line comes from the game of football, while *up for grabs* derives from the jump ball in basketball.

A *kingpin* is the number-one pin in bowling, the one that stands in front of all the others. Hit correctly, it causes all the other pins to fall. That's why we also use the word *kingpin* to refer to the most critical person—the leader or the chief—in a business or project.

No holds barred, meaning "without restriction," originates from wrestling matches, in which no holds were disallowed, producing a wild, unstructured contest.

When we say *this is where I draw the line,* we lay down a definite limit. The phrase started in tennis. When the sport was first introduced in the fourteenth century, there were no exact dimensions for the court, so players drew lines and agreed that the ball couldn't be hit beyond those lines.

ACTIVITY 1 Identify the sport from which each of these phrases comes.
1. saved by the bell
2. behind the eight ball
3. hit the bullseye
4. the ball's in your court
5. below par
6. take the bull by the horns

Extended Reading Opportunities

Trouble—and someone's response to it—can reveal a person's character, culture, and creativity. Explore the imaginative ways that the characters in these novels solve their troubles.

Suggested Titles

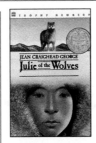

The Adventures of Tom Sawyer
Mark Twain

In this classic tale of a boyhood in nineteenth-century Mississippi, you'll follow Tom Sawyer as he plays pranks and gets caught up in one adventure after another. Tom is full of energy and a natural leader among his friends. His life seems charmed, until he witnesses a murder one night. Knowing his life is in danger, he runs away from home. Yet Tom's luck holds as he plays pirate on a deserted island, attends his own funeral, and even steals the murderer's treasure.

Julie of the Wolves
Jean Craighead George

At the age of thirteen, Julie leaves her home village in Alaska to travel on her own to San Francisco. When she gets lost in the wilderness, she has to rely on wolves—animals she has befriended—to help her survive. In one scene, all the wolves join together to fight a bear. While hiking through the cold landscape, Julie must decide what truly matters to her. This thrilling adventure story of her struggle will have you on the edge of your seat!

Words by Heart
Ouida Sebestyen

In this moving novel of a twelve-year-old girl's struggle with racism, you'll see how conflict can challenge personal actions and beliefs. Lena wants to win a contest at school, but when she does, someone plunges a butcher knife into the family's kitchen table. Suddenly, Lena wonders if she has overstepped the bounds set for her as the only African American girl in a small town. The knife's implied threat is only the beginning, and Lena must solve the problem of how to confront her enemy—with vengeance or forgiveness.

Other Possibilities

The Kid's Guide to Service Projects	Barbara A. Lewis
What I Had Was Singing: The Story of Marian Anderson	Jeri Ferris
One Proud Summer	Marsha Hewitt and Claire McKay
Profiles in Courage	John F. Kennedy

Snap the Whip, Winslow Homer, Butler Institute of American Art,
Youngstown, Ohio

Just for Fun

Words have the power to spark emotion—fear, sadness, surprise—even anger. In this unit, you'll find literature to make you laugh. You'll meet an unusual cat, a stubborn child, and a curious shopkeeper. The behavior of each of these quirky characters produces amusing results. Read on to see how the most common activities can be funny when they are seen through the eyes of a writer with a sense of humor.

Guide for Reading

Meet the Author:

Charles Osgood (1933–)

As a reporter, Charles Osgood has covered such serious topics as politics, the economy, and war. However, lighter subjects and everyday experiences interest him most. In addition to the formal news pieces he writes for radio and television, his special broadcasts —called *Newsbreak* and *The Osgood File*—highlight his unique, humorous slant on life. Osgood may be best known for his rhyming commentaries that poke fun at current events. For example, he once wrote in rhyme, "We've all really had it with trouble and woe. And if those things exist, why, we don't want to know."

Man of the Media Born before television came into people's homes, Osgood grew up loving radio. He eventually got a job announcing the Army Band during his years in the service. From professional radio work, Osgood moved into television, becoming the anchor on the *CBS Evening News* in 1972. When Charles Kuralt retired as anchor of the CBS news program *Sunday Morning* in 1994, Osgood's style earned him the job as the new anchor.

THE STORY BEHIND THE ESSAY

Osgood usually covers news stories—describing the *who, what, where, when, how,* and *why* of events. In "Our Finest Hour," he turns the reporter's lens on himself to describe a chaotic newscast he once anchored.

◆ LITERATURE AND YOUR LIFE

CONNECT YOUR EXPERIENCE

At one time or another, you've probably had a carefully planned event turn into a disaster. Just imagine what it would be like to have such an experience on live television in front of millions of viewers. This is the type of situation that Osgood describes in his essay about a newscast that went terribly wrong.

THEMATIC FOCUS: Just For Fun

This essay shows you that you can have fun even when a simple plan goes completely wrong.

◆ Background for Understanding

MEDIA

The people who report the news may seem relaxed, but because their work is broadcast live, they are actually under a great deal of pressure. The newsroom buzzes with activity until the broadcast is over. When a story changes, copy is written and rewritten until the moment it is read. Teleprompters roll scripts as the anchors read. Pre-recorded stories are cued, waiting for precisely the right moment before the tapes roll. Earphones allow directors and producers to communicate with the anchors even during the broadcast. Since this all happens live, anchors must handle any mistakes—mispronunciations, incorrect graphics, technical difficulties with live interviews, or even more unexpected disasters—as they occur.

◆ Our Finest Hour ◆

◆ Literary Focus

HUMOR

Humor is writing that is meant to evoke laughter. One of the best ways to create humor is to describe real-life bloopers and blunders. In this essay, for example, Charles Osgood recounts a disastrous live newscast in which just about everything goes wrong. While the situation he describes is clearly funny to readers, Osgood takes a subtle approach. He never admits that the events he endured were humorous. Indeed, he probably did not find them humorous until later.

◆ Build Vocabulary

SUFFIXES: -ment

Charles Osgood admits his bewilderment in the face of disaster. The word *bewilderment* contains the suffix *-ment*, meaning "the condition of." When combined with *bewilder*, meaning "to confuse or perplex," the suffix *-ment* produces the word *bewilderment*, meaning "the condition of confusion."

WORD BANK

Which of these words from the essay names a person who contributes stories to the news?

correspondent
bewilderment

Reading for Success

Strategies for Reading Critically

Some people think that being critical is the same as being negative. However, being a critical reader doesn't mean that you necessarily respond negatively to what you read. It means that you take the time to analyze carefully what you read and to consider how effectively an author has put together a piece of writing.

Understand the author's bias.

▶ Recognize that writers often present an issue through their own bias—their unique perspective on a subject. Look for details that might reveal a writer's opinion. Use what you know about the writer's background and knowledge. For example, each of the people shown in the chart below might describe a disastrous newscast differently.

A writer's bias influences the details he or she presents. Keep this in mind as you read—you might be getting only half the story.

Recognize the author's purpose.

▶ Authors generally write to achieve a purpose, such as the following:
• to entertain • to inform • to call to action • to reflect on experiences
Notice the author's choice of words and the details he or she includes. These clues will help you determine an author's purpose.

Evaluate the author's message.

▶ When you evaluate an author's message, you make a judgment about how effectively the writer has proved his or her point. First, identify the writer's message. Then, look to see whether this message has been supported. Also, consider whether the writer is qualified to write on a subject.

Distinguish fact from opinion.

▶ It's important to distinguish facts from opinions.
Fact: A statement that can be proved true by consulting a reliable source.
Opinion: A belief that is based on a writer's attitude or values.
Writers should back up their opinions with facts, not simply cite a series of opinions without any support.

As you read this essay by Charles Osgood, look at the notes along the sides. The notes demonstrate how to apply these strategies to a work of literature.

MODEL

Our Finest Hour

Charles Osgood

Only occasionally do most reporters or correspondents get to "anchor" a news broadcast. Anchoring, you understand, means sitting there in the studio and telling some stories into the camera and introducing the reports and pieces that other reporters do. It looks easy enough. It is easy enough, most of the time . . .

It was back when I was relatively new at CBS News. I'd been in the business a while, but only recently had moved over to CBS News. I was old, but I was new. It was a Saturday night and I was filling in for Roger Mudd[1] on the *CBS Evening News.* Roger was on vacation. The regular executive producer[2] of the broadcast, Paul Greenberg, was on vacation, too.

> Comical repetition of the word *regular* indicates Osgood's purpose—to entertain.

And so was the regular cameraman and the regular editor and the regular director. Somewhere along the line we had one too many substitutes that night.

I said "Good evening" and introduced the first report and turned to the monitor to watch it. What I saw was myself looking at the monitor. Many seconds passed. Finally there was something on the screen. A reporter was beginning a story. It was not the story I had introduced. Instead, it was a different story by a different reporter. This was supposed to be the second item in the newscast. So I shuffled my script around and made the first piece second and the second piece first. When I came back on camera, I explained what it was we had seen and reintroduced the first piece. Again there was a long, awkward pause. I shuffled my

papers. I scribbled on the script. I turned to the monitor. Finally, the floor director, who was filling in for the regular floor director, cued me to go on. So I introduced the next report. It didn't come up either, so I said we'd continue in just a moment. Obvious cue for a commercial, I thought, but it took a while to register in the control room. When a commercial did come up, there was a frantic scramble in the studio to reorganize what was left of the broadcast. But by now everything had come undone.

> It is a **fact** that a commercial was shown. It is an **opinion** that the studio became frantic.

When the commercial was over, I introduced a piece from Washington. What came up was a series of pictures of people who seemed to be dead. One man was slumped over a car wheel. Two or three people were lying in the middle of the street. Another man was propped up against the wall of the building, his eyes staring vacantly into space. Then came the voice of Peter Kalisher. "This was the town where everyone died," he said. I knew nothing whatsoever about this piece. It was not scheduled for the broadcast. Peter Kalisher was in Paris as far as I knew. But there had been nothing on the news wires about everybody in Paris having died. In the "fishbowl," the glassed-in office where the executive producer sits, there were at least three people yelling into telephones. Nobody in there knew anything about this piece either. The story was

> The **author's bias** as anchor influences the way he describes the "fishbowl."

---

1. **Roger Mudd:** *CBS News* reporter from 1961 to 1980. He was a backup anchorperson for Walter Cronkite during the time of this story.
2. **executive producer:** Person responsible for the quality of the newscast.

◆ **Build Vocabulary**

correspondent (kôr′ ə spän′ dənt) *n.*: Person hired by a news organization to provide news from a distant place

Our Finest Hour ◆ 375

Guide for Reading

Meet the Author:

James Herriot (1916–1995)

At the early age of 24, James Herriot became a trained veterinarian. However, it wasn't until he was in his fifties that he combined his two loves—animals and writing—into the first of his books, *All Creatures Great and Small.* This work served as the basis for a television series.

Dual Dedication Herriot was so dedicated to both of his passions that he never even took a day off at Christmas. At the time he was writing, British veterinarians were not allowed to advertise, so although he was born James Alfred Wight, he adopted the pen name of James Herriot. This allowed him to publish accounts of his experiences.

Herriot continued his veterinary practice into his seventies, splitting his time between treating his animal patients and signing autographs for his many fans.

THE STORY BEHIND THE ESSAY

Herriot's books—written directly from his experience—are widely known for their lively descriptions of characters he met, both animal and human. "Cat on the Go," from his book *All Things Wise and Wonderful*, describes an unforgettable cat that he and his wife adopted.

◆ LITERATURE AND YOUR LIFE

CONNECT YOUR EXPERIENCE

If you've ever had a pet or have interacted with someone else's pet, you know that animals have distinctive personalities. Some pets can even perform tricks or behave in ways that will amaze you. In this story, you'll meet Oscar, a very unusual cat with a surprising habit.

THEMATIC FOCUS: Quirky Characters

As you read about this cat's adventures, notice how his strange behavior charms most of the people he meets.

◆ Background for Understanding

SCIENCE

James Herriot's veterinary practice gave him endless material for his writing. Veterinarians have a strong scientific education and complete a four-year postgraduate program before becoming licensed. Usually, they specialize in either small animals, such as house pets, or large animals, such as horses and farm animals. Like doctors, veterinarians sometimes have to perform surgery to save an animal's life. Through medical advances, veterinarians now have access to sophisticated equipment and a wide range of medicines. As you'll discover, the medicine and equipment available at the time of the story wasn't so advanced.

◆ Build Vocabulary

PREFIXES: *in-*

In this story, an infection seems *inevitable*. *Evitable* means "avoidable." When the prefix *in-* meaning "not" is added, it creates "inevitable," meaning "not avoidable."

WORD BANK

Which of these words from the story might you use to describe an action that is completed in a disgusting way?

grotesquely
emaciated
inevitable
sauntered
distraught
despondent
intrigued
surreptitiously

◆ Cat on the Go ◆

Happy Cat, Christian Pierre

◆ Literary Focus

CHARACTER TRAITS

Character traits are the qualities that make a person, or even an animal, an individual. For example, one person may seem calm; another, excitable. One person may be musical; another, athletic. It is these character traits that determine how each person behaves and interacts with others.

Use a chart like the one below to record the traits of each real-life person and animal in Herriot's essay.

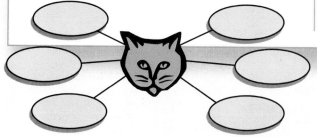

◆ Reading Strategy

UNDERSTAND BIAS

Just like the characters in a literary work, every writer has unique personality traits that contribute to that writer's **bias**—the knowledge and interest that a writer brings to a subject. You can see bias through the author's choice of words. For example, Herriot describes the cat's fur as "auburn and copper-gold," not plain brown. From this choice of words, you can tell that he thinks this is a special cat. As you read, look for more evidence of bias. Think about how Herriot's bias affects the way information is presented and the way you respond to it.

Cat on the Go

James Herriot

One winter evening Tristan shouted up the stairs from the passage far below.

"Jim! Jim!"

I went out and stuck my head over the bannisters. "What is it, Triss?"

"Sorry to bother you, Jim, but could you come down for a minute?" The upturned face had an anxious look.

I went down the long flights of steps two at a time and when I arrived slightly breathless on the ground floor Tristan beckoned me through to the consulting room at the back of the house. A teenage girl was standing by the table, her hand resting on a stained roll of blanket.

"It's a cat," Tristan said. He pulled back a fold of the blanket and I looked down at a large, deeply striped tabby. At least he would have been large if he had had any flesh on his bones, but ribs and pelvis stood out painfully through the fur and as I passed my hand over the motionless body I could feel only a thin covering of skin.

Tristan cleared his throat. "There's something else, Jim."

▶ **Critical Viewing** What human emotions does the cat in this photograph seem to convey? Explain your response. [Speculate]

I looked at him curiously. For once he didn't seem to have a joke in him. I watched as he gently lifted one of the cat's hind legs and rolled the abdomen into view. There was a gash on the ventral surface[1] through

_____

1. **ventral** (ven´ trəl) **surface:** Surface near or on the belly.

which a coiled cluster of intestines spilled grotesquely onto the cloth. I was still shocked and staring when the girl spoke.

"I saw this cat sittin' in the dark, down Brown's yard. I thought 'e looked skinny, like, and a bit quiet and I bent down to give 'im a pat. Then I saw 'e was badly hurt and I went home for a blanket and brought 'im round to you."

"That was kind of you," I said. "Have you any idea who he belongs to?"

The girl shook her head. "No, he looks like a stray to me."

"He does indeed." I dragged my eyes away from the terrible wound. "You're Marjorie Simpson, aren't you?"

"Yes."

"I know your Dad well. He's our postman."

"That's right." She gave a half smile then her lips trembled.

"Well, I reckon I'd better leave 'im with you. You'll be going to put him out of his misery. There's nothing anybody can do about . . . about that?"

I shrugged and shook my head. The girl's eyes filled with tears, she stretched out a hand and touched the emaciated animal then turned and walked quickly to the door.

"Thanks again, Marjorie," I called after the retreating back. "And don't worry—we'll look after him."

In the silence that followed, Tristan and I looked down at the shattered animal. Under the surgery lamp it was all too easy to see. He had almost been disemboweled[2] and the pile of intestines was covered in dirt and mud.

"What d'you think did this?" Tristan said at length. "Has he been run over?"

"Maybe," I replied. "Could be anything. An attack by a big dog or somebody could have kicked him or struck him." All things were possible with cats because some people seemed to regard them as fair game for any cruelty.

Tristan nodded. "Anyway, whatever happened, he must have been on the verge of starvation. He's a skeleton. I bet he's wandered

miles from home."

"Ah well," I sighed. "There's only one thing to do. Those guts are perforated in several places. It's hopeless."

Tristan didn't say anything but he whistled under his breath and drew the tip of his forefinger again and again across the furry cheek. And, unbelievably, from somewhere in the scraggy chest a gentle purring arose.

The young man looked at me, round eyed. "My God, do you hear that?"

"Yes . . . amazing in that condition. He's a good-natured cat."

Tristan, head bowed, continued his stroking. I knew how he felt because, although he preserved a cheerfully hard-boiled attitude to our patients he couldn't kid me about one thing: he had a soft spot for cats. Even now, when we are both around the sixty mark, he often talks to me about the cat he has had for many years. It is a typical relationship— they tease each other unmercifully—but it is based on real affection.

"It's no good, Triss," I said gently. "It's got to be done." I reached for the syringe but something in me rebelled against plunging a needle into that mutilated body. Instead I pulled a fold of the blanket over the cat's head.

"Pour a little ether onto the cloth," I said. "He'll just sleep away."

Wordlessly, Tristan unscrewed the cap of the ether bottle and poised it above the head. Then from under the shapeless heap of blanket we heard it again: the deep purring which increased in volume till it boomed in our ears like a distant motorcycle.

Tristan was like a man turned to stone, hand gripping the bottle rigidly, eyes staring

◆ **Literary Focus**
Both men believe the situation is hopeless, yet they operate anyway. What character traits does this decision reveal?

---

2. **disemboweled** (dis´ im bou´ əld) v.: Lost its intestines.

◆ **Build Vocabulary**
grotesquely (grō tesk´ le) adv.: In a strange or distorted way

emaciated (ē mā´ shē āt´ id) adj.: Extremely thin; starving

down at the mound of cloth from which the purring rose in waves of warm friendly sound.

At last he looked up at me and gulped. "I don't fancy this much, Jim. Can't we do something?"

"You mean, put that lot back?"

"Yes."

"But the bowels are damaged—they're like a sieve in parts."

"We could stitch them, couldn't we?"

I lifted the blanket and looked again. "Honestly, Triss, I wouldn't know where to start. And the whole thing is filthy."

He didn't say anything, but continued to look at me steadily. And I didn't need much persuading. I had no more desire to pour ether onto that comradely purring than he had.

"Come on, then," I said. "We'll have a go."

With the oxygen bubbling and the cat's head in the anesthetic mask we washed the whole prolapse[3] with warm saline.[4] We did it again and again but it was impossible to remove every fragment of caked dirt. Then we started the painfully slow business of stitching the many holes in the tiny intestines, and here I was glad of Tristan's nimble fingers which seemed better able to manipulate the small round-bodied needles than mine.

Two hours and yards of catgut[5] later, we dusted the patched up peritoneal[6] surface with sulfanilamide[7] and pushed the entire mass back into the abdomen. When I had sutured muscle layers and skin everything looked tidy but I had a nasty feeling of sweeping undesirable things under the carpet. The extensive damage, all that contamination—peritonitis[8] was <u>inevitable</u>.

---

3. **prolapse** (prō´ laps) *n.*: Internal organ—here, the intestines—that has fallen out of place.
4. **saline** (sā´ lĭn) *n.*: Salt solution.
5. **catgut** (kat´ gut´) *n.*: Tough string or thread used in surgery.
6. **peritoneal** (per´ i tō nē´ əl) *adj.*: Having to do with the membrane that lines the abdomen.
7. **sulfanilamide** (sul´ fə nil´ ə mĭd) *n.*: Sulfa drugs were used to treat infections before penicillin and other antibiotics were discovered.
8. **peritonitis** (per´ i tō nīt´ is) *n.*: Inflammation of the abdominal lining.

"He's alive, anyway, Triss," I said as we began to wash the instruments. "We'll put him onto sulfapyridine and keep our fingers crossed." There were still no antibiotics at that time but the new drug was a big advance.

The door opened and Helen came in. "You've been a long time, Jim." She walked over to the table and looked down at the sleeping cat. "What a poor skinny little thing. He's all bones."

"You should have seen him when he came in." Tristan switched off the sterilizer and screwed shut the valve on the anesthetic machine. "He looks a lot better now."

She stroked the little animal for a moment. "Is he badly injured?"

"I'm afraid so, Helen," I said. "We've done our best for him but I honestly don't think he has much chance."

"What a shame. And he's pretty, too. Four white feet and all those unusual colors." With her finger she traced the faint bands of auburn and copper-gold among the gray and black.

Tristan laughed. "Yes, I think that chap has a ginger Tom somewhere in his ancestry."

Helen smiled, too, but absently, and I noticed a broody look about her. She hurried out to the stock room and returned with an empty box.

"Yes . . . yes . . ." she said thoughtfully. "I can make a bed in this box for him and he'll sleep in our room, Jim."

"He will?"

"Yes, he must be warm, mustn't he?"

"Of course."

Later, in the darkness of our bed-sitter,[9] I looked from my pillow at a cozy scene. Sam in his basket on one side of the flickering fire and the cat cushioned and blanketed in his box on the other.

As I floated off into sleep it was good to know that my patient was so comfortable, but I wondered if he would be alive in the morning. . . .

◆ **Reading Strategy**
How does this passage reveal the author's bias toward cats?

---

9. **bed-sitter:** British term for a one-room apartment.

I knew he was alive at 7:30 a.m. because my wife was already up and talking to him. I trailed across the room in my pajamas and the cat and I looked at each other. I rubbed him under the chin and he opened his mouth in a rusty miaow. But he didn't try to move.

"Helen," I said. "This little thing is tied together inside with catgut. He'll have to live on fluids for a week and even then he probably won't make it. If he stays up here you'll be spooning milk into him umpteen times a day."

"Okay, okay." She had that broody look again.

It wasn't only milk she spooned into him over the next few days. Beef essence, strained broth and a succession of sophisticated baby foods found their way down his throat at regular intervals. One lunch time I found Helen kneeling by the box.

"We shall call him Oscar," she said.

"You mean we're keeping him?"

"Yes."

I am fond of cats but we already had a dog in our cramped quarters and I could see difficulties. Still I decided to let it go.

"Why Oscar?"

"I don't know." Helen tipped a few drops of chop gravy onto the little red tongue and watched intently as he swallowed.

One of the things I like about women is their mystery, the unfathomable part of them, and I didn't press the matter further. But I was pleased at the way things were going. I had been giving the sulfapyridine every six hours and taking the temperature night and morning, expecting all the time to encounter the roaring fever, the vomiting and the tense abdomen of peritonitis. But it never happened.

It was as though Oscar's animal instinct told him he had to move as little as possible because he lay absolutely still day after day and looked up at us—and purred.

His purr became part of our lives and when he eventually left his bed, sauntered through to our kitchen and began to sample Sam's dinner of meat and biscuit it was a moment of triumph. And I didn't spoil it by wondering if he was ready for solid food; I felt he knew.

From then on it was sheer joy to watch the furry scarecrow fill out and grow strong, and as he ate and ate and the flesh spread over his bones the true beauty of his coat showed in the glossy medley of auburn, black and gold. We had a handsome cat on our hands.

Once Oscar had fully recovered, Tristan was a regular visitor.

He probably felt, and rightly, that he, more than I, had saved Oscar's life in the first place and he used to play with him for long periods. His favorite ploy was to push his leg round the corner of the table and withdraw it repeatedly just as the cat pawed at it.

Oscar was justifiably irritated by this teasing but showed his character by lying in wait for Tristan one night and biting him smartly[10] in the ankle before he could start his tricks.

From my own point of view Oscar added many things to our menage.[11] Sam was delighted with him and the two soon became firm friends. Helen adored him and each evening I thought afresh that a nice cat washing his face by the hearth gave extra comfort to a room.

Oscar had been established as one of the family for several weeks when I came in from a late call to find Helen waiting for me with a stricken face.

"What's happened?" I asked.

"It's Oscar—he's gone!"

"Gone? What do you mean?"

"Oh, Jim, I think he's run away."

I stared at her. "He wouldn't do that. He often goes down to the garden at night. Are you sure he isn't there?"

◆ Build Vocabulary

inevitable (in evʹ ə tə bəl) *adj.*: Certain to happen

sauntered (sônʹ tərd) *v.*: Strolled

---

10. **smartly** (smartʹ lē) *adv.*: Sharply.
11. **menage** (mā näzhʹ) *n.*: Household.

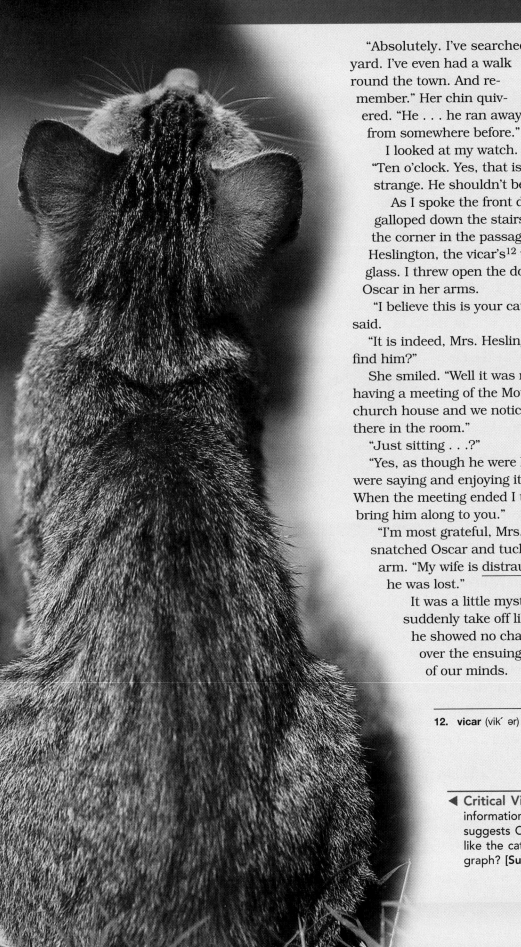

"Absolutely. I've searched right into the yard. I've even had a walk round the town. And remember." Her chin quivered. "He . . . he ran away from somewhere before."

I looked at my watch. "Ten o'clock. Yes, that is strange. He shouldn't be out at this time."

◆ Literary Focus
What character traits are revealed by Helen's quivering chin?

As I spoke the front door bell jangled. I galloped down the stairs and as I rounded the corner in the passage I could see Mrs. Heslington, the vicar's[12] wife, through the glass. I threw open the door. She was holding Oscar in her arms.

"I believe this is your cat, Mr. Herriot," she said.

"It is indeed, Mrs. Heslington. Where did you find him?"

She smiled. "Well it was rather odd. We were having a meeting of the Mothers' Union at the church house and we noticed the cat sitting there in the room."

"Just sitting . . .?"

"Yes, as though he were listening to what we were saying and enjoying it all. It was unusual. When the meeting ended I thought I'd better bring him along to you."

"I'm most grateful, Mrs. Heslington." I snatched Oscar and tucked him under my arm. "My wife is distraught—she thought he was lost."

It was a little mystery. Why should he suddenly take off like that? But since he showed no change in his manner over the ensuing week we put it out of our minds.

---

12. **vicar** (vik´ ər) *n.*: Parish priest.

◀ Critical Viewing What information in the essay suggests Oscar might look like the cat in this photograph? [Support]

Then one evening a man brought in a dog for a distemper[13] inoculation and left the front door open. When I went up to our flat I found that Oscar had disappeared again. This time Helen and I scoured the marketplace and side alleys in vain and when we returned at half past nine we were both despondent. It was nearly eleven and we were thinking of bed when the doorbell rang.

It was Oscar again, this time resting on the ample stomach of Jack Newbould. Jack was a gardener at one of the big houses. He hiccuped gently and gave me a huge benevolent smile. "Brought your cat, Mr. Herriot."

"Gosh, thanks, Jack!" I said, scooping up Oscar gratefully. "Where the devil did you find him?"

"Well, s'matter o' fact 'e sort of found me."

"What do you mean?"

Jack closed his eyes for a few moments before articulating carefully. "Thish is a big night, tha knows, Mr. Herriot. Darts championship. Lots of t'lads round at t'Dog and Gun—lotsh and lotsh of 'em. Big gatherin'."

"And our cat was there?"

"Aye, he were there, all right. Sitting among t'lads. Shpent t'whole evenin' with us."

"Just sat there, eh?"

"That 'e did." Jack giggled reminiscently. "By gaw 'e enjoyed 'isself. Ah gave 'em a drop out of me own glass and once or twice ah thought 'e was going to have a go at chuckin' a dart. He's some cat." He laughed again.

As I bore Oscar upstairs I was deep in thought. What was going on here? These sudden desertions were upsetting Helen and I felt they could get on my nerves in time.

I didn't have long to wait till the next one. Three nights later he was missing again. This time Helen

◆ **Literary Focus**
What can you tell about Oscar's personality from his actions?

and I didn't bother to search—we just waited.

He was back earlier than usual. I heard the door bell at nine o'clock. It was the elderly Miss Simpson peering through the glass. And she wasn't holding Oscar—he was prowling on the mat waiting to come in.

Miss Simpson watched with interest as the cat stalked inside and made for the stairs. "Ah, good, I'm so glad he's come home safely. I knew he was your cat and I've been intrigued by his behavior all evening."

"Where . . . may I ask?"

"Oh, at the Women's Institute. He came in shortly after we started and stayed there till the end."

"Really? What exactly was your program, Miss Simpson?"

"Well, there was a bit of committee stuff, then a short talk with lantern slides by Mr. Walters from the water company and we finished with a cake-making competition."

"Yes . . . yes . . . and what did Oscar do?"

She laughed. "Mixed with the company, apparently enjoyed the slides and showed great interest in the cakes."

"I see. And you didn't bring him home?"

"No, he made his own way here. As you know, I have to pass your house and I merely rang your bell to make sure you knew he had arrived."

"I'm obliged to you, Miss Simpson. We were a little worried."

I mounted the stairs in record time. Helen was sitting with the cat on her knee and she looked up as I burst in.

"I know about Oscar now," I said.

"Know what?"

◆ **Build Vocabulary**

distraught (dis trôt´) *adj.*: Extremely upset

despondent (di spän´ dənt) *adj.*: Lacking hope; depressed

intrigued (in trēg d´) *v.*: Fascinated

---

13. **distemper** (dis tem´ pər) *adj.*: Infectious viral disease of young dogs.

"Why he goes on these nightly outings. He's not running away—he's visiting."

"Visiting?"

"Yes," I said. "Don't you see? He likes getting around, he loves people, especially in groups, and he's interested in what they do. He's a natural mixer."

Helen looked down at the attractive mound of fur curled on her lap. "Of course . . . that's it . . . he's a socialite!"

"Exactly, a high stepper!"

"A cat-about-town!"

It all afforded us some innocent laughter and Oscar sat up and looked at us with evident pleasure, adding his own throbbing purr to the merriment. But for Helen and me there was a lot of relief behind it; ever since our cat had started his excursions there had been the gnawing fear that we would lose him, and now we felt secure.

From that night our delight in him increased. There was endless joy in watching this facet of his character unfolding. He did the social round meticulously, taking in most of the activities of the town. He became a familiar figure at whist drives,[14] jumble sales,[15] school concerts and scout bazaars. Most of the time he was made welcome, but was twice ejected from meetings of the Rural District Council who did not seem to relish the idea of a cat sitting in on their deliberations.

At first I was apprehensive about his making his way through the streets but I watched him once or twice and saw that he looked both ways before tripping daintily across. Clearly he had excellent traffic sense and this made me feel that his original injury had not been caused by a car.

Taking it all in all, Helen and I felt that it was a kind stroke of fortune which had brought Oscar to us. He was a warm and cherished part of our home life. He added to our happiness.

When the blow fell it was totally unexpected.

I was finishing the evening surgery.[16] I looked round the door and saw only a man and two little boys.

"Next, please," I said.

The man stood up. He had no animal with him. He was middle-aged, with the rough weathered face of a farm worker. He twirled a cloth cap nervously in his hands.

"Mr. Herriot?" he said.

"Yes, what can I do for you?"

He swallowed and looked me straight in the eyes. "Ah think you've got ma cat."

"What?"

"Ah lost ma cat a bit since." He cleared his throat. "We used to live at Missdon but ah got a job as plowman to Mr. Horne of Wederly. It was after we moved to Wederly that t'cat went missin'. Ah reckon he was tryin to find 'is way back to his old home."

"Wederly? That's on the other side of Brawton—over thirty miles away."

"Aye, ah knaw, but cats is funny things."

"But what makes you think I've got him?"

He twisted the cap around a bit more. "There's a cousin o' mine lives in Darrowby and ah heard tell from 'im about this cat that goes around to meetin's. I 'ad to come. We've been huntin' everywhere."

"Tell me," I said. "This cat you lost. What did he look like?"

"Gray and black and sort o' gingery. Right bonny[17] 'e was. And 'e was allus goin' out to gatherin's."

A cold hand clutched at my heart. "You'd better come upstairs. Bring the boys with you."

◆ Literature and Your Life
What would you do in Jim and Helen's place?

---

14. **whist** (hwist) **drives:** Attempts to raise money for charities and other purposes by playing the card game whist.

15. **jumble sales:** British term for sales of contributed articles to raise money for charity.

---

16. **surgery** (sur´ jer ē) *n.*: British term for "office hours."

17. **bonny** (bän´ ē) *adj.*: Pretty.

Helen was putting some coal on the fire of the bed-sitter.

"Helen," I said. "This is Mr.—er—I'm sorry, I don't know your name."

"Gibbons, Sep Gibbons. They called me Septimus because ah was the seventh in family and it looks like ah'm goin' t'same way 'cause we've got six already. These are our two youngest." The two boys, obvious twins of about eight, looked up at us solemnly.

I wished my heart would stop hammering. "Mr. Gibbons thinks Oscar is his. He lost his cat some time ago."

My wife put down her little shovel. "Oh . . . oh . . . I see." She stood very still for a moment then smiled faintly. "Do sit down. Oscar's in the kitchen, I'll bring him through."

She went out and reappeared with the cat in her arms. She hadn't got through the door before the little boys gave tongue.

"Tiger!" they cried. "Oh, Tiger, Tiger!"

The man's face seemed lit from within. He walked quickly across the floor and ran his big work-roughened hand along the fur.

"Hullo, awd lad," he said, and turned to me with a radiant smile. "It's 'im, Mr. Herriot. It's 'im awright, and don't 'e look well!"

"You call him Tiger, eh?" I said.

"Aye," he replied happily. "It's them gingery stripes. The kids called 'im that. They were brokenhearted when we lost 'im."

As the two little boys rolled on the floor our Oscar rolled with them, pawing playfully, purring with delight.

Sep Gibbons sat down again. "That's the way 'e allus went on wi' the family. They used to play with 'im for hours. By gaw we did miss 'im. He were a right favorite."

I looked at the broken nails on the edge of the cap, at the decent, honest, uncomplicated Yorkshire[18] face so like the many I had grown to like and respect. Farm men like him got thirty shillings a week in those days and it

was reflected in the threadbare jacket, the cracked, shiny boots and the obvious hand-me-downs of the boys.

◆ Reading Strategy
Do you think the author respects people like Sep Gibbons? Explain.

But all three were scrubbed and tidy, the man's face like a red beacon, the children's knees gleaming and their hair carefully slicked across their foreheads. They looked like nice people to me. I didn't know what to say.

Helen said it for me. "Well, Mr. Gibbons." Her tone had an unnatural brightness. "You'd better take him."

The man hesitated. "Now then, are ye sure, Missis Herriot?"

"Yes . . . yes, I'm sure. He was your cat first."

"Aye, but some folks 'ud say finders keepers or summat like that. Ah didn't come 'ere to demand 'im back or owt of t'sort."

"I know you didn't, Mr. Gibbons, but you've had him all those years and you've searched for him so hard. We couldn't possibly keep him from you."

He nodded quickly. "Well, that's right good of ye." He paused for a moment, his face serious, then he stooped and picked Oscar up.

"We'll have to be off if we're goin' to catch the eight o'clock bus."

Helen reached forward, cupped the cat's head in her hands and looked at him steadily for a few seconds. Then she patted the boys' heads. "You'll take good care of him, won't you?"

"Aye, missis, thank ye, we will that." The two small faces looked up at her and smiled.

"I'll see you down the stairs, Mr. Gibbons," I said.

On the descent I tickled the furry cheek resting on the man's shoulder and heard for the last time the rich purring. On the front door step we shook hands and they set off down the street. As they rounded the corner of Trengate they stopped and waved, and I waved back at the man, the two children and the cat's head looking back at me over the shoulder.

It was my habit at that time in my life to

18. **Yorkshire:** Region of northern England.

▲ Critical Viewing Which of Oscar's qualities are shown in this photograph? Which qualities are not represented? [Connect]

mount the stairs two or three at a time but on this occasion I trailed upwards like an old man, slightly breathless, throat tight, eyes prickling.

I cursed myself for a sentimental fool but as I reached our door I found a flash of consolation. Helen had taken it remarkably well. She had nursed that cat and grown deeply attached to him, and I'd have thought an unforeseen calamity like this would have upset her terribly. But no, she had behaved calmly and rationally.

It was up to me to do as well. I adjusted my features into the semblance of a cheerful smile and marched into the room.

Helen had pulled a chair close to the table and was slumped face down against the wood. One arm cradled her head while the other was stretched in front of her as her body shook with an utterly abandoned weeping.

I had never seen her like this and I was appalled. I tried to say something comforting but nothing stemmed the flow of racking sobs.

Feeling helpless and inadequate I could only sit close to her and stroke the back of her head. Maybe I could have said something if I hadn't felt just about as bad myself.

You get over these things in time. After all, we told ourselves, it wasn't as though Oscar had died or got lost again—he had gone to a good family who would look after him. In fact he had really gone home.

And of course, we still had our much-loved Sam, although he didn't help in the early stages by sniffing disconsolately where Oscar's bed used to lie then collapsing on the rug with a long lugubrious sigh.

There was one other thing, too. I had a little notion forming in my mind, an idea which I would spring on Helen when the time was right. It was about a month after that shattering night and we were coming out of the cinema at Brawton at the end of our half day. I looked at my watch.

"Only eight o'clock," I said. "How about going to see Oscar?"

Helen looked at me in surprise. "You mean—drive on to Wederly?"

"Yes, it's only about five miles."

A smile crept slowly across her face. "That would be lovely. But do you think they would mind?"

"The Gibbons? No, I'm sure they wouldn't. Let's go."

Wederly was a big village and the plowman's cottage was at the far end a few yards beyond the Methodist chapel. I pushed open the garden gate and we walked down the path.

A busy-looking little woman answered my knock. She was drying her hands on a striped towel.

"Mrs. Gibbons?" I said.

"Aye, that's me."

"I'm James Herriot—and this is my wife."

Her eyes widened uncomprehendingly. Clearly the name meant nothing to her.

"We had your cat for a while," I added.

Suddenly she grinned and waved her towel at us. "Oh aye, ah remember now. Sep told me about you. Come in, come in!"

The big kitchen-living room was a tableau[19] of life with six children and thirty shillings a week. Battered furniture, rows of much-mended washing on a pulley, black cooking range and a general air of chaos.

Sep got up from his place by the fire, put down his newspaper, took off a pair of steel-rimmed spectacles and shook hands.

He waved Helen to a sagging armchair. "Well, it's right nice to see you. Ah've often spoke of ye to t'missis."

His wife hung up her towel. "Yes, and I'm glad to meet ye both. I'll get some tea in a minnit."

She laughed and dragged a bucket of muddy water into a corner. "I've been washin' football jerseys. Them lads just handed them to me tonight—as if I haven't enough to do."

As she ran the water into the kettle I peeped

---

19. **tableau** (tab´ lō) *n.*: Dramatic scene or picture.

surreptitiously around me and I noticed Helen doing the same. But we searched in vain. There was no sign of a cat. Surely he couldn't have run away again? With a growing feeling of dismay I realized that my little scheme could backfire devastatingly.

It wasn't until the tea had been made and poured that I dared to raise the subject.

"How—" I asked diffidently. "How is—er—Tiger?"

"Oh, he's grand," the little woman replied briskly. She glanced up at the clock on the mantelpiece. "He should be back any time now, then you'll be able to see 'im."

As she spoke, Sep raised a finger. "Ah think ah can hear 'im now."

He walked over and opened the door and our Oscar strode in with all his old grace and majesty. He took one look at Helen and leaped onto her lap. With a cry of delight she put down her cup and stroked the beautiful fur as the cat arched himself against her hand and the familiar purr echoed round the room.

"He knows me," she murmured. "He knows me."

Sep nodded and smiled. "He does that. You were good to 'im. He'll never forget ye, and we won't either, will we mother?"

"No, we won't, Mrs. Herriot," his wife said as she applied butter to a slice of gingerbread. "That was a kind thing ye did for us and I 'ope you'll come and see us all whenever you're near."

"Well, thank you," I said. "We'd love to—we're often in Brawton."

I went over and tickled Oscar's chin, then I turned again to Mrs. Gibbons. "By the way, it's after nine o'clock. Where has he been till now?"

She poised her butter knife and looked into space.

"Let's see, now," she said. "It's Thursday, isn't it? Ah yes, it's 'is night for the Yoga class."

◆ **Build Vocabulary**

surreptitiously (sʉr´ əp tish´ əs lē) *adv.*: Secretly

Beyond Literature

Science Connection

Cats—Domestic and Wild You may be familiar with the many breeds of cats that are domesticated. These cats are trainable and friendly to humans. However, there are some species of cat that live in the wild, scavenging food for themselves and marking out a space to call their own. While Oscar is treated as a house cat, his roaming demonstrates some behaviors of wild cats.

All felines are solitary creatures who travel a specific range or territory. They spend a large portion of their day covering this range, searching for food and defending their territory from invaders.

Wildcats—like the bobcat and Canada lynx—are generally longer and stronger than house cats. They have shorter tails and tufts of fur on their ears. These cats prowl at night and may be more vicious than a typical house cat.

Cross-Curricular Activity

Categorizing Cats Conduct research to learn the species of cats common in your region. Identify the breeds of cats your friends and neighbors keep as pets, and collect information on as many breeds as possible. Find out about wildcats that may roam free in your state.

Create an illustrated report to share your findings with classmates.

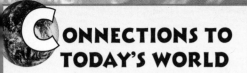
Garfield

Jim Davis

From the Herriots' home in England to the homes of many of your friends and neighbors, cats are beloved by people the world over. Those of us who don't own a furry feline may enjoy the witty commentary of Jim Davis's Garfield, a cat who visits our homes in daily newspapers and in collections of Davis's funny cartoons.

GARFIELD ©Paws, Inc. Dist. by UNIVERSAL PRESS SYNDICATE. Reprinted with permission. All rights reserved.

1. According to the cartoon, what happened to Hubert?
2. Compare the characterization of Garfield with that of Oscar in "Cat on the Go."

Guide for Responding

◆ LITERATURE AND YOUR LIFE

Reader's Response How have you felt when, like the Herriots, you've had to give up something that meant a lot to you?

Thematic Focus What do the Herriots discover about the cat that makes them laugh?

Journal Writing Is it better that the Herriots had the chance to know Oscar, or would they have been better off not meeting him? In a journal entry, explore your response.

☑ Check Your Comprehension

1. Explain how Doctor Herriot helped the cat.
2. What is Helen Herriot's response to the cat?
3. Where does the cat go each time it wanders off from the Herriots' home?
4. How does the community react to the cat?
5. How is the cat reunited with its owners?
6. Where is the cat when the Herriots go to visit?

◆ Critical Thinking

INTERPRET

1. What effect does the injured cat's purring have on Herriot and Tristan? **[Analyze Cause and Effect]**
2. (a) Identify three places where neighbors spot the cat. (b) What do these places have in common? **[Generalize]**
3. Why do the Herriots give up the cat instead of claiming "finders keepers"? **[Analyze]**
4. After the cat leaves, what details of their life tell you the Herriots had become attached to him? **[Support]**

EVALUATE

5. How does Herriot's enjoyment of the cat increase your interest in the essay? **[Assess]**
6. Do you think that the Herriots did the right thing in returning Oscar to the Gibbons family? Explain your answer. **[Evaluate]**

APPLY

7. Why do you think that many people enjoy having pets? **[Generalize]**

Guide for Responding (continued)

◆ Reading Strategy

UNDERSTAND BIAS

A writer's **bias** is the knowledge, background, interests, and attitude that he or she brings to a piece of writing. You can detect a writer's bias through the details a writer includes. If you remember that bias affects the information the writer presents, you can read a piece of literature objectively.

1. What bias do the italicized words in this statement reveal? "His purr became a *part of our lives* and when he eventually left his bed, *sauntered* . . . to our kitchen and began to *sample* Sam's dinner of meat and biscuit *it was a moment of triumph*."
2. Find two other examples in the story that show Herriot's bias. Explain each one.

◆ Build Vocabulary

USING THE PREFIX *in-*

Add the prefix *in-*, meaning "not," to the following words. Then, write sentences using the new words.

1. consistent (following the same pattern)
2. capable (able; skilled)
3. sincere (honest; truthful)

SPELLING STRATEGY

In words like *distraught*, the letters *gh* are silent. Finish the sentences with words that follow this rule.

1. I th___?___ I asked you to feed the cat.
2. Mrs. Herriot f___?___ back tears.
3. The dr___?___ caused a terrible water shortage.

USING THE WORD BANK

Use the Word Bank to complete these sentences.

1. The cat ___?___ into the room gracefully.
2. The movie's complicated plot ___?___ me.
3. The child became so ___?___ he cried.
4. After a crash diet, he looked ___?___.
5. Intestines spilled ___?___ onto the table.
6. Despite all my excuses, the speeding ticket was ___?___.
7. Stealing glances, she looked at him ___?___.
8. When the cat left, the family became ___?___.

◆ Literary Focus

CHARACTER TRAITS

Character traits are the qualities that make a person or an animal an individual. As the events unfold, Oscar, Tristan, Doctor Herriot, and Helen reveal their special traits in what they do and say.

1. Tristan brings an injured and starving cat to James Herriot. What traits does this behavior reveal?
2. Herriot includes technical details about the operation, even though they might seem unpleasant. What does this say about him?
3. Which character traits make Oscar so well loved by the Herriots?

◆ Build Grammar Skills

COMPOUND SUBJECTS AND PREDICATES

A **compound subject** is two or more subjects that have the same verb. Similarly, a **compound predicate** contains two or more verbs that have the same subject. Both compound subjects and compound predicates are joined by conjunctions, such as *and* or *or*. Look at these examples:

compound subject

Tristan and *I* looked down at the shattered animal.

compound predicate

I *shrugged* and *shook* my head.

Practice Write these sentences on your paper. Underline compound subjects once and compound predicates twice.

1. Tristan unscrewed the cap and poised it above the head.
2. Beef essence, strained broth, and baby food found their way down his throat.
3. I galloped downstairs and rounded the corner.
4. Helen and I felt that it was a kind stroke of fortune that brought Oscar to us.
5. He would either fill out or have trouble surviving.

Writing Application Create sentences using the following items as directed.

1. Herriot and Tristan (compound subject)
2. give or take (compound predicate)
3. Oscar or Tiger (compound subject)

Build Your Portfolio

Idea Bank

Writing

1. **Pet Story** Using "Cat on the Go" as a model, write an amusing episode featuring your pet or an animal you know. Include, as Herriot did, realistic dialogue and vivid descriptions.

2. **Monologue** Write a speech from Oscar's point of view. Describe your injury, your feelings about the Herriots, and your evening habits. Explain your feelings about returning to the Gibbonses.

3. **Biographical Sketch** Using the details provided in "Cat on the Go" and the author information on page 380, write a biographical sketch of James Herriot. In your essay, identify the character traits that made him a good doctor.

Speaking and Listening

4. **Career Interview** Interview a veterinarian to find out more about the job Herriot describes. Ask questions to learn what makes the job tough and what makes it rewarding. Share your findings with the class. **[Career Link]**

5. **Musical Retelling [Group Activity]** With a group, set this story to music. Review the piece to determine where the mood changes. For each section, write a summary of the action, and identify music that captures the mood. Combine your summaries with the music, and perform your retelling for the class. **[Music Link]**

Projects

6. **Training Profile** Use the Internet and the library to research the educational requirements needed to get into a school of veterinary medicine. For each school you find, learn what it takes to get a D.V.M. degree. **[Career Link]**

7. **Pet-Care Brochure** Visit an animal shelter or pet store to find out about the responsibilities of pet ownership. In a pamphlet, teach others the daily tasks that need to be done, and offer suggestions for making a pet feel at home. Illustrate your brochure, and share it with classmates.

Writing Mini-Lesson

Directory of Places

Oscar's habit of visiting meetings and groups reveals not only his sociable side but also his resourcefulness. Imagine how much easier his travel would have been if he had used a directory of places to visit. Research your community to find clubs or meetings Oscar might have liked to visit. Then, create a directory of community information.

Writing Skills Focus: Supply Background Information

Your directory will be more useful if it provides more than just names and addresses. **Supply background information on local clubs**—details such as history, goals, major accomplishments, and special programs. These details will make the directory a good resource for any newcomer to your community.

Model

Wederly Art Club: 2-07 High Street. Celebrating its fiftieth year, the Art Club offers classes in a variety of media, including painting, sculpting, and computer animation. Each year, the club creates the floats for the summer parade.

Prewriting Check the library and telephone book to find interesting places in your community. Jot down phone numbers, addresses, and information describing their activities. Decide whether you will organize your directory alphabetically or by category.

Drafting Use your notes to create entries on clubs and activities. Keep directory entries brief.

> ◆ **Grammar Application**
> Compound subjects or predicates can help you avoid short, choppy sentences.

Revising Confirm the accuracy of your information against your notes. Add illustrations, colors, logos, or bullets to make your directory attractive.

Guide for Reading

Meet the Authors:

Lucille Clifton (1936–)

Lucille Clifton has worked hard to overcome discrimination and become a successful writer. Whether in poetry or prose, she often writes about the value of sharing family traditions.

Lewis Carroll (1832–1898)

Lewis Carroll is the pen name of Charles Dodgson, a mathematics professor who was born in England. Under his pen name, Dodgson wrote *Alice's Adventures in Wonderland* and *Through the Looking Glass*. His poems are noted for their clever wordplay, nonsensical meanings, and delightfully zany fantasy worlds.

Maxine Kumin (1925–)

Maxine Kumin writes children's books, as well as volumes of poetry, fiction, and nonfiction. She often plays with the lines in her poems to create a look that reflects the subject of her writing.

E. E. Cummings (1894–1962)

Edward Estlin Cummings's poetry shows his original use of language and uncommon use of punctuation. His style caused much controversy during his lifetime—a controversy that continues today.

Shel Silverstein (1932–1999)

Shel Silverstein is a cartoonist, a composer, a folk singer, and a writer. He is best known to people of all ages for two books of poetry, *Where the Sidewalk Ends* and *A Light in the Attic*. Although his poems are humorous, they contain a message for all.

◆ LITERATURE AND YOUR LIFE

CONNECT YOUR EXPERIENCE

There are many reasons to look for humor and happiness in daily life. You may joke to relieve the tension of a bad day, or you may smile with joy on the first warm spring morning. Like you, characters in these selections find comedy and satisfaction in life's daily experiences.

THEMATIC FOCUS: Quirky Characters

As you encounter the quirky characters in each selection, think about whether they remind you of anyone you know.

◆ Background for Understanding

LITERATURE

Dialect is the form of a language spoken by people in a specific region or group. Dialects differ from the standard language in pronunciation, grammar, and word choice. For example, the varieties of English spoken in Boston, Chicago, or Dallas are quite different from each other. In "The Luckiest Time of All," Clifton uses a dialect from the rural South. Because she uses words like *usta* for "used to" and *nothin* for "nothing," she lets readers enjoy the unique way her narrator tells a story.

◆ Build Vocabulary

WORDS WITH MULTIPLE MEANINGS

Sage is one of many English words that have multiple meanings. In "Father William," the word means "a very wise person." *Sage*, however, is also the name of an herb used in cooking.

WORD BANK

Look over these words from the selections. How might *rancid* food smell?

incessantly
sage
supple
withered
curdled
rancid

◆ Literary Focus

HYPERBOLE

"I'm so hungry I could eat a horse!"

"I haven't seen you for ages."

Everyday speech is full of examples of **hyperbole,** or exaggeration for effect. Writers use hyperbole to create humor or to emphasize a point. For example, when a character in "The Luckiest Time of All" describes a dog chasing after her, she says, "He lit out after me and I flew!" As you read, keep a list like the one below to note examples of hyperbole in these selections.

HYPERBOLE — I flew!

◆ Reading Strategy

RECOGNIZE AUTHOR'S PURPOSE

When you are prepared for a strange reflection as you face a fun-house mirror, you can enjoy the view. However, you might be terrified if you were expecting a realistic image. **Recognizing an author's purpose,** or reason, for writing can be equally helpful as you face a piece of literature. This purpose might be to influence you, to educate you, to make you laugh, or to make you think. A purpose shapes the language and details a writer uses. For example, in "Father William," Lewis Carroll creates a ridiculous character in an old man who turns somersaults and offers to sell his son his healing ointment. These details enhance the humor of the poem.

The Luckiest Time of All

Lucille Clifton

Mrs. Elzie F. Pickens was rocking slowly on the porch one afternoon when her Great-granddaughter, Tee, brought her a big bunch of dogwood blooms, and that was the beginning of a story.

"Ahhh, now that dogwood reminds me of the day I met your Great-granddaddy, Mr. Pickens, Sweet Tee.

"It was just this time, spring of the year, and me and my best friend Ovella Wilson, who is now gone, was goin to join the Silas Greene. Usta be a kinda show went all through the South, called it the Silas Greene show. Somethin like the circus. Me and Ovella wanted to join that thing and see the world. Nothin wrong at home or nothin, we just wanted to travel and see new things and have high times. Didn't say nothin to nobody but one another. Just up and decided to do it.

"Well, this day we plaited our hair and put a dress and some things in a croka-sack[1] and started out to the show. Spring day like this.

"We got there after a good little walk and it was the world, Baby, such music and wonders as we never had seen! They had everything there, or seemed like it.

"Me and Ovella thought we'd walk around for a while and see the show before goin to the office to sign up and join.

"While we was viewin it all we come up on this dancin dog. Cutest one thing in the world next to you, Sweet Tee, dippin and movin and

head bowin to that music. Had a little ruffly skirt on itself and up on two back legs twistin and movin to the music. Dancin dancin dancin till people started throwin pennies out of they pockets.

"Me and Ovella was caught up too and laughin so. She took a penny out of her pocket and threw it to the ground where that dog was dancin, and I took two pennies and threw 'em both.

"The music was faster and faster and that dog was turnin and turnin. Ovella reached in her sack and threw out a little pin she had won from never being late at Sunday school. And me, laughin and all excited, reached in my bag and threw out my lucky stone!

"Well, I knew right off what I had done. Soon as it left my hand it seemed like I reached back out for it to take it back. But the stone was gone from my hand and Lord, it hit that dancin dog right on his nose!

"Well, he lit out after me, poor thing. He lit out after me and I flew! Round and round the Silas Greene we run, through every place me and Ovella had walked before, but now that dancin dog was a runnin dog and all the people was laughin at the new show, which was us!

"I felt myself slowin down after a while and I thought I would turn around a little bit to see how much gain that cute little dog was makin on me. When I did I got such a surprise! Right behind me was the dancin dog and right behind him was the finest fast runnin hero in the bottoms of Virginia.

---

1. **crokasack** (krō´ kər sak) *usually spelled croker sack, n.*: Bag made of burlap or similar material.

▲ Critical Viewing Why would an activity like the quilting shown here provide a good opportunity for sharing family stories? [Analyze]

"And that was Mr. Pickens when he was still a boy! He had a length of twine in his hand and he was twirlin it around in the air just like the cowboy at the Silas Greene and grinnin fit to bust.

"While I was watchin how the sun shined on him and made him look like an angel come to help a poor sinner girl, why, he twirled that twine one extra fancy twirl and looped it right around one hind leg of that dancin dog and brought him low.

"I stopped then and walked slow and shy to where he had picked up that poor dog to see if he was hurt, cradlin him and talkin to him soft and sweet. That showed me how kind and gentle he was, and when we walked back to the dancin dog's place in the show he let the dog loose and helped me to find my stone. I told him how shiny black it was and how it had the letter *A* scratched on one side. We searched and searched and at last he spied it!

"Ovella and me lost heart for shows then and we walked on home. And a good little way, the one who was gonna be your Great-granddaddy was walkin on behind. Seein us safe. Us walkin kind of slow. Him seein us safe. Yes." Mrs. Pickens' voice trailed off softly and Tee noticed she had a little smile on her face.

"Grandmama, that stone almost got you bit by a dog that time. It wasn't so lucky that time, was it?"

Tee's Great-grandmother shook her head and laughed out loud.

"That was the luckiest time of all, Tee Baby. It got me acquainted with Mr. Amos Pickens, and if that ain't luck, what could it be! Yes, it was luckier for me than for anybody, I think. Least mostly I think it."

Tee laughed with her Great-grandmother though she didn't exactly know why.

"I hope I have that kind of good stone luck one day," she said.

"Maybe you will someday," her Great-grandmother said.

And they rocked a little longer and smiled together.

Guide for Responding

◆ LITERATURE AND YOUR LIFE

Reader's Response Have you ever met someone "by chance"? What happened?

Thematic Focus Would you describe Great-grandmother as quirky? Explain.

Journal Writing Great-grandmother's story sounds as if it has been told countless times. In a journal entry, tell a story about yourself that you have heard others tell many times.

☑ Check Your Comprehension

1. Who tells the story about the lucky stone and the Silas Greene show?
2. Who is listening to the story?
3. Why does Tee think Great-grandmother's stone was not so lucky at first?
4. What is Great-grandmother's reason for believing that the stone was lucky for her?

◆ Critical Thinking

INTERPRET

1. What details show that Great-grandmother and Ovella were adventurous? **[Support]**
2. Mr. Pickens cradles the dog and speaks softly to it. What can you tell about his character from these actions? **[Infer]**
3. What was Mr. Pickens's real intention in saving Great-grandmother from the dog and in following her home? **[Draw Conclusions]**
4. Would you say that Great-grandmother is happy with her life? Support your opinion with examples. **[Speculate]**

APPLY

5. What does this story suggest about the importance of family stories? **[Apply]**

Father William

Lewis Carroll

You Are Old, Father William, 1865, Sir John Tenniel

"You are old, Father William," the young man said,
   "And your hair has become very white;
And yet you <u>incessantly</u> stand on your head—
   Do you think, at your age, it is right?"

5   "In my youth," Father William replied to his son,
   "I feared it might injure the brain;
But, now that I'm perfectly sure I have none,
   Why, I do it again and again."

▲ **Critical Viewing** Which stanza or group of lines does this drawing illustrate? **[Connect]**

"You are old," said the youth, "as I mentioned before.
10   And have grown most uncommonly[1] fat;
Yet you turned a back-somersault in at the door—
     Pray, what is the reason of that?"

"In my youth," said the sage, as he shook his gray locks,
     "I kept all my limbs very supple
15   By the use of this ointment—one shilling[2] the box—
     Allow me to sell you a couple?"

"You are old," said the youth, "and your jaws are too weak
     For anything tougher than suet;[3]
Yet you finished the goose, with the bones and the beak—
20   Pray, how did you manage to do it?"

---

1. **uncommonly** (un käm´ ən lē) *adv.*: Remarkably.
2. **shilling** (shil´ iŋ) *n.*: British coin.
3. **suet** (sōō´ it) *n.*: Fat used in cooking.

You Are Old Father William II, 1865, Sir John Tenniel

◆ Build Vocabulary

incessantly (in ses´ ənt lē) *adv.*: Without stopping

sage (sāj) *n.*: Very wise man

supple (sup´ əl) *adj.*: Flexible

▲ **Critical Viewing** How do the illustrations contribute to the humor of the characters? **[Assess]**

"In my youth," said his father, "I took to the law,
    And argued each case with my wife;
And the muscular strength, which it gave to my jaw
    Has lasted the rest of my life."

25   "You are old," said the youth, "one would hardly suppose
    That your eye was as steady as ever;
Yet you balanced an eel on the end of your nose—
    What made you so awfully clever?"

"I have answered three questions, and that is enough,"
30   Said his father. "Don't give yourself airs!
Do you think I can listen all day to such stuff?
    Be off, or I'll kick you downstairs!"

Guide for Responding

◆ LITERATURE AND YOUR LIFE

Reader's Response Which of Father William's replies do you think is the most ridiculous? Why?

Thematic Focus Identify three things about Father William that make him an unusual man.

Journal Writing Record a question that someone has asked recently about your behavior. Then, create a reply as zany as those of Father William.

☑ Check Your Comprehension

1. What reason does Father William give for incessantly standing on his head?
2. What enables him to do back-somersaults?
3. Why is he able to eat an entire goose— bones and all?
4. Why does the son think his father should not be able to do the things that he does?
5. How does the poem end?

◆ Critical Thinking

INTERPRET

1. What is it about Father William's physical condition that makes his behavior so absurd? **[Infer]**
2. In general, how does the son regard his father? **[Interpret]**
3. What does the father think about his own behavior? **[Infer]**
4. Do you think the poem presents a typical conversation between this father and son? Explain. **[Speculate]**
5. Why is it comical that Father William refuses to answer any more questions? **[Analyze]**

APPLY

6. How would the poem's humor change if Father William had different physical characteristics? **[Hypothesize]**

COMPARE LITERARY WORKS

7. Compare the relationship between generations in "The Luckiest Time of All" with the one in "Father William." **[Compare and Contrast]**

THE MICROSCOPE

Maxine Kumin

Anton Leeuwenhoek was Dutch.
He sold pincushions, cloth, and such.
The waiting townsfolk fumed and fussed
As Anton's dry goods gathered dust.

5   He worked, instead of tending store,
At grinding special lenses for
A microscope. Some of the things
He looked at were:
            mosquitoes' wings,
the hairs of sheep, the legs of lice,
10 the skin of people, dogs, and mice;
ox eyes, spiders' spinning gear,
fishes' scales, a little smear
of his own blood,
          and best of all,
the unknown, busy, very small
15 bugs that swim and bump and hop
inside a simple water drop.

Impossible! Most Dutchmen said.
This Anton's crazy in the head.
We ought to ship him off to Spain.
20 He says he's seen a housefly's brain.
He says the water that we drink
Is full of bugs. He's mad, we think!

They called him *dumkopf,* which means dope.
That's how we got the microscope.

▶ **Critical
Viewing** How
might Leeuwen-
hoek's microscope
have compared
with the one
pictured here?
Explain.
[Speculate]

in Just-
E. E. Cummings

in Just-
spring   when the world is mud-
luscious the little
lame balloonman

5   whistles   far   and wee[1]

and eddieandbill come
running from marbles and
piracies and it's
spring

10   when the world is puddle-wonderful

the queer
old balloonman whistles
far   and   wee
and bettyandisbel come dancing

15   from hop-scotch and jump-rope and

it's
spring
and
      the

20   goat-footed[2]

balloonMan   whistles
far
and
wee

---

1. **wee** (wē) *adj.*: Very small; tiny.
2. **goat-footed:** Like the Greek god Pan, who had the legs of a goat and was associated with fields, forests, and wild animals.

Guide for Responding

◆ LITERATURE AND YOUR LIFE

Reader's Response What memories of spring does "in Just-" call up for you?

Thematic Focus Use "The Microscope" to explain Anton Leeuwenhoek's quirkiness.

Group Activity With a partner, choose a season and brainstorm for the words you'd use to describe it. To make your list vivid, include words that appeal to all five senses.

☑ Check Your Comprehension

1. Who is the main character in the poem "The Microscope"?
2. What is this person's occupation?
3. What is this person's hobby?
4. What event does the poem "in Just-" describe?
5. What are the children doing when they hear the whistle?

◆ Critical Thinking

INTERPRET

1. What was unusual about the items Leeuwenhoek studied in "The Microscope"? **[Infer]**
2. Why did the townsfolk think Leeuwenhoek was "crazy in the head"? **[Interpret]**
3. In "in Just-," what is the effect of the poet's writing "eddieandbill" instead of "Eddie and Bill"? **[Analyze]**
4. How does the description of the balloonman change as the poem progresses? **[Interpret]**
5. The Greek god Pan inspired people with his flute playing. What effect does the balloonman's whistling have on the children? **[Analyze]**

APPLY

6. What reasons might poets have for playing with the physical arrangements of words, phrases, or lines in poetry? **[Synthesize]**

EXTEND

7. In what ways did the "dumkopf," Anton Leeuwenhoek, change the world? **[Science Link]**

Sarah Cynthia Sylvia Stout Would Not Take the Garbage Out

Shel Silverstein

Sarah Cynthia Sylvia Stout
Would not take the garbage out!
She'd scour[1] the pots and scrape the pans,
Candy[2] the yams and spice the hams,
5   And though her daddy would scream and shout,
She simply would not take the garbage out.
And so it piled up to the ceilings:
Coffee grounds, potato peelings,
Brown bananas, rotten peas,
10   Chunks of sour cottage cheese.
It filled the can, it covered the floor,
It cracked the window and blocked the door
With bacon rinds[3] and chicken bones,
Drippy ends of ice cream cones,
15   Prune pits, peach pits, orange peel,
Gloppy glumps of cold oatmeal,
Pizza crusts and <u>withered</u> greens,
Soggy beans and tangerines,
Crusts of black burned buttered toast,
20   Gristly bits of beefy roasts . . .
The garbage rolled on down the hall,
It raised the roof, it broke the wall . . .

◀ **Critical Viewing**
Does the exaggerated style of the cartoon on this page better suit this poem than a realistic photograph might? Explain. [**Make a Judgment**]

◆ **Build Vocabulary**
withered (with´ ərd) *adj.*: Dried up

---

1. **scour** (skour) *v.*: Clean by rubbing vigorously.
2. **candy** (kan´ dē) *v.*: Coat with sugar.
3. **rinds** (rindz) *n.*: Tough outer layers or skins.

Greasy napkins, cookie crumbs,
Globs of gooey bubblegum,
25 Cellophane from green baloney,
Rubbery blubbery macaroni,
Peanut butter, caked and dry,
Curdled milk and crusts of pie,
Moldy melons, dried up mustard,
30 Eggshells mixed with lemon custard,
Cold french fries and rancid meat,
Yellow lumps of Cream of Wheat.
At last the garbage reached so high
That finally it touched the sky.
35 And all the neighbors moved away,
And none of her friends would come to play.
And finally Sarah Cynthia Stout said,
"OK, I'll take the garbage out!"
But then, of course, it was too late
40 The garbage reached across the state,
From New York to the Golden Gate
And there, in the garbage she did hate,
Poor Sarah met an awful fate,
That I cannot right now relate[4]
45 Because the hour is much too late.
But children, remember Sarah Stout
And always take the garbage out!

---

4. **relate** (ri lāt´) *v.:* Tell.

◀ **Critical Viewing** The author created
the illustrations accompanying the
poem. How does this art enhance the
humor of the poem? **[Assess]**

◆ **Build Vocabulary**

curdled (kur´ dəld) *adj.:* Thickened; clotted
rancid (ran´ sid) *adj.:* Spoiled and smelling bad

Beyond Literature

Technology Connection

New Uses for Recycled Materials
Sarah Cynthia may not have cared about the garbage she was accumulating, but more and more products are being made from recycled—and recyclable—materials. You probably know that glass and plastic bottles are recycled into new containers. However, you may not have known that some plastic is converted into insulation for maintaining an even temperature in homes and offices. In addition, recycled glass is used in road pavement, and coal ashes are used in cement.

Cross Curricular Activity
Community Research If your community has a recycling program, find out more about it. Call local officials to get information about what happens to recycling materials that are collected. Then, create a flowchart to show the path from curb side to new product. Refer to your chart as you make a presentation to classmates.

Guide for Responding

◆ LITERATURE AND YOUR LIFE

Reader's Response Do you sympathize more with Sarah or her father? Why?

Thematic Focus If you were asked to describe Sarah with one word, what word would you choose?

Group Activity In a small group, brainstorm for a list of chores that young people are often asked to complete. Then, vote to rank these jobs on a scale from least pleasant to most fun.

☑ Check Your Comprehension

1. Name four chores that Sarah Cynthia Sylvia Stout does at home.
2. What does her father do when Sarah refuses to take out the garbage?
3. What happens to the garbage?
4. What do Sarah's friends and neighbors do as the situation progresses?
5. What finally happens to Sarah?

◆ Critical Thinking

INTERPRET
1. At what point in the poem does the poet begin to use exaggeration? **[Distinguish]**
2. What is the effect of the continuing exaggeration? **[Analyze]**
3. What reason might the poet have—besides the fact that it is "late"—for not telling readers what happened to Sarah? **[Infer]**
4. What do you think was Sarah's "awful fate"? **[Speculate]**

APPLY
5. Find two lines in the poem that do not rhyme. What is the effect of this break in rhyme? **[Synthesize]**

EXTEND
6. What local rules exist in your area to prevent Sarah's situation from actually happening? **[Community Link]**

Guide for Responding (continued)

◆ Reading Strategy

RECOGNIZE AUTHOR'S PURPOSE

All of the pieces in this grouping were written for a similar purpose—to entertain and amuse readers. This purpose is evident in the writers' choice of language, details, and events.

1. Identify two examples in "The Luckiest Time of All" that show that the narrator tells the story to entertain her listener.
2. What do you find humorous about the name Sarah Cynthia Sylvia Stout?
3. Imagine that Kumin's purpose were to provide scholarly information about the microscope. How would her poem "The Microscope" be different?

◆ Build Vocabulary

USING WORDS WITH MULTIPLE MEANINGS

Like *sage,* which can refer to a wise person or an herb, many words in English have multiple meanings. On your paper, explain the different meanings of the italicized words in each set of sentences.

1. Rice is a *staple* in their diet.
   One *staple* can't hold that many pages!
2. Fill the *pitcher* with iced tea.
   Give the *pitcher* the ball.

SPELLING STRATEGY

The *ses* sound in *incessantly* is spelled *cess.* On your paper, write a word that contains *cess* to complete each of the following sentences.

1. To avoid disaster, it is n___?___ to take the garbage out.
2. The boys play marbles during r___?___ at school.
3. Without a password, you can't a___?___ the file.

USING THE WORD BANK

Answer each question, and explain your answer.

1. Will a faucet that *incessantly* drips waste water?
2. Is a baseball bat smooth and *supple*?
3. Is *curdled* milk good for drinking?
4. Would you listen to the advice of a *sage*?
5. Might black bananas be *rancid*?
6. Would a *withered* salad be appetizing?

◆ Literary Focus

HYPERBOLE

Hyperbole is exaggeration for effect. For example, "Butter doesn't melt in her mouth" and "I'm walking on air" each overstate an idea. Hyperbole is used to create emphasis, humor, or drama. Without hyperbole, the poem about Sarah Stout would not be nearly so funny and dramatic, and "Father William" might simply become a charming character sketch.

1. In your opinion, which of Father William's behaviors is exaggerated the most? Explain.
2. Find an example of hyperbole in "The Microscope." Explain your choice.
3. Find three examples of hyperbole in "Sarah Cynthia Sylvia Stout . . ." Explain each example.
4. Why does hyperbole make people laugh?

◆ Build Grammar Skills

COMPLETE AND INCOMPLETE SENTENCES

A **complete sentence** contains both a subject and a verb. It expresses a complete thought. If a sentence does not meet these requirements, it is **incomplete** and may not be understood. Because people often do not speak in complete sentences, dialogue may include incomplete sentences.

Complete: Elzie rocked gently on the porch.

Incomplete: Spring day like this

Practice Copy these examples on your paper. If an item is a complete sentence, underline the subject once and the verb twice. If it is not a sentence, write *incomplete.*

1. Tee brought her great-grandmother a bunch of dogwood blooms.
2. Something like the circus.
3. Between you and me, Father William.
4. When the world is puddle-wonderful.
5. He looked through the lenses of a microscope.

Writing Application Rewrite each incomplete sentence above, adding a subject or a verb to make the sentence complete.

Build Your Portfolio

 ## Idea Bank

Writing

1. **Postcard From Sarah** Write a postcard or letter from Sarah Cynthia Sylvia Stout that explains what happened to her.

2. **Seasonal Description** Cummings joined words like *mud* and *luscious* together to make *mud-luscious*. Create combinations of words like these to capture the essence of a season. Then, use these words in an essay about your favorite season.

3. **Literary Review** Write a review of one of the selections you've just read. Summarize the poem or story, state the author's message, and then explain whether you think the author successfully conveyed that message.

Speaking and Listening

4. **Dramatization [Group Activity]** With a group, choose a scene from "The Luckiest Time of All" to bring to life. After a planning meeting, assign these tasks: write the script, plan the costumes and set, and direct the rehearsal. Perform your scene for the class. **[Performing Arts Link]**

5. **Interview** Work with a partner to plan and stage an interview with a character from one of the selections. Develop a series of questions and answers, and present the interview to classmates.

Projects

6. **Report on Good-Luck Charms** Elzie had her lucky stone, baseball players have their rally caps, and many of your classmates have their own good-luck charms. In an illustrated report, explain the variety of modern good-luck objects. Include quotations from friends and family about why they believe these items bring them luck.

7. **Microscope Presentation** Using library resources, learn about Leeuwenhoek's invention. Include photographs, a microscope, and Kumin's poem. If possible, demonstrate use of the microscope as part of your presentation. **[Science Link]**

 ## Writing Mini-Lesson

Humorous Poem

In their work, writers often describe everyday experiences with comic results. Lewis Carroll creates a silly conversation between a father and his son. Shel Silverstein imagines the absurd consequences of a child's decision to avoid her chores. Choose a memorable experience or event from your life, and write a humorous poem about it.

> **Writing Skills Focus:**
> **Use Imaginative Words**
>
> In your poem, **use imaginative words** to add humor to the story you tell. Consider these techniques as you experiment:
> - Lucille Clifton adds humor by spelling words as Elzie pronounces them. "Usta be a kinda show went all through the South," she says.
> - E. E. Cummings creates new words, such as "puddle-wonderful," to describe spring.
> - Shel Silverstein chooses words beginning with the same sound to make his poem fun: "Crusts of black burned buttered toast/Gristly bits of beefy roasts . . ."

Prewriting List words and phrases that will bring the experience to life. If you like, choose the key words to use as the start of rhyming lists.

Drafting Set the pattern of rhyme you wish to use. If you plan to write without regular rhyme, consider how to shape your poem on the page. Then, refer to your list as you draft your poem.

Revising Fine-tune words, phrases, and lines to correct rhyme or physical shape. Feel free to create new words if you need them—or create them just for fun.

> ◆ **Grammar Application**
>
> If your poem is written in complete sentences, check to be sure that each sentence contains a subject and a verb.

Humorous Anecdote

Writing Process Workshop

An old expression says that "laughter is the best medicine." It's true that sometimes when you're feeling down, hearing a funny story can pick you right up again.

Brighten someone's day by writing a **humorous anecdote,** a short, funny story that will make your audience laugh. The following skills, introduced in this section's Writing Mini-Lessons, will help you.

Writing Skills Focus

▶ **Answer the five W's.** Help your audience get the most enjoyment from your humorous anecdote: tell *who* was involved, *what* happened, *when* and *where* the action took place, and *why* the whole thing was so funny. (See p. 378.)

▶ **Supply the background.** Just as every good joke has a "setup," every humorous anecdote needs details and background that build to a funny "punch line." (See p. 395.)

▶ **Use imaginative words** to add to the humor of your story and make it come to life. (See p. 409.)

Notice how Charles Osgood uses these skills in his essay "Our Finest Hour."

MODEL FROM LITERATURE

from "Our Finest Hour" by Charles Osgood

When the commercial was over, I introduced a piece from Washington. What came up was a series of pictures of people who seemed to be dead. . . . I knew nothing whatsoever about this piece. It was not scheduled for the broadcast. . . . In the "fishbowl," the glassed-in office where the executive producer sits, ① there were at least three people yelling into telephones. Nobody in there knew anything about this piece either. ②

① This sentence tells *when, who, what,* and *where.*

② By giving background that explains what the "fishbowl" is, Osgood helps readers picture this funny scene.

Prewriting

Decide What's Funny A humorous anecdote is short, funny, and often tells about real people. If you have trouble coming up with an idea, try one of the following strategies:

Brainstorming Suggestions

- Skim your journal for funny stories about you and people you know.
- Ask friends and family members to share hilarious stories.
- Flip through photo albums or scrapbooks to stir up amusing memories.
- Read a biography to find a funny episode in the life of a famous person.

Jot Down the Five W's Use a chart like the one below to record the *who, what, where, when,* and *why* of your story. Once you have all these facts on paper, writing your humorous anecdote will be a breeze!

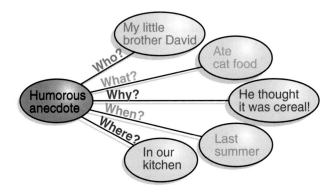

Brainstorm for Wacky Words Before you begin to write, brainstorm for words that will add zing to your anecdote. For example, if a little boy ate cat food by mistake, he might *squinch* up his face in disgust.

Drafting

Use a Humorous Technique There are several ways to make a funny story even funnier. Choose one of the following techniques, and work it into your anecdote as you draft.

▶ Add an unexpected twist at the end.
▶ Use exaggeration.
▶ Contrast a serious tone with a ridiculous situation.
▶ Include unusual details of setting and character.

APPLYING LANGUAGE SKILLS: Specific vs. Vague Words

Some words are **vague** and general. They are commonly used and are broad in meaning. Other words are **specific.** They are unusual, crisp, and precise. In most writing, especially in storytelling, it's better to use words that are specific.

Vague:
It tasted bad.

Precise:
It tasted revolting.

Practice Replace the italicized vague words in these sentences with more specific ones.

1. My brother *ate* the *stuff.*
2. He *reacted.*
3. My mother *moved* toward him.
4. It was so *funny,* I had to *laugh.*

Writing Application As you write your humorous anecdote, replace vague words with words that are more specific.

Writer's Solution Connection
Writing Lab

To avoid using vague adjectives, use the Revision Checker in the tutorial on Description.

APPLYING LANGUAGE SKILLS:
Spelling Contractions With *Have*

Several **contractions** are made from the word *have*. Here are a few:

would've	would have
could've	could have
should've	should have

In writing contractions, be careful not to write *would of* or *could of* when you mean *would've* or *could've*.

Practice On your paper, rewrite these sentences using contractions with *have*. Correct any errors.

1. You would of been amazed.
2. I should of put the cat food away.
3. I could of laughed for hours.
4. He could of been sick!

Writing Application As you write your humorous anecdote, spell all contractions with *have* correctly.

Writer's Solution Connection
Language Lab

For more instruction on writing dialogue, see the lesson on Quotation Marks in the Language Lab.

Include Dialogue A good story includes dialogue. Include questions and exclamations. Keep the dialogue short, crisp, and easy to read.

Time Your Punch Line Your anecdote will be funniest if you don't give away your ending too early in the story. Keep your audience guessing. Build suspense. Then, serve up a hilarious punch line.

Revising

Include Necessary Information Your audience won't "get" the joke if you don't give them all the information they need. Have a friend read your anecdote. Then, ask if more background information could make it funnier.

Replace Weak Words Don't settle for boring, everyday words. When you notice them, circle them. Use a dictionary, thesaurus, peer reviewer, or your own imagination to replace them.

REVISION MODEL

① horrified and disgusted.   howled with laughter.

He looked surprised and sick. I started to laugh.

② As soon as he could talk,

He grabbed a glass, ran to the sink, and screamed,

"Yick! How could Fluffy eat this stuff?!"

① The writer adds interest and flair by replacing dull words with vivid and precise ones.
② The writer provides more detail to tell *when* events happened.

Publishing and Presenting

▶ **Tell It** Plan a Funny Stories Festival for a slow afternoon. Take turns telling your anecdotes aloud, using voice, gesture, and movement to add to the humor. If possible, videotape your performances and share the tape with another class.

▶ **Find a Magazine** Many magazines—for example, *Reader's Digest*—publish humorous anecdotes sent in by their readers. Submit your anecdote for publication. This could be the beginning of a career in comedy writing!

Real-World Reading Skills Workshop

Interpreting Charts and Graphs

Strategies for Success

Whether you are researching a report or reading the newspaper, you may find information in charts and graphs. Charts and graphs can help you compare several pieces of related information quickly. Follow these guidelines for interpreting charts and graphs:

Identify the Topic Use the title, captions, and label of the chart or graph to identify its topic. The article in which the chart or graph appears will also provide information. Understanding the purpose of the graph will help you to read it accurately.

Study the Elements Follow these steps to study all the information given in the chart or graph:

► Identify the type of chart or graph: The most common types are bar graphs, line graphs, and pie charts.

► Read the key, which tells you what the elements on the graph represent.

► Note the labels and units of measurement on the graph.

► Identify the number of items shown on the graph.

Read the Graph To read a pie chart, compare the values represented by the "wedges" to the value of the whole "pie."

To read a bar or line graph:

1. Start at the left side, and locate the first point or bar on the graph.
2. Trace your finger downward to the horizontal axis to see what the point or bar represents.
3. Look across from the point or top of the bar to the vertical axis, and find the unit of measurement.
4. Repeat this process for each point or bar.

Apply the Strategies

Your teacher has asked you to help plan activities for this year's school fair based on the events that were most popular last year. Use the graph to answer the questions that follow.

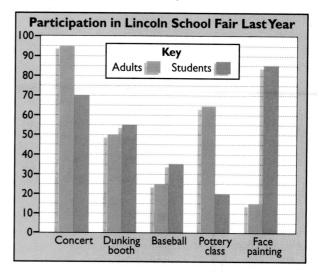

Participation in Lincoln School Fair Last Year

1. Which activity was most popular with adults? With students?

2. Which activity came closest to having the same number of adult and student participants?

3. Which activity had the greatest difference in interest between adults and students?

4. In order to please the most people, which three events would you recommend holding again at this year's fair?

✔ *Here are other situations in which you need to interpret charts and graphs:*
► *Comparing sports statistics*
► *Reading newspapers and magazines*
► *Doing research*

Subjects and Predicates

Grammar Review

SEND

sen·tence (sen'təns) *n.* **1** a group of words that is used to tell, ask, command, or exclaim something, usually having a subject and a predicate: a sentence begins with a capital letter and ends with a period, question mark, or exclamation point

A sentence is a group of words that expresses a complete thought. Every sentence consists of two parts: the **subject** and the **predicate.** The subject states whom or what the sentence is about. The predicate tells what the subject is or does. (See page 377.)

           subject | *predicate*

The young Sarah Stout | refused to take out the garbage.

Simple Subject and Simple Predicate Each complete subject and predicate contains a simple subject and simple predicate. The simple subject is the main word in the complete subject, and the simple predicate is the verb or verb phrase in the predicate. (See page 377.)

       subject | *predicate*

The young (Sarah Stout)|(refused) to take out the garbage.

Compound Subjects and Compound Verbs Some sentences may have more than one subject or verb. A **compound subject** is two or more subjects that have the same verb and are linked by a coordinating conjunction such as *and* or *or*. A **compound predicate** is two or more verbs that have the same subject and are linked by a coordinating conjunction such as *and* or *or*. (See page 394.)

> **Compound Subject:** The *producers* and *technicians* were panicking in the control room.

> **Compound Verb:** They *looked* at the monitors and *gasped* at the video.

Every complete sentence has both a subject and a verb. (See page 408.)

Practice 1 Copy the following sentences into your notebook. Underline the complete subject once and the complete predicate twice. Then, circle the simple subject and the simple predicate, and label those that are compound.

1. Sarah scoured the pots and scraped the pans.

2. The garbage reached across the state.

3. You are old, Father William.

4. In my youth, I took to the law and argued each case with my wife.

5. This day, we plaited our hair and put a dress and some things in a crokasack and started out to the show.

Practice 2 In a paragraph, describe someone you would label a "quirky character." In your paragraph, use two sentences with compound subjects and two with compound verbs.

Grammar in Writing

✔ *You can cut down on wordiness and repetition by combining sentences using compound subjects and verbs.*

Repetitive: Father William turned somersaults. Father William stood on his head.

Revised: Father William turned somersaults and stood on his head.

PART 2 *Mixed Messages*

Central Park, Gustavo Novoa, Wally Findlay Galleries, New York

Guide for Reading

Meet the Authors:

Edward D. Hoch (1930–)

After Edward Hoch graduated from college, he worked as a researcher and copy writer for an advertising agency. He uses these skills in science-fiction and mystery writing. A sense of humor has come in handy, too, as you'll see in his story "Zoo."

Ogden Nash (1902–1971)

Ogden Nash became famous for his ability to look at life from an unusual angle. Packed with a comical punch, his wise and witty poems continue to delight. Readers of all ages look to his work for fun and insight into life's absurdities.

John Godfrey Saxe (1816–1887)

John Godfrey Saxe lived during a time when writers and readers enjoyed poems that told stories. Saxe added humor to his verse, which has remained popular to this day. "The Blind Men and the Elephant," his most famous verse, is based on a tale from ancient India.

Zora Neale Hurston (1891–1960)

In addition to forging a successful career writing her own stories and essays, Zora Neale Hurston traveled throughout the South collecting African American folk tales. When she wrote the tales on paper, she preserved the exact language in which they had been told. This allowed her to honor the oral tradition and made the tales available to a wider audience.

◆ LITERATURE AND YOUR LIFE

CONNECT YOUR EXPERIENCE

Science-fiction writers like to invent wild beings who live in the outer reaches of space, but creatures here on Earth are pretty amazing, too. Observe a caterpillar up close or an elephant from afar. These selections may help you see the animal kingdom in a completely new way.

THEMATIC FOCUS: Mixed Messages

In their confusion, the characters in these selections expend a lot of misplaced energy. Imagine how their experiences would be different if they understood everything the first time!

◆ Background for Understanding

SCIENCE

In this grouping, you'll encounter only a few of the millions of animals who roam the Earth. To help their study of the animal kingdom, scientists have developed a classification system. Animals are classed together based on features they share. For example, the mammal class includes such diverse species as humans, cats, elephants, and dolphins. The 4,500 species of mammals have backbones, warm blood, and well-developed brains.

◆ Build Vocabulary

RELATED WORDS: FORMS OF *wonder*

Wonder and its related words convey a sense of surprise and amazement. *Wonder* can be a noun or a verb. *Wonderment* is also a noun, and *wondrous* and *wonderful* are adjectives.

WORD BANK

Which of these words from the selections might mean hugeness?

interplanetary
wonderment
awe
inclined
observation
wondrous
immensity

Zoo ◆ The Hippopotamus ◆ The Caterpillar ◆ The Blind Men and the Elephant ◆ How the Snake Got Poison

◆ Reading Strategy

EVALUATE AUTHOR'S MESSAGE

A message is the idea that a writer wants to convey. In "Hippopotamus," for example, Nash weighs an animal's perspective against his own to decide that animals and humans each find beauty in their own species. You **evaluate an author's message** by first identifying the message and then judging whether it is true, clearly reasoned, and well supported.

◆ Literary Focus

CHARACTER'S PERSPECTIVE

You might laugh when people in movies make fools of themselves. Yet if you were in the same situation, you might feel more like crying. The same is true of characters in a story or poem. A **character's perspective,** or the position from which he or she views events, will affect his or her actions, reactions, and attitudes. This perspective can be based on knowledge, ability, and former experiences. As you read, use a chart like the one below to track the ways each character's perspective affects his or her understanding of events.

Perspective	Understanding of Events	Actions

ZOO
Edward D. Hoch

The children were always good during the month of August, especially when it began to get near the twenty-third. It was on this day that the great silver spaceship carrying Professor Hugo's <u>Interplanetary</u> Zoo settled down for its annual six-hour visit to the Chicago area.

Before daybreak the crowds would form, long lines of children and adults both, each one clutching his or her dollar and waiting with <u>wonderment</u> to see what race of strange creatures the Professor had brought this year.

In the past they had sometimes been treated to three-legged creatures from Venus, or tall, thin men from Mars, or even snakelike horrors from somewhere more distant. This year, as the great round ship settled slowly to earth in the huge tri-city parking area just outside of Chicago, they watched with <u>awe</u> as the sides slowly slid up to reveal the familiar barred cages. In them were some wild breed of nightmare—small, horse-like animals that moved with quick, jerking motions and constantly chattered in a high-pitched tongue. The citizens of Earth clustered around as Professor Hugo's crew quickly collected the waiting dollars, and soon the good Professor himself made an appearance, wearing his many-colored rainbow cape and top hat. "Peoples of Earth," he called into his microphone. The crowd's noise died down and he continued. "Peoples of Earth, this year you see a real treat for your single dollar—the little-known horse-spider people of Kaan—brought to you across a million miles of space at great expense. Gather around, see them, study them, listen to them, tell your friends about them. But hurry! My ship can remain here only six hours!"

And the crowds slowly filed by, at once horrified and fascinated by these strange creatures that looked like horses but ran up the walls of their cages like spiders. "This is certainly worth a dollar," one man remarked, hurrying away. "I'm going home to get the wife."

All day long it went like that, until ten thousand people had filed by the barred cages set into the side of the spaceship. Then, as the six-hour limit ran out, Professor Hugo once more took the microphone in hand. "We must go now, but we will return next year on this date. And if you enjoyed our zoo this year, telephone your friends in other cities about it. We will land in New York tomorrow, and next week on to London, Paris,

♦ **Build Vocabulary**

interplanetary (in´ tər plan´ ə ter´ ē) *adj.*: Between planets

wonderment (wun´ dər ment) *n.*: Astonishment

awe (ô) *n.*: Mixed feelings of fear and wonder

Rome, Hong Kong, and Tokyo. Then on to other worlds!"

He waved farewell to them, and as the ship rose from the ground, the Earth peoples agreed that this had been the very best Zoo yet. . . .

Some two months and three planets later, the silver ship of Professor Hugo settled at last onto the familiar jagged rocks of Kaan, and the odd horse-spider creatures filed quickly out of their cages. Professor Hugo was there to say a few parting words, and then they scurried away in a hundred different directions, seeking their homes among the rocks.

In one house, the she-creature was happy to see the return of her mate and offspring. She babbled a greeting in the strange tongue and hurried to embrace them. "It was a long time you were gone. Was it good?"

And the he-creature nodded. "The little one enjoyed it especially.

We visited eight worlds and saw many things."

The little one ran up the wall of the cave. "On the place called Earth it was the best. The creatures there wear garments over their skins, and they walk on two legs."

"But isn't it dangerous?" asked the she-creature.

"No," her mate answered. "There are bars to protect us from them. We remain right in the ship. Next time you must come with us. It is well worth the nineteen commocs it costs."

And the little one nodded. "It was the very best Zoo ever. . . ."

◆ Reading Strategy
Why does she think human beings are dangerous?

▼ Critical Viewing After you've read "Zoo," suggest two captions for this illustration—one from the people's perspective and one from the animals'. [Summarize]

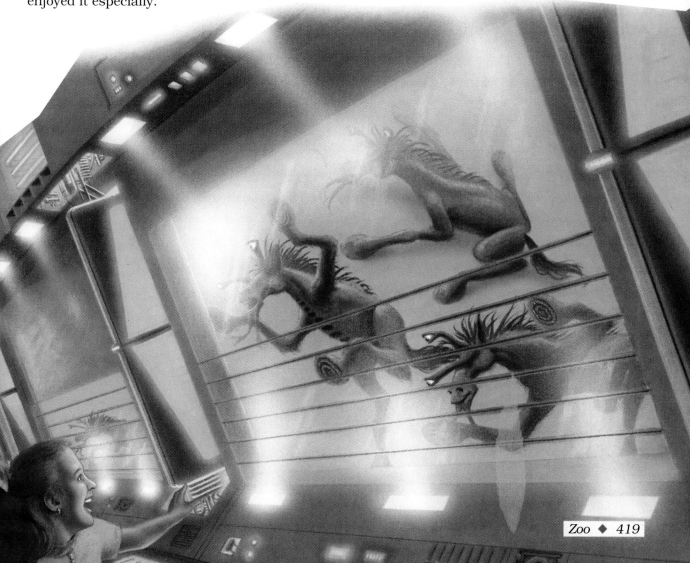

The Hippopotamus

Ogden Nash

Behold the hippopotamus!
We laugh at how he looks to us,
And yet in moments dank and grim
I wonder how we look to him.
5   Peace, peace, thou hippopotamus!
We really look all right to us,
As you no doubt delight the eye
Of other hippopotami.

▲ Critical Viewing What features of the hippopotamus might someone find funny? [Connect]

The Caterpillar
Ogden Nash

I find among the poems of Schiller[1]
No mention of the caterpillar,
Nor can I find one anywhere
In Petrarch[2] or in Baudelaire,[3]
5 So here I sit in extra session
To give my personal impression.
The caterpillar, as it's called,
Is often hairy, seldom bald;
It looks as if it never shaves;
10 When as it walks, it walks in waves;
And from the cradle to the chrysalis
It's utterly speechless, songless, whistleless.

---

1. **Schiller:** Friedrich von Schiller (1759–1805);
German dramatist, poet, and historian.
2. **Petrarch:** Francesco Petrarca (1304–1374);
Italian poet and scholar.
3. **Baudelaire:** Charles Pierre Baudelaire
(1821–1867); French poet.

▲ Critical Viewing Why might a caterpillar,
like the one pictured here, be overlooked
by the poets that Nash names? **[Speculate]**

Guide for Responding

◆ **LITERATURE AND YOUR LIFE**

Reader's Response Were you surprised by
the ending of Hoch's story? Explain.

Thematic Focus How do "Zoo," "The Hippopotamus," and "The Caterpillar" each illustrate the concept of mixed messages?

Journal Writing What other animal do you
think would make a good subject for a poem by
Ogden Nash? In a journal entry, explain your
choice.

☑ **Check Your Comprehension**

1. In "Zoo," what impression do earthlings have
of the creatures from Kaan?
2. How do the Kaanians describe humans?
3. What does the speaker of "The Hippopotamus" imagine that the animal thinks?
4. Where has the speaker of "The Caterpillar"
looked to find poetry about the animal?

◆ **Critical Thinking**

INTERPRET

1. Based on what he tells the earthlings, how do
you think Professor Hugo entices the Kaanians to visit Earth? **[Speculate]**
2. What does the way Professor Hugo runs his
zoo suggest about him? **[Infer]**
3. (a) In "The Hippopotamus," why does the
speaker want to console the animal? (b) What
does he say to console him? **[Interpret]**
4. In "The Caterpillar," what qualities of the insect does the speaker celebrate? **[Analyze]**
5. What elements of Nash's poetry tell you the
poems are meant to amuse? **[Support]**

EVALUATE

6. (a) Do you think Nash likes his subjects?
(b) What details in the poems help you
decide? **[Assess]**

EXTEND

7. What facts about the hippopotamus and the
caterpillar would you stress in a scientific
description? **[Science Link]**

The Blind Men and the Elephant

John Godfrey Saxe

It was six men of Indostan
    To learning much <u>inclined</u>,
Who went to see the Elephant
    (Though all of them were blind),
5 That each by <u>observation</u>
    Might satisfy his mind.

The *First* approached the Elephant,
    And happening to fall
Against his broad and sturdy side,
10   At once began to bawl:
"God bless me! but the Elephant
    Is very like a wall!"

The *Second*, feeling of the tusk,
    Cried, "Ho! what have we here
15 So very round and smooth and sharp?
    To me 'tis mighty clear
This wonder of an Elephant
    Is very like a spear!"

The *Third* approached the animal,
20   And happening to take
The squirming trunk within his hands,
    Thus boldly up and spake:
"I see," quoth he, "the Elephant
    Is very like a snake!"

25 The *Fourth* reached out an eager hand,
    And felt about the knee.
"What most this <u>wondrous</u> beast is like
    Is mighty plain," quoth he;
"'Tis clear enough the Elephant
30   Is very like a tree!"

The *Fifth*, who chanced to touch the ear,
    Said; "E'en the blindest man
Can tell what this resembles most;
    Deny[1] the fact who can,
35 This marvel of an Elephant
    Is very like a fan!"

---

1. **deny** (dē nī´) *v.*: Say is untrue; reject.

◆ **Build Vocabulary**

inclined (in klīnd´) *adj.*: Interested in

observation (äb´ zər vā´ shən) *n.*: The act of noticing details

wondrous (wun´ drəs) *adj.*: Extraordinary

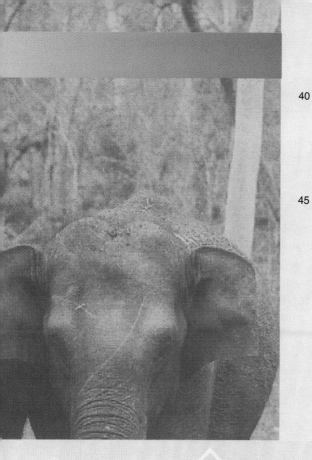

The *Sixth* no sooner had begun
    About the beast to grope.
Than, seizing[2] on the swinging tail
40   That fell within his scope,[3]
"I see," quoth he, "the Elephant
    Is very like a rope!"

And so these men of Indostan
    Disputed[4] loud and long,
45 Each in his own opinion
    Exceeding[5] stiff and strong,
Though each was partly in the right,
    And all were in the wrong!

---

2. **seizing** (sēz´ iŋ) *v.*: Quickly grabbing.
3. **scope** (skōp) *n.*: Reach or range.
4. **disputed** (di spyo͞ot´ id) *v.*: Argued.
5. **exceeding** (ek sēd´ iŋ) *adv.*: Going beyond.

◀ **Critical Viewing** The blind men observe six different parts of an elephant. Which of these elements can you see in this photograph? **[Connect]**

Guide for Responding

◆ LITERATURE AND YOUR LIFE

Reader's Response Explain which description of the elephant was funniest to you.

Thematic Focus Each man receives a different message about the elephant's nature. How might the men arrive at the whole truth?

Journal Writing In a brief journal entry, write about a time when you got only part of a story. Explain the problems this created.

☑ Check Your Comprehension

1. What did the blind men want to find out?
2. How did they observe the elephant without actually seeing it?
3. What did each of the men think the elephant was like? What part did each observe?
4. What did each blind man think of the others' interpretations?

◆ Critical Thinking

INTERPRET

1. What is the purpose of each of the separate sections, or stanzas, of the poem? **[Analyze]**
2. The men of Indostan are physically blind. In what other ways are they blind? **[Infer]**
3. If the men each observed a part of the elephant accurately, how can each man's conclusion be so wrong? **[Analyze Cause and Effect]**

APPLY

4. What advice would you give to these men to help them resolve their conflict? **[Resolve]**

EXTEND

5. The men of Indostan are not alone in their problematic methods of getting at the truth. Identify a situation in current events that was brought about in the same way. **[Social Studies Link]**

HOW THE SNAKE GOT POISON

Zora Neale Hurston

Well, when God made de snake he put him in de bushes to ornament de ground. But things didn't suit de snake so one day he got on de ladder and went up to see God.

"Good mawnin', God."

"How do you do, Snake?"

"Ah[1] ain't so many, God, you put me down here on my belly in de dust and everything trods upon me and kills off my generations. Ah ain't got no kind of protection at all."

God looked off towards immensity and thought about de subject for awhile, then he said, "Ah didn't mean for nothin' to be stompin' you snakes lak dat. You got to have some kind of a protection. Here, take dis poison and put it in yo' mouf and when they tromps on you, protect yo'self."

So de snake took de poison in his mouf and went on back.

So after awhile all de other varmints went up to God.

"Good evenin', God."

"How you makin' it, varmints?"

"God, please do somethin' 'bout dat snake. He' layin' in de bushes there wid poison in his mouf and he's strikin' everything dat shakes de bushes. He's killin' up our generations. Wese skeered to walk de earth."

◆ **Literary Focus**
Notice how both the snake and the varmints see themselves as victims.

So God sent for de snake and tole him:

"Snake, when Ah give you dat poison, Ah didn't mean for you to be hittin' and killin' everything dat shake de bush. I give you dat poison and tole you to protect yo'-self when they tromples on you. But you killin' everything dat moves. Ah didn't mean for you to do dat."

De snake say, "Lawd, you know Ah'm down here in de dust. Ah ain't got no claws to fight wid, and Ah ain't got no feets

1. **Ah:** Dialect for "I."

to git me out de way. All Ah kin see is feets comin' to tromple me. Ah can't tell who my enemy is and who is my friend. You gimme dis protection in my mouf and Ah uses it."

God thought it over for a while then he says:

"Well, snake, I don't want yo' generations all stomped out and I don't want you killin' everything else dat moves. Here take dis bell and tie it to yo' tail. When you hear feets comin' you ring yo' bell and if it's yo' friend, he'll be keerful. If it's yo' enemy, it's you and him."

So dat's how de snake got his poison and dat's how come he got rattles.

◆ Build Vocabulary

immensity (i men´ si tē) *n.*: Something extremely large or immeasurably vast

Guide for Responding

◆ LITERATURE AND YOUR LIFE

Reader's Response In this folk tale, God weighs arguments from two conflicting sides. Would you have made the same decision?

Thematic Focus What mixed message does God give the snake? Explain.

Journal Writing The snake complains about his lot in life. In a journal entry, use another animal's physical traits and write the complaint it might voice if it could.

☑ Check Your Comprehension

1. Why does the snake ask God for protection?
2. (a) Why do the other animals complain to God? (b) How does God respond to their problem?
3. What natural fact does this story explain?

◆ Critical Thinking

INTERPRET

1. The snake's problem could have been solved if God gave him legs or claws. Why couldn't the story end this way? **[Infer]**
2. Reread God's final decision. What seems most important to him? **[Analyze]**

EVALUATE

3. By imitating the exact pronunciation, sentence structure, and language of some African Americans in the South, Zora Neale Hurston used dialect in her writing. How did this choice affect your appreciation of the story? **[Assess]**

EXTEND

4. What does this folk tale illustrate about people and their ways of interacting? **[Social Studies Link]**

Guide for Responding (continued)

◆ Reading Strategy

EVALUATE AUTHOR'S MESSAGE

You **evaluate an author's message** by first identifying the message, then examining how well it is supported. In "Zoo," Hoch suggests that people often feel superior to others who are different from them. He supports this message by presenting Kaanians, who like a fence to protect them from "dangerous" humans. Your experience will help you decide whether this message rings true.

1. (a) What is the message of "The Blind Men and the Elephant"? (b) How does Saxe support his message? (c) Explain whether you agree or disagree with it.
2. Choose one other selection from this grouping. (a) Identify the message. (b) Identify the reasoning the writer provides to support this message. (c) Explain whether you agree or disagree with it.

◆ Build Vocabulary

USING FORMS OF *wonder*

On your paper, complete the following sentences with the appropriate form of *wonder*. Choose from *wonderment, wonderful, wondrous,* and *wondrously*.

1. The hippopotamus gazed at me with ____?____.
2. Snake's poison was ____?____ effective.
3. An elephant is a most ____?____ creature.

SPELLING STRATEGY

Before you add the suffix *-ity* to nouns ending in *e*, drop the *e*: *immense* becomes *immensity*. Add *-ity* to each of the following words, and use each new word in a sentence.

1. dense   2. insane   3. scarce

USING THE WORD BANK

Explain your answer to each of these questions.

1. Do varmints view the snake with *wonderment*?
2. Do the people of Earth think the people of Kaan are *wondrous*?
3. Would you be struck by an elephant's *immensity*?
4. Is a flight from New York to Rome *interplanetary*?
5. What inspires a sense of *awe* in you?
6. Would you be *inclined* to help your best friend?
7. Should doctors expect to do a lot of *observation*?

◆ Literary Focus

CHARACTER'S PERSPECTIVE

Each character in these stories views events from a unique **perspective,** or position. For example, in "How the Snake Got Poison," the snake feels victimized without feet. This affects the way he thinks. The other animals—each with its own perspective—are less understanding about his behavior.

1. How does your understanding of the story "Zoo" change when you see things from the perspective of the creatures of Kaan?
2. Six varying perspectives create conflict in "The Blind Men and the Elephant." Explain.

◆ Build Grammar Skills

DIRECT AND INDIRECT OBJECTS

A subject and a verb may require more to complete their meaning. A **direct object** is the noun or pronoun that receives the action of a verb. It answers *whom* or *what* after the verb.

> verb   D.O.
> The creatures wear *garments*. (*Wear what?*)

> verb   D.O.
> Professor Hugo invited *them*. (*Invited whom?*)

A sentence with a direct object can also contain an **indirect object,** which names the person or thing that something is given to or done for. It answers the question *to or for whom* or *to or for what.* Indirect objects appear only before direct objects.

> verb   I.O.   D.O.
> Snake told *God* his trouble. (*Told to whom?*)

Practice Identify the direct and indirect objects that appear in the following sentences.

1. We enjoyed our zoo visit this year.
2. The third man gave the elephant a shake.
3. You showed me this protection.
4. The message reached an interplanetary audience.
5. They bought the children tickets to the show.

Writing Application Use the following verbs in sentences with direct and indirect objects. For each, identify the objects you use.

1. write   2. send   3. tell   4. bake   5. sell

Build Your Portfolio

 ## Idea Bank

Writing

1. **Advertising Flyer** Professor Hugo has re- cruited a group of humans for an exhibit he'll bring to other planets. Write an advertising flyer telling about these amazing creatures.

2. **Humorous Poem** Using Ogden Nash's verse as a model, write a short poem about an animal. Choose an animal with unusual characteristics or one that is often overlooked.

3. **Comparison-and-Contrast Essay** In "The Blind Men and the Elephant," six men see one object in six different ways. Use the information in the poem to write an essay in which you com- pare and contrast the accuracy of the conclu- sions they draw.

Speaking and Listening

4. **Zoo Commercial** Imagine that you are the public relations director for Hugo's Zoo. Create a radio commercial to be aired in several cities. Appeal to a wide audience. **[Career Link]**

5. **Animal Game** Team up with a partner to find out ten unusual facts about an animal. Playing against another team of two, take turns reporting a fact and trying to identify the animal. The first group that guesses an animal correctly wins.

Projects

6. **Pet Show [Group Activity]** As these selections remind you, animals come in many shapes and sizes. With several classmates, research the variety of animals that people keep as pets. Interview pet owners, collect photos and videos, and learn more about these animals. Then, present a report to the class. Each group member can describe the unique characteristics of a specific pet. **[Science Link]**

7. **Metamorphosis** Research the care and feeding of caterpillars. Collect specimens and raise them in an indoor exhibit tank or cage. Track their de- velopment as they shed their chrysalises and emerge as butterflies or moths. **[Science Link]**

 ## Writing Mini-Lesson

Report

The stories and poems you've just read focus on animals, but they don't provide much factual infor- mation. Take a different approach by writing a non- fiction report about an animal that interests you. In your report, focus on the animal's three most out- standing characteristics.

Writing Skills Focus: Topic Sentences and Supporting Details

Keep your writing clear and focused by organ- izing every paragraph of your report. The **topic sentence** is a general statement that tells the reader what the paragraph is going to be about. **Supporting details** prove the point made in the topic sentence. Look at this outline:

Topic Sentence: Seal pups are hardy animals.

> **Detail:** They swim in ocean water from birth.
>
> **Detail:** A thick layer of fat protects them.
>
> **Detail:** At age five weeks, pups are able to catch fish on their own.

Prewriting Use a library, the Internet, or a nearby zoo to research the animal you've chosen. When you've collected enough data, choose the animal's three outstanding characteristics. Make an outline, organizing your report according to these traits.

Drafting In your introduction, provide general facts about the animal. In each of the next three paragraphs, discuss one of the animal's most out- standing characteristics. In your conclusion, summa- rize and extend by mentioning the animal's value.

Revising Review your notes to make sure your facts are correct. If necessary, add details to support your topic sentences and to make the report more interesting.

> ◆ **Grammar Application**
> With a highlighter pen, identify any direct or indirect objects you have used.

Guide for Reading

Meet the Authors:

Charles Dickens (1812–1870)

With *Oliver Twist*, *A Christmas Carol*, and *Great Expectations* to his credit, Charles Dickens is one of the world's best-known novelists.

A Childhood of Poverty Born in Portsmouth, England, Dickens began supporting his family at the age of twelve. For the rest of his life, he could not forget what it was like to be poor. As a young man, Dickens became a law apprentice in London, but his main interest was in journalism. He took a job as a political reporter and then began his career as a fiction writer.

In addition to his novels, Dickens wrote many comical sketches and letters. The letter you are about to read shows off the grace and wit of his writing style. [For more about Charles Dickens, see page 642.]

Paul Reiser (1957–   )

Of all his accomplishments, Paul Reiser's biggest claim to fame may be the hit television comedy *Mad About You*. The show, produced by and starring Reiser, details the lives of Paul and Jamie Buchman, a young married couple living in New York. Following the birth of Reiser's real-life son, Ezra, a daughter was added to the television family, offering more opportunities for laughs based on Reiser's "honest" comedy.

◆ LITERATURE AND YOUR LIFE

CONNECT YOUR EXPERIENCE

Such daily chores as doing the laundry, baby sitting, or mowing the lawn might really annoy you. However, as these selections reveal, such routine tasks as fixing a clock and taking an infant on a walk can be a source of humor.

THEMATIC FOCUS: Mixed Messages

Notice how these writers discover humor by exploring everyday experiences from unusual angles.

◆ Background for Understanding

SCIENCE

Recent research in early childhood development stresses the need to stimulate children at an early age. Scientists now believe that the brain development that occurs within the first years is critical. Every experience helps introduce the brain to new ways of interpreting information. For this reason, parents are encouraged to interact with their new babies as much as they can. Experts suggest playing classical music, reading aloud, hanging mobiles over a baby's crib, and talking to babies as much as possible. In "Stepping Out With My Baby," Paul Reiser tries to follow this advice.

◆ Build Vocabulary

PREFIXES: *auto-*

Automatically contains the prefix *auto-* meaning "self." When Reiser reports that he responds *automatically* to an idea, he means that he answers like a self-run machine would—without thinking.

WORD BANK

Which of these words from the selections might mean "secret"?

reluctance
confidential
automatically

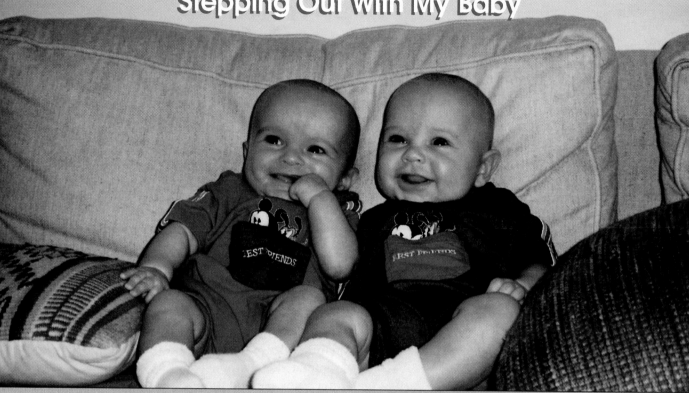

◆ A Letter to a Clockmaker ◆
Stepping Out With My Baby

◆ Literary Focus
HUMOROUS COMMENTARY

Laughter forms bonds between people. It can sometimes turn strangers into friends or break the tension in uncomfortable situations. Writers use **humorous commentary,** writing that contains amusing personal observations or opinions, to help readers look at life a little less seriously. You are about to see how this technique works in two different forms of writing—a letter and an essay. As you read each selection, notice the topics the writers address, paying attention to the points they make about these topics.

◆ Reading Strategy
DISTINGUISH FACT FROM OPINION

To show the humor in the subjects they tackle, these writers combine **facts** (statements that can be proved true) and **opinions** (statements that can be supported but not proved). For instance, Reiser starts with a fact: "We arrive at the mailbox." He adds opinion to create comedy: "an exhausting block and a half from home." By **distinguishing fact from opinion,** you form your interpretation of an event rather than just accepting what the author says. Use a chart like the one below to separate facts from opinions.

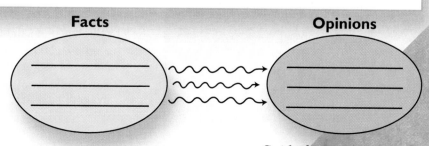

Facts   Opinions

A Letter to a Clockmaker

Charles Dickens

My dear Sir:

Since my hall clock was sent to your establishment to be cleaned it has gone (as indeed it always has) perfectly, but has struck with great <u>reluctance</u>, and after enduring internal agonies of a most distressing nature it has now ceased striking altogether. Though a happy release for the clock, this is not a convenience for the household. If you can send down any <u>confidential</u> person with whom the clock can confer, I think it may have something on its works that it would be glad to make a clean breast of.

Faithfully yours,
Charles Dickens.

Higham by Rochester, Kent,
Monday night, Sep. 14, 1863

◀ **Critical Viewing** How might the size and shape of a grandfather clock like the one pictured here prompt Dickens to write "A Letter to a Clockmaker"? [**Hypothesize**]

◆ Build Vocabulary

reluctance (ri luk´ təns) *n.*: Unwillingness

confidential (kän´ fə den´ shəl) *adj.*: Entrusted with private or secret matters

automatically (ôt´ ə mat´ ik lē) *adv.*: Without thought; by reflex

Stepping Out With My Baby

Paul Reiser

On his first trip outside the house with his infant son, Paul Reiser describes the stressful experience of being outdoors. Armed with advice from his wife and worried about the opinions of the people who pass him on the street, Reiser endures a barrage of panicked thoughts.

Finally we arrive at the mailbox—an exhausting block and a half from home. Dizzy with the victory of arriving at our destination in more or less one piece, I reach into my pocket, retrieve the now sweaty envelopes, and am about to toss them into the mailbox when I hear a voice. It's my wife's voice, echoing in my head.

"Talk to him."

"Hmm?" I say <u>automatically</u>, totally accepting that my wife might in fact be physically standing next to me, just for a follow-up evaluation on my performance.

"Talk to him. Explain to him what you're doing," the voice in my head suggests.

Sometimes I forget that part—talking to my child. Actually *being* with him. When I'm in charge of the kid, I tend to either stare at him like he's television or drift totally into a world of my own, running through my list of things-I-have-to-do-later-when-I'm-not-taking-care-of-the-kid. Or I take the job *so* seriously I become blinded by the severity of the responsibility, and panic. What I seem to miss is the middle

▲ **Critical Viewing** Using the text to help you, describe the action suggested by this illustration. **[Analyze]**

ground—the part where you share, teach, learn, play—the part you can actually enjoy.

"Right. Talk to him. I'll do that. Thanks," I say to myself, and the voice of the Nice Lady in My Head leaves me alone again.

"So," I say to my buckled-up Beautiful Boy. "This is a mailbox."

And in response, he takes a hearty bite out of his little red corduroy clown's terry-cloth head.

"See? Daddy's going to put these letters into the mailbox. See? . . . What else can I tell you . . . The mailbox is blue."

When in doubt, mention the color. They can't get enough of colors, these kids.

"It's a blue mailbox."

Another ferocious bite-and-tug almost removes the corduroy clown's left ear. Clearly the boy is not that interested—I'll just mail the letters.

Guide for Responding (continued)

◆ Reading Strategy

DISTINGUISH FACT FROM OPINION

To add humor, these writers combine their comical opinions with facts that set up the situations they describe. When you **distinguish fact from opinion,** you ask whether a given statement could be proved to be true. If the answer is yes, the statement is a fact. If the answer is no, the statement is an opinion.

1. Identify one fact and one opinion from Dickens's letter. Explain.
2. Read the last paragraph of Reiser's essay. (a) Identify three facts. (b) Identify two opinions. Explain your answers.

◆ Build Vocabulary

USING THE PREFIX: *auto-*

The prefix *auto-* means "self." Knowing this prefix can help you determine the meaning of many other English words. Explain how *auto-* affects the meaning of these words:

1. autobiography
2. autopilot
3. autograph (*graph* means writing)
4. autonomy (*nomy* means government or management)

SPELLING STRATEGY

The letter *t* combines with the suffix *-ial* to produce the *shul* sound that you hear in the word *confidential*. The *shul* sound can also be spelled *cial*, but the *tial* spelling is more common. On your paper, complete each sentence with a word that ends with *tial*.

1. Karate and judo are m____?____ arts.
2. Your i____?____ is the first letter of your name.
3. His mansion on the beach is p____?____.

USING THE WORD BANK

For each of the following pairs of words, write *S* on your paper if the words are synonyms and *A* if they are antonyms.

1. reluctance, eagerness
2. confidential, private
3. automatically, deliberately

◆ Literary Focus

HUMOROUS COMMENTARY

Stand-up comedians often deliver **humorous commentaries,** or amusing observations and opinions, about everyday experiences and events. Humorous commentaries also appear in written form. They are frequently found in newspapers.

1. What amusing comments about his clock does Dickens make in his letter?
2. What amusing observations about babies does Reiser make in his essay?
3. Would either selection be as effective if it were written without humor? Explain.

◆ Build Grammar Skills

SUBJECT COMPLEMENTS

Linking verbs like *be, is,* and *am* show a state of being. They are followed by **subject complements** to complete an idea about a subject. A **predicate noun** renames or identifies the subject; a **predicate adjective** describes the subject. Look at these examples:

<pre>
          L.V.   P.N.
Dickens is a world-famous writer. (renames subject)
                        L.V.   P.A.
Reiser's new work will be funny. (describes subject)
</pre>

To help you identify complements, note the kind of verb in a sentence. Only linking verbs can have subject complements. Action verbs take direct and indirect objects.

Practice Identify the predicate noun (P.N.) or the predicate adjective (P.A.) in each sentence.

1. Charles Dickens was once a reporter.
2. His family became confused when the clock stopped striking.
3. Reiser's show has been popular for years.
4. It is our favorite situation comedy.
5. Many of the jokes seem original.

Writing Application Write sentences using the following linking verbs. Then, identify the subject complements you use.

1. is   2. will be   3. has been   4. were   5. are

Build Your Portfolio

Idea Bank

Writing

1. **Letter of Response** If you were the clock-maker who received Dickens's letter, how might you respond? Write a brief note replying to Dickens's request.

2. **Personal Narrative** Write an essay describing an experience you've had with an infant or tod-dler who couldn't use language to communicate. In your narrative, explain how the child conveyed his or her needs to you.

3. **Comparison-and-Contrast Essay** Rewrite Dickens's letter in more modern English. Then, write an essay in which you compare and con-trast these two versions.

Speaking and Listening

4. **Charles Dickens Presentation** Use Internet or library sources to find more samples of Charles Dickens's famous work. Then, choose a brief piece to read aloud to the class. Give an introduction to explain your choice.

5. ***Mad About You* Review** Watch an episode of Reiser's sitcom *Mad About You*. As you watch, take notes about the comic techniques the show uses. Share your insights with the class. **[Media Link]**

Projects

6. **Report on the 1850's [Group Activity]** With several classmates, research and report on life in Dickens's time—the 1850's in London. Each per-son can address a specific question. For example, How did people travel around town? What was the cost of common necessities? What were typ-ical jobs? Share your findings in an illustrated re-port. **[Social Studies Link]**

7. **Sitcom Guide** Prepare a list of your favorite sitcoms. For each, write a summary that explains the show's basic premise. Identify the stars and the night and time the show appears. Devise a system to rate each show. **[Media Link]**

Writing Mini-Lesson

Letter of Complaint

If you're like most people, you probably ignore the little frustrations you face every day. What if you could write someone a letter about that finicky locker combination or that bicycle chain that keeps slipping even though it was supposedly fixed? Write a complaint letter about a frustrating or annoying experience that you've had.

> **Writing Skills Focus: Letter Format**
> A **formal letter** contains five parts:
> 1. Heading, including your address and the date, at the top of the page
> 2. Salutation, or greeting
> 3. Body
> 4. Closing
> 5. Signature
>
> Notice that Dickens chooses the words "My dear Sir" for the salutation and "Faithfully yours" for the closing of his letter to the clockmaker.

Prewriting Choose an annoying incident or expe-rience to describe. Jot down details about it. For example, note what happened, how you felt at the time, and what action you would like taken.

Drafting Write the heading of your letter. Then, choose a salutation. Refer to your notes as you write the body of your letter. Finally, choose a clos-ing phrase and sign your letter.

> ◆ **Grammar Application**
> Let subject complements work for you. Make them as specific as possible.

Revising Make sure you have explained the situa-tion thoroughly. If necessary, add details to clarify your experience and your request.

Connecting Literature to Social Studies
EASTERN EUROPE

Let's Steal the Moon *by Blanche Serwer-Bernstein*

Water Carrier by Moonlight, Marc Chagall,
© 1989 by The Metropolitan Museum of Art

"DID YOU HEAR THE ONE ABOUT . . . ?"

Even before comedy clubs offered people a chance to laugh at their mistakes, humor was part of most cultures. For enjoyment and education, people passed funny stories from one generation to the next. Such tales can be found in many cultural traditions, including the rich folk heritage of the Jewish people.

A History of Wandering The Jews settled in Palestine more than 3,000 years ago. In 63 B.C., their kingdom, Judea, was conquered by the Roman Empire. In A.D. 70, the Romans destroyed the temple in Jerusalem. From that time until the establishment of Israel in 1947, no Jewish state existed.

A Changing Map Many Jews settled in Russia and Eastern Europe—a part of the world where countries and borders were constantly shifting as groups entered, crossed, or settled in the region. For example, in 1795, Russia, Prussia, and Austria moved into Poland, dividing it among themselves. Poland was not independent again until 1918.

Ethnic Conflicts In some Eastern European countries, people of different ethnic groups live together in harmony. For example, in 1993, the Czechs and the Slovaks peacefully agreed to separate Czechoslovakia into two countries. However, in other places, tension between different populations has led to ethnic conflicts. As a result, the map continues to change.

A Town Full of Fools This folk tale comes from Eastern Europe. It was originally told in Yiddish, a language that mixes elements of Hebrew and German. In Jewish folklore, Chelem is a fictional town whose inhabitants are known for their stupidity. The Chelemites, however, consider themselves to be clever, which makes their foolish behavior even funnier.

Let's Steal the Moon

A Yiddish Tale

Blanche Serwer-Bernstein

The people of Chelem[1] loved their city and tried to improve it in every way. Whenever they heard of something new and different in another city, they wanted it for themselves. What is good for others is good for us, they reasoned.

Imagine how excited they became when they learned that in some towns the streets were lighted at night. What a brilliant idea! With street lamps there would be no need to stumble in the dark or to come right up to a person and peer closely into his face to recognize him, or guess when you came to a street corner, or lose your way because you made a wrong turn. A wonderful improvement, lamps in the streets! Why hadn't they thought of this before?

Connecting Literature to Social Studies
How is the city of Chelem governed?

As was the custom, all the citizens of Chelem came together to discuss the appealing new notion of installing lights on their street corners.

As they sat in council, thinking the matter through, a white-bearded patriarch stood up and spoke, "Street lights, my friends, would cost us a great deal of money and where would the money come from? From our fund for the poor? That is forbidden!

"On the other hand, there is a luminary up in the sky that helps us for part of the month and leaves us in the dark for part of the month. There are nights when the moon shines and Chelem has enough light. There are other nights when there is no moon and Chelem is dark. Now, why can't the moon shine for us every night?"

"Why not?" wondered the people of Chelem, looking skyward and shaking their heads thoughtfully.

Then they drew closer to the old man, delighting in his great wisdom as he unfolded his plan. The wise patriarch persuaded the people of Chelem to wait for a night when the moon was large and full, shedding light into every nook and cranny of their dark streets. Then, to put it simply and directly, they would steal the moon and guard her safely until the dark nights of the month, when they would hang her in the skies to light up their streets.

"Steal the moon? Why not?" reasoned the people of Chelem, rubbing their chins in deepest contemplation.

Gimpel, who always had the most advanced ideas, suggested, "While we have it down, why not clean and polish it so that it will be brighter than ever?"

"Polish the moon? Why not?" agreed the people of Chelem, bewildered by the onrush of their own creative ideas.

They had no difficulty at all in capturing the moon. It was a simple matter. They filled a barrel with water and left it open, exposed to the moon's light. Then ten Chelemites stood ready with sackcloth.

The moon, unaware of the plot, moved into the barrel of water. When it was clearly trapped, the Chelemites covered the barrel with the heavy sackcloth and bound it down with thick strong rope. To make certain that everything was as it should be, they put the official seal of Chelem on the barrel and carried it carefully into the Synagogue[2] where it would be safe from all harm. They checked every night to make sure the seal was not broken.

---

2. **Synagogue** (sin´ ə gäg): Place of worship in the Jewish religion.

◆ **Build Vocabulary**
patriarch (pā´ trē ärk) *n.*: Old, dignified man
luminary (lo͞o´ mə ner´ ē) *n.*: Something that gives off light

---

1. **Chelem** (khel´ əm)

Reading for Success

Strategies for Reading Fiction

Fiction is writing that tells about imaginary characters and events. Short stories are brief works of fiction; novels are longer works of fiction. In fiction, the author creates a whole new world for you to explore. Sometimes, this world is strongly based on the real world of today or some time in the past. Other times, this world may be wildly inventive. In order to get the most out of the world the author has created, use the following strategies:

Predict.

As the events of the story unfold, ask yourself what will happen next. Be on the lookout for clues that hint of events to come. To find out whether your predictions are correct, read on.

> **Event:** Policeman walks an isolated beat at night.
>
> **Predictions:** He will meet someone; he may arrest someone.

Identify with the characters or the situation.

Fiction not only allows you to visit new worlds, but also allows you to experience other lives. By putting yourself in the characters' places or imagining yourself in their situation, you get to live the story with the characters.

Make inferences.

▶ Writers seldom tell you everything directly. As a result, you need to make inferences, or draw conclusions based on the details the author provides.

▶ An inference map is a useful way to organize details that the author provides and the inferences you draw from them. A partial inference map for one of the characters in "After Twenty Years" is shown below.

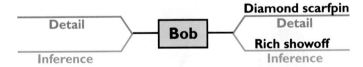

Question.

Stories are more interesting when you ask questions about characters and events. Ask: Why did he or she do that? What does this mean? How does this relate to what's already happened? Is this a hint about events to come? As you read, look for the answers to your questions.

As you read "After Twenty Years," read the side notes, which demonstrate how to apply these strategies to your reading.

After Twenty Years

O. Henry

The policeman on the beat moved up the avenue impressively. The impressiveness was habitual and not for show, for spectators were few. The time was barely 10 o'clock at night, but chilly gusts of wind with a taste of rain in them had well nigh[1] depeopled the streets.

> From the policeman's swagger and careful attention to his duty even when there was no one to admire him, you might **infer** that he is proud of his job.

Trying doors as he went, twirling his club with many intricate and artful movements, turning now and then to cast his watchful eye adown the pacific thoroughfare,[2] the officer, with his stalwart form and slight swagger, made a fine picture of a guardian of the peace. The vicinity was one that kept early hours. Now and then you might see the lights of a cigar store or of an all-night lunch counter; but the majority of the doors belonged to business places that had long since been closed.

When about midway of a certain block the policeman suddenly slowed his walk. In the doorway of a darkened hardware store a man leaned, with an unlighted cigar in his mouth. As the policeman walked up to him the man spoke up quickly.

"It's all right, officer," he said, reassuringly. "I'm just waiting for a friend. It's an appointment made twenty

> **Predict** what the man is going to tell the policeman.

1. **well nigh** (nī): Very nearly.
2. **pacific thoroughfare:** Calm street.

◆ **Build Vocabulary**

spectators (spek´ tāt´ ərz) *n.*: People who watch something without taking part; onlookers

intricate (in´ tri kit) *adj.*: Complex; full of complicated detail

years ago. Sounds a little funny to you, doesn't it? Well, I'll explain if you'd like to make certain it's all straight. About that long ago there used to be a restaurant where this store stands—'Big Joe' Brady's restaurant."

"Until five years ago," said the policeman. "It was torn down then."

The man in the doorway struck a match and lit his cigar. The light showed a pale, square-jawed face with keen eyes, and a little white scar near his right eyebrow. His scarfpin was a large diamond, oddly set.

"Twenty years ago tonight," said the man, "I dined here at 'Big Joe' Brady's with Jimmy Wells, my best chum, and the finest chap in the world. He and I were raised here in New York, just like two brothers, together. I was

> The diamond scarf-pin might lead you to **infer** that the man is wealthy and likes to show off.

◀ Critical
Viewing What
details in this
painting match
the setting of the
story? [Connect]

Nighthawks, 1942, Edward Hopper, The Art Institute of Chicago

To **identify** with the man, think about the way you feel about very close friends that you have known for a long time.

eighteen and Jimmy was twenty. The next morning I was to start for the West to make my fortune. You couldn't have dragged Jimmy out of New York; he thought it was the only place on earth. Well, we agreed that night that we would meet here again exactly twenty years from that date and time, no matter what our conditions might be or from what distance we might have to come. We figured that in twenty years each of us ought to have our <u>destiny</u> worked out and our fortunes made, whatever they were going to be."

◆ Build Vocabulary

destiny (des´ tə nē) *n.*: What will necessarily happen to any person or thing; fate

After Twenty Years ◆ 455

"It sounds pretty interesting," said the policeman. "Rather a long time between meets, though, it seems to me. Haven't you heard from your friend since you left?"

"Well, yes, for a time we corresponded," said the other. "But after a year or two we lost track of each other. You see, the West is a pretty big proposition, and I kept hustling around over it pretty lively. But I know Jimmy will meet me here if he's alive, for he always was the truest, stanchest old chap in the world. He'll never forget. I came a thousand miles to stand in this door to-night, and it's worth it if my old partner turns up."

The waiting man pulled out a handsome watch, the lids of it set with small diamonds.

"Three minutes to ten," he announced. "It was exactly ten o'clock when we parted here at the restaurant door."

"Did pretty well out West, didn't you?" asked the policeman.

"You bet! I hope Jimmy has done half as well. He was a kind of plodder, though, good fellow as he was. I've

> Up to this point, the man has said only good things about his friend. However, you can infer from these statements that the man feels superior to Jimmy.

had to compete with some of the sharpest wits going to get my pile. A man gets in a groove in New York. It takes the West to put a razor-edge on him."

The policeman twirled his club and took a step or two.

"I'll be on my way. Hope your friend comes around all right. Going to call time on him sharp?"

"I should say not!" said the other. "I'll give him half an hour at least. If Jimmy is alive on earth he'll be here by that time. So long, officer."

> The long conversation with the policeman might cause you to ask the **question**: Why is the policeman so interested in the man?

"Good-night, sir," said the policeman, passing on along his beat, trying doors as he went.

There was now a fine, cold drizzle falling, and the wind had risen from its uncertain puffs into a steady blow. The few foot passengers astir in that quarter hurried dismally and silently along with coat collars turned high and pocketed hands. And in the door of the hardware store the man who had come a thousand miles to fill an appointment, uncertain almost to absurdity, with the friend of his youth, smoked his cigar and waited.

About twenty minutes he waited, and then a tall man in a long overcoat, with collar turned up to his ears, hurried across from the opposite side of the street. He went directly to the waiting man.

"Is that you, Bob?" he asked, doubtfully.

"Is that you, Jimmy Wells?" cried the man in the door.

"Bless my heart!" exclaimed the new arrival, grasping both the other's hands with his own. "It's Bob, sure as fate. I was certain I'd find you here if you were still in existence. Well, well, well!—twenty years is a long time. The old restaurant's gone, Bob; I wish it had lasted, so we could have had another dinner there. How has the West treated you, old man?"

"Bully;[3] it has given me everything I asked it for. You've changed lots, Jimmy. I never thought you were so tall by two or three inches."

"Oh, I grew a bit after I was twenty."

"Doing well in New York, Jimmy?"

"Moderately. I have a position in one of the city departments. Come on, Bob; we'll go around to a place I know of, and have a good long talk about old times."

The two men started up the street, arm in arm. The man from the West, his egotism enlarged by success, was beginning to outline the history of his career. The other, submerged in his overcoat, listened with interest.

At the corner stood a drug store, brilliant with electric lights. When they came into this glare each of them turned <u>simultaneously</u> to gaze upon the other's face.

> **Predict** what the brilliant lights of the drugstore might reveal.

The man from the West stopped suddenly and released his arm.

"You're not Jimmy Wells," he snapped. "Twenty years is a long time, but not long enough to change a man's nose from a Roman to a pug."[4]

"It sometimes changes a good man into a bad one," said the tall man. "You've been under arrest for ten minutes, 'Silky' Bob. Chicago thinks you

> You might **question** why the tall man's statement is important to the action of the story and to the author's message.

---

3. **Bully:** Very well.
4. **change a man's nose from a Roman to a pug:** A Roman nose has a high, prominent bridge; a pug nose is short, thick, and turned up at the end.

◆ **Build Vocabulary**

dismally (diz′ məl lē) *adv.*: Gloomily; miserably

absurdity (ab sur′ də tē) *n.*: Nonsense; foolishness

simultaneously (sī məl tā′ nē əs lē) *adv.*: At the same time

Build Your Portfolio

 ## Idea Bank

Writing

1. **Friendship List** Make a list of the ten qualities you think are most important in a friend. For each item on your list, write a sentence or two explaining why you included it.

2. **Letter From Prison** Write a letter to Patrolman Wells from "Silky" Bob. In your letter, describe the events of the story from Bob's point of view. Express Bob's feelings about his friend's actions. Is he angry, or does he understand why Jimmy had to turn him in?

3. **Police Report** Imagine that you are Jimmy Wells. Write a report on the arrest of "Silky" Bob. Explain how you discovered the wanted criminal and arranged for him to be brought into police custody. **[Career Link]**

Speaking and Listening

4. **News Bulletin** Write a brief radio news bulletin about the arrest of "Silky" Bob. In the role of a radio announcer, read your bulletin to the class.

5. **Tabloid Television [Group Activity]** With a group, act out an interview of Jimmy and Bob on a daytime talk show after the arrest. Roles for your performance might include Jimmy, Bob, the talk-show host, and members of the studio audience. **[Performing Arts Link]**

Projects

6. **Wanted Poster** Create a wanted poster for "Silky" Bob. Make a drawing that shows what he looks like. Provide information about his real name and aliases, distinguishing characteristics, and crimes. **[Art Link]**

7. **New York in 1900** Create an illustrated report describing life in New York City at the time of "After Twenty Years." Where did people live and work? What did they do for fun? What did the buildings look like? Present your findings to the class. **[Social Studies Link]**

 ## Writing Mini-Lesson

Prequel

In this story, Bob talks fondly of his old friend Jimmy and describes how they were raised together "just like two brothers." The things Bob says, together with the surprise ending, might make you wonder what the friendship was really like, twenty years before. Using what you know about the events and characters, write a prequel, or story before a story, about Bob and Jimmy.

> #### Writing Skills Focus: Use Dialogue
> To make your prequel more engaging and realistic, **use dialogue** to show the relationship between Jimmy and Bob. You can also use dialogue to reveal the personalities of the two characters. Notice how O. Henry uses dialogue to hint at Bob's shady activities:
>
> ##### Model From the Story
> "You see, the West is a pretty big proposition, and I kept hustling around over it pretty lively."

Prewriting Prepare a two-column chart. In one column, list Bob's characteristics. In the other column, list Jimmy's characteristics.

Drafting Build your prequel around revealing conversations between the two characters. Make sure that what the characters say and how they say it are consistent with their personalities.

Revising Revise your prequel by looking for the passages where you simply describe the characters. Replace these passages with dialogue that shows the characters' personalities and relationships.

◆ **Grammar Application**

Vary your sentences by using independent and subordinate clauses. You can also show supporting or modifying ideas by attaching them as subordinate clauses to an independent clause.

---

garden path, very <u>draggled</u> indeed, and a small boy was saying: "Here's a dead mongoose. Let's have a funeral."

"No," said his mother; "let's take him in and dry him. Perhaps he isn't really dead."

They took him into the house, and a big man picked him up between his finger and thumb and said he was not dead but half choked; so they wrapped him in cotton wool, and warmed him, and he opened his eyes and sneezed.

"Now," said the big man (he was an Englishman who had just moved into the bungalow); "don't frighten him, and we'll see what he'll do."

It is the hardest thing in the world to frighten a mongoose, because he is eaten up from nose to tail with curiosity. The motto of all the mongoose family is, "Run and find out"; and Rikki-tikki was a true mongoose. He looked at the cotton wool, decided that it was not good to eat, ran all round the table, sat up and put his fur in order, scratched himself, and jumped on the small boy's shoulder.

"Don't be frightened, Teddy," said his father. "That's his way of making friends."

"Ouch! He's tickling under my chin," said Teddy.

Rikki-tikki looked down between the boy's collar and neck, snuffed at his ear, and climbed down to the floor, where he sat rubbing his nose.

"Good gracious," said Teddy's mother, "and that's a wild creature! I suppose he's so tame because we've been kind to him."

"All mongooses are like that," said her husband. "If Teddy doesn't pick him up by the tail, or try to put him in a cage, he'll run in and out of the house all day long. Let's give him something to eat."

They gave him a little piece of raw meat. Rikki-tikki liked it immensely, and when it was finished he went out into the veranda and sat in the sunshine and fluffed up his fur to make it dry to the roots. Then he felt better.

"There are more things to find out about in this house," he said to himself, "than all my family could find out in all their lives. I shall certainly stay and find out."

He spent all that day roaming over the house. He nearly drowned himself in the bathtubs, put his nose into the ink on a writing table, and burned it on the end of the big man's cigar, for he climbed up in the big man's lap to see how writing was done. At nightfall he ran into Teddy's nursery to watch how kerosene lamps were lighted, and when Teddy went to bed Rikki-tikki climbed up too; but he was a restless companion, because he had to get up and attend to every noise all through the night, and find out what made it. Teddy's mother and father came in, the last thing, to look at their boy, and Rikki-tikki was awake on the pillow. "I don't like that," said Teddy's mother; "he may bite the child." "He'll do no such thing," said the father. "Teddy's safer with that little beast than if he had a bloodhound to watch him. If a snake came into the nursery now—"

But Teddy's mother wouldn't think of anything so awful.

Early in the morning Rikki-tikki came to early breakfast in the veranda riding on Teddy's shoulder, and they gave him banana and some boiled egg; and he sat on all their laps one after the other, because every well-brought-up mongoose always hopes to be a house mongoose some day and have rooms to run about in, and Rikki-tikki's mother (she used to live in the General's house at Segowlee) had carefully told Rikki what to do if ever he came across Englishmen.

Then Rikki-tikki went out into the garden to see what was to be seen. It was a large garden,

◆ **Reading Strategy**
Teddy's father praises Rikki as a guardian. Based on this detail, what do you predict might happen later in the story?

◀ **Critical Viewing** Does the mongoose shown here appear friendly or hostile? Explain. [Assess]

◆ **Build Vocabulary**

revived (ri vīvd´) v.: Came back to consciousness
draggled (drag´ əld) adj.: Wet and dirty

only half cultivated, with bushes as big as summer houses of Marshal Niel roses, lime and orange trees, clumps of bamboos, and thickets of high grass. Rikki-tikki licked his lips. "This is a splendid hunting ground," he said, and his tail grew bottlebrushy at the thought of it, and he scuttled up and down the garden, snuffing here and there till he heard very sorrowful voices in a thornbush.

It was Darzee, the tailorbird, and his wife. They had made a beautiful nest by pulling two big leaves together and stitching them up the edges with fibers, and had filled the hollow with cotton and downy fluff. The nest swayed to and fro, as they sat on the rim and cried.

"What is the matter?" asked Rikki-tikki.

"We are very miserable," said Darzee. "One of our babies fell out of the nest yesterday and Nag[3] ate him."

"H'm!" said Rikki-tikki, "that is very sad—but I am a stranger here. Who is Nag?"

Darzee and his wife only cowered down in the nest without answering, for from the thick grass at the foot of the bush there came a low hiss—a horrid cold sound that made Rikki-tikki jump back two clear feet. Then inch by inch out of the grass rose up the head and spread hood of Nag, the big black cobra, and he was five feet long from tongue to tail. When he had lifted one third of himself clear of the ground, he stayed balancing to and fro exactly as a dandelion tuft balances in the wind, and he looked at Rikki-tikki with the wicked snake's eyes that never change their expression, whatever the snake may be thinking of.

"Who is Nag?" he said. "*I* am Nag. The great god Brahm[4] put his mark upon all our people when the first cobra spread his hood to keep the sun off Brahm as he slept. Look, and be afraid!"

---

3. **Nag** (Näg)
4. **Brahm** (bräm): Abbreviation of Brahma, the name of the chief god in the Hindu religion.

▼ **Critical Viewing** How might a mongoose like Rikki-tikki-tavi know that the cobra pictured here is in a state of attack? [Interpret]

◆ Literary Focus
What part of the plot is Rikki's meeting with Nag?

He spread out his hood more than ever, and Rikki-tikki saw the spectacle mark on the back of it that looks exactly like the eye part of a hook-and-eye fastening. He was afraid for the minute; but it is impossible for a mongoose to stay frightened for any length of time, and though Rikki-tikki had never met a live cobra before, his mother had fed him on dead ones, and he knew that all a grown mongoose's business in life was to fight and eat snakes. Nag knew that too, and at the bottom of his cold heart he was afraid.

"Well," said Rikki-tikki, and his tail began to fluff up again, "marks or no marks, do you think it is right for you to eat fledglings out of a nest?"

Nag was thinking to himself, and watching the least little movement in the grass behind Rikki-tikki. He knew that mongooses in the garden meant death sooner or later for him and his family; but he wanted to get Rikki-tikki off his guard. So he dropped his head a little, and put it on one side.

"Let us talk," he said. "You eat eggs. Why should not I eat birds?"

"Behind you! Look behind you!" sang Darzee.

Rikki-tikki knew better than to waste time in staring. He jumped up in the air as high as he could go, and just under him whizzed by the head of Nagaina,[5] Nag's wicked wife. She had crept up behind him as he was talking, to make an end of him; and he heard her savage

5. **Nagaina** (nə gī´ nə)

hiss as the stroke missed. He came down almost across her back, and if he had been an old mongoose he would have known that then was the time to break her back with one bite; but he was afraid of the terrible lashing return stroke of the cobra. He bit, indeed, but did not bite long enough, and he jumped clear of the whisking tail, leaving Nagaina torn and angry.

"Wicked, wicked Darzee!" said Nag, lashing up high as he could reach toward the nest in the thornbush; but Darzee had built it out of reach of snakes; and it only swayed to and fro.

Rikki-tikki felt his eyes growing red and hot (when a mongoose's eyes grow red, he is angry), and he sat back on his tail and hind legs like a little kangaroo, and looked all around him, and chattered with rage. But Nag and Nagaina had disappeared into the grass. When a snake misses its stroke, it never says anything or gives any sign of what it means to do next. Rikki-tikki did not care to follow them, for he did not feel sure that he could manage two snakes at once. So he trotted off to the gravel path near the house, and sat down to think. It was a serious matter for him.

If you read the old books of natural history, you will find they say that when the mongoose fights the snake and happens to get bitten, he runs off and eats some herb that cures him. That is not true. The victory is only a matter of quickness of eye and quickness of foot— snake's blow against mongoose's jump—and as no eye can follow the motion of a snake's head when it strikes, that makes things much more wonderful than any magic herb. Rikki-tikki knew he was a young mongoose, and it made him all the more pleased to think that he had managed to escape a blow from behind. It gave him confidence in himself, and when Teddy came running down the path, Rikki-tikki was ready to be petted.

But just as Teddy was stooping, something <u>flinched</u> a little in the dust, and a tiny voice said: "Be careful. I am death!" It

◆ **Build Vocabulary**
flinched (flincht) v.: Moved back, as if away from a blow

was Karait,[6] the dusty brown snakeling that lies for choice on the dusty earth; and his bite is as dangerous as the cobra's. But he is so small that nobody thinks of him, and so he does the more harm to people.

Rikki-tikki's eyes grew red again, and he danced up to Karait with the peculiar rocking, swaying motion that he had inherited from his family. It looks very funny, but it is so perfectly balanced a gait that you can fly off from it at any angle you please; and in dealing with snakes this is an advantage. If Rikki-tikki had only known, he was doing a much more dangerous thing than fighting Nag, for Karait is so small, and can turn so quickly, that unless Rikki bit him close to the back of the head, he would get the return stroke in his eye or lip. But Rikki did not know: his eyes were all red, and he rocked back and forth, looking for a good place to hold. Karait struck out. Rikki jumped sideways and tried to run in, but the wicked little dusty gray head lashed within a fraction of his shoulder, and he had to jump over the body, and the head followed his heels close.

Teddy shouted to the house: "Oh, look here! Our mongoose is killing a snake"; and Rikki-tikki heard a scream from Teddy's mother. His father ran out with a stick, but by the time he came up, Karait had lunged out once too far, and Rikki-tikki had sprung, jumped on the snake's back, dropped his head far between his fore legs, bitten as high up the back as he could get hold, and rolled away. That bite paralyzed Karait, and Rikki-tikki was just going to eat him up from the tail, after the custom of his family at dinner, when he remembered that a full meal makes a slow mongoose, and if he wanted all his strength and quickness ready, he must keep himself thin.

He went away for a dust bath under the castor-oil bushes, while Teddy's father beat the dead Karait. "What is the use of that?" thought Rikki-tikki. "I have settled it all"; and then Teddy's mother picked him up from the dust and hugged him, crying that he had saved Teddy from death, and Teddy's father said that he was a providence,[7] and Teddy looked on with big scared eyes. Rikki-tikki was rather amused at all the fuss, which, of course, he did not understand. Teddy's mother might just as well have petted Teddy for playing in the dust. Rikki was thoroughly enjoying himself.

That night, at dinner, walking to and fro among the wineglasses on the table, he could have stuffed himself three times over with nice things; but he remembered Nag and Nagaina, and though it was very pleasant to be patted and petted by Teddy's mother, and to sit on Teddy's shoulder, his eyes would get red from time to time, and he would go off into his long war cry of "*Rikk-tikk-tikki-tikki-tchk!*"

Teddy carried him off to bed, and insisted on Rikki-tikki sleeping under his chin. Rikki-tikki was too well bred to bite or scratch, but as soon as Teddy was asleep he went off for his nightly walk round the house, and in the dark he ran up against Chuchundra the muskrat, creeping round by the wall. Chuchundra is a brokenhearted little beast. He whimpers and cheeps all the night, trying to make up his mind to run into the middle of the room, but he never gets there.

"Don't kill me," said Chuchundra, almost weeping. "Rikki-tikki don't kill me."

"Do you think a snake-killer kills muskrats?" said Rikki-tikki scornfully.

"Those who kill snakes get killed by snakes," said Chuchundra, more sorrowfully than ever. "And how am I to be sure that Nag won't mistake me for you some dark night?"

"There's not the least danger," said Rikki-tikki; "but Nag is in the garden, and I know you don't go there."

"My cousin Chua, the rat, told me—" said Chuchundra, and then he stopped.

"Told you what?"

"H'sh! Nag is everywhere, Rikki-tikki. You should have talked to Chua in the garden."

"I didn't—so you must tell me. Quick,

6. **Karait** (kə rīt´)

7. **a providence** (präv´ ə dəns): A godsend; a valuable gift.

Chuchundra, or I'll bite you!"

Chuchundra sat down and cried till the tears rolled off his whiskers. "I am a very poor man," he sobbed. "I never had spirit enough to run out into the middle of the room. H'sh! I mustn't tell you anything. Can't you *hear*, Rikki-tikki?"

Rikki-tikki listened. The house was as still as still, but he thought he could just catch the faintest *scratch-scratch* in the world—a noise as faint as that of a wasp walking on a windowpane—the dry scratch of a snake's scales on brickwork.

"That's Nag or Nagaina," he said to himself; "and he is crawling into the bathroom sluice.[8] You're right, Chuchundra; I should have talked to Chua."

He stole off to Teddy's bathroom, but there was nothing there, and then to Teddy's mother's bathroom. At the bottom of the smooth plaster wall there was a brick pulled out to make a sluice for the bath water, and as Rikki-tikki stole in by the masonry curb where the bath is put, he heard Nag and Nagaina whispering together outside in the moonlight.

"When the house is emptied of people," said Nagaina to her husband, "*he* will have to go away, and then the garden will be our own again. Go in quietly, and remember that the big man who killed Karait is the first one to bite. Then come out and tell me, and we will hunt for Rikki-tikki together."

"But are you sure that there is anything to be gained by killing the people?" said Nag.

"Everything. When there were no people in the bungalow, did we have any mongoose in the garden? So long as the bungalow is empty, we are king and queen of the garden; and remember that as soon as our eggs in the melon bed hatch (as they may tomorrow), our children will need room and quiet."

"I had not thought of that," said Nag. "I will go, but there is no need that we should hunt for Rikki-tikki afterward. I will kill the big man and his wife, and the child if I can, and come away quietly. Then the bungalow will be empty, and Rikki-tikki will go."

Rikki-tikki tingled all over with rage and hatred at this, and then Nag's head came through the sluice, and his five feet of cold body followed it. Angry as he was, Rikki-tikki was very frightened as he saw the size of the big cobra. Nag coiled himself up, raised his head, and looked into the bathroom in the dark, and Rikki could see his eyes glitter.

"Now, if I kill him here, Nagaina will know;—and if I fight him on the open floor, the odds are in his favor. What am I to do?" said Rikki-tikki-tavi.

Nag waved to and fro, and then Rikki-tikki-tikki heard him drinking from the biggest water jar that was used to fill the bath. "That is good," said the snake. "Now, when Karait was killed, the big man had a stick. He may have that stick still, but when he comes in to bathe in the morning he will not have a stick. I shall

---

8. **sluice** (slo͞os) Drain.

▲ **Critical Viewing** What role does Darzee, the tailor-bird, play in the conflict between Rikki-tikki-tavi and Nag? [Analyze]

wait here till he comes. Nagaina—do you hear me?—I shall wait here in the cool till daytime."

There was no answer from outside, so Rikki-tikki knew Nagaina had gone away. Nag coiled himself down, coil by coil, round the bulge at the bottom of the waterjar, and Rikki-tikki stayed still as death. After an hour he began to move, muscle by muscle, toward the jar. Nag was asleep, and Rikki-tikki looked at his big back, wondering which would be the best place for a good hold. "If I don't break his back at the first jump," said Rikki, "he can still fight; and if he fights—O Rikki!" He looked at the thickness of the neck below the hood, but that was too much for him; and a bite near the tail would only make Nag savage.

"It must be the head," he said at last; "the head above the hood; and, when I am once there, I must not let go."

Then he jumped. The head was lying a little clear of the water jar, under the curve of it; and, as his teeth met, Rikki braced his back against the bulge of the red earthenware to hold down the head. This gave him just one second's purchase,[9] and he made the most of it. Then he was battered to and fro as a rat is shaken by a dog—to and fro on the floor, up and down, and round in great circles: but his eyes were red, and he held on as the body cart-whipped over the floor, upsetting the tin dipper and the soap dish and the fleshbrush, and banged against the tin side of the bath. As he held he closed his jaws tighter and tighter, for he made sure he would be banged to death, and, for the honor of his family, he preferred to be found with his teeth locked. He was dizzy, aching, and felt shaken to pieces when something went off like a thunderclap just behind him; a hot wind knocked him senseless and red fire singed his fur. The big man had been wakened by the noise, and had fired both barrels of a shotgun into Nag just behind the hood.

---

9. **purchase** (pʉr´ chəs): In this case, an advantage.

▼ **Critical Viewing** Basing your answer on the details of this photograph, which animal would you expect to win a match to the death—the cobra or the mongoose? Explain. **[Evaluate]**

Rikki-tikki held on with his eyes shut, for now he was quite sure he was dead; but the head did not move, and the big man picked him up and said: "It's the mongoose again, Alice; the little chap has saved *our* lives now." Then Teddy's mother came in with a very white face, and saw what was left of Nag, and Rikki-tikki dragged himself to Teddy's bedroom and spent half the rest of the night shaking himself tenderly to find out whether he really was broken into forty pieces, as he fancied.

When morning came he was very stiff, but well pleased with his doings. "Now I have Nagaina to settle with, and she will be worse than five Nags, and there's no knowing when the eggs she spoke of will hatch. Goodness! I must go and see Darzee," he said.

Without waiting for breakfast, Rikki-tikki ran to the thornbush where Darzee was singing a song of triumph at the top of his voice. The news of Nag's death was all over the garden, for the sweeper had thrown the body on the rubbish heap.

"Oh, you stupid tuft of feathers!" said Rikki-tikki, angrily. "Is this the time to sing?"

"Nag is dead—is dead—is dead!" sang Darzee. "The valiant Rikki-tikki caught him by the head and held fast. The big man brought the bang-stick and Nag fell in two pieces! He will never eat my babies again."

◆ **Literary Focus**
Why is the death of Nag considered part of the rising action of the plot?

"All that's true enough; but where's Nagaina?" said Rikki-tikki, looking carefully round him.

"Nagaina came to the bathroom sluice and called for Nag," Darzee went on; "and Nag came out on the end of a stick—the sweeper picked him up on the end of a stick and threw him upon the rubbish heap. Let us sing about the great, the red-eyed Rikki-tikki!" and Darzee filled his throat and sang.

"If I could get up to your nest, I'd roll all your babies out!" said Rikki-tikki "You don't know when to do the right thing at the right time. You're safe enough in your nest there, but it's war for me down here. Stop singing a minute, Darzee."

Guide for Responding (continued)

◆ Reading Strategy

PREDICT

To make a **prediction,** you examine clues in the text, and then make an educated guess about what is going to happen next. Review the story to find clues that helped you to predict each of the following:

1. Rikki would eventually fight Nag.
2. The cobra eggs would be destroyed.

◆ Build Vocabulary

USING THE WORD ROOT -viv-

Use your knowledge of the word root -viv-, meaning "life," to complete each sentence with one of the words below. Use each word once.

vivacious   revival   vivid

1. The toys came in a variety of _____?_____ colors.
2. She has an outgoing, _____?_____ personality.
3. During the _____?_____ of disco music, the fashions of the 1970's made a comeback.

SPELLING STRATEGY

Mourning and *morning* are homophones—they are spelled differently and mean different things, but they have the same pronunciation. On a piece of paper, write the following sentences, correcting the misused homophones.

1. He sat on a peer, fishing.
2. She does everything with stile and flare.

USING THE WORD BANK

On your paper, write the Word Bank word that best completes each of the following sentences.

1. The contest winner received a trophy, and all the other entrants received _____?_____ prizes.
2. He _____?_____ when he saw the dentist's drill.
3. Her hair was _____?_____ from her fall into the pond.
4. He was gloomy because he was _____?_____ the death of his pet turtle.
5. The pirate's treasure chest was _____?_____ concealed in a cave behind a waterfall.
6. The wilted plant _____?_____ when I watered it.

◆ Literary Focus

PLOT

A story's **plot**—the sequence of events—usually begins with the *exposition*. Next, the conflict is introduced and intensifies during the *rising action*. The *climax,* or high point of the story, is followed by the *falling action*, which leads to the *resolution* of the conflict and the tying up of loose ends.

1. What happens during the exposition in "Rikki-tikki-tavi"?
2. What is the conflict in the story?
3. List three events that occur during the rising action of the story.
4. At what point is the climax reached?
5. How is the conflict resolved?

◆ Build Grammar Skills

SIMPLE AND COMPOUND SENTENCES

A **simple sentence** consists of one independent clause (a group of words that has a subject and a verb and can stand by itself as a complete sentence). A **compound sentence** consists of two or more independent clauses. These clauses may be linked by semicolons or by words such as *and, but, or, yet,* and *so.*

Simple Sentence: Rikki fights snakes.
Compound Sentence:

Independent Clause	Independent Clause
Rikki was afraid of Nag, but	he fought him anyway.

Practice On your paper, split the following compound sentences into simple sentences.

1. Rikki-tikki is curious; he is also brave.
2. Teddy's family might remain in India, or they might return to England.
3. The cobras plotted, and then Nag slipped inside.
4. Rikki was not afraid, nor did he hesitate.
5. The mongoose leapt; it bit the snake, but it did not bite long enough, for the snake broke loose.

Writing Application Write a paragraph summarizing one of the scenes in "Rikki-tikki-tavi." Use only simple sentences. Then, revise your paragraph, combining some of the simple sentences to form compound sentences.

Build Your Portfolio

 ## Idea Bank

Writing

1. Picture Book for First Graders Create a book for first graders about Rikki-tikki-tavi. To make your book easy to read, simplify the story and use short words and sentences. You may either draw the illustrations for your book or describe what they should look like.

2. Letter As Teddy, write a letter to your grandmother in England about your pet mongoose. Describe your pet and his adventures. Keep in mind that Teddy did not see all of the events. Feel free to add details that are not in the story.

3. Comparison-and-Contrast Essay Write an essay in which you compare and contrast two of the characters from the story.

Speaking and Listening

4. Play-by-Play Account Imagine that you are a radio sportscaster. Prepare and perform an exciting play-by-play description to accompany video footage of the big fight between Rikki-tikki-tavi and Nag. **[Performing Arts Link]**

5. First-Aid Demonstration Consult the school nurse and other health experts to find out the steps for giving first aid for snake bites. Explain these steps as you demonstrate them for the class. **[Health Link]**

Projects

6. Wildlife Collage Use pictures from old magazines, drawings, and other objects to create a collage about wildlife in a specific part of the world, such as southern India or your state. Create a key to explain the images you use. **[Science Link]**

7. Multimedia Report **[Group Activity]** With a group, create a multimedia report on life in India. Gather maps, charts, photographs, and, if possible, video. Combine these materials with written text in a report that you can present to the class. **[Social Studies Link; Media Link]**

 ## Writing Mini-Lesson

Report on Natural Enemies

In "Rikki-tikki-tavi," the conflict between natural enemies is described in the form of a fictional story. Another way to describe such a conflict is in the form of a factual report. Choose another pair of natural enemies, and write a report about them.

Writing Skills Focus: Details to Describe the Environment

To help your readers understand the conflict between the enemies described in your report, you need to show how they fit into the natural world. Notice how Kipling provides **details about the environment** to help readers picture Rikki-tikki-tavi's tropical surroundings:

Model From the Story
It was a large garden, only half cultivated, with bushes as big as summer houses of Marshal Niel roses, lime and orange trees, clumps of bamboos, and thickets of high grass.

Prewriting With a partner, brainstorm for a list of natural enemies. Then, conduct research in the library or on the Internet to gather information about one of these pairs of enemies. Collect at least ten facts about the animals.

Drafting As you draft your report, make sure you include plenty of details about what the enemies look like, how they behave, and how they interact. Thoroughly describe the environment in which the enemies are found.

◆ **Grammar Application**
As you write, be sure to use a mixture of simple and compound sentences in your report.

Revising Revise your report by looking for places where you can improve your descriptions. Replace vague words with more vivid ones and add details.

Guide for Reading

Meet the Authors:

Cynthia Rylant (1954–)

Cynthia Rylant, who grew up in a West Virginia mountain town, was originally planning to be a nurse. However, she fell in love with literature in college, and switched her major to English.

Surrounded by Books Later, while working as a librarian, Rylant discovered children's books and was hooked. Her love of books inspired her to write one of her own. Her first book, *When I Was Young in the Mountains*, was published in 1982. It was soon followed by works of many types—picture books, novels, short stories, poetry, and biographies.

Sherwood Anderson (1876–1941)

As a teenager, Sherwood Anderson was able to attend school only part of the time because he had to work to help support his family. Despite his lack of formal education, Anderson became a successful business-man, the manager of a paint factory.

Change of Scenery In 1912, he shocked those who knew him by moving from Elyria, Ohio, to Chicago, where he devoted himself to writing. His most famous book, *Winesburg, Ohio*, was published in 1921. Anderson and his work had a powerful influence on such writers as Ernest Hemingway and William Faulkner.

◆ LITERATURE AND YOUR LIFE

CONNECT YOUR EXPERIENCE

At times, you may have made up wild excuses for not doing something you were supposed to do, or maybe you simply avoided doing something and chose not to offer any explanation at all. Both of these stories focus on characters who avoid responsibility and learn important lessons as a consequence of their actions.

THEMATIC FOCUS: Personal Codes

These stories illustrate how the mistakes we make can lead to important insights about our actions. As you read, ask yourself how the lessons the characters learn will affect how they act in the future.

◆ Background for Understanding

SCIENCE

Medical problems affect events in both these stories. In "Papa's Parrot," a character suffers a heart attack. Heart attacks are caused by a blockage in a blood vessel that supplies blood to the heart muscle. In "Stolen Day," a character says he has "inflammatory rheumatism." The term *rheumatism* is used to describe a number of different diseases, including rheumatoid arthritis. In this disease, the joints swell painfully and gradually break down.

◆ Build Vocabulary

WORD ROOTS: -flam-

In "Stolen Day," a boy is convinced he has "inflammatory rheumatism." Once you know that the word root -*flam*- means "flame" or "burn," it's not surprising to learn that a symptom of this disease is that affected joints feel hot.

WORD BANK

Which of these words do you think describes someone who is serious?

resumed
inflammatory
rheumatism
solemn

Papa's Parrot ◆ Stolen Day

◆ Literary Focus

CHARACTERIZATION

A writer can reveal characters' personalities in two basic ways. When using **direct characterization,** the writer tells you the character's traits: *Rocky was good company.* When using **indirect characterization,** the writer reveals the characters' personalities through the characters' own words, thoughts, and actions and by what other characters say to or about them. In these stories, the authors rely mainly on indirect characterization.

◆ Reading Strategy

IDENTIFY WITH A CHARACTER

Stories give you a chance to live another life for a while. To do this, you **identify with a character.** You put yourself in a character's place and think about how you would react to the situations that the character experiences.

As you read each story, fill out a chart like the one below to help you identify with the main character. List each major event, and record the character's reaction to it. Then, note what you might have said or done in the character's place.

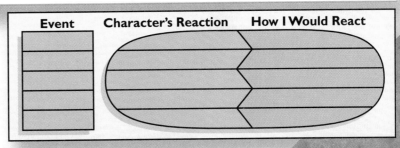

Event	Character's Reaction	How I Would React

Papa's Parrot

Cynthia Rylant

*T*hough his father was fat and merely owned a candy and nut shop, Harry Tillian liked his papa. Harry stopped liking candy and nuts when he was around seven, but, in spite of this, he and Mr. Tillian had remained friends and were still friends the year Harry turned twelve.

For years, after school, Harry had always stopped in to see his father at work. Many of Harry's friends stopped there, too, to spend a few cents choosing penny candy from the giant bins or to sample Mr. Tillian's latest batch of roasted peanuts. Mr. Tillian looked forward to seeing his son and his son's friends every day. He liked the company.

When Harry entered junior high school, though, he didn't come by the candy and nut shop as often. Nor did his friends. They were older and they had more spending money. They went to a burger place. They played video games. They shopped for records. None of them were much interested in candy and nuts anymore.

A new group of children came to Mr. Tillian's shop now. But not Harry Tillian and his friends.

The year Harry turned twelve was also the year Mr. Tillian got a parrot. He went to a pet store one day and bought one for more money than he could really afford. He brought the parrot to his shop, set its cage near the sign for maple clusters, and named it Rocky.

Harry thought this was the strangest thing his father had ever done, and he told him so, but Mr. Tillian just ignored him.

Rocky was good company for Mr. Tillian. When business was slow, Mr. Tillian would turn on a small color television he had sitting in a corner, and he and Rocky would watch the soap operas. Rocky liked to scream when the romantic music came on, and Mr. Tillian

would yell at him to shut up, but they seemed to enjoy themselves.

The more Mr. Tillian grew to like his parrot, and the more he talked to it instead of to people, the more embarrassed Harry became. Harry would stroll past the shop, on his way somewhere else, and he'd take a quick look inside to see what his dad was doing. Mr. Tillian was always talking to the bird. So Harry kept walking.

At home things were different. Harry and his father joked with each other at the dinner table as they always had—Mr. Tillian teasing Harry about his smelly socks; Harry teasing Mr. Tillian about his blubbery stomach. At home things seemed all right.

◆ **Reading Strategy**
Put yourself in Harry's place. How would you react to Mr. Tillian talking to his parrot?

But one day, Mr. Tillian became ill. He had been at work, unpacking boxes of caramels, when he had grabbed his chest and fallen over on top of the candy. A customer had found him, and he was taken to the hospital in an ambulance.

Mr. Tillian couldn't leave the hospital. He lay in bed, tubes in his arms, and he worried about his shop. New shipments of candy and nuts would be arriving. Rocky would be hungry. Who would take care of things?

Harry said he would. Harry told his father that he would go to the store every day after school and unpack boxes. He would sort out all the candy and nuts. He would even feed Rocky.

So, the next morning, while Mr. Tillian lay in his hospital bed, Harry took the shop key to school with him. After school he left his friends and walked to the empty shop alone. In all the days of his life, Harry had never seen the shop closed after school. Harry didn't even remember what the CLOSED sign looked like. The key stuck in the lock three times, and inside he had to search all the walls for the light switch.

◀ **Critical Viewing** What unique ability of parrots is suggested by the combination of the photograph and the title of the story? **[Apply Prior Knowledge]**

The shop was as his father had left it. Even the caramels were still spilled on the floor. Harry bent down and picked them up one by one, dropping them back in the boxes. The bird in its cage watched him silently.

Harry opened the new boxes his father hadn't gotten to. Peppermints. Jawbreakers. Toffee creams. Strawberry kisses. Harry traveled from bin to bin, putting the candies where they belonged.

"Hello!"

Harry jumped, spilling a box of jawbreakers.

"Hello, Rocky!"

Harry stared at the parrot. He had forgotten it was there. The bird had been so quiet, and Harry had been thinking only of the candy.

"Hello," Harry said.

"Hello, Rocky!" answered the parrot.

Harry walked slowly over to the cage. The parrot's food cup was empty. Its water was dirty. The bottom of the cage was a mess.

Harry carried the cage into the back room.

"Hello, Rocky!"

"Is that all you can say, you dumb bird?" Harry mumbled. The bird said nothing else.

Harry cleaned the bottom of the cage, re-filled the food and water cups, and then put the cage back in its place and <u>resumed</u> sorting the candy.

"Where's Harry?"

Harry looked up.

"Where's Harry?"

Harry stared at the parrot.

"Where's Harry?"

Chills ran down Harry's back. What could the bird mean? It was something from "The Twilight Zone."[1]

"Where's Harry?"

Harry swallowed and said, "I'm here. I'm here, you stupid bird."

---

1. **"The Twilight Zone":** Science-fiction television series from the 1960's.

◆ Build Vocabulary

resumed (ri zo͞omd´) *v.:* Began again; continued

"You stupid bird!" said the parrot.

Well, at least he's got one thing straight, thought Harry.

"Miss him! Miss him! Where's Harry? You stupid bird!"

Harry stood with a handful of peppermints. "What?" he asked.

"Where's Harry?" said the parrot.

"I'm *here*, you stupid bird! I'm here!" Harry yelled. He threw the peppermints at the cage, and the bird screamed and clung to its perch.

Harry sobbed, "I'm here." The tears were coming.

Harry leaned over the glass counter.

"Papa." Harry buried his face in his arms.

"Where's Harry?" repeated the bird.

Harry sighed and wiped his face on his sleeve. He watched the parrot. He understood now: someone had been saying, for a long time, "Where's Harry? Miss him."

Harry finished his unpacking and then swept the floor of the shop. He checked the furnace so the bird wouldn't get cold. Then he left to go visit his papa.

> ◆ **Literary Focus**
> What does Harry's reaction to Rocky reveal about his character?

Guide for Responding

◆ LITERATURE AND YOUR LIFE

Reader's Response Should Harry tell his father what he learned from Rocky? Why or why not?

Thematic Focus How might his experience change the way Harry allows himself to interact with others? Explain.

Journal Writing Write about a time when, like Harry, you had an experience that led to a moment of insight. Tell what happened and what the event taught you about yourself.

☑ Check Your Comprehension

1. What does Mr. Tillian do for a living?
2. Why do Harry and his friends visit Harry's father after school?
3. Why do Harry and his friends stop visiting Harry's father?
4. Who is Rocky?
5. Why does Harry have to take care of the shop?
6. What does Rocky say that upsets Harry?

◆ Critical Thinking

INTERPRET

1. What is Mr. Tillian's motivation, or reason, for buying a parrot? **[Analyze Cause and Effect]**
2. Why is it significant that Mr. Tillian paid "more money than he could really afford" for his parrot? **[Infer]**
3. What can you tell about what motivates Harry from the fact that he walks by his father's shop, looks in, but doesn't stop? **[Interpret]**
4. What motivates Harry to throw peppermints at Rocky? **[Infer]**
5. What does this story suggest about the motivations for people's behavior? **[Draw Conclusions]**

EVALUATE

6. In what ways was Harry's behavior irresponsible? Explain. **[Criticize]**

APPLY

7. Why might doctors recommend parrots or other pets for older people who are alone? **[Health Link]**

Stolen Day

Sherwood Anderson

It must be that all children are actors. The whole thing started with a boy on our street named Walter, who had inflammatory rheumatism. That's what they called it. He didn't have to go to school.

Still he could walk about. He could go fishing in the creek or the waterworks pond. There was a place up at the pond where in the spring the water came tumbling over the dam and formed a deep pool. It was a good place. Sometimes you could get some big ones there.

I went down that way on my way to school one spring morning. It was out of my way but I wanted to see if Walter was there.

He was, inflammatory rheumatism and all. There he was, sitting with a fish pole in his hand. He had been able to walk down there all right.

It was then that my own legs began to hurt. My back too. I went on to school but, at the recess time, I began to cry. I did it when the teacher, Sarah Suggett, had come out into the schoolhouse yard.

She came right over to me.

"I ache all over," I said. I did, too.

I kept on crying and it worked all right.

"You'd better go on home," she said.

So I went. I limped painfully away. I kept on limping until I got out of the schoolhouse street.

Then I felt better. I still had inflammatory rheumatism pretty bad but I could get along better.

I must have done some thinking on the way home.

"I'd better not say I have inflammatory rheumatism," I decided. "Maybe if you've got that you swell up."

I thought I'd better go around to where Walter was and ask him about that, so I did—but he wasn't there.

"They must not be biting today," I thought.

I had a feeling that, if I said I had inflammatory rheumatism, Mother or my brothers and my sister Stella might laugh. They did laugh at me pretty often and I didn't like it at all.

"Just the same," I said to myself, "I have got it." I began to hurt and ache again.

I went home and sat on the front steps of our house. I sat there a long time. There wasn't anyone at home but Mother and the two little ones. Ray would have been four or five then and Earl might have been three.

It was Earl who saw me there. I had got tired sitting and was lying on the porch. Earl was always a quiet, solemn little fellow.

He must have said something to Mother for presently she came.

"What's the matter with you? Why aren't you in school?" she asked.

I came pretty near telling her right out that I had inflammatory rheumatism but I thought I'd better not. Mother and Father had been speaking of Walter's case at the table just the day before. "It affects the heart," Father had said. That frightened me when I thought of it. "I might die," I thought. "I might just suddenly die right here; my heart might stop beating."

On the day before I had been running a race with my brother Irve. We were up at the

◆ Literary Focus
Is the narrator's description of Earl an example of direct characterization or indirect characterization? Explain.

◆ **Build Vocabulary**

inflammatory (in flam′ ə tôr ē) adj.: Characterized by pain and swelling

rheumatism (r$\overline{oo}$′ mə tiz′ əm) n.: Painful condition of the joints and muscles

solemn (säl′ əm) adj.: Serious; somber

The Pond, 1985, Adele Alsop, Courtesy of Schmidt Bingham Gallery, NYC

▲ **Critical Viewing** Why might Walter or the narrator enjoy spending time at a lake like the one in this painting? **[Speculate]**

fairgrounds after school and there was a half-mile track.

"I'll bet you can't run a half-mile," he said. "I bet you I could beat you running clear around the track."

And so we did it and I beat him, but afterwards my heart did seem to beat pretty hard. I remembered that lying there on the porch. "It's a wonder, with my inflammatory rheumatism and all, I didn't just drop down dead," I thought. The thought frightened me a lot. I ached worse than ever.

"I ache, Ma," I said. "I just ache."

She made me go in the house and upstairs and get into bed.

It wasn't so good. It was spring. I was up there for perhaps an hour, maybe two, and then I felt better.

I got up and went downstairs. "I feel better, Ma," I said.

Mother said she was glad. She was pretty busy that day and hadn't paid much attention to me. She had made me get into bed upstairs and then hadn't even come up to see how I was.

I didn't think much of that when I was up there but when I got downstairs where she was, and when, after I had said I felt better and she only said she was glad and went right on with her work, I began to ache again.

I thought, "I'll bet I die of it. I bet I do."

I went out to the front porch and sat down. I was pretty sore at Mother.

"If she really knew the truth, that I have the inflammatory rheumatism and I may just drop down dead any time, I'll bet she wouldn't care about that either," I thought.

I was getting more and more angry the more thinking I did.

"I know what I'm going to do," I thought; "I'm going to go fishing."

I thought that, feeling the way I did, I might be sitting on the high bank just above the deep pool where the water went over the dam, and suddenly my heart would stop beating.

And then, of course, I'd pitch forward, over the bank into the pool and, if I wasn't dead when I hit the water, I'd drown sure.

They would all come home to supper and they'd miss me.

"But where is he?"

Then Mother would remember that I'd come home from school aching.

She'd go upstairs and I wouldn't be there. One day during the year before, there was a child got drowned in a spring. It was one of the Wyatt children.

Right down at the end of the street there was a spring under a birch tree and there had been a barrel sunk in the ground.

Everyone had always been saying the spring ought to be kept covered, but it wasn't.

So the Wyatt child went down there, played around alone, and fell in and got drowned.

Mother was the one who had found the drowned child. She had gone to get a pail of water and there the child was, drowned and dead.

This had been in the evening when we were all at home, and Mother had come running up the street with the dead, dripping child in her arms. She was making for the Wyatt house as hard as she could run, and she was pale.

She had a terrible look on her face, I remembered then.

"So," I thought, "they'll miss me and there'll be a search made. Very likely there'll be someone who has seen me sitting by the pond fishing, and there'll be a big alarm and all the town will turn out and they'll drag the pond."

I was having a grand time, having died. Maybe, after they found me and had got me out of the deep pool, Mother would grab me up in her arms and run home with me as she had run with the Wyatt child.

I got up from the porch and went around the house. I got my fishing pole and lit out for the pool below the dam. Mother was busy—she always was—and didn't see me go. When I got there I thought I'd better not sit too near the edge of the high bank.

By this time I didn't ache hardly at all, but I thought.

"With inflammatory rheumatism you can't tell," I thought.

"It probably comes and goes," I thought.

"Walter has it and he goes fishing," I thought.

I had got my line into the pool and suddenly I got a bite. It was a regular whopper. I knew that. I'd never had a bite like that.

I knew what it was. It was one of Mr. Fenn's big carp.

Mr. Fenn was a man who had a big pond of his own. He sold ice in the summer and the pond was to make the ice. He had bought some big carp and put them into his pond and then, earlier in the spring when there was a freshet, his dam had gone out.

So the carp had got into our creek and one or two big ones had been caught—but none of them by a boy like me.

The carp was pulling and I was pulling and I was afraid he'd break my line, so I just tumbled down the high bank holding onto the line and got right into the pool. We had it out, there in the pool. We struggled. We wrestled. Then I got a hand under his gills and got him out.

He was a big one all right. He was nearly half

◆ Literary Focus
What do the narrator's thoughts about drowning reveal about his personality?

as big as I was myself. I had him on the bank and I kept one hand under his gills and I ran.

I never ran so hard in my life. He was slippery, and now and then he wriggled out of my arms; once I stumbled and fell on him, but I got him home.

So there it was. I was a big hero that day. Mother got a washtub and filled it with water. She put the fish in it and all the neighbors came to look. I got into dry clothes and went down to supper—and then I made a break that spoiled my day.

There we were, all of us, at the table, and suddenly Father asked what had been the matter with me at school. He had met the teacher, Sarah Suggett, on the street and she had told him how I had become ill.

"What was the matter with you?" Father asked, and before I thought what I was saying I let it out.

◆ **Reading Strategy**
How would you feel at this moment?

"I had the inflammatory rheumatism," I said—and a shout went up. It made me sick to hear them, the way they all laughed.

It brought back all the aching again, and like a fool I began to cry.

"Well, I *have* got it—I *have*, I *have*," I cried, and I got up from the table and ran upstairs.

I stayed there until Mother came up. I knew it would be a long time before I heard the last of the inflammatory rheumatism. I was sick all right, but the aching I now had wasn't in my legs or in my back.

Guide for Responding

◆ LITERATURE AND YOUR LIFE

Reader's Response Do you find the narrator's behavior and ideas realistic? Explain.

Thematic Focus How does his experience affect the way the narrator feels about being honest with himself and others?

Journal Writing The boy knows he has done something wrong, yet he tries to justify his actions. In your journal, consider why people try to convince themselves that they've done the right thing, even when they know they haven't.

☑ Check Your Comprehension

1. What inspires the narrator to think he has "inflammatory rheumatism"?
2. What happens to the narrator in school?
3. What does the narrator do after he gets home?
4. How does his father learn that the narrator left school that day?
5. How does the narrator's family respond when he tells them he has inflammatory rheumatism?

◆ Critical Thinking

INTERPRET

1. Why does the narrator stop limping once he gets away from the schoolhouse street? **[Interpret]**
2. Why is it significant that the boy decides not to tell his family he has inflammatory rheumatism? **[Infer]**
3. (a) What does the narrator mean when he says, "I was having a grand time, having died"? (b) What is his motivation for feeling this way? **[Analyze Causes and Effects]**
4. Do you think that the narrator is fully conscious of his motives? Explain. **[Deduce]**
5. What does this story say about the motivations for people's behavior? **[Draw Conclusions]**

EVALUATE

6. Should the narrator be punished for stealing a day? Why or why not? **[Make a Judgment]**

COMPARE LITERARY WORKS

7. How would you state the theme, or main idea, that lies at the center of "Papa's Parrot" and "Stolen Day"? **[Generalize]**

Guide for Responding (continued)

◆ Reading Strategy

IDENTIFY WITH A CHARACTER

To fully appreciate a character's experiences, put yourself in his or her place. As the events of the story unfold, **identify with a character** by asking yourself what you would do or how you would feel under the circumstances.

1. If you were in Harry's place, how would you change your behavior in the future?
2. If you were in the narrator's place in "Stolen Day," what would you learn from your feelings at the end of the story?
3. What can you learn from these characters' experiences that might help you in your own life?

◆ Build Vocabulary

USING THE WORD ROOT -flam-

Knowing that the word root -flam- means "burn" or "flame" can help you figure out the meaning of words that contain this root. Define each of the following words, incorporating the meaning of -flam-. If necessary, use a dictionary for assistance.

1. inflame   2. flammable   3. flamboyant

SPELLING STRATEGY

Almost all words that end with the m sound end with -m or -me. However, a few end with -mn. In these words, the letter n is silent. There are fewer than a dozen such words. On your paper, complete each of the following words to form a list of the most common -mn words.

1. autu_ _   3. conde_ _   5. sole_ _
2. colu_ _   4. hy_ _

USING THE WORD BANK

On your paper, write the following paragraph, filling in each of the blanks with the appropriate Word Bank word.

The doctor was ____?____ as she examined the sick boy. She had asked him to stop treatment, but he was not improving. Following her instructions, Walter ____?____ taking an anti-____?____ medicine when ____?____ made his joints swollen, feverish, and painful. The medicine reduced his symptons.

◆ Literary Focus

CHARACTERIZATION

In **direct characterization,** the writer tells you about the character's traits. In **indirect characterization,** the writer shows you a character's personality through what he or she says, does, and thinks and by how others interact with the character.

1. Find two examples of indirect characterization of Harry in "Papa's Parrot."
2. Find two examples of indirect characterization of the narrator in "Stolen Day." Rewrite each of the examples you identified as direct characterization.
3. Which is more effective: direct characterization or indirect characterization? Explain.

◆ Build Grammar Skills

COMPLEX SENTENCES

A **complex sentence** contains one independent clause, which can stand by itself as a complete sentence, and one or more subordinate clauses. A subordinate clause contains a subject and a verb but cannot stand alone. A subordinate clause starts with a word (or words) that links it to the rest of the sentence. Words that introduce subordinate clauses include *after, although, as, as if, because, before, despite, if, so that, that, until, what, when, where, which, while,* and *who.*

Practice Copy the following sentences. Underline the independent clause. Circle the word that introduces the subordinate clause.

1. While Mr. Tillian lay in his hospital bed, Harry took the shop key to school with him.
2. Harry stopped liking candy when he was seven.
3. It was Earl who saw me there.
4. I stayed there until Mother came up.
5. It would be a long time before I heard the last of the inflammatory rheumatism.

Writing Application Copy the following sentences, adding subordinate clauses that provide additional information about *who, where,* or *why.*

1. The boy sat on the riverbank.
2. Mr. Tillian bought a parrot.

Build Your Portfolio

 ## Idea Bank

Writing

1. **Diary Entry** As the narrator of "Stolen Day," compose a diary entry in which you explain your behavior on this day. Discuss the reasons for what you thought and what you did.

2. **Review** Write a review of one of these stories for a student literary magazine. Summarize the events of the story. Then explain why you would or would not recommend the story to your audience. Cite passages from the story for support.

3. **Comparing Literary Works** Write an essay in which you compare and contrast the experiences of the main characters in the two stories.

Speaking and Listening

4. **Television Interview [Group Activity]** Imagine that years after the incidents described in the story, Harry Tillian and his father are asked to appear on a talk show to describe the events in the story. With two other classmates, dramatize this talk-show appearance for the class.

5. **Dramatic Reading** Present a dramatic reading of "Papa's Parrot" to the class. Take some time to practice before your presentation. Vary the tone and volume of your voice to match the main character's feelings about the events described.

Projects

6. **Health Statistics** Through research, gather statistics about rheumatoid arthritis, heart disease, or another health condition. Find out the number of people affected, the age groups they fit into, and cure rates. Then, create a series of graphs to chart your findings. Present your graphs to the class. **[Health Link; Math Link]**

7. **Report [Group Activity]** With a group, create a report on the heart. Divide up topics like these among the members of your group: heart-healthy diets, heart structure, artificial hearts, and heart attacks. **[Science Link]**

 ## Writing Mini-Lesson

Continuation

Both stories end with a conversation just about to take place between a parent and a child. In "Papa's Parrot," Harry is going to visit his father. In "Stolen Day," the narrator's mother is coming upstairs after the narrator has fled to his room. Write a continuation of one of the stories that shows what happens next.

Writing Skills Focus: Show, Don't Tell

As you write your continuation, focus on providing details that get your point across, rather than simply stating what's going on. In other words, **show, don't tell.** Through dialogue and description, lead your readers to the conclusions or insights you want to express.

Prewriting List the emotions you'll want to convey in your continuation. For each, identify actions or dialogue that show this emotion. For example, to convey anger, characters might raise their voices. To show embarrassment, characters might bow their heads or avoid eye contact.

Drafting Sometimes a character's actions say more than his or her actual words. As you relate the conversation, refer to your notes. Then, make sure you include details about the character's gestures and how they speak.

> ◆ **Grammar Application**
> Use complex sentences to show cause-and-effect relationships, to indicate when actions happened relative to one another, or to provide less important details about people or events.

Revising Revise your continuation by looking for places in the description where you can replace statements about the characters with events that reveal the characters' needs and personalities.

CONNECTING LITERATURE TO SOCIAL STUDIES

LATIN AMERICA

Lather and Nothing Else *by Hernando Téllez*

CAN YOU KEEP A SECRET? Imagine that you are living during America's Civil War. You support one side— maybe even spy for its cause—but you live among the other side. Some Americans did face this problem, as did some Colombians during that South American country's years of civil unrest.

Two Histories As in many Latin American nations, the political divisions in Colombia are rooted in the events of the 1500's, when Europeans colonized the land. Native Americans, who had lived in Colombia for thousands of years, lost their land to Spaniards. Spanish landowners became wealthy and helped build big cities like Bogotá, the capital of Colombia.

A Growing Gap Though Colombia became independent from Spain in the early 1800's, the gap between poor peasants of Native American heritage and wealthy, educated city dwellers of European heritage grew wider. Conflict also arose over how to organize the government.

Civil War Breaks Out In the late 1800's, Colombians' anger and frustration finally erupted in civil war. After years of fighting, 100,000 Colombians were dead. Still, the main problems were not solved. During the twentieth century, violence has regularly pierced calm times. One very rocky period from 1948 through the mid-1960's was filled with such fierce fighting that it was known as *La Violencia* (The Violence). In "Lather and Nothing Else," you'll meet a barber who must choose his own role in this violent time.

Lather and Nothing Else

Hernando Téllez

He came in without a word. I was stropping[1] my best razor. And when I recognized him, I started to shake. But he did not notice. To cover my nervousness, I went on honing the razor. I tried the edge with the tip of my thumb and took another look at it against the light.

Meanwhile, he was taking off his cartridge-studded belt with the pistol holster suspended from it. He put it on a hook in the wardrobe and hung his cap above it. Then he turned full around toward me and, loosening his tie, remarked, "It's hot as the devil. I want a shave." With that he took his seat.

I estimated he had a four-days' growth of beard, the four days he had been gone on the last foray after our men. His face looked burnt, tanned by the sun.

I started to work carefully on the shaving soap. I scraped some slices from the cake, dropped them into the mug, then

---

1. **stropping** (sträp´ iŋ) v.: Sharpening a blade to a fine edge on a thick band of leather called a strop.

◆ **Build Vocabulary**

foray (fôr´ ā) n.: Sudden attack or raid

◀ **Critical Viewing** Use the title and illustrations on this page to predict the setting of this story. **[Predict]**

added a little lukewarm water, and stirred with the brush. The lather soon began to rise.

"The fellows in the troop must have just about as much beard as I." I went on stirring up lather.

"But we did very well, you know. We caught the leaders. Some of them we brought back dead; others are still alive. But they'll all be dead soon."

Connecting Literature to Social Studies Given Colombia's political problems, who do you think the customer has been chasing?

"How many did you take?" I asked.

"Fourteen. We had to go pretty far in to find them. But now they're paying for it. And not one will escape; not a single one."

He leaned back in the chair when he saw the brush in my hand, full of lather. I had not yet put the sheet on him. I was certainly flustered. Taking a sheet from the drawer, I tied it around my customer's neck.

He went on talking. He evidently took it for granted that I was on the side of the existing regime.

"The people must have gotten a scare with what happened the other day," he said.

"Yes," I replied, as I finished tying the knot against his nape, which smelt of sweat.

"Good show, wasn't it?"

"Very good," I answered, turning my attention now to the brush. The man closed his eyes wearily and awaited the cool caress of the lather.

I had never had him so close before. The day he ordered the people to file through the schoolyard to look upon the four rebels hanging there, my path had crossed his briefly. But the sight of those mutilated bodies kept me from paying attention to the face of the man who had been directing it all and whom I now had in my hands.

It was not a disagreeable face, certainly. And the beard, which aged him a bit, was not unbecoming. His name was Torres. Captain Torres.

I started to lay on the first coat of lather. He kept his eyes closed.

"I would love to catch a nap," he said, "but there's a lot to be done this evening."

I lifted the brush and asked, with pretended indifference: "A firing party?"

"Something of the sort," he replied, "but slower."

"All of them?"

"No, just a few."

I went on lathering his face. My hands began to tremble again. The man could not be aware of this, which was lucky for me. But I wished he had not come in. Probably many of our men had seen him enter the shop. And with the enemy in my house I felt a certain responsibility.

I would have to shave his beard just like any other, carefully, neatly, just as though he were a good customer, taking heed that not a single pore should emit a drop of blood. Seeing to it that the blade did not slip in the small whorls. Taking care that the skin was left clean, soft, shining, so that when I passed the back of my hand over it not a single hair should be felt. Yes. I was secretly a revolutionary, but at the same time I was a conscientious barber, proud of the way I did my job. And that four-day beard presented a challenge.

Connecting Literature to Social Studies Why do you think the barber feels so responsible for how he treats Captain Torres?

I took up the razor, opened the handle wide, releasing the blade, and started to work, downward from one sideburn. The blade responded to perfection. The hair was tough and hard; not very long, but thick. Little by little the skin began to show through. The razor gave out its usual sound as it gathered up layers of soap mixed with bits of hair. I paused to wipe it clean, and

◆ Build Vocabulary

regime (rə zhēm´) *n*.: System or rule of government

nape (nāp) *n*.: Back of the neck

rejuvenated (ri jōō´ və nāt´ id) *v*.: Made to feel refreshed; revitalized taking up the strop once more went about improving its edge, for I am a painstaking barber.

The man, who had kept his eyes closed, now opened them, put a hand out from under the sheet, felt of the part of his face that was emerging from the lather, and said to me, "Come at six o'clock this evening to the school."

"Will it be like the other day?" I asked, stiff with horror.

"It may be even better," he replied.

"What are you planning to do?"

"I'm not sure yet. But we'll have a good time."

Once more he leaned back and shut his eyes. I came closer, the razor on high.

"Are you going to punish all of them?" I timidly ventured.

"Yes, all of them."

The lather was drying on his face. I must hurry. Through the mirror, I took a look at the street. It appeared about as usual; there was the grocery shop with two or three customers. Then I glanced at the clock, two-thirty.

The razor kept descending. Now from the other sideburn downward. It was a blue beard, a thick one. He should let it grow like some poets, or some priests. It would suit him well. Many people would not recognize him. And that would be a good thing for him, I thought, as I went gently over all the throat line. At this point you really had to handle your blade skillfully, because the hair, while scantier, tended to fall into small whorls. It was a curly beard. The pores might open, minutely, in this area and let out a tiny drop of blood. A good barber like myself stakes his reputation on not permitting that to happen to any of his customers.

And this was indeed a special customer. How many of ours had he sent to their death? How many had he mutilated? It was best not to think about it. Torres did not know I was his

General With Sword, Francisco Vidal, Courtesy of the artist

▲ Critical Viewing What details in this painting suggest both the revolution and the barber shop? [Connect]

enemy. Neither he nor the others knew it. It was a secret shared by very few, just because that made it possible for me to inform the revolutionaries about Torres's activities in the town and what he planned to do every time he went on one of his raids to hunt down rebels. So it was going to be very difficult to explain how it was that I had him in my hands and then let him go in peace, alive, cleanshaven.

His beard had now almost entirely disappeared. He looked younger, several years younger than when he had come in. I suppose that always happens to men who enter and leave barbershops. Under the strokes of my razor, Torres was rejuvenated; yes, because I am a good barber, the best in this town, and I say this in all modesty.

Mexican Market, Ira Moskowitz, Courtesy of the artist

A little more lather here under the chin, on the Adam's apple, right near the great vein. How hot it is! Torres must be sweating just as I am. But he is not afraid. He is a tranquil man, who is not even giving thought to what he will do to his prisoners this evening. I, on the other hand, polishing his skin with this razor but avoiding the drawing of blood, careful with every stroke—I cannot keep my thoughts in order.

> **Connecting Literature to Social Studies**
> What do you think may be the special challenges of fighting for change in your own country?

Confound the hour he entered my shop! I am a revolutionary but not a murderer. And it would be so easy to kill him. He deserves it. Or does he? No! No one deserves the sacrifice others make in becoming assassins. What is to be gained by it? Nothing. Others and still others keep coming, and the first kill the second, and then these kill the next, and so on until everything becomes a sea of blood. I could cut his throat, so, swish, swish! He would not even have time to moan, and with his eyes shut he would not even see the shine of the razor or the gleam in my eye.

But I'm shaking like a regular murderer. From his throat a stream of blood would flow on the sheet, over the chair, down on my hands, onto the floor. I would have to close the door. But the blood would go flowing, along the floor, warm, indelible, not to be <u>stanched</u>, until it reached the street like a small scarlet river.

I'm sure that with a good strong blow, a deep cut, he would feel no pain. He would not suffer at all. And what would I do then with the body? Where would I hide it? I would have to flee, leave all this behind, take shelter far away, very far away. But they would follow until they caught up with me. "The murderer of Captain Torres. He slit his throat while he was shaving him. What a cowardly thing to do." And others would say, "The <u>avenger</u> of our people. A name to

◆ Build Vocabulary

stanched (stônchd) *v.*: Stopped or slowed down
avenger (ə venj´ ər) *n.*: One who gets even for a wrong or injury

◀ **Critical Viewing** How does this market scene represent what could be taking place outside the barber's shop? [**Analyze**]

remember"—my name here. "He was the town barber. No one knew he was fighting for our cause."

And so, which will it be? Murderer or hero? My fate hangs on the edge of this razor blade. I can turn my wrist slightly, put a bit more pressure on the blade, let it sink in. The skin will yield like silk, like rubber, like the strop. There is nothing more tender than a man's skin, and the blood is always there, ready to burst forth. A razor like this cannot fail. It is the best one I have.

But I don't want to be a murderer. No, sir. You came in to be shaved. And I do my work honorably. I don't want to stain my hands with blood. Just with lather, and nothing else. You are an executioner; I am only a barber. Each one to his job. That's it. Each one to his job.

The chin was now clean, polished, soft. The man got up and looked at himself in the glass. He ran his hand over the skin and felt its freshness, its newness.

"Thanks," he said. He walked to the wardrobe for his belt, his pistol, and his cap. I must have been very pale, and I felt my shirt soaked with sweat. Torres finished adjusting his belt buckle, straightened his gun in its holster, and, smoothing his hair mechanically, put on his cap. From his trousers pocket he took some coins to pay for the shave. And he started toward the door. On the threshold he stopped for a moment, and turning toward me he said,

"They told me you would kill me. I came to find out if it was true. But it's not easy to kill. I know what I'm talking about."

Guide for Responding

◆ LITERATURE AND YOUR LIFE

Reader's Response Did you think the barber would kill Captain Torres? Why or why not?

Thematic Focus Each of us has a set of rules by which we live. How does the barber's personal code dictate his behavior?

☑ Check Your Comprehension

1. How does the barber feel when Captain Torres enters the shop?
2. What has Captain Torres been doing for the past four days?
3. What role does the barber have in the civil war?

◆ Critical Thinking

INTERPRET

1. Why does the barber consider what would "be a good thing" for his enemy? **[Infer]**
2. Why does the barber decide not to kill Captain Torres? **[Interpret]**
3. What message does this story suggest about the effects of civil war on people and their community? **[Draw Conclusions]**

EVALUATE

4. Do you think the barber made the right choice? Why or why not? **[Criticize]**

EXTEND

5. The barber decides that though he is a revolutionary, he is not a murderer. How do you think war might change people's views of their roles—or jobs—in society? Explain. **[Social Studies Link]**

Meet the Author

Hernando Téllez (1908–1966)

Growing up surrounded by Colombia's political unrest shaped Hernando Téllez's life. He became a politician himself and worked as a senator on resolving his country's problems. Téllez also served as a delegate to UNESCO, an organization that uses education and the arts to help people everywhere learn to get along better.

Politics led Téllez toward another main focus of his life—writing. He wrote about politics often, in nonfiction essays and in fictional stories such as "Lather and Nothing Else."

CONNECTING LITERATURE TO SOCIAL STUDIES

Colombia is not the only Latin American country to face revolution and civil war. Many of her neighboring countries share a history of conflict between different groups in society.

Though Latin American countries gained independence from Europe one by one in the 1800's, many were then ruled by dictators. Elections have occurred infrequently in most Latin American nations, and citizens have had little say in how their country is run. In addition, governments have sometimes jailed those who speak out for change.

In this century, revolution has broken out in many Latin American nations; for example, Peru, Chile, and Argentina. Like the barber and the captain in this story, these civil wars have set neighbor against neighbor, businessperson against customer.

1. In what ways are the story's setting and characters typical of the political situation in Latin America?

2. How might this story help readers understand the personal and political stakes of revolution and civil war?

 Idea Bank

Writing

1. **Letter** As the barber, write a letter to your fellow revolutionaries. Explain why you did not kill your common enemy even though you had the perfect opportunity.

2. **Internal Monologue** Describe the thoughts running through Captain Torres's mind as the barber worked. Consider the captain's view of the political situation and his reasons for behaving as he does.

3. **Story Sequel** What do you think will happen to the barber now? Incorporating what you know about the characters and Latin American history, write a sequel to the story.

Speaking and Listening

4. **Speech** Learn more about the political ideas on both sides of Colombia's civil unrest. Then, deliver a speech asking people to support one side's position. **[Social Studies Link]**

Projects

5. **Gallery of Leaders** Find out about the leader of a Latin American nation—either living today or earlier in the twentieth century. Create a museum exhibit about this person's political and personal life. As a class, assemble all the exhibits into one presentation. **[Social Studies Link]**

6. **Time Capsule [Group Activity]** Within a group, divide the task of researching Colombia's current political and social situation through the Internet, media, and library sources. Identify problems the nation faces. Consider whether the issues raised in the story have been resolved. Then, work together to create a time capsule telling future Colombians about what their nation was like in your lifetime. Where has the country been and where is it headed? **[Social Studies Link]**

Further Reading, Listening, and Viewing

- Marion Morrison's *Enchantment of the World: Colombia* (1990) offers text and pictures about Colombia's past and present.
- Naomi Shihab Nye edited *This Same Sky* (1992), which includes poems by many Latin Americans.
- Lori M. Carlson and Cynthia L. Ventura edited *Where Angels Glide at Dawn: New Stories from Latin America* (1990). This collection includes works by recent Latin American writers.

Writing Process Workshop

This unit contains short stories written by the masters. Try your hand at writing a **short story** of your own. Your story should be fiction, not fact. You can base it on something that you know—a family, a conflict, or a person—but let your imagination mix with reality to create an original story that no one else could write.

To keep your story short, include only a few events and keep the number of characters down to five or fewer. The following skills, covered in the Writing Mini-Lessons in this part, will help you write your short story.

Writing Skills Focus

▶ To make your story more interesting and engaging, **use dialogue** to help you reveal the personalities of your characters and to move the plot along. (See p. 460.)

▶ **Include descriptive details** to make your setting vivid and real to your readers. (See p. 477.)

▶ **Show, don't tell** what your characters are like, how they behave, and what happens. (See p. 489.)

Cynthia Rylant uses all these skills in this scene from "Papa's Parrot."

MODEL FROM LITERATURE

from "Papa's Parrot" by Cynthia Rylant

Harry opened the new boxes his father hadn't gotten to. Peppermints. Jawbreakers. Toffee creams. Strawberry kisses. ① Harry traveled from bin to bin, putting the candies where they belonged.

"Hello!"

Harry jumped, spilling a box of jawbreakers. ②

"Hello, Rocky!" ③

① Rylant doesn't simply *tell* us that there are many different kinds of candy. She *shows* us.

② Descriptive details make the story come to life.

③ Dialogue also adds life and realism to the story.

Prewriting

Choose an Idea Perhaps you already have an idea for a story. For example, you might want to add fictional details to tell the story of an actual event. You could write a comic tale like the kind you like to read. If you don't already have the spark for your story, consider one of the ideas listed here.

Topic Ideas

- Surviving a storm
- Taming an animal
- Solving a mystery
- Losing—or making—a friend

Devise a Story Plan Think about your story before you start to write. Use the questions below to generate the information you'll need. Make your answers as detailed as possible.

▶ Who will be in your story? (character)
▶ What will happen? (plot)
▶ When and where will it happen? (setting)
▶ What is the main character's problem? (conflict)
▶ What will be the turning point? (climax)

Drafting

Start Strong Experiment with the first sentence of your story. Make it a hook that catches your readers' attention. Here are a few suggestions and examples. Which of them would hook you?

Dialogue:	"Richard, I have something to tell you." Once these words were out, Stacey began to feel better.
An Intriguing Description:	The river rushed past Mia's bare feet, chilling her bones.
A Sound or Noise:	The helicopter's whir stopped our conversation.
A Memory:	When I was three, I gave my teddy bear a haircut.
A Question:	Have you ever insulted someone without realizing it?

Choose a Voice Some stories are told using the first-person voice. ("I answered the phone.") If you choose this voice, decide which character will tell the story. Other stories are told using the third-person voice. ("He answered the phone.") Once you make this choice, stick with it.

APPLYING LANGUAGE SKILLS: Vary Tag Words

Dialogue is a key part of many short stories. While *said* is straightforward and accurate, avoid attaching the same tag words to identify speakers. Choose words that communicate emotion. Notice how each of these examples conveys a different meaning.

Weak Tag Word:
"Stop that," he said.

Stronger Tag Words:
"Stop that," he whined.
"Stop that," he laughed.
"Stop that," he hissed angrily.

Practice Wake up these sentences by replacing the dull tag words with more vivid ones.

1. She said, "Would you go to the store?"
2. "I can't wait for that!" he said.
3. "Please be careful," she said.

Writing Application In your short story, use *said* sparingly. When you can, use other words to convey the emotion of the dialogue.

Writer's Solution Connection Writing Lab

For more on developing characters, use the Character Trait Word Bin in the Prewriting section of the Narration tutorial.

Grammar Review

A **sentence** is a group of words that expresses a complete thought. Each sentence contains one or more **clauses,** groups of words with their own subjects and verbs (see page 459). The two major types of clauses are independent clauses and subordinate clauses. An independent (main) clause can stand by itself as a complete sentence. A subordinate clause is only part of a sentence. Sentences can be classified according to the number and types of clauses they contain.

SEND

sen·tence (sen'təns) *n.* **1** a group of words that is used to tell, ask, command, or exclaim something, usually having a subject and a predicate: a sentence begins with a capital letter and ends with a period, question mark, or exclamation point

Sentence Type	Types of Clause(s) in the Sentence
Simple (See p. 476.)	One main clause only
Compound (See p. 476.)	Two or more main clauses
Complex (See p. 488.)	One main clause plus one or more subordinate clauses

Practice 1 Copy these sentences on a piece of paper. Underline main clauses once. Underline subordinate clauses twice. Then, identify each sentence as *simple, compound,* or *complex.*

1. Bob and Jimmy, who were best friends as kids, agreed to meet again in exactly twenty years.

2. Rikki is a mongoose that lives with a family in India.

3. The brave little mongoose killed the deadly cobra.

4. Mr. Tillian will get out of the hospital soon, but he will rest at home for a few weeks.

5. Although the boy was sent home from school because he said that he was sick, he did not stay in bed.

Practice 2

Rewrite the following sentence pairs, combining the ideas to form the types of sentences indicated.

1. (a) This unit features short stories.
   (b) Short stories are brief works of fiction. (*complex*)

2. (a) Some stories are closely based on real people and events.
   (b) Others are wildly fanciful. (*compound*)

3. (a) Elements of a short story include the plot.
   (b) Elements of a short story include the characters. (*simple*)

Grammar in Writing

✔ Using the same type of sentence over and over again is boring. When you write, use a mixture of different types of sentences. This will help make your writing more lively and interesting.

✔ Be careful not to write a subordinate clause as if it were a sentence on its own. Subordinate clauses must always be attached to an independent clause.

PART 2 *Setting and Theme*

Looking Along Broadway Towards Grace Church (detail), 1981, Red Grooms, Courtesy Marlborough Gallery

Guide for Reading

Meet the Authors:

Anton Chekhov (1860–1904)

While still a teen, Anton Chekhov began writing articles and humorous sketches to help support his family. Even though he graduated from medical school and became a successful doctor, writing remained Chekhov's primary career throughout his life.

A Russian Treasure Chekhov is widely considered to be the greatest Russian playwright and short-story writer. His greatest masterpieces are four plays written during the last decade of his life: *The Seagull, Uncle Vanya, Three Sisters,* and *The Cherry Orchard.*

Jane Yolen (1939–   )

Jane Yolen's storytelling career began in first grade, when she wrote a class musical about vegetables. Since then, Yolen has written more than a hundred books. She has produced novels, short stories, poems, plays, and essays.

THE STORY BEHIND THE STORY

Although Yolen is known mainly for her fantasy stories, she found inspiration in her Jewish heritage to write "Suzy and Leah," the story of a Holocaust survivor. Yolen wrote about the Holocaust so that her own children could understand and remember.

◆ LITERATURE AND YOUR LIFE

CONNECT YOUR EXPERIENCE

When you have a problem, you probably reach out to people close to you for comfort or guidance. Neither of the main characters in these stories has the benefit of such support. In "Heartache," a carriage driver needs to share his sorrow, but he cannot get anyone to listen to him. In "Suzy and Leah," a young girl is afraid to reach out to others and ask for help.

THEMATIC FOCUS: Finding Solutions

As you read these stories, you may find yourself wondering how people can make themselves heard.

◆ Background for Understanding

HISTORY

"Suzy and Leah" is based on true events. Before and during World War II, the Nazi government of Germany persecuted Jews. At first, Jews were forced to identify themselves with yellow stars. Eventually, many Jews were forced to leave their homes. Many were herded into concentration camps, where they were starved, overworked, and killed. Six million Jews died in the Holocaust. Some Jews, however, survived. One group gathered the few belongings they still had and came to a refugee camp in Oswego, New York. The fictional character Leah lives in this camp.

◆ Build Vocabulary

SUFFIXES: -ee

Leah is a *refugee.* The word *refugee* is formed by adding the suffix -ee, meaning "one who," to the word *refuge.* Thus, a refugee is a person who seeks or has taken refuge.

WORD BANK

Which of these words means "not important"? Check the Build Vocabulary boxes to see if you've chosen correctly.

conspiring
ponderous
indignantly
quavering
insignificant
refugee

Heartache ◆ Suzy and Leah

◆ Literary Focus

SETTING

The **setting** of a story is the time and place of the action. The importance of the setting varies. In some stories, the setting is little more than a background. In others, such as "Heartache," the setting highlights the action. In still others, such as "Suzy and Leah," the setting shapes the action.

◆ Reading Strategy

MAKE INFERENCES

Short-story writers don't tell you everything there is to know about the characters, setting, and events. Instead, they leave it to you to fill in missing information by **making inferences,** or drawing conclusions, based on the material that is provided. For example, the first paragraph of "Heartache" describes a character and his horse waiting motionless in the snow. From this detail, you might infer that the character is deep in thought or depressed. As you read the stories, jot down key details and record your inferences in a table like the one below.

Details   **Inferences**

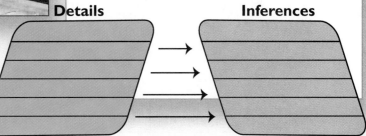

Heartache

Anton Chekhov

Evening twilight. Large wet flakes of snow circle lazily around the just lighted streetlamps and lie on roofs, horses' backs, caps, and shoulders in a thin, soft layer. Cabby Iona Potapov is all white as a ghost. As hunched over as a living body can be hunched, he sits on the box and does not stir. If a whole snowdrift were to fall on him, even then, it seems, he would not find it necessary to shake the snow off himself. . . . His nag, too, is white and motionless. In her motionlessness, angularity of shape, and stick-like straightness, even up close she looks like a penny gingerbread horse. In all probability she is sunk in thought. One who has been torn away from the plow, from the customary grey scenes, and been cast here, into this whirlpool of monstrous light, unceasing din, and rushing people, cannot help thinking. . . .

It has been a long time since Iona and his horse have moved from their place. They left the stable before supper, and still there is no fare. But now evening darkness is descending on the city. The pale light of the streetlamps is surrendering its place to vivid color, and the bustle in the street is becoming noisier.

"Cabby, to the Vyborg District!" hears Iona, "Cabby!"

Iona starts, and through eyelashes pasted over with snow he sees an officer in a cloak with a hood.

"To the Vyborg District!" repeats the officer. "What's the matter, are you asleep? To the Vyborg District!"

As a sign of assent Iona tugs the reins, causing the layers of snow to pour off the horse's back and his own shoulders. . . . The officer gets in. The cabby clucks to the horse, stretches his neck out swan-like, raises up, and more from habit than

◆ **Literary Focus**
How does the setting of the story reflect Iona's emotional state?

◀ **Critical Viewing** What details in the first three paragraphs of this story are shown in the photograph? **[Analyze]**

need, waves his whip. The nag stretches her neck too, crooks her stick-like legs, and moves irresolutely from her place . . .

"Where are you heading, you gnome!" almost immediately Iona hears shouts from the dark mass of people moving back and forth. "Where are you going? Keep to the r-r-right!"

"You don't know how to drive! Keep to the right!" says the officer angrily.

The driver of a carriage curses him; a passer-by who was crossing the road and has his shoulder bumped by the nag's muzzle looks at him fiercely and shakes the snow from his sleeve. Iona fidgets on the box, as if on pins and needles, shoves his elbows out to the side and rolls his eyes like a madman, as if he does not understand where he is and why he is here.

"What scoundrels they all are!" jokes the officer. "They are all trying to bump into you or fall under the horse. They're conspiring."

Iona looks around at the passenger and moves his lips . . . Apparently he wants to say something, but nothing comes from his throat except a wheeze.

"What?" asks the officer.

Iona twists his mouth with a smile, strains his throat and wheezes:

"My son, sir . . . er, he died this week."

"Hm! What did he die of?"

Iona turns his whole body around toward the passenger and says:

"Well who knows? From a fever, probably . . . He lay in the hospital three days and died . . . God's will."

"Turn off, you scoundrel!" rings out in the dark. "Where yah crawled out of, you old dog? Use your eyes!"

"Get going, get going . . ." says the passenger. "At this rate we won't get there before tomorrow. Use the whip!"

The cabby again stretches out his neck, raises up, and waves the whip with ponderous grace. Then he looks back at the passenger, but he has closed his eyes and apparently is not disposed to listen. When he has let him out in the Vyborg District, Iona stops by a tavern, hunches over on the box, and again he does not stir . . . The wet snow again paints him and his nag white. One hour passes, another . . .

Cursing each other and stomping their boots loudly on the sidewalk, three young men walk by: two of them are tall and thin, the third is short and hunchbacked.

"Driver, to Policemen's Bridge!" shouts the hunchback in a cracking voice. "Three of us . . . a twenty-kopek piece!"

Iona tugs the reins and clucks. A twenty-kopek piece is not a proper fare, but he's not interested in the price . . . A ruble or a five-kopek piece, it's all the same to him, as long as he has passengers . . . Bumping into each other and swearing, the young men walk up to the sleigh and all three immediately try to sit down. They begin to solve the question of which two are to sit and which one to stand. After lengthy abuse, capriciousness, and rebukes, they reach the conclusion that since the hunchback is the smallest, he ought to stand.

"Well, drive on," cracks the hunchback, taking his place and breathing down Iona's neck. "Shove off! And, brother, your cap! A worse one couldn't be found in all of Petersburg . . ."

"He, he . . . He, he . . ." laughs Iona. "Whatever you say . . ."

"Well, you 'whatever you say,' drive on! You gonna drive like this the whole way? Yes? And how about a sock in the neck? . . ."

"My head is bursting . . ." says one of the gangly ones. "Yesterday at the Dukmasovs' Vaska and I drank four bottles of cognac between the two of us."

"I don't see why he lies!" the other gangly one says angrily. "He lies like a pig!"

"Really, God punish me . . ."

"That's about as true as that louse's coughs."

"He, he!" snickers Iona. "Jolly fellows!"

"Faugh," says the hunchback indignantly. "Are you going to get going or not, you old rat? Is this the way to drive?"

Behind his back Iona can feel the twisting body and quavering voice of the hunchback.

▲ Critical Viewing Find evidence in this photograph to support the fact that it was taken in Russia during the time the story takes place. **[Support]**

"And this week my . . . er . . . son died!"

"We'll all die . . ." sighs the hunchback, wiping his lips after the coughing. "Well, drive on, drive on! Gentlemen, I absolutely cannot go any further like this! When will he get us there?"

He hears the abuse directed at him, he sees the men, and little by little the feeling of loneliness begins to lift from his heart. The hunchback goes on abusing him until he is choked by a six-story-high oath and breaks off coughing. The gangly ones begin to talk about a certain Nadezhda Petrovna. Iona looks around at them. Waiting for a short pause, he looks around again and mutters:

◆ Build Vocabulary

conspiring (kən spīr´ iŋ) *v.*: Planning in secret to do something bad

ponderous (pän´ dər əs) *adj.*: Large; heavy

indignantly (in dig´ nənt lē) *adv.*: Angrily

quavering (kwā´ vər iŋ) *adj.*: Shaking; trembling

"You encourage him a little—in the neck!"

"Hear that you old rat? Why I'll whack your neck! . . . If we're going to stand on ceremony with your kind, we might as well go on foot . . . You hear, Snake Gorynych? Or do you spit on your words?"

And Iona hears more than feels the thud of a blow on the neck.

"He, he . . ." he laughs. "Jolly fellows . . . God grant you health!"

"Driver, are you married?" asks a tall one.

"Me? He, he . . . Jo-ol-ly fellows! Now I got one wife—the damp earth . . . Ho, ho, ho . . . The grave, that is! . . . My son's died now, and I'm alive . . . Queer thing, death knocked at the wrong door . . . In-stead of coming to me, it went to my son . . ."

And Iona turns around to tell how his son died, but the hunchback sighs lightly and announces that, thank God, they've finally arrived. Receiving his twenty-kopek piece, Iona looks after the carousers disappearing in a dark entrance for a long time. Again he is alone, and again there is silence for him . . . The heartache which had eased for a while, appears again and rends the breast with even greater force. Iona's eyes run anxiously and tormentedly over the crowd surging along both sides of the street: from these thousands of people, can't even one be found who would hear him out? But the crowds run along, not noticing him or his heartache . . . Vast, boundless heartache. If Iona's breast burst and the heartache poured out, it seems it would flood the entire world—but nevertheless people do not see it. It managed to fit into such an insignificant shell that you would not see it in the daylight with a torch . . .

Iona sees a doorkeeper with a sack and de-cides to talk to him.

"What time would it be now, friend?" he asks.

"After nine . . . Why you stopping here? Move along!"

Iona drives a few steps away, hunches up and surrenders to the heartache . . . He con-siders it useless to turn to people. But five minutes do not pass before he straightens up, shakes his head as if he felt a sharp pain, and yanks the reins . . . He can't bear it.

"To the stable," he thinks, "to the stable."

And as if she has understood his thought, the nag begins to run at a trot. An hour and a half later Iona is already sitting by a big dirty stove. On the stove, floor, and benches people are snoring. The air is stuffy and full of smells . . . Iona looks at the sleepers, scratches him-self and regrets returning home so early . . .

"And I didn't make enough for oats," he thinks. "That's the reason for the heartache. A man who knows his stuff . . . who's full him-self and whose horse is full, is always at ease."

In one of the corners a young driver gets up, croaks sleepily, and heads for the waterbucket.

"You want a drink?" asks Iona.

"Obviously!"

"So . . . Your health . . . And, friend, my son died. Did you hear? This week in the hospital . . . A story!"

Iona looks for what effect his words have produced, but sees nothing. The young man has covered his head and is already sleeping. The old man sighs and scratches himself . . . He wants to talk, just as the young man wanted to drink. It will soon be a week since his son died, and he still hasn't talked to any-one about it properly . . . He should speak with good sense, in measured tones . . . He must tell how his son got sick, how he suffered, what he said before death, how he died . . . He should describe the funeral and the trip to the hospital for the deceased's clothes. A daughter, Anisya, remained in the country . . . He should talk about her too . . . Does he have any dearth of things he can talk about now? The listener should moan, sigh, lament . . . And it's even better to talk to women. Even though they are fools, they wail after two words.

"Go see after the horse," thinks Iona. "You'll always manage some sleep . . . You'll probably get enough sleep."

He gets dressed and goes into the stable where his horse is standing. He thinks about oats, hay, about the weather . . . About his son, when he is alone, he cannot think . . . It is possible to talk to someone about him, but by himself it is unbearably painful to think about him and draw his picture.

"Chewing?" Iona asks his horse, seeing her shining eyes. "Well, chew, chew . . . If we didn't get enough for oats, we'll eat hay . . . Yes . . . I've already got too old to go out . . . My son should drive, not me . . . He was a real driver . . . If only he were alive . . ."

Iona is silent for a while and continues:

"So, my girl . . . Kozma Ionych is gone . . .

He left this life . . . Went and died for nothing . . . Now, let's say, you have a little colt, and you are the natural mother of this little colt . . . And suddenly, let's say, this little colt left this life . . . Wouldn't you be sorry?"

The nag chews, listens, and breathes on the hands of her master . . .

Iona is carried away and tells her everything . . .

◆ **Build Vocabulary**

insignificant (in′ sig nif′ i kənt) *adj.*: Small; unimposing

Guide for Responding

◆ LITERATURE AND YOUR LIFE

Reader's Response Would you stop to hear Iona Potapov's story? Explain.

Thematic Focus What should Iona do to deal with his heartache more productively?

Journal Writing When a friend needs someone to talk to, are you a good listener? In a brief journal entry, write about the qualities you think a good listener needs. Then, evaluate your strengths and weaknesses with these skills.

☑ Check Your Comprehension

1. Identify the time of day and season of the year in which this story is set.
2. What is Iona's occupation?
3. How do Iona's passengers treat him?
4. What happened to Iona's son?
5. Who listens to Iona's story in the end?

◆ Critical Thinking

INTERPRET

1. In the first paragraph, Chekhov writes that Iona seems as if he wouldn't bother to shake the snow off himself even if a whole snowdrift were to fall on him. What does this tell you about Iona's state of mind? **[Interpret]**
2. After the officer gets in the cab, why does Iona drive so poorly? **[Infer]**
3. Why do Iona's passengers treat him badly? **[Analyze]**
4. In what ways are Iona and his horse similar? **[Support]**
5. What message about people does "Heartache" convey? **[Draw Conclusions]**

EVALUATE

6. How effective do you find the ending of the story? Explain. **[Make a Judgment]**

APPLY

7. What can individuals and society do to help people who are in situations similar to Iona's? **[Speculate]**

Suzy and Leah

Jane Yolen

August 5, 1944

Dear Diary,

Today I walked past *that* place, the one that was in the newspaper, the one all the kids have been talking about. Gosh, is it ugly! A line of rickety wooden buildings just like in the army. And a fence lots higher than my head. With barbed wire[1] on top. How can anyone—even a refugee—live there?

I took two candy bars along, just like everyone said I should. When I held them up, all those kids just swarmed over to the fence, grabbing. Like in a zoo. Except for this one girl, with two dark braids and bangs nearly covering her eyes. She was just standing to one side, staring at me. It was so creepy. After a minute I looked away. When I looked back, she was gone. I mean gone. Disappeared as if she'd never been.

Suzy

August 5, 1944

My dear Mutti,[2]

I have but a single piece of paper to write on. And a broken pencil. But I will write small so I can tell all. I address it to you, *Mutti*, though you are gone from me forever. I write in English, to learn better, because I want to make myself be understood.

Today another girl came. With more sweets. A girl with yellow hair and a false smile. Yonni and Zipporah and Ruth, my friends, all grabbed for the sweets. Like wild animals. Like . . . like prisoners. But we are not wild animals. And we are no longer prisoners. Even though we are still penned in.

I stared at the yellow-haired girl until she was forced to look down. Then I walked away. When I turned to look back, she was gone. Disappeared. As if she had never been.

Leah

September 2, 1944

Dear Diary,

I brought the refugee kids oranges today. Can you believe it—they didn't know you're supposed to peel oranges first. One boy tried to eat one like an apple. He made an awful face, but then he ate it anyway. I showed them how to peel oranges with the second one. After I stopped laughing.

Mom says they are going to be coming to school. Of course they'll have to be cleaned up first. Ugh. My hand still feels itchy from where one little boy grabbed it in his. I wonder if he had bugs.

Suzy

> ◆ **Reading Strategy**
> What can you infer about Suzy's understanding of the refugees from her thoughts and feelings?

September 2, 1944

My dear Mutti,

Today we got cereal in a box. At first I did not know what it was. Before the war we ate such lovely porridge with milk straight from our cows. And eggs fresh from the hen's nest,

---

1. **barbed wire:** Twisted wire with sharp points all along it, used for fences and barriers.
2. **Mutti** (mŏŏ′ tē): German equivalent of Mommy.

though you know how I hated that nasty old chicken. How often she pecked me! In the German camp, it was potato soup—with onions when we were lucky, without either onion or potato when we were not. And after, when I was running from the Nazis, it was stale brown bread, if we could find any. But cereal in a box—*that* is something.

I will not take a sweet from that yellow-haired girl, though. She laughed at Yonni. I will not take another orange fruit.

Leah

September 5, 1944

Dear Diary,

So how are those refugee kids going to learn? Our teachers teach in English. This is America, after all.

I wouldn't want to be one of them. Imagine going to school and not being able to speak English or understand anything that's going on. I can't imagine anything worse.

Suzy

September 5, 1944

My dear Mutti,

The adults of the Americans say we are safe now. And so we must go to their school. But I say no place is safe for us. Did not the Germans say that we were safe in their camps? And there you and baby Natan were killed.

And how could we learn in this American school anyway? I have a little English. But Ruth and Zipporah and the others, though they speak Yiddish[3] and Russian and German, they have no English at all. None beyond *thank you* and *please* and *more sweets*. And then there is little Avi. How could he go to this school? He will speak nothing at all. He stopped speaking, they say, when he was hidden away in a cupboard by his grandmother who was taken by the Nazis after she swore there was no child in the house. And he was almost three days in that cupboard without food, without water, without words to comfort him. Is English a safer language than German?

There is barbed wire still between us and the world.

Leah

---

3. **Yiddish** (yid´ ish) *n:* Language spoken by eastern European Jews and their descendants. It is written with Hebrew letters and contains words from Hebrew, Russian, Polish, and English.

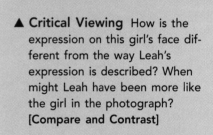

▲ **Critical Viewing** How is the expression on this girl's face different from the way Leah's expression is described? When might Leah have been more like the girl in the photograph? **[Compare and Contrast]**

◆ **Build Vocabulary**

refugee (ref´ yoo jē) *n.:* Person who flees home or country to seek shelter from war or cruelty

Suzy and Leah ◆ 513

▲ **Critical Viewing** This photograph shows the Nazi government overseeing Jews leaving their homes. What do you find most surprising about the picture? **[Respond]**

September 14, 1944

Dear Diary,

At least the refugee kids are wearing better clothes now. And they all have shoes. Some of them still had those stripy pajamas on when they arrived in America.

The girls all wore dresses to their first day at school, though. They even had hair bows, gifts from the teachers. Of course I recognized my old blue pinafore. The girl with the dark braids had it on, and Mom hadn't even told me she was giving it away. I wouldn't have minded so much if she had only asked. It doesn't fit me anymore, anyway.

The girl in my old pinafore was the only one without a name tag, so all day long no one knew her name.

Suzy

September 14, 1944

My dear Mutti,

I put on the blue dress for our first day. It fit me well. The color reminded me of your eyes and the blue skies over our farm before the smoke from the burning darkened it. Zipporah braided my hair, but I had no mirror until we got to the school and they showed us the toilets. They call it a bathroom, but there is no bath in it at all, which is strange. I have never been in a school with boys before.

They have placed us all in low grades. Because of our English. I do not care. This way I do not have to see the girl with the yellow hair who smiles so falsely at me.

But they made us wear tags with our names printed on them. That made me afraid. What next? Yellow stars?[4] I tore mine off and threw it behind a bush before we went in.

Leah

September 16, 1944

Dear Diary,

Mr. Forest has assigned each of us to a refugee to help them with their English. He gave me the girl with the dark braids, the one without the name tag, the one in my pinafore. Gee, she's as prickly as a porcupine. I asked if I could have a different kid. He said I was the best English student and she already spoke the best English. He wants her to learn as fast as possible so she can help the others. As if she would, Miss Porcupine.

Her name is Leah. I wish she would wear another dress.

Suzy

September 16, 1944

My dear Mutti,

Now I have a real notebook and a pen. I am writing to you at school now. I cannot take the notebook back to the shelter. Someone there will surely borrow it. I will instead keep it here. In the little cupboard each one of us has been given.

I wish I had another dress. I wish I had a different student helping me and not the yellow-haired girl.

Leah

September 20, 1944

Dear Diary,

Can't she ever smile, that Leah? I've brought her candy bars and apples from home. I tried to give her a handkerchief with a yellow flower on it. She wouldn't take any of them.

Her whole name is Leah Shoshana Hershkowitz. At least, that's the way she writes it. When she says it, it sounds all different, low and growly. I laughed when I tried to say it, but she wouldn't laugh with me. What a grouch.

And yesterday, when I took her English paper to correct it, she shrank back against her chair as if I was going to hit her or something. Honestly!

Mom says I should invite her home for dinner soon. We'll have to get her a special pass for that. But I don't know if I want her to come. It's not like she's any fun at all. I wish Mr. Forest would let me trade.

Suzy

◆ Literature and Your Life
How would you feel if you had to help someone who didn't act grateful? Would you be understanding or irritated?

September 20, 1944

My dear Mutti,

The girl with the yellow hair is called Suzy Ann McCarthy. It is a silly name. It means nothing. I asked her who she was named for, and she said, "For a book my mom liked." A book! I am named after my great-grandmother on my mother's side, who was an important woman in our village. I am proud to carry on her name.

This Suzy brings many sweets. But I must call them candies now. And a handkerchief. She expects me to be grateful. But how can I be grateful? She treats me like a pet, a pet she does not really like or trust. She wants to feed me like an animal behind bars.

If I write all this down, I will not hold so much anger. I have much anger. And terror besides. *Terror.* It is a new word for me, but an old feeling. One day soon this Suzy and her people will stop being nice to us. They will remember we are not just refugees but Jews, and they will turn on us. Just as the Germans did. Of this I am sure.

Leah

---

4. **yellow stars:** Jews were forced to wear fabric stars during the Holocaust to distinguish them from others.

October 12, 1944

Dear Diary,

I did a terrible thing. I read Leah's diary. I'd kill anyone who did that to me!

At first it made no sense. Who were *Mutti* and Natan, and why were they killed? What were the yellow stars? What does kosher mean? And the way she talked about *me* made me furious. Who did she think she was, little Miss Porcupine? All I did was bring candy and fruit and try to make those poor refugee kids feel at home.

Then, when I asked Mom some questions, carefully, so she wouldn't guess I had read Leah's diary, she explained. She said the Nazis killed people, mothers and children as well as men. In places called concentration camps. And that all the Jews—people who weren't Christians like us—had to wear yellow stars on their clothes so they could be spotted blocks and blocks away. It was so awful I could hardly believe it, but Mom said it was true.

How was I supposed to know all that? How can Leah stand any of us? How could she live with all that pain?

Suzy

▼ **Critical Viewing** The girls pictured here are looking out of a ship's porthole as they prepare to go to America. Which girl has an expression you'd expect to see on Leah's face? Explain. **[Connect]**

◆ **Literary Focus**
Setting includes the historical context of the story's action. How has this shaped Leah's thoughts and behavior?

October 12, 1944

My dear Mutti,

Suzy and her mother came to see me in the hospital. They brought me my notebook so now I can write again.

I was so frightened about being sick. I did not tell anyone for a long time, even though it hurt so much. In the German camp, if you were sick and could not do your work, they did not let you live.

But in the middle of the night, I had so much fever, a doctor was sent for. Little Avi found me. He ran to one of the guards. He spoke out loud for the first time. He said, "Please, for Leah. Do not let her go into the dark."

The doctor tells me I nearly died, but they saved me. They have given me much medicines and soon I will eat the food and they will be sure it is kosher, too. And I am alive. This I can hardly believe. *Alive!*

Then Suzy came with her *Mutti*, saying, "I am sorry. I am so sorry. I did not know. I did not understand." Suzy did a bad thing. She read my notebook. But it helped her understand. And then, instead of making an apology, she did a strange thing. She took a red book with a lock out of her pocket and gave it to me. "Read this," she said. "And when you are out of the hospital, I have a green dress with white trim I want you to have. It will be just perfect with your eyes."

I do not know what this trim may be. But I like the idea of a green dress. And I have a new word now, as well. It is this: *diary*.

A new word. A new land. And—it is just possible—a new friend.

Leah

Beyond Literature

Social Studies Connection

The U.S. Holocaust Museum Created to keep the memory of the Holocaust alive, the U. S. Holocaust Museum was built in Washington, D.C. One exhibit, "Daniel's Story," is for younger visitors. Through photos and film, children see events through the eyes of a Jewish boy growing up in Nazi Germany. Like Leah, Daniel is fictional, but his story is based on the stories of real people.

Cross Curricular Activity
On-Line Visit Use the Internet to access the U.S. Holocaust Memorial Museum Home Page. Learn more about the Holocaust, and share your findings with the class.

Guide for Responding

◆ LITERATURE AND YOUR LIFE

Reader's Response How do you think you would have reacted if you had tried to help Leah and she had rejected you?

Thematic Focus Do you think it was wise of Suzy to admit that she had read Leah's diary and to let Leah read her diary? Explain.

Group Discussion This story is about a way in which two people from different worlds learn to understand each other. With classmates, discuss ways in which kids your age can bridge the gaps between different cultures.

☑ Check Your Comprehension

1. What happened to Leah's mother and brother?
2. How are Suzy and Leah forced to get to know each other?
3. Why doesn't Leah eat the food she is given?
4. Why is Leah afraid to go to the hospital?
5. How does Suzy find out that she has misjudged Leah?

◆ Critical Thinking

INTERPRET
1. (a) What do Suzy's reactions to Leah tell you about Suzy? (b) What do Leah's reactions to Suzy tell you about Leah? **[Analyze]**
2. What does Leah mean when she says, "There is barbed wire still between us and the world"? **[Interpret]**
3. How do Suzy's motivations for offering candy to Leah at the story's beginning differ from her motivations for offering her diary to Leah at the end of the story? **[Distinguish]**
4. What has each girl learned from her experience with the other? **[Draw Conclusions]**

EVALUATE
5. Suzy reads Leah's diary and then calls her action "a terrible thing." However, this action leads Suzy to understand Leah better. Would you forgive Suzy? Explain. **[Assess]**

EXTEND
6. How has this story affected your understanding of the Holocaust? **[Social Studies Link]**

Guide for Responding (continued)

◆ Reading Strategy

MAKE INFERENCES

To fully understand a story's characters and grasp its message, you have to **make inferences** about the underlying significance of details the author provides. For example, you can make inferences about a character's personality based on details about his or her appearance and actions.

1. What can you infer from Iona's reaction to his three rude passengers:"He hears the abuse directed at him ... and little by little the feeling of loneliness begins to lift from his heart."
2. Suzy and Leah's first observations of each other end with nearly identical words:"When I looked back, she was gone.... Disappeared as if she'd never been." What can you infer from this?

◆ Build Vocabulary

USING THE SUFFIX -ee

The suffix -ee indicates a person who is or receives something. Copy the following sentences on your paper. Add -ee to a word from the first sentence to create the word that completes the second sentence.

1. Is he employed there? Yes, he's an ___?___ .
2. Is she retired? Yes, she's a ___?___ .
3. Was he inducted in the army? Yes, he's an ___?___ .

SPELLING STRATEGY

When you add -ee to a word that ends in the letter e, drop the final e before adding the suffix: escape + e = escapee. If the word ends in a consonant, simply add -ee: appoint + -ee = appointee.

On your paper, add -ee to the following words.

1. devote   2. award   3. trust   4. absent   5. examine

USING THE WORD BANK

On your paper, write the letter of the word closest in meaning to the first word.

1. refugee: (a) soldier, (b) escapee, (c) teacher
2. conspiring: (a) plotting, (b) finding, (c) hiding
3. quavering: (a) steady, (b) shaky, (c) heavy
4. insignificant: (a) unimportant, (b) huge, (c) costly
5. ponderous: (a) simple, (b) heavy, (c) sweet
6. indignantly: (a) quietly, (b) sharply, (c) furiously

◆ Literary Focus

SETTING

The **setting** is the time and place in which a story unfolds. The setting may help to set the mood of a story and may even shape the characters and events.

1. Describe the setting of "Heartache."
2. Why is the setting of "Heartache" significant?
3. Describe the setting of "Suzy and Leah."
4. Why is the setting of "Suzy and Leah" essential to the story?

◆ Build Grammar Skills

ADVERB CLAUSES

An **adverb clause** is a subordinate clause (a group of words that has a subject and verb but cannot stand alone as a sentence) that functions as an adverb. The entire clause modifies a verb, adjective, or other adverb. Like one-word adverbs, adverb clauses answer the questions *when, where, how, why,* and *to what extent.* Adverb clauses begin with subordinating conjunctions. Common subordinating conjunctions are *after, as, although, because, if, since, when, unless,* and *until.*

When I held them up, all those kids just swarmed over to the fence, grabbing. **(Tells when)**

Practice Copy the following sentences. Underline each adverb clause, and draw an arrow to the word it modifies. Then, tell what question the adverb clause answers.

1. I write in English because I want to be understood.
2. I stared at the yellow-haired girl until she was forced to look down.
3. He stopped speaking when he was hidden away in a cupboard.
4. If I write all this down, I will not hold so much anger.
5. I had no mirror until we got to the school.

Writing Application Write each of the following sentences on your paper, adding to each an adverb clause that answers the question.

1. The snow fell on Iona. *(To what extent?)*
2. Only his horse listened to him. *(How?)*

Build Your Portfolio

 ## Idea Bank

Writing

1. **Sympathy Note** Imagine that you are a friend of Iona Potapov's son, Kozma. Write a note to comfort Iona. In your note, show that you understand how Iona must be feeling.

2. **Diary Entries** Write a new pair of diary entries for Suzy and Leah describing events after Leah leaves the hospital. Try to write with each girl's style and tone.

3. **Analytic Essay** Yolen chose to tell her story through letters. In an essay, evaluate the success of that decision. What are the benefits and disadvantages of telling a story this way?

Speaking and Listening

4. **Questions and Answers** With a classmate, stage a question-and-answer session between Suzy and Leah in which they ask each other honest questions about their behavior. Base both your questions and answers on information from the story.

5. **Talk Radio** [Group Activity] Imagine that the characters from "Heartache" called in to a radio talk show to share their opinions about the events in the story and their views on life. Role-play the conversations. Possible roles include: one or two talk-show hosts, Iona, the passengers, and Iona's horse. [Media Link; Performing Arts Link]

Projects

6. **Snow Statistics** To get a better understanding of the setting in "Heartache," use library resources to find the amount of snowfall in the Russian cities of Moscow and St. Petersburg. Construct a bar graph to compare snowfall in those cities with that in your hometown. [Science Link; Math Link]

7. **Research Report** Use Internet, library, and community resources to collect information on the Holocaust. Share what you learn with the class. [Social Studies Link]

 ## Writing Mini-Lesson

Introduction to an Exhibition

Imagine that you are helping your local historical museum prepare an exhibit relating to the setting of either "Heartache" or "Suzy and Leah." Write an introductory brochure to help visitors understand what they will see in the exhibits.

> #### Writing Skills Focus: Necessary Context/Background
>
> Your job is to provide the **necessary context or historical background** in your introduction so that museum visitors can understand the photographs and artifacts in your exhibition. Otherwise, visitors will misunderstand or fail to appreciate what they are seeing—just as Suzy misjudged Leah because she did not know much about Leah's background.

Prewriting Select the topic for your exhibition: City Life in Nineteenth-Century Russia or The Holocaust. Then, make a list of questions the introduction to the exhibition should answer. To answer these questions, you may need to do library or Internet research. Record key pieces of information on separate note cards. Remember to include information about your source (author, title, publication information, and page) on each note card.

Drafting Organize your most important findings in logical paragraphs. Begin with the most important facts first. End by explaining how the exhibit relates to this historical background.

> ◆ **Grammar Application**
> Use adverb clauses to clarify the descriptions in your introduction to an exhibition.

Revising Reread your introduction to make sure that you have provided the background needed to understand the exhibit. Make sure you present accurate information in a logical order. Check that the facts and language are interesting.

Guide for Reading

Meet the Authors:

Laurence Yep (1948–)

Laurence Yep was born in San Francisco and grew up in an apartment above his family's grocery store. When a high-school teacher encouraged Yep to send out his stories for publication, he decided to become a professional writer. He is the author of more than a dozen books, including the Newbery Honor Book *Dragonwings*.

THE STORY BEHIND THE STORY

Yep learned about his Chinese heritage from his maternal grandmother. Her influence is seen in "Ribbons" and other works featuring a wise, beloved, strong-willed grandmother.

Walter Dean Myers (1937–)

Born in West Virginia, Myers grew up in the New York City community of Harlem. Although he dreamed of being a professional writer, this seemed impossible because of his poverty and lack of formal education. In 1969, however, his first book won a writing contest and was published. Since then, Myers has published dozens of books and won numerous awards.

◆ LITERATURE AND YOUR LIFE

CONNECT YOUR EXPERIENCE

Think about a time when you learned something from an older member of your family or community. In these stories, characters discover that by drawing upon an older person's experiences, they gain ideas, information, and skills that can shape their future.

THEMATIC FOCUS: Community Ties

These stories may prompt you to wonder: What can people my age learn from older people in my community? What can my generation teach older generations?

◆ Background for Understanding

MUSIC

In "The Treasure of Lemon Brown," a teenager meets a man who was once a famous blues musician. Blues, which have strongly influenced other forms of music, such as jazz and rock, are part of the African American musical heritage. Blues lyrics typically deal with loneliness, sorrow, and life's troubles. As you will discover in the story, Lemon Brown's life has certainly given him the right to sing the blues.

◆ Build Vocabulary

WORD ROOTS: -sens-

In "Ribbons," a mother warns her daughter that her grandmother is sensitive about her feet. The word *sensitive* contains the word root -sens-, meaning "feel." Knowing this, you can correctly conclude that *sensitive* has something to do with feelings. In "Ribbons," the grandmother is quick to feel offended or angry when anyone mentions her feet.

WORD BANK

Which words from the stories are adjectives? Check the Build Vocabulary boxes to see if you are right.

sensitive
meek
coax
laborious
exertion
impromptu
ajar
tentatively

Ribbons ◆ The Treasure of Lemon Brown

Four Piece Orchestra, 1944, Ben Shahn, 17 1/2 by 23 1/2 inches © Estate of Ben Shahn/Licensed by VAGA, New York, NY

◆ Literary Focus

THEME

A story's **theme** is its central message or insight into life. Occasionally, the theme is stated directly. More often, however, the theme is implied. The writer provides clues to the theme in the words and experiences of the characters, in the events and setting of the story, and in significant objects that represent ideas or people. For example, if a person in a story comes to accept and love an heirloom, the theme might be an insight into the relationships between generations.

◆ Reading Strategy

ASK QUESTIONS

By **asking questions** as you read, you will be better able to understand a story and figure out its theme. For example, you might ask questions like the following:

- Why is the author telling me this?
- Why did the character do or say that?
- How does this event fit into what has happened so far?

As you read these stories, jot down questions in a chart like the one below. Fill in answers as you find them or figure them out for yourself.

Question	Answer
Why is Grandmother sensitive about her feet?	

Ribbons

Laurence Yep

The sunlight swept over the broad grassy square, across the street, and onto our living-room rug. In that bright, warm rectangle of light, I practiced my ballet. Ian, my little brother, giggled and dodged around me while I did my exercises.

A car stopped outside, and Ian rushed to the window. "She's here! She's here!" he shouted excitedly. "Paw-paw's here!" *Paw-paw* is Chinese for grandmother—for "mother's mother."

I squeezed in beside Ian so I could look out the window, too. Dad's head was just disappearing as he leaned into the trunk of the car. A pile of luggage and cardboard boxes wrapped in rope sat by the curb. "Is that all Grandmother's?" I said. I didn't see how it would fit into my old bedroom.

Mom laughed behind me. "We're lucky she had to leave her furniture behind in Hong Kong." Mom had been trying to get her mother to come to San Francisco for years. Grandmother had finally agreed, but only because the British were going to return the city to the Chinese Communists in 1997. Because Grandmother's airfare and legal expenses had been so high, there wasn't room in the family budget for Madame Oblomov's ballet school. I'd had to stop my daily lessons.

The rear car door opened, and a pair of carved black canes poked out like six-shooters. "Wait, Paw-paw," Dad said, and slammed the trunk shut. He looked sweaty and harassed.

Grandmother, however, was already using her canes to get to her feet. "I'm not helpless," she insisted to Dad.

Ian was relieved. "She speaks English," he said.

"She worked for a British family for years," Mom explained.

Turning, Ian ran toward the stairs. "I've got the door," he cried. Mom and I caught up with him at the front door and made him wait on the porch. "You don't want to knock her over," I said. For weeks, Mom had been rehearsing us for just this moment. Ian was supposed to wait, but in his excitement he began bowing to Grandmother as she struggled up the outside staircase.

Grandmother was a small woman in a padded silk jacket and black slacks. Her hair was pulled back into a bun behind her head. On her small feet she wore a pair of quilted cotton slippers shaped like boots, with furred tops that hid her ankles.

"What's wrong with her feet?" I whispered to Mom.

"They've always been that way. And don't mention it," she said. "She's <u>sensitive</u> about them."

I was instantly curious. "But what happened to them?"

"Wise grandchildren wouldn't ask," Mom warned.

Mom bowed formally as Grandmother reached the porch. "I'm so glad you're here," she said.

Grandmother gazed past us to the stairway leading up to our second-floor apartment. "Why do you have to have so many steps?" she said.

Mom sounded as <u>meek</u> as a child. "I'm sorry, Mother," she said.

Dad tried to change the subject. "That's Stacy, and this little monster is Ian."

"*Joe sun, Paw-paw,*" I said. "Good morning, Grandmother." It was afternoon, but that was the only Chinese I knew, and I had been practicing it.

Mother had coached us on a proper Chinese greeting for the last two months, but I thought Grandmother also deserved an American-style bear hug. However, when I tried to put my arms around her and kiss her, she stiffened in surprise. "Nice children don't drool on people," she snapped at me.

To Ian, anything worth doing was worth repeating, so he bowed again. "*Joe sun, Paw-paw.*"

Grandmother brightened in an instant. "He has your eyes," she said to Mom.

Mom bent and hefted Ian into her arms. "Let me show you our apartment. You'll be in Stacy's room."

Grandmother didn't even thank me. Instead, she stumped up the stairs after Mom, trying to <u>coax</u> a smile from Ian, who was staring at her over Mom's shoulder.

Grandmother's climb was long, slow, <u>laborious</u>. *Thump, thump, thump.* Her canes struck the boards as she slowly mounted the

♦ **Build Vocabulary**

sensitive (sen´ sə tiv´) *adj.*: Easily hurt or irritated; touchy

meek (mēk) *adj.*: Timid; humble; not showing anger

coax (kōks) *v.*: Use gentle persuasion

laborious (la bôr´ ē əs) *adj.*: Taking much work or effort; difficult

steps. It sounded like the slow, steady beat of a mechanical heart.

Mom had told us her mother's story often enough. When Mom's father died, Grandmother had strapped my mother to her back and walked across China to Hong Kong to escape the Communists who had taken over her country. I had always thought her trek was heroic, but it seemed even braver when I realized how wobbly she was on her feet.

I was going to follow Grandmother, but Dad waved me down to the sidewalk. "I need you to watch your grandmother's things until I finish bringing them up," he said. He took a suitcase in either hand and set off, catching up with Grandmother at the foot of the first staircase.

While I waited for him to come back, I inspected Grandmother's pile of belongings. The boxes, webbed with tight cords, were covered with words in Chinese and English. I could almost smell their exotic scent, and in my imagination I pictured sunlit waters lapping at picturesque docks. Hong Kong was probably as exotic to me as America was to Grandmother. Almost without thinking, I began to dance.

Dad came back out, his face red from exertion. "I wish I had half your energy," he said. Crouching, he used the cords to lift a box in each hand.

I pirouetted,[1] and the world spun round and round. "Madame Oblomov said I should still practice every day." I had waited for this day not only for Grandmother's sake but for my own. "Now that Grandmother's here, can I begin my ballet lessons again?" I asked.

Dad turned toward the house. "We'll see, hon."

Disappointment made me protest. "But you said I had to give up the lessons so we could bring her from Hong Kong," I said. "Well, she's here."

Dad hesitated and then set the boxes down. "Try to understand, hon. We've got to set your grandmother up in her own apartment. That's going to take even more money. Don't you want your room back?"

Poor Dad. He looked tired and worried. I should have shut up, but I loved ballet almost as much as I loved him. "Madame put me in the fifth division even though I'm only eleven. If I'm absent much longer, she might make me start over again with the beginners."

"It'll be soon. I promise." He looked guilty as he picked up the boxes and struggled toward the stairs.

Dad had taken away the one hope that had kept me going during my exile[2] from Madame. Suddenly I felt lost, and the following weeks only made me more confused. Mom started laying down all sorts of new rules. First, we couldn't run around or make noise because Grandmother had to rest. Then we couldn't watch our favorite TV shows because Grandmother couldn't understand them. Instead, we had to watch Westerns on one of the cable stations because it was easier for her to figure out who was the good guy and who was the bad one.

Worst of all, Ian got all of her attention—and her candy and anything else she could bribe him with. It finally got to me on a warm Sunday afternoon a month after she had arrived. I'd just returned home from a long walk in the park with some friends. I was looking forward to something cool and sweet, when I found her giving Ian an ice cream bar I'd bought for myself. "But that was *my* ice cream bar," I complained as he gulped it down.

"Big sisters need to share with little brothers," Grandmother said, and she patted him on the head to encourage him to go on eating.

When I complained to Mom about how Grandmother was spoiling Ian, she only sighed. "He's a boy, Stacy. Back in China, boys are everything."

> ◆ **Literary Focus**
> How might this incident relate to the theme of the story?

---

2. **exile** (eg′ zīl′) *n*.: Forced absence.

◆ **Build Vocabulary**

exertion (eg zʉr′ shən) *n*.: Physical work

---

1. **pirouetted** (pir′ o͞o et′ əd) *v*.: Whirled around on the point of the toe.

Three Studies of a Dancer in Fourth Position, ©1879/80, Edgar Degas, Art Institute of Chicago

▲ **Critical Viewing** Which character would be most interested in this painting? Find a sentence on this page to support your answer. **[Connect]**

It wasn't until I saw Grandmother and Ian together the next day that I thought I really understood why she treated him so much better. She was sitting on a kitchen chair with her head bent over next to his. She had taught Ian enough Chinese so that they could hold short, simple conversations. With their faces so close, I could see how much alike they were.

Ian and I both have the same brown eyes, but his hair is black, while mine is brown, like Dad's. In fact, everything about Ian looks more Chinese. Except for the shape of my eyes, I look as Caucasian as Dad. And yet people sometimes stare at me as if I were a freak. I've always told myself that it's because they're ignorant and never learned manners, but it was really hard to have my own grandmother make me feel that way.

Even so, I kept telling myself: Grandmother is a hero. She saved my mother. She'll like me just as much as she likes Ian once she gets to know me. And, I thought in a flash, the best way to know a person is to know what she loves. For me, that was the ballet.

Ever since Grandmother had arrived, I'd been practicing my ballet privately in the room I now shared with Ian. Now I got out the special

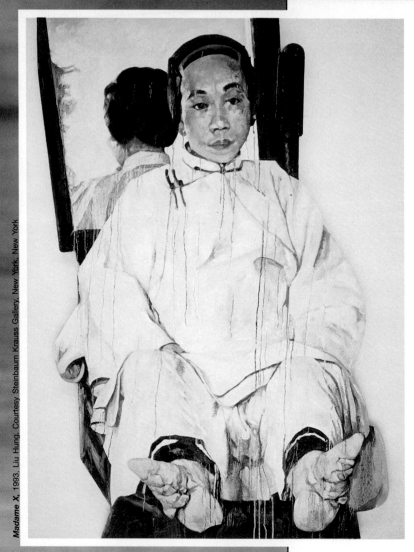

Madame X, 1993, Liu Hung. Courtesy Steinbaum Krauss Gallery, New York, New York

▲ **Critical Viewing** Review Grandmother's actions as described on this page and the next one. Then, analyze this painting to draw a conclusion about Grandmother's experiences with ribbons. [Draw Conclusions]

box that held my satin toe shoes. I had been so proud when Madame said I was ready to use them. I was the youngest girl on pointe[3] at Madame's school. As I lifted them out, the satin ribbons fluttered down around my wrists as if in a welcoming caress. I slipped one of the shoes onto my foot, but when I tried to tie the ribbons around my ankles, the ribbons came off in my hands.

I could have asked Mom to help me reattach them, but then I remembered that at one time Grandmother had supported her family by being a seamstress.

Grandmother was sitting in the big recliner in the living room. She stared uneasily out the window as if she were gazing not upon the broad, green lawn of the square but upon a Martian desert.

"Paw-paw," I said, "can you help me?"

Grandmother gave a start when she turned around and saw the ribbons dangling from my hand. Then she looked down at my bare feet, which were callused from three years of daily lessons. When she looked back at the satin ribbons, it was with a hate and disgust that I had never seen before.

◆ **Reading Strategy** Grandmother's reaction might prompt you to ask the question: Why does she hate the ribbons so much?

"Give those to me." She held out her hand.

I clutched the ribbons tightly against my stomach. "Why?"

"They'll ruin your feet." She lunged toward me and tried to

---

3. on pointe (pwant) *n.*: Dancing on the tip of the toe.

snatch them away.

Angry and bewildered, I retreated a few steps and showed her the shoe. "No, they're for dancing!"

All Grandmother could see, though, was the ribbons. She managed to totter to her feet without the canes and almost fell forward on her face. Somehow, she regained her balance. Arms reaching out, she stumbled clumsily after me. "Lies!" she said.

"It's the truth!" I backed up so fast that I bumped into Mom as she came running from the kitchen.

Mom immediately assumed it was my fault. "Stop yelling at your grandmother!" she said.

By this point, I was in tears. "She's taken everything else. Now she wants my toe-shoe ribbons."

Grandmother panted as she leaned on Mom. "How could you do that to your own daughter?"

"It's not like you think," Mom tried to explain.

However, Grandmother was too upset to listen. "Take them away!"

Mom helped Grandmother back to her easy chair. "You don't understand," Mom said.

All Grandmother did was stare at the ribbons as she sat back down in the chair. "Take them away. Burn them. Bury them."

Mom sighed. "Yes, Mother."

As Mom came over to me, I stared at her in amazement. "Aren't you going to stand up for me?"

But she acted as if she wanted to break any ties between us. "Can't you see how worked up Paw-paw is?" she whispered. "She won't listen to reason. Give her some time. Let her cool off." She worked the ribbons away from my stunned fingers. Then she also took the shoe.

For the rest of the day, Grandmother just turned away every time Mom and I tried to raise the subject. It was as if she didn't want to even think about satin ribbons.

That evening, after the dozenth attempt, I finally said to Mom, "She's so weird. What's so bad about satin ribbons?"

"She associates them with something awful that happened to her," Mom said.

That puzzled me even more. "What was that?"

She shook her head. "I'm sorry. She made me promise never to talk about it to anyone."

The next morning, I decided that if Grandmother was going to be mean to me, then I would be mean to her. I began to ignore her. When she entered a room I was in, I would deliberately turn around and leave.

For the rest of the day, things got more and more tense. Then I happened to go into the bathroom early that evening. The door wasn't locked, so I thought it was unoccupied, but Grandmother was sitting fully clothed on the edge of the bathtub. Her slacks were rolled up to her knees and she had her feet soaking in a pan of water.

"Don't you know how to knock?" she snapped, and dropped a towel over her feet.

However, she wasn't quick enough, because I saw her bare feet for the first time. Her feet were like taffy that someone had stretched out and twisted. Each foot bent downward in a way that feet were not meant to, and her toes stuck out at odd angles, more like lumps than toes. I didn't think she had all ten of them, either.

"What happened to your feet?" I whispered in shock.

Looking ashamed, Grandmother flapped a hand in the air for me to go. "None of your business. Now get out."

She must have said something to Mom, though, because that night Mom came in and sat on my bed. Ian was outside playing with Grandmother. "Your grandmother's very upset, Stacy," Mom said.

"I didn't mean to look," I said. "It was horrible." Even when I closed my eyes, I could see her mangled feet.

I opened my eyes when I felt Mom's hand on my shoulder. "She was so ashamed of them that she didn't like even me to see them," she said.

"What happened to them?" I wondered.

Mom's forehead furrowed as if she wasn't sure how to explain things. "There was a time back in China when people thought women's feet had to be shaped a certain way to look beautiful. When a girl was about five, her mother would gradually bend her toes under the sole of her foot."

"Ugh." Just thinking about it made my own feet ache. "Her own mother did that to her?"

Mom smiled apologetically. "Her mother and father thought it would make their little girl attractive so she could marry a rich man. They were still doing it in some of the back areas of China long after it was outlawed in the rest of the country."

I shook my head. "There's nothing lovely about those feet."

"I know. But they were usually bound up in silk ribbons." Mom brushed some of the hair from my eyes. "Because they were a symbol of the old days, Paw-paw undid the ribbons as soon as we were free in Hong Kong—even though they kept back the pain."

I was even more puzzled now. "How did the ribbons do that?"

Mom began to brush my hair with quick, light strokes. "The ribbons kept the blood from circulating freely and bringing more feeling to her feet. Once the ribbons were gone, her feet ached. They probably still do."

I rubbed my own foot in sympathy. "But she doesn't complain."

"That's how tough she is," Mom said.

Finally the truth dawned on me. "And she mistook my toe-shoe ribbons for her old ones."

Mom lowered the brush and nodded solemnly. "And she didn't want you to go through the same pain she had."

◆ Literary Focus
How might Stacy's insight relate to the theme of the story?

I guess Grandmother loved me in her own way. When she came into the bedroom with Ian later that evening, I didn't leave. However, she tried to ignore me—as if I had become tainted by her secret.

When Ian demanded a story, I sighed. "All right. But only one."

Naturally, Ian chose the fattest story he could, which was my old collection of fairy tales by Hans Christian Andersen. Years of reading had cracked the spine so that the book fell open automatically in his hands to the story that had been my favorite when I was

small. It was the original story of "The Little Mermaid"—not the cartoon. The picture illustrating the tale showed the mermaid posed like a ballerina in the middle of the throne room.

"This one," Ian said, and pointed to the picture of the Little Mermaid.

When Grandmother and Ian sat down on my bed, I began to read. However, when I got to the part where the Little Mermaid could walk on land, I stopped.

Ian was impatient. "Come on, read," he ordered, patting the page.

"After that," I went on, "each step hurt her as if she were walking on a knife." I couldn't help looking up at Grandmother.

This time she was the one to pat the page. "Go on. Tell me more about the mermaid."

So I went on reading to the very end, where the Little Mermaid changes into sea foam. "That's a dumb ending," Ian said. "Who wants to be pollution?"

"Sea foam isn't pollution. It's just bubbles," I explained. "The important thing was that she wanted to walk even though it hurt."

"I would rather have gone on swimming," Ian insisted.

"But maybe she wanted to see new places and people by going on the land," Grandmother said softly. "If she had kept her tail, the land people would have thought she was odd. They might even have made fun of her."

When she glanced at her own feet, I thought she might be talking about herself—so I seized my chance. "My satin ribbons aren't like your old silk ones. I use them to tie my toe shoes on when I dance." Setting the book down, I got out my other shoe. "Look."

Grandmother fingered the dangling ribbons and then pointed at my bare feet. "But you already have calluses there."

I began to dance before Grandmother could stop me. After a minute, I struck a pose on half-toe. "See? I can move fine."

She took my hand and patted it clumsily. I think it was the first time she had showed me any sign of affection. "When I saw those ribbons, I didn't want you feeling pain like I do."

I covered her hands with mine. "I just wanted to show you what I love best—dancing."

"And I love my children," she said. I could hear the ache in her voice. "And my grandchildren. I don't want anything bad to happen to you."

Suddenly I felt as if there were an invisible ribbon binding us, tougher than silk and satin, stronger even than steel; and it joined her to Mom and Mom to me.

I wanted to hug her so badly that I just did. Though she was stiff at first, she gradually softened in my arms.

"Let me have my ribbons and my shoes," I said in a low voice. "Let me dance."

"Yes, yes," she whispered fiercely.

I felt something on my cheek and realized she was crying, and then I began crying, too.

"So much to learn," she said, and began hugging me back. "So much to learn."

Beyond Literature

Community Connection

Bridging the Generation Gap Just like Stacy and her grandmother can learn from each other, communities are finding good reasons to bring their oldest and youngest citizens together. In some cities, adopt-a-senior programs allow people your age to build friendships with senior citizens. Students learn about history from those who've actually witnessed it, and the seniors get a chance to enjoy the steady companionship of a new friend.

Cross-Curricular Activity
Volunteer Opportunities Find out about volunteer opportunities to work and interact with senior citizens in your community. You might talk to people in nursing homes and community centers and to senior citizens you know, to learn more about intergenerational programs.

Guide for Responding

◆ LITERATURE AND YOUR LIFE

Reader's Response What do you think is the hardest part of Stacy's experiences with her grandmother? Why?

Thematic Focus In this story, conflict is created because Stacy and her grandmother come from unique communities and cultures. How are such conflicts resolved?

Journal Writing Stacy may soon enjoy having her grandmother living with her family. In your journal, list the benefits of her situation.

☑ Check Your Comprehension

1. What sacrifices does Stacy make as a result of Grandmother's visit?
2. What changes occur in Stacy's house as a result of Grandmother's visit?
3. How does Stacy learn the secret about Grandmother's feet?
4. Why does Grandmother react so violently to Stacy's ribbons?

◆ Critical Thinking

INTERPRET
1. What are Stacy's reasons for feeling a little resentful of her grandmother? **[Analyze Cause and Effect]**
2. Why doesn't Grandmother do anything to make Stacy feel better? **[Speculate]**
3. How do her mother's explanations of Chinese culture affect Stacy's attitude toward her grandmother? **[Connect]**
4. How do Stacy and her grandmother eventually come to appreciate each other? **[Deduce]**

APPLY
5. What can you learn from this story about getting along with people from different generations? **[Generalize]**

EXTEND
6. How might an understanding of cultural differences—like those between Stacy and her grandmother—be helpful in the workplace? **[Career Link]**

The Treasure of Lemon Brown

Walter Dean Myers

The dark sky, filled with angry, swirling clouds, reflected Greg Ridley's mood as he sat on the stoop of his building. His father's voice came to him again, first reading the letter the principal had sent to the house, then lecturing endlessly about his poor efforts in math.

"I had to leave school when I was thirteen," his father had said, "that's a year younger than you are now. If I'd had half the chances that you have, I'd . . ."

Greg had sat in the small, pale green kitchen listening, knowing the lecture would end with his father saying he couldn't play ball with the Scorpions. He had asked his father the week before, and his father had said it depended on his next report card. It wasn't often the Scorpions took on new players, especially fourteen-year-olds, and this was a chance of a lifetime for Greg. He hadn't been allowed to play high school ball, which he had really wanted to do, but playing for the Community Center team was the next best thing. Report cards were due in a week, and Greg had been hoping for the best. But the principal had ended the suspense early when she sent that letter saying Greg would probably fail math if he didn't spend more time studying.

"And you want to play *basketball*?" His father's brows knitted over deep brown eyes. "That must be some kind of a joke. Now you just get into your room and hit those books."

That had been two nights before. His father's words, like the distant thunder that

Morning at the Jackson Ave. Ferry, Gilbert Fletcher, Courtesy of the artist

now echoed through the streets of Harlem, still rumbled softly in his ears.

It was beginning to cool. Gusts of wind made bits of paper dance between the parked cars. There was a flash of nearby lightning, and soon large drops of rain splashed onto his jeans. He stood to go upstairs, thought of the lecture that probably awaited him if he did anything except shut himself in his room with his math book, and started walking down the street instead. Down the block there was an old tene-

---

▼ **Critical Viewing** How do the colors of this painting compare with the mood and description in the story? [**Compare and Contrast**]

ment[1] that had been abandoned for some months. Some of the guys had held an impromptu checker tournament there the week before, and Greg had noticed that the door, once boarded over, had been slightly ajar.

Pulling his collar up as high as he could, he checked for traffic and made a dash across the street. He reached the house just as another flash of lightning changed the night to day for an instant, then returned the graffiti-scarred building to the grim shadows. He vaulted over the outer stairs and pushed tentatively on the door. It was open, and he let himself in.

The inside of the building was dark except for the dim light that filtered through the dirty windows from the streetlamps. There was a room a few feet from the door, and from where he stood at the entrance, Greg could see a squarish patch of light on the floor. He entered the room, frowning at the musty smell. It was a large room that might have been someone's parlor at one time. Squinting, Greg could see an old table on its side against one wall, what looked like a pile of rags or a torn mattress in the corner, and a couch, with one side broken, in front of the window.

He went to the couch. The side that wasn't broken was comfortable enough, though a little creaky. From the spot he could see the blinking neon sign over the bodega[2] on the corner.

◆ **Reading Strategy**
What questions might this description prompt you to ask?

---

1. **tenement** (ten´ əh mənt) *n.*: Old, run-down apartment house.
2. **bodega** (bō dä´ gə) *n.*: Small grocery store serving a Latino neighborhood.

◆ **Build Vocabulary**

impromptu (im prämp´ tōō) *adj.*: Unscheduled; unplanned

ajar (ə jär´) *adj.*: Open

tentatively (ten´ tə tiv lē) *adv.*: Hesitantly; with uncertainty

He sat awhile, watching the sign blink first green then red, allowing his mind to drift to the Scorpions, then to his father. His father had been a postal worker for all Greg's life, and was proud of it, often telling Greg how hard he had worked to pass the test. Greg had heard the story too many times to be interested now.

For a moment Greg thought he heard something that sounded like a scraping against the wall. He listened carefully, but it was gone.

Outside the wind had picked up, sending the rain against the window with a force that shook the glass in its frame. A car passed, its tires hissing over the wet street and its red taillights glowing in the darkness.

Greg thought he heard the noise again. His stomach tightened as he held himself still and listened intently. There weren't any more scraping noises, but he was sure he had heard something in the darkness—something breathing!

He tried to figure out just where the breathing was coming from; he knew it was in the room with him. Slowly he stood, tensing. As he turned, a flash of lightning lit up the room, frightening him with its sudden brilliance. He saw nothing, just the overturned table, the pile of rags and an old newspaper on the floor. Could he have been imagining the sounds? He continued listening, but heard nothing and thought that it might have just been rats. Still, he thought, as soon as the rain let up he would leave. He went to the window and was about to look when he heard a voice behind him.

"Don't try nothin' 'cause I got a razor here sharp enough to cut a week into nine days!"

Greg, except for an involuntary tremor[3] in his knees, stood stock still. The voice was high and brittle, like dry twigs being broken, surely not one he had ever heard before. There was a shuffling sound as the person who had been

---

▼ **Critical Viewing** What role does music play in this story? **[Connect]**

---

3. **involuntary** (in väl´ ən ter´ ē) **tremor** (trem´ ər) *n.*: Automatic trembling or shaking.

Four Piece Orchestra, 1944, Ben Shahn, 17 1/2 by 23 1/2 inches © Estate of Ben Shahn/Licensed by VAGA, New York, NY

speaking moved a step closer. Greg turned, holding his breath, his eyes straining to see in the dark room.

The upper part of the figure before him was still in darkness. The lower half was in the dim rectangle of light that fell unevenly from the window. There were two feet, in cracked, dirty shoes from which rose legs that were wrapped in rags.

"Who are you?" Greg hardly recognized his own voice.

"I'm Lemon Brown," came the answer. "Who're you?"

"Greg Ridley."

"What you doing here?" The figure shuffled forward again, and Greg took a small step backward.

"It's raining," Greg said.

"I can see that," the figure said.

The person who called himself Lemon Brown peered forward, and Greg could see him clearly. He was an old man. His black, heavily wrinkled face was surrounded by a halo of crinkly white hair and whiskers that seemed to separate his head from the layers of dirty coats piled on his smallish frame. His pants were bagged to the knee, where they were met with rags that went down to the old shoes. The rags were held on with strings, and there was a rope around his middle. Greg relaxed. He had seen the man before, picking through the trash on the corner and pulling clothes out of a Salvation Army box. There was no sign of the razor that could "cut a week into nine days."

"What are you doing here?" Greg asked.

"This is where I'm staying," Lemon Brown said. "What you here for?"

"Told you it was raining out," Greg said, leaning against the back of the couch until he felt it give slightly.

"Ain't you got no home?"

"I got a home," Greg answered.

"You ain't one of them bad boys looking for my treasure, is you?" Lemon Brown cocked his head to one side and squinted one eye. "Because I told you I got me a razor."

> Greg turned, holding his breath, his eyes straining to see in the dark room.

"I'm not looking for your treasure," Greg answered, smiling. "*If* you have one."

"What you mean, *if* I have one," Lemon Brown said. "Every man got a treasure. You don't know that, you must be a fool!"

"Sure," Greg said as he sat on the sofa and put one leg over the back. "What do you have, gold coins?"

"Don't worry none about what I got," Lemon Brown said. "You know who I am?"

"You told me your name was orange or lemon or something like that."

"Lemon Brown," the old man said, pulling back his shoulders as he did so, "they used to call me Sweet Lemon Brown."

"Sweet Lemon?" Greg asked.

"Yessir. Sweet Lemon Brown. They used to say I sung the blues so sweet that if I sang at a funeral, the dead would commence to rocking with the beat. Used to travel all over Mississippi and as far as Monroe, Louisiana, and east on over to Macon, Georgia. You mean you ain't never heard of Sweet Lemon Brown?"

◆ Literature
and Your Life
Think about the times you have met strange people. In a similar situation, do you think your attitude would be similar to Greg's?

"Afraid not," Greg said. "What . . . what happened to you?"

"Hard times, boy. Hard times always after a poor man. One day I got tired, sat down to rest a spell and felt a tap on my shoulder. Hard times caught up with me."

"Sorry about that."

"What you doing here? How come you didn't go on home when the rain come? Rain don't bother you young folks none."

"Just didn't." Greg looked away.

"I used to have a knotty-headed boy just like you." Lemon Brown had half walked, half shuffled back to the corner and sat down against the wall. "Had them big eyes like you got, I used to call them moon eyes. Look into them moon eyes and see anything you want."

"How come you gave up singing the blues?" Greg asked.

"Didn't give it up," Lemon Brown said. "You don't give up the blues; they give you up. After a while you do good for yourself, and it ain't nothing but foolishness singing about how hard you got it. Ain't that right?"

"I guess so."

"What's that noise?" Lemon Brown asked, suddenly sitting upright.

Greg listened, and he heard a noise outside. He looked at Lemon Brown and saw the old man pointing toward the window.

Greg went to the window and saw three men, neighborhood thugs, on the stoop. One was carrying a length of pipe. Greg looked back toward Lemon Brown, who moved quietly across the room to the window. The old man looked out, then beckoned frantically for Greg to follow him. For a moment Greg couldn't move. Then he found himself following Lemon Brown into the hallway and up darkened stairs. Greg followed as closely as he could. They reached the top of the stairs, and Greg felt Lemon Brown's hand first lying on his shoulder, then probing down his arm until he finally took Greg's hand into his own as they crouched in the darkness.

"They's bad men," Lemon Brown whispered. His breath was warm against Greg's skin.

"Hey! Rag man!" A voice called. "We know you in here. What you got up under them rags? You got any money?"

Silence.

"We don't want to have to come in and hurt you, old man, but we don't mind if we have to."

Lemon Brown squeezed Greg's hand in his own hard, gnarled fist.

There was a banging downstairs and a light as the men entered. They banged around noisily, calling for the rag man.

"We heard you talking about your treasure." The voice was slurred. "We just want to see it, that's all."

"You sure he's here?" One voice seemed to come from the room with the sofa.

"Yeah, he stays here every night."

"There's another room over there; I'm going to take a look. You got that flashlight?"

"Yeah, here, take the pipe too."

Greg opened his mouth to quiet the sound of his breath as he sucked it in uneasily. A beam of light hit the wall a few feet opposite him, then went out.

"Ain't nobody in that room," a voice said. "You think he gone or something?"

"I don't know," came the answer. "All I know is that I heard him talking about some kind of treasure. You know they found that shopping bag lady with that money in her bags."

"Yeah. You think he's upstairs?"

"HEY, OLD MAN, ARE YOU UP THERE?"

Silence.

"Watch my back, I'm going up."

There was a footstep on the stairs, and the beam from the flashlight danced crazily along the peeling wallpaper. Greg held his breath. There was another step and a loud crashing noise as the man banged the pipe against the wooden banister.[4] Greg could feel his temples throb as the man slowly neared them. Greg thought about the pipe, wondering what he would do when the man reached them—what he *could* do.

> ◆ Reading Strategy
> This tense situation might prompt you to ask what Greg and Lemon Brown will do. How would you expect to find out the answer to this question?

Then Lemon Brown released his hand and moved toward the top of the stairs. Greg looked around and saw stairs going up to the next floor. He tried waving to Lemon Brown, hoping the old man would see him in the dim light and follow him to the next floor. Maybe, Greg thought, the man wouldn't follow them up there. Suddenly, though, Lemon Brown stood at the top of the stairs, both arms raised high above his head.

"There he is!" A voice cried from below.

"Throw down your money, old man, so I won't have to bash your head in!"

Lemon Brown didn't move. Greg felt himself near panic. The steps came closer, and still Lemon Brown didn't move. He was an eerie

---

4. **banister** (ban´ is tər) *n*.: Railing along a staircase.

Disequilibrium, 1987, Catherine Redmond, Courtesy of the artist

▲ Critical Viewing How does a dismal setting like the one in the story and the one in this painting add to the tension of "The Treasure of Lemon Brown"? [Analyze]

sight, a bundle of rags standing at the top of the stairs, his shadow on the wall looming over him. Maybe, the thought came to Greg, the scene could be even eerier.

Greg wet his lips, put his hands to his mouth and tried to make a sound. Nothing came out. He swallowed hard, wet his lips once more and howled as evenly as he could.

"What's that?"

As Greg howled, the light moved away from Lemon Brown, but not before Greg saw him hurl his body down the stairs at the men who had come to take his treasure. There was a crashing noise, and then footsteps. A rush of warm air came in as the downstairs door opened, then there was only an ominous silence.

Greg stood on the landing. He listened, and after a while there was another sound on the staircase.

"Mr. Brown?" he called.

"Yeah, it's me," came the answer. "I got their flashlight."

Greg exhaled in relief as Lemon Brown made his way slowly back up the stairs.

"You OK?"

"Few bumps and bruises," Lemon Brown said.

"I think I'd better be going," Greg said, his breath returning to normal. "You'd better leave, too, before they come back."

"They may hang around outside for a while," Lemon Brown said, "but they ain't getting their nerve up to come in here again. Not with crazy old rag men and howling spooks. Best you stay a while till the coast is clear. I'm heading out west tomorrow, out to east St. Louis."

"They were talking about treasures," Greg said. "You *really* have a treasure?"

"What I tell you? Didn't I tell you every man got a treasure?" Lemon Brown said. "You want to see mine?"

"If you want to show it to me," Greg shrugged.

"Let's look out the window first, see what them scoundrels be doing," Lemon Brown said.

They followed the oval beam of the flashlight into one of the rooms and looked out the window. They saw the men who had tried to take the treasure sitting on the curb near the corner. One of them had his pants leg up, looking at his knee.

"You sure you're not hurt?" Greg asked Lemon Brown.

"Nothing that ain't been hurt before," Lemon Brown said. "When you get as old as me all you say when something hurts is, 'Howdy, Mr. Pain, sees you back again.' Then when Mr. Pain see he can't worry you none, he go on mess with somebody else."

Greg smiled.

"Here, you hold this." Lemon Brown gave Greg the flashlight.

He sat on the floor near Greg and carefully untied the strings that held the rags on his right leg. When he took the rags away, Greg saw a piece of plastic. The old man carefully took off the plastic and unfolded it. He revealed some yellowed newspaper clippings and a battered harmonica.

"There it be," he said, nodding his head. "There it be."

Greg looked at the old man, saw the distant look in his eye, then turned to the clippings. They told of Sweet Lemon Brown, a blues singer and harmonica player who was appearing at different theaters in the South. One of the clippings said he had been the hit of the show, although not the headliner. All of the clippings were reviews of shows Lemon Brown had been in more than 50 years ago. Greg looked at the harmonica. It was dented badly on one side, with the reed holes on one end nearly closed.

"I used to travel around and make money for to feed my wife and Jesse—that's my boy's name. Used to feed them good, too. Then his mama died, and he stayed with his mama's sister. He growed up to be a man, and when the war come he saw fit to go off and fight in it. I didn't have nothing to give him except these things that told him who I was, and what he come from. If you know your pappy did something, you know you can do something too.

"Anyway, he went off to war, and I went off still playing and singing. 'Course by then I wasn't as much as I used to be, not without somebody to make it worth the while. You know what I mean?"

"Yeah," Greg nodded, not quite really knowing.

"I traveled around, and one time I come home, and there was this letter saying Jesse got killed in the war. Broke my heart, it truly did.

"They sent back what he had with him over there, and what it was is this old mouth fiddle and these clippings. Him carrying it around with him like that told me it meant something to him. That was my treasure, and when I give it to him he treated it just like that, a treasure. Ain't that something?"

"Yeah, I guess so," Greg said.

"You *guess* so?" Lemon Brown's voice rose an octave as he started to put his treasure back into the plastic. "Well, you got to guess 'cause you sure don't know nothing. Don't know enough to get home when it's raining."

"I guess . . . I mean, you're right."

"You OK for a youngster," the old man said as he tied the strings around his leg, "better than those scalawags[5] what come here looking for my treasure. That's for sure."

"You really think that treasure of yours was worth fighting for?" Greg asked. "Against a pipe?"

"What else a man got 'cepting what he can

> " 'Course by then I wasn't as much as I used to be, not without somebody to make it worth the while. You know what I mean?"

◆ **Literary Focus**
What might the details about Lemon Brown's treasure tell you about the theme of the story?

---

5. scalawags (skal´ ə wagz´) *n.*: People who cause trouble; scoundrels.

pass on to his son, or his daughter, if she be his oldest?" Lemon Brown said. "For a big-headed boy you sure do ask the foolishest questions."

Lemon Brown got up after patting his rags in place and looked out the window again.

"Looks like they're gone. You get on out of here and get yourself home. I'll be watching from the window so you'll be all right."

Lemon Brown went down the stairs behind Greg. When they reached the front door the old man looked out first, saw the street was clear and told Greg to scoot on home.

"You sure you'll be OK?" Greg asked.

"Now didn't I tell you I was going to east St. Louis in the morning?" Lemon Brown asked. "Don't that sound OK to you?"

"Sure it does," Greg said. "Sure it does. And you take care of that treasure of yours."

"That I'll do," Lemon said, the wrinkles about his eyes suggesting a smile. "That I'll do."

The night had warmed and the rain had stopped, leaving puddles at the curbs. Greg didn't even want to think how late it was. He thought ahead of what his father would say and wondered if he should tell him about Lemon Brown. He thought about it until he reached his stoop, and decided against it. Lemon Brown would be OK, Greg thought, with his memories and his treasure.

Greg pushed the button over the bell marked Ridley, thought of the lecture he knew his father would give him, and smiled.

Guide for Responding

◆ LITERATURE AND YOUR LIFE

Reader's Response Do you agree with Greg's decision not to tell his father about Lemon Brown?

Thematic Focus Using Lemon Brown's life experience as a guide, what do you think this story says about the value of family and community ties?

☑ Check Your Comprehension

1. List five facts you learn about Greg at the beginning of the story.
2. Why is Greg upset and angry at the beginning of the story?
3. How does Greg meet Lemon Brown?
4. Why do three men break into the building where Brown is?
5. What is the "treasure" of Lemon Brown?
6. What happened to Brown's son?
7. What is Brown planning to do next?

◆ Critical Thinking

INTERPRET

1. Why doesn't Greg go home when it starts to rain? **[Analyze]**
2. Why does Greg go into the old tenement building? **[Infer]**
3. How does Greg's opinion of Lemon Brown change over the course of the story? **[Compare and Contrast]**
4. What does Brown teach Greg? **[Interpret]**
5. Why do you think Greg smiles at the end of the story? **[Analyze Cause and Effect]**

APPLY

6. If you were to talk to someone younger about what's important in life, what treasures would you share? **[Synthesize]**

COMPARE LITERARY WORKS

7. How are the relationships between Greg and Brown and Stacy and her grandmother similar? How are they different? **[Compare and Contrast]**

Blues music—the sort played by Lemon Brown on his treasured harmonica—inspired other forms of American music, including rhythm-and-blues and rock-and-roll. At the Rock and Roll Hall of Fame and Museum, located in Cleveland, Ohio, exhibits celebrate American popular music and show the influence of one generation of musicians upon the next. This press release announces one such exhibit.

Rhythm and Blues,
Let the Good Times Roll

Rock and Roll Hall of Fame

The roots of rhythm and blues are complex and deeply woven into the fabric of American history and culture. Like blues, jazz, and country, R&B was, in part, shaped by events far removed from the music. A look at America in the 1940's and '50's reveals how R&B not only was impacted by the many things going on in this country during these two important post-war decades, but also how R&B reflected them in song and sound.

Rhythm & blues evolved into a generic term describing all forms of black popular music: down home blues, big city jump bands, vocal groups, jazz, urban shouters and torchy night club singers. It was rhythm & blues that provided one of the foundations for rock and roll in the early 1950's and, while rock and roll became the mainstream of popular music, rhythm & blues continued its development into an easily recognizable music form.

From R&B came soul, funk, disco and rap—all important African American music forms that still resonate with energy and excitement today.

The Rock and Roll Hall of Fame and Museum honors the men and women who have made unique contributions to the evolution of rock and roll in our new exhibit, "Let the Good Times Roll: A Tribute to Rhythm & Blues."

Facts About The Rock And Roll Hall Of Fame And Museum

The Museum:

The Rock and Roll Hall of Fame and Museum is a 150,000 square-foot facility that serves as the permanent home of the Rock and Roll Hall of Fame. It provides dynamic interactive exhibits, intimate performance spaces, displays from the museum's permanent collection. Exhibits change periodically and showcase specific rock'n'roll eras, styles, milestones and the many facets of the music's evolution. It also houses research facilities and features public programming dedicated to the exploration of the music's enduring impact on global culture. It is the world's first museum dedicated to the living heritage of rock and roll music.

◀ **Critical Viewing** This photograph of Chuck Berry is on the cover of an exhibit brochure. What does it suggest about Berry's importance in rhythm-and-blues music? [Infer]

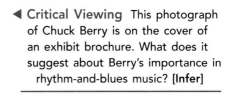

Special Features:

- Exhibits on the roots of rock-and-roll include Gospel, Country, Folk, Blues, and Rhythm-and-Blues, featuring the Museum's collections.
- Working studio from which visiting radio stations can conduct live broadcasts
- 200-seat indoor theater
- Outdoor area for concerts
- Dramatic new multimedia gallery for the Rock and Roll Hall of Fame

Exhibits:

The Museum's exhibits are designed to give the visitor a unique, interactive experience. The Museum's collection is brought to life through a combination of high-tech wizardry and innovative film and video. The Museum offers a comprehensive retrospective on the music's origins, its development, its legends, and its immense impact on global culture.

The exhibitions will take the visitor on a fast-paced journey through the history of rock and roll. They will bring the visitor into the experience, showcasing rock and roll and its impact on society. Major music scenes, specific artists and the music's impact on the way we live will be examined.

◆ **Build Vocabulary**

retrospective (reˊ trə spekˊ tiv) *n*.: Look on the past

1. What types of music have their origin in rhythm-and-blues?
2. What do the exhibits in the museum show?
3. What can you learn from this article and the stories about the importance of learning from older generations?

Critical Review

Writing Process Workshop

"Did you read the review?" Lots of reviews appear in writing these days: reviews of books, movies, television shows, restaurants, plays, CDs, video games, concerts—you name it. **Critical reviews** describe their subjects in detail and give opinions about their quality. If a reviewer likes something, he or she will rave and sales may sky-rocket. On the other hand, a poor review can discourage others from buying, visiting, reading, or viewing. Now, it's your turn to play critic. The following skills, introduced in Writing Mini-Lessons in this part, will help you write an effective critical review.

Writing Skills Focus

▶ **Give the necessary context.** Provide the background information that your readers will need to understand your review and what you are reviewing. (See p. 521.)

▶ **Support with evidence.** Give specific reasons or examples to back up your opinion. (See p. 541.)

▶ **Elaborate** to convey your reactions to your subject.

Notice how this writer uses all the skills in a review of a blues album.

MODEL

Bubba Bailey's Blues, a new CD by Ben Bailey (Ragan Records, 1997), is a great introduction to the blues because it includes blues ① of all kinds. For example, "Bubba's Romp" is a playful tune picked on a solo steel-stringed guitar with lyrics that will make you laugh. In contrast, "My Mama's Piano" is a slow, sad song with a beautiful piano riff in the middle that will bring tears to your eye. ② Later, "A Penny for Your Thoughts" rocks wildly in loud, hard rhythms. ③

① This provides necessary information—identifying the CD, the date of its release, and the reviewer's opinion.

② Notice how the writer elaborates by showing how the music evokes playfulness or tears.

③ The writer offers specific examples of songs to support her opinion about the album.

Prewriting

Choose a Subject Choose a subject that you know a lot about. It will be easier to describe, and you'll probably find that you have a strong opinion worth supporting. Here are a few suggestions:

> ### Topic Ideas
> - Compact disk
> - Film you've seen recently
> - Play or concert
> - Book you've read
> - Restaurant you've visited
> - Work of art or an exhibit

Include Opinions and Facts State your opinion early in your review. Use facts to support your opinion: statistics, examples, specific details, quotations, even an anecdote. Each piece of evidence makes your case stronger.

Pack In Words That Describe In your review, show, don't tell. For example, don't simply tell your readers that a meal was good. Provide details so that readers see it, taste it, and smell it. If a movie's monster was scary, let your reader feel the ground shake when he passes by.

Drafting

Show Your Reasoning Work carefully on your opinion. Don't settle for simply, "It was good" or "I didn't like it." Elaborate with specific explanations. Once you've written your review, everything in it should support that opinion. Here are some examples:

> Amber's new CD is her best yet because she goes beyond rap.
>
> *Hatchet* was the most suspenseful, exciting, and realistic novel I've ever read.
>
> *Dr. Doolittle* was so funny I never stopped laughing.
>
> The service at Eddie's Diner was great, but the hamburgers were overcooked.

Keep to a Set Length Some reviews are lengthy essays; others are single paragraphs. The length of your review depends on your purpose, audience, and the subject you are reviewing.

DRAFTING/REVISING

APPLYING LANGUAGE SKILLS: Vary Sentence Beginnings

To keep your writing from falling into a dull and predictable pattern, vary the ways you start your sentences. Consider shaking up your writing with these sentence starters:

Phrase:
In his restaurant, Maurice prepares omelets with salsa.

Clause:
Although the flavor is strong, it is not too spicy.

Single-Word Modifier:
Luckily, people love his recipe.

Practice Add phrases, clauses, or single-word modifiers to vary the beginnings of these sentences.

1. He serves side dishes of rice and beans.
2. The burritos are served on hand-painted plates.
3. Prices are reasonable, too.

Writing Application As you draft your critical review, vary your sentence beginnings to avoid a predictable pattern.

Writer's Solution Connection Writing Lab

To help you gather details for your review, use the Cluster Diagram activity in the Exposition: Giving Information tutorial.

EDITING/PROOFREADING

APPLYING LANGUAGE SKILLS:
Writing Titles Correctly

If you refer to a novel, short story, song, or other work, be sure to punctuate the title correctly. Follow these rules:

- Capitalize the first word and all other important words.
- Place quotation marks around titles of short works.
- Underline or italicize the titles of long works.

Look at these examples:

Novel:
A Separate Peace

Short Story:
"The Treasure of Lemon Brown"

Album:
Rites of Passage

Song:
"Closer to Fine"

Practice Rewrite these titles correctly:

1. ribbons (short story)
2. the grapes of wrath (novel)
3. america the beautiful (song)

Writing Application In your critical review, be sure to refer to titles correctly.

Writer's Solution Connection
Writing Lab

For more information on writing titles, see the instruction on punctuation in the Revising and Editing section of the Response to Literature tutorial.

Include the Facts Depending on your subject, you'll want to include certain necessary background information. Here are some questions your review should address:

Restaurant:	Address? Cost? Menu? Atmosphere? Accessibility? Comfort?
Book:	Author? Publisher? Date? Length? Ease of Reading?
Music:	Artist? Producer? Recording Company? Date? Specific Songs?
Film:	Title? Director? Date? Studio? Actors?

Revising

Check Sentence Variety Vary the lengths of your sentences. Combine short sentences into longer ones—or break up longer sentences into shorter ones for emphasis. Inserting a question, a quotation, or an exclamation can jazz up your review.

Don't Repeat Be careful not to repeat words unnecessarily. Also, be on the lookout for redundancy, the unnecessary repetition of an idea.

REVISION MODEL

① , located at 307 Anchorage Way,
Elaine's Schooner provides seafood fare served in a
② Time your reservation so you can
friendly, warm setting. As you order the savory Clams

and
Casino or the hearty chowder take in a beautiful sunset

overlooking the bay.

① The writer provides the restaurant's address.
② This advice tells diners the best time to visit.

Publishing and Presenting

Bulletin Board of Reviews Use a bulletin board in a common area of your school to display written reviews. Create an eye-catching title and design for your display.

Review Broadcast Often, critics read their reviews on television and radio programs. Choose an appropriate piece of music to introduce and end your review. Then, work with a partner to record both of your reviews with the accompanying music. Share the recordings with your class.

Strategies for Success

Consider the variety of ways you approach the nonfiction you encounter every day. You may read your science textbook one way, the box scores another, and a humorous narrative still another. Beyond your changing attitude and interest level about the content of these items, you actually change the speed with which you absorb each one's meaning based on your purpose for reading. To get the most from the nonfiction that you take the time to read, it's important to adjust your reading rate.

Get Your Mind in Gear As your mind rides across the page, make sure it has all the gears it needs to meet your goals. These are some of the ways you might approach nonfiction:

▶ **Reading for mastery** Slow reading to memorize facts, understand ideas, and test what is said against your own experience

▶ **Attentive reading** Somewhat quicker reading to take in the main ideas and the facts that support them

▶ **Skimming** Quick reading to capture the main ideas without focusing on details

▶ **Scanning** Quick reading to find specific information by looking for key words in the headings and the text

Learn How to Shift Some kinds of reading require you to be able to shift rapidly from one gear to another. Keep your purpose in mind, and allow yourself to scan at some times and read more attentively at others.

Apply the Strategies

1. You have just picked up Dr. Robert D. Ballard's *The Discovery of the* Titanic. You want to identify the chapter in which Ballard finds the *Titanic*. In looking at the table of contents, what reading rate would you use to do this? Explain.

2. On this page, you'll find an excerpt from Ballard's book. What reading rate would you use to discover the main idea of this passage from the book? Explain your choice.

3. State the main idea of this passage in your own words.

Titanic Found!

Suddenly, out of the gloom, the Boat Deck of the ship came into view. We were on the port side looking at what appeared to be a stack opening—but the funnel was gone, the same forward funnel that had fallen into the water a few minutes before the ship sank, nearly hitting collapsible B, to which a handful of survivors—including Second Officer Lightoller, Colonel Gracie, and Marconi Operator Bride—had been clinging for dear life. Miraculously, its wash had pushed them clear of the hull just in time.

Then I saw it, just off to the starboard side of the bridge—the unmistakable image of a boat davit; and suddenly it hit me square in the stomach. Empty davits: not enough lifeboats.

Before we knew it, Argo had safely passed out over the starboard bow railing and back into the featureless murk. All at once, the bottled-up excitement in the crowded van exploded. People were whooping, hugging, and dancing around . . .

✔ *These types of nonfiction often call for varied reading rates:*
▶ Newspaper articles
▶ Essays in magazines
▶ Written directions

Grammar Review

Two types of subordinate clauses are **adverb clauses** and **adjective clauses**. Adverb clauses are used as adverbs, modifying a verb, an adjective, or an adverb (see page 520). Adjective clauses are used as adjectives to modify a noun or pronoun in another clause (see page 540).

There are a number of different words that introduce adverb and adjective clauses, linking them to the rest of the sentence.

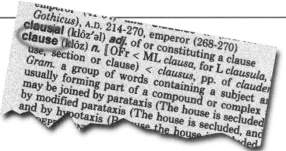

Introductory Words for Adverb Clauses

Relationship Expressed	Subordinating Conjunctions
Time (when?)	after, as, as soon as, before, until, when, whenever, while
Place (where?)	where, wherever
Reason (why?)	because, in order that, since, so that
Condition (under what circumstances?)	although, even if, even though, if, provided that, though, unless
Manner (how?)	as, as if, as though, than

Introductory Words for Adjective Clauses

Relative Pronouns	that, which, who, whoever, whom, whose
Relative Adverbs	where, when

Practice 1 On your paper, write the subordinate clauses in the sentences that follow. Identify each as an adverb or adjective clause. Then, underline the word that introduces each clause. Beside each clause, write the word or phrase it modifies.

1. Although Iona, who is a cab driver, wants to talk about his son, none of his passengers will listen.

2. Leah distrusts everyone because she cannot forget the concentration camp where her mother and brother died.

3. When the Communists took over China, Stacy's grandmother fled to Hong Kong, which was under British rule.

4. Lemon Brown still carries the harmonica that he played when he was a famous blues musician.

Practice 2 Rewrite each set of sentences as one sentence. Use the word given in parentheses to make one sentence an adverb or adjective clause.

1. Elements of short stories include setting and theme. Short stories are a type of fiction. (which)

2. The setting is very important. It drives the action. (when)

3. To determine the theme, you must look for the clues. The clues are found throughout the story. (that)

Grammar in Writing

✔ If a clause starts with a word that introduces an adverb or adjective clause, it cannot stand by itself as a complete sentence. Adverb and adjective clauses must be linked to main clauses.

Speaking, Listening, and Viewing Workshop

Every day, your teachers, parents, and friends pass along important information. In some situations, you are specifically told that they are giving you directions; in other cases, you just know that they'll expect you to know how to do something very soon. Whether your sister is telling you to be home for dinner at six o'clock or your friend is asking to borrow your math or your history notes, careful listening is the key. If you follow directions, you'll avoid any confusion or trouble down the road.

Pay Attention to Key Words
Every sentence spoken to you contains key words that get to the heart of the message. If your teacher tells you, "Be sure to bring two pencils and a blue notebook to class tomorrow," the words *two, pencils,* and *blue notebook* should jump out at you. Different commands or instructions will contain key words. By listening closely, you'll be able to pick them out.

Apply the Strategies

With a group of three, follow the directions in each example below.

1. As one of you gives instructions on how to check out a book from the library, the other two should take notes identifying the key steps. Compare the listeners' notes against each other and then against the speaker's.

2. One group member should create a combination of shapes on a piece of paper. Then, to help the other two create the same design, the first person

should give directions. Next, compare the designs on all three pages.

Tips for Following Oral Directions

✔ *For help in following oral directions, use these hints:*

▶ Pay attention to every word spoken.
▶ Look directly at the person speaking to you.
▶ Repeat the instructions to yourself out loud to make sure you understand them.
▶ If you have questions, ask.

What's Behind the Words

Words
Vocabulary Adventures With Richard Lederer

Clipped Words

During a typical day in your life as a student, you may attend classes and take exams in *math, lit,* or *phys ed.* You may hang out in the *gym, lab,* or *libe,* and, if you have a typical American appetite, your menu at lunch may consist of a *burger* or *frank.*

In each italicized example, people have substituted a part of the word for the whole word by clipping off the back part—*math* (ematics), *lab*(oratory), *lunch*(eon)—or the front part (ham)*burger.* Very occasionally, only the middle part of the word is retained, as in *flu* (influenza) and *fridge* (refrigerator).

Compact words

There are scores of words that are clipped in our language. Their popularity arises because people want to communicate as concisely and quickly as possible. They will take advantage of the opportunity to speak or write only part of a word to make themselves understood, especially when the word is one that people use frequently.

The name is the game

You can see this theory at work in the formations of nicknames. When we come to know people well, we usually address them using a familiar clipping of their first name. Most often we lop off the back part, as in *Al, Ben, Doug, Nick, Pam, Rich, Sam,* and *Sue.* We may clip the front of the name, as in *Beth, Becca, Gene,* and *Tina.* Or we may clip away both the front and the back, as in *Liz, Trish,* and *Zeke* (Ezekiel).

It's an ad, ad world

Advertisers often bestow upon their products a clipped name in order to suggest, in a snappy and space-saving way, some outstanding quality of their particular concoction—*Fab, Coke, Fedex, Jell-O, Jif, Lux, Spray 'n Vac,* and *Tums.*

The clip art

It's safe to predict that clipping will remain a productive process for forming new words—an emblem of our impulse as a modern society to scrunch the most meaning into the smallest space.

ACTIVITY 1 From which longer words do the following common clippings derive?

1. ad
2. deli
3. memo
4. phone
5. auto
6. fan
7. op-ed
8. teen
9. bus
10. gas
11. pants
12. zoo

ACTIVITY 2 Make a list of clipped first names of students in your class.

ACTIVITY 3 Identify the longer words from which the brand names mentioned above are coined. How many more examples can you find in your local supermarket?

ACTIVITY 4 In a group, brainstrom for a list of other clipped words you know.

Extended Reading Opportunities

Short stories allow you to take a brief journey to another time or place or to take a quick step in another person's shoes. These collections of stories offer you endless chances for such armchair travel.

Suggested Titles

The Red Pony
John Steinbeck

Written by the Nobel Prize-winning American author John Steinbeck, *The Red Pony* is a book of four related stories that trace the growing pains of a young boy named Jody. In the best-known story, "The Gift," Jody's father gives him a red pony. Jody trains and cares for the pony he loves. However, he discovers there are some tragedies from which he cannot protect the animal. Combined, the four stories show Jody's growth and maturity as he learns to respect life and the land and the people he knows.

Fifty Short Science Fiction Tales
Isaac Asimov and Groff Conklin, Editors

Isaac Asimov—the man who helped make science fiction what it is today—brings to-gether fifty tales of wonder and delight. He presents tales that inspire us with their original views of the future or faraway places. He includes stories that amaze us with their unique technological advances and all the problems these advances bring. Contributing authors to this collection include such favorites as Jack Finney, Isaac Asimov, Robert Heinlein, Arthur Clarke, and Antony Boucher.

Baseball in April and Other Stories
Gary Soto

In a collection of eleven short stories, Gary Soto focuses on the everyday lives of Hispanic young people growing up in Fresno, California. Through such ordinary events as Little League tryouts, a first date, and a performance in the school talent show, each story shows readers the hopes, desires, and troubles that go along with being a teenager.

Other Possibilities

American Eyes: New Asian American Short Stories for Young Adults   Lori M. Carlson, Editor

Connections: Short Stories   Donald Gallo

8 Plus 1   Robert Cormier

The Mellow Pad, 1945–51, Stuart Davis, The Brooklyn Museum, © Estate of Stuart Davis/Licensed by VAGA, New York, NY

Nonfiction

Many people who love reading believe that the most interesting literature being written today is nonfiction. The subjects of nonfiction writing are real people, and the events are actual happenings. There are many specific types of nonfiction. Following are the types you'll encounter in this unit:

- A **biography** is the life story of someone written by another person.

- An **autobiography** is a writer's own life story.

- An **expository essay** provides information about a single subject.

- A **narrative essay** tells the story of an actual event.

- A **personal essay** is an informal account of a person's experiences.

- A **reflective essay** reveals a writer's thoughts about an idea or experience.

- A **persuasive essay** presents an argument and attempts to convince readers of this position.

Guide for Reading

Meet the Author:

James Dickey (1923–1997)

The poet who speaks to you in this essay about the joys of poetry and real experience lived a life packed with adventure.

A Life of Action Born in Atlanta, Georgia, Dickey was a football player and motorcycle enthusiast as a young man. During World War II, he served as a radar operator. Then, for a period in the 1950's, he worked for advertising agencies in Atlanta and New York.

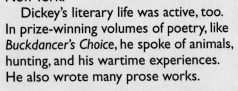

Dickey's literary life was active, too. In prize-winning volumes of poetry, like *Buckdancer's Choice*, he spoke of animals, hunting, and his wartime experiences. He also wrote many prose works.

The Poet as Movie Star Dickey's most famous prose work is the novel *Deliverance*, which was also made into a movie. At the end of the movie, a Southern sheriff comes to interview some crime victims. The actor who plays that big but soft-spoken sheriff is the poet himself!

THE STORY BEHIND THE STORY

Just as Dickey urges you to take a chance with poetry, he himself took a chance by plunging into it at age 24. He hadn't yet mastered poetic techniques, but he was full of enthusiasm.

◆ LITERATURE AND YOUR LIFE

CONNECT YOUR EXPERIENCE

The picture on the next page, *The Starry Night*, is familiar and strange at the same time. The artist has taken a sight familiar to you—the sky at night—and given it the strangeness of his own powerful way of seeing.

This essay explains that poets also show you common things with a strange new shine on them. As Dickey says, you can even see the sun with new eyes, through "the special spell that poetry brings to the *fact* of the sun."

THEMATIC FOCUS: Lessons Learned

How does Dickey surprise you into a better understanding of poetry?

◆ Background for Understanding

LITERATURE

As James Dickey says, poetry has been around a long time. It began not with the printed page but with the memory, the breath, and the spoken word. Thousands of years ago, before writing was invented, poets composed and recited long story-poems. They used rhythms, rhymes, and other devices to remember and compose these works. In this essay, Dickey offers advice to modern readers approaching one of the oldest literary forms.

How to Enjoy Poetry

The Starry Night, 1889, Vincent van Gogh, Oil on canvas, 29 x 36 1/4", Collection, The Museum of Modern Art, New York

◆ Literary Focus

EXPOSITORY ESSAY

An essay is a short piece of nonfiction in which a writer presents a personal view of a topic. There are many types of essays. One of these is the **expository essay,** in which a writer explains or gives information about a subject. The title of this expository essay, "How to Enjoy Poetry," may remind you of magazine articles that explain a process. However, unlike many how-to articles, this one does not give you rules or steps to follow.

◆ Build Vocabulary

PREFIXES: *inter-*

The prefix *inter-*, meaning "between" or "among," suits our computer age. Just think of the *Inter*net, a system of connections "among" computers. In his essay, Dickey uses the word *interacts,* meaning "to affect and be affected by each other."

Gather other *inter-* words with a chart like the one below.

WORD BANK

Which of these words from the essay has the same root as the word *vitamin?*

prose
inevitability
interacts
vital

Inter-

interfere

Which Sun? Whose Stars?

These boldface headings are clues to the **organization.** Each section gives different tips for enjoying poetry.

The sun is new every day, the ancient philosopher Heraclitus[1] said. The sun of poetry is new every day, too, because it is seen in different ways by different people who have lived under it, lived with it, responded to it. Their lives are different from yours, but by means of the special spell that poetry brings to the *fact* of the sun—everybody's sun; yours, too—you can come into possession of many suns: as many as men and women have ever been able to imagine. Poetry makes possible the deepest kind of personal possession of the world.

The most beautiful constellation in the winter sky is Orion,[2] which ancient poets thought looked like a hunter, up there, moving across heaven with his dog Sirius.[3] What is this hunter made out of stars hunting for? What does he mean? Who owns him, if anybody? The poet Aldous Huxley[4] felt that he did, and so, in Aldous Huxley's universe of personal emotion, he did.

> Up from among the emblems of the
>   wind into its heart of power,
> The Huntsman climbs, and all his
>   living stars
> Are bright, and all are mine.

Where to Start

The beginning of your true encounter with poetry should be simple. It should bypass all classrooms, all textbooks, courses, examinations, and libraries and go straight to the things that make your own existence exist: to your body and nerves and blood and

Dickey continues to say that poetry is not just a classroom subject. One of his **main points** seems to be that readers should find their "own way" to poetry.

muscles. Find your own way—a secret way that just maybe you don't know yet—to open yourself as wide as you can and as deep as you can to the moment, the *now* of your own existence and the endless mystery of it, and perhaps at the same time to one other thing that is not you, but is out there: a handful of gravel is a good place to start. So is an ice cube—what more mysterious and beautiful *interior* of something has there ever been?

As for me, I like the sun, the source of all living things, and on certain days very good-feeling, too. "Start with the sun," D. H. Lawrence[5] said, "and everything will slowly, slowly happen." Good advice. And a lot *will* happen.

What is more fascinating than a rock, if you really feel it and *look* at it, or more interesting than a leaf?

> *Horses, I mean; butterflies, whales;*
> *Mosses, and stars; and gravelly*
> *Rivers, and fruit.*
>
> *Oceans, I mean; black valleys; corn;*
> *Brambles, and cliffs; rock, dirt, dust,*
> *ice . . .*

Go back and read this list—it is quite a list, Mark Van Doren's[6] list!—item by item. Slowly. Let each of these things call up an image out of your own life.

Think and feel. What moss do you see? Which horse? What field of corn? What brambles are *your* brambles? Which river is most yours?

The Poem's Way of Going

Part of the spell of poetry is in the rhythm of language, used by poets who understand how powerful a factor rhythm can be, how compelling and unforgettable. Almost anything put into rhythm and rhyme is more memorable than the same thing said in prose. Why this is, no one knows completely,

---

1. **Heraclitus** (her´ ə klī´ təs): Greek philosopher who lived about 500 B.C.
2. **Orion** (ō rī´ ən)
3. **Sirius** (sir´ ē əs)
4. **Aldous Huxley:** English poet, essayist, and novelist (1894–1963).

5. **D. H. Lawrence:** English poet and novelist (1885–1930).
6. **Mark Van Doren:** American poet, teacher, and critic (1894–1972).

The Starry Night, 1889, Vincent van Gogh, Oil on canvas, 29 x 36 1/4", Collection, The Museum of Modern Art, New York

▲ **Critical Viewing** Dickey says that a poet in some ways "owns" what he or she describes. In Dickey's sense of the word, does Vincent Van Gogh "own" the night sky he painted here? **[Assess]**

though the answer is surely rooted far down in the biology by means of which we exist; in the circulation of the blood that goes forth from the heart and comes back, and in the repetition of breathing. Croesus[7] was a rich Greek king, back in the sixth century before Christ, but this tombstone was not his:

> *No Croesus lies in the grave you see;*
> *I was a poor laborer, and this suits me.*

That is plain-spoken and definitive. You believe it, and the rhyme helps you believe it and keep it.

Some Things You'll Find Out

Writing poetry is a lot like a contest with yourself, and if you like sports and games

and competitions of all kinds, you might like to try writing some. Why not?

The possibilities of rhyme are great. Some of the best fun is in making up your own limericks. There's no reason you can't invent limericks about anything that comes to your mind. No reason. Try it.

The problem is to find three words that rhyme and fit into a meaning. "There was a young man from . . ." *Where* was he from? What situation was he in? How can these things fit into the limerick form—a form everybody knows—so that the rhymes "pay off," and give that sense of completion and inevitability

◆ **Build Vocabulary**

prose (prōz) *n.*: Nonpoetic language
inevitability (in ev′ ə tə bil′ i tē) *n.*: Certainty

7. **Croesus** (krē′ səs)

Build Your Portfolio

 ## Idea Bank

Writing

1. **Reader's Log** List the nonfiction you've read during a week. Include newspaper and magazine articles, information on packages, books, and CD liner notes.

2. **Limerick** Write a limerick—a five-line poem with three beats in the rhyming first, second, and fifth lines and two beats in the rhyming third and fourth lines. Here's an example: "A puppy whose hair was so flowing/There really was no means of knowing/Which end was his head,/Once stopped me and said,/'Please, sir, am I coming or going?'"

3. **How-to Essay** Write a step-by-step explanation of a process. It can involve anything you do, such as cooking a meal, playing a musical instrument, or assembling a model airplane.

Speaking and Listening

4. **Poetry Listening** Play recordings of poets reading from their work. Hand out copies of the poems so students can follow along. Then, discuss how readers vary their speed and emphasis to convey a message. **[Performing Arts Link]**

5. **Choral Reading [Group Activity]** Choose a poem for choral reading, like "The Cremation of Sam McGee." Give a reading of the poem, with different people or groups of people reading different parts of it. **[Performing Arts Link]**

Projects

6. **Anthology of Essays** Find several essays in which a person deeply involved in a field explains it to beginners. Collect the essays in an anthology, and write a brief introduction explaining what the essays have in common.

7. **Poetry Home Page** Using Dickey's essay, design an Internet Home Page for poetry. Include ideas from the essay and quotations from poems, to encourage people to read more poetry. Also, indicate the kind of graphics that would go on the page. **[Media Link]**

 ## Writing Mini-Lesson

Essay of Praise

Think of a sport, hobby, or subject that you love as much as James Dickey loves poetry. Then, write an essay in praise of this pursuit. Imagine that you're writing for classmates who don't necessarily share your interest or knowledge. Tell them why this activity is so rewarding and what they can do to appreciate it.

Writing Skills Focus: Clearly Express the Main Points

Get your message across by clearly expressing two or three **main points** about your interest. At the beginning of his essay, Dickey alerts readers to a main point by using the phrase "The first thing to understand . . ."

Model From the Essay

The first thing to understand about poetry is that it comes to you from outside you, in books or in words, but that for it to live, something from within you must come to it and meet it and complete it.

Prewriting After choosing the activity you'll write about, jot down three main points to convey. Also, brainstorm to gather experiences you've had that support your main points.

Drafting Imagine that you're talking to a friend about your chosen activity. Tell your friend why this pursuit is so rewarding and what he or she can do to learn more about it. Hook your friend by describing what this activity *feels* like. Add explanations later.

> ◆ **Grammar Application**
> In your draft, highlight examples of the different sentence functions.

Revising Scan your Prewriting notes, making sure you've included the main points you wanted to convey. Check that you've supported these points with descriptions of your own experience and feelings.

PART 1

Biography and Autobiography

Self-Portrait, 1967, Andy Warhol, The Andy Warhol Foundation, Inc.

Guide for Reading

Meet the Authors:

Russell Baker (1925–)

Nonfiction is about facts, but no one says that it can't be funny. As a newspaper columnist and author, Russell Baker has found humor in news stories and in his own life story.

Facing Economic Trouble You'll see how Baker's humor emerges even as he writes about problems he faced early in life. As a result of the country's failing economy, his family moved often in search of better opportunities.

Eventually, Baker went on to a successful career in journalism. He won a Pulitzer Prize for his "Observer" column in the *The New York Times* and another for his autobiography *Growing Up,* from which this essay comes.

Annie Dillard (1945–)

As a child, Annie Dillard loved reading, drawing, and observing the natural world. While attending college in Virginia, she lived near a creek in a valley of the Blue Ridge Mountains. In 1974, she published *Pilgrim at Tinker Creek,* which describes her exploration of that environment. The book won the Pulitzer Prize for Nonfiction.

This essay comes from *An American Childhood,* Dillard's autobiographical account of growing up in Pittsburgh, Pennsylvania.

◆ LITERATURE AND YOUR LIFE

CONNECT YOUR EXPERIENCE

Imagine trying to paint someone you see only in mirrors—yourself! That's what artist Norman Rockwell did when he created the painting on the next page. Perhaps your self-portrait would include humorous touches, like Rockwell's. These selections by Russell Baker and Annie Dillard are self-portraits that use words instead of paint. Like the brush strokes of a humorous painting, some of their words will tickle your funny bone.

THEMATIC FOCUS: Moments of Insight

As you read, ask yourself what these authors discover about themselves or about life.

◆ Background for Understanding

SOCIAL STUDIES

"No Gumption" is set during the Depression, a period of economic troubles that began in 1929 when the value of stocks fell rapidly. By 1933, one out of every three workers in the United States was unemployed! That's why Baker's mother considers a good job so important. It wasn't until the early 1940's that the economy recovered completely.

◆ Build Vocabulary

WORD ROOTS: -pel-

Since the root *-pel-* means "to drive," it gives a push to words in which it appears. Dillard writes, for example, "we compelled him to follow our route." *Compelled* means "forced." It combines *com-* ("together") and *-pelled* ("drove").

WORD BANK

Which of these words from the essays appears in the titles of certain kinds of tests?

gumption
paupers
crucial
aptitude
translucent
compelled
perfunctorily

◆ No Gumption ◆
The Chase *from* An American Childhood

The Deadline, Norman Rockwell, Photo Courtesy of The Norman Rockwell Museum at Stockbridge

◆Literary Focus

AUTOBIOGRAPHY

Every day you tell people stories from your own life history. In an **autobiography**—the story of a person's life written by that person—a writer does the same thing in a more formal way. An autobiography includes the key events of a person's life and reveals his or her struggles, values, and ideas.

In reading these two autobiographical essays, enjoy the stories that the authors tell you, but also look deeper. Ask yourself who or what the author struggles against and what the author wants from life.

◆Reading Strategy

UNDERSTAND THE AUTHOR'S PURPOSE

An **author's purpose** is his or her reason for writing. Writers of autobiography could have many different reasons for telling their life story. Their purposes might include explaining themselves and their values, teaching lessons in life, entertaining, boasting, or a combination of these.

As you read the essays, use a chart like the one below to figure out the writer's purpose or purposes:

Passage	Possible Purpose
The flaw in my character . . . was lack of "gumption."	To explain himself. To entertain by making fun of himself.

NO GUMPTION

Russell Baker

I began working in journalism when I was eight years old. It was my mother's idea. She wanted me to "make something" of myself and, after a level-headed appraisal[1] of my strengths, decided I had better start young if I was to have any chance of keeping up with the competition.

The flaw in my character which she had already spotted was lack of "gumption." My idea of a perfect afternoon was lying in front of the radio rereading my favorite Big Little Book,[2] *Dick Tracy Meets Stooge Viller*. My mother despised inactivity. Seeing me having a good time in repose, she was powerless to hide her disgust. "You've got no more gumption than a bump on a log," she said. "Get out in the kitchen and help Doris do those dirty dishes."

My sister Doris, though two years younger than I, had enough gumption for a dozen people. She positively enjoyed washing dishes, making beds, and cleaning the house. When she was only seven she could carry a piece of short-weighted cheese back to the A&P, threaten the manager with legal action, and

come back triumphantly with the full quarter-pound we'd paid for and a few ounces extra thrown in for forgiveness. Doris could have made something of herself if she hadn't been a girl. Because of this defect, however, the best she could hope for was a career as a nurse or schoolteacher, the only work that capable females were considered up to in those days.

This must have saddened my mother, this twist of fate that had allocated all the gumption to the daughter and left her with a son who was content with Dick Tracy and Stooge Viller. If disappointed, though, she wasted no energy on self-pity. She would make me make something of myself whether I wanted to or not. "The Lord helps those who help themselves," she said. That was the way her mind worked.

She was realistic about the difficulty. Having sized up the material the Lord had given her to mold, she didn't overestimate what she

---

1. **appraisal** (ə prā´ zəl) *n.*: Judgment of something's or someone's quality.
2. **Big Little Book:** A small, inexpensive illustrated book that often portrayed the adventures of comic-strip heroes like Dick Tracy.

◆ Reading Strategy
Which portions of this paragraph indicate that Baker is showing himself as less than perfect in order to entertain the reader?

◆ **Build Vocabulary**
gumption (gump´ shən) *n.*: Courage; enterprise

◀ Critical Viewing These magazine covers are from the 1930's, when Russell Baker was a boy. What can you infer about his childhood based on these illustrations? [Infer]

could do with it. She didn't insist that I grow up to be President of the United States.

Fifty years ago parents still asked boys if they wanted to grow up to be President, and asked it not jokingly but seriously. Many parents who were hardly more than paupers still believed their sons could do it. Abraham Lincoln had done it. We were only sixty-five years from Lincoln. Many a grandfather who walked among us could remember Lincoln's time. Men of grandfatherly age were the worst for asking if you wanted to grow up to be President. A surprising number of little boys said yes and meant it.

I was asked many times myself. No, I would say, I didn't want to grow up to be President. My mother was present during one of these interrogations.[3] An elderly uncle, having posed the usual question and exposed my lack of interest in the Presidency, asked, "Well, what *do* you want to be when you grow up?"

I loved to pick through trash piles and collect empty bottles, tin cans with pretty labels, and discarded magazines. The most desirable job on earth sprang instantly to mind. "I want to be a garbage man," I said.

My uncle smiled, but my mother had seen the first distressing evidence of a bump budding on a log.

◆ **Literary Focus**
What do these details reveal about Russell's character?

▲ **Critical Viewing** Baker's description of himself probably creates an image of a boy in your mind. How does your image compare with this photograph of Russell and his sister? [**Compare and Contrast**]

"Have a little gumption, Russell," she said. Her calling me Russell was a signal of unhappiness. When she approved of me I was always "Buddy."

When I turned eight years old she decided that the job of starting me on the road toward making something of myself could no longer be safely delayed. "Buddy," she said one day, "I want you to come home right after school this afternoon. Somebody's coming and I want you to meet him."

When I burst in that afternoon she was in conference in the parlor with an executive of the Curtis Publishing Company. She introduced me. He bent low from the waist and shook my hand. Was it true as my mother had told him, he asked, that I longed for the opportunity to conquer the world of business?

My mother replied that I was blessed with a rare determination to make something of myself.

"That's right," I whispered.

"But have you got the grit, the character, the never-say-quit spirit it takes to succeed in business?"

My mother said I certainly did.

"That's right," I said.

He eyed me silently for a long pause, as though weighing whether I could be trusted to keep his confidence, then spoke man-to-man. Before taking a crucial step, he said, he wanted to advise me that working for the Curtis Publishing Company placed enormous responsibility on a young man. It was one of the great companies of America. Perhaps the

---

3. **interrogations** (in ter′ ə gā′ shənz) *n.*: Situations where a person is formally questioned.

greatest publishing house in the world. I had heard, no doubt, of the *Saturday Evening Post*?

Heard of it? My mother said that everyone in our house had heard of the *Saturday Post* and that I, in fact, read it with religious devotion.

Then doubtless, he said, we were also familiar with those two monthly pillars of the magazine world, the *Ladies Home Journal* and the *Country Gentleman.*

Indeed we were familiar with them, said my mother.

Representing the *Saturday Evening Post* was one of the weightiest honors that could be bestowed in the world of business, he said. He was personally proud of being a part of that great corporation.

My mother said he had every right to be.

Again he studied me as though debating whether I was worthy of a knighthood. Finally: "Are you trustworthy?"

My mother said I was the soul of honesty.

"That's right," I said.

The caller smiled for the first time. He told me I was a lucky young man. He admired my spunk. Too many young men thought life was all play. Those young men would not go far in this world. Only a young man willing to work and save and keep his face washed and his hair neatly combed could hope to come out on top in a world such as ours. Did I truly and sincerely believe that I was such a young man?

"He certainly does," said my mother.

"That's right," I said.

He said he had been so impressed by what he had seen of me that he was going to make me a representative of the Curtis Publishing Company. On the following Tuesday, he said, thirty freshly printed copies of the *Saturday Evening Post* would be delivered at our door. I would place these magazines, still damp with the ink of the presses, in a handsome canvas bag, sling it over my shoulder, and set forth through the streets to bring the best in journalism, fiction, and cartoons to the American public.

He had brought the canvas bag with him. He presented it with reverence fit for a chasuble.[4] He showed me how to drape the sling over my left shoulder and across the chest so that the pouch lay easily accessible[5] to my right hand, allowing the best in journalism, fiction, and cartoons to be swiftly extracted and sold to a citizenry whose happiness and security depended upon us soldiers of the free press.

The following Tuesday I raced home from school, put the canvas bag over my shoulder, dumped the magazines in, and, tilting to the left to balance their weight on my right hip, embarked on the highway of journalism.

We lived in Belleville, New Jersey, a commuter town at the northern fringe of Newark. It

▲ **Critical Viewing** What details tell you that this is an old photograph? **[Analyze]**

◆ **Build Vocabulary**

paupers (pô′ pərz) *n.*: People who are very poor
crucial (kroo′ shəl) *adj.*: Of great importance

---

4. **chasuble:** (chaz′ ə bəl) *n.*: Sleeveless outer garment worn by priests.
5. **accessible** (ak ses′ ə bəl) *adj.*: Easy to get.

was 1932, the bleakest year of the Depression. My father had died two years before, leaving us with a few pieces of Sears, Roebuck furniture and not much else, and my mother had taken Doris and me to live with one of her younger brothers. This was my Uncle Allen. Uncle Allen had made something of himself by 1932. As salesman for a soft-drink bottler in Newark, he had an income of $30 a week; wore pearl-gray spats,[6] detachable collars, and a three-piece suit; was happily married; and took in threadbare relatives.

With my load of magazines I headed toward Belleville Avenue. That's where the people were. There were two filling stations at the intersection with Union Avenue, as well as an A&P, a fruit stand, a bakery, a barber shop, Zuccarelli's drugstore, and a diner shaped like a railroad car. For several hours I made myself highly visible, shifting position now and then from corner to corner, from shop window to shop window, to make sure everyone could see the heavy black lettering on the canvas bag that said *The Saturday Evening Post.* When the angle of the light indicated it was suppertime, I walked back to the house.

"How many did you sell, Buddy?" my mother asked.

"None."

"Where did you go?"

"The corner of Belleville and Union Avenues."

"What did you do?"

"Stood on the corner waiting for somebody to buy a *Saturday Evening Post.*"

"You just stood there?"

"Didn't sell a single one."

"For God's sake, Russell!"

Uncle Allen intervened. "I've been thinking about it for some time," he said, "and I've about decided to take the *Post* regularly. Put me down as a regular customer." I handed him a magazine and he paid me a nickel. It was the first nickel I earned.

Afterwards my mother instructed me in salesmanship. I would have to ring doorbells, address adults with charming self-confidence, and break down resistance with a sales talk pointing out that no one, no matter how poor, could afford to be without the *Saturday Evening Post* in the home.

I told my mother I'd changed my mind about wanting to succeed in the magazine business.

"If you think I'm going to raise a good-for-nothing," she replied, "you've got another think coming." She told me to hit the streets with the canvas bag and start ringing doorbells the instant school was out next day. When I objected that I didn't feel any aptitude for salesmanship, she asked how I'd like to lend her my leather belt so she could whack some sense into me. I bowed to superior will and entered journalism with a heavy heart.

My mother and I had fought this battle almost as long as I could remember. It probably started even before memory began, when I was a country child in northern Virginia and my mother, dissatisfied with my father's plain workman's life, determined that I would not grow up like him and his people, with calluses on their hands, overalls on their backs, and fourth-grade educations in their heads. She had fancier ideas of life's possibilities. Introducing me to the *Saturday Evening Post,* she was trying to wean me as early as possible from my father's world where men left with lunch pails at sunup, worked with their hands until the grime ate into the pores, and died with a few sticks of mail-order furniture as their legacy. In my mother's vision of the better life there were desks and white collars, well-pressed suits, evenings of reading and lively talk, and perhaps—if a man were very, very lucky and hit the jackpot, really made something important of himself—perhaps there might be a fantastic salary of $5,000 a year to support a big house and a Buick with a rumble seat[7] and a vacation in Atlantic City.

---

6. **spats** (spats) *n.:* Pieces of cloth or leather that cover the upper part of the shoe or ankle.

7. **rumble seat:** In early automobiles, an open seat in the rear of the car that could be folded shut.

And so I set forth with my sack of magazines. I was afraid of the dogs that snarled behind the doors of potential buyers. I was timid about ringing the doorbells of strangers, relieved when no one came to the door, and scared when someone did. Despite my mother's instructions, I could not deliver an engaging sales pitch. When a door opened I simply asked, "Want to buy a *Saturday Evening Post*?" In Belleville few persons did. It was a town of 30,000 people, and most weeks I rang a fair majority of its doorbells. But I rarely sold my thirty copies. Some weeks I canvassed the entire town for six days and still had four or five unsold magazines on Monday evening; then I dreaded the coming of Tuesday morning, when a batch of thirty fresh *Saturday Evening Posts* was due at the front door.

"Better get out there and sell the rest of those magazines tonight," my mother would say.

I usually posted myself then at a busy intersection where a traffic light controlled commuter flow from Newark. When the light turned red I stood on the curb and shouted my sales pitch at the motorists.

"Want to buy a *Saturday Evening Post*?"

One rainy night when car windows were sealed against me I came back soaked and with not a single sale to report. My mother beckoned to Doris.

©The Curtis Publishing Company, Illustrator: Frances Tipton Hunter

▲ **Critical Viewing** How are the boys in this illustration from the 1930's different from you? How are they the same? **[Compare and Contrast]**

"Go back down there with Buddy and show him how to sell these magazines," she said.

Brimming with zest, Doris, who was then seven years old, returned with me to the corner. She took a magazine from the bag, and when the light turned red she strode to the nearest car and banged her small fist against the closed window. The driver, probably startled at what he took to be a midget assaulting his car, lowered the window to stare, and Doris thrust a *Saturday Evening Post* at him.

"You need this magazine," she piped, "and it only costs a nickel."

Her salesmanship was irresistible. Before the light changed half a dozen times she disposed of the entire batch. I didn't feel humiliated. To the contrary. I was so happy I decided to give her a treat. Leading her to the vegetable store on Belleville Avenue, I bought three apples, which cost a nickel, and gave her one.

"You shouldn't waste money," she said.

"Eat your apple." I bit into mine.

"You shouldn't eat before supper," she said. "It'll spoil your appetite."

Back at the house that evening, she dutifully reported me for wasting a nickel. Instead of a scolding, I was rewarded with a pat on the back for having the good sense to buy fruit instead of candy. My mother reached into her bottomless supply of maxims[8] and told Doris, "An apple a day keeps the doctor away."

◆ **Reading Strategy**
How does the contrast between Baker and his sister help Baker to explain what he was like?

8. **maxims** (mak′ simz) *n.*: Wise sayings.

By the time I was ten I had learned all my mother's maxims by heart. Asking to stay up past normal bedtime, I knew that a refusal would be explained with, "Early to bed and early to rise, makes a man healthy, wealthy, and wise." If I whimpered about having to get up early in the morning, I could depend on her to say, "The early bird gets the worm."

The one I most despised was, "If at first you don't succeed, try, try again." This was the battle cry with which she constantly sent me back into the hopeless struggle whenever I moaned that I had rung every doorbell in town and knew there wasn't a single potential buyer left in Belleville that week. After listening to my explanation, she handed me the canvas bag and said, "If at first you don't succeed . . ."

Three years in that job, which I would gladly have quit after the first day except for her insistence, produced at least one valuable result. My mother finally concluded that I would never make something of myself by pursuing a life in business and started considering careers that demanded less competitive zeal.

One evening when I was eleven I brought home a short "composition" on my summer vacation which the teacher had graded with an A. Reading it with her own schoolteacher's eye, my mother agreed that it was top-drawer seventh grade prose and complimented me. Nothing more was said about it immediately, but a new idea had taken life in her mind. Halfway through supper she suddenly interrupted the conversation.

"Buddy," she said, "maybe you could be a writer."

◆ **Literature and Your Life**
Why does this discovery help solve a conflict Baker has experienced?

I clasped the idea to my heart. I had never met a writer, had shown no previous urge to write, and hadn't a notion how to become a writer, but I loved stories and thought that making up stories must surely be almost as much fun as reading them. Best of all, though, and what really gladdened my heart, was the ease of the writer's life. Writers did not have to trudge through the town peddling from canvas bags, defending themselves against angry dogs, being rejected by surly strangers. Writers did not have to ring doorbells. So far as I could make out, what writers did couldn't even be classified as work.

©The Curtis Publishing Company, Illustrator: G. Brehm

▲ **Critical Viewing** Which character in this illustration seems the most like Doris? Explain. **[Connect]**

I was enchanted. Writers didn't have to have any gumption at all. I did not dare tell anybody for fear of being laughed at in the schoolyard, but secretly I decided that what I'd like to be when I grew up was a writer.

Beyond Literature

<hr/>

Career Connection

Careers in Journalism Russell Baker didn't enjoy selling newspapers, but he found writing rewarding. He eventually made newspapers into a career. Journalists inform people about what is happening in the world and help to shape what the public thinks about these events.

Journalists work in one of five main branches of media: newspapers, news services, magazines, radio, and television. Jobs available include columnists, copy editors, editorial writers, feature writers, news editors, photojournalists, reporters, and

newscasters. Many of these jobs require at least a college degree in liberal arts or journalism, along with experience on a college paper or radio.

Cross-Curricular Activity

Job Research Research a particular job field of journalism. Find out what the requirements and responsibilities of this job are. If you can, interview a local journalist to get a more accurate idea of the work journalists do. Share your findings with the class through a written or oral report.

<hr/>

Guide for Responding

◆ LITERATURE AND YOUR LIFE

Reader's Response Do you agree with Baker's mother that he has no "gumption"? Why or why not?

Thematic Focus In what ways does Baker's mother lead him to a discovery of his true talents?

Role Play With a partner, act out a situation in which Baker tries to sell the *Saturday Evening Post* to an adult in Belleville.

☑ Check Your Comprehension

1. Describe how Baker's mother gets him started in "journalism."
2. Explain what success Baker has as a magazine salesman.
3. How does his sister's performance as a salesperson contrast with his?
4. What does his mother conclude after he has worked at the job for three years?
5. What inspires his mother's new plan for his career?

◆ Critical Thinking

INTERPRET
1. What qualities prevent Baker from being a good salesperson? **[Analyze]**
2. Give two examples that show Baker's sense of humor about his poor salesmanship. **[Support]**
3. Compare Baker's aims in life as a child with the goals his mother sets for him. **[Compare and Contrast]**
4. How much of the idea for Baker's new career plan comes from him, and how much comes from his mother? **[Draw Conclusions]**

APPLY
5. What interests of yours could lead to a career? **[Apply]**

EXTEND
6. What does "No Gumption" reveal about the different expectations people had for boys and for girls in the 1930's? **[Social Studies Link]**

CONNECTIONS TO TODAY'S WORLD

In the 1930's, Russell Baker sold copies of *The Saturday Evening Post* on street corners. Since then, a technology explosion has dramatically changed the way people get information. In addition to all-news radio and 24-hour cable news channels, millions of people worldwide have logged onto the Internet. An electronic information network introduced to the American public in the 1990's, the Internet makes vast amounts of information readily available. This essay provides strategies for making the most of this new technology.

Let the Reader Beware

Reid Goldsborough

Tips for Verifying Information on the Internet

The fact is, the Internet is chock full of rumors, gossip, hoaxes, exaggerations, falsehoods, ruses, and scams. Although the Net can reveal useful, factual information that you'd be hard pressed to find elsewhere, it can also appear to be a gigantic electronic tabloid.[1]

Can you ever trust the Internet? Sure you can. You just need to apply critical thinking in evaluating the information and advice you come across. Here's a six-step approach to doing this.

1. Don't judge a Web site by its appearance.

Sure, if a Web site looks professional rather than slopped together, chances are greater that the information within it will be accurate and reliable.

But looks can and do deceive. A flashy site can merely be a marketing front for quack health remedies or an illegal pyramid scheme.

2. Try to find out who's behind the information.

If you're looking at a Web site, check if the author or creator is identified. See if there are links to a page listing professional credentials[2] or affiliations.[3] Be very skeptical if no authorship information is provided.

If you're looking at a message in a Usenet newsgroup or Internet mailing list, see if the author has included a signature—a short, often biographical, description that's automatically appended to the end of messages. Many people include their credentials in their signature or point to their home page, where they provide biographical information.

---

1. tabloid (tab′ loid′) *n.*: Newspaper with many pictures and often sensationalized stories.

2. credentials (kri den′ shəlz) *n.*: Information that indicates position or authority.
3. affiliations (ə fil′ ē ā′ shənz) *n.*: Organizational membership.

3. Try to determine the reason the information was posted.

Among those who create Web sites are publishing companies, professional and trade organizations, government agencies, non-profit organizations, for-profit companies, educational institutions, individual research-ers, political and advocacy groups, and hobbyists.

Each has its own agenda—sometimes ex-plicit, sometimes hidden. Unearth the agenda and keep it in mind when evaluating the in-formation presented.

Similarly, look behind and between the words posted in Usenet and mailing list dis-cussions. Is the author trying to promote his or her own ends, or be helpful? You can often do both, but not always.

4. Look for the date the information was created or modified.

Unless you're doing historical research, current information is usually more valid and useful than older material.

If the Web site doesn't provide a "last up-dated" message or otherwise date its content, check out some of its links. If more than a couple are no longer working, the informa-tion at the site may no longer be up to date either.

5. Try to verify the same information elsewhere.

This is particularly important if the infor-mation is at odds with your previous under-standing or if you intend to use it for critical purposes such as an important health, fam-ily, or business decision.

Ideally, you should confirm the informa-tion with at least two other sources. Librari-ans and information scientists call this the "principle of triangulation of data." Spending a bit of time validating the material, through the Internet or at a local library, can be well worth the investment.

6. Try to find out how others feel about the reliability and professionalism of the Web site you're looking at.

There are a number of review guides that offer evaluations of other sites. Here are three excellent, relatively new review guides that you may not have heard of:

Argus Clearinghouse
http://www.clearinghouse.net/

Mining Company
http://miningco.com/

Readers Digest's LookSmart
http://www.looksmart.com/

With any information you come across on the Net, the watchword is "Caveat lector"—Let the reader beware.

If you'd like to delve further into the issue of information credibility on the Internet, there are Web sites out there that let you do just that. Here are four good ones.

Evaluating Internet Information
http://www-medlib.med.utah.edu/navigator/discovery/eval.html

Evaluating Quality on the Net
http://www.tiac.net/users/hope/findqual.html

Thinking Critically About World Wide Web Resources
http://www.library.ucla.edu/libraries/college/instruct/critical.htm

Internet Source Validation Project
http://www.stemnet.nf.ca/Curriculum/Validate/validate.html

1. Why does the writer warn people to read in-formation on the Internet critically?
2. Which tip do you think is most useful? Explain.

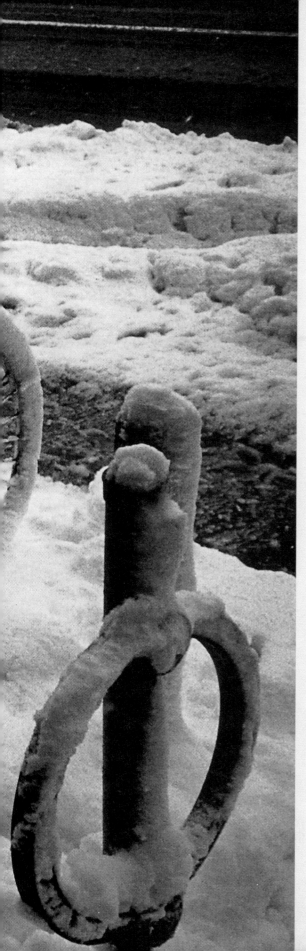

The Chase

from An American Childhood

Annie Dillard

Some boys taught me to play football. This was fine sport. You thought up a new strategy for every play and whispered it to the others. You went out for a pass, fooling everyone. Best, you got to throw yourself mightily at someone's running legs. Either you brought him down or you hit the ground flat out on your chin, with your arms empty before you. It was all or nothing. If you hesitated in fear, you would miss and get hurt: you would take a hard fall while the kid got away, or you would get kicked in the face while the kid got away. But if you flung yourself wholeheartedly at the back of his knees—if you gathered and joined body and soul and pointed them diving fearlessly—then you likely wouldn't get hurt, and you'd stop the ball. Your fate, and your team's score, depended on your concentration and courage. Nothing girls did could compare with it.

◆ Reading Strategy
What lesson in life might Dillard be trying to teach in this passage?

Boys welcomed me at baseball, too, for I had, through enthusiastic practice, what was weirdly known as a boy's arm. In winter, in the snow, there was neither baseball nor football, so the boys and I threw snowballs at passing cars. I got in trouble throwing snowballs, and have seldom been happier since.

◀ **Critical Viewing** In what two ways is this photograph of a snow-covered bicycle a good choice for this selection? **[Support]**

On one weekday morning after Christmas, six inches of new snow had just fallen. We were standing up to our boot tops in snow on a front yard on trafficked Reynolds Street, waiting for cars. The cars traveled Reynolds Street slowly and evenly; they were targets all but wrapped in red ribbons, cream puffs. We couldn't miss.

I was seven; the boys were eight, nine, and ten. The oldest two Fahey boys were there—Mikey and Peter— polite blond boys who lived near me on Lloyd Street, and who already had four brothers and sisters. My parents approved Mikey and Peter Fahey. Chickie McBride was there, a tough kid, and Billy Paul and Mackie Kean too, from across Reynolds, where the boys grew up dark and furious, grew up skinny, knowing, and skilled. We had all drifted from our houses that morning looking for action, and had found it here on Reynolds Street.

It was cloudy but cold. The cars' tires laid behind them on the snowy street a complex trail of beige chunks like crenellated castle walls.[1] I had stepped on some earlier; they squeaked. We could have wished for more traffic. When a car came, we all popped it one. In the intervals between cars we reverted to the natural solitude of children.

I started making an iceball—a perfect iceball, from perfectly white snow, perfectly spherical, and squeezed perfectly <u>translucent</u> so no snow remained all the way through. (The Fahey boys and I considered it unfair actually to throw an iceball at somebody, but it had been known to happen.)

I had just embarked on the iceball project when we heard tire chains come clanking from afar. A black Buick was moving toward us down the street. We all spread out, banged together some regular snowballs, took aim, and, when the Buick drew nigh, fired.

A soft snowball hit the driver's windshield right before the driver's face. It made a smashed star with a

---

1. **chunks like crenellated** (kren´ əl āt´ əd) **castle walls:** The snow was in rows of square clumps like the notches along the top of castle walls.

◆ **Build Vocabulary**

translucent (trans lō͞o´ sənt) *adj.*: Able to transmit light but no detail of that light

---

▶ **Critical Viewing** Compare the amount of snow in this photograph with the amount of snow Dillard describes. **[Compare and Contrast]**

Guide for Responding (continued)

◆ Reading Strategy

UNDERSTAND THE AUTHOR'S PURPOSE

These authors write about their own lives, but their **purposes,** their reasons for writing, all relate to you. The writers want to share details of their lives to teach you, charm you, convince you, or impress you. Dillard, for example, begins "The Chase" by teaching you about herself and what she valued most in life: "concentration and courage."

1. What might Baker be trying to teach by showing his failures as well as his successes?
2. What does Dillard herself seem to learn about "concentration and courage" from the chase?
3. Why do you think she wants to share this lesson?

◆ Build Vocabulary

USING THE WORD ROOT -pel-

The root -pel- in the word *compelled* means "to push" or "to drive." Explain the meaning of each of these words:

1. *repel* (re- means "back" or "away")
2. *propel* (pro- means "forward" or "toward")
3. *expel* (ex- means "out")

SPELLING STRATEGY

Compel ends in a single consonant coming after a single vowel. It also has the accent on the final syllable. In this case, you usually double the final consonant when adding a suffix starting with a vowel: *compelled.* On your paper, correctly spell the following combinations:

1. impel + -ed   2. admit + -ing   3. refer + -ed

USING THE WORD BANK

Choose the word or phrase that is most nearly opposite in meaning to each first word:

1. gumption: (a) spunk, (b) laziness, (c) loveliness
2. paupers: (a) clerks, (b) puppets, (c) billionaires
3. crucial: (a) unimportant, (b) essential, (c) facial
4. aptitude: (a) test, (b) inability, (c) capacity
5. translucent: (a) admitting light, (b) filled with light, (c) not admitting light
6. compelled: (a) jailed, (b) ignored, (c) dreamed
7. perfunctorily: (a) excitedly, (b) deliberately, (c) jokingly

◆ Literary Focus

AUTOBIOGRAPHY

These essays come from **autobiographies,** narratives in which the authors tell their life stories. Interestingly, these authors portray themselves in opposite ways. Baker shows himself as a charming loser, a no-gumption kid who stumbles into success at the end. Dillard reveals herself as a girl *with* gumption who dives fearlessly into everything she does.

1. Explain how Baker's humorous confession of his faults makes him more appealing to readers.
2. Show how the chase Dillard describes reveals her passionate approach to life.

◆ Build Grammar Skills

PARTICIPLES AND PARTICIPIAL PHRASES

A **participle** is a verb form that acts as an adjective, modifying a noun or a pronoun. **Present participles** end in -*ing*, and **past participles** usually end in -*ed* but may have an irregular ending such as -*t* or -*en*. A **participial phrase** consists of a participle and its modifiers. Look at these examples:

present participle ⟶ noun
I could not deliver an *engaging* sales pitch.

past participle ⟶ noun
The snowball made a *smashed* star on the window.

participial phrase ⟶ pronoun
Brimming with zest, she returned with me.

Practice Identify the participles and participial phrases in these sentences. Indicate the nouns or pronouns that they modify.

1. Doris raised her fist against the closed window.
2. She threw herself mightily at his running legs.
3. Dazed by exhaustion, we froze in our tracks.
4. They ran up the sliding woodpile.
5. After an exalting pursuit, he finally caught them.

Writing Application Combine each pair of sentences by using a participle or participial phrase.

Example: He received a grade. It was passing.
He received a *passing* grade.

1. He dreaded the magazines. They were wrapped.
2. She went back. She was angry about the cheese.

Build Your Portfolio

 Idea Bank

Writing

1. **Personality Profile** Review one of these auto-biographical accounts. Then, use it to write a profile of the author, summarizing his or her qualities in a paragraph.

2. **Personal Narrative** Like Baker and Dillard, write about a brief episode from your life. Use language that appeals to the senses so that readers can share your experience. Also, tell readers why the events were important to you.

3. **Extended Definition** Write an extended definition of the word *gumption* as it is used in "No Gumption." Summarize what the word means, and draw on both essays and your own experience to give examples of this quality.

Speaking and Listening

4. **Dialogue of Authors** With a partner, act out a scene in which the young Russell Baker meets the young Annie Dillard. Review their autobiographical accounts for clues about how they would relate to each other. **[Performing Arts Link]**

5. **Oral Interpretation** You can hear the rhythm of the chase in Dillard's description of it. Capture that rhythm as you read her narrative aloud, starting from the moment that the man gets out of his car. **[Performing Arts Link]**

Projects

6. **Book Report** Read Russell Baker's *Growing Up* or Annie Dillard's *An American Childhood*, and report on it to the class. Explain how well the book reveals the author's struggles, values, and ideas about life.

7. **Multimedia Presentation** **[Group Activity]** Join with classmates to give a presentation on the Depression, the time in which Baker spent his childhood. Use film clips, recordings, photographs, news stories, and speeches to explain that time of economic hardship. **[Social Studies Link; Media Link]**

 Writing Mini-Lesson

Comparison-and-Contrast Essay

These autobiographies offer portraits of two young people. Although they grew up twenty years apart, you can introduce them in the pages of your own essay. Write a comparison-and-contrast essay of the young Russell Baker and the young Annie Dillard. Choose three or four points to show how Baker and Dillard are similar or different.

Writing Skills Focus: Clear and Logical Organization

Give your essay a **clear and logical organization** so that readers can understand your ideas. Include an introduction and a conclusion. Also, devote a paragraph to each point of comparison or contrast. Within the paragraph, you can discuss how Baker and Dillard are similar or different with regard to that point.

Model Paragraph Outline:

Paragraph Comparing Their "Gumption"
- Baker lacks it—give examples
- Dillard has it—give examples

Prewriting Focus on three or four points, and jot down similarities or differences for each. Points of comparison or contrast might include gumption, favorite activities, and interaction with adults.

Drafting Referring to your notes, write a paragraph for each point of comparison or contrast. Write the introduction and conclusion after you have written the body of your essay.

> ◆ **Grammar Application**
> Use participles and participial phrases to combine short sentences.

Revising Be sure that your essay has an introduction that explains your purpose and a conclusion that summarizes your findings. The body of your essay should contain separate paragraphs for each point on which you compare or contrast the authors.

Guide for Reading

Meet the Authors:

H.N. Levitt (1920–   )

H.N. Levitt was born and raised in New York City. During World War II, he was a naval officer. After the war, he pursued a career as a playwright and a college professor of drama.

THE STORY BEHIND THE ESSAY

Levitt has always loved the visual arts as well as drama. He learned how to paint at a well-known art school, and he has written often about painters. In this essay, he describes the life and career of the nineteenth-century American artist Winslow Homer.

William W. Lace (1942–   )

A native of Fort Worth, Texas, William W. Lace worked for newspapers before joining the University of Texas at Arlington as sports information director. Later, he became the director of college relations for a junior college in Fort Worth.

Lace and his wife, Laura, a public school librarian, live in Arlington, Texas, with their two children. His wife and her book-hungry students inspired Lace to write about Nolan Ryan for young people.

◆ LITERATURE AND YOUR LIFE

CONNECT YOUR EXPERIENCE

What do you see in the painting on the opposite page? Do you see the work of a contemporary artist or the achievements of all-time strikeout king Nolan Ryan? If you combine these answers, you might see the artist's power—through broad strokes and bright colors—to shape the way you see the athlete. As you read these biographies, think about the way the writers shape your understanding of their subjects.

THEMATIC FOCUS: Wishes, Hopes, Dreams

What do these essays tell you about the goals and ambitions of their subjects?

◆ Background for Understanding

MATHEMATICS

Numbers don't tell the whole story of a life. However, you can suggest people's achievements with statistics, a numerical measure of what they've accomplished. Nolan Ryan's statistics include 5,714 strikeouts, the major league record. The artist Winslow Homer used his arm more gently but just as effectively. He created about 1,000 paintings.

◆ Build Vocabulary

PREFIXES: *sub-*

Levitt's essay explains that many nineteenth-century American painters depicted African Americans in "subservient poses." *Subservient*, meaning "inferior," combines the prefix *sub-*, meaning "under" or "below," with a word part meaning "to serve."

cantankerous
subtle
brutality
vanquished
serenity
subservient
hostility

WORD BANK

Which three words from the essays have the same suffix, indicating that they are nouns?

Winslow Homer: America's Greatest Painter
◆ Nolan Ryan, Texas Treasure ◆

Nolan Ryan, LeRoy Neiman

◆ Literary Focus

BIOGRAPHY

A **biography** is the story of someone's life told by someone else. Usually, authors write about a famous subject—someone known and of interest to many people. Biographers not only tell you the facts of their subject's lives, they also explain what these facts mean.

◆ Reading Strategy

SET A PURPOSE FOR READING

Setting a purpose, or goal, for reading will help you get the most out of a biography or any other piece of writing. Often, you can phrase your purpose in terms of a question. The titles of these two biographical essays suggest purpose-setting questions to guide your reading. You might ask about Homer, "What makes him America's greatest painter?" You might ask about Ryan, "Why is he a Texas treasure?" Use a KWL chart like the one below to record your answers:

K	W	L
What do I know about Homer?	**What do I want to know about Homer?**	**What have I learned about Homer?**
(Fill this in before you read.)	**Purpose-setting question:** Why is he America's greatest painter?	(Fill this in by answering your question as you read.)

Winslow Homer:
America's Greatest Painter   H. N. Levitt

Prisoners from the Front, 1866, Winslow Homer, The Metropolitan Museum of Art

▲ **Critical Viewing** What can you learn about the Civil War from this painting by Homer? **[Infer]**

*H*is oil paintings and watercolors are in all major American museums and collections today. But even when Winslow Homer was alive, they called him America's greatest painter.

That wasn't all they said about him. They also called him crusty, bad-tempered, <u>cantankerous</u>, grouchy, sour as a crab, and surly as a bear. He was all those things, and more.

His brother's wife—and Winslow's only female friend—thought Homer the most courteous gentleman she ever knew. She said he knew what he wanted in life, and he went about getting it without any fuss or feathers.

When it came to painting, he took five lessons, decided that was enough, then went on to become a self-taught genius.

Homer was born into a middle-class family on Feb. 24, 1836. The family lived near the harbor in Boston, so Homer's earliest memories were of ships, sailors, fishermen and the sea.

When he was six, the family moved to Cambridge, directly across the street from Harvard College. Sometimes Winslow's dad would suggest that the boy consider attending Harvard someday. But it was no use. All young Winslow wanted to do was fish and draw.

After a while, the family realized there was something special about Winslow, because that's all he would do—fish and draw, day in and day out, all year long.

But even if Homer had wanted to go to college, there would have been no money for it. When Homer was 13, his dad sold all and left to make his fortune in the California gold rush. He came back a few years later empty-handed.

But the family remained close. And once they realized how important art was to Homer, they encouraged it. In fact, his brothers secretly bought up his paintings at early exhibitions so he wouldn't get discouraged if no one else bought them. Those two brothers remained his best friends all his life.

When the Civil War broke out in 1861, Homer was a young artist already on his way to fame. As a freelance illustrator for *Harper's Weekly,* America's most important news magazine, he was considered one of the country's finest wood-block engravers.

In those days, an artist would cut illustrations into a wood block, which was then inked in black and printed on sheets of paper. Techniques like <u>subtle</u> shadowing and distant perspective were hard to achieve, but Homer's illustrations were unusually lively and strong.

Harper's Weekly offered Homer a good job, and he could have remained a weekly illustrator all his life. But he wanted to work for no one but himself, so he turned the offer down.

Homer left New York to paint the war. He joined Gen. George McClellan's Army of the Potomac[1] as a freelance artist-correspondent. He painted scenes at the siege of Yorktown[2] and did many drawings of Abraham Lincoln, the tall, gaunt, serious president who was desperately trying to keep the Union together.

In a few short years, Homer's Civil War paintings brought him fame at home and abroad. He painted war as no other artist ever had. He emphasized not <u>brutality</u> but rather scenes of loneliness, camp life, endless waiting, and even horseplay on the battlefield.

Homer was a Yankee,[3] but he showed equal concern for soldiers from both the North and South. His paintings did not glorify war; they seemed to cry out for it to end.

◆ Literary Focus
What do you learn about Homer from the way in which he depicted the Civil War?

His *Prisoners from the Front* made a reputation overnight. This one painting, done in Homer's honest, realistic style, showed the common humanity that linked North and South, victor and <u>vanquished</u>, Americans all. Homer's war paintings give us the best record we have of how the Civil War soldier actually looked and acted.

After the war, railroads and new industries changed America from a rural to an industrial society almost overnight. But Homer paid no attention. He went back to painting the things he liked: country scenes, farmers, beautiful women in fashionable clothes, and kids at play.

He never painted kids with the gushy sentimentalism of other American painters. And he didn't look down on young people. His paintings showed what was then a typical American upbeat attitude marked by humor and innocence. The public loved it.

And then something strange happened. Homer stopped painting. For three years, his brushes sat idle. He left his studio for Europe, but avoided the art world in Paris. Instead, he went to Tynemouth, England, a small fishing port on the North Sea.

It was there, at Tynemouth, that Winslow Homer witnessed the fierce, day-to-day struggle of men and women against the sea. Their

---

3. **Yankee:** Native or inhabitant of a northern state.

---

1. **Gen. George McClellan's Army of the Potomac:** McClellan served for a time as the general in chief of the Union Army during the Civil War. The Union Army in the East was known as the Army of the Potomac.
2. **Yorktown:** Yorktown, Virginia, which Gen. McClellan occupied on May 4, 1862.

◆ **Build Vocabulary**
cantankerous (kan taŋ′ kər əs) *adj.*: Quarrelsome; argumentative
subtle (sut′ əl) *adj.*: Delicately skillful or clever
brutality (broō tal′ ə tē) *n.*: Violence; harshness
vanquished (vaŋ′ kwisht) *n.*: The person defeated (usually a verb)

The Gulf Stream, 1899, Winslow Homer, The Metropolitan Museum of Art

▲ Critical Viewing What is conveyed more strongly to you in this painting—the man's predicament or the power of the sea? Explain. [Assess]

hard, bitter, dangerous lives made him think critically about his own life and work.

After that, women, children and country life appeared less often in his paintings. What replaced them was the harsh existence of men of the sea. These heroic people became, in his mind, the best examples of mankind. That's apparent in his famous painting *The Life Line*. To Homer, the sea had lost its serenity and had become a powerful force of nature.

Homer began painting larger pictures too, and his style became more bold and powerful. Some complained that his paintings now looked unfinished. But he didn't care. Nice finishing touches were no longer important.

Besides the sea and its people, Homer started painting scenes of the American wilderness. He did big, masculine pictures of hunting and fishing, canoeing the rapids, sitting around the campfire and trekking over rugged trails.

He painted large oils, but he also painted many watercolors. By the time he had hit his stride, he had become America's first great watercolor painter. It was he who developed the technique of using the white, unpainted paper as sparkling highlight.

Then, at 48, when he was selling just about everything he painted, he did another about-face.

He surprised his family, friends and fellow artists by turning his back on the city and the world of art. He packed up and left to spend the rest of his life—27 years—as a hermit on a rocky cliff overlooking the sea in Prouts Neck, Maine.

In typical, cantankerous, Yankee fashion, when asked how he could leave New York, the scene of his success, he said, "I left New York to escape jury duty."

In a more serious mood, he told his brother that his new, lonely life was the only setting in which he could do his work in peace, free from visitors and publicity seekers.

◆ **Literature and Your Life**
Have you ever made a snap decision to change—like the one described here?

Winslow Homer finally came to love his life. It was at Prouts Neck that he finished one of his great masterpieces, *The Gulf Stream*, in 1899.

This painting showed a black man marooned in a broken-masted boat circled by sharks in the Gulf Stream.[4] It was an immediate sensation, but only one of a long series of oils and watercolors that Homer painted of American blacks. This was at a time when blacks were usually depicted as minstrel singers and servants, or in other <u>subservient</u> poses.

In his last years, Homer made another big change. Instead of painting scenes of men struggling against the sea and wilderness, he started painting the sea and wilderness alone.

Like a stubborn tree growing out of a rock, he stood on his lonely cliff and painted the sea, forever untamed and uncontrolled by man.

In 1910, just before he died, he wrote in a letter, "All is lovely outside my house and inside my house and myself." Winslow Homer was a simple, modest, unsentimental man—the kind of American we Americans like.

---

4. **Gulf Stream:** Warm ocean current flowing from the Gulf of Mexico along the east coast of the United States.

◆ **Build Vocabulary**

serenity (sə ren′ ə tē) *n.*: Calmness
subservient (səb sur′ vē ənt) *adj.*: Inferior

Guide for Responding

◆ LITERATURE AND YOUR LIFE

Reader's Response Would you like to have known Winslow Homer? Why or why not?

Thematic Focus What do you think Homer wanted to achieve with his art when he reached old age?

Journal Writing Study one of the paintings that accompany this essay. In a journal entry, describe your response to the work.

☑ Check Your Comprehension

1. What caused Homer's family to realize there was "something special" about him?
2. In what ways did Homer's Civil War pictures differ from those of other artists?
3. How did Homer's work change after he lived in England?
4. Why did Homer leave New York to live in Maine?
5. What change occurred in his painting during his "last years"?

◆ Critical Thinking

INTERPRET

1. In what ways did Homer gain strength from his family? **[Infer]**
2. In your own words, summarize the direction that Homer's art took from the time he returned from the Civil War until his death. **[Analyze]**
3. What do you think might have caused Homer to stop painting for three years? **[Hypothesize]**
4. How does the essay show that Homer "knew what he wanted in life"? **[Support]**

EVALUATE

5. Levitt suggests that simplicity, modesty, and lack of sentimentality are values that most Americans share. Explain why you agree or disagree. **[Make a Judgment]**

EXTEND

6. How would you describe the mood of Homer's painting *The Gulf Stream*? Support your answer with details from the picture. **[Art Link]**

Nolan Ryan, TEXAS TREASURE

William W. Lace

A generation has passed since Nolan Ryan threw his first major league pitch. His fellow players are sometimes just as eager as fans to get his autograph. Texas third baseman Steve Buchele, a southern California native, said, "There wasn't anything more exciting than coming to the games and watching Nolan pitch."

How has Ryan lasted so long? He claims that it's a combination of physical condition and mental attitude.

Ryan has always taken good care of his body. Even after the biggest of games, like his seventh no-hitter, he was up early, working out. "We're working against the clock," he told a reporter. "I can't do this forever. I haven't got much time."

◆ **Reading Strategy**
What clues in this passage help answer the purpose-setting question "Why is Ryan a treasure?"

He learned a balanced, healthy diet from his mother, who took pride in putting wholesome meals on the Ryan family table. Even as a young player he was careful about what he ate. He's even more careful now, avoiding meats like bacon or sausage, cream soups, and any other food high in fat. He doesn't eat fried foods and doesn't often eat large meals. When he snacks, he usually chooses fruit.

Ryan's physical conditioning has kept him going long after most players his age have retired. He stays fit during the winter, and during the season, maintains a workout schedule

of weightlifting, throwing, and running that almost never changes. The times are very different from his early days in baseball, when all a pitcher did between starts was throw enough each day to stay loose.

Mental fitness probably has been just as important. Even after 26 major-league seasons, baseball is still fun and challenging to Ryan. Yet, even though it's his living, baseball isn't his whole life. He spends as much time at home with his family as he can. He is keenly interested in cattle raising and operates three ranches in addition to his property near Alvin. He has many other business interests and spends much time on charity work.

The talented pitcher has not allowed fame and fortune to change his personality, as many star athletes have. Ryan remains what he always was—a modest, uncomplicated, man from a middle-class, family-centered background.

"I still represent small-town Texas, and that's fine with me," he once said. "I'm still like the people who lived where I grew up. I've kept my roots. I'm proud of that."

If you didn't know differently, you'd think Ryan was the man next door, working hard to put food on the table and tires on the car. "If you saw him in a shopping mall or talked

▼ Critical Viewing Ryan is carried off the field after throwing his record-breaking seventh no-hitter. What details in this photograph tell you this is a historic moment? [Analyze]

Guide for Responding (continued)

◆ Reading Strategy

SET A PURPOSE FOR READING

When you **set a purpose** for reading by deciding what you want to learn, you help yourself to get the information you want. If your purpose was to discover why Homer was America's greatest painter, you learned several facts to support this idea. For instance, Homer's paintings of the Civil War showed the "humanity" of soldiers on both sides.

Name two facts that each of these purpose-setting questions would have uncovered.

1. In what ways did Homer's family influence him?
2. Why was Ryan able to have such a long career?

◆ Build Vocabulary

USING THE PREFIX *sub-*

Use the meaning of the prefix *sub-* ("under" or "below") to define the italicized words in this paragraph:

His performance was *subnormal* tonight. Now, he's *submerging* his arm in ice water. Even if he's not aware of them, questions must be going through the levels of his *subconscious* mind. Can he rise above his *substandard* performance?

SPELLING STRATEGY

When adding suffixes to words ending with e, you usually keep the e when the suffix begins with a consonant but drop the e when the suffix begins with a vowel:

subtle + -ty = subtlety   hostile + -ity = hostility
noise + -less = noiseless   like + -able = likable

On your paper, spell these combinations:

1. place + -ment =
2. voice + -ing =
3. space + -ious =
4. survive + -ing =

USING THE WORD BANK

On your paper, match each word in the first column with its definition in the second column

1. subtle
2. brutality
3. vanquished
4. serenity
5. cantankerous
6. subservient
7. hostility

a. person defeated
b. calmness
c. feeling of unfriendliness
d. delicately skillful
e. argumentative
f. violence
g. inferior

◆ Literary Focus

BIOGRAPHY

A **biography** is an author's account of the facts and meaning of another person's life. The biographical essay on Ryan, for example, tells you about the facts of his career with the Texas Rangers. It weaves these facts together to present a general idea of the man: He is an ordinary guy with extraordinary skills.

1. Find three examples in Homer's biography that show him as a talented but stubborn loner.
2. Name three facts in Ryan's biography that depict him as ordinary off the field and extraordinary on it.

◆ Build Grammar Skills

APPOSITIVES AND APPOSITIVE PHRASES

An **appositive** is a noun placed near another noun or pronoun to explain it. An **appositive phrase** is an appositive and the words that modify it. Appositives and appositive phrases are often set off from the sentence by commas or dashes. Look at these examples:

Appositive: Ryan, *the pitcher*, reached the mound.
Appositive Phrase: Homer loved to paint scenes of the ocean, *the most untamed part of nature*.

Practice On your paper, identify the appositive phrase in each of these sentences. Then, indicate what it explains.

1. His brother's wife, Winslow's only female friend, called Homer a courteous gentleman.
2. Homer left New York, the scene of his success.
3. He finished one of his great masterpieces, *The Gulf Stream*, in 1899.
4. Ryan's seventh no-hitter—one for the records—brought the team a victory over Toronto.
5. Texas third baseman Steve Buchele, a southern California native, was Ryan's teammate.

Writing Application Rewrite these sentences, inserting an appositive or an appositive phrase.

1. Winslow Homer painted in watercolors and oils.
2. During the Civil War, Homer did many drawings of Abraham Lincoln.
3. Ryan is an inspiration to many young athletes.

Build Your Portfolio

 ## Idea Bank

Writing

1. **Baseball Card** Using the following information and the essay on Ryan, design and write the text for a baseball card that summarizes his career: lifetime wins—324; lifetime losses—292; strike-outs—5,714; walks—2,795. **[Art Link]**

2. **Song of Praise** Write a song honoring the achievements of a person you admire. Describe some of those achievements in the song. Also, create a catchy phrase about this person that you can repeat in your lyrics.

3. **Proposal for a Documentary** Write to a television station proposing a documentary film on Homer, Ryan, or a person of your choice. Convince the station's director that the person is worth the attention and that his or her life could inspire a dramatic film. **[Media Link; Career Link]**

Speaking and Listening

4. **Gallery Talk** Imagine that you're giving a talk about the Homer paintings on pages 586 and 588. Explain to museum visitors what is worth noticing about the subjects and about Homer's portrayal of them. **[Art Link; Career Link]**

5. **Award Presentation** As the emcee at a formal dinner, present Winslow Homer or Nolan Ryan with a lifetime achievement award. In your speech, explain why the prize is well deserved.

Projects

6. **Book Circle [Group Activity]** Form a group to read and discuss a biography of a well-known person. Each student should read the book with a different purpose, in order to bring a fresh point of view to the discussion. Then, a group member can sum up the discussion for the class.

7. **Biographical Report** Research the life of someone who interests you. Collect facts and photographs about your subject's career and achievements. Share your report with the class.

 ## Writing Mini-Lesson

Instructional Guide

Nolan Ryan probably knows all the tricks of the trade when it comes to pitching. However, you know the secrets for success in the activities that you do. Publish those secrets in a manual, giving a step-by-step explanation of how to perform a task or a feat that you have mastered.

Writing Skills Focus: Thoroughness

Readers who aren't as familiar with the task as you are may stumble if you leave out some of the steps. That's why **thoroughness,** a complete presentation of details, is essential in a how-to essay. H. N. Levitt shows thoroughness in his biographical essay by explaining wood-block engraving.

Model From the Essay

In those days, an artist would cut illustrations into a wood block, which was then inked in black and printed on sheets of paper.

Prewriting Choose an activity that you understand completely, and jot down all the steps that go into it. Also, jot down positive phrases you can use to encourage readers.

Drafting Remember that you're writing for beginners. Make the activity seem worthwhile, and describe the steps that you might take for granted because of your experience.

Revising Have a classmate who isn't familiar with the activity read your essay. Whenever a passage confuses your classmate, add further explanations or insert steps you may have left out.

◆ **Grammar Application**

Use appositive phrases to clarify your explanations. Here's an example:

Attach the kite frame, *the two crossed sticks*, to the paper.

Biographical Report

Writing Process Workshop

Certain people intrigue us. Maybe for you, it's sports heroes, political leaders, great explorers, or famous artists. One way to learn more about a person you admire is to research and write a **biographical report.** This kind of writing gives information about a person's life and achievements. Though this report will convey mostly facts, it should also include your own ideas about what makes the person noteworthy. These skills, covered in the Writing Mini-Lessons in this part, will help:

Writing Skills Focus

▶ **Clarify your main points.** Decide what is most interesting or important about your subject, and then focus on those ideas. (See p. 562.)

▶ **Use a clear and logical organization** to help readers follow the story of your subject's life. Chronological order—from first event to last event—may be best. (See p. 583.)

▶ **Tell the story thoroughly.** Be sure you've covered the most important elements of your subject's life. Don't leave out key events. (See p. 595.)

"Winslow Homer: America's Greatest Painter" inspired this writer to study another American great. She uses the skills above in the introduction to a report on Georgia O'Keeffe.

MODEL

Everyone has a different idea about who is America's greatest painter. In my opinion, it's a woman who began a new style and gave women artists a new role model. ① That woman was Georgia O'Keeffe (1887–1986). ② O'Keeffe painted hundreds of masterpieces in her very long life. ③

① This sentence expresses the two main ideas of this report: O'Keeffe began a new style, and she served as a role model.

② All facts—including dates—are 100 percent accurate.

③ This sentence suggests that this report will trace her very long life, from beginning to end, in clear, chronological order.

Prewriting

Identify Your Subject The first step, of course, is to choose a person to study. You'll want to choose someone whom you admire and want to write about. It's also important that there is ample information available. Here are some general ideas:

> ### Topic Ideas
> - World leader
> - Sports star
> - Writer or artist
> - Great entertainer

Research Use more than one source to find your information: library reference books, on-line sources, biographies, video documentaries. Keep track of exactly what sources you use. Include facts that answer questions such as these:

- When and where was he/she born?
- When did he/she get interested in his/her life work?
- How did he/she begin his/her career?
- What were the highlights of his/her life?
- For what is he/she most known or remembered?

Make a Timeline With any writing that is organized chronologically, it's helpful to make a timeline to organize details. Begin with your subject's birth, and move through the years.

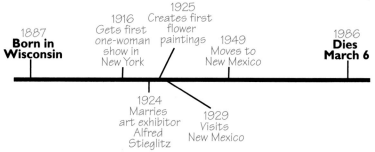

Include a Portrait Sometimes, a picture can say a thousand words. If possible, include a copy of a photograph or portrait of your subject.

Drafting

Write Your Main Idea Before you begin to draft, pause and think: What quality or idea is most important about this person? Write a sentence that expresses your original idea. Use this sentence in your report.

APPLYING LANGUAGE SKILLS: Documenting Sources

At the end of your report, include a **bibliography**—a list of all the sources you've used. Bibliographies are arranged alphabetically. Look at the format and the information included in these examples:

Encyclopedia: "O'Keeffe, Georgia," *Encyclopedia Britannica,* Vol. 25, 1990, pp. 49–74.

Book: Moore, Lisa. *Artists of Courage: Georgia O'Keeffe.* New York: Acme Publishing, 1997.

Article: Brown, Sherrill. "Flowers and Bones: The Art of Georgia O'Keeffe." *Painters and Gardeners Monthly,* November 1992, pp. 90–98.

Practice Make corrections in this bibliography entry for a book. There are four mistakes.

> Smith, Thale, American Painters. Boston, Brown Publishing, Inc.

Writing Application When writing your biographical report, be sure to document your sources accurately and completely.

Writer's Solution Connection Writing Lab

For more about documenting sources, see the Drafting section of the Reports tutorial.

APPLYING LANGUAGE SKILLS: Avoiding Double Negatives

Negative words, such as *never* or *not,* are used in sentences to deny something. Some writers mistakenly use **double negatives**—two negative words—when one alone is needed. Notice how this example can be corrected in two ways.

Double Negative:
She didn't learn from no one.

Corrected Sentence:
She didn't learn from anyone.

She learned from no one.

Practice Correct the double negatives in these sentences.

1. O'Keeffe never suggests nothing original.
2. She didn't make no excuses for her art.
3. She hasn't got no competition.

Writing Application As you edit your biographical report, correct any double negatives you have included.

Writer's Solution Connection Language Lab

For more practice, see the Avoiding Double Negatives lesson on the Language Lab CD-ROM.

Choose Active Verbs As you draft your report, choose your verbs carefully. Don't settle for too many *be* verbs. Avoid common, bland verbs like *make, have, do, go,* or *say.* Picture your verbs moving your reader along through the person's life.

Include Time Transitions Words and phrases such as the ones listed here will help your reader keep track of the passage of time, an important factor in biographical writing.

Time Transitions			
after two years	during	formerly	second
as soon as	earlier	in the end	since
at first	eventually	later	soon
at the same time	finally	meanwhile	then
before	first	next	while

Revising

Check Facts and Document Sources As you revise, be your own best editor. Go back to your notes or the books, magazines, or on-line sites you used. Check all your facts. Confirm dates and names. As you fact-check, prepare your bibliography. Be careful and complete.

Create a Catchier Title Take a second look at your title. Many biography titles include the subject's name and a phrase that suggests the main idea. It's a good chance for some word play, but don't go overboard.

Use a Peer Reviewer Ask a classmate to read your report. Together, discuss the following:
▶ Does the title fit?
▶ Does the writing flow smoothly?
▶ Where should information be added? Deleted?
▶ What was the essay's strongest part? Weakest?

Publishing and Presenting

Anthology of Biographies Combine your report with those of others in a class anthology. Include portraits, if possible. Choose a title, and prepare a table of contents. Make your anthology available to students in other classes.

Ballad Ballads are songs that tell stories—often tales of legendary or famous people. Take the information from your report, and add a sense of humor, rhyme, and rhythm. Write a refrain, or set of lines to be repeated. You might even set your ballad to music. Then, share your poetic biography with classmates.

Strategies for Success

Wouldn't it be great to have a *User's Guide to Your Life*—a book that gave you all the answers? It would tell you how to make the baseball team, how to do better in math, or how to tell jokes. In reality, the answers to your questions are scattered in hundreds of manuals, books, and encyclopedias. You can find these answers by reading for specific information.

Practice the Moves Learn the moves that will get you through the maze of a reference book. For example, use the sections of a book that may seem as dull as a telephone directory: the table of contents (in the front) and the index (at the back). The table of contents outlines the book's organization. The index is an alphabetized list of the book's subjects. Use them both to get fast facts.

Let Your Fingers Do the Walking Most reference books are not meant to be read cover to cover. By moving your finger and scanning down the table of contents or the index, you'll find the page numbers to direct you to the specific information you need.

Find Key Words When you turn to the page you need, look again for the key word you need, especially in the headings or captions or boldfaced in the text.

Apply the Strategies

Use the table of contents and the index on this page to answer these questions about information in an arts and literature almanac:

1. Which chapter will probably have information on prime-time television? On which page does that chapter begin?

2. Which chapter will probably have information on Andy Warhol and other popular painters? On which page does that chapter begin?

3. On what pages will you find information on the movie *E.T.?*

4. On what pages will you find information about the Academy Awards?

✔ You may also read for specific information in:
► Atlases
► Textbooks
► Works of nonfiction
► Encyclopedias

Almanac of the Arts and Literature of Our Time

Contents

Index

Grammar Review

A **phrase** is a group of words that functions in a sentence as a single part of speech. Phrases do not contain subjects or verbs.

An appositive is a noun or a pronoun placed next to another noun or pronoun to identify or explain it. An **appositive phrase** contains an appositive and its modifiers. (See page 594.)

> ┌── appositive phrase ──┐
> Russell Baker, *an award-winning journalist,* sold magazines as a boy.

A **participial phrase** functions as an adjective. (See page 582.) A participle is a verb form that acts as an adjective. Present participles end in *-ing,* and past participles usually end in *-ed,* but they may have an irregular ending such as *-t* or *-en.* A participial phrase contains a participle and its modifiers.

> ┌participial phrase┐
> *Blazing past batters,* the ball can't be hit.

> ┌participial phrase┐
> *Amazed by its speed,* hitters stand motionless.

Practice 1 Identify the appositive phrases and participial phrases in the sentences below. Identify which word each participial phrase modifies, and tell what word each appositive phrase identifies.

1. Biographies, the written stories of people's lives, can teach readers.

2. Engrossed in someone else's struggles, you might understand yourself better.

3. Disappointed by events, Winslow Homer made several changes in his life.

4. Even he, a world-famous painter, had to re-evaluate his work.

5. Reading about his courage, we may feel more inclined to make changes.

phrase (frāz) *n.* 1 a group of words that is not a complete sentence, but that gives a single idea, usually as a separate part of a sentence ["Drinking fresh milk," "with meals," and "to be healthy" are phrases.]

Practice 2 Write original sentences using the following phrases, as indicated.

1. the captain of the ship (appositive phrase)

2. a beautiful song (appositive phrase)

3. a mistake with serious consequences (appositive phrase)

4. laughing uncontrollably (participial phrase)

5. wondering about tomorrow (participial phrase)

6. pleased with the news (participial phrase)

Grammar in Writing

✔ *Phrases can help you pack meaning into a sentence. Notice how two sentences can become a single, more informative, one:*

Short Sentences:

Annie Dillard threw snowballs.

She experienced an exciting adventure.

Combined With a Participial Phrase:

While throwing snowballs, Annie Dillard experienced an exciting adventure.

Look for places in your writing to add sophistication with phrases.

Part 2 *Types of Essays*

Untitled, Ivan Lee Sanford

Guide for Reading

Meet the Authors:

Charles Kuralt (1934–1997)

Charles Kuralt was the youngest correspondent ever to work at CBS News. Though he anchored with the network, he is probably best remembered for a series he did called *On the Road*. For 13 years, he crossed the country, filing stories that would reveal the flavor of the nation. "Independence Hall" is one of those reports.

Marjorie Kinnan Rawlings (1896–1953)

After starting out as a journalist, Rawlings moved to rural Florida. Later, she would use this region as the setting of her novel *The Yearling*. "Rattlesnake Hunt" introduces you to a scary inhabitant of this area.

Ernesto Galarza (1905–1984)

As a child, Ernesto Galarza moved from Mexico to California. His family struggled to make ends meet, but Galarza eventually became a teacher and writer. In *Barrio Boy*, he tells about his childhood.

Chief Dan George (1899–1981)

A member of the Squamish Indian Band in Canada, Chief Dan George became an actor late in life. He received an Academy Award nomination for his role in *Little Big Man* (1971).

Barbara Jordan (1936–1996)

Barbara Jordan was the first black Texan elected to Congress. She served three terms and gave a major speech at the 1976 Democratic National Convention.

◆ LITERATURE AND YOUR LIFE

CONNECT YOUR EXPERIENCE

Everywhere you look, words leap out at you: STOP, GO, BUY, TURN LEFT, PAY HERE. Nobody speaks these words. They're just written on signs, advertisements, and machines.

An essay is the opposite of these impersonal messages. It contains the words of an individual who speaks to you quietly, directly, and personally.

THEMATIC FOCUS: Wishes, Hopes, Dreams

How do the essays express each author's viewpoint or goals?

◆ Background for Understanding

LITERATURE

In 1580, the Frenchman Montaigne (män tän´) first used the word *essai* to describe a brief prose work. This French word means "try," and Montaigne's essays were "tries" at understanding. The form caught on, finding its way into the earliest magazines. Today, not only can you read essays in magazines and newspapers, you can "see" them on television.

◆ Build Vocabulary

WORD ROOTS: -mort-

The word root *-mort-*, meaning "death," is usually associated with life-and-death matters. In "Rattlesnake Hunt," Rawlings refers to a snake's "mortality," meaning "the fact that it must die": *mortal* ("having to die") + *-ity* ("the fact of").

WORD BANK

Which word from these essays replaces the author's name when the author of a piece is unknown? Check the Build Vocabulary boxes to see if you chose correctly.

anonymous
unanimously
desolate
mortality
formidable
communal
tolerant

Independence Hall ◆ Rattlesnake Hunt
from Barrio Boy ◆ I Am a Native of North America
All Together Now

◆ Literary Focus

ESSAY

An **essay** is a brief prose work in which an author expresses his or her view of a subject. These are the most common types of essays:

- A **narrative essay** is a true story that may focus on a character other than the writer.
- A **descriptive essay** uses vivid sensory details to describe people or places.
- A **personal essay** is an informal account of an episode from a person's own life.
- A **reflective essay** presents a writer's thoughts about ideas or experiences.
- A **persuasive essay** is a series of arguments presented to convince readers to believe or act in a certain way.

In reading, notice the qualities that help you categorize the essays in this group.

◆ Reading Strategy

IDENTIFY MAIN POINTS

Many essays have several **main points,** important ideas that the author wants to convey. The rest of the essay contains ideas, examples, stories, or statistics that support these points. By finding and keeping in mind the main points, you'll be sure to get the message that the author wanted to send.

Most of these authors state their main points directly or give you a clue to them at the beginning or the end of the essay. Use a chart like the one below to identify the main points:

Passage	Hint in Passage	Main Point
John Adams... said, "... The bridge is cut away."	Cutting a bridge means you can't go back.	There was no turning back once the Declaration of Independence was signed.

Independence Hall
Charles Kuralt

The Declaration of Independence, John Trumball, Yale University Art Gallery

▲ **Critical Viewing** What details of this painting convey the importance of the moment that the Declaration of Independence was signed? **[Infer]**

"I say let us wait." John Dickinson of Pennsylvania stood in this hall, July 1st, 1776, and begged the Continental Congress to be reasonable. "The time is not yet ripe for proclaiming independence. Instead of help from foreign powers, it will bring us disaster. I say we ought to hold back any declaration and remain the masters of our fate and our fame. All of Great Britain is armed against us. The wealth of the Empire is poured into her treasury. We shall weep at our folly."

John Dickinson was not a timid or frightened man. He was a great old Quaker patriot, and he had a good argument. At the moment he spoke, British grenadiers[1] were sweeping down from Canada, British guns were bombarding Charleston, and just ninety miles away an incredible British armada was entering New York harbor—five hundred ships carrying thirty-two thousand troops, the best army in the world. That army could march to Philadelphia and take this building and arrest this Congress any afternoon it chose to do so. So John

◆ **Literary Focus**
How can you tell that this essay tells a story?

---

1. **grenadiers** (gren´ ə dirz´) *n.*: Soldiers in a special unit of the British Army attached to the royal household.

Dickinson pleaded, "Let us not brave the storm in a paper boat."

The delegates paid him respectful attention. John Adams and his cousin, Sam, hot for independence, impatient with the delay, sat listening. Thomas Jefferson sat back in the corner. He had already written the Declaration of Independence. It spoke his thoughts. Beside him, old Benjamin Franklin, also silent, his mind made up.

But every mind was not made up. Pennsylvania and South Carolina were opposed to independence; Delaware divided; New York undecided. All through the spring and into the summer they had sat here and wrangled, their tempers growing hot with the season. Young Edward Rutledge of South Carolina had said of John Adams and the New Englanders, "They will bring us ruin. I dread their low cunning and those leveling principles which men without character and without fortune possess." And John Adams had said of Rutledge, "Rutledge is a perfect bobolink, a swallow, a sparrow, a peacock, excessively vain, excessively weak."

Now, Rutledge and Adams and the rest listened to John Dickinson speaking gravely from the heart: "Declaring our independence at a time like this is like burning down our house before we have another."

It was John Adams who rose to his feet. He was not John Dickinson's equal as a speaker, and everything he had to say he had said before. He never said it better than on that July afternoon: "We've been duped and bubbled by the phantom of peace. What is the real choice before us? If we postpone the declaration, do we mean to submit? Do we consent to yield and become a conquered people? No, we do not! We shall fight! We shall fight with whatever means we have—with rusty muskets and broken flints, with bows and arrows, if need be. Then why put off the declaration? For myself, I can only say this: I have crossed the Rubicon.[2] All that I have, all that I am, all that I hope for in this life, I stake on our cause. For me, the die is cast. Sink or swim, live or die, to survive or perish with my country—that is my unalterable resolution!"

That night, John Dickinson went home, put on his militia uniform, and rode away to join his regiment. He could not vote for independence, but he could fight the British. That night, Edward Rutledge changed his mind. South Carolina would not stand in the way of unanimity. That night, Caesar Rodney, a man dying of cancer, rode through the night on horseback in a storm to Philadelphia to cast the deciding vote for Delaware. And so, when Secretary Charles Thomson called the roll on July 2nd, of the twelve colonies voting, all twelve voted for Independence. It was done. What remained was the declaring it.

The next morning, July 3rd, an <u>anonymous</u> note was found on President Hancock's table. It said, "You have gone too far. Take care. A plot is framed for your destruction, and all of you shall be destroyed." It suddenly occurred to them that there might be a lighted powder keg under the floor; there was an uproar. There were volunteers to search the cellar. Then crusty old Joseph Hewes of North Carolina stood up to say, "Mr. President, I am against wasting any time searching cellars. I would as soon be blown to pieces as proclaim to the world that I was frightened by a note."

Without searching any cellars, the Continental Congress proceeded to a consideration of the Declaration of Independence. They're immortal words now, but of course they weren't when Charles Thomson read them for the first time: "When in the Course of human events . . ." And for two days Jefferson sat back in the corner and fumed as they all toyed with his masterpiece. "Did we really have to call the King a tyrant quite so often?" They changed some of the "tyrants" back to "King." "Did we have to bid the British people our everlasting adieu?" They

> ◆ **Reading Strategy**
> How does this passage suggest that the delegates may have been uncertain about the outcome of events?

---

2. **Rubicon** (roo͞´ bə kän) *n.*: A limiting line that when crossed commits a person to an unchangeable decision.

◆ **Build Vocabulary**

anonymous (ə nän´ ə məs) *adj.*: Unsigned; written by a person whose name is unknown

struck that out. And Jefferson's mightiest passage, his denunciation[3] of slavery, that was struck out, too, at the insistence of Georgia and South Carolina. Jefferson wrote elsewhere, "Nothing is more certainly written in the book of fate than that these people are to be free."

But finally, all the cuts and changes were done, and what remained was a document still noble enough to inspire the tired delegates and bold enough to hang them all. It was read through one more time to the end: ". . . And for the support of this Declaration, with a firm reliance on the Protection of Divine Providence, we mutually pledge to each other our Lives, our Fortunes and our sacred Honor." There was one final vote, and President Hancock announced the result with the use of a new

phrase: "The Declaration of the United States of America is unanimously agreed to." There was no cheering, no fireworks; not yet. The delegates simply walked out into the night of the Fourth of July thinking their own thoughts, some of them no doubt remembering what John Dickinson had said: "This is like burning down our house before we have another." Others hearing Tom Paine: "The birthday of a new world is at hand. We have it in our power to begin the world all over again."

John Adams walked to his boardinghouse to write a letter to a friend. "Well," he said, "the river is passed. The bridge is cut away."

◆ **Build Vocabulary**

unanimously (yoo nan′ ə məs lē) *adv.*: Overwhelmingly; without disagreement

---

3. **denunciation** (dē nun′ sē ā′ shən) *n.*: Strong criticism.

Guide for Responding

◆ Literature and Your Life

Reader's Response Which of the men named in the essay do you admire most? Why?

Thematic Focus What does this essay indicate about the difficulty of stating and realizing a national dream or goal?

Speech Read aloud the speech that John Adams gave in response to John Dickinson's warnings. (See page 605.) Express not only the ideas but the feelings behind them.

☑ Check Your Comprehension

1. What immediate threats from the British prompted John Dickinson to warn against declaring independence?
2. What did John Adams say in answer to John Dickinson?
3. Give the results of the final vote on the issue of independence.
4. Identify three changes that the Continental Congress made in Jefferson's draft of the Declaration of Independence.

◆ Critical Thinking

Interpret

1. Give two examples from the essay of divisions between northern colonies and southern colonies. **[Analyze]**
2. What do you think persuaded the delegates to vote unanimously for independence? **[Speculate]**
3. Explain how Adams's letter summarizes the situation of the colonies after independence was declared: "the river is passed. The bridge is cut away." **[Interpret]**

Evaluate

4. Do you agree with Joseph Hewes that there was no point in searching the cellar for a bomb? Why or why not? **[Make a Judgment]**

Extend

5. In what ways does Kuralt show that living through a historic event is not as easy as looking back on it? **[Social Studies Link]**

Rattlesnake Hunt

Marjorie Kinnan Rawlings

Ross Allen, a young Florida herpetologist,[1] invited me to join him on a hunt in the upper Everglades[2]—for rattlesnakes. Ross and I drove to Arcadia in his coupé[3] on a warm January day.

I said, "How will you bring back the rattlesnakes?"

"In the back of my car."

My courage was not adequate to inquire whether they were thrown in loose and might be expected to appear between our feet. Actually, a large portable box of heavy close-meshed wire made a safe cage. Ross wanted me to write an article about his work and on our way to the unhappy hunting grounds I took notes on a mass of data that he had accumulated in years of herpetological research. The scientific and dispassionate detachment of the material and the man made a desirable approach to rattlesnake territory. As I had discovered with the insects and varmints,[4] it is difficult to be afraid of anything about which enough is known, and Ross' facts were fresh from the laboratory.

The hunting ground was Big Prairie, south of Arcadia and west of the northern tip of Lake Okeechobee. Big Prairie is a <u>desolate</u> cattle country, half marsh, half pasture, with islands of palm trees and cypress and oaks. At that time of year the cattlemen and Indians were burning the country, on the theory that the young fresh wire grass that springs up from the roots after a fire is the best cattle forage. Ross planned to hunt his rattlers in the forefront of the fires. They lived in winter, he said, in gopher holes, coming out in the midday warmth to forage, and would move ahead of the flames and be easily taken. We joined forces with a big man named Will, his snake-hunting companion of the territory, and set out in early morning, after a long rough drive over deep-rutted roads into the open wilds.

I hope never in my life to be so frightened as I was in those first few hours. I kept on Ross' footsteps, I moved when he moved, sometimes jolting into him when I thought he might leave me behind. He does not use the forked stick of conventional snake hunting, but a steel prong, shaped like an L, at the end of a long stout stick. He hunted casually, calling my attention to the varying vegetation, to hawks overhead, to a pair of the rare whooping cranes that flapped over us. In mid-morning he stopped short, dropped his stick, and brought up a five-foot rattlesnake draped limply over the steel L. It seemed to me that I should drop in my tracks.

"They're not active at this season," he said

◆ **Literary Focus**
Which words and phrases give you a picture of the plant life in this region?

---

1. **herpetologist** (hʉr′ pə täl′ ə jist) *n.*: Someone who studies reptiles and amphibians.
2. **Everglades:** Large region of swampland in southern Florida, about 100 miles long and 50–75 miles wide.
3. **coupé** (ko͞o pā′) *n.*: Small two-door automobile.
4. **varmints** (vär′ mənts) *n.*: Animals regarded as troublesome.

◆ **Build Vocabulary**

desolate (des′ ə lit) *adj.*: Lonely; solitary

quietly. "A snake takes on the temperature of its surroundings. They can't stand too much heat for that reason, and when the weather is cool, as now, they're sluggish."

The sun was bright overhead, the sky a translucent blue, and it seemed to me that it was warm enough for any snake to do as it willed. The sweat poured down my back. Ross dropped the rattler in a crocus sack and Will carried it. By noon, he had caught four. I felt faint and ill. We stopped by a pond and went swimming. The region was flat, the horizon limitless, and as I came out of the cool blue water I expected to find myself surrounded by a ring of rattlers. There were only Ross and Will, opening the lunch basket. I could not eat. Will went back and drove his truck closer, for Ross expected the hunting to be better in the afternoon. The hunting was much better. When we went back to the truck to deposit two more rattlers in the wire cage, there was a rattlesnake lying under the truck.

Ross said, "Whenever I leave my car or truck with snakes already in it, other rattlers always appear. I don't know whether this is because they scent or sense the presence of other snakes, or whether in this arid[5] area they come to the car for shade in the heat of the day."

The problem was scientific, but I had no interest.

That night Ross and Will and I camped out in the vast spaces of the Everglades prairies. We got water from an abandoned well and cooked supper under buttonwood bushes by a flowing stream. The camp fire blazed cheerfully under the stars and a new moon lifted in the sky. Will told tall tales of the cattlemen and the Indians and we were at peace.

Ross said, "We couldn't have a better night for catching water snakes."

After the rattlers, water snakes seemed innocuous[6] enough. We worked along the edge of the stream and here Ross did not use his L-shaped steel. He reached under rocks and along the edge of the water and brought out

harmless reptiles with his hands. I had said nothing to him of my fears, but he understood them. He brought a small dark snake from under a willow root.

"Wouldn't you like to hold it?" he asked. "People think snakes are cold and clammy, but they aren't. Take it in your hands. You'll see that it is warm."

♦ **Literature and Your Life**
How would you feel at a moment like this?

Again, because I was ashamed, I took the snake in my hands. It was not cold, it was not clammy, and it lay trustingly in my hands, a thing that lived and breathed and had <u>mortality</u> like the rest of us. I felt an upsurgence of spirit.

The next day was magnificent. The air was crystal, the sky was aquamarine, and the far horizon of palms and oaks lay against the sky. I felt a new boldness and followed Ross bravely. He was making the rounds of the gopher holes. The rattlers came out in the mid-morning warmth and were never far away. He could tell by their trails whether one had come out or was still in the hole. Sometimes the two men dug the snake out. At times it was down so long and winding a tunnel that the digging was hopeless. Then they blocked the entrance and went on to other holes. In an hour or so they made the original rounds, unblocking the holes. The rattler in every case came out hurriedly, as though anything were preferable to being shut in. All the time Ross talked to me, telling me the scientific facts he had discovered about the habits of the rattlers.

"They pay no attention to a man standing perfectly still," he said, and proved it by letting Will unblock a hole while he stood at the entrance as the snake came out. It was exciting to watch the snake crawl slowly beside and past the man's legs. When it was at a safe distance he walked within its range of vision, which he had proved to be no higher than a man's knee, and the snake whirled and drew back in an attitude[7] of fighting defense. The rattler strikes only for paralyzing and killing

---

5. arid (ar′ id) *adj.*: Dry and barren.
6. innocuous (in näk′ yōo əs) *adj.*: Harmless.

7. attitude: (at′ ə tōōd′) *n.*: A position or posture of the body.

its food, and for defense.

"It is a slow and heavy snake," Ross said. "It lies in wait on a small game trail and strikes the rat or rabbit passing by. It waits a few minutes, then follows along the trail, coming to the small animal, now dead or dying. It noses it from all sides, making sure that it is its own kill, and that it is dead and ready for swallowing."

A rattler will lie quietly without revealing itself if a man passes by and it thinks it is not seen. It slips away without fighting if given the chance. Only Ross' sharp eyes sometimes picked out the gray and yellow diamond pattern, camouflaged among the grasses. In the cool of the morning, chilled by the January air, the snakes showed no fight. They could be looped up limply over the steel L and dropped in a sack or up into the wire cage on the back of Will's truck. As the sun mounted in the sky and warmed the moist Everglades earth, the snakes were warmed too, and Ross warned that it was time to go more cautiously. Yet having learned that it was we who were the aggressors; that immobility meant complete safety; that the snakes, for all their lightning flash in striking, were inaccurate in their aim, with limited vision; having watched again and again the liquid grace of movement, the beauty of pattern, suddenly I understood that I was drinking in freely the magnificent sweep of the horizon, with no fear of what might be at the moment under my feet. I went off hunting by myself, and though I found no snakes, I should have known what to do.

The sun was dropping low in the west. Masses of white cloud hung above the flat marshy plain and seemed to be tangled in the tops of distant palms and cypresses. The sky turned orange, then saffron. I walked leisurely back toward the truck. In the distance I could see Ross and Will making their way in too. The season was more advanced than at the Creek, two hundred miles to the north, and I noticed that spring flowers were blooming among the lumpy hummocks. I leaned over to pick a white violet. There was a rattlesnake under the violet.

If this had happened the week before, if it had happened the day before, I think I should have lain down and died on top of the rattlesnake, with no need of being struck and poisoned. The snake did not coil, but lifted its head and whirred its rattles lightly. I

◆ Build Vocabulary

mortality (môr tal´ ə tē) *n.*: The condition of being mortal; having to die eventually

◀ **Critical Viewing**
Why was the author afraid of rattlesnakes, like the one pictured here? **[Analyze]**

stepped back slowly and put the violet in a buttonhole. I reached forward and laid the steel L across the snake's neck, just back of the blunt head. I called to Ross:

"I've got one."

He strolled toward me.

"Well, pick it up," he said.

I released it and slipped the L under the middle of the thick body.

"Go put it in the box."

He went ahead of me and lifted the top of the wire cage. I made the truck with the rattler, but when I reached up the six feet to drop it in the cage, it slipped off the stick and dropped on Ross' feet. It made no effort to strike.

"Pick it up again," he said. "If you'll pin it down lightly and reach just back of its head with your hand, as you've seen me do, you can drop it in more easily."

I pinned it and leaned over.

"I'm awfully sorry," I said, "but you're pushing me a little too fast."

He grinned. I lifted it on the stick and again as I had it at head height, it slipped off, down Ross' boots and on top of his feet. He stood as still as a stump. I dropped the snake on his feet for the third time. It seemed to me that the most patient of rattlers might in time resent being hauled up and down, and for all the man's quiet certainty that in standing motionless there was no danger, would strike at whatever was nearest, and that would be Ross.

I said, "I'm just not man enough to keep this up any longer," and he laughed and reached down with his smooth quickness and lifted the snake back of the head and dropped it in the cage. It slid in among its mates and settled in a corner. The hunt was over and we drove back over the uneven trail to Will's village and left him and went on to Arcadia and home. Our catch for the two days was thirty-two rattlers.

I said to Ross, "I believe that tomorrow I could have picked up that snake."

Back at the Creek, I felt a new lightness. I had done battle with a great fear, and the victory was mine.

◆ **Reading Strategy**

Explain how this passage comes close to stating one of the essay's main points.

Guide for Responding

◆ LITERATURE AND YOUR LIFE

Reader's Response Would you like to go on a rattlesnake hunt? Why or why not?

Thematic Focus In what ways does the rattlesnake hunt change how Rawlings thinks about nature and about herself?

☑ Check Your Comprehension

1. Why does Rawlings go on the hunt?
2. Identify three facts Rawlings learns about rattlers.
3. Note two ways in which Rawlings shows that she has partly overcome her fears.

◆ Critical Thinking

INTERPRET

1. Why do Rawlings's feelings about snakes change when she holds one? **[Infer]**
2. What might contribute to Rawlings's feeling of "boldness" on the second day? **[Speculate]**
3. Describe the "victory" that Rawlings has won by the end of the hunt. **[Draw Conclusions]**

APPLY

4. In what way does this essay support the idea that knowledge drives away fear? **[Defend]**

from Barrio Boy

Ernesto Galarza

▶ **Critical Viewing** Does this photograph effectively convey the emotions that Ernesto might have felt as he enrolled in a new school? Explain. **[Evaluate]**

My mother and I walked south on Fifth Street one morning to the corner of Q Street and turned right. Half of the block was occupied by the Lincoln School. It was a three-story wooden building, with two wings that gave it the shape of a double-T connected by a central hall. It was a new building, painted yellow, with a shingled roof that was not like the red tile of the school in Mazatlán. I noticed other differences, none of them very reassuring.

We walked up the wide staircase hand in hand and through the door, which closed by itself. A mechanical contraption screwed to the top shut it behind us quietly.

Up to this point the adventure of enrolling me in the school had been carefully rehearsed. Mrs. Dodson had told us how to find it and we had circled it several times on our walks.

Friends in the *barrio*[1] explained that the director was called a principal, and that it was a lady and not a man. They assured us that there was always a person at the school who could speak Spanish.

Exactly as we had been told, there was a sign on the door in both Spanish and English: "Principal." We crossed the hall and entered the office of Miss Nettie Hopley.

Miss Hopley was at a roll-top desk to one side, sitting in a swivel chair that moved on wheels. There was a sofa against the opposite wall, flanked by two windows and a door that opened on a small balcony. Chairs were set around a table and framed pictures hung on the walls of a man with long white hair and

---

1. barrio (bär′ ē ō) *n.*: Part of a town or city where most of the people are Hispanic.

◀ **Critical Viewing** How does the classroom in this photograph compare with Miss Ryan's classroom? **[Compare and Contrast]**

another with a sad face and a black beard.

The principal half turned in the swivel chair to look at us over the pinch glasses crossed on the ridge of her nose. To do this she had to duck her head slightly as if she were about to step through a low doorway.

What Miss Hopley said to us we did not know but we saw in her eyes a warm welcome and when she took off her glasses and straightened up she smiled wholeheartedly, like Mrs. Dodson. We were, of course, saying nothing, only catching the friendliness of her voice and the sparkle in her eyes while she said words we did not understand. She signaled us to the table. Almost tiptoeing across the office, I maneuvered myself to keep my mother between me and the gringo lady. In a matter of seconds I had to decide whether she was a possible friend or a menace.[2] We sat down.

◆ **Literary Focus**
In what way does Galarza's honesty about his feelings make the essay seem more personal?

Then Miss Hopley did a <u>formidable</u> thing. She stood up. Had she been standing when we entered she would have seemed tall. But rising from her chair she soared. And what she carried up and up with her was a buxom superstructure,[3] firm shoulders, a straight sharp nose, full cheeks slightly molded by a curved line along the nostrils, thin lips that moved like steel springs, and a high forehead topped by hair gathered in a bun. Miss Hopley was not a giant in body but when she mobilized[4] it to a standing position she seemed a match for giants. I decided I liked her.

She strode to a door in the far corner of the office, opened it and called a name. A boy of about ten years appeared in the doorway. He sat down at one end of the table. He was brown like us, a plump kid with shiny black hair combed straight back, neat, cool, and faintly obnoxious.

Miss Hopley joined us with a large book and some papers in her hand. She, too, sat down and the questions and answers began by way of our interpreter.[5] My name was Ernesto. My mother's name was Henriqueta. My birth

---

2. menace (men´ is) *n.*: Danger; threat.

3. buxom superstructure: Full figure.

4. mobilized (mō´ bə līzd´) *v.*: Put into motion.

5. interpreter (in tur´ prə tər) *n.*: Someone who translates from one language into another.

certificate was in San Blas. Here was my last report card from the Escuela Municipal Numero 3 para Varones of Mazatlán,[6] and so forth. Miss Hopley put things down in the book and my mother signed a card.

As long as the questions continued, Doña[7] Henriqueta could stay and I was secure. Now that they were over, Miss Hopley saw her to the door, dismissed our interpreter and without further ado took me by the hand and strode down the hall to Miss Ryan's first grade.

Miss Ryan took me to a seat at the front of the room, into which I shrank—the better to survey her. She was, to skinny, somewhat runty me, of a withering height when she patrolled the class. And when I least expected it, there she was, crouching by my desk, her blond radiant face level with mine, her voice patiently maneuvering me over the awful idiocies of the English language.

During the next few weeks Miss Ryan overcame my fears of tall, energetic teachers as she bent over my desk to help me with a word in the pre-primer. Step by step, she loosened me and my classmates from the safe anchorage of the desks for recitations at the blackboard and consultations at her desk. Frequently she burst into happy announcements to the whole class. "Ito can read a sentence," and small Japanese Ito, squint-eyed and shy, slowly read aloud while the class listened in wonder: "Come, Skipper, come. Come and run." The Korean, Portuguese, Italian, and Polish first graders had similar moments of glory, no less shining than mine the day I conquered "butterfly," which I had been persistently pronouncing in standard Spanish as boo-ter-flee. "Children," Miss Ryan called for attention. "Ernesto has learned how to pronounce *butterfly*!" And I proved it with a perfect imitation of Miss Ryan. From that celebrated success, I was soon able to match Ito's progress as a sentence reader with "Come, butterfly, come fly with me."

Like Ito and several other first graders who did not know English, I received private lessons from Miss Ryan in the closet, a narrow hall off the classroom with a door at each end. Next to one of these doors Miss Ryan placed a large chair for herself and a small one for me. Keeping an eye on the class through the open door she read with me about sheep in the meadow and a frightened chicken going to see the king, coaching me out of my phonetic ruts in words like *pasture, bow-wow-wow, hay,* and *pretty,* which to my Mexican ear and eye had so many unnecessary sounds and letters. She made me watch her lips and then close my eyes as she repeated words I found hard to read. When we came to know each other better, I tried interrupting to tell Miss Ryan how we said it in Spanish. It didn't work. She only said "oh" and went on with *pasture, bow-wow-wow,* and *pretty.* It was as if in that closet we were both discovering together the secrets of the English language and grieving[8] together over the tragedies of Bo-Peep. The main reason I was graduated with honors from the first grade was that I had fallen in love with Miss Ryan. Her radiant, no-nonsense character made us either afraid not to love her or love her so we would not be afraid, I am not sure which. It was not only that we sensed she was with it, but also that she was with us.

Like the first grade, the rest of the Lincoln School was a sampling of the lower part of town where many races made their home. My pals in the second grade were Kazushi, whose parents spoke only Japanese; Matti, a skinny Italian boy; and Manuel, a fat Portuguese who would never get into a fight but wrestled you to the ground and just sat on you. Our assortment of nationalities included Koreans, Yugoslavs, Poles, Irish, and home-grown Americans.

At Lincoln, making us into Americans did not mean scrubbing away what made us

---

6. **Escuela Municipal Numero 3 para Varones of Mazatlán** (es kwä lə moo nē sē päl noo´ me rô träs pärä vä rō´ nas mä sät län´): Municipal School Number 3 for Boys of Mazatlán.

7. **Doña** (dô´ nyä): Spanish title of respect meaning "lady" or "madam."

8. **grieving** (grēv´ iŋ) *v.*: Feeling sorrow for a loss.

◆ **Build Vocabulary**

formidable (fôr´ mi də bəl) *adj.*: Impressive

originally foreign. The teachers called us as our parents did, or as close as they could pronounce our names in Spanish or Japanese. No one was ever scolded or punished for speaking in his native tongue on the playground. Matti told the class about his mother's down quilt, which she had made in Italy with the fine feathers of a thousand geese. Encarnación acted out how boys learned to fish in the Philippines. I astounded the third grade with the story of my travels on a stagecoach, which nobody else in the class had seen except in the museum at Sutter's Fort. After a visit to the Crocker Art Gallery and its collection of heroic paintings of the golden age of California, someone showed a silk scroll with a Chinese painting. Miss Hopley herself had a way of expressing wonder over these matters before a class, her eyes wide open until they popped slightly. It was easy for me to feel that becoming a proud American, as she said we should, did not mean feeling ashamed of being a Mexican.

Guide for Responding

◆ LITERATURE AND YOUR LIFE

Reader's Response Have you ever felt the way Ernesto felt in his new school? Explain.

Thematic Focus In what way did the Lincoln School help Galarza realize his dream of "becoming a proud American"?

Journal Writing In your journal, write about the ways you might make a new student feel comfortable at school.

☑ Check Your Comprehension

1. What is the purpose of Galarza's first visit to the Lincoln School?
2. Why does Galarza decide he likes Miss Hopley?
3. Why is Galarza afraid of Miss Ryan at first?
4. In what ways does Miss Ryan help him overcome his fears of her and of the new class?

◆ Critical Thinking

INTERPRET
1. Why did Galarza feel he had to decide immediately whether Miss Hopley "was a possible friend or a menace"? **[Infer]**
2. What does Galarza mean when he says Miss Ryan "was with it" and "with us"? **[Interpret]**
3. In what ways were the seeds of Galarza's success planted in the first grade? **[Speculate]**

APPLY
4. Using this essay, explain the qualities a person needs to help someone feel at home in a new situation. **[Generalize]**

COMPARE LITERARY WORKS
5. In what ways are "Rattlesnake Hunt" and "Barrio Boy" both about overcoming fears? **[Connect]**

belonging to him and he expected to share them with others and to take only what he needed.

Everyone likes to give as well as receive. No one wishes only to receive all the time. We have taken much from your culture . . . I wish you had taken something from our culture . . . for there were some beautiful and good things in it.

Soon it will be too late to know my culture, for integration[5] is upon us and soon we will have no values but yours. Already many of our young people have forgotten the old ways. And many have been shamed of their Indian ways by scorn[6] and ridicule. My culture is like a wounded deer that has crawled away into the forest to bleed and die alone.

The only thing that can truly help us is genuine love. You must truly love us, be patient with us and share with us. And we must love you—with a genuine love that forgives and forgets . . . a love that forgives the terrible sufferings your culture brought ours when it swept over us like a wave crashing along a beach . . . with a love that forgets and lifts up its head and sees in your eyes an answering love of trust and acceptance.

This is brotherhood . . . anything less is not worthy of the name.

I have spoken.

---

5. **integration** (in tə grā´ shən) *n.*: The mingling of different ethnic or racial groups.
6. **scorn** (skôrn) *n.*: Complete lack of respect.

◆ **Reading Strategy**
What point does Chief Dan George state directly in this paragraph? Summarize it in your own words.

Guide for Responding

◆ LITERATURE AND YOUR LIFE

Reader's Response Do you agree that "the power to love" is the most important human quality? Why or why not?

Thematic Focus How would the world change if the dream that Chief Dan George expresses came true?

☑ Check Your Comprehension

1. Name three things that people learned from growing up in communal houses.
2. What three things puzzle Chief Dan George about his "white brother"?
3. According to Chief Dan George, what important values could modern society learn from Chief Dan George's culture?
4. Describe the "brotherhood" that Chief Dan George talks about at the end of the essay.
5. According to the author, what makes humans the "greatest of all" creatures?

◆ Critical Thinking

INTERPRET

1. Sum up the differences between the "two distinct cultures" in which Chief Dan George lived. **[Compare and Contrast]**
2. When Chief Dan George says, "My white brother . . . is more clever than my people," what does he mean by *clever*? **[Interpret]**
3. What values does Chief Dan George think are lacking in modern society? **[Analyze]**

EVALUATE

4. Why do you think Chief Dan George wrote about his culture only in the past tense? **[Assess]**

EXTEND

5. Where might you look to find out if the Squamish people and culture are still alive today? **[Social Studies Link]**

ALL TOGETHER NOW

BARBARA JORDAN

When I look at race relations today I can see that some positive changes have come about. But much remains to be done, and the answer does not lie in more legislation. We *have* the legislation we need; we have the laws. Frankly, I don't believe that the task of bringing us all together can be accomplished by government. What we need now is soul force—the efforts of people working on a small scale to build a truly <u>tolerant</u>, harmonious society. And parents can do a great deal to create that tolerant society.

We all know that race relations in America have had a very rocky history. Think about the 1960s when Dr. Martin Luther King, Jr., was in his heyday and there were marches and protests against segregation[1] and discrimination. The movement culminated in 1963 with the March on Washington.

Following that event, race relations reached an all-time peak. President Lyndon B. Johnson pushed through the Civil Rights Act of 1964, which remains the fundamental piece of civil rights legislation in this century. The Voting Rights Act of 1965 ensured that everyone in our country could vote. At last, black people and white people seemed ready to live together in peace.

But that is not what happened. By the 1990's the good feelings had diminished. Today the nation seems to be suffering from compassion fatigue, and issues such as race relations and civil rights have never regained momentum.

Those issues, however, remain crucial. As our society becomes more diverse, people of all races and backgrounds will have to learn to live together. If we don't think this is important, all we have to do is look at the situation in Bosnia[2] today.

How do we create a harmonious society out of so many kinds of people? The key is tolerance—the one value that is indispensable in creating community.

---

1. **segregation** (seg′ rə gā′ shən) *n.*: The practice of forcing racial groups to live apart from each other.

2. **Bosnia** (bäz′ nē ə) *n.*: Country, located on the Balkan Peninsula in Europe, that was the site of a bloody civil war between Muslims and Christians during the 1990's.

If we are concerned about community, if it is important to us that people not feel excluded, then we have to do something. Each of us can decide to have one friend of a different race or background in our mix of friends. If we do this, we'll be working together to push things forward.

One thing is clear to me: We, as human beings, must be willing to accept people who are different from ourselves. I must be willing to accept people who don't look as I do and don't talk as I do. It is crucial that I am open to their feelings, their inner reality.

What can parents do? We can put our faith in young people as a positive force. I have yet to find a racist baby. Babies come into the world as blank as slates and, with their beautiful innocence, see others not as different but as enjoyable companions. Children learn ideas and attitudes from the adults who nurture them. I absolutely believe that children do not adopt prejudices unless they absorb them from their parents or teachers.

The best way to get this country faithful to the American dream of tolerance and equality is to start small. Parents can actively encourage their children to be in the company of people who are of other racial and ethnic backgrounds. If a child thinks, "Well, that person's color is not the same as mine, but she must be okay because she likes to play with the same things I like to play with," that child will grow up with a broader view of humanity.

I'm an incurable optimist. For the rest of the time that I have left on this planet I want to bring people together. You might think of this as a labor of love. Now, I know that love means different things to different people. But what *I* mean is this: I care about you because you are a fellow human being and I find it okay in my mind, in my heart, to simply say to you, I love you. And maybe that would encourage you to love me in return.

It is possible for all of us to work on this—at home, in our schools, at our jobs. It is possible to work on human relationships in every area of our lives.

◆ Build Vocabulary

tolerant (täl′ ər ənt) *adj.*: Free from bigotry or prejudice

◇Guide for Responding

◆ LITERATURE AND YOUR LIFE

Reader's Response Does this essay inspire you to change your thinking? Explain.

Thematic Focus How does the word *tolerance* express Jordan's American dream?

☑ Check Your Comprehension

1. How does Jordan summarize the history of race relations from the 1960's to the 1990's?
2. What "one value" is necessary to create "a harmonious society"?
3. According to Jordan, what can parents do to foster a sense of community?

◆ Critical Thinking

INTERPRET

1. In your own words, describe what Jordan means by "compassion fatigue." **[Interpret]**
2. How does the phrase "start small" express two ideas for promoting tolerance? **[Analyze]**

EVALUATE

3. Do you think that Jordan's ideas could work to promote tolerance? Explain. **[Evaluate]**

APPLY

4. In what ways can you apply Jordan's ideas in your life? **[Community Link]**

Guide for Responding (continued)

◆ Literary Focus

ESSAY

An **essay** is a brief prose work expressing an author's view of a subject. You often know what type it is right away. For example, the first paragraph of the narrative essay "Independence Hall" reveals that the writer will tell a true story.

1. Find three details to confirm that "Rattlesnake Hunt" is a descriptive essay.
2. What elements of the essay from *Barrio Boy* show that it is a personal essay?
3. What ideas or experiences does the writer reflect on in "I Am a Native of North America"?
4. In "All Together Now," what does the writer want to persuade her audience to do?

◆ Build Vocabulary

USING THE WORD ROOT -mort-

Explain how the word root -mort-, meaning "death," helps you understand the meaning of these words. Then, use each word in a sentence.

mortician *n.*: funeral director
mortal *n.*: a being that will eventually die
immortal *adj.*: deathless; living forever

SPELLING STRATEGY

When spelling the *it* sound at the end of multi-syllable adjectives, you often use the letters *ate*: *desolate, temperate*. Write the words containing the *ate* spelling that fit the following definitions:

1. average, comfortable: mod____?____
2. complex, involved: intri____?____
3. popular flavor: choc____?____

USING THE WORD BANK

On your paper, explain your answer to each question.

1. Was the Declaration of Independence *anonymous*?
2. When do delegates vote *unanimously*?
3. Will rattlers be disturbed in a *desolate* place?
4. Do we share *mortality* with all creatures?
5. Does Galarza seem *formidable* to Miss Ryan?
6. Do *communal* houses have things to be shared?
7. Can a *tolerant* attitude help resolve conflicts?

◆ Reading Strategy

IDENTIFY MAIN POINTS

You can't fully understand these essays until you identify their **main points,** their most important ideas. Often, these ideas appear at the beginning or end of an essay. For example, "Rattlesnake Hunt" states a main point at the end, concluding that by facing fears, you can free yourself of them.

1. Find a stated or suggested main point in *Barrio Boy,* "I Am a Native of North America," and "All Together Now." Express each in your own words.
2. What point does Kuralt hint at in "Independence Hall" by telling about the disagreements among the delegates as well as their unanimous vote?

◆ Build Grammar Skills

SUBJECT AND OBJECT PRONOUNS

Some pronouns change forms depending on their use in a sentence.

Subjective Case	Use in Sentence
I, we	Subject of a verb
you	Subject complement
he, she, it, they	
Objective Case	**Use in Sentence**
me, us	Direct object
you	Indirect object
him, her, it, them	Object of a preposition

Practice On your paper, identify the case of each italicized pronoun.

1. *We* mutually pledge to each other our lives.
2. It was *they* who went hunting for rattlesnakes.
3. *He* could see *her* rise above *him*.
4. Jordan gave *us* her ideas on the subject.
5. George says, "It is hard for *me* to understand."
6. The classroom was a good one for *them*.
7. *She* had a way of making *us* feel welcome.

Writing Application On your paper, write sentences using personal pronoun forms according to the directions given.

1. Use two subject pronouns.
2. Use one subject and one object pronoun.
3. Use two object pronouns.

Build Your Portfolio

 ## Idea Bank

Writing

1. **Anecdote** Write an anecdote—a brief story—based on one of these essays. For example, you might tell what happened to Rawlings on another rattlesnake hunt or what Galarza did on his first day in the second grade.

2. **Essay for a Broadcast** Use one of these essays as the basis for a televised response. Write a narrative or a persuasive essay for a reporter to read on the air. Remember that short sentences with catchy phrases work better on television.

3. **Introduction to an Anthology** Imagine that the essays in this section will be collected in a book. Write an introduction to this anthology. Define what an essay is, and tell about the types of essays that readers will find in the book.

Speaking and Listening

4. **Press Conference [Group Activity]** With a group, stage a press conference in which one of these writers answers reporters' questions about his or her essay. **[Performing Arts Link]**

5. **Book Talk** Give a talk to your class on a recently published book of essays. Gather facts by reading all or part of the book, the information from the inside cover, and reviews of the book in newspapers. **[Performing Arts Link]**

Projects

6. **Essay "Fortune Cookies"** Choose your favorite essay, and write its main points on small strips of paper. Wrap each strip in a package together with a cookie. Then, exchange these essay "fortune cookies" with classmates.

7. **Timeline** Present the history of the essay in the form of an illustrated timeline. Include birth, death, and publication dates for such essayists as Montaigne, Francis Bacon, and Charles Lamb. Also, include information on well-known media "essayists," like Edward R. Murrow and Charles Kuralt. **[Art Link; Media Link]**

 ## Writing Mini-Lesson

Reflective Essay

In "I Am a Native of North America," Chief Dan George reflects on what is important in life. You can write a reflective essay also—by thinking your own thoughts on paper. Start by choosing a subject that has caused you to wonder. It can be anything from the clothing styles of athletes to a concept you've learned in school. Remember that you don't have to know all the answers. It's enough to think about interesting questions.

Writing Skills Focus: Necessary Background

You'll want to take readers along on your reflective journey. That's why you must give them the **necessary background,** the facts they need to follow your thoughts. For example, Chief Dan George gives you background on his childhood so you can understand his comparison of cultures.

Prewriting Flip through the pages of your journal for an idea. Then, choose a subject that has already made you thoughtful. Don't worry if it isn't a life-and-death matter. Big thoughts can grow from little subjects. Freewrite for five to ten minutes, creating a cluster diagram to record your ideas.

Drafting Refer to your diagram as you write. Remember to include information that readers must know in order to understand your thoughts. As you conclude, leave something for the reader to continue thinking about.

Revising Have several classmates read your essay. If they can't follow your thinking, insert more explanations and background material.

◆ **Grammar Application**

Be sure that you have correctly used subject and object pronouns.

CONNECTING LITERATURE TO SOCIAL STUDIES

GEOGRAPHY

Tenochtitlan: Inside the Aztec Capital *by Jacqueline Dineen*

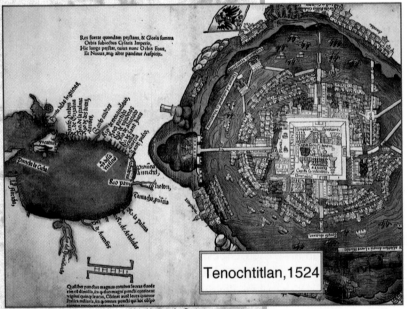

Tenochtitlan, 1524

Map of Tenochtitlan, 1524, Hernando Cortes, The Newberry Library, Chicago

PLANNING A CITY To create a city, what problems would you face? You'd need food, shelter, and ways to earn a living for thousands of people. Geography—the region's land, climate, and vegetation—would guide your plans.

A High Valley Mexico is a plateau guarded by two long mountain chains. Some of these mountains are taller than 18,000 feet! A few are volcanic. Even the plateau sits on very high ground—often, more than 4,000 feet above sea level! Along the plateau, there were once many lakes—including Lake Texcoco, where the Aztecs, a native people who controlled the region until the arrival of the Spaniards, built their capital city of Tenochtitlan (te nōch tēt län´) in the 1300's. Set on islands in the lake, Tenochtitlan was safe from invaders, had a mild climate, and offered fertile soil for crops.

The Lake of the Moon Mexico City, which today sits on the drained remains of Lake Texcoco, owes its name to Aztec words meaning "city in the center of the lake of the moon." The city enjoys a fairly dry climate with rainy summers. Limited rain in the winter means farmers must either irrigate or plant crops suited to dry climates.

Window to Another Place The piece you're about to read is a visual essay—a nonfiction piece that blends text and images—that will tell you how the Aztecs built the ancient city of Tenochtitlan on the site where Mexico City stands today. How did the geography of the region shape the way the Aztecs built their city?

TENOCHTITLAN: Inside the Aztec Capital

Jacqueline Dineen

The Lake City of Tenochtitlan[1]

The city of Tenochtitlan began on an island in the middle of a swampy lake. There the Aztecs built their first temple to Huitzilopochtli.[2] The place was given the name Tenochtitlan, which means "The Place of the Fruit of the Prickly Pear Cactus." Later on the name was given to the city that grew up around the temple. The Aztecs rebuilt their temples on the same site every 52 years, so the first temple eventually became the great Temple Mayor[3] that stood at the center of the city.

The city started as a collection of huts. It began to grow after 1385, while Acamapichtli[4] was king. The Aztecs were excellent engineers. They built three causeways over the swamp to link the city with the mainland. These were raised roads made of stone supported on wooden pillars. Parts of the causeways were bridges. These bridges could be removed to leave gaps and this prevented enemies from getting to the city. Fresh water was brought from the mainland to the city along stone aqueducts.[5]

<table>
<tr><td>

Connecting Literature to Social Studies
Why might fresh water be so important to a growing city?

</td></tr>
</table>

from *THE AZTECS* by Jacqueline Dineen (Worlds of the Past), Heinemann Educational Books Ltd., an imprint of Reed Educational and Professional Publishing.

▲ Critical Viewing
How does this city map compare with modern maps? [Compare and Contrast]

The Lake City of Tenochtitlan.

Each grouping of houses in Tenochtitlan was planned so that the houses could be reached through the many waterways. These canals crisscrossed the city, and some are still in and around Mexico City today.

---

1. **Tenochtitlan** (te nōch tēt län´) *n.*: Ancient Aztec capital located in what is now Mexico City.
2. **Huitzilopochtli** (wēt sē pōch´ tlē)
3. **Mayor** (mä yōr´)
4. **Acamapichtli** (ä kä mä pēch´ tlē)
5. **aqueducts** (ak´ wə dukts´) *n.*: Large pipes made for bringing water from a distant source.

Maguey cactus plants, like these in front of a rebuilt Aztec temple, had many uses. Parts of the plants were used to make medicines. The thorns were used as sewing needles, and fibers of the maguey were spun together and woven into coarse cloth. Pulque, a popular drink, comes from this plant. The maguey even had its own goddess— Mayahuel!

▲ **Critical Viewing** Why do you think the Aztecs found so many uses for the cactus plants, like those in this photograph? **[Infer]**

Inside the City

The Spaniards' first view of Tenochtitlan was described by one of Cortés's[6] soldiers, Bernal Diaz: "And when we saw all those towns and level causeway leading into Mexico, we were astounded. These great towns and buildings rising from the water, all made of stone, seemed like an enchanted vision."

By that time Tenochtitlan was the largest city in Mexico. About 200,000 people lived there. The houses were one story high and had flat roofs. In the center of the city was a large square. The twin temple stood on one side, and the king's palace on another. Officials' houses made of white stone also lined the square. There were few roads. People traveled in canoes along canals.

Floating Gardens

Tenochtitlan was built in a huge valley, the Valley of Mexico, which was surrounded by mountains. Rivers flowed from the mountains into Lake Texcoco, where Tenochtitlan

---

6. **Hernando Cortés** (er nän´ dō kōr tes´): Spanish adventurer (1485–1547) who conquered what is now central and southern Mexico.

stood. The lake was linked to four other shallow, swampy lakes. The land around the lakes was dry because there was very little rain.

Connecting Literature to Social Studies
What problems might a dry climate cause?

The Aztecs dug ditches and piled up the earth to make islands in the shallow parts of the lake. These chinampas, or swamp gardens, could be farmed. The ditches carried water into larger canals that were used for irrigation[7] and as waterways to the city.

Texcoco and the lake to the south contained fresh water, but the northern lakes contained salt water, which was no good for irrigation. The Aztecs built an embankment[8] 10 miles long to keep out the salt water and also to protect the city from flooding.

---

7. irrigation (ir´ ə gā´ shən) *n.*: Act of supplying water by means of ditches, canals, or sprinklers.
8. embankment (em bank´ mənt) *n.*: Bank of earth to keep water back.

▼ **Critical Viewing** What does seeing a codex like this one add to your understanding of Aztec culture? **[Connect]**

This Aztec codex (the first manuscript presented in modern book form) shows the life of a corn plant over four years. Corn was so precious to the Aztecs that special gods and goddesses were in charge of it. Tlaloc, the God of Rain; Xipe Totec, the God of Planting; and Spring, and the Storm Goddess, are all featured with the corn in this codex.

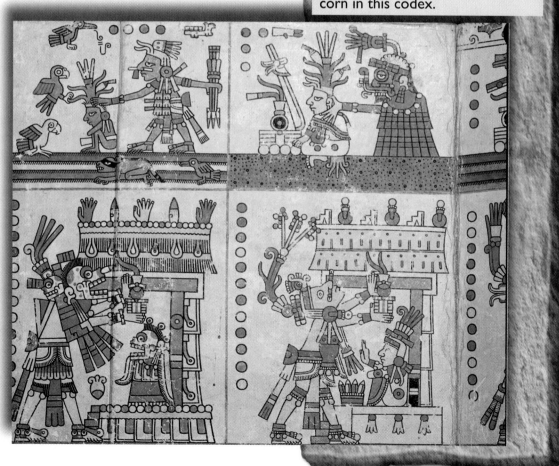

Codex Fejervary-Mayer (detail). The life of a corn plant over four years, Werner Forman Archive, Liverpool Museum, Liverpool

Drawing of the King's Palace from the Codex Mendoza, The Bodleian Library, Oxford

This drawing from the Codex Mendoza
shows what the Aztec emperor Montezuma's palace looked like. Practically a small town, it had a main palace and smaller surrounding palaces, council offices, courts of law, and store-rooms.

◀ **Critical Viewing** What details in the drawing suggest the emperor's importance? **[Analyze]**

half of the population. The rest were the nobility, crafts-people, and others. Each chinampa was only big enough to grow food for one family. Most people in Tenochtitlan depended on food from outside the city.

As the city grew, more and more land was drained for farming and for building. Farmers had no tools except simple hoes and digging sticks, but the loose soil was fertile and easy to turn. The main crop was corn, but farmers also grew tomatoes, beans, chili peppers, and prickly pears. They grew maguey cactus for its fibers and to make a drink called pulque. Cacao trees were grown in the hottest areas. The seeds were used for trading and to make a chocolate drink.

Feeding the People
Archaeologists think that when Tenochtitlan was at its greatest, about one million people lived in the Valley of Mexico. That included Tenochtitlan and the 50 or 60 city-states on the mainland surrounding the lakes. Food for all these people had to come from farming.

Historians are not sure how many people in Tenochtitlan were farmers, but they think it may have been between one third and one

Inside an Aztec Home
There were big differences between a rich Aztec home and a poor one. The nobles' houses were like palaces. They were one story high and built

around a courtyard. Each of the four sides contained four or five large rooms. The courtyards were planted with flower and vegetable gardens. Some houses on the island in the center of the city were built of adobe—bricks made from mud and dried in the sun. Adobe is still used for building in Mexico today. These grand houses and palaces were whitewashed so that they shone in the sun. The Spanish soldier Bernal Diaz described buildings that looked like "gleaming white towers and castles: a marvelous sight."

There is very little evidence about the buildings in Tenochtitlan and hardly any about the poor people's houses. What we do know has been pieced together from scattered historical records such as documents that record the sale of building sites on the chinampa

gardens. All of the poorer people's homes were built on the chinampas on the <u>outskirts</u> of the city. Because the chinampas would not take the weight of stone, houses had to be built of lighter materials such as wattle-and-daub. This was made by weaving <u>reeds</u> together and then plastering them with mud. We know that the outskirts of the city were divided into groups of houses inside walled areas, or compounds. A whole family lived in each compound. The

> **Connecting Literature to Social Studies**
> Why wouldn't chinampas support stone houses and buildings?

◆ Build Vocabulary

outskirts (out´ skʉrtz´) *n.*: Part of a district far from the center of a city

reeds (rēdz) *n.*: Tall, slender grasses that grow in marshy land

---

▶ **Critical Viewing** What can you learn about Aztec technology and skills by examining these stone structures? **[Infer]**

This priest's house is located at Teotihuacan, an Aztec ruin site outside Mexico City. It is probably similar to the homes of Aztec nobles. A doorway opened onto a central courtyard, and the outside walls are decorated with carvings. The houses had flat roofs that were often decorated with flower gardens.

family consisted of a couple, their married children, and their grandchildren. Every married couple in the family had a separate house of one or two rooms. All the houses opened onto an outdoor patio that belonged to the whole family.

Outside the house, the families often kept turkeys in pens. The turkeys provided eggs and meat. There was also a beehive for honey. Most families had a bathhouse in the garden.

Furniture and Decoration

Aztec houses were very plain inside. Everyone slept on mats of reeds that were spread on the dirt floor at night. Families had cooking pots and utensils made of clay. There were goblets for pulque and other drinks, graters for grinding chilis, and storage pots of various designs. Reed baskets were also used for storage. Households had grinding stones for grinding corn into flour. There was also a household shrine with statues of the gods.

Connecting Literature to Social Studies
What do you learn about the role religion played in Aztec culture? Explain.

The houses had no windows or chimneys, so they must have been dark and smoky from the cooking fire. There were no doors, just an open doorway. Even the palaces had open doorways with cloths hanging over them.

◆ Build Vocabulary

goblets (gäb´ lits) *n.*: Bowl-shaped drinking containers without handles

Guide for Responding

◆ LITERATURE AND YOUR LIFE

Reader's Response Would you have enjoyed living in Tenochtitlan? Why or why not?

Thematic Focus Given the resources available to them, how could the leaders of Tenochtitlan have improved community life?

☑ Check Your Comprehension

1. Describe Tenochtitlan's location.
2. Where did both wealthy and poor Aztec people live?
3. Identify three problems faced by the Aztecs, and explain how they solved them.

◆ Critical Thinking

INTERPRET
1. What do the removable bridges suggest about the relationship between the Aztecs and neighboring peoples? **[Infer]**
2. For what main reason might the Aztecs have created codexes? **[Infer]**
3. Did the city of Tenochtitlan meet the basic needs of its people? Why or why not? **[Draw Conclusions]**

EXTEND
4. Archaeologists studying Tenochtitlan use artifacts to piece together the puzzle of the past. What skills do you think such a job requires? **[Career Link]**

Meet the Author
Jacqueline Dineen

Jacqueline Dineen probably wishes she could travel back in time to see Tenochtitlan and other ancient civilizations. Bringing these worlds to life for children has been a longtime interest of hers. Dineen pursued that interest during her years as an editor for a London educational publisher and in more than fifty books for children. Sometimes she has focused on specific cultures, as with *The Aztecs* (from which this essay comes) and *The Romans*. In such books as *The Early Inventions* and *Art and Technology Through the Ages*, she's highlighted common human problems and explored how ancient peoples solved them.

CONNECTING LITERATURE TO SOCIAL STUDIES

You might wonder how and why the highly advanced city of Tenochtitlan disappeared. In 1519, Hernando Cortés, the Spanish conquistador, arrived in the beautiful Aztec capital. Because the superstitious emperor Montezuma believed Cortés was a god, the Aztecs did not use geographic defenses but instead welcomed Cortés.

Cortés kidnapped Montezuma and took over his government. In 1521, the Spaniards seized Tenochtitlan and quickly destroyed it. On its main island, they built their city around a square. The Aztecs had to live on the outer islands.

The Spaniards, like the Aztecs before them and the Mexicans after them, had to manage the water around their city. They had to bring in fresh water and irrigate crops. To stop flooding, they filled in Lake Texcoco. Modern Mexico City now sits on this soft lake bottom. As a result, it is sinking—more than 20 feet since 1900! In this essay about the geographic challenges facing the Aztecs, you can see the seeds of these later difficulties.

1. What were some geographic advantages and disadvantages of Tenochtitlan?
2. Explain how geography might have helped the Aztecs succeed in creating their empire.
3. Who has or has had a harder task in maintaining a city: ancient Aztecs or modern Mexicans? Explain.

 Idea Bank

Writing

1. **Community Events Poster** Create a poster announcing community happenings in Tenochtitlan. Include as many details about daily life as possible, and illustrate your poster to fit the ancient city's appearance. **[Art Link]**
2. **Ancient Call-in Show** With a partner, write a dialogue for a call-in radio show in which people ask advice about solving life's problems in Tenochtitlan. **[Media Link]**
3. **Campaign Speech** Imagine that you want to be Tenochtitlan's next emperor. Write a speech outlining the main issues that you see facing the city and how you would address these issues. **[Social Studies Link]**

Speaking and Listening

4. **Interview** Call the planning office in your city. Talk to officials there about the jobs of city planners and builders. Find out about the skills these occupations require. Then, determine whether the Aztecs used such skills in making their city. **[Career Link]**

Projects

5. **Visual Essay** Choose a culture that thrived between the years 500 and 1789, and create a visual essay about it. In addition to the running text, include drawings, photographs, and captions. Make your visual essay available for class viewing. **[Social Studies Link]**

Further Reading, Listening, and Viewing

- Elizabeth Baquedano, *Eyewitness: Aztec, Inca, and Maya* (1993) is a book-length picture essay about ancient Latin American cultures.
- John Bierhorst, *Mythology of Mexico and Central America* (1990) shares legends and folk tales of the Aztecs and other ancient peoples.

Report on a Current Event

Writing Process Workshop

What's happening in the world? A **report on a current event** is a short piece of informative writing that answers the question by summarizing a recent news item. In this workshop, you'll research something in the news that catches your eye. Then, you'll write a report to explain the event to others. The following skills will help you write your report.

Writing Skills Focus

▶ **Provide necessary background** to help readers understand the events you describe in your report. (See p. 621.)

▶ **Follow your interests** as you search for a current event. Choose something that catches your eye—something you would like to learn more about.

▶ **Use the Five W's** to identify the information you'll want to include: *who, what, where, when,* and *why.*

One writer was hooked by a headline that read: **It's Dry, Dry, Dry.** Here's the beginning of her report on wildfires in Florida:

MODEL

This summer has been Florida's worst fire season in over 50 years. ① From Jacksonville to Orlando, new fires have ignited and continued to burn. ② More than 200,000 acres have burned, and many buildings and crops have been destroyed. "The number of fires and the size of them are unbelievable," said one fire lieutenant. The fires are a result of drought plus lightning from storms that dump little or no rain. ③

① This sentence provides background by placing the severity of the fire in context.

② The writer provides information to tell *what* and *where.*

③ This sentence tells *why* the fires are starting.

Prewriting

Shop Around Find an event that interests you. Browse through newspapers, listen to the radio, watch television news, or talk to friends about what's happening. Consider these categories to help you pinpoint a current event you'd like to research.

Topic Ideas

- Local or national government
- Business
- Extreme weather conditions
- Conflict
- Trends in fashion or music

Get the Facts Find information about the event you've chosen. Read slowly and carefully. Take notes. Look for answers to questions that begin with the five W's.

Find Another Source Base your report on more than one source. Here are some avenues for information:

Jot Down Key Words Make a list of three to five important ideas about your current event. You'll want to use them as key words in your report.

Drafting

Report All the Facts As you draft, think about the five W's. Make sure you include information that answers each question: *Who? What? Where? When?* and *Why?*

APPLYING LANGUAGE SKILLS: Use Synonyms for Variety

You'll want to thread certain ideas through your report, but you don't want to repeat the words over and over. For variety, use **synonyms,** words that are similar in meaning. A dictionary or thesaurus might help. Here are some examples:

Instead of repeating . . .	Try . . .
mayor	leader; official
mountain	peak; summit
solution	cure; answer

Practice Replace the italicized words in these sentences with synonyms that make sense.

1. Lightning bolts *start* many fires in dry *places*.
2. The Bulls *beat* the Jazz because of their *better speed*.
3. *Shopping* on the Internet is *common today*.

Writing Application When writing your report on a current event, use synonyms to avoid repetition.

Writer's Solution Connection Writing Lab

For more instruction on considering your audience, see the Reports tutorial on the Writing Lab CD-ROM.

APPLYING LANGUAGE SKILLS: Capitalize Proper Nouns

A **proper noun** is the exact name of a person, place, or thing. Often, proper nouns are one of a kind—and proper nouns are *always* capitalized. Flip through a newspaper, noticing the proper nouns.

People:

Charles Kuralt, Nolan Ryan, Barbara Jordan

Places:

New York City, North America, Tenochtitlan, Independence Hall

Things:

Internet, Statue of Liberty, Godzilla, January

Practice Capitalize the proper nouns in these sentences.

1. President clinton visited china in june 1998.
2. He debated with jiang zemin in the great hall of the people.
3. People in washington and beijing watched on television.

Writing Application As you edit your report, be sure all proper nouns are capitalized.

Writer's Solution Connection
Language Lab

For more practice with capitalization, see the Proper Nouns lesson on the Language Lab CD-ROM.

Remember Your Audience Imagine that your audience is your class: teenagers like you. To help you inform them, consider the answers to these questions:

- Would a map help clarify the location of the event?
- Are there key words that need defining?
- Are there key people who must be identified?

Revising

Read Aloud Now that you've written the facts, here's your chance to make your writing smooth and precise. Reading your report aloud will help you hear a word or phrase you've used too often. Be alert to the sound of sentences, and revise those that seem awkward or clunky.

Combine Short Sentences Work to edit short, choppy sentences. Combine them whenever the points they make are closely related. Look at this example:

Short and Choppy:	Smooth and Combined
The mayor announced a new airport. It will be built north of town. It will cost $20 million. The project will take four years.	The mayor announced a four-year project to build a $20 million airport north of town.

Check Facts Confirm the spelling of names and places, especially those that are unfamiliar. Double-check dates, statistics, and any direct quotations you use. Make sure your report is 100 percent accurate.

Use a Peer Reviewer Ask someone to read your report. Use these questions to help get the most out of your reader.

▶ Have I included enough information?
▶ Can you picture what I'm writing about?
▶ Are my sentences clear?
▶ Do you see errors in spelling, grammar, or mechanics?

Publishing and Presenting

Newscast Use a video camera to record your report as if you were a television reporter. Watch the news for some tips. Then, rehearse to look and sound like a news anchor.

Current Events Board Find a bulletin board somewhere in your school and label it "In the News." Divide it into four parts: Local, State, National, World. Display your reports, using big, bold headlines for each one. Include copies of photographs if possible. Be sure to keep the board up to date.

Real-World Reading Skills Workshop

Strategies for Success

Daily newspapers are an excellent source of information on a wide range of topics. They provide up-to-date articles or subjects as varied as politics, business, sports, human interest, leisure time, and travel. Most newspapers are arranged so that readers can easily find the information they need. Here are some suggestions about how to read a newspaper:

Read Headlines Headlines are written in bold type and announce the major point of the news story that follows. Headlines often use short, attention-getting sentences to catch the reader's eye. Scan these to determine whether an article relates to you.

Notice Subheads Newspaper articles can be quite long, so they are usually divided into sections. Subheads, or mini-headlines, before each section of a long article let the reader know what information will be covered in the section that follows.

Find the Section You Want Most newspapers are divided into several different sections. A table of contents, or index, may list the sections by name. For instance, there is often a sports section, an arts and entertainment section, and a business section. Don't feel overwhelmed by all the categories—read only what you want or need to know.

Apply the Strategies

Read the front page of the newspaper at left. Then, answer the questions that follow.

1. What headlines do you see?
2. Identify the subheads in each story.
3. Why did the mayor cancel the parade?
4. What caused the forest fires?
5. In which section of the paper could you find baseball scores?
6. How many different sections does this newspaper have?

The Daily News

Mayor Cancels Parade

Monday, May 1. Mayor Daniels announced today that this year's Memorial Day parade would be canceled because of the traffic jams that were caused by last year's parade.

Protests Voiced Parade organizers protested the mayor's decision and hoped to find another site for the event.

Forest Fires Continue to Burn

Monday, May 1. Forest fires raged through several acres of land on the north side of the city. Firefighters from towns and cities all over the county have been called in to help put out the blaze.

Dry Weather Blamed Fire Chief Dave Monore blamed the recent spell of dry weather for creating conditions that led to the fires. Forecasters have predicted a period of rain by the weekend that should help the problem.

Index

World News.......A		Local News........D
Sports..............B		Entertainment...E
Business...........C		

✔ Here are other situations in which using headlines and text structure can be helpful:
- ▶ Reading a magazine
- ▶ Reading an article on the Internet
- ▶ Reading an encyclopedia or atlas
- ▶ Reading a textbook

𝒢rammar Review

Pronouns are words that replace nouns. Some pronouns change form depending on their use in a sentence. (See page 620.) Case is the form of the pronoun that shows its use in a sentence.

nominal adjective "our"] —pro·nom'i·nal·ly adv.
pro·noun (prō'noun') *n.* [altered (infl. by NOUN) < *pronomen* < *pro*, for + *nomen*, NOUN] *Gram.* any relationship or signal words that assume the fu within clauses or phrases while referring to othe the sentence or in other sentences: *I, you, them, it,* *myself, anybody, etc.* pronouns

Subjective Case	Use in Sentence	Example
I, we you he, she, it, they	Subject of a Verb	*She* caught a snake.
	Predicate Pronoun	It was *she.*

Objective Case	Use in Sentence	Example
me, us you him, her, it, them	Direct Object	Miss Ryan invited *us.*
	Indirect Object	She taught *them* tolerance.
	Object of a Preposition	She was happy with *him.*

Practice 1 Identify the case of the italicized pronouns in these sentences.

1. Nonfiction can teach *us* about the world and our interaction with *it.*

2. *I* read two articles on the Internet.

3. *They* could offer *us* more help.

4. After reading *them, she* will write two essays about the Internet.

5. *You* will find *them* useful.

6. We should learn from each other.

7. Let *us* take our experiences and share *them.*

8. *It* will make some events seem easier.

9. Let *me* tell you my opinion.

10. When *you* hit trouble, *you'll* see what *I* mean.

Practice 2 Complete each sentence with the correct pronoun.

1. Charles Kuralt gave (we, us) a vision of the past.

2. (He, him) brought a historic event to life.

3. Between you and (me, I), I liked that essay about the founders best.

4. It was (they, them) who granted (we, us) freedom.

5. (We, us) should be more aware of how (they, them) affected history.

6. Without (they, them), the nation might be different for (we, us).

7. If you ask my classmates and (I, me), I'd guess that (we, us) might not want to take the same risks that they did.

Grammar in Writing

✔ *Mistakes usually occur when a pronoun is part of a compound subject or object. To test whether the form of a pronoun is correct, use the pronoun by itself after the verb or preposition.*

Incorrect: The essay inspired Sam and I.

Test: The essay inspired I.

Correct: The essay inspired Sam and me.

Speaking, Listening, and Viewing Workshop

Speaking Persuasively

Candidates for public office use persuasion to convince voters to elect them. Trial lawyers use persuasion to sway juries toward specific verdicts. While you may not be delivering a closing argument anytime soon, you use persuasive tactics every day. Mastering these skills will help you convey your opinions to others—and it should help you change people's minds in the process.

Speak Clearly and Confidently One of the best ways to get someone to believe in your ideas is to believe in them yourself. If you speak clearly and confidently, listeners are more likely to agree with what you say. Use body language and tone of voice to convey your enthusiasm.

Consider Your Audience Persuading your parents to let you see a movie may be a tougher sell than convincing your friend to go with you. Choose the reasons that will sway the person you're addressing.

Organize Your Thoughts Thinking before speaking is always a good rule, especially if you are trying to persuade someone. Keep your goal in mind, and decide the best way to win another person over. Then, present your points in a clear, logical way.

Apply the Strategies

Get together with a small group to role-play the following situations. After two group members act out a scene, the others can give feedback about what worked and what didn't. Share your findings with the class.

1. You argue with a friend over whether you should see a movie or go bicycle riding.
2. You try to persuade a parent to allow you to get an after-school job.
3. You want a salesperson to give you a refund.

Tips for Speaking Persuasively

✔ *To persuade another person to agree with your opinions, follow these suggestions:*

▶ Use an upbeat tone of voice.
▶ Listen to objections, and address them in your argument.
▶ Control your emotions. Don't get angry or shout. Be persuasive, but remain in control.
▶ Let the facts speak for themselves.

What's Behind the Words

Vocabulary Adventures With Richard Lederer

Idioms From Land, Sea, and Sky

If someone says a concept comes from *out of left field*, you understand the idea is wacky, but you might not expect it to have anything to do with baseball. Like *out of left field*, many of the expressions we use in everyday speech are idioms—they have meanings different from what they actually say. Many English idioms come from farming, shipping, and the weather.

Down-to-Earth Words

The floor of the house we all share on this planet is the soil. Because the vast majority of Americans now live in cities, we have to some extent lost contact with that soil. Our down-to-earth English words and phrases, however, constantly remind us of our dependence on the earth that supports us:

▶ Like well-farmed land, the fertile mind of a cultured person is carefully tended and yields a bountiful harvest. We describe such people as *cultivated*.
▶ Late spring frosts or pests of the insect or human variety can kill a young tree or flower before it has a chance to develop. When we stop a problem in its early stages, we say that we *nip it in the bud*.

Our Seaworthy Language

Four fifths of our planet consists of water, and most of that is ocean. The salt of the sea is indeed on our tongues in phrases like these: I don't wish to *make waves, rock the boat, go overboard, lower the boom* on you, or make you feel *at sea*. I'd rather you *stay on an even keel* and have *smooth sailing*.

▶ The phrase that old sailors used to describe a ship in shallow water that touches land from time to time was *touch and go*. Today, the expression describes any dangerous situation.
▶ On the high seas, when the weather gets rough, travelers go below deck to ride out the storm and avoid becoming seasick. Thus, they retreat to a location *under the weather,* which gradually has come to mean "feeling ill."

Weather or Not

Now, explore how our language breathes in the air that sustains us all: I don't want to create a *tempest in a teapot* and cause *gales of laughter* in you. Nor do I wish to make a *lightning-quick* decision and *steal your thunder*. But I'm not just *shooting the breeze* either. I'm hoping that your awareness of the weather patterns that stream across our language will put you on *cloud nine*.

ACTIVITY 1 Explain the earthy metaphors embedded in the following expressions: (1) *a budding movie star*, (2) *to crop up*, (3) *a farm team*, (4) *a grass-roots campaign*, (5) *a needle in a haystack*, (6) *to weed out*.

ACTIVITY 2 Explain the sea and sailing metaphors in the following words and expressions: (1) *bitter end*, (2) *the doldrums*, (3) *hard and fast*, (4) *a landmark*, (5) *take the wind out of her sails*, (6) *the tide is turning*.

ACTIVITY 3 Certain people strike us as *cold*, while others radiate a *sunny* disposition. List additional moods and personalities that reflect the weather.

Extended Reading Opportunities

From biographies to history to personal narratives, nonfiction has something to satisfy every interest. Take a look at these suggestions:

Suggested Titles

Eleanor Roosevelt, A Life of Discovery
Russell Freedman

In a biography of one of the most influential twentieth-century Americans, the author traces the life of Eleanor Roosevelt, the former First Lady. Readers follow this strong woman from her childhood, through the troubled period of World War II, to her role in the founding of the United Nations. Throughout his telling, Freedman remains faithful to the spirit of Roosevelt's life.

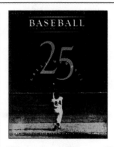

Twenty-Five Great Moments
Geoffrey C. Ward and Ken Burns With S. A. Kramer

Don Larsen pitches a perfect game in the 1956 World Series. Roberto Clemente pounds his 3,000th hit in 1972. Ken Griffey, Sr., and Ken Griffey, Jr., set a record when they hit back-to-back homers in 1990. Exciting moments like these are described in detail in a companion book to the PBS *Baseball* series. Written expressly for young people, Ward and Burns's book brings the history of baseball to life.

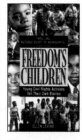

Freedom's Children: Young Civil Rights Activists Tell Their Own Stories
Ellen Levine

From the 1955 Montgomery bus boycott to the 1965 march from Selma to Montgomery, civil rights activity in the South challenged the beliefs, determination, and courage of African Americans. In a book that chronicles these turbulent times, Ellen Levine provides the firsthand accounts of young adults fighting to make a difference.

Other Possibilities

A Summer Life	Gary Soto
Close Encounters: Exploring the Universe With the Hubble Telescope	Elaine Scott
Zlata's Diary: A Child's Life in Sarajevo	Zlata Filipovic

Performers, Freshman Brown

Drama

When you read drama—literature meant to be performed—you give your imagination a workout. Use the plays presented in this unit to hear and see the scenes acted before you. As you read, notice the elements that make drama a unique form of writing:

- **Dialogue** is a conversation among characters.

- **Stage directions** are the playwright's notes to actors, directors, and readers. They reveal information about sets, movements, and emotion.

- **Characterization** is the playwright's technique of creating believable characters. The writer can't speak directly to an audience, so dialogue, costume, and gestures show you who each person really is.

- **Theme** is the central message the dramatist shares with the audience.

Reading for Success

Strategies for Reading Drama

Although drama shares many elements with stories, essays, and poetry, it is fundamentally different from these forms because it is designed to be performed for an audience. The story is told mostly through what the actors say (dialogue) and what they do (action). Stage directions in the script indicate when and how the actors should move and how they should deliver their lines. Most of the time, stage directions also include descriptions of sets, costumes, props, and sound and lighting effects. In screenplays (dramas written for film or television), the script may also include camera directions. When you read drama, keep in mind that it was written to be performed.

The following strategies will help you interact with the text of drama:

Envision the action and setting.

Reading a drama without envisioning the action and setting is like trying to watch your favorite television program with the picture turned off. To understand and appreciate drama, read the stage directions and use the details to turn on a mental picture.
- ▶ How do the actors move? What tone of voice do they use? What goes on between the characters?
- ▶ When and where do the events of the drama take place? What do the characters' surroundings look like?

Predict.

As you read, make predictions, or educated guesses, about what you think will happen. Look for hints in the dialogue and action that seem to suggest a certain outcome. As you read on, you will see if your predictions are correct.

Question.

Ask questions about what you read. Some questions that might come to mind as you read a drama may include:

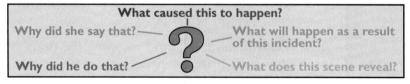

What caused this to happen?
Why did she say that? — ? — What will happen as a result of this incident?
Why did he do that? — What does this scene reveal?

Summarize.

Dramas are often broken into acts or scenes. These natural breaks give you an opportunity to review the action and sum up what has happened.

When you read the selections in this unit, use these general strategies, as well as those specifically suggested with each drama. They will help you gain a better understanding and appreciation for the dramas.

Part 1 *Classic Voices*

Henry Samary (1865–1902), de la Comedie Francaise, 1889, Henri de Toulouse-Lautrec, Musee d'Orsay, Paris, France

Guide for Reading

Meet the Author:

Charles Dickens (1812–1870)

The works of Charles Dickens were immensely popular during his lifetime and have remained so. His novels have been made into films, television movies, and even Broadway musicals!

A Difficult Childhood
Dickens spent most of his life in London. When Dickens was twelve, his father was sent to jail for not paying his debts. For several months, the burden of supporting the family fell on young Charles. He had to quit school and work in a factory for ten hours a day, six days a week.

When he was fifteen, Dickens went to work as a law clerk. Later, he became a reporter. In 1833, he began writing humorous pieces for newspapers and magazines under the pen name Boz.

The Turning Point The year 1836 was an eventful one for Dickens. His first book, *Sketches by Boz,* was published in February. Soon after, the first installment of his first novel, *The Pickwick Papers,* was published. Within a few months, *Pickwick,* which was published in twenty monthly installments, was all the rage, and Dickens had become England's most popular author.

THE STORY BEHIND THE STORY

Dickens loved Christmas and longed to see the Christmas spirit of kindness persist throughout the year. This was a driving force behind *A Christmas Carol* and is reflected in many of his other works. [For more on Dickens, see page 428.]

◆ LITERATURE AND YOUR LIFE

CONNECT YOUR EXPERIENCE

You probably know people who are inconsiderate, self-centered, even cruel. Imagine that there were some way to teach these people a lesson that would lead them to change their behavior. In this play, a greedy, mean-spirited character is taught a lesson he'll never forget.

THEMATIC FOCUS: Personal Codes

As you read, take note of how this drama illustrates the importance of being fair and considerate.

◆ Background for Understanding

HISTORY

Like most of Dickens's works, *A Christmas Carol* is set in England during the 1800's. This period was characterized by rapid industrial growth and a booming economy. The wealthy lived in great luxury. For the poor and the working class, however, life was hard. Factory workers put in long hours and endured brutal working conditions for low wages. Dickens had great sympathy for the poor and working classes, and you'll find this sympathy reflected in *A Christmas Carol*.

◆ Build Vocabulary

WORD ROOTS: -bene-

Scrooge, the main character in *A Christmas Carol,* is not known for his *benevolence*. This word is formed from the word roots -bene-, meaning "good," and -volen-, meaning "to wish." Thus, you might guess that *benevolence* means "wishing or wanting to do good," or "kindliness."

WORD BANK

Which of the Word Bank words do you think means "living in poverty"? Check the Build Vocabulary boxes to find out.

implored
morose
destitute
misanthrope
void
ponderous
benevolence

◆ A Christmas Carol, Act I ◆

◆ Literary Focus

ELEMENTS OF DRAMA

As in a movie or television program, the characters in a play are developed entirely through *dialogue* (what the characters say) and actions. Dialogue is one of the two main **elements of drama.** The other main element of drama is *stage directions.* Stage directions, which are printed in italics and enclosed in square brackets, describe what the characters, costumes, and sets look like. They also give instructions about special effects and how the actors should move and speak.

◆ Reading Strategy

ENVISION

Reading a drama is quite different from seeing a performance on stage. However, you can use the details the playwright provides, along with your imagination, to **envision,** or picture in your mind, what a performance might be like. To help you do so, pay close attention to the stage directions. Look for details that describe how the characters and the setting look. You might use a chart like the one below to help you keep track of these details in each scene.

	Setting:
Character:	**Scrooge:**
	Marley:
	Cratchit:

A Christmas Carol: Scrooge and Marley

Israel Horovitz

from
A Christmas Carol
by Charles Dickens

Act I

THE PEOPLE OF THE PLAY

JACOB MARLEY, a specter

EBENEZER SCROOGE, not yet dead, which is to say still alive

BOB CRATCHIT, Scrooge's clerk

FRED, Scrooge's nephew

THIN DO-GOODER

PORTLY DO-GOODER

SPECTERS (VARIOUS), carrying money-boxes

THE GHOST OF CHRISTMAS PAST

FOUR JOCUND TRAVELERS

A BAND OF SINGERS

A BAND OF DANCERS

LITTLE BOY SCROOGE

YOUNG MAN SCROOGE

FAN, Scrooge's little sister

THE SCHOOLMASTER

SCHOOLMATES

FEZZIWIG, a fine and fair employer

DICK, young Scrooge's co-worker

YOUNG SCROOGE

A FIDDLER

MORE DANCERS

SCROOGE'S LOST LOVE

SCROOGE'S LOST LOVE'S DAUGHTER

SCROOGE'S LOST LOVE'S HUSBAND

THE GHOST OF CHRISTMAS PRESENT

SOME BAKERS

MRS. CRATCHIT, Bob Cratchit's wife

BELINDA CRATCHIT, a daughter

MARTHA CRATCHIT, another daughter

PETER CRATCHIT, a son

TINY TIM CRATCHIT, another son

SCROOGE'S NIECE, Fred's wife

THE GHOST OF CHRISTMAS FUTURE, a mute Phantom

THREE MEN OF BUSINESS

DRUNKS, SCOUNDRELS, WOMEN OF THE STREETS

A CHARWOMAN

MRS. DILBER

JOE, an old second-hand goods dealer

A CORPSE, very like Scrooge

AN INDEBTED FAMILY

ADAM, a young boy

A POULTERER

A GENTLEWOMAN

SOME MORE MEN OF BUSINESS

THE PLACE OF THE PLAY
Various locations in and around the City of London, including Scrooge's Chambers and Offices; the Cratchit Home; Fred's Home; Scrooge's School; Fezziwig's Offices; Old Joe's Hide-a-Way.

THE TIME OF THE PLAY
The entire action of the play takes place on Christmas Eve, Christmas Day, and the morning after Christmas, 1843.

Scene 1

[*Ghostly music in auditorium. A single spotlight on* JACOB MARLEY, D.C. *He is ancient; awful, dead-eyed. He speaks straight out to auditorium.*]

MARLEY. [*Cackle-voiced*] My name is Jacob Marley and I am dead. [*He laughs.*] Oh, no, there's no doubt that I am dead. The register of my burial was signed by the clergyman, the clerk, the undertaker . . . and by my chief mourner . . . Ebenezer Scrooge . . . [*Pause; remembers*] I am dead as a doornail.

[*A spotlight fades up, Stage Right, on* SCROOGE, *in his counting-house,[1] counting. Lettering on the window behind* SCROOGE *reads:* "SCROOGE AND MARLEY, LTD." *The spotlight is tight on* SCROOGE's *head and shoulders. We shall not yet see into the offices and setting. Ghostly music continues, under.* MARLEY *looks across at* SCROOGE; *pitifully. After a moment's pause*]

I present him to you: Ebenezer Scrooge . . . England's most tightfisted hand at the grindstone, Scrooge! a squeezing, wrenching, grasping, scraping, clutching, covetous, old sinner! secret, and self-contained, and solitary as an oyster. The cold within him freezes his old features, nips his pointed nose, shrivels his cheek, stiffens his gait; makes his eyes red, his thin lips blue; and speaks out shrewdly in his grating voice. Look at him. Look at him . . .

▲ **Critical Viewing** Marley is the first character to appear on stage. What mood would the lighting shown above create for an audience? [**Interpret**]

[SCROOGE *counts and mumbles.*]

SCROOGE. They owe me money and I will collect. I will have them jailed, if I have to. They owe me money and I will collect what is due me.

[MARLEY *moves towards* SCROOGE; *two steps. The spotlight stays with him.*]

MARLEY. [*Disgusted*] He and I were partners for I don't know how many years. Scrooge was my sole executor, my sole administrator, my sole assign, my sole residuary legatee,[2] my sole friend and my sole mourner. But Scrooge was

---

1. **counting house:** Office for keeping financial records and writing business letters.

2. **my sole executor** (ig zek´ yə tər), **my sole administrator, my sole assign** (ə sīn´), **my sole residuary legatee** (ri zij´ oo wer´ ē leg´ ə tē´): Legal terms giving one person responsibility to carry out the wishes of another who has died.

◆ Literary Focus
What key background information is provided in this dialogue?

not so cut up by the sad event of my death, but that he was an excellent man of business on the very day of my funeral, and solemnized[3] it with an undoubted bargain. [*Pauses again in disgust*] He never painted out my name from the window. There it stands, on the window and above the warehouse door: Scrooge and Marley. Sometimes people new to our business call him Scrooge and sometimes they call him Marley. He answers to both names. It's all the same to him. And it's cheaper than painting in a new sign, isn't it? [*Pauses; moves closer to* SCROOGE] Nobody has ever stopped him in the street to say, with gladsome looks, "My dear Scrooge, how are you? When will you come to see me?" No beggars implored him to bestow a trifle, no children ever ask him what it is o'clock, no man or woman now, or ever in his life, not once, inquire the way to such and such a place. [MARLEY *stands next to* SCROOGE *now. They share, so it seems, a spotlight.*] But what does Scrooge care of any of this? It is the very thing he likes! To edge his way along the crowded paths of life, warning all human sympathy to keep its distance.

[*A ghostly bell rings in the distance.* MARLEY *moves away from* SCROOGE, *now, heading* D. *again. As he does, he "takes" the light:* SCROOGE *has disappeared into the black void beyond.* MARLEY *walks* D.C., *talking directly to the audience. Pauses*]

The bell tolls and I must take my leave. You must stay a while with Scrooge and watch him play out his scroogey life. It is now the story: the once-upon-a-time. Scrooge is busy in his counting-house. Where else? Christmas eve and Scrooge is busy in his counting-house. It is cold, bleak, biting weather outside: foggy withal: and, if you listen closely, you can hear the people in the court go wheezing up and down, beating their hands upon their breasts, and stamping their feet upon the pavement stones to warm them . . .

---

3. **solemnized** (säl´ əm nizd´) *v.:* Honored or remembered. Marley is being ironic.

[*The clocks outside strike three.*]

Only three! and quite dark outside already: it has not been light all day this day.

[*This ghostly bell rings in the distance again.* MARLEY *looks about him. Music in.* MARLEY *flies away.*]

[N.B. *Marley's comings and goings should, from time to time, induce the explosion of the odd flash-pot.* I.H.]

Scene 2

[*Christmas music in, sung by a live chorus, full. At conclusion of song, sound fades under and into the distance. Lights up in set: offices of Scrooge and Marley, Ltd.* SCROOGE *sits at his desk, at work. Near him is a tiny fire. His door is open and in his line of vision, we see* SCROOGE'S *clerk,* BOB CRATCHIT, *who sits in a dismal tank of a cubicle, copying letters.*

◆ Reading Strategy
How do the stage directions help you envision Scrooge's office?

Near CRATCHIT *is a fire so tiny as to barely cast a light: perhaps it is one pitifully glowing coal?* CRATCHIT *rubs his hands together, puts on a white comforter[4] and tries to heat his hands around his candle.* SCROOGE'S NEPHEW *enters, unseen.*]

SCROOGE. What are you doing, Cratchit? Acting cold, are you? Next, you'll be asking to replenish your coal from my coal-box, won't you? Well, save your breath, Cratchit! Unless you're prepared to find employ elsewhere!

NEPHEW. [*Cheerfully; surprising* SCROOGE] A merry Christmas to you, Uncle! God save you!

SCROOGE. Bah! Humbug![5]

NEPHEW. Christmas a "humbug," Uncle? I'm sure you don't mean that.

SCROOGE. I do! Merry Christmas? What right do you have to be merry? What reason have you to be merry? You're poor enough!

NEPHEW. Come, then. What right have you

---

4. **comforter** (kum´ fər tər) *n.:* Long, woolen scarf.
5. **Humbug** (hum´ bug´) *interj.:* Nonsense!

to be dismal? What reason have you to be morose? You're rich enough.

SCROOGE. Bah! Humbug!

NEPHEW. Don't be cross, Uncle.

SCROOGE. What else can I be? Eh? When I live in a world of fools such as this? Merry Christmas? What's Christmastime to you but a time of paying bills without any money; a time for finding yourself a year older, but not an hour richer. If I could work my will, every idiot who goes about with "Merry Christmas" on his lips, should be boiled with his own pudding, and buried with a stake of holly through his heart. He should!

NEPHEW. Uncle!

SCROOGE. Nephew! You keep Christmas in your own way and let me keep it in mine.

NEPHEW. Keep it! But you don't keep it, Uncle.

SCROOGE. Let me leave it alone, then. Much good it has ever done you!

NEPHEW. There are many things from which I have derived good, by which I have not profited,

▲ **Critical Viewing** Bob Cratchit heats his hands over a small flame in his office. What does this action communicate to the audience about the setting? **[Infer]**

I daresay. Christmas among the rest. But I am sure that I always thought of Christmas time, when it has come round—as a good time: the only time I know of, when men and women seem to open their shut-up hearts freely, and to think of people below them as if they really were fellow-passengers to the grave, and not another race of creatures bound on other journeys. And therefore, Uncle, though it has never put a scrap of gold or silver in my pocket, I believe that it *has* done me good, and that it *will* do me good; and I say, God bless it!

[*The* CLERK *in the tank applauds, looks at the furious* SCROOGE *and pokes out his tiny fire, as if in exchange for the moment of impropriety.* SCROOGE *yells at him.*]

◆ **Build Vocabulary**

implored (im plôrd´) *v.*: Asked or begged earnestly

morose (mə rōs´) *adj.*: Gloomy; ill-tempered

SCROOGE. [*To the* CLERK] Let me hear another sound from you and you'll keep your Christmas by losing your situation. [*To the* NEPHEW] You're quite a powerful speaker, sir. I wonder you don't go into Parliament.[6]

NEPHEW. Don't be angry, Uncle. Come! Dine with us tomorrow.

SCROOGE. I'd rather see myself dead than see myself with your family!

NEPHEW. But, why? Why?

SCROOGE. Why did you get married?

NEPHEW. Because I fell in love.

SCROOGE. That, sir, is the only thing that you have said to me in your entire lifetime which is even more ridiculous than "Merry Christmas"! [*Turns from* NEPHEW] Good afternoon.

NEPHEW. Nay, Uncle, you never came to see me before I married either. Why give it as a reason for not coming now?

SCROOGE. Good afternoon, Nephew!

NEPHEW. I want nothing from you; I ask nothing of you; why cannot we be friends?

SCROOGE. Good afternoon!

NEPHEW. I am sorry with all my heart, to find you so resolute. But I have made the trial in homage to Christmas, and I'll keep my Christmas humor to the last. So A Merry Christmas, Uncle!

SCROOGE. Good afternoon!

NEPHEW. And A Happy New Year!

SCROOGE. Good afternoon!

NEPHEW. [*He stands facing* SCROOGE.] Uncle, you are the most . . . [*Pauses*] No, I shan't. My Christmas humor is intact . . . [*Pause*] God bless you, Uncle . . . [NEPHEW *turns and starts for the door; he stops at* CRATCHIT's *cage.*] Merry Christmas, Bob Cratchit . . .

CRATCHIT. Merry Christmas to you sir, and a very, very happy New Year . . .

SCROOGE. [*Calling across to them*] Oh, fine, a perfection, just fine . . . to see the perfect pair of you: husbands, with wives and children to support . . . my clerk there earning fifteen shillings a week . . . and the perfect pair of you, talking about a Merry Christmas! [*Pauses*] I'll retire to Bedlam![7]

NEPHEW. [*To* CRATCHIT] He's impossible!

CRATCHIT. Oh, mind him not, sir. He's getting on in years, and he's alone. He's noticed your visit. I'll wager your visit has warmed him.

NEPHEW. Him? Uncle Ebenezer Scrooge? *Warmed?* You are a better Christian than I am, sir.

CRATCHIT. [*Opening the door for* NEPHEW; *two* DO-GOODERS *will enter, as* NEPHEW *exits*] Good day to you, sir, and God bless.

NEPHEW. God bless . . . [*One man who enters is portly, the other is thin. Both are pleasant.*]

CRATCHIT. Can I help you, gentlemen?

THIN MAN. [*Carrying papers and books; looks around* CRATCHIT *to* SCROOGE] Scrooge and Marley's, I believe. Have I the pleasure of addressing Mr. Scrooge, or Mr. Marley?

SCROOGE. Mr. Marley has been dead these seven years. He died seven years ago this very night.

PORTLY MAN. We have no doubt his liberality[8] is well represented by his surviving partner . . . [*Offers his calling card*]

SCROOGE. [*Handing back the card; unlooked at*] . . . Good afternoon.

THIN MAN. This will take but a moment, sir . . .

PORTLY MAN. At this festive season of the year, Mr. Scrooge, it is more than usually desirable that we should make some slight provision for the poor and <u>destitute</u>, who suffer greatly at the present time. Many thousands are in want of common necessities; hundreds of thousands are in want of common comforts, sir.

SCROOGE. Are there no prisons?

PORTLY MAN. Plenty of prisons.

---

6. **Parliament** (pär′ lə mənt): National legislative body of Great Britain, in some ways like the American Congress.

7. **Bedlam** (bed′ ləm): Hospital in London for the mentally ill.

8. **liberality** (lib′ ər al′ i tē): Generosity.

SCROOGE. And aren't the Union workhouses still in operation?

THIN MAN. They are. Still. I wish that I could say that they are not.

SCROOGE. The Treadmill[9] and the Poor Law[10] are in full vigor, then?

THIN MAN. Both very busy, sir.

SCROOGE. Ohhh, I see. I was afraid, from what you said at first, that something had occurred to stop them from their useful course. [*Pauses*] I'm glad to hear it.

PORTLY MAN. Under the impression that they scarcely furnish Christian cheer of mind or body to the multitude, a few of us are endeavoring to raise a fund to buy the Poor some meat and drink, and means of warmth. We choose this time, because it is a time, of all others, when Want is keenly felt, and Abundance rejoices. [*Pen in hand; as well as notepad*] What shall I put you down for, sir?

SCROOGE. Nothing!

PORTLY MAN. You wish to be left anonymous?

SCROOGE. I wish to be left alone! [*Pauses; turns away; turns back to them*] Since you ask me what I wish, gentlemen, that is my answer. I help to support the establishments that I have mentioned: they cost enough: and those who are badly off must go there.

THIN MAN. Many can't go there; and many would rather die.

SCROOGE. If they would rather die, they had better do it, and decrease the surplus population. Besides—excuse me—I don't know that.

THIN MAN. But you might know it!

SCROOGE. It's not my business. It's enough for a man to understand his own business, and not to interfere with other people's. Mine

---

9. **the Treadmill** (tred´ mil´): Kind of mill wheel turned by the weight of persons treading steps arranged around it; this device was used to punish prisoners in jails.
10. **the Poor Law:** The original 17th-century Poor Laws called for overseers of the poor in each parish to provide relief for the needy. The New Poor Law of 1834 made the workhouses in which the poor sometimes lived and worked extremely harsh and unattractive. They became a symbol of the misery of the poor.

occupies me constantly. Good afternoon, gentlemen! [SCROOGE *turns his back on the gentlemen and returns to his desk.*]

PORTLY MAN. But, sir, Mr. Scrooge . . . think of the poor.

SCROOGE. [*Turns suddenly to them. Pauses*] Take your leave of my offices, sirs, while I am still smiling.

◆ **Reading Strategy**
How would you expect these visitors to react to Scrooge's comments? What expressions might they show?

[*The* THIN MAN *looks at the* PORTLY MAN. *They are undone. They shrug. They move to the door.* CRATCHIT *hops up to open it for them.*]

THIN MAN. Good day, sir . . . [*To* CRATCHIT] A merry Christmas to you, sir . . .

CRATCHIT. Yes. A Merry Christmas to both of you . . .

PORTLY MAN. Merry Christmas . . .

[CRATCHIT *silently squeezes something into the hand of the* THIN MAN.]

THIN MAN. What's this?

CRATCHIT. Shhhh . . .

[CRATCHIT *opens the door; wind and snow whistle into the room.*]

THIN MAN. Thank you, sir, thank you.

[CRATCHIT *closes the door and returns to his workplace.* SCROOGE *is at his own counting table. He talks to* CRATCHIT *without looking up.*]

SCROOGE. It's less of a time of year for being merry, and more a time of year for being loony . . . if you ask me.

CRATCHIT. Well, I don't know, sir . . .

[*The clock's bell strikes six o'clock.*]

Well, there it is, eh, six?

SCROOGE. Saved by six bells, are you?

◆ **Build Vocabulary**

destitute (des´ tə tōōt´) *adj. used as n.*: People living in complete poverty

▲ **Critical Viewing** What emotion does each actor express in this photograph? Describe the tone of voice that the actors might use to convey this emotion. **[Speculate]**

CRATCHIT. I must be going home . . . [*He snuffs out his candle and puts on his hat.*] I hope you have a . . . very very lovely day tomorrow, sir . . .

SCROOGE. Hmmm. Oh, you'll be wanting the whole day tomorrow, I suppose?

CRATCHIT. If quite convenient, sir.

SCROOGE. It's not convenient, and it's not fair. If I was to stop half-a-crown for it, you'd think yourself ill-used, I'll be bound?

[CRATCHIT *smiles faintly.*]

CRATCHIT. I don't know, sir . . .

SCROOGE. And yet, you don't think me ill-used when I pay a day's wages for no work . . .

CRATCHIT. It's only but once a year . . .

SCROOGE. A poor excuse for picking a man's pocket every 25th of December! But I suppose you must have the whole day. Be here all the earlier the next morning!

CRATCHIT. Oh, I will, sir. I will. I promise you. And, sir . . .

SCROOGE. Don't say it, Cratchit.

CRATCHIT. But let me wish you a . . .

SCROOGE. Don't say it, Cratchit. I warn you . . .

CRATCHIT. Sir!

SCROOGE. Cratchit!

[CRATCHIT *opens the door.*]

CRATCHIT. All right, then, sir . . . well . . . [*Suddenly*] Merry Christmas, Mr. Scrooge!

> ◆ **Literary Focus**
> How does this dialogue help reveal Scrooge's personality?

[*And he runs out the door, shutting same behind him.* SCROOGE *moves to his desk; gathering his coat, hat, etc. A* BOY *appears at his window. . . .*]

BOY. [*Singing*] "Away in a manger . . ."

[SCROOGE *seizes his ruler and whacks at the image of the* BOY *outside. The* BOY *leaves.*]

SCROOGE. Bah! Humbug! Christmas! Bah! Humbug! [*He shuts out the light.*]

A note on the crossover, following Scene 2:

[SCROOGE *will walk alone to his rooms from his offices. As he makes a long slow cross of the stage, the scenery should change. Christmas music will be heard, various people will cross by* SCROOGE, *often smiling happily.*

    There will be occasional pleasant greetings tossed at him.

    SCROOGE, *in contrast to all, will grump and mumble. He will snap at passing boys, as might a horrid old hound.*

    In short, SCROOGE'S *sounds and movements will define him in contrast from all other people who cross the stage: he is the* <u>misanthrope</u>, *the malcontent, the miser. He is* SCROOGE.

    This statement of SCROOGE'S *character, by contrast to all other characters, should seem comical to the audience.*

During SCROOGE'S *crossover to his rooms, snow should begin to fall. All passers-by will hold their faces to the sky, smiling, allowing snow to shower them lightly.* SCROOGE, *by contrast, will bat at the flakes with his walking-stick, as might an insomniac swat at a sleep-stopping, middle-of-the-night swarm of mosquitoes. He will comment on the blackness of the night, and, finally, reach his rooms and his encounter with the magical specter:*[11] MARLEY, *his eternal mate.*]

Scene 3

SCROOGE. No light at all . . . no moon . . . *that* is what is at the center of a Christmas Eve: dead black: <u>void</u> . . .

[SCROOGE *puts his key in the door's keyhole. He has reached his rooms now. The door knocker changes and is now* MARLEY'S *face. A musical sound; quickly: ghostly.* MARLEY'S *image is not at all angry, but looks at* SCROOGE *as did the old* MARLEY *look at* SCROOGE. *The hair is curiously stirred; eyes wide open, dead: absent of focus.* SCROOGE *stares wordlessly here. The face, before his very eyes, does* deliquesce.[12] *It is a knocker again.* SCROOGE *opens the door and checks the back of same, probably for* MARLEY'S *pigtail. Seeing nothing but screws and nuts,* SCROOGE *refuses the memory.*]

Pooh, pooh!

[*The sound of the door closing resounds throughout the house as thunder. Every room echoes the sound.* SCROOGE *fastens the door and walks across the hall to the stairs, trimming his candle as he goes; and then he goes slowly up the staircase. He checks each room: sitting room, bedrooms, slumber-room. He looks under the sofa, under the table: nobody there. He fixes his evening gruel on the hob,*[13] *changes his jacket.* SCROOGE *sits near the tiny low-flamed fire, sipping his gruel. There are various pictures on the walls: all of them now show likenesses of* MARLEY. SCROOGE *blinks his eyes.*]

---

11. **specter** (spek´ tər) *n.:* Ghost.
12. **deliquesce** (del´ ə kwes´) *v.:* Melt away.
13. **gruel** (grōō´ əl) **on the hob** (häb): Thin broth warming on a ledge at the back or side of the fireplace.

Bah! Humbug!

[SCROOGE *walks in a circle about the room. The pictures change back into their natural images. He sits down at the table in front of the fire. A bell hangs overhead. It begins to ring, of its own accord. Slowly, surely, begins the ringing of every bell in the house. They continue ringing for nearly half a minute.* SCROOGE *is stunned by the phenomenon. The bells cease their ringing all at once. Deep below* SCROOGE, *in the basement of the house, there is the sound of clanking, of some enormous chain being dragged across the floors; and now up the stairs. We hear doors flying open.*]

Bah still! Humbug still! This is not happening! I won't believe it!

[MARLEY'S GHOST *enters the room. He is horrible to look at: pigtail, vest, suit as usual, but he drags an enormous chain now, to which is fastened cash-boxes, keys, padlocks, ledgers, deeds, and heavy purses fashioned of steel. He is transparent.* MARLEY *stands opposite the stricken* SCROOGE.]

How now! What do you want of me?

MARLEY. Much!

SCROOGE. Who are you?

MARLEY. Ask me who I *was.*

SCROOGE. Who *were* you then?

MARLEY. In life, I was your business partner: Jacob Marley.

SCROOGE. I see . . . can you sit down?

MARLEY. I can.

SCROOGE. Do it then.

MARLEY. I shall. [MARLEY *sits opposite* SCROOGE, *in the chair across the table, at the front of the fireplace.*] You don't believe in me.

SCROOGE. I don't.

MARLEY. Why do you doubt your senses?

◆ Build Vocabulary

misanthrope (mis´ ən *thrōp*´) *n.:* Person who hates or distrusts everyone

void (void) *n.:* Total emptiness

SCROOGE. Because every little thing affects them. A slight disorder of the stomach makes them cheat. You may be an undigested bit of beef, a blot of mustard, a crumb of cheese, a fragment of an underdone potato. There's more of gravy than of grave about you, whatever you are!

[*There is a silence between them.* SCROOGE *is made nervous by it. He picks up a toothpick.*]

Humbug! I tell you: humbug!

[MARLEY *opens his mouth and screams a ghosty, fearful scream. The scream echoes about each room of the house. Bats fly, cats screech, lightning flashes.* SCROOGE *stands and walks backwards against the wall.* MARLEY *stands and screams again. This time, he takes his head and lifts it from his shoulders. His head continues to scream.* MARLEY'S *face again appears on every picture in the room: all screaming.* SCROOGE, *on his knees before* MARLEY.]

◆ **Reading Strategy**
How do the stage directions help you picture the frightening appearance and actions of Marley's ghost?

Mercy! Dreadful apparition,[14] mercy! Why, O! why do you trouble me so?

MARLEY. Man of the worldly mind, do you believe in me, or not?

SCROOGE. I do. I must. But why do spirits such as you walk the earth? And why do they come to me?

MARLEY. It is required of every man that the spirit within him should walk abroad among his fellow-men, and travel far and wide; and if that spirit goes not forth in life, it is condemned to do so after death. [MARLEY *screams again; a tragic scream; from his ghosty bones.*] I wear the chain I forged in life. I made it link by link, and yard by yard. Is its pattern strange to

14. **apparition** (ap´ ə rish´ ən) *n.:* Ghost.

◀ **Critical Viewing** What music might a director choose to enhance the mood of this scene? Explain. [**Extend**]

you? Or would you know, you, Scrooge, the weight and length of the strong coil you bear yourself? It was full as heavy and long as this, seven Christmas Eves ago. You have labored on it, since. It is a <u>ponderous</u> chain.

[*Terrified that a chain will appear about his body,* SCROOGE *spins and waves the unwanted chain away. None, of course, appears. Sees* MARLEY *watching him dance about the room.* MARLEY *watches* SCROOGE; *silently.*]

SCROOGE. Jacob. Old Jacob Marley, tell me more. Speak comfort to me, Jacob . . .

MARLEY. I have none to give. Comfort comes from other regions, Ebenezer Scrooge, and is conveyed by other ministers, to other kinds of men. A very little more, is all that is permitted to me. I cannot rest, I cannot stay, I cannot linger anywhere . . . [*He moans again.*] my spirit never walked beyond our counting-house —mark me!—in life my spirit never roved beyond the narrow limits of our money-changing hole; and weary journeys lie before me!

SCROOGE. But you were always a good man of business, Jacob.

MARLEY. [*Screams word "business"; a flashpot explodes with him.*] BUSINESS!!! Mankind was my business. The common welfare was my business; charity, mercy, forbearance, <u>benevolence</u>, were, all, my business. [SCROOGE *is quaking.*] Hear me, Ebenezer Scrooge! My time is nearly gone.

SCROOGE. I will, but don't be hard upon me. And don't be flowery, Jacob! Pray!

MARLEY. How is it that I appear before you in a shape that you can see, I may not tell. I have sat invisible beside you many and many a day. That is no light part of my penance. I am here tonight to warn you that you have yet a chance and hope of escaping my fate. A chance and hope of my procuring, Ebenezer.

◆ **Build Vocabulary**

ponderous (pän´ dər əs) *adj.:* Very heavy; bulky
benevolence (bə nev´ ə lens) *n.:* Kindliness

SCROOGE. You were always a good friend to me. Thank'ee!

MARLEY. You will be haunted by Three Spirits.

SCROOGE. Would that be the chance and hope you mentioned, Jacob?

MARLEY. It is.

SCROOGE. I think I'd rather not.

MARLEY. Without their visits, you cannot hope to shun the path I tread. Expect the first one tomorrow, when the bell tolls one.

SCROOGE. Couldn't I take 'em all at once, and get it over, Jacob?

MARLEY. Expect the second on the next night at the same hour. The third upon the next night when the last stroke of twelve has ceased to vibrate. Look to see me no more. Others may, but you may not. And look that, for your own sake, you remember what has passed between us!

[MARLEY *places his head back upon his shoulders. He approaches the window and beckons to* SCROOGE *to watch. Outside the window, specters fly by, carrying money-boxes and chains. They make a confused sound of lamentation.* MARLEY, *after listening a moment, joins into their mournful dirge. He leans to the window and floats out into the bleak, dark night. He is gone.*]

SCROOGE. [*Rushing to the window*] Jacob! No, Jacob! Don't leave me! I'm frightened!

[*He sees that* MARLEY *has gone. He looks outside. He pulls the shutter closed, so that the scene is blocked from his view. All sound stops. After a pause, he re-opens the shutter and all is quiet, as it should be on Christmas Eve. Carolers carol out of doors, in the distance.* SCROOGE *closes the shutter and walks down the stairs. He examines the door by which* MARLEY *first entered.*]

No one here at all! Did I imagine all that? Humbug! [*He looks about the room.*] I did imagine it. It only happened in my foulest dream-mind, didn't it? An undigested bit of . . .

[*Thunder and lightning in the room; suddenly*]

Sorry! Sorry!

[*There is silence again. The lights fade out.*]

Scene 4

[*Christmas music, choral, "Hark the Herald Angels Sing," sung by an onstage choir of children, spotlighted,* D.C. *Above,* SCROOGE *in his bed, dead to the world, asleep, in his darkened room. It should appear that the choir is singing somewhere outside of the house, of course, and a use of scrim*[15] *is thus suggested. When the singing is ended, the choir should fade out of view and* MARLEY *should fade into view, in their place.*]

MARLEY. [*Directly to audience*] From this point forth . . . I shall be quite visible to you, but invisible to him. [*Smiles*] He will feel my presence, nevertheless, for, unless my senses fail me completely, we are—you and I—witness to the changing of a miser: that one, my partner in life, in business, and in eternity: that one: Scrooge. [*Moves to staircase, below* SCROOGE] See him now. He endeavors to pierce the darkness with his ferret eyes.[16] [*To audience*] See him, now. He listens for the hour.

[*The bells toll.* SCROOGE *is awakened and quakes as the hour approaches one o'clock, but the bells stop their sound at the hour of twelve.*]

SCROOGE. [*Astonished*] Midnight! Why this isn't possible. It was past two when I went to bed. An icicle must have gotten into the clock's works! I couldn't have slept through the whole day and far into another night. It isn't possible that anything has happened to the sun, and this is twelve at noon! [*He runs to window; unshutters same; it is night.*] Night, still. Quiet, normal for the season, cold. It is certainly not noon. I cannot in any way afford to lose my days. Securities come due, promissory notes,[17] interest on investments: these are things that happen in the daylight! [*He returns to his bed.*] Was this a dream?

---

15. scrim (skrim) *n.:* Light, semitransparent curtain.
16. ferret eyes: A ferret is a small, weasellike animal used for hunting rabbits; this expression means to look persistently, the way a ferret hunts.
17. promissory (präm′ i sôr′ ē) **notes:** Written promises to pay someone a certain sum of money.

[MARLEY *appears in his room. He speaks to the audience.*]

MARLEY. You see? He does not, with faith, believe in me fully, even still! Whatever will it take to turn the faith of a miser from money to men?

SCROOGE. Another quarter and it'll be one and Marley's ghosty friends will come. [*Pauses; listens*] Where's the chime for one? [*Ding, dong*] A quarter *past* [*Repeats*] Half-past! [*Repeats*] A quarter to it! But where's the heavy bell of the hour one? This is a game in which I lose my senses! Perhaps, if I allowed myself another short doze . . .

MARLEY . . . Doze, Ebenezer, doze.

[*A heavy bell thuds its one ring; dull and definitely one o'clock. There is a flash of light.* SCROOGE *sits up, in a sudden. A hand draws back the curtains by his bed. He sees it.*]

SCROOGE. A hand! Who owns it! Hello!

[*Ghosty music again, but of a new nature to the play. A strange figure stands before* SCROOGE— *like a child, yet at the same time like an old man: white hair, but unwrinkled skin, long, muscular arms, but delicate legs and feet. Wears white tunic; lustrous belt cinches waist. Branch of fresh green holly in its hand, but has its dress trimmed with fresh summer flowers. Clear jets of light spring from the crown of its head. Holds cap in hand. The Spirit is called* PAST.]

Are you the Spirit, sir, whose coming was foretold to me?

PAST. I am.

MARLEY. Does he take this to be a vision of his green grocer?

SCROOGE. Who, and what are you?

PAST. I am the Ghost of Christmas Past.

SCROOGE. Long past?

PAST. Your past.

SCROOGE. May I ask, please, sir, what business you have here with me?

PAST. Your welfare.

SCROOGE. Not to sound ungrateful, sir, and

really, please do understand that I am plenty obliged for your concern, but, really, kind spirit, it would have done all the better for my welfare to have been left alone altogether, to have slept peacefully through this night.

PAST. Your reclamation, then. Take heed!

SCROOGE. My what?

PAST. [*Motioning to* SCROOGE *and taking his arm*] Rise! Fly with me! [*He leads* SCROOGE *to the window.*]

SCROOGE. [*Panicked*] Fly, but I am a mortal and cannot fly!

PAST. [*Pointing to his heart*] Bear but a touch of my hand *here* and you shall be upheld in more than this!

[SCROOGE *touches the* SPIRIT's *heart and the lights dissolve into sparkly flickers. Lovely crystals of music are heard. The scene dissolves into another. Christmas music again*]

Scene 5

[SCROOGE *and the* GHOST OF CHRISTMAS PAST *walk together across an open stage. In the background, we see a field that is open; covered by a soft, downy snow: a country road.*]

SCROOGE. Good Heaven! I was bred in this place. I was a boy here!

[SCROOGE *freezes, staring at the field beyond.* MARLEY's *ghost appears beside him; takes* SCROOGE's *face in his hands, and turns his face to the audience.*]

MARLEY. You see this Scrooge: stricken by feeling. Conscious of a thousand odors floating in the air, each one connected with a thousand thoughts, and hopes, and joys, and care long, long forgotten. [*Pause*] This one—this Scrooge—before your very eyes, returns to life, among the living. [*To audience, sternly*] You'd best pay your most careful attention. I would suggest rapt.[18]

[*There is a small flash and puff of smoke and* MARLEY *is gone again.*]

---

18. rapt (rapt) *adj.*: Giving complete attention; totally carried away by something.

PAST. Your lip is trembling, Mr. Scrooge. And what is that upon your cheek?

SCROOGE. Upon my cheek? Nothing . . . a blemish on the skin from the eating of over-much grease . . . nothing . . . [*Suddenly*] Kind Spirit of Christmas Past, lead me where you will, but *quickly!* To be stagnant in this place is, for me, *unbearable!*

PAST. You recollect the way?

SCROOGE. Remember it! I would know it blindfolded! My bridge, my church, my winding river! [*Staggers about, trying to see it all at once. He weeps again.*]

PAST. These are but shadows of things that have been. They have no consciousness of us.

[*Four jocund travelers enter, singing a Christmas song in four-part harmony—"God Rest Ye Merry Gentlemen."*]

SCROOGE. Listen! I know these men! I know them! I remember the beauty of their song!

PAST. But, why do you remember it so happily? It is Merry Christmas that they say to one another! What is Merry Christmas to you, Mr. Scrooge? Out upon Merry Christmas, right? What good has Merry Christmas ever done you, Mr. Scrooge? . . .

SCROOGE. [*After a long pause*] None. No good. None . . . [*He bows his head.*]

PAST. Look, you, sir, a school ahead. The schoolroom is not quite deserted. A solitary child, neglected by his friends, is left there still.

[SCROOGE *falls to the ground; sobbing as he sees, and we see, a small boy, the young* SCROOGE, *sitting and weeping, bravely, alone at his desk: alone in a vast space, a void.*]

SCROOGE. I cannot look on him!

PAST. You must, Mr. Scrooge, you must.

SCROOGE. It's me. [*Pauses; weeps*] Poor boy. He lived inside his head . . . alone . . . [*Pauses; weeps*] poor boy. [*Pauses; stops his weeping*] I wish . . . [*Dries his eyes on his cuff*] ah! it's too late!

PAST. What is the matter?

SCROOGE. There was a boy singing a Christmas Carol outside my door last night. I should like to have given him something: that's all.

PAST. [*Smiles; waves his hand to* SCROOGE] Come. Let us see another Christmas.

[*Lights out on little boy. A flash of light. A puff of smoke. Lights up on older boy*]

SCROOGE. Look! Me, again! Older now! [*Realizes*] Oh, yes . . . still alone.

[*The boy—a slightly older* SCROOGE —*sits alone in a chair, reading. The door to the room opens and a young girl enters. She is much, much younger than this slightly older* SCROOGE. *She is, say, six, and he is, say, twelve. Elder* SCROOGE *and the* GHOST OF CHRISTMAS PAST *stand watching the scene, unseen.*]

FAN. Dear, dear brother, I have come to bring you home.

BOY. Home, little Fan?

FAN. Yes! Home, for good and all! Father is so much kinder than he ever used to be, and home's like heaven! He spoke so gently to me one dear night when I was going to bed that I was not afraid to ask him once more if you might come home; and he said "yes" . . . you should; and sent me in a coach to bring you. And you're to be a man and are never to come back here, but first, we're to be together all the Christmas long, and have the merriest time in the world.

BOY. You are quite a woman, little Fan!

[*Laughing; she drags at* BOY, *causing him to stumble to the door with her. Suddenly we hear a mean and terrible voice in the hallway, Off. It is the* SCHOOLMASTER.]

SCHOOLMASTER. Bring down Master Scrooge's travel box at once! He is to travel!

FAN. Who is that, Ebenezer?

BOY. O! Quiet, Fan. It is the Schoolmaster, himself!

[*The door bursts open and into the room bursts with it the* SCHOOLMASTER.]

▲ **Critical Viewing** Without knowing about the action of the scene, what can you infer about the relationship of the characters? **[Infer]**

SCHOOLMASTER. Master Scrooge?

BOY. Oh, Schoolmaster. I'd like you to meet my little sister, Fan, sir . . .

[*Two boys struggle on with* SCROOGE'S *trunk.*]

FAN. Pleased, sir . . . [*She curtsies.*]

SCHOOLMASTER. You are to travel, Master Scrooge.

SCROOGE. Yes, sir. I know sir . . .

[*All start to exit, but* FAN *grabs the coattail of the mean old* SCHOOLMASTER.]

BOY. Fan!

SCHOOLMASTER. What's this?

FAN. Pardon, sir, but I believe that you've forgotten to say your goodbye to my brother, Ebenezer, who stands still now awaiting it . . . [*She smiles, curtsies, lowers her eyes.*] pardon, sir.

SCHOOLMASTER. [*Amazed*] I . . . uh . . . harumph . . . uhh . . . well, then . . . [*Outstretches hand*] Goodbye, Scrooge.

BOY. Uh, well, goodbye, Schoolmaster . . .

[*Lights fade out on all but* BOY *looking at* FAN; *and* SCROOGE *and* PAST *looking at them.*]

SCROOGE. Oh, my dear, dear little sister, Fan . . . how I loved her.

PAST. Always a delicate creature, whom a breath might have withered, but she had a large heart . . .

SCROOGE. So she had.

PAST. She died a woman, and had, as I think, children.

SCROOGE. One child.

PAST. True. Your nephew.

SCROOGE. Yes.

PAST. Fine, then. We move on, Mr. Scrooge. That warehouse, there? Do you know it?

SCROOGE. Know it? Wasn't I apprenticed[19] there?

PAST. We'll have a look.

[*They enter the warehouse. The lights cross-fade with them, coming up on an old man in Welsh wig:* FEZZIWIG.]

SCROOGE. Why, it's old Fezziwig! Bless his heart; it's Fezziwig, alive again!

[FEZZIWIG *sits behind a large, high desk, counting. He lays down his pen; looks at the clock: seven bells sound.*]

Quittin' time . . .

FEZZIWIG. Quittin' time . . . [*He takes off his waistcoat and laughs; calls off*] Yo ho, Ebenezer! Dick!

◆ **Literature and Your Life**
What scene from your life might you enjoy seeing again?

---

19. **apprenticed** (ə pren′ tist) *v.*: Receiving financial support and instruction in a trade in return for work.

[DICK WILKINS and EBENEZER SCROOGE —a young man version—enter the room. DICK and EBENEZER are FEZZIWIG's apprentices.]

SCROOGE. Dick Wilkins, to be sure! My fellow-'prentice! Bless my soul, yes. There he is. He was very much attached to me, was Dick. Poor Dick! Dear, dear!

FEZZIWIG. Yo ho, my boys. No more work tonight. Christmas Eve, Dick. Christmas, Ebenezer!

[They stand at attention in front of FEZZIWIG; laughing]

Hilli-ho! Clear away, and let's have lots of room here! Hilli-ho, Dick! Chirrup, Ebenezer!

[The young men clear the room, sweep the floor, straighten the pictures, trim the lamps, etc. The space is clear now. A fiddler enters, fiddling.]

Hi-ho, Matthew! Fiddle away . . . where are my daughters?

[The FIDDLER plays. Three young daughters of FEZZIWIG enter followed by six young male suitors. They are dancing to the music. All employees come in: workers, clerks, housemaids, cousins, the baker, etc. All dance. Full number

◆ **Reading Strategy**
Why are these stage directions necessary for you to envision what is happening in the play?

wanted here. Throughout the dance, food is brought into the feast. It is "eaten" in dance, by the dancers. EBENEZER dances with all three of the daughters, as does DICK. They compete for the daughters, happily, in the dance. FEZZIWIG dances with his daughters. FEZZIWIG dances with DICK and EBENEZER. The music changes: MRS. FEZZIWIG enters. She lovingly scolds her husband. They dance. She dances with EBENEZER, lifting him and throwing him about. She is enormously fat. When the dance is ended, they all dance off, floating away, as does the music. SCROOGE and the GHOST OF CHRISTMAS PAST stand alone now. The music is gone.]

PAST. It was a small matter, that Fezziwig made those silly folks so full of gratitude.

SCROOGE. Small!

PAST. Shhh!

[Lights up on DICK and EBENEZER]

DICK. We are blessed, Ebenezer, truly, to have such a master as Mr. Fezziwig!

YOUNG SCROOGE. He is the best, best, the very and absolute best! If ever I own a firm of my own, I shall treat my apprentices with the same dignity and the same grace. We have learned a wonderful lesson from the master, Dick!

DICK. Ah, that's a fact, Ebenezer. That's a fact!

PAST. Was it not a small matter, really? He spent but a few pounds[20] of his mortal money on your small party. Three or four pounds, perhaps. Is that so much that he deserves such praise as you and Dick so lavish now?

SCROOGE. It isn't that! It isn't that, Spirit. Fezziwig had the power to make us happy or unhappy; to make our service light or burdensome; a pleasure or a toil. The happiness he gave is quite as great as if it cost him a fortune.

PAST. What is the matter?

SCROOGE. Nothing particular.

PAST. Something, I think.

SCROOGE. No, no. I should like to be able to say a word or two to my clerk just now! That's all!

[EBENEZER enters the room and shuts down all the lamps. He stretches and yawns. The GHOST OF CHRISTMAS PAST turns to SCROOGE; all of a sudden.]

PAST. My time grows short! Quick!

[In a flash of light, EBENEZER is gone, and in his place stands an OLDER SCROOGE, this one a man in the prime of his life. Beside him stands a young woman in a mourning dress. She is crying. She speaks to the man, with hostility.]

WOMAN. It matters little . . . to you, very little. Another idol has displaced me.

MAN. What idol has displaced you?

---

20. pounds (poundz) *n.*: Common type of money used in Great Britain.

WOMAN. A golden one.

MAN. This is an even-handed dealing of the world. There is nothing on which it is so hard as poverty; and there is nothing it professes to condemn with such severity as the pursuit of wealth!

WOMAN. You fear the world too much. Have I not seen your nobler aspirations fall off one by one, until the master-passion, Gain, engrosses you? Have I not?

SCROOGE. No!

MAN. What then? Even if I have grown so much wiser, what then? Have I changed towards you?

WOMAN. No . . .

MAN. Am I?

WOMAN. Our contract is an old one. It was made when we were both poor and content to be so. You *are* changed. When it was made, you were another man.

MAN. I was not another man: I was a boy.

WOMAN. Your own feeling tells you that you were not what you are. I am. That which promised happiness when we were one in heart is fraught with misery now that we are two . . .

SCROOGE. No!

WOMAN. How often and how keenly I have thought of this, I will not say. It is enough that I *have* thought of it, and can release you . . .

SCROOGE. [*Quietly*] Don't release me, madame . . .

MAN. Have I ever sought release?

WOMAN. In words. No. Never.

MAN. In what then?

WOMAN. In a changed nature; in an altered spirit. In everything that made my love of any worth or value in your sight. If this has never been between us, tell me, would you seek me out and try to win me now? Ah, no!

SCROOGE. Ah, yes!

MAN. You think not?

WOMAN. I would gladly think otherwise if I could, heaven knows! But if you were free

today, tomorrow, yesterday, can even I believe that you would choose a dowerless girl[21] —you who in your very confidence with her weigh everything by Gain; or, choosing her, do I not know that your repentance and regret would surely follow? I do; and I release you. With a full heart, for the love of him you once were.

SCROOGE. Please, I . . . I . . .

MAN. Please, I . . . I . . .

WOMAN. Please. You may—the memory of what is past half makes me hope you will—have pain in this. A very, very brief time, and you will dismiss the memory of it, as an unprofitable dream, from which it happened well that you awoke. May you be happy in the life that you have chosen for yourself . . .

SCROOGE. No!

WOMAN. Yourself . . . alone . . .

SCROOGE. No!

WOMAN. Goodbye, Ebenezer . . .

SCROOGE. Don't let her go!

MAN. Goodbye.

SCROOGE. No!

[*She exits.* SCROOGE *goes to younger man: himself.*]

You fool! Mindless loon! You fool!

MAN. [*To exited woman*] Fool. Mindless loon. Fool . . .

SCROOGE. Don't say that! Spirit, remove me from this place.

PAST. I have told you these were shadows of the things that have been. They are what they are. Do not blame me, Mr. Scrooge.

SCROOGE. Remove me! I cannot bear it!

[*The faces of all who appeared in this scene are now projected for a moment around the stage: enormous, flimsy, silent.*]

---

21. a dowerless (dou´ ər les) **girl:** A girl without a dowery, the property or wealth a woman brought to her husband at marriage.

Leave me! Take me back! Haunt me no longer!

[*There is a sudden flash of light: a flare. The* GHOST OF CHRISTMAS PAST *is gone.* SCROOGE *is, for the moment, alone onstage. His bed is turned down, across the stage. A small candle burns now in* SCROOGE'S *hand. There is a child's cap in his other hand. He slowly crosses the stage to his bed, to sleep.* MARLEY *appears behind* SCROOGE *, who continues his long, elderly cross to bed.* MARLEY *speaks directly to the audience.*]

MARLEY. Scrooge must sleep now. He must surrender to the irresistible drowsiness caused by the recognition of what was. [*Pauses*] The cap he carries is from ten lives past: his boyhood cap . . . donned atop a hopeful hairy head . . . askew, perhaps, or at a rakish angle. Doffed now in honor of regret.[22] Perhaps even too heavy to carry in his present state of weak remorse . . .

[SCROOGE *drops the cap. He lies atop his bed. He sleeps. To audience*]

He sleeps. For him, there's even more trouble ahead. [*Smiles*] For you? The play house tells me there's hot cider, as should be your anticipation for the specter Christmas Present and Future, for I promise you both. [*Smiles again*] So, I pray you hurry back to your seats refreshed and ready for a miser—to turn his coat of gray into a blazen Christmas holly-red.

[*A flash of lightning. A clap of thunder. Bats fly. Ghosty music.* MARLEY *is gone.*]

---

22. **donned . . . regret:** To *don* and *doff* a hat means to put it on and take it off; *askew* means "crooked," and *at a rakish angle* means "having a dashing or jaunty look."

◇ Guide for Responding

◆ LITERATURE AND YOUR LIFE

Reader's Response What do you think is the meanest thing Scrooge does in Act I? Explain your answer.

Thematic Focus What aspects of Scrooge's personal code of conduct do you find the most unacceptable? Why?

☑ Check Your Comprehension

1. Who is Marley?
2. What is Marley's purpose in the play?
3. How does Scrooge treat his clerk, Bob Cratchit?
4. For what purpose does Scrooge's nephew come to see Scrooge?
5. Why do the portly man and the thin man visit Scrooge?
6. Which scenes from his past does Scrooge revisit?
7. How does Scrooge react to each one of the episodes from his past?

◆ Critical Thinking

INTERPRET

1. Why does the Ghost of Christmas Past show Scrooge "shadows of things that have been"? **[Infer]**
2. How do the episodes at the school explain Scrooge's dislike of people? **[Connect]**
3. What does the scene with the young woman reveal about how Scrooge changed as he got older? **[Interpret]**
4. What hints are there that Scrooge may still change for the better? **[Analyze]**
5. Compare and contrast the young Scrooge and the old Scrooge. **[Compare and Contrast]**

EVALUATE

6. Assess Scrooge's personality. In what areas does he need improvement? In what areas is he strong? **[Criticize]**

APPLY

7. Do you think people like Scrooge are ever really happy? Why or why not? **[Generalize]**

Guide for Responding (continued)

◆ Literary Focus

ELEMENTS OF DRAMA

Dialogue and stage directions are two of the main **elements of drama.**

1. How does the dialogue in Scene 2 reveal the personalities of Scrooge, his nephew, and Cratchit?
2. Explain what stage directions in Scene 4 would be particularly important to the lighting crew and the costume designer.

◆ Reading Strategy

ENVISION

The stage directions in a play can help you **envision,** or picture, what is happening.

1. How do the stage directions help you envision the party at Fezziwig's?
2. Why are the stage directions necessary for you to envision Scrooge's reaction to his younger self alone in the schoolroom?

◆ Build Grammar Skills

SUBJECT AND VERB AGREEMENT

A **verb** must **agree** with its **subject** in number (singular or plural) and person.

A singular subject must take a singular form of a verb, and a plural subject must use a plural form of the verb. Verbs in the present tense change form to agree with singular or plural subjects.

Practice Copy the following sentences. Underline the subject once and the verb twice. Then, identify the number of the subject.

EXAMPLE: They <u>owe</u> me money. (plural)

1. He answers to both names.
2. I wish to be left alone!
3. The ghosts terrify Scrooge.
4. A heavy bell thuds its one ring.
5. Scrooge and the Ghost of Christmas Past walk together across an open stage.

Writing Application Choose the correct verb to complete each sentence.

1. The party at Fezziwig's (is, are) fun.
2. Scrooge's relatives (feel, feels) sorry for him.
3. The scenes (frighten, frightens) him.

◆ Build Vocabulary

USING THE WORD ROOT -bene-

Knowing that the word root -bene- means "good" can help you figure out the meaning of words that contain it. On a piece of paper, write a definition for each italicized word.

1. Exercising is beneficial to your health.
2. We benefited from her wise advice.

SPELLING STRATEGY

Words that end with the letters -stitute, such as destitute, originally come from a Latin word that means "place" or "stand." The word ending is always spelled -stitute. On your paper, write the word that results from adding -stitute to each of the following.

1. con____?____   2. in____?____
3. sub____?____   4. recon____?____

USING THE WORD BANK

Write the following paragraph on your paper, filling in each blank with the appropriate word from the Word Bank.

The ____?____ beggar ____?____ the sad but wealthy-looking man to show some ____?____. "Don't be a ____?____! Helping others will make your troubles feel less ____?____. You won't feel so ____?____ if you let compassion fill the ____?____ in your heart."

 Idea Bank

Writing

1. **Invitation** In the role of Scrooge's nephew, write a letter to Scrooge to persuade him to join you and your wife for Christmas dinner.
2. **Dramatic Scene** Write a scene that shows Bob Cratchit's job interview with Scrooge. Use dialogue to reveal Scrooge's stinginess.

Project

3. **Set Design** Choose a scene from Act 1. Using the descriptions in the stage directions as a starting point, sketch the sets, costumes, and props for the scene. Provide labels and notes on your drawings to help explain your ideas. **[Art Link]**

Guide for Reading, Act II

◆ Review and Anticipate

In Act I, you met grumpy, miserly Ebenezer Scrooge. Although the people around him are cheerful and charitable in anticipation of Christmas, Scrooge is as bad-tempered and selfish as ever. However, Scrooge is forced to reexamine his attitude and behavior by the ghost of his old partner, Marley, and by the Ghost of Christmas Past.

From Marley's warning, you know that two more spirits will visit Scrooge. What do you think the Ghosts of Christmas Present and Future will show him? How will Scrooge react? Do you think he will take the Ghosts' lessons to heart? With a partner, jot down your predictions about the outcome of the play.

◆ Literary Focus

CHARACTERIZATION AND THEME IN DRAMA

Characterization is the means through which a writer reveals a character's personality. In drama, characters are revealed mainly through what they say, through what others say about them, and through their actions. A character's physical appearance and gestures may also offer insights into what he or she is like as a person.

The **theme** of a play is its central idea or insight into life. One way to arrive at the theme of a play is to notice how the main character changes. If you can explain why the main character changes for the better—or for the worse—you are probably very close to understanding the theme.

◆ Reading Strategy

QUESTION

You will be able to better understand what is going on in a play—or any work of literature —if you ask **questions** as you read. Some questions you might ask include these:

- Why did he do that?
- What did she mean by that comment?
- How might this incident be significant?

As you read Act II, jot down your questions in a chart like the one on this page. Record the answers to your questions as you encounter them in your reading.

◆ Build Vocabulary

WORD ROOTS: -aud-

In Scene 4, Scrooge pleads, "Make me *audible*! I want to talk with my nephew and my niece!" Using the word's context and the knowledge that the word root *-aud-* means "hear," you can determine that *audible* means "able to be heard."

WORD BANK

Look over these words from Act II. Which one might describe the knees in your oldest, most worn-out pair of jeans?

astonish
compulsion
severe
meager
threadbare
audible
gnarled
dispelled

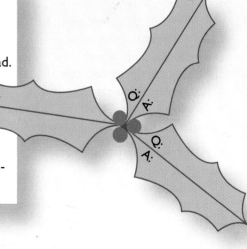

A CHRISTMAS CAROL: SCROOGE AND MARLEY

Act II

Scene 1

[*Lights. Choral music is sung. Curtain.* SCROOGE, *in bed, sleeping, in spotlight. We cannot yet see the interior of his room.* MARLEY, *opposite, in spotlight equal to* SCROOGE'S. MARLEY *laughs. He tosses his hand in the air and a flame shoots from it, magically, into the air. There is a thunder clap, and then another; a lightning flash, and then another. Ghostly music plays under. Colors change.* MARLEY'S *spotlight has gone out and now reappears, with* MARLEY *in it, standing next to the bed and the sleeping* SCROOGE. MARLEY *addresses the audience directly.*]

MARLEY. Hear this snoring Scrooge! Sleeping to escape the nightmare that is his waking day. What shall I bring to him now? I'm afraid nothing would astonish old Scrooge now. Not after what he's seen. Not a baby boy, not a rhinoceros, nor anything in between would astonish Ebenezer Scrooge just now. I can think of nothing . . . [*Suddenly*] that's it! Nothing! [*He speaks confidentially.*] I'll have the clock strike one and, when he awakes expecting my second messenger, there will be no one . . . nothing. Then I'll have the bell strike twelve. And then one again . . . and then nothing. Nothing . . . [*Laughs*] nothing will . . . astonish him. I think it will work.

[*The bell tolls one.* SCROOGE *leaps awake.*]

◆ **Build Vocabulary**

astonish (ə stän´ ish) *v.*: Amaze

SCROOGE. One! One! This is it: time! [*Looks about the room*] Nothing!

[*The bell tolls midnight.*]

Midnight! How can this be? I'm sleeping backwards.

[*One again*]

Good heavens! One again! I'm sleeping back and forth! [*A pause.* SCROOGE *looks about.*] Nothing! Absolutely nothing!

[*Suddenly, thunder and lightning.* MARLEY *laughs and disappears. The room shakes and glows. There is suddenly springlike music.* SCROOGE *makes a run for the door.*]

MARLEY. Scrooge!

SCROOGE. What?

MARLEY. Stay you put!

SCROOGE. Just checking to see if anyone is in here.

[*Lights and thunder again: more music.* MARLEY *is of a sudden gone. In his place sits the* GHOST OF CHRISTMAS PRESENT—*to be called in the stage directions of the play,* PRESENT—*center of room. Heaped up on the floor, to form a kind of throne, are turkeys, geese, game, poultry, brawn, great*

◆ **Reading Strategy**
What questions might the appearance of the Ghost of Christmas Present prompt you to ask about Christmas celebrations in Dickens's time?

joints of meat, suckling pigs, long wreaths of sausages, mince-pies, plum puddings, barrels of oysters, red hot chestnuts, cherry-cheeked apples, juicy oranges, luscious pears, immense twelfth cakes, and seething bowls of punch, that make the chamber dim with their delicious steam. Upon this throne sits PRESENT, *glorious to see. He bears a torch, shaped as a Horn of Plenty.*[1] SCROOGE *hops out of the door, and then*

1. **Horn of Plenty:** A horn overflowing with fruits, flowers, and grain, standing for wealth and abundance.

peeks back again into his bedroom. PRESENT *calls to* SCROOGE.]

PRESENT. Ebenezer Scrooge. Come in, come in! Come in and know me better!

SCROOGE. Hello. How should I call you?

PRESENT. I am the Ghost of Christmas Present. Look upon me.

[PRESENT *is wearing a simple green robe. The walls around the room are now covered in greenery, as well. The room seems to be a perfect grove now: leaves of holly, mistletoe and ivy reflect the stage lights. Suddenly, there is a mighty roar of flame in the fireplace and now the hearth burns with a lavish, warming fire. There is an ancient scabbard girdling the* GHOST'S *middle, but without sword. The sheath is gone to rust.*]

You have never seen the like of me before?

SCROOGE. Never.

PRESENT. You have never walked forth with younger members of my family; my elder brothers born on Christmases past.

SCROOGE. I don't think I have. I'm afraid I've not. Have you had many brothers, Spirit?

PRESENT. More than eighteen hundred.

SCROOGE. A tremendous family to provide for! [PRESENT *stands*] Spirit, conduct me where you will. I went forth last night on compulsion, and learnt a lesson which is working now. Tonight, if you have aught to teach me, let me profit by it.

PRESENT. Touch my robe.

[SCROOGE *walks cautiously to* PRESENT *and touches his robe. When he does, lightning flashes, thunder claps, music plays. Blackout*]

Scene 2

[PROLOGUE: MARLEY *stands spotlit,* L. *He speaks directly to the audience.*]

MARLEY. My ghostly friend now leads my living partner through the city's streets.

[*Lights up on* SCROOGE *and* PRESENT]

See them there and hear the music people make when the weather is <u>severe</u>, as it is now.

[*Winter music. Choral group behind scrim, sings. When the song is done and the stage is re-set, the lights will fade up on a row of shops, behind the singers. The choral group will hum the song they have just completed now and mill about the streets,[2] carrying their dinners to the bakers' shops and restaurants. They will, perhaps, sing about being poor at Christmastime, whatever.*]

PRESENT. These revelers, Mr. Scrooge, carry their own dinners to their jobs, where they will work to bake the meals the rich men and women of this city will eat as their Christmas dinners. Generous people these . . . to care for the others, so . . .

[PRESENT *walks among the choral group and a sparkling incense[3] falls from his torch on to their baskets, as he pulls the covers off of the baskets. Some of the choral group become angry with each other.*]

MAN #1. Hey, you, watch where you're going.

MAN #2. Watch it yourself, mate!

[PRESENT *sprinkles them directly, they change.*]

MAN #1. I pray go in ahead of me. It's Christmas. You be first!

MAN #2. No, no, I must insist that YOU be first!

MAN #1. All right, I shall be, and gratefully so.

MAN #2. The pleasure is equally mine, for being able to watch you pass, smiling.

---

2. **mill about the streets:** Walk around aimlessly.
3. **incense** (in′ sens) *n.:* Any of various substances that produce a pleasant odor when burned.

MAN #1. I would find it a shame to quarrel on Christmas Day . . .

MAN #2. As would I.

MAN #1. Merry Christmas then, friend!

MAN #2. And a Merry Christmas straight back to you!

[*Church bells toll. The choral group enter the buildings: the shops and restaurants; they exit the stage, shutting their doors closed behind them. All sound stops.* SCROOGE *and* PRESENT *are alone again.*]

SCROOGE. What is it you sprinkle from your torch?

PRESENT. Kindness.

SCROOGE. Do you sprinkle your kindness on any particular people or on all people?

PRESENT. To any person kindly given. And to the very poor most of all.

SCROOGE. Why to the very poor most?

PRESENT. Because the very poor need it most. Touch my heart . . . here, Mr. Scrooge. We have another journey.

[SCROOGE *touches the* GHOST'S *heart and music plays, lights change color, lightning flashes, thunder claps. A choral group appears on the street, singing Christmas carols.*]

Scene 3

[MARLEY *stands spotlit in front of a scrim on which is painted the exterior of* CRATCHIT'S *four-roomed house. There is a flash and a clap and* MARLEY *is gone. The lights shift color again, the scrim flies away, and we are in the interior of the* CRATCHIT *family home.* SCROOGE *is there, with the* SPIRIT (PRESENT), *watching* MRS. CRATCHIT

◆ **Literature and Your Life**

Why are some people nicer to each other on holidays?

◆ **Build Vocabulary**

compulsion (kəm pul′ shən) *n.:* A driving, irresistible force

severe (sə vir′) *adj.:* Harsh

set the table, with the help of BELINDA CRATCHIT *and* PETER CRATCHIT, *a baby, pokes a fork into the mashed potatoes on his highchair's tray. He also chews on his shirt collar.*]

SCROOGE. What is this place, Spirit?

PRESENT. This is the home of your employee, Mr. Scrooge. Don't you know it?

SCROOGE. Do you mean Cratchit, Spirit? Do you mean this is Cratchit's home?

PRESENT. None other.

SCROOGE. These children are his?

PRESENT. There are more to come presently.

SCROOGE. On his <u>meager</u> earnings! What foolishness!

PRESENT. Foolishness, is it?

SCROOGE. Wouldn't you say so? Fifteen shillings⁴ a week's what he gets!

PRESENT. I would say that he gets the pleasure of his family, fifteen times a week times the number of hours a day! Wait, Mr. Scrooge. Wait, listen and watch. You might actually learn something . . .

MRS. CRATCHIT. What has ever got your precious father then? And your brother, Tiny Tim? And Martha warn't as late last Christmas by half an hour!

[MARTHA *opens the door, speaking to her mother as she does.*]

MARTHA. Here's Martha, now, Mother! [*She laughs. The* CRATCHIT CHILDREN *squeal with delight.*]

BELINDA. It's Martha, Mother! Here's Martha!

PETER. Marthmama, Marthmama! Hullo!

BELINDA. Hurrah! Martha! Martha! There's such an enormous goose for us, Martha!

MRS. CRATCHIT. Why, bless your heart alive, my dear, how late you are!

MARTHA. We'd a great deal of work to finish up

---

4. **fifteen shillings:** A small amount of money for a week's work.

---

last night, and had to clear away this morning, Mother.

MRS. CRATCHIT. Well, never mind so long as you are come. Sit ye down before the fire, my dear, and have a warm, Lord bless ye!

BELINDA. No, no! There's Father coming. Hide, Martha, hide!

[MARTHA *giggles and hides herself.*]

MARTHA. Where? Here?

PETER. *Hide, hide!*

BELINDA. Not there! *THERE!*

[MARTHA *is hidden.* BOB CRATCHIT *enters, carrying* TINY TIM *atop his shoulder. He wears a <u>threadbare</u> and fringeless comforter hanging down in front of him.* TINY TIM *carries small crutches and his small legs are bound in an iron frame brace.*]

BOB and **TINY TIM.** Merry Christmas.

BOB. Merry Christmas my love, Merry Christmas Peter, Merry Christmas Belinda. Why, where is Martha?

MRS CRATCHIT. Not coming.

BOB. Not coming: Not coming upon Christmas Day?

MARTHA. [*Pokes head out*] Ohhh, poor Father. Don't be disappointed.

BOB. What's this?

MARTHA. 'Tis I!

BOB. Martha! [*They embrace.*]

TINY TIM. Martha! Martha!

MARTHA. Tiny Tim!

[TINY TIM *is placed in* MARTHA'S *arms.* BELINDA *and* PETER *rush him offstage.*]

BELINDA. Come, brother! You must come hear the pudding singing in the copper.

TINY TIM. The pudding? What flavor have we?

PETER. Plum! Plum!

TINY TIM. Oh, Mother! I love plum!

[*The children exit the stage, giggling.*]

MRS CRATCHIT. And how did little Tim behave?

BOB. As good as gold, and even better. Somehow he gets thoughtful sitting by himself so much, and thinks the strangest things you ever heard. He told me, coming home, that he hoped people saw him in the church, because he was a cripple, and it might be pleasant to them to remember upon Christmas Day, who made lame beggars walk and blind men see. [*Pauses*] He has the oddest ideas sometimes, but he seems all the while to be growing stronger and more hearty . . . one would never know. [*Hears* TIM's *crutch on floor outside door*]

PETER. The goose has arrived to be eaten!

BELINDA. Oh, mama, mama, it's beautiful.

MARTHA. It's a perfect goose, Mother!

TINY TIM. To this Christmas goose, Mother and Father I say . . . [*Yells*] Hurrah! Hurrah!

OTHER CHILDREN. [*Copying* TIM] Hurrah! Hurrah!

[*The family sits round the table.* BOB *and* MRS. CRATCHIT *serve the trimmings, quickly. All sit; all bow heads; all pray.*]

BOB. Thank you, dear Lord, for your many gifts . . . our dear children; our wonderful meal; our love for one another; and the warmth of our small fire—[*Looks up at all*] A merry Christmas to us, my dear. God bless us!

ALL. [*Except* TIM] Merry Christmas! God bless us!

TINY TIM. [*In a short silence*] God bless us every one.

[*All freeze. Spotlight on* PRESENT *and* SCROOGE]

SCROOGE. Spirit, tell me if Tiny Tim will live.

◆ **Build Vocabulary**

meager (mē´ gər) *adj.*: Of poor quality; small in amount

threadbare (*th*red´ ber) *adj.*: Worn; shabby

PRESENT. I see a vacant seat . . . in the poor chimney corner, and a crutch without an owner, carefully preserved. If these shadows remain unaltered by the future, the child will die.

SCROOGE. No, no, kind Spirit! Say he will be spared!

PRESENT. If these shadows remain unaltered by the future, none other of my race will find him here. What then? If he be like to die, he had better do it, and decrease the surplus population.

[SCROOGE *bows his head. We hear* BOB's *voice speak* SCROOGE's *name.*]

BOB. Mr. Scrooge . . .

SCROOGE. Huh? What's that? Who calls?

BOB. [*His glass raised in a toast*] I'll give you Mr. Scrooge, the Founder of the Feast!

SCROOGE. Me, Bob? You toast *me*?

PRESENT. Save your breath, Mr. Scrooge. You can't be seen or heard.

MRS. CRATCHIT. The Founder of the Feast, indeed! I wish I had him here, that miser Scrooge. I'd give him a piece of my mind to feast upon, and I hope he'd have a good appetite for it!

BOB. My dear! Christmas Day!

MRS. CRATCHIT. It should be Christmas Day, I am sure, on which one drinks the health of such an odious, stingy, unfeeling man as Mr. Scrooge . . .

SCROOGE. Oh, Spirit, must I? . . .

MRS. CRATCHIT. You know he is, Robert! Nobody knows it better than you do, poor fellow!

BOB. This is Christmas Day, and I should like to drink to the health of the man who employs me and allows me to earn my living and our support and that man is Ebenezer Scrooge . . .

MRS. CRATCHIT. I'll drink to his health for your sake and the day's, but not for his sake . . . a

◆ **Literary Focus**
How does Scrooge's concern for Tiny Tim reflect a change in Scrooge's character?

Merry Christmas and a Happy New Year to you, Mr. Scrooge, wherever you may be this day!

SCROOGE. Just here, kind madam . . . out of sight, out of sight . . .

BOB. Thank you, my dear. Thank you.

SCROOGE. Thank *you*, Bob . . . and Mrs. Cratchit, too. No one else is toasting me, . . . not now . . . not ever. Of that I am sure . . .

BOB. Children . . .

ALL. Merry Christmas to Mr. Scrooge.

BOB. I'll pay you sixpence, Tim, for my favorite song.

TINY TIM. Oh, Father, I'd so love to sing it, but not for pay. This Christmas goose—this

▲ **Critical Viewing** Why might a director stage the scene this way, with Tiny Tim standing on the table? [Interpret]

feast—you and Mother, my brother and sisters close with me: that's my pay—

BOB. Martha, will you play the notes on the lute,[5] for Tiny Tim's song.

BELINDA. May I sing, too, Father?

BOB. We'll all sing.

[*They sing a song about a tiny child lost in the snow—probably from Wordsworth's poem.* TIM *sings the lead vocal; all chime in for the*

5. **lute** (lo͞ot) *n.*: Stringed instrument like a guitar.

chorus. Their song fades under, as THE GHOST OF CHRISTMAS PRESENT *speaks.*]

PRESENT. Mark my words, Ebenezer Scrooge. I do not present the Cratchits to you because they are a handsome, or brilliant family. They are not handsome. They are not brilliant. They are not well-dressed, or tasteful to the times. Their shoes are not even waterproofed by virtue of money or cleverness spent. So when the pavement is wet, so are the insides of their shoes and the tops of their toes. These are the Cratchits, Mr. Scrooge. They are not highly special. They are happy, grateful, pleased with one another, contented with the time and how it passes. They don't sing very well, do they? But, nonetheless, they do sing . . . [*Pauses*] think of that, Scrooge. Fifteen shillings a week and they do sing . . . hear their song until its end.

SCROOGE. I am listening.

[*The chorus sings full volume now, until . . . the song ends here.*]

Spirit, it must be time for us to take our leave. I feel in my heart that it is . . . that I must think on that which I have seen here . . .

PRESENT. Touch my robe again . . .

[SCROOGE *touches* PRESENT'S *robe. The lights fade out on the* CRATCHITS, *who sit, frozen, at the table.* SCROOGE *and* PRESENT *in a spotlight now. Thunder, lightning, smoke. They are gone.*]

Scene 4

[MARLEY *appears* D.L. *in single spotlight. A storm brews. Thunder and lightning.* SCROOGE *and* PRESENT *"fly" past,* U. *The storm continues, furiously, and, now and again,* SCROOGE *and* PRESENT *will zip past in their travels.* MARLEY *will speak straight out to the audience.*]

MARLEY. The Ghost of Christmas Present, my co-worker in this attempt to turn a miser, flies about now with that very miser, Scrooge, from street to street, and he points out partygoers on their way to Christmas parties. If one were to judge from the numbers of people on their way to friendly gatherings, one might think that no one was left at home to give anyone welcome . . . but that's not the case, is it? Every home is expecting company and . . . [*He laughs.*] Scrooge is amazed.

[SCROOGE *and* PRESENT *zip past again. The lights fade up around them. We are in the* NEPHEW'S *home, in the living room.* PRESENT *and* SCROOGE *stand watching the* NEPHEW: FRED *and his wife, fixing the fire.*]

SCROOGE. What is this place? We've moved from the mines!

PRESENT. You do not recognize them?

SCROOGE. It is my nephew! . . . and the one he married . . .

[MARLEY *waves his hand and there is a lightning flash. He disappears.*]

FRED. It strikes me as sooooo funny, to think of what he said . . . that Christmas was a humbug, as I live! He believed it!

WIFE. More shame for him, Fred!

FRED. Well, he's a comical old fellow, that's the truth.

WIFE. I have no patience with him.

FRED. Oh, I have! I am sorry for him; I couldn't be angry with him if I tried. Who suffers by his ill whims? Himself, always . . .

SCROOGE. It's me they talk of, isn't it, Spirit?

FRED. Here, wife, consider this. Uncle Scrooge takes it into his head to dislike us, and he won't come and dine with us. What's the consequence?

WIFE. Oh . . . you're sweet to say what I think you're about to say, too, Fred . . .

FRED. What's the consequence? He don't lose much of a dinner by it, I can tell you that!

WIFE. Ooooooo, Fred! Indeed, I think he loses a very good dinner . . . ask my sisters, or your bachelor friend, Topper . . . ask any of them. They'll tell you what old Scrooge, your uncle, missed: a dandy meal!

FRED. Well, that's something of a relief, wife. Glad to hear it! [*He hugs his wife. They laugh. They kiss.*] The truth is, he misses much yet. I mean to give him the same chance every year, whether he likes it or not, for I pity him. Nay, he is my only uncle and I feel for the old miser . . . but, I tell you, wife: I see my dear and perfect mother's face on his own wizened cheeks and brow: brother and sister they were, and I cannot erase that from each view of him I take . . .

WIFE. I understand what you say, Fred, and I am with you in your yearly asking. But he never will accept, you know. He never will.

FRED. Well, true, wife. Uncle may rail at Christmas till he dies. I think I shook him some with my visit yesterday . . . [*Laughing*] I refused to grow angry . . . no matter how nasty he became . . . [*Whoops*] It was HE who grew angry, wife! [*They both laugh now.*]

SCROOGE. What he says is true, Spirit . . .

FRED and **WIFE.** Bah, humbug!

FRED. [*Embracing his wife*] There is much laughter in our marriage, wife. It pleases me. You please me . . .

WIFE. And you please me, Fred. You are a good man . . . [*They embrace.*] Come now. We must have a look at the meal . . . our guests will soon arrive . . . my sisters, Topper . . .

◆ **Reading Strategy**

What questions might you ask about the episode with Fred and his wife?

FRED. A toast first . . . [*He hands her a glass.*] A toast to Uncle Scrooge . . . [*Fills their glasses*]

WIFE. A toast to him?

FRED. Uncle Scrooge has given us plenty of merriment, I am sure, and it would be ungrateful not to drink to his health. And I say . . . *Uncle Scrooge!*

WIFE. [*Laughing*] You're a proper loon,[6] Fred . . . and I'm a proper wife to you . . . [*She raises her glass.*] Uncle Scrooge! [*They drink. They embrace. They kiss.*]

---

6. **a proper loon:** A silly person.

SCROOGE. Spirit, please, make me visible! Make me <u>audible</u>! I want to talk with my nephew and my niece!

[*Calls out to them. The lights that light the room and* FRED *and wife fade out.* SCROOGE *and* PRESENT *are alone, spotlit.*]

PRESENT. These shadows are gone to you now, Mr. Scrooge. You may return to them later tonight in your dreams. [*Pauses*] My time grows short, Ebenezer Scrooge. Look you on me! Do you see how I've aged?

SCROOGE. Your hair has gone gray! Your skin, wrinkled! Are spirits' lives so short?

PRESENT. My stay upon this globe is very brief. It ends tonight.

SCROOGE. Tonight?

PRESENT. At midnight. The time is drawing near!

[*Clock strikes 11:45.*]

Hear those chimes? In a quarter hour, my life will have been spent! Look, Scrooge, man. Look you here.

[*Two <u>gnarled</u> baby dolls are taken from* PRESENT'S *skirts.*]

SCROOGE. Who are they?

PRESENT. They are Man's children, and they cling to me, appealing from their fathers. The boy is Ignorance; the girl is Want. Beware them both, and all of their degree, but most of all beware this boy, for I see that written on his brow which is doom, unless the writing be erased. [*He stretches out his arm. His voice is now amplified: loudly and oddly.*]

SCROOGE. Have they no refuge or resource?

PRESENT. Are there no prisons? Are there no workhouses? [*Twelve chimes*] Are there no prisons? Are there no workhouses?

[*A* PHANTOM, *hooded, appears in dim light,* D., *opposite.*]

Are there no prisons? Are there no workhouses?

[PRESENT *begins to deliquesce.* SCROOGE *calls after him.*]

SCROOGE. Spirit, I'm frightened! Don't leave me! Spirit!

PRESENT. Prisons? Workhouses? Prisons? Workhouses . . .

[*He is gone.* SCROOGE *is alone now with the* PHANTOM, *who is, of course, the* GHOST OF CHRISTMAS FUTURE. THE PHANTOM *is shrouded in black. Only its outstretched hand is visible from under his ghostly garment.*]

SCROOGE. Who are you, Phantom? Oh, yes, I think I know you! You are, are you not, the Spirit of Christmas Yet to Come? [*No reply*] And you are about to show me the shadows of the things that have not yet happened, but will happen in time before us. Is that not so, Spirit?

[*The* PHANTOM *allows* SCROOGE *a look at his face. No other reply wanted here. A nervous giggle here.*]

Oh, Ghost of the Future, I fear you more than any Specter I have seen! But, as I know that your purpose is to do me good and as I hope to live to be another man from what I was, I am prepared to bear you company.

> ◆ **Literary Focus**
> What do Scrooge's words to the Ghost of Christmas Future tell you about the play's theme?

[FUTURE *does not reply, but for a stiff arm, hand and finger set, pointing forward.*]

Lead on, then, lead on. The night is waning fast, and it is precious time to me. Lead on, Spirit!

[FUTURE *moves away from* SCROOGE *in the same rhythm and motion employed at its arrival.* SCROOGE *falls into the same pattern, a considerable space apart from the* SPIRIT. *In the space between them,* MARLEY *appears. He looks to* FUTURE *and then to* SCROOGE. *He claps his hands. Thunder and lightning. Three* BUSINESSMEN *appear, spotlighted singularly: One is* D.L.; *one is* D.R.; *one is* U.C. *Thus, six points of the stage should now be spotted in light.* MARLEY *will watch this scene from his position,* C. SCROOGE *and* FUTURE *are* R. *and* L. *of* C.]

FIRST BUSINESSMAN. Oh, no, I don't know much about it either way, I only know he's dead.

SECOND BUSINESSMAN. When did he die?

FIRST BUSINESSMAN. Last night, I believe.

SECOND BUSINESSMAN. Why, what was the matter with him? I thought he'd never die, really . . .

FIRST BUSINESSMAN. [*Yawning*] Goodness knows, goodness knows . . .

THIRD BUSINESSMAN. What has he done with his money?

SECOND BUSINESSMAN. I haven't heard. Have you?

FIRST BUSINESSMAN. Left it to his Company, perhaps. Money to money; you know the expression . . .

THIRD BUSINESSMAN. He hasn't left it to me. That's all I know . . .

FIRST BUSINESSMAN. [*Laughing*] Nor to me . . . [*Looks at* SECOND BUSINESSMAN] You, then? You got his money???

SECOND BUSINESSMAN. [*Laughing*] Me, me, his money? Nooooo! [*They all laugh.*]

THIRD BUSINESSMAN. It's likely to be a cheap funeral, for upon my life, I don't know of a living soul who'd care to venture to it. Suppose we make up a party and volunteer?

SECOND BUSINESSMAN. I don't mind going if a lunch is provided, but I must be fed, if I make one.

FIRST BUSINESSMAN. Well, I am the most disinterested among you, for I never wear black gloves, and I never eat lunch. But I'll offer to go, if anybody else will. When I come to think of it, I'm not all sure that I wasn't his most

◆ **Build Vocabulary**
audible (ô′ də bəl) *adj.*: Loud enough to be heard
gnarled (närld) *adj.*: Knotty and twisted

particular friend; for we used to stop and speak whenever we met. Well, then . . . bye, bye!

SECOND BUSINESSMAN. Bye, bye . . .

THIRD BUSINESSMAN. Bye, bye . . .

[*They glide offstage in three separate directions. Their lights follow them.*]

SCROOGE. Spirit, why did you show me this? Why do you show me businessmen from my streets as they take the death of Jacob Marley. That is a thing past. You are *future!*

[JACOB MARLEY *laughs a long, deep laugh. There is a thunder clap and lightning flash, and he is gone.* SCROOGE *faces* FUTURE, *alone on stage now.* FUTURE *wordlessly stretches out his arm-hand-and-finger-set, pointing into the distance,* U. *There, above them.*

◆ **Reading Strategy**
How would you find out the answer to the question "Who has died"?

Scoundrels "fly" by, half-dressed and slovenly. When this scene has passed, a woman enters the playing area. She is almost at once followed by a second woman; and then a man in faded black; and then, suddenly, an old man, who smokes a pipe. The old man scares the other three. They laugh, anxious.]

FIRST WOMAN. Look here, old Joe, here's a chance! If we haven't all three met here without meaning it!

OLD JOE. You couldn't have met in a better place. Come into the parlor. You were made free of it long ago, you know; and the other two an't strangers [*He stands; shuts a door. Shrieking*] We're all suitable to our calling. We're well matched. Come into the parlor. Come into the parlor . . .

[*They follow him* D. SCROOGE *and* FUTURE *are now in their midst, watching; silent. A truck comes in on which is set a small wall with fireplace and a screen of rags, etc. All props for the scene.*]

Let me just rake this fire over a bit . . .

[*He does. He trims his lamp with the stem of his pipe. The* FIRST WOMAN *throws a large bundle*

on to the floor. She sits beside it crosslegged, defiantly.*]

FIRST WOMAN. What odds then? What odds, Mrs. Dilber? Every person has a right to take care of themselves. HE always did!

MRS. DILBER. That's true indeed! No man more so!

FIRST WOMAN. Why, then, don't stand staring as if you was afraid, woman! Who's the wiser? We're not going to pick holes in each other's coats, I suppose?

MRS. DILBER. No, indeed! We should hope not!

FIRST WOMAN. Very well, then! That's enough. Who's the worse for the loss of a few things like these? Not a dead man, I suppose?

MRS. DILBER. [*Laughing*] No, indeed!

FIRST WOMAN. If he wanted to keep 'em after he was dead, the wicked old screw, why wasn't he natural in his lifetime? If he had been, he'd have had somebody to look after him when he was struck with Death, instead of lying gasping out his last there, alone by himself.

MRS. DILBER. It's the truest word that was ever spoke. It's a judgment on him.

FIRST WOMAN. I wish it were a heavier one, and it should have been, you may depend on it, if I could have laid my hands on anything else. Open that bundle, old Joe, and let me know the value of it. Speak out plain. I'm not afraid to be the first, nor afraid for them to see it. We knew pretty well that we were helping ourselves, before we met here, I believe. It's no sin. Open the bundle, Joe.

FIRST MAN. No, no, my dear! I won't think of letting you being the first to show what you've . . . earned . . . earned from this. I throw in mine. [*He takes a bundle from his shoulder, turns it upside down, and empties its contents out on to the floor.*] It's not very extensive, see . . . seals . . . a pencil case . . . sleeve buttons . . .

MRS. DILBER. Nice sleeve buttons, though . . .

FIRST MAN. Not bad, not bad . . . a brooch there . . .

OLD JOE: Not really valuable, I'm afraid . . .

FIRST MAN. How much, old Joe?

OLD JOE: [*Writing on the wall with chalk*] A pitiful lot, really. Ten and six and not a sixpence more!

FIRST MAN. You're not serious!

OLD JOE. That's your account and I wouldn't give another sixpence if I was to be boiled for not doing it. Who's next?

MRS. DILBER. Me! [*Dumps out contents of her bundle*] Sheets, towels, silver spoons, silver sugar-tongs . . . some boots . . .

OLD JOE. [*Writing on wall*] I always give too much to the ladies. It's a weakness of mine and that's the way I ruin myself. Here's your total comin' up . . . two pounds-ten . . . if you asked me for another penny, and made it an open question, I'd repent of being so liberal and knock off half-a-crown.

FIRST WOMAN. And now do MY bundle, Joe.

OLD JOE. [*Kneeling to open knots on her bundle*] So many knots, madam . . . [*He drags out large curtains; dark*] What do you call this? Bed curtains!

FIRST WOMAN. [*Laughing*] Ah, yes, bed curtains!

OLD JOE. You don't mean to say you took 'em down, rings and all, with him lying there?

FIRST WOMAN. Yes, I did, why not?

OLD JOE. You were born to make your fortune and you'll certainly do it.

FIRST WOMAN. I certainly shan't hold my hand, when I can get anything in it by reaching it out, for the sake of such a man as he was, I promise you, Joe. Don't drop that lamp oil on those blankets, now!

OLD JOE. His blankets?

FIRST WOMAN. Whose else's do you think? He isn't likely to catch cold without 'em, I daresay.

OLD JOE. I hope that he didn't die of anything catching? Eh?

FIRST WOMAN. Don't you be afraid of that. I ain't so fond of his company that I'd loiter about him for such things if he did. Ah! You may look through that shirt till your eyes ache, but you won't find a hole in it, nor a threadbare place. It's the best he had, and a fine one, too. They'd have wasted it, if it hadn't been for me.

OLD JOE. What do you mean 'They'd have wasted it?'

FIRST WOMAN. Putting it on him to be buried in, to be sure. Somebody was fool enough to do it, but I took it off again . . . [*She laughs, as do they all, nervously.*] If calico[7] ain't good enough for such a purpose, it isn't good enough then for anything. It's quite as becoming to the body. He can't look uglier than he did in that one!

SCROOGE. [*A low-pitched moan emits from his mouth; from the bones.*] OOOOOOOoo oooOOOOOoooooOOOOOOOOooooOOOOOOoo oooOO!

OLD JOE. One pound six for the lot. [*He produces a small flannel bag filled with money. He divvies it out. He continues to pass around the money as he speaks. All are laughing.*] That's the end of it, you see! He frightened every one away from him while he was alive, to profit us when he was dead! Hah ha ha!

ALL. HAHAHAHAhahahahahahah!

SCROOGE. OOOoooOOOoooOOOoooOOOooo OOoooOOoooOOOooo! [*He screams at them.*] Obscene demons! Why not market the corpse itself, as sell its trimming??? [*Suddenly*] Oh, Spirit, I see it, I see it! This unhappy man— this stripped-bare corpse . . . could very well be my own. My life holds parallel! My life ends that way now!

[SCROOGE *backs into something in the dark behind his spotlight.* SCROOGE *looks at* FUTURE, *who points to the corpse.* SCROOGE *pulls back the blanket. The corpse is, of course,* SCROOGE, *who screams. He falls aside the bed; weeping.*]

Spirit, this is a fearful place. In leaving it, I shall not leave its lesson, trust me. Let us go!

[FUTURE *points to the corpse.*]

---

7. **calico** (kal′ ə kō) *n.*: Coarse and cheap cloth.

Spirit, let me see some tenderness connected with a death, or that dark chamber, which we just left now, Spirit, will be forever present to me.

[FUTURE *spreads his robes again. Thunder and lightning. Lights up,* U., *in the* CRATCHIT *home setting.* MRS. CRATCHIT *and her daughters, sewing*]

TINY TIM'S VOICE. [*Off*] And He took a child and set him in the midst of them.

SCROOGE. [Looking about the room; to FUTURE] Huh? Who spoke? Who said that?

MRS. CRATCHIT. [*Puts down her sewing*] The color hurts my eyes. [*Rubs her eyes*] That's better. My eyes grow weak sewing by candle-light. I shouldn't want to show your father weak eyes when he comes home . . . not for the world! It must be near his time . . .

PETER. [*In corner, reading. Looks up from book*] Past it, rather. But I think he's been walking a bit slower than usual these last few evenings, Mother.

MRS. CRATCHIT. I have known him walk with . . .

▲ **Critical Viewing** Why might a director choose to place the actors playing the Cratchits this way? What does their position reveal about their family? **[Analyze]**

[*Pauses*] I have know him walk with Tiny Tim upon his shoulder and very fast indeed.

PETER. So have I, Mother! Often!

DAUGHTER. So have I.

MRS. CRATCHIT. But he was very light to carry and his father loved him so, that it was not trouble—no trouble.

[BOB, *at door*]

And there is your father at the door.

[BOB CRATCHIT *enters. He wears a comforter. He is cold, forlorn.*]

PETER. Father!

BOB. Hello, wife, children . . .

[*The daughter weeps; turns away from* CRATCHIT.]

Children! How good to see you all! And you, wife. And look at this sewing! I've no doubt, with all your industry, we'll have a quilt to set down upon our knees in church on Sunday!

MRS. CRATCHIT. You made the arrangements today, then, Robert, for the . . . service . . . to be on Sunday.

BOB. The funeral. Oh, well, yes, yes, I did. I wish you could have gone. It would have done you good to see how green a place it is. But you'll see it often. I promised him that I would walk there on Sunday, after the service. *[Suddenly]* My little, little child! My little child!

ALL CHILDREN. *[Hugging him]* Oh, Father . . .

BOB. *[He stands]* Forgive me. I saw Mr. Scrooge's nephew, who you know I'd just met once before, and he was so wonderful to me, wife . . . he is the most pleasant-spoken gentleman I've ever met . . . he said "I am heartily sorry for it and heartily sorry for your good wife. If I can be of service to you in any way, here's where I live." And he gave me this card.

PETER. Let me see it!

BOB. And he looked me straight in the eye, wife, and said, meaningfully, "I pray you'll come to me, Mr. Cratchit, if you need some help. I pray you do." Now it wasn't for the sake of anything that he might be able to do for us, so much as for his kind way. It seemed as if he had known our Tiny Tim and felt with us.

MRS. CRATCHIT. I'm sure that he's a good soul.

BOB. You would be surer of it, my dear, if you saw and spoke to him. I shouldn't be at all surprised, if he got Peter a situation.

MRS. CRATCHIT. Only hear that, Peter!

MARTHA. And then, Peter will be keeping company with someone and setting up for himself!

PETER. Get along with you!

BOB. It's just as likely as not, one of these days, though there's plenty of time for that,

◆ Literary Focus
How might the differences in the reactions to the two deaths tie in to the theme of the play?

my dear. But however and whenever we part from one another, I am sure we shall none of us forget poor Tiny Tim—shall we?—or this first parting that was among us?

ALL CHILDREN. Never, Father, never!

BOB. And when we recollect how patient and mild he was, we shall not quarrel easily among ourselves, and forget poor Tiny Tim in doing it.

ALL CHILDREN. No, Father, never!

LITTLE BOB. I am very happy, I am, I am, I am very happy.

[BOB *kisses his little son, as does* MRS. CRATCHIT, *as do the other children. The family is set now in one sculptural embrace. The lighting fades to a gentle pool of light, tight on them.*]

SCROOGE. Specter, something informs me that our parting moment is at hand. I know it, but I know not how I know it.

[FUTURE *points to the other side of the stage. Lights out on Cratchits.* FUTURE *moves slowing, gliding.* SCROOGE *follows.* FUTURE *points opposite.* FUTURE *leads* SCROOGE *to a wall and a tombstone. He points to the stone.*]

Am *I* that man those ghoulish parasites[8] so gloated over? [*Pauses*] Before I draw nearer to that stone to which you point, answer me one question. Are these the shadows of things that will be, or the shadows of things that MAY be, only?

[FUTURE *points to the gravestone.* MARLEY *appears in light well* U. *He points to grave as well. Gravestone turns front and grows to ten feet high. Words upon it:* EBENEZER SCROOGE: *Much smoke billows now from the grave. Choral music here.* SCROOGE *stands looking up at gravestone.* FUTURE *does not at all reply in mortals' words, but points once more to the gravestone. The stone undulates and glows. Music plays, beckoning* SCROOGE. SCROOGE *reeling in terror*]

Oh, no. Spirit! Oh, no, no!

---

8. ghoulish parasites (gōōl′ ish par′ ə sīts): Man and women who stole and divided Scrooge's goods after he died.

[FUTURE'S *finger still pointing*]

Spirit! Hear me! I am not the man I was. I will not be the man I would have been but for this intercourse. Why show me this, if I am past all hope?

[FUTURE *considers* SCROOGE'S *logic. His hand wavers.*]

Oh, Good Spirit, I see by your wavering hand that your good nature intercedes for me and pities me. Assure me that I yet may change these shadows that you have shown me by an altered life!

[FUTURE'S *hand trembles; pointing has stopped.*]

I will honor Christmas in my heart and try to keep it all the year. I will live in the Past, the Present, and the Future. The Spirits of all Three shall strive within me. I will not shut out the lessons that they teach. Oh, tell me that I may sponge away the writing that is upon this stone!

◆ **Literary Focus**

How does this passage reveal the theme of the play?

[SCROOGE *makes a desperate stab at grabbing* FUTURE'S *hand. He holds firm for a moment, but* FUTURE, *stronger than* SCROOGE, *pulls away.* SCROOGE *is on his knees, praying.*]

Spirit, dear Spirit, I am praying before you. Give me a sign that all is possible. Give me a sign that all hope for me is not lost. Oh, Spirit, kind Spirit, I beseech thee: give me a sign . . .

[FUTURE *deliquesces, slowly, gently. The* PHANTOM'S *hood and robe drop gracefully to the ground in a small heap. Music in. There is nothing in them. They are mortal cloth. The Spirit is elsewhere.* SCROOGE *has his sign.* SCROOGE *is alone. Tableau. The lights fade to black.*]

Scene 5

[*The end of it.* MARLEY, *spotlighted, opposite* SCROOGE, *in his bed, spotlighted.* MARLEY *speaks to audience, directly.*]

MARLEY. [*He smiles at* SCROOGE:] The firm of Scrooge and Marley is doubly blessed; two misers turned; one, alas, in Death, too late; but the other miser turned in Time's penultimate nick.[9] Look you on my friend, Ebenezer Scrooge . . .

SCROOGE. [*Scrambling out of bed; reeling in delight*] I will live in the Past, in the Present, and in the Future! The Spirits of all Three shall strive within me!

MARLEY. [*He points and moves closer to* SCROOGE'S *bed.*] Yes, Ebenezer, the bedpost is your own. Believe it! Yes, Ebenezer, the room is your own. Believe it!

SCROOGE. Oh, Jacob Marley! Wherever you are, Jacob, know ye that I praise you for this! I praise you . . . and heaven . . . and Christmastime! [*Kneels facing away from* MARLEY] I say it to ye on my knees, old Jacob, on my knees! [*He touches his bed curtains.*] Not torn down. My bed curtains are not at all torn down! Rings and all, here they are! They are here: I am here: the shadows of things that would have been, may now be dispelled. They will be, Jacob! I know they will be! [*He chooses clothing for the day. He tries different pieces of clothing and settles, perhaps on a dress suit, plus a cape of the bed clothing: something of color.*] I am light as a feather, I am happy as an angel, I am as merry as a schoolboy. [*Yells out window and then out to audience*] Merry Christmas to everybody! Merry Christmas to everybody! A Happy New Year to all the world! Hallo here! Whoop! Whoop! Hallo! Hallo! I don't know what day of the month it is! I don't care! I don't know anything! I'm quite a baby! I don't care! I don't care a fig! I'd much rather be a baby than be an old wreck like me or Marley! (Sorry, Jacob, wherever ye be!) Hallo! Hallo there!

[*Church bells chime in Christmas Day. A small boy, named* ADAM, *is seen now* D.R., *as a light fades up on him.*]

Hey, you boy! What's today? What day of the year is it?

---

9. **in Time's penultimate nick:** Just at the last moment.

ADAM. Today, sir? Why, it's Christmas Day!

SCROOGE. It's Christmas Day, is it? Whoop! Well, I haven't missed it after all, have I? The Spirits did all they did in one night. They can do anything they like, right? Of course they can! Of course they can!

ADAM. Excuse me, sir?

SCROOGE. Huh? Oh, yes, of course, what's your name, lad?

[SCROOGE *and* ADAM *will play their scene from their own spotlights.*]

ADAM. Adam, sir.

SCROOGE. Adam! What a fine, strong name! Do you know the poulterer's[10] in the next street but one, at the corner?

▲ **Critical Viewing** How does Scrooge's costume reveal the change in his character? [**Compare and Contrast**]

ADAM. I certainly should hope I know him, sir!

SCROOGE. A remarkable boy! An intelligent boy! Do you know whether the poulterer's have sold the prize turkey that was hanging up there? I don't mean the little prize turkey, Adam. I mean the big one!

ADAM. What, do you mean the one they've got that's as big as me?

SCROOGE. I mean, the turkey the size of Adam: that's the bird!

ADAM. It's hanging there now, sir.

◆ **Build Vocabulary**

dispelled (dis peld′) *v.*: Scattered and driven away; made to vanish

SCROOGE. It is? Go and buy it! No, no, I am absolutely in earnest. Go and buy it and tell 'em to bring it here, so that I may give them the directions to where I want it delivered, as a gift. Come back here with the man, Adam, and I'll give you a shilling. Come back here with him in less than five minutes, and I'll give you half-a-crown!

ADAM. Oh, my sir! Don't let my brother in on this.

[ADAM *runs offstage.* MARLEY *smiles.*]

MARLEY. An act of kindness is like the first green grape of summer: one leads to another and another and another. It would take a queer man indeed to not follow an act of kindness with an act of kindness. One simply whets the tongue for more . . . the taste of kindness is too too sweet. Gifts—goods—are lifeless. But the gift of goodness one feels in the giving is full of life. It . . . is . . . a . . . wonder.

◆ **Literature and Your Life**

Give an example from your experience to support Marley's statements.

[*Pauses; moves closer to* SCROOGE, *who is totally occupied with his dressing and arranging of his room and his day. He is making lists, etc.* MARLEY *reaches out to* SCROOGE:]

ADAM. [*Calling, off*] I'm here! I'm here!

[ADAM *runs on with a man, who carries an enormous turkey.*]

Here I am, sir. Three minutes flat! A world record! I've got the poultryman and he's got the poultry! [*He pants, out of breath.*] I have earned my prize, sir, if I live . . .

[*He holds his heart, playacting.* SCROOGE *goes to him and embraces him.*]

SCROOGE. You are truly a champion, Adam . . .

MAN. Here's the bird you ordered, sir . . .

SCROOGE. *Oh, my, MY!!!* look at the size of that turkey, will you! He never could have stood upon his legs, that bird! He would have

snapped them off in a minute, like sticks of sealingwax! Why you'll never be able to carry that bird to Camden-Town. I'll give you money for a cab . . .

MAN. Camden-Town's where it's goin', sir?

SCROOGE. Oh, I didn't tell you? Yes, I've written the precise address down just here on this . . . [*Hands paper to him*] Bob Cratchit's house. Now he's not to know who sends him this. Do you understand me? Not a word . . . [*Handing out money and chuckling*]

MAN. I understand, sir, not a word.

SCROOGE. Good. There you go then . . . this is for the turkey . . . [*Chuckle*] and this is for the taxi. [*Chuckle*] . . . and this is for your world-record run, Adam . . .

ADAM. But I don't have change for that, sir.

SCROOGE. Then keep it, my lad. It's Christmas!

ADAM. [*He kisses* SCROOGE'S *cheek, quickly.*] Thank you, sir. Merry, Merry Christmas! [*He runs off.*]

MAN. And you've given me a bit overmuch here, too, sir . . .

SCROOGE. Of course I have, sir. It's Christmas!

MAN. Oh, well, thanking you, sir. I'll have this bird to Mr. Cratchit and his family in no time, sir. Don't you worry none about that. Merry Christmas to you, sir, and a very happy New Year, too . . .

[*The man exits.* SCROOGE *walks in a large circle about the stage, which is now gently lit. A chorus sings Christmas music far in the distance. Bells chime as well, far in the distance. A gentlewoman enters and passes.* SCROOGE *is on the streets now.*]

SCROOGE. Merry Christmas, madam . . .

WOMAN. Merry Christmas, sir . . .

[*The portly businessman from the first act enters.*]

SCROOGE. Merry Christmas, sir.

PORTLY MAN. Merry Christmas, sir.

SCROOGE. Oh, you! My dear sir! How do you do? I do hope that you succeeded yesterday! It was very kind of you. A Merry Christmas.

PORTLY MAN. Mr. Scrooge?

SCROOGE. Yes, Scrooge is my name though I'm afraid you may not find it very pleasant. Allow me to ask your pardon. And will you have the goodness to—[*He whispers into the man's ear.*]

PORTLY MAN. Lord bless me! My dear Mr. Scrooge, are you *serious!?!*

SCROOGE. If you please. Not a farthing[11] less. A great many back payments are included in it, I assure you. Will you do me that favor?

PORTLY MAN. My dear sir, I don't know what to say to such munifi—

---

11. **farthing** (fär thin) *n.*: Small British coin.

▲ **Critical Viewing** How do the color and movement in this photo convey Scrooge's new attitude? **[Analyze Cause and Effect]**

SCROOGE. [*Cutting him off*] Don't say anything, please. Come and see me. Will you?

PORTLY MAN. I will! I will! Oh I will, Mr. Scrooge! It will be my pleasure!

SCROOGE. Thank'ee, I am much obliged to you. I thank you fifty times. Bless you!

[*Portly man passes offstage, perhaps by moving backwards.* SCROOGE *now comes to the room of his* NEPHEW *and* NIECE. *He stops at the door, begins to knock on it, loses his courage, tries again, loses his courage again, tries again, fails again, and then backs off and runs at the door, causing a tremendous bump against it. The*

NEPHEW and NIECE are startled. SCROOGE, poking head into room]

Fred!

NEPHEW. Why, bless my soul! Who's that?

NEPHEW and **NIECE.** [Together] How now? Who goes?

SCROOGE. It's I. Your Uncle Scrooge.

NIECE. Dear heart alive!

SCROOGE. I have come to dinner. May I come in, Fred?

NEPHEW. May you come in???!!! With such pleasure for me you may, Uncle!!! What a treat!

NIECE. What a treat, Uncle Scrooge! Come in, come in!

[They embrace a shocked and delighted SCROOGE: FRED calls into the other room.]

NEPHEW. Come in here, everybody, and meet my Uncle Scrooge! He's come for our Christmas party!

[Music in. Lighting here indicates that day has gone to night and gone to day again. It is early, early morning. SCROOGE walks alone from the party, exhausted, to his offices, opposite side of the stage. He opens his offices. The offices are as they were at the start of the play. SCROOGE seats himself with his door wide open so that he can see into the tank, as he awaits CRATCHIT, who enters, head down, full of guilt. CRATCHIT starts writing almost before he sits.]

SCROOGE. What do you mean by coming in here at this time of day, a full eighteen minutes late, Mr. Cratchit? Hallo, sir? Do you hear me?

BOB. I am very sorry, sir. I *am* behind my time.

SCROOGE. You are? Yes, I certainly think you are. Step this way, sir, if you please . . .

BOB. It's only but once a year, sir . . . it shall not be repeated. I was making rather merry yesterday and into the night . . .

SCROOGE. Now, I'll tell you what, Cratchit. I am

not going to stand this sort of thing any longer. And therefore . . .

[He stands and pokes his finger into BOB's chest.]

I am . . . about . . . to . . . raise . . . your salary.

BOB. Oh, no, sir, I . . . [Realizes] what did you say, sir?

SCROOGE. A Merry Christmas, Bob . . . [He claps BOB's back.] A merrier Christmas, Bob, my good fellow! than I have given you for many a year. I'll raise your salary and endeavor to assist your struggling family and we will discuss your affairs this very afternoon over a bowl of smoking bishop.[12] Bob! Make up the fires and buy another coal scuttle before you dot another i, Bob. It's too cold in this place! We need warmth and cheer, Bob Cratchit! Do you hear me? DO . . . YOU . . . HEAR . . . ME?

[BOB CRATCHIT stands, smiles at SCROOGE: BOB CRATCHIT faints. Blackout. As the main lights black out, a spotlight appears on SCROOGE: C. Another on MARLEY: He talks directly to the audience.]

MARLEY. Scrooge was better than his word. He did it all and infinitely more; and to Tiny Tim, who did NOT die, he was a second father. He became as good a friend, as good a master, as good a man, as the good old city knew, or any other good old city, town, or borough in the good old world. And it was always said of him that he knew how to keep Christmas well, if any man alive possessed the knowledge. [Pauses] May that be truly said of us, and all of us. And so, as Tiny Tim observed . . .

TINY TIM. [Atop SCROOGE's shoulder] God Bless Us, Every One . . .

[Lights up on chorus, singing final Christmas Song. SCROOGE and MARLEY and all spirits and other characters of the play join in. When the song is over, the lights fade to black.]

12. **smoking bishop:** Hot sweet orange-flavored drink.

Beyond Literature

Language Connection

Don't Be a Scrooge Ebenezer Scrooge is such a memorable character that his name has become part of the English language. The term *scrooge* means "a miser who doesn't like people." In other words, a *scrooge* is a person who has the attitude and personality that Ebenezer Scrooge had before Marley's ghost and the ghosts of Christmas Past, Present, and Future showed him the error of his ways.

Cross-Curricular Activity
Famous Names *Scrooge* is not the only name from literature and history to become an everyday expression. For example, a romantic man might be called a *romeo*, after the character in Shakespeare's *Romeo and Juliet*. With a group of classmates, use library and Internet resources to learn more about names that have become part of the language. Share your findings with the class.

Guide for Responding

◆ LITERATURE AND YOUR LIFE

Reader's Response Do you believe in Scrooge's change of heart? Explain.

Thematic Focus How is Dickens's personal code reflected in Scrooge's transformation?

Journal Writing Do you think that knowing what you'll be like in twenty years would change the way you act now? In a journal entry, explore your response.

☑ Check Your Comprehension

1. Where does Scrooge go with the Ghost of Christmas Present?
2. What fate does the Ghost of Christmas Present foretell for Tiny Tim?
3. What are the dolls that the Ghost of Christmas Present carries?
4. What five scenes does the Ghost of Christmas Future show Scrooge?
5. List five good deeds Scrooge performs at the end of the drama.

◆ Critical Thinking

INTERPRET

1. How does hearing his own cruel words about "surplus population" and "workhouses" echoed by the Ghost of Christmas Present affect Scrooge? **[Infer]**
2. What does this reaction suggest about Scrooge? **[Assess]**
3. What does Scrooge's desire to talk with his nephew and his niece reveal? **[Interpret]**
4. How does Marley's speech in which he compares acts of kindness to grapes summarize what has happened to Scrooge? **[Connect]**

EVALUATE

5. How well does Scrooge live up to the promise he makes at the beginning of Scene 5? **[Make a Judgment]**

APPLY

6. How does the Ghost of Christmas Present's explanation about why he gives more kindness to the poor tie to Dickens's experiences and concerns? **[Social Studies Link]**

Guide for Reading

Meet the Author:

Rod Serling (1924–1975)

Rod Serling once said that he didn't have much imagination. This is an odd statement from a man who wrote more than 100 television scripts, many of which were highly imaginative science-fiction fantasies.

Beginnings as a Writer Although he worked on his school's newspaper as a teenager, Serling didn't become serious about writing until college, after serving as a paratrooper in World War II. Driven by a love for radio drama, Serling earned second place in a national script contest. Soon after, he landed his first staff job as a radio writer.

Quick Success Serling branched out into writing for a new medium—television—and rocketed to fame. Just five years after he won the contest, everyone wanted to watch—and perform— Serling's work. To speed up production, he began recording his stories on tape instead of typing them.

THE STORY BEHIND THE STORY

In the 1950's and 1960's, television censors banned any script that appeared to question American society. In order to examine society and human nature in his work, Serling disguised social criticism with a science-fiction mask. For example, "The Monsters Are Due on Maple Street" addresses the Cold War mentality. However, by substituting an alien threat for a communist one, Serling avoided censorship.

◆ LITERATURE AND YOUR LIFE

CONNECT YOUR EXPERIENCE

Rumors can spread quickly and become increasingly distorted with each retelling. Sometimes, as in this screenplay, wild rumors have terrible effects.

THEMATIC FOCUS: Community Ties

As the rumors in Serling's drama spread, community ties are stretched to the breaking point. How might your community react in such a situation?

◆ Background for Understanding

HISTORY

This screenplay was written during the Cold War, a period of intense rivalry between the United States and the Soviet Union that lasted from the mid-1940's through the 1980's. Because the Soviet Union had a communist government, the two countries had conflicting political, economic, and social views. Both countries feared that the other was seeking to change its rival's way of life. This suspicion resulted in a massive nuclear arms race and an atmosphere of fear in which people's allegiances were sometimes questioned. As you read Serling's screenplay, think about what sort of statement the author seems to be making about Cold War attitudes.

◆ Build Vocabulary

WORD ROOTS: -sist-

In Serling's screenplay, you'll encounter the word *persistently*. The root -sist- means "stand." *Persistently* means "standing firmly, especially in the face of an obstacle."

WORD BANK

Which of these words might describe the actions of someone who moves very slowly?

flustered
sluggishly
assent
persistently
defiant
metamorphosis
scapegoat

The Monsters Are Due on Maple Street

◆ Literary Focus

CONFLICT IN DRAMA

Conflict is a struggle between opposing forces that drives the action in a literary work. The conflict can occur within a character or between a character and an outside force, such as another character. Because playwrights can't reveal a character's thoughts the same way a short-story writer would, a conflict that occurs within a character must be presented through what the character says or through what other characters say about him or her. In addition, because dramas tend to be longer works, there may be more than one conflict. As you read, note the conflicts that occur at different levels—between individuals, between groups and individuals, and between groups.

◆ Reading Strategy

PREDICT

One of the qualities that makes this screenplay successful is Serling's ability to build suspense, a feeling of intense curiosity about the outcome of events. To get the most out of this screenplay or any other piece of suspenseful literature, pause every now and then to **predict,** or make an educated guess, about where the story is headed. Base your predictions on clues that the author provides. You may want to note the clues and your predictions in a chart like the one below, revising as you encounter new information.

The Monsters Are Due on Maple Street

Rod Serling

CHARACTERS

NARRATOR
FIGURE ONE
FIGURE TWO

RESIDENTS OF MAPLE STREET

STEVE BRAND
CHARLIE'S WIFE
MRS. GOODMAN
MRS. BRAND
TOMMY
WOMAN
DON MARTIN
SALLY, Tommy's Mother
MAN ONE
MAN TWO
PETE VAN HORN
CHARLIE
LES GOODMAN

ACT I

[*Fade in on a shot of the night sky. The various nebulae and planet bodies stand out in sharp, sparkling relief, and the camera begins a slow pan across the Heavens.*]

NARRATOR'S VOICE. There is a fifth dimension beyond that which is known to man. It is a dimension as vast as space, and as timeless as infinity. It is the middle ground between light and shadow—between science and superstition. And it lies between the pit of man's fears and the summit of his knowledge. This is the dimension of imagination. It is an area which we call The Twilight Zone.

[*The camera has begun to pan down until it passes the horizon and is on a sign which reads "Maple Street." Pan down until we are shooting down at an angle toward the street below. It's a tree-lined, quiet residential American street, very typical of the small town. The houses have front porches on which people sit and swing on gliders, conversing across from house to house.* STEVE BRAND *polishes his car parked in front of his house. His neighbor,* DON MARTIN, *leans against the fender watching him. A Good Humor man rides a bicycle and is just in the process of stopping to sell some ice cream*] to a couple of kids. Two women gossip on the front lawn. Another man waters his lawn.]

NARRATOR'S VOICE. Maple Street, U.S.A., late summer. A tree-lined little world of front porch gliders, hop scotch, the laughter of children, and the bell of an ice cream vendor.

[*There is a pause and the camera moves over to a shot of the Good Humor man and two small boys who are standing alongside, just buying ice cream.*]

NARRATOR'S VOICE. At the sound of the roar and the flash of light it will be precisely 6:43 P.M. on Maple Street.

[*At this moment one of the little boys,* TOMMY, *looks up to listen to a sound of a tremendous screeching roar from overhead. A flash of light plays on both their faces and then it moves* down the street past lawns and porches and rooftops and then disappears.

♦ **Reading Strategy**
What do you think the flash is? Predict what effect this event will have on the community.

Various people leave their porches and stop what they're doing to stare up at the sky. STEVE BRAND, the man who's been polishing his car, now stands there transfixed, staring upwards. He looks at DON MARTIN, *his neighbor from across the street.*]

STEVE. What was that? A meteor?

DON. [*Nods*] That's what it looked like. I didn't hear any crash though, did you?

STEVE. [*Shakes his head*] Nope. I didn't hear anything except a roar.

MRS. BRAND. [*From her porch*] Steve? What was that?

STEVE. [*Raising his voice and looking toward porch*] Guess it was a meteor, honey. Came awful close, didn't it?

MRS. BRAND. Too close for my money! Much too close.

[*The camera pans across the various porches to* people who stand there watching and talking in low tones.]

NARRATOR'S VOICE. Maple Street. Six-forty-four P.M. on a late September evening. [*A pause*] Maple Street in the last calm and reflective moment . . . before the monsters came!

[*The camera slowly pans across the porches again. We see a man screwing a light bulb on a front porch, then getting down off the stool to flick the switch and finding that nothing happens.*

Another man is working on an electric power mower. He plugs in the plug, flicks on the switch of the power mower, off and on, with nothing happening.

Through the window of a front porch, we see a woman pushing her finger back and forth on the dial hook. Her voice is indistinct and distant, but intelligible and repetitive.]

WOMAN. Operator, operator, something's wrong on the phone, operator!

[MRS. BRAND *comes out on the porch and calls to* STEVE.]

MRS. BRAND. [*Calling*] Steve, the power's off. I had the soup on the stove and the stove just stopped working.

WOMAN. Same thing over here. I can't get anybody on the phone either. The phone seems to be dead.

[*We look down on the street as we hear the voices creep up from below, small, mildly disturbed voices highlighting these kinds of phrases:*]

VOICES.

Electricity's off.

Phone won't work.

Can't get a thing on the radio.

My power mower won't move, won't work at all.

Radio's gone dead!

[PETE VAN HORN, *a tall, thin man, is seen standing in front of his house.*]

VAN HORN. I'll cut through the back yard . . . See if the power's still on on Floral Street. I'll be right back!

[*He walks past the side of his house and disappears into the back yard.*

The camera pans down slowly until we're looking at ten or eleven people standing around the street and over-flowing to the curb and sidewalk. In the background is STEVE BRAND'S *car.*]

STEVE. Doesn't make sense. Why should the power go off all of a sudden, and the phone line?

DON. Maybe some sort of an electrical storm or something.

CHARLIE. That don't seem likely. Sky's just as blue as anything. Not a cloud. No lightning. No thunder. No nothing. How could it be a storm?

WOMAN. I can't get a thing on the radio. Not even the portable.

[*The people again murmur softly in wonderment and question.*]

CHARLIE. Well, why don't you go downtown and check with the police, though they'll probably think we're crazy or something. A little power failure and right away we get all <u>flustered</u> and everything.

STEVE. It isn't just the power failure, Charlie. If it was, we'd still be able to get a broadcast on the portable.

[*There's a murmur of reaction to this.* STEVE *looks from face to face and then over to his car.*]

STEVE. I'll run downtown. We'll get this all straightened out.

[*He walks over to the car, gets in it, turns the key. Looking through the open car door, we see the crowd watching him from the other side.* STEVE *starts the engine. It turns over <u>sluggishly</u> and then just stops dead. He tries it again and*

▲ **Critical Viewing** What impression does this illustration convey about life on Maple Street? [Analyze]

this time he can't get it to turn over. Then, very slowly and reflectively, he turns the key back to "off" and slowly gets out of the car.

The people stare at STEVE. *He stands for a moment by the car, then walks toward the group.*]

◆ **Build Vocabulary**

flustered (flus′ terd) *adj.:* Nervous; confused
sluggishly (slug′ ish lē) *adv.:* As if lacking energy

STEVE. I don't understand it. It was working fine before . . .

DON. Out of gas?

STEVE. [*Shakes his head*] I just had it filled up.

WOMAN. What's it mean?

CHARLIE. It's just as if . . . as if everything had stopped. [*Then he turns toward* STEVE.] We'd better walk downtown. [*Another murmur of assent at this.*]

STEVE. The two of us can go, Charlie. [*He turns to look back at the car.*] It couldn't be the meteor. A meteor couldn't do *this*.

[*He and* CHARLIE *exchange a look, then they start to walk away from the group.*

We see TOMMY, *a serious-faced fourteen-year-old in spectacles who stands a few feet away from the group. He is halfway between them and the two men, who start to walk down the sidewalk.*]

TOMMY. Mr. Brand . . . you better not!

STEVE. Why not?

TOMMY. They don't want you to.

[STEVE *and* CHARLIE *exchange a grin, and* STEVE *looks back toward the boy.*]

STEVE. Who doesn't want us to?

> ◆ **Literary Focus**
> What opposing force is introduced here? What kinds of conflicts might result?

TOMMY. [*Jerks his head in the general direction of the distant horizon*] Them!

STEVE. Them?

CHARLIE. Who are them?

TOMMY. [*Very intently*] Whoever was in that thing that came by overhead.

[STEVE *knits his brows for a moment, cocking his head questioningly. His voice is intense.*]

STEVE. What?

TOMMY. Whoever was in that thing that came

over. I don't think they want us to leave here.

[STEVE *leaves* CHARLIE *and walks over to the boy. He kneels down in front of him. He forces his voice to remain gentle. He reaches out and holds the boy.*]

STEVE. What do you mean? What are you talking about?

TOMMY. They don't want us to leave. That's why they shut everything off.

STEVE. What makes you say that? Whatever gave you that idea?

WOMAN. [*From the crowd*] Now isn't that the craziest thing you ever heard?

TOMMY. [*Persistently but a little intimidated by the crowd*] It's always that way, in every story I ever read about a ship landing from outer space.

WOMAN. [*To the boy's mother,* SALLY, *who stands on the fringe of the crowd*] From outer space, yet! Sally, you better get that boy of yours up to bed. He's been reading too many comic books or seeing too many movies or something.

SALLY. Tommy, come over here and stop that kind of talk.

STEVE. Go ahead, Tommy. We'll be right back. And you'll see. That wasn't any ship or anything like it. That was just a . . . a meteor or something. Likely as not—[*He turns to the group, now trying to weight his words with an optimism he obviously doesn't feel but is desperately trying to instill in himself as well as the others.*] No doubt it did have something to do with all this power failure and the rest of it. Meteors can do some crazy things. Like sunspots.

DON. [*Picking up the cue*] Sure. That's the kind of thing—like sunspots. They raise Cain[1] with radio reception all over the world. And this thing being so close—why, there's no telling the sort of stuff it can do. [*He wets his lips,*

---

1. **raise Cain with:** Badly disturb.

smiles nervously.] Go ahead, Charlie. You and Steve go into town and see if that isn't what's causing it all.

[STEVE and CHARLIE again walk away from the group down the sidewalk. The people watch silently.

    TOMMY stares at them, biting his lips, and finally calling out again.]

TOMMY. *Mr. Brand!*

[The two men stop again. TOMMY takes a step toward them.]

TOMMY. Mr. Brand . . . please don't leave here.

[STEVE and CHARLIE stop once again and turn toward the boy. There's a murmur in the crowd, a murmur of irritation and concern as if the boy were bringing up fears that shouldn't be brought up; words which carried with them a strange kind of validity that came without logic but nonetheless registered and had meaning and effect. Again we hear a murmur of reaction from the crowd.

    TOMMY is partly frightened and partly <u>defiant</u> as well.]

TOMMY. You might not even be able to get to town. It was that way in the story. Nobody could leave. Nobody except—

STEVE. Except who?

TOMMY. Except the people they'd sent down ahead of them. They looked just like humans. And it wasn't until the ship landed that—

[The boy suddenly stops again, conscious of the parents staring at them and of the sudden hush of the crowd.]

SALLY. [In a whisper, sensing the antagonism of the crowd] Tommy, please son . . . honey, don't talk that way—

MAN ONE. That kid shouldn't talk that way . . . and we shouldn't stand here listening to him. Why this is the craziest thing I ever heard of. The kid tells us a comic book plot and here we stand listening—

[STEVE walks toward the camera, stops by the boy.]

STEVE. Go ahead, Tommy. What kind of story was this? What about the people that they sent out ahead?

TOMMY. That was the way they prepared things for the landing. They sent four people. A mother and a father and two kids who looked just like humans . . . but they weren't.

[There's another silence as STEVE looks toward the crowd and then toward TOMMY. He wears a tight grin.]

STEVE. Well, I guess what we'd better do then is to run a check on the neighborhood and see which ones of us are really human.

[There's laughter at this, but it's a laughter that comes from a desperate attempt to lighten the atmosphere. It's a release kind of laugh. The people look at one another in the middle of their laughter.]

CHARLIE. There must be somethin' better to do than stand around makin' bum jokes about it.

[Rubs his jaw nervously] I wonder if Floral Street's got the same deal we got. [He looks past the houses.] Where is Pete Van Horn anyway? Didn't he get back yet?

[Suddenly there's the sound of a car's engine starting to turn over.

    We look across the street toward the driveway of LES GOODMAN's house. He's at the wheel trying to start the car.]

SALLY. Can you get it started, Les? [He gets out of the car, shaking his head.]

GOODMAN. No dice.

◆ Build Vocabulary

assent (ə sent´) n.: Agreement

persistently (pər sist´ ənt lē) adv.: Firmly and steadily

defiant (dē fī´ ənt) adj.: Boldly resisting

Overview of family walking dog on the street, William Low, Courtesy of the artist

▲ **Critical Viewing** How do the colors in this illustration contrast with the mood of the drama? Explain. **[Compare and Contrast]**

[*He walks toward the group. He stops suddenly as behind him, inexplicably and with a noise that inserts itself into the silence, the car engine starts up all by itself.* GOODMAN *whirls around to stare toward it.*

The car idles roughly, smoke coming from the exhaust, the frame shaking gently.

GOODMAN'S *eyes go wide, and he runs over to his car.*

The people stare toward the car.]

MAN ONE. He got the car started somehow. He got his car started!

[*The camera pans along the faces of the people as they stare, somehow caught up by this revelation and somehow, illogically, wildly, frightened.*]

WOMEN. How come his car just up and started like that?

SALLY. All by itself. He wasn't anywhere near

it. It started all by itself.

[DON *approaches the group, stops a few feet away to look toward* GOODMAN'S *car and then back toward the group.*]

DON. And he never did come out to look at that thing that flew overhead. He wasn't even interested. [*He turns to the faces in the group, his face taut and serious.*] Why? Why didn't he come out with the rest of us to look?

CHARLIE. He always was an oddball. Him and his whole family. Real oddball.

DON. What do you say we ask him?

[*The group suddenly starts toward the house. In this brief fraction of a moment they take the first step toward performing a metamorphosis that changes people from a group into a mob. They begin to head purposefully across the street toward the house at the end.* STEVE *stands in front of them. For a moment their fear almost*

♦ **Literary Focus**
What forces are in conflict now? How has the nature of the conflict changed?

turns their walk into a wild stampede, but STEVE'S *voice, loud, incisive, and commanding, makes them stop.*]

STEVE. Wait a minute . . . wait a minute! Let's not be a mob!

[*The people stop as a group, seem to pause for a moment, and then much more quietly and slowly start to walk across the street.* GOODMAN *stands alone facing the people.*]

GOODMAN. I just don't understand it. I tried to start it and it wouldn't start. You saw me. All of you saw me.

[*And now, just as suddenly as the engine started, it stops and there's a long silence that is gradually intruded upon by the frightened murmuring of the people.*]

GOODMAN. I don't understand. I swear . . . I don't understand. What's happening?

DON. Maybe you better tell us. Nothing's working on this street. Nothing. No lights, no power, no radio. [*And then meaningfully*] Nothing except one car—yours!

[*The people pick this up and now their murmuring becomes a loud chant filling the air with accusations and demands for action. Two of the men pass* DON *and head toward* GOODMAN, *who backs away, backing into his car and now at bay.*]

GOODMAN. Wait a minute now. You keep your distance—all of you. So I've got a car that starts by itself—well, that's a freak thing, I admit it. But does that make me some kind of a criminal or something? I don't know why the car works—it just does!

[*This stops the crowd momentarily and now* GOODMAN, *still backing away, goes toward his front porch. He goes up the steps and then stops*

◆ **Build Vocabulary**

metamorphosis (met′ ə môr′ fə sis) *n.:* Change of form

to stand facing the mob.

We see a long shot of STEVE *as he comes through the crowd.*]

STEVE. [*Quietly*] We're all on a monster kick, Les. Seems that the general impression holds that maybe one family isn't what we think they are. Monsters from outer space or something. Different than us. Fifth columnists[2] from the vast beyond. [*He chuckles.*] You know anybody that might fit that description around here on Maple Street?

GOODMAN. What is this, a gag or something? This a practical joke or something?

[*We see a close-up of the porch light as it suddenly goes out. There's a murmur from the group.*]

GOODMAN. Now I suppose that's supposed to incriminate me! The light goes on and off. That really does it, doesn't it? [*He looks around the faces of the people.*] I just don't understand this—[*He wets his lips, looking from face to face.*] Look, you all know me. We've lived here five years. Right in this house. We're no different from any of the rest of you! We're no different at all. Really . . . this whole thing is just . . . just weird—

WOMAN. Well, if that's the case, Les Goodman, explain why—[*She stops suddenly, clamping her mouth shut.*]

GOODMAN. [*Softly*] Explain what?

STEVE. [*Interjecting*] Look, let's forget this—

CHARLIE. [*Overlapping him*] Go ahead, let her talk. What about it? Explain what?

WOMAN. [*A little reluctantly*] Well . . . sometimes I go to bed late at night. A couple of times . . . a couple of times I'd come out on the porch and I'd see Mr. Goodman here in the wee hours of the morning standing out in front of his house . . . looking up at the sky. [*She looks around*

---

2. **Fifth columnists:** People who help an invading enemy from within their own country.

the circle of faces.] That's right, looking up at the sky as if . . . as if he were waiting for something. [*A pause*] As if he were looking for something.

[*There's a murmur of reaction from the crowd again.*

We cut suddenly to a group shot. As GOODMAN *starts toward them, they back away frightened.*]

GOODMAN. You know really . . . this is for laughs. You know what I'm guilty of? [*He laughs.*] I'm guilty of insomnia. Now what's the penalty for insomnia? [*At this point the laugh, the humor, leaves his voice.*] Did you hear what I said? I said it was insomnia. [*A pause as he looks around, then shouts.*] I said it was insomnia! You fools. You scared, frightened rabbits, you. You're sick people, do you know that? You're sick people—all of you! And you don't even know what you're starting because let me tell you . . . let me tell you—this thing you're starting—that should frighten you. As God is my witness . . . you're letting something begin here that's a nightmare!

◆ **Reading Strategy**
How do you think the crowd will treat Les Goodman?

ACT II

[*We see a medium shot of the* GOODMAN *entry hall at night. On the side table rests an unlit candle.* MRS. GOODMAN *walks into the scene, a glass of milk in hand. She sets the milk down on the table, lights the candle with a match from a box on the table, picks up the glass of milk, and starts out of scene*

MRS. GOODMAN *comes through her porch door, glass of milk in hand. The entry hall, with table and lit candle, can be seen behind her.*

Outside, the camera slowly pans down the sidewalk, taking in little knots of people who stand around talking in low voices. At the end of each conversation they look toward LES GOOD-MAN'S *house. From the various houses we can see candlelight but no electricity, and there's an* all-pervading quiet that blankets the whole area, disturbed only by the almost whispered voices of the people as they stand around. The camera pans over to one group where CHARLIE stands. He stares across at GOODMAN'S house.

We see a long shot of the house. Two men stand across the street in almost sentry-like poses. Then we see a medium shot of a group of people.]

SALLY. [*A little timorously*] It just doesn't seem right, though, keeping watch on them. Why . . . he was right when he said he was one of our neighbors. Why, I've known Ethel Goodman ever since they moved in. We've been good friends—

CHARLIE. That don't prove a thing. Any guy who'd spend his time lookin' up at the sky early in the morning—well, there's something wrong with that kind of person. There's something that ain't legitimate. Maybe under normal circumstances we could let it go by, but these aren't normal circumstances. Why, look at this street! Nothin' but candles. Why, it's like goin' back into the dark ages or somethin'!

[STEVE *walks down the steps of his porch, walks down the street over to* LES GOODMAN'S *house, and then stops at the foot of the steps.* GOODMAN *stands there, his wife behind him, very frightened.*]

GOODMAN. Just stay right where you are, Steve. We don't want any trouble, but this time if anybody sets foot on my porch, that's what they're going to get—trouble!

STEVE. Look, Les—

GOODMAN. I've already explained to you people. I don't sleep very well at night sometimes. I get up and I take a walk and I look up at the sky. I look at the stars!

MRS. GOODMAN. That's exactly what he does. Why this whole thing, it's . . . it's some kind of madness or something.

STEVE. [*Nods grimly*] That's exactly what it is—some kind of madness.

Streetlight, 1930, Constance Coleman Richardson, Indianapolis Museum of Art

▲ **Critical Viewing** Why does night's darkness, shown in this illustration, make people more fearful? **[Hypothesize]**

CHARLIE'S VOICE. [*Shrill, from across the street*] You best watch who you're seen with, Steve! Until we get this all straightened out, you ain't exactly above suspicion yourself.

STEVE. [*Whirling around toward him*] Or you, Charlie. Or any of us, it seems. From age eight on up!

WOMAN. What I'd like to know is—what are we gonna do? Just stand around here all night?

CHARLIE. There's nothin' else we can do! [*He turns back looking toward* STEVE *and* GOODMAN *again.*] One of 'em'll tip their hand. They got to.

STEVE. [*Raising his voice*] There's something you can do, Charlie. You could go home and keep your mouth shut. You could quit strutting around like a self-appointed hanging judge and just climb into bed and forget it.

CHARLIE. You sound real anxious to have that happen, Steve. I think we better keep our eye on you too!

DON. [*As if he were taking the bit in his teeth, takes a hesitant step to the front*] I think everything might as well come out now. [*He turns toward* STEVE.] Your wife's done plenty of talking, Steve, about how odd you are!

CHARLIE. [*Picking this up, his eyes widening*] Go ahead, tell us what she's said.

[*We see a long shot of* STEVE *as he walks toward them from across the street.*]

STEVE. Go ahead, what's my wife said? Let's get it all out. Let's pick out every idiosyncrasy of every single man, woman, and child on the street. And then we might as well set up some kind of kangaroo court.[3] How about a firing squad at dawn, Charlie, so we can get rid of all the suspects? Narrow them down. Make it easier for you.

DON. There's no need gettin' so upset, Steve. It's just that . . . well . . . Myra's talked about how there's been plenty of nights you spent hours down in your basement workin' on some kind of radio or something. Well, none of us have ever seen that radio—

[*By this time* STEVE *has reached the group. He stands there defiantly close to them.*]

CHARLIE. Go ahead, Steve. What kind of "radio set" you workin' on? I never seen it. Neither has anyone else. Who you talk to on that radio set? And who talks to you?

STEVE. I'm surprised at you, Charlie. How come you're so dense all of a sudden? [*A pause*] Who do I talk to? I talk to monsters from outer space. I talk to three-headed green men who fly over here in what look like meteors.

[STEVE'S *wife steps down from the porch, bites her lip, calls out.*]

MRS. BRAND. Steve! Steve, please. [*Then looking around, frightened, she walks toward the group.*] It's just a ham radio set, that's all. I bought him a book on it myself. It's just a ham radio set. A lot of people have them. I can show it to you. It's right down in the basement.

STEVE. [*Whirls around toward her*] Show them nothing! If they want to look inside our house—let them get a search warrant.

CHARLIE. Look, buddy, you can't afford to—

---

3. **kangaroo court:** Unofficial court that does not follow normal rules.

STEVE. [*Interrupting*] Charlie, don't tell me what I can afford! And stop telling me who's dangerous and who isn't and who's safe and who's a menace. [*He turns to the group and shouts.*] And you're with him, too—all of you! You're standing here all set to crucify—all set to find a scapegoat—all desperate to point some kind of a finger at a neighbor! Well now look, friends, the only thing that's gonna happen is that we'll eat each other up alive—

[*He stops abruptly as* CHARLIE *suddenly grabs his arm.*]

CHARLIE. [*In a hushed voice*] That's not the only thing that can happen to us.

[*Cut to a long shot looking down the street. A figure has suddenly materialized in the gloom and in the silence we can hear the clickety-clack of slow, measured footsteps on concrete as the figure walks slowly toward them. One of the women lets out a stifled cry. The young mother grabs her boy as do a couple of others.*]

TOMMY. [*Shouting, frightened*] It's the monster! It's the monster!

[*Another woman lets out a wail and the people fall back in a group, staring toward the darkness and the approaching figure.*

We see a medium group shot of the people as they stand in the shadows watching. DON MARTIN *joins them, carrying a shotgun. He holds it up.*]

DON. We may need this.

STEVE. A shotgun? [*He pulls it out of* DON'S *hand.*] Good Lord—will anybody think a thought around here? Will you people wise up? What good would a shotgun do against—

◆ **Literature and Your Life**
Why do people often need to blame a scapegoat for unexplainable events?

◆ **Build Vocabulary**

scapegoat (skāp´ gōt´) *n.*: Person or group blamed for the mistakes or crimes of others

[*Now* CHARLIE *pulls the gun from* STEVE'S *hand.*]

CHARLIE. No more talk, Steve. You're going to talk us into a grave! You'd let whatever's out there walk right over us, wouldn't yuh? Well, some of us won't!

[*He swings the gun around to point it toward the sidewalk.*
The dark figure continues to walk toward them.
The group stands there, fearful, apprehensive, mothers clutching children, men standing in front of wives. CHARLIE *slowly raises the gun. As the figure gets closer and closer he suddenly pulls the trigger. The sound of it explodes in the stillness. There is a long angle shot looking down at the figure, who suddenly lets out a small cry, stumbles forward onto his knees and then falls forward on his face.* DON, CHARLIE, *and* STEVE *race forward over to him.* STEVE *is there first and turns the man over. Now the crowd gathers around them.*]

STEVE. [*Slowly looks up*] It's Pete Van Horn.

DON. [*In a hushed voice*] Pete Van Horn! He was just gonna go over to the next block to see if the power was on—

WOMAN. You killed him, Charlie. You shot him dead!

CHARLIE. [*Looks around at the circle of faces, his eyes frightened, his face contorted*] But . . . but I didn't know who he was. I certainly didn't know who he was. He comes walkin' out of the darkness—how am I supposed to know who he was? [*He grabs* STEVE.] Steve—you know why I shot! How was I supposed to know he wasn't a monster or something? [*He grabs* DON *now.*] We're all scared of the same thing. I was just tryin' to . . . tryin' to protect my home, that's all! Look, all of you, that's all I was tryin' to do. [*He looks down wildly at the body.*] I didn't know it was somebody we knew! I didn't know—

[*There's a sudden hush and then an intake of breath. We see a medium*

◆ **Reading Strategy**
Do you think the blackout will be resolved? How?

shot of the living room window of CHARLIE'S house. The window is not lit, but suddenly the house lights come on behind it.]

WOMAN. [*In a very hushed voice*] Charlie . . . Charlie . . . the lights just went on in your house. Why did the lights just go on?

DON. What about it, Charlie? How come you're the only one with lights now?

GOODMAN. That's what I'd like to know.

[*A pause as they all stare toward* CHARLIE.]

GOODMAN. You were so quick to kill, Charlie, and you were so quick to tell us who we had to be careful of. Well, maybe you had to kill. Maybe Peter there was trying to tell us something. Maybe he'd found out something and came back to tell us who there was amongst us we should watch out for—

[CHARLIE *backs away from the group, his eyes wide with fright.*]

CHARLIE. No . . . no . . . it's nothing of the sort! I don't know why the lights are on. I swear I don't. Somebody's pulling a gag or something.

[*He bumps against* STEVE, *who grabs him and whirls him around.*]

STEVE. A gag? A gag? Charlie, there's a dead man on the sidewalk and you killed him! Does this thing look like a gag to you?

[CHARLIE *breaks away and screams as he runs toward his house.*]

CHARLIE. No! No! Please!

[*A man breaks away from the crowd to chase* CHARLIE.
We see a long angle shot looking down as the man tackles CHARLIE *and lands on top of him. The other people start to run toward them.* CHARLIE *is up on his feet, breaks away from the other man's grasp, lands a couple of desperate punches that push the man aside. Then he forces his way, fighting, through the crowd to once again break free, jumps up on his front*

porch. A rock thrown from the group smashes a window alongside of him, the broken glass flying past him. A couple of pieces cut him. He stands there perspiring, rumpled, blood running down from a cut on the cheek. His wife breaks away from the group to throw herself into his arms. He buries his face against her. We can see the crowd converging on the porch now.]

VOICES.

It must have been him.
He's the one.
We got to get Charlie.

[Another rock lands on the porch. Now CHARLIE *pushes his wife behind him, facing the group.]*

CHARLIE. Look, look I swear to you . . . it isn't me . . . but I do know who it is . . . I swear to you, I do know who it is. I know who the monster is here. I know who it is that doesn't belong. I swear to you I know.

GOODMAN. *[Shouting]* What are you waiting for?

WOMAN. *[Shouting]* Come on, Charlie, come on.

MAN ONE. *[Shouting]* Who is it, Charlie, tell us!

DON. *[Pushing his way to the front of the crowd]* All right, Charlie, let's hear it!

*[*CHARLIE'S *eyes dart around wildly.]*

CHARLIE. It's . . . it's . . .

MAN TWO. *[Screaming]* Go ahead, Charlie, tell us.

CHARLIE. It's . . . it's the kid. It's Tommy. He's the one!

[There's a gasp from the crowd as we cut to a shot of SALLY *holding her son* TOMMY. *The boy at first doesn't understand and then, realizing the eyes are all on him, buries his face against his mother.]*

SALLY. *[Backs away]* That's crazy! That's crazy! He's a little boy.

WOMAN. But he knew! He was the only one who knew! He told us all about it. Well, how did he know? How *could* he have known?

[The various people take this up and repeat the question aloud.]

VOICES.

How could he know?
Who told him?
Make the kid answer.

DON. It was Charlie who killed old man Van Horn.

WOMAN. But it was the kid here who knew what was going to happen all the time. He was the one who knew!

[We see a close-up of STEVE.]*

STEVE. Are you all gone crazy? *[Pause as he looks about]* Stop.

[A fist crashes at STEVE'S *face, staggering him back out of the frame of the picture.*
  There are several close camera shots suggesting the coming of violence. A hand fires a rifle. A fist clenches. A hand grabs the hammer from VAN HORN'S *body, etc. Meanwhile, we hear the following lines.]*

DON. Charlie has to be the one—Where's my rifle—

> ◆ **Reading Strategy**
> What do you think will happen next on Maple Street?

WOMAN. Les Goodman's the one. His car started! Let's wreck it.

MRS. GOODMAN. What about Steve's radio—He's the one that called them—

MRS. GOODMAN. Smash the radio. Get me a hammer. Get me something.

STEVE. Stop—Stop—

CHARLIE. Where's that kid—Let's get him.

MAN ONE. Get Steve—Get Charlie—They're working together.

[The crowd starts to converge around the mother, who grabs the child and starts to run with him. The crowd starts to follow, at first

▲ Critical Viewing How does this manipulated photograph help to communicate the ideas of the play? [Connect]

walking fast, and then running after him.

We see a full shot of the street as suddenly CHARLIE'S *lights go off and the lights in another house go on. They stay on for a moment, then from across the street other lights go on and then off again.*]

MAN ONE. [*Shouting*] It isn't the kid . . . it's Bob Weaver's house.

WOMAN. It isn't Bob Weaver's house. It's Don Martin's place.

CHARLIE. I tell you it's the kid.

DON. It's Charlie. He's the one.

[*We move into a series of close-ups of various people as they shout, accuse, scream, interspersing these shots with shots of houses as the lights go on and off, and then slowly in the middle of this nightmarish morass of sight and sound the camera starts to pull away, until once again we've reached the opening shot looking at the Maple Street sign from high above.*

The camera continues to move away until we dissolve to a shot looking toward the metal side of a space craft, which sits shrouded in darkness. An open door throws out a beam of light from the illuminated interior. Two figures silhouetted against the bright lights appear. We get only a vague feeling of form, but nothing more explicit than that.]

FIGURE ONE. Understand the procedure now? Just stop a few of their machines and radios and telephones and lawn mowers . . . throw them into darkness for a few hours, and then you just sit back and watch the pattern.

FIGURE TWO. And this pattern is always the same?

FIGURE ONE. With few variations. They pick the most dangerous enemy they can find . . . and it's themselves. And all we need do is sit back . . . and watch.

FIGURE TWO. Then I take it this place . . . this Maple Street . . . is not unique.

FIGURE ONE. [*Shaking his head*] By no means. Their world is full of Maple Streets. And we'll go from one to the other and let them destroy themselves. One to the other . . . one to the other . . . one to the other—

[*Now the camera pans up for a shot of the starry sky and over this we hear the* NARRATOR'S *voice.*]

NARRATOR'S VOICE. The tools of conquest do not necessarily come with bombs and explosions and fallout. There are weapons that are simply thoughts, attitudes, prejudices—to be found only in the minds of men. For the record, prejudices can kill and suspicion can destroy and a thoughtless frightened search for a scapegoat has a fallout all its own for the children . . . and the children yet unborn. [*A pause*] And the pity of it is . . . that these things cannot be confined to . . . The Twilight Zone!

CONNECTIONS TO TODAY'S WORLD

The possibility of aliens visiting Earth has sparked the imaginations of writers and artists to develop many scenarios. Rod Serling spun tales of fear and conspiracy. In contrast, cartoonist Gary Larson imagined a funnier interaction between humans and creatures from outer space.

The Far Side
by Gary Larson

"Hello, Emily. This is Gladys Murphy up the street. Fine, thanks . . . Say, could you go to your window and describe what's in my front yard?"

"Wonderful! Just wonderful! . . . So much for instilling them with a sense of awe."

1. What impression of aliens does the cartoon to the left convey?
2. Using the cartoon above, what would you expect Emily to tell Gladys?
3. Why do you think Larson chooses aliens as a subject for his comedy?

Media Connection

The Twilight Zone "You unlock this door with the key of imagination. Beyond it is another dimension, a dimension of sound, a dimension of sight, a dimension of mind." So began Rod Serling's narration of *The Twilight Zone*, one of the most popular TV shows of all time. The series, whose 156 episodes aired for the first time between 1959 and 1965, combined fantasy and science fiction to examine serious themes such as prejudice, identity, and the effects of technology on society.

The premise was so popular that a second series was produced from 1985 to 1987.

Cross-Curricular Activity

TV Review Locate and watch an episode of *The Twilight Zone*. In a review, summarize the plot of the show, and tell readers what the episode suggests about human behavior. Finally, express your opinion about the success of the episode you saw. Share your review with the class.

Guide for Responding

◆ LITERATURE AND YOUR LIFE

Reader's Response If you were a resident of Maple Street, how would you have responded to the strange events?

Thematic Focus Why does the community turn into an angry and suspicious mob?

Skit In a group, role-play the scene in which the crowd begins to suspect there is an alien among them. Discuss how each of you feels as the scene progresses.

☑ Check Your Comprehension

1. What are the first signs that something strange is happening on Maple Street?
2. How does Tommy explain the strange happenings?
3. How do the other neighborhood residents react to these events?
4. Why does Charlie shoot Pete Van Horn?
5. What happens after the shooting?
6. What is the real cause of the strange occurrences on Maple Street?

◆ Critical Thinking

INTERPRET
1. How does the appearance of the aliens at the end affect your view of the preceding action? **[Analyze]**
2. What qualities in Les Goodman and Steve Brand cause people to become suspicious of them? **[Interpret]**
3. What do the crowd's accusations suggest about how clearly they are thinking? **[Infer]**
4. How does fear contribute to the conflict on Maple Street? **[Analyze Cause and Effect]**
5. How do the events of the play prove the narrator's statement: "The tools of conquest do not necessarily come with bombs and explosions and fallout"? **[Connect]**
6. Who are the real monsters in this play? **[Draw Conclusions]**

APPLY
7. What warning should readers take away from this play? **[Generalize]**

EXTEND
8. Why do you think people's behaviors change when they're in a group? **[Social Studies Link]**

Guide for Responding (continued)

◆ Reading Strategy

PREDICT

The outcome of this play is not easy to **predict,** or figure out in advance. Still, if you watched for the clues Serling offered, you may have had some idea where the story was headed.

1. Based on Steve Brand's responses to Tommy and the others, what role did you expect him to play in the story? Why?
2. When the crowd begins suspecting Les Goodman and the others, did you think that the crowd's fears would be confirmed? Explain how your own experiences helped you predict.
3. How did you think the play would end? Did you at any point think there might actually be aliens? Why or why not?

◆ Build Vocabulary

USING THE WORD ROOT -sist-

The word root -sist- means "stand." Complete these sentences with -sist- words from this list:

consist   resist   assist

1. He begged them to ____?____ acting like a mob.
2. His wife tried to ____?____ him, pointing out that the rumors did not ____?____ of any real facts.

SPELLING STRATEGY

The f sound is sometimes spelled ph, as in meta-morphosis. On your paper, use the definitions provided to complete the words containing the ph spelling of the f sound.

1. Equipment used to listen to music: he____?____
2. A person's life story: bi____?____
3. Letters in ordered sequence: al____?____

USING THE WORD BANK

Choose the word most opposite in meaning to the first word.

1. defiant: (a) agreeable, (b) angry, (c) curious
2. persistently: (a) quickly, (b) sadly, (c) occasionally
3. metamorphosis: (a) bloom, (b) choice, (c) stability
4. scapegoat: (a) hero, (b) victim, (c) director
5. flustered: (a) shy, (b) confident, (c) sleepy
6. sluggishly: (a) energetically, (b) newly, (c) dimly
7. assent: (a) confusion, (b) approval, (c) denial

◆ Literary Focus

CONFLICT IN DRAMA

Conflict is a struggle between opposing forces in a work of literature. In "The Monsters Are Due on Maple Street," several different kinds of conflicts move the play toward its surprising conclusion.

1. How does Serling's play show conflict between individuals?
2. How does the play show conflict between individuals and society?
3. What other conflict occurs in the play?
4. What is the central conflict of the play?

◆ Build Grammar Skills

PRONOUN AND ANTECEDENT AGREEMENT

A **pronoun** takes the place of a noun. An **antecedent** is the noun for which a pronoun stands. Pronouns should agree with their antecedents in number and gender. *Number* indicates whether a pronoun is singular (referring to one) or plural (referring to more than one). *Gender* indicates whether a pronoun refers to a male or a female. In this example, the plural pronoun *their* agrees with its plural antecedent *neighbors:*

The *neighbors* have lost *their* ability to think.

Here, the singular pronoun *his* agrees with its singular antecedent *Tommy.*

Tommy gave *his* opinion.

Practice On your paper, complete each sentence with a pronoun that matches the antecedent.

1. The aliens had planned ____?____ game carefully.
2. Each woman did what ____?____ could.
3. Pete showed ____?____ fear.
4. Charlie became angry, while Steve tried to solve the puzzle with ____?____ mind.
5. The shooting shocked the crowd. ____?____ was unexpected.

Writing Application On your paper, write a sentence with a pronoun that refers to each of the following words as antecedents. Underline the pronoun.

1. Tommy   2. everyone   3. each wife   4. Les

Build Your Portfolio

 Idea Bank

Writing

1. **Neighborhood Code** Write a set of rules outlining the way neighbors should treat one another. Use the actions of the Maple Street residents as examples. **[Social Studies Link]**

2. **Aliens' Report** Write a report on the events that Figure One and Figure Two give to their leader on returning. Include recommendations for further action.

3. **Drama Review** In a review for a television guide, write a critique of "The Monsters Are Due on Maple Street." Tell readers whether they should tune in for this episode, and explain why. **[Media Link]**

Speaking and Listening

4. **Performance [Group Activity]** With a group, perform a scene from "The Monsters . . ." If possible, use a video camera to film the scene as the camera directions suggest—or try your own camera angles! If a camera is not available, stage the scene for a live audience. **[Performing Arts Link]**

5. **Conflict-Resolution Meeting [Group Activity]** Learn about conflict-resolution techniques from school counselors or peer mediators. Then, discuss with a group how these techniques could be used to resolve the conflicts on Maple Street. Summarize your findings for the class.

Projects

6. **The Scientific View** What are some possible scientific explanations for the ways Maple Street machines fail? Talk with electricians or car mechanics. Share their ideas with the class, and discuss which make the most sense. **[Science Link]**

7. **Casting Sketches** To help the actors who will perform the television play, create a series of sketches of different scenes. Think about how people look and move when they are afraid. Capture the movement of the crowd and its growing sense of panic. **[Art Link]**

Writing Mini-Lesson

Final Scene

The end of "The Monsters Are Due . . ." may leave you wondering what happens next. Imagine that you are the television writer hired to create a sequel to the episode. Write the opening scene for a sequel that begins the next morning. Include realistic dialogue and descriptions of camera shots.

Writing Skills Focus: Script Format

Make sure that actors and other crew members can understand the scene you have in mind. Using **script format,** which identifies who is speaking and includes camera angles and stage directions, will help.

Model From the Play

ACT I

[*Fade in on a shot of the night sky. The various nebulae and planet bodies stand out in sharp, sparkling relief, and the camera begins a slow pan across the Heavens.*]

NARRATOR'S VOICE. There is a fifth dimension beyond that which is known to man.

Prewriting Write a list of events that will occur in the scene. Put them in time sequence. Next to each event, briefly describe how the characters are likely to respond. Identify setting elements that should be described in the stage or camera directions.

Drafting Begin by setting the morning scene. Then, show how events have moved forward since the previous night.

Revising Review your scene to make sure characters' actions are consistent with their behavior earlier in the play. Then, look at your script formatting to check that you have identified each character speaking and that the camera angles and stage directions are clear.

◆ **Grammar Application**

As you draft and revise, make sure your pronouns and antecedents agree.

Radio Script

Writing Process Workshop

When you go to see a drama, the gestures of the actors, the costumes, and the set help you to understand the events of the play. When you hear a radio play, you have to rely on sounds—those of the actors' voices and of any special effects that convey action. A **radio script** includes the dialogue that characters say and sound-effect advice that will help listeners imagine the action they will never see. Put your imaginations in gear as you write a radio script. The following skills will help you write a script alive with action:

Writing Skills Focus

▶ **Use the proper script format** so readers and actors can understand the directions you provide. (See p. 713.)

▶ **Let your dialogue work for you.** What the characters say—and how they say it—is at the heart of a radio script. Choose each character's dialogue wisely and well.

▶ **Include sounds and noises** of all kinds to bring your script to life.

The following passage from a radio script uses these skills to tell the story of a town that gets hit by a tornado.

MODEL

SAM. ① Look in the sky just past the horizon! Is that a funnel cloud? [*Sound of wind in the distance.*] ②

LUTHER. Quick! Get inside! Get everyone inside! [*As wind gets stronger and louder, sounds of running feet and slamming doors.*]

SAM. [*Nervously*] Luther! Where are you going? Get back here! [*Now completely panicked and breathless.*] Stay inside, you've got to save yourself! ③

① Script format uses capitalization to identify speakers.

② This precise sound description offers helpful direction.

③ Dialogue develops the conflict of the scene.

Prewriting

Plan the Plot Think about what will happen in the radio script you write. Choose a conflict that will be dramatic. Here are a few suggestions:

> ### Script Ideas
> - Group of friends hikes up a mountain
> - Child gets lost at a carnival
> - Misunderstanding turns into a comedy

Tune In Many public radio stations still offer radio plays to their audiences. Call a local station to ask when a play is being broadcast, or get a recording from a local library. As you listen, notice how the characters are developed, how the story grows from the dialogue, and how sound effects are used.

Build Suspense Start out in a normal, comfortable way. Let your audience learn about the characters and the setting. Then, introduce the problem, and let the tension grow. Remember that good plots build to a dramatic moment of action or insight. Look at this example:

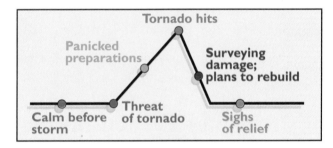

Drafting

Use Realistic Spoken Language To make your dialogue sound like real speech, take note of the way people actually talk. Go to a busy place and listen—on a bus, in the cafeteria, in a school hallway. As you draft, use what you've learned.

Include Stage Directions In brackets in your script, include information about sound effects and how characters should deliver each line.

Find Ways to Add Sound Decide which sounds will enhance the action. A creaky cabinet, a heavy knock on a door, or the ring of a telephone can bring the scenes to life.

APPLYING LANGUAGE SKILLS: Spoken vs. Written Language

Spoken language is loose and free-flowing. We often speak in fragments and use slang. We slur words together and cut things short. In contrast, **written language** is more formal and structured. Look at these examples:

Spoken:
The time? Um, I dunno.

Written:
What time is it? I don't know.

Spoken:
Gotta run. I'm gonna be late.

Written:
I've got to run. I'm going to be late.

Practice Rewrite these spoken sentences into correct written language.

1. When ya comin' home?
2. Any tickets left? We gotta have three.
3. The play was like totally awesome!
4. Wanna go again?

Writing Application When writing a radio script, use spoken language to make dialogue seem real.

Writer's Solution Connection Writing Lab

For more topic ideas, see the Inspirations in the Creative Writing tutorial.

APPLYING LANGUAGE SKILLS: Use Punctuation to Show Emotion

In a radio script, you need to describe the emotion the actors should convey. Consider the power of these punctuation marks:

Exclamation points show strong emotion.

Run for your life!

Question marks show direct questions.

Where are you going?

Ellipses create pauses that can show uncertainty or breathlessness.

I can't . . . keep up! . . . Wait . . . for . . me!

Practice Add punctuation to make these sentences more powerful.

1. Give me your hand. I'll save you.
2. How can we get out.
3. Um, what are you doing.

Writing Application Let the punctuation direct the emotions in your radio script.

Writer's Solution Connection Language Lab

For more practice with end marks, see the Language Lab unit on Punctuation.

Revising

Read Aloud It's essential to hear a script read aloud during the revision process. Ask two or three friends to help you read. They can tell you which lines seemed uncomfortable, awkward, or unbelievable. After the reading, ask the actors to discuss your draft, telling what they liked and did not like.

Add More Sometimes, it's important to add words while you are revising, especially if a character's reasons for action seem unclear. If a line has someone wondering "Why?", add more dialogue to answer the question.

REVISION MODEL

MICHAEL. Turn up the television—I want to hear the score. ① *and changing channels* [*Sound of static.*] Great! They won! We're going to the playoffs!

PATTI. We'd better get tickets to that soccer match. ② *definitely* It'll sell out soon.

① Stage directions add more information about sound effects.

② This word makes the dialogue more realistic.

Publishing and Presenting

Tape It Radio scripts are meant to be heard! Share your work with an audience by capturing it on tape. Follow these suggestions to record your production successfully:

▶ Use the stage directions to direct actors and sound effects technicians.

▶ Rehearse each scene in your script. Plan how actors will deliver the lines, and make sure you are happy with the results on the tape. Run through the action a few times before your final recording.

▶ Don't take the technology for granted. Be sure the recorder is working, that the sound is clear, and that effects don't overpower voices.

▶ When you're finished, play the recording for your class—or send it in to a local radio station.

Strategies for Success

Television, magazines, and the Internet give us lots of information. Messages from these media can entertain us and help us make decisions. Since they can also influence us in subtle ways, it is important to read media messages with a critical eye. Use these skills to help you critically evaluate media messages:

Identify the Writer Try to find out who wrote the message. That will help you figure out the point of view being expressed. It can also reveal a message's intent, even if it isn't stated outright. For example, the makers of Toasty Crispy O's want you to buy their cereal, even if they don't come out and say it directly.

Separate Fact From Opinion Facts are statements that can be checked. If an article says the stock market crashed in 1929, you can look it up and find out whether that's true: It's a fact. If the article says the market crashed because brokers weren't doing their jobs, you can't check that: It's an opinion. Pay attention to the statements you read. Ask yourself: *Is that a fact?*

Ask Questions When you read a media message, ask yourself what information is missing. Is there another point of view? Do you need to know more about the subject? Presenting only one side of the story can change its impact. Ask questions, and get the full story.

Apply the Strategies

Read the accompanying paid advertisement. Then, answer the questions that follow.

1. Who wrote the message? How might that person's position and motivation affect the content of the text?
2. List three facts and three opinions that appear in the text.
3. What information is missing from the article? How would the inclusion of this information change the character of the text?

Stop Bill 4135A

In June, California voters wisely agreed to give more money to schools to buy delicious dairy products for school cafeterias. That new law made sense. After all, $40 million a year is not a lot to spend when you're buying the healthiest food product around.

Now, Senator Smalley proposes a bill to endanger the health of young people by cutting spending for dairy products. On June 17, the California Senate will vote on Bill 4135A, which would cut dairy spending for public schools to $32 million per year. He says the money can be put to better use. I say you should call your senator and tell him or her to vote against this unhealthy bill.

C.K. Skoda
President, California Dairy League

✔ *Here are other situations in which you can apply strategies for evaluating media messages:*
▶ **Listening to political speeches**
▶ **Watching infomercials**
▶ **Reading letters to the editor**
▶ **Surfing Web sites**

Pronoun and Antecedent Agreement

a·gree (ə grē') v. 1 to be healthful or proper: followed by with /This climate agrees with me./ 6 Grammar to have the same number, person, case, or gender /A verb should agree with its subject in number./ a·greed', a·gree'ing

A **pronoun** takes the place of a noun. An **antecedent** is the noun for which a pronoun stands. A pronoun must agree with its antecedent in both person and number. (See page 712.) Singular pronouns refer to singular antecedents. Plural pronouns agree with plural antecedents. Look at this example:

Rod Serling achieved *his* fame with *The Twilight Zone* series.

The pronoun *his* is third person, singular, and masculine. It agrees with its antecedent, Rod Serling, which is also third person, singular, and masculine.

	Singular	Plural
First Person	*I* brought *my* lunch.	*We* brought *our* lunches.
Third Person	*He* brought *his* lunch. *She* brought *her* lunch.	*They* brought *their* lunches.

Practice 1 On your paper, write each of the following sentences, filling in the blanks with the correct pronoun.

1. Two women noticed that ___?___ phones weren't working.

2. Pete went to the next block. ___?___ wanted to see what was happening there.

3. The car wouldn't start. ___?___ engine wouldn't turn over.

4. Tommy yelled out a warning, "Mr. Brand . . . ___?___ better not!"

5. Tommy warned ___?___ neighbors about aliens. He told ___?___ what he had heard.

Practice 2 Revise each sentence according to the directions that follow. Correct pronouns to agree with their new antecedents.

1. Rod Serling's audience loved his plays. (Change *Rod Serling* to *Wendy Wasserstein*.)

2. The play showed average people acting in a way that was strange for them. (Change *average people* to *a young man*.)

3. Since citizens were worried about invasions, the play struck a chord with them. (Change *citizens* to *my friends and I*.)

Grammar in Writing

✔ *A common error in agreement occurs when a writer uses* you *to refer to a noun.*

Incorrect: The *neighbors* are trying to place blame, a mistake *you* shouldn't make when *you're* frightened.

Revised: The *neighbors* are trying to place blame, a mistake *they* shouldn't make when *they're* frightened.

Whenever you use *you* in your writing, make sure it refers only to the person you are addressing—your reader. It should never be used to refer to the person about whom you are writing.

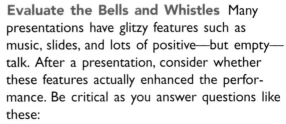
When you watch an infomercial, attend a school assembly, or participate in a walking tour, you experience a presentation on a variety of levels. First, listen for the information presented. Once you've done that, however, take time to judge the quality of the presentation. Use these strategies to help you evaluate a presentation:

Summarize the Message To help you assess whether a presentation was successful, take a moment to sum up what you learned. The simplicity—or difficulty—of this task may reveal the angle of your evaluation. If you can't state briefly what you learned, the presentation may not have been effective.

Be Thorough Many elements combine in a good presentation. Use the following questions to assess a presentation:

▶ Was the organization of the presentation clear and logical?

▶ Did the presentation contain accurate, interesting information?

▶ Did the presenter speak in a way that everyone in the audience could hear?

Evaluate the Bells and Whistles Many presentations have glitzy features such as music, slides, and lots of positive—but empty—talk. After a presentation, consider whether these features actually enhanced the performance. Be critical as you answer questions like these:

▶ Did the music fit the message?

▶ Did visuals enhance your understanding?

▶ Did a humorous anecdote serve a purpose?

Apply the Strategies

With a group, watch a news report, an infomercial, or a live presentation. Then, answer these questions:

1. What was the main idea of the presentation?

2. Identify at least three elements of the presentation that were effective.

3. Identify at least one element of the presentation that could have been improved.

4. In a paragraph, explain whether you would recommend that a friend watch this presentation. Provide evidence to support your evaluation.

Tips for Evaluating a Presentation

✔ *When evaluating a presentation, follow these strategies:*

▶ *Note the reaction of other members of the audience.*

▶ *Don't get caught up in an emotional reaction. Be sure that your assessment can be supported by evidence.*

What's Behind the Words

Vocabulary Adventures With Richard Lederer

Numerical Prefixes

Let's play a numbers game. Can you name the numbers embedded in each of the following words? What numbers can you find in hexagon, September, octopus, nonagenarian, and decathlon?

Doing a Number on Words

The numbers in the words above are *6, 7, 8, 9,* and *10*. Each of the words contains a Greek or Latin prefix that stands for the numbers six through ten. A hexagon (Latin, *hexa*) is a six-sided figure. September (Latin, *sept*) was once the seventh month of the year. Before the Romans changed their calendar, March was the first month, so September, October, November, and December were suitable names. An octopus (Latin, *octo*) has eight legs. A nonagenarian (Latin, *non, nov*) has reached at least ninety years of age, and a decathlon (Greek, *deka*) consists of exactly ten athletic events.

Counting Off With Prefixes

To discover other numbers hiding in our words, try counting from one to five with prefixes from the classical languages:

Number	Latin	Greek
one	uni	mono
two	duo	di
three	tri	tri
four	quadr	tetra
five	quint	penta

One, Two, Three . . .

The universe is made from two Latin word parts that mean "one world." *Twilight* is literally "the time of two lights," the fading sunset and the emerging light of the moon and stars.

Have you ever wondered if the *tri-* in *trivial* is the same as the *tri-* in *triple*? In fact, *trivial* does derive from the Latin *tri* (three) and *via* (way) and literally means "like something found at a place where three roads meet." In ancient times, shoppers returning from the market often stopped at intersections where three roads converged to exchange idle gossip. Hence, the modern meaning of *trivial*: "common; insignificant."

The Latin *quadr* is in *quarantine,* originally a period of forty days during which ships suspected of carrying disease were banned from port. The *Pentagon* in Washington, D.C., is a famous five-sided building.

ACTIVITY 1 *One* is a unique number. It stands for the smallest number—one of any kind—and for the largest number—everything rolled into one unified whole, or union—like the United States or the universe. List as many words as you can that begin with *uni* and *mono,* and tell what they mean.

ACTIVITY 2 The motto of our nation is *E pluribus unum.* Use a dictionary to translate those Latin words into English.

ACTIVITY 3 Find the meanings of ten words that begin with the numerical prefixes you have learned in this lesson.

Extended Reading Opportunities

Reading a play allows you to enjoy a play at any time, in any place. Consider reading these plays as you extend your exploration of drama.

Suggested Titles

Brian's Song
William Blinn

In a screenplay based on the biography of Brian Piccolo, dramatist William Blinn shares the comic and tragic moments in the life of an athlete dying young. Along with Piccolo, Gale Sayers joined the Chicago Bears in 1965. The two men competed with each other, roomed with each other, and helped each other through injury. The play takes a tragic turn when Piccolo is diagnosed with cancer.

Center Stage: One-Act Plays for Teenage Readers and Actors
Donald R. Gallo, Editor

From an aerobics class for college freshmen to the schoolyard of a city school, this collection of high-interest short plays features young people in a variety of settings. One play, "The War of the Words," pits the "Grunts" against the "Notes" and calls for the audience to vote on the outcome. Chosen especially for young adults, the selections in *Center Stage* feature something for every interest.

Short Dramas and Teleplays

This anthology of dramas includes classics, one-act plays, and television scripts for readers of all ability levels. In addition to such favorites as *Robin Hood*, *Oliver Twist,* and *Frankenstein,* you'll find dramatic versions of *The Bishop's Candlesticks, The Red Badge of Courage,* and *I Remember Mama.*

Other Possibilities

¡Aplauso! Hispanic Children's Theater   Joe Rosenberg, Editor

Modern Monologues for Young People   John Murray

Our Town   Thornton Wilder

Effect of the Sun on the Water, 1905, Andre Derain, © Artists Rights Society (ARS), NY/Giraudon

Poetry

Whether telling a story, capturing a single moment, or describing nature in a whole new way, poetry is the most musical of all literary forms. These terms will help you discuss the variety of poetry you'll encounter in this unit:

- **Narrative poetry** tells a story.

- **Lyric poetry** expresses thoughts and feelings.

- **Form** describes the structure of a poem. Some poems are written in regular groups of lines called *stanzas*. Others, like *haiku*, follow strict syllable and line counts.

- **Rhythm, rhyme, and sound devices,** such as *alliteration* and *onomatopoeia*, give poetry its musical quality.

- **Figurative language**—such as *simile, metaphor,* and *personification*—allows the poet to draw vibrant and creative comparisons.

UNIT 9

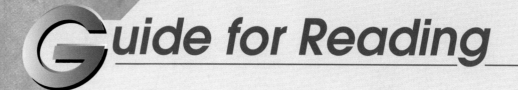

Guide for Reading

Meet the Author:

Sir Walter Scott (1771–1832)

When Sir Walter Scott died, people in his native Scotland and in England mourned as if a king had died.

A Varied Life Born into an old and wealthy Scottish family, Scott grew to love his country's history while listening to elderly relatives' stories and accounts. After working briefly—and without much interest—for his lawyer father, Scott explored many different interests. He traveled widely, collected antiques, translated German poetry, and worked as a journalist.

Inventing a New Form of Fiction As "Lochinvar" and his other works show, Scott was a talented poet. In 1813, he was offered the prestigious position of Poet Laureate of England, but he declined the honor; poetry no longer interested him. Instead, he began writing novels based on people and events in Scottish and English history. In the process, he created such classics as *Ivanhoe* and a type of fiction that has remained popular ever since—the historical novel.

THE STORY BEHIND THE STORY

"Lochinvar," like many of Scott's works, reflects his love for the Scottish border ballads, or storytelling songs. His keen ear for the way people spoke and his knowledge of history enabled him to make the past come alive with romance, heroism, and adventure.

◆ LITERATURE AND YOUR LIFE

CONNECT YOUR EXPERIENCE

You've probably seen many movies in which a dashing hero defeats all enemies and walks away with his or her love interest. The poem "Lochinvar" tells such a story, set in the distant past when people fought with swords and the world seemed to be filled with hidden dangers.

THEMATIC FOCUS: Personal Codes

Heroes often live by their own codes of honor. As you read, think about how you would describe Lochinvar's personal code.

◆ Background for Understanding

LITERATURE

In this poem, a knight in shining armor comes to declare his love to a beautiful maiden. Knights were members of the nobility, or upper class, in Europe's Medieval period, which lasted from about 400 to 1400. Their primary duty was to defend the estates of wealthy lords, who provided them with lands in return for their service. In addition, knights were sometimes called upon to travel to distant lands to fight for the king. As a result of their travels, knights were viewed as great adventurers. Because they helped people feel safe in dangerous times, they were also viewed as gallant and romantic heroes.

◆ Lochinvar ◆

A procession of knights and their squires on their way to do battle, ms. illumination c. 1450

◆ Literary Focus

BALLAD

A **ballad** is a song or songlike poem that tells a story, often dealing with adventure or romance. Ballads usually have rhyming lines with a strong, musical rhythm. They are divided into stanzas, or groups, of four or six lines. Ballads usually have a refrain, which is a repeated line or set of lines. In many ballads, including "Lochinvar," the refrain changes a little each time it appears.

◆ Build Vocabulary

WORDS WITH MULTIPLE MEANINGS

In "Lochinvar," Scott uses the word *bar* as a verb, meaning "to prevent access." The word *bar* has many other meanings, including "a piece of wood or metal used as a barrier." As you read this poem, watch for other words with multiple meanings. Note each word and what you think it means in a chart like the one below.

WORD BANK

Which of these words do you think means "to worry"? Check the Build Vocabulary box to see if you chose correctly.

dauntless
consented
laggard
bar
tread
fret

Multiple Meaning Word	What You Think It Means in Poem
brake	
suit	
lead	
bank	

Reading for Success

Strategies for Reading Poetry

Sometimes reading poetry is like watching a whodunit movie. It can take a while until you really grasp the story line. You have to listen carefully to what is said (and notice who says it), survey the surroundings to find clues, and keep restating what you know as you put the pieces together. These strategies will help you make poetry less of a mystery:

Identify the speaker.

The speaker is the imaginary voice assumed by the poet. Sometimes, the speaker is the poet. Other times, the speaker is a character created by the poet. Whenever you read a poem, look for clues that will help you make inferences about the speaker's personality, experiences, and attitudes.

Read lines according to punctuation.

▶ Pause at commas, dashes, semicolons, and ellipsis marks (three or four dots). Stop longer at end marks. Don't stop at the end of a line unless the punctuation indicates that you should.

slight pause   full pause

He rode all unarmed, and he rode all alone.

▶ When sentences end in question marks, read them as questions. When they end with exclamation points, read them with emphasis.

Use your senses.

▶ Use your senses—sight, hearing, smell, taste, and physical sensation—to understand and experience the poem's world fully.
▶ Envision the setting and action by painting a mental picture from the poem's words.

Paraphrase the lines.

If you're unsure of the poem's meaning, you may want to restate a line or passage in your own words to help you understand it.

Scott's Version:	So faithful in love, and so dauntless in war, There never was knight like the young Lochinvar.
Paraphrased:	Lochinvar was a great knight. He was a brave soldier and remained true to the woman he left behind while at war.

As you read "Lochinvar," look at the notes in the boxes. They will help you apply the reading strategies to the poem.

Lochinvar

SIR WALTER SCOTT

A knight and a lady on horseback. Breviary with calendar, May, Flemish School (end 15th)

▲ **Critical Viewing** What details in this painting tell you it is set in the Medieval period? **[Analyze]**

O, young Lochinvar is come out of the
West,
Through all the wide Border his steed[1] was
the best,
And save his good broadsword[2] he weapons
had none;
He rode all unarmed, and he rode all
alone.
5   So faithful in love, and so <u>dauntless</u> in war,
There never was knight like the young
Lochinvar.

He stayed not for brake, and he stopped
not for stone,
He swam the Eske river[3] where ford there
was none;
But, ere he alighted at Netherby[4] gate,
10 The bride had <u>consented</u>, the gallant came
late:
For a <u>laggard</u> in love, and a dastard in war,
Was to wed the fair Ellen of brave
Lochinvar.

So boldly he entered the Netherby hall,
Among bridesmen and kinsmen, and
brothers and all;
15 Then spoke the bride's father, his hand
on his sword
(For the poor craven[5] bridegroom said
never a word),
"O come ye in peace here, or come ye in
war,
Or to dance at our bridal, young Lord
Lochinvar?"

"I long wooed your daughter, my suit you
denied;—
20 Love swells like the Solway, but ebbs like
its tide—
And now I am come, with this lost love of
mine,

> You can **paraphrase** lines 9–14
> as: Before Lochinvar reached
> Netherby manor, his love,
> Ellen, had agreed to marry
> someone else. This other man
> was slow-moving in love and a
> cowardly soldier.

> **Read** lines 17–18 **according
> to the punctuation,** pausing
> briefly after "here," "war,"
> and "bridal," but not after
> "in." Noting the final end
> mark, read the entire sen-
> tence as a question.

---

1. **steed** (stēd) *n.*: Horse.
2. **broadsword** *n.*: Sword with a wide
double-edged blade used for slashing
rather than thrusting.
3. **Eske river** (esk) *n.*: River near border
between England and Scotland.
4. **Netherby** *n.*: Name of the manor
where the poem is set.
5. **craven** (krā´ vən) *adj.*: Very cowardly.

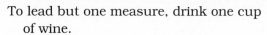

To lead but one measure, drink one cup
    of wine.
There are maidens in Scotland more lovely
    by far,
That would gladly be bride to the young
    Lochinvar."

25 The bride kissed the goblet;[6] the knight
    took it up,
He quaffed off the wine, and he threw
    down the cup,
She looked down to blush, and she looked
    up to sigh,
With a smile on her lips and a tear in her
    eye.
He took her soft hand, ere her mother
    could <u>bar</u>—

30 "Now <u>tread</u> we a measure!" said young
    Lochinvar.

So stately his form, and so lovely her face,
That never a hall such a galliard[7] did grace;
While her mother did <u>fret</u>, and her father
    did fume,
And the bridegroom stood dangling his
    bonnet and plume;[8]

35 And the bridesmaidens whispered, " 'Twere
    better by far
To have matched our fair cousin with
    young Lochinvar."

One touch to her hand, and one word in
    her ear,
When they reached the hall door, and the
    charger stood near;
So light to the croupe the fair lady he
    swung,

40 So light to the saddle before her he sprung!
"She is won! we are gone, over bank, bush,
    and scaur;[9]
They'll have fleet steeds that follow,"
    quoth young Lochinvar.

▲ **Critical Viewing** What lines from "Lochinvar" would make the best caption for this tapestry? Explain. **[Connect]**

Bag with scenes of "Minne" (Love) French, c. 1340, Museum fur Kunst und Gewerb, Hamburg, Germany

Use your senses to see the blush on Ellen's cheek and to hear her soft sigh. Picture her smiling lips and a slow-moving tear on her cheek.

◆ **Build Vocabulary**

dauntless (dônt′ lis) *adj.*: Fearless

consented (kən sent′ id) *v.*: Agreed

laggard (lag′ ərd) *n.*: One who is slow to move, follow, or respond

bar (bär) *v.*: To stop or prevent

tread (tred) *v.*: Walk; dance; step

fret (fret) *v.*: Worry

6. **goblet** (gäb′ lit) *n.*: Drinking cup.
7. **galliard** (gal′ yərd) *n.*: Lively French dance.
8. **plume** (ploom) *n.*: Decoration made of a large feather or feathers.
9. **scaur** (skär) *n.*: Steep, rocky hill.

There was mounting 'mong Græmes of the
    Netherby clan;
Forsters, Fenwicks, and Musgraves,[10] they
    rode and they ran;
45 There was racing, and chasing, on Can-
    nobie Lee,
But the lost bride of Netherby ne'er did
    they see.
So daring in love, and so dauntless in war,
Have ye e'er heard of gallant like young
    Lochinvar?

> Use the details in this stanza to infer that the **speaker** is impressed by Lochinvar's actions.

---

10. **Græmes . . . Forsters, Fenwicks, and Musgraves:** Family names.

Guide for Responding

◆ LITERATURE AND YOUR LIFE

Reader's Response Did you hope that Lochinvar and Ellen would get away? Explain why you did or did not.

Thematic Focus What do the events in the poem tell you about Lochinvar's personal code?

Journal Writing In your journal, explain whether you think Lochinvar is a hero or a scoundrel.

☑ Check Your Comprehension

1. Where had Lochinvar been before arriving at Netherby hall?
2. What event is taking place as he arrives?
3. Describe Lochinvar's previous relationship with Ellen.
4. What do Lochinvar and Ellen do at the end of the poem?

◆ Critical Thinking

INTERPRET

1. Why do you think Ellen went with Lochinvar, even though she'd agreed to marry another? **[Interpret]**
2. How do the female characters and male characters differ in their response to Lochinvar? **[Compare and Contrast]**
3. What does Lochinvar's behavior at the wedding reveal about his values? **[Infer]**

EVALUATE

4. Do you think Lochinvar's actions were justified? Why or why not? **[Evaluate]**

APPLY

5. In literature, knightly behavior is characterized by bravery and a romantic attitude toward women. How does this poem illustrate such characteristics? **[Relate]**

Guide for Responding (continued)

◆ Reading for Success

STRATEGIES FOR READING POETRY

Review the reading strategies and the notes showing how to read poetry. Then, apply these strategies to answer the following:

1. Indicate where the pauses and stops should occur in reading the poem's sixth stanza.
2. List three sensory details that suggest Lochinvar's heroic qualities.
3. Paraphrase the poem's fifth stanza.

◆ Build Vocabulary

USING WORDS WITH MULTIPLE MEANINGS

The word *bar*, which appears in "Lochinvar," has more than one meaning. Several other words with multiple meanings are listed below. With a partner, brainstorm for several definitions for each word. Check your ideas in a dictionary. Then, write a sentence for one definition of the word.

1. brake   3. lead
2. suit   4. bank

SPELLING STRATEGY

The short and long e sounds can be spelled with the letters *ea*, as in *tread* (rhymes with *bed*) or *bead* (rhymes with *feed*). Choose an *ea* word below to complete each sentence. Then, write the complete word on your paper.

s_ _t   l_ _d   h_ _d   r_ _d

1. Yesterday, I ____?____ Walter Scott's poem "Lochinvar."
2. Now I can picture Lochinvar in my ____?____.
3. I can see Ellen in her ____?____ upon Lochinvar's horse.
4. Did Lochinvar ____?____ Ellen toward a good choice?

USING THE WORD BANK

On your paper, complete the paragraph with Word Bank words.

No one dared to ____?____ the way of the ____?____ knight. After all, Ellen had ____?____ to go with him. Her mother did ____?____ some. This worry led her to ____?____ anxiously back and forth across the floor. At least, she knew, he was no ____?____.

◆ Literary Focus

BALLAD

A **ballad**, like Scott's poem about Lochinvar, relates a romantic and adventurous story. Structural features, such as a refrain, a strong rhythm, and rhyming lines, give ballads a musical quality.

1. Describe the pattern of rhyming lines in the poem "Lochinvar."
2. Identify the poem's refrain, and explain how it changes each time it is repeated.
3. Do you think that this poem lends itself to being set to music? Explain.

◆ Build Grammar Skills

DEGREES OF COMPARISON

Most adjectives and adverbs have three **degrees of comparison:** the positive, the comparative, and the superlative. The positive degree is used when no comparison is being made: *brave*. The comparative is used when two things are being compared: Lochniver was *braver* than the bridegroom. The superlative is used when three or more things are being compared: Lochniver was the *bravest* of all the men there.

To create the comparative form of short (one- or two-syllable) adjectives and adverbs, add *-er* to the positive form. To create the superlative form, add *-est*. For most adjectives and adverbs with two or more syllables, use *more* or *most* with the positive form.

Positive	Comparative	Superlative
young	younger	youngest
late	later	latest
lovely	lovelier	loveliest
boldly	more boldly	most boldly

Practice Write the comparative and superlative forms of these adjectives and adverbs.

1. wide 2. stately 3. daring 4. gladly 5. light

Writing Application Use the following line as the starting point for a brief summary of the poem. Include all five modifiers listed in parentheses, and use all three forms of comparison.

The Scottish knight Lochinvar rode his horse . . .
(*brave, challenging, beautiful, quick, early*)

Build Your Portfolio

 ## Idea Bank

Writing

1. **Farewell Letter** As Ellen, write a letter to your family, explaining why you left with Lochinvar.

2. **Editorial** Write a column for the Netherby newspaper that supports or criticizes the actions taken by Lochinvar and Ellen. Explain your views, using specific examples from the poem.

3. **Sequel** In ballad form, continue the story of Lochinvar in a few more stanzas. Tell readers what happens to Lochinvar and Ellen. How do they escape their pursuers? Where do they go?

Speaking and Listening

4. **Skit [Group Activity]** With a group of classmates, perform the events of the poem. Use gestures and facial expressions to capture the emotions of the story. **[Performing Arts Link]**

5. **Missing Persons Description** As a representative of Ellen's family, create descriptions of Lochinvar and Ellen to help people in other towns search for them. Present these descriptions as they would be used for radio or television announcements. **[Media Link]**

Projects

6. **Search Report** Using library and community resources, such as the local police department, find out what methods are used to locate people who have disappeared. Explain how technology is used in such searches, and identify some organizations focused on locating people. Present your findings in a pamphlet format. **[Social Studies Link]**

7. **Illustrated Storyboard** Using the Background for Understanding on page 724 and further research about knights, create historically accurate illustrations to accompany the poem. Mount these in sequential storyboard form, with lines from the poem included as captions. **[Art Link]**

 ## Writing Mini-Lesson

Updated Ballad

The ballad "Lochinvar" tells the story of a gallant hero from long ago. Like most ballads, the story is one of adventure and romance. Think about someone today—either real or imagined—who could be the hero of a modern-day ballad. Then, tell his or her story in ballad format, using "Lochinvar" as a model.

Writing Skills Focus: Refrain

Ballads have a songlike rhythm. To anchor that rhythm in readers' (or listeners') minds, use a **refrain,** or repeated line or lines. Refrains, which often appear at the end of a stanza, bring readers or listeners back to the main character or idea. For example, notice how Walter Scott ends every stanza with his hero's name, Lochinvar, almost always preceded by "young."

Prewriting Choose a real or imaginary hero for your ballad and list some of his or her personal and physical features. Then, plot the central event you will recount in your ballad. What adventure will occur? How will romance arise?

Drafting Begin by introducing your hero and setting the scene. Then, follow your hero step by step through his or her adventure. As you write, experiment with text that might work as a refrain.

◆ **Grammar Application**

To paint a vivid picture of your hero and his or her adventures, use comparative and superlative forms of modifiers.

Revising Revise your ballad by adding descriptive details to enhance the sense of romance and adventure. Also, read your refrain aloud. If it seems flat or unmusical, rearrange words or replace it with more rhythmic text.

PART 1 *Structure of Poetry*

Le Bassin aux Nympheas—harmonie verte (green harmony), Claude Monet

Guide for Reading

Meet the Author

Robert Service (1874–1959)

Robert Service established himself as a poet by introducing readers to the exciting life of Canada's northern wilderness. He could paint a vivid picture of this life because he'd spent many years there himself.

From Banking to Poetry Service came to Canada at age twenty to work for a bank. Sent by the bank to the Yukon Territory, Canada's northernmost territory, Service came face-to-face with the rough world of trappers and gold prospectors. Soon, he was writing poems about these lively characters.

It didn't take Service long to leave banking for a full-time life of writing. He traveled the Yukon and other Arctic areas for eight years, recording his adventures. Later, Service worked as a newspaper correspondent during both world wars. Though he returned to Canada only briefly during World War II, Service wrote his most popular story poems and novels during this stay.

THE STORY BEHIND THE STORY

Written during Service's brief stay in Canada during World War II, "The Cremation of Sam McGee" is probably the author's best-known poem. As you read, you'll see how the poem reflects Service's firsthand experience with the bitter cold of the Yukon Territory.

◆ LITERATURE AND YOUR LIFE

CONNECT YOUR EXPERIENCE

When you're too cold or too hot, it can be hard to think about anything but how to get warmer (or cooler)! Imagine what it would be like to spend time out in the wilderness in one of the coldest places in the world. Read this poem, and you'll find out.

THEMATIC FOCUS: Personal Codes

When people are placed in life-threatening situations, such as being pitted against extreme cold, they may make desperate promises or requests. As you read, consider the importance of fulfilling such a request.

◆ Background for Understanding

GEOGRAPHY

In this poem, two men prospect for gold in Canada's far northwestern Yukon Territory. As you can see from the map on the next page, Yukon's geography is a challenge. Located just east of Alaska, the Yukon stretches to well north of the Arctic Circle. The land is made of high plateaus and even higher mountains. In winter, the temperature reaches -60°F, and much of the ground is permanently frozen. Still, miners have long struggled to get at the territory's mineral wealth.

◆ Build Vocabulary

SHADES OF MEANING

Loathed is defined as "disliked intensely," "hated," and "abhorred." Each of these definitions gets at the meaning, but none can convey exactly the intensity of the word itself. An awareness of words' shades of meaning can help you appreciate the word choices poets make.

WORD BANK

Which two of these words from the poem might you use to describe a horrible sight?

cremated
whimper
ghastly
stern
loathed
grisly

The Cremation of Sam McGee

Alaska

Yukon R.   Porcupine R.

Peel R.

UNITED STATES

CANADA

Yukon
Territory

Mackenzie R.

Great Bear
Lake

FRANKLIN MTNS.

MACKENZIE MOUNTAINS

SELWYN MOUNTAINS

Northwest
Territories

0   100   200   300
Scale in miles

Yukon R.

L. Laberge

ST. ELIAS MTNS.

Gulf of Alaska

YUKON TERRITORY

British Columbia

Alaska   Yukon
Terr.

CANADA

PACIFIC
OCEAN

U.S.A.

N   W   E   S

◆ Literary Focus

NARRATIVE POETRY

Narrative poetry is poetry that tells a story. Like a short story, a narrative poem has a plot, characters, and a setting. However, narrative poems generally make much more use of sound than short stories do. Often, rhythm and repetition are used to create a musical effect and to draw your attention to the most important details in the poem.

◆ Reading Strategy

IDENTIFY THE SPEAKER

In a narrative poem, the **speaker** is the voice that relates the story. Because the speaker's perspective affects how the story is told, identifying the speaker is one of the keys to unlocking a narrative poem's meaning. As you read "The Cremation of Sam McGee," look for details that reveal the speaker's personality, and take note of his perspective of events. You might use a chart like the one below.

Clues	Inferences About the Speaker

The Cremation of Sam McGee

Robert Service

There are strange things done in the midnight sun[1]
    By the men who moil[2] for gold;
The Arctic trails have their secret tales
    That would make your blood run cold;
5 The Northern Lights have seen queer sights,
    But the queerest they ever did see
Was that night on the marge[3] of Lake Lebarge
    I <u>cremated</u> Sam McGee.

Now Sam McGee was from Tennessee,
    where the cotton blooms and blows.
10 Why he left his home in the South to roam
    'round the Pole, God only knows.
He was always cold, but the land of gold
    seemed to hold him like a spell;
Though he'd often say in his homely way
    that "he'd sooner live in hell."

On a Christmas Day we were mushing[4] our way
    over the Dawson trail.
Talk of your cold! through the parka's fold
    it stabbed like a driven nail.
15 If our eyes we'd close, then the lashes froze
    til sometimes we couldn't see;
It wasn't much fun, but the only one
    to <u>whimper</u> was Sam McGee.

And that very night, as we lay packed tight
    in our robes beneath the snow,
And the dogs were fed, and the stars o'erhead
    were dancing heel and toe,

---

1. **the midnight sun:** The sun visible at midnight in the Arctic or Antarctic regions during their summers.
2. **moil** (moil) v.: To toil and slave.
3. **marge** (märj) n.: Poetic word for the shore of the lake.
4. **mushing** (mush´ iŋ) v.: Traveling by foot over snow, usually with a dog sled. "Mush" is a command to sled dogs to start or to go faster.

◆ **Build Vocabulary**

cremated (krē´ māt id) v.: Burned to ashes

whimper (hwim´ pər) v.: Make low, crying sounds; complain

He turned to me, and "Cap," says he,
    "I'll cash in[5] this trip, I guess;
20 And if I do, I'm asking that you
    won't refuse my last request."

Well, he seemed so low that I couldn't say no;
    then he says with a sort of moan:
"It's the cursed cold, and it's got right hold
    till I'm chilled clean through to the bone.
Yet 'tain't being dead—it's my awful dread
    of the icy grave that pains;
So I want you to swear that, foul or fair,
    you'll cremate my last remains."

25 A pal's last need is a thing to heed,
    so I swore I would not fail;
And we started on at the streak of dawn;
    but God! he looked <u>ghastly</u> pale.
He crouched on the sleigh, and he raved all day
    of his home in Tennessee;
And before nightfall a corpse was all
    that was left of Sam McGee.

There wasn't a breath in that land of death,
    and I hurried, horror-driven,
30 With a corpse half hid that I couldn't get rid,
    because of a promise given;
It was lashed to the sleigh, and it seemed to say:
    "You may tax your brawn[6] and brains,
But you promised true, and it's up to you
    to cremate those last remains."

Now a promise made is a debt unpaid,
    and the trail has its own <u>stern</u> code.
In the days to come, though my lips were dumb,
    in my heart how I cursed that load.

---

5. **cash in:** Slang expression meaning "die."
6. **brawn:** (brôn) *n.*: Physical strength.

35   In the long, long night, by the lone firelight,
        while the huskies,[7] round in a ring,
    Howled out their woes to the homeless snows—
        O God! how I <u>loathed</u> the thing.

    And every day that quiet clay
        seemed to heavy and heavier grow;
    And on I went, though the dogs were spent
        and the grub was getting low;
    The trail was bad, and I felt half mad,
        but I swore I would not give in;
40   And I'd often sing to the hateful thing,
        and it hearkened with a grin.

    Till I came to the marge of Lake Lebarge,
        and a derelict[8] there lay;
    It was jammed in the ice, but I saw in a trice
        it was called the "Alice May."
    And I looked at it, and I thought a bit,
        and I looked at my frozen chum;
    Then "Here," said I, with a sudden cry,
        "is my cre-ma-tor-eum."

45   Some planks I tore from the cabin floor,
        and I lit the boiler fire;
    Some coal I found that was lying around,
        and I heaped the fuel higher;
    The flames just soared, and the furnace roared—
        such a blaze you seldom see;
    And I burrowed a hole in the glowing coal,
        and I stuffed in Sam McGee.

---

7. **huskies** (hus´ kēs) *n.*: Strong dogs used for pulling sleds over the snow.
8. **derelict** (der´ ə likt´) *n.*: Abandoned ship.

◆ Build Vocabulary

ghastly (gast´ lē) *adv.*: Ghostlike; frightful
stern (stʉrn) *adj.*: Strict; unyielding
loathed (lōthd) *v.*: Hated

Then I made a hike, for I didn't like
 to hear him sizzle so;
50 And the heavens scowled, and the huskies howled,
 and the wind began to blow.
It was icy cold, but the hot sweat rolled
 down my cheeks, and I don't know why;
And the greasy smoke in an inky cloak
 went streaking down the sky.

I do not know how long in the snow
 I wrestled with <u>grisly</u> fear;
But the stars came out and they danced about
 ere again I ventured near;
55 I was sick with dread, but I bravely said:
 "I'll just take a peep inside.
I guess he's cooked, and it's time I looked"; . . .
 then the door I opened wide.

And there sat Sam, looking cool and calm,
 in the heart of the furnace roar;
And he wore a smile you could see a mile,
 and he said: "Please close that door.
It's fine in here, but I greatly fear
 you'll let in the cold and storm—
60 Since I left Plumtree, down in Tennessee,
 it's the first time I've been warm."

There are strange things done in the midnight sun
 By the men who moil for gold;
The Arctic trails have their secret tales
 That would make your blood run cold;
65 *The Northern Lights have seen queer sights,*
 But the queerest they ever did see
Was that night on the marge of Lake Lebarge
 I cremated Sam McGee.

◆ Build Vocabulary

grisly (griz´ lē) *adj.*: Horrible

History Connection

The Gold Rush Is On! Just like Sam McGee and his buddy, thousands of real people went searching for Yukon gold during the Klondike Gold Rush. Beginning in 1896, when three explorers found gold in a tributary of the Klondike River, the rush took off at breakneck speed. The town of Dawson sprang up to house and serve nearly 25,000 miners. However, the Klondike Gold Rush didn't last long. Few individual prospectors could get at the gold, especially in the Yukon's frozen climate. Big mining groups quickly took over, and the population shrank.

Cross-Curricular Activity
Mining the Past Use encyclopedias, library reference books, and sites on the World Wide Web to find out about mining in the Yukon—in the past and in the present. Focus on how Klondike prospectors searched for gold. Identify the kind of equipment that was used, and find out how the land was manipulated to make mining possible. Then, study the way Yukon mining works today. Create a comparison-and-contrast chart showing the relationship between mining then and now.

Guide for Responding

◆ LITERATURE AND YOUR LIFE

Reader's Response What was your reaction to the ending of the poem? Why?

Thematic Focus Do you admire the narrator for keeping his promise? Why or why not?

One-Liner Ask your classmates what they think their first words would be if they discovered a revived Sam in the furnace.

☑ Check Your Comprehension

1. What problem does Sam McGee have with his surroundings?
2. Why doesn't he go home?
3. What does Sam ask the narrator to promise?
4. How is the narrator supposed to keep his promise?
5. Describe what the narrator finds when he opens the furnace door.

◆ Critical Thinking

INTERPRET
1. What do Sam's fears reveal about his personality? **[Infer]**
2. Why is the speaker so determined to keep his promise? **[Interpret]**
3. What conflicting emotions drive the speaker as he works to fulfill his promise? **[Analyze]**
4. How do you think each character feels at the end of the poem? **[Draw Conclusions]**

APPLY
5. Do you agree with the narrator that "a promise made is a debt unpaid"? Why or why not? **[Make a Judgment]**

EXTEND
6. Speculate about the ways in which modern prospectors might use special equipment and clothing to make their Yukon journeys safer and more comfortable. **[Science Link]**

Guide for Reading

Meet the Authors:

James Stephens (1880–1950)

Growing up in a poor neighborhood in Dublin, James Stephens read everything he could get his hands on. He came to love Ireland's powerful legends and fairy tales. Later, he began to write poetry and novels. "Washed in Silver" captures the magical quality of Irish legends.

Sara Teasdale (1884–1933)

Although her life was short and unhappy, Sara Teasdale left behind a body of poetry charged with emotional intensity. Born in St. Louis, Missouri, Teasdale led a sheltered childhood of carefully chosen schools and travel. She began to write while still young and was quickly successful, winning a Pulitzer Prize in 1918.

Nikki Giovanni (1943–   )

Nikki Giovanni's poems share the major events in her life—working for civil rights, celebrating the birth of her son, and experiencing the joys of African American family life. In "Winter," she writes about a universal subject: the changing of the seasons.

William Butler Yeats (1865–1939)

Irish poet William Butler Yeats is regarded as one of the finest poets the world has ever known. His poems offer evidence of his keen powers of observation, a talent sharpened by his study of painting.

◆ LITERATURE AND YOUR LIFE

CONNECT YOUR EXPERIENCE

Waterfalls cascading downward, mountains rising to the heavens, flowers blooming in a city park—scenes from nature have the power to stir our emotions and imaginations. As these poems reveal, nature can also help people discover themselves.

THEMATIC FOCUS: Nature's Wonders

As you read, take note of what each poet discovers by exploring nature's wonders. How do these discoveries compare with one you've made?

◆ Background for Understanding

SCIENCE

Nikki Giovanni describes the ways people and animals prepare for winter. If you live in a wintry environment, you can turn up the heat and eat hearty foods, but animals don't have this luxury. Some animals—like bears, frogs, and hedgehogs—go into hibernation to survive the cold. Their bodies slip into a state of inactivity. Such life functions as heartbeat, breathing rate, and growth slow until they are almost stopped. In this sleeplike state, hibernating animals burn energy very slowly. That way, the food they have stored as fat can last until the spring.

◆ Build Vocabulary

WORD ROOTS: -rad-

James Stephens describes the *radiance* of the moon's light. The root of this word is *-rad-*, which means "spoke or branch." This root offers an important clue to the meaning of *radiance*: "quality of sending out rays of light."

WORD BANK

Which of these words from the poems would you use to describe a place where a groundhog lives?

radiance
strife
ecstasy
burrow

Washed in Silver ◆ Barter ◆ Winter
◆ Down by the Salley Gardens ◆

◆ Literary Focus
LYRIC POETRY

Nature is a common subject of **lyric poetry,** verse that expresses a poet's personal thoughts and feelings. Once sung to the music of a stringed instrument called a lyre (which gives lyric poetry its name), lyric poetry sweeps you into the poet's world with vivid, musical language. For example, when Sara Teasdale commands "spend all you have for loveliness," you feel the strength of her longing for beauty. These memorable words and phrases echo in your mind like song lyrics (named for the same historical instrument), and the poet's emotions take hold in your mind.

◆ Reading Strategy
USE YOUR SENSES

Most lyric poetry is filled with vivid images, or word pictures. To experience the imagery, **use your senses**—close your eyes and try to see, hear, touch, taste, and smell what the poet describes. For example, you might feel the cool mud around a burrowing frog or hear the lilt of a young woman's voice. Give this process a trial run by studying the photograph above. As you look at it, feel the frigid air around you and see the silvery reflections of sunlight on the icy water. As you read, use a chart like the one below to record the sensations you experience through the poetry.

	Sight	Hearing	Touch	Taste	Smell
Washed in Silver					

Washed In Silver

James Stephens

Gleaming in silver are the hills!
Blazing in silver is the sea!

And a silvery <u>radiance</u> spills
Where the moon drives royally!

5   Clad in silver tissue, I
March magnificently by!

◀ **Critical Viewing** Which details in the poem are represented in the photograph? Which are not? **[Compare and Contrast]**

◆ **Build Vocabulary**

radiance (rā´ dē əns) *n.*: Quality of shining brightly

strife (strīf) *n.*: Fighting; conflict

ecstasy (ek´ stə sē) *n.*: Overpowering joy

Barter

Sara Teasdale

Life has loveliness to sell,
　　All beautiful and splendid things,
Blue waves whitened on a cliff,
　　Soaring fire that sways and sings,
5　And children's faces looking up
Holding wonder like a cup.

Life has loveliness to sell,
　　Music like a curve of gold,
Scent of pine trees in the rain,

10　　Eyes that love you, arms that hold,
And for your spirit's still delight,
Holy thoughts that star the night.

Spend all you have for loveliness,
　　Buy it and never count the cost;
15　For one white singing hour of peace
　　Count many a year of <u>strife</u> well lost,
And for a breath of <u>ecstasy</u>
Give all you have been, or could be.

Guide for Responding

◆ LITERATURE AND YOUR LIFE

Reader's Response Which poem do you like better—"Washed in Silver" or "Barter"? Why?

Thematic Focus Both poems celebrate the beauty in nature. "Washed in Silver" focuses on one aspect of nature's beauty, while "Barter" mentions several. Based on the details in the poems and the speaker's attitude, explain what you think nature means to each of the poets.

☑ Check Your Comprehension

1. What natural scene does Stephens describe in "Washed in Silver"?
2. What does the speaker in "Barter" say life has to offer people?
3. Name three examples of natural beauty that are mentioned in "Barter."

◆ Critical Thinking

INTERPRET

1. In "Washed in Silver," what does the speaker mean by saying he is "Clad in silver tissue"? **[Interpret]**
2. Explain what the poem's title, "Washed in Silver," means. **[Draw Conclusions]**
3. There is no money in a barter system. Instead, goods and services are used as currency. What are the units of exchange in "Barter"? **[Interpret]**
4. What advice does the speaker give to readers in "Barter?" **[Infer]**

EVALUATE

5. Do you think that the speaker gives good advice in "Barter"? Explain. **[Assess]**

COMPARE LITERARY WORKS

6. Do you think the speaker in "Washed in Silver" would agree with the advice in "Barter"? Explain. **[Literature Link]**

Winter

Nikki Giovanni

Frogs <u>burrow</u> the mud
snails bury themselves
and I air my quilts
preparing for the cold

5   Dogs grow more hair
mothers make oatmeal
and little boys and girls
take Father John's Medicine[1]

Bears store fat
10   chipmunks gather nuts
and I collect books
For the coming winter

—————————————————
1. **Father John's Medicine:** An old-fashioned cough syrup.

◆ **Build Vocabulary**

burrow (bʉr´ ō) *v.*: To dig a hole or tunnel, especially for shelter

▶ Critical Viewing Why is winter, as pictured here, a time that demands the preparations the poem describes? [Relate]

Down by the Salley[1] Gardens

William Butler Yeats

Les Adieux (The Good-bye), James L. Tissot, City of Bristol Museum and Art Gallery, England

Down by the salley gardens my love and I did meet;
She passed the salley gardens with little snow-white feet.
She bid me take love easy, as the leaves grow on the tree;
But I, being young and foolish, with her would not agree.

5   In a field by the river my love and I did stand,
And on my leaning shoulder she laid her snow-white hand.
She bid me take life easy, as the grass grows on the weirs;[2]
But I was young and foolish, and now am full of tears.

---

1. **salley** (sal´ ē) *n.*: Type of willow tree.
2. **weirs** (wirz) *n.*: Low dams in a river.

▶ **Critical Viewing** How does the mood of the people in the painting reflect the events of the poem? **[Connect]**

Guide for Responding

◆ LITERATURE AND YOUR LIFE

Reader's Response What do you think of the speaker of "Down by the Salley Gardens"? Why?

Thematic Focus What pictures of nature's processes do "Winter" and "Down by the Salley Gardens" create?

Journal Writing In a brief journal entry, describe your impressions of winter.

☑ Check Your Comprehension

1. In "Winter," why are all the characters making preparations?
2. What two things does the speaker do to prepare for this coming season?
3. In Yeats's poem, where do the speaker and his love go?
4. What does the speaker's love ask him to do?
5. How does the speaker respond to her request?
6. What is the result of the speaker's actions?

◆ Critical Thinking

INTERPRET
1. In "Winter," how do the speaker's actions suggest the coming of winter? **[Connect]**
2. In what ways does this poem suggest that people and animals are alike? **[Compare and Contrast]**
3. In "Down by the Salley Gardens," how does the speaker's love use nature to support her request? **[Connect]**
4. Explain how the speaker and his love differ. **[Compare and Contrast]**
5. What do you think has happened to the love between the two people in "Down by the Salley Gardens"? **[Speculate]**

EVALUATE
6. Is it wiser to "take life easy"? Explain. **[Criticize]**

APPLY
7. How might an acceptance of natural cycles help people improve their lives? **[Relate]**

Guide for Responding (continued)

◆ Literary Focus

LYRIC POETRY

Lyric poetry expresses a poet's thoughts and emotions about a topic in lively and musical language.

1. What feelings does each poet communicate?
2. Find an example of repetition in each poem. Explain its effect in the poem.
3. Choose one of the poems, and explain why you think it would be effective if set to music.

◆ Reading Strategy

USE YOUR SENSES

Each of these poets uses vivid images, or word pictures, to capture the wonders of nature and to connect nature to the poet's own experiences. By **using your senses** to see, hear, smell, touch, and taste what the poets are describing, you can fully experience the poems.

1. Identify two details from each poem that appeal to your senses. Name the sense you used for each detail.
2. For each poem, tell which sense you used most in reading.

◆ Build Vocabulary

USING THE WORD ROOT -rad-

The root -rad-, meaning "spoke or branch," usually indicates that the word in which it is found relates to something spreading out from a center. With this meaning in mind, define the words below.

1. radius   2. radiology   3. radiator

SPELLING STRATEGY

When the see sound appears at the end of a word, it may be spelled sy, as in ecstasy. On your paper, correctly spell each of the following words.

1. fanta_ _   2. courte_ _   3. jealou_ _   4. curt_ _

USING THE WORD BANK

Identify the best synonym for each word.

1. radiance: (a) darkness, (b) silliness, (c) glow
2. ecstasy: (a) bliss, (b) misery, (c) boredom
3. strife: (a) agreement, (b) conflict, (c) goal
4. burrow: (a) tunnel, (b) emerge, (c) hurdle

◆ Build Grammar Skills

CORRECT USE OF good AND well

Good is an adjective (a word that describes a noun or pronoun). **Well** can be an adjective, but it is usually an adverb (a word that describes a verb, an adjective, or another adverb). In the following line, the adverb well modifies the adjective lost:

> Count many a year of strife well lost.

A common mistake is to use good rather than well after an action verb. Look at this example:

Incorrect: Teasdale wrote good even as a girl.
Correct: Teasdale wrote well even as a girl.

Practice On your paper, complete each sentence correctly with either good or well.

1. The scent of pine trees smelled ___?___.
2. The moon lit the hills ___?___ last night.
3. Winter is described ___?___ in the poem.
4. I think a change of season is ___?___ for us all.
5. If you prepare ___?___, you can survive the season.

Writing Application Write four sentences: two using good correctly and two using well correctly.

Beyond Literature

History Connection

The Barter System Teasdale's poem "Barter" refers to an economy in which people use goods and services as currency. For example, you might trade a cow for fruit, cloth, or other goods. You might trade several cows to pay for a carpenter's work. Throughout history, and even today, people in some cultures use barter to meet their needs.

Cross-Curricular Activity
A Barter Community With a group, plan a barter system for a community. What skills or products could the people in the group offer? Which skills would be problematic? Summarize the pros and cons of bartering.

Build Your Portfolio

 ## Idea Bank

Writing

1. **Recommendation** If you were to recommend one of these poems, which one would it be? Choose one of the poems. Then, write a note to a friend recommending that he or she read it. Be sure to explain why you are recommending it.

2. **Nature Poem** Write a nature poem of your own. Use vivid imagery to capture one or more scenes from nature that stand out in your memory. You might also include personal reflections about the scene or scenes you describe.

3. **Literary Response** Choose one of the poems that you think presents a meaningful message. In an essay, explain how the poem conveys this message, and tell why the message is important to you. Cite details from the poem for support.

Speaking and Listening

4. **Lyrics Presentation** Find some song lyrics you find especially meaningful. Read them aloud to your classmates. Explain what the lyrics convey to you, and identify language that is vivid and memorable. **[Music Link]**

5. **Dramatic Reading** Read one of these poems aloud to the class. Use the punctuation to guide where you pause, and use your voice to add emphasis to the most important lines and images. **[Performing Arts Link]**

Projects

6. **Seasonal Preparations [Group Activity]** With a group, discuss the economic preparations individuals and businesses in your community make for each season. Each of you can generate a list for one season. Review each other's ideas before creating a single list. **[Social Studies Link]**

7. **Nature Walk** Nature can be viewed and enjoyed even in cities. Plan a nature walk in your area. Create a map showing your route, and identify sites of particular interest. **[Science Link]**

 ## Writing Mini-Lesson

Introduction to a Poetry Collection

While some people enjoy reading the collected works of a specific writer, others prefer to read poems organized by theme. For example, a book of sports poems or an anthology of poems about facing challenges would appeal to many readers. Write an introduction to a collection that includes the four poems presented here. In your introduction, explain how each poem relates to a theme.

Writing Skills Focus: Elaborate on an Idea

To show readers the connection among the poems in your collection, **elaborate on the ideas** you present. Use these tips to develop your points:

- Gather details that support the idea you'll present.
- Provide vivid examples that make your explanation clear.
- Be sure every general statement is supported by a fact.

Prewriting As you review the poems in this group, consider the ideas that tie them together. Decide on the theme of your collection. Then, jot down details that support this theme.

Drafting Begin with a general statement about the poems and the theme you've chosen. Focus each body paragraph on an individual poem, using your notes to develop the theme of your collection.

> ◆ **Grammar Application**
> When you describe the poems, make sure to use *good* and *well* correctly.

Revising Remember, your introduction should encourage people to read the collection. As you revise, look for places where you can make each poem's connection to the theme more clear.

Guide for Reading

Meet the Authors:

William Jay Smith (1918–   )

William Smith was born in Winnfield, Louisiana. He has led a busy life—teaching college students, writing poetry and essays, translating Russian and French poetry, and even serving in the Vermont State Legislature for three years. His most successful writing has been his poetry for young people. When you read "Seal," you will see why. Lively and amusing, it shows that poetry can be pure and simple fun.

Robert Frost (1875–1963)

Born in San Francisco, Robert Frost spent most of his life in New England. At different times, he worked as a farmer and as a part-time teacher. He was not well known as a writer until his first book of poetry, *A Boy's Will* (1913), appeared in Great Britain. Then, almost overnight, he became famous for his poems about New England people and landscapes. Frost had a long and distinguished career as a poet, winning the Pulitzer Prize four times—more than any other poet. [For more information on Robert Frost, see page 258.]

Matsuo Bashō (1644–1694)

Matsuo Bashō was born near Kyoto, Japan. In his three-line poems, he presents a scene in which a momentary feature stands out against an unchanging background. He evokes a whole landscape or an entire season by describing just a few details.

◆ LITERATURE AND YOUR LIFE

CONNECT YOUR EXPERIENCE

Although we don't always notice, amazing and beautiful events in nature happen all around us—common events, like the appearance of a colorful butterfly or a beautiful sunset, or rare occurrences, like a sun shower or the sighting of a bald eagle. Each of these poems celebrates some aspect of nature. Reading them may help you appreciate natural occurrences you encounter in your life.

THEMATIC FOCUS: Nature's Wonders

How do these poets' feelings about and observations of nature compare with your own?

◆ Background for Understanding

LITERATURE

The Japanese consider poetry to be the highest form of literature. As you'll discover when you read the three haiku by Matsuo Bashō—perhaps the most famous of all Japanese poets—Japanese verse is characterized by its brevity and simplicity. In addition, most traditional Japanese poetry presents vivid images of nature that spark associations in the reader's mind. As you read Bashō's haiku, note the thoughts and emotions that each image sparks in your mind.

◆ Build Vocabulary

SYNONYMS

One way to study a word is to memorize its definition. To become comfortable with a new word, you can also learn its synonyms, the words that mean the same thing. In "The Pasture," a calf *totters* when its mother licks it. Some synonyms of *totter* are *quake, shake,* and *tremble.*

WORD BANK

Which of these words do you think might mean "to turn aside from a straight line"?

| swerve |
| utter |
| pasture |
| totters |

Seal ◆ The Pasture
◆ Three Haiku ◆

◆ Literary Focus
FORM IN POETRY

Poetry can take many different forms. Most traditional English poems are divided into stanzas. A **stanza** is a group of lines that might be thought of as corresponding to a paragraph in prose. A **concrete poem** is one with a shape that suggests its subject. The poet arranges the letters and lines to create an image on the page. **Haiku** is a traditional form of Japanese poetry. Haiku always have three lines and seventeen syllables. There are five syllables in the first and third lines, and seven syllables in the second line.

◆ Reading Strategy
READ ACCORDING TO PUNCTUATION

Poets use punctuation the same way prose writers do: to show where thoughts begin and end and how they relate. The structure of poetry, however, can take many forms. Very often the structure of a poem doesn't correspond to the punctuation. You can get around this by **reading according to the punctuation.** Let the punctuation, rather than the line structure, be your guide. If a line ends without a punctuation mark, keep reading until you get to one. Ignore the capital letter at the beginning of a line if it is not also the beginning of a sentence.

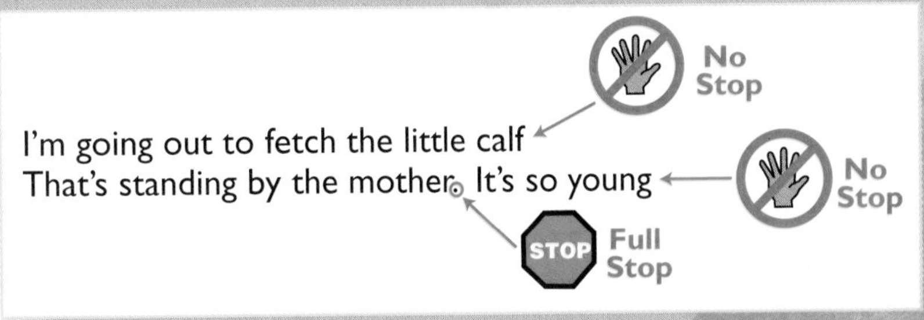

No Stop

I'm going out to fetch the little calf
That's standing by the mother. It's so young

No Stop

STOP Full Stop

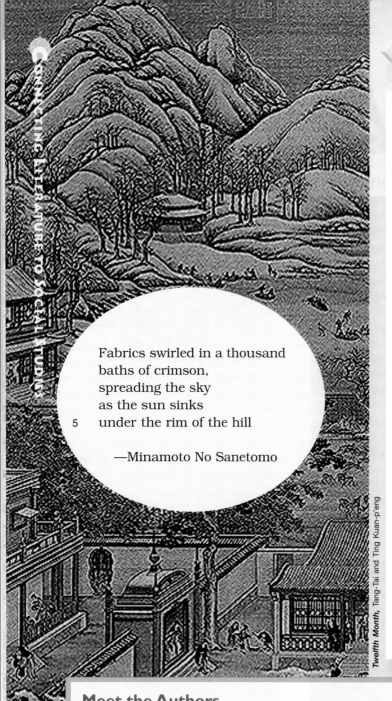

Fabrics swirled in a thousand
baths of crimson,
spreading the sky
as the sun sinks
5 under the rim of the hill

—Minamoto No Sanetomo

Twelfth Month, Tang-Tai and Ting Kuan-p'eng

Guide for Responding

◆ LITERATURE AND YOUR LIFE

Reader's Response Which tanka creates the stronger picture in your mind? Explain.

Thematic Focus How does each poem capture the wonder of nature?

☑ Check Your Comprehension

1. At what time of day does each tanka take place?
2. What natural feature does Myoe describe?
3. Explain the swirling "fabrics" in Minamoto No Sanetomo's tanka.
4. What natural event does Minamoto No Sanetomo describe?

◆ Critical Thinking

INTERPRET

1. How does each poet's language show movement and change? Give two examples. **[Analyze]**
2. What mood does each poem suggest? Explain. **[Draw Conclusions]**

COMPARE LITERARY WORKS

3. How is the point of view different in the two tanka? **[Compare and Contrast]**

EXTEND

4. Why might tanka be especially appreciated by people interested in protecting the environment? **[Science Link; Career Link]**

Meet the Authors

Myoe (1173–1232) One of the main ways that China changed Japanese culture was through the teachings of Buddhist monks. These priests came to Japan and built great monasteries in which to pray and study. Many were skilled artists, architects, and poets. One such monk was the poet Myoe. He was much admired as a man of great faith. In this poem, he seems to connect to nature in a moment of thoughtful solitude.

Minamoto No Sanetomo (1192–1219) Minamoto No Sanetomo was an important figure in his town. He studied with well-known court poet Fujiwara No Teika, and his poems often appeared in collections. As a shogun, he was a military general and also ruler of a region. Though his military role didn't stop him from writing poetry, it resulted in his death in a famous political murder.

CONNECTING LITERATURE TO SOCIAL STUDIES

Through all Japan's historical changes, nature has remained a central focus of the nation's poetry—and of daily life. Respect for nature, which is important in a place where only a tiny bit of land can be farmed, has helped Japan become and remain a strong nation. You can see that respectful attitude even in these poems from long ago.

1. How do you think Japan's isolation contributed to the development of the tanka form?

2. In what ways do you think these poems show a respect for nature?

3. How does Japanese history help you explain that a lifelong soldier—who solves problems by fighting—and a priest—who solves problems by praying—would share a view of nature?

 Idea Bank

Writing

1. **Directions** Imagine that you are meeting a friend at either of the places described in these tanka. Write a set of directions to help your friend find the meeting place. Remember that he or she must travel to Japan first.

2. **Tanka** Write a tanka about a natural scene. You should have five syllables in the first and third lines and seven syllables in the second, fourth, and fifth lines. The lines should not rhyme.

3. **Artistic Goals** Many countries have poet laureates who represent the nation and help set goals for all artists to work toward. As Japan's poet laureate, write a set of guidelines describing goals for Japanese tanka poets.

Speaking and Listening

4. **Group Reading [Group Activity]** In many periods of Japanese history, poetry was performed at the court. With a few classmates, review a collection of Japanese poetry to explore the poetry of different time periods. Then, vote on a small sampling to perform for the class.

Projects

5. **Illustrations** If a picture speaks a thousand words, surely you can capture 31 syllables with one picture. Using these or other tanka, create illustrations showing the poet's image. Set your picture in thirteenth-century Japan. **[Art Link]**

6. **A Poet's Life** Both soldiers and priests were poets in medieval Japan. Find out about the life of a Japanese shogun or a Buddhist monk. How did they dress? Where did they live? What were their values and goals in life? Present your findings in an oral report. **[Social Studies Link]**

Further Reading, Listening, and Viewing

- *The Essential Haiku: Versions of Bashō, Buson, and Issa* (1995), edited by Robert Hass, contains a wealth of Japanese poetry.
- Lensey Namioka's *Den of the White Fox* (1997) is an adventure story set in feudal Japan.
- In Myra Cohn Livingston's *Cricket Never Does: A Collection of Haiku and Tanka* (1997), the poet uses Japanese forms to address modern subjects.

Guide for Reading

Meet the Authors:

Raymond Richard Patterson (1929–   )

Raymond Patterson's poetry appears in numerous anthologies, as well as in individual collections such as *Elemental Blues*. Patterson's passion for sharing his knowledge of African American history is shown in his newspaper column, "From Our Past," and poems like "Martin Luther King."

Edgar Allan Poe (1809–1849)

Edgar Allan Poe's life is a story of great literary achievement, some literary fame, and much personal loss. His parents were impoverished traveling actors. When Poe was three, his mother died, and Poe went to live with the Allans of Richmond, Virginia.

Although his writing won recognition, it did not bring financial success. Two years after the death of his beloved wife, Virginia, Poe died poor and alone.

THE STORY BEHIND THE POEM

Poe's biographer Kenneth Silverman believes that the heroine of "Annabel Lee" "represents all of the women he loved and lost." Poe finished the poem about a year after his wife's death and published it in a New York newspaper. He always had a special feeling for the poem. His mother-in-law said, "Oh! How he cried!" as he read it aloud to her.

Mary O'Neill (1908–1990)

Mary O'Neill published many stories and poems for young people. Her sense of the magic of words is clear in "Feelings About Words."

◆ LITERATURE AND YOUR LIFE

CONNECT YOUR EXPERIENCE

Your sense of who you are depends on memory. You'd be incomplete if you couldn't remember those who have loved you or recall those who have contributed to this country.

One role of poetry is to keep memory alive. For example, Poe's fictional "Annabel Lee" is a tribute to a woman or women he had loved. In "Martin Luther King," Patterson honors a national hero.

THEMATIC FOCUS: People in Their Variety

As you read, notice the different types of people you meet in these poems.

◆ Background for Understanding

HISTORY

Martin Luther King, Jr. (1929–1968), honored in Raymond Richard Patterson's poem, was a great civil rights leader. Using nonviolent methods, he helped end legal discrimination against African Americans in the South and elsewhere in the United States. In 1968, he was shot and killed by an assassin in Memphis, Tennessee.

◆ Build Vocabulary

WORD ROOT: -found-

When you use words with the root *-found-*, meaning "bottom," you're probably talking about something deep. Patterson, for example, calls Martin Luther King Jr.'s passion "profound," meaning "deeply felt": *pro-* means "forward to" and *-found* means "the bottom."

WORD BANK

Which of these words from the poems looks as if it's closely related to the verb *prune,* meaning "to trim"?

beset
profound
coveted
squat
saunter
preen
pomp

Martin Luther King ◆ Annabel Lee
◆ Feelings About Words ◆

◆ Literary Focus

RHYTHM AND RHYME

Like a song, a poem has patterns of beats and sounds that make it memorable. **Rhythm** is a poem's pattern of stressed (´) and unstressed (˘) syllables. Notice the drumbeat rhythm here:

> Hĕ cáme ŭpón ăn áge
> Bĕsét bў gríef, bў ráge—

Rhyme is the repetition of a sound at the ends of nearby words—*age/rage*, for example. The pattern of rhyming words at the ends of lines creates the poem's rhyme scheme.

◆ Reading Strategy

PARAPHRASE

To help you understand the meaning of a poem, you may want to **paraphrase,** or restate, some or all of it. A paraphrase can't replace the music of a poem. However, it can give you a better grip on what a poem is about. The chart below shows how a reader might paraphrase the first stanza, or group of lines, in "Martin Luther King."

Stanza	Paraphrase
1. He came upon an age Beset by grief, by rage—	King was born in a troubled time.
2.	
3.	
4.	

Martin Luther King

Raymond Richard Patterson

He came upon an age
Beset by grief, by rage—

His love so deep, so wide,
He could not turn aside.

5   His passion, so profound,
He would not turn around.

He taught this suffering Earth
The measure of Man's worth.

He showed what Man can be
10 Before death sets him free.

◆ **Build Vocabulary**
beset (bē set´) *adj.*: Covered; set thickly with
profound (prō found´) *adj.*: Deeply or intensely felt

▶ **Critical Viewing** The photograph on page 773 shows Martin Luther King, Jr., the subject of Patterson's poem. How might the poet describe the leader's expression? **[Connect]**

Guide for Responding

◆ LITERATURE AND YOUR LIFE

Reader's Response Do you think this poem captures the spirit of Martin Luther King, Jr.? Why or why not?

Thematic Focus What clues to Martin Luther King Jr.'s personality can you find in this poem?

Journal Writing What political heroes inspire you? In a journal entry, explain what this leader has accomplished or what he or she represents to you. **[Social Studies Link]**

☑ Check Your Comprehension

1. Describe the "age" into which King was born.
2. What are two personal qualities that King brought to this "age"?
3. What did King teach "this suffering Earth"?

◆ Critical Thinking

INTERPRET
1. What does the poet mean by King's "passion, so profound"? **[Interpret]**
2. In your own words, explain the phrases in lines 8–9 that describe King's achievement. **[Draw Conclusions]**

EVALUATE
3. Would this poem be suitable for an epitaph, an inscription on King's grave? Explain. **[Make a Judgment]**

EXTEND
4. If King were alive today, what are the causes for which he might be fighting? **[Hypothesize]**
5. Where might you go to find out more about Martin Luther King Jr.'s life? **[Social Studies Link]**

Martin Luther King Jr.'s life inspired millions. His death caused shock and sadness and moved poets, songwriters, and the public alike. In this song, Richard Holler honors King and three other important Americans who were assassinated.

Abraham, Martin and John

Richard Holler

Has anybody here seen my old friend
   Abraham,[1]
Can you tell me where he's gone?
He freed a lotta people,
but it seems the good die young,
5 But I just looked around and he's
   gone.

Has anybody here seen my old friend
   John,[2]
Can you tell me where he's gone?
He freed a lotta people,
but it seems the good die young,
10 But I just looked around and he's
   gone.

Has anybody here seen my old friend
   Martin,[3]
Can you tell me where he's gone?
He freed a lotta people,
but it seems the good die young,
15 But I just looked around and he's
   gone.

Didn't you love the things they stood
   for?
Didn't they try to find some good for
   you and me?
And we'll be free.
Someday soon,
20 It's gonna be one day.

Has anybody here seen my old friend
   Bobby?[4]
Can you tell me where he's gone?
I thought I saw him walkin' up over
   the hill,
with Abraham, Martin and John.

---

4. **Bobby:** Robert Kennedy (1925–68), a brother of John F. Kennedy, was a political leader and presidential candidate involved in the civil rights movement.

---

1. **Abraham:** Abraham Lincoln (1809–65), the 16th President of the United States, freed the slaves during the Civil War.
2. **John:** John F. Kennedy (1917–63) was the 35th President of the United States.
3. **Martin:** Martin Luther King, Jr. (1929–68), was a famous civil rights leader in the 1960's.

1. What two things do Abraham, Martin, John, and Bobby have in common?
2. What conclusion does the songwriter draw based on their deaths?

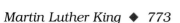

Annabel Lee

Edgar Allan Poe

It was many and many a year ago,
    In a kingdom by the sea.
That a maiden there lived whom you may know
    By the name of Annabel Lee;—
And this maiden she lived with no other thought
    Than to love and be loved by me.

She was a child and *I* was a child,
    In this kingdom by the sea.
5 But we loved with a love that was more than love—
    I and my Annabel Lee—
With a love that the wingèd seraphs[1] of Heaven
    <u>Coveted</u> her and me.

And this was the reason that, long ago,
    In this kingdom by the sea,
A wind blew out of a cloud by night
    Chilling my Annabel Lee;
So that her highborn kinsmen[2] came
    And bore her away from me,
10 To shut her up in a sepulcher[3]
    In this kingdom by the sea.

The angels, not half so happy in Heaven,
    Went envying her and me:—
Yes! that was the reason (as all men know,
    In this kingdom by the sea)
That the wind came out of a cloud, chilling
    And killing my Annabel Lee.

But our love it was stronger by far than the love
    Of those who were older than we—
    Of many far wiser than we—
15 And neither the angels in Heaven above
    Nor the demons down under the sea,
Can ever dissever[4] my soul from the soul
    Of the beautiful Annabel Lee:—

---

1. seraphs (ser´ əfs) *n.*: Angels.
2. highborn kinsmen: Relatives of noble birth.
3. sepulcher (sep´ əl kər) *n.*: Vault for burial; grave; tomb.
4. dissever (di sev´ ər) *v.*: Separate.

For the moon never beams without bringing
    me dreams
Of the beautiful Annabel Lee;
And the stars never rise but I see the bright eyes
    Of the beautiful Annabel Lee;
20 And so, all the nighttide,[5] I lie down by the side
Of my darling, my darling, my life and my bride,
    In her sepulcher there by the sea—
    In her tomb by the side of the sea.

---

5. **nighttide** (nīt′ tīd′) *n.*: An old-fashioned way of saying nighttime.

◆ Build Vocabulary

coveted (kuv′ it id) *v.*: Wanted greatly

Guide for Responding

◆ LITERATURE AND YOUR LIFE

Reader's Response Do you think this poem would make a good song? Why or why not?

Thematic Focus Do people today still experience the type of love that the speaker describes in this poem? Explain.

Retelling Review what happens in the poem, and retell the events to classmates as if you were presenting a fairy tale. **[Performing Arts Link]**

☑ Check Your Comprehension

1. At what stage in life did the speaker in the poem fall in love?
2. What caused the death of Annabel Lee?
3. What did Annabel Lee's kinsmen do when she died?
4. Why will nothing be able to separate the speaker's soul from the soul of Annabel Lee?
5. What does the speaker do "all the nighttide"?

◆ Critical Thinking

INTERPRET

1. In your own words, describe the love between the speaker and Annabel Lee. **[Interpret]**
2. In what way does Poe make the events of the story seem distant, like those in a fairy tale? **[Analyze]**
3. How does the last stanza make the sense of sadness in the poem seem immediate and never-ending? **[Support]**

EVALUATE

4. Is the story in this poem realistic? Why or why not? **[Criticize]**

APPLY

5. The poet Countee Cullen once wrote, "Never love with all your heart,/It only ends in aching." Would the speaker in "Annabel Lee" agree? Why or why not? **[Apply]**

COMPARE LITERARY WORKS

6. "Martin Luther King" and "Annabel Lee" are similar in honoring someone who has died. In what ways do they differ? **[Compare and Contrast]**

Dominant Curve, Vasily Kandinsky, Solomon R. Guggenheim Museum, New York, New York

FEELINGS ABOUT WORDS
Mary O'Neill

Some words clink
As ice in drink.
Some move with grace
A dance, a lace.
5   Some sound thin:
Wail, scream and pin.
Some words are squat:
A mug, a pot,
And some are plump,
10   Fat, round and dump.
Some words are light:
Drift, lift and bright.
A few are small:
A, is and all.

▲ **Critical Viewing** The poet says that every word has a personality. What words would you choose to describe this painting? **[Analyze]**

15 And some are thick,
    Glue, paste and brick.
    Some words are sad:
    "I never had . . ."
    And others gay:
20 Joy, spin and play.
    Some words are sick:
    Stab, scratch and nick.
    Some words are hot:
    Fire, flame and shot.
25 Some words are sharp,
    Sword, point and carp.
    And some alert:
    Glint, glance and flirt.
    Some words are lazy:
30 Saunter, hazy.
    And some words preen:
    Pride, pomp and queen.
    Some words are quick,
    A jerk, a flick.
35 Some words are slow:
    Lag, stop and grow,
    While others poke
    As ox with yoke.
    Some words can fly—
40 There's wind, there's high:
    And some words cry:
    "Goodbye . . .
    Goodbye . . ."

◆ Build Vocabulary

squat (skwät) *adj.*: Short and heavy

saunter (sôn´ tər) *v.*: Walk about idly; stroll

preen (prēn) *v.*: Dress up; show pride in one's appearance

pomp (pämp) *n.*: Impressive show or display

Guide for Responding

◆ LITERATURE AND YOUR LIFE

Reader's Response Name three of your favorite words, and explain the feelings you have about them.

Thematic Focus O'Neill describes the "personalities" of different words. Do you agree that words can be categorized this way? Explain.

Word Search [Group Activity] With a group, brainstorm for two more examples for each of these kinds of words: "squat," "plump," "light," and "sharp."

☑ Check Your Comprehension

1. List five of the types or categories of words that O'Neill describes.
2. Give one example she uses for each of the five types you have chosen.

◆ Critical Thinking

INTERPRET

1. Why is *flick* a good example of a word that is quick? **[Support]**
2. Name two ways in which *goodbye* is a word that cries. **[Analyze]**
3. Why does O'Neill call the poem "Feelings About Words"? **[Draw Conclusions]**

EVALUATE

4. Do you disagree with any of O'Neill's choices to illustrate certain types of words? Explain. **[Criticize]**

APPLY

5. Can two words with the same dictionary definition call up different feelings? Explain. **[Synthesize]**
6. Look at the painting by Wassily Kandinski on page 776. In what way is a poet's love of words similar to an artist's love of color and form? **[Art Link]**

Guide for Responding (continued)

◆ Reading Strategy

PARAPHRASE

By **paraphrasing** a poem, you can clarify its meaning.

1. Paraphrase each stanza of "Martin Luther King."
2. Paraphrase lines 34–41 of "Annabel Lee."
3. Paraphrase lines 1–6 of "Feelings About Words."
4. Compare one of your paraphrases to the original poem, and find a rhyme or a rhythm that you had to leave out.

◆ Build Vocabulary

USING THE WORD ROOT -found-

Use your knowledge of the word root -found- ("bottom") to match each numbered word with its definition:

1. profound
2. foundation
3. founder

  a. one who begins something from the bottom up
  b. deeply or intensely felt
  c. a structure's support at the bottom

SPELLING STRATEGY

When you spell the *kw* sound in a word, you use the letters *qu,* not a combination with the letter *w:*

    squat   quality   squirm

On your paper, identify and correct the misspelled words.

1. quantity **2.** akwire **3.** quench **4.** kwarrel

USING THE WORD BANK

On your paper, choose the lettered word or phrase that is closest in meaning to the numbered word.

1. beset: (a) placed in, (b) surrounded by, (c) set again
2. profound: (a) strongly felt, (b) hardly felt, (c) quietly felt
3. coveted: (a) chilled, (b) refused, (c) envied
4. squat: (a) high and mighty, (b) short and heavy, (c) short and sweet
5. saunter: (a) stroll, (b) loaf, (c) hurry
6. preen: (a) take off, (b) dress up, (c) cut with
7. pomp: (a) big display, (b) small ritual, (c) full feast

◆ Literary Focus

RHYTHM AND RHYME

Poems create patterns with **rhythm,** an arrangement of stressed and unstressed syllables, and **rhyme,** the repetition of a sound at the ends of words:

- Mark rhythms with (˘) for an unstressed syllable and (´) for a stressed syllable. Example: The word *aside* would be marked ăsíde.
- Rhymes that fall at the ends of lines create a rhyme scheme, which you can analyze by using letters for each rhyme, starting with *a.* For example, the rhyme scheme for "Martin Luther King" is *aa bb cc dd ee.*

1. Mark the rhythm of the first stanza of "Annabel Lee." You'll need the pattern ˘ ˘ ´ as well as ˘ ´.
2. Indicate the rhyme scheme of "Feelings About Words."

◆ Build Grammar Skills

PRONOUNS IN COMPARISONS

When **pronouns** appear in **comparisons** using *than* or *as,* sometimes words are suggested rather than stated. If you mentally supply the missing words, you can easily select the correct pronoun form to use. When you supply the missing word *were* in the following example, it is clear why Poe used the subject pronoun *we.*

> But our love it was stronger by far than the love/Of those who were older than we [*were*]

Practice On your paper, fill in the unstated word(s), and then choose the correct pronoun.

1. Angels weren't as happy as (them, they) ____?____.
2. The highborn kinsmen weren't as noble as (her, she) ____?____.
3. No one was sadder than (he, him) ____?____.
4. King achieved more than (her, she) ____?____.
5. Which leaders were more active than (they, them) ____?____?

Writing Application Write three comparisons using *than* or *as,* pronouns, and a word that's only suggested.

Build Your Portfolio

 ## Idea Bank

Writing

1. **Couplet** Write two rhyming lines that can be included in "Feelings About Words." Follow this pattern: Some words are _____: / _____, _____, and _____.

2. **Liner Notes** A singing group has just recorded "Annabel Lee." Write a paraphrase of the poem for the liner notes that will accompany the CD. Your paraphrase will help listeners understand the story told in the poem. **[Career Link]**

3. **Critical Review** Organizers of a King Day celebration are considering whether to include a reading of Patterson's poem. Review the poem to help them. Decide whether its rhythm, rhymes, mood, and message make it suitable.

Speaking and Listening

4. **Oral Interpretation** Read one of these poems aloud for the class, stopping at the ends of lines only where there is punctuation. Convey the poet's mood, whether sad or funny. **[Performing Arts Link]**

5. **Poetry Drumbeat** Drum out the beat of one of these poems as you read it aloud. Give a weak beat to unstressed syllables and a strong one to stressed syllables. Have classmates follow the text silently as they listen. **[Music Link]**

Projects

6. **Missing Person Investigation [Group Activity]** If possible, find the real identity of Poe's Annabel Lee. Check Web sites on Poe and biographies like Kenneth Silverman's *Mournful and Never-Ending Remembrance*. Present the findings of your investigation to the class.

7. **Multimedia Presentation** Give a presentation on the life of Martin Luther King, Jr. In addition to an oral report, include news clips, recordings of speeches, photographs, and readings of poems like Patterson's. **[Social Studies Link]**

 ## Writing Mini-Lesson

Remembrance of a Person

Two of these poems, "Annabel Lee" and "Martin Luther King," are types of remembrance. Write a prose remembrance of someone who has been important in your life. Describe this person, your relationship with him or her, and some of the experiences you had together. Above all, show why this person has meant a great deal to you.

Writing Skills Focus: Specific Examples

Use **specific examples,** precise descriptions and detailed stories, to bring your subject to life and show his or her importance to you. For example, don't just say that someone was kind to you. Back up your statement with a story illustrating this person's kindness.

Prewriting Use an outline form like this one to gather information for your remembrance:

I. Description of Person	II. Our Relationship
A. Her clothes	A. Her kindness
1. Example #1	1. Example #1
2. Example #2	2. Example #2
B. Her ____?____	B. Her ____?____

Drafting Refer to your outline as you write. However, don't hesitate to add examples and descriptions that occur to you while you are drafting.

> ◆ **Grammar Application**
> To be sure you've used the correct form of the pronoun in *than* or *as* comparisons, mentally fill in the missing words.

Revising Ask a classmate to read your remembrance and describe your subject as specifically as possible. If your reader's description is too general, consider adding more specific examples to your remembrance.

Guide for Reading

Meet the Author:

William Shakespeare (1564–1616)

Many people regard William Shakespeare as the greatest writer in the English language. In all, Shakespeare wrote 37 plays, many of which are still performed. These include *Romeo and Juliet* and *Hamlet*. He also wrote sonnets and other lyric poems. The song "Full Fathom Five" appears in his play *The Tempest,* which may have been his last work. [For more on Shakespeare, see page 228.]

THE STORY BEHIND THE POEM

The Tempest was inspired by European exploration in the Americas. The sense of wonder in the play and in "Full Fathom Five" reflects the wonder that Shakespeare felt about this "new world." In fact, the shipwreck referred to in "Full Fathom Five" was based on the wreck of an English ship in Bermuda in 1609.

Eve Merriam (1916–1992)

Eve Merriam's fascination with words began at an early age: "I remember being enthralled by the sound of words." This love, which led her to write poetry, fiction, nonfiction, and drama, is reflected in the poem "Onomatopoeia."

Pat Mora (1942–   )

Pat Mora grew up in El Paso, Texas, on the United States/Mexico border. She has written many award-winning stories and poems about her experiences as a Mexican American.

◆ LITERATURE AND YOUR LIFE

CONNECT YOUR EXPERIENCE

There's something that can quickly change your mood. It doesn't cost any money. You can't hold it in your hands, but it travels in the air and can make different people move to the same rhythm. It's called music.

If you take time to hear it, the music in these poems can make you laugh or feel a sense of wonder.

THEMATIC FOCUS: People in Their Variety

How do the people and things in these poems reveal their personalities through the sounds they make?

◆ Background for Understanding

LITERATURE

In Shakespeare's *The Tempest,* a spirit named Ariel sings "Full Fathom Five" to the young prince Ferdinand. The prince and his father, King Alonso, were traveling in a ship that was wrecked on a magical island. Now Ferdinand, wandering the island, hears Ariel sing that his father has drowned. However, Alonso is really alive and will appear at the end of the play.

◆ Build Vocabulary

WORDS BASED ON *onomatopoeia*

Onomatopoeia refers to the creation of words to imitate sounds. As you might expect, you'll find examples of this kind of word in the poem "Onomatopoeia": "The rusty spigot/sputters ... " The dictionary shows that *sputters* was invented long ago to imitate the sound of something that "spits out in small particles."

WORD BANK

Which of these words from the poems might describe someone who has *mastered* the art of music?

knell
sputters
maestro
snare

◆ Literary Focus

SOUND DEVICES

Poets use **sound devices,** ways of making a work more musical, to appeal to your ear. One device is **onomatopoeia,** the use of words whose sound suggests their meaning, like *sputter.* Another device is **alliteration,** the repetition of sounds at the beginning of words or in stressed syllables: "*F*ull *f*athom *f*ive thy *f*ather lies."

Before you read, tune your ear to these devices by completing this chart:

Onomatopoeia	With Alliteration Added
Sputter	Sprinkly Sputter
Hiss	
Buzz	
Plop	

◆ Reading Strategy

LISTEN AS YOU READ POETRY

You'll get more out of poetry if you **listen as you read,** hearing a poem's sounds and rhythms. Many poets speak their poems aloud as they write them. Their ear, not their eye, tells them whether a word or line is working.

If possible, read each of these poems softly to yourself, or at least "hear" it in your mind. Listen for the music of the vowel sounds and the sharper music of consonants, like the *t, p,* and *g* sounds in "rusty spigot." Also, hear the chimes of rhymes, like "knell" and "bell."

Full Fathom Five

WILLIAM SHAKESPEARE

Full fathom[1] five thy father lies,
Of his bones are coral made,
Those are pearls that were his eyes.
Nothing of him that doth fade
5   But doth suffer a sea change
Into something rich and strange.
Sea nymphs hourly ring his <u>knell</u>.
Ding-dong.
"Hark! Now I hear them—ding-dong, bell."

---

1. **fathom** (fath´ əm) *n.*: Length of six feet used to measure water depth.

◆ **Build Vocabulary**

knell (nel) *n.*: Funeral bell

sputters (sput´ ərz) *v.*: Makes hissing or spitting sounds

ONOMATOPOEIA
Eve Merriam

The rusty spigot
<u>sputters</u>,
utters
a splutter,
5   spatters a smattering of drops,
gashes wider;
slash,
splatters,
scatters,
10   spurts,
finally stops sputtering
and plash!
gushes rushes splashes
clear water dashes.

▶ **Critical Viewing** What onomatopoeia would you use to describe the water flowing from this spigot? **[Synthesize]**

◇ Guide for Responding

◆ LITERATURE AND YOUR LIFE

Reader's Response Which of these poems was more unusual to you? Why?

Thematic Focus Contrast the "personalities" of the spigot in "Onomatopoeia" and the father in "Full Fathom Five."

Partner Poetry Reading Now that you've listened to these poems yourself, read them aloud to a partner.

☑ **Check Your Comprehension**

1. What is happening to the father in "Full Fathom Five"?
2. On what object does "Onomatopoeia" focus?
3. In your own words, describe the action in "Onomatopoeia."

◆ Critical Thinking

1. What does Shakespeare mean when he says the father is changing "Into something rich and strange"? **[Interpret]**
2. Which words in "Onomatopoeia" sound most like water? Explain. **[Analyze]**

EVALUATE

3. Do the brief lines in "Onomatopoeia" help contribute to the effect of the poem? Explain. **[Criticize]**

APPLY

4. In addition to a "rusty spigot," what other thing would be a good subject for a poem entitled "Onomatopoeia"? Why? **[Hypothesize]**

Maestro

Pat Mora

He hears her
when he bows.
Rows of hands clap
again and again he bows
5 to stage lights and upturned faces
but he hears only his mother's voice

years ago in their small home
singing Mexican songs
one phrase at a time
10 while his father strummed the guitar
or picked the melody with quick fingertips.
Both cast their music in the air
for him to <u>snare</u> with his strings,
songs of *lunas*[1] and *amor*[2]
15 learned bit by bit.
She'd nod, smile, as his bow slid
note to note, then the trio
    voz,[3] *guitarra,*[4] *violín*[5]
would blend again and again
20 to the last pure note
sweet on the tongue.

---

1. **lunas** (loō´ näs) *n.*: Spanish for "moons."
2. **amor** (ä môr´) *n.*: Spanish for "love."
3. **voz** (vōs) *n.*: Spanish for "voice."
4. **guitarra** (gē tär´ rä) *n.*: Spanish for "guitar."
5. **violín** (vē ō lēn´) Spanish for "violin."

◆ Build Vocabulary

maestro (mīs´ trō) *n.*: Great musician

snare (snar) *v.*: Catch or trap

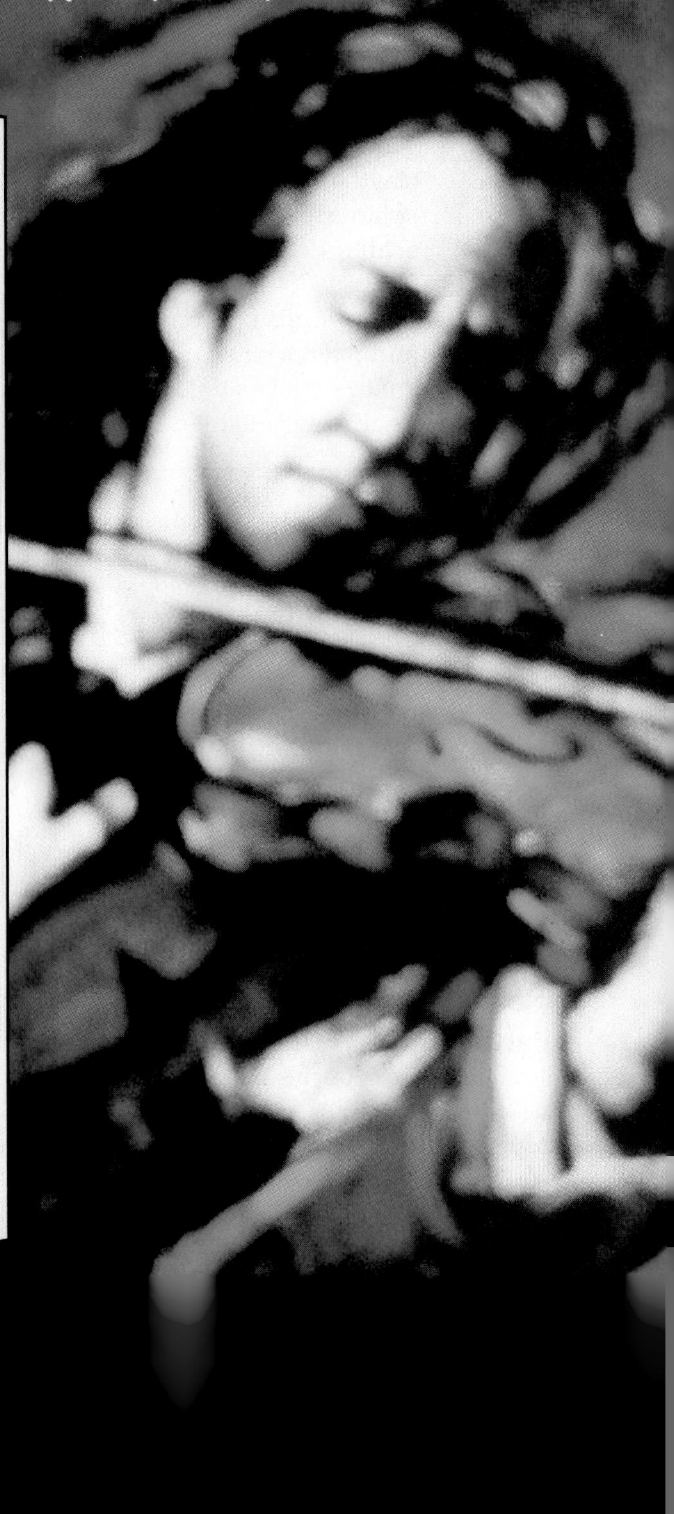

Untitled, Mike Reed

◄ Critical Viewing In what ways
do both the poem and the photograph convey the energy of music?
[Compare and Contrast]

Guide for Responding

◆ LITERATURE AND YOUR LIFE

Reader's Response Would you like to
know the family described in "Maestro"? Why
or why not?

Thematic Focus How is the musical trio in
the poem an example of three different
"voices" working together as one?

Group Activity With several classmates,
discuss the music you like to hear. Explain your
taste in music, and listen to others as they
explain theirs.

☑ Check Your Comprehension

1. What is the profession of the person named
   in the title?
2. What does he recall when he hears the audience's applause?
3. What is his ethnic background?
4. What did each family member contribute to
   the musical trio?

◆ Critical Thinking

1. Why does the performer hear "only his
   mother's voice" when he bows? **[Infer]**
2. Which words in the poem convey the feelings in the family without mentioning these
   feelings directly? **[Analyze]**
3. In what way does this poem use the past to
   explain the present? **[Draw Conclusions]**

EVALUATE

4. Is Mora's use of Spanish words effective?
   Explain. **[Criticize]**

APPLY

5. What does this poem suggest about the
   importance of the parents' influence on a
   child? **[Generalize]**

Guide for Responding (continued)

◆ Reading Strategy
LISTEN AS YOU READ POETRY
By **listening as you read these poems,** you heard the rich patterns of sounds in them. Now tune your ears and test your listening skills by answering these questions:

1. Read aloud lines 1–6 of "Onomatopoeia." Which consonant sounds leap out at you? Explain.
2. Reread "Full Fathom Five," listening for the short o sound (as in "doth"). In which words do you hear it?
3. "Maestro" creates music with repeated words. Listen for them as you read the poem aloud. Then, write them down.

◆ Build Vocabulary
USING WORDS BASED ON *onomatopoeia*
A word based on onomatopoeia sounds like what it describes. For each of these words, fill in a type of sound that it imitates (the first has been done for you).

1. sputter   water being coughed from a faucet
2. sizzle   _____
3. hiss   _____
4. zing   _____
5. whiz   _____

SPELLING STRATEGY
In some words, you spell an initial n sound kn: *knell.* Other words with this silent k before an n include *knowledge, knight,* and *knuckle.*

On your paper, write the words with initial kn that fit these definitions:

1. A blow, as on a door: ____?____
2. A tool for cutting food: ____?____
3. A handle on a door: ____?____

USING THE WORD BANK
On your paper, answer each question with *yes* or *no.* Then, explain your answer.

1. Could a *maestro* supervise an orchestra?
2. Does a *knell* usually sound joyful?
3. Would you call a plumber to fix a faucet that *sputters*?
4. Could you use cheese to *snare* a mouse?

◆ Literary Focus
SOUND DEVICES
These poets use a number of **sound devices,** ways to make their poems more musical. One of these is **onomatopoeia,** the use of words that sound like what they mean. You'll find this device not only in "Onomatopoeia" but also in "Maestro." There the word *strummed* imitates the sound of long strokes across the strings of a guitar.

Another sound device is **alliteration,** the repetition of sounds at the beginning of words or in stressed syllables.

1. In addition to the word *sputters* in "Onomatopoeia," how does the whole poem imitate a "rusty spigot"?
2. Find the example of onomatopoeia in "Full Fathom Five," and tell what sound it imitates.
3. Identify an example of alliteration in a line from "Maestro."

◆ Build Grammar Skills
COMMONLY CONFUSED VERBS: *lay* AND *lie*
Lay is a verb meaning "to set or put something down." Its principal parts are *lay, laying, laid, laid. Lay* always takes a direct object. In contrast, *lie* is a verb meaning "to recline." Its principal parts are *lie, lying, lay, lain. Lie* never takes a direct object. Shakespeare uses the present tense of *lie*: "Full fathom five thy father *lies* ..."

Practice On your paper, choose the correct verb for each sentence.

1. (Lay, Lie) that copy of *The Tempest* on the table.
2. You can (lie, lay) on the couch and listen to the maestro.
3. As he worked on the spigot, he (laid, lay) his wrench down.
4. "I have (lay, lain) underwater for hours," said King Alonso.
5. The maestro has (lain, laid) down his baton for the night.

Writing Application Write a paragraph inspired by one of these poems. Use at least two forms of *lie* and two of *lay.*

Build Your Portfolio

 ## Idea Bank

Writing

1. **School Cheer** Write a cheer to encourage one of your school's athletic teams. Include examples of onomatopoeia and alliteration to give your cheer zing and zest.

2. **Radio Spot** Write a brief radio ad for a product of your choice. Use both onomatopoeia and alliteration to grab listeners' attention. **[Media Link; Career Link]**

3. **Poem With Artful Alliteration** Just as Merriam wrote a poem entitled "Onomatopoeia," write a poem called "Alliteration." In your poem, include examples of alliteration, such as *skittish skateboard*, *noisy neighbors*, and *wondrous winter*.

Speaking and Listening

4. **Silly, Sensational Storytelling** With a circle of classmates, tell a silly, sensational story about someone or something in one of the poems. Each teller should add a sentence with alliteration before passing the story to the next teller in the circle. **[Performing Arts Link]**

5. **Poetry Singing** Listen to a recording of an actor singing "Full Fathom Five" in Act I, Scene ii of *The Tempest*. Then, imitating the actor, sing the poem for the class. **[Performing Arts Link]**

Projects

6. **Onomatopoeia Factory** **[Group Activity]** With classmates, set up a "factory" to create sound words. Add to our stock of sound words (like *hiss*) by assembling words to imitate such sounds as heavy scraping and hearty laughing.

7. **Shakespeare and Exploration** Summarize *The Tempest* for your class. Then, explain how Shakespeare used details from exploration in the Americas in the play. Use the preface to an edition of the play to research this subject. **[Social Studies Link]**

 ## Writing Mini-Lesson

Analysis of a Poem

You analyze when you break something down to see how it works—whether it's a car's engine or a friend's behavior. Now choose one of these poems to analyze. Discuss two of its different elements, like sound devices and characters. Show how these work in the poem and how they work together to create a single feeling or idea.

Writing Skills Focus: Clear and Logical Organization

Your analysis will be easier to read and to write if you use **clear and logical organization:**

- **Introduction**—a paragraph to identify the poem you'll analyze and the elements you'll discuss
- **Body**—two paragraphs to discuss the elements of the poem
- **Conclusion**—a paragraph to explain how the elements of the poem work together

Prewriting Figure out two elements of the poem you can discuss. Among the elements you could discuss are sound devices, rhyme, appearance, images, or characters. Review the poem, and jot down ideas about these elements.

Drafting You don't have to write the sections in the order that they'll appear. Start with the body if you want to get into your discussion right away. You can write the introduction later.

> ◆ **Grammar Application**
> Be sure that you haven't confused *lie* and *lay*.

Revising Check that your analysis contains an introduction, body, and conclusion. Also, be sure that the conclusion shows how the elements work together. In discussing "Maestro," for example, indicate how the music of the sound devices helps you better understand the musical people in the poem.

Guide for Reading

Meet the Authors:

Mary Oliver (1935–   )

As a poet, Mary Oliver is known for her fresh perceptions of nature. She received the Pulitzer Prize in Poetry for her book *American Primitive*.

Carl Sandburg (1878–1967)

The son of Swedish immigrants, Carl Sandburg was born in Illinois. Although he won the Pulitzer Prize in both poetry and history, he was not a typical scholar. By the time his first book appeared, he had been a farm worker, a stagehand, a railroad worker, a soldier, and a cook, among other things.

THE STORY BEHIND THE POEM

Sandburg was working as a reporter when he wrote "Fog." He jotted down the poem one day while waiting to interview a Chicago judge for his paper.

Naomi Long Madgett (1923–   )

Naomi Long Madgett once said, "I would rather be a good poet than anything else." This ambition has led her to write seven collections of poetry.

Wendy Rose (1948–   )

Wendy Rose was born in California, to a Hopi father and a Scots-Irish-Miwok mother. Besides being a poet, she is a painter and a scientist who studies customs and beliefs. "Loo-Wit" is based on legends of the Cowlitz people of Washington State.

◆ LITERATURE AND YOUR LIFE

CONNECT YOUR EXPERIENCE

You've heard people refer to nature as a person: Mother Nature. Although she has her quiet moments, Mother Nature can also get angry. The picture on the facing page shows that you don't want to be there when she blows her top! These poems are like home movies of Mother Nature. They show both her quiet and her angry moods.

THEMATIC FOCUS: Nature's Wonders

How do these poems help you see nature with fresh eyes?

◆ Background for Understanding

SCIENCE

"Loo-Wit" describes the May 18, 1980, eruption of the Mount St. Helens volcano in Washington State. A volcano is an opening in the Earth's crust through which rocks, dust, and ash, or hot liquid rock, can shoot out. The Mount St. Helens eruption killed about 60 people and destroyed about 10,000,000 trees. Hundreds of miles away, volcanic ash "like gray talcum powder" rained down on cities.

◆ Build Vocabulary

PREFIXES: *dis-*

You may have heard the phrase, "don't dis me!" The prefix *dis-*, meaning "away, apart, not, or the opposite," disses every word it can. In "Loo-Wit," it changes *lodge* ("to stay in a resting place") to *dislodge* ("to go away from a resting place").

WORD BANK

Which of these words from the poems describes what a runner does just before starting the 100-yard dash?

haunches
buttes
crouches
unravel
dislodge

Aunt Leaf ◆ Fog ◆ Life ◆ Loo-Wit

◆ Reading Strategy

RESPOND TO POETRY

A poem is an open invitation for you to think and feel. **Respond** to its invitation by bringing your understanding to its words, your heartbeat to its rhythms, and your senses to its descriptions. Agree or disagree with its statements, and tap out the beat of its stressed syllables. Enrich its descriptions with your own memories and experiences.

These questions, and those you make up yourself, will help you respond to the poems:

- "Aunt Leaf"—What natural creature would I most like to be?
- "Fog"—When have I seen fog? Did it move or stand still?
- "Life"—To what would I compare life?
- "Loo-Wit"—Is it fun to think of a volcano as a person? Why or why not?

◆ Literary Focus

FIGURATIVE LANGUAGE

You can expect to see figurative language in poetry. **Figurative language** is language that is not meant to be interpreted literally. The following chart lists and describes the major types of figurative language. As you read the poems, look for examples of these types of figurative language.

Type	Description	Example
Simile	Comparison using *like* or *as* to note a similarity in two apparently unlike items	"We'd travel cheerful as birds."
Metaphor	Direct comparison that describes one item as if it were another	"Life is but a toy."
Extended Metaphor	Metaphor that continues past a phrase or sentence	The poem "Fog" develops an extended metaphor.
Personification	Language that gives human traits to something nonhuman	"Loo-Wit" describes a volcano as a woman.

Aunt Leaf

Mary Oliver

Needing one, I invented her—
the great-great-aunt dark as hickory
called Shining-Leaf, or Drifting-Cloud
or The-Beauty-of-the-Night.

5   Dear aunt, I'd call into the leaves,
and she'd rise up, like an old log in a pool,
and whisper in a language only the two of us knew
the word that meant *follow*,

and we'd travel
10 cheerful as birds
out of the dusty town and into the trees
where she would change us both into something quicker—
two foxes with black feet,
two snakes green as ribbons,
15 two shimmering fish—
and all day we'd travel.

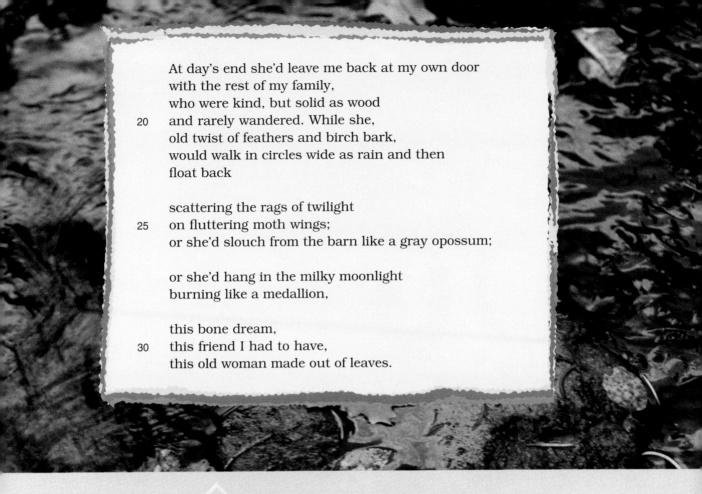

At day's end she'd leave me back at my own door
with the rest of my family,
who were kind, but solid as wood
20 and rarely wandered. While she,
old twist of feathers and birch bark,
would walk in circles wide as rain and then
float back

scattering the rags of twilight
25 on fluttering moth wings;
or she'd slouch from the barn like a gray opossum;

or she'd hang in the milky moonlight
burning like a medallion,

this bone dream,
30 this friend I had to have,
this old woman made out of leaves.

Guide for Responding

◆ LITERATURE AND YOUR LIFE

Reader's Response Have you ever "traveled" the way the poem's speaker does? Explain.

Thematic Focus Find a word or phrase in the poem that conveys the wonder of nature, and explain your choice.

Journal Writing In your journal, describe an imaginary friend who would suit your personality.

☑ Check Your Comprehension

1. What names did the speaker give her invented great-great-aunt?
2. How did the speaker call to her "aunt," and how did the "aunt" respond?
3. Describe the adventures the speaker had with her "aunt."

◆ Critical Thinking

INTERPRET

1. In your own words, describe the "aunt" that the speaker invented. **[Interpret]**
2. Contrast the "travel" that the speaker did with ordinary travel. **[Compare and Contrast]**
3. In what way is the speaker different from her family? **[Infer]**
4. Why do you think the speaker "had to have" a friend like this? **[Draw Conclusions]**

EVALUATE

5. Is *shimmering* (line 15) a good word to describe a fish? Explain. **[Criticize]**

APPLY

6. What does this poem suggest about the power of the imagination? **[Generalize]**

FOG

Carl Sandburg

The fog comes
on little cat feet.

It sits looking
over harbor and city
5 on silent <u>haunches</u>
and then moves on.

◆ Build Vocabulary

haunches (hônch´ iz) *n.*:
An animal's legs

Beyond Literature

Science Connection

Fog vs. Smog Both fog and smog can cloud your vision, but they are very different in nature. Fog is a mass of microscopic water droplets that hug the ground as a low-flying cloud. Smog, whose name was created by combining the words *smoke* and *fog,* is a form of air pollution. Despite the origins of its name, smog has no relationship to real fog other than being similar in appearance. Smog results from large amounts of pollutants in the air. These pollutants come from the exhausts from automobiles, factory smokestacks, and chimneys. Smog is dangerous and even deadly to people, animals, and plants.

Cross-Curricular Activity

Group Report [Group Activity] With a group, prepare a report on smog. Divide up topics like these: causes of smog; smog prevention; air quality in major cities such as London, Los Angeles, Tokyo, and Beijing; effects of smog on human health. Share your findings with the class in an illustrated report.

▶ Critical Viewing In what ways is life like a pocket-watch? [Connect]

Life

Naomi Long Madgett

Life is but a toy that swings on a bright gold chain
Ticking for a little while
To amuse a fascinated infant,
Until the keeper, a very old man,
5   Becomes tired of the game
And lets the watch run down.

Guide for Responding

◆ LITERATURE AND YOUR LIFE

Reader's Response Do you agree with the statement in "Life" that "Life is but a toy"? Why or why not?

Thematic Focus Would you call fog one of nature's wonders? Explain.

Pantomime Using gestures, expressions, and movements but not words, express the action in one of these poems.

☑ Check Your Comprehension

1. Describe the setting of "Fog."
2. Identify three things the fog does.
3. In your own words, describe what happens in "Life."

◆ Critical Thinking

INTERPRET

1. What overall impression of fog does the poet create in "Fog"? [Draw Conclusions]
2. In your own words, explain what the poem "Life" suggests about life. [Draw Conclusions]

EVALUATE

3. Is a ticking watch a good image for life? Why or why not? [Make a Judgment]

APPLY

4. What is it about fog that makes it a good subject for a poem? [Speculate]

COMPARE LITERARY WORKS

5. What is similar or different about the overall feeling that each of these poems creates? [Compare and Contrast]

Loo-Wit[1]

Wendy Rose

The way they do
this old woman
no longer cares
what others think
5   but spits her black tobacco
any which way
stretching full length
from her bumpy bed.
Finally up
10 she sprinkles ashes
on the snow,
cold buttes
promise nothing
but the walk
15 of winter.
Centuries of cedar
have bound her
to earth,
huckleberry ropes
20 lay prickly
on her neck.
Around her
machinery growls,
snarls and plows
25 great patches
of her skin.
She crouches
in the north,
her trembling
30 the source
of dawn.
Light appears
with the shudder

of her slopes,
35 the movement
of her arm.
Blackberries unravel,
stones dislodge;
it's not as if
40 they weren't
warned.

She was sleeping
but she heard the boot
scrape,
45 the creaking floor,
felt the pull of the blanket
from her thin
    shoulder.
With one free hand
50 she finds her weapons
and raises them high;
clearing the twigs from her
throat
she sings, she
55 sings,
shaking the sky
like a blanket about her
Loo-wit sings and sings and
sings!

---

1. **Loo-Wit:** The name given
by the Cowlitz People to
Mount St. Helens, an active
volcano in Washington State.
It means "lady of fire."

◆ **Build Vocabulary**

buttes (byo͞ots) *n*.: Steep hills standing in flat land

crouches (krouch′ iz) *v*.: Stoops or
bends low

unravel (un rav′ əl) *v*.: Become
untangled or separated

dislodge (dis läj′) *v*.: Leave a resting
place

◆ LITERATURE AND YOUR LIFE

Reader's Response When have you thought of nature—or something in it—as having a personality? Explain.

Thematic Focus Find a word or phrase in "Loo-Wit" that surprised you into seeing a volcano in a new way. Then, explain your choice.

Volcano's Monologue As Loo-Wit, give a speech expressing what you're feeling and what you intend to do. Combine your speech with appropriate gestures.

☑ Check Your Comprehension

1. To what kind of person does the poet compare Loo-Wit?
2. How does Loo-Wit show that she doesn't care what others think of her?
3. What has bound Loo-Wit to the earth?
4. Describe what Loo-Wit does in lines 46–53.

◆ Critical Thinking

INTERPRET

1. Who are "they" in line 40? **[Infer]**
2. What picture of humans and their activities does the poem convey? **[Analyze]**
3. What overall impression of Loo-Wit do you get from the poem? Explain. **[Draw Conclusions]**

APPLY

4. Why do you think people speak of volcanoes and other natural forces as if they were people? **[Speculate]**

EXTEND

5. Contrast this poem with a scientific description of a volcano. **[Science Link]**

COMPARE LITERARY WORKS

6. Compare and contrast the portrayal of nature in "Aunt Leaf" and "Loo-Wit." **[Compare and Contrast]**

▲ Critical Viewing Which lines of the poem best capture the action of this photograph? Explain. **[Assess]**

Guide for Responding *(continued)*

◆ Reading Strategy

RESPOND TO POETRY

You **responded** to these poems by thinking about the ideas they stated, feeling the emotions they called up, and using your senses to experience the scenes they described. Now, recall and develop some of your responses to the poems.

1. Which of these poems stated or suggested an idea that made you think more deeply? Explain.
2. To which poem did you have the strongest emotional response? Why?
3. Which poem appealed to three of your senses? Explain.

◆ Build Vocabulary

USING THE PREFIX *dis-*

Here's your chance to be *dis*respectful and get away with it. Add the prefix *dis-* ("away, apart, not, or the opposite") to these words, and explain the meaning of the word that results.

1. dis- + lodge =
2. dis- + respect =
3. dis- + honor =
4. dis- + similar =

SPELLING STRATEGY

If the last syllable of a word ending with a consonant-vowel-consonant is not stressed, you usually don't double the final consonant when adding an ending:

un rav´ el + -ing = unraveling
ben´ e fit + -ed = benefited

On your paper, correctly spell these combinations.

1. benefit + -ing =
2. travel + -ed =
3. unravel + -ed =
4. shovel + -er =

USING THE WORD BANK

On your paper, fill in each blank with an appropriate word from the Word Bank. Do not use any word more than once.

I am a proud thunderstorm. I'm not a storm that ___?___ behind the ___?___, squatting on my ___?___. I approach boldly, wanting to ___?___ everything you've tied together. Even boulders will ___?___ when they hear my thunder-footsteps.

◆ Literary Focus

FIGURATIVE LANGUAGE

Figurative language is not to be taken literally. Types of figurative language include simile, metaphor, and personification.

1. Identify two similes in "Aunt Leaf." Do they indicate that the aunt is a real person or imagined? Explain.
2. How do the similes in "Aunt Leaf" help you see the world as a child would see it?
3. What object is a metaphor for life in "Life"?
4. For either "Fog" or "Life," show how the metaphor continues from the beginning of the poem to the end.
5. (a) How does the poem "Loo-Wit" show the use of personification? (b) Find three details which develop this personification.

◆ Build Grammar Skills

CORRECT USE OF *like* AND *as*

As (including *as if* and *as though*) introduces a clause, or group of words that contains a subject and its verb:

> s v
> They ate their lunch *as* they sat on the grass.

Like introduces a noun or pronoun:

> noun
> The lemonade tasted *like* sunshine.

Do not use *like* to introduce a clause:

> The sandwiches, however, seemed *as if*
> ——— clause ———
> [not *like*] they needed more mustard.

Practice On your paper, choose the word or words that correctly complete each sentence.

1. It looks (like, as if) the girl is imaginative.
2. (As, Like) a child, a poet sees things in fresh ways.
3. The baby is acting (like, as if) he needs a nap.
4. He cooks lasagna (like, as) they do in Italy.
5. The volcano erupts (like, as though) it were spitting.

Writing Application Write a short description of a natural object or event. In your description, include sentences that demonstrate the correct use of both *like* and *as*.

Build Your Portfolio

 ## Idea Bank

Writing

1. **E-mail Response** Write an e-mail note to one of these poets, explaining what you liked or disliked about his or her poem. Be sure to mention the use of figurative language.

2. **Personified Weather Report** Write a television weather report. However, change the usual approach by describing storms and other weather systems as if they were human. **[Media Link]**

3. **Analysis** "Life" compares life to a watch. In other metaphors, life is a bowl of cherries, a fleeting melody, a race to the finish, or a climb up a mountain. Choose three of these, and analyze the attitude toward life expressed by each of them.

Speaking and Listening

4. **Television Newscast** Read the Background for Understanding on page 788 and magazine articles to find out more about the Mount St. Helens eruption. Then, deliver a telecast on the volcano, using figurative language in your report. **[Media Link]**

5. **Simile Slam** Enter a figurative language contest by choosing your favorite simile from "Aunt Leaf" or another poem you know. Read it to the class, and explain why the simile works so well. Ask the class to select a winner, based on the best reading and the most convincing explanation. **[Performing Arts Link]**

Projects

6. **Illustrated Figure of Speech** Draw a picture that will help other students understand the concept of a simile, metaphor, or personification. For example, show a volcano that is also an "old woman." **[Art Link]**

7. **Dancing With "Aunt Leaf"** **[Group Activity]** With several classmates, create and perform a dance showing the adventures of the girl in "Aunt Leaf." **[Performing Arts Link]**

 ## Writing Mini-Lesson

Extended Definition

The poem "Life" is not only a metaphor but also a kind of extended definition. Using prose, write your own extended definition of a great idea, like justice or love. Start with an explanation of the concept. Then, support your explanation with facts, stories, and examples from your reading, viewing, and personal experience.

> **Writing Skills Focus:**
> **Topic Statement**
> Begin with a **topic statement** that summarizes your main idea or ideas. The first sentence in this model is a topic statement:
>
> *Model*
> Justice means that people get what they truly deserve, not what a government is willing to give them. Too often, justice is confused with the existing court system. . . .

Prewriting Use an organizer like the one below to gather support for your definition (write your topic statement in the center):

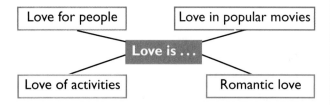

Drafting Write your topic statement. Then, develop your main ideas further in your explanation. Support your ideas with stories and examples from the organizer.

Revising Be sure that your topic statement accurately expresses your main idea, that the explanation develops it, and that your examples support it.

> ◆ **Grammar Application**
> Check to see that you haven't mistakenly used *like* as a conjunction.

Writing Process Workshop

It's often helpful to think carefully about two things—two poems, two works of art, two people, or two events. Somehow, when you compare and contrast them, both things come into better focus. In a **comparison-and-contrast essay,** you write about how two things are alike and how they are different. These writing skills, covered in the Writing Mini-Lessons in this part, will help you write an effective comparison-and-contrast essay:

Writing Skills Focus

▶ **Specific examples** will make your essay interesting and meaningful. (See p. 779.)

▶ **A clear and logical organization** will help readers follow your argument. Make your case point by point or subject by subject. (See p. 787.)

▶ **Strong topic statements** will guide your writing—and your readers. (See p. 797.)

After reading "Fog," one student decided to look for other poems by Carl Sandburg. He chose to compare and contrast "Fog" with another short poem of Sandburg's: "Grass."

MODEL

I enjoyed reading both "Fog" and "Grass" by Carl Sandburg. Although they didn't rhyme, they were easy to read. They are similar in their language and style but very different in their meanings. ①

Both poems look short and simple. ② "Fog" has only eight lines. "Grass" has eleven. The words in "Fog" are very simple. The poem almost looks like a children's poem. The words and concepts in "Grass" are a little more advanced, especially the place names, but most of the words and sentences in the poem are short and simple. ③

① This is the topic statement.

② The writer uses a point-by-point organization. This paragraph focuses on the language and length of each poem.

③ By referring to the place names in "Grass," the writer uses a specific example to prove a point.

Prewriting

Make a Choice You'll need to choose two items that are worth comparing and contrasting. Your subjects should be both alike and different. They must be alike enough to warrant a comparison, but they must also be different enough to make contrasts interesting. Here are a few suggestions:

> ## Topic Ideas
> ■ Two poems or stories by the same poet or writer
> ■ Two ways to do something
> ■ Two famous people who have something important in common
> ■ Two shows or films about the same subject

Use a Venn Diagram In a Venn diagram, each circle represents an item being compared and contrasted. In the overlapping part of the circles, write the similarities. In the two nonoverlapping parts, write the differences. This Venn diagram compares and contrasts two types of bicycles:

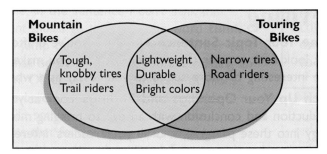

Mountain Bikes
Tough, knobby tires
Trail riders

Lightweight
Durable
Bright colors

Touring Bikes
Narrow tires
Road riders

Get Organized There are two general ways to organize a comparison-and-contrast essay. Look at these outlines, showing subject-by-subject and point-by-point organization. Choose the organization that best suits your topic.

Subject by Subject
○ I. Introduction
II. Mountain Bikes
Frames; Tires
III. Touring Bikes
Frames; Tires
IV. Conclusion
Uses of both bikes

Point by Point
○ I. Introduction
II. Frames
Mountain Bikes
Touring Bikes
III. Tires
Mountain Bikes
Touring Bikes
IV. Conclusion
Uses of both bikes

APPLYING LANGUAGE SKILLS: Vary Sentence Length

When comparing two items, it is easy to use a predictable pattern of sentences. Take care to avoid writing sentences that repeat the same format.

Short Sentences:
The French Open is played on clay courts.

Wimbledon is played on grass.

Try these suggestions to vary sentences:

Combine Sentences:
The French Open is played on clay, but Wimbledon is played on grass.

Use a Subordinate Clause:
While both tournaments are grand slam events, the French Open is played on clay and Wimbledon is played on grass.

Practice Vary the length of the sentences in this paragraph:

The U.S. Open is played in September. The French Open is played in June. Wimbledon is played in July.

Writing Application As you draft, vary the length of sentences in your essay.

Writer's Solution Connection Writing Lab

To gather details, use the Venn diagram in the Prewriting section of the Exposition tutorial.

Sleeping Beauty, John Dixon Batten, Christie's Images, London

Myths, Legends, and Folk Tales

Gods and goddesses, talking animals, strange and wondrous events—these are some of the elements of myths, legends, and folk tales. Although writers retell these stories in print, most of the tales originated long before reading and writing began. They have survived by being handed down from generation to generation. Taken together, these forms make up what is known as the oral tradition of literature:

- **Myths** are anonymous stories involving gods and goddesses. They stress cultural ideals or explain natural occurrences.

- **Legends** are stories that are believed to be based on real-life events and feature larger-than-life people.

- **Folk tales** are stories about ordinary people. Like myths, these stories reveal the traditions and values of a culture.

- **Fables** are stories that feature animals that speak and act like humans. Fables teach morals, or lessons about how to live.

Guide for Reading

◆ LITERATURE AND YOUR LIFE

CONNECT YOUR EXPERIENCE

Even in today's technologically advanced society, natural events occur that are beyond our comprehension. We can't accurately predict when a volcano will erupt or explain what determines the exact time that an earthquake will strike. Just imagine how hard it was to understand and predict nature in ancient times. In their efforts to understand and explain events, people came up with fantastic stories like the one you're about to read.

THEMATIC FOCUS: Wishes, Hopes, Dreams

This fantastic tale deals with the struggles of a young couple to overcome obstacles that prevent them from fulfilling their dream of being together. What do you expect will be the outcome of their struggles? Why?

◆ Background for Understanding

CULTURE

This legend comes to us from the Aztec Indians, who controlled a great empire in Mexico about 500 years ago. They were great builders and engineers who constructed cities larger than European cities of that time. Their capital city of Tenochtitlan (te nôch´ tē tlän´), built on a lake, contained an incredible system of canals for transportation and floating gardens for crops. The Spanish conquered the Aztec empire in 1521, but the influence of Aztec culture has continued in Mexico's art, language, and food.

◆ Popocatepetl and Ixtlaccihuatl ◆

◆ Literary Focus

LEGEND

"Popocatepetl and Ixtlaccihuatl" is a **legend,** a traditional story about the past believed to be based on real events or people. Legends are part of the oral tradition—they were passed down by word of mouth from generation to generation. The details in a legend become increasingly exaggerated over time. As a result, legends often contain fantastic details and involve larger-than-life characters performing amazing feats.

Legends reveal the values and attitudes of the cultures from which they come. For example, this legend reflects the Aztec belief in loyalty and bravery.

◆ Build Vocabulary

PREFIXES: *be-*

In reading this legend, you'll come across the word *besieged*. Its opening prefix *be-*, meaning "make" or "be," is a clue to its meaning, "be under siege." To help get you thinking about other *be-* words, work with a partner to complete a word web like the one below.

WORD BANK

Which of these words from the legend do you think is a noun?

besieged
decreed
relished
brandishing
unanimous
refute
routed
edifice

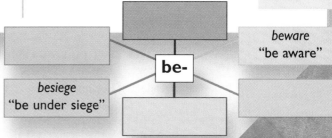

besiege
"be under siege"

be-

beware
"be aware"

Reading for Success

Strategies for Reading Legends, Folk Tales, and Myths

Reading legends, folk tales, and myths is a bit like writing a newspaper article about the history of a culture. You must ask: *Who* was important? *What* did they do? *Why* did it matter? *Where* and *when* did the events happen? *What* may happen next? The following strategies can help you find the meaning in a legend, folk tale, or myth:

Identify the cultural context.

▶ Read the accompanying notes, such as the Background for Understanding on Aztec culture for this legend, to better understand the culture from which the work originated.

▶ Look for details that suggest how the ancient Aztecs lived and what they found important. You may want to record cultural clues in a chart:

Clue	What This Suggests About the Culture
Ixtla is her father's heir.	The Aztecs believed that a woman could rule.

Reread or read ahead.

▶ Skim the story for the names of places and characters. Make a list with brief descriptions or notes to help you remember unfamiliar names.

▶ If you don't understand a certain passage, reread it to look for connections among the words and sentences. It might also help to read ahead, because a word or idea may be clarified further on.

Predict.

Look for clues to help you predict, or make educated guesses about, how the events will unfold. While you read, revise your predictions as you encounter new information.

Recognize the storyteller's purpose.

▶ Remember that legends, myths, and folk tales are traditional stories that people used to communicate shared beliefs and to explain their world.

▶ Identify the original storyteller's audience. Knowing that a legend was told by community elders to youngsters around the fire, for example, will help you determine that its purpose was to teach cultural values.

As you read the following Aztec legend, look at the notes in the boxes. These notes demonstrate how to apply reading strategies to a legend.

POPOCATEPETL AND IXTLACCIHUATL

Mexican Legend

Juliet Piggott

Before the Spaniards came to Mexico and marched on the Aztec capital of Tenochtitlan[1] there were two volcanoes to the southeast of that city. The Spaniards destroyed much of Tenochtitlan and built another city in its place and called it Mexico City. It is known by that name still, and the pass through which the Spaniards came to the ancient Tenochtitlan is still there, as are the volcanoes on each side of that pass. Their names have not been changed. The one to the north is Ixtlaccihuatl[2] and the one on the south of the pass is Popocatepetl.[3] Both are snowcapped and beautiful, Popocatepetl being the taller of the two. That name means Smoking Mountain. In Aztec days it gushed forth smoke and, on occasion, it does so still. It erupted too

> Recognize that the original Aztec storytellers' **purpose** is to explain something about the two volcanoes.

---

1. **Tenochtitlan** (te nôch´ tē tlän´): The Spanish Conquered the Aztec capital in 1521.

2. **Ixtlaccihuatl** (ēs´ tä sē´ wät´ əl)
3. **Popocatepetl** (pô pô kä tē´ pet´ əl)

The Volcanos, 1905, Jose Maria Velasco, Courtesy of CDS Gallery, New York

▲ **Critical Viewing** Use the details in the legend to identify each volcano in this painting. **[Connect]**

in Aztec days and has done so again since the Spaniards came. Ixtlaccihuatl means The White Woman, for its peak was, and still is, white.

Perhaps Ixtlaccihuatl and Popocatepetl were there in the highest part of the Valley of Mexico in the days when the earth was very young, in the days when the new people were just learning to eat and grow corn. The Aztecs claimed the volcanoes as their own, for they possessed a legend about them and their creation, and they believed that legend to be true.

There was once an Aztec Emperor in Tenochtitlan. He was very powerful. Some thought he was wise as well, whilst others doubted his wisdom. He was both a ruler and a warrior and he kept at bay those tribes living in and beyond the mountains surrounding the Valley of Mexico, with its huge lake called Texcoco[4] in which Tenochtitlan was built. His power was absolute and the splendor in which he lived was very great.

Read ahead to see if the emperor makes wise decisions.

It is not known for how many years the Emperor ruled in Tenochtitlan, but it is known that he lived to a great age. However, it was not until he was in his middle years that his wife gave him an heir, a girl. The Emperor and Empress loved the princess very much and she was their only child. She was a dutiful daughter and learned all she could from her father about the art of ruling, for she knew that when he died she would reign in his stead in Tenochtitlan.

Her name was Ixtlaccihuatl. Her parents and her friends called her Ixtla. She had a pleasant disposition and, as a result, she had many friends. The great palace where she lived with the Emperor and Empress rang with their laughter when they came to the parties her parents gave for her. As well as being a delightful companion Ixtla was also very pretty, even beautiful.

Her childhood was happy and she was content enough when she became a young woman. But by then she was fully aware of the great responsibilities which would be hers when her father died and she became serious and studious and did not enjoy parties as much as she had done when younger.

Another reason for her being so serious was that she was in love. This in itself was a joyous thing, but the Emperor forbade her to marry. He wanted her to reign and rule alone when he died, for he trusted no one, not even his wife, to rule as he did except his much loved only child, Ixtla. This was why there were some who doubted the wisdom of the Emperor for, by not allowing his heiress to marry, he showed a selfishness and shortsightedness towards his daughter and his empire which many considered was not truly wise. An emperor, they felt, who was not truly wise could not also be truly great. Or even truly powerful.

The man with whom Ixtla was in love was also in love with her. Had they been allowed to marry their state could have been doubly joyous. His name was Popocatepetl and Ixtla and his friends all called him Popo. He was a warrior in the service of the Emperor, tall and strong, with a capacity for gentleness, and very brave. He and Ixtla loved each other very much and while they were content and even happy when they were together, true joy was not theirs because the Emperor continued to insist that Ixtla should not be married when the time came for her to take on her father's responsibilities.

This unfortunate but moderately happy relationship between Ixtla and Popo continued for several years, the couple pleading with the Emperor at regular intervals and the Emperor remaining constantly adamant. Popo loved Ixtla no less for her father's stubbornness and she loved him no less while she studied, as her father demanded she should do, the art of ruling in preparation for her reign.

When the Emperor became very old he also became ill. In his feebleness he channeled all his failing energies towards instructing Ixtla in statecraft, for he was no longer able to exercise that craft himself. So it was that his enemies, the tribes who lived in the mountains and beyond, realized that the great Emperor in Tenochtitlan was great no longer, for he was only teaching his daughter to rule and not ruling himself.

---

4. **Texcoco** (tā skō′ kō)

The tribesmen came nearer and nearer to Tenochtitlan until the city was besieged. At last the Emperor realized himself that he was great no longer, that his power was nearly gone and that his domain was in dire peril.

Warrior though he long had been, he was now too old and too ill to lead his fighting men into battle. At last he understood that, unless his enemies were frustrated in their efforts to enter and lay waste to Tenochtitlan, not only would he no longer be Emperor but his daughter would never be Empress.

Instead of appointing one of his warriors to lead the rest into battle on his behalf, he offered a bribe to all of them. Perhaps it was that his wisdom, if wisdom he had, had forsaken him, or perhaps he acted from fear. Or perhaps he simply changed his mind. But the bribe he offered to whichever warrior succeeded in lifting the siege of Tenochtitlan and defeating the enemies in and around the Valley of Mexico was both the hand of his daughter and the equal right to reign and rule, with her, in Tenochtitlan. Furthermore, he decreed that directly he learned that his enemies had been defeated he would instantly cease to be Emperor himself. Ixtla would not have to wait until her father died to become Empress and, if her father should die of his illness or old age before his enemies were vanquished, he further decreed that he who overcame the surrounding enemies should marry the princess whether he, the Emperor, lived or not.

> Based on your personal experiences and other stories you've read, you might **predict** that the Emperor's bribe may not have the outcome he intends.

Ixtla was fearful when she heard of her father's bribe to his warriors, for the only one whom she had any wish to marry was Popo and she wanted to marry him, and only him, very much indeed.

> From these details, you can **identify** an important element of the tale's **cultural context:** The Aztecs were a warrior society.

The warriors, however, were glad when they heard of the decree: there was not one of them who would not have been glad to have the princess as his wife and they all relished the chance of becoming Emperor.

And so the warriors went to war at their ruler's behest, and each fought trebly[5] hard for each was fighting not only for the safety of Tenochtitlan and the surrounding valley, but for the delightful bride and for the right to be the Emperor himself.

Even though the warriors fought with great skill and even though each one exhibited a courage he did not know he possessed, the war was a long one. The Emperor's enemies were firmly entrenched around Lake Texcoco and Tenochtitlan by the time the warriors were sent to war, and as battle followed battle the final outcome was uncertain.

The warriors took a variety of weapons with them; wooden clubs edged with sharp blades of obsidian,[6] obsidian machetes,[7] javelins which they hurled at their enemies from troughed throwing boards, bows and arrows, slings and spears set with obsidian fragments, and lances, too. Many of them carried shields woven from wicker[8] and covered in tough hide and most wore armor made of thick quilted cotton soaked in brine.

The war was long and fierce. Most of the warriors fought together and in unison, but some fought alone. As time went on natural leaders emerged and, of these, undoubtedly Popo was the best. Finally it was he, brandishing his club and shield, who led the great charge of running warriors across the valley, with their enemies

> At this point, you might be able to **predict** the story's outcome.

---

5. **trebly** (tre´ blē) *adv.*: Three times as much; triply.
6. **obsidian** (əb sid´ ē ən) *n.*: Hard, usually dark-colored or black, volcanic glass.
7. **machetes** (mə shet´ ēs) *n.*: Large, heavy-bladed knives.
8. **wicker** (wik´ ər) *n.*: Thin, flexible twig.

◆ Build Vocabulary

besieged (bi sējd´) *adj.*: Surrounded
decreed (di krēd´) *v.*: Officially ordered
relished (rel´ isht) *v.*: Especially enjoyed
brandishing (bran´ dish iŋ) *adj.*: Waving in a menacing way

fleeing before them to the safety of the coastal plains and jungles beyond the mountains.

The warriors acclaimed Popo as the man most responsible for the victory and, weary though they all were, they set off for Tenochtitlan to report to the Emperor and for Popo to claim Ixtla as his wife at last.

But a few of those warriors were jealous of Popo. Since they knew none of them could rightly claim the victory for himself (the decision among the Emperor's fighting men that Popo was responsible for the victory had been unanimous), they wanted to spoil for him and for Ixtla the delights which the Emperor had promised.

These few men slipped away from the rest at night and made their way to Tenochtitlan ahead of all the others. They reached the capital two days later, having traveled without sleep all the way, and quickly let it be known that, although the Emperor's warriors had been successful against his enemies, the warrior Popo had been killed in battle.

It was a foolish and cruel lie which those warriors told their Emperor, and they told it for no reason other than that they were jealous of Popo.

When the Emperor heard this he demanded that Popo's body be brought to him so that he might arrange a fitting burial. He knew the man his daughter had loved would have died courageously. The jealous warriors looked at one another and said nothing. Then one of them told the Emperor that Popo had been killed on the edge of Lake Texcoco and that his body had fallen into the water and no man had been able to retrieve it. The Emperor was saddened to hear this.

After a little while he demanded to be told which of his warriors had been responsible for the victory but none of the fighting men before him dared claim the successful outcome of the war for himself, for each knew the others would refute him. So they were silent. This puzzled the Emperor and he decided to wait for the main body of his warriors to return and not to press the few who had brought the news of the victory and of Popo's death.

Then the Emperor sent for his wife and his daughter and told them their enemies had been overcome. The Empress was thoroughly excited and relieved at the news. Ixtla was only apprehensive. The Emperor, seeing her anxious face, told her quickly that Popo was dead. He went on to say that the warrior's body had been lost in the waters of Lake Texcoco, and again it was as though his wisdom had left him, for he spoke at some length of his not being able to tell Ixtla who her husband would be and who would become

Emperor when the main body of warriors returned to Tenochtitlan.

But Ixtla heard nothing of what he told her, only that her beloved Popo was dead. She went to her room and lay down. Her mother followed her and saw at once she was very ill. Witch doctors were sent for, but they could not help the princess, and neither could her parents. Her illness had no name, unless it was the illness of a broken heart. Princess Ixtlaccihuatl did not wish to live if Popocatepetl was dead, and so she died herself.

Rereading the descriptions of Ixtla's feelings for Popo will help you understand her actions.

The day after her death Popo returned to Tenochtitlan with all the other surviving warriors. They went straight to the palace and, with much cheering, told the Emperor that his enemies had been <u>routed</u> and that Popo was the undoubted victor of the conflict.

The Emperor praised his warriors and pronounced Popo to be the new Emperor in his place. When the young man asked first to see Ixtla, begging that they should be married at once before being jointly proclaimed Emperor and Empress, the Emperor had to tell Popo of Ixtla's death, and how it had happened.

Popo spoke not a word.

He gestured the assembled warriors to follow him and together they sought out the few jealous men who had given the false news of his death to the Emperor. With the army of warriors watching, Popo killed each one of them in single combat with his obsidian studded club. No one tried to stop him.

That task accomplished Popo returned to the palace and, still without speaking and still wearing his stiff cotton armor, went to Ixtla's room. He gently lifted her body and carried it out of the palace and out of the city, and no one tried to stop him doing that either. All the warriors followed him in silence.

When he had walked some miles he gestured to them again and they built a huge pile of stones in the shape of a pyramid. They all worked together and they worked fast while Popo stood and watched, holding the body of the princess in his arms. By sunset the mighty <u>edifice</u> was finished. Popo climbed it alone, carrying Ixtla's corpse with him. There, at the very top, under a heap of stones, he buried the

---

◆ Build Vocabulary

unanimous (yoo nan′ ə məs) *adj.*: Based on complete agreement

refute (ri fyoot′) *v.*: Prove someone wrong

routed (rout′ əd) *v.*: Completely defeated

edifice (ed′ ə fis) *n.*: Large structure

young woman he had loved so well and for so long, and who had died for the love of him.

That night Popo slept alone at the top of the pyramid by Ixtla's grave. In the morning he came down and spoke for the first time since the Emperor had told him the princess was dead. He told the warriors to build another pyramid, a little to the southeast of the one which held Ixtla's body and to build it higher than the other.

He told them too to tell the Emperor on his behalf that he, Popocatepetl, would never reign and rule in Tenochtitlan. He would keep watch over the grave of the Princess Ixtlacci-huatl for the rest of his life.

The messages to the Emperor were the last words Popo ever spoke. Well before the evening the second mighty pile of stones was built. Popo climbed it and stood at the top, taking a torch of resinous pine wood with him.

And when he reached the top he lit the torch and the warriors below saw the white smoke rise against the blue sky, and they watched as the sun began to set and the smoke turned pink and then a deep red, the color of blood.

So Popocatepetl stood there, holding the torch in memory of Ixtlaccihuatl, for the rest of his days.

The snows came and, as the years went by, the pyramids of stone became high white-capped mountains.

This reference to the volcanoes confirms the **storyteller's purpose:** to explain the origins of the volcanoes.

Even now the one called Popocatepetl emits smoke in memory of the princess whose body lies in the mountain which bears her name.

Guide for Responding

◆ LITERATURE AND YOUR LIFE

Reader's Response If you were either Ixtla or Popo, how would you have responded to the news of the other's death?

Thematic Focus Do you think the dream of love that Ixtla and Popo shared was a realistic one? Explain.

Journal Writing In your journal, share your reactions to the events in the story.

☑ Check Your Comprehension

1. Why are Ixtla and Popo unable to marry?
2. How do the Emperor's actions show his selfishness?
3. What effect does the Emperor's selfishness have on the safety of his kingdom?
4. What leads to Ixtla's death at the end of the war?
5. Why does Popo refuse to become emperor and rule in Tenochtitlan?

◆ Critical Thinking

INTERPRET

1. What qualities make the two lovers well suited to each other? **[Analyze]**
2. Is the Emperor a wise man? Why or why not? **[Make a Judgment]**
3. In what ways are events caused by the characters' selfishness, jealousy, and love? **[Connect]**
4. How does this story turn tragedy into something positive? **[Interpret]**
5. Based on this legend, what traits do you think the Aztecs admired? **[Draw Conclusions]**

APPLY

6. What do you think this legend indicates about the power of love? **[Generalize]**

EXTEND

7. What kinds of professionals do you think could have helped Ixtla, her father, and Popo resolve their conflict more happily? **[Career Link; Health Link]**

Guide for Responding (continued)

◆ Reading for Success

STRATEGIES FOR READING MYTHS, LEGENDS, AND FOLK TALES

Review the reading strategies and the notes showing how to read myths, legends, and folk tales. Then, apply them to answer the following:

1. (a) At what point were you able to predict the story's outcome? (b) On what did you base your predictions?
2. What does this legend reveal about how the Aztec government worked and how the Aztecs made war?
3. What do you think the original storyteller's main purposes were in creating this legend?

◆ Build Vocabulary

USING THE PREFIX be-

Words that start with the prefix be- are usually verbs (action words). They tell you something has been "made" to happen. With this information in mind, work with a partner (and a dictionary, if necessary) to define each of these words:

1. becalm
2. befriend
3. bewitch
4. belittle

SPELLING STRATEGY

Use i before e except after c in words containing the long e sound: besiege. Complete the spelling of these words.

1. bel_ _ve
2. f_ _ld
3. th_ _f
4. p_ _ce

USING THE WORD BANK

Write the letter of the definition that best matches each word.

1. besieged
2. decreed
3. relished
4. brandishing
5. unanimous
6. refute
7. routed
8. edifice

a. all in agreement
b. prove wrong
c. large building
d. surrounded by armies
e. waving in a menacing way
f. especially enjoyed
g. completely defeated
h. officially ordered

◆ Literary Focus

LEGEND

Legends are tales handed down orally from generation to generation that are believed to have some basis in fact. Like other types of folk literature, legends reveal the values and the beliefs of the culture from which they originate.

1. Which events in this legend might have been based on historical events?
2. Which events are highly imaginative and probably not based on historical events?
3. What inferences can you make about Aztec values and beliefs based on this legend?

◆ Build Grammar Skills

COMMAS WITH INTERRUPTERS

Writers use **commas** to set off **interrupters**—words or phrases that help relate ideas to one another but that are not essential to the meaning—from the rest of the sentence.

> She was kind and, as a result, she had many friends.

Practice Rewrite the following sentences with correctly placed commas.

1. In Aztec days the volcano gushed forth smoke and on occasion it does so still.
2. Ixtlaccihuatl means The White Woman, for its peak was and still is white.
3. An emperor they felt who was not truly wise could not also be truly great.
4. As time went on natural leaders emerged and of these undoubtedly Popo was the best.
5. He told them too to tell the Emperor on his behalf that he Popocatepetl would never reign and rule in Tenochtitlan.

Writing Application For each of the following interrupters, write a sentence that contains it. Use commas to correctly set off the interrupting text.

1. therefore   2. on the other hand   3. some felt

Build Your Portfolio

 ## Idea Bank

Writing

1. **Diary Entry** Imagine that you are either Ixtla, Popo, or a jealous soldier. Choose a critical point in the story. Then, write a journal entry describing the situation and your feelings about it.

2. **New Ending** Like many stories of doomed love, this legend turns on a communication failure. Rewrite the story's ending as if a messenger from Popo had brought Ixtla news of his safety. How might the story end now? Give another explanation of the creation of the two volcanoes.

3. **Essay About Cultural Context** Write a brief essay explaining what this legend reveals about Aztec citizens' values and beliefs, their form of government, and the region in which they lived. Support your points with passages from the legend.

Speaking and Listening

4. **TV News Report** Imagine that you're a war correspondent reporting for a TV station in Tenochtitlan. Using maps and diagrams, describe to your viewers how the war between the Aztec army and its enemies is going. **[Social Studies Link]**

5. **Musical Accompaniment** Choose a piece of music that captures the feelings of Popo and Ixtla upon the discovery of each other's death. Play the piece for the class, and explain why you chose it. **[Music Link]**

Projects

6. **Aztec City** Conduct research to find out what the Aztec city of Tenochtitlan looked like. Then, draw a map of such a city, showing the arrangement of the buildings. **[Art Link]**

7. **Volcano Model** The volcanoes in this tale really exist, about 30 miles from Mexico City. Find out more about volcanoes. Then, build a model of one using the medium of your choice. Ask your science teacher to help find a way to make your volcano "erupt" safely. **[Science Link]**

 ## Writing Mini-Lesson

Explanation of a Natural Wonder

The Aztecs didn't have the scientific knowledge we have today, so they invented stories to explain things that frightened them or made them wonder. Often, these stories explained the origins of objects in nature, such as volcanoes. Now it's your turn to create a tale about how something came to be. Consider writing about a local landmark or a natural feature.

> #### Writing Skills Focus: Sequence of Events
> Readers won't understand exactly *how* your natural feature was created unless they can follow the **sequence of events** in your explanation. To help them keep track of this sequence, tell your story in time order. Use signal words like *before* and *still* to help clarify the sequence.
>
> #### Model From the Story
> There was *once* an Aztec Emperor in Tenochtitlan. . . . However, it was not until he was *in his middle years* that his wife gave him an heir, a girl.

Prewriting On separate note cards, list events you can imagine leading up to the creation of your natural feature. Then, arrange your note cards in chronological order.

Drafting If you like, begin your story by introducing the feature you are explaining. Then, referring to your note cards, write your first draft in time order. Clarify the events with time-order words like *in the early days* or *after many seasons*.

> ◆ **Grammar Application**
> Be sure you've used commas correctly to set apart interrupting material.

Revising Read your story aloud to a classmate. If he or she can't follow the sequence of events, reorganize and add details to make it clearer.

PART 1 *Folk Tales and Legends From Around the World*

Illustration from "Russkie Volshebnuie Skazki" by Kochergin, Victoria & Albert Museum, London

Guide for Reading

Meet the Authors:

Virginia Hamilton (1936–   )

In her many award-winning novels for young readers, Virginia Hamilton uses elements of history, myth, folklore, legend, and dream to bring to life her African American heritage.

Idries Shah (1924–1996)

Idries Shah published more than 30 books in his lifetime, winning six first prizes from the UNESCO International Book Year competition in 1972.

Ai-Ling Louie

When Ai-Ling Louie was a child, her grandmother told her the story "Yeh-Shen," the Chinese version of "Cinderella." Louie later learned that the tale was first written down by Tuan Cheng-shi during the Tang dynasty (A.D. 618–906) and had probably been handed down orally for centuries before that.

Lone Thygesen-Blecher and George Blecher

In 1982, Lone Thygesen-Blecher and George Blecher won an award for their translation of the Swedish novel *The Battle Horse.* They have also written *Swedish Folktales,* a collection of tales passed down through the generations.

Inea Bushnaq

Growing up in Jerusalem, Inea Bushnaq was frightened and charmed by the folk tales of her Arabic culture's oral tradition. As an adult, she returned to her homeland to record variations of those tales she heard as a child.

◆ LITERATURE AND YOUR LIFE

CONNECT YOUR EXPERIENCE

In a difficult situation, you can sometimes look within yourself and find reserves of strength you didn't know you had. Such is the case for many of the characters you're about to meet.

THEMATIC FOCUS: Lessons Learned

In these stories, some characters learn lessons, while others teach them. As you read, identify the lesson in each story.

◆ Background for Understanding

HISTORY

One way that enslaved Africans kept their hopes alive despite the tremendous hardships they faced was to tell freedom tales—folk tales about the fight for freedom. These tales served an important function: They helped people to believe that they would eventually find freedom from slavery and injustice. As you'll notice in the freedom tale "The People Could Fly," these stories are full of references to the storytellers' native Africa.

◆ Build Vocabulary

RELATED WORDS: *undaunted*

The word *daunted* means "afraid or frightened of." Add the prefix *un-*, which means "not," and you'll get the related word *undaunted,* meaning "not afraid or frightened of." You'll encounter the word *undaunted* in "Yeh-Shen: A Cinderella Story From China."

WORD BANK

Which word from the selections means "walk with dragging feet"? Check the Build Vocabulary boxes to see if you chose correctly.

croon
shuffle
sage
undaunted

The People Could Fly ◆ The Algonquin Cinderella ◆ Yeh-Shen: A Cinderella Story From China ◆ His Just Reward ◆ Djuha Borrows a Pot

◆ Literary Focus

FOLK TALES

Many cultures have **folk tales** that communicate important values and ideas. A folk tale is a story that was composed orally and then passed from person to person by word of mouth. Most folk tales are anonymous: No one knows who first composed them. When modern writers retell a folk tale, they try to capture the feeling and spirit of the tale as it has been told for hundreds of years.

The Ride for Liberty - the Fugitive Slaves, Eastman Johnson

◆ Reading Strategy

RECOGNIZE CULTURAL CONTEXT

One way to appreciate a folk tale is to recognize its **cultural context**—details about the time and place of the story and information about the customs and beliefs of its characters. The following selections were first told in many different places and times—from China in the seventh century to the United States during the time of slavery. Keep track of the cultural context of each folk tale by using a chart like the one shown. It will provide a window of understanding into what you read.

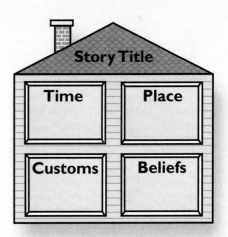

Story Title

Time	Place
Customs	Beliefs

The People Could Fly

African American Folk Tale

❧ Virginia Hamilton ❧

They say the people could fly. Say that long ago in Africa, some of the people knew magic. And they would walk up on the air like climbin up on a gate. And they flew like blackbirds over the fields. Black, shiny wings flappin against the blue up there.

Then, many of the people were captured for Slavery. The ones that could fly shed their wings. They couldn't take their wings across the water on the slave ships. Too crowded, don't you know.

The folks were full of misery, then. Got sick with the up and down of the sea. So they forgot about flyin when they could no longer breathe the sweet scent of Africa.

Say the people who could fly kept their power, although they shed their wings. They kept their secret magic in the land of slavery. They looked the same as the other people from Africa who had been coming over, who had dark skin. Say you couldn't tell anymore one who could fly from one who couldn't.

One such who could was an old man, call him Toby. And standin tall, yet afraid, was a young woman who once had wings. Call her Sarah. Now Sarah carried a babe tied to her back. She trembled to be so hard worked and scorned.

The slaves labored in the fields from sunup to sundown. The owner of the slaves callin himself their Master. Say he was a hard lump of clay. A hard, glinty[1] coal. A hard rock pile, wouldn't be moved. His Overseer[2] on horseback pointed out the slaves who were slowin down. So the one called Driver[3] cracked his whip over the slow ones to make them move faster. That whip was a slice-open cut of pain. So they did move faster. Had to.

Sarah hoed and chopped the row as the babe on her back slept.

Say the child grew hungry. That babe started up bawling too loud. Sarah couldn't stop to feed it. Couldn't stop to soothe and quiet it down. She let it cry. She didn't want to. She had no heart to croon to it.

"Keep that thing quiet," called the Overseer. He pointed his finger at the babe. The woman scrunched low. The Driver cracked his whip across the babe anyhow. The babe hollered like any hurt child, and the woman fell to the earth.

The old man that was there, Toby, came and helped her to her feet.

"I must go soon," she told him.

"Soon," he said.

Sarah couldn't stand up straight any longer. She was too weak. The sun burned her face. The babe cried and cried, "Pity me, oh, pity me," say it sounded like. Sarah was so sad and starvin, she sat down in the row.

"Get up, you black cow," called the Overseer. He pointed his hand, and the Driver's whip snarled around Sarah's legs. Her sack dress tore into rags. Her legs bled onto the earth. She couldn't get up.

Toby was there where there was no one to help her and the babe.

"Now, before it's too late," panted Sarah. "Now, Father!"

"Yes, Daughter, the time is come," Toby answered. "Go, as you know how to go!"

---

1. **glinty** (glint′ ē) *adj.*: Shiny; reflecting light.
2. **Overseer** (ō′ vər sir′) *n.*: Someone who watches over and directs the work of others.

3. **Driver** *n.*: Someone who forced (drove) the slaves to work harder.

From THE PEOPLE COULD FLY by Virginia Hamilton, illustrated by Leo and Diane Dillon

▲ **Critical Viewing** How does the folk tale explain the unique way the people in this illustration fly? [Interpret]

He raised his arms, holding them out to her. "*Kum . . . yali, kum buba tambe*," and more magic words, said so quickly, they sounded like whispers and sighs.

The young woman lifted one foot on the air. Then the other. She flew clumsily at first, with the child now held tightly in her arms. Then she felt the magic, the African mystery. Say she rose just as free as a bird. As light as a feather.

The Overseer rode after her, hollerin. Sarah flew over the fences. She flew over the woods. Tall trees could not snag her. Nor could the Overseer. She flew like an eagle now, until she was gone from sight. No one dared speak about it. Couldn't believe it. But it was, because they that was there saw that it was.

Say the next day was dead hot in the fields. A young man slave fell from the heat. The Driver come and whipped him. Toby come over and spoke words to the fallen one. The words of ancient Africa once heard are never remembered completely. The young man forgot them as soon as he heard them. They went way

inside him. He got up and rolled over on the air. He rode it awhile. And he flew away.

Another and another fell from the heat. Toby was there. He cried out to the fallen and reached his arms out to them. "*Kum kunka yali, kum . . . tambe*!" Whispers and sighs. And they too rose on the air. They rode the hot breezes. The ones flyin were black and shinin sticks, wheelin above the head of the Overseer. They crossed the rows, the fields, the fences, the streams, and were away.

"Seize the old man!" cried the Overseer. "I heard him say the magic *words*. Seize him!"

The one callin himself Master come runnin. The Driver got his whip ready to curl around old Toby and tie him up. The slaveowner took his hip gun from its place. He meant to kill old, black Toby.

But Toby just laughed. Say he threw back his head and said, "Hee, hee! Don't you know who I am? Don't you know some of us in this field?" He said it to their faces. "We are ones who fly!"

And he sighed the ancient words that were a dark promise. He said them all around to

◆ **Build Vocabulary**

croon (kro͞on) *v.*: Sing or hum quietly, soothingly

the others in the field under the whip,

" . . . *buba yali . . . buba tambe. . . .*"

There was a great outcryin. The bent backs straightened up. Old and young who were called slaves and could fly joined hands. Say like they would ring-sing.[4] But they didn't shuffle in a circle. They didn't sing. They rose on the air. They flew in a flock that was black against the heavenly blue. Black crows or black shadows. It didn't matter, they went so high. Way above the plantation, way over the slavery land. Say they flew away to *Free-dom*.

And the old man, old Toby, flew behind them, takin care of them. He wasn't cryin. He wasn't laughin. He was the seer.[5] His gaze fell on the plantation where the slaves who could not fly waited.

---

4. **ring-sing:** Joining hands in a circle to sing and dance.
5. **seer** (sē´ ər) *n.*: One who has supposed power to see the future; prophet.

"Take us with you!" Their looks spoke it but they were afraid to shout it. Toby couldn't take them with him. Hadn't the time to teach them to fly. They must wait for a chance to run.

"Goodie-bye!" The old man called Toby spoke to them, poor souls! And he was flyin gone.

So they say. The Overseer told it. The one called Master said it was a lie, a trick of the light. The Driver kept his mouth shut.

The slaves who could not fly told about the people who could fly to their children. When they were free. When they sat close before the fire in the free land, they told it. They did so love firelight and *Free-dom*, and tellin.

They say that the children of the ones who could not fly told their children. And now, me, I have told it to you.

Guide for Responding

◆ LITERATURE AND YOUR LIFE

Reader's Response Who do you think is the most important character in the story? Why?

Thematic Focus Do you think that the Master learned anything in this story? Why or why not?

Group Activity Read the story aloud, switching readers at each paragraph. Is the story more effective when read aloud?

☑ Check Your Comprehension

1. How did the people lose their wings?
2. Why does Sarah tell Toby that she must leave soon?
3. How does Toby help Sarah?
4. Who kept alive the story of the people who could fly?

◆ Critical Thinking

INTERPRET
1. Describe three details that help you understand the harsh living conditions of the enslaved Africans. **[Support]**
2. Why do you think the author includes African words in the story? **[Interpret]**
3. What do you think "flying" really refers to? **[Draw Conclusion]**

APPLY
4. How do you think it would feel to hear this tale if you were an enslaved African? **[Relate]**

EXTEND
5. Do you think that African American freedom tales were still told after the abolition of slavery in 1865? Why? **[History Link]**

The Algonquin Cinderella

Native American Folk Tale

Retold by Idries Shah

There was once a large village of the MicMac Indians of the Eastern Algonquins,[1] built beside a lake. At the far end of the settlement stood a lodge, and in it lived a being who was always invisible. He had a sister who looked after him, and everyone knew that any girl who could see him might marry him. For that reason there were very few girls who did not try, but it was very long before anyone succeeded.

This is the way in which the test of sight was carried out: at evening-time, when the Invisible One was due to be returning home, his sister would walk with any girl who might come down to the lakeshore. She, of course, could see her brother, since he was always visible to her. As soon as she saw him, she would say to the girls:

"Do you see my brother?"

"Yes," they would generally reply—though some of them did say "No."

To those who said that they could indeed see him, the sister would say:

"Of what is his shoulder strap made?" Some people say that she would enquire:

"What is his moose-runner's haul?" or "With what does he draw his sled?"

And they would answer:

"A strip of rawhide" or "a green flexible branch," or something of that kind.

Then she, knowing that they had not told the truth, would say:

"Very well, let us return to the wigwam!"[2]

When they had gone in, she would tell them not to sit in a certain place, because it belonged to the Invisible One. Then, after they had helped to cook the supper, they would wait with great curiosity, to see him eat. They could be sure that he was a real person, for when he took off his moccasins they became visible, and his sister hung them up. But beyond this they saw nothing of him, not even when they stayed in the place all night, as many of them did.

---

1. **Algonquins** (al gän′ kwinz) n.: Native Americans living near the Ottawa River in Canada.

2. **wigwam** (wig′ wäm′) n.: Indian dwelling made by a dome-shaped framework of poles covered by rush mats or sheets of bark.

Now there lived in the village an old man who was a widower, and his three daughters. The youngest girl was very small, weak and often ill: and yet her sisters, especially the elder, treated her cruelly. The second daughter was kinder, and sometimes took her side: but the wicked sister would burn her hands and feet with hot cinders, and she was covered with scars from this treatment. She was so marked that people called her *Oochigeaskw*,[3] the Rough-Faced-Girl.

When her father came home and asked why she had such burns, the bad sister would at once say that it was her own fault, for she had disobeyed orders and gone near the fire and fallen into it.

These two elder sisters decided one day to try their luck at seeing the Invisible One. So they dressed themselves in their finest clothes,

▲ **Critical Viewing** This woven fabric demonstrates Algonquin attention to beauty—even in functional items. What details in the folk tale confirm this concern? [Connect]

and tried to look their prettiest. They found the Invisible One's sister and took the usual walk by the water:

When he came, and when they were asked if they could see him, they answered, "Of course." And when asked about the shoulder strap or sled cord, they answered, "A piece of rawhide."

But of course they were lying like the others, and they got nothing for their pains.

The next afternoon, when the father returned home, he brought with him many of the pretty little shells from which wampum[4] was made, and they set to work to string them.

---

3. **Oochigeaskw** (ō shē´ gā shkə)

4. **wampum** (wäm´ pəm) *n.*: Small beads made of shells used as money by Native Americans.

That day, poor little Oochigeaskw, who had always gone barefoot, got a pair of her father's moccasins, old ones, and put them into water to soften them so that she could wear them. Then she begged her sisters for a few wampum shells. The elder called her a 'little pest,' but the younger one gave her some. Now, with no other clothes than her usual rags, the poor little thing went into the woods and got herself some sheets of birch bark, from which she made a dress, and put marks on it for decoration, in the style of long ago. She made a petticoat and a loose gown, a cap, leggings and a handkerchief. She put on her father's large old moccasins, which were far too big for her, and went forth to try her luck. She would try, she thought, to discover whether she could see the Invisible One.

She did not begin very well. As she set off, her sisters shouted and hooted, hissed and yelled, and tried to make her stay. And the loafers around the village, seeing the strange little creature, called out "Shame!"

The poor little girl in her strange clothes, with her face all scarred, was an awful sight, but she was kindly received by the sister of the Invisible One. And this was, of course, because this noble lady understood far more about things than simply the mere outside which all the rest of the world knows. As the brown of the evening sky turned to black, the lady took her down to the lake.

"Do you see him?" the Invisible One's sister asked.

"I do, indeed—and he is wonderful!" said Oochigeaskw.

The sister asked:
"And what is his sled-string?"
The little girl said:
"It is the Rainbow."
"And, my sister, what is his bow-string?"
"It is The Spirit's Road—the Milky Way."
"So you *have* seen him," said his sister. She took the girl home with her and bathed her. As she did so, all the scars disappeared from her

▼ **Critical Viewing** In what ways do the rainbow and the Milky Way help readers imagine the size and power of the Invisible One? **[Relate]**

body. Her hair grew again, as it was combed, long, like a blackbird's wing. Her eyes were now like stars: in all the world there was no other such beauty. Then, from her treasures, the lady gave her a wedding garment, and adorned her.

Then she told Oochigeaskw to take the *wife's* seat in the wigwam: the one next to where the Invisible One sat, beside the entrance. And when he came in, terrible and beautiful, he smiled and said:

"So we are found out!"

"Yes," said his sister. And so Oochigeaskw became his wife.

Beyond Literature

Culture Connection

Cinderella Around the World The story of a poor hard-working girl suffering under an evil stepmother is known and loved around the world. There are more than nine hundred versions of this classic tale—the oldest has been traced back more than a thousand years to China. The story most Americans are familiar with was written in the 1600's by Charles Perrault, a French writer, and it is the only one with a fairy godmother and a warning to be home by midnight. Yet for all the differences between the stories, the poor girl always manages to escape her stepmother, marry the prince, and live happily ever after.

Cross-Curricular Activity
Comparing Stories Read the Cinderella stories in this book. Then, using library resources, locate one or two others. In a report to classmates, share the stories, describe the similarities and differences among them, and explain why you think the Cinderella model is so popular.

Guide for Responding

◆ LITERATURE AND YOUR LIFE

Reader's Response What image from the story had the greatest impact on you? Why?

Thematic Focus What lesson does this tale teach its audience?

Group Activity Work with a group to plan and create a comic-book version of "The Algonquin Cinderella."

☑ Check Your Comprehension

1. What task must a girl accomplish in order to marry the mysterious brother?
2. How did Oochigeaskw get her name?
3. What happens when Oochigeaskw's sisters visit the Invisible One?
4. What happens when Oochigeaskw visits the mysterious brother and sister?

◆ Critical Thinking

INTERPRET
1. How does the Invisible One's sister protect him? **[Interpret]**
2. Why do people in the story pretend to be able to see the Invisible One? **[Infer]**
3. Why do you think Oochigeaskw succeeds where others failed? **[Speculate]**

EVALUATE
4. Do you think that the stepsisters should be punished for their behavior? Explain your answer. **[Make a Judgment]**

EXTEND
5. What do you think is the most important difference between Oochigeaskw's story and the European tale known as "Cinderella"? **[Literature Link]**

Yeh-Shen: A Cinderella Story From China

Chinese Folk Tale

Retold by Ai-Ling Louie

In the dim past, even before the Ch'in and the Han dynasties, there lived a cave chief of southern China by the name of Wu. As was the custom in those days, Chief Wu had taken two wives. Each wife in her turn had presented Wu with a baby daughter. But one of the wives sickened and died, and not too many days after that Chief Wu took to his bed and died too.

Yeh-Shen, the little orphan, grew to girlhood in her stepmother's home. She was a bright child and lovely too, with skin as smooth as ivory and dark pools for eyes. Her stepmother was jealous of all this beauty and goodness, for her own daughter was not pretty at all. So in her displeasure, she gave poor Yeh-Shen the heaviest and most unpleasant chores.

The only friend that Yeh-Shen had to her name was a fish she had caught and raised. It was a beautiful fish with golden eyes, and every day it would come out of the water and rest its head on the bank of the pond, waiting for Yeh-Shen to feed it. Step-mother gave Yeh-Shen little enough food for herself, but the orphan child always found something to share with her fish, which grew to enormous size.

◆ **Reading Strategy**
In China, many people catch and raise fish as pets. How does this context help you understand Yeh-Shen's situation?

Somehow the stepmother heard of this. She was terribly angry to discover that Yeh-Shen had kept a secret from her. She hurried down to the pond, but she was unable to see the fish, for Yeh-Shen's pet wisely hid itself. The stepmother, however, was a crafty woman, and she soon thought of a plan. She walked home and called out, "Yeh-Shen, go and collect some firewood. But wait! The neighbors might see you. Leave your filthy coat here!" The minute the girl was out of sight, her stepmother slipped on the coat herself and went down again to the pond. This time the big fish saw Yeh-Shen's familiar jacket and heaved itself onto the bank, expecting to be fed. But the stepmother, having hidden a dagger in her sleeve, stabbed the fish, wrapped it in her garments, and took it home to cook for dinner.

When Yeh-Shen came to the pond that evening, she found her pet had disappeared. Overcome with grief, the girl collapsed on the ground and dropped her tears into the still waters of the pond.

"Ah, poor child!" a voice said.

Yeh-Shen sat up to find a very old man looking down at her. He wore the coarsest of clothes, and his hair flowed down over his shoulders.

"Kind uncle,[1] who may you be?" Yeh-Shen asked.

"That is not important, my child. All you must know is that I have been sent to tell you of the wondrous powers of your fish."

"My fish, but sir . . ." The girl's eyes filled with tears, and she could not go on.

The old man sighed and said, "Yes, my child, your fish is no longer alive, and I must tell you that your stepmother is once more the cause of your sorrow." Yeh-Shen gasped in horror, but the old man went on. "Let us not dwell on things that are past," he said, "for I have come bringing you a gift. Now you must listen carefully to this: The bones of your fish are filled with a powerful spirit. Whenever you are in serious need, you must kneel before them and let them know your heart's desire. But do not waste their gifts."

Yeh-Shen wanted to ask the old sage many more questions, but he rose to the sky before she could utter another word. With heavy heart, Yeh-Shen made her way to the dung heap to gather the remains of her friend.

Time went by, and Yeh-Shen, who was often left alone, took comfort in speaking to the bones of her fish. When she was hungry, which happened quite often, Yeh-Shen asked the bones for food. In this way, Yeh-Shen managed to live from day to day, but she lived in dread that her stepmother would discover her secret and take even that away from her.

So the time passed and spring came. Festival time was approaching: It was the busiest time of the year. Such cooking and cleaning and sewing there was to be done! Yeh-Shen had hardly a moment's rest. At the spring festival young men and young women from the village hoped to meet and to choose whom they would marry. How Yeh-Shen longed to go! But her stepmother had other plans. She hoped to find a husband for her own daughter and did not want any man to see the beauteous Yeh-Shen first. When finally the holiday arrived, the stepmother and her daughter dressed themselves in their finery and filled their baskets with sweetmeats. "You must remain at home now, and watch to see that no one steals fruit from our trees," her stepmother told Yeh-Shen, and then she departed for the banquet with her own daughter.

As soon as she was alone, Yeh-Shen went to speak to the bones of her fish. "Oh, dear friend," she said, kneeling before the precious bones, "I long to go to the festival, but I cannot show myself in these rags. Is there somewhere I could borrow clothes fit to wear to the feast?" At once she found herself dressed in a gown of

> "Kind uncle, who may you be?" Yeh-Shen asked. "That is not important, my child. All you must know is that I have been sent to tell you of the wondrous powers of your fish."

---

1. **uncle:** In this case, *uncle* is a term of respect given to an older man and not a blood relation.

◆ **Build Vocabulary**

sage (sāj) *n.*: Very wise man

undaunted (ən dônt′ id) *adj.*: Not stopping because of fear or failure

azure blue, with a cloak of kingfisher feathers draped around her shoulders. Best of all, on her tiny feet were the most beautiful slippers she had ever seen. They were woven of golden threads, in a pattern like the scales of a fish, and the glistening soles were made of solid gold. There was magic in the shoes, for they should have been quite heavy, yet when Yeh-Shen walked, her feet felt as light as air.

"Be sure you do not lose your golden shoes," said the spirit of the bones. Yeh-Shen promised to be careful. Delighted with her transformation, she bid a fond farewell to the bones of her fish as she slipped off to join in the merrymaking.

That day Yeh-Shen turned many a head as she appeared at the feast. All around her people whispered, "Look at that beautiful girl! Who can she be?"

But above this, Stepsister was heard to say, "Mother, does she not resemble our Yeh-Shen?"

Upon hearing this, Yeh-Shen jumped up and ran off before her stepsister could look closely at her. She raced down the mountainside, and in doing so, she lost one of her golden slippers. No sooner had the shoe fallen from her foot than all her fine clothes turned back to rags. Only one thing remained—a tiny golden shoe. Yeh-Shen hurried to the bones of her fish and returned the slipper, promising to find its mate. But now the bones were silent. Sadly Yeh-Shen realized that she had lost her only friend. She hid the little shoe in her bedstraw, and went outside to cry. Leaning against a fruit tree, she sobbed and sobbed until she fell asleep.

The stepmother left the gathering to check on Yeh-Shen, but when she returned home she found the girl sound asleep, with her arms wrapped around a fruit tree. So thinking no

> It wasn't until the blackest part of night, while the moon hid behind a cloud, that Yeh-Shen dared to show her face at the pavilion, and even then she tiptoed timidly across the wide floor.

more of her, the stepmother rejoined the party. Meantime, a villager had found the shoe. Recognizing its worth, he sold it to a merchant, who presented it in turn to the king of the island kingdom of T'o Han.

The king was more than happy to accept the slipper as a gift. He was entranced by the tiny thing, which was shaped of the most precious of metals, yet which made no sound when touched to stone. The more he marveled at its beauty, the more determined he became to find the woman to whom the shoe belonged. A search was begun among the ladies of his own kingdom, but all who tried on the sandal found it impossibly small. Undaunted, the king ordered the search widened to include the cave women from the countryside where the slipper had been found. Since he realized it would take many years for every woman to come to his island and test her foot in the slipper, the king thought of a way to get the right woman to come forward. He ordered the sandal placed in a pavilion by the side of the road near where it had been found, and his herald announced that the shoe was to be returned to its original owner. Then from a nearby hiding place, the king and his men settled down to watch and wait for a woman with tiny feet to come and claim her slipper.

All that day the pavilion was crowded with cave women who had come to test a foot in the shoe. Yeh-Shen's stepmother and stepsister were among them, but not Yeh-Shen—they had told her to stay home. By day's end, although many women had eagerly tried to put on the slipper, it still had not been worn. Wearily, the king continued his vigil into the night.

It wasn't until the blackest part of night, while the moon hid behind a cloud, that Yeh-Shen dared to show her face at the pavilion, and even then she tiptoed timidly across the wide floor. Sinking down to her knees, the girl in rags examined the tiny shoe. Only when she was sure that this was the missing mate to her own golden slipper did she dare pick it up. At last she could return both little shoes to the fish bones. Surely then her beloved spirit would speak to her again.

Now the king's first thought, on seeing Yeh-Shen take the precious slipper, was to throw the girl into prison as a thief. But when she turned to leave, he caught a glimpse of her face. At once the king was struck by the sweet harmony of her features, which seemed so out of keeping with the rags she wore. It was then that he took a closer look and noticed that she walked upon the tiniest feet he had ever seen.

With a wave of his hand, the king signaled that this tattered creature was to be allowed to depart with the golden slipper. Quietly, the king's men slipped off and followed her home.

All this time, Yeh-Shen was unaware of the excitement she had caused. She had made her way home and was about to hide both sandals in her bedding when there was a pounding at the door. Yeh-Shen went to see who it was— and found a king at her doorstep. She was very frightened at first, but the king spoke to her in a kind voice and asked her to try the golden slippers on her feet. The maiden did as she was told, and as she stood in her golden shoes, her rags were transformed once more into the feathered cloak and beautiful azure gown.

Her loveliness made her seem a heavenly being, and the king suddenly knew in his heart that he had found his true love.

Not long after this, Yeh-Shen was married to the king. But fate was not so gentle with her stepmother and stepsister. Since they had been unkind to his beloved, the king would not permit Yeh-Shen to bring them to his palace. They remained in their cave home, where one day, it is said, they were crushed to death in a shower of flying stones.

Guide for Responding

◆ LITERATURE AND YOUR LIFE

Reader's Response Which character in the story would you most like to meet? Why?

Thematic Focus If you told this tale to a group of young children, what lesson do you think they would learn?

☑ Check Your Comprehension

1. Why was Yeh-Shen treated so badly in her own home?
2. What happens to the fish that Yeh-Shen loves?
3. How does the king find Yeh-Shen?
4. How does fate treat the stepmother and stepsister?

◆ Critical Thinking

INTERPRET

1. What three words would you use to describe Yeh-Shen? **[Interpret]**
2. Why does the king want to meet Yeh-Shen? **[Infer]**
3. Why do you think Yeh-Shen is described as beautiful? **[Draw Conclusions]**

APPLY

4. How do you think Yeh-Shen will treat her own children? **[Speculate]**

COMPARE LITERARY WORKS

5. What basic story elements do both "The Algonquin Cinderella" and "Yeh-Shen" share? **[Compare and Contrast]**

HIS JUST REWARD

SWEDISH FOLK TALE

LONE THYGESEN-BLECHER AND GEORGE BLECHER

A man went out into the forest one day looking for a runaway horse. At one point he had to climb across a cleft in the mountain, and that was when he found that a large snake had got its rear end caught in the crevice.

The snake said to the man, "If you help free me, I'll see that you get your just reward!"

The man took his staff and pried the rocks apart so that the snake could get out.

"Thanks," said the snake. "Now come over here and I'll give you your just reward."

The man asked what his just reward might be.

"Death," said the snake.

The man said that he wasn't sure that he wanted that, and he suggested that they ask the first creature who came along what one's just reward ought to be.

A bear came along, and the man asked the bear what one's just reward ought to be.

"Death," said the bear.

"You see?" said the snake. "Death *is* one's just reward! So now I'm going to take you."

"But then the man replied, "Let's just walk a little farther and ask someone else."

After a while they met a wolf. And the man asked him what one's just reward ought to be.

"Death," answered the wolf. "That's everybody's just reward."

"There it is," said the snake. "Now you're mine!"

"Just a minute," said the man. "Let us say that the third creature we meet is the final judge, whoever it turns out to be."

In a little while they met a fox. The man asked the fox what one's just reward ought to be, and the fox answered just like the others.

"Death," he said.

"So now I'll bite you to death," said the snake.

When the fox heard that, he said, "Now wait just a moment. We must consider this case more carefully. First of all, what really happened?"

"Well," said the man, " the snake got its tail caught in a crevice."

Then the fox said, "Why don't we go back there to see exactly how it was."

Well, they went back, and the fox asked the man to pry open the rocks again with his staff, and then the snake should put his rear end right in between, just the way it'd been before. Then the man should let the rocks slip back a little.

"Was it tighter than this before?" asked the fox.

"Yes," said the snake.

"Let go a little more," said the fox to the man. "Was it tighter than this?"

"Yes."

"Then let go completely. Now, are you in good and tight?"

"It's worse than it was before!" said the snake.

"Well then, you might as well stay there. That way the two of you are even."

So the snake had to stay, and the man avoided getting his just reward.

Djuha Borrows a Pot

Syrian Folk Tale Inea Bushnaq

One day Djuha[1] wanted to entertain his friends with a dinner of lamb stewed whole with rice stuffing, but he did not have a cooking pot large enough. So he went to his neighbor and borrowed a huge, heavy caldron of fine copper.

Promptly next morning, Djuha returned the borrowed pot. "What is this?" cried the neighbor, pulling a small brass pot from inside the caldron. "Oh yes," said Djuha, "congratulations and blessings upon your house! While your caldron was with me it gave birth to that tiny pot." The neighbor laughed delightedly. "May Allah[2] send blessings your way too," he told Djuha, and carried the two cooking pots into his house.

A few weeks later Djuha knocked on his

Bronze cauldron from Daghestan decorated with equestrian figure and two eagles, © The Board of Trustees of the Victoria and Albert Museum, London

---

1. **Djuha** (jōō´ ə)
2. **Allah** (al´ ə): Name for God in the Muslim religion.

neighbor's door again to ask for the loan of the caldron. And the neighbor hurried to fetch it for him. The next day came and went, but Djuha did not return the pot. Several days passed and the neighbor did not hear from Djuha. At last he went to Djuha's house to ask for his property. "Have you not heard, brother?" said Djuha looking very grave. "The very evening I borrowed it from you, your un-fortunate caldron—God grant you a long life—died!" "What do you mean, 'died'?" shouted the neighbor. "Can a copper cooking pot die?" "If it can give birth," said Djuha, "it can surely die."

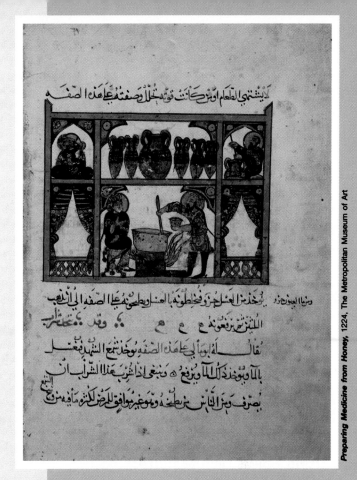

Preparing Medicine from Honey, 1224, The Metropolitan Museum of Art

▶ **Critical Viewing** This Arabic illustration originally accompanied an ancient pharmacology text. In what ways does the artist's style differ from "Western" illustrations you have seen? **[Compare and Contrast]**

Guide for Responding

◆ LITERATURE AND YOUR LIFE

Reader's Response How do you feel about letting people borrow your possessions?

Thematic Focus What lesson does the man learn in "His Just Reward"?

☑ Check Your Comprehension

1. In "His Just Reward," how does the man help the snake?
2. How does the snake plan to reward the man for his help?
3. In "Djuha Borrows a Pot," what happens when Djuha returns the pot for the first time?
4. What happens the second time he borrows the same pot?

◆ Critical Thinking

INTERPRET
1. Which character gets "his just reward" in the story with that title? **[Interpret]**
2. In "Djuha Borrows a Pot," why is the neighbor willing to lend Djuha the pot a second time? **[Infer]**
3. On what human frailty does Djuha count to play his trick? **[Analyze]**

COMPARE LITERARY WORKS
4. Does the neighbor who lends Djuha a pot get his "just reward"? Explain. **[Make a Judgment]**

APPLY
5. Why do you think that many cultures tell tales about tricksters like Djuha who use their cunning and wits to get ahead? **[Hypothesize]**

Guide for Responding (continued)

◆ Literary Focus

FOLK TALES

Many cultures communicate their values and traditions through **folk tales,** stories passed through the generations by word of mouth. One characteristic of many folk tales is the use of repetition: words, phrases, or events that occur more than once. Repetition makes key events easy to remember. As folk tales were passed from generation to generation, these key repeated events were likely to stay the same, while other details might change with each telling.

1. What event is repeated in "The Algonquin Cinderella"?
2. What similar event is repeated in "Yeh-Shen"?
3. How does repetition contribute to the humor of "Djuha Borrows a Pot"?

◆ Build Vocabulary

USING FORMS OF *undaunted*

The word *undaunted,* which means "not frightened or afraid of," is related to several other words. Paraphrase each of the following sentences in your own words. Use a dictionary to check the meanings of words related to *undaunted.*

1. Even the *dauntless* girl felt nervous as she looked at the king.
2. Defending your life is a *daunting* task.

SPELLING STRATEGY

The sound *aw* can be spelled *au,* as in the words *undaunted* and *cause.* Rewrite each sentence below, correcting the spelling of words with the *aw* sound.

1. The stepmother opened the secret vawlt.
2. The snake was mawled by a hungry bear.
3. The neighbor eagerly hawled out the pot.

USING THE WORD BANK

On your paper, write the word from the Word Bank that best completes each sentence.

1. The flying woman was ____?____ by the shouting man on the ground.
2. She began to ____?____ a happy tune.
3. I saw the old men ____?____ slowly away.
4. The ____?____ gives wise advice to young visitors.

◆ Reading Strategy

RECOGNIZE CULTURAL CONTEXT

When you understand the **cultural context** of folk tales—the time and culture from which they come—you will not only understand the tales better, but you will also learn a lot about the people who created them.

1. What does "The People Could Fly" tell you about the spiritual lives of enslaved people in the United States?
2. The brother in "The Algonquin Cinderella" is invisible. What does this tell you about the values of the Algonquin people?
3. What do you learn about Chinese values from the fate of the stepmother and stepsister in "Yeh-Shen"?

◆ Build Grammar Skills

COMMAS IN A SERIES

Use **commas** to separate items that are listed together. Place a comma before the word *and* when three or more things are listed:

> The youngest girl was very small, weak, and often ill.

Practice On your paper, rewrite the sentences, adding commas to separate items listed in a series.

1. Yeh-Shen lived with her father stepmother and two stepsisters.
2. The stepmother was jealous of Yeh-Shen's beauty kindness and grace.
3. The fish bones granted Yeh-Shen's wishes desires and dreams.
4. Yeh-Shen wore a blue gown a feather cloak and golden slippers.
5. The stepmother and stepsister were punished for their jealousy unkindness and cruelty.

Writing Application Write a sentence that contains each of the following groups of words as a series. Separate the words with commas.

1. shirt, pants, belt, shoes
2. brave, powerful, noble
3. swimming, running, climbing

Build Your Portfolio

 ## Idea Bank

Writing

1. **Book Jacket** Create a book jacket for a collection of folk tales that includes the stories you have just read. Choose a title, create an illustration, and write a couple of paragraphs about the collection that will make others want to read it.

2. **Story Sequel** Write a continuation of one of the stories. You might choose to introduce new characters, settings, and events as you create your sequel.

3. **Reader Review** Choose one of these stories, and write a short review for others who might want to read it. Include a brief summary that will interest someone in reading the tale.

Speaking and Listening

4. **Retelling** In your own words, retell one of these stories. Review the story to remember the most important events, but add details of your own. Remember that part of the oral tradition involves adding your own personality to your retelling. **[Performing Arts Link]**

5. **Role Play** With a partner, role-play a discussion between Yeh-Shen, the Chinese Cinderella, and Oochigeaskw, the Algon-quin Cinderella. Discuss similarities and differences between the two girls' lives and their experiences.

Projects

6. **Folk-Tale Festival [Group Activity]** Hold a class storytelling festival. Each student or team can prepare a story to share with the group. Choose stories from several cultures, and consider using props and music to enhance your presentations. **[Performing Arts Link; Social Studies Link]**

7. **Puzzle Challenge** Djuha and the fox trick others with their cleverness. Stump your classmates with number puzzles. Research brain teasers in puzzle books, and choose the best ones. Then, challenge your classmates to solve them. **[Math Link]**

 ## Writing Mini-Lesson

Essay on Cultural Context

Writing an essay can help you organize your thoughts and share them with others. Think about the cultural context of one of these folk tales. Write an essay explaining how the cultural context influences the story and what the story tells you about the culture it is from. Your essay can include your own reactions to the tale as well.

> **Writing Skills Focus: Elaborate to Support an Idea**
>
> In an essay, it is important to **support your ideas.** After you make a statement, follow it with an example or illustration that shows *why* your statement is true. This will make your writing stronger and more effective. If you have trouble finding details that support a statement, your statement may be too general or it may not be accurate. Try restating your idea. Then, elaborate to support it.

Prewriting Choose a folk tale to study. Then, use a chart or table to jot down ideas about its cultural context. Use reference sources to find out more about the culture.

Drafting Begin each paragraph by clearly stating a main idea. For example, you might say that "The Algonquin Cinderella" reveals values that are important to the Algonquin people. In the body of the paragraph, support this statement with specific details from the story and your research.

> ◆ **Grammar Application**
>
> If your draft contains three or more words in a series, separate them with commas.

Revising As you revise, look for ideas that can be further supported with examples. Go back to the folk tale to look for details you might use as support for the ideas in your essay.

The folk-tale form is nearly universal—most cultures tell stories to pass on traditions, beliefs, and values. In "The Princess and the Tin Box," American humorist James Thurber (1894–1961) updates the traditional folk-tale format by using a marriage contest similar to the one in "Popocatepetl and Ixtlaccihuatl." The results are surprising; however, the story still serves to reveal something about the values of the society in which Thurber wrote.

The Princess and the Tin Box

◆ James Thurber

Portrait of a Young Woman, c. 1470, Piero del Pollaiuolo, The Metropolitan Museum of Art

Once upon a time, in a far country, there lived a king whose daughter was the prettiest princess in the world. Her eyes were like the cornflower, her hair was sweeter than the hyacinth, and her throat made the swan look dusty.

From the time she was a year old, the princess had been showered with presents. Her nursery looked like Cartier's[1] window. Her toys were all made of gold or platinum or diamonds or emeralds. She was not permitted to have wooden blocks or china dolls or rubber dogs or linen books, because such materials were considered cheap for the daughter of a king.

▲ **Critical Viewing** What details of this portrait reveal that the woman pictured has lived a life like the princess in the story? **[Support]**

When she was seven, she was allowed to attend the wedding of her brother and throw real pearls at the bride instead of rice. Only the nightingale, with his lyre[2] of gold, was permitted to sing for the princess. The common blackbird, with his boxwood flute, was kept out of the palace grounds. She walked in silver-and-samite slippers to a sapphire-and-topaz bathroom and slept in an ivory bed inlaid with rubies.

On the day the princess was eighteen,

---

1. **Cartier's:** Well-known upscale jewelry store.

2. **lyre** (lĩr) *n.*: Harp.

the king sent a royal ambassador to the courts of five neighboring kingdoms to announce that he would give his daughter's hand in marriage to the prince who brought her the gift she liked most.

The first prince to arrive at the palace rode a swift white stallion and laid at the feet of the princess an enormous apple made of solid gold which he had taken from a dragon who had guarded it for a thousand years. It was placed on a long ebony table set up to hold the gifts of the princess's suitors. The second prince, who came on a gray charger, brought her a nightingale made of a thousand diamonds, and it was placed beside the golden apple. The third prince, riding on a black horse, carried a great jewel box made of platinum and sapphires, and it was placed next to the diamond nightingale. The fourth prince, astride a fiery yellow horse, gave the princess a gigantic heart made of rubies and pierced by an emerald arrow. It was placed next to the platinum-and-sapphire jewel box.

Now the fifth prince was the strongest and handsomest of all the five suitors, but he was the son of a poor king whose realm had been overrun by mice and locusts and wizards and mining engineers so that there was nothing much of value left in it. He came plodding up to the palace of the princess on a plow horse and he brought her a small tin box filled with mica and feldspar and hornblende[3] which he had picked up on the way.

The other princes roared with <u>disdainful</u> laughter when they saw the <u>tawdry</u> gift the fifth prince had brought to the princess. But she examined it with great interest and squealed with delight, for all her life she had been <u>glutted</u> with precious stones and priceless metals, but she had never seen tin before or mica or feldspar or hornblende. The tin box was placed next to the ruby

---

3. **mica** (mī′ kəh), **feldspar** (feld′ spär′), **hornblende** (hôrn′ blend′) *n.*: Common minerals found in rocks.

heart pierced with an emerald arrow.

"Now," the king said to his daughter, "you must select the gift you like best and marry the prince that brought it."

The princess smiled and walked up to the table and picked up the present she liked the most. It was the platinum-and-sapphire jewel box, the gift of the third prince.

"The way I figure it," she said, "is this. It is a very large and expensive box, and when I am married, I will meet many admirers who will give me the precious gems with which to fill it to the top. Therefore, it is the most valuable of all the gifts my suitors have brought me and I like it the best."

The princess married the third prince that very day in the midst of great merriment and high <u>revelry</u>. More than a hundred thousand pearls were thrown at her and she loved it.

Moral: All those who thought the princess was going to select the tin box filled with worthless stones instead of one of the other gifts will kindly stay after class and write one hundred times on the blackboard, "I would rather have a hunk of aluminum silicate than a diamond necklace."

◆ Build Vocabulary

disdainful (dis dān′ fəl) *adj.*: Showing arrogance or scorn for someone considered beneath oneself

tawdry (tô′ drē) *adj.*: Cheap and showy; gaudy

glutted (glut′ əd) *v.*: Given more than is needed or wanted

revelry (rev′ əl rē) *n.*: Celebration; noisy merrymaking

1. (a) What choice does the princess make? (b) How does she defend her decision?
2. What details in the moral reveal that the story is meant to amuse?
3. What conclusions can you draw from this story about the values of the society in which Thurber wrote?

CONNECTING LITERATURE TO SOCIAL STUDIES

AFRICA

All Stories Are Anansi's *Retold by Harold Courlander*

BRAINS BEAT MUSCLES The person with the greatest physical strength doesn't always win. Sometimes a quick-thinking, clever mind can overpower a mighty opponent. Throughout history, people have enjoyed seeing the underdog come out on top. Maybe this is why the clever trickster is so popular in folk tales from Africa and other cultures. A trickster is a character who relies on brains to outwit those who are bigger and stronger. The Ashanti (ə shän´ tē) of western Africa have passed down trickster tales through the generations.

A Powerful Empire The Ashanti ruled a large empire in western Africa during the 1700's and 1800's. At its height, the Ashanti empire included parts of three modern-day countries—much of Ghana, eastern Ivory Coast, and western Togo.

The Empire Falls During the late nineteenth century, the Ashanti and the British fought each other for control of trade in western Africa. In 1901, the British defeated the Ashanti and made their lands a British colony.

Today, the Ashanti region makes up a large part of Ghana, an independent country. The Ashanti play a major role in Ghana's economic and political development. Most Ashanti work in farming, mining, or forestry. The Ashanti have also earned a reputation as skillful weavers of colorful *kente* cloth. Over the years, the Ashanti have also woven many wonderful stories.

A Sneaky Spider In Ashanti folklore, the slyest trickster is Kwaku Anansi (kwä´ ko͞o ə nän´ sē), the spider. He's so clever, he even tries to trick the most important god—Nyame, the supreme Sky God. As you read about Kwaku Anansi, notice the ways in which he appeals to the fears and vanities of his victims in order to fool them.

Western Africa

SENEGAL
GAMBIA
GUINEA-BISSAU
GUINEA
SIERRA LEONE
LIBERIA
CÔTE D'IVOIRE (IVORY COAST)
BURKINA FASO
GHANA
TOGO
BENIN
NIGERIA
EQUATORIAL GUINEA
SAO TOME AND PRINCIPE
CAMEROON
GABON

N

0   500 mi
0   500 km

area of map

All Stories Are Anansi's

African Folk Tale

Harold Courlander

In the beginning, all tales and stories belonged to Nyame,[1] the Sky God. But Kwaku Anansi,[2] the spider, yearned to be the owner of all the stories known in the world, and he went to Nyame and offered to buy them.

The Sky God said: "I am willing to sell the stories, but the price is high. Many people have come to me offering to buy, but the price was too high for them. Rich and powerful families have not been able to pay. Do you think you can do it?"

Anansi replied to the Sky God: "I can do it. What is the price?"

"My price is three things," the Sky God said. "I must first have Mmoboro,[3] the hornets. I must then have Onini,[4] the great python. I must then have Osebo,[5] the leopard. For these things I will sell you the right to

---

1. **Nyame** (nē ä′ mē)
2. **Kwaku Anansi** (kwä′ kōō ə nän′ sē)
3. **Mmoboro** (mō bô′ rō)
4. **Onini** (ō nē′ nē)
5. **Osebo** (ō sä′ bō)

◆ **Build Vocabulary**

yearned (yʉrnd) *v.:* Wanted very much

▼ **Critical Viewing** This nineteenth-century pendant from the Ivory Coast shows a snake catching a frog. What role does the snake play in this folk tale? [**Analyze**]

Pendant in the form of a snake catching a frog, Brooklyn Museum

tell all stories."

Anansi said: "I will bring them."

He went home and made his plans. He first cut a <u>gourd</u> from a vine and made a small hole in it. He took a large calabash[6] and filled it with water. He went to the tree where the hornets lived. He poured some of the water over himself, so that he was dripping. He threw some water over the hornets, so that they too were dripping. Then he put the calabash on his head, as though to protect himself from a storm, and called out to the hornets: "Are you foolish people? Why do you stay in the rain that is falling?"

The hornets answered: "Where shall we go?"

"Go here, in this dry gourd," Anansi told them.

The hornets thanked him and flew into the gourd through the small hole. When the last of them had entered, Anansi plugged the hole with a ball of grass, saying: "Oh, yes, but you are really foolish people!"

He took the gourd full of hornets to Nyame, the Sky God. The Sky God accepted them. He said: "There are two more things."

Anansi returned to the forest and cut a long bamboo pole and some strong vines. Then he walked toward the house of Onini, the python, talking to himself. He said: "My wife is

---

6. **calabash** (kal′ ə bash′) *n.*: Large fruit that is dried and made into a bowl or cup.

stupid. I say he is longer and stronger. My wife says he is shorter and weaker. I give him more respect. She gives him less respect. Is she right or am I right? I am right, he is longer. I am right, he is stronger."

When Onini, the python, heard Anansi talking to himself, he said: "Why are you arguing this way with yourself?"

The spider replied: "Ah, I have had a dispute with my wife. She says you are shorter and weaker than this bamboo pole. I say you are longer and stronger."

Onini said: "It's useless and silly to argue when you can find out the truth. Bring the pole and we will measure."

So Anansi laid the pole on the ground, and

> **Connecting Literature to Social Studies**
> What can you conclude about the animal and plant life in Ghana from the characters in this folk tale?

▼ **Critical Viewing** What characteristic of the leopard does Anansi use in his trick? **[Connect]**

the python came and stretched himself out beside it.

"You seem a little short," Anansi said.

The python stretched further.

"A little more," Anansi said.

"I can stretch no more," Onini said.

"When you stretch at one end, you get shorter at the other end," Anansi said. "Let me tie you at the front so you don't slip."

He tied Onini's head to the pole. Then he went to the other end and tied the tail to the pole. He wrapped the vine all around Onini, until the python couldn't move.

"Onini," Anansi said, "it turns out that my wife was right and I was wrong. You are shorter than the pole and weaker. My opinion wasn't as good as my wife's. But you were even more foolish than I, and you are now my prisoner."

Anansi carried the python to Nyame, the Sky God, who said: "There is one thing more."

Osebo, the leopard, was next. Anansi went into the forest and dug a deep pit where the leopard was accustomed to walk. He covered it with small branches and leaves and put dust on it, so that it was impossible to tell where the pit was. Anansi went away and hid. When Osebo came prowling in the black of night, he stepped into the trap Anansi had prepared and fell to the bottom. Anansi heard the sound of the leopard falling, and he said: "Ah, Osebo, you are half-foolish!"

When morning came, Anansi went to the pit and saw the leopard there.

"Osebo," he asked, "what are you doing in this hole?"

"I have fallen into a trap," Osebo said.

"Help me out."

"I would gladly help you," Anansi said. "But I'm sure that if I bring you out, I will have no thanks for it. You will get hungry, and later on you will be wanting to eat me and my children."

"I swear it won't happen!" Osebo said.

"Very well. Since you swear it, I will take you out," Anansi said.

He bent a tall green tree toward the ground, so that its top was over the pit, and

▼ Critical Viewing Anansi, the spider, is the clever one in this folk tale. What traits of a spider lend themselves to this characterization? [Defend]

◆ **Build Vocabulary**

gourd (gôrd) *n.*: Fruit of a certain kind of plant; the dried, hollowed shell of this fruit is used as a drinking cup or dipper

CONNECTING LITERATURE TO SOCIAL STUDIES

he tied it that way. Then he tied a rope to the top of the tree and dropped the other end of it into the pit.

"Tie this to your tail," he said.

Osebo tied the rope to his tail.

"Is it well tied?" Anansi asked.

"Yes, it is well tied," the leopard said.

"In that case," Anansi said, "you are not merely half-foolish, you are all-foolish."

And he took his knife and cut the other rope, the one that held the tree bowed to the ground. The tree straightened up with a snap, pulling Osebo out of the hole. He hung in the air head downward, twisting and turning. And while he hung this way, Anansi killed him with his weapons.

Then he took the body of the leopard and carried it to Nyame, the Sky God, saying: "Here is the third thing. Now I have paid the price."

Nyame said to him: "Kwaku Anansi, great warriors and chiefs have tried, but they have been unable to do it. You have done it. Therefore, I will give you the stories. From this day onward, all stories belong to you. Whenever a man tells a story, he must acknowledge that it is Anansi's tale."

In this way Anansi, the spider, became the owner of all stories that are told. To Anansi all these tales belong.

> **Connecting Literature to Social Studies**
> Based on this folk tale, do you think the Ashanti feel that their stories hold great value? Why or why not?

◆ **Build Vocabulary**

acknowledge (ak näl´ ij) v.: Recognize and admit

Guide for Responding

◆ **LITERATURE AND YOUR LIFE**

Reader's Response Which of Anansi's accomplishments impressed you the most? Why?

Thematic Focus How would you describe Anansi's personal code of behavior? Do you agree or disagree with this code? Explain.

☑ **Check Your Comprehension**

1. What does Anansi want from Nyame?
2. What does Nyame want to fill this request?
3. How does Anansi capture the hornets, the python, and the leopard?
4. What does Nyame do in the end?

◆ **Critical Thinking**

INTERPRET

1. What can you infer about the hornets, the python, and the leopard from the fact that they listen to Anansi? **[Infer]**
2. What is Anansi's attitude toward the other animals? **[Interpret]**
3. Why is Anansi able to do what warriors and chiefs have failed to do? **[Draw Conclusions]**

APPLY

4. What lessons does this folk tale teach? Explain. **[Generalize]**

EXTEND

5. Cultures have focused on many different animals in the trickster role. What animal from your natural surroundings would make a good trickster? Why? **[Science Link]**

Meet the Author

Harold Courlander (1908–   )

Harold Courlander has studied and written about African, West Indian, Native American, and African American cultures. He has written books on literature and music, novels, and several collections of folk tales from around the world. Courlander is interested in folk tales, he says, because "they convey human values, philosophical outlook, and cultural heritage."

CONNECTING LITERATURE TO SOCIAL STUDIES

As an Ashanti folk tale, "All Stories Are Anansi's" reveals information about the Ashanti's physical environment, their beliefs, and their traditions. For example, the characters in the story are animals common in western Africa—hornets, pythons, and leopards. In addition, the story's main conflict demonstrates the Ashanti's religious beliefs. The Ashanti people believe that a supreme god, Nyame, created the universe. Nyame has many descendants, who are the gods of villages or geographic regions and features. In this story, Anansi, the trickster, meets with Nyame in order to buy all the stories known. Through cleverness and deceit, Anansi gets his wish.

1. What animal characteristics do you think the Ashanti and other cultures looked for when choosing an animal as their trickster?
2. Note two examples of how Anansi displays trickster traits.
3. Why do you think tricksters like Djuha and Anansi have been such popular characters in folklore?

 Idea Bank

Writing

1. **Help-Wanted Ad** Write a help-wanted ad for a trickster. Include a description of qualities the trickster should have.
2. **Argument** Imagine that Anansi now wants to take over Nyame's job. Write the argument he might make to Nyame to explain why the Sky God should allow him to run the universe.
3. **Folk Tale** Write your own folk tale about a trickster like Anansi. Give your character a goal and at least three characters to deceive.

Speaking and Listening

4. **Performance** [Group Activity] With a group of classmates, prepare a performance of "All Stories Are Anansi's." Decide who will play each role. Then, create costumes and sets to fit the western African location. Videotape your play, or perform it live.

Projects

5. **Storytelling Festival** With a group, collect folk tales from different cultures. Look for stories that share similar story lines or characters. For example, you might collect Cinderella stories or trickster tales from around the world. In a presentation, explain the similarities and differences among the stories. Then, retell selected stories to the class. Add music to bring the stories to life.
6. **Spider Profile** Using Internet and library sources, find out about the spiders that live in the western African tropical forests. Describe what they look like, how they behave, and what they eat. Include your own drawing of one such spider or of the fictional Anansi in your report. [Science Link; Art Link]

Further Reading, Listening, and Viewing

- Jane Yolen's *Favorite Folktales From Around the World* (1986) is a collection of popular versions of this and other folk tales.
- *Come With Me to Africa* (1993) by Gregory Scott Kreikemeier takes you along on Kreikemeier's African travels while a student.
- *Ghana* (1987) by Martin Hintz offers an overview in pictures and text.

Cause-and-Effect Essay

Writing Process Workshop

In "Popocatepetl and Ixtlaccihuatl," a cause—a young couple's enduring love—leads to an effect—the emergence of a pair of volcanic mountains. Legends and myths often tell *why* a particular event or situation occurred. Another type of writing that answers the question, "Why?" is a **cause-and-effect essay.** Write your own cause-and-effect essay on a topic that interests you. The following skills, introduced in this section's Writing Mini-Lessons, will help you:

Writing Skills Focus

▶ **Clearly explain the sequence of events.** Often, one cause leads to an effect, which in turn leads to its own effect. Make this chain of causes and effects clear in your essay. (See p. 818.)

▶ **Elaborate to support your ideas.** Use specific details and facts that show the connections between events. Be sure to offer reasons for the results you describe. (See p. 837.)

Notice how the writer uses these skills in "Popocatepetl and Ixtlaccihuatl."

MODEL FROM LITERATURE

from "Popocatepetl and Ixtlaccihuatl" by Juliet Piggott

The snows came and, as the years went by, the pyramids of stone became high white-capped mountains. ① Even now the one called Popocatepetl emits smoke in memory of the princess whose body lies in the mountain which bears her name. ②

① This sentence shows a clear sequence of events—over time, the pyramids became mountains.

② Details here support the main idea—that Popocatepetl emits smoke in memory of Ixtlaccihuatl.

Prewriting

Start With a Question What causes the common cold? Why is the ocean salty? Why did the Union army win the Civil War? Beginning with a good question will give you a strong start.

Topic Ideas

- What causes a disease?
- Why did a historical event happen?
- Why does a rule or law exist?
- Why is a species endangered?
- What causes a certain kind of pollution?

Gather Details Write a list of questions about your topic. Then, conduct research to find the answers. Use the library, on-line resources, or interview an expert on the subject.

Use a Cluster Diagram To clarify the relationships between details, create a cluster diagram. The diagram might consist of a central effect surrounded by several causes, or—as shown below—a central cause surrounded by several effects.

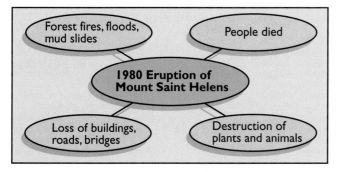

Organize Your Details To show how each cause leads to an effect, organize your details into a flowchart or timeline. Another idea is to write each detail on a separate note card and arrange the cards in the proper order.

Drafting

Write a Strong Introduction Your introduction is the first thing your audience will read, so be sure to grab their attention. You should also explain the importance of your topic and touch on the main points you'll make in your essay.

Write Notes to Yourself Use asterisks (*) to mark places in your draft where you need more information, want to find a better word, or notice a gap in your logic. Write yourself a note in the margin or—if you're working on a computer—in brackets. Later, you can search for the asterisks.

DRAFTING/REVISING

APPLYING LANGUAGE SKILLS: Transitions to Show Cause and Effect

Transitions are like bridges. They connect ideas and sentences. Some transitions show time, and others show location. The ones below show cause and effect.

as a result	meanwhile
as soon as	next
consequently	then
further	therefore
furthermore	when

Practice On your paper, connect the pairs of sentences below with the transitions from the list above.

1. Sam poured birdseed along the path. We provided a bird buffet.
2. I play with the chess club once a week. I've made a lot of new friends.
3. I studied hard. I passed the test.

Writing Application When writing your cause-and-effect essay, use transitions to show the relationships between your sentences.

Writer's Solution Connection
Writing Lab

For additional help, use the Transition Word Bin in the tutorial on Exposition.

Writing Process Workshop

EDITING/PROOFREADING

APPLYING LANGUAGE SKILLS: Punctuating Introductory Elements

Some introductory elements are not critical to a sentence. Use a comma to separate the introductory material if the main clause can stand alone.

Prepositional Phrase:
At first light, Columbus landed on San Salvador.

Participle Phrase:
Claiming the land for Spain, he planted a flag.

Transitional Word:
Finally, a European had sailed to the Western Hemisphere.

Subordinate Clause:
When he returned, Columbus was a hero.

Practice Correct the errors in these sentences—if necessary.

1. In 1492 Columbus "discovered" America.
2. Of course there were people here already.
3. In his log Columbus wrote that the people were friendly.

Writing Application When revising, use commas after introductory elements.

Writer's Solution Connection Writing Lab

If you work with a peer reviewer, refer to the Peer Editing Worksheet in the tutorial on Exposition.

Revising

Use a Checklist As you revise your work, ask yourself the following questions:

▶ What is the main idea of my essay? How can I make it clearer?
▶ Have I clearly shown the sequence of causes and effects in my essay? Can I add or change details or transition words to make causes and effects clearer?
▶ Is there any unnecessary information I should drop from my essay?
▶ Are there any errors in spelling, grammar, or punctuation?

Answer these questions thoughtfully and thoroughly. Then, use your responses to guide your revision.

REVISION MODEL

When the volcano became active, it made the earth shake, set off avalanches, and sparked an intense series of noises. It ① The first eruption spread a thick layer of volcanic ash over a wide area ② , destroying plant and animal life.

① The writer elaborates to add clarity.
② The writer adds an effect.

Publishing and Presenting

Informative Poster Write the question your essay answers at the top of a big posterboard. Then, use visuals and captions to answer the question based on the information in your essay. Display your poster somewhere in your school.

Talk Show Imagine that your topic is the subject for a talk show. Work with a partner, taking turns being the talk-show host and the guest expert. Answer questions about your topic. Then, ask questions about your partner's topic. Videotape your show if you can.

848 ◆ *Myths, Legends, and Folk Tales*

Real-World Reading Skills Workshop

Evaluating an Argument

Strategies for Success

An argument is more than just a quarrel between people. For example, a written argument in a book or a magazine is a formal presentation of an opinion. When a lawyer makes closing statements in a court case, he or she is presenting an argument. Here are some strategies for evaluating the strength of an argument:

Evaluate the Balance Between Logic and Emotion Both logic and emotion play important roles in argument because they are important in how people think. Logical arguments use reasoning to outline an argument clearly. Logical arguments may include pros and cons that need to be considered. An emotional argument offers the writer's feelings on a topic. Although emotional points have merit, an argument that uses only emotional points is usually weak. As you consider the strength of a writer's opinion, look to see that the argument—whether logical or emotional—is supported by reason.

Look for Backup A strong argument will back up its claims with supporting information. This might be in the form of facts, statistics, illustrations, or quotes. For example, the argument that "everybody wants curbside recycling" would be weak unless it offered support. Quotes from residents, poll results, or studies conducted by outside researchers would provide support for the argument.

Apply the Strategies

Read the following persuasive argument. Then, answer the questions that follow.

> Michael Jordan is the best basketball player in the history of the game. In 1998, his team, the Chicago Bulls, beat the Utah Jazz in a six-game championship series. It was the second time in ten years that the team won three championships in a row!
>
> They couldn't have done it without Jordan. His playing was breathtaking, even after 13 years in the league. In the last game of the series, he scored 45 of the Bulls' 87 points and was named the most valuable player of the championship series. That must have been an easy decision.
>
> There have been many other great players in the history of the game, but none have had the combination of skills, power, know-how, and drive of Michael Jordan.

1. What point does the argument make?
2. What does it offer for support?
3. (a) What details appeal to emotion? (b) What details appeal to logic?
4. (a) Overall, do you think the writer presents a strong argument? (b) How could it be stronger?

✔ *Here are other situations in which you'll need to evaluate a written argument:*
- ▶ Information about an election issue
- ▶ Critique of a book or a movie
- ▶ Newspaper editorial

While an end mark signals a full stop, a **comma** signals a brief pause.

Commas With Interrupters Commas are used to set off interrupters. These are words and phrases that interrupt the flow of a sentence to add information that is not essential to the meaning of the sentence. Commas separate these words from the rest of the sentence. (See page 817.)

Kinds of Interrupters:	
Names of People Being Addressed	I warn you, *Ixtla,* rethink your plan.
Common Expressions	You'll regret your choice, *I believe.*

Commas With a Series Use commas to separate three or more words, phrases, or clauses in a series. (See page 836.)

Series of Words: The Cinderella tale is told in *Europe, North America,* and *Africa.*

Series of Phrases: It is told to *teach a lesson, pass on values,* and *entertain children.*

Series of Clauses: It's interesting to compare *how the stories differ, how they are the same,* and *what each story says about the culture that tells it.*

Practice 1 Write the following sentences, adding commas to set off interrupters.

1. Yeh-Shen of course was blessed with joy.

2. Many women in the Algonquin Cinderella story on the other hand did not find happiness.

3. These stories many believe are worth comparing.

4. Both of them it seems contain evil characters and good ones.

5. Please tell us Mr. Thurber why the princess chose as she did.

Practice 2 On your paper, write the following sentences, adding commas to separate items listed in a series.

1. Popocatepetl and Ixtlaccihuatl loved each other were committed to each other and died for their beliefs.

2. Ixtla asked begged and pleaded with her father to reconsider his decision.

3. The emperor announced that warriors would compete for Ixtla's hand the leadership of the kingdom and the chance at power.

4. Some warriors were jealous short-sighted and mean-spirited.

5. When Popo learned what truly happened, he wondered who could be so cruel why Ixtla lost faith and what he should do with his life.

Grammar in Writing

✔ *Commas in a series can be critical to a correct reading. Notice that the following instructions are unclear when commas are omitted:*

Confusing: Review A B and C.

Could mean: Review AB and review C.
    or
    Review A, review B, and review C.

Clear: Review A, B, and C.

In your writing, use commas to separate items in a series.

PART 2 Myths and Fables From Ancient Greece

All the evils flying forth into the world on the opening of *Pandora's box,* colored engraving, 19th-century

Guide for Reading

Meet the Authors:

Olivia E. Coolidge (1908–   )

Although she is best known for writing biographies, Olivia Coolidge has also written a number of books on myths from ancient Greece, Rome, and Egypt.

Anne Terry White (1896–1980)

Anne Terry White was an authority on ancient Greece. She shares this knowledge in retelling the myth of "Demeter and Persephone." White also explored science, biography, and other topics in her many books for children and young adults.

Jay Macpherson (1931–   )

Jay Macpherson is best known for her poetry, which celebrates the power of imagination. Because her poems feature many symbols from myths and legends, it's no surprise that Macpherson has also written a retelling of the Greek myth "Narcissus." Although born in England, Jay Macpherson has lived most of her life in Canada.

Josephine Preston Peabody (1874–1922)

Josephine Preston Peabody was a quick starter. She began writing at thirteen and published her first book—*Old Greek Folk Stories*—when she was twenty-three. "Icarus and Daedalus" is from this collection. Peabody went on to write many poems and plays.

◆ LITERATURE AND YOUR LIFE

CONNECT YOUR EXPERIENCE

You may know stories—either true or made up—about people who have suffered the consequences of thinking too highly of themselves. As you'll learn from these myths, the ancient Greeks believed that a person was almost sure to be punished for being overly proud or arrogant.

THEMATIC FOCUS: Lessons Learned

Sometimes knowledge comes at a price. In these myths, the characters learn their lessons the hard way. As you read, think about easier ways they could have learned the same lessons.

◆ Background for Understanding

LITERATURE

Each of these myths comes from ancient Greece, where people believed in a complex collection of gods and goddesses. The supreme god was Zeus. Zeus ruled with his wife, Hera, from atop Mount Olympus. Beneath Zeus in rank were many lesser gods and goddesses, each linked to ideas or qualities in nature. For example, the goddess Demeter protected the harvest. The god Apollo was linked to poetry, music, and the sun.

◆ Build Vocabulary

WORD ROOTS: -domin-

In "Demeter and Persephone," you'll encounter the word *dominions*. Based on the root -*domin*-, meaning "master," *dominions* means "regions over which someone rules."

WORD BANK

Which of these words from the myths do you think is the opposite of *persuade*? Check the Build Vocabulary boxes to see if you're correct.

mortal
dissuade
dominions
avenging
deluded
lament
vacancy
sustained

Phaëthon, Son of Apollo
◆ Demeter and Persephone ◆
Narcissus ◆ Icarus and Daedalus

Le Char D'Apollon (Apollo's Chariot) (detail), Odilon Redon, Musée D'Orsay, Paris/Giraudon, Paris

◆ Literary Focus

MYTH

Since time began, people have tried to understand the world around them—from how it began to the origins of fire. To help them do so, ancient peoples created **myths,** stories about gods and heroes that explain natural occurrences and express beliefs about right and wrong. Built on an imaginative understanding of nature, myths make sense to us because they explain the world in human terms. In these myths, for example, you will learn how the Greeks explained the sun's daily travel across the sky, the season of winter, and the risks of human pride.

◆ Reading Strategy

PREDICT

In some myths, characters get into trouble because they happen to be in the wrong place at the wrong time. Most of the time, however, a character's troubles are the result of his or her own actions. As you read, look for clues about what is going to happen and **predict,** or make educated guesses about, where events will lead. Then, read on to see if your predictions were correct. Use a chart like the one below to record clues and your predictions based on these clues.

Clue	Prediction

PHAËTHON, SON OF APOLLO

Olivia E. Coolidge

The Chariot of Phaëthon racing through the skies, Copper engraving, 1606

Though Apollo always honored the memory of Daphne she was not his only love. Another was a <u>mortal</u>, Clymene,[1] by whom he had a son named Phaëthon.[2] Phaëthon grew up with his mother, who, since she was mortal, could not dwell in the halls of Olympus[3] or in the palace of the sun. She lived not far from the East in the land of Ethiopia, and as her son grew up, she would point to the place where Eos,[4] goddess of the dawn, lighted up the sky and tell him that there his father dwelt. Phaëthon loved to boast of his divine father as he saw the golden chariot riding high through the air. He would remind his comrades of other sons of gods and mortal women who, by virtue of their great deeds, had themselves become gods at last. He must always be first in everything, and in most things this was easy, since he was in truth stronger, swifter, and more daring than the others. Even if he were not victorious, Phaëthon always claimed to be first in honor. He could never bear to be beaten, even if he must risk his life in some rash way to win.

Most of the princes of Ethiopia willingly paid Phaëthon honor, since they admired him greatly for his fire and beauty. There was one boy, however, Epaphos,[5] who was rumored to be a child of Zeus himself. Since this was not certainly proved, Phaëthon chose to disbelieve it and to demand from Epaphos the deference that he obtained from all others. Epaphos was proud too, and one day he lost his temper with Phaëthon and turned on him, saying, "You are a fool to believe all that your mother tells you. You are all swelled up with false ideas about your father."

Crimson with rage, the lad rushed home to his mother and demanded that she prove to him the truth of the story that she had often told. "Give me some proof," he implored her, "with which I can answer this insult of Epaphos. It is a matter of life and death to me, for if I cannot, I shall die of shame."

"I swear to you," replied his mother solemnly, "by the bright orb of the sun itself that you are his son. If I swear falsely, may I never look on the sun again, but die before the next time he mounts the heavens. More than this I cannot do, but you, my child, can go to the eastern palace of Phoebus[6] Apollo—it lies not far away—and there speak with the god himself."

The son of Clymene leaped up with joy at his mother's words. The palace of Apollo was indeed not far. It stood just below the eastern horizon, its tall pillars glistening with bronze and gold. Above these it was white with gleaming ivory, and the great doors were flashing silver, embossed with pictures of earth, sky, and sea, and the gods that dwelt therein. Up the steep hill and the bright steps climbed Phaëthon, passing unafraid through the silver doors, and stood in the presence of the sun. Here at last he was forced to turn away his face, for Phoebus sat in state on his golden throne. It gleamed with emeralds and precious stones, while on the head of the god was a brilliant diamond crown upon which no eye could look undazzled.

Phaëthon hid his face, but the god had recognized his son, and he spoke kindly,

---

1. **Clymene** (klim´ ə nē)
2. **Phaëthon** (fā´ ə tän)
3. **Olympus** (ō lim´ pəs): Mountain in northern Greece that was known as the home of the gods.
4. **Eos** (ē´ äs)
5. **Epaphos** (ep´ ə fəs)

6. **Phoebus** (fē´ bəs): Means "bright one" in Greek.

◀ Critical Viewing Basing your answer on the details in this illustration, what can you infer about the settings, characters, and events of this myth? [Infer]

◆ **Build Vocabulary**
mortal (môr´ təl) n.: Being who must eventually die

asking him why he had come. Then Phaëthon plucked up courage and said, "I come to ask you if you are indeed my father. If you are so, I beg you to give me some proof of it so that all may recognize me as Phoebus' son."

The god smiled, being well pleased with his son's beauty and daring. He took off his crown so that Phaëthon could look at him, and coming down from his throne, he put his arms around the boy, and said, "You are indeed my son and Clymene's, and worthy to be called so. Ask of me whatever thing you wish to prove your origin to men, and you shall have it."

Phaëthon swayed for a moment and was dizzy with excitement at the touch of the god. His heart leaped; the blood rushed into his face. Now he felt that he was truly divine, unlike other men, and he did not wish to be counted with men any more. He looked up for a moment at his radiant father. "Let me drive the chariot of the sun across the heavens for one day," he said.

◆ Literary Focus
How do the Greeks explain the sun's daily travel across the sky?

Apollo frowned and shook his head. "I cannot break my promise, but I will dissuade you if I can," he answered. "How can you drive my chariot, whose horses need a strong hand on the reins? The climb is too steep for you. The immense height will make you dizzy. The swift streams of air in the upper heaven will sweep you off your course. Even the immortal gods could not drive my chariot. How then can you? Be wise and make some other choice."

The pride of Phaëthon was stubborn, for he thought the god was merely trying to frighten him. Besides, if he could guide the sun's chariot, would he not have proved his right to be divine rather than mortal? For that he would risk his life. Indeed, once he had seen Apollo's splendor, he did not wish to go back and live among men.

Therefore, he insisted on his right until Apollo had to give way.

When the father saw that nothing else would satisfy the boy, he bade the Hours bring forth his chariot and yoke the horses. The chariot was of gold and had two gold-rimmed wheels with spokes of silver. In it there was room for one man to stand and hold the reins. Around the front and sides of it ran a rail, but the back was open. At the end of a long pole there were yokes for the four horses. The pole was of gold and shone with precious jewels: the golden topaz, the bright diamond, the green emerald, and the flashing ruby. While the Hours were yoking the swift, pawing horses, rosy-fingered Dawn hastened to the gates of heaven to draw them open. Meanwhile Apollo anointed his son's face with a magic ointment, that he might be able to bear the heat of the fire-breathing horses and the golden chariot. At last Phaëthon mounted the chariot and grasped the reins, the barriers were let down, and the horses shot up into the air.

At first the fiery horses sped forward up the accustomed trail, but behind them the chariot was too light without the weight of the immortal god. It bounded from side to side and was dashed up and down. Phaëthon was too frightened and too dizzy to pull the reins, nor would he have known anyway whether he was on the usual path. As soon as the horses felt that there was no hand controlling them, they soared up, up with fiery speed into the heavens till the earth grew pale and cold beneath them. Phaëthon shut his eyes, trembling at the dizzy, precipitous height. Then the horses dropped down, more swiftly than a falling stone, flinging themselves madly from side to side in panic because they

◆ **Build Vocabulary**

dissuade (di swād´) v.: Advise someone against an action

were masterless. Phaëthon dropped the reins entirely and clung with all his might to the chariot rail. Meanwhile as they came near the earth, it dried up and cracked apart. Meadows were reduced to white ashes, cornfields smoked and shriveled, cities perished in flame. Far and wide on the wooded mountains the forests were ablaze, and even the snowclad Alps were bare and dry. Rivers steamed and dried to dust. The great North African plain was scorched until it became the desert that it is today. Even the sea shrank back to pools and caves, until dried fishes were left baking upon the white-hot sands. At last the great earth mother called upon Zeus to save her from utter destruction, and Zeus hurled a mighty thunderbolt at the unhappy Phaëthon, who was still crouched in the chariot, clinging desperately to the rail. The dart cast him out, and he fell flaming in a long trail through the air. The chariot broke in pieces at the mighty blow, and the maddened horses rushed snorting back to the stable of their master, Apollo.

Unhappy Clymene and her daughters wandered over the whole earth seeking the body of the boy they loved so well. When they found him, they took him and buried him. Over his grave they wept and could not be comforted. At last the gods in pity for their grief changed them into poplar trees, which weep with tears of amber in memory of Phaëthon.

Guide for Responding

◆ LITERATURE AND YOUR LIFE

Reader's Response Have you ever regretted that you didn't take someone's advice? Explain.

Thematic Focus Why do you think Phaëthon rejects Apollo's advice and has to learn his lesson from personal experience?

Journal Writing Phaëthon insists on driving his father's chariot. In a journal entry, explain what you might have wished for in a similar situation.

☑ Check Your Comprehension

1. Why does Phaëthon go to Apollo's palace?
2. Why does Apollo urge Phaëthon to choose a different wish?
3. What is Phaëthon's secret reason for his request?
4. What is the result of this request?
5. What natural features are explained in this myth?

◆ Critical Thinking

INTERPRET

1. What does Phaëthon's need to "always be first in everything" reveal about his character? **[Infer]**
2. Describe two ways that Phaëthon displays his pride. **[Connect]**
3. How might this story have been different if Phaëthon had resembled his father less? **[Speculate]**
4. What lessons does this myth teach? **[Draw Conclusions]**

APPLY

5. Besides refusing to grant Phaëthon's request, how might Apollo have avoided his son's tragic end? **[Modify]**

EXTEND

6. How do modern scientists explain the sun's movement across the sky? **[Science Link]**

DEMETER
AND
PERSEPHONE

Anne Terry White

Demeter Mourning for Persephone, 1906, Evelyn de Morgan, The De Morgan Foundation, London

▲ **Critical Viewing** What symbols in this painting convey
Demeter's role as goddess of the harvest? **[Analyze]**

Deep under Mt. Aetna, the gods had buried alive a number of fearful, fire-breathing giants. The monsters heaved and struggled to get free. And so mightily did they shake the earth that Pluto, the king of the underworld, was alarmed.

"They may tear the rocks asunder and leave the realm of the dead open to the light of day," he thought. And mounting his golden chariot, he went up to see what damage had been done.

Now the goddess of love and beauty, fair Aphrodite,[1] was sitting on a mountainside playing with her son, Eros.[2] She saw Pluto as he drove around with his coal-black horses and she said:

"My son, there is one who defies your power and mine. Quick! Take up your darts! Send an arrow into the breast of that dark monarch. Let him, too, feel the pangs of love. Why should he alone escape them?"

At his mother's words, Eros leaped lightly to his feet. He chose from his quiver[3] his sharpest and truest arrow, fitted it to his bow, drew the string, and shot straight into Pluto's heart.

The grim King had seen fair maids enough in the gloomy underworld over which he ruled. But never had his heart been touched. Now an unaccustomed warmth stole through his veins. His stern eyes softened. Before him was a blossoming valley, and along its edge a charming girl was gathering flowers. She was Persephone,[4] daughter of Demeter,[5] goddess of the harvest. She had strayed from her companions, and now that her basket overflowed with blossoms, she was filling her apron with lilies and violets. The god looked at Persephone and loved her at once. With one sweep of his arm he caught her up and drove swiftly away.

"Mother!" she screamed, while the flowers fell from her apron and strewed the ground. "Mother!"

And she called on her companions by name. But already they were out of sight, so fast did Pluto urge the horses on. In a few moments they were at the River Cyane.[6] Persephone struggled, her loosened girdle[7] fell to the ground, but the god held her tight. He struck the bank with his trident.[8] The earth opened, and darkness swallowed them all—horses, chariot, Pluto, and weeping Persephone.

From end to end of the earth Demeter sought her daughter. But none could tell her where Persephone was. At last, worn out and despairing, the goddess returned to Sicily. She stood by the River Cyane, where Pluto had cleft[9] the earth and gone down into his own <u>dominions</u>.

Now a river nymph[10] had seen him carry off his prize. She wanted to tell Demeter where her daughter was, but fear of Pluto kept her dumb. Yet she had picked up the girdle Persephone had dropped, and this the nymph wafted[11] on the waves to the feet of Demeter.

The goddess knew then that her daughter was gone indeed, but she did not suspect Pluto of carrying her off. She laid the blame on the innocent land.

---

6. **River Cyane** (sī´ an): A river in Sicily, an island just south of Italy.
7. **girdle** (gər´ dəl) *n*.: Belt or sash for the waist.
8. **trident** (trīd´ ənt) *n*.: Spear with three points.
9. **cleft** (kleft) *v*.: Split or opened.
10. **river nymph** (nimf): Goddess living in a river.
11. **wafted** (wäft´ əd) *v*.: Carried.

◆ **Build Vocabulary**

dominions (də min´ yənz) *n*.: Regions over which someone rules

---

1. **Aphrodite** (af´ rə dīt´ ē)
2. **Eros** (er´ äs): In Greek mythology, the god of love. identified by the Romans with Cupid.
3. **quiver** (kwiv´ ər) *n*.: Case for arrows.
4. **Persephone** (pər sef´ ə nē)
5. **Demeter** (di mēt´ ər)

NARCISSUS

Jay Macpherson

As beautiful as Adonis[1] was the ill-fated Narcissus,[2] who from his childhood was loved by all who saw him but whose pride would let him love no one in return. At last one of those who had hopelessly courted him turned and cursed him, exclaiming: "May he suffer as we have suffered! May he too love in vain!" The avenging goddess Nemesis[3] heard and approved this prayer.

There was nearby a clear pool, with shining silvery waters. No shepherd had ever come there, nor beast nor bird nor falling branch marred its surface: the grass grew fresh and green around it, and the sheltering woods kept it always cool from the midday sun.

Here once came Narcissus, heated and tired from the chase, and lay down by the pool to drink. As he bent over the water, his eyes met the eyes of another young man, gazing up at him from the depth of the pool. Deluded by his reflection, Narcissus fell in love with the beauty that was his own. Without thought of food or

Narcissus at the Spring, Caravaggio, Scala

◆ **Reading Strategy**
What do you predict will happen to Narcissus because of his vanity and pride?

▲ **Critical Viewing** What personality traits does this painting of Narcissus convey? Explain. **[Interpret]**

rest he lay beside the pool addressing cries and pleas to the image, whose lips moved as he spoke but whose reply he could never catch. Echo came by, the most constant of his disdained lovers. She was a nymph who had once angered Hera, the wife of Zeus, by talking too much, and in consequence was deprived of the use of her tongue for ordinary conversation: all she could do was repeat the last words of others. Seeing

---

1. **Adonis** (ə dän′ is): Handsome young man loved by Aphrodite, the goddess of love.
2. **Narcissus** (när sis′ əs)
3. **Nemesis** (nem′ ə sis)

Narcissus lying there, she pleaded with him in his own words. "I will die unless you pity me," cried Narcissus to his beloved. "Pity me," cried Echo as vainly to hers. Narcissus never raised his eyes to her at all, though she remained day after day beside him on the bank, pleading as well as she was able. At last she pined away, withering and wasting with unrequited[4] love, till nothing was left of her but her voice, which the traveler still hears calling unexpectedly in woods and waste places.

As for the cruel Narcissus, he fared no better. The face that looked back at him from the water became pale, thin and haggard,[5] till at last poor Echo caught and repeated his last "Farewell!" But when she came with the other nymphs to lament over his body, it was nowhere to be found. Instead, over the pool bent a new flower, white with a yellow center, which they called by his name. From this flower the Furies, the avengers of guilt, twist garlands to bind their hateful brows.

---

4. **unrequited** (un ri kwīt′ əd) *adj.*: Unreturned.
5. **haggard** (hag′ ərd) *adj.*: Looking worn from grief or illness.

◆ **Build Vocabulary**

avenging (ə venj′ iŋ) *adj.*: Taking revenge for an injury or wrong

deluded (di lōōd′ əd) *adj.*: Fooled; misled

lament (lə ment′) *v.*: Express deep sorrow for; mourn

Guide for Responding

◆ **LITERATURE AND YOUR LIFE**

Reader's Response Do you think Narcissus receives a fitting punishment? Why or why not?

Thematic Focus In this myth, Narcissus pays a huge price to learn his lesson. How else might Narcissus have been taught to love others?

Journal Writing Write about a time when you were proud of your skills or personal qualities. How did your pride affect the situation?

☑ **Check Your Comprehension**

1. What does Narcissus do that causes him to be cursed?
2. How does Narcissus finally fall in love?
3. In what way has Echo's voice been changed and why?
4. How are Echo and Narcissus changed at the end of the myth?

◆ **Critical Thinking**

INTERPRET

1. Why is it appropriate that Narcissus becomes a flower? **[Interpret; Support]**
2. Explain how the myth's effect would be different if Narcissus simply died, without undergoing a magical change. **[Speculate]**
3. What does this myth suggest about the risks of human pride? **[Draw Conclusions]**
4. What two facts of nature are explained by this myth? **[Connect]**

APPLY

5. Do you think there is a little bit of Narcissus in each of us? Explain. **[Relate; Generalize]**

COMPARE LITERARY WORKS

6. Which of these myths—"Phaëthon, Son of Apollo," "Demeter and Persephone," or "Narcissus"—offers the most appealing explanation of a natural occurrence? **[Evaluate]**

Daedalus and Icarus, French colored engraving, 1660

ICARUS *and* DAEDALUS

Josephine Preston Peabody

Among all those mortals who grew so wise that they learned the secrets of the gods, none was more cunning[1] than Daedalus.[2]

He once built, for King Minos of Crete,[3] a wonderful Labyrinth[4] of winding ways so cunningly tangled up and twisted around that, once inside, you could never find your way out again without a magic clue. But the king's favor veered[5] with the wind, and one day he had his master architect imprisoned in a tower. Daedalus managed to escape from his cell; but it seemed impossible to leave the island, since every ship that came or went was well guarded by order of the king.

At length, watching the sea-gulls in the air—the only creatures that were sure of liberty—he thought of a plan for himself and his young son Icarus,[6] who was captive with him.

1. **cunning** (kun´ iŋ) *adj.*: Skillful; clever.
2. **Daedalus** (ded´ əl əs)
3. **King Minos** (mī´ nəs) **of Crete**: King Minos was a son of the god Zeus. Crete is a Greek island in the eastern Mediterranean Sea, southeast of Greece.
4. **Labyrinth** (lab´ ə rinth´) *n.*: Maze.
5. **veered** (vird) *v.*: Changed directions.
6. **Icarus** (ik´ ə rəs)

◀ **Critical Viewing** Use the title of this myth, your knowledge of Greek mythology, and this illustration to predict what will happen to the two mortals in the story. **[Predict]**

Little by little, he gathered a store of feathers great and small. He fastened these together with thread, molded them in with wax, and so fashioned two great wings like those of a bird. When they were done, Daedalus fitted them to his own shoulders, and after one or two efforts, he found that by waving his arms he could winnow[7] the air and cleave it, as a swimmer does the sea. He held himself aloft, wavered this way and that with the wind, and at last, like a great fledgling,[8] he learned to fly.

Without delay, he fell to work on a pair of wings for the boy Icarus, and taught him carefully how to use them, bidding him beware of rash adventures among the stars. "Remember," said the father, "never to fly very low or very high, for the fogs about the earth would weigh you down, but the blaze of the sun will surely melt your feathers apart if you go too near."

For Icarus, these cautions went in at one ear and out by the other. Who could remember to be careful when he was to fly for the first time? Are birds careful? Not they! And not an idea remained in the boy's head but the one joy of escape.

The day came, and the fair wind that was to set them free. The father bird put on his wings, and, while the light urged them to be gone, he waited to see that all was well with Icarus, for the two could not fly hand in hand. Up they rose, the boy after his father. The hateful ground of Crete sank beneath them; and the country folk, who caught a glimpse of them when they were high above the treetops, took it for a vision of the gods—Apollo, perhaps, with Cupid after him.

At first there was a terror in the joy. The wide vacancy of the air dazed them—a glance downward made their brains reel.

But when a great wind filled their wings, and Icarus felt himself sustained, like a halcyon bird[9] in the hollow of a wave, like a child uplifted by his mother, he forgot everything in the world but joy. He forgot Crete and the other islands that he had passed over: he saw but vaguely that wingèd thing in the distance before him that was his father Daedalus. He longed for one draft of flight to quench the thirst of his captivity: he stretched out his arms to the sky and made towards the highest heavens.

Alas for him! Warmer and warmer grew the air. Those arms, that had seemed to uphold him, relaxed. His wings wavered, drooped. He fluttered his young hands vainly—he was falling—and in that terror he remembered. The heat of the sun had melted the wax from his wings; the feathers were falling, one by one, like snowflakes; and there was none to help.

He fell like a leaf tossed down the wind, down, down, with one cry that overtook Daedalus far away. When he returned, and sought high and low for his poor boy, he saw nothing but the birdlike feathers afloat on the water, and he knew that Icarus was drowned.

The nearest island he named Icaria, in memory of the child; but he, in heavy grief, went to the temple of Apollo in Sicily, and there hung up his wings as an offering. Never again did he attempt to fly.

> ◆ **Reading Strategy**
> Predict what will happen as the result of Icarus' failure to follow his father's instructions.

9. **halcyon** (hal´ sē ən) **bird** n.: Legendary bird, identified with the kingfisher, which could calm the sea by resting on it.

◆ **Build Vocabulary**
vacancy (vā´ kən sē) n.: Emptiness
sustained (sə stānd´) adj.: Supported

7. **winnow** (win´ ō) v.: Beat as with wings.
8. **fledgling** (flej´ liŋ) n.: Young bird.

Beyond Literature

Art Connection

Leonardo da Vinci's Flying Machines Daedalus wasn't the only man to ever attempt flight. People have wanted to fly since the beginning of time. In the 1440's, Italian artist and inventor Leonardo da Vinci worked long and hard to design a human flying machine. He sketched wings that could attach to a person, who would then generate power by flapping his or her arms. In time, Da Vinci gave up on human-powered flight and began to design other flying machines, such as the flying screw, a predecessor of today's helicopter.

Cross-Curricular Connection
Sketch Your Way to the Sky Forget about airplanes and rockets—invent your own flying machine. As you plan your machine, consider the story of Icarus and Daedalus. Think about how the weight of fog affects Icarus' flight and what happens when air can penetrate his wings. Explore different ways to power your machine. Then, sketch your ideas and build your machine from clay, balsa wood, or another medium. Display your finished model, along with those of classmates, in a school hallway.

Guide for Responding

◆ LITERATURE AND YOUR LIFE

Reader's Response In the same situation, would you have done what Icarus did? Why or why not?

Thematic Focus Do you think that Daedalus was punished by the gods for taking too much pride in his own cleverness? Explain.

Sketch Make a sketch of Icarus—either in his moment of joyful flight or as he realizes his mistake.

☑ Check Your Comprehension

1. Where is Daedalus when the story begins?
2. How does Daedalus plan to escape?
3. Who is Icarus?
4. Summarize the warning Daedalus gives to Icarus.
5. What happens to Icarus at the end of the myth?

◆ Critical Thinking

INTERPRET
1. In what ways does Daedalus display his "cunning"? **[Analyze]**
2. What does Daedalus reveal about himself in his words to his son? **[Infer]**
3. Icarus flies too close to the sun. What do his actions reveal about his character? **[Infer]**
4. Compare and contrast the reactions of Icarus and Daedalus to the experience of flying. **[Compare and Contrast]**
5. What lesson does this myth teach? **[Draw Conclusions]**

APPLY
6. What does the myth suggest about the way people change as they age? **[Generalize]**

EXTEND
7. To what modern-day professions would Icarus and Daedalus be well suited? Explain. **[Career Link]**

Guide for Responding (continued)

◆ Reading Strategy

PREDICT

By putting together the clues in a story or myth, you can **predict,** or make educated guesses about, what will happen next.

1. What clues in "Demeter and Persephone" helped you predict the ending of the myth?
2. How did the personality traits of both Phaëthon and Narcissus provide clues about their fates?
3. How does Daedalus' warning to Icarus provide a clue about Icarus' fate?

◆ Build Vocabulary

USING THE WORD ROOT -domin-

Complete the paragraph with the listed words containing the root -domin-. Explain how the meaning, "master," occurs in each.

dominates   domain   dominant

Zeus is the ____?____ Greek god. He rules a ____?____ of lesser gods and goddesses. Each of them ____?____ a part of nature or human life.

SPELLING STRATEGY

In some words, like *dissuade,* the *sw* sound is spelled *su.* On your paper, complete the spelling of each word. Use the definitions as a guide.

1. soft and fuzzy type of leather: s _ _ de
2. to convince: pers _ _ de
3. two or more connected rooms: s _ _ te

USING THE WORD BANK

Write sentences according to the directions below. Use context to clearly demonstrate the meaning of the italicized words.

1. Use the words *mortal, dominions, dissuade,* and *avenging* to describe the relationship between the Greek gods and people.
2. Use the words *deluded* and *lament* to describe Narcissus.
3. Use the words *vacancy* and *sustained* to describe Clymene's reaction to Phaëthon's disappearance.

◆ Literary Focus

MYTH

People of many cultures have created **myths,** stories about gods or heroes, to explain natural occurrences or to express beliefs. Often in myths the explanation of natural occurrences has its roots in the actions of the gods and goddesses involved. The story "Demeter and Persephone," for example, explains why the Earth is unproductive in winter but blooms again in spring.

1. List the natural occurrences and objects that each of these myths explain.
2. Give an example from "Narcissus" and from "Phaëthon, Son of Apollo" of how a god or goddesses's emotions resulted in a natural occurrence.
3. What beliefs about the relationship between humans and gods are expressed in these myths?

◆ Build Grammar Skills

COMMAS AFTER INTRODUCTORY PHRASES

Use a comma after **introductory phrases** in sentences. The phrases may be adjectives, adverbs, prepositional phrases, participial phrases, or appositive phrases. Notice the commas Josephine Preston Peabody uses after introductory phrases:

> *Little by little,* he gathered a store of feathers....
> *Without delay,* he fell to work....

Practice On your paper, rewrite each sentence, placing a comma after the introductory phrase.

1. Deep under Mt. Aetna the gods had buried alive a number of fearful, fire-breathing giants.
2. At his mother's words Eros leaped lightly to his feet.
3. Deluded by his reflection Narcissus fell in love with the beauty that was his own.
4. Crimson with rage the lad rushed home.
5. As for the cruel Narcissus he fared no better.

Writing Application On your paper, write sentences containing these introductory phrases.

1. Before you know it
2. After a while
3. Actually

Build Your Portfolio

 ## Idea Bank

Writing

1. **News Article** Write a news article relating the events that occur in one of the myths. Make sure your article answers the reporter's basic questions: *who, what, when, where,* and *why.* **[Career Link]**

2. **Autobiography** Imagine that Icarus survived his fall and has lived for years in hiding. As the elderly Icarus, tell the story about your famous flight from your point of view.

3. **Myth** Compare and contrast two Greek myths that teach a lesson about human behavior. Use at least one myth from this grouping. Compare the lessons learned in the myths, and explain how the myths reflect the values and beliefs of ancient Greece.

Speaking and Listening

4. **Oral Reading [Group Activity]** With a small group, give a dramatic reading of a portion of one of the myths. After assigning roles, practice reading aloud the passages you've chosen. Present your group's interpretation of the myth to the class. **[Performing Arts Link]**

5. **Radio Advice Show** Using examples from these myths, create a radio advice show outlining acceptable human behavior in ancient Greece. Have a partner "phone in" advice requests or questions. **[Social Studies Link]**

Projects

6. **Model** Create a model or drawing of either Pluto's underworld or Phaëthon's chariot ride. Use any medium you wish. Let your imagination fill in details that are not supplied in the retellings of the myths. **[Art Link]**

7. **Comparison Chart** Choose one of the natural occurrences explained in these myths. Then, research the scientific explanation. Create a chart using both text and pictures to compare and contrast the two explanations. **[Science Link]**

 ## Writing Mini-Lesson

Modern Myth

The ancient Greeks created myths to explain natural occurrences. Choose a dramatic natural occurrence, such as a destructive earthquake, or a small occurrence, such as the appearance of dew on the grass. Write a modern myth about the gods or heroes—and their actions—behind this occurrence.

> **Writing Skills Focus: Use an Outline**
>
> Creating an **outline** can help you organize details and events in your myth. In your outline, each Roman numeral might cover a paragraph. Look at this outline of the first paragraph of "Phaëthon, Son of Apollo."
>
> I. Phaëthon
>   A. Son of Apollo and Clymene
>   1. Father a god
>   2. Mother a mortal
>   B. Boastful of divine father
>   1. Believes mortals can become gods

Prewriting Choose a natural occurrence, flipping through nature magazines for ideas if you like. Then, brainstorm for some ways a god could create this occurrence. For example, an earthquake might be caused by a god stamping his foot. Outline your myth using the model shown above.

Drafting Begin by identifying the natural occurrence or vividly describing human reactions to it. Then, follow your outline to write the myth in greater detail. Be sure to link a god's or hero's action to the resulting occurrence.

Revising Read your myth aloud, listening for unclear links between characters' actions and the plot. Add details or cause-and-effect words such as *because, when,* or *next* to cement these links.

> ◆ **Grammar Application**
> Make sure the introductory phrases in your myth are set off with commas.

Guide for Reading

Meet the Author:

Aesop (about 620–560 B.C.)

Aesop's fables have been enjoyed for centuries. However, we know very little about the origin of these famous stories—including who actually wrote them.

A Man of Mystery There are different theories about Aesop's identity. Some believe he was a slave who lived on the Greek island of Samos during the sixth century. Others believe that he was a spokesman who defended criminals in court. Still others believe that he was either an advisor or a riddle solver for one of the Greek kings. The most widely held theory, however, is that Aesop wasn't an actual individual at all. Rather, because certain stories in ancient Greece were told over and over, people invented an imaginary author for them.

What We Do Know About Aesop's Fables About 200 years after Aesop's supposed death, a fellow Greek created the first written version of the tales. In the centuries that have followed, the fables have remained very popular and have been enjoyed by people all over the world.

◆ LITERATURE AND YOUR LIFE

CONNECT YOUR EXPERIENCE

Some stories grab our attention—and our hearts—because they tell about an idea or experience we can all understand. This is true of Aesop's fables, including the ones you're about to read. It is the unusual quality of these stories and their messages that has made them popular for centuries.

THEMATIC FOCUS: Community Ties

Stories such as these fables provide a vehicle for communities to share common values and beliefs. As you read, think about how the morals the fables convey apply to your own community.

◆ Background for Understanding

SOCIAL STUDIES

Aesop's fables bring us a small piece of ancient Greek life. From this faraway civilization, we have inherited not only suggestions about manners and conduct, but also a framework for democracy. In Athens during the 400's B.C., men had the right to vote, to serve in an assembly, and to serve on a jury. Every year, citizens participated in the random election of a council of 500 men who debated policy and set law. Although the election of United States leaders is not random, Congress takes many of its practices from the success of Athenian government.

◆ Build Vocabulary

PREFIXES: sur-

In "The Fox and the Crow," you'll encounter the word *surpass*. Given that the prefix *sur-* means "above" or "over," it makes sense that *surpass* means "be superior to" or "be above all others."

WORD BANK

Which of these words from the fables might describe the shiny feathers of a crow?

glossy
surpass
flatterers

The Lion and the Statue ◆ The Fox and the Crow

The Lion and the Statue ◆ The Fox and the Crow

◆ Literary Focus

FABLE

A **fable** is a brief story that teaches a lesson. In Aesop's fables and in many others, the lesson or **moral** is clearly stated as a wise saying at the end of the story.

Fables are short and simple, with relatively undeveloped characters, situations, and conflicts. Fable characters are often animals that act like human beings and illustrate human failings and weaknesses. As you read, look for connections between these animals' attitudes and behaviors and the beliefs and actions of people you know. Keep a chart like the one below to record your reactions.

Behavior in Fable	Reminds Me of . . .

◆ Reading Strategy

RECOGNIZE STORYTELLER'S PURPOSE

When you **recognize a storyteller's purpose,** you can determine how best to read a story. Fables are written for two specific purposes: to teach a lesson and to entertain. As you read, notice how these fables include only those details that achieve one of these purposes. For example, be aware of how characters and situations are sketched briefly enough to set up the problem, relate the outcome, and report the moral.

The Lion and the Statue Aesop

▲ **Critical Viewing** Why would the Lion be bothered by his species' portrayal in the statue shown here? **[Speculate]**

A Man and a Lion were discussing the relative[1] strength of men and lions in general. The Man contended[2] that he and his fellows were stronger than lions by reason of their greater intelligence. "Come now with me," he cried, "and I will soon prove that I am right." So he took him into the public gardens and showed him a statue of Hercules[3] overcoming the Lion and tearing his mouth in two.

"That is all very well," said the Lion, "but proves nothing, for it was a man who made the statue."

We can easily represent things as we wish them to be.

◆ **Build Vocabulary**

glossy (glôs′ ē) *adj.*: Smooth and shiny

surpass (sər pas′) *v.*: Be superior to

flatterers (flat′ ər ərz) *n.*: Those who praise a person insincerely in order to gain something for themselves

---

1. **relative** (rel′ ə tiv) *adj.*: Related to another; comparative.
2. **contended** (kən tend′ id) *v.*: Argued.
3. **Hercules** (hʉr′ kyōō lēz′): Hero of Ancient Greek mythology known for his strength.

The Fox and the Crow

Aesop

A Fox once saw a Crow fly off with a piece of cheese in its beak and settle on a branch of a tree. "That's for me, as I am a Fox," said Master Reynard,[1] and he walked up to the foot of the tree.

"Good day, Mistress Crow," he cried. "How well you are looking today: how glossy your feathers; how bright your eye. I feel sure your voice must surpass that of other birds, just as your figure does; let me hear but one song from you that I may greet you as the Queen of Birds."

The Crow lifted up her head and began to caw her best, but the moment she opened her mouth the piece of cheese fell to the ground, only to be snapped up by Master Fox. "That will do," said he. "That was all I wanted. In exchange for your cheese I will give you a piece of advice for the future—

Do not trust flatterers."

---

1. **Master Reynard** (ren´ ərd): The fox in the medieval beast epic *Reynard the Fox*; therefore, a proper name for the fox in other stories.

Guide for Responding

◆ LITERATURE AND YOUR LIFE

Reader's Response What is your reaction to the moral of each fable? Explain.

Thematic Focus Explain how fables like these might help a community express its values, teach its members how to behave, and create a sense of community identity.

Journal Writing In your journal, write about a time—real or imagined—when someone told you a fable in order to help you understand something.

☑ Check Your Comprehension

1. Summarize the discussion in "The Lion and the Statue."
2. How does the Crow in "The Fox and the Crow" lose the cheese?

◆ Critical Thinking

INTERPRET
1. What might the statue in "The Lion and the Statue" look like if it were created by a lion? **[Deduce]**
2. In "The Fox and the Crow," how does the Fox's attitude change when he gets the piece of cheese? **[Infer]**
3. What human character traits do the characters in these fables represent? **[Draw Conclusions]**
4. How do the actions of the characters support each fable's moral? **[Connect]**

EVALUATE
5. Why might a fable with animal characters teach a lesson better than a tale with human characters? **[Make a Judgment]**

COMPARE LITERARY WORKS
6. How well does each fable teach its lesson? Consider whether or not you find the characters memorable and the lesson important. **[Make a Judgment]**

Guide for Responding (continued)

◆ Literary Focus

FABLE

A **fable** is a brief tale that teaches a lesson called a **moral**. Often, as in the fables you've just read, fables include animal characters that possess human traits.

1. What is the moral of each Aesop fable presented here?
2. Restate the moral of each fable in your own words.
3. Explain why you agree or disagree with each moral.

◆ Build Vocabulary

USING THE PREFIX sur-

The prefix *sur-* means "above" or "over." In each sentence, replace the italicized words with a *sur-* word from this list:

surrenders surprise survey

1. From the Acropolis, you can *look over* Athens.
2. Aesop's stories sometimes *take over with an unexpected reaction for* you at the end.
3. The Crow *gives over* the cheese to the Fox.

SPELLING STRATEGY

Use the ending -er to describe people who participate in a specific activity: *flatterer*. For each clue below, provide a word ending in -er.

1. One who votes
2. One who hairdresses
3. One who takes photographs
4. One who believes
5. One who writes
6. One who sings
7. One who paints
8. One who fights

USING THE WORD BANK

On your paper, write a sentence that answers each question.

1. Would a car *surpass* a bicycle in speed?
2. If you wanted *flatterers*, might you seek a fan club?
3. Would polishing a table make it *glossy*?

◆ Reading Strategy

RECOGNIZE A STORYTELLER'S PURPOSE

Recognizing a storyteller's purpose can help you get the most from these fables. Intended to teach a lesson and to entertain, these fables keep the tension light and the stories short.

1. What part of each fable best supports the storyteller's purpose of entertainment? Explain.
2. What part best supports the purpose of education? Explain.
3. In what ways would the fables be different if they were meant to persuade?

◆ Build Grammar Skills

QUOTATION MARKS

Quotation marks are punctuation marks that set off someone else's exact words. Writers use quotation marks to set off dialogue, or conversations between characters. When the dialogue appears inside a sentence, commas are used to separate the quotation. Notice how Aesop uses quotation marks to indicate that the Crow is speaking:

> Quotation marks enclose the Fox's words.
>
> "Good day, Mistress Crow," he cried.
>
> A comma separates the Fox's words from the rest of the sentence.

Practice Rewrite each sentence with correctly placed quotation marks and commas.

1. What other fables have you read? he asked.
2. I've read some modern fables by James Thurber she said. They were very funny.
3. I like the fables by La Fontaine he said.
4. My favorite, he said, is the one about not counting your chickens before they're hatched.
5. I like that one, too, she said. I also like the one about belling the cat.

Writing Application Continue the conversation between the characters from one of the fables. Make sure you use quotation marks correctly.

Build Your Portfolio

 ## Idea Bank

Writing

1. **Journal Entry** In the role of a character from one of the fables, explain what you learned from the events in the story.

2. **Fable** Choose a saying that teaches a lesson about life, and write a fable to illustrate it. Examples of possible sayings include: "Look before you leap" and "He who hesitates is lost."

3. **Fable Essay** Write an essay explaining whether or not you think that fables are useful for teaching children about proper attitudes and behaviors. Support your ideas with specific examples from actual fables.

Speaking and Listening

4. **Television Dialogue [Group Activity]** What if two characters from one of these fables decided to air their differences on a televised talk show? With two classmates, write a dialogue that lets each character explain his or her side. Remember to include a talk-show host. Decide which roles each of you will take. Then, perform your dialogue for the class. **[Performing Arts Link]**

5. **Monologue** Write and perform a monologue—a speech by one character—as either the Crow or the Lion. Talk about the lesson you learned, how you learned it, and how you can apply that lesson to your life in the future. **[Performing Arts Link]**

Projects

6. **Multicultural Fables [Group Activity]** Work with a group to collect fables from different countries. Conduct research to gather the fables. Develop a table of contents. Then, illustrate each fable. **[Social Studies Link]**

7. **Web Site Review** Go on-line to find a Web site of fables. Study its organization and content. Then, in a presentation to the class, evaluate the site. Explain what worked well and how you might improve the collection. **[Technology Link]**

 ## Writing Mini-Lesson

Introduction to a Collection of Fables

In addition to Aesop, fables have been written by many other storytellers from around the world and through the ages. Choose a group of fables—by a certain storyteller or from a specific time period or part of the world. Write an introduction to a collection of these fables.

> **Writing Skills Focus: Use Appropriate Sources**
>
> Your introduction should define the fable form and provide historical background. Find accurate information quickly by **using appropriate sources.** Try some of these:
> - Encyclopedias
> - Literary reference books such as *Benet's Reader's Encyclopedia*
> - Introductions to published fable collections

Prewriting Use note cards to record information from your source materials. Jot down the source for each fact or quotation you include in your notes.

Drafting Begin by explaining what a fable is. Then, share some historical or cultural information about the fables in your collection. Finally, tell readers why they might find these stories from other times and places easy to understand.

> ◆ **Grammar Application**
> Make sure that you have correctly placed quotation marks when quoting a source's exact words.

Revising Reread your draft for organization and content. Do your ideas flow smoothly? Will your introduction help readers understand the collection? If necessary, return to your sources for additional information. Also, confirm that you have correctly credited any sources used.

Research Report

Writing Process Workshop

One way to learn about a topic—and to share what you've learned—is to write a **research report.** In this workshop, you'll choose and narrow a topic, develop an outline, and conduct research. You'll put it all together into a finished piece of writing, complete with documentation of your sources. The following skills will help you write your report:

Writing Skills Focus

▶ **Narrow your topic** by dividing your subject into subtopics and choosing one on which to focus your report.

▶ **Use an outline** to help you organize your ideas before you begin to write. (See p. 869.)

▶ **Use appropriate sources** that supply accurate information on your topic. Cite these sources in your report. (See p. 875.)

▶ **Use a clear organization.** State your topic in a strong introduction. Offer information about your topic in the body of your report. Summarize your main points in your conclusion.

After reading the myths in this section, one student decided to research growing up in ancient Greece.

MODEL

Like middle-school students today, students in ancient Greece studied a wide variety of subjects and were taught by several different teachers. ① A *grammatistes* taught reading, writing, and arithmetic. A *kitharistes* taught poetry and music. A *paidotribes* ② taught sports.[1]

① In this body paragraph, the writer focuses on one aspect of the topic—education.

② The writer will cite the source of this information in a footnote at the bottom of the page.

Prewriting

Narrow Your Topic Some topics are so broad, you could write *several* research reports about them. For example, "Greece" is too big a topic to cover in a brief report. To narrow your topic, keep dividing it into subtopics. Then, choose the one that interests you most. If the subtopic you've chosen can stand alone as a topic, you're ready to begin.

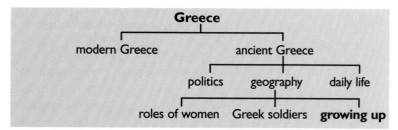

Gather Information In the library, look for information in reference books, nonfiction books, magazines, and on-line services. Consult up-to-date sources to get the most accurate information. Also, try to find the same facts in at least two different sources.

Use Note Cards Record facts and details on note cards, which should also include information about your sources. You'll need this source information when you draft your footnotes and bibliography.

Make an Outline Organize your notes into an outline. The more detailed your outline, the easier your job will be when you begin to draft. Look at this writer's working outline:

> Topic: Growing Up in Ancient Greece
>
> I. Education
>   A. Education for boys
>   1. School: subjects and teachers
>   2. Military training
>   3. Observational walks
>   B. Education for girls
>   1. Domestic training

Drafting

Write a Thesis Statement Begin with a thesis statement—a sentence that expresses the main idea of your report. Your thesis statement might be a quotation, fact, description, or question that grabs your readers' attention and makes them want to read more.

DRAFTING/REVISING

APPLYING LANGUAGE SKILLS: Sentence Variety

Your report will be more interesting to read if you vary the length and structure of your sentences. Use both long and short sentences, and include simple, compound, and complex sentences. Notice the variety in this paragraph:

Both boys and girls wore sandals. They also wore chitons, or tunics. The Doric chiton wrapped around the body, while the Ionic chiton fastened across the shoulders.

Practice Revise this paragraph by varying the sentences:

Children played board games. There were games similar to checkers, chess, and dice. Knucklebones was played with animal bones. Knucklebones was popular with girls. Children had other toys, too. They played with yo-yos, hoops, spinning tops, dolls, and balls.

Writing Application Combine shorter sentences with conjunctions and appropriate punctuation to create longer, more complex sentences.

Writer's Solution Connection Language Lab

For more practice, see the lesson on Varying Sentence Structure in the unit on Styling Sentences.

APPLYING LANGUAGE SKILLS: Bibliographic Form

In your bibliography, you will present information about each source you used:

Article:

Baxter, Zoe. "Fun and Games in Ancient Greece." *National Geographic Explorer,* December 1, 1999: 35.

Encyclopedia Entry:

"Greece (Ancient)." *The World Book Encyclopedia.* 2000 ed.

Book:

Ganeri, Anita. *Ancient Greeks.* New York: Shooting Star Press, 1994.

Interview:

Professor Dina Costalas, interviewed April 20, 2000.

CD-ROM:

"World Wonders: The Acropolis." *Planet Earth.* Macmillan Digital: 1998.

Writing Application As you research your topic, keep a list of the sources you consult. Use proper bibliographic form to create a bibliography of the sources you used. Alphabetize your entries, and then attach your bibliography to the end of your report.

Writer's Solution Connection
Writing Lab

For additional information on citing sources, consult the tutorial on Reports.

Cite Sources Whenever you use another person's exact words or when you use another person's idea, even if you rephrase it in your own words, you must credit your source. There are two ways to do this. You can cite a source in parentheses in the body of your report, or you can cite the source in a footnote at the bottom of the page. Failure to cite a source is called plagiarism—presenting someone else's ideas as your own. Plagiarism is a serious offense.

Parenthetical Citation:	"Life was very different for boys and girls in ancient Greece." (Smith, p. 98)
Footnote:	"Life was very different for boys and girls in ancient Greece."[1]
(bottom of page)	**1.** Smith, p. 98.

Write the Body Develop and support your thesis in the body of your report. Each body paragraph can focus on one aspect of your thesis. Refer to your outline as you draft.

Write the Conclusion Wrap up your report in a conclusion that summarizes your main idea and reemphasizes your thesis.

Revising

Use a Peer Reviewer Ask a classmate who doesn't know much about your subject to read your draft. Take a few minutes to discuss the answers to these questions:

▶ Is the thesis presented in an interesting way?
▶ Do the body paragraphs support the thesis statement?
▶ Is the information clearly presented? Is there enough information?
▶ Have all sources been accurately cited?

Publishing and Presenting

Class Magazine Combine your report with others into a magazine called *Everything You Always Wanted to Know.* Have volunteers write an introduction, prepare a table of contents, and create illustrations.

Presentation for a Younger Class Before a class of younger students, explain what a research report is and present your report as an example. Show students some of your sources. Encourage them to ask questions after you've finished your presentation.

Strategies for Success

Research is often the most time-consuming part of preparing a report. In your quest for information, you may look at encyclopedias, books, magazines, and newspapers. Not all sources of information, however, are equally valuable. Follow these guidelines for evaluating your sources:

Investigate the Source Suppose you find a source of information for your report, but it turns out to be a comic book. The information may not be trustworthy. Consider the reputation of a publication before accepting it as a source. For example, not all newspapers are equally reliable. A tabloid—a paper with many pictures and short, sensational stories—is generally less reliable than a large city newspaper.

Consider the Author Before deciding to use a source, investigate its author. Is he or she an expert on the subject? Look in the book for the author's biography. The book jacket may provide more information on the author. Review the author's experience and qualifications to determine whether he or she is knowledgeable enough to write on the subject.

Check the Date The information in older books might not be accurate. For example, if you look for information on Russia in a book from 1990, you might read that Russia is part of the Soviet Union. The book would not say that the Soviet Union was dissolved in 1991.

Apply the Strategies

You are writing a report about the intelligence of dolphins. Look at these sources as you answer the questions that follow:

> *The World Book Encyclopedia*, Volume D, copyright 1998
>
> *Dolphins: Geniuses of the Sea*, by John Gerald, copyright 1960 by Forest Publishing
>
> "New Research on Dolphin Communication," *The New York Times*, May 5, 1998
>
> "Man Says Dolphin Spoke to Him," *Weekly Examiner*, May 5, 1998
>
> *The Lives of Dolphins*, by Susan Mendez, copyright 1998 by Prentice Hall

1. Which source would you prefer to use—the encyclopedia or *The New York Times* article? Why?

2. Which of the newspapers would you use? Why?

3. Which of the books would you prefer to use? Why?

✔ *Here are other situations in which it is helpful to evaluate sources of information:*
  ▶ Listening to television news interviews
  ▶ Reading an advertisement
  ▶ Reading newspaper editorials

Grammar Review

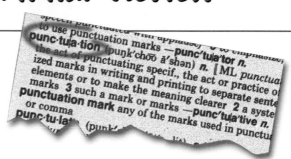

A **comma** separates introductory phrases from the rest of a sentence. (See page 868.)

Introductory Phrases:	Inside the shining palace, Phaëthon saw his father.
	Impressed by the splendor, Phaëthon wanted more.

Quotation marks enclose a person's exact words. A comma separates a direct quotation from the rest of the sentence. (See page 874.)

"You really ought to reconsider," his mother warned.

Phaëthon said, "You can't stop me!"

"You'll see," she said, "you could get hurt."

Practice 1 Rewrite the following sentences, adding commas and quotation marks where needed.

1. For years Narcissus spent his days loving only himself.

2. In their anger the gods took vengeance on him.

3. Remember said Daedalus never to fly very low or very high.

4. Mourning his son Daedalus never attempted to fly again.

5. You have no flowers here Demeter told Pluto.

6. This cannot go on said mighty Zeus.

7. Oh how can I survive without my daughter Demeter cried.

8. Happy once again Demeter welcomed Persephone with springtime and warmth.

Practice 2 Write sentences containing the following introductory words and phrases:

1. Under the setting sun

2. Gazing at his reflection

3. For many days and nights

4. Dazed by the power of the horses

5. After six paralyzing minutes

6. Grabbing the reins

Grammar in Writing

✔ When writing dialogue, begin a new paragraph with each change of speaker. Look at this example:

"Come now with me," cried the man, "and I will prove that I am right."

"Where are we going?" asked the Lion.

"I want you to look at this statue," the man said.

"That is all very well," said the Lion, "but proves nothing."

From time to time, you may be called upon to give an oral presentation. Being able to speak confidently in front of a group of people is an important skill to learn. With practice and attention to the following guidelines, you'll be able to give skillful and interesting oral presentations.

Know Your Material Before giving any type of oral presentation, take some time to review the material you will be presenting. You might spend time rehearsing—by practicing the actual words you'll use in your presentation, you may become more comfortable with the material. This will give you more confidence and make you less likely to lose your place or get confused.

Speak Up Without shouting, use a strong, clear voice that can be heard in the back of the room. Speak slowly enough for listeners to understand what you're saying.

Don't Just Stand There A speaker who appears bored and stiff won't give a successful oral presentation. Use gestures and body language to make your points. To prevent yourself from standing absolutely still, consider incorporating pictures, maps, charts, or graphs. Then, refer to these props as you speak. If you are lively and interested, your listeners will be, too.

Make Eye Contact During your presentation, make eye contact with your audience. Even if you use notes, be sure to glance up at your listeners from time to time.

Apply the Strategies

Take turns giving oral presentations to your classmates about the following topics:

1. News event about which you feel strongly
2. Report on a place you have visited
3. Your favorite relative or friend

Ask your classmates for feedback on your presentation.

Tips for Giving an Oral Presentation

✔ *To give an effective oral presentation to a small or large group, follow these strategies:*

▶ Know your material.
▶ Speak loudly and clearly enough for everybody to hear.
▶ Maintain good eye contact.
▶ Use body language where appropriate. Be lively, but remain in control.

What's Behind the Words

Vocabulary Adventures With Richard Lederer

Words From Myths

Of all the literary sources that feed into our English language, ancient mythology is one of the richest. Today, we constantly speak, hear, write, and read the names of ancient gods and goddesses, heroes and heroines—even if we don't always know it.

Words to Honor Heroes

Because many myths assign supernatural causes to natural occurrences, myths often tell about gods. The ancient gods and heroes of Greek and Roman mythology are not dead at all. Rather, they reside in our English language.

One of the greatest heroes of Greek literature was Hercules, who needed all his power to complete twelve amazingly difficult labors. Today, we use the word *herculean* to describe a mighty effort or a very challenging task.

During his journeys, Hercules met a giant named Atlas, who was condemned to support the heavens on his shoulders. Today, a book of maps is called an *atlas* because the title pages of such collections traditionally show the figure of Atlas with the world on his back.

According to Greek mythology, the Titans were the first children of Mother Earth. They were giants. Once Zeus was born to rule over Olympus, the Titans became his direct enemies. As a result, they posed a threat to all the gods and goddesses of Olympus, and the two groups were frequently at war. Today, we use the word *titanic* to describe anything that is powerful or huge.

A Tantalizing Story

Tantalus, King of Lydia, was such a vile villain that the gods banished him to Hades. In that underworld, he is condemned to stand in a sparkling pool of water with boughs of luscious fruit overhead. When he stoops to drink, the water drains away through the bottom of the pool, and when he reaches to eat, the branches of fruit sway just out of his grasp. Ever since, when something presents itself temptingly to our view but we can't have it, we say it *tantalizes* us.

ACTIVITY 1 A Greek herald in Homer's *Iliad* was a human public-address system, for his voice could be heard all over camp. Today, the adjective *stentorian* means "loud-voiced; bellowing." Locate the sources of the following words that come down to us from mythology. Be sure you know what the word means today, as well as the story of the person from which it comes.

1. flora and fauna
2. hermetic
3. mentor
4. phobia
5. fury
6. martial
7. nemesis

ACTIVITY 2 Go on a scouting expedition to find some of the other myths hiding in everyday English. With a group, complete one of the following scavenger hunts:

1. See what mythology you can find lurking behind the names of our planets or the names of flowers.
2. Take a trip to your local supermarket, and identify the mythological inspiration for many brand names.

Extended Reading Opportunities

By describing the creation of the world, the adventures of ancient gods and heroes, or the traditions of a culture, folk tales, myths, and legends share timeless stories. Continue your study of folklore with any of these titles.

Suggested Titles

In the Beginning: Creation Stories from Around the World
Virginia Hamilton
Where did we come from, and how did the world begin? These questions have puzzled every culture that ever existed. This illustrated collection of twenty-five creation myths shows some of the answers people once believed and presents a few stories some still hold to be true. Each tale reflects the diverse people who created them and the awe of the universe they shared.

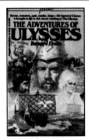

The Adventures of Ulysses
Bernard Evslin
A hero of the brutal Trojan War, Ulysses wants nothing more than to return to his wife and son. But the anger of the gods descends upon him, and he is forced off his course, hopelessly lost. A classic tale of the wandering hero, this story shows how Ulysses must struggle against the elements and battle monsters to return to those he loves.

Myths and Legends From Ancient Greece and Around the World
To extend your enjoyment of the genre, this collection provides a wide sampling of ancient folklore. Among the classical myths presented here are the story of Zeus and the creation of mankind; a retelling of Jason and the Golden Fleece; and a narrative about the wanderings of Aeneas. The collection also includes Norse myths describing the death of Balder and a variety of stories from the mythology of world cultures.

Other Possibilities

Ride With the Sun   Harold Courlander

*African Folktales: Traditional
Stories of the Black World*   Roger D. Abrahams, Editor

The Dancing Fox: Arctic Folktales   John Bierhorst, Editor

Greek Myths   Robert Graves

GLOSSARY

absurdity (ab sur´ də tē) *n.*: Nonsense; foolishness

afflicted (ə flik´ tid) *v.*: Received pain or suffering

agitated (aj´ i tāt id) *adj.*: Shaken or upset

ajar (ə jär´) *adj.*: Open

allay (a lā´) *v.*: Put to rest; calm

anguish (aŋ´ gwish) *n.*: Great suffering; agony

anonymous (ə nän´ ə məs) *adj.*: Unsigned; written by a person whose name is unknown

apprehensions (ap´ rē hen´ shənz) *n.*: Fears; anxious feelings

aptitude (ap´ tə tōōd´) *n.*: Talent; ability

arched (ärcht) *adj.*: Curved

assent (ə sent´) *n.*: Agreement

assume (ə sōōm´) *v.*: Believe to be a fact

astonish (ə stän´ ish) *v.*: Amaze

audible (ô´ də bəl) *adj.*: Loud enough to be heard

automatically (ôt´ ə mat´ ik lē) *adv.*: Without thought; by reflex

avenger (ə venj´ ər) *n.*: One who gets even for a wrong or injury

avenging (ə venj´ iŋ) *adj.*: Taking revenge for an injury or wrong

awe (ô) *n.*: Mixed feelings of fear and wonder

banish (ban´ ish) *v.*: Send away; exile

bar (bär) *v.*: To stop or prevent

base (bās) *adj.*: Lowly; inferior

benevolence (bə nev´ ə ləns) *n.*: Kindliness

besieged (bi sējd´) *adj.*: Surrounded

bewilderment (bē wil´ dər mənt) *n.*: State of confusion

bigots (big´ əts) *n.*: Narrow-minded, prejudiced people

blundered (blun´ dərd) *v.*: Made a foolish mistake

bog (bäg) *n.*: Small marsh or swamp

bound (bound) *v.*: Tied

brandished (bran´ dishd) *adj.*: Waved in a threatening way

brandishing (bran´ dish iŋ) *adj.*: Waving in a menacing way

brawny (brôn´ ē) *adj.*: Strong and muscular

brooch (brōch) *n.*: Large ornamental pin worn on a blouse or dress

brutality (brōō tal´ ə tē) *n.*: Violence; harshness

burrow (bur´ ō) *v.*: To dig a hole or tunnel, especially for shelter

buttes (byōōts) *n.*: Steep hills standing in flat land

cantankerous (kan taŋ´ kər əs) *adj.*: Quarrelsome; argumentative

cascade (kas kād´) *n.*: Waterfall or anything tumbling like water

cherished (cher´ ishd) *adj.*: Beloved; valued

chortle (chor´ təl) *n.*: Amused chuckling or snorting sound

coalition (kō ə lish´ ən) *n.*: Association or organization formed for a specific purpose

coax (kōks) *v.*: Use gentle persuasion

communal (kə myōō´ nəl) *adj.*: Shared by all

compelled (kəm peld´) *v.*: Forced

composure (kəm pō´ zhər) *n.*: Calmness of mind

compulsion (kəm pul´ shən) *n.*: A driving, irresistible force

concussion (kən kush´ ən) *n.*: Violent shaking

confidential (kän fə den´ shəl) *adj.*: Entrusted with private or secret matters

consented (kən sent´ id) *v.*: Agreed

consolation (kän´ sə lā´ shən) *n.*: Something that makes you feel better

console (kən sōl´) *v.*: Comfort; make less sad

conspired (kən spīrd´) *v.*: Planned together secretly

conspiring (kən spīr´ iŋ) *v.*: Planning in secret to do something bad

content (kən tent´) *adj.*: Happy enough

conviction (kən vik´ shən) *n.*: Belief

correspondent (kôr´ ə spän´ dənt) *n.*: Person hired by a news organization to provide news from a distant place

cremated (krē´ māt id) *v.*: Burned to ashes

croon (krōōn) *v.*: Sing or hum quietly, soothingly

crouches (krouch´ iz) *v.*: Stoops or bends low

crucial (krōō´ shəl) *adj.*: Of great importance

culprit (kul´ prit) *n.*: Guilty person

cunningly (kun´ iŋ lē) *adv.*: Cleverly

curdled (kur´ dəld) *adj.*: Thickened; clotted

currency (kur´ ən sē) *n.*: Money

dauntless (dônt´ lis) *adj.*: Fearless

debut (dā byōō´) *n.*: First performance in public

declined (dē klīnd´) *v.*: Bent or sank downward

decreed (dē krēd´) *v.*: Officially ordered

defiant (dē fī´ ənt) *adj.*: Boldly resisting

dejectedly (dē jek´ tid lē) *adv.*: Sadly; showing discouragement

delicacies (del´ i ke sēz) *n.*: Foods that are rare and tasty

deluded (di lōōd´ əd) *adj.*: Fooled; misled

deluge (del´ yōōj) *n.*: Great flood or rush of anything

denigrate (den´ ə grāt´) *v.*: Discredit; put down; belittle

desolate (des´ ə lit) *adj.*: Lonely; solitary

despondent (di spän´ dənt) *adj.*: Lacking hope; depressed

destination (des´ tə nā´ shən) *n.*: The place to which something is being sent

destitute (des´ tə tōōt´) *adj.*: Living in complete poverty

devastated (dev´ ə stā tid) *v.*: Destroyed; completely upset

devastating (dev´ əs tāt´ iŋ) *adj.*: Destructive; overwhelming

devotion (di vō´ shən) *n.*: Loyalty or deep affection

disdainful (dis dān´ fəl) *adj.*: Showing arrogance or scorn for someone considered beneath oneself

dislodge (dis läj´) *v.*: Leave a resting place

dismally (diz´ məl lē) *adv.*: Gloomily; miserably

dismayed (dis mād´) *adj.*: Afraid; without confidence

dispelled (dis peld´) *v.*: Driven away; made to disappear

dispelled (dis peld´) *v.*: Scattered and driven away; made to vanish

distinct (di stiŋkt´) *adj.*: Separate and different

distraught (dis trôt´) *adj.*: Extremely upset

domestic (dō mes´ tik) *adj.*: Of the home and family

domestic (dō mes´ tik) *n.*: Servant for the home

dominions (də min´ yənz) *n.*: Regions over which someone rules

downy (doun´ ē) *adj.*: Soft and fluffy

draggled (drag´ əld) *adj.*: Wet and dirty

ecstasy (ek´ stə sē) *n.*: Overpowering joy

edifice (ed´ ə fis) *n.*: Large structure

elective (ē lek´ tiv) *n.*: Optional course or subject in a school or college curriculum

emaciated (ē mā´ shē āt´ id) *adj.*: Extremely thin; starving

emblems (em´ bləmz) *n.*: Symbols, signs, or badges

eminent (em´ ə nənt) *adj.*: Distinguished or outstanding

emitting (ē mit´ iŋ) *adj.*: Sending out or uttering

enthralled (en thrôld´) *v.*: Fascinated; charmed

epidemic (ep´ ə dem´ ik) *n.*: Outbreak of a contagious disease

equal (ē´ kwəl) *adj.*: Of the same amount

evading (ē vād´ iŋ) *adj.*: Keeping away from or avoiding

evidently (ev´ ə dent´ lē) *adv.*: Clearly; obviously

exertion (eg zur´ shən) *n.*: Physical work

exquisite (eks kwi´ zit) *adj.*: Very beautiful, especially in a delicate way

extricate (eks´ tri kāt) *v.*: To set free; disentangle

ferocious (fə rō´ shəs) *adj.*: Fierce; savage

ferocity (fə räs´ ə tē) *n.*: Fierceness; wild force

fiasco (fē as´ cō) *n.*: Complete failure

flatterers (flat´ ər ərz) *n.*: Those who praise a person insincerely in order to gain something for themselves

flinched (flincht) *v.*: Moved back, as if away from a blow

fluent (flōō´ ənt) *adj.*: Able to write or speak easily and smoothly

flustered (flus´ terd) *adj.*: Nervous; confused

foray (fôr´ ā) *n.*: Sudden attack or raid

forlorn (fôr lôrn´) *adj.*: Alone and miserable

formidable (fôr´ mi də bəl) *adj.*: Impressive

fortitude (fôrt´ ə tōōd´) *n.*: Firm courage

frail (frāl) *adj.*: Delicate or weak

fret (fret) *v.*: Worry

furtive (fur´ tiv) *adj.*: Sneaky

gaunt (gônt) *adj.*: Thin and bony

ghastly (gast´ lē) *adv.*: Ghostlike; frightful

glossy (glôs´ ē) *adj.*: Smooth and shiny

glutted (glut´ əd) *v.*: Given more than is needed or wanted

gnarled (närld) *adj.*: Knotty and twisted

goblets (gäb´ lits) *n.*: Bowl-shaped drinking containers without handles

gourd (gôrd) *n.*: Fruit of a certain kind of plant; the dried, hollowed shell of this fruit is used as a drinking cup or dipper

gratify (grat´ i fī) *v.*: To please

grieved (grēvd) *adj.*: Saddened; overcome by grief

grisly (griz´ lē) *adj.*: Horrible

grotesquely (grō tesk´ le) *adv.*: In a strange or distorted way

gumption (gump´ shən) *n.*: Courage; enterprise

harassed (hə rast´) *adj.*: Troubled

haunches (hônch´ iz) *n.*: An animal's legs

hindered (hin´ dərd) *adj.*: Held back

hissing (his´ iŋ) *adj.*: Making a sound like a prolonged *s*

hostility (häs til´ ə tē) *n.*: Anger; unfriendliness

illuminates (i lōō´ mə nāts´) *v.*: Brightens; sheds light on

immensity (i men´ si tē) *n.*: Something extremely large or immeasurably vast

implore (im plôr´) *v.*: Ask or beg earnestly

implored (im plôrd´) *v.*: Asked or begged earnestly

impostors (im päs´ terz) *n.*: People who trick or deceive others by pretending to be what they are not

impromptu (im prämp´ tōō) *adj.*: unscheduled; unplanned

incessantly (in ses´ ənt lē) *adv.*: Without stopping

inclined (in klīnd´) *adj.*: Interested in

incomprehensible (in´ käm pri hen´ sə bəl) *adj.*: Not able to be understood

incorporate (in kôr´ pôr āt) *v.*: Form into a legal business

indignantly (in dig´ nənt lē) *adv.*: Angrily

inevitability (in ev´ ə tə bil´ i tē) *n.*: Certainty

inevitable (in ev´ ə tə bəl) *adj.*: Certain to happen

inflammatory (in flam´ ə tôr´ ē) *adj.*: Characterized by pain and swelling

interacts (in´ tər akts´) *v.*: Affects and is affected by

interloper (in´ tər lō´ pər) *n.*: Person who intrudes on another's rights or territory

interplanetary (in´ tər plan´ ə ter´ ē) *adj.*: Between planets

intimidating (in tim′ ə dāt′ iŋ) *adj.*: Causing fear

intricate (in′ tri kit) *adj.*: Complex; full of complicated detail

intrigue (in′ trēg′) *n.*: Curiosity and interest

intrigued (in trēgd′) *v.*: Fascinated

irksome (ʉrk′ səm) *adj.*: Tiresome or annoying

knell (nel) *n.*: Funeral bell

laborious (lə bôr′ ē əs) *adj.*: Taking much work or effort; difficult

laggard (lag′ ərd) *n.*: One who is slow to move or follow

lament (lə ment′) *v.*: Express deep sorrow for; mourn

landlord (land′ lôrd) *n.*: Person who keeps a rooming house, inn, etc.

loaf (lōf) *v.*: Spend time idly

loathed (lōthd) *v.*: Hated

luminary (lōō′ mə ner′ ē) *n.*: Something that gives off light

maestro (mīs′ trō) *n.*: Great musician

majestic (mə jes′ tik) *adj.*: Grand; lofty

malady (mal′ ə dē) *n.*: Illness; disease

malevolent (mə lev′ ə lənt) *adj.*: Wishing evil or harm to others

malicious (mə lish′ əs) *adj.*: Spiteful; hateful

marauders (mə rôd′ ərs) *n.*: Roaming attackers

martial (mär′ shəl) *adj.*: Suitable for war

meager (mē′ gər) *adj.*: Of poor quality; small in amount

meek (mēk) *adj.*: Timid; humble; not showing anger

melancholy (mel′ ən käl′ ē) *adj.*: Sad; gloomy

mesmerizing (mez′ mər īz′ iŋ) *adj.*: Hypnotizing

metamorphosis (met′ ə môr′ fə sis) *n.*: Change of form

methodical (mə thäd′ i kəl) *adj.*: Orderly; organized

misanthrope (mis′ ən throp′) *n.*: Person who hates or distrusts everyone

morose (mə rōs′) *adj.*: Gloomy; ill-tempered

mortal (môr′ təl) *adj.*: Being who must eventually die

mortality (môr tal′ ə tē) *n.*: The condition of being mortal; having to die eventually

mourning (môrn′ iŋ) *adj.*: Feeling sorrow for the death of a loved one

nape (nāp) *n.*: Back of the neck

nimble (nim′ bəl) *adj.*: Moving quickly and lightly

observation (äb′ zər vā′ shən) *n.*: The act of noticing details

ominous (äm′ ə nəs) *adj.*: Threatening

ordained (ôr dānd′) *v.*: Ordered; decreed

outskirts (out′ skʉrts′) *n.*: Part of a district far from the center of a city

pathetic (pə thet′ ik) *adj.*: Arousing pity, sorrow, and sympathy

pathological (path′ ə läj′ i kəl) *adj.*: Due to or related to disease

patriarch (pā′ trē ärk) *n.*: Old, dignified man

pauper (pô′ pər) *n.*: Extremely poor person

perfunctorily (per fuŋk′ tə rə lē) *adv.*: Without enthusiasm; routinely

perilous (per′ ə ləs) *adj.*: Dangerous

perpetual (pər pech′ ōō əl) *adj.*: Constant; unending

persistently (pər sist′ ənt lē) *adv.*: Firmly and steadily

pomp (pämp) *n.*: Impressive show or display

ponderous (pän′ dər əs) *adj.*: Very heavy; bulky

preen (prēn) *v.*: Dress up; show pride in one's appearance

premium (prē′ mē əm) *n.*: Additional charge

presumptuous (prē zump′ chōō əs) *adj.*: Overconfident; arrogant

prodigy (präd′ ə jē) *n.*: Child of unusually high talent

profusely (prō fyōōs′ lē) *adv.*: Freely or plentifully

prone (prōn) *adj.*: Lying face downward

prose (prōz) *n.*: Nonpoetic language

protruded (prō trōōd′ id) *v.*: Stuck out; extended

psychiatrist (sī kī′ ə trist) *n.*: Medical doctor specializing in illnesses of the mind

pummeled (pum′ əld) *v.*: Beat

pungent (pun′ jənt) *adj.*: Sharp-smelling

quarried (kwôr′ ēd) *adj.*: Carved out of the ground

quavering (kwā′ vər iŋ) *adj.*: Shaking; trembling

queried (kwir′ ēd) *v.*: Asked

radiance (rā′ dē əns) *n.*: Quality of shining brightly

radiant (rā′ dē ənt) *adj.*: Filled with light; shining brightly

rancid (ran′ sid) *adj.*: Spoiled and smelling bad

rash (rash) *adj.*: Thoughtless

realign (rē′ ə līn′) *v.*: Readjust into a straight line or into proper coordination

reconnoiter (rē kə noit′ ər) *v.*: Look around

reeds (rēdz) *n.*: Tall, slender grasses that grow in marshy land

reeled (rēld) *v.*: Fell back from a blow

refugee (ref′ yōō jē) *n.*: Person who flees home or country to seek shelter from war or cruelty

refute (ri fyōōt′) *v.*: Prove someone wrong

regime (rə zhēm′) *n.*: System or rule of government

rejuvenated (ri jōō′ və nāt′ id) *v.*: Made to feel refreshed; revitalized

relished (rel′ isht) *v.*: Especially enjoyed

reluctance (ri luk′ təns) *n.*: Unwillingness

remedy (rem′ ə dē) *n.*: Medicine or treatment that cures illness

remote (ri mōt′) *adj.*: Far away from everything else

reproach (ri prōch′) *n.*: Disgrace; blame

resilient (ri zil′ yənt) *adj.*: Springing back into shape

resumed (ri zōōmd′) *v.*: Began again; continued

retrospective (re′ trə spek′ tiv) *n.*: Look on the past

revelry (rev′ əl rē) *n.*: Celebration; noisy merrymaking

revived (ri vīvd′) *v.*: Came back to consciousness

rheumatism (rōō′ mə tiz′ əm) *n.*: Painful condition of the joints and muscles

roamed (rōmd) *v.*: Wandered

rouge (rōōzh) *n.*: Reddish cosmetic used to color cheeks

routed (rout′ əd) *v.*: Completely defeated

sage (sāj) *n.*: Very wise person

sauciness (sô′ sē nes) *n.*: Liveliness; boldness; spirit

saunter (sôn′ tər) *v.*: Walk about idly; stroll

savored (sā′ vərd) *v.*: Enjoyed

scapegoat (skāp′ gōt′) *n.*: Person or group blamed for the mistakes or crimes of others

scowl (skoul) *v.*: Lower eyebrows and corners of the mouth; look angry or irritated

sensitive (sen′ sə tiv) *adj.*: Easily hurt or irritated; touchy

serenity (sə ren′ ə tē) *n.*: Calmness

severe (sə vir′) *adj.*: Harsh

sheepishly (shēp′ ish lē) *adv.*: In a shy or embarrassed way

shuffle (shuf′ əl) *v.*: Walk with dragging feet

simultaneously (sī məl tā′ nē əs lē) *adv.*: At the same time

slackening (slak′ ən iŋ) *v.*: Easing; becoming less active

sluggishly (slug′ ish lē) *adv.*: As if lacking energy

snare (snar) *v.*: Catch or trap

solemn (säl′ əm) *adj.*: Serious; somber

spectators (spek′ tāt′ ərz) *n.*: People who watch something without taking part; onlookers

sputters (sput′ ərz) *v.*: Makes hissing or spitting sounds

squat (skwät) *adj.*: Short and heavy

stamina (stam′ ə nə) *n.*: Endurance

stanched (stônchd) *v.*: Stopped or slowed down

stern (stʉrn) *adj.*: Strict; unyielding

strife (strīf) *n.*: Trouble; conflict; struggle

strive (strīv) *v.*: Struggle

subservient (səb sʉr′ vē ənt) *adj.*: Inferior

subtle (sut′ əl) *adj.*: Delicately skillful or clever

sundered (sun′ dərd) *v.*: Broken apart

superimposed (sōō′ pər im pōzd′) *adj.*: Put or stacked on top of something else

supple (sup′ əl) *adj.*: Flexible

surged (sʉrjd) *v.*: Moved in a violent, swelling motion

surpass (sər pas′) *v.*: Be superior to

surreptitiously (sʉr′ əp tish′ əs lē) *adv.*: Secretly

sustained (sə stānd′) *adj.*: Supported

swerve (swʉrv) *n.*: Curving motion

taut (tôt) *adj.*: Tightly stretched

tawdry (tô′ drē) *adj.*: Cheap and showy; gaudy

tawny (tô′ nē) *adj.*: Tan; yellowish brown

tentatively (ten′ tə tiv lē) *adv.*: Hesitantly; with uncertainty

threadbare (thred′ ber) *adj.*: Worn; shabby

tiered (tird) *adj.*: Stacked in rows

tolerant (täl′ ər ənt) *adj.*: Free from bigotry or prejudice

torrent (tôr′ ənt) *n.*: Flood

tourniquets (tʉr′ ni kits) *n.*: Devices used to stop bleeding in an emergency, as a bandage tightly twisted to stop the flow of blood.

transformation (trans′ fər mā′ shən) *n.*: Change in condition or outward appearance

translucent (trans lōō′ sənt) *adj.*: Able to transmit light but no detail of that light

tread (tred) *v.*: Walk; dance; step

tumultuously (tōō mul′ chōō əs lē) *adv.*: Noisily and violently

unanimous (yōō nan′ ə məs) *adj.*: Based on complete agreement

uncanny (un kan′ ē) *adj.*: Strange; eerie

undaunted (ən dônt′ id) *adj.*: Not stopping because of fear or failure

unique (yōō nēk′) *adj.*: Unlike any other; singular

unravel (un rav′ əl) *v.*: Become untangled or separated

utter (ut′ ər) *v.*: Speak

vacancy (vā′ kən sē) *n.*: Emptiness

vanity (van′ ə tē) *n.*: The quality of being very proud of one's appearance

vanquished (vaŋ′ kwisht) *n.*: The person defeated (usually a verb)

virtue (vʉr′ chōō) *n.*: Moral goodness

vital (vīt′ əl) *adj.*: Necessary to life; critically important

void (void) *n.*: Total emptiness

volleyed (väl′ ēd) *v.*: Fired together

whimper (hwim′ pər) *v.*: Make low, crying sounds; complain

wielding (wēld′ iŋ) *v.*: Using with skill

wistfully (wist′ fəl lē) *adv.*: With longing

withered (with′ ərd) *adj.*: Dried up

wonderment (wun′ dər mənt) *n.*: Astonishment

wondrous (wun′ drəs) *adj.*: Extraordinary

yearned (yʉrnd) *v.*: Wanted very much

yield (yēld) *v.*: Give way to pressure or force

LITERARY TERMS HANDBOOK

ALLITERATION *Alliteration* is the repetition of initial consonant sounds. Writers use alliteration to draw attention to certain words or ideas, to imitate sounds, and to create musical effects. Shel Silverstein uses alliteration for humorous effect in the title of his poem "Sarah Cynthia Sylvia Stout," on page 405.

ALLUSION An *allusion* is a reference to a well-known person, place, event, literary work, or work of art. Understanding what a writer is saying often depends on recognizing allusions. E. E. Cummings's "goat-footed balloonMan" in the poem "in Just-," on page 404, is an allusion to Greek myths about the god Pan. Pan was a goat-footed god associated with spring.

ANECDOTE An *anecdote* is a brief story about an interesting, amusing, or strange event. Writers tell anecdotes to entertain or to make a point. For example, in "Cat on the Go," on page 382, James Herriot tells several anecdotes about the character named Oscar. Herriot tells these anecdotes to amuse the reader and to reveal Oscar's unusual personality.
See *Narration.*

ANTAGONIST An *antagonist* is a character or force in conflict with a main character, or protagonist. In "Rikki-tikki-tavi," on page 464, there are two antagonists, the cobras Nag and Nagaina. The protagonist is the mongoose, Rikki.
See *Conflict* and *Protagonist.*

ATMOSPHERE See *Mood.*

AUTOBIOGRAPHY An *autobiography* is a form of nonfiction in which a person tells his or her own life story. An autobiography may tell about the person's whole life or only a part of it. This text contains several excerpts from autobiographies, including the selections from Ernesto Galarza's *Barrio Boy,* on page 611.
See *Biography* and *Nonfiction.*

BALLAD A *ballad* is a songlike poem that tells a story, often one dealing with adventure and romance. Most ballads are written in four- to six-line stanzas and have regular rhythms and rhyme schemes. A ballad often features a refrain—a regularly repeated line or group of lines.

Originally, ballads were not written down. They were composed orally and then sung. As these early *folk ballads* passed from singer to singer, they often changed dramatically.

Many writers of the modern era have used the ballad form to create *literary ballads*—written imitations of folk ballads. The influence of the ballad tradition can be seen in Alfred Noyes's "The Highwayman," on page 300.
See *Oral Tradition* and *Refrain.*

BIOGRAPHY A *biography* is a form of nonfiction in which a writer tells the life story of another person. Biographies have been written about many famous historical and contemporary people, but they can also be written about ordinary people. An example of a biography of a famous historical person in the text is "Winslow Homer: America's Greatest Painter," on page 586. Because biographies deal with real people and real events, they are classified as nonfiction.
See *Autobiography* and *Nonfiction.*

BLANK VERSE *Blank verse* is poetry written in unrhymed iambic pentameter lines. The following lines from Robert Frost's "Birches" are written in blank verse:

> When I see birches bend to left and right
> Across the lines of straighter darker trees,
> I like to think some boy's been swinging them.

See *Meter.*

CHARACTER A *character* is a person or animal who takes part in the action of a literary work. The main character is the most important character in a story, poem, or play. A minor character is one who takes part in the action, but who is not the focus of attention.

Characters are sometimes classified as flat or round. A *flat character* is one-sided and often stereotypical. A *round character,* on the other hand, is fully developed and exhibits many traits—often both faults and virtues. Teddy's mother, in Rudyard Kipling's story "Rikki-tikki-tavi," on page 464, is an example of a flat character. In Washington Irving's "Rip Van Winkle," on page 144, the title character is round, or fully developed.

Characters can also be classified as dynamic or static. A *dynamic character* is one who changes or grows during the course of the work. A *static character* is one who does not change. Rip Van Winkle is a dynamic character, while Rip's overbearing wife is a static character.
See *Characterization, Hero/Heroine,* and *Motivation.*

CHARACTERIZATION *Characterization* is the act of creating and developing a character. Writers use two major methods of characterization—*direct* and *indirect.*

When describing a character *directly,* a writer states the character's traits, or characteristics. In "Rip Van Winkle," on page 145, Washington Irving describes Rip directly:

> He inherited, however, but little of the martial character of his ancestors. I have observed that he was a simple good-natured man; he was, moreover, a kind neighbor, and an obedient henpecked husband.

When describing a character *indirectly,* a writer depends on the reader to draw conclusions about the character's traits. Sometimes, the writer describes the character's appearance, actions, or speech. At other times, the writer tells what other participants in the story say and think about the character. The reader then draws his or her own conclusions.
See *Character* and *Motivation.*

CLIMAX See *Conflict* and *Plot.*

CONCRETE POEM A *concrete poem* is one with a shape that suggests its subject. The poet arranges the letters, punctuation, and lines to create an image, or picture, on the page. William Jay Smith's "Seal," on page 754, is a concrete poem. Its swirling shape suggests the form of a seal's body and the way the seal moves.

CONFLICT A *conflict* is a struggle between opposing forces. Conflict is one of the most important elements of stories, novels, and plays because it causes the action.

There are two kinds of conflict: external and internal. An *external conflict* is one in which a character struggles against some outside force. For example, in "A Boy and a Man," on page 210, the character Rudi struggles against nature to save the life of a man who has fallen into a crevasse.

An *internal conflict* is one that takes place within the mind of a character. The character struggles to make a decision, take an action, or overcome a feeling. For example, in "A Day's Wait," on page 72, the boy struggles with his feelings of fear and despair because he believes he is dying.
See *Plot.*

DESCRIPTION A *description* is a portrait, in words, of a person, place, or object. Descriptive writing uses images that appeal to the five senses—sight, hearing, touch, taste, and smell.
See *Image.*

DEVELOPMENT See *Plot.*

DIALECT *Dialect* is the form of a language spoken by people in a particular region or group. The English language is divided into many dialects. British English differs from American English. The English spoken in Boston differs from that spoken in Charleston, Chicago, Houston, or San Francisco. This variety adds richness to the language. Dialects differ in pronunciation, grammar, and word choice.

Writers use dialects to make their characters seem realistic. In "The Luckiest Time of All," on page 398, the narrator uses a dialect from the rural southern United States.

DIALOGUE A *dialogue* is a conversation between characters. In poems, novels, and short stories, dialogue is usually set off by quotation marks to indicate a speaker's exact words. In a play, dialogue follows the names of the characters, and no quotation marks are used.
See *Drama.*

DRAMA A *drama* is a story written to be performed by actors. Although a drama is meant to be performed, one can also read the script, or written version, and imagine the action. The script of a drama is made up of dialogue and stage directions. The *dialogue* is the words spoken by the actors. The *stage directions,* usually printed in italics, tell how the actors should look, move, and speak. They also describe the setting, sound effects, and lighting.

Dramas are often divided into parts called *acts.* The acts are often divided into smaller parts called *scenes.*

DYNAMIC CHARACTER See *Character.*

ESSAY An *essay* is a short nonfiction work about a particular subject. Most essays have a single major focus and a clear introduction, body, and conclusion.

There are many types of essays. A *narrative essay* tells a story about a real-life experience. An *expository essay* relates information or provides explanations. A *persuasive essay,* like "I Am a Native of North America," on page 615, presents and supports an opinion. Most essays contain passages that describe people, places, or objects. However, there are very few purely descriptive essays.
See *Description, Exposition, Narration,* and *Persuasion.*

EXPOSITION *Exposition* is writing or speech that explains a process or presents information. This Literary Terms Handbook is an example of exposition. So are the introductions to the selections in this text. In the plot of a story or drama, the *exposition,* or introduction, introduces the characters, setting, and basic situation.
See *Plot.*

EXTENDED METAPHOR In an *extended metaphor,* as in a regular metaphor, a subject is described as though it were something else. However, extended metaphor differs from regular metaphor in that several comparisons are made. Carl Sandburg uses extended metaphor in his poem "Fog," on page 792. The poem points out a number of similarities between fog and a cat. See *Metaphor*.

FABLE A *fable* is a brief story or poem, usually with animal characters, that teaches a lesson, or moral. The moral is usually stated at the end of the fable.

The fable is an ancient literary form found in many cultures. The fables written by Aesop, a Greek slave who lived in the sixth century B.C., are still popular with children today. Other famous writers of fables include La Fontaine, the seventeenth-century French poet, and James Thurber, the twentieth-century American humorist. See the fables by Aesop on pages 872–873.
See *Moral*.

FANTASY A *fantasy* is highly imaginative writing that contains elements not found in real life. Examples of fantasy include stories that involve supernatural elements, stories that resemble fairy tales, stories that deal with imaginary places and creatures, and science-fiction stories. In Jack Finney's "The Third Level," on page 50, traveling through time is a fantastic element.
See *Science Fiction*.

FICTION *Fiction* is prose writing that tells about imaginary characters and events. Short stories and novels are works of fiction. Some writers base their fiction on actual events and people, adding invented characters, dialogue, settings, and plots. Other writers of fiction rely on imagination alone to provide their materials.
See *Narration, Nonfiction,* and *Prose*.

FIGURATIVE LANGUAGE *Figurative language* is writing or speech that is not meant to be taken literally. The many types of figurative language are known as *figures of speech*. Common figures of speech include hyperbole, metaphor, personification, and simile. Writers use figurative language to state ideas in vivid and imaginative ways. Carl Sandburg uses figurative language to creatively describe the fog in his poem "Fog," on page 792.
See *Metaphor, Personification, Simile,* and *Symbol*.

FLASHBACK A *flashback* is a section of a literary work that interrupts the sequence of events to relate an event from an earlier time.

FLAT CHARACTER See *Character*.

FOLK TALE A *folk tale* is a story composed orally and then passed from person to person by word of mouth. Folk tales originated among people who could neither read nor write. These people entertained one another by telling stories aloud, often about heroes, adventure, magic, or romance. Eventually, modern scholars like Wilhelm and Jakob Grimm began collecting these stories and writing them down. In this way, folk tales have survived into the present day. In the United States, scholars have also collected folk tales. These tales deal with such legendary heroes as Pecos Bill, Paul Bunyan, Mike Fink, and Davy Crockett. See *Fable, Legend, Myth,* and *Oral Tradition*.

FOOT See *Meter*.

FORESHADOWING *Foreshadowing* is the use, in a literary work, of clues that suggest events that have yet to occur. Writers use foreshadowing to build their readers' expectations and to create suspense. For example, at the beginning of *The Monsters Are Due on Maple Street*, on page 698, the narrator makes the following statement:

> **NARRATOR'S VOICE.** Maple Street. Six-forty-four P.M. on a late September evening. [*A pause*] Maple Street in the last calm and reflective moment . . . before the monsters came!

The narrator's comment foreshadows, or predicts, what will happen later in the play. It leads the reader or audience to expect the arrival of monsters. Later, the reader or audience is surprised to find out who the monsters really are.

FREE VERSE *Free verse* is poetry not written in a regular rhythmical pattern, or meter. In a free verse poem, the poet is free to write lines of any length or with any number of stresses, or beats. Free verse is therefore less constraining than *metrical verse,* in which every line must have a certain length and a certain number of stresses. Walt Whitman's "Miracles," on page 262, is written in free verse.
See *Meter*.

GENRE A *genre* is a division or type of literature. Literature is commonly divided into three major genres: poetry, prose, and drama. Each major genre is in turn divided into lesser genres, as follows:

1. *Poetry:* lyric poetry, concrete poetry, dramatic poetry, narrative poetry, epic poetry
2. *Prose:* fiction (novels and short stories) and nonfiction (biography, autobiography, letters, essays, and reports)
3. *Drama:* serious drama and tragedy, comic drama, melodrama, and farce

See *Drama, Poetry,* and *Prose*.

HAIKU The *haiku* is a three-line Japanese verse form. The first and third lines of a haiku each have five syllables. The second line has seven syllables. A writer of haiku uses images to create a single vivid picture. See examples of haiku on page 756.

HERO/HEROINE A *hero* or *heroine* is a character whose actions are inspiring or noble. Often, heroes and heroines struggle mightily to overcome foes or to escape difficulties. This is true, for example, of Demeter in "Demeter and Persephone," on page 858. The most obvious examples of heroes and heroines are the larger-than-life characters in myths and legends. However, characters who are more ordinary than Demeter can also act heroically. For example, in Alfred Noyes's poem on page 300, the landlord's daughter, Bess, sacrifices her own life to save that of the highwayman. This is a heroic deed, and Bess is therefore a heroine.

HUBRIS *Hubris* is excessive pride. In "Phaëthon, Son of Apollo," on page 854, the central character is guilty of hubris.

IAMB See *Meter*.

IMAGE An *image* is a word or phrase that appeals to one or more of the five senses. Writers use images to describe how their subjects look, sound, feel, taste, and smell. In "Aunt Leaf" on page 791, Mary Oliver uses the image of a medallion to describe her companion.

IRONY *Irony* is the general name given to literary techniques that involve surprising, interesting, or amusing contradictions. In *verbal irony*, words are used to suggest the opposite of their usual meanings. In *dramatic irony*, there is a contradiction between what a character thinks and what the reader or audience knows to be true. In *irony of situation*, an event occurs that directly contradicts the expectations of the characters, the reader, or the audience.

LEGEND A *legend* is a widely told story about the past, one that may or may not have a foundation in fact. Every culture has its own legends—its familiar, traditional stories. An example of a legend is "Popocatepetl and Ixtlaccihuatl," on page 811. This legend comes from the Aztec Indians of Mexico.
See *Oral Tradition*.

LYRIC POEM A *lyric poem* is a highly musical verse that expresses the observations and feelings of a single speaker. Examples of lyric poems in the text include "Washed in Silver," on page 746, and "Winter," on page 748.

MAIN CHARACTER See *Character*.

METAPHOR A *metaphor* is a figure of speech in which something is described as though it were something else. A metaphor, like a simile, works by pointing out a similarity between two unlike things. In her poem "Life," on page 793, Naomi Long Madgett describes life with metaphors, comparing it to a watch, a toy, and a game. See *Extended Metaphor* and *Simile*.

METER The *meter* of a poem is its rhythmical pattern. This pattern is determined by the number of stresses, or beats, in each line. To describe the meter of a poem, you must *scan* its lines. *Scanning* involves marking the stressed and unstressed syllables, as follows:

> The life | Ĭ lead | Ĭ wănt | tŏ bé

As you can see, each stress is marked with a slanted line (´) and each unstressed syllable with a horseshoe symbol (˘). The stressed and unstressed syllables are then divided by vertical lines (|) into groups called feet. The following types of feet are common in English poetry:

1. *Iamb:* a foot with one unstressed syllable followed by one stressed syllable, as in the word "begín"
2. *Trochee:* a foot with one stressed syllable followed by one unstressed syllable, as in the word "péople"
3. *Anapest:* a foot with two unstressed syllables followed by one stressed syllable, as in the phrase "ŏn thĕ séa"
4. *Dactyl:* a foot with one stressed syllable followed by two unstressed syllables, as in the word "háppinĕss"
5. *Spondee:* a foot with two stressed syllables, as in the word "dówntówn"

Depending on the type of foot that is most common in them, lines of poetry are described as *iambic, trochaic, anapestic,* or *dactylic*.

Lines are also described in terms of the number of feet that occur in them, as follows:

1. *Monometer:* verse written in one-foot lines:
   > Thŭs Í
   > Păss bý
   > Ănd díe
   >> —Robert Herrick, "Upon His Departure"

2. *Dimeter:* verse written in two-foot lines:
   > Thĕre wás | ă wómăn
   > Whŏ lived | ŏn ă híll.
   > Ĭf shé's | nŏt góne,
   > Shĕ lives | thĕre stíll.
   >> —Anonymous

3. *Trimeter:* verse written in three-foot lines:
   > Whĕre dips | thĕ rock | y̆ highland

Of Sleuth | Wood in | the lake,
There lies | a leaf | y island
Where flap | ping her | ons wake
The drows | y wat | er rats;
—W. B. Yeats, "The Stolen Child"

4. *Tetrameter:* verse written in four-foot lines:
When wear | y with | the long | day's care,
And earth | ly change | from pain | to pain,
And lost, | and read | y to | despair,
Thy kind | voice calls | me back | again
—Emily Brontë, "To Imagination"

5. *Pentameter:* verse written in five-foot lines:
Amidst | these scenes, | O Pil | grim, seek'st |
thou Rome?
Vain is | thy search |—the pomp | of Rome | is fled
—Francisco de Quevedo, "Rome in Her Ruins"

A complete description of the meter of a line tells the kinds of feet each line contains, as well as how many feet of each kind. Thus, the lines from Quevedo's poem would be described as *iambic pentameter* with one variation, a trochee, in the second line. Blank verse is poetry written in unrhymed iambic pentameter. Poetry that does not have a regular meter is called free verse.
See *Blank Verse* and *Free Verse.*

MINOR CHARACTER See *Character.*

MOOD
Mood, or *atmosphere,* is the feeling created in the reader by a literary work or passage. Writers use many devices to create mood, including images, dialogue, setting, and plot. Often, a writer creates a mood at the beginning of a work and then sustains this mood throughout. Sometimes, however, the mood of the work changes dramatically. For example, the mood of most of "A Boy and a Man," on page 210, is tense and suspenseful. This mood changes after the man is rescued from the crevasse.

MORAL
A *moral* is a lesson taught by a literary work. A fable usually ends with a moral that is directly stated. For example, Aesop's fable "The Fox and the Crow," on page 873, ends with the moral "Do not trust *flatterers.*" A poem, novel, short story, or essay often suggests a moral that is not directly stated. The moral must be drawn by the reader, based on other elements in the work.
See *Fable.*

MOTIVATION
A *motivation* is a reason that explains or partially explains a character's thoughts, feelings, actions, or speech. Writers try to make their characters' motivations, or motives, as clear and believable as possible.

Characters are often motivated by needs, such as food and shelter. They are also motivated by feelings, such as fear, love, and pride. In "Suzy and Leah," on page 512, dislike for Leah motivates Suzy to keep her dresses, even though they are too small to fit her well.

MYTH
A *myth* is a fictional tale that explains the actions of gods or heroes or the origins of elements of nature. Myths are part of the oral tradition. They are composed orally and then passed from generation to generation by word of mouth. Every ancient culture has its own mythology, or collection of myths. The stories on pages 854–866 are retellings, in writing, of myths from ancient Greece. These Greek myths are known collectively as *classical mythology.*
See *Oral Tradition.*

NARRATION
Narration is writing that tells a story. Fictional works, such as novels and short stories, are examples of narration. So are poems that tell stories, such as "The Cremation of Sam McGee," on page 736. Narration can also be found in many kinds of nonfiction, including autobiographies, biographies, and newspaper reports. A story told in fiction, nonfiction, poetry, or even in drama is called a narrative.
See *Narrative Poem* and *Narrator.*

NARRATIVE POEM
A *narrative poem* is a story told in verse. Narrative poems often have all the elements of short stories, including characters, conflict, and plot. An example of a narrative poem is "The Highwayman," on page 300.

NARRATOR
A *narrator* is a speaker or character who tells a story. A *third-person narrator* is one who stands outside the action and speaks about it. A *first-person narrator* is one who tells a story and participates in its action.

In some dramas, like *The Monsters Are Due on Maple Street,* on page 696, there is a separate character called "The Narrator," who introduces, comments on, and concludes the play.
See *Point of View.*

NONFICTION
Nonfiction is prose writing that presents and explains ideas or that tells about real people, places, objects, or events. Autobiographies, biographies, essays, reports, letters, memos, and newspaper articles are all types of nonfiction.
See *Fiction.*

NOVEL
A *novel* is a long work of fiction. Novels contain all the elements of short stories, including characters, plot, conflict, and setting. However, novels are much longer

than short stories. The writer of novels, or the novelist, can therefore develop these elements more fully than a writer of short stories can. In addition to its main plot, a novel may contain one or more subplots, or independent, related stories. A novel may also have several themes.
See *Fiction.*

ONOMATOPOEIA *Onomatopoeia* is the use of words that imitate sounds. *Crash, buzz, screech, hiss, neigh, jingle,* and *cluck* are examples of onomatopoeia.

In her poem "Onomatopoeia," on page 783, Eve Merriam uses words like *sputters, spatters, spurts,* and *plash* to re-create the sounds of water splashing from a faucet.

ORAL TRADITION *Oral tradition* is the passing of songs, stories, and poems from generation to generation by word of mouth. Folk songs, folk tales, legends, and myths all come from the oral tradition. No one knows who first created these stories and poems. The authors are *anonymous.*
See *Folk Tale, Legend,* and *Myth.*

PERSONIFICATION *Personification* is a type of figurative language in which a nonhuman subject is given human characteristics. In "Feelings About Words," on page 776, Mary O'Neill personifies words, describing some as "lazy" and some as full of "pride" and "pomp."

PERSUASION *Persuasion* is writing or speech that attempts to convince the reader or listener to adopt a particular opinion or course of action. Newspaper editorials, letters to the editor, advertisements, and campaign speeches use persuasion.

PLOT *Plot* is the sequence of events in a literary work. In most novels, dramas, short stories, and narrative poems, the plot involves both characters and a central conflict. The plot usually begins with an *exposition* that introduces the setting, the characters, and the basic situation. This is followed by the introduction of the central conflict. The conflict then increases during the *rising action* until it reaches a high point of interest or suspense, the *climax.* The climax is followed by the *falling action,* or end, of the central conflict. Any events that occur during the falling action make up the *resolution,* or *denouement.*

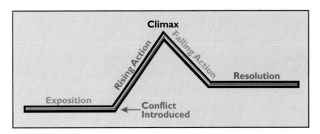

Some plots do not have all these parts. Some stories begin with the inciting incident and end with the resolution. In some, the inciting incident has occurred before the opening of the story.
See *Conflict.*

POETRY *Poetry* is one of the three major types of literature, the others being prose and drama. Defining poetry more precisely isn't easy, for there is no single, unique characteristic that all poems share. Poems are often divided into lines and stanzas and often employ regular rhythmical patterns, or meters. However, some poems are written out just like prose, and some are written in free verse. Most poems make use of highly concise, musical, and emotionally charged language. Many also make use of imagery, figurative language, and special devices of sound such as rhyme.

Major types of poetry include *lyric poetry, narrative poetry,* and *concrete poetry.* Other forms of poetry include *dramatic poetry,* in which characters speak in their own voices, and *epic poetry,* in which the poet tells a long, involved tale about gods or heroes.
See *Concrete Poem, Genre, Lyric Poem,* and *Narrative Poem.*

POINT OF VIEW *Point of view* is the perspective, or vantage point, from which a story is told. Three commonly used points of view are first person, omniscient third person, and limited third person.

In stories told from the *first-person point of view,* the narrator is a character in the story and refers to himself or herself with the pronoun "I." In "Ribbons," on page 524, the character Stacy serves as a first-person narrator.

The two kinds of *third-person point of view,* limited and omniscient, are called "third person" because the narrator uses third-person pronouns such as "he" and "she" to refer to the characters. There is no "I" telling the story.

In stories told from the *omniscient third-person point of view,* the narrator knows and tells about what each character feels and thinks. "Rikki-tikki-tavi," on page 464, is written from the omniscient third-person point of view.

In stories told from the *limited third-person point of view,* the narrator relates the inner thoughts and feelings of only one character, and everything is viewed from this character's perspective. "A Boy and a Man," on page 210, is written from the limited third-person point of view.
See *Narrator.*

PROSE *Prose* is the ordinary form of written language. Most writing that is not poetry, drama, or song is considered prose. Prose is one of the major genres of literature

and occurs in two forms: fiction and nonfiction.
See *Fiction, Genre,* and *Nonfiction.*

PROTAGONIST The *protagonist* is the main character in a literary work. In "Rikki-tikki-tavi," on page 464, the protagonist, or main character, is Rikki, the mongoose. See *Antagonist* and *Character.*

REFRAIN A *refrain* is a regularly repeated line or group of lines in a poem or song. In "The Dying Cowboy," on page 306, these lines separate the song's verses and stress the song's main idea:

> "Oh, bury me not on the lone prairie
> Where the wild coyotes will howl o'er me,
> In a narrow grave just six by three.
> Oh, bury me not on the lone prairie."

In some cases, the refrain varies slightly each time it appears.

REPETITION *Repetition* is the use, more than once, of any element of language—a sound, word, phrase, clause, or sentence. Repetition is used in both prose and poetry. In prose, a situation or character may be repeated with some variations. A subplot, for example, may repeat, with variations, the circumstances presented in the main plot.

Poets make use of many varieties of repetition. *Rhyme, alliteration,* and *rhythm* are all repetitions of sounds or sound patterns. A *refrain* is a repeated line.
See *Alliteration, Meter, Plot, Rhyme,* and *Rhyme Scheme.*

RESOLUTION See *Plot.*

RHYME *Rhyme* is the repetition of sounds at the ends of words. Poets use rhyme to lend a songlike quality to their verses and to emphasize certain words and ideas. Many traditional poems contain *end rhymes,* or rhyming words at the ends of lines. See, for example, the end rhymes in Robert Frost's "The Pasture," on page 755. Another common device is the use of *internal rhymes,* or rhyming words within lines. Notice, for example, the internal rhymes in the following passage from Edgar Allan Poe's "Annabel Lee," on page 775:

> For the moon never beams without
>   bringing me dreams
> Of the beautiful Annabel Lee;

See *Rhyme Scheme.*

RHYME SCHEME A *rhyme scheme* is a regular pattern of rhyming words in a poem. To indicate the rhyme scheme of a poem, use lowercase letters. Each rhyme is assigned a different letter, as follows:

> Under a spreading chestnut tree   *a*
> The village smithy stands;   *b*
> The smith, a mighty man is he,   *a*
> With large and sinewy hands;   *b*
> And the muscles of his brawny arms   *c*
> Are strong as iron bands.   *b*
> —Henry Wadsworth Longfellow,
>   "The Village Blacksmith"

The rhyme scheme of these lines is thus *ababcb.*

RHYTHM *Rhythm* is the pattern of beats, or stresses, in spoken or written language.
See *Meter.*

ROUND CHARACTER See *Character.*

SCIENCE FICTION *Science fiction* is writing that tells about imaginary events that involve science or technology. Many science-fiction stories are set in the future. "All Summer in a Day," on page 288, is a science-fiction story. In this story, Ray Bradbury describes events that take place in the future on the planet Venus.

SENSORY LANGUAGE *Sensory language* is writing or speech that appeals to one or more of the five senses. See *Image.*

SETTING The *setting* of a literary work is the time and place of the action. The time includes not only the historical period—the past, present, or future—but also the year, the season, the time of day, and even the weather. The place may be a specific country, state, region, community, neighborhood, building, institution, or home. Details such as dialects, clothing, customs, and modes of transportation are often used to establish setting.

In most stories the setting serves as a backdrop—a context in which the characters interact. In some stories, the setting is crucial to the plot. For example, the weather on the planet Venus is central to the plot of Ray Bradbury's story "All Summer in a Day," on page 288. Setting can also help to create a mood, or feeling. In "The Third Level," on page 52, the writer's description of a summer evening in a small Illinois town creates a mood of peace and innocence.
See *Mood.*

SHORT STORY A *short story* is a brief work of fiction. Like a novel, a short story presents a sequence of events, or plot. The plot usually deals with a central conflict faced by a main character, or protagonist. Like a lyric poem, a short story is concise and creates a single effect, or dominant impression, on its reader. The events in a short story usually communicate a message about life or human nature. This message, or central idea, is the story's theme. See *Conflict, Plot,* and *Theme.*

SIMILE A *simile* is a figure of speech that uses *like* or *as* to make a direct comparison between two unlike ideas. Everyday speech often contains similes, such as "pale as a ghost," "good as gold," and "clever as a fox."

Writers use similes to describe people, places, and things vividly. Poets, especially, create similes to point out new and interesting ways of viewing the world.

SPEAKER The *speaker* is the imaginary voice assumed by the writer of a poem. The speaker is the character who tells the poem. This character, or voice, often is not identified by name. The speaker's voice in Robert Frost's poem "Stopping by Woods on a Snowy Evening," on page 260, carries a sense of quiet sadness, but also mystery. See *Narrator.*

STAGE DIRECTIONS *Stage directions* are notes included in a drama to describe how the work is to be performed or staged. Stage directions are usually printed in italics and enclosed within parentheses or brackets. Some stage directions describe the movements, costumes, emotional states, and ways of speaking of the characters. This example of stage directions can be found in "The Dying Detective," on page 329.

> **MRS. HUDSON.** He's asleep, sir.
> [*They approach the bed.* WATSON *comes round to the audience's side and looks down at* HOLMES *for a moment. He shakes his head gravely, then he and* MRS. HUDSON *move away beyond the foot of the bed.*]

See *Drama.*

STANZA A *stanza* is a formal division of lines in a poem, considered as a unit. Many poems are divided into stanzas that are separated by spaces. Stanzas often function just like paragraphs in prose. Each stanza states and develops a single main idea.

Stanzas are commonly named according to the number of lines found in them, as follows:

1. *Couplet:* two-line stanza
2. *Tercet:* three-line stanza
3. *Quatrain:* four-line stanza
4. *Cinquain:* five-line stanza
5. *Sestet:* six-line stanza
6. *Heptastich:* seven-line stanza
7. *Octave:* eight-line stanza

Robert Frost's "Stopping by Woods on a Snowy Evening," on page 260, is written in quatrains:

> Whose woods these are I think I know.
> His house is in the village, though;
> He will not see me stopping here
> To watch his woods fill up with snow.

Division into stanzas is common in traditional poetry and is often accompanied by rhyme. Notice, for example, that in the stanzas from the Frost poem, the first, second, and fourth lines rhyme. However, some rhyming poems are not divided into stanzas, and some poems divided into stanzas do not contain rhyme.

STATIC CHARACTER See *Character.*

SURPRISE ENDING A *surprise ending* is a conclusion that is unexpected. Sometimes, a surprise ending follows a false resolution. The reader thinks that the conflict has already been resolved but then is confronted with a new twist that changes the outcome of the plot. Often, a surprise ending is *foreshadowed,* or subtly hinted at, in the course of the work.
See *Foreshadowing* and *Plot.*

SUSPENSE *Suspense* is a feeling of anxious uncertainty about the outcome of events in a literary work. Writers create suspense by raising questions in the minds of their readers. For example, in "A Day's Wait," on page 72, Ernest Hemingway raises questions about whether the boy will recover from his illness.

SYMBOL A *symbol* is anything that stands for or represents something else. Symbols are common in everyday life. A dove with an olive branch in its beak is a symbol of peace. A blindfolded woman holding a balanced scale is a symbol of justice.

THEME A *theme* is a central message, concern, or purpose in a literary work. A theme can usually be expressed as a generalization, or general statement, about people or about life. The theme of a work is not a summary of its plot. The theme is the central idea that the writer communicates.

A theme may be stated directly by the writer, although this is unusual. Instead, most themes are not directly stated but are implied. When the theme is implied, the reader must figure out what the theme is by looking carefully at what the work reveals about people or about life.

WRITING HANDBOOK

THE WRITING PROCESS

The writing process can be roughly divided into a series of stages: prewriting, drafting, revising, editing, proofreading, and publishing. It is important to remember that the writing process is one that moves backward as well as forward. Even while you are moving forward in the creation of your composition, you may still return to a previous stage—to rethink or rewrite.

Following are stages of the writing process, with key points to address during each stage.

Prewriting

In this stage, you plan out the work to be done. You prepare to write by exploring ideas, gathering information, and working out an organization plan. Following are the key steps to take at this stage:

Step 1: Analyze the writing situation. Before writing, analyze the writing assignment. To do this, ask yourself the following questions about each element:

- *Topic (the subject you will be writing about):* What exactly are you going to write about? Can you state your subject in a sentence? Is your subject too broad or too narrow?
- *Purpose (what you want your writing to accomplish):* Do you want your writing to explain? To describe? To persuade? To tell a story? To entertain? What do you want your audience to learn or to understand?
- *Audience (the people who will read or listen to your writing):* Who is your audience? What might they already know about your subject? What basic facts will you have to provide for them?

Step 2: Gather ideas and information. After thinking about the writing situation, you may find that you need more information. If so, you must decide how to gather this information. On the other hand, you may find that you already have too much information—that your topic is too broad. If this is the case, then you must decide how to narrow your topic.

There are many ways to gather information and to narrow a topic. Consider these strategies:

- *Brainstorm.* Discuss the topic with a group of people. Try to generate as many ideas as possible. Not all of your brainstormed ideas will be useful or

suitable. You'll need to evaluate them later.
- *Consult other people about your topic.* Speaking with others may suggest an idea or an approach you did not see at first.
- *Make a list of questions about your topic.* Begin your questions with words like *who, what, where, when, why,* and *how.* Then, find the answers to your questions.

Step 3: Organize your notes. Once you have gathered enough information, you will have to organize it. Sort your ideas and notes; decide which points are most important. You can make an outline to show the order of ideas, or you can use some other organizing plan that works for you.

There are many ways to organize and develop your material. Careful organization will make your writing easy to read and understand. The following are common methods of organizing information:

- *Time Order or Chronological Order* Events are organized in order of occurrence (from earliest to latest, for example).
- *Spatial Order* Details are organized by position in space (from left to right, for example).
- *Degree Order* This order is organization by size, amount, or intensity (from coldest to warmest, for example).
- *Priority Order* This is organization by importance, value, usefulness, or familiarity (from worst to best, for example).

Drafting

Drafting follows prewriting and is the second stage in the writing process. Working from your prewriting notes and your outline or plan, you develop and present your ideas in sentences and paragraphs. The following are important points to remember about drafting:

- Do not try to make your rough draft perfect. Concentrate on getting your ideas on paper. Once this is done, you can make improvements in the revision and proofreading stages.
- Keep your audience and purpose in mind as you write. This will help you determine what you say and how you say it.
- Don't be afraid to set aside earlier ideas if later

ones work better. Some of the best ideas are those that were not planned at the beginning.

Most papers, regardless of the topic, are developed with an introduction, a body, and a conclusion. Here are tips for developing these parts of a paper:

Introduction In the introduction to a paper, you want to engage your readers' attention and let them know the purpose of your paper. You might use the following strategies in your introduction:

- State your main idea.
- Take a stand.
- Use an anecdote.
- Quote someone.
- Startle your readers.

Body of the paper In the body of your paper, you present your information and make your points. Your *organization* is an important factor in leading readers through your ideas. Your elaboration on your main ideas is also important. *Elaboration* is the development of ideas to make your written work precise and complete. You can use the following kinds of details to elaborate your main ideas:

- Facts and statistics
- Anecdotes
- Sensory details
- Examples
- Explanation and definition
- Quotations

Conclusion The ending of your paper is the final impression you leave with your readers. Your conclusion should give readers the sense that you have pulled everything together. Following are some effective ways to end your paper:

- Summarize and restate.
- Ask a question.
- State an opinion.
- Call for action.
- Tell an anecdote.

Revising

Once you have a draft, you can look at it critically or have others review it. This is the time to make changes on many levels. Revising is the process of reworking what you have written to make it as good as it can be. You may change some details so that your ideas flow smoothly and are clearly supported. You may discover that some details don't work, and you'll need to discard them. Try these strategies:

- Read your work aloud. This is an excellent way to catch any ideas or details that have been left out and to notice errors in logic.
- Ask someone else to read your work. Choose someone who can point out how to improve it.

How do you know what to look for and what to change? Here is a checklist of major writing issues. If the answer to any of these questions is no, then that is an area that needs revision.

1. Does the writing achieve my purpose?
2. Does the paper have a single focus, with all details and information contributing to that focus?
3. Is the arrangement of information clear and logical?
4. Have I elaborated enough to give my audience adequate information?

Editing

When you edit, you look more closely at the language you have used so that the way you express your ideas is most effective.

- Replace dull language with vivid, precise words.
- Cut or change unnecessary repetition.
- Check passive voice; active voice is more effective.
- Replace wordy expressions with shorter, more precise ones.

Proofreading

After you finish your final draft, the last step is to proofread the draft to make it ready for a reader. You may do this on your own or with the help of a partner.

It's useful to have handy both a dictionary and a usage handbook to help you check for correctness. Here are the tasks in proofreading:

- Correct errors in grammar and usage.
- Correct errors in punctuation and capitalization.
- Correct errors in spelling.

Publishing and Presenting

These are some of the many ways in which you can share your work:

- Share your writing in a small group by reading it aloud or by passing it around for others to read.
- Read your work aloud to the class.
- Display your work on a classroom bulletin board.
- Submit your writing to the school literary magazine, or start a literary magazine for your school or for your class.
- Submit your writing to your school or community newspaper.
- Enter your writing in literary contests for student writers.
- Submit your writing to a magazine that publishes work by young people.

THE MODES OF WRITING

Expression

Expression is writing that captures your thoughts, feelings, or experiences. Some expressive writing is private, written only for you to read. Some is written to be shared with an audience—friends, family, or other interested readers. Expressive writing is another way to communicate how you think and feel. You can share your experiences and emotions and reflect on memorable moments in your life. Through expressive writing, you can capture on paper what is most meaningful to you. Expressive writing takes many forms. Here are a few of them:

Personal Letter Writing a personal letter is a good way to share your thoughts and experiences with a friend or family member. In a personal letter, you can express feelings or thoughts you have difficulty talking about directly to the person.

Personal Journal A journal is a book with blank pages in which you record your personal feelings, thoughts, or observations over a period of time. As you write in your journal, you will have a record of the day-to-day happenings or most important events of your own life. Most personal journals are kept private because they are very personal, although some journals have been published to be read by the public.

Personal Memoir In a memoir, you write about significant events from your past and include your thoughts and feelings about those experiences. A memoir may be brief and focus on a single event or it may describe a larger part of your life.

Description

Description is writing that creates a vivid picture for readers, draws readers into a scene, and makes readers feel as if they are meeting a character or experiencing an event firsthand. A description may stand on its own or be part of a longer work, such as a short story.

When you write a description, bring it to life with sensory details, which tell you how your subject looks, smells, sounds, tastes, or feels. You'll want to choose your details carefully, so that you create a single main impression of your subject. These are a few types of descriptions:

Observation In an observation, you describe an event that you have witnessed firsthand, often over an extended period of time. You may focus on an aspect of daily life or on a scientific phenomenon, such as a storm or an eclipse.

Remembrance of People and Places When you write a remembrance, you use vivid descriptive details to bring to life memorable people, places, or events from your past. You include details that convey your feelings about your subject.

Narration

Whenever writers tell any type of story, they are using narration. Most narratives share certain elements—characters, a setting, a sequence of events (or plot, in fiction), and, often, a theme. You might be asked to write one of these types of narration:

Firsthand Biography In a firsthand biography, you tell about the life of a person whom you know personally. You can use your close relationship with the person to help you include personal insights not found in biographies based solely on research.

Short Story Short stories are short fictional narratives in which a main character faces a conflict that is resolved by the end of the story. In planning a short story, focus on developing plot, setting, and characters.

Autobiographical Incident An autobiographical incident tells a true story about a specific event in the writer's life. Because you are the writer and the central figure in an autobiographical incident, this type of writing reveals more about you than about other people.

Exposition: Giving Information

Exposition to give information is writing that informs or explains. In writing expositions that give information, the information you include is factual and the opinions you express should be based on factual information. Here are some types of exposition you may be asked to write:

Summary To write a summary or synopsis of a story, write as few words as possible to give the reader basic information about the plot, characters, and setting without going into detail. To write a summary of an event, present the details as factually as possible and avoid giving personal opinions about what happened.

Classification When writing classification, you put groups of items into categories and define the groups, using facts and examples. For example, you might group animals into categories, such as mammals and reptiles, and define them according to their characteristics.

How-to Composition In a how-to essay, you provide detailed, step-by-step directions that explain a process.

Exposition: Making Connections

Exposition can **make connections** for readers by comparing and contrasting two subjects, by examining a problem and its solution, or by connecting information to an opinion about something. Here are some types of exposition that make connections:

Comparison-and-Contrast Essay A comparison-and-contrast essay points out the similarities and differences between two subjects. For example, when you compare and contrast two objects, you point out the similarities and differences in their physical qualities—how they look and what they're made of—and their functions—how they're used and how they work.

Written Solution to a Problem Writers use exposition to present or explain a problem and to provide a solution. In a written solution to a problem, you identify a specific problem and then suggest one or more solutions supported with facts and examples.

Persuasion

Persuasion is writing or speaking that attempts to convince people to agree with a position or take a desired action. When used effectively, persuasive writing has the power to change people's lives. As a reader and a writer, you will find yourself engaged in many forms of persuasion. Here are a few of them:

Advice Column An advice column provides readers with suggestions for solving problems or improving their lives. When writing an advice column, include facts and other information to support your advice.

Advertisement The purpose of an advertisement is to persuade people to buy something, accept an idea, vote for someone, or support a cause. When you write an advertisement, include imaginative, lively writing that will catch your readers' or viewers' attention. Present your information in an appealing way to make your product or service seem desirable.

Essay Supporting an Opinion In writing an essay to support an opinion, you build an argument and support your opinions with a variety of evidence: facts, statistics, examples, and statements from experts.

Reports

A **report** is writing based on research. People write reports to present information and ideas, to share findings and research, and to explain subjects they have studied. Here are some types of reports:

Biographical Sketch When you write a biographical sketch, include facts about a person's character and achievements. Include the dates and details of the main events in the person's life, presenting the information in chronological order beginning with childhood.

Lab/Experiment Report In a lab/experiment report, you define or explain the purpose of your experiment, describe the materials used, and outline the procedures followed. You also describe your observations and state the conclusions you reached.

Library Research Report When you write a library research report, put together information from books and other library sources. Include details from the research to support a main idea. Also, include footnotes, or credits, to cite your sources.

Creative

Creative Writing blends imagination, ideas, and emotions, and allows you to present your own view of the world. Poems, songs, and dramas are examples of creative writing. The literature in this anthology may inspire you to create your own works, such as these:

Song Lyrics In writing lyrics, or words, for a song, you use many elements of poetry—rhyme, rhythm, repetition, and imagery. Song lyrics convey emotions and make the reader think.

Poem Writing a poem is a way to express thoughts and feelings about a subject. Poems present ideas and stir emotions in readers. In writing poems, use figurative language and sensory images to create strong impact or rhyme; use rhythm and repetition to create a musical quality.

Monologue A monologue is a dramatic speech by a single character. In writing a monologue, choose a subject, and write the details from your subject's point of view.

Response to Literature

In a **response to literature,** you express your thoughts and feelings about a work and often, in so doing, gain a better understanding of the work. Response to literature can take many forms—oral or written, formal or informal. Here are two typical forms:

Reader's Response Journal Entry Your reader's response journal is a record of your feelings about works you've read. Use it to remind yourself of works that you liked or disliked or to provide a source of writing ideas.

Letter to an Author People sometimes respond to a work of literature by writing a letter to the author. You can praise the work, ask questions, or offer constructive criticism.

GRAMMAR AND MECHANICS HANDBOOK

Nouns A **noun** is the name of a person, place, thing, or idea. A **common noun** names any one of a class of people, places, or things. A **proper noun** names a specific person, place, or thing.

Common Nouns	Proper Nouns
writer	Russell Baker
city	Los Angeles

Pronouns A **pronoun** is a word that stands for a noun or for a word that takes the place of a noun.

A **personal pronoun** refers to (1) the person speaking, (2) the person spoken to, or (3) the person, place, or thing spoken about.

	Singular	Plural
First Person	I, me, my, mine	we, us, our, ours
Second Person	you, your, yours	you, your, yours
Third Person	he, him, his, she, her, hers, it, its	they, them, their, theirs

She is involved in work her soul must have.

> —from "In Search of Our Mothers' Gardens," Walker, p. 115

They would sit at dinner tables, cool drinks in their hands, and *scowl.*

> —"Seventh Grade," Soto, p. 123

A **demonstrative pronoun** directs attention to a specific person, place, or thing.

this lamp   *these* rugs

An **interrogative pronoun** is used to begin a question.

What is the title of the story?

Who is the author of "Mother to Son"?

An **indefinite pronoun** refers to a person, place, or thing, often without specifying which one.

Many of the players were tired.

Everyone brought something.

Verbs A **verb** is a word that shows an action, a condition, or the fact that something exists.

An **action verb** indicates the action of someone or something.

Bears store fat

Chipmunks gather nuts. . . .

> —"Winter," Giovanni, p. 748

A **linking verb** connects the subject of a sentence with a noun or a pronoun that renames or describes the subject.

She was a very frail girl. . . .

> —"All Summer in a Day," Bradbury, p. 290

A **helping verb** can be added to another verb to make a single verb phrase.

They had read in class about the sun.

> —"All Summer in a Day," Bradbury, p. 290

Adjectives An **adjective** describes a noun or a pronoun, or gives a noun or a pronoun a more specific meaning. Adjectives answer these questions:

What kind?	*red* rose, *small* bowl
Which one?	*this* spoon, *those* pots
How many?	*four* hours, *many* tomatoes
How much?	*no* rain, *little* money

The **articles** *the, a,* and *an* are adjectives. *An* is used before a word beginning with a vowel sound.

A noun may sometimes be used as an adjective.

family home   *science* fiction

Adverbs An **adverb** modifies a verb, an adjective, or another adverb. Adverbs answer the questions *where, when, in what way,* or *to what extent.*

He ran *outside.* (modifies verb *ran*)

She *never* wrote us. (modifies verb *wrote*)

Close the window *quickly.* (modifies verb *close*)

We were *very* sad. (modifies adjective *sad*)

They left *too* suddenly. (modifies adverb *suddenly*)

Prepositions A **preposition** relates a noun or a pronoun following it to another word in the sentence.

across the road   *near* the corner

except me   *during* the show

Conjunctions A **conjunction** connects other words or groups of words.

A **coordinating conjunction** connects similar kinds or groups of words.

lions *and* tigers   small *but* strong

Correlative conjunctions are used in pairs to connect similar words or groups of words.

> *both* Zachary *and* Justin   *neither* they *nor* I

Interjections An **interjection** is a word that expresses feeling or emotion and functions independently of a sentence.

> "Ssh! He's waking."
> > —"The Dying Detective," Hardwick
> > and Hardwick, p. 330
>
> "Now, look here, Holmes!"
> > —"The Dying Detective," Hardwick
> > and Hardwick, p. 330

Sentences A **sentence** is a group of words with two main parts: a complete subject and a complete predicate. Together, these parts express a complete thought.

A **fragment** is a group of words that does not express a complete thought.

> Into the room quietly.
> Strolled until night came.

Subject-Verb Agreement To make a **subject** and a **verb agree**, make sure that both are singular or both are plural. Two or more singular subjects joined by *or* or *nor* must have a singular verb. When singular and plural subjects are joined by *or* or *nor,* the verb must agree with the closest subject.

> *He is* at the door.
> *They drive* home every day.
> *Jeff* or *Sam is* absent.
> Both *pets are* hungry.
> Either the *chairs* or the *table is* on sale.
> Neither the *tree* nor the *shrubs were* in bloom.

Phrases A **phrase** is a group of words without a subject and a verb that functions in a sentence as one part of speech.

A **prepositional phrase** is a group of words that includes a preposition and a noun or a pronoun that is the object of the preposition.

> near the town   with them
> inside our house   beneath the floor

An **adjective phrase** is a prepositional phrase that modifies a noun or a pronoun by telling *what kind, which one,* or *how many.*

> Friends *in the barrio* explained that the director
> was called a principal . . .
> > —from *Barrio Boy,* Galarza, p. 611

An **adverb phrase** is a prepositional phrase that modifies a verb, an adjective, or an adverb by pointing out *where, when, in what way,* or *to what extent.*

> I had not yet put the sheet *on him.*
> > —"Lather and Nothing Else,"
> > Téllez, p. 492

An **appositive phrase** is a noun or a pronoun with modifiers, placed next to a noun or a pronoun to add information and details.

> As a freelance illustrator for *Harper's Weekly, America's most important news magazine,* he was considered one of the country's finest woodblock engravers.
> > —"Winslow Homer: America's
> > Greatest Painter," Levitt, p. 587

A **participial phrase** is a participle modified by an adjective or an adverb phrase or accompanied by a complement. The entire phrase acts as an adjective.

> *Finding no takers,* Felix decided to split to his aunt's.
> > —"Amigo Brothers," Thomas, p. 354

An **infinitive phrase** is an infinitive with modifiers, complements, or a subject, all acting together as a single part of speech.

> He came into the room *to shut the windows* while we were still in bed and I saw he looked ill.
> > —"A Day's Wait," Hemingway, p. 72

Clause A **clause** is a group of words with its own subject and verb.

An **independent clause** can stand by itself as a complete sentence.

A **subordinate clause** has a subject and a verb, but it cannot stand by itself as a complete sentence; it can only be part of a sentence.

An **adjective clause** is a subordinate clause that modifies a noun or a pronoun by telling *what kind, which one,* or *how many.*

> He was a descendant of the Van Winkles *who figured so gallantly in the chivalrous days of Peter Stuyvesant . . .*
> > — "Rip Van Winkle," Irving, p. 145

An **adverb clause** modifies a verb, an adjective, or an adverb by telling *where, when, in what way, to what extent, under what condition,* or *why.*

> "*When I look at race relations today,* I can see that some positive changes have come about."
> > —"All Together Now," Jordan, p. 618

Summary of Capitalization and Punctuation

Capitalization

Capitalize the first word of a sentence.

> At the corner stood a drugstore, brilliant with electric lights.
>
> —"After Twenty Years,"
> O. Henry, p. 457

Capitalize all proper nouns and adjectives.

> Amy Tan   Amazon River   Thanksgiving Day
> Florida   October   Italian

Capitalize a person's title when it is followed by the person's name or when it is used in direct address.

> Doctor   Chief Wu   Dame Van Winkle

Capitalize titles showing family relationships when they refer to a specific person, unless they are preceded by a possessive noun or pronoun.

> Aunt Sarah Shoaf   Teddy's mother

Capitalize the first word and all other key words in the titles of books, periodicals, poems, stories, plays, paintings, and other works of art.

> from *Into Thin Air*
>
> "All Summer in a Day"   "Valediction"

Capitalize the first word and all nouns in letter salutations and the first word in letter closings.

> Dear Mr. Herriot,   Yours truly,

Punctuation

End Marks Use a **period** to end a declarative sentence, an imperative sentence, and most abbreviations.

> We read the haiku.
>
> Review the tanka before you recite it.

Use a **question mark** to end a direct question or an incomplete question in which the rest of the question is understood.

> Has spring come indeed?
>
> —"Haiku," Bashō, p. 756
>
> "Go ahead, let her talk. What about it?"
>
> —*The Monsters Are Due on Maple Street*, Serling, p. 703

Use an **exclamation mark** after a statement showing strong emotion, an urgent imperative sentence, or an interjection expressing strong emotion.

> "It's Oscar—he's gone!"
>
> —"Cat on the Go," Herriot, p. 385
>
> "Get me out of this!"
>
> —"The Night the Bed Fell," Thurber, p. 281
>
> "Bah! Humbug!"
>
> —"A Christmas Carol: Scrooge and Marley," Horovitz, p. 650

Commas Use a **comma** before the coordinating conjunction to separate two independent clauses in a compound sentence.

> They were among the last students to arrive in class, so all the good desks in the back had already been taken.
>
> —"Seventh Grade," Soto, p. 125

Use commas to separate three or more words, phrases, or clauses in a series.

> There were two filling stations at the intersection with Union Avenue, as well as an A&P, a fruit stand, a bakery, a barber shop, Zuccarelli's drugstore, and a diner shaped like a railroad car.
>
> —"No Gumption," Baker, p. 570

Use commas to separate adjectives of equal rank. Do not use commas to separate adjectives that must stay in a specific order.

> He did big, masculine pictures of hunting and fishing. . . .
>
> —"Winslow Homer: America's Greatest Painter," Levitt, p. 588

Use a comma after an introductory word, phrase, or clause.

> Naturally, Ian chose the fattest story he could . . .
>
> —"Ribbons," Yep, p. 530
>
> In his corner, Antonio was doing what all fighters do when they are hurt.
>
> —"Amigo Brothers," Thomas, p. 358
>
> Outside the wind had picked up, sending the rain against the window with a force that shook the glass in its frame.
>
> —"The Treasure of Lemon Brown," Myers, p. 534

Use commas to set off parenthetical and nonessential expressions.

We were, of course, saying nothing. . . .

—from *Barrio Boy*, Galarza, p. 612

Use commas with places and dates made up of two or more parts.

Ray Bradbury was born in Waukegan, Illinois.

On July 20, 1969, American astronauts first set foot on the moon.

Use commas after items in addresses, after the salutation in a personal letter, after the closing in all letters, and in numbers of more than three digits.

Linden Lane, Durham, N.C.   My dear Sam,

Sincerely yours,   1,372,597

Use a comma to set off a direct quotation.

"Very good," I answered, turning my attention now to the brush.

—"Lather and Nothing Else," Téllez, p. 492

Semicolons Use a **semicolon** to join independent clauses that are not already joined by a conjunction.

The motto of all the mongoose family is, "Run out and find out"; and Rikki-tikki was a true mongoose.

—"Rikki-tikki-tavi," Kipling, p. 465

Use a semicolon to join independent clauses or items in a series that already contain commas.

Your response with your own mind and body and memory and emotions gives the poem its ability to work its magic; if you give to it, it will give to you, and give plenty.

—"How to Enjoy Poetry," Dickey, p. 557

Colons Use a **colon** before a list of items following an independent clause.

The following words are examples of onomatopoeia: *buzz, hiss, jingle,* and *cluck.*

Use a colon in numbers giving the time, in salutations in business letters, and in labels used to signal important ideas.

4:30 A.M.   Dear Ms. Mazzilli:

Danger: Landslide Area Ahead

Quotation Marks A **direct quotation** represents a person's exact speech or thoughts and is enclosed in quotation marks.

In 1910, just before he died, he wrote in a letter, "All is lovely outside my house and inside my house and myself."

—"Winslow Homer: America's Greatest Painter," Levitt, p. 589

An **indirect quotation** reports only the general meaning of what a person said or thought and does not require quotation marks.

Mom says I should invite her home for dinner soon.

—"Suzy and Leah," Yolen, p. 515

Always place a comma or a period inside the final quotation mark of a direct quotation.

"It's no good, Triss," I said gently. "It's got to be done."

—"Cat on the Go," Herriot, p. 383

Place a question mark or exclamation mark inside the final quotation mark if the end mark is part of the quotation; if it is not part of the quotation, place it outside the final quotation mark.

As Rikki-tikki went up the path, he heard his "attention" notes like a tiny dinner gong; and then the steady "*Ding-dong-tock!* Nag is dead—*dong!* Nagaina is dead! *Ding-dong-tock!*"

—"Rikki-tikki-tavi," Kipling, pp. 474–475

Does that poem by Robert Frost start with the line, "I'm going out to clean the pasture spring"?

—"The Pasture," Frost, p. 755

Underline or italicize the titles of long written works, movies, television and radio series, lengthy works of music, paintings, and sculptures.

A Christmas Carol   *Star Trek*

The Mona Lisa

Use quotation marks around the titles of short written works, episodes in a series, songs, and titles of works mentioned as parts of collections.

"Winter"   "Cat on the Go"

"Let's Steal the Moon"   "Annabel Lee"

Hyphens Use a **hyphen** with certain numbers, after certain prefixes, with two or more words used as one word, and with a compound modifier that comes before a noun.

fifty-four   self-employed

daughter-in-law   happy-go-lucky friend

Apostrophes Add an **apostrophe** and -s to show the possessive case of most singular nouns.

> Aesop's fables   the author's story
>
> Dickens's novels

Add an apostrophe to show the possessive case of plural nouns ending in -s and -es.

> the bats' squeaks   the Brookses' home

Add an apostrophe and -s to show the possessive case of plural nouns that do not end in -s or -es.

> the women's hats   the mice's whiskers

Use an apostrophe in a contraction to indicate the position of the missing letter or letters.

> "I'd better not say I have inflammatory rheumatism," I decided.
>
>   —"Stolen Day," Anderson, p. 484

GLOSSARY OF COMMON USAGE

accept, except

Accept is a verb that means "to receive" or "to agree to." *Except* is a preposition that means "other than" or "leaving out." Do not confuse these two words.

> The Amigo brothers *accepted* the challenge and prepared for the match.
>
> All the children *except* Margot played.

affect, effect

Affect is normally a verb meaning "to influence" or "to bring about a change in." *Effect* is usually a noun, meaning "result."

> The death of his son deeply *affects* Iona.
>
> In James Thurber's essay, the collapse of the bed has many humorous *effects*.

among, between

Among is usually used with three or more items. *Between* is generally used with only two items.

> "Zoo" was *among* the stories I liked best.
>
> There was a special relationship *between* Felix and Antonio in "Amigo Brothers."

amount, number

Amount refers to a mass or a unit, whereas *number* refers to individual items that can be counted. Therefore, *amount* generally appears with singular nouns, and *number* appears with plural nouns.

> To climb Mt. Everest, Jon Krakauer needed a huge *amount* of determination.

In "The Night the Bed Fell," the family members draw a *number* of mistaken conclusions.

bad, badly

Use the predicate adjective *bad* after linking verbs such as *feel, look,* and *seem*. Use *badly* whenever an adverb is required.

> At the beginning of "Amigo Brothers," Felix and Antonio feel *bad* about the upcoming fight.
>
> When Charley finds he's stepped back in time to 1894, he is *badly* confused at first.

because of, due to

Use *due to* if it can logically replace the phrase *caused by*. In introductory phrases, however, *because of* is better usage than *due to*.

> Washington Irving's popularity was largely *due to* his use of setting to re-create early America.
>
> *Because* of the parrot's ability to mimic, Harry learns what his father had said.

beside, besides

Do not confuse these two prepositions, which have different meanings. *Beside* means "at the side of" or "close to." *Besides* means "in addition to."

> In Hemingway's "A Day's Wait," the father sits *beside* his son to comfort him.
>
> No one *besides* me had read Twain's "The Californian's Tale."

can, may

The verb *can* generally refers to the ability to do something. The verb *may* generally refers to permission to do something.

> Anansi *may* tell all stories if he *can* deliver the hornets, the python, and the leopard to Nyame.

compare, contrast

The verb *compare* can involve both similarities and differences. The verb *contrast* always involves differences. Use *to* or *with* after *compare*. Use *with* after *contrast*.

> Stan *compared* Nikki Giovanni's "Winter" *with* Carl Sandburg's "Fog."
>
> Marianna and her daughters' opinions of themselves after they look in the mirror *contrast with* their feelings before seeing the mirror.

different from, different than

Different from is generally preferred over *different than*.

> Similes are *different from* metaphors because similes use the words *like* or *as* to make comparisons.

farther, further
Use *farther* when you refer to distance. Use *further* when you mean "to a greater degree or extent" or "additional."

> The speaker in Robert Frost's poem is tempted to ride *farther* into the snowy woods.

> Reference to age *further* irritates Father William.

fewer, less
Use *fewer* for things that can be counted. Use *less* for amounts or quantities that cannot be counted.

> Which animals have *fewer* fangs: sharks or rattlesnakes?

> Rikki-tikki-tavi is *less* fearful of the cobra than are the other animals.

good, well
Use the predicate adjective *good* after linking verbs such as *feel, look, smell, taste,* and *seem.* Use *well* whenever you need an adverb.

> The speaker in "Oranges" feels *good* about his meeting with the girl.

> Rudyard Kipling describes Indian animals *well.*

hopefully
You should not loosely attach this adverb to a sentence, as in *"Hopefully,* the rain will stop by noon." Rewrite the sentence so *hopefully* modifies a specific verb. Other possible ways of revising such sentences include using the adjective *hopeful* or a phrase like "everyone *hopes* that."

> James Dickey writes *hopefully* about everyone's ability to enjoy poetry.

> At the end of "The Third Level," Charley seems *hopeful* that he will find the third level again.

its, it's
Do not confuse the possessive pronoun *its* with the contraction *it's,* standing for "it is" or "it has."

> If a rattler thinks *it's* not seen, it will lie quietly without revealing *its* location.

lay, lie
Do not confuse these verbs. *Lay* is a transitive verb meaning "to set or put something down." Its principal parts are *lay, laying, laid, laid. Lie* is an intransitive verb meaning "to recline." Its principal parts are *lie, lying, lay, lain.*

> The seal *lays* its flipper on a rock.

> Sam McGee *lies* down in his sleigh.

leave, let
Leave means "to go away" or "to allow to remain." *Let* means "to permit."

> After the fox had eaten the cheese, he *left* the crow sitting forlorn and hungry in the tree.

> The aliens *let* the people destroy themselves.

like, as
Like is a preposition that usually means "similar to" or "in the same way as." *Like* should always be followed by an object. Do not use *like* before a subject and a verb. Use *as* or *that* instead.

> A story *like* "A Boy and a Man" by James Ramsey Ullman uses suspense to hold the reader's interest.

> The journey of Icarus does not end *as* he expected.

loose, lose
Loose can be either an adjective (meaning "unattached") or a verb (meaning "to untie"). *Lose* is always a verb (meaning "to fail to keep, have, or win").

> There is often only a *loose* connection between the speaker of a poem and the poem's author; sometimes there is no link whatever between the two.

> When no one recognizes him, Rip Van Winkle feels that he is *losing* his mind.

many, much
Use *many* to refer to a specific quantity. Use *much* for an indefinite amount or for an abstract concept.

> Winslow Homer painted *many* Civil War scenes.

> Seamus Heaney has won *much* praise for his poetry about Ireland.

of, have
Do not use *of* in place of *have* after auxiliary verbs like *would, could, should, may, might,* or *must.*

> Russell Baker writes that his lack of gumption *must have* saddened his mother.

raise, rise
Raise is a transitive verb that usually takes a direct object. *Rise* is intransitive and never takes a direct object.

> All the miners' visits *raise* the speaker's expectations about meeting the lady in "The Californian's Tale."

> Rip rubs his eyes, *rises* from the ground, and looks around for his gun.

set, sit

Do not confuse these verbs. *Set* is a transitive verb meaning "to put (something) in a certain place." Its principal parts are *set, setting, set, set. Sit* is an intransitive verb meaning "to be seated." Its principal parts are *sit, sitting, sat, sat.*

> The speaker *sets* the planks in the furnace.
>
> Nicholas Vedder would *sit* all day in the doorway to his inn.

than, then

The conjunction *than* is used to connect the two parts of a comparison. Do not confuse *than* with the adverb *then,* which usually refers to time.

> Rena liked "Aunt Leaf" more *than* "Life."
>
> Mark Twain worked on a riverboat and *then* moved to California to search for gold.

that, which, who

Use the relative pronoun *that* to refer to things or people. Use *which* only for things and *who* only for people.

> The season *that* E. E. Cummings describes is spring.
>
> Lyric poems, *which* express personal emotions, are often brief.
>
> One writer *who* has vividly described the experiences of African Americans is Alice Walker.

their, there, they're

Do not confuse the spelling of these three words. *Their* is a possessive adjective and always modifies a noun. *There* is usually used either at the beginning of a sentence or as an adverb. *They're* is a contraction for "they are."

> Teddy and his parents are very happy about *their* new pet.
>
> For most people, *there* are few creatures more terrifying than sharks.
>
> Ron and Nan are in the class production of *The Monsters Are Due on Maple Street,* and *they're* rehearsing in the auditorium right now.

to, too, two

Do not confuse the spelling of these words. *To* is a preposition that begins a prepositional phrase or an infinitive. *Too,* with two *o's,* is an adverb and modifies adjectives and other adverbs. *Two* is a number.

> The barber pays close attention *to* the Captain's skin as he gives him a shave.
>
> Josh thought that his paper on Greek myths was *too* short, so he added another paragraph.
>
> *Two* poems that Thelma especially liked were Edgar Allan Poe's "Annabel Lee" and Nikki Giovanni's "Winter."

unique

Because *unique* means "one of a kind," you should not use it carelessly to mean "interesting" or "unusual." Avoid such illogical expressions as *most unique, very unique,* and *extremely unique.*

> Mark Twain's experiences in California gave him a *unique* insight into the gold-mining camps.

when, where, why

Do not use *when, where,* or *why* directly after a linking verb such as *is.* Reword the sentence.

> **Faulty:** Suspense is *when* an author increases the reader's tension.
>
> **Revised:** An author uses suspense to increase the reader's tension.
>
> **Faulty:** Mexico is *where* the legend "Popocatepetl and Ixtlaccihuatl" is told.
>
> **Revised:** The legend "Popocatepetl and Ixtlaccihuatl" is told in Mexico.

who, whom

In formal writing, remember to use *who* only as a subject in clauses and sentences and *whom* only as an object.

> Amy Tan, *who* writes about the two worlds of her life, grew up in San Francisco's Chinatown.
>
> Langston Hughes, *whom* we discussed yesterday, was a leader in an important cultural movement during the 1920's called the Harlem Renaissance.

Speaking, Listening, and Viewing Handbook

Communication is the way in which people convey their ideas and interact with one another. The literature in this book is written, which is one form of communication, but much of your personal communication is probably oral or visual. Oral communication involves both speaking and listening. Visual communication involves both conveying messages through physical expression or pictorial representations and interpreting images. Developing strong communication skills can benefit your school life and your life outside of school.

Many of the assignments accompanying the literature in this textbook involve speaking, listening, viewing, and representing. This handbook identifies some of the terminology related to the oral and visual communication you experience every day and the assignments you may do in conjunction with the literature in this book.

Communication

You use many different kinds of communication every day. When you communicate with your friends, your teachers, or your parents, or when you interact with a cashier in a store, you are communicating orally. In addition to ordinary conversation, oral communication includes class discussions, speeches, interviews, presentations, and debates. When you communicate face to face, you usually use more than your voice to get your message across. If you communicate by telephone, however, you must rely solely on your verbal skills. At times, you may use more visual communication than any other kind. For example, when you paint a picture, participate in a dance recital, or prepare a multimedia presentation, you use strategies of visual communication.

The following terms will give you a better understanding of the many elements that are part of oral and visual communication:

BODY LANGUAGE refers to the use of facial expressions, eye contact, gestures, posture, and movement to communicate a feeling or an idea.

CONNOTATION is the set of associations a word calls to mind. The connotations of the words you choose influence the message you send. For example, most people respond more favorably to being described as "slim" rather than as "skinny." The connotation of *slim* is more appealing than that of *skinny*.

EYE CONTACT is direct visual contact with another person's eyes.

FEEDBACK is the set of verbal and nonverbal reactions that indicate to a speaker that a message has been received and understood.

GESTURES are the movements made with arms, hands, face, and fingers to communicate.

LISTENING is understanding and interpreting sound in a meaningful way. You listen differently for different purposes.
Listening for key information: For example, when a teacher gives an assignment, or when someone gives you directions to a place, you listen for key information.
Listening for main points: In a classroom exchange of ideas or information, or while watching a television documentary, you listen for main points.
Listening critically: When you evaluate a performance, song, or a persuasive or political speech, you listen critically, questioning and judging the speaker's message.

MEDIUM is the material or technique used to present a visual image. Common media include paint, clay, and film.

NONVERBAL COMMUNICATION is communication without the use of words. People communicate nonverbally through gestures, facial expressions, posture, and body movements. Sign language is an entire language based on nonverbal communication.

VIEWING is observing, understanding, analyzing, and evaluating information presented through visual means. You might use the following questions to help you interpret what you view:
- What subject is presented?
- What is communicated about the subject?
- Which parts are factual? Which are opinion?
- What mood, attitude, or opinion is conveyed?
- What is your emotional response?

VOCAL DELIVERY is the way in which you present a message. Your vocal delivery involves all of the following elements:
Volume: the loudness or quietness of your voice
Pitch: the high or low quality of your voice
Rate: the speed at which you speak; also called pace
Stress: the amount of emphasis placed on different syllables in a word or on different words in a sentence

All of these elements individually, and the way in which they are combined, contribute to the meaning of a spoken message.

Speaking, Listening, and Viewing Situations

Here are some of the many types of situations in which you apply speaking, listening, and viewing skills:

AUDIENCE Your audience in any situation refers to the person or people to whom you direct your message. An audience can be a group of people sitting in a classroom or auditorium observing a performance or just one person to whom you address a question or a comment. When preparing for any speaking situation, it's useful to analyze your audience, learning what you can about their background, interests, and attitudes so that you can tailor your message to them.

CHARTS AND GRAPHS are visual representations of statistical information. For example, a pie chart might indicate how the average dollar is spent by government, and a bar graph might compare populations in cities over time.

DEBATE A debate is a formal public-speaking situation in which participants prepare and present arguments on opposing sides of a question, stated as a **proposition.**

The two sides in a debate are the *affirmative* (pro) and the *negative* (con). The affirmative side argues in favor of the proposition, while the negative side argues against it. The affirmative side begins the debate, since it is seeking a change in belief or policy. The opposing sides take turns presenting their arguments, and each side has an opportunity for *rebuttal,* in which they may challenge or question the other side's argument.

DOCUMENTARIES are nonfiction films that analyze news events or other focused subjects. You can watch a documentary for the information on its subject.

GROUP DISCUSSION results when three or more people meet to solve a common problem, arrive at a decision, or answer a question of mutual interest. Group discussion is one of the most widely used forms of interpersonal communication in modern society.

INTERVIEW An interview is a form of interaction in which one person, the interviewer, asks questions of another person, the interviewee. Interviews may take place for many purposes: to obtain information, to discover a person's suitability for a job or a college, or to inform the public of a notable person's opinions.

MAPS are visual representations of the Earth's surface. Maps may show political boundaries or physical features. They can also provide information on a variety of other topics. A map's title and its key identify the content of the map.

ORAL INTERPRETATION is the reading or speaking of a work of literature aloud for an audience. Oral interpretation involves giving expression to the ideas, meaning, or even the structure of a work of literature. The speaker interprets the work through his or her vocal delivery. **Storytelling,** in which a speaker reads or tells a story expressively, is a form of oral interpretation.

PANEL DISCUSSION is a group discussion on a topic of interest common to all members of a panel and to a listening audience. A panel is usually composed of four to six experts on a particular topic who are brought together to share information and opinions.

PANTOMIME is a form of nonverbal communication in which an idea or a story is communicated completely through the use of gesture, body language, and facial expressions, without any words at all.

POLITICAL CARTOONS are drawings that comment on important political or social issues. Often, these cartoons use humor to convey a message about their subject. Viewers use their own knowledge of events to evaluate the cartoonist's opinion.

READERS THEATRE is a dramatic reading of a work of literature in which participants take parts from a story or play and read them aloud in expressive voices. Unlike a play, however, sets and costumes are not part of the performance, and the participants remain seated as they deliver their lines.

ROLE PLAY To role-play is to take the role of a person or character and, as that character, act out a given situation, speaking, acting, and responding in the manner of the character.

SPEECH A speech is a talk or address given to an audience. A speech may be **impromptu**—delivered on the spur of the moment with no preparation—or formally prepared and delivered for a specific purpose or occasion.

- *Purposes:* The most common purposes of speeches are to persuade (for example, political speeches), to entertain, to explain, and to inform.
- *Occasions:* Different occasions call for different types of speeches. Speeches given on these occasions could be persuasive, entertaining, or informative, as appropriate. The following are common occasions for speeches:

Introduction: Introducing a speaker at a meeting
Presentation: Giving an award or acknowledging the contributions of someone
Acceptance: Accepting an award or tribute
Keynote: Giving an inspirational address at a large meeting or convention
Commencement: Honoring the graduates of a school

Test Preparation Handbook

Contents

Test Preparation Workshop 1

Reading Comprehension — Using Context Clues

Strategies for Success

The reading sections of standardized tests ask you to read a passage and answer questions about word meanings. Some questions require you to figure out the meanings of words by using context clues. Use the following strategies to help you answer this type of test question:

Look for Synonyms and Antonyms Context clues are the words or phrases around an unfamiliar word that give you clues to that word's meaning. Sometimes a passage contains a synonym (word with the same meaning) or an antonym (word with the opposite meaning) for the unfamiliar word. Look at these examples:

> Helen didn't always mean to be **facetious**; still, almost everything she said was humorous. She charmed the audience, who had come in looking **dour** but went away with cheerful smiles on their faces.

1 In this passage, the word **facetious** means—
   A funny   C flattering
   B upsetting   D sad

2 The word **dour** in this passage means—
   A relieved   C gloomy
   B expectant   D happy

For Question 1: From the context, it is clear that *facetious* and *humorous* are synonyms. The correct answer is another synonym, *funny*.

For Question 2: The context suggests that *dour* is the opposite of *cheerful*, so **C** is correct.

Look for Definitions, Explanations, Descriptions, or Examples When you are asked to define an unfamiliar word, reread the passage to see if the word is explained or defined or if a description or examples in the passage can

help you figure out the meaning. Look at these examples.

> We went to a **retrospective** of the work of a local artist and saw samples of her lifetime work. She had expressed herself in several **media,** including oils, charcoal, pastels, and watercolor.

1 In this passage, **retrospective** means—
   A biographical movie   C critical lecture
   B representative   D art store
     exhibition

2 The word **media** in this passage means—
   A names   C materials
   B shows   D decades

For Question 1: The words "samples of her lifetime work" explain what a retrospective is. **B** is correct.

For Question 2: Oils, charcoal, pastels, and watercolor are examples of materials used in art. **C** is correct.

Apply the Strategies

Answer these test questions based on the passage.

> After her car accident, we visited my aunt in the hospital. She is a bit **prolix,** fond of using twenty words where two would do. Still, her **veracity** is admirable. She admitted with charming honesty that the accident had been her fault entirely.

1 In this passage, the word **prolix** means—
   A angry   C distant
   B wordy   D cheerful

2 The word **veracity** in this passage means—
   A truthfulness   C dishonesty
   B strength   D conversation

Test Preparation Workshop 2

Reading Comprehension — Arranging Details in Sequential Order

Strategies for Success

The reading sections of standardized tests require you to read a passage and answer multiple-choice questions about the sequence of details. Use the following strategies to help you answer test questions about sequence:

Read Carefully A passage is not always written in chronological, or time, order. Some passages may start with the most recent event and then go back to tell the story leading up to that event. Other passages may start in the middle of a story and then use a flashback to give background information. You must read carefully to determine sequence. Look at the following example:

> In 1986, the Statue of Liberty got new steel supports, a new torch, and a thorough cleaning. Other than those details, she was in good shape for a hundred-year-old woman. Her story began in 1865 when a group of Frenchmen decided to give the United States a monument to freedom. Sculptor Frederic-Auguste Bartholdi designed and built the monument. Bartholdi sought help from engineer Gustave Eiffel, who years later designed Paris's Eiffel Tower. When Bartholdi finished the Statue of Liberty, it was taken apart, and shipped to New York City. It arrived in 1885 and was dedicated in 1886.

Which event described in the passage happened most recently?

  A The Statue of Liberty was dedicated.
  B Some Frenchmen decided to build a monument to freedom.
  C The Statue of Liberty was taken apart.
  D The Statue of Liberty was cleaned.

A happened in 1886, **B** in 1865, **C** in 1885, and **D** in 1986. **D** is correct.

Look for Word Clues When you are asked a question about the sequence of events, look for words that signal the order of events, such as *first, next, lately,* and *last,* to help you determine the sequence. Look at the following question based on the passage above.

Gustave Eiffel advised the sculptor Bartholdi—
  A while Eiffel was designing the Eiffel Tower
  B before Eiffel designed the Eiffel Tower
  C after Eiffel designed the Eiffel Tower
  D after 1885

The words "years later designed Paris's Eiffel Tower" tell you that **B** is correct.

Apply the Strategies

Answer the questions based on this passage.

> Justin couldn't believe how much work it was just to get his baby brother ready for an outing in the park. After changing Scott's diaper, he'd put sunscreen on him and found a cap to keep the sun out of his eyes. As they were about to leave, Justin realized he should probably take an extra diaper. Then he thought Scott might get hungry, so he packed a snack. Finally, Justin remembered that Dad always took a few toys in case Scott got bored. By the time Justin had squeezed everything into his backpack, Scott needed another diaper change!

1 Before Justin put sunscreen on Scott, he—
  A changed his diaper
  B packed some toys
  C gave Scott a snack
  D found his baseball cap

2 The last thing Justin remembered to pack was—
  A a cap **B** toys **C** diaper **D** sunscreen

Test Preparation Workshop 3

Reading Comprehension

Identify Main Idea

Strategies for Success

The reading sections of standardized tests require you to read a passage and answer multiple-choice questions about main ideas. Use the following strategies to help you answer such questions:

Identify the Stated Main Idea The main idea, the most important point of a passage, is often stated in a topic sentence that summarizes the details in the passage. The topic sentence may be located anywhere in the passage. In some tests, identifying the main idea means finding a restatement of the topic sentence. Read the following:

> Mrs. Gomez always does nice things for the young people of the neighborhood. For your birthday, she might present you with a home-baked goodie or a bouquet from her garden. She welcomes youngsters to cool off under her lawn sprinklers. Visitors are encouraged to pick flowers in her garden.

What is the main idea of this passage?
   A Mrs. Gomez gives the neighborhood children birthday presents.
   B Mrs. Gomez is always doing nice things for the young people of the neighborhood.
   C Mrs. Gomez wants you to enjoy her garden.
   D Mrs. Gomez welcomes children to cool off under her lawn sprinklers.

A and **D** are details. **C** does not take in all the details in the passage. **B** is correct.

Identify the Implied Main Idea If a main idea is not stated, it is implied or suggested. To identify an implied main idea, look for the answer choice that best summarizes the details in the passage. Look at this example:

> One summer Nilda noticed that the weeds were taking over Mrs. Gomez's garden. The day before the woman's eighty-fifth birthday, Nilda had an inspiration. She called eight young people to weed Mrs. Gomez's garden. After three hours, the garden was weed-free and nine happy people were drinking lemonade and eating cake on the porch.

What is the main idea of this passage?
   A People over eighty need help gardening.
   B Mrs. Gomez's garden needed weeding.
   C Several young people pitched in to weed Mrs. Gomez's garden for her birthday.
   D Mrs. Gomez loved to celebrate birthdays.

A and **D** do not summarize the information in the passage. **B** is a detail. **C** is correct.

Apply the Strategies

Read this passage and then answer the questions that follow.

> Even though they are predators, octopuses would rather flee than fight. Sometimes they avoid enemies by changing their skin patterns to blend in with their surroundings. If this doesn't work, an alarmed octopus can retreat at remarkable speeds.
>
> Just how smart are octopuses? In experiments, some have learned to solve simple puzzles and problems. One scientist has seen an octopus dismantle a dead crab in order to get the food back to its den.

1 What is the main idea of the first paragraph?
   A Octopuses would rather flee than fight.
   B Octopuses can blend in with their surroundings.
   C Octopuses are rapid swimmers.
   D Octopuses are predators.

2 What is the main idea of the second paragraph?
   A Octopuses can learn to solve puzzles.
   B Octopuses exhibit intelligence.
   C Octopuses eat crabs.
   D An octopus can dismantle a crab.

Test Preparation Workshop 4

Reading Comprehension — Author's Point of View and Purpose

Strategies for Success

The reading sections of standardized tests require you to read a passage and answer multiple-choice questions about the author's point of view and purpose. Use these strategies to help you answer such questions:

Recognize the Author's Purpose An author may write primarily to inform, persuade, or entertain readers. To identify an author's purpose, look at the language he or she uses. Facts and details can be presented plainly, or in a way that attempts to convince readers of something. Likewise, if an author aims to entertain, the language may be dramatic or humorous.

Recognize Authors' Points of View Authors' points of view are the way they think and feel about their subjects. Authors may state their point of view directly or imply it through the language they use. If a test question asks you to identify an author's point of view, look for the ways he or she expresses feelings.

Use the following editorial to practice recognizing an author's purpose and point of view.

Though some may not know it, our class will soon vote on whether formal wear will be required at the annual dance. Many have said that they want to continue the tradition of formal attire. Others say that formal wear is uncomfortable, and too expensive for most students. Though the outcome of the vote means a great deal to all of us, the most important thing is for everyone to cast their votes.

1 In writing this, the author's purpose was to—
  A inform readers about the upcoming vote and its importance
  B offer an entertaining view of school politics
  C encourage a vote for formal clothing

  D persuade others to dress up for the dance

Since the letter is neither primarily entertaining nor persuasive, **B**, **C**, and **D** are incorrect. **A** is correct.

2 What is the author's point of view?
  A The author wants the tradition of formal wear to continue.
  B The author dislikes formal dress.
  C The author likes dressing formally.
  D The author thinks it is important to be informed and to vote.

The author appears neutral about the outcome of the vote, so **A** and **B** are wrong. There is no evidence supporting **C**. **D** is correct.

Apply the Strategies

Answer the questions based on this passage.

Bill wrote his parents from camp:

I love this place. There is so much to do and I get to choose my activities. I've tried pottery and working in stained glass. The food is plain but plentiful, and desserts are great. I can't wait to see you on Visitors' Day.

His sister Lillian wrote:

I'm not really enjoying camp. My cabin mates are mean. The activities are OK, but we do the same thing everyday. One good thing is the food. Please write back and say I can come home with you after Visitors' Day.

1 The purpose of Lillian's letter is to—
  A inform her parents about camp activities
  B complain about the food
  C persuade her parents to let her come home
  D express her feelings about her cabin mates

2 Lillian and Bill differ in their views of—
  A camp activities **C** seeing their parents
  B camp food **D** their cabin mates

Test Preparation Workshop 5

Reading Comprehension — Making Generalizations

Strategies for Success

The reading sections of standardized tests require you to read a passage and answer multiple-choice questions about generalizations. Use the following strategies to help you answer such questions:

Consider the Evidence A generalization is a broad statement that sums up or describes an array of facts and details. A generalization should always be based on facts and details that can be checked for accuracy. Read this example, then answer the question that follows.

> Clara Barton was much younger than her four brothers and sisters. Because she had few playmates, she was very shy as a child. When she was nine, her parents sent her to boarding school, hoping she would overcome her shyness. The opposite happened. After some students laughed at her lisp, she refused to stay at the school. Remarkably, Clara Barton became a teacher herself. When she was refused promotion to the job of principal, she left teaching. She later worked at the U.S. Patent Office, nursed soldiers during the Civil War, and founded the American Red Cross.

The author provides evidence to show that—
 A Clara Barton saved many lives
 B Clara Barton overcame childhood shyness to achieve many things
 C Clara Barton could not stick with one job
 D everyone admired Clara Barton

There is no evidence to support **A**, **C**, or **D**. Evidence does show that Barton was shy and accomplished many things. **B** is correct.

Avoid Overgeneralizations An overgeneralization is a statement that is too broad to be supported by the relevant facts. Words like *all*, *every*, and *always* may signal overgeneralizations. Review the passage above and answer the following question.

Information in the passage shows that—
 A Clara Barton was always successful
 B Clara Barton had wonderful relationships with all her family
 C all people with lisps are shy
 D as a child, Clara Barton was mainly with adults

Evidence contradicts **A**. No evidence supports **B**. **C** is an overgeneralization. **D** is correct.

Apply the Strategies

Use the strategies you have learned to answer the questions based on this passage.

> My granddad says that when he was growing up, most people in the United States had never seen a soccer game. Now most towns have leagues for all ages of boys and girls. I read that more young people in the United States play soccer than Little League baseball. Our town even has a soccer league for adults. Granddad watches us play and wonders what sport our children will be playing that we haven't even heard of yet.

1 The author provides evidence to show that—
 A his family likes soccer more than baseball
 B soccer has increased in popularity in the United States
 C baseball is more popular than soccer
 D baseball and soccer are the most popular sports in the United States

2 Information in the passage indicates that—
 A people in different age groups play soccer
 B people of all ages play soccer
 C new sports are constantly being developed
 D most older people dislike soccer

Test Preparation Workshop 6

Reading Comprehension

Predicting Probable Actions and Outcomes

Strategies for Success

The reading sections of standardized tests require you to read a passage and answer questions about probable outcomes and actions. Use the following strategies to help you answer such questions:

Analyze the Facts Look at the details, facts, and information in the passage. Notice how characters behave and what circumstances surround the actions or dialogue of the passage.

Make Logical Assumptions Remember that writers must make their stories unfold according to some believable logic or pattern. For instance, if you know about one character's personality, you can predict how he or she will behave in future scenes. Look at this example:

> Todd slid into a seat just as the newspaper's representative began to talk. "I have just a few suggestions for you new deliverers. First, look at the map that we have attached to your route list, which is alphabetical by customer's last name. Then plan the most efficient route. Finally, rewrite the list in the order you will deliver the papers."
>
> Todd had just begun to follow these directions when Kristina passed his seat. "Are you actually doing that? That's a waste of time. I can figure out my route in my head." Kristina's list, like Todd's, had at least thirty customers on ten different streets. He doubted that anyone could figure out the best route at a glance. But he also knew better than to argue with Kristina. "Come on, my mom will give you a lift," she said. Gratefully Todd accepted.

I After he gets home, Todd will most likely—
  A deliver his papers
  B throw away the map he received
  C finish rewriting his route list
  D call Kristina to thank her for the ride

Evidence suggests that Todd thinks rewriting the list is a good idea, so **C** is correct.

2 The first time Kristina delivers her papers, she will probably—
  A not take the most efficient route
  B run into Todd
  C ask Todd for help
  D ask her mother to drive her around

There is no evidence to support **B**, **C**, or **D**. Based on the evidence that Kristina seems determined not to rewrite her list and Todd says her route is long and complicated, **A** is correct.

Apply the Strategies

Answer the questions based on this passage.

> Marcie slammed her locker shut and hurried down the hall. She wanted to walk home with Chaney to discuss their weekend plans. Then she remembered that Ms. Weaver was offering extra help in German that afternoon. Marcie hadn't done well on the quiz that day. Ahead she spied Chaney. "Wait up!" she yelled. Chaney turned. "Oh, hi," she smiled. "I wish we could walk home together, Marcie, but I have to go to Ms. Weaver for some extra help. Today's quiz was murder."

I Marcie will probably—
  A walk home alone
  B never understand German verbs
  C not see Chaney on the weekend
  D suggest they both go for extra help

2 If she gets extra help from Ms. Weaver, Marcie will probably—
  A miss walking home with Chaney
  B do poorly on her next quiz
  C understand German verbs better
  D neglect her other subjects

Test Preparation Workshop 7

Reading Comprehension

Fact and Opinion

Strategies for Success

The reading sections of standardized tests require you to read a passage and answer multiple-choice questions about facts and opinions. Use the following strategies to help you answer such questions:

Recognize Facts A fact can be proven to be true by consulting a reliable source, such as a book or an unbiased expert. When you are asked to identify a fact, ask yourself, "Is it possible to find out whether or not this is true?" Look at this example:

> There are many things to see and do in Washington D.C. You can visit the Washington Monument, the Capitol, and the White House. You could spend weeks exploring the many museums that are part of the Smithsonian Institution. The best is the National Museum of American History, where you can see George Washington's false teeth. Some of the city's spots, such as the Vietnam War Memorial, are thought-provoking. For a blend of fun and education, everyone should see Washington, D.C., at least once.

Which of these is a FACT in the passage?

   A Washington, D.C., is a fascinating city.
   B At the National Museum of American History, you can see George Washington's false teeth.
   C The Vietnam War Memorial is thought-provoking and fun.
   D Everyone should see Washington, D.C., once.

A, **C**, and **D** cannot be shown to be true. They are the speaker's opinions. **B** is correct.

Recognize Opinions Opinions are statements of belief expressing a writer's attitudes or feelings. A writer may use facts to support opinions, but opinions themselves cannot be proven. When you are asked to identify an opinion, look for a statement that cannot be checked against any objective source. Look at this question based on the passage above:

Which is an OPINION expressed in the passage?

   A Washington, D.C., has many attractions.
   B Everyone should see Washington, D.C., once.
   C The Vietnam War Memorial is in Washington, D.C.
   D The Smithsonian Institution includes many museums.

A, **C**, and **D** can be proven to be true by research. **B** is the writer's opinion.

Apply the Strategies

Read the following passage and answer the questions.

> No student at my school should ever have a boring afternoon. There are after-school activities for every interest. Athletes can run track or play basketball. The Math Team challenges mathematicians to put their skills to work. There are clubs for readers, history buffs, and cooks. The chess club is best. I've improved my game tremendously since joining. With all these activities, maybe we need a Free-Time Club, for those who just want to relax!

1 Which of these statements is an OPINION?
   A There is a club for readers.
   B Athletes can run track.
   C No student at my school should ever have a boring afternoon.
   D I have improved my chess game since joining the Chess Club.

2 Which is a FACT expressed in the passage?
   A The best activity is the Chess Club.
   B The Math Team challenges mathematicians.
   C Maybe we need a Free-Time Club.
   D After-school activities cover every interest.

Test Preparation Workshop 8

Writing Skills — Sentence Construction

Strategies for Success

The writing sections of standardized tests require you to read a passage and answer multiple-choice questions about sentence construction. Use the following strategies to help you answer such questions:

Recognize Incomplete Sentences and Run-on Sentences Sentences should express complete, unified thoughts. Incomplete sentences lack either a subject or a predicate. Run-on sentences include two or more sentences without proper punctuation between them. You can correct an incomplete sentence by adding to it or by combining it with a sentence or another incomplete sentence. Run-on sentences can be corrected by adding the proper punctuation.

Combine Sentences Sometimes two short sentences that are closely related sound better if they are combined to make a single sentence. Look at the following sample test item:

(1) In 1984, two men were cutting peat They were cutting it from a bog in Lindow Moss, England. Suddenly, they saw a human foot sticking up out of the peat. (2) The men called the police they needed an archaeologist instead. Lindow Man had been dead for about 2,300 years.

Choose the best way to write each underlined section. If it needs no change, choose **D**.

1 **A** In 1984, two men cutting peat from a bog in Lindow Moss, England.
  B In 1984, two men were cutting peat they were cutting it from a bog in Lindow Moss, England.
  C In 1984, two men were cutting peat from a bog in Lindow Moss, England.
  D Correct as is

A is incomplete. **B** is a run-on sentence. **C** is correct because it properly combines two short related sentences.

2 **A** The men called the police, but they needed an archaeologist instead.
  B The men called the police, and they needed an archaeologist instead.
  C The men called. The police they need an archaeologist instead.
  D Correct as is

B corrects the run-on sentence, but the conjunction *and* doesn't work. **C** is punctuated incorrectly. **A** is correct because it properly punctuates a run-on sentence.

Apply the Strategies

Choose the best way to write each underlined section. If it needs no change, choose **D**.

(1) When you eat breakfast cereal. You are actually getting muscle power. From the sun. (2) Plants absorb the sun's energy. They use it to produce glucose. Glucose is changed to starch, which gives humans energy when eaten.

1 **A** When you eat breakfast cereal, you are actually getting muscle power. From the sun.
  B When you eat breakfast. Cereal you are actually getting muscle power from the sun.
  C When you eat breakfast cereal, you are actually getting muscle power from the sun.
  D Correct as is

2 **A** Plants absorb the sun's energy and use it to produce glucose.
  B Plants absorb the sun's energy. Using it to produce glucose.
  C Plants absorbing the sun's energy. They using it to produce energy.
  D Correct as is

Test Preparation Workshop 9

Writing Skills | Appropriate Usage

Strategies for Success

The writing sections of standardized tests require you to read a passage and answer multiple-choice questions about appropriate usage. Use the following strategies to help you answer such questions:

Use the Correct Form of a Word Some test questions will ask you to choose the correct part of speech, the appropriate form of an adjective or adverb, the correct case of a pronoun, or the correct way to express a negative. Look at these examples:

1 After a _____ performance at the trials, Mark did very well at the meet.
   A disappoint   **C** disappointment
   B disappointed   **D** disappointing

An adjective is needed. **B** and **D** are adjectives, but *disappointed* cannot modify *performance*. **D** is correct.

2 The child played _____ in the sandbox.
   A happier   **C** more happy
   B happily   **D** happiest

An adverb is needed to modify the verb *played*. **B** is correct.

3 Emily and _____ gave a report about Egypt.
   A her   **B** him   **C** she   **D** herself

The correct answer must be in the same case as *Emily*. The answer is **C**.

4 No one _____ that sign.
   A ever sees   **C** doesn't ever see
   B hardly never sees **D** never sees

B, **C**, and **D** form double negatives. **A** is correct.

Use Correct Agreement A verb must agree with its subject in number. A pronoun must agree with its antecedent (the word it stands

for). Look at these examples:

5 The brown dog _____ to visit every day.
   A come   **C** comes
   B have come   **D** were coming

The verb must agree with the singular subject *dog*. **C** is correct.

6 Luanne lost _____ wallet at the game.
   A her   **B** its   **C** their   **D** him

The antecedent, Luanne, is third person singular feminine, so **A** is correct.

Use Correct Verb Tense and Form Some test questions will require you to choose the correct tense of a verb or the correct form of an irregular verb. Look at this example:

7 By the time we got home, the wind _____ down several trees.
   A had blew   **C** had blown
   B blown   **D** blowed

The verb describes past action that happened before another past action, so the past perfect tense is needed. **C** is correct.

Apply the Strategies

Choose the words that belong in each space.

About one person in ten __(1)__ left-handed. Nobody __(2)__ for sure why people prefer one hand over the other. Lefties have __(3)__ difficulties in a right-handed world. They may be __(4)__ with objects like scissors and cameras designed for righties.

1 **A** were   **B** is   **C** are   **D** have been

2 **A** don't never know   **C** knows
   B hardly knows   **D** won't never know

3 **A** their   **B** them   **C** there   **D** they

4 **A** awkwardly   **C** awkward
   B awkwarder   **D** most awkwardly

Test Preparation Workshop 10

Writing Skills — Spelling, Capitalization, Punctuation

Strategies for Success

The writing sections of standardized tests often require you to read a passage and answer multiple-choice questions about spelling, capitalization, and punctuation. Use the following strategies to help you answer such questions:

Recognize Spelling Errors Check the spelling of the words in the passage you are being tested on. Pay special attention to homophones (to, too, two), double vowels (squeak, not squeek), suffixes (-ness, not –nes), and words containing –ie- or –ei-.

Recognize Capitalization Errors Make sure that the first word in a sentence or a quotation is capitalized, that proper nouns are capitalized, and that no words are capitalized unnecessarily. All the words in a compound proper noun should be capitalized (Middletown City Council).

Recognize Punctuation Errors Check end punctuation, make sure that all necessary commas and no unnecessary commas are there, and notice if both pairs of quotation marks are present. Look at this example:

Read the passage and decide which type of error, if any, appears in each underlined section.

(1) What's it like two hundred miles above Earth (2) Astronaut and Senator John glenn says, (3) "Space is completely black, even when the son is shining." Glenn was the first American to orbit Earth in 1962. (4) Thirty-six years later he went back into space on the space shuttle.

1 **A** Spelling error   **C** Punctuation error
   B Capitalization error   **D** No error

2 **A** Spelling error   **C** Punctuation error
   B Capitalization error   **D** No error

3 **A** Spelling error   **C** Punctuation error
   B Capitalization error   **D** No error

4 **A** Spelling error   **C** Punctuation error
   B Capitalization error   **D** No error

For question 1: The sentence has no end punctuation, so **C** is correct.

For question 2: *Glenn* is a proper noun and should be capitalized, so **B** is correct.

For question 3: *Son* is a homophone for *sun,* so **A** is correct.

For question 4: There are no errors, so **D** is correct.

Apply the Strategies

Read the passage and decide which type of error, if any, appears in each underlined section.

(1) If you are looking for extreme weather, here's a gide for where to go. (2) In Death Valley California, the temperature has been known to reach 134 degrees Fahrenheit. (3) To cool off, try Prospect Creek Camp, Alaska, where it can go down to eighty degrees below zero. (4) For high winds, climb Mount Washington, new Hampshire, where winds have reached 231 miles per hour.

1 **A** Spelling error   **C** Punctuation error
   B Capitalization error   **D** No error

2 **A** Spelling error   **C** Punctuation error
   B Capitalization error   **D** No error

3 **A** Spelling error   **C** Punctuation error
   B Capitalization error   **D** No error

4 **A** Spelling error   **C** Punctuation error
   B Capitalization error   **D** No error

Test Preparation Workshop 11

Research Skills — Using Information Resources

Strategies for Success

Some tests require you to review a packet of information resources, and to respond to questions about how you would use these resources to gather information and plan a report on a given subject. Use these strategies:

Review the Packet of Information Skim through the packet to see what types of material are included, such as articles from encyclopedias and computer information.

Scan the Questions Look through the questions to see which types of information are required to answer the questions. Focus on each question separately. The questions are not necessarily related to each other. Locate the best example or piece of information in the packet to answer each question.

Use Correct Sentence Form Write responses to the short-answer questions in complete sentences and include key words. Look at these examples:.

Directions: Suppose that you are writing a report on the life and times of Thomas Alva Edison (1847–1931). Edison is one of the world's most important inventors.

This packet includes several information resources about Thomas Alva Edison:

- an excerpt from an encyclopedia article, "Inventions of the Nineteenth Century"
- a biographical dictionary entry
- *Thomas Alva Edison*, a biography of the inventor: a short excerpt, table of contents, and a list of key dates in Edison's life and career
- Computer screen: on-line index of library books about Thomas Edison

Excerpt from Encyclopedia Article: "Inventions of the Nineteenth Century"

A flood of inventions swept the United States in the late 1800's. By the 1890's Americans were patenting 21,000 new inventions a year. These inventions helped industry to grow and become more efficient. New devices also made daily life easier in many American homes.

Advanced Communication Some remarkable new devices filled the need for faster communication. The telegraph speeded communication within the United States. It still took weeks, however, for news from Europe to arrive by boat. In 1866, Cyrus Field ran an underwater telegraph cable across the Atlantic Ocean, bringing the United States and Europe closer together.

Thomas Edison In an age of invention, Thomas Edison was right at home. In 1876, he opened a research laboratory in Menlo Park, New Jersey. There, Edison boasted that he and his 15 co-workers set out to create "minor" inventions every 10 days and "a big thing every 6 months or so."

Biographical Dictionary

Edison, Thomas Alva A poor student, Thomas Edison grew up to invent the light bulb, the phonograph, and dozens of other devices. Edison once went without sleep for three days working on his phonograph. At last, he heard his own voice reciting "Mary Had a Little Lamb." Edison said, "Genius is one percent inspiration and ninety-nine percent perspiration."

Table of Contents from *Thomas Alva Edison*

Test Preparation Workshop 11

Research Skills — Using Information Resources (cont.)

Short Excerpt from *Thomas Alva Edison*

The key to Edison's success was his approach. He turned inventing into a system. Teams of experts refined Edison's ideas and turned them into practical inventions. Menlo Park became an "invention factory." The results were amazing. Edison became knows as the "Wizard of Menlo Park" for inventing the light bulb, the phonograph, and hundreds of other devices.

Lists of Key Dates from *Thomas Alva Edison*

1847: Born in Milan, Ohio

1852: Moved to Port Huron, Michigan

1869: Was paid $40,000 for improvements to the stock ticker. Opened his first workshop in Newark, New Jersey

1874: Improved the typewriter

1877: Invented the phonograph

1879: Perfected the electric light

1887: Moved to West Orange, New Jersey. Worked on such inventions as the motion picture, a storage battery, a cement mixer, the Dictaphone, and a duplicating machine.

1931: Died at 84 in West Orange, New Jersey

Computer Screen

Library Online Catalog

Subject Search: Thomas Alva Edison

Line	Titles	Subjects
1	2	Edison, Thomas: Early Life
2	4	Edison, Thomas: Bibliography
3	1	Edison, Thomas: Biography

Sample Questions and Explanations

1 Which information given in the encyclopedia article would be LEAST useful for your report?

A the number of patents in the 1890's

B the date Edison opened his laboratory

C Cyrus Field's contributions to communication

D the description of Edison's workshop

The correct answer is **C.** Cyrus Field's contributions are not important to a report on Edison.

2 In which chapter of *Thomas Alva Edison* would you find information about Edison's schooling? ("Early Years" would provide the information.)

3 Which of these sources would you use to find books written about Thomas Alva Edison?

A the encyclopedia article

B the biographical dictionary article

C computer screen

D the biography *Thomas Alva Edison*

The correct answer is **C.** The other sources do not reference other books about Edison.

Apply the Strategies

4 Suppose you are going to write an outline of your report on the life of Thomas Alva Edison. What three main topics would you include?

5 State the main idea of your report.

6 In which source would you find detailed information about Edison's marriage?

A the encyclopedia article

B the biographical dictionary entry

C the main body of the biography

D the list of key dates from the biography

Test Preparation Workshop 12

Writing Skills — Proofreading

Strategies for Success

The writing sections of some standardized tests assess your ability to edit, proofread, and use other writing processes. You are required to look for mistakes in passages and then to choose the best way to correct them.

Check for Incorrect Verb Tense and Errors in Subject-Verb Agreement Check to see that the correct verb tense is used and make the verb agree in number with its subject. If the parts of the subject name more than one thing, use a plural verb. If the parts of the subject refer to the same thing, use a singular verb.

Correct Run-on Sentences Use an end mark and a capital letter to separate main clauses. Use a semicolon between clauses.

Correct Sentence Fragments Add a subject or verb to make a sentence fragment a complete sentence.

Use Supporting Details Effectively Avoid the use of details that interrupt the flow of the passage, and that do not support the main idea.

Sample Passage and Questions:

Directions: A student wrote a paper about Alaska. There are mistakes that need correcting.

(1) Susan Butcher win the Iditarod dog-sled race several times. (2) A large strip of mountains cross Alaska. (3) Despite its challenges, the race attracts more and more racers every year. (4) In the years ahead, racers may come from such far-off countries as Sweden Norway and Denmark.

I Select the best way to write sentence 1.
   A Susan Butcher won the Iditarod dog-sled race several times.
   B Susan Butcher will win the Iditarod dog-sled race several times.
   C Susan Butcher would have won the Iditarod dog-sled race several times.
   D Best as it is

The correct answer is **A**. *Won* is the past tense of the irregular verb *win*.

2 Select the best way to write sentence 2.
   A A large strip of mountains crosses Alaska.
   B A large strip of mountains do cross Alaska.
   C A mountainous strip crosses Alaska.
   D Best as it is.

The correct answer is **A**. A large strip of mountains crosses Alaska. The subject is singular and requires a singular verb.

Apply the Strategies

(1) Secretary of State Seward bought Alaska from Russia the deal was mocked as "Seward's Folly." (2) Seward's $7.2 million purchase proved to be a bargain; gold deposits were discovered there three decades later. (3) My uncle told me about a trip he took to Alaska when he was only 12 years old. (4) Prospectors first struck gold in 1889.

I Which is the best way to write the underlined section in sentence one?
   A Secretary of State Seward bought Alaska from Russia. The deal was mocked as "Seward's Folly."
   B Secretary of State Seward bought Alaska from Russia, and the deal was mocked.
   C Secretary of State Seward bought Alaska. The deal was "Seward's Folly."
   D Best as it is

2 Which is the correct way to fix the flow of the passage?
   A Delete sentence 3.
   B Move sentence 4 to the beginning.
   C Switch sentences 1 and 2.
   D Move sentence 1 to the end.

Test Preparation Workshop 13

Writing Skills — Responding to Writing Prompts

Strategies for Success

The writing sections of many standardized tests require you to write an essay based on a writing prompt. Your essay usually is evaluated as a whole, on a 1–6 point scale from *outstanding* to *deficient,* and assessed for focus, content, organization, grammar, usage, and mechanics. Use the following strategies to help you with a writing assessment:

Read the writing prompt The writing prompt consists of two parts. The first part explains the topic you are asked to write about, or the writing situation. The second part provides specific instructions on how to respond to the prompt.

Look for Key Words As you examine the writing prompt, look for key words such as *define, explain, classify,* and *contrast.* These words indicate the purpose of your essay. It is essential that you keep these key words in mind as you develop your essay.

Budget Your Time When writing for a test, you need to be aware of how much time you have. Allow one quarter of your time for gathering ideas, half your time for writing your first draft, and one quarter of your time for revising.

Collect Your Ideas Before you begin writing, jot down key ideas and details that you plan to include. Then, review your ideas and decide on the best organization.

Draft Carefully Because you'll have less time to revise than you might in other writing situations, take care in the words and sentences you use as you draft your essay. Begin with an introduction that presents your main point. Follow with body paragraphs, each focusing on a single subtopic. Then, end with a conclusion restating your point.

Use Transitions As you draft, use transitional words to indicate the connections between ideas. The following words show comparison-and-contrast relationships: *however; nevertheless; yet; likewise; in like manner; on the contrary; similarly; instead;* and *nonetheless.*

Proofread Make sure your descriptions are clear. Check that there are no errors in spelling, grammar, usage, or mechanics.

Key Strategies:

- Focus on the topic and do not include unnecessary information.
- Present the material in an organized manner.
- Provide supporting ideas.
- Write with sentence variety.
- Proofread your work.

Apply the Strategies

Practice the preceding strategies by writing an essay in response to the following prompt.

Sample Writing Prompt

Everyone looks forward to weekends and a break from the weekday routine. Think about one thing that you like to do on weekends and why. It could be a community activity, an opportunity to be by yourself to play video games or watch television, or it could be sharing time with family members and friends.

Now explain in an essay why this event or activity is important to you. Support your ideas with examples and details.

Reading Comprehension

Describing Plot, Setting, Character, and Mood

Read the passage, and then answer the questions that follow. Mark the letter of your answer on a bubble sheet if your teacher provides one; otherwise, number from 1 to 6 on a separate sheet of paper, and write the letter of the correct answer next to each number.

> While they ate their bread-and-bacon supper, while Alyce helped Edward mound up straw in a corner of the kitchen, while she sat by watching for him to go to sleep, all the while Edward talked of life on the manor. . . . And he complained at his lot, doing all the smallest tasks, . . . being teased for being so little and frail and tied to Cook's skirts and fit for nothing but gathering eggs. Finally as his eyes looked near to closing, he said, "Tell me a story, Alyce."
>
> ". . . [O]nce there was a boy who for all he was so small and puny was brave enough to do what he must although he didn't like it and was sometimes teased. Is that a story?"
>
> "Close enough, Alyce." And he closed his eyes.
>
> —*The Midwife's Apprentice* by Karen Cushman

1 What is the most likely setting of this passage?
  A a suburban home in the 1950s
  B an army hospital in World War II
  C a country house in medieval times
  D an abandoned hotel in the Old West

2 What is the central problem Edward faces?
  A He has to gather straw.
  B He wants to stay awake.
  C He does not like being teased.
  D He does not like Alyce's story.

3 Which of these words best describes the mood of the passage?
  A bright
  B familial
  C jubilant
  D suspenseful

4 In this passage, Edward's character is primarily revealed by—
  A his words and thoughts
  B Alyce's story
  C his surroundings
  D Alyce's thoughts

5 Based on the passage, which of these words best describes Alyce?
  A brilliant
  B irritable
  C jolly
  D motherly

6 How does Alyce's story relate to Edward?
  A It recalls how Edward used to behave.
  B It explains why Edward is often teased.
  C It restates Edward's own story.
  D It describes a boy worse off than Edward.

Reading Comprehension

Making Generalizations

Read each passage, and then answer the questions that follow. Mark the letter of your answer on a bubble sheet if your teacher provides one; otherwise, number from 1 to 4 on a separate sheet of paper, and write the letter of the correct answer next to each number.

It is believed that people began creating zoos as early as 4500 B.C. Rulers sometimes designed zoos themselves. In China, in about 1000 B.C., Wen Wang established a 1,500-acre zoological garden, which he named "The Garden of Intelligence." The Greeks also had collections of captive animals, and Alexander the Great collected animals on his expeditions. In Mexico during the 1500's, Hernán Cortés came upon a zoo so large it needed a staff of 300. One zoo in Vienna, Austria, has been open since 1752.

1 Based on the passage, which of these is an accurate generalization about the history of zoos?
  A The first zoos were primarily in America.
  B Early zoos were sometimes quite elaborate.
  C Most zoos were designed by political leaders.
  D Most zoos were founded hundreds of years ago.

2 Which of these is an accurate generalization about "The Garden of Intelligence"?
  A It contained more animals than European zoos.
  B It required more keepers than zoos in Mexico.
  C It was the oldest zoo in China.
  D It was a large zoo for its time.

Anton van Leeuwenhoek (1632–1723) was among the first people to observe microscopic life. Leeuwenhoek, a cloth merchant, first developed the microscope to examine the quality of cloth. Later, he began to use his microscope to observe drops of water, where he was amazed to find tiny moving organisms. These microorganisms included bacteria, protozoa, and rotifers.

3 Based on the passage, which of these is an accurate generalization about the organisms Leeuwenhoek observed with his microscope?
  A They were larger than cloth fibers.
  B They consisted mainly of bacteria.
  C They could not be seen by unaided human eyes.
  D They could easily survive without water.

4 Which of these is an accurate generalization about the career of Anton van Leeuwenhoek?
  A He was interested in science as well as business.
  B He had an extremely limited knowledge of science.
  C He is best known for his work as a cloth merchant.
  D He was the first person to observe microorganisms.

Reading Comprehension

Predicting Probable Actions and Outcomes

Read each passage, and then answer the questions that follow. Mark the letter of your answer on a bubble sheet if your teacher provides one; otherwise, number from 1 to 4 on a separate sheet of paper, and write the letter of the correct answer next to each number.

[Rikki-tikki-tavi] was a mongoose, rather like a little cat in his fur and his tail, but quite like a weasel in his head and his habits. . . .

One day, a high summer flood washed him out of the burrow where he lived with his father and mother, and carried him, kicking and clucking, down a roadside ditch. He found a little wisp of grass floating there, and clung to it till he lost his senses. When he revived, he was lying in the hot sun on the middle of a garden path, very draggled indeed, and a small boy was saying: "Here's a dead mongoose. Let's have a funeral."

"No," said his mother, "let's take him in and dry him. Perhaps he isn't really dead."

—"Rikki-tikki-tavi" by Rudyard Kipling

1 What will probably happen to the mongoose next?
   A He will follow the boy home.
   B He will be buried near the path.
   C He will be taken to the boy's house.
   D He will return to his parents' burrow.

2 How will the boy probably react to his mother's suggestion?
   A He will refuse to believe her.
   B He will try to change her mind.
   C He will want to sell the mongoose.
   D He will attempt to help the mongoose.

It has been a long time since Iona and his horse have moved from their place. They left the stable before supper, and still there is no fare. But now evening darkness is descending on the city. The pale light of the streetlamps is surrendering its place to vivid color, and the bustle in the street is becoming noisier.

"Cabby, to the Vyborg District!" hears Iona, "Cabby!"

Iona starts, and through eyelashes pasted over with snow he sees an officer in a cloak with a hood.

—"Heartache" by Anton Chekhov

3 What will Iona probably do next?
   A He will move his cab away from the officer.
   B He will pick up the officer in his cab.
   C He will return his horse to the stable.
   D He will leave his cab to eat supper.

4 How will the officer probably react if Iona does not respond?
   A He will repeat his order in a louder voice.
   B He will quietly walk to his destination.
   C He will apologize for making a scene.
   D He will offer to take Iona to supper.

Reading Comprehension

Distinguishing Fact and Opinion

Read each passage, and then answer the questions that follow. Mark the letter of your answer on a bubble sheet if your teacher provides one; otherwise, number from 1 to 4 on a separate sheet of paper, and write the letter of the correct answer next to each number.

Winslow Homer was not the only artist to cover the Civil War. Because photography at that time was too slow to capture battle action, newspapers and magazines sent artists to draw the battles. Henry Walke was one illustrator who, like Homer, got close enough to the action to make pen-and-ink sketches of it. These images provide a wrenching record of the war.

Photographs, too, were important. They illustrated the Civil War personalities and landscapes as well as the unthinkable aftermath of battle. Pioneer photographers like Mathew Brady and Alexander Gardner made significant contributions to coverage of the war.

1 Which of these is a FACT from the passage?
  A Photographs were unimportant in documenting the war.
  B Winslow Homer was not the only artist to cover the war.
  C Henry Walke's illustrations are a wrenching record of the war.
  D Photographs illustrated the aftermath of battles.

2 Which of these is an OPINION expressed in the passage?
  A Henry Walke made pen-and-ink sketches of the war.
  B Magazines sent artists to draw what the battles looked like.
  C Photography was too slow to capture battle action.

  D Alexander Gardner made significant contributions to the coverage of the war.

The Florida Everglades is a vast marsh area. It may be the world's most precious wetlands. It covers about 5,000 square miles, but the water averages less than a foot in depth. One of the most fascinating animals there is the rattlesnake. The Everglades is also home to alligators, panthers, and many types of birds.

Today, with the need to supply south Florida's water, the natural balance of the Everglades is at risk. Steps should be taken to protect this treasure.

3 Which of these is a FACT from the passage?
  A The Everglades' most fascinating animal is the rattlesnake.
  B People should protect the irreplaceable Everglades.
  C South Florida uses too much of the Everglades' water.
  D The Everglades is home to many types of birds.

4 Which of these is an OPINION expressed in the passage?
  A The Everglades is panther habitat.
  B The Everglades is one of the most precious wetlands.
  C The Everglades is covered by less than a foot of water.
  D The Everglades covers about 5,000 square miles of land.

Reading Comprehension

Drawing Inferences and Conclusions

Read the passage, and then answer the questions that follow. Mark the letter of your answer on a bubble sheet if your teacher provides one; otherwise, number from 1 to 6 on a separate sheet of paper, and write the letter of the correct answer next to each number.

> Though Apollo always honored the memory of Daphne she was not his only love. Another was a mortal, Clymene, by whom he had a son named Phaëthon. Phaëthon grew up with his mother, who, since she was mortal, could not dwell in the halls of Olympus or in the palace of the sun. She lived not far from the East in the land of Ethiopia, and as her son grew up, she would point to the place where Eos, goddess of the dawn, lighted up the sky and tell him that there his father dwelt. Phaëthon loved to boast of his divine father as he saw the golden chariot riding high through the air. He would remind his comrades of other sons of gods and mortal women who, by virtue of their great deeds, had become gods at last. . . . He could never bear to be beaten, even if he had to risk his life in some rash way to win.
>
> —"Phaëthon, Son of Apollo" by Olivia E. Coolidge

1 Which of these statements is a sound inference about Phaëthon?
A His father is a god.
B He was once mortal.
C He owns a golden chariot.
D His mother is named Daphne.

2 From what type of literature was this passage taken?
A a ballad
B a biography
C a drama
D a myth

3 What does Phaëthon hope will happen if he is first in everything?
A He will earn his mother's respect.
B He will be transformed into a god.
C He will win a mortal woman's love.
D He will be allowed to visit Ethiopia.

4 Which of these statements is a logical inference about the halls of Olympus?
A Phaëthon was born there.
B Clymene once lived there.
C Only gods may enter there.
D They were built by Apollo.

5 What does Apollo's golden chariot represent?
A the air   **C** the land
B the East   **D** the sun

6 What is implied by the last sentence of the passage?
A Phaëthon may take great risks because of his success.
B Phaëthon may come to harm as he strives to be godlike.
C Phaëthon may become arrogant if he behaves dangerously.
D Phaëthon may become discouraged if he behaves recklessly.

Reading Comprehension

Identifying Cause and Effect

Read the passage, and then answer the questions that follow. Mark the letter of your answer on a bubble sheet if your teacher provides one; otherwise, number from 1 to 5 on a separate sheet of paper, and write the letter of the correct answer next to each number.

The highwayman whistled a tune to the window, and Bess, the landlord's daughter, appeared to greet him. Someone else had heard the whistle, too, though: a door squeaked as Tim, the stableman, came close to listen. Tim loved Bess too, and he overheard the robber's promise to return to her by morning. Tim slipped away and set off toward town.

Waiting for the highwayman's return, Bess heard a noise, but not the familiar gait of her sweetheart's horse. Suddenly, there were soldiers at her window. In a moment they were tying her up, and setting a musket aimed at her heart. As the soldiers hid, Tim watched with satisfaction.

Bess struggled with the knots around her wrists and managed to free one hand. Suddenly, she heard the horse's hooves in the distance. What to do? They would surely catch him! Drawing one last breath, she moved her free hand to the trigger of the musket. The silence at the inn was shattered by the gun's roar.

Hearing the sound, the highwayman turned away and headed west. He would come back for Bess another day. He knew she would understand, but he did not know who was slumped on the floor of the inn, her head bowed over a musket.

—adapted from the poem "The Highwayman" by Alfred Noyes

---

1 What effect did the highwayman's whistle have?
   A to signal his sweetheart
   B to keep himself awake
   C to signal his arrival to Tim
   D to alert the soldiers

2 What causes the noise in the yard of the inn when the highwayman and Bess are at the window?
   A Bess firing a musket
   B Soldiers sneaking into the yard
   C Tim entering the yard to listen
   D The highwayman whistling

3 Why do the soldiers come to the inn?

   A to find a place to stay
   B to alert the landlord
   C to catch the highwayman
   D to protect Bess

4 What causes Tim to leave the yard?
   A He has no more work to do.
   B He is afraid of the highwayman.
   C He is angry at Bess.
   D He wants to tell the soldiers about the highwayman's return.

5 Why does Bess fire the musket?
   A to frighten the soldiers
   B to warn the highwayman
   C to show her anger with Tim
   D to help catch the highwayman

Combined Reading and Literary Skills

Read the passage, and then answer the questions that follow. Mark your answers to questions 1 to 9 on a bubble sheet if your teacher provides one; otherwise, number from 1 to 9 on a separate sheet of paper, and write the letter of the correct answer next to each number. Answer number 10 on a separate sheet of paper.

He was as thin as a steel shaft and lighter than graphite.[1] He stood five-feet-five and weighed one hundred seven pounds, which, if a fair fight was the objective, would have required he be matched against a 4-iron. In this instance, his opponent was a heavyweight, John Daly, the Arkansas Player of the Year in 1986 and 1987, and already a legend, on a local scale, for his prodigious length.

The site was Texarkana Country Club in Texarkana, Arkansas. . . .Tiger was there to play in the Big I, short for the Insurance Youth Gold Classic, a prestigious event on the American Junior Gold Association tour. The Big I created excitement among the juniors: in the final round they were paired with professional golfers. Daly was among the twenty pros recruited to participate with the sixty juniors, and he was paired with Woods. Through four holes, Woods was ahead of Daly, who turned to a friend and said loud enough to be heard by those in the gallery, "I can't let this thirteen-year-old beat me."

Tiger remained ahead at the turn, three-under par to Daly's one-under par. But Daly's four birdies on the back nine and three on the last four holes enabled him to defeat Woods. Still, Tiger's score was better than those posted by eight of the twenty professionals, and he finished second in the tournament.

Three years later, Tiger was asked what he recalled about playing with Daly that day. "I don't remember too much, except he wasn't a smart player," he said. "He'd take his driver and go over trees. He's got to throttle back."[2]

Daly, conversely, had been indelibly[3] impressed. "That kid is great," he said. "Everybody was applauding him and nobody applauded me. He's better than I'd heard."

—"Tiger: A Biography of Tiger Woods" by John Strege

---

1. graphite: Lightweight material used to make golf clubs.
2. throttle back: Ease up.
3. indelibly: Lastingly; permanently.

1 The word *prestigious* in this passage means—
A casual
B questionable
C unexpected
D renowned

2 In this passage, the word *conversely* means—
A in contrast
B in confusion
C lacking control
D without confidence

3 Which of these is an OPINION expressed in this passage?

   A Tiger finished second in the tournament.

   B Tiger competed against a legend in the Big I.

   C Tiger led Daly after four holes.

   D Daly had three birdies on the last four holes.

4 What is the main idea of the first paragraph?

   A Tiger had to compete against a stronger golfer.

   B Although Tiger was thin, he was a powerful golfer.

   C Tiger and John Daly were evenly matched opponents.

   D John Daly was famous for hitting balls a great distance.

5 What will likely be John Daly's reaction if he plays against Tiger in the future?

   A Daly will insist on going first.

   B Daly will take Tiger less seriously as a player.

   C Daly will ask to compete as a junior.

   D Daly will be less confident of winning.

6 You can conclude from the passage that Tiger Woods—

   A played well but lacked confidence

   B had great skill but rarely practiced

   C demonstrated leadership despite being young

   D showed great talent for such a young golfer

7 The author's main purpose is to—

   A entertain readers with an amusing story about golf

   B convince readers to begin playing golf at a young age

   C explain why Tiger Woods was not able to beat John Daly

   D describe an event from early in Tiger Woods's golfing career

8 What happened during the first four holes of the final round of the Big I?

   A Daly scored three birdies.

   B Tiger scored better than Daly.

   C Tiger recalled golfing with Daly.

   D Daly became Player of the Year.

9 Which of these BEST describes the main events of the passage?

   A Tiger played against John Daly at the Texarkana Country Club. The crowd applauded Tiger rather than Daly.

   B John Daly was much stronger than Tiger. Tiger criticized Daly's playing, but Daly was impressed by Tiger's talent.

   C John Daly was determined not to be beaten by Tiger. Daly hit several birdies, which allowed him to defeat Tiger.

   D Tiger was paired with John Daly in a golf tournament. Daly beat Tiger, but Tiger showed great promise.

10 Why was Tiger Woods's performance in the Big I so impressive? Support your answer with evidence from the text.

Writing Skills

Sentence Construction

Read the passage. Some sections are underlined. The underlined sections may be one of the following: incomplete sentences, run-on sentences, correctly written sentences that should be combined, correctly written sentences that do not need to be rewritten. Choose the best way to write each underlined section. Mark the letter of your answer on a bubble sheet if your teacher provides one; otherwise, number from 1 to 3 on a separate sheet of paper, and write the letter of the correct answer next to each number.

> (1) Good nonfiction is created by men and women. Who use words well what they write has clarity, liveliness, interest, and style. When you read nonfiction, look for these qualities. (2) A persuasive essay is one type of nonfiction. In which a writer tries to convince you to accept a certain idea, or to act a certain way. (3) Writers often state their opinion at the start of the essay and then present a variety of arguments to back up the idea.

1 **A** Good nonfiction is created by men and women: who use words well what they write has clarity, liveliness, interest, and style.

 B Good nonfiction is created by men and women who use words well. What they write has clarity, liveliness, interest, and style.

 C Good nonfiction is created by men and women who use words well, what they write has clarity, liveliness, interest, and style.

 D Correct as is

2 **A** A persuasive essay is one type of nonfiction in which a writer tries to convince you to accept a certain idea or to act a certain way.

 B A persuasive essay is one type of nonfiction; in which a writer tries to convince you to accept a certain idea, or

to act a certain way.

 C A persuasive essay is one type of nonfiction, in which a writer tries to convince you to accept a certain idea. Or to act a certain way.

 D Correct as is

3 **A** Writers often state their opinion at the start of the essay; and then they present a variety of arguments, to back up the idea.

 B Writers often state their opinion, at the start of the essay and, then, present a variety of arguments to back up the idea.

 C Writers, often state their opinion at the start of the essay, and then, present a variety of arguments to back up the idea.

 D Correct as is

Writing Skills

Appropriate Usage

Read the passage, and choose the word or group of words that best fits each space. Mark the letter of your answer on a bubble sheet if your teacher provides one; otherwise, number from 1 to 6 on a separate sheet of paper, and write the letter of the correct answer next to each number.

The poet Oliver Herford (1863–1935) was born in England but __(1)__ most of his life in the United States. There are many stories about Herford's sense of humor and carefree nature. Once, passing a schoolhouse at night, he imagined the typical school day that lay ahead for the teacher and pupils. He entered the school and covered the chalkboard with drawings of animals. The next day, the teachers and pupils __(2)__ both surprised and amused to see the animals cavorting on the board. Another time, after some of his poems were repeatedly rejected by the editor of a magazine, Herford sent __(3)__ back to the editor along with the following note: "Sir: Your office boy __(4)__ continually rejecting these masterpieces. Kindly see that they receive the attention of the editor." The editor __(5)__ by accepting several of the poems. These incidents __(6)__ two of Herford's most beloved qualities: his sense of humor and his fondness for animals as subjects.

---

1 **A** live
   B lived
   C will live
   D living

2 **A** is
   B are
   C will be
   D were

3 **A** them
   B those
   C this
   D they

4 **A** has been
   B will have been
   C having been
   D are being

5 **A** responds
   B will respond
   C responded
   D should respond

6 **A** have revealed
   B will reveal
   C revealing
   D reveal

Writing

Spelling, Capitalization, and Punctuation

Read the passage, and decide which type of error, if any, appears in each underlined section. Mark the letter of your answer on a bubble sheet if your teacher provides one; otherwise, number from 1 to 6 on a separate sheet of paper, and write the letter of the correct answer next to each number.

Their are more people living to be 100 than ever before. Alot of the
  (1)   (2)

reason for this is diet, people are simply getting better nutrition throughout
        (3)

their lives. Another reason is: that health care is improving all the time, as
             (4)

the Medical profession is getting better at prevention and early diagnosis of
  (5)

disease. Many doctors now believe that most people will be able to reach the
        (6)

century mark within the next generation.

---

1 **A** Spelling error
    B Capitalization error
    C Punctuation error
    D No error

2 **A** Spelling error
    B Capitalization error
    C Punctuation error
    D No error

3 **A** Spelling error
    B Capitalization error
    C Punctuation error
    D No error

4 **A** Spelling error
    B Capitalization error
    C Punctuation error
    D No error

5 **A** Spelling error
    B Capitalization error
    C Punctuation error
    D No error

6 **A** Spelling error
    B Capitalization error
    C Punctuation error
    D No error

Writing Tasks

The following activity is designed to assess your writing ability. The prompts will ask you to explain something. You may think of your audience as being any reader other than yourself.

In "Tiger Woods," the author shows the golfer as an exceptionally promising thirteen-year-old player. Living up to such promise is never easy, though.

Write an essay exploring the good and bad aspects of placing such high expectations on young people who excel in their field.

When Tiger Woods played his match against John Daly, he didn't think of the older player as "smart." Was Woods being arrogant, or just confident of his own golf judgement?

Write an essay that defines arrogance and shows the difference between arrogance and confidence. Use Tiger Woods's behavior as an example, but feel free to draw on other examples as well.

A tight, hard-fought match like the one between Tiger Woods and John Daly can remain in the minds of viewers for years.

Write an essay about the attraction of sports for so many viewers. Why do athletic events draw such large crowds? Why do fans get so involved in the actions of their favorite players or teams? Use examples from your own experience.

Scoring Rubric

Use this scoring rubric to assess the composition you write in response to the prompts on the previous page. The scale runs from **0** (the poorest) to **4** (the best).

0	1	2	3	4
Blank paper	Vague or brief	Correct purpose, audience, and mode	Correct purpose, audience, and mode	Correct purpose, audience, and mode
In a foreign language	Poorly organized			
Unreadable because of incoherence or illegibility	Wrong purpose, audience, or mode	Organization has lapses	Fair organization	Full, appropriate elaboration
On wrong topic	Loses focus; rambles	Some elaboration and detail	Moderate elaboration and detail	Logical, effective organization
Content too scant to score	Lacks elaboration, detail, language control	Language control is limited	Clear, effective language	Fluent, clear, effective language

INDEX OF AUTHORS AND TITLES

WRITING

Writing Opportunities

Lawyer's argument, 341
Lecture, 10, 297
Leisure-time presentation, 55
Listening, 905
Lyrics presentation, 751
Mad About You review, 435
Medal presentation speech, 77
Missing person description, 732
Modernization, 683
Monologue, 27, 541, 875
Musical accompaniment, 818
Musical retelling, 395
Neighborhood meeting, 133
News bulletin, 460
Nonverbal communication, 905
Oral directions, 549
Oral history, 55
Oral interpretation, 583, 779, 906
Oral presentation, 779, 881
Oral reading, 869
Panel discussion, 77, 906
Performance, 713, 759, 845
Pitch, 905
Play-by-play account, 477
Poetry contest, 35
Poetry drumbeat, 779
Poetry listening, 562
Poetry reading, 141, 237, 313, 759
Poetry singing, 787
Press conference, 621
Public reading, 255
Questions and answers, 521
Radio advice show, 869
Radio drama, 206
Rate, 905
Readers Theatre, 906
Rescue interview, 221
Retelling, 395, 837
Role play, 91, 837, 906
School interview, 361
Silly, sensational storytelling, 787
Simile slam, 797
Skit, 284, 732
Song, 177
Song lyrics, 85, 206, 751
"Sounds of Home" tape, 265
Speaker's introduction, 47
Speaking persuasively, 635
Speech, 77, 118, 497, 906
Stand-up routine, 91
Storytellers' circle, 47
Storytelling, 439, 787, 906
Stress, 905
Tabloid television, 460
Talk radio, 521
Talk-show appearance, 159
Telephone conversation, 35
Telephone interview, 227, 803
Television commercial, 118
Television dialogue, 875
Television interview, 489
Television news report, 818
Television newscast, 797
Three-way poetry contest, 35
Unexpected meeting, 177
Vocal delivery, 905
Volume, 905
Weather commentary, 265
Weather report, 743
Zoo commercial, 427

LIFE AND WORK SKILLS

Archaeology, 628
Bravery, 75
Charts, 906
Cultural differences in the workplace, 531
Detective methods, 339
Documentary, 906
Drama critic's review, 683
Film director's memo, 77
Gallery talk, 595
Graphs, 906
Internet, 574
Interview about city planners, 629
Interview veterinarian, 395
Jobs meeting conditions of the poem, 139
Lawyer's argument, 341
Liner notes, 779
Map, 906
Map reading, 163
Modern-day professions for Icarus and
    Daedalus, 867
Music review, 27
News article, 10, 159, 869
News reporters, 376, 378
Police report, 460
Political cartoon, 906
Proposal for a documentary, 595
Protecting the environment, 762
Radio spot, 787
Resolving conflicts, 816
Telephone interview, 227
Training profile, 395
Travel brochure, 541
Values in the United States, 171
Viewing, 905
World Wide Web, 574
Zoo commercial, 427

PROJECTS

Advice pamphlet, 77
Anthology of essays, 562
Aquarium lecture, 759
Aztec city, 818
Biographical report, 595
Biography, 141, 341, 595
Book circle, 595
Book report, 583
Casting sketches, 713
Chart, 265
Chinese customs report, 27
Coat of arms, 63
Collage, wildlife, 477
Comic strip, 91
Community participation, 361
Community work, 133
Comparison chart, 77, 869
Crime-solvers' club, 341
Dancing with "Aunt Leaf," 797
Eastern Europe report, 10
Essays:
    anthology of, 562
    "Fortune Cookies," 621
    visual, 629
Family chart, 47
Film review, 47
Flag, 687
Flowchart, 361
Folk-tale festival, 837
Food festival, 133
Gallery of leaders, 497

Game collection, 284
Garden plan, 118
Geography comparison, 313
Geography update, 159
Glacier research, 221
Good-luck charms, 409
Health statistics, 489
How-to guide, 221
Illustrated chart, 85
Illustrated figure of speech, 797
Illustrated storyboard, 732
Illustrations, 763
Informative brochure, 85
Internet research, 177, 297
Jewish emigration, 439
Living biography, 141
Lizard presentation, 319
Map, 743
Map research, 439
Medieval festival, 185
Metamorphosis, 427
Microscope presentation, 409
Missing person investigation, 779
Model, 869
Model tools, 227
Multicultural fables, 875
Multimedia biography, 341
Multimedia presentation, 35, 255, 583, 779
Multimedia report, 10, 206, 297, 477
Museum exhibit, 237
Nature walk, 751
New York in 1900, 460
News report, 378
News show, 378
Onomatopoeia factory, 787
Oral history, 237
Oral presentation, 159
Oral report on legendary figures, 313
Pet-care brochure, 395
Pet show, 427
Picture of miracles, 265
Poetry Home Page, 562
Poet's life, 763
Portrait of a lady, 255
Poster on the number three, 206
Poster series on train travel, 55
Puzzle challenge, 837
Report, 489, 541
    on Chinese customs, 27
    on Eastern Europe, 10
    on good-luck charms, 409
    on the news, 378
    on the 1850's, 435
    on Vietnamese history, 319
Research, 227
    project, 759
    report, 521
Science fair, 35
Scientific view, 713
Scrapbook of heroes, 91
Search report, 732
Seasonal preparations, 751
Set design, 661
Set model, 683
Shakespeare and exploration, 787
Sharecropping report, 118
Sitcom guide, 435
Sleep research, 284
Snow statistics, 521
Spider profile, 845

STAFF CREDITS

The people who made up the *Prentice Hall Literature: Timeless Voices, Timeless Themes* team—representing design services, editorial, editorial services, managing editor, manufacturing and inventory planning, market research, marketing services, on-line services/multimedia development, permissions, product marketing, production services, and publishing processes—are listed below. Bold type denotes core team members.

Laura Bird, Betsy Bostwick, Pam Cardiff, **Megan Chill,** Rhett Conklin, Carlos Crespo, Gabriella Della Corte, Ed de Leon, Donna C. DiCuffa, **Amy E. Fleming, Holly Gordon, Rebecca Z. Graziano, William J. Hanna, Rick Hickox,** Jim Jeglikowski, John Kingston, **Perrin Moriarty,** James O'Neill, **Jim O'Shea, Maureen Raymond,** Rob Richman, Doris Robinson, Gerry Schrenck, Ann Shea, Melissa Shustyk, Annette Simmons, **Rita M. Sullivan, Elizabeth Torjussen**

ADDITIONAL CREDITS

Ernie Albanese, Robert H. Aleman, Diane Alimena, Michele Angelucci, Rosalyn Arcilla, Penny Baker, Anthony Barone, Rui Camarinha, Tara Campbell, Amy Capetta, Lorena Cerisano, Kam Cheng, Elizabeth Crawford, Mark Cryan, Paul Delsignore, Robert Dobaczewski, Irene Ehrmann, Kathryn Foot, Joe Galka, Catalina Gavilanes, Elaine Goldman, Joe Graci, Stacey Hosid, Leanne Korszoloski, Jan Kraus, Gregory Lynch, Mary Luthi, Vickie Menanteaux, John McClure, Frances Medico, Omni-Photo Communications, Inc., Photosearch, Inc., Linda Punskovsky, David Rosenthal, Laura Ross, Rose Sievers, Gillian Speeth/Picture This, Cindi Talocci, Mark Taylor, Lashonda Williams, Jeff Zoda

ACKNOWLEDGMENTS (continued)

Susan Essoyan From "Nosing Around U.S. Borders" by Susan Essoyan. First appeared in *Dog Fancy* magazine, June 1997. Used by permission of the author.

Farrar, Straus & Giroux, Inc. "The Cat Who Thought She Was a Dog and the Dog Who Thought He Was a Cat" from *Naftali the Storyteller and His Horse, Sus* by Isaac Bashevis Singer. Pictures by Margot Zemach. Copyright © 1973, 1976 by Isaac Bashevis Singer. Pictures copyright © 1976 by Margot Zemach. "Seal" from *Laughing Time: Collected Nonsense* by William Jay Smith. Copyright © 1990 by William Jay Smith. Reprinted by permission of Farrar, Straus & Giroux, Inc.

Farrar, Straus & Giroux, Inc., and Faber and Faber Limited "Valediction" by Seamus Heaney. Published by Farrar, Straus & Giroux in the U.S. in *Poems 1965–1975* by Seamus Heaney, copyright © 1966, 1980 by Seamus Heaney. Published by Faber and Faber Ltd. in the U.K. in *Death of a Naturalist* by Seamus Heaney. Reprinted by permission.

M.W. Farrell, executrix for the Estate of Juliet Piggott Wood "Popocatepetl and Ixtlaccihuatl" from *Mexican Folk Tales* by Juliet Piggott. Copyright © 1973 by Juliet Piggott. Reprinted by permission.

Golden Books Family Entertainment "The Bride of Pluto" (retitled "Demeter and Persephone") from *Golden Treasury of Myths and Legends* by Anne Terry White. Copyright © 1959 Western Publishing Company, Inc. All rights reserved. Reprinted by permission.

Reid Goldsborough "Let the reader beware" by Reid Goldsborough (reidgold@ netaxs.com) syndicated columnist, which appeared in *Reading Today*, August/September 1997. Used by permission of the author.

Hal Leonard Corporation "On My Own," music by Claude-Michel Schonberg, lyrics by Alain Boublil, Herbert Kretzmer, John Caird, Trevor Nunn and Jean-Marc Natel. Music and lyrics copyright © 1980 by Editions Musicales Alain Boublil. English lyrics copyright © 1986 by Alain Boublil Music Ltd. (ASCAP). Mechanical and publication rights for the U.S.A. administered by Alain Boublil Music Ltd. (ASCAP) c/o Stephen Tenenbaum & Co., Inc., 1775 Broadway, Suite 708, New York, NY 10019, Tel. (212) 246-7204, Fax (212) 246-7217. International Copyright Secured. All Rights Reserved. This music is copyrighted. Photocopying is illegal. All Performance Rights Restricted.

Harcourt Brace & Company "The Writer" from *The Mind-Reader,* copyright © 1971 by Richard Wilbur. "Seventh Grade" from *Baseball in April and Other Stories,* copyright © 1990 by Gary Soto. "Primer Lesson" from *Slabs of the Sunburnt West* by Carl Sandburg, copyright 1922 by Harcourt Brace & Company and renewed 1950 by Carl Sandburg. "Fog" from *Chicago Poems* by Carl Sandburg, copyright 1916 by Holt, Rinehart and Winston and renewed 1944 by Carl Sandburg. "The Algonquin Cinderella" from *World Tales: The Extraordinary Coincidence of Stories Told In All Times, In All Places* by Idries Shah, copyright © 1979 by Technographia, S.A., and Harcourt Brace & Company. "Lonely Particular" from *Revolutionary Petunias & Other Poems,* copyright © 1972 by Alice Walker. Excerpt from *In Search Of Our Mothers' Gardens: Womanist Prose,* copyright © 1983 by Alice Walker, and "Women" from *Revolutionary Petunias & Other Poems,* copyright © 1970 by Alice Walker. "The Enemy" from *Once,* copyright © 1968 by Alice Walker. Reprinted by permission of Harcourt Brace & Company.

HarperCollins Publishers, Inc. Selected excerpts from *An American Childhood* by Annie Dillard. Copyright © 1987 by Annie Dillard. "How the Snake Got Poison" from *Mules and Men* by Zora Neale Hurston. Copyright © 1935 by Zora Neale Hurston. Copyright renewed 1963 by John C. Hurston and Joel Hurston. "Sarah Cynthia Sylvia Stout Would Not Take The Garbage Out" from *Where The Sidewalk Ends* by Shel Silverstein. Copyright © 1974 by Evil Eye Music, Inc. "A Boy and a Man" from *Banner in the Sky* by James Ramsey Ullman. Copyright 1954 by James Ramsey Ullman. Reprinted by permission of HarperCollins Publishers, Inc. "Rikki-tikki-tavi" from *The Jungle Book* by Rudyard Kipling. Excerpt from "King Arthur: The Marvel of the Sword" from *The Book of King Arthur and His Noble Knights* by Mary MacLeod (J. B. Lippincott).

Harvard University Press and the Trustees of Amherst College "I'm Nobody" (poem #288) from *The Poems of Emily Dickinson,* Thomas H. Johnson, editor, Cambridge, Mass.: The Belknap Press of Harvard University Press, Copyright © 1951, 1955, 1979, 1983 by the President and Fellows of Harvard College. Reprinted by permission of the publishers and the Trustees of Amherst College.

John Hawkins & Associates, Inc. "My Furthest-Back Person—The African" by Alex Haley, published July 16, 1972, by *The New York Times Magazine.* Copyright © 1972 by Alex Haley. Reprinted by permission of John Hawkins & Associates, Inc.

Heinemann Educational Publishers, division of Reed Educational & Professional Publishing Ltd. "Tenochtitlan: Inside the Aztec Capital" from *The Aztecs* by Jacqueline Dineen. Copyright © 1992 by Heinemann Educational Publishers. Reprinted by permission of the publisher.

Bill Hilgers, Esq., for the Estate of Barbara Jordan "All Together Now" by Barbara Jordan, orginally published in *Sesame Street Parents,* July/August 1994. Reprinted by permission.

Henry Holt and Company, Inc. "The Pasture," copyright 1939, © 1967, 1969 by Holt, Rinehart and Winston, Inc. "Stopping by Woods on a Snowy Evening," copyright 1923, © 1969 by Holt, Rinehart and Winston, Inc. From *The Poetry of Robert Frost* edited by Edward Connery Lathem. Reprinted by permission of Henry Holt and Company, Inc. From "Birches" by Robert Frost. Copyright © 1969 by Holt, Rinehart and Wilson, Inc.; copyright © 1962 by Robert Frost; copyright © 1975 by Leslie Frost Ballantine.

D. Hoch "Zoo" by Edward D. Hoch, copyright © 1958 by ... Publications, Inc.; © renewed 1986 by Edward D. Hoch. ... ed by permission of the author.

Houghton Mifflin Company From "St. Crispian's Day Speech" from *Henry V* by William Shakespeare, G. Blakemore Evans (Editor), *The Riverside Shakespeare.* Copyright © 1974 by Houghton Mifflin Company. "Phaethon, Son of Apollo," from *Greek Myths.* Copyright 1949, © renewed 1977 by Olivia E. Coolidge. "Icarus and Daedalus" from *Old Greek Folk Stories Told Anew* by Josephine Preston Peabody, The Riverside Press. "The Village Blacksmith" from *The Poetical Works of Longfellow,* Cambridge Edition, 1975. Reprinted by permission of Houghton Mifflin Company. All rights reserved.

Indiana University Press "Heartache" by Anton Chekhov from pp. 328–333 of *From Karamzin to Bunin* edited by Carl Proffer. Published by Indiana University Press. Reprinted by permission of the publisher.

International Paper Company "How to Enjoy Poetry" by James Dickey from the Power of the Printed Word Program. Reprinted by permission of International Paper Company.

Japan Publications, Inc. "On sweet plum blossoms," "Has spring come indeed?" and "Temple bells die out" by Bashō. Reprinted from *One Hundred Famous Haiku* by Daniel C. Buchanan, with permission from Japan Publications, copyright © 1973.

Alfred A. Knopf, Inc. "Mother to Son" from *Collected Poems* by Langston Hughes. Copyright © 1994 by the Estate of Langston Hughes. "The People Could Fly" from *The People Could Fly* by Virginia Hamilton. Text copyright © 1985 by Virginia Hamilton. Illustrations copyright © 1995 by Leo and Diane Dillon. "Annabel Lee" from *The Complete Poems and Stories of Edgar Allan Poe, with Selections from His Writings,* edited by Arthur Hobson Quinn. Reprinted by permission of Alfred A. Knopf, Inc.

Trustees of Leland Stanford Junior University c/o William Saroyan Foundation "The Hummingbird That Lived Through Winter" from *Dear Baby* by William Saroyan. Copyright 1935, 1936, 1939, 1941, 1942, 1943, 1944 by William Saroyan. Reprinted by permission of the Trustees of Leland Stanford Junior University c/o William Saroyan Foundation.

H.N. Levitt "Winslow Homer: America's Greatest Painter" by H. N. Levitt from *Boy's Life,* September 1986. Copyright H. N. Levitt 1986. Reprinted by permission of the author.

Little, Brown and Company From *Let's Steal the Moon* by Blanche Serwer Bernstein. Copyright © 1970, 1987 by Blanche L. Serwer (text). "The Real Story of a Cowboy's Life" from *The West: An Illustrated History* by Geoffrey Ward. Copyright © 1997 by The West Company. "Justin Lebo" from *It's Our World, Too!* by Phillip Hoose. Copyright © 1993 by Phillip Hoose. Used by permission of Little, Brown and Company. "Aunt Leaf" from *Twelve Moons* by Mary Oliver, copyright © 1972, 1973, 1974, 1976, 1977, 1978, 1979 by Mary Oliver. "The Hippopotamus" and "The Caterpillar" from *Verses from 1929 On* by Ogden Nash. Both first appeared in *The Saturday Evening Post.* Copyright 1) 1935 by the Curtis Publishing Company. Copyright 2) 1949 by Ogden Nash; renewed 1976 by Frances Nash, Isabel Nash Eberstadt, and Linell Nash Smith. Used by permission of Little, Brown and Company.

Liveright Publishing Corporation "In Just" by E. E. Cummings, copyright 1923, 1951, © 1991 by the Trustees for the E. E. Cummings Trust. Copyright © 1976 by George James Firmage, from *Complete Poems: 1904–1962* by E.E. Cummings, edited by George J. Firmage. Reprinted by permission of Liveright Publishing Corporation.

Alan Lomax "The Dying Cowboy" from *Cowboy Songs and Other Frontier Ballads* collected by John A. Lomax and Alan Lomax. Copyright © 1910, 1916, 1938 by The Macmillan Company. Copyright © 1938 by John A. Lomax. Used by permission of Alan Lomax.

Louisiana State University Press "Flint" by Christina Rossetti from *The Complete Poems of Christina Rossetti,* edited by R.W. Crump, © 1986, Louisiana State University Press. Reprinted by permission.

Jay Macpherson "Narcissus" by Jay Macpherson from *Four Ages of Man: The Classical Myths.* Copyright © 1962 by Jay Macpherson. Used by permission of the author.

Naomi Long Madgett "Life" from *One and Many* by Naomi Long Madgett. Copyright 1956; from *Remembrances of Spring,* 1993. Reprinted by permission of the author.

The Edna St. Vincent Millay Society c/o Elizabeth Barnett, Literary Executor "The Courage That My Mother Had" by Edna St. Vincent Millay, from *Collected Poems,* HarperCollins. Copyright © 1954 by Norma Millay Ellis. All rights reserved. Used by permission of Elizabeth Barnett, Literary Executor.

William Morrow & Company, Inc. "Winter" from *Cotton Candy On A Rainy Day* by Nikki Giovanni. Copyright © 1978 by Nikki Giovanni. Used by permission of William Morrow & Company, Inc.

John Murray (Publishers) Ltd. "The Dying Detective" from *The Game's Afoot* by Michael and Mollie Hardwick. Copyright © 1969 by Michael & Mollie Hardwick. Reprinted by permission of John Murray (Publishers) Ltd.

New American Library "Miracles" from *Leaves of Grass* by Walt Whitman.

W.W. Norton & Company for the author "The Microscope" by Maxine Kumin. Copyright © 1963 by The Atlantic Monthly Company, Boston, Mass. Reprinted by permission of the author.

Hugh Noyes on behalf of the Trustees of Alfred Noyes Literary Estate. "The Highwayman" from *Collected Poems* by Alfred Noyes (J. B. Lippincott). Reprinted by permission.

NTC Contemporary Books "No Gumption" from *Growing Up* by Russell Baker. Copyright © 1982 by Russell Baker. Reprinted by permission of NTC Contemporary Books.

Naomi Shihab Nye "The Rider" by Naomi Shihab Nye. Copyright © Naomi Shihab. First appeared in *Invisible,* a chapbook from Tribolite Press, Denton, TX. By permission of the author, Naomi Shihab Nye.

Harold Ober Associates Incorporated "Stolen Day" by Sherwood Anderson, originally published in *This Week* Magazine. Copyright 1941 by United Newspapers Magazine Corp. Copyright renewed 1968 by Eleanor Copenhaver Anderson. Reprinted by permission of Harold Ober Associates Incorporated.

Pantheon Books, a division of Random House, Inc. "His Just Reward" from *Swedish Folktales and Legends* by Lone Thygesen Blecher and George Blecher. Copyright © 1993 by G & L Blecher Inc. "Djuha Borrows a Pot" from *Arab Folktales* by Inea Bushnaq. Copyright © 1986 by Inea Bushnaq. Reprinted by permission of Pantheon Books, a division of Random House, Inc.

Raymond R. Patterson "Martin Luther King" by Raymond R. Patterson. Copyright © 1971 by Raymond R. Patterson. Reprinted by permission of the author.

Philomel Books, a division of Penguin Putnam Inc. From *Yeh Shen: A Cinderella Story from China* by Ai-Ling Louie. Copyright © 1982 by Ai-Ling Louie. Used by permission of Philomel Books, a division of Penguin Putnam Inc.

Penguin Putnam, Inc. "Independence Hall" from *On The Road With Charles Kuralt* by Charles Kuralt. Copyright © 1985 by CBS Inc. "Our Finest Hour" from *The Osgood Files* by Charles Osgood. Copyright © 1986, 1987, 1988, 1989, 1990, 1991 by Charles Osgood. Reprinted by permission of Penguin Putnam, Inc. *Ribbons* by Laurence Yep, copyright © 1992 by Laurence Yep from *American Girl Magazine,* Jan/Feb 1992. An expanded version of *Ribbons* by Laurence Yep is available from G.P. Putnam's Sons.

G.P. Putnam's Sons, a division of Penguin Putnam Inc. "Two Kinds" by Amy Tan from *The Joy Luck Club* by Amy Tan. Copyright © 1989 by Amy Tan. From "Was Tarzan a Three-Bandage Man?" from *Childhood* by Bill Cosby. Copyright © 1991 by Bill Cosby. Reprinted by permission of G.P. Putnam's Son, a division of Penguin Putnam, Inc.

The Putnam Publishing Group "Rip Van Winkle" from *A Legend of the Kaatskill Mountains* by Washington Irving. G.P. Putnam & Sons, 1871.

Random House, Inc. "Melting Pot" from *Living Out Loud* by Anna Quindlen. Copyright © 1987 by Anna Quindlen. Reprinted by permission of Random House, Inc. "Father William" from *The Complete Works of Lewis Carroll* by Lewis Carroll.

Regent Music Corporation "Abraham, Martin, and John" by Richard Holler. © 1968, 1970 (Renewed) Regent Music Corporation. All Rights Reserved. Used by permission of Regent Music Corporation. International Copyright Secured.

Marian Reiner "Feelings About Words" from *Words, Words, Words* by Mary O'Neill. Copyright © 1966 by Mary O'Neill. Copyright renewed 1994 by Erin Baroni and Abigail Hagler. "Thumbprint" from *A Sky Full of Poems* by Eve Merriam. Copyright © 1964, 1970, 1973 Eve Merriam. Copyright renewed 1992 Eve Merriam, 1998 Dee Michel and Guy Michel. "Onomatopoeia" from *It Doesn't Always Have To Rhyme* by Eve Merriam. Copyright © 1964, 1992 Eve Merriam. Reprinted by permission of Marian Reiner.

Rock and Roll Hall of Fame and Museum From "Rhythm and Blues: Let the Good Times Roll" and from *Joel Whitburn's Top R&B Singles 1942–1988*, Menomonee Falls, Wis., Record Research, Inc. 1988. Reprinted by kind permission of the Rock and Roll Hall of Fame and Museum, Cleveland, Ohio.

Wendy Rose "Loo-wit" from *The Halfbreed Chronicles and Other Poems* (West End Press) by Wendy Rose. Copyright © 1985 by Wendy Rose. Reprinted by permission of the author.

St. Martin's Press, Incorporated, and Harold Ober Associates Incorporated "Cat on the Go" from *All Things Wise and Wonderful* by James Herriot. Copyright © 1976, 1977 by James Herriot. Reprinted by permission.

Scribner, a division of Simon & Schuster Excerpts from "The Ancient Enmity," retitled "Rattlesnake Hunt," from *Cross Creek* by Marjorie Kinnan Rawlings. Copyright 1942 by Marjorie Kinnan Rawlings; copyright renewed © 1970 by Norton Baskin and Charles Scribner's Sons. "A Day's Wait" from *Winner Take Nothing* by Ernest Hemingway. Copyright 1933 Charles Scribner's Sons. Copyright renewed © 1961 by Mary Hemingway. Reprinted with the permission of Scribner, a division of Simon & Schuster, Inc.

The Rod Serling Trust "The Monsters Are Due On Maple Street" by Rod Serling. Copyright © 1960 Rod Serling; © 1988 by Carolyn Serling, Jodi Serling and Anne Serling. Reprinted by permission of The Rod Serling Trust. All rights reserved.

Estate of Robert Service c/o William Krasilovsky, Esq., Feinman & Krasilovsky "The Cremation of Sam McGee" by Robert Service. 1910 Dodd Mead & Co. Reprinted by permission.

Simon & Schuster Books for Young Readers, an imprint of Simon & Schuster Children's Publishing Division "Papa's Parrot" by Cynthia Rylant from *Every Living Thing* by Cynthia Rylant. Copyright © 1985 Cynthia Rylant. "The Lion and the Statue" and "The Fox and the Crow" from *The Fables of Aesop*, Selected, Told Anew and Their History Traced by Joseph Jacobs. Copyright © 1964 Macmillan Publishing Company. Reprinted with the permission of Simon & Schuster Books for Young Readers, an imprint of Simon & Schuster Children's Publishing Division

Society of Authors as the Literary Representative of the Estate of James Stephens "Washed In Silver" by James Stephens from *Collected Poems*. Copyright © 1943 by James Stephens. Reprinted by permission of the Society of Authors as the Literary Representative of the Estate of James Stephens.

Society of Authors as Representative of The Literary Trustees of Walter de la Mare "Me" by Walter de la Mare from *The Complete Poems of Walter de la Mare*. Copyright © 1969, published by Faber and Faber. Reprinted by permission of The Literary Trustees of Walter de la Mare, and The Society of Authors as their representative.

Gary Soto and Poetry "Oranges" by Gary Soto. First appeared in *Poetry*, copyright © 1983 by The Modern Poetry Association and is reprinted by permission of the author and the Editor of *Poetry*.

Sports Illustrated Magazine Reprinted courtesy of *Sports Illustrated* March 2, 1998. Copyright © 1998, Time Inc. "Golden Girls" by Johnette Howard. All rights reserved.

Stoddart Publishing Co. Limited "I Am a Native of North America" by Chief Dan George, from *My Heart Soars*. Copyright © 1974 by Clarke Irwin. Reprinted by permission of Stoddart Publishing Co.. Limited.

Piri Thomas "Amigo Brothers" by Piri Thomas from *El Barrio*. Copyright © 1978 by Piri Thomas. Reprinted by permission of the author, Piri Thomas.

Rosemary A. Thurber "The Night the Bed Fell" by James Thurber. Copyright © 1933, 1961 James Thurber, from *My Life and Hard Times*, published by Harper & Row. Reprinted by permission.

Rosemary A. Thurber and the Barbara Hogensen Agency "The Princess and the Tin Box" from *The Beast in Me and Other Animals* by James Thurber. Copyright © 1948 by James Thurber. Copyright © renewed 1976 by Helen Thurber and Rosemary A. Thurber. Reprinted by arrangement with Rosemary A. Thurber and the Barbara Hogenson Agency.

Time Life Syndication From "Thanksgiving Inventory" by Roger Rosenblatt, published in *Time*, December 1, 1997. Copyright © 1997 Time Inc. Reprinted by permission of Time, Inc.

University of Notre Dame Press From *Barrio Boy* by Ernesto Galarza. Copyright © 1971 by University of Notre Dame Press. Reprinted by permission.

Villard Books, a division of Random House, Inc. From *Into Thin Air* by Jon Krakauer. Copyright © 1997 by Jon Krakauer. Reprinted by permission of Villard Books, a division of Random House, Inc.

Mai Vo-Dinh "The Little Lizard's Sorrow" from *The Toad is the Emperor's Uncle, Animal Folktales from Viet-Nam*, told and illustrated by Mai Vo-Dinh. Copyright © 1970 by Mai Vo-Dinh. Reprinted by permission of the author.

Warner Bros. Publications U.S. Inc. "Bring Back Nelson Mandela" by Hugh Masekela. © 1988 Kalahari Music (BMI). All Rights o/b/o Kalahari Music for the World administered by Warner Chappell Music Ltd. (PRS). All Rights o/b/o Warner Chappell Music Ltd. for the Western Hemisphere administered by Warner-Tamerlane Publishing Corp. (BMI) All Rights Reserved. Used by permission of Warner Bros. Publications U.S. Inc., Miami, Fla. 33014

Rob Weisbach Books, a division of William Morrow & Company "Stepping Out With My Baby" from *Babyhood* by Paul Reiser. Copyright © 1997 by Paul Reiser. Reprinted by permission.

Writers & Artists Agency *A Christmas Carol: Scrooge and Marley* by Israel Horovitz, an adaptation of Charles Dickens's *A Christmas Carol*. Copyright © 1994 by Fountain Pen, Inc. All rights reserved. Reprinted by permission.

Note: Every effort has been made to locate the copyright owner of material reprinted in this book. Omissions brought to our attention will be corrected in subsequent editions.

ART CREDITS

Cover © Jerry Driendl/FPG International Corp.; **vii t.:** *Portrait*, Pamela Chin Lee, Courtesy of the artist; **vii b.:** *La Grande Famille (The Great Family)*, René Magritte, Private Collection/Lauros-Giraudon, Paris, ©2000 C. Herscovici, Brussels/Artists Rights Sociey (ARS), New York; **viii:** Chris Thomaidis/Tony Stone Images; **ix t.:** Corel Professional Photos CD-ROM™; **ix b.:** *La Bonne Aventure (Good Fortune)*, 1939, René Magritte, Gouache on paper, 33.5 x 40.7 cm., Museum Boymans-van Beuningen, Rotterdam, ©2000 C. Herscovici, Brussels/Artists Rights Society (ARS), New York; **x t.:** Corel Professional Photos CD-ROM™; **x b.:** Bryce Flynn/Stock, Boston/PNI; **xi t.:** *Happy Cat*, Christian Pierre, Private Collection/SuperStock; **xii t.:** image ©Copyright 1997 PhotoDisc, Inc.; **xii b.:** © 1990 Terry Heffernan; **xiii t.:** *Simultaneous Contrasts: Sun and Moon*, 1913, Robert Delaunay, Oil on canvas, 53" diameter, Collection, The Museum of Modern Art, New York, Mrs. Simon Guggenheim Fund; **xiii b.:** *Nolan Ryan* by LeRoy Neiman, Copyright ©1981 LeRoy Neiman, Inc. All Rights Reserved; **xiv l.:** Ebenezer Scrooge celebrating in the Guthrie Theater's 1994 production of *A Christmas Carol* adapted by Barbara Field. Photo credit: Michal Daniel.; **xiv r.:** *Over view of family walking dog on the street*, William Low, Courtesy of the artist; **xv t.:** image ©Copyright 1997 PhotoDisc, Inc.; **xv b.:** ©The Stock Market/Peter Steiner; **xvi:** *The Chariot of Phaeton racing through the skies*. Copper engraving, 1606, Corbis-Bettmann; **1:** © Stock Illustration Source, Inc.; **2:** Thomas Victor; **3:** The Bettmann Archive; **5:** "Then Came a Dog and Bit the Cat" from *Had Gadya (Tale of a Goat)*, 1919, E. Lissitzky, The Jewish Museum/Art Resource, NY. ©1997 Artists Rights Society (ARS), New York/VG Bild-

Bonn.; **6:** *La Cour d'un Ferme,* June 28, 1983, London, Christie's (armyard)/The Bridgeman Art Library, London/New York, ©2000 Artists Rights Society (ARS), New York/ADAGP, Paris; **11:** *Untitled,* Jean-Francois Podevin, © Stock Illustration Source, Inc.; **12:** Robert Foothorap; **13:** *Portrait,* Pamela Chin Lee, Courtesy of the artist; **14:** UPI/Corbis-Bettmann; **17:** *Mandarin Square: Badge with peacock-insignia-3rd civil rank. China,* 17th–20th century, Unknown artist, Yale University Art Gallery; **18–19:** Corbis-Bettmann; **20:** *Chinese Girl under Lanterns,* Winson Trang, Courtesy of the artist; **23:** *Portrait,* Pamela Chin Lee, Courtesy of the artist; **24:** Courtesy of Amy Tan; **28 t.:** Courtesy of the Library of Congress; **28 m.:** The Granger Collection, New York; **28 b.:** © Faber & Faber Ltd; **29:** Corel Professional Photos CD-ROM™; **30–31:** Frank Orel/Tony Stone Images; **32–33:** Michael P. Gadomski/Photo Researchers, Inc.; **36:** AP/Wide World Photos; **37:** © Faith Ringgold, 1986, The Purple Quilt (detail), 91" x 72", acrylic on canvas with pieced fabric borders; **38–39:** Betty Press/Panos Pictures; **41:** © 1998 ABC, Inc. All rights reserved.; **43:** © 1998 ABC, Inc. All rights reserved.; **49:** Culver Pictures, Inc.; **51:** Corel Professional Photos CD-ROM™; **52:** Corbis-Bettmann; **58:** *Drawing from an 1894 edition of Sir Thomas Malory's Le Morte D'arthur,* Aubrey Beardsley, The Granger Collection, New York; **61:** The Print and Picture Collection, Free Library of Philadelphia; **64:** Tracy Frankel/ The Image Bank; **69:** Diana Ong/SuperStock; **70:** Larry Burrows/Life Magazine © Time Warner Inc.; **71:** Oscar Burriel/Photo Researchers, Inc.; **73:** Herve Pelletier/SuperStock; **78 t.:** Corbis-Bettmann; **78 m.:** *Christina Rossetti (1830–1894),* english poet, wood engraving after Dante Gabriel Rossitti, The Granger Collection, New York; **78 b.:** Dianne Trejo; **79:** Corel Professional Photos CD-ROM™; **81:** *La Grande Famille (The Great Family),* René Magritte, Private Collection/Lauros-Giraudon, Paris, ©2000 C. Herscovici, Brussels/SuperStock Artists Rights Society (ARS), New York; **82:** *Three Fruit,* Ashton Hinrichs/SuperStock; **86:** Globe Photos; **87:** The Granger Collection, New York; **89:** Culver Pictures, Inc.; **92:** Courtesy Broadway Books; **93:** © Allsport/Alan Levenson; **95:** © Allsport/Ken Levine; **96:** AP/Wide World Photos; **98:** Paul Berger/Tony Stone Images; **103:** Francisco Cruz/SuperStock; **106:** © David Ridley/Stock Illustration Source, Inc.; **108:** Thomas Victor; **109:** Corel Professional Photos CD-ROM™; **112–113:** Corel Professional Photos CD-ROM™; **114:** Corel Professional Photos CD-ROM™; **119:** Private Collection/Diana Ong/Superstock; **120 t.:** Courtesy of the Author. Photo by Carolyn Soto.; **120 b.:** John Barrett/Globe Photos; **121:** Vicky Kasala/The Image Bank; **122–123:** D. Young-Wolfe/PhotoEdit; **122:** Mary Kate Denny/PhotoEdit; **123 b.:** Photo Courtesy of Will Faller; **123 inset:** Mary Kate Denny/PhotoEdit; **124:** Bob Daemmrich/The Image Works; **128 t.:** Corel Professional Photos CD-ROM™; **128 b.:** Corel Professional Photos CD-ROM™; **129 t.:** Corel Professional Photos CD-ROM™; **129 b.:** Corel Professional Photos CD-ROM™; **130:** Corel Professional Photos CD-ROM™; **134 t.:** Courtesy of the Library of Congress; **134 m.:** Photo by Bachrach; **134 b.:** *Rudyard Kipling,* oil on canvas, P. Burne-Jones, Courtesy of the National Portrait Gallery, London; **135:** Corel Professional Photos CD-ROM™; **136:** Photo Researchers, Inc.; **138–139:** Chris Thomaidis/ Tony Stone Images; **142:** *Washington Irving* (detail): Daniel Huntington, National Portrait Gallery, Smithsonian Institution, Washington, D.C./Art Resource, NY; **144:** *Rip in the Mountains,* Albertus Del Orient Brower, Shelburne Museum, Shelburne, Vt.; **146:** *Rip at the Inn,* Albertus Del Orient Brower, Shelburne Museum, Shelburne, Vt., Photograph by Ken Burris; **151:** *Rip Van Winkle Asleep,* Albertus Del Orient Brower, Shelburne Museum, Shelburne, Vt.; **152:** John Quidor, *Return of Rip Van Winkle,* 1849, Andrew W. Mellon Collection, © Board of Trustees, National Gallery of Art, Washington; **160:** Corel Professional Photos CD-ROM™; **163:** MBTA Marketing Communications; **165:** *Untitled (Two Girls Talking),* Pierre-Auguste Renoir/SuperStock; **166 t.:** New York Public Library; **166 m.t.:** Nationwide News Service; **166 m.b.:** Courtesy of the Library of Congress; **166 b.:** Corbis-Bettmann; **167:** *The Banjo Lesson,* c. 1894, pastel, 28" x 22 ½", Virginia Museum of Fine Arts, Richmond, The Adolf D. and Wilkins C. Williams Fund. Photo: Katherine Wetzel. © 2000 Virginia Museum of Fine Arts; **168:** *Organdy Collar,* 1936, Edmund Archer, Collection of Whitney Museum of American Art; **170:** Colonial Williamsburg Foundation; **172–173:** Corel Professional Photos CD-ROM™; **182:** *Farmyard with woman milking cow, from the Da Costa Book of Hours,* Bruges, c. 1515, The Pierpont Morgan Library/Art Resource, NY; **186:** Corel Professional Photos CD-ROM™; **191:** Michael Newman, PhotoEdit; **194–195:** *Couple on the Road,* Diana Ong/SuperStock; **197 t.:**

Corel Professional Photos CD-ROM™; **197 b.:** Garden in the interior of a palace: a young lady and her servant, from Recueil de miniatures, Giraudon/Art Resource, NY; **199:** SuperStock; **200–201:** border Hideki Fujii/The Image Bank; **202–204 border:** Hideki Fujii/The Image Bank; **202–203:** Pal Hermansen/Tony Stone Images; **207:** *Untitled,* © Antar Dayal/Stock Illustration Source, Inc.; **208 t.:** AP/Wide World Photos; **208 b.:** Villard Books; **209:** Alex Stewart/The Image Bank; **210–211:** Tony Stone Images; **215:** © Jean-Marc Boivin/Photo Research-ers, Inc.; **218:** Corel Professional Photos CD-ROM™; **225:** Reuters/Gary Caskey/ Archive Photos; **228 t.:** *Alfred Lord Tennyson,* c.1840, S. Laurence, Courtesy of the National Portrait Gallery, London; **228 m.:** *William Shakespeare,* (detail), Artist unknown, Courtesy of the National Portrait Gallery, London; **228 b.:** Thomas Victor; **229:** Courtesy of the Director, National Army Museum, London; **230:** *Charge of the Light Brigade at the Battle of Balaklava,*1854, Artist Unknown/SuperStock; **232–233:** © United Artists/Archive Photos; **238:** Corel Professional Photos CD-ROM™; **243:** *The Voice,* 1930, Agnes Pelton, Collection of the Jonson Gallery of the University of New Mexico Art Museum, Albuquerque. Bequest of Raymond Jonson; **244 t.:** The Mark Twain House, Hartford, Conn.; **244 b.:** Thomas Victor; **245:** © The Stock Market/Jeffrey W. Myers; **252–253:** Corel Professional Photos CD-ROM™; **256:** Corel Professional Photos CD-ROM™; **258 t.:** Dimitri Kessel/Life Magazine; **258 m.:** AP/Wide World Photos; **258 b.:** Courtesy of the Library of Congress; **259:** *The White Veil,* 1909, William L. Metcalf, Museum of Art, Rhode Island School of Design, Gift of Mrs. Gustav Radeke; **260:** Philip F. Chaudoir/Tranquality; **263:** *La Bonne Aventure (Good Fortune),*1939, René Magritte, Gouache on paper, 33.5 x 40.7 cm., Museum Boymans-van Beuningen, Rotterdam, ©2000 C. Herscovici/ARS, New York; **266:** © Phyllis Picard, Stock, Boston/PNI; **271:** Lynn Saville; **274–275:** *The Fight Interrupted,* William Mulready, Victoria & Albert Museum/Art Resource, NY; **276:** Corbis-Bettmann; **277:** "Briggs Suffocating" by James Thurber, Barbara Hogenson Agency, Photo by Eric H. Antoniou; **280:** My Life and Hard Times Copyright ©1933 by James Thurber. Copyright © renewed 1961 by James Thurber. Reprinted by arrangement with Rosemary A. Thurber and The Barbara Hogenson Agency.; **281:** "Briggs and Rex," by James Thurber, Barbara Hogenson Agency, Photo by Eric H. Antoniou; **285:** *View of Toledo,* Domenikos Theotokopoulos, The Metropolitan Museum of Art, H. O. Havemeyer Collection, Bequest of Mrs. H.O. Havemeyer, 1929. (29.100.6).; **286 t.:** Thomas Victor; **286 b.:** *Carl Sandburg,* Miriam Svet, The National Portrait Gallery, Smithsonian Institution, Washington, D.C./Art Resource, NY; **287:** Greg Martin/SuperStock; **288–289:** Dr. E.R. Degginger; **290–291 border:** Dr. E.R. Degginger; **290:** *Untitled,* Rob Wood, Illustration by Wood Ronsaville Harlin, Inc.; **292–293 border:** Dr. E.R. Degginger; **292–293 border:** Dr. E.R. Degginger; **292:** *A New Planet,* K.F.Yuon, Tretiakov Gallery, Moscow, Russia/SuperStock; **294–295 border:** Dr. E.R. Degginger; **294–295 border:** Dr. E.R. Degginger; **294:** *Sunrise IV,* 1937, Arthur Dove, Hirshhorn Museum and Sculpture Garden, Smithsonian Institution; **298 t.:** UPI/ Corbis-Bettmann; **298 b.:** Villard Books, Photo © John Isaac; **299:** image © Copyright 1997 PhotoDisc, Inc.; **306–307:** Image © Copyright 1997 PhotoDisc, Inc.; **308–309 t.:** Kansas State Historical Society, Topeka, Kans.; **308–309 b.:** Courtesy of the Library of Congress; **310–311 border:** Courtesy of the Library of Congress; **315:** Corel Professional Photos CD-ROM™; **316:** Corel Professional Photos CD-ROM™; **320:** PhotoEdit; **325:** *The Cabinetmaker,* Jacob Lawrence, Hirshhorn Museum and Sculpture Garden, Smithsonian Institution, Gift of Joseph H. Hirshhorn, 1966. Photo by Lee Stalsworth; **326 t.:** *Sir Arthur Conan Doyle* (detail), H. L. Gates, The National Portrait Gallery, London; **326 m.:** John Murray Publishers, London; **326 b.:** John Murray Publishers, London; **327:** *Sherlock Holmes,* Frederic Dorr Steele, The Granger Collection, New York; **328 t.:** Culver Pictures, Inc.; **328 b.:** *The Death of Theodore Gericault (1791–1824) with his friends Colonel Bro de Comeres and the painter Pierre-Joseph Dedreux-Dorcy (1789–1874),* 1824 by Ary Scheffer (1795–1858), Louvre, Paris, France/The Bridgeman Art Library International Ltd., London/New York; **331:** Culver Pictures, Inc.; **334:** The Granger Collection, New York; **336:** Culver Pictures, Inc.; **343:** Hawaii Department of Agriculture; **344 t.:** Richard Connelly; **344 m.t.:** Photo by Michael Nye; **344 m.b.:** Arte Publico Press; **344 b.:** *Thomas Hardy* (detail), R.G. Eres, Courtesy of the National Portrait Gallery, London; **345:** Bryce Flynn/Stock, Boston/PNI; **346–347 border:** Bryce Flynn/Stock, Boston/PNI; **347:** Bill Bachmann/New England Stock Photo; **348–349 border:** SuperStock; **349:** *Bicycles,* Robert Vickrey, 32 ½" x 46"

ni-Photo Communications, Inc.; **612:** Richard Hutchings/Photo ...: *Buffalo,* 1992, Jaune Smith, Collection Eleanor and Len Flomen- ...ourtesy Steinbaum Krauss Gallery, NYC; **618:** UPI/Corbis-Bettmann; **622:** Photo Courtesy of the Edward E. Ayer Collection, The Newberry Library, Chicago; **623:** from THE AZTECS by Jacqueline Dineen (Worlds of the Past), Heinemann Educational Books Ltd, an imprint of Reed Educational and Professional Publishing.; **624:** Werner Forman Archive/Art Resource, NY; **625:** Werner Forman Archive, Liverpool Museum, Liverpool/Art Resource NY; **626:** The Bodleian Library, Oxford, MS. Arch. Selden, A.1, fol. 69r; **627:** Erich Lessing/Art Resource, NY; **630:** Corel Professional Photos CD-ROM™; **635:** Jonathan Nourok/PhotoEdit; **638–639:** *Performers,* Freshman Brown, SuperStock; **641:** *Henry Samary (1865–1902), de la Comedie Francaise,* 1889, Musee d'Orsay, Paris, France, Erich Lessing/Art Resource, NY; **642:** Corbis-Bettmann; **643:** Richard Ooms as Ebenezer Scrooge in the Guthrie Theater's 1994 production of *A Christmas Carol* adapted by Barbara Field. Photo credit: Michal Daniel; **645:** John Carroll Lynch as Marley in the Guthrie Theater's 1994 production of *A Christmas Carol* adapted by Barbara Field. Photo credit: Michal Daniel; **647:** Charles Janasz as Bob Cratchit in the Guthrie Theater's 1992 production of *A Christmas Carol* adapted by Barbara Field. Photo credit: Michal Daniel; **650:** Bob Davis as Bob Cratchit and Nathaniel Fuller in the Guthrie Theater's 1994 production of *A Christmas Carol* adapted by Barbara Field. Photo credit: Michal Daniel; **652:** John Carroll Lynch as Marley and Richard Ooms as Ebenezer Scrooge in the Guthrie Theater's 1994 production of *A Christmas Carol* adapted by Barbara Field. Photo credit: Michal Daniel; **657:** Bob Davis as Bob Cratchit, Kevin James Kelly as Charles Dickens and Richard Ooms as Ebneezer Scrooge in the Guthrie Theater's 1994 production of *A Christmas Carol* adapted by Barbara Field. Photo credit: Michal Daniel; **664:** Jim Baker as Ghost of Christmas Present in the Guthrie Theater's 1975 production of *A Christmas Carol* adapted by Barbara Field. Photo credit: Michal Daniel; **668:** The Guthrie Theatre; **674:** The Cratchit family and Ebenezer Scrooge in the Guthrie Theater's 1994 production of *A Christmas Carol* adapted by Barbara Field. Photo credit: Michal Daniel; **677:** Richard Ooms as Ebenezer Scrooge in the Guthrie Theater's 1994 production of *A Christmas Carol* adapted by Barbara Field. Photo credit: Michal Daniel; **679:** Ebenezer Scrooge celebrating in the Guthrie Theater's 1994 production of *A Christmas Carol* adapted by Barbara Field. Photo credit: Michal Daniel; **685:** Photofest; **688:** Corel Professional Photos CD-ROM™; **693:** *Tukoer-Ter-Ur,* 1989, Victor de Vasarely, © ARS, Private Collection, Monaco, Photo by Erich Lessing/Art Resource, NY; **694:** UPI/Corbis-Bettmann; **695:** Mark C.Burnett/Stock, Boston; **696–697:** Jean-Pierre Pieuchot/The Image Bank; **699:** *Woman on telephone as seen through window,* William Low, Courtesy of the artist.; **702:** *Over view of family walking dog on the street,* William Low, Courtesy of the artist; **705:** *Streetlight,* 1930, Constance Coleman Richardson, © Indianapolis Museum of Art, Gift of Mrs. James W. Fesler; **709:** Donald Carroll/The Image Bank; **710 l.:** THE FAR SIDE ©1983 FARWORKS, INC. Used by permission of Universal Press Syndicate. All rights reserved.; **710 r.:** THE FAR SIDE ©1982 FARWORKS, INC. Used by permission of Universal Press Syndicate. All rights reserved.; **714:** Peter Rauter/Tony Stone Images; **719:** Corel Professional Photos CD-ROM™; **722–723:** *Effect of the Sun on the Water,* 1905, Andre Derain, © ARS/Giraudon/Art Resource, NY; **724:** © Archive Photos; **725:** *A procession of knights and their squires on their way to do battle,* ms. illumination, c. 1450, The Granger Collection, New York; **727:** *A knight and a lady on horseback. Breviary with calendar, May.* Flemish School (end 15th), Bibliothoque Nationale, Paris, France, Erich Lessing/Art Resource, NY; **729:** Erich Lessing/Art Resource, NY; **733:** *Le bassin aux Nympheas—harmonie verte (green harmony),* Claude Monet, © Photo by Erich Lessing/Art Resource, NY; **734:** AP/Wide World Photos; **736:** Corel Professional Photos CD-ROM™; **736–737:** inset © Jeff Schultz/ Alaska Stock Images; **738–739:** Corel Professional Photos CD-ROM™; **740–741:** Corel Professional Photos CD-ROM™; **744 t.:** *James Stephens* (detail), Sir William Rothenstein, The Tate Gallery, London/Art Resource, NY; **744 m.t.:** Corbis-Bettmann; **744 m.b.:** Courtesy of the author; **744 b.:** The Granger Collection, New York; **745:** Ragnar Sigurdsson/Tony Stone Images; **746:** Chad Ehlers/Tony Stone Images; **748:** *Cross Country,* 1989, Karl J. Kuerner III, David David Gallery/SuperStock; **749:** *Les Adieux (The Good-bye),* James L.

Tissot, City of Bristol Museum and Art Gallery, England/Bridgeman Art Library, London/Superstock; **749:** City of Bristol Museum and Art Gallery, England/Bridgeman Art Library, London/Superstock; **752 t.:** Sonja H. Smith; **752 m.:** Dimitri Kessel/Life Magazine; **752 b.:** *Basho, Watanahe Kwasan,* The Granger Collection, New York; **753:** Garry McMichael/ Photo Researchers, Inc.; **755:** Brian Yarvin/Photo Researchers, Inc.; **756:** *Ravens in Moonlight,* 1882, Gengyo, Photo by John Lei/ Omni-Photo Communications, © Lea,; **757:** *Ravens in Moonlight,* 1882, Gengyo, Photo by John Lei/Omni-Photo Communications, © Lea,; **761:** Corel Professional Photos CD-ROM™; **762:** Corel Professional Photos CD-ROM™; **764:** Epic Records; **769:** *Double Bass,* Triple Head, Gil Mayers, Private Collection/Gil Mayers/SuperStock; **770 t.:** William E. Stafford; **770 m.:** Corbis-Bettmann; **770 b.:** Mary O'Neil, John Gannon, Courtesy of the artist; **771:** Corbis-Bettmann; **773:** Courtesy of the Library of Congress; **776:** *Dominant Curve,* April 1936, Vasily Kandinsky, Solomon R. Guggenheim Museum/Artists Rights Society (ARS), New York; **780 t.:** *William Shakespeare* (detail), Artist unknown, Courtesy of the National Portrait Gallery, London; **780 m.:** Photo by Bachrach; **780 b.:** Arte Publico Press; **781:** Robert Fried/Stock, Boston/ PNI; **782:** Larry Lipsky/Tom Stack & Associates; **783:** © The Stock Market/Peter Steiner; **784–785:** *Untitled,* © Mike Reed/Stock Illustration Source, Inc.; **788 t.:** AP/Wide World Photos; **788 m.t.:** *Carl Sandburg,* Miriam Svet, The National Portrait Gallery, Smithsonian Institution, Washington, D.C./Art Resource, NY; **788 m.b.:** Courtesy of Naomi Long Madgett; **788 b.:** Patricia Allen-Wolk; **789:** ©The Stock Market/Jim Foster; **790–791:** Image © Copyright 1997 PhotoDisc, Inc.; **792–793:** © The Stock Market/Jim Foster; **793 inset:** Image © Copyright 1997 PhotoDisc, Inc.; **794–795:** Roger Werth/ Woodfin Camp & Associates; **798:** Howard Bluestein/ Photo Researchers, Inc.; **803:** David Young-Wolff/ Photo Edit; **806–807:** Christie's Images, London/Bridgeman Art Library, London/SuperStock; **808:** Courtesy of the author; **809:** Robert Frerck/ Odyssey Productions/Chicago; **811:** *The Volcanos,* 1905, Jose Maria Velasco, Galeria Arvil, Mexico. Courtesy of CDS Gallery, New York. Private Collection; **812–813:** © Robert & Linda Mitchell; **819:** Illustration from "Russkie Volshebnuie Skazki" by Kochergin, Victoria & Albert Museum, London/Art Resource, NY; **820 t.:** Prentice Hall; **820 b.:** Courtesy of the authors; **821:** *The Ride for Liberty—the Fugitive Slaves,* Eastman Johnson, The Granger Collection, New York; **823:** From THE PEOPLE COULD FLY by Virginia Hamilton, illustrated by Leo and Diane Dillon. Cover art copyright © 1985 by Leo and Diane Dillon. Reprinted by permission of Alfred A. Knopf, Inc.; **826:** Maria Szadziuk; **827:** Phil Jude/Photo Researchers, Inc.; **834:** © The Board of Trustees of the Victoria and Albert Museum, London; **835:** *Preparing Medicine from Honey,* 1224, The Metropolitan Museum of Art, Cora Timken Burnett Collection of Persian Miniatures and Other Persian Art Objects, Bequest of Cora Timken Burnett, 1957. (57.51.21). Copyright ©1986 by The Metropolitan Museum of Art; **838:** *Portrait of A Young Woman,* c. 1470, Piero del Pollaiuolo, Copyright ©1979/95 by the Metropolitan Museum of Art, Bequest of Edward S. Harkness, 1950. (50.135.3); **841:** Pendant in the form of a snake catching a frog, Ebrie people, Côte d'Ivoire, 19th century, gold., Brooklyn Museum, Frank L. Babbott Fund.; **842:** Corel Professional Photos CD-ROM™; **843:** Image © Copyright 1997 PhotoDisc, Inc.; **846:** Soames Summerhays/Photo Researchers, Inc.; **851:** All the evils flying forth into the world on the opening of Pandora's box: colored engraving, 19th century, The Granger Collection Ltd., New York; **852 t.:** Courtesy, Houghton Mifflin Company; **852 m.:** Courtesy of the author; **852 b.:** From Christina Hopkinson Baker, "Diary and Letters of Josephine Preston Peabody," Riverside Press, Mass.; **853:** *Le Char D'Apollon (Apollo's Chariot),* (detail), Odilon Redon, Musee D'Orsay, Paris/Giraudon, Paris/SuperStock; **854:** *The Chariot of Phaeton racing through the skies.* Copper engraving, 1606, Corbis-Bettmann; **858:** *Demeter Mourning for Persephone,* 1906, Evelyn de Morgan, The De Morgan Foundation, London/The Bridgeman Art Library, London; **862:** *Narcissus at the Spring,* Caravaggio, Scala/Art Resource, NY; **864–865:** *Daedalus and Icarus:* French colored engraving, 1660, The Granger Collection, New York; **870:** The Granger Collection, New York; **871:** George Grigoriou/ Tony Stone Images; **876:** Corel Professional Photos CD-ROM™; **879:** Brian Parker/Tom Stack & Associates; **881:** Lynn Saville